CW00925391

Endorsements

"Understandings of Mark's Gospel have changed enormously over the decades. Once seen as a simplistic narrative by an untutored believer, Mark is now understood as the work of a subtle writer who used a deceptively simple literary style to present profound theological truths. The modern literature on Mark is so vast that a learned guide is essential for anyone wishing to make sense of it. Fortunately, we now have this work of exemplary scholarship in which David Garland offers his carefully considered thoughts on Mark, and on the gospel's theological arguments. Both scholars and general readers will benefit greatly from Garland's illuminating study, which is presented in such a clear, accessible writing style."

—Philip Jenkins, Institute for Studies of Religion, Baylor University

"As usual, David Garland provides an insightful and well-researched reading into the biblical text. In this book, however, he offers an additional benefit: a model for how to write a helpful theology of a narrative work. By exploring Mark thematically and theologically, Garland provides a distinctively new contribution."

—Craig Keener, F. M. and Ada Thompson Professor of Biblical Studies, Asbury Theological Seminary

"David Garland offers a 'one-stop shop' on the Gospel of Mark, with treatments of introductory questions, analysis of the literary structure, and cogent discussion of major theological emphases. Conducted in ample dialogue with current and past scholarship on all matters dealt with, this is a rich resource for anyone seeking an up-to-date and wide-ranging analysis of Mark."

—L. W. Hurtado, Emeritus Professor of New Testament Language, Literature & Theology, School of Divinity, University of Edinburgh

"Having written two excellent commentaries on Mark's Gospel, David Garland is well suited to write a comprehensive work on Markan theology. This clear, accurate, and engaging volume is a welcome addition at a time when scholars are more and more celebrating the unique theological contributions of each of the four Evangelists."

—Mark L. Strauss, Professor of New Testament, Bethel Seminary in San Diego

"Simply put, this is a magnificent, major resource for the study of Mark. It is both comprehensive and detailed. It is impressive for the depth and range of its scholarship, as well as its careful argumentation. David Garland's approach to Mark reflects the perfect blend of believing and responsibly critical scholarship. It is hard to imagine a better or more helpful volume on the theology of Mark than this."

—Donald A. Hagner, George Eldon Ladd Professor Emeritus of New Testament, Fuller Theological Seminary

A Theology of Mark's Gospel

Good News about Jesus the Messiah,
the Son of God

A THEOLOGY OF MARK'S GOSPEL

BIBLICAL THEOLOGY OF THE NEW TESTAMENT

DAVID E. GARLAND
ANDREAS J. KÖSTENBERGER,
GENERAL EDITOR

ZONDERVAN

ZONDERVAN

A Theology of Mark's Gospel
Copyright © 2015 by David E. Garland
This title is also available as a Zondervan ebook. Visit www.zondervan.com/ebooks.

Requests for information should be addressed to:
Zondervan, *3900 Sparks Dr. SE, Grand Rapids, Michigan 49546*

Library of Congress Cataloging-in-Publication Data

Garland, David E.
A theology of Mark's Gospel : good news about Jesus the Messiah, the Son of God / David E. Garland, Andreas J. Kostenberger, general editor.
pages cm
Includes bibliographical references and indexes.
ISBN 978-0-310-27088-1 (hardcover)
1. Jesus Christ – Divinity – Biblical teaching. 2. Jesus Christ – Person and offices – Biblical teaching. 3. Bible. Mark – Theology. I. Kostenberger, Andreas J., 1957- II.Title.
BT216.3.G37 2014 226.3'06 - dc23

All Scripture quotations, unless otherwise indicated, are taken from The Holy Bible, *New International Version*®, *NIV*®. Copyright © 1973, 1978, 1984, 2011 by Biblica, Inc.® Used by permission. All rights reserved worldwide.

Any Scripture quotations from the Apocrypha, unless otherwise noted, are taken from the *New Revised Standard Version of the Bible*, copyright © 1989 by the Division of Christian Education of the National Council of Churches of Christ in the United States of America, and are used by permission. All rights reserved.

Any Internet addresses (websites, blogs, etc.) and telephone numbers in this book are offered as a resource. They are not intended in any way to be or imply an endorsement by Zondervan, nor does Zondervan vouch for the content of these sites and numbers for the life of this book.

All rights reserved. No part of this publication may be reproduced, stored in a retrieval system, or transmitted in any form or by any means — electronic, mechanical, photocopy, recording, or any other — except for brief quotations in printed reviews, without the prior permission of the publisher.

Cover photography: The Convent of Saint Elizabeth the Grand Duchess of Russia, www.conventofsaintelizabeth.org

Printed in the United States of America

15 16 17 18 19 20 21 22 23 24 25 /DCI/ 20 19 18 17 16 15 14 13 12 11 10 9 8 7 6 5 4 3 2 1

To Aurora, Azalea, and Tess

CONTENTS

CONTENTS (DETAILED)

CHAPTER 5

CHAPTER 6

CHAPTER 7

CHAPTER 13

Series Preface

The Biblical Theology of the New Testament series consists of eight distinct volumes covering the entire New Testament. Each volume is devoted to an in-depth exploration of a given New Testament writing, or group of writings, within the context of the theology of the New Testament, and ultimately of the entire Bible. While each corpus requires an approach that is suitable for the writing(s) studied, all volumes include:

(1) a survey of recent scholarship and of the state of research
(2) a treatment of the relevant introductory issues
(3) a thematic commentary following the narrative flow of the document(s)
(4) a treatment of important individual themes
(5) discussions of the relationship between a particular writing and the rest of the New Testament and the Bible

While Biblical Theology is a relatively new academic discipline and one that has often been hindered by questionable presuppositions, doubtful methodology, and/or flawed execution, the field is one of the most promising avenues of biblical and theological research today. In essence, Biblical Theology engages in the study of the biblical texts while giving careful consideration to the historical setting in which a given piece of writing originated. It seeks to locate and relate the contributions of the respective biblical documents along the lines of the continuum of God's salvation-historical program centered in the coming and salvific work of Christ. It also endeavors to ground the theological exploration of a given document in a close reading of the respective text(s), whether narrative, discourse, or some other type of literature.

By providing in-depth studies of the diverse, yet complementary perspectives of the New Testament writings, the Biblical Theology of the New Testament series aims to make a significant contribution to the study of the major interrelated themes of Scripture in a holistic, context-sensitive, and spiritually nurturing manner. Each volume is written by a scholar who has written a major commentary or monograph on the corpus covered. The generous page allotment allows for an in-depth investigation. While coming from diverse academic backgrounds and institutional affiliations, the contributors share a commitment to an evangelical faith and a respect for the authority of Scripture. They also have in common a conviction that the canon of Scripture is ultimately unified, not contradictory.

In addition to contributing to the study of individual New Testament writings and to the study of the New Testament and ultimately of Scripture as a whole, the series also seeks to make a methodological contribution, showing how Biblical Theology ought to be conducted. In each case, the way in which the volume is conceived reflects careful consideration of the nature of a given piece or body of writings. The complex interrelationships between the three so-called "Synoptic Gospels"; the two-volume nature of Luke-Acts; the relationship between John's gospel, letters, and the book of Revelation; the thirteen letters making up the Pauline corpus; and the theologies of Peter, James, and Jude, as well as Hebrews, each present unique challenges and opportunities.

In the end, it is hoped that the volumes will pay tribute to the multifaceted nature of divine revelation contained in Scripture. As G. B. Caird put it:

> The question we must ask is not whether these books all say the same thing, but whether they all bear witness to the same Jesus and through him to the many splendoured wisdom of the one God.... We shall neither attempt to press all our witnesses into a single mould nor captiously complain that one seems at some points deficient in comparison with another. What we shall do is rejoice that God has seen fit to establish His gospel at the mouth of so many independent witnesses. The music of the New Testament choir is not written to be sung in unison.[1]

In this spirit, the contributors offer their work as a humble aid to a greater appreciation of the magnificent scriptural symphony of God.

Andreas J. Köstenberger, series editor
Wake Forest, NC

1. G. B. Caird, *New Testament Theology* (ed. L. D. Hurst; Oxford: Clarendon, 1994), 24.

Author's Preface

The stream of literature on the Gospel of Mark is so voluminous and so unremittingly fast-moving that an attempt to digest it all is like stepping into the rapids of a river and trying to analyze each water molecule. For every exegetical decision made, I am aware that one can find a battery of scholars who conclude otherwise and who offer a multitude of other options. The mass of literature and diversity of opinion can drive a student to distraction. Since writing a commentary on Mark that was published in 1996, I have changed my views on several points, in particular, the significance of the ending of the gospel. I am therefore acutely aware that I can be wrong, but I try as best I can to be judicious in the exegesis of Mark's text that leads to my understanding of its theological implications. I am firmly convinced that it is mistaken to read the gospel from the model of mirror reading in the same way Paul's letters are read to imagine the position of Paul's opponents. The gospel was not written to counteract heresy or any group. Mark's primary purpose was to present Jesus to his readers as the Messiah and Son of God and to show that his shameful death on a cross was part of God's plan for the redemption of humanity. God vindicated him in the resurrection and his exaltation. Mark, however, is an enigmatic gospel, and Taylor captures this mystery in this statement:

> We ask who He is and He gives us no answer. Enigmatic as in the days of His flesh, He is enigmatic still to the questing mind. But He so works in history and life that, after He has left us "in suspense," we come to know of a surety who He is. He makes Himself known in His deeds, in the breaking of bread, in the Cross, in prayer and worship. He is what He does. His secret cannot be read; it must be found.[1]

I have many to thank. I am grateful to Andreas Köstenberger for the invitation to contribute to this important series, and I am also most appreciative to the editors at Zondervan for the work on this book—in particular, Verlyn Verbrugge. I am deeply indebted to Tia Park-Kim, my teaching assistant, for her tireless diligence in tracking down various works, proofing several drafts, sharing her own insights, and providing encouragement. I also must thank her family, her children, Grace and Daniel, and her husband, Andrew, who is working on his PhD at Baylor, for supporting her during this project in which she spent so much time. She has been an incredible assistant. I must also thank Angela Bailey, my most able and gracious administrative assistant when I served as Dean of George W. Truett Theological Seminary at Baylor University, and Erin Shoemake, my most able and gracious administrative assistant when I served as Interim Provost of Baylor University.

1. Vincent Taylor, "Unsolved New Testament Problems: The Messianic Secret in Mark," *ExpTim* 59 (1948): 151.

Baylor is filled with most able and gracious people, and I have been particularly blessed to be able to work with these three. I also give thanks to my wife, Diana, who serves as Dean of the Baylor School of Social Work and has her own research agenda and administrative duties, but never has failed to support me in my work.

ABBREVIATIONS

1 Apol.	*First Apology* (Justin)
2 Bar.	*2 Baruch*
1 Clem.	*1 Clement*
2 Clem.	*2 Clement*
1 En.	*1 Enoch*
2 En.	*2 Enoch*
1 Serv. lib.	*De servitute et libertate i (Or. 14)* (Dio Chrysostom)
AASF	Annales Academiae Scientiarum Fennicae
ʾAbot R. Nat.	*ʾAbot de Rabbi Nathan*
AB	Anchor Bible
ABD	*The Anchor Bible Dictionary* (ed. David Noel Freedman)
ABR	*Australian Biblical Review*
ABRL	Anchor Bible Reference Library
ACCS NT	Ancient Christian Commentary on Scripture, New Testament
ACNT	Augsburg Commentary on the New Testament
Aen.	*Aeneid* (Virgil)
Ag. Ap.	*Against Apion* (Josephus)
AGJU	Arbeiten zur Geschichte des antiken Judentums und des Urchristentums
AGSU	Arbeiten zur Geschichte des Spätjudentums und Urchristentums
AJT	*The American Journal of Theology*
Alleg. Interp.	*Allegorical Interpretation* (Philo)
AnBib	Analecta biblica
Ann.	*Annales* (Tacitus)
ANRW	*Aufstieg und Niedergang der römischen Welt: Geschichte und Kultur Roms im Spiegel der neueren Forschung*
Ant.	*Jewish Antiquities* (Josephus)
Apoc. Ab.	*Apocalypse of Abraham*
Apoc. El.	*Apocalypse of Elijah*
ASNU	Acta Seminarii Neotestamentici Upsaliensis
ASV	American Standard Version
ATANT	Abhandlungen zur Theologie des Alten und Neuen Testaments
AYB	Anchor Yale Bible
b. ʿArak.	Babylonian Talmud, *ʿArakin*
b. B. Bat.	Babylonian Talmud, *Baba Batra*
b. B. Qam.	Babylonian Talmud, *Baba Qamma*
b. Bek.	Babylonian Talmud, *Bekorot*
b. Ber.	Babylonian Talmud, *Berakot*
b. ʿErub.	Babylonian Talmud, *ʿErubin*

b. Giṭ.	Babylonian Talmud, *Giṭṭin*
b. Ḥag.	Babylonian Talmud, *Ḥagigah*
b. Ḥul.	Babylonian Talmud, *Ḥullin*
b. Ker.	Babylonian Talmud, *Keritot*
b. Ketub.	Babylonian Talmud, *Ketubbot*
b. Meg.	Babylonian Talmud, *Megillah*
b. Menaḥ.	Babylonian Talmud, *Menaḥot*
b. Moʿed Qaṭ.	Babylonian Talmud, *Mo'ed Qaṭan*
b. Ned.	Babylonian Talmud, *Nedarim*
b. Nid.	Babylonian Talmud, *Niddah*
b. Pesaḥ.	Babylonian Talmud, *Pesaḥim*
b. Qidd.	Babylonian Talmud, *Qiddušin*
b. Šabb.	Babylonian Talmud, *Šabbat*
b. Sanh.	Babylonian Talmud, *Sanhedrin*
b. Soṭah	Babylonian Talmud, *Soṭah*
b. Sukkah	Babylonian Talmud, *Sukkah*
b. Taʿan.	Babylonian Talmud, *Taʿanit*
b. Yebam.	Babylonian Talmud, *Yebamot*
b. Yoma	Babylonian Talmud, *Yoma*
Barn.	*Barnabas*
BAR	*Biblical Archaeology Review*
BASP	*Bulletin of the American Society of Papyrologists*
BBR	*Bulletin for Biblical Research*
BCBC	Believers Church Bible Commentary
BDAG	Bauer, W., F. W. Danker, W. F. Arndt, and F. W. Gingrich. *Greek-English Lexicon of the New Testament and Other EarlyChristian Literature.* 3rd ed. Chicago, 2000
BECNT	Baker Exegetical Commentary on the New Testament
Ben.	*De beneficiis* (Seneca)
BETL	Bibliotheca ephemeridum theologicarum lovaniensium
BEvT	Beiträge zur evangelischen Theologie
BGBE	Beiträge zur Geschichte der biblischen Exegese
Bib	*Biblica*
BibInt	*Biblical Interpretation*
BibS(N)	Biblische Studien (Neukirchen)
BIS	Biblical Interpretation Series
BJRL	*Bulletin of John Rylands University Library*
BNTC	Black's New Testament Commentary
BR	*Biblical Research*
BRev	*Bible Review*
BT	*The Bible Translator*
BTB	*Biblical Theology Bulletin*
BTS	Biblical Tools and Studies

BWANT	Beiträge zur Wissenschaft vom Alten und Neuen Testament
BZ	*Biblische Zeitschrift*
BZNW	Beihefte zur Zeitschrift für die neutestamentliche Wissenschaft
CBET	Contributions to Biblical Exegesis and Theology
CBQ	*Catholic Biblical Quarterly*
CBQMS	Catholic Biblical Quarterly Monograph Series
Cels.	*Contra Celsum* (Origen)
CGTC	Cambridge Greek Testament Commentary
Comm	*Communio*
Cons.	*Harmony of the Gospels* (Augustine)
ConBNT	Coniectanea biblica, New Testament Series
CTJ	*Calvin Theological Journal*
CTM	*Concordia Theological Monthly*
CurBS	*Currents in Research: Biblical Studies*
Curios.	*De curiositate* (Plutarch)
CurTM	*Currents in Theology and Mission*
Def. orac.	*De defectu oraculorum* (Plutarch)
Deut. Rab.	*Deuteronomy Rabbah*
Dial.	*Dialogue with Trypho* (Justin)
Did	*Didaskalia*
Did.	*Didache*
DJG	*Dictionary of Jesus and the Gospels* (ed. Joel B. Green, Scot McKnight, and I. Howard Marshall; Downers Grove, IL: InterVarsity Press, 1992)
EBib	Études biblique
Ecl.	*Eclogae* (Virgil)
EDNT	*Exegetical Dictionary of the New Testament* (ed. H. Balz and G. Schneider; Grand Rapids: Eerdmans, 1991)
EKKNT	Evangelisch-katholischer Kommentar zum Neuen Testament
Ep.	*Epistulae Morales* (Seneca)
ETL	*Ephemerides theologicae lovanienses*
ETR	*Etudes théologiques et religieuses*
EvK	Evangelische Kommentare
EvQ	*Evangelical Quarterly*
EvT	*Evangelische Theologie*
Exod. Rab.	*Exodus Rabbah*
ExpTim	*Expository Times*
FB	Forschung zur Bibel
FBBS	Facet Books Biblical Series
FN	*Filologia neotestamentaria*
FoiVie	*Foi et Vie*
FRLANT	Forschungen zur Religion und Literatur des Alten und Neuen Testaments
FTS	Frankfurter Theologische Studien

GBSNTS	Guides to Biblical Scholarship New Testament Series
Gen. Rab.	*Genesis Rabbah*
Geogr.	*Geography* (Strabo)
GTA	Göttinger theologischer Arbeiten
Haer.	*Against Heresies* (Irenaeus)
HBT	*Horizons in Biblical Theology*
Heir	*Who Is the Heir?* (Philo)
Herm. Sim.	*Shepherd of Hermas, Similitudes*
Herm.Vis.	*Shepherd of Hermas, Visions*
Hist.	*Historiae* (Tacitus)
Hist. eccl.	*Ecclesiastical History* (Eusebius)
HNT	Handbuch zum Neuen Testament
Hom. Matt.	*Homiliae in Matthaeum* (John Chrysostom)
HTKNT	Herders theologischer Kommentar zum Neuen Testament
HTR	*Harvard Theological Review*
HTS	Harvard Theological Studies
HUCA	*Hebrew Union College Annual*
HUT	Hermeneutische Untersuchungen zur Theologie
HvTSt	*Hervormde teologiese studies*
HvTStSup	Hervormde teologiese studies supplements
IBS	*Irish Biblical Studies*
IBT	Interpreting Biblical Texts
ICC	International Critical Commentary
Idol.	*Idolatry* (Tertullian)
IEJ	*Israel Exploration Journal*
Ign. *Eph.*	Ignatius, *To the Ephesians*
Il.	*Iliad* (Homer)
Inst.	*Institutio oratoria* (Quintilian)
Int	*Interpretation*
IVPNTC	InterVarsity Press New Testament Commentary
JAAR	*Journal of the American Academy of Religion*
JAJ	*Journal of Ancient Judaism*
JBR	*Journal of Bible and Religion*
JETS	*Journal of the Evangelical Theological Society*
JGRChJ	*Journal of Greco-Roman Christianity and Judaism*
JJS	*Journal of Jewish Studies*
Jos. Asen.	*Joseph and Aseneth*
JAR	*Jewish Quarterly Review*
JR	*Journal of Religion*
JRH	*Journal of Religious History*
JSHJ	*Journal for the Study of the Historical Jesus*
JSJ	*Journal for the Study of Judaism*

JSJSup	Journal for the Study of Judaism in the Persian, Hellenistic, and Roman Periods Supplement Series
JSNT	*Journal for the Study of the New Testament*
JSNTSup	Journal for the Study of the New Testament Supplements Series
JSOTSup	Journal for the Study of the Old Testament Supplements Series
JSP	*Journal for the Study of the Pseudepigrapha*
JSS	*Journal for the Study of Judaism*
JTI	*Journal of Theological Interpretation*
JTS	*Journal of Theological Studies*
JTSA	*Journal of Theology for South Africa*
Jub.	*Jubilees*
J.W.	*Jewish Wars* (Josephus)
KBANT	Kommentare und Beiträge zum Alten und Neuen Testament
KEK	Kritisch-exegetischer Kommentar über das Neue Testament
KJV	King James Version
L.A.B.	*Liber antiquitatum biblicarum* (Pseudo-Philo)
LD	Lectio divina
LEC	Library of Early Christianity
Embassy	*On the Embassy to Gaius* (Philo)
Let. Aris.	*Letter of Aristeas*
Lev. Rab.	*Leviticus Rabbah*
LNTS	Library of New Testament Studies
LQ	*Lutheran Quarterly*
LS	*Louvain Studies*
LXX	Septuagint (Greek translation of the Old Testament)
m. ʿAbod. Zar.	Mishnah, *ʿAbodah Zarah*
m. ʾAbot	Mishnah, *ʾAbot*
m. Ber.	Mishnah, *Berakot*
m. Giṭ.	Mishnah, *Giṭṭin*
m. Ḥag.	Mishnah, *Ḥagigah*
m. Naz.	Mishnah, *Nazir*
m. Neg.	Mishnah, *Negaʿim*
m. Nid.	Mishnah *Niddah*
m. Pesaḥ.	Mishnah, *Pesaḥim*
m. Qidd.	Mishnah, *Qiddušin*
m. Šabb.	Mishnah, *Šabbat*
m. Sanh.	Mishnah, *Sanhedrin*
m. Šeqal.	Mishnah, *Šeqalim*
m. Tamid	Mishnah, *Tamid*
m. Ṭehar.	Mishnah, *Ṭeharot*
m. Yad.	Mishnah, *Yadayim*
m. Yoma	Mishnah, *Yoma*
m. Zebaḥ	Mishnah, *Zebaḥim*

Marc.	*Against Marcion* (Tertullian)
Mart. Isa.	*Martyrdom and Ascension of Isaiah*
Mart. Pol.	*Martyrdom of Polycarp*
Midr. Ps.	*Midrash I Psalm*
Moses	*On the Life of Moses* (Philo)
MT	Masoretic Text
MTZ	*Münchener theologische Zeitschrift*
NASB	New American Standard Bible
NASV	New American Standard Version
Nat.	*Natural History* (Pliny the Elder)
NCB	New Century Bible
NEB	New English Bible
NedTT	*Nederlands theologisch tijdschrift*
Beot	*Neotestamentica*
NIBC	New International Biblical Commentary
NICNT	New International Commentary on the New Testament
NICOT	New International Commentary on the Old Testament
NIGTC	New International Greek Testament Commentary
NIV	New International Version
NIVAC	New International Version Application Commentary
NJB	New Jerusalem Bible
NovT	*Novum Testamentum*
NovTSup	*Novum Testamentum* Supplements
NRSV	New Revised Standard Version
NRTh	*La nouvelle revue théoligique*
NSBT	New Studies in Biblical Theology
NTAbh	Neutestamentliche Abhandlungen
NTL	New Testament Library
NTM	New Testament Monographs
NTS	*New Testament Studies*
NTTS	New Testament Tools and Studies
OBO	Orbis biblicus et orientalis
Od.	*Odyssey* (Homer)
Odes Sol.	*Odes of Solomon*
OGIS	*Orientis graeci inscriptions selectae*
OrChrAn	Orientalia christiana analecta
ÖTK	Ökumenischer Taschenbuch-Kommentar
OTL	Old Testament Library
Pan.	*Refutation of All Heresies* (Epiphanius)
Pelag.	*Adversus Pelagianos dialogi III* (Jerome)
PEQ	*Palestine Exploration Quarterly*
PGM	*Papyri graecae magicae: Die griechischen Zauberpapyri*
Pillar	Pillar New Testament Commentaries

Poet.	*Poetica* (Aristotle)
Posterity	*On the Posterity of Cain* (Philo)
Praef.	*Compositiones* (Scribonius Largus)
Princ.	*First Principles* (Origen)
Pr. Man.	*Prayer of Manasseh*
PRSt	*Perspectives in Religious Studies*
Pss. Sol.	*Psalms of Solomon*
QG	*Questions and Answers on Genesis* (Philo)
Qoh. Rab.	*Qoheleth Rabbah*
Quaest. rom.	*Quaestiones romanae et grecae* (Plutarch)
RA	*Revue d'assyriologie et d'archéologie orientale*
Rab. Post.	*Pro Rabirio Postumo* (Cicero)
RB	*Revue biblique*
REB	Revised English Bible
Refut.	*Refutation of All Heresies* (Hippolytus)
ResQ	*Restoration Quarterly*
RevExp	*Review and Expositor*
Rewards	*On Rewards and Punishments* (Philo)
RHPR	*Revue d'histoire et de philosophie religieuses*
RNT	Regensburger Neues Testament
Rom. Hist.	*Roman History* (Cassius Dio)
RSV	Revised Standard Version
RTR	*Reformed Theological Review*
SANT	Studien zum Alten und Neuen Testaments
Sat.	*Satirae* (Juvenal)
SBG	Studies in Biblical Greek
SBLDS	Society of Biblical Literature Dissertation Series
SBLSP	Society of Biblical Literature Seminar Papers
SBLSymS	Society of Biblical Literature Symposium Series
SBM	Stuttgarter biblische Monographien
SBS	Stuttgarter Bibelstudien
SBT	Studies in Biblical Theology
ScEs	*Science et esprit*
SE	*Studia evangelica*
SEÅ	*Svensk exegetisk årsbok*
SemeiaSt	Semeia Studies
Sera	*De sera numinis vindicta* (Plutarch)
SFSHJ	South Florida Studies in the History of Judaism
SHAW	Sitzungsberichte der heidelberger Akademie der Wissenschaften
Sib. Or.	*Sibylline Oracles*
SJLA	Studies in Judaism in Late Antiquity
SJT	*Scottish Journal of Theology*
SKKNT	Stuttgarter kleiner Kommentar, Neues Testament

SNTSMS	Society of New Testament Studies Monograph Series
SNTSU	Studien zum neuen Testament und seiner Umwelt
SP	Sacra Pagina
Spec. Laws	*On the Special Laws* (Philo)
STDJ	Studies on the Texts of the Desert of Judah
STRev	*Sewanee Theological Review*
Strom.	*Stromata* (Clement of Alexandria)
SUNT	Studien zur Umwelt des Neuen Testaments
T. 12 Patr.	*Testaments of the Twelve Patriarchs*
T. Ab.	*Testament of Abraham*
T. Adam	*Testament of Adam*
T. Jos.	*Testament of Joseph*
T. Jud.	*Testament of Judah*
T. Levi	*Testament of Levi*
T. Mos.	*Testament of Moses*
T. Naph.	*Testament of Naphtali*
T. Sol.	*Testament of Solomon*
t. Meʿil.	Tosefta, *Meʿilah*
t. Neg.	Tosefta, *Negʿaim*
t. Šabb.	Tosefta, *Šabbat*
t. Sanh.	Tosefta, *Sanhedrin*
t. Šeqal.	Tosefta, *Šheqalim*
t. Sukkah	Tosefta, *Sukkah*
t. Ter.	Tosefta, *Terumot*
TBT	*The Bible Today*
TDNT	*Theological Dictionary of the New Testament*
THKNT	*Theologischer Handkommentar zum Neuen Testament*
Tg. Isa.	*Targum Isaiah*
ThEv	*Theologica evangelica*
TLZ	*Theologische Literaturzeitung*
TS	*Theological Studies*
TynBul	*Tyndale Bulletin*
TZ	*Theologische Zeitschrift*
VC	*Vigiliae christianae*
WBC	Word Biblical Commentary
WMANT	Wissenschaftliche Monographien zum Alten und Neuen Testament
WPC	Westminster Pelican Commentaries
WTJ	*Westminster Theological Journal*
WUNT	Wissenschaftliche Untersuchungen zum Neuen Testament
y. Ber.	Jerusalem Talmud, *Berakot*
y. Sanh.	Jerusalem Talmud, *Sanhedrin*
y. Šeb.	Jerusalem Talmud, *Šebiʿit*

y. Ta'an.	Jerusalem Talmud, *Ta'anit*
y. Ter.	Jerusalem Talmud, *Terumot*
ZDPV	*Zeitschrift des deutschen Palästina-Vereins*
ZKT	*Zeitschrift für katholische Theologie*
ZNW	*Zeitschrift für die neutestamentliche Wissenschaft und die Kunde der älteren Kirche*
ZTK	*Zeitschrift für Theologie und Kirche*

Part 1

INTRODUCTORY MATTERS

Chapter 1

THE ORIENTATION OF THIS STUDY AND THE HISTORICAL FRAMEWORK FOR MARK'S THEOLOGY

BIBLIOGRAPHY

Aune, David E. "Genre Theory and the Genre-Function of Mark and Matthew." Pp. 145–75 in *Mark and Matthew I: Comparative Readings: Understanding the Earliest Gospels in Their First-Century Settings*. WUNT 2/271. Ed. Eve-Marie Becker and Anders Runesson. Tübingen: Mohr Siebeck, 2011. **Bauckham, Richard.** "For Whom Were Gospels Written?" Pp. 9–48 in *The Gospels for All Christians: Rethinking the Gospel Audiences*. Ed. Richard Bauckham. Grand Rapids: Eerdmans, 1998. Idem. "The Gospel of Mark: Origins and Eyewitness." Pp. 145–69 in *Earliest Christian History: History, Literature, and Theology: Essays from the Tyndale Fellowship in Honor of Martin Hengel*. WUNT 2/320. Ed. Michael F. Bird and Jason Maston. Tübingen: Mohr Siebeck, 2012. **Best, Ernest.** "Mark's Readers: A Profile." Pp. 839–58 in *The Four Gospels 1992: Festschrift Frans Neirynck*. Vol. 2. BETL 100. Ed. Frans van Segbroeck et al. Leuven: Leuven University Press, 1992. **Bird, Michael F.** "The Markan Community, Myth or Maze? Bauckham's *The Gospel for All Christians* Revisited." *JTS* 57 (2006): 474–86. Idem. "Mark: Interpreter of Peter and Disciple of Paul." Pp. 30–61 in *Paul and the Gospels: Christologies, Conflicts, and Convergences*. LNTS 411. Ed. Michael F. Bird and Joel Willitts. London/New York: T&T Clark International, 2011. **Black, C. Clifton.** "Was Mark a Roman Gospel?" *ExpTim* 105 (1993): 36–40. Idem. *Mark: Images of an Apostolic Interpreter*. Columbia, SC: University of South Carolina Press, 1994. **Breytenbach, Cilliers.** "Current Research on the Gospel according to Mark: A Report on Monographs Published from 2000–2009." Pp. 13–32 in *Mark and Matthew I: Comparative Readings: Understanding the Earliest Gospels in their First-Century Settings*. WUNT 2/271. Ed. Eve-Marie Becker and Anders Runesson. Tübingen: Mohr Siebeck, 2011. **Bruce, F. F.** "The Date and Character of Mark." Pp. 69–89 in *Jesus and the Politics of His Day*. Ed. Ernst Bammel and C. F. D. Moule. Cambridge: Cambridge University Press, 1984. **Collins, Adela Yarbro.** *The Beginning of the Gospel: Probings of Mark in Context*. Minneapolis: Fortress, 1992. **Cook, John G.** *The Structure and Persuasive Power of Mark: A Linguistic Approach*. Semeia Studies. Atlanta: Scholars Press, 1995. **Dahl, Nils Alstrup.** "The Purpose of Mark's Gospel." Pp. 52–65 in *Jesus in the Memory of the Early Church*. Minneapolis: Augsburg,

1976. **Damm, Alex.** *Ancient Rhetoric and the Synoptic Problem: Clarifying Markan Priority*. BETL 252. Leuven: Peeters, 2013. **Dawsey, James.** *Peter's Last Sermon: Identity and Discipleship in the Gospel of Mark*. Macon, GA: Mercer University Press, 2010. **Donahue, John R.** "The Quest for the Community of Mark's Gospel." Pp. 817–38 in *The Four Gospels 1992: Festschrift Frans Neirynck*. Vol. 2. BETL 100. Ed. Frans van Segbroeck et al. Leuven: Leuven University Press, 1992. Idem. "Windows and Mirrors: The Setting of Mark's Gospel." *CBQ* 57 (1995): 1–26. **Dormeyer, Detlev and Hubert Frankemölle.** "Evangelium als literarischer und als theologischer Begriff: Tendenzen und Aufgaben der Evangelienforschung im 20. Jahrhundert, mit einer Untersuchung des Markusevangeliums in seinem Verhältnis zur griechischen Biographie." Pp. 1541–704 in *ANRW Vol. II.25.2*. Ed. H. Temporini. Berlin/New York: de Gruyter, 1972. **Elliott, J. K.** *The Language and Style of the Gospel of Mark: An Edition of C. H. Turner's "Notes on Marcan Usage" Together with Other Comparable Studies*. NovTSup 71. Leiden: Brill, 1993. **Ellis, E. Earle.** "The Date and Purpose of Mark's Gospel." Pp. 810–15 in *The Four Gospels 1992: Festschrift Frans Neirynck*. Vol. 2. BETL 100. Ed. Frans van Segbroeck et al. Leuven: Leuven University Press, 1992. **Evans, Craig A.** "How Mark Writes." Pp. 135–48 in *The Written Gospel*. Ed. Markus Bockmuehl and Donald A. Hagner. Cambridge: Cambridge University Press, 2005. **Goodacre, Mark.** *The Case Against Q: Studies in Markan Priority and the Synoptic Problem*. Harrisburg, PA: Trinity Press International, 2002. **Harrington, Daniel J.** *What Are They Saying about Mark?* New York/Mahwah, NJ: Paulist, 2004. **Head, Ivan.** "Mark as a Roman Document from the Year 69: Testing Martin Hengel's Thesis." *JRH* 28 (2004): 240–59. **Head, Peter M.** *Christology and the Synoptic Problem: An Argument for Markan Priority*. SNTSMS 94. Cambridge: Cambridge University Press, 1997. **Hengel, Martin.** *Studies in the Gospel of Mark*. Trans. John Bowden. London: SCM, 1985. **Hooker, Morna D.** "Mark." Pp. 220–30 in *It Is Written—Scripture Citing Scripture: Essays in Honour of Barnabas Lindars, SSF*. Ed. D. A. Carson and H. G. M. Williamson. Cambridge: Cambridge University Press, 1988. **Incigneri, Brian J.** *The Gospel to the Romans: The Setting and Rhetoric of Mark's Gospel*. BIS 65. Leiden/Boston/Köln: Brill, 2003. **Kealy, Sean P.** *A History of the Interpretation of the Gospel of Mark. Volume I. Through the Nineteenth Century*. Lewiston/Queenston/Lampeter: Mellen, 2008. Idem. *A History of the Interpretation of the Gospel of Mark. Volume II. The Twentieth Century Book 1*. Lewiston/Queenston/Lampeter: Mellen, 2008. Idem. *A History of the Interpretation of the Gospel of Mark. Volume II. The Twentieth Century Book 2*. Lewiston/Queenston/Lampeter: Mellen, 2008. **Kloppenborg, John S.** "Evocatio Deorum and the Date of Mark." *JBL* 124 (2005): 419–50. **Lane, William L.** "From Historian to Theologian: Milestones in Markan Scholarship." *RevExp* 75 (1978): 601–17. **Martin, Ralph P.** *Mark: Evangelist and Theologian*. Grand Rapids: Zondervan, 1972. **Peterson, Dwight N.** *The Origins of Mark: The Markan Community in Current Debate*. BIS 48. Leiden/Boston/Köln: Brill, 2000. **Senior, Donald P.** "'With Swords and Clubs ...'—The Setting of Mark's Community and His Critique of Abusive Power." *BTB* 17 (1987): 10–20.

Idem. "The Gospel of Mark in Context." *TBT* 34 (1996): 215–21. **Styler, G. M.** "Excursus IV: The Priority of Mark." Pp. 285–316 in C. F. D. Moule, *The Birth of the New Testament*. 3rd ed. San Francisco: Harper & Row, 1982. **Telford, William R.** *The Interpretation of Mark*. 2nd ed. Edinburgh: T&T Clark, 1995. Idem. *Writing on the Gospel of Mark*. Guides to Advanced Biblical Research 1. Dorset: Deo, 2009. **Van Iersel, Bas M. F.** "The Gospel According to Mark—Written for a Persecuted Community?" *NedTT* 34 (1980): 15–36. **Williams, Joel F.** "Is Mark's Gospel an Apology for the Cross?" *BBR* 12 (2002): 97–122. Idem. "Does Mark's Gospel Have an Outline?" *JETS* 49 (2006): 505–25. **Winn, Adam.** *The Purpose of Mark's Gospel: An Early Christian Response to Roman Imperial Propaganda*. WUNT 2/245. Tübingen, Mohr Siebeck, 2008.

1.1 THE ORIENTATION OF THIS STUDY

Given the history of the interpretation of Mark's gospel, one might justifiably wonder, why write a book on Mark's theology? Readers over the centuries generally have not esteemed the gospel for its theological profundity. Early interpreters had little interest in Mark and were attracted to the more doctrinally evocative gospels. Mark's reputation was further diminished by Augustine, who discounted the gospel as only "an abridgment of Matthew."[1] Why bother with a digest when one could consult the original? Much later in the nineteenth century, Mark drew more attention as a window on the historical life of Jesus, but it was not viewed as having a theological message of its own.[2] According to Black, in contrast to John and Paul, who are championed as the pivotal theologians in the NT, Mark "has been stereotyped as little more than an unsophisticated storyteller whose interests were more historical, or historicist, than theological."[3] The gospel was considered to be a string of isolated units that portrayed raw history.

The pendulum began to swing in the other direction when the historicity of the gospel was called into question by William Wrede. He contended that Mark devised the fiction of the secrecy theme that is so prominent in his gospel to explain the incongruity between the early Christian confession that Jesus was the Messiah and the historical non-messianic nature of his ministry.[4] Wrede's conclusions, while seriously challenged at many points, ultimately changed the perspective on Mark. Beavis summarizes in a nutshell the current appraisal of Mark: "Mark is not a transcript of apostolic memoirs but a mosaic of pre-Gospel traditions from various sources, artfully edited together into a connected narrative."[5]

My approach differs to the extent that I consider that Mark faithfully organized

1. Ian D. Mackay, *John's Relationship with Mark* (WUNT 2/182; Tübingen: Mohr Siebeck, 2004), 47.

2. Ibid., 52.

3. C. Clifton Black, "Christ Crucified in Paul and in Mark: Reflections on an Intracanonical Conversation," in *Theology and Ethics in Paul and His Interpreters: Essays in Honor of Victor Paul Furnish* (ed. Eugene H. Lovering Jr. and Jerry L. Sumney; Nashville: Abingdon, 1996), 184.

4. William Wrede, *The Messianic Secret* (trans. J. C. G. Greig; London: James Clarke, 1971).

5. Mary Ann Beavis, *Mark* (Paideia; Grand Rapids: Baker Academic, 2011), 9.

into a narrative the historical tradition about Jesus' ministry, which he gleaned from Peter's preaching and from other traditions. Paul Simon, the American pop singer, said, "Facts can be turned into art if one is artful enough," and I believe that Mark has artfully transmitted the historical facts to "present (or re-present) Jesus to his readers so that his significance for their lives becomes clear."[6] If, as I will argue below, the author Mark was a close associate of Peter and Paul, he wrote when Christians already believed in Christ's divinity, and the gospel displays a high Christology. Benoit states, "Granted the properly divine sense which Paul gave to the title 'Son of God,' it is unthinkable that Mark, who had been his disciple and been influenced by him, should have understood the title differently when he uses it in his gospel."[7] Mark inherited a Christian theological tradition and did not invent it; rather, he shaped the material for his context and stamped it with his own distinctive theological watermark.

This gospel was not intended by its author to be a vessel of theological truths waiting to be quarried but a story in which Jesus is the central figure. Mark's theology is unfurled through narrative development. He shows rather than tells. Perkins rightly recognizes that to understand Mark's Christology, for example, one cannot focus on the use of a particular theme or title: "It depends on the unfolding impact of the story. None of the titles can express the paradoxes imaged in that story."[8] In fact, one of the features that sets this gospel apart from the others is that it is filled with enigmas, paradoxes, and unresolved questions.[9] These puzzles and mysteries can cause some readers to undervalue the gospel while they strike others as a sign of the gospel's theological depth. I would concur with the latter opinion. Boring observes:

> While propositional discursive language has difficulty with contrary statements and images, narrative can embrace sets of contrary statements and images without denying either member of the pair. The narrative form may be chosen intentionally in order to make affirmations that pose difficulties for logic. The interpreters should thus be wary of such constructions as "Since Jesus is clearly and explicitly human in Mark, Mark cannot have also affirmed Christ's divinity," or "Since Jesus is clearly and explicitly distinguished from the one God in Mark, Mark cannot have also affirmed Christ's deity."[10]

In my view, Mark's narrative reveals that Jesus is both fully human and fully divine.

The incipit and the introduction (1:1–13) prepare the audience for the narrative by giving a theological preview to which none of the characters in the narrative are

6. Robert C. Tannehill, "The Gospel of Mark as Narrative Christology," *Semeia* 16 (1979): 57.

7. Pierre Benoit, *Jesus and the Gospel Volume 1* (trans. Benet Weatherhead; New York: Seabury, 1973), 47–48.

8. Pheme Perkins, "Mark as Narrative Christology," in *Who Is This Christ? Gospel Christology and Contemporary Faith* (ed. Reginald Fuller and Pheme Perkins; Philadelphia: Fortress, 1983), 76.

9. Robert M. Fowler, *Let the Reader Understand: Reader-Response Criticism and the Gospel of Mark* (Minneapolis: Fortress, 1991), 155–237. Geert Van Oyen, "The Vulnerable Authority of the Author of the Gospel of Mark: Re-Reading the Paradoxes," *Bib* 91 (2010): 161–86.

10. M. Eugene Boring, "Markan Christology: God-Language for Jesus?" *NTS* 45 (1999): 462.

privy. Jesus is the Messiah, the Son of God, who hails from Nazareth in Galilee and accepts the baptism of repentance of John the Baptist, but who also is imbued with the Holy Spirit and announced as God's Son by a heavenly voice. The audience is therefore in the know from the beginning and can appreciate the ironies as the characters, who largely remain in the dark, interact with Jesus. The narrative only incrementally reveals who Jesus is and what he has come to do.[11] Many remain blind. The disciples receive special coaching from Jesus, but their growth in understanding progresses at a snail's pace, and they seem to fail utterly at the end. Ironically, the revelatory moment occurs when Jesus dies and his chief executioner recognizes him to be truly the Son of God. Mark's vivid storytelling is intended to draw the audience into the story so that they have the same experiences as the disciples, as the mystery about Jesus is revealed paradoxically through secrets.

Mark's gospel represents a dramatic shift in the gospel tradition. The deeds and teaching of the historical Jesus were first disseminated via oral tradition (see 1 Cor 11:23; 15:3) and shaped by being preached and taught in different contexts. Mark is the first to arrange this tradition into a written narrative of Jesus' ministry, and my work begins with an investigation of the historical framework for Mark's theology in the conviction that history and theology cannot be divorced. It is important to understand, as best as one can, who created this gospel.[12] This first chapter surveys the tradition behind the attribution of the gospel to Mark as Peter's interpreter and rehearses the arguments for the location and date of its writing. I conclude that the author of this gospel was not an unknown person named Mark but the Mark who is known from the casual references in the NT. He was the first to pen a narrative that later became known as a gospel, and his narrative devotedly encapsulated the teaching and preaching of Peter, an eyewitness and a notable influence on the tradition.

Recent reader-oriented approaches give the reader the autonomy to determine the meaning of a text and, in their most extreme expressions, pronounce "the death of the author," so that "the reader, and the reader alone, constructs the meaning of a text utterly indifferent to whatever meaning its author might have intended."[13] My approach assumes that the gospel's meaning cannot be restricted to what an ancient Roman, a modern American, or anyone else might understand from their experiences and culture. Readers may not understand the Jewish context in which Jesus lived, acted, and reacted. They may not catch all of the scriptural allusions that pepper the narrative and are vital for understanding Mark's intent.[14] For Mark, the Scriptures provide the crucial key to unravel the mysterious elements in the life of

11. R. T. France, *The Gospel of Mark* (NIGTC; Grand Rapids: Eerdmans, 2002), 24–25.

12. Many interpreters have concluded that identifying the author of the gospel of Mark is unnecessary. Dennis E. Nineham, *St. Mark* (WPC; Philadelphia: Westminster, 1963), 39, for one, claims that the question "is a *comparatively* unimportant one."

13. Philip Esler, *New Testament Theology: Communion and Community* (Minneapolis: Fortress, 2005), 88. He argues that "the New Testament documents are practical messages intended to directly impact their audiences. They were written to bring their addressees to faith in Christ or to confirm them in that faith in the distinctive cultural context in which they were first published" (p. 118).

14. Esler (ibid., 88–118) strongly refutes those who reject the notion of authorial intent and label it the "intentional fallacy."

Jesus, the Messiah and Son of God, and to unlock God's purposes behind his death and resurrection.[15] Hay notes, "Jesus is first of all *the one who died and rose again*, and, since the narrative is quickly concluded after a brief announcement of the resurrection (16:6), the bulk of the material is devoted to a history which culminates in the cross, which is to say, a history of the Son's *humiliation*."[16] To understand this humiliation and how victory looks like a defeat,[17] Mark requires the audience to interpret it in light of God's purposes secreted in Scripture.

Mark's theological presuppositions emerge in the way he develops the story. Chapter 2 provides a literary reading of the narrative, the way Mark intended for the story to be experienced. The text has a certain kaleidoscopic quality as different facets of Mark's theology take on varying features and emerge in different passages. This characteristic makes it necessary to cover a particular passage more than once in the various sections to draw out fully Mark's theological message.

As noted, Mark provides a brief preview of his theology in the incipit and the introduction (1:1–13) so that the audience has clues about Jesus' divine identity and the fulfillment of God's purposes. Because this section is so important for unveiling Mark's theology, and in particular his Christology, it receives a careful exegetical analysis in chapter 3. While Mark notifies the audience that Jesus is the Messiah and the Son of God, he does not disclose everything to the audience in these extraordinary opening scenes. It serves only as an introduction, in many ways like an orchestral overture that sets the stage for what follows.

Mark's use of christological titles is addressed in chapter 4. Because the titles can be nebulous with different associations and implications, they fail to reveal the whole story about Jesus' identity. Minette de Tillesse concludes that although the Gospel of Mark was not written in order to demonstrate that Jesus is the Son of God in a metaphysical sense, it seems that this is presupposed.[18]

This truth becomes most clear in the enacted Christology, a term I have borrowed from Malbon.[19] It refers to how Mark presents Jesus' identity to his audience through his words and actions. It requires a meticulous exegesis of various passages

15. I fully agree with the conclusions of A. B. Caneday, "Mark's Provocative Use of Scripture in Narration: 'He Was with the Wild Animals and Angels Ministered to Him,'" *BBR* 9 (1999): 20–21:

> Mark, the narrator, uses the Hebrew Bible much as Jesus, in the narrative, uses parables, miracles, and symbolic acts. His use is principally allusive rather than explicit quotation, so that only those who know the Hebrew Scriptures recognize either the biblical references or their significance within the present context. If Mark's readers are to have ears that hear and eyes that see who Jesus truly is, they must exercise their spiritual senses, especially with reference to the Hebrew Scriptures. Proper understanding of Mark's symbols and scriptural allusions does not lie on the surface any more than the explanation of Jesus' parables and miracles does. Mark's technique of telling the story imitates the method of Jesus. As Jesus discloses who he is by way of parables, whether in his teachings or actions, so Mark writes in parables. On the basis of his narrative technique, Mark expects his readers to be able to answer correctly Jesus' question: "Who do you say I am?" (Mark 8:29).

16. Lewis S. Hay, "The Son-of-God Christology in Mark," *JBR* 32 (1964): 108.

17. Martin Hengel, *Crucifixion in the Ancient World and the Folly of the Message of the Cross* (Philadelphia: Fortress, 1977), 7, notes, "The real gods of Greece and Rome could be distinguished from mortal men by the very fact that they were *immortal*—they had absolutely nothing in common with the cross as a sign of shame (αἰσχύνη)."

18. G. Minette de Tillesse, *Le secret messianique dans l'évangile de Marc* (Paris: Cerf, 1968), 362–63.

19. Elizabeth Struthers Malbon, "'Reflected Christology': An Aspect of Narrative 'Christology' in the Gospel of Mark," *PRSt* 26 (1999): 127–45; idem, *Mark's Jesus: Characterization as Narrative Christology* (Waco, TX: Baylor University Press, 2009).

to unpack the high Christology, which has often been unnoticed but is presupposed in the various scenes. The exegesis revealing Mark's enacted Christology comprises chapter 5. Mark presents Jesus through his words and actions as possessing a status that transcends the human. He is God incarnate.

Chapter 6 deals with Mark's presentation of God. Origen (*Princ.* 4.3.14) wrote regarding 1 Corinthians 2:

> Paul did not say that God's judgments were hard to search out but that they could not be searched out at all. He did not say that God's ways were hard to find out but that they were impossible to find out. For however far one may advance in the search and make progress through an increasingly earnest study, even when aided and enlightened in the mind by God's grace, he will never be able to reach the final goal of his inquiries.

Mark's account of God's role in the narrative suggests that he would share Paul's and Origen's judgment. Mark understands God to be wholly other and operating mysteriously behind the scenes. God can be known, however, through the promises in the Jewish Scriptures that find their fulfillment in history in the coming of Jesus as God's Son. Marcus writes, "The God whose advent the Markan Jesus announces, to whom he calls his hearers to turn in penitence and faith, the God whom he trusts to raise him from the dead (an un-Hellenistic concept), is the God of Abraham, Isaac, and Jacob (cf. 12:26), and not of the philosophers (cf. Pascal, 'Memorial,' *Pensées*)."[20] But only the eyes of faith can see in Jesus' ministry, death, and resurrection the revelation of God's power for salvation. Only the eyes of faith can see that God has deigned to take on human flesh and entered this world with its sin and shame. Only the eyes of faith can see God's glory in the paradox of allowing God's Son, the Messiah, to be treated ingloriously and to die on a cross.

For Mark, this world is God's world where God reigns as King, but the godless, in collusion with and under the thrall of satanic powers, resist God's reign. Jesus proclaims at the outset of his ministry in Mark that God's reign is invading the world in a new way; the kingdom of God is the topic examined in chapter 7. The kingdom of God is not some far-off, future hope or a cataclysmic world-ending irruption but a divine reality at work within history and not simply outside of time. It is so near that it can be experienced in this world through the preaching and miracles of Jesus. It transcends and excludes all nationalistic and political connotations and brings a different kind of liberation than political freedom. It is liberation from demonic powers and the stranglehold of human sin.

The so-called messianic secret that has dominated discussion of Mark since Wrede is addressed in chapter 8. In my view, Jesus' identity is not kept secret but is fully revealed through his miraculous deeds and authoritative teaching. The problem, however, is that Jesus, the Messiah and Son of God, was crucified. Justin

20. Joel Marcus, *Mark 1–8* (AB 27; New York: Doubleday, 2000), 71.

Martyr has Rabbi Trypho respond: "It is just this that we cannot comprehend, that you set your hope on one crucified" (*Dial.* 10.3). The mystery is that one cannot understand who Jesus is apart from his destiny to undergo the cross, and only believers recognize this reality after the resurrection.

Many recent studies on Mark consider discipleship to be the gospel's major theme. The nature of discipleship and its requirements, costs, and rewards do take up a major portion of the gospel, and these topics are dealt with in chapters 9 and 10, followed by an analysis of the mission of the church in chapter 11. The invasion of the kingdom of God into this world brings with it enormous claims on individuals who must radically restructure their lives according to God's will. The cosmic battle against Satan and Satan's minions is one battlefield that is pictured in the gospel, but it is not the only one. The kingdom of God confronts humans in the person of Jesus and meets with a divided response. Some submit; others try to repel the invading King. Some will take up their cross and follow Jesus; others will desert him, deride him, or try to destroy him.

Jesus summons and commissions disciples who are his constant companions. They witness his mighty works, receive his public teaching and private instruction, and are given authority. Matera writes, "Just as one cannot understand who Jesus is apart from the cross, so one cannot grasp the true meaning of discipleship unless he or she is willing to follow Jesus 'on the way.' That way, of course, leads to the cross."[21] Therefore doing "God's will" (in 3:35) and becoming a member of Jesus' family is in its most radical sense being willing, like Jesus, to accept even suffering and rejection as being willed by God. This is what Peter fails to do in 8:32, which Jesus characterizes as thinking human thoughts, not the thoughts of God (8:33).

Mark portrays Jesus' disciples as slow on the uptake, laden with a false sense of superiority and self-importance, prone to quarreling, easily discouraged, and just as easily fainthearted in the face of danger. The disciples' various shortcomings in Mark, however, serve to teach the nature and requirements of discipleship to the audience. They can see their own foibles mirrored in those of the disciples. But Mark also drops clear hints about the disciples' subsequent success after Jesus' death and resurrection. Mark's presentation of discipleship makes it clear that success does not hinge on humans mustering faith and courage on their own. Understanding is God's gift (4:11), and success in discipleship and in mission "is ultimately God's act."[22]

The disciples' mission is to take the gospel to the entire world because Jesus came to give his life as a ransom for many (10:45). Mark's theology of atonement, in my opinion, has been largely neglected because it only surfaces explicitly in 10:45 and 14:22–24. This issue is addressed in chapter 12. Once again, Mark conveys his theology through narrative, and a thorough exegesis of various passages is required to bring to light his theological presuppositions about the new epoch in the history of salvation established by Jesus' death and resurrection.

Mark's eschatology becomes the focus of chapter 13, and, like so many issues

21. Frank J. Matera, *What Are They Saying about Mark?* (New York/Mahwah, NJ: Paulist, 1987), 54.

22. Michael Trainor, "The Women, the Empty Tomb, and *That* Final Verse," *TBT* 34 (1996): 181.

in Markan interpretation, no consensus exists. Nevertheless, this topic impinges on Mark's view of God, discipleship, and the task of the church before the end, and therefore is vital for understanding the gospel.

Chapter 14 deals with the gospel's abrupt and puzzling ending and what it means. I understand the intended ending of the gospel to be 16:8, which ties into the incipit or title of the gospel in 1:1, "The beginning of the good news about Jesus the Messiah, the Son of God." The empty tomb is not the end of the gospel, only the beginning. While some see the ending as showing the contrast between the dazzling intensity of God's act and the darkness of human perception in response, I agree instead with Meye that "the gospel concludes, even as it begins, with fulfilled prophecy" (see 1:2–4; 8:31; 9:31; 10:33–34).[23] Jesus' prophecy that he will reunite with his disciples after his resurrection (14:27–28; 16:7) is also certain to be fulfilled.

1.2 The Historical Framework for Mark's Theology

1.2.1 Authorship

The author of this gospel did not identify himself or announce his purposes or methods as other ancient historians did, but Collins thinks that he probably was following the precedent of biblical historians, who also did none of these things.[24] Marcus claims he had no need to do so because he would have been known to the original addressees.[25] This conjecture may be true if Mark was originally intended to be circulated only for a local community, but I would argue that this reserve also stems from a sense of humility. While the majority of writers today want to be given credit for their work and exult in being well reviewed or even becoming a footnote, it is unlikely that an author would attach his own name to a narrative about Jesus, as if to say that this narrative about Jesus Christ is "my gospel."[26]

Is it important to try to unearth the identity of the author of the second gospel? Grant says no:

> It adds nothing to our knowledge of John Mark—of whom we know practically nothing—to attribute this Gospel to him; it adds nothing to our understanding of the Gospel to call him its author, since he is too shadowy a figure; and it adds nothing to our knowledge of the Gospel's content, or to our knowledge of the historical Jesus, to make this attribution.[27]

23. Robert P. Meye, "Mark 16:8—The Ending of Mark's Gospel," *BR* 15 (1969): 41.

24. Adela Yarbro Collins, *Mark: A Commentary* (Hermeneia; Minneapolis: Fortress, 2007), 41. See also Robert A. Guelich, *Mark 1–8:26* (WBC 34a; Dallas: Word, 1989), xxvi.

25. Marcus, *Mark 1–8*, 17.

26. This is quite different from Paul's reference to "my gospel" in Rom 2:16; 16:25; and 2 Tim 2:8, which refers to his proclamation (see 1 Cor 9:18).

27. F. C. Grant, "Gospel according to St. Mark," in *Interpreters Bible* (Nashville: Abingdon, 1951), 7:632. France, *Mark*, 35, argues similarly: "Just when and where the book was written, and by whom, interesting as they must be to historical scholarship, are not questions which are likely to have a major impact on its exegesis." Timothy J. Geddert, *Mark* (BCBC; Scottdale, PA: Herald, 2001), 20, argues that identifying the author is unnecessary because he was not an eyewitness.

He thinks the gospel is to be regarded as an anonymous collection of common tradition. Guelich may be correct that "the identity of the author is more a historical curiosity than an exegetical necessity."[28] Anderson concurs: "The power of the Gospel does not reside in the credentials of the writer.... The gospel carries its own authority as Gospel, as the Evangelist, hiding himself behind his witness to Jesus Christ, surely wanted it to do."[29] But Black recognizes that the effort to identify the author of the gospel is not an antiquarian fool's errand: "If the figure of Mark informed, in some sense and to some degree, the church's 'apostolic tradition,' then the reclamation of that figure's contribution is not religiously irrelevant, even if, for Christians, it is not religiously essential."[30]

The work of form critics fostered a widespread assumption that "there was an indefinite number of totally unrecorded and unremembered figures in the history of early Christianity who have left absolutely no mark except as the supposed authors of much of its greatest literature."[31] The collections of oral tradition in the community, not a literary personality, according to form criticism, shaped the gospel framework.[32] Hengel challenges this widespread supposition. He claims, "The history of earliest Christianity in the first sixty or seventy years ... did not get lost in an anonymous, unbounded, and imaginary setting; it can still be traced and was influenced by the authority of particular persons who were generally known at the time."[33] The Gospel of Mark may have been little read and little esteemed in the early church, but it did attract more statements regarding its authorship than any other work. The patristic tradition unanimously attributes this gospel to Mark, Peter's close associate. It makes sense. Who else would have such a repository of Jesus' teaching and actions? This link to an eyewitness may suggest, for example, that the messianic claims of Jesus and his interpretation of the meaning of his death as a redemptive act of God may go back to Jesus' own self-understanding. Riesner contrasts this view with that of Bultmann in one of his last publications. Bultmann believed that the only certainty about Jesus' death was that he was crucified by the Romans, which was the death of a political criminal. He theorizes:

> This execution can hardly be understood as the internal necessary consequence of his work; rather, it happened because of a misunderstanding of his work as political. It was then—historically speaking—senseless fate. Whether or how Jesus found some sense in it, we cannot know. The possibility that he broke down should not be dismissed.[34]

28. Guelich, *Mark 1–8:26*, xxix.

29. Hugh Anderson, *The Gospel of Mark* (NCB; London: Oliphants, 1976), 31–32.

30. C. Clifton Black, *Mark: Images of an Apostolic Interpreter* (Columbia, SC: University of South Carolina Press, 1994), 15.

31. John A. T. Robinson, *Redating the New Testament* (Philadelphia: Westminster, 1976), 347.

32. Martin Dibelius, *From Tradition to Gospel* (trans. Bertram Lee Woolf; New York: Scribner's, 1935), 2–3.

33. Martin Hengel, *Acts and the History of Earliest Christianity* (trans. John Bowden; Philadelphia: Fortress, 1980), 27.

34. Rainer Riesner, "Martin Hengel's Quest for Jesus and the Synoptic Question," in *Earliest Christian History: History, Literature, and Theology: Essays from the Tyndale Fellowship in Honor of Martin Hengel* (ed. Michael F. Bird and Jason Maston; WUNT 2/320; Tübingen: Mohr Siebeck, 2012), 177, citing and translating Rudolf Bultmann, *Das Verhältnis der urchristlichen Christusbotschaft zum historischen Jesus* (SHAW, Philosophisch-Historische Klasse 1960/3; Heidelberg: C. Winter, 1962), 12.

If it can be reasonably established that an historical continuity exists between the tradition about Jesus and the historical Jesus, then the tradition regarding Jesus' understanding of his death that is found in Mark's gospel should not be dismissed simply as the inventive and wishful thinking of anonymous post-Easter Christian communities. The historicity of the tradition recorded in this gospel does not depend on its author being John Mark, who was Peter's interpreter. But it does strengthen the case.

1.2.1.1 Arguments for the Conventional View That the Author Was John Mark

1.2.1.1.1 The Title "According to Mark"

The phrase "According to Mark" (א B) or "Gospel (or Good News) according to Mark" (A D L W Θ f^{13}) appears in most extant manuscripts either at the beginning and/or end of the text or in a side margin. This title would not have been in the original copy but was added by copyists at a later point when the gospel was being circulated to other communities. Practical necessity prompted it, since churches would have needed a title to distinguish this gospel from other works on the shelf or in the book chest and to inform hearers which gospel was being read in worship. This development likely would have occurred early on and certainly by the late first century when other gospels were in circulation.[35]

The prepositional phrase "according to Mark" would have differentiated it from Matthew's, Luke's, or John's gospels and would have helped organize the library. Hengel observes that if the gospels had circulated anonymously, we would expect that "because of the pressing need to distinguish them in community libraries a variation of titles would have inevitably arisen, whereas in the case of the canonical Gospels (in contrast to that of countless apocryphal writings) we can detect nothing of this."[36] The title serves as early testimony that the gospel was widely attributed to Mark.

1.2.1.1.2 Mark in the New Testament

It is often repeated that "Mark" (*Marcus*) was one of the most common names in the Roman world (e.g., Marcus Tullius Cicero, Marcus Junius Brutus, Marcus Anthony, Marcus Aurelius).[37] It is then assumed that there would have been several "Marks" in the primitive church, so the author could be an unknown Mark. Nineham therefore claims that it is precarious to make assumptions about the identity of Mark.[38]

35. Martin Hengel, *Studies in the Gospel of Mark* (trans. John Bowden; London: SCM, 1985), 74–81. He argues that people would have been suspicious of anonymous works missing titles (pp. 170–72, n. 57). Black, *Images*, 151, mistakenly claims that some copies circulated anonymously. Richard Bauckham, "The Gospel of Mark: Origins and Eyewitness," in *Earliest Christian History: Essays from the Tyndale Fellowship in Honor of Martin Hengel* (ed. Michael F. Bird and Jason Maston; WUNT 2/320; Tübingen: Mohr Siebeck, 2012), 147, n. 15, shows that this conclusion results from a misreading of Adamantius' *De recta in deum fide*. James G. Crossley, *The Date of Mark's Gospel: Insight from the Law in Earliest Christianity* (JSNTSup 266; London/New York: T&T Clark, 2004), 15–17, tries, unsuccessfully in my view, to counter Hengel's arguments.

36. Hengel, *Studies*, 82.

37. See Henry Barclay Swete, *The Gospel according to Mark* (London: Macmillan, 1913), xiii–xiv, for the inscriptional evidence.

38. Nineham, *St. Mark*, 39.

References to Mark in the NT, however, do not distinguish him from some other "Mark," which suggests that Mark was well known. Luke does give his name as John Mark (Acts 12:12, 25; 15:37), a Hebrew name and a second Latin name, and the addition of "Mark" serves to tell him apart from the other John who was the brother of James (Acts 12:2). In Acts 13:5 and 13, he is identified only as John. In Acts 15:39, he is identified only as Mark. Black notes that when Mark is first introduced in Acts, it is "in order to identify his mother, Mary; it is not the other way around, as we might have anticipated."[39] This debut implies that Mark is the better-known figure, since it is rare for persons to be identified by their offspring (see Mark 15:40). It may suggest that when Luke wrote Acts, Mark was already associated with the gospel and was known beyond his local community.

The argument that "Mark" was too common a name to assume that the author of the gospel was the same John Mark mentioned elsewhere in the NT has been seriously challenged by Bauckham. First, he points out that it may have been a common praenomen, "but no Roman citizen would be known by his praenomen alone." He states, "If Cicero or Brutus or Marcus Aurelius, Mark Antony (Marcus Antonius) had written a Gospel, it would not have been called the Gospel according to Mark."[40] He infers from this evidence that the Mark behind the gospel must have been either a slave or a non-Roman. It is highly unlikely that he was a slave and more likely that he was a non-Roman. Second, the collection of the Jewish inscriptions from the western Diaspora before AD 200 reveals that the name Mark, including John Mark in Acts, appears only five times out of the 2,500 named male individuals.[41] The name was rare among Jews! He concludes from this evidence, "Among Jewish Christian leaders or teachers, such as could have written a Gospel or were likely to have a Gospel attributed to them, there may well have been only one Mark."[42]

That one Mark would be the Mark mentioned in Acts and in Paul's and Peter's letters. In Acts 12:25 and 13:5, John Mark is reintroduced as the junior member of the missionary team of Paul and Barnabas. He is colorlessly described as their "helper" or "assistant." One can only speculate if the term in Acts 13:5 for "assistant" (*hypēretēs*) is an allusion to Luke 1:2, "just as they were handed down to us by those who from the first were eyewitnesses and servants of the word." Since the term was used in the papyri "for a man who handles documents and delivers their contents" to others,[43] Byrskog suggests that he "served Barnabas and Paul with material that aided them in their preaching activity."[44]

This abrupt mention of Mark as the missionaries head out from Antioch to Cyprus prepares for the notice in 13:13 that he leaves them when they set sail for

39. Black, *Images*, 27.

40. Bauckham, "The Gospel of Mark: Origins and Eyewitness," 159.

41. Ibid., 160.

42. Ibid., 161. This fact explains why Marcus, *Mark 1–8*, 18, could say that "there is only one Mark known to us from early church history."

43. B. T. Holmes, "Luke's Description of John Mark," *JBL* 54 (1935): 68 (63–72); see also R. O. P. Taylor, "The Ministry of Mark," *ExpTim* 54 (1942–43): 136–38.

44. Samuel Byrskog, *Story as History, History as Story* (WUNT 123; Tübingen: Mohr Siebeck, 2000), 279.

Pamphylia and returns to Jerusalem. Luke offers no reason at this point to explain why he departs from Barnabas and Paul, and it seems to be a fruitless exercise to try to guess why.[45] When it is first narrated, Mark's return does not seem to be of any consequence, but it emerges later as a bone of contention between Barnabas and Paul. A potentially ruinous breach in the unity of the church over the Gentile issue is averted by the Jerusalem Council (Acts 15), but a rupture does occur in Paul's relationship with Barnabas when Barnabas desires to take Mark with them on their next missionary venture (Acts 15:36–41). It creates a sharp disagreement as Paul interprets Mark's earlier leave-taking as desertion (Acts 15:38; see the use of the verb in Luke 8:13), and he considers him unfit for their new task. As a result of the split, Barnabas sets sail for Cyprus with Mark, and Paul sets off for Syria, Cilicia, and beyond with Silas.

Barnabas and Mark drop out of Luke's story in Acts at this point, and he does not narrate what happened to them. Luke does not record this break-up episode to vilify Mark any more than the gospel accounts of Peter's denial of Jesus were recorded to disparage him. Factors other than their disagreement over Mark may have also caused Paul and Barnabas to go their separate ways. In Gal 2:11–14, Paul recounts a crisis when Jewish Christians in Antioch abandoned eating with Gentile Christians after the arrival of certain men from James. He despairs, "By their hypocrisy even Barnabas was led astray" (2:13). Luke does not narrate this incident in Acts, and he has no interest in dissecting the disagreement between Paul and Barnabas to delineate all of its causes. He may have used the clash between Paul and Barnabas over Mark simply to portray the sovereignty of God working through human weakness[46] or to show that even division between leading missionaries will not ultimately hinder the mission.[47]

Paul's mention of Mark in his letters, assuming that he refers to the same Mark, which I think is reasonable, reveals that Mark must have redeemed himself in Paul's eyes. In Col 4:10, Mark is included in greeting the Colossians and is identified as the cousin of Barnabas. The readers have received instructions about him and are urged to welcome him if he comes to them. He is also mentioned in the greeting to Philemon (v. 24) and identified with Aristarchus, Demas, and Luke as Paul's fellow workers. In 2 Tim 4:11, Paul asks Timothy to get Mark and bring him along

45. Speculation that Mark was homesick, lost his enthusiasm, could not bear the danger and rigors of the journey, was frightened by strange places, or resented his cousin Barnabas playing second fiddle to Paul reads too much into the text. Nor is there any warrant in the proposal that he sparked the conflict recounted in Acts 15 by informing those in Judea what happened on the missionary journey recorded in Acts 13. The *Acts of Barnabas*, pseudonymously ascribed to John Mark, attributes his actions to a miraculous vision and the direction of the Holy Spirit. Black, *Images*, 40, argues that Mark disapproved of the increasing shift toward Gentiles. He contends that the statement in Acts 15:37 that Mark "had not continued with them in the work" refers to the "work for which Barnabas and Saul were specially set apart by the Holy Spirit," namely, "the propagation of faith among Gentiles." In Acts 14:27, Luke records that God had opened a door of faith for the Gentiles, and Black infers from this that Mark recoiled at this change of course. He did not "throw in the towel" but "recalcitrantly had given up on the Christian mission to Gentiles." If this explanation is accurate, and if the account in Acts refers to the same Mark who wrote the gospel, then the gospel with its positive perspective on the Gentile mission shows that at some point a dramatic change in his views occurred.

46. Ajith Fernando, *Acts* (NIVAC; Grand Rapids: Zondervan, 1998), 431.

47. Jacob Jervell, *Die Apostelgeschichte* (KEK; Göttingen: Vandenhoeck & Ruprecht, 1998), 409.

"because he is helpful to me in my ministry."[48] Both Silas (Silvanus) and Mark are mentioned together as being with Peter in 1 Pet 5:12–13. In giving greetings to the recipients, Silvanus is identified as "a faithful brother," who wrote the letter, and Mark is distinguished as "my son," who joins the sister church in Babylon (presumably Rome, see Rev 14:8; 16:19; 17:5; 18:1–24).[49] Barnabas had significant contact with Peter in Jerusalem (Acts 4:32–37; Gal 2:1–10) and in Antioch (Gal 2:11–13). Since he was Mark's cousin (Col 4:10), it is not a stretch to assume that Mark would have developed a significant association with Peter. Peter goes to Mark's mother's house in Acts 12:12 after his release from prison.[50] Even if Colossians and 1 Peter were pseudonymous, they provide first-century evidence of Mark's good reputation and involvement in the Gentile mission.

Acts describes the transformation of Peter's views toward the propagation of the faith among the Gentiles through a vision (Acts 10:1–48). It is likely that Mark was influenced by Peter and changed his view, and it is also likely that he and Paul reconciled.[51] Dunn concludes, "Mark must rank as one of the few effective bridge figures between different strands of the early Christian mission (perhaps having been one of the casualties of the earlier disagreements)."[52] Bird goes further in his contention that the gospel of Mark represents "*Petrine testimony shaped into an evangelical narrative conducive to Pauline proclamation.*"[53]

1.2.1.1.3 Ancient Testimony about the Authorship of the Gospel

The ancient testimony unanimously links this gospel to Mark. In the NT references, he ranks at best as a minor figure, which makes it improbable that he would have risen to the top as the choice for the pseudonymous authorship of this gospel. Why would someone make up a tradition about Mark as the author of this gospel were it not true since in the NT he is not identified as a disciple or a leading figure in the early church? Even as a minor deputy of Paul and Peter, he played a less-than-heroic role in Acts as a source of discord between Paul and Barnabas.[54] The apocryphal gospels are identified with apostles or notable figures in the NT: Philip, Thomas, Bartholomew, Peter, Judas, James, Mary, and Nicodemus. Mark hardly compares. Mark's obscurity in the NT, then, might incline one to take at face value the tradition

48. Paul uses the same term "helpful" (*euchrēstos*; see 2 Tim 2:21) in Phlm 11 with a play on words to describe Onesimus, which means "useful": "Formerly he was useless to you, but now he has become useful both to you and to me." Paul does not summon Mark to work as his domestic servant but to work in his ministry.

49. As Paul called Onesimus "my son" (Phlm 10) because he came to faith through his preaching, Peter may call Mark "my son" for the same reason when he was preaching in Jerusalem.

50. Detlev Dormeyer, *Das Markus-Evangelium* (Darmstadt: Wissenschaftliche Buchgesellschaft, 2005), 147.

51. Ron Chernow, *Alexander Hamilton* (New York: Penguin, 2004), 151–53, narrates that a bitter Alexander Hamilton left George Washington as his aide-de-camp during the Revolutionary War after a slight reprimand. Despite General Washington's displeasure and dismay over his departure, they later reconciled, and he gave Hamilton a coveted field command. When Washington became President, he chose Hamilton to be his Secretary of the Treasury.

52. James D. G. Dunn, *Colossians and Philemon* (NIGTC; Grand Rapids: Eerdmans, 1996), 276.

53. Michael F. Bird, "Mark: Interpreter of Peter and Disciple of Paul," in *Paul and the Gospels: Christologies, Conflicts, and Convergences* (ed. Michael F. Bird and Joel Willitts; LNTS 411; London/New York: T&T Clark, 2011), 32. The italics are his.

54. Collins, *Mark*, 5, states it more boldly: Acts "presents a fairly negative portrait of Mark as a backslider or reluctant missionary to the Gentiles."

that Mark was the author of the gospel bearing his name. What that tradition says about Mark's authorship of the gospel, however, is difficult to untangle.

1.2.1.1.3.1 The Evidence of Papias

Papias, Bishop of Hierapolis, in the vicinity of Colossae and Laodicea, wrote *Exposition of the Lord's Oracles* in five books near the beginning of the second century. His writings are now lost, but fragments of his comments about Mark have been passed on by Eusebius.[55] Irenaeus, writing around AD 180, identified Papias as a "hearer of John and companion of Polycarp" (*Haer.* 5.33.4).[56] Eusebius, writing around AD 324 in Caesarea, also places him during the time of Polycarp and Ignatius (*Hist. eccl.* 3.36.1–2; 3.39.1). The date for Papias's work was probably around AD 110 or possibly as early as 101, but the sources for his statements about Mark would have lived in the first century.[57] Eusebius records that Papias preferred "the word of a living and surviving voice" (*Hist. eccl.* 3.39.4) to that which could be gotten from books. Hierapolis was on a main road between Syria and Ephesus, and Papias would query those passing through who had been followers of the elders to learn "what Andrew or Peter or Philip or Thomas or James or John or Matthew, or any other of the Lord's disciples, had said, and what Aristion and the presbyter John, the Lord's disciples, were saying" (*Hist. eccl.* 3.39.1–4).[58] Gundry notes, "If Papias writes 101–108, then, the tradition that he passes on reaches back into the first century," and "the chain of tradition" is "(1) the apostles; (2) those who heard the apostles; and (3) Papias."[59] Bauckham points out that the relevant passage from Papias that is quoted below refers to "an earlier period in his life, the time during which he was collecting oral reports of the words and deeds of Jesus," which Bauckham dates to around AD 80. He contends that few have appreciated the significance of the relatively short difference in time between Papias's completion of his writing and the time about which he reminisces.[60]

Eusebius (*Hist. eccl.* 3.39.15) records Papias's report from the "elder," presumably the apostle John, regarding Mark and Matthew to support his view regarding apostolic succession, "the successions of the sacred apostles, covering the period stretching from our Saviour to ourselves" (*Hist. eccl.* 1.1.1).[61]

55. For an extensive discussion of research on Papias, see William R. Schoedel, "Papias," in *ANRW* Part 2, *Principat* 27/1 (ed. W. Haase; Berlin/New York: de Gruyter, 1992), 235–70; and Charles E. Hill, "Papias of Hierapolis," *ExpTim* 117 (2006): 309–15.

56. The area of Phrygia, where Hierapolis is located, was Christianized early (Acts 16:6; 18:23). Eusebius (*Hist. eccl.* 8.11.1) reports that a little town in Phrygia whose "inhabitants were all Christians, every man of them" was attacked during the time of the Diocletian persecution, and the Christians, along with young children and women, were burned for refusing to commit idolatry.

57. Vernon Bartlet, "Papias's 'Exposition': Its Date and Contents," in *Amicitiae Corolla: A Volume of Essays Presented to James Rendel Harris, D.Litt. on the Occasion of His Eightieth Birthday* (ed. H. G. Wood; London: University of London Press, 1933), 15–44, dates his work to A.D. 110. Robert W. Yarbrough, "The Date of Papias: A Reassessment," *JETS* 26 (1983): 181–91, dates it even earlier.

58. Papias does not appear to distinguish between the terms "elders" and "the disciples of the Lord," see Robert H. Gundry, *Mark: A Commentary on His Apology for the Cross* (Grand Rapids: Eerdmans, 1993), 1029–30.

59. Gundry, *Mark*, 1029.

60. Richard Bauckham, *Jesus and the Eyewitnesses* (Grand Rapids: Eerdmans, 2006), 14.

61. Pieter J. J. Botha, "The Historical Setting of Mark's Gospel: Problems and Possibilities," *JSNT* 51 (1993): 36. Papias does not claim to have heard this tradition directly from John, but from those close to John who reported what he had said. Eusebius does express contempt for Papias's "very little intelligence" (*Hist. eccl.* 3.39.13) because of the latter's belief in a literal thousand-year utopian reign of Christ on earth after the general resurrection. Eusebius reflects a strong bias against the book of Revelation: see Gundry, *Mark*, 1032–34; and Schoedel, "Papias," 248–49.

> And this the presbyter [elder] used to say: "Having become the interpreter of Peter, Mark wrote accurately—not, indeed, in order—as much as he remembered of the things said or done by the Lord. For he had neither heard the Lord nor followed him, though later on, as I said, [he followed] Peter, who gave teaching in the form of *chreiai*,[62] but not making, as it were, an arrangement of the Lord's oracles, so that Mark did nothing wrong in thus writing down single points as he remembered. For to one thing he gave attention, to leave out nothing of what he had heard and to falsify nothing in them.[63]

Many have challenged the credibility of these statements. Marxsen calls them "historically worthless,"[64] and Conzelmann dismisses them as "twaddle."[65] Niederwimmer contends that Papias invented this fiction "to endow the Gospel with apostolic authority."[66] Marcus agrees that Papias seems to protest too much Mark's connection with Peter to confer a secondhand apostolicity on the gospel.[67] That aim may arouse suspicion, but Marcus concedes that Papias's defensive stance does not negate the truth of what he says.[68]

It is telling, however, that in the same breath that Papias affirms the gospel's apostolic connection to Peter, he implicitly criticizes this gospel. He defends Mark in a rather backhanded way. Mark was not an original disciple and not an eyewitness of the events he records, but he did the best he could, accurately writing down points as he remembered the teaching of Peter without falsifying them. Papias remarks that Mark's compilation of Peter's teaching was not "in order," however. He seems to imply that "*Peter* spoke ad hoc and incompletely, and we should not fault *Mark* for recording unconnected bits of information."[69] Kennedy contends that Mark followed the procedures of ancient composition and made notes on Peter's preaching and teaching as he remembered it. What is not in order are these preliminary notes. He asserts:

62. Marion C. Moeser, *The Anecdote in Mark, the Classical World and the Rabbis* (JSNTSup 227; Sheffield: Sheffield Academic, 2002), 20–21, proposes this definition of the "anecdote": "a brief narrative, either oral or written, describing an incident, including its setting, which involves one or more persons and which focuses on an action, saying, or dialogue; the function of an anecdote is to entertain, instruct, relate an historical incident, characterize a person, or authoritatively legitimate a specific opinion, a specific practice, or a broader view of reality." Seneca (*Ep.* 33.7) states that what the Greeks call *chreia* are simple, easily comprehended by the young mind that cannot as yet hold more, and can be learned by heart.

63. Eusebius, *Hist. eccl.* 3.39.15. This more literal translation comes from Byrskog, *Story as History*, 272.

64. Willi Marxsen, *Introduction to the New Testament* (trans. G. Buswell; Philadelphia: Fortress, 1968), 143.

65. Hans Conzelmann, *History of Primitive Christianity* (trans. John E. Steely; Nashville: Abingdon, 1973), 153.

66. Kurt Niederwimmer, "Johannes Markus und die Frage nach dem Verfasser des zweiten Evangeliums," *ZNW* 58 (1967): 185–88. See also Rudolf Pesch, *Das Markusevangelium* (HTKNT; Freiburg/Basel/Vienna: Herder, 1984), 1:4–7. Raymond E. Brown, *An Introduction to the New Testament* (New York: Doubleday, 1997), 160, who seems to grant limited credibility to Papias, contends, "Papias could … be reporting in a dramatized and simplified way that in his writing about Jesus, Mark reorganized and rephrased a content derived from a standard type of preaching that was considered apostolic."

67. Since other writings that emerged in the second century attempt to link their origins to Peter, for example, the *Gospel of Peter*, *the Apocalypse of Peter*, *the Acts of Peter*, Walter Bauer, *Orthodoxy and Heresy in Earliest Christianity* (ed. Robert Kraft and Gerhard Krodel; Philadelphia: Fortress, 1971), argues that Papias was trying to counter gnostic attempts to co-opt Peter as the guarantor of their tradition. Papias, however, shows no evidence of anti-Gnostic apologetic. Gundry, *Mark*, 1027, comments, "The failure of Irenaeus and Eusebius to quote Papias against Gnosticism is best explained by Papias's having said nothing against Gnosticism because he wrote before it became a serious threat." These writings attributed to Peter also appear much later than Mark.

68. Marcus, *Mark 1–8*, 22–23. Hengel, *Studies*, 47–53, and Gundry, *Mark*, 1026–45, defend Papias's veracity.

69. Hugh M. Humphrey, *From Q to "Secret" Mark: A Composition History of the Earliest Narrative Theology* (London/New York: T&T Clark, 2006), 13.

> Papias is not describing the actual composition of Mark's Gospel; he is describing the note-taking that was preliminary to composition. Mark's note-taking may have been in Aramaic, and the result was an abstract of Peter's sermons. Subsequently, of course, Mark put the material into narrative order, thus forming a gospel in Greek on the basis of these notes, but Papias is not here telling us about this latter stage.[70]

Eusebius, however, who transmits this tradition, seems to understand that he was talking about the Gospel of Mark. Others point out that Papias refers to "the things said and done by the Lord," which more aptly describes a version of Mark without the Passion Narrative.[71] But why would "the things said and done by the Lord" exclude what is recorded in the Passion Narrative in which Mark records Jesus also saying and doing many things that were foreshadowed in the early chapters of Mark? The matter is complicated, but if Papias were indeed describing the final composition of the gospel, then Black explains his reasoning: "If Mark's account seems lacking or disordered, then that actually redounds to the fidelity of his reporting and attests to a premeditated decision 'to falsify nothing [what he had heard].'"[72]

Those who find Papias's testimony to be of no value may do so because it controverts their own theories. One can be skeptical of the skepticism of NT scholars, because if one dismisses Papias's testimony, "then only speculation as to the geographical and authorial origin is left."[73] Bird expresses optimism about Papias's testimony "if only for the reason that no serious alternative ever presented itself for consideration in the early church."[74] Whether Papias refers to Mark taking down notes from Peter's preaching and teaching or commenting on the final composition of the gospel, he provides plausible evidence that Mark's gospel is fundamentally linked to an eyewitness, namely, Peter.

1.2.1.1.3.1.1 Mark's Lack of "Order." That Mark compared poorly to the orderly structure of Matthew or to the chronology of John's gospel with its record of a three-year ministry may be behind Papias's comments about Mark's lack of order. "Order" (*taxis*), however, need not refer to chronological order but may be used here as a rhetorical term that denotes a "rhetorically and logically effective order."[75] In stressing Mark's accuracy in recording Peter's teaching, Papias uses language that is reminiscent of Luke 1:1–4. Luke insists that he writes an "orderly account" (Luke

70. George Kennedy, "Classical and Christian Source Criticism," in *The Relationships among the Gospels: An Interdisciplinary Dialogue* (ed. William O. Walker Jr.; San Antonio: Trinity University Press, 1978), 148.

71. Humphrey, *From Q to "Secret" Mark*, believes that Mark's gospel in its present form represents a number of different stages in its composition by Mark. He cites Martin Kähler's, *The So-Called Historical Jesus and the Historic, Biblical Christ* (trans. Carl E. Braaten; Philadelphia: Fortress, 1964), 80, much repeated one-liner that Mark is a Passion Narrative with an extended introduction. What Kähler actually writes is this: "To state the matter somewhat provocatively, one could call the Gospels passion narratives with extended introductions." He uses the plural to refer to all the Gospels but then cites Mark 8:27–9:13 as the prime example.

72. Black, *Images*, 92.

73. John Granger Cook, *Roman Attitudes toward the Christians: From Claudius to Hadrian* (WUNT 2/261; Tübingen: Mohr Siebeck, 2010), 102.

74. Bird, "Mark: Interpreter of Peter and Disciple of Paul," 31.

75. Ben Witherington, III, *The Gospel of Mark: A Socio-Rhetorical Commentary* (Grand Rapids: Eerdmans, 2001), 22.

1:3). He does not refer to a chronological sequence of what happened but to a coherent, sequential arrangement of the material so that the reader has clear impressions.[76] The objective is to present the reader with the truth in a plotted narrative and to convince the reader of that truth, not to present just the facts.[77]

Papias's observations suggest that according to his standards Mark's work consisted of a collage of traditions faithfully passed on but rhetorically ineffectual.[78] Witherington attributes the problem of a lack of "order" to Mark's use of *chreiai*. The term appears in Papias's statement that Peter adapted his teachings to "the needs" [*chreiai*] of his hearers. Witherington states that Peter used "the most elemental rhetorical way of condensing material into a persuasive historical, biographical anecdote."[79] Gundry believes that the lack of order refers to "gaps" in the narrative and tallies with Papias's statement that Peter told in his oral addresses "as much as he remembered of the things said or done by the Lord" and Mark wrote "as he remembered." The result, he claims, is what Aristotle classified as "an episodic narrative of loose-knit anecdotes whose progression from one to another is ungoverned by the laws of inevitability or even of probability (*Poet.* 9.11–13; contrast the elder's going on to say that by contrast with Mark, Matthew 'arranged' [*synetazato*] the oracles)."[80] Witherington believes that Mark followed the lead of Peter and did not adhere to the dictates found in elementary rhetorical handbooks[81] by using the *chreia* as a "thesis statement followed by elaboration of arguments in rhetorically effective order."[82] Witherington also notes that Papias's affirmation that Mark "took forethought for one thing, not to omit any of the things that he had heard nor to state them falsely," which matches the concern of Theon that "the two greatest faults *chreiai* can have are either leaving out essential information or telling what is false."[83]

A careful reading of this excerpt from Papias reveals that his purpose, as opposed to Eusebius's purpose, was not to attempt to prove that Mark's gospel was connected to Peter and was therefore apostolic. Hengel comments that Papias's statements are "far too detached and critical" if they were meant "to guarantee that apostolic derivation of the Second Gospel."[84] From his perspective, Mark's gospel fell short by being disordered. Black, I think, correctly reads Papias's intent. He sought "to

76. Richard Longenecker, "Acts," in *The Expositor's Bible Commentary: Luke-Acts* (rev. ed.; ed. Tremper Longman III and David E. Garland; Grand Rapids: Zondervan, 2007), 10:672.

77. David E. Garland, *Luke* (ZECNT; Grand Rapids: Zondervan, 2011), 55. David P. Moessner, "The Appeal and Power of Poetics (Luke 1:1–4)," in *Jesus and the Heritage of Israel: Luke's Narrative Claim upon Israel's Legacy* (ed. David P. Moessner; Harrisburg, PA: Trinity Press International, 1999), 118, notes that three key terms ("to compile," "followed," and "closely") in Luke's preface appear in Papias's comparison of Mark and Matthew (Eusebius, *Hist. eccl.* 3.39.15–16). He contends that Luke's "'proper' narrative ... has set the standard for the critique."

78. He may also have regarded Mark's gospel to be woefully incomplete with its abrupt ending.

79. Witherington, *Mark*, 22. He argues that ancient biographers "edited source material *down* to *chreia* form, not creating the material out of thin air" (pp. 11–12).

80. Gundry, *Mark*, 1036–37.

81. The *progymnasmata* were a set of graduated, from rudimentary to complex, exercises designed to prepare students in the concepts and strategies of rhetoric. See George A. Kennedy, ed. and trans.; *Progymnasmata: Greek Textbooks of Prose Composition and Rhetoric* (Writings from the Greco-Roman World 10; Atlanta: Society of Biblical Literature, 2003).

82. Witherington, *Mark*, 23.

83. Ibid. See Ralph P. Martin, *Mark: Evangelist and Theologian* (Grand Rapids: Zondervan, 1972), 82.

84. Hengel, *Studies*, 4.

justify his [Mark's] literary technique by appealing to its fidelity to Petrine teaching, as it was heard and remembered (*Hist. eccl.* 3.39.14–15)."[85] He tentatively suggests that Papias defends

> Markan literature not so much against the proposed superiority of other written documents, as against the acknowledged superiority of *oral traditions* about the Lord. Therefore, "Mark did not miss the mark *in writing down* individual items as he remembered them" (emphasis added). Why? Because "[Mark left] out nothing *of what he had heard*" (again, my emphasis). For Papias, Mark's very disorganization was the clearest, positive evidence that his literary endeavor had falsified nothing in an oral tradition that was equally disordered.[86]

1.2.1.1.3.1.2 Mark's Connection to the Apostle Peter. What is important to note is that Papias accepts the report from the elder John that Mark's gospel derives from the preaching and teaching of the apostle Peter. If this connection were not historically accurate, how and why did it arise? It would be odd if the impetus for it came from the brief reference to Mark in 1 Pet 5:13. Silvanus is also mentioned in 1 Pet 5:12 as a faithful brother and the one through whom Peter wrote "briefly." He would have been a far more likely candidate than Mark if someone were seeking an imagined author of this gospel to pass on Peter's traditions. Silvanus (Silas) was also an intrepid associate of Paul (Acts 15:22, 27, 32, 40; 16:19, 25, 29; 17:4, 10, 14–15; 18:5; 2 Cor 1:19; 1 Thess 1:1; and 2 Thess 1:1) and did not bear the onus of having left Paul and Barnabas on mission as did Mark (Acts 13:13).

What Papias meant by describing Mark as "the interpreter of Peter" is also disputed. Did Mark translate his preaching into Greek or Latin from Aramaic?[87] Since Peter lived in Galilee, he was probably bilingual and may not have needed someone to translate his preaching. Did Mark's interpreting imply that he adapted and explained what he heard Peter teach, as Ezra did in interpreting the law for the people (Neh 8:8)? The phrase "as much as he remembered of the things said or done by the Lord" implies that Mark heard Peter's teaching and only transmitted it later to others. It may also intimate that he composed his narrative from Peter's anecdotes about Jesus after the apostle had died.[88]

To conclude, Papias's statement asserts that Mark was not an eyewitness, depended primarily on the preaching of Peter, perhaps rephrasing it, and laid it out according to his own order.

1.2.1.1.3.2 Other Ancient Testimony

Mark's connection to Peter is taken for granted in later tradition. An enigmatic link between the gospel of Mark and Peter is found in Justin Martyr (*Dial.* 106.3; c. AD 100–165). He appears to refer to Mark 3:16–17 when he writes:

85. Black, *Images*, 92.
86. Ibid., 92–93.
87. Terence Y. Mullins, "Papias on Mark's Gospel," *VC* 14 (1960): 216–24, argues that Mark translated Peter's written testimony.
88. It does not exclude the probability that Mark also used sources other than Peter.

> And ... it is said that [Jesus] changed the name of one of the apostles to Peter; and ... it is written in his memoirs that this so happened, as well that he changed the names of two other brothers, the sons of Zebedee, to Boanerges, which means "the sons of thunder."

The phrase "his memoirs" probably refers to Peter's memoirs about Jesus. The moniker Boanerges occurs only in Mark.

The details from other statements from this era seem to be no more than "embellishments" of the Papias tradition with "no factual basis," but they do testify to the overall acceptance of Mark's relationship to Peter and that he was author of the gospel attributed to him.[89] Eusebius (*Hist. eccl.* 2.15.1–2) also cites a tradition from Clement, Bishop of Alexandria (c. AD 150–215), which, he says, is quoted in the sixth book of his *Hypotyposes* and is confirmed by Papias:

> But a great light of religion shone on the minds of the hearers of Peter, so that they were not satisfied with a single hearing or with the unwritten teaching of the divine proclamation, but with every kind of exhortation besought Mark, whose Gospel is extant, seeing that he was Peter's follower, to leave them a written statement of the teaching given them verbally, nor did they cease until they had persuaded him, and so became the cause of the Scripture called the Gospel of Mark. And they say that the Apostle, knowing by the revelation of the spirit to him what had been done, was pleased at their zeal, and ratified the scripture for study in the churches.[90]

He adds (*Hist. eccl.* 2.15.2) that Clement gives this account:

> He also says that Peter mentions Mark in his first Epistle, and that he composed this in Rome itself, which they say that he himself indicates, referring to the city metaphorically as Babylon, in the words: "the elect one in Babylon greets you, and Marcus my son" [1 Pet 5:13].

89. F. F. Bruce, "The Date and Character of Mark," in *Jesus and the Politics of His Day* (ed. Ernst Bammel and C. F. D. Moule; Cambridge: Cambridge University Press, 1984), 75.

90. Eusebius (*Hist. eccl.* 2.16.1–2.17.1) continues his account with a tradition about Mark establishing churches in Alexandria and Peter preaching in Rome that is not attributed to anyone in particular:

> They say that Mark was the first to be sent to preach in Egypt the Gospel which he had also put into writing, and was the first to establish churches in Alexandria itself. The number of men and women who were there converted at the first attempt was so great and their asceticism was so extraordinarily philosophic, that Philo thought it right to describe their conduct and assemblies and meals and all the rest of their manner of life. Tradition says that he came to Rome in the time of Claudius to speak to Peter, who was at that time preaching to those there.

Eusebius (*Hist. eccl.* 6.14.5–7) again cites from the *Hypotyposes* of Clement of Alexandria, who assumes that Mark wrote the gospel during Peter's lifetime:

> And again in the same books Clement has inserted a tradition of the primitive elders with regard to the order of the Gospels, as follows. He said that those Gospels were first written which include the genealogies, but that the Gospel according to Mark came into being in this manner: When Peter had publicly preached the word at Rome, and by the Spirit had proclaimed the Gospel, that those present, who were many, exhorted Mark, as one who had followed him for a long time and remembered what had been spoken, to make a record of what was said; and that he did this, and distributed the Gospel among those that asked him. And that when the matter came to Peter's knowledge he neither strongly forbade it nor urged it forward. But that John, last of all, conscious that the outward facts had been set forth in the Gospels, was urged on by his disciples, and, divinely moved by the Spirit, composed a spiritual Gospel.

In his *Adumbrationes* in 1 Peter 5:13, Clement states:

> When Peter was openly preaching the Gospel in Rome, in front of certain imperial *equites* [men of the equestrian order], and furnishing for them many testimonies of Christ, Mark, a follower of Peter, having been petitioned by these men (so that they might be able to commit to memory what had been said), wrote the Gospel called "According to Mark" from the things which were spoken by Peter.[91]

Morton Smith claimed to discover a letter purportedly from Clement of Alexandria to Theodore containing the so-called "Secret Gospel of Mark."[92] Carlson, Jeffery, and Watson have argued that it is a hoax perpetrated by the discoverer to advance his own unconventional views.[93]

Eusebius (*Hist. eccl.* 6.25.5) also cites Origen's (AD 185–254) testimony that Mark wrote his gospel in accordance with Peter's instructions. Irenaeus (c. AD 135–202; *Haer.* 3.1.1, quoted by Eusebius, *Hist. eccl.* 5.8.2–3) writes:

> Now Matthew published a written Gospel among the Hebrews a written gospel also in their own tongue, while Peter and Paul were preaching in Rome and founding the church. But after their departure [*exodon*] Mark also, the disciple and interpreter of Peter, himself handed down to us in writing the things which were preached by Peter, and Luke also, who was a follower of Paul, put down in a book the gospel which was preached by him. Then John, the disciple of the Lord, who had even rested on his breast, himself also gave forth the gospel, while he was living at Ephesus at Asia.

Eusebius implies that Mark wrote in Rome since he mentions that both Peter and Paul preached in Rome.[94] Some conjecture that Irenaeus "lived and studied for a time in Rome," and "he may have taken these additional details from local tradition."[95] His comments defending the fourfold Gospels are better known. He argues that "Mark takes his beginning from the prophetic Spirit who comes on men from on high, saying, 'The beginning of the good news of Jesus Christ, as it is written in the

91. Translated by Michael Peppard, *The Son of God in the Roman World: Divine Sonship in its Social and Political Context* (New York: Oxford University Press, 2011), 90. Peppard claims that "this testimony encourages us to read Mark not only in light of Roman provenance, but even in light of Roman imperial ideology."

92. Morton Smith, *Clement of Alexandria and a Secret Gospel of Mark* (Cambridge: Harvard University Press, 1973), and *The Secret Gospel: The Discovery and Interpretation of the Secret Gospel according to Mark* (New York: Harper & Row, 1973).

93. Stephen C. Carlson, *The Gospel Hoax: Morton Smith's Invention of Secret Mark* (Waco, TX: Baylor University Press, 2005); Peter Jeffery, *The Secret Gospel of Mark Unveiled: Imagined Rituals of Sex, Death, and Madness in a Biblical Forgery* (New Haven, CT: Yale University Press, 2007); and Francis Watson, "Beyond Suspicion: On the Authorship of the Mar Saba Letter and the Secret Gospel of Mark," *JTS* 61 (2010): 128–70. It is suspicious that the manuscript's current whereabouts are unknown. Only photographs of it exist, so that the actual manuscript has never been subjected to scientific analysis. Philip Jenkins, *Hidden Gospels: How the Search for Jesus Lost Its Way* (Oxford: Oxford University Press, 2001), 101, notes, "The location of the find is fascinating, since this was the scene of the forgery described only a few years before in the then-popular novel *The Mystery of Mar Saba* [by James H. Hunter]." It suggests either proof of its authenticity since "nobody would have dared invent such a thing in the 1950's, or else it is a tribute to the unabashed *chutzpah* of a forger." See the essays in Tony Burke, ed., *Ancient Gospel or Modern Forgery? The Secret Gospel of Mark in Debate* (Eugene, OR: Cascade, 2013), which present both sides of the argument.

94. Michael D. Goulder, "Did Peter Ever Go to Rome?" *SJT* 57 (2004): 377–96, dismisses Peter's presence in Rome as a legend with no historical basis.

95. Collins, *Mark*, 7.

prophet Isaiah,' showing a winged image of the Gospel. Therefore, he made his message compendious and cursory, for such is the prophetic character" (*Haer.* 3.11.8).

An odd tradition about Mark as the author of this gospel is found in Hippolytus (*Refut.* 7.30.1) in his attack on Marcion:

> Whenever Marcion or any of those dogs would howl about the demiurge, fobbing off contrasting statements of good and evil, one must say of them that neither Paul the apostle nor Mark the stumpy-fingered [*ho kolobodaktylos*] corroborated such things—for nothing of this is written in the Markan Gospel—but rather Empedocles of Acragas, whose appropriation has until now gone unnoticed. [Marcion] seized upon the arrangement of every one of his heresies, transferring these sayings from Sicily over to the evangelical words.[96]

Why does it mention that Mark was called stump-fingered? Was it a reference to some deformity? If so, Stein fittingly asks, "Why would a completely fictional tradition attribute such a negative comment to the author of one of the sacred Gospels?"[97] Or worse, does it derive from a pun from a military context that refers negatively to his desertion of duty when he left Paul and Barnabas?[98] Or, does it refer to Mark's gospel as truncated? It is impossible to decide.

Tertullian (AD 160–225), also writing against Marcion, wrote: "That gospel which Mark edited may be affirmed to be of Peter, whose interpreter Mark was" (*Marc.* 4.5). The later testimony reveals that Papias's assertion that Mark's gospel was linked to Peter had become conventional understanding. Things have since changed.

1.2.1.2 Response to Arguments against Mark's Connection to Peter

Telford notes that in Markan studies since the 1960s "a direct and uniform Petrine connection has not in practice been a basic premise." He attributes it to a "new look" characterized "by an open mind or even lack of interest in such historical questions."[99] The ancient testimony is treated with great skepticism, if not contempt, and as completely unreliable, and some dismiss those who do accept it as trustworthy as precritical romantics.[100] Black counters, "It would be fatuous, however, to suggest

96. This statement introduces a curiosity that is also found in the so-called Anti-Marcionite Prologue (ca. AD 160–180): "Mark declared, who is called 'stump-fingered,' because he had rather small fingers in comparison with the stature of the rest of his body. He was the interpreter of Peter. After the death [or departure, *post excessionem*] of Peter himself, the same man wrote down this same gospel in the regions of Italy." Engelbert Gutwenger, "The Anti-Marcionite Prologues," *TS* 7 (1946): 393–409, argues that the prologues should not be used "in the same manner as the documents of well-known writers of the early patristic literature" (p. 409).

97. Robert H. Stein, *Mark* (BECNT; Grand Rapids: Baker Academic, 2008), 8.

98. J. L. North, "ΜΑΡΚΟΣ Ο ΚΟΛΟΒΑΔΑΚΤΥΛΟΣ: Hippolytus, *Elenchus* VII.30," *JTS* 28 (1977): 498–507.

99. William R. Telford, "Introduction," in *The Interpretation of Mark* (ed. William R. Telford; 2nd ed.; Edinburgh: T&T Clark, 1995), 2. John R. Donahue, "The Quest for the Community of Mark's Gospel," in *The Four Gospels 1992: Festschrift Frans Neirynck* (ed. Frans Van Segbroeck et al.; BETL 100; Leuven: Leuven University Press, 1992), 2:817, writes that prior to the publication of Willi Marxsen's redaction critical studies in Mark in 1956 (Eng. trans.: *Mark the Evangelist: Studies on the Redaction History of the Gospel* [trans. James Boyce; Nashville: Abingdon, 1969]), "there existed a rare thing in New Testament studies—a near consensus on the dating and setting of a specific gospel."

100. James Dawsey, *Peter's Last Sermon: Identity and Discipleship in the Gospel of Mark* (Macon, GA: Mercer University Press, 2010), 18–21, draws an interesting contrast between the widespread skepticism of Markan scholars concerning the traditions about the name and situation of the author and the approach to traditions about the authorship of Plato's writings, for example, by classical scholars.

that Markan scholars were a generally gullible lot until around 1950, at which time the scales fell from their eyes and their vision became critical."[101] It is assumed by many of those who are suspicious of any Petrine connection to the gospel of Mark that to accept uncritically such testimony smacks of a predisposition to fundamentalism. Black makes the astute observation, "One of the really curious paradoxes of contemporary scholarship is its insistence on ambitious speculations concerning the traditions about Jesus, prior to Mark's Gospel, and its comparative disparagement of the actual traditions that came to be attached to that book in the early history of the church."[102] The theories that have arisen around the so-called Q document and its imagined community that are accepted with complete assurance provide a prime example of this paradox. One may venture to propose that a reverse gullibility exists that dismisses patristic traditions as apostolic fiction and as "misbegotten attempts to validate Christian faith through the forging of a spurious historical continuity between Jesus and the church that succeeded him."[103]

Martin challenges the general rejection of eyewitness testimony in the Gospels, which stems from the influence of form criticism that assumes all gospel material derives from traditions shaped primarily by the community. He writes, "Community tradition, however, may well include the report of eyewitness testimony in its first stage; after all, *someone* had to set the process in motion, unless these stories are spun out of the fertile imagination of that anonymous entity, the faceless 'community.'"[104] Byrskog argues that ancient historians did

> weigh and select the material with critical care, but from the very beginning of history writing their objective stance was always combined with literary and ideological ambitions reflecting their subjectivity and interpretive ambition. Although the ancient historians mostly regarded the reports of eyewitnesses as of prime importance, they intermingled carefully fact and interpretation into coherent narratives. The Markan author, as well as the other gospel writers, did very much the same, and *the internal theological profile of his narrative is therefore no indication that he did not appreciate and use eyewitness testimony.*[105]

Others argue against a Petrine connection from internal evidence, which tends to be subjective. Although Mark contains a high frequency of references to Peter, some ask why the stories recorded in the other gospels in which Peter appears prominently are absent from Mark (see Matt 14:28–31; 16:17–19; 17:24–27; Luke 5:1–11; 22:32; 24:12; John 13:3–10; 21:1–22). Some also point out that he seems to be portrayed as the typical disciple rather than as a living individual. He also comes off badly in the gospel. It is argued by some that Peter could ill afford to pass on stories that put himself in a bad light given "the ideological battles within the early church" (Gal 2:11–14).[106]

101. Black, *Images*, 7.

102. Ibid., 11.

103. Ibid., 10.

104. Ralph P. Martin, *New Testament Foundations* (Grand Rapids: Eerdmans, 1975), 1:204.

105. Byrskog, *Story as History*, 275.

106. His name is used among the combatants at Corinth (1 Cor 1:12), but see David E. Garland, *1 Corinthians* (BECNT; Grand Rapids: Baker, 2003), 44–51, for arguments that the so-called slogans in 1 Cor 1:12 are purely hypothetical impersonations.

In response to these objections, Mark's references to Peter are disproportionately large compared to the other gospels.[107] James and John as well as Judas have bit parts, but the other members of the Twelve serve merely as extras. The best explanation for his prominence in Mark is because of his "foundational importance," not only to the tradition of Jesus that is passed on but also to the theology it reflects.[108] The gospel is not about Peter, however, and he is often presented as a foil to clarify the nature of discipleship. He is not presented as a hero because only one, Jesus, can play that role as the model of faithful obedience to God. Peter's portrayal in the gospel conveys the theological truth that as a fallible human being he stands in need of God's saving grace and that God redeems both him and his failures. The frank portrayal of the weaknesses of one known to have become a faithful martyr could only serve as an encouragement to the average Christian. This less than flattering picture of Peter in the gospel parallels what Paul's heart-burning self-reproach does in his letters. Bockmuehl observes concerning the depiction of Paul:

> Far from either glossing or passing over his former life in silence, he explicitly highlights and disowns his previous enmity to Christ and the church in order to accentuate the nature of his new life. It is a point also amply documented in Acts and the Pastoral Epistles that Paul's earliest followers understood and embraced his rehearsal of pre-Christian errors as theologically vital to his practice of evangelism and catechesis: Jesus came to save even the chief of sinners (e.g., 1 Tim. 1:15).[109]

The unfavorable portrayal of Peter in Mark corresponds not only to Paul's view of his own past reflected in his letters (1 Cor 15:8–9; 2 Cor 5:16; Gal 1:13–14; Phil 3:6; Eph 3:8; 1 Tim 1:15–16) but also to Paul's theology regarding boasting. Paul asserts that only fools boast, and if he must boast, it will be only about things that show his weakness (2 Cor 11:29–33; 12:5), because the one who boasts is only to boast in the Lord (10:17). God's power is shown to be most evident in weakness (12:9). This theological perspective is mirrored in the gospel of Mark.

Marcus lists three other reasons against the traditional view of Markan authorship:[110] (1) the Gentile orientation of the gospel; (2) the supposed mistakes and/or unconcern about Jewish laws and customs;[111] and (3) the supposed errors of Palestinian geography.[112] These objections are not weighty and will be addressed in reverse order.

Mark lived in a mapless culture, and it may be too much to expect precision in this area.[113] Many of the so-called geographical errors, however, can be explained.

107. Reinhard Feldmeier, "The Portrayal of Peter in the Synoptic Gospels," in Hengel, *Studies*, 59, provides these statistics from Robert Morgenthaler, *Statistik des neutestamentlichen Wortschatzes* (Zürich: Gotthelf, 1958): "Out of the total 11,078 words in Mark, the ratio of Peter being named is 1:443; out of 19,448 words in Luke the ratio is 1:648; out of 18,298 words in Matthew the ratio is 1:722."

108. Martin Hengel, *Saint Peter: The Underestimated Apostle* (trans. Thomas H. Trapp; Grand Rapids: Eerdmans, 2010), 37–40.

109. Markus Bockmuehl, *Simon Peter in Scripture and Memory* (Grand Rapids: Baker, 2012), 140.

110. Marcus, *Mark 1–8*, 19.

111. See Pierson Parker, "The Posteriority of Mark," in *New Synoptic Studies: The Cambridge Gospel Conference and Beyond* (ed. William R. Farmer; Macon, GA: Mercer University Press, 1983), 73–75.

112. See Kurt Niederwimmer, "Johannes Markus," 178–83; Parker, "The Posteriority of Mark," 68–70.

113. See Hengel, *Studies*, 148, n. 51.

For example, identifying the site of the expulsion of the demons into the swine as Gerasa (5:1–17), modern Jerash, which was thirty miles from the lake, prompted the textual variants that locate the incident at Gadara or Gergesa. The text, however, allows it to be a reference to territory controlled by Gerasa. Or, the original reference was to a town that is now called Kersa or Koursi on the eastern shore of the lake, which was later mistaken for the better known Gerasa, a member of the Decapolis.

The journey described in 7:31 that has Jesus return from the region of Tyre, by way of Sidon toward the Sea of Galilee, into the region of the Decapolis seems to be an unusual detour, which Collins compares to travelling from Chicago to Indiana "by going north through Wisconsin and then east and south through Michigan to Indiana."[114] Collins explains that the problem lies with scholars who have the wrong picture of the extent of the Decapolis, and she cites Pliny (*Nat.* 5.16.74), who includes Damascus among the ten cities. It extends the northern border "a bit farther north than is usual in today's scholarly maps."[115] It is unlikely that Mark included this territory because the community for which he wrote was located there.[116] The journey may prefigure the mission to the Gentiles, though the population of the area also included Jews and not just Gentiles.

Stein, however, offers the best solution with a stylistic explanation, comparing the itinerary in both 7:31 and 11:1, where a similar alleged geographical error occurs. He concludes that in both instances Mark lists "the ultimate goal of the journey" first and the intervening places of the journey second. Jesus left Tyre for the Sea of Galilee passing through Sidon and the Decapolis (7:31). He left Jericho (10:46) for Jerusalem passing through Bethpage and Bethany near the Mount of Olives (11:1).[117] The pattern also occurs in 10:1 except that "the place of departure is mentioned first ('there,' i.e. Capernaum [9:33]), the ultimate goal second ('the region of Judea'), and the intervening route last ('across the Jordan')."[118] Gundry also observes that the topographical notations grow clearer and denser in the Jerusalem area.[119] This greater precision may be attributable to Mark's residence in Jerusalem (Acts 12:12).[120]

Mark does not intend to provide an introduction to Jewish customs. When he says that "all the Jews" wash their hands (7:3), it is certainly an exaggeration,[121] but the purpose of mentioning the custom of washing hands is to explain to non-Jewish

114. Collins, *Mark*, 9.

115. Ibid.

116. Contra Gerd Theissen, *The Gospels in Context: Social and Political History in the Synoptic Tradition* (trans. Linda M. Maloney; Edinburgh: T&T Clark, 1992), 244–45.

117. Stein, *Mark*, 6. Friedrich Gustav Lang, "'Über Sidon mitten ins Gebiet der Dekapolis': Geographie und Theologie in Markus 7,31," *ZDPV* 94 (1978): 145–60, argues that this verse does not describe a route actually taken by Jesus but a theological itinerary that is related to Mark's interest in and anticipation of the mission to the Gentiles. He notes, however, that traveling from Tyre to Sidon to Damascus and south and west to the east shore of the Sea of Galilee was technically conceivable. He concludes that this verse should not be used to discredit Mark's familiarity with Palestinian geography.

118. Stein, *Mark*, 6, n. 12.

119. Gundry, *Mark*, 1039.

120. In 11:1, Mark has Jesus approach Jerusalem from Jericho through Bethphage, which is closer to Jerusalem, and Bethany, which is to the southeast. James R. Edwards, *The Gospel according to Mark* (Pillar; Grand Rapids: Eerdmans, 2002), 334, explains that the ancient Roman road passed through Bethphage before Bethany, and Bethany is mentioned because that is where Jesus spent his nights when he was in Jerusalem (11:11).

121. This same exaggeration can also be found in the *Let. Aris.* 305.

readers why flouting this practice would have created such a row. Collins notes that our knowledge of Jewish customs in Palestine during this period is "quite limited." Since the Gospels serve as a primary source for our knowledge, she appropriately asks on what grounds one challenges Mark's accuracy.[122]

Mark appears to have known Hebrew and Aramaic, using many Aramaic names, phrases, and terms: "*Boanerges*" (3:17); "*talitha koum*" (5:41); "*Corban*" (7:11); "*Ephphatha*" (7:34); "*Bartimaeus*" (10:46); "*Abba*" (14:36); "*Golgotha*" (15:22); "*Eloi, Eloi, lema sabachthani*" (15:34).[123] Bauckham singles out Aramaic utterances of Jesus in two miracles that are distinctive. Jesus says to Jairus's daughter when he takes her by the hand, "'*Talitha koum*!' (which means 'Little girl, I say to you, get up!')" (5:41). He puts his fingers into the ears of the deaf man who could hardly talk, touches his tongue, and says "'*Ephphatha*!' (which means 'Be opened!')" (7:34). Since they are translated, Mark does not present these words as magical incantations used for healing. The translations diminish their mysterious aura, because they reveal that "Jesus speaks rather ordinary and obvious words in the language understood by his hearers within the narrative."[124]

Mark records many other healings in his gospel when Jesus does not speak in Aramaic, so it is evident that the use of Aramaic has no miraculous effect. Mark's purpose was to recreate a vivid narrative of the scene.[125] But recording what Jesus spoke in Aramaic also makes "a claim to *historical authenticity*."[126] It conveys a sense that Jesus actually said this as reported by eyewitness testimony. The same can be said of the last words Jesus speaks in the gospel when he is dying on the cross: "'*Eloi, Eloi, lema sabachthani*?' (which means 'My God, my God, why have you forsaken me?')" (15:34). This cry is not a direct quote from the Hebrew of Ps 22:1 but is in Aramaic, and it may derive from the way Jesus regularly prayed in Aramaic. If so, it conveys that it derives from eyewitness testimony from one who remembered what Jesus actually said.[127]

Stein contends that the vigorous debate over Markan authorship "does not involve a simple, objective pursuit of knowledge. Various presuppositions are often

122. Collins, *Mark*, 6.

123. Hengel, *Studies*, 46, comments that he does not know "any other in Greek which has as many Aramaic or Hebrew words and formulae in so narrow a space as does the second Gospel." See Hans-Peter Rüger, "Die lexikalischen Aramaismen im Markusevangelium," in *Markus-Philologie: Historische, literargeschichtliche und stilistische Untersuchungen zum zweiten Evangelium* (ed. Hubert Cancik; WUNT 33; Tübingen: Mohr Siebeck, 1984), 73–84.

124. Bauckham, "The Gospel of Mark: Origins and Eyewitness," 164.

125. Ibid., 165, citing France, *Mark*, 240.

126. Bauckham, "The Gospel of Mark: Origins and Eyewitness," 165–66.

127. Ibid., 166–67. Since Matthew omits most of these transliterations of Aramaic and Luke omits all of them, Howard Clark Kee, *Community of the New Age: Studies in Mark's Gospel* (Philadelphia: Westminster, 1977), 101, argues that the most plausible explanation is that the "readers in some way identified with the Semitic linguistic background." He thinks that this inference is supported by the fact that the Aramaic terms appear at "especially sensitive points in his narrative, such as the raising of the little daughter (5.41), the prayer in the garden (14.36), and above all, the cry from the cross (15.34)." I would argue quite the opposite. Paul's retention of "Abba" in Rom 8:15 and Gal 4:6, written to a Gentile audience, serves no purpose and probably reflects the strong impression that Jesus' unconventional approach to God in prayer made on the tradition. If Antioch, which is a prime candidate for the place where Matthew was written, contained a large number of Aramaic speakers, why did Matthew omit Mark's use of Aramaic words? I would argue that the Aramaic in these dramatic points in Mark's narrative is the result of the foothold it had in the tradition, and that it has nothing to do with the audience's Semitic linguistic background. It also explains why Jesus' unusual use of "*amēn*" that introduces a statement would be included thirteen times in Mark and left untranslated (3:28; 8:12; 9:1, 41; 10:15, 29; 11:23; 12:43; 13:30; 14:9, 18, 25, 30).

involved that are seldom discussed and at times may not even be consciously recognized but predispose scholars to a particular viewpoint."[128] He states boldly,

> If one brings to the study of Mark naturalistic presuppositions and denies the historicity of much or all of the miracles recorded in Mark, then how can one attribute the authorship of Mark to the John Mark of Acts 12:12 and 1 Pet 5:13, whose main source for this information was the apostle Peter, an eyewitness of the events? One must conclude either that the author was not John Mark but an anonymous author who believed the fictional accounts created by the anonymous community and incorporated them into his Gospel or that John Mark was an unabashed deceiver who created fictional accounts to deceive or to edify the church.

Stein continues that "those who believe in the historicity in the miracle accounts of the Second Gospel and/or believe that it was in some way divinely inspired see support for this in the view that the Gospel was written by Mark and that he obtained his information from an eyewitness, the apostle Peter."[129] Unquestionably, the importance and meaning of the Gospel of Mark are not determined by authorship, but Stein puts his finger on an important point. "Antisupernaturalist" presuppositions tend to require that John Mark was not the author or that the eyewitness testimony of the apostle Peter stand behind the accounts recorded. Markan authorship in association with the eyewitness testimony of Peter would be nice, but it is not necessary, because the truthfulness of its testimony does not require Markan authorship.[130]

If Mark did not compose this gospel on the basis of Peter's teaching, then we have no idea who wrote it. The origin of this gospel would be consigned to an "ill-defined fog."[131] Hengel's arguments are persuasive. The writing of this gospel would not have been undertaken or entrusted to an unknown "Mr. Nobody" but to a recognized teacher in the church who could appeal to an even greater authority, and this "could explain the initial success of his work."[132] He declares, "His unusual work *cannot* have been circulated *anonymously* from the beginning, for that would have disqualified it from the start."[133] If one assumes that Matthew and Luke allowed themselves to be guided completely by Mark, it attests to their conviction of its reliability and authority. Luke identifies his sources as "those who from the first were eyewitnesses and servants of the word" (Luke 1:2). They were present "from the first" (see Acts 1:21–22; John 15:27). Why would Luke use Mark unless he regarded it as coming from a trustworthy eyewitness source, from a minister of the word who witnessed things from the beginning?[134] Hengel also concludes that the

128. Stein, *Mark*, 7.

129. Ibid.

130. Ibid., 7–8.

131. Hengel, *Saint Peter*, 37.

132. Hengel, *Studies*, 52.

133. Martin Hengel, "Eye-witness Memory and the Writing of the Gospels: Form-Criticism, Community Tradition and the Authority of the Authors," in *The Written Gospel* (ed. Markus Bockmuehl and Donald A. Hagner; Cambridge: Cambridge University Press, 2005), 80.

134. Vernon K. Robbins, "The Claims of the Prologues and Greco-Roman Rhetoric: The Prefaces to Luke and Acts in Light of Greco-Roman Rhetorical Strategies," in *Jesus and the Heritage of Israel: Luke's Narrative Claim upon Israel's Legacy* (ed. David P. Moessner; Harrisburg, PA: Trinity Press International 1999), 83. What Luke does differently from his predecessors is to write a "'continuous' account—one that tells the story from the beginning to Rome."

events recorded in the last week of Jesus' life cannot be attributed to the "novelistic creativity" of the evangelist or theologically driven fantasy. He writes,

> If Mark has invented all this material—historically appropriate in style to an incredible degree—then he has done it with ingenious empathy, intuition, and understanding. But in the opinion of many critics he was a simple anonymous Gentile Christian. How is this supposed to have come about?[135]

It would seem beyond strange that Peter did not leave a legacy of tradition about Jesus' historical ministry in a gospel and most likely in the earliest gospel. He would have been a significant fount of knowledge about Jesus' ministry, and he is the most likely source of the traditions found in this gospel. Bauckham adds an interesting point from internal evidence. Simon Peter is the first and last mentioned disciple in the gospel (1:16, where his name is mentioned twice in the Greek text; and 16:7). These "two references form an *inclusio* around the whole story, suggesting that Peter is the witness whose testimony includes the whole."[136] This last mention of Peter is interesting because he is mentioned second *after* the disciples, "Go, tell his disciples and Peter." Elsewhere, Peter is always listed first when other disciples are mentioned (3:16; 5:37; 9:2; 13:3; 14:33, 37). The addition of his name as an addendum in 16:7 serves to accentuate his importance. Bauckham identifies the *inclusio* as a literary device in other Greco-Roman literary sources to identify eyewitness sources.[137] Hengel also identifies this *inclusio* as "a signature, by means of which Mark indicates the one who for him is the most important guarantor of the tradition, an individual who at the same time was the most authoritative disciple of Jesus."[138]

Paul recognized that Peter was an authoritative repository of information about Jesus' historical ministry when he visited with him for fifteen days (Gal 1:18). The NIV translates the verb "to get acquainted with" Cephas, but it is better to interpret it to mean to "*visit* a person for the purpose of inquiry" or to "*inquire into* a thing or *about* a person."[139] We may assume that Paul and Peter did not spend two weeks talking about the weather.[140] Paul recites the tradition behind the Lord's Supper (1 Cor 11:23–25), Jesus' resurrection appearances (15:3–7), and Jesus' teaching on divorce (7:10–11), and he had to have learned it from someone. Galatians 1:18 makes it likely that he heard it directly from Peter, the most significant eyewitness mediator of the tradition.[141]

---

135. Martin Hengel, "Jesus, the Messiah of Israel," in *Studies in Early Christology* (Edinburgh: T&T Clark, 1995), 57, see pp. 41–58.

136. Bauckham, *Eyewitnesses*, 125. Martin Hengel, *The Four Gospels and the One Gospel of Jesus Christ* (trans. John Bowden; Harrisburg: Trinity Press International, 2000), 82, made this argument earlier.

137. Bauckham, *Eyewitnesses*, 132–47, develops this argument citing Lucian's *Alexander* and Porphyry's *Life of Plotinus*.

138. Hengel, *Saint Peter*, 42.

139. G. D. Kilpatrick, "Galatians 1:18 ἹΣΤΟΡΗΣΑΙ ΚΗΦΑΝ," in *New Testament Essays: Studies in Memory of T. W. Manson, 1893–1958* (ed. A. J. B. Higgins; Manchester: Manchester University Press, 1959), 144–49.

140. W. D. Davies, *The Setting of the Sermon on the Mount* (Cambridge: Cambridge University Press, 1966), 453–54.

141. Receiving eyewitness testimony from Peter about what happened and what Jesus taught is quite different from receiving an apostolic commission or seeking recognition from him. Nor did Paul ask for an interpretation of the meaning of the gospel.

The scholarly consensus is that Matthew incorporated much of Mark in composing his gospel, and Peter is especially singled out as an apostolic foundational figure (Matt 16:17–19). According to John 21:15–17, Jesus commissions Peter three times to "feed my sheep," which suggests an authoritative teaching role. It would be amazing if Peter's eyewitness testimony were not conserved in one of the gospels, and all of the evidence points to Mark as that gospel. Mark leaves the impression that it records eyewitness testimony. Bockmuehl declares:

> It seems reasonable to assume ... that most of this exotic material would be largely meaningless to a gentile Roman audience. Even for Greek speakers in Rome, of course, the very clumsiness of outlandish places, phrases, and expressions intruding into the narrative would reinforce the impression of verisimilitude: like the other evangelists, Mark underscores the sense that these "memoirs" record real events and are not mere literary playthings. Herein lies an important difference between Christian and pagan belief: the remembered Peter roots the Gospel episodes in actual experiences and not in stereotyped timeless myths that "always are" (as pagan apologists liked to put it).[142]

In my view, Mark is to be credited with organizing the wealth of previously unrelated stories from Peter into a historical narrative that also has a distinctive theological point of view.

1.2.2 The Provenance and Date of the Gospel

Papias does not mention where Mark wrote or when he wrote. Those scholars who dismiss the early church tradition that Mark was written in Rome propose various other locales from Galilee, the Decapolis, Tyre, Sidon, Syria, the East, and Alexandria, a tradition that goes back to John Chrysostom (*Hom. Matt.* 1.3). The range of proposals reveals that the gospel itself does not provide clear evidence for determining its original setting. Aune asserts that the proliferation and diversity of attempts to profile Mark's community "invalidates the entire enterprise."[143] Bird contends that even if a Markan community existed, which he questions, it is almost impossible to identify its setting and situation with any degree of certainty.[144] The evidence is so limited that it prompts Peterson to conclude that the entire enterprise is "not worth the trouble."[145] I would agree with his conclusion that at "the very least, the present state of affairs should make it impossible simply to assume that

142. Bockmuehl, *Simon Peter*, 137.

143. David E. Aune, "Genre Theory and the Genre-Function of Mark and Matthew," in *Mark and Matthew I: Comparative Readings: Understanding the Earliest Gospels in Their First-Century Settings* (ed. Eve-Marie Becker and Anders Runesson; WUNT 2/271; Tübingen: Mohr Siebeck, 2011), 165.

144. Michael F. Bird, "The Markan Community, Myth or Maze? Bauckham's *The Gospel for All Christians* Revisited," *JTS* 57 (2006): 476.

145. Dwight N. Peterson, *The Origins of Mark: The Markan Community in Current Debate* (BIS 48; Leiden/Boston/Köln: Brill, 2000), 202. Mary Ann Tolbert, *Sowing the Gospel: Mark's World in Literary-Historical Perspective* (Minneapolis: Fortress, 1989), 303, expresses skepticism about the search for an "identifiable, individualized local group—that is a *specific* community" as the setting from Mark much earlier.

reconstructed communities behind Gospels are hermeneutically necessary to read Gospels rightly."[146] Nevertheless, inferences can be drawn about the setting of the community or communities addressed that do not rely on circular reasoning.

1.2.2.1 Inferences from Mark about the Audience

1.2.2.1.1 An Audience Acquainted with Persecution

One can infer from the prominence given to the issue of persecution in Mark that the gospel was composed in a context where being a follower of Christ was laden with danger.[147] The interpretation of the parable of the Sower equates the seed sown on rocky ground with those who hear the word and immediately receive it with joy, but they endure only for a while and just as immediately fall away when trouble or persecution arises on account of the word (4:16–17). Jesus promises those who have left everything to follow him that they will receive rewards of hundredfold now in this age, but they will come "with persecutions," and in the age to come, eternal life (10:30). His predictions of his own suffering are tied to predictions that his disciples will suffer as well (8:31–38; 10:38–39). The situation of persecution may explain the frequent references to the disciples' fear (4:40; 6:50; 10:32; 16:8). It clearly explains the warning that is unique to Mark that everyone will be salted with fire and that salt that loses its savor could not be resalted (9:49–50).

The consequence of having faith in Christ in a world where the authorities make competing claims and do not brook any rivalry is that Christ's followers will be hated by all (13:13). For Jesus to assert that those who offer Christians something as modest as a cup of water to drink will not lose their reward (9:41) reveals that he foresees that they will be living in desperate circumstances. Only those who endure to the end will be saved (13:13). This declaration is more than a warning but an assurance that eternal salvation awaits those who pass through severe tribulation. These statements suggest that Mark is acutely aware that persecution will not only create faithful martyrs among Jesus' followers but will also beget failure, as terror and the fear of public rejection lead to apostasy and betrayal.

In 13:9–13, Jesus becomes more specific and warns that they will be handed over to councils, beaten in synagogues, and stand in the dock before governors and kings because of their commitment to him. He assures them that when they are brought to trial, they need not worry what to say; the Holy Spirit will speak through them (13:11). He then gives a dire picture of family turmoil as the universal loathing of Christians (13:13) spills over into family life. Family members will betray them and hand them over to death (13:12).

146. Peterson, *Origins*, 202.

147. Crossley, *The Date of Mark's Gospel*, 125, 207–8, argues that since Mark presents Jesus as Sabbath observant (2:23–28), does not shelve biblical food laws (7:1–23), and endorses a strict interpretation of the law of divorce (10:1–12), the gospel was written before Paul contested the law, sometime before AD 50. His conclusions have not been well received, and they suggest that using internal evidence does not provide solid proof for dating the gospel since it is so open to alternative interpretations.

1.2.2.1.2 A Gentile Audience

There are intimations in the gospel that Mark has in view a Gentile audience.[148] The translation of Aramaisms (5:41; 7:11, 34; 14:36; 15:22, 34) suggests that the evangelist takes for granted that many, if not all, in the audience do not know Aramaic. They also need to be informed about the customs of Pharisees (7:3–4). The explanation, "the Pharisees and all the Jews," drops a clear hint that Mark envisions a Gentile audience only vaguely familiar with Jewish traditions. One does not need to tell Jews what every Jew does. The audience also is not expected to know that the Sadducees did not believe in resurrection (12:18). Apparently, they also need to be informed that "Preparation Day" is "the day before the Sabbath" (15:42). The favorable examples of Gentiles in the gospel—the humble faith of the Syrophoenician mother in 7:24–30 and the confession of the centurion when Jesus dies in 15:39—and the emphasis that the gospel will include and be preached to the nations in 11:17; 13:10; 14:9, suggest that Mark has a special interest in Gentiles as the audience of his gospel, but this interest does not exclude the possibility that Jews also composed a significant part of the audience.

1.2.2.1.3 An Audience Familiar with Scripture and the Gospel Story

The audience is made up of Christians who are assumed to be familiar with the Jewish Scriptures, which are referred to simply as "the Scriptures" or "Scripture" (12:10, 24; 14:49) and to what "is written" or "Moses wrote" (1:2; 7:6; 9:12–13; 10:4–5; 11:17; 12:19; 14:21, 27). Isaiah is mentioned without explanation (1:2; 7:6–7), as are Elijah (1:6 implied; 6:15; 8:28; 9:4–5; 9:11–13; 15:35–36); Moses (1:44; 7:10; 9:4–5; 10:3–4; 12:19, 26); David (2:25; 10:47–48; 11:10; 12:35–37); and Abraham, Isaac, and Jacob (12:26). The audience also does not need explanations for the various titles for Jesus that crop up in the gospel, "Christ," "Son of Man," "son of David," and "Son of God."[149] They apparently know many of the characters beforehand, such as John the Baptist, because the author does not introduce them. Mark also does not explain what "baptize ... with the Holy Spirit" (1:8) means, and one may assume that the readers understand that it refers to the coming of Spirit into the life of the believer at conversion that empowers them to witness to the world.

Explicit quotations appear in 1:2–3 (Isa 40:3); 7:10 (Exod 20:12; 21:17; Deut 5:16; Lev 20:9); 10:6–8 (Gen 1:27; 2:24; 5:2); 10:19–20 (Exod 20:12–16; Deut 5:16–20); 11:17 (Isa 56:7); 12:10–11 (Ps 118:22–23); 12:26 (Exod 3:6); 12:29–30 (Deut 6:4–5; Josh 22:5); 12:31 (Lev 19:18); 12:36 (Ps 110:1); and 14:27 (Zech 13:7). Some of the implicit references to Scripture appear in 1:2–3 (Exod 23:20; Mal 3:1); 4:12 (Isa 6:9–10); 4:32 (Ps 104:12); 8:18 (Jer 5:21; Ezek 12:2; Isa 6:10); 9:11 (Mal 3:1); 9:48 (Isa 66:24); 11:9–10 (Pss 118:25–26; 148:1); 11:17–18 (Jer 7:11);

148. Ernest Best, "Mark's Readers: A Profile," in *The Four Gospels 1992: Festschrift Frans Neirynck* (ed. Frans van Segbroeck et al.; BETL 100; Leuven: Leuven University Press, 1992), 2:839–58.

149. H. Douglas Buckwalter, *The Character and Purpose of Luke's Christology* (SNTSMS 89; Cambridge/New York: Cambridge University Press, 1996), 81.

12:32–33 (Deut 4:35; 6:4–5; LXX Josh 22:5; Isa 45:21); 13:14 (Dan 9:27; 11:31; 12:11); 13:25 (Isa 13:10; 34:4); 13:26 (Dan 7:13–14); 14:34 (Pss 42:5–6, 11; 43:5; 116:3); 14:62 (Dan 7:13); 15:24 (Ps 22:18); 15:34 (Ps 22:1).

1.2.2.2 Various Proposals for Mark's Provenance

1.2.2.2.1 Rome

The bond between Peter and Mark that is presumed in the tradition about Mark may have led many church fathers to assume that the gospel was composed in Rome (Eusebius, *Hist. eccl.* 2.25.7).[150] Black writes, "*Nowhere in patristic testimony ... is a link between Mark and Rome ever wrought in the absence of a coincident coupling of Mark and Peter.*"[151] The exception might be Irenaeus's remark (*Haer.* 3.1.1) that Mark "himself handed down to us in writing the things which were preached by Peter." The "us" may refer to the church in Rome. The tradition of a Roman provenance for the gospel, however, is also supported by internal evidence in Mark.

1.2.2.2.1.1 The Persecution of Christians in Rome

The situation of persecution corresponds well with Tacitus's description (*Ann.* 15.44) of the Neronian persecution that specifically singled out Christians. After the fire broke out in Rome on July 19, AD 64, and raged for nine days, Tacitus reports:

> But neither all human endeavor, nor all imperial largess, nor all the modes of placating the gods, could stifle the scandal or banish the belief that the [great Roman] fire had taken place by order. Therefore to scotch the rumor, Nero substituted as culprits, and punished with the utmost exquisite cruelty, a class loathed for their abominations, whom the crowd styled Christians. Christus, from whom the name is derived, had undergone the death penalty in the reign of Tiberius, by sentence of the procurator Pontius Pilate. Checked for the moment, this pernicious superstition again broke out, not only in Judea, the home of the disease, but in the capital itself [Rome]—that receptacle for everything hideous and degraded from every quarter of the globe, which there finds a vogue. Accordingly, arrest was first made of those who confessed [to being Christians]; next, on their disclosures, vast numbers were convicted, not so much on the charge of arson as for hatred of the human race.[152] Every sort of derision was added to their deaths: they were wrapped in the skins of wild beasts and dismembered by dogs, others were nailed to crosses; others when daylight failed, were set afire to serve as lamps by night. Nero had offered his gardens for

150. Bruce, "The Date and Character of Mark," 77–78, speculates that Peter might have gone to Rome after the church was being reconstituted after Claudius had expelled the Jews from Rome and he was helping in the effort. He suggests that it might explain Paul's language in Rom 15:20 that he did not want to "build on someone else's foundation."

151. C. Clifton Black, "Was Mark a Roman Gospel?" *ExpTim* 105 (1993): 36 (italics original). The title of the article resembles that of the work of B. W. Bacon, *Is Mark a Roman Gospel?* (HTS 7; Cambridge: Harvard University Press, 1919), who argues for the Roman provenance of Mark, and Black's title reveals that the question has not been resolved.

152. Persons could prove their loyalty to Rome by turning in those, including family members (13:12), whom the Romans perceived as disruptive influences.

> the spectacle and gave an exhibition in the circus, mingling with the people in the costume of a charioteer or mounted on a car. Hence even for criminals who merited extreme and exemplary punishment, there arose a feeling of pity, due to the impression that they were being destroyed, not for the public good, but to gratify the cruelty of a single man.[153]

While Jews had experienced persecution across the empire for years,[154] what is significant and unparalleled is that Tacitus describes Roman persecution that is specifically aimed at Christians *as Christians*. His description of their abuse reveals their low social standing, because Roman law forbade that Roman citizens could be treated in this way. Black comments, "Trastevere, the harbour in which many poor Christians were concentrated, suffered no damage from the fire, which may partially explain how Nero was able to make his scapegoating stick."[155] The church in Rome was subject to vicious gossip and hostility (see also 1 Pet 2:15; 3:13–16; 4:12). The Roman populace may have associated Christians with murderers, thieves, criminals, and mischief makers (4:15) since the latter were commonly exposed to beasts to provide more entertaining public executions.[156]

Christians undergoing this persecution could hear in Mark's narrative that Jesus was also falsely accused of being in league with the devil (3:21, 30). He, too, was framed by trumped-up charges by false witnesses (14:56–59) and was betrayed by an intimate friend, one of the Twelve (14:43–46). They could also hear Jesus speaking bluntly of his own suffering and death and warning his disciples that they would not escape tribulation. Jesus insists that bearing a cross and following him was fundamental to becoming his disciple (8:34–38), and for those in Rome it had become a reality. Santos claims, "Such an environment of persecution, hatred, betrayal and turmoil within Rome and among Roman Christians works well with Mark's use of the authority–servanthood paradox."[157]

To be sure, persecution against Christians reared its ugly head in a variety of locales throughout the Roman Empire (see Rom 8:35; 12:14; 1 Cor 4:12; Phil 1:29–30; 2 Thess 1:4–7). Stein warns of the danger of "mirror reading" the text to discover clues about the audience's provenance.[158] But Incigneri is on target when he argues that the strong motif of persecution in the gospel "has to be explained, not in relation to random attacks by mobs, but to executions by legal authorities for

153. For a commentary on this passage, see Cook, *Roman Attitudes*, 39–83.

154. The Emperor Claudius expelled the Jews from Rome. The Jews of Alexandria suffered vicious oppression in AD 38, as reviewed by Philo in his *Against Flaccus* and his *Embassy to Gaius*.

155. Black, "Was Mark a Roman Gospel?" 37.

156. Brian J. Incigneri, *The Gospel to the Romans: The Setting and Rhetoric of Mark's Gospel* (BIS 65; Leiden/Boston/Köln: Brill, 2003), 111. Citing Donald G. Kyle (*Spectacles of Death in Ancient Rome* [London: Routledge, 1998], 53–54), he reports (111, n. 206), "Victims were tied to posts or just left without weapons before beasts, naked or near naked, sometimes with the verdict (*titulus*) attached to them. It was a common penalty for slaves, foreign enemies and 'free men guilty of a few heinous offences.'" Incigneri proposes "that Mark empathised deeply with his readers in their questioning and in their suffering, because he lived among them" (56). It is not an "imagined audience" but real "flesh-and-blood readers ... many of whom were prepared to give up their flesh and blood for the sake of the gospel" (58).

157. Narry F. Santos, *Slave of All: The Paradox of Authority and Servanthood in the Gospel of Mark* (JSNTSup 237; London/New York: Sheffield Academic, 2003), 287. He cites John R. Donahue, "Windows and Mirrors: The Setting of Mark's Gospel," *CBQ* 57 (1995): 26: "Mark's narrative world offers his community a vision of hope, divorced from dominating power."

158. Stein, *Mark*, 14.

being a Christian, because Mark's text demands this."[159] He argues that the verb "put to death" in 13:12 "relates to an execution by legal authorities (cf. 14:55; Exod 21:12, 14–17; 1 Macc 1:57; Rom 8:36; 2 Cor 6:9; Matt 27:1)."[160] He also argues that if the text refers to crucifixion, it "could only be carried out by Roman authorities throughout the Empire," and there is "no evidence at all of Roman executions of Christians in the East at this time."[161]

The situation of turmoil fits well the description of Roman upheaval before Vespasian was named emperor. From a Roman perspective, the whole world seemed to be running amok with the tumult of civil war and international threats. Tacitus (*Hist.* 1.2–3) gravely describes the chaotic times of the late 60s:

> The history on which I am entering is that of a period rich in disasters, terrible with battles, torn by civil struggles, horrible even in peace. Four emperors fell by the sword; there were three civil wars, more foreign wars, and often both at the same time.... Italy was distressed by disasters unknown before or returning after the lapse of the ages.... Beside the manifold misfortunes that befell mankind, there were prodigies in the sky and on the earth, warnings given by thunderbolts, and prophecies of the future, both joyful and gloomy, uncertain and clear.

If Mark wrote after the martyrdom of so many Christians in Rome, including Peter and Paul, during the political chaos in Rome when the imperial realm seemed to be hitting the skids, and during the crisis of the Jewish revolt against Rome when things had taken a turn for the worse and the fall of Jerusalem had occurred or was inevitable, then Jesus' warnings about "wars and rumors of wars" and "nation [rising] against nation, and kingdom against kingdom" (13:7–8) and his prophecy about "the abomination that causes desolation" (13:14–20) would have struck a chord. These were precarious times, and these were watershed events. The gospel would have braced the audience to endure the catastrophes and to keep their eyes peeled for Christ's return without being panicked, knowing that this was only the beginning, not the end.

The connections between the discourse in Mark 13 and the situation in Rome do not mean that Mark 13 was tailored to apply to the author's current context. To counter the Roman theory, Marcus uses the phrase "we would expect" to introduce his arguments.[162] Why should "our" expectations determine what is probable or improbable, particularly when our expectations are so closely tied to our particular theories? He argues that if Mark stems "from personal reminiscence, we would expect more detail."[163] For example, if the gospel came out of the Neronian persecution, should we not expect Mark 13 to focus more on "a bestial, anti-God figure" as in Daniel or Revelation?[164] I would argue instead that Mark 13 accurately preserves Jesus' teaching on the subject of the coming destruction of Jerusalem that

159. Incigneri, *Gospel*, 90. Hengel, *Four Gospels*, 79, claims that we know of no clear example of Roman persecution other than what occurred under Nero in the mid-60s.

160. Incigneri, *Gospel*, 91.

161. Ibid., 92.

162. Marcus, *Mark 1–8*, 33–37.

163. Ibid., 23.

164. Ibid., 33.

he envisioned and the turmoil that would arise throughout the world. Mark is not crafting an apocalyptic work, using indirect imagery to comment on current events. He recognizes that what Jesus prophesied is remarkably relevant for his audience's situation, and he does not need to tweak it or expand on it.

Marcus also argues that bitterness is directed against the Jews, not the Romans.[165] Again, this assumes that Mark's portrayal of the roles of the Jewish priestly hierarchy and the Roman governor in the death of Jesus is not historically accurate. The gospel is not a political pamphlet denouncing the unjust death of Jesus or the unjust persecution of his followers by the Jews or by the Romans. Persecution, according to Mark's account of Jesus' teaching, was to be expected as normative for Christians before the end, and that it would come from all circles. As Jesus said, "Everyone will hate you because of me" (13:13).

1.2.2.2.1.2 Linguistic Arguments

Many argue that the frequency of Latinisms, more numerous than in any other writing in the NT, suggests "that the Evangelist wrote in a Roman environment."[166]

"to make their way" (2:23; *iter facere*)
"mat" (2:4, 9, 11, 12; 6:55; *grabatus*)
"to plot" ["took counsel"] (3:6; 15:1; *concilium*)
"basket" (4:21; *modius*)
"legion" (5:9, 15; *legio*)
"at the point of death" (5:23; *in extremis esse*)
"soldier of the guard" (6:27; *speculator*)
"denarius" (6:36; 12:15; 14:5; *denarius*)
"fist" (7:3; *pugnus*)
"pitcher" (7:4; *sextarius*)
"Caesar" (12:14; *Caesar*)
"tax" (12:14; *census*)
"penny" (12:42; *quadrans*), in which the Greek *lepta* is explained in terms of a Roman coin
"centurion" (15:39, 44, 45; *centurio*)
"to satisfy" (15:15; *satisfacere*)
"scourge" (15:15; *flagellare*)
"praetorium" (15:16; *praetorium*), in which the Greek expression "palace" is explained in Latin

Note too that the "fourth watch" (in the Greek text) in 6:48 reflects a Roman reckoning of time since Jews normally referred to three watches of the night.

Others contend that the Latinisms and Latin loan words derive from Roman

165. Ibid.

166. Stein, *Mark*, 11–12. Gundry, *Mark*, 1043–45, has a more extensive list of Latinisms.

political, military, and economic influences that had expanded throughout the world and do not help to narrow the options for the gospel's origin.[167] Many of the expressions had crept into colloquial Greek usage in places that were occupied by Roman forces and engaged in trade with Rome. But there are telltale signs that point to a context in Rome. Mark translates the widow's two *lepta*, the smallest coin in circulation, as a *quadrans*, the smallest Roman coin (12:42). Collins thinks that the use of "*lepton*" suggests a provenance in one of the eastern provinces, since it was "the smallest denomination of coins in the Syrian-Nabatean region."[168] If that were the case, however, why would Mark feel the need to translate what it was for his audience? The *quadrans* was not in circulation throughout the entire Roman Empire, was familiar to Latin-speaking people, and was *not* familiar in Syria.[169] It makes more sense, then, that Mark felt the need to interpret the coinage for a Roman audience.

Van Iersel detects the influence of a Latin-speaking milieu from the position of the verb in the sentence where Mark deviates from normal Greek word order and follows a Latin word order in thirty-seven cases compared to twelve in Matthew and five in Luke. He also cites the cases where the Greek *hina* is used in a nonfinal sense ("that is") of the Latin *ut* after verbs of speaking: "Of the thirty-one occurrences of this Latinism in Mark only eight have been preserved in the parallels of Matthew and only four in those of Luke."[170] These Latinisms increase the probability that the gospel was composed where the author would have been exposed to Latin in everyday life, which makes Rome more likely than Galilee or Syria.

The use of the term "Syrophoenician" in the Greek text of 7:26 (NIV renders it "born in Syrian Phoenicia) is also telling. This ethnic designation would have been unnecessary in Palestine or Syria but would clarify for Romans that the woman who came to appeal to Jesus to help her demonized daughter was not a "Libo-Phoenician" from the Carthage area of North Africa (Libya) but a Phoenician from the Levant (see Strabo, *Geogr.* 17.3). This district was called "Syrophoenicia" to distinguish it from the North African Libyophoenicia.[171] Theissen counters that the term was used instead to distinguish the northern part of Syria (Syria Coele) from the southern part (Syria Phoenice).[172] Marcus asserts that it does not distinguish her as a particular kind of Phoenician but subtly distinguishes her as a particular kind of Syrian who comes from the Palestinian coast rather than the Coele-Syrian region.[173] Both Theissen and Marcus contend that Mark was written in Syria, but why would

167. Theissen, *The Gospels in Context*, 247–49; Collins, *Mark*, 10, 99–100; Marcus, *Mark 1–8*, 32–33.

168. Collins, *Mark*, 10, 589.

169. See the debate between F. Blass, "On Mark xii.42 and xv.16," *ExpTim* 10 (1898): 185–87; idem, "On Mark xii.42," *ExpTim* 10 (1898): 286–87; and W. M. Ramsay, "On Mark xii.42," *ExpTim* 10 (1898–99): 232, 336, which I believe Ramsay wins.

170. Bastiaan van Iersel, *Mark: A Reader-Response Commentary* (trans. W.H. Bisscheroux; JSNTSup 164; Sheffield: Sheffield Academic, 1998), 34–35.

171. Hengel, *Studies*, 29–30, 137–38. Benoît Standaert, *L'Évangile selon Marc: deuxième partie Marc 6,14 à 10,52* (EBib; Pendé: Gabalda, 2010), 559.

172. Theissen, *The Gospels in Context*, 245–47. Pablo Alonso, *The Woman Who Changed Jesus: Crossing Boundaries in Mk 7,24–30* (BTS 11; Leuven: Peeters, 2011), 151–59, believes that the term is part of the historical tradition and does not derive from Mark's redaction, but also does not find proof that it has a Latin derivation. He therefore does not consider it conclusive evidence for identifying the gospel's provenance.

173. Marcus, *Mark 1–8*, 32, 36.

a Syrian audience need this clarification if it has been made clear that Jesus has come to the district of Tyre where the woman appears to reside? Matthew, which many think was written in Antioch, omits the reference altogether and identifies her instead as a "Canaanite" (Matt 15:22). Mark's use of this term, however, may or may not tip the scales toward a Roman provenance.

According to Mark, Jesus prohibits not just a husband but also a wife from divorcing and remarrying (10:11–12). The prohibition in Matt 5:32 and 19:9 and Luke 16:18 mentions only the husband. A woman could not divorce her husband except in special circumstances in the Palestinian context. Mark may have adapted Jesus' teaching to his Roman setting where women did have the right to divorce. If Seneca (*Ben.* 3.16.2) is to be believed, the divorce rate of upper-class Roman matrons was scandalous in this era. He writes, "Surely no woman will blush to be divorced now that some distinguished and noble ladies count the years not by the consuls but by their own marriages, and divorce in order to be married, marry in order to be divorced." Mark understands Jesus to have laid down the fundamental principles that may be adjusted to different cultural circumstances, and this additional prohibition fits particularly well with a Roman context.

The identification of Rufus and Alexander as the sons of Simon of Cyrene may also be suggestive of a Roman context. Their names are omitted by Matthew and Luke. Since they play no role in the narrative, their mention may suggest that Mark assumes his audience knows who these men are. Both were common names, but Paul singles out a "Rufus" and his mother, who is also mentioned in Rom 16:13, as well known to him. If 16:13 is addressed to Rome, which I think is most likely, it is possible that the name surfaces here to draw a connection with the readers.[174] Best surmises, however, that Mark may only be preserving names that came to him in the tradition, reflecting a pattern of "positive respect for the material which he used."[175] More likely is Bauckham's argument that Mark cites the names of the sons of Simon of Cyrene because he "is appealing to Simon's eyewitness testimony, known in the early Christian movement not from his own firsthand account but through his sons."[176]

1.2.2.2.2 Galilee

If the patristic evidence tying the gospel to Peter and Rome is dismissed as unreliable, another locus for home of the gospel must be found, and some have proposed Galilee.[177] Lohmeyer contends that early Christianity in Palestine had two primary centers, Jerusalem and Galilee, and that Mark writes from the perspective of

174. Nahman Avigad, "A Depository of Inscribed Ossuaries in the Kidron Valley," *IEJ* 12 (1962): 9–12, published an ossuary inscription that identifies the bones as those of "Alexander, son of Simon," and there are suggestions that other persons in these ossuaries came from Cyrene. Pieter W. van der Horst, *Ancient Jewish Epitaphs* (CBET 2; Kampen: Kok Pharos, 1991), 140–41, notes the uncertainties of making a connection with Mark's story.

175. Ernest Best, "Mark's Preservation of the Tradition," in *The Interpretation of Mark* (ed. William R. Telford; 2nd ed.; Edinburgh: T&T Clark, 1995), 162–63.

176. Bauckham, *Eyewitnesses*, 52.

177. See Ernst Lohmeyer, *Galiläa und Jerusalem* (FRLANT 34; Göttingen: Vandenhoeck & Ruprecht, 1936); and R. H. Lightfoot, *Locality and Doctrine in the Gospels* (London: Hodder & Stoughton, 1938).

Galilean Christianity with its emphasis on Son of Man eschatology over against the perspective of Jerusalem Christianity, which, he claims, adhered to a nationalistic messianic hope, Christ Jesus, the sacrificial cult, and world mission. Lightfoot adapts Lohmeyer's arguments and states:

> Galilee and Jerusalem therefore stand in opposition to each other, as the story of the Gospel runs in Mark. The despised and more or less outlawed Galilee is shewn to have been chosen by God as the seat of the gospel and the revelation of the Son of Man, while the sacred city of Jerusalem, the home of Jewish piety and patriotism, has become the centre of relentless hostility and sin. Galilee is the sphere of revelation, Jerusalem the scene only of rejection. Galilee is the scene of the beginning and middle of the Lord's ministry; Jerusalem only of its end.[178]

There is little historical evidence to back up these broad assertions, and this kind of interpretation treats the text as if it were an allegory about the community rather than an account of the life, death, and resurrection of Jesus.

Marxsen also argues that Galilee is the home of the gospel and claims that its geographical outline is primarily theological in intent. He writes, "To overstate the case, Mark does not intend to say: Jesus worked in Galilee, but rather: Where Jesus worked there is Galilee."[179] He associates the gospel with the oracle reported in Eusebius that the people of the church in Jerusalem should leave to go to Pella in Perea.[180] The end would come soon and Jerusalem would be destroyed. The prophecy in 14:28 that Jesus will go before the disciples to Galilee, and the announcement in 16:7 that he is going ahead of them to Galilee are key passages for him. That the disciples will see him in Galilee implies for Marxsen that a community already exists there and that they expect the Parousia, which is assumed to be imminent, to occur there.[181] The two prophecies about Galilee in 14:28 and 16:7, however, refer to resurrection appearances rather than to the Parousia, and his arguments are not convincing.

The argument that Mark was composed in Galilee is continued by Kelber, who reemphasizes the polarity between Galilee and Jerusalem.[182] Van Eck adds sociological trappings to Lohmeyer's conclusions.[183] Roskam most recently claims that the gospel was written in Galilee and dates it after the Jewish revolt. In a situation of persecution, Mark wrote to downplay any hint that Jesus was subversive in his teaching or activity and to highlight the unjust malevolence of the Jewish authorities who engineered the execution of a righteous man.[184] Roskam considers the external evidence insufficient to establish the provenance and date of the gospel and instead

178. Lightfoot, *Locality and Doctrine*, 124–25.

179. Marxsen, *Mark the Evangelist*, 93–94.

180. Ibid., 114–15.

181. Ibid., 92, 107.

182. Werner Kelber, *The Kingdom in Mark: A New Place and a New Time* (Philadelphia: Fortress, 1974), 130; idem, *Mark's Story of Jesus* (Philadelphia: Fortress, 1979), 13–14. See also Pierson Parker, "Mark, Acts and Galilean Christianity," *NTS* 16 (1970): 295–304; Theodore J. Weeden, *Mark: Traditions in Conflict* (Philadelphia: Fortress, 1971).

183. Ernest van Eck, *Galilee and Jerusalem in Mark's Story of Jesus: A Narratological and Social-Scientific Reading* (HvTStSup 7; Pretoria: University of Pretoria, 1995).

184. Hendrika Nicoline Roskam, *The Purpose of the Gospel of Mark in its Historical and Social Context* (NovTSup 114; Leiden: Brill, 2004), 17–21, 237–38.

relies on internal evidence. Her conclusions about the situation of the community, which she thinks the gospel addresses, particularly in 13:9, could apply to multiple locales and do not narrow the gospel's origin to Galilee. For example, Paul faces persecution, presumably at the instigation of Jews in Damascus, and must flee King Aretas (2 Cor 11:32). He is turned over to the Roman governor in Caesarea and stands before the two governors and King Agrippa and is ultimately sent to Rome to defend himself before the emperor (Acts 23:24–26:32). In 1 Pet 2:13–14, written from "Babylon," which is a cryptic reference to Rome, the Christians there who are facing persecution are urged to accept the authority of the emperor and governors. Why Roskam thinks that emphasizing the malice of the Jewish authorities in the gospel would help to quell their suspicions of Christians and stop them from handing them over to the Romans is puzzling.

Galilee's prominence in Mark's plot is undeniable, but its importance can be explained simply by the historical fact that the majority of Jesus' ministry took place there (see Acts 10:37) and that some resurrection appearances were to take place there. "The correct and detailed geographical references to places in Galilee," noted by Roskam,[185] may simply reflect the accuracy of the tradition that Mark records and need not mean that the gospel was composed there. There is no external evidence that a major Christian community existed in Galilee or faced persecution.[186] That Mark needed to translate Aramaic names and phrases for his audience implies that the gospel was written outside of Palestine. The important critique of this theory by Stemberger has too often been ignored, perhaps because it appears only as an appendix in Davies's *The Gospel and the Land*, but he makes the strongest case that rules out Galilee as an option.[187] The prominence of Galilee is not because the gospel was composed there but because that is the region where Jesus conducted most of his ministry and many of his followers were Galileans.

1.2.2.2.3 Syria

Bartlet was one of the first to champion Antioch in Syria as the setting for the gospel. He contends that it was composed by Mark when he returned there after the martyrdom of Peter in Rome.[188] He argues that Peter was connected to and held in honor by the Antiochene church, that Alexander and Rufus, the sons of Simon of Cyrene, who was forced into carrying Jesus' cross (15:21), may have belonged to the men of Cyrene who helped plant the church there (Acts 11:20); that Antioch was a great center of Roman culture and the place where the term "Christian" was coined; and that this location may best explain how Mark came to be used by Matthew and Luke.

185. Ibid., 113–14.

186. Collins, *Mark*, 101, 658–67.

187. Günter Stemberger, "Appendix IV: Galilee—Land of Salvation?" in W. D. Davies, *The Gospel and the Land: Early Christianity and Jewish Territorial Doctrine* (Berkeley: University of California Press, 1974), 409–38.

188. J. Vernon Bartlet, *St Mark* (rev. ed.; The Century Bible; Edinburgh: T. C. & E. C. Jack, 1922), 36–38. W. C. Allen, *The Gospel according to St. Mark* (Oxford Church Bible Commentary; New York: Macmillan, 1915), contends that the gospel was first written in Jerusalem in Aramaic shortly after AD 44 and translated into Greek in Antioch in AD 44–47.

Others have refined the arguments for a Syrian provenance.[189] Theissen argues that someone familiar with the wider Mediterranean world would hardly call the little Galilean lake a "sea" (2:13; 3:7; 4:1; 5:1, 21, and with a genitive attribute in 1:16; 7:31) as if it were comparable to the great Mediterranean Sea.[190] This usage, however, may indicate the provenance of the tradition that Mark uses instead of the provenance of where the gospel was composed. Van Iersel argues that the word "sea" is used in the LXX for the great sea but also for an inland lake (Num 34:3, 11, 12; Josh 3:16; 8:9; 12:3, 7; 13:27; 18:19; 19:46), an artificial water basin (2 Kgdms 8:8; 3 Kgdms 3:1; 7:23–44; 1 Chr 18:8; 2 Chr 4:2–15), and a reservoir (3 Kgdms 18:32–38). Mark's usage probably reflects the influence of the LXX rather than his locale.[191]

Collins connects the gospel's emphasis on persecution to a report in Josephus (*J.W.* 2.18.1–5 §§457–480) that records Jews being persecuted in nearly all of the cities of Syria.[192] The persecution Josephus mentions, however, is directed against Jews in general and not against Christians as Christians, who in Mark are persecuted "on account of me" (13:9) and "because of me" (13:13).[193] Van Iersel notes that all of the reports of the persecutions of Jews that Josephus mentions are carried out by civilians, not by the authorities who are presumed to be behind the persecution mentioned in 13:9–11.[194]

Boring argues that Mark reflects no awareness of the theology of the Roman Christian community or awareness of Paul's letter to the Romans with its emphasis on the "righteousness of God" and the law. Nor do later writings associated with Rome (1 Peter or *1 Clement*), which he claims come from Rome near the first century, reflect any awareness of Mark's gospel.[195] But why should Pauline theology and terminology be expected to surface in a historical narrative about the ministry, death, and resurrection of Jesus? This expectation assumes a unidirectional influence of the community on the text, which is hardly warranted, and a gospel that is primarily engaged in resolving sectarian theological issues at a particular time rather

189. So Kee, *Community*, 100–105, who ventures that it was written in a "rural and small-town southern Syria"; Burton L. Mack, *Myth of Innocence: Mark and Christian Origins* (Philadelphia: Fortress, 1988), 315–18; Theissen, *The Gospels in Context*, 235–58; Marcus, *Mark 1–8*, 33–37; Collins, *Mark*, 7–10.

190. Theissen, *The Gospels in Context*, 237–38. Lars Hartman, *Mark for the Nations: A Text-and Reader-Oriented Commentary* (Eugene, OR: Pickwick, 2010), 250, cites Porphyry (*Contra Christianos*, Fragment 55), who mocks Mark's characterization of this body of water as a "sea": "Those who tell the truth about the place say that there is no sea but only a little lake.... Mark goes far from the truth and concocts this ridiculous story ... in which Jesus finds the disciples on that pool. He calls it a sea and, in addition, a storm-beaten one and with terrifying enormous, raging waves, in order to be able to present Jesus as performing a great sign."

191. Van Iersel, *Mark*, 37–38.

192. Collins, *Mark*, 12–13. Joel Marcus, "The Jewish War and the *Sitz im Leben* of Mark," *JBL* 111 (1992): 441–62, claims that the prophecies in Mark 13 are shaped after the events and that this intimate familiarity with what happened during the Jewish War against Rome reflects the geographical proximity of the community to Jerusalem. In my view, it is precarious to start from Mark 13 to look for clues for the setting of the gospel, since this approach can be treacherously circular.

193. See Incigneri, *Gospel*, 84–86.

194. Van Iersel, *Mark*, 40. See Josephus, *J.W.* 2.13.7 §§266–270; 2.14.4–5 §§284–292; 2.18.1–8 §§457–498; 2.20.2 §§559–561; 3.2.1–3 §§9–28; 7.3.2–4 §§41–62; *Ant.*18.9.1 §§374–379.

195. M. Eugene Boring, *Mark A Commentary* (NTL; Louisville: Westminster John Knox, 2006), 18–19. Thomas Söding, "Der Evangelist in seiner Zeit: Voraussetzungen, Hintergründe und Schwerpunkte markinischer Theologie," in *Der Evangelist als Theologe: Studien zum Markusevangelium* (ed. Thomas Söding; SBS 163; Stuttgart: Katholisches Bibelwerk, 1995), 29–30, believes that if Mark were written in Rome, we should expect the gospel to exhibit more echoes of Paul's letter to the Romans and more evidence of the problems between the weak and the strong that comes out in Romans 14.

than imparting historical information that will serve the church beyond a limited situation.[196] The assumption that the evangelists bend the narrative toward the theology of the community in which they are writing is completely unwarranted. It is curious that some think that Paul's letters should be more like gospels and would have included more traditions about Jesus had he known them, while others think that the gospels are more like letters and are written to address the particular needs of the author's community rather than passing on the traditions about Jesus.

Finally, no external evidence supports Syria as the provenance for the gospel, which is surprising if it were correct. Black notes, "The figure of Peter played a significant role in Syrian Christianity, but none of the early fathers—even those from Syria themselves—located the composition of the Second Gospel there."[197] If Mark's provenance were unsure from the beginning, why would they have not claimed Mark as their own?

1.2.2.2.4 A Local or Universal Community?

Marcus admits that "most of the exegesis" in his commentary "would work just as well if the setting were Rome or some other place where Christians were under pressure."[198] The influence of redaction criticism leads many to assume that the gospels were written with the needs of a particular community uppermost in the mind of the authors and that they should be read through the prism of some historically identifiable, local group, for example, the Markan community.[199] This community is constructed from various hypotheses which are both read out of *and* read into the text.

After examining the various pictures of the Markan community in current debate, however, Peterson concludes that this methodology "never actually provides reliable interpretative control."[200] It may be an exaggeration to say as Peterson does that there are "as many so-called Markan communities as there are scholars to produce them,"[201] but the number of proposals does suggest that this research produces a "highly speculative, viciously circular and ultimately unpersuasive and inconclusive reading."[202] He contends that the "lack of agreement among Gospel community constructors is related more to the futility of the entire enterprise than to a need for further study."[203] The gospel was not intended to be read as a window

196. Michael F. Bird, "The Formation of the Gospels in the Setting of Early Christianity: The Jesus Tradition as Corporate Memory," *WTJ* 67 (2005): 116, astutely observes that if someone "is attempting to validate a certain teaching, enforce a particular vision of community, marginalize an opposing faction, or dictate a theological agenda, then writing a Gospel (i.e., a connected narrative about Jesus) appears to be a rather convoluted way of doing it and is highly susceptible to being misunderstood. Why not write a list of community rules (1QS, CD, 4QMMT), quote the Hebrew Scriptures repeatedly in an epistle (1 Clement, Hebrews), compose a list of sapiential sayings of Jesus (e.g. Gospel of Thomas, Q), make some creative exegetical notes (Targums, Pesher, Midrash, Allegory), appeal to episcopal authority (Clement, Ignatius), or even refer to sayings of venerated leaders (Mishnah)?"

197. Black, "Was Mark a Roman Gospel?" 39–40.

198. Marcus, *Mark 1–8*, 36.

199. C. Clifton Black, *The Disciples according to Mark: Markan Redaction in Current Debate* (JSNTSup 27; Sheffield: JSOT, 1989), 17–38, 60; and "The Quest of Mark the Redactor: Why Has It Been Pursued, and What Has It Taught Us?" *JSNT* 33 (1988): 19–39, demonstrates through his examination of redaction-critical studies on the role of the disciples in Mark that redaction criticism of Mark's gospel has produced less than dependable results. The speculative efforts to demarcate Mark's editorial influence when we do not know Mark's sources have led to an abundance of mutually exclusive hypotheses.

200. Peterson, *Origins*, 194.

201. Ibid., 196.

202. Ibid.

203. Ibid., 4.

into the community in which it was produced. That so-called window seems too often to reflect the image of the scholar trying to look through it than it does the image of the actual community.

Bauckham therefore asserts that "the enterprise of reconstructing an evangelist's community is . . . doomed to failure."[204] He claims that to assume that "each Gospel addresses a localized community in its own, quite specific context and character"[205] turns the gospel into an allegory by which the church tells its own story rather than the story of Jesus Christ.[206] This is not to say that the local context would not have exerted some influence on the composition of the gospel, but I am inclined to agree with Bauckham that the gospel was intended to be applicable for all Christians whatever their local setting. Bird insists,

> Mark could have been written nearly anywhere in the Greco-Roman world, because it seeks to engage the mind, heart, fears, and hopes of Christians spread throughout the Greco-Roman world. The inability to locate an exact provenance for Mark is directly attributable to the literary purpose of Mark that aims to engender attitudes, patterns of behaviour, hope, and an ethos of discipleship in a broad and undefined audience of Greek-speaking Christians.[207]

Mark's gospel was used and valued by Matthew and Luke, not as a work focused on the particular circumstances of Mark's community, but as a work generally useful to various different churches. According to Bauckham, the early Christian movement did not consist of scattered, isolated, and self-sufficient communities with little or no communication between them, but rather of a network of communities with constant and close communication. He writes, "In other words, the social character of early Christianity was such that the idea of writing a Gospel purely for one's own community is unlikely to have occurred to anyone."[208] Relative ease of travel and the evidence of wide-ranging Christian mobility and extensive networks lend credibility to idea that the gospels would have been written for general circulation.

I believe that Rome as the provenance of the gospel of Mark makes good historical sense. I also assume that the gospel was composed not only for this community but was intended for wider circulation that would contribute to the good news being proclaimed to all nations (13:10; see 14:9). As a result, this gospel transcends its original setting and the setting of all of its readers throughout the eons because of the power of the theological truth it narrates.

---

204. Richard Bauckham, "For Whom Were Gospels Written?" in *The Gospels for All Christians: Rethinking the Gospel Audiences* (ed. Richard Bauckham; Grand Rapids: Eerdmans, 1998), 45.

205. Ibid., 11. It is to be expected that Bauckham's theory would spark a strong reaction since it challenges one of the fundamental principles of gospel study. Those who have made significant investments in their theories regarding particular settings for the gospels and their readings resulting from them have naturally challenged this argument. See, e.g., Philip F. Esler, "Community and Gospel in Early Christianity: A Response to Richard Bauckham's *Gospel for All Christians*," *SJT* 51 (1998): 235–48; and Margaret M. Mitchell, "Patristic Counter-Evidence to the Claim that 'The Gospels Were Written for All Christians,'" *NTS* 51 (2005): 36–79.

206. Bauckham, "For Whom Were Gospels Written?" 19–20.

207. Bird, "The Markan Community, Myth or Maze?" 485.

208. Bauckham, "For Whom Were Gospels Written?" 30.

1.2.2.3 Dating: Before or After AD 70?

John A. T. Robinson attacked the scholarly consensus regarding the dating of the NT books and tried to make the case that all of these books were produced in the two decades before AD 70. He includes a private letter from C. H. Dodd regarding the NT dating game:

> I should agree with you that much of this late dating is quite arbitrary, even wanton, the offspring not of any argument that can be presented, but rather of the critic's prejudice that if he appears to assent to the traditional position of the early church he will be thought no better than a stick-in-the-mud.[209]

Nevertheless, most scholars assume that Mark was written just before, during, or shortly after the trauma of the Jewish War against Rome that led to the temple's destruction.[210]

1.2.2.3.1 After AD 70

Brandon argues that Mark 13 utilizes an earlier Jewish apocalyptic flyleaf and that 13:14 refers to Caligula's design to erect a statue of himself in the temple. That plan was aborted when he was assassinated in the year 41, but the memory of that threat lived on. The text was applied to the time when Jerusalem was sacked and Titus's triumphant legionaries erected their standards in the courtyard of the temple, sacrificed to them, and acclaimed Titus as imperator (Josephus, *J.W.* 6.6.1 §316). The "abomination that causes desolation" standing where it does not belong (13:14), he claims, refers to Titus's standing (the participle in Greek is masculine) in the temple.[211] When this event happened, however, the chance to flee, as Jesus enjoins in this verse, was long gone. Those who remained in the city were either slaughtered or captured to be led away in slavery. It makes sense that it would only apply in a time when it was possible to flee Jerusalem. Flight would only have been possible before the impending Roman siege of the city and before they built a wall around the whole city that was patrolled by sentries to block any exit (Josephus, *J.W.* 5.12.1–2 §§499–511), that is, before AD 70.[212]

209. Robinson, *Redating*, 360.

210. Morna D. Hooker, *The Gospel according to Saint Mark* (BNTC; Peabody, MA: Hendrickson, 1991), 8, states that Mark is usually dated between AD 65 and 75.

211. S. G. F. Brandon, "The Date of the Markan Gospel," *NTS* 7 (1960): 126–41.

212. In my view, Jesus' prediction of the temple's destruction in 13:1–2 is not decisive for dating the composition of the gospel, contra John S. Kloppenborg, "*Evocatio Deorum* and The Date of Mark," *JBL* 124 (2005): 419–50. Kloppenborg (450) claims: "The extraordinary prediction made in Mark 13:2—the complete and final demolition of the temple—should be regarded not as a fortunate guess about the accidents of war. It presupposes awareness of Roman siege tactics and, in particular, the ritual of *evocatio* and the separation of an enemy from its protective deity preliminary to the razing of a town and its temples. Mark's forecast ... entails a claim that the divine presence is no longer there; accordingly Mark 13:2 should be read in concert with Q 13:35a and the oracle of Jesus ben Hananiah, both uttered before the revolt."

The cluster of references to its destruction (11:15–19, 27; 12:35, 41; 13:1–2, 14; 14:58; 15:29, 38) need not reflect a perspective after the event. It may accurately reflect Jesus' prescience about its destruction during his ministry (see the parallels with the threats against the temple by Jesus ben Ananias that provoked the Jewish authorities to turn him over to the Roman governor). It may also reflect the perspective of those who, during the war, recognize the inevitability of the temple's destruction and have resigned themselves to it theologically.

Incigneri argues that the gospel was composed in AD 71 after the triumphal ceremonies of Titus and Vespasian in Rome. The spoils of war plundered from Jerusalem — the prisoners of war, the golden temple vessels and furnishings, a copy of the law, and the purple hangings from the sanctuary — were paraded through Rome in a grand triumph (see Josephus, *J.W.* 7.5.5–7 §§132–162).[213]

1.2.2.3.2 Before AD 70

If the tradition is to be credited that Mark's gospel was composed in Rome, Hengel makes a strong case that it might have occurred after the deaths of Peter and Paul in that city (*1 Clem* 5:2–7). The death of central eyewitnesses would have affected the oral rendition of the gospel and would have provided an impetus to create a written narrative. Hengel offers AD 69 as the date of composition during an exceptionally chaotic time. Civil war had broken out in Rome after Nero's suicide on June 9, AD 68, as aspirants to the throne battled for ascendancy. Despite this disarray, the Roman military juggernaut was slowly but surely crushing the Jewish revolt and the fate of Jerusalem was sealed.[214]

If Mark 13 is considered to offer any evidence concerning the gospel's date, Stein lists several things that suggest that it was not composed after the destruction of Jerusalem. First, it contains no prophecy of fire that Josephus said incinerated the city and the temple (*J.W.* 6.4.5 §§249–287).[215] There is no prophecy of "the violent, intramural fighting" among the various Jewish factions during the siege. There is no prophecy "of the thousands of Jews that were crucified by the Romans outside the city walls."[216] The absence of these parallels to what Josephus describes in his account of the city's ruin may simply mean that the discourse faithfully records Jesus' teaching and that Mark did not fine-tune that teaching to fit later events.[217]

A date for Mark prior to the destruction of Jerusalem seems to be the best option. The evidence does not permit a definitive answer, however.

1.2.3 The Priority of Mark

The Griesbach hypothesis that contended that Matthew was the first gospel, that Luke made use of Matthew and additional sources, and that Mark wrote his

213. Incigneri, *Gospel*, 202–7; see also Ivan Head, "Mark as a Roman Document from the Year 69: Testing Martin Hengel's Thesis," *JRH* 28 (2004): 240–59.

214. Hengel, *Studies*, 26–30. The election of Vespasian, the general who commanded the Roman army in the battle with the Jewish rebels, as emperor, began the Flavian dynasty. His son Titus directed the siege of Jerusalem and its final destruction.

215. Kathleen and Leen Ritmeyer, *Reconstructing Herod's Temple Mount in Jerusalem* (Washington, DC: Biblical Archaeological Society, 1990), 45, 48, explain the archaeological discovery of the imprint of arches burnt into the bedrock foundations of chambers adjoining the southern retaining wall, east of the Triple Gate: "Before the arches collapsed, the fire burnt into the back wall of the chambers, leaving the imprint of the arches as evocative testimony to the dreadful inferno."

216. Robert H. Stein, *Jesus, the Temple and the Coming of the Son of Man* (Downers Grove, IL: InterVarsity Press, 2014), 35–36.

217. Stein, *Jesus, the Temple and the Coming of the Son of Man*, 51, recognizes that "Mark considered the Jesus traditions he was reporting as sacred traditions: 'Heaven and earth will pass away, but [Jesus'] words will not pass away' (13:31)."

gospel by condensing both Matthew and Luke had somewhat of a revival in the 1960s,[218] but now has few supporters.[219] To argue that Mark epitomized Matthew and Luke turns this gospel into an odd account. It is difficult to explain why, for example, Mark would leave out so much from these other gospels but would add the healing of a deaf mute (7:33–36) and the healing of the blind man of Bethsaida (8:22–26). In both cases, Jesus uses saliva, the only time he employs a physical agent in healing in the Synoptics; and in the second case, the effect of the miracle is not immediate but requires a second try. Davies and Allison ask a reasonable question that the supporters of the Griesbach hypothesis cannot answer adequately:

> Can one seriously envision someone rewriting Matthew and Luke so as to omit the miraculous birth of Jesus, the sermon on the mount, and the resurrection appearances, while, on the other hand, adding the tale of the naked young man, a healing miracle in which Jesus has trouble healing, and the remark that Jesus' family thought him mad?[220]

Or, why would Mark change Matthew's conclusion to Jesus' visit to his hometown of Nazareth, "he did not do many miracles there because of their lack of faith" (Matt 13:58) to "he could not do any miracles there" (Mark 6:5), which strangely draws attention to his impotence in this situation?[221]

In addition to the many arguments that have been raised against the Griesbach thesis,[222] Goodacre identifies numerous examples of "editorial fatigue" or "docile reproduction" that he argues conclusively establishes that Matthew and Luke used Mark's gospel in which incoherencies are introduced when Matthew and Luke make changes in the early part of the narrative they have taken over from Mark that they

---

218. Bernard Orchard and Thomas R. W. Longstaff, eds., *J. J. Griesbach: Synoptic and Text-Critical Studies 1776–1976* (SNTSMS 34; Cambridge: Cambridge University Press, 1978); William R. Farmer, "Modern Developments of Griesbach's Hypothesis," *NTS* 23 (1977): 275–95; Hans-Herbert Stoldt, *History and Criticism of the Markan Hypothesis* (trans. Donald L. Niewyk; Macon, GA: Mercer University Press, 1980); and David B. Peabody, Lamar Cope, and Allan J. McNicol, *One Gospel from Two: Mark's Use of Matthew and Luke* (Harrisburg: Trinity Press International, 2002). David J. Neville, *Mark's Gospel: Prior or Posterior? A Reappraisal of the Phenomenon of Order* (JSNTSup 222; London/New York: Sheffield Academic, 2002), tries to sort through the problem of order looking at it from the perspectives of both theories. C. S. Mann, *Mark: A New Translation with Introduction and Commentary* (AB 27; Garden City, NY: Doubleday, 1986), wrote a commentary assuming the Griesbach hypothesis that was fairly quickly replaced by the commentary by Marcus, *Mark 1–8*, in 2000. Delbert R. Burkett, *Rethinking the Gospel Sources: From Proto-Mark to Mark* (London/New York: T&T Clark International, 2004), 5–6, offers a multisource theory that proposes the priority of a pre-Markan gospel and suggests that Mark and Matthew were written about the same time, around AD 80–100, and independently using the Synoptic material.

219. Christopher M. Tuckett, *The Revival of the Griesbach Hypothesis: Analysis and Appraisal* (SNTSMS 44; Cambridge: Cambridge University Press, 1983), has been influential in invalidating the arguments of the Griesbach Hypothesis. See also Peter M. Head, *Christology and the Synoptic Problem: An Argument for Markan Priority* (SNTSMS 94; Cambridge: Cambridge University Press, 1997); and Paul Foster et al., eds., *New Studies in the Synoptic Problem: Oxford Conference, April 2008: Essays in Honour of Christopher M. Tuckett* (BETL 239; Leuven: Peeters, 2011).

220. W. D. Davies and Dale Allison Jr., *The Gospel According to Saint Matthew* (ICC; Edinburgh: T&T Clark, 1988), 1:109.

221. Head, *Christology and the Synoptic Problem*, 66–83, while arguing for Markan priority, contends that this particular passage is a weak link in supporting it.

222. E. P. Sanders, *The Tendencies of the Synoptic Tradition* (SNTSMS 9; Cambridge: Cambridge University Press, 1969), shows that Matthew and Luke edit down their source material.

are unable to maintain throughout the narrative.[223] Damm has added another nail in the coffin of the Griesbach hypothesis by approaching the problem from the perspective of Greco-Roman rhetoric. He examines the triple tradition and double tradition *chreia* and concludes that Mark's reasoning is often clumsy according to rhetorical conventions but that Matthew and Luke adapt Mark's account to increase clarity and suitability. He concludes from this research that Markan priority is more plausible than Matthean priority.[224] Mark's textual tradition has undergone more scribal corrections than have Matthew's or Luke's, and Gamble conjectures that they could be attributable to Mark being in circulation for a longer period.[225] Goodacre's analysis concludes that Matthew and Luke

> are simultaneously enthralled and concerned by Mark. While inspired by the notion of writing this kind of narrative of Jesus' life culminating in the Passion, they nevertheless see it as only "the beginning of the Gospel of Jesus Christ" and want to fill it out with stories of Jesus' origin at one end and his resurrection at the other, adding much material in between focusing on Jesus' teaching, correcting what they perceive to be its rough literary style and, more important, its theological idiosyncrasies.[226]

I would only disagree with the reference to "theological idiosyncrasies." To my mind, Matthew and Luke do not so much correct Mark's theology as miss some of Mark's theological subtlety.

The Synoptic Problem remains a problem because of the complexity of the issues related to the sources used by the gospel.[227] Allowances must be made for the continuing influence of oral tradition and varying textual traditions. When all is said and done, however, Markan priority remains the best hypothesis for explaining features in Mark, Matthew, and Luke.

---

223. Mark Goodacre, "Fatigue in the Synoptics," *NTS* 44 (1998): 45–58. G. M. Styler, "Excursus IV: The Priority of Mark," in C. F. D. Moule, *The Birth of the New Testament* (3rd ed.; San Francisco: Harper & Row, 1982), 285–316, cites six examples (Matt 9:14/Mark 2:18; Matt 14:3–12/Mark 6:17–29; Matt 19:16–17/Mark 10:17–18; Matt 22:41–45/Mark 12:35–37a; Matt 24:3/Mark 13:3; and Matt 27:15–18/Mark 15:6–10) where Matthew retained Mark's wording without assimilating it and as a result blurring the logic. He then cites three examples (Luke 8:51/Mark 5:37, 40; Luke 20:39/Mark 12:28, 32; and Luke 9:21/Mark 8:30) that show that Luke must be secondary to Mark.

David C. Sim, "Matthew's Use of Mark: Did Matthew Intend to Supplement or to Replace His Primary Source?" *NTS* 57 (2011): 182–83, argues that since Matthew reproduces 90 percent of Mark's content he "composed his Gospel to render Mark redundant." He also argues (180) that "Matthew often edited the Marcan texts he did retain either to remove offence or to correct unpalatable theological features in Mark's account." Ulrich Luz, "The Gospel of Matthew: A New Story of Jesus, or a Rewritten One?" in *Studies in Matthew* (trans. Rosemary Selle; Grand Rapids: Eerdmans, 2005), 18–36, contends, however, that Matthew left Mark's gospel largely untouched and wrote to supplement it, not to replace it. Matthew, he says, is the author of "a rewritten Markan Gospel" (35). Kari Syreeni, *The Making of the Sermon on the Mount: A Procedural Analysis of Matthew's Redactional Activity: Part 1: Method and Compositional Analysis (*AASF 44; Helsinki: Suomalainen Tiedeakatemia, 1987), 113, maintains that the basic characteristic of Matthew's gospel is the combination of Mark and Q to produce a "'double' gospel with the complete story of Jesus and the whole of Jesus' authoritative teaching." Whether or not one accepts the two-document hypothesis and the existence of Q, Matthew clearly develops Mark.

224. Alex Damm, *Ancient Rhetoric and the Synoptic Problem: Clarifying Markan Priority* (BETL 252; Leuven: Peeters, 2013).

225. Harry Y. Gamble, *The New Testament Canon: Its Making and Meaning* (GBSNTS; Philadelphia: Fortress, 1985): 27.

226. Mark Goodacre, *The Case Against Q: Studies in Markan Priority and the Synoptic Problem* (Harrisburg, PA: Trinity Press International, 2002), 44.

227. See Paul Foster et al., eds., *New Studies in the Synoptic Problem: Oxford Conference, April 2008: Essays in Honour of Christopher M. Tuckett* (BETL 239; Leuven: Peeters, 2011).

1.2.4 The Genre of Mark

Mark was the first evangelist to compose a connected narrative from a plethora of stories about Jesus. Was he influenced by a particular genre in undertaking this task? Hirsch defines genre as "a system of expectations" that affect how a work is understood.[228] Identifying the genre of Mark has been touted as an important hermeneutical key for understanding how this gospel functioned in the lives of the readers, the church, and society.[229] The efforts to pinpoint Mark's genre, however, have failed to produce a real consensus. Telford's survey of the research leads him to observe that "attempts to identify the genre of Mark ... in terms of its literary antecedents or ancient literary parallels, have produced mixed results."[230] The array of proposals suggests that the genre is not that obvious.

1.2.4.1 Sui Generis

For some time, it was thought that the gospels were unique (*sui generis*).[231] Aune comments that this view is true "in the sense that no other ancient composition, Greco-Roman or Jewish, is precisely like them."[232] The "gospel" as it is understood in the NT is a message, and Mark turned it into a type of book, conserving traditions and editing them into a coherent narrative. Mark may be considered the father of the gospel genre in the same way that Herodotus was the father of history-writing (ca. 440 BC). The title of Herodotus's *History*, "This is the Exposition of the History of Herodotus of Halicarnassus," in which the word "history" or "inquiry" (*historia*) later became a general term for works of historiography, is analogous to what happened with the opening lines of Mark's work, "The beginning of the good news about Jesus the Messiah, the Son of God." The term "good news" (*euangelion*) became the general term for works about Jesus.[233] Knight comments, however, "The Gospel form was an innovation in first-century Christianity but it is broadly related to other ancient literary types."[234] This fact may explain why scholars can find so many parallels with other ancient literature. Downing also observes that there is a "flexibility of and overlap between all the genres we or the ancients discern."[235]

228. E. D. Hirsch, *Validity in Interpretation* (New Haven, CT: Yale University Press, 1967), 83.

229. Adela Yarbro Collins, *The Beginning of the Gospel: Probings of Mark in Context* (Minneapolis: Fortress, 1992), 2.

230. William R. Telford, *Writing on the Gospel of Mark* (Guides to Advanced Biblical Research 1; Dorset: Deo, 2009), 9.

231. See Rudolf Bultmann, *The History of the Synoptic Tradition* (trans. John Marsh; New York: Harper and Row, 1963), 346–50, 371; Robert A. Guelich, "The Gospel Genre," in *Das Evangelium und die Evangelien 1982* (ed. Peter Stuhlmacher; WUNT 2/28; Tübingen: Mohr Siebeck, 1983), 183–219; Eve-Marie Becker, *Das Markus-Evangelium im Rahmen antiker Historiographie* (WUNT 194; Tübingen: Mohr Siebeck, 2006), 50, 52.

232. David E. Aune, *The Westminster Dictionary of the New Testament and Early Christian Literature* (Louisville: Westminster John Knox, 2003), 204.

233. Silke Petersen, "Die Evangelienüberschriften und die Entstehung des neutestamentlichen Kanons," *ZNW* 97 (2006): 269, n. 66. See Michel Bouttier, "Commencement, force et fin de l'évangile," *ETR* 28 (1977): 465–93, who compares it to the originality of the work of the Yahwist, or the Deuteronomist.

234. Jonathan Knight, *Luke's Gospel* (New Testament Readings; London/New York: Routledge, 1998), 4.

235. F. Gerald Downing, "Theophilus's First Reading of Luke-Acts," in *Luke's Literary Achievement: Collected Essays* (ed. Christopher M. Tuckett; JSNTSup 116; Sheffield: Sheffield Academic, 1995), 99.

1.2.4.2 Biography

Many interpreters assume that Mark understands himself to be writing biography.[236] Brower states, "Mark's gospel is a narrative in the pattern of ancient *bios*. This is crucial because it takes as its default position that the gospel is coherent and has its focus primarily on Jesus."[237] This genre should not be understood in terms of a modern biography that provides a detailed description of a person's life, delving into his or her background and formative influences and often engaging in psychological speculation to shed light on the individual's personality. In the ancient world, biography primarily had a didactic function. Votaw said that biographies eulogize and idealize their subjects, collecting their best sayings and most dramatic deeds for "hortatory" aims, "to teach uprightness and usefulness by example."[238] Collins notes, however, that "there is no ancient definition and no ancient literary-critical discussion of how a biography should be written, what its essential features are, and what its purpose is."[239] Mark's resemblance to ancient biography, then, may only be a family resemblance that is difficult to pin down.

Hemer cautions regarding genre criticism related to Luke-Acts:

> Contemporary Roman literature, in particular, was an aristocratic avocation pursued within the confines of a social and cultural élite, whereas the Christian movement seems to have been concerned from the outset with popular proclamation. It is wholly probable that their writers, and especially one with the literary ability and aspiration of Luke, were influenced by its cultural environment and reflect their trends, but by no means certain how closely or consciously.[240]

If that is true for Luke, then how much more is it true for Mark, who shows no sign of literary aspirations? Hemer also cautions, "We can find almost whatever we seek, and we can see significance in what we find. In such a case the study of literary forms is a task to be pursued with special caution, with a care not to use categories which arise out of imposed, rather than inherent, classifications."[241]

As a result, Aune states that "we must be prepared to forego simplistic answers and entertain the possibility that Mark has been recycled from elements of several

236. See Clyde Weber Votaw, "The Gospels and Contemporary Biographies," *AJT* 19 (1915): 45–73, 217–49; repr. *The Gospels and Contemporary Biographies in the Greco-Roman World* (FBBS 27; Philadelphia: Fortress, 1970). See also Charles H. Talbert, *What Is a Gospel? The Genre of the Canonical Gospels* (Philadelphia: Fortress, 1977); and Richard A. Burridge, *What Are the Gospels? A Comparison with Graeco-Roman Biography* (2nd ed.; Grand Rapids: Eerdmans, 2004).

237. Kent E. Brower, "'Who Then Is This?'—Christological Questions in Mark 4:35–5:43," *EvQ* 81 (2009): 292.

238. Votaw, "The Gospels and Contemporary Biographies," 51.

239. Collins, *Mark*, 25. Collins (26–33) provides a valuable history of the question and helpfully classifies six types of biography: (1) encomiastic, typically of high ranking, prominent persons such as kings, generals, and statesmen, which tends to ignore any embarrassing facts; (2) scholarly, typically of literary authors and philosophers; (3) didactic, typically of religious leaders and philosophers, which is designed to instruct the reader about the subject's life and a virtuous way of life and contains extensive teaching; (4) ethical, which is designed to encourage imitation of ethical virtues and avoidance of vices; (5) entertainment, which intends to satisfy curiosity about past heroes or tyrants; and (6) historical, which, like historiography, lists and explains the causes for important series of events. She claims that Mark's gospel has the greatest affinity with the didactic type and the historical type.

240. Colin J. Hemer, *The Book of Acts in the Setting of Hellenistic History* (ed. Conrad H. Gempf; Winona Lake, IN: Eisenbrauns, 1990), 34.

241. Ibid.

genres."[242] He points out the contrast between Mark and Greco-Roman biography. The latter recorded the lives of renowned politicians, generals, philosophers, and poets and "was written largely by and for members of the educated upper classes of Greek and Roman society, reflecting the humanistic values of those social strata."[243] Mark was "written in a much lower register of Koine Greek than most extant Greco-Roman biographies." Mark's gospel "reflects the countercultural social and religious values of first-century Christians, often marked by a subversive rejection of the values of the dominant culture."[244]

Aune maintains that Mark is a "parody" of Greco-Roman biography rather than "a simple emulation of it."[245] He uses Dentith's definition of parody as including "any cultural practice which provides a relatively polemical allusive imitation of another cultural production or practice."[246] How could a narrative in which the hero is offered mock homage as a king robed in purple and crowned with thorns and then crucified as a common criminal be anything else? If this is correct, then parody has a serious side. Aune concludes: "Mark was not modeled after a single identifiable textual prototype. Mark is an episodic text based on linking earlier oral and written gospel tradition into a relative large-scale narrative that functions as a complex genre with an ideological function."[247] It adopts features from many different genres, and parodies ancient biography "by subverting the social values enshrined in typical performances of Greco-Roman biography." It thereby "expanded the repertoire of what was thought appropriate for ancient biography."[248] Collins, however, demurs that Mark does not simply "invert and parody" but utilizes the techniques and values of Roman historiography and biography,[249] but she "re-places them in an implied, biblical, master-narrative, constructed from the Septuagint, which culminates in an apocalyptic scenario."[250]

Collins helpfully reminds us that Mark writes from a biblical perspective, which is often ignored. She asserts, "The author of Mark has taken the model of biblical sacred history and transformed it, first, by infusing it with an eschatological and apocalyptic perspective and, second, by adapting it to Hellenistic historiographical and biographical traditions. The latter was accomplished by the focus on the person of Jesus and by the presentation of his life and teaching in a way that assimilated

242. Aune, "Genre Theory and the Genre-Function of Mark and Matthew," 165.

243. Ibid., 167.

244. Ibid., 167–68.

245. Ibid., 168. This view explains why Mark lacks some of the features that appear in Greco-Roman biography that are highlighted by Michael E. Vines, *The Problem of Markan Genre: The Gospel of Mark and the Jewish Novel* (Academia biblica 3; Atlanta: Society of Biblical Literature, 2002), 10–13.

246. Aune, "Genre Theory and the Genre-Function of Mark and Matthew,"169, citing Simon Dentith, *Parody* (London/New York: Routledge, 2000), 9.

247. Aune, "Genre Theory and the Genre-Function of Mark and Matthew," 175.

248. Ibid.

249. Becker, *Das Markus-Evangelium*, argues that the gospel is more historiographical than biographical and is more closely related to the broad category of historical monograph. See also her "The Gospel of Mark in the Context of Ancient Historiography," in *The Function of Ancient Historiography in Biblical and Cognate Studies* (ed. Patricia G. Kirkpatrick and Timothy D. Goltz; London/New York: T&T Clark, 2008), 124–34.

250. Adela Yarbro Collins, "Reflections on the Conference at the University of Aarhus, July 25–27, 2008," in *Mark and Matthew I: Comparative Readings: Understanding the Earliest Gospels in Their First-Century Settings* (ed. Eve-Marie Becker and Anders Runesson; WUNT 2/271; Tübingen: Mohr Siebeck, 2011), 414.

him to the Hellenistic philosophers."[251] She argues that Greek and Roman literature are important, "but it is equally essential to interpret them in light of Jewish literature."[252] Sabin further contends that "it does not make sense to look to a genre that comes from a purely secular context."[253]

1.2.4.3 A Revelatory, Scriptural Book

The dizzying debate over Mark's genre in my opinion has not been repaying. Kennedy asserts regarding the genre of the gospels that there is no "perfect classical analogue."[254] Davies makes this observation in her review of Richard Burridge's, *What Are the Gospels? A Comparison with Graeco-Roman Biography*: "From reading Burridge's list of features, no one would guess that the gospels are theological narratives, and that they set the life of Jesus in the context of what God, the Creator and Sustainer of the world, is achieving through him."[255] I am inclined to agree with Pavur that Mark understands himself to be writing a "scriptural book" that is a "truly revelational, truly authoritative writing."[256] Mark presumes that his gospel will be read with the same expectations that his audience brought to their reading of Scripture.

The beginning of Mark's work reveals that he intends to narrate the fulfillment of divine promises foretold in Scripture and to present Jesus as the agent of God's saving purposes for the world. He presents God's reign as fully present in Jesus, who has come to bring about the defeat of Satan and provide atonement for humanity. Mark presents the coming of Jesus and his death and resurrection as the climactic moment in the unfolding of the divine plan of salvation. It narrates a renewed covenant that is sealed by Jesus' blood poured out for the many (14:24). The transfiguration shows Jesus to be superior to Moses, the lawgiver, and Elijah, the wonder-working prophet. The disciples are to "listen to him" (9:2–8). Mark presents Jesus clarifying how the Sabbath laws are to be applied and redefining the implication of food laws, the law on divorce, and God's relationship to the temple. Jesus breaks the shackles of unforgiven sins (2:1–10) and therefore also redefines how one can find forgiveness from God apart from the temple cult (11:25). While Jesus is akin to David, the anointed king, he is also mysteriously superior to him. Mark's story is therefore unique. Boring avers, "Though Mark does not invent an absolutely new genre, the narrative he composes is so distinctive from existing genres as to be considered a quantum leap, a mutation rather than merely a Christian example of an existing genre or an evolution from preceding models."[257] Since this

---

251. Collins, *Mark*, 1.

252. Ibid., 29.

253. Marie Noonan Sabin, *Reopening the Word: Reading Mark as Theology in the Context of Early Judaism* (New York: Oxford University Press, 2002), 11.

254. Kennedy, "Classical and Christian Source Criticism," 129.

255. Meg Davies, review of Richard A. Burridge, *What Are the Gospels? A Comparison with Graeco-Roman Biography*," *New Blackfriars* 74 (1993): 110.

256. Claude Nicholas Pavur, "'As It Is Written': The Nature, Purpose, and Meaning of Mark's Gospel" (M.S.T. thesis, The Jesuit School of Theology at Berkeley, 1985; rev., 2011), 5.

257. Boring, *Mark*, 7–9, lists five elements that set Mark apart from Hellenistic biographies and comments that these distinctive features are all "christological." (1) Mark's narrative "presents a tensive juxtaposition of pictures of Jesus as truly human and truly divine." (2) The gospel has an apocalyptic perspective as "the story of Jesus is presented as the definitive segment of universal history that extends from creation to eschaton; Jesus the Christ and Son of Man who has already appeared in history will appear at the end of

gospel is about saving events in history, it is analogous to the biblical history and should be read as such.

1.2.5 Markan Style

Deissmann characterizes Mark as a book written "in cosmopolitan Greek with marks of Semitic origin."[258] Mark writes a simple Greek that lacks sophistication,[259] but Sandmel declares that "whoever wrote Mark was neither a simple writer, nor a simpleton, but an artful writer usually in full control of his pen."[260] Stein offers that the simplicity of Mark's Greek may be due to his own lack of sophistication or to his accommodation to his intended readers, who were relatively uneducated.[261] When we speak of Mark's "readers," however, we should not envision a group of "readers" silently reading Mark's original codex [or scroll] but a group of *hearers* listening to Mark's text being read to them.

1.2.5.1 Action

Mark's gospel is characterized by a "paratactic, anecdotal style."[262] The narrative has a staccato, quick-fire character. In the first half of the gospel, Jesus and the disciples dart from event to event.[263] His ministry, as Mark presents it, consists of an impressive sequence of dramatic incidents, relentlessly pressing upon each other without any pause between.[264] The rush of activity only begins to slow down when Jesus heads south with his disciples for Jerusalem. When Jesus reaches Jerusalem, the days and hours are logged as they pass by during this last week. Mark tolls the hours during the crucifixion: It was the third hour (9:00 a.m.) when they crucified

---

history as its goal and judge." (3) "The main character is presented as both a figure of past history who once spoke and the present Lord of the community who still speaks." (4) The individual units of tradition previously had been used in "preaching and teaching the gospel" before Mark connected them into a narrative. "Many of the incidents and sayings that make up the content of Mark had been proclaimed and taught previously." (5) "As Jesus spoke of the kingdom in parables, so Mark speaks in the new narrative form that is an extended parable."

258. Adolf Deissmann, *Light from the Ancient East* (rev. ed.; trans. Lionel R. M. Strachan; New York: Doran, 1927), 392. Various scholars have addressed Mark's stylistic features, and some believe that it is useful for detecting Mark's editing of sources. Vincent Taylor, *The Gospel according to St. Mark* (2nd ed.; London: Macmillan, 1966), 44–54; Nigel Turner, *A Grammar of New Testament Greek. IV. Style.* (Edinburgh: T&T Clark, 1976), 11, 21; E. J. Pryke, *Redactional Style in the Marcan Gospel: A Study of Syntax and Vocabulary as Guides to Redaction in Mark* (SNTSMS 33; Cambridge: Cambridge University Press, 1978); Peter Dschulnigg, *Sprache, Redaktion und Intention des Markus-Evangeliums: Eigentümlichkeiten der Sprache des Markus-Evangeliums und ihre Bedeutung für die Redaktionskritik* (SBS 11; Stuttgart: Katholisches Bibelwerk, 1984); Marius Reiser, *Syntax und Stil des Markusevangeliums im Licht der hellenistischen Volksliteratur* (WUNT 2/11; Tübingen: Mohr Siebeck, 1984); J. K. Elliott, *The Language and Style of the Gospel of Mark: An Edition of C. H. Turner's "Notes on Marcan Usage" Together with Other Comparable Studies* (NovTSup 71; Leiden: Brill, 1993); and Craig A. Evans, "How Mark Writes," in *The Written Gospel* (ed. Markus Bockmuehl and Donald A. Hagner; Cambridge: Cambridge University Press, 2005), 135–48.

259. Richard A. Burridge, "The Gospels and Acts," in *Handbook of Classical Rhetoric in the Hellenistic Period, 330 B.C.–A.D. 400* (ed. Stanley E. Porter; Leiden: Brill, 1997), 526, comments on Mark's unrefined style: "Unlike pure rhetorical Greek which prized conjunction and the period, Mark's writing has little connection: eighty-eight sections begin paratactically merely with καί [and] (often used incorrectly where δέ would have been better) and there are nineteen examples of asyndeton, no linking at all."

260. Samuel Sandmel, "Prolegomena to a Commentary on Mark," in *New Testament Issues* (ed. Richard Batey; New York: Harper & Row, 1970), 54.

261. Robert H. Stein, "Is Our Reading the Bible the Same as the Original Audience's Hearing It? A Case Study in the Gospel of Mark," *JETS* 46 (2003): 71.

262. Guelich, *Mark 1–8:26*, xxvii.

263. See the discussion of this issue in §2.4.1.2 and §13.1.

264. Gilbert G. Bilezikian, *The Liberated Gospel: A Comparison of the Gospel of Mark and Greek Tragedy* (Grand Rapids: Baker, 1977), 105.

him (15:25); darkness covers the land beginning at the sixth hour, high noon (15:33); and Jesus cries out in a loud voice at the ninth hour (3:00 p.m., 15:34).

1.2.5.2 Vividness

Mark uses the historical present tense (using the present tense to refer to a past action) around 150 times instead of the simple past tense. The historical present enlivens a narrative and "was common in Hellenistic Greek in its literary, technical, and more popular styles."[265]

Mark also tends to add minute observations that add vividness to an account, such as the description of the men breaking up a roof to lower a paralytic down to Jesus (2:4); the nicknames of James and John as the "sons of thunder" (3:17); Jesus laying his head on a pillow in the stern of the boat (4:38); the arrangement of the crowds in ranks "on the green grass" (6:39); the healing of a deaf and mute man by sticking his fingers into the man's ears and spitting and touching his tongue (7:33); putting saliva on the blind man's eyes and recording his partial healing so that he only sees people looking like trees walking around (8:23–24); taking a child in his arms (9:36); and Peter warming himself by the fire (14:54).

1.2.5.3 An Omniscient Point of View

The narrator's point of view is omniscient. He tells "the story as though present in the wilderness, by the sea, in a private home, in Herod's palace, in the synagogue or Temple, on a mountain, in a boat, in Galilee, in the area of Tyre and Sidon, in Caesarea Philippi, in the Decapolis, in Bethany, and in Jerusalem."[266] He knows the thoughts, feelings, emotions, and intentions of the various characters. Guelich contends, "This knowledge allows him as an 'intrusive narrator' to intrude into the world of the characters or into any scene to give additional comments and explanations to the reader."[267] Clear examples of parenthetical comments appear in 7:19 concerning what defiles a person, "In saying this, Jesus declared all foods clean," and in 13:14 concerning the desolating sacrilege, "let the reader understand."

1.2.5.4 Framing

Mark's use of framing may help interpret his intention in the narrative. The healing of two paralyzed men in 2:1–12 and 3:1–6 frames a section of sayings and controversies related to Jewish practices. In between these two healings, the teachers of the law and Pharisees complain about Jesus eating with sinners and toll collectors such as Levi (2:13–17); the question about fasting, which the disciples of John the Baptist and the Pharisees observe and Jesus' disciples do not, arises (2:18–22); and a controversy over Jesus' disciples plucking grain on the Sabbath surfaces (2:23–28).

---

265. Elliott C. Maloney, "The Historical Present in the Gospel of Mark," in *To Touch the Text: Biblical and Related Studies in Honor of Joseph A. Fitzmyer, S.J.* (ed. Maurya P. Horgan and Paul J. Kobelski; New York: Crossroad, 1989), 70. He shows (70–73) that its use is not the result of Semitic interference, and that its use "is so widespread and so uniform in the Gospel, it is unlikely that the phenomenon is the chance result of the oral traditions that gave rise to a written Gospel."

266. Guelich, *Mark 1–8:26*, xxx–xxxi.

267. Ibid., xxiii.

Jesus' healing of a man with a withered hand on the Sabbath tips the balance, and the Pharisees and Herodians resolve to destroy Jesus (3:1–6). These incidents framed by the healing of men paralyzed depict Jesus' opponents as paralyzed by their traditions and that they need healing as well.

In 8:22–26 and 10:46–52, the healing of two blind men frames Jesus' three announcements of his death and resurrection and the disciples' inability to comprehend what he is saying. Their thickheaded or insensitive response to these announcements leads to specific instructions from Jesus about the requirements of discipleship, which involves the willingness to suffer and to serve others. The disciples consistently demonstrate that they are blind to all of this. The framing suggests that they are like blind men and holds out hope that they, too, will be given sight.

The passion and resurrection narrative is framed by the references to Jesus' burial. An anonymous woman anoints Jesus with expensive perfume, made of pure nard poured out from an alabaster jar. Jesus interprets this gesture as preparing his body for burial beforehand. Jesus announces to those who grumbled about her extravagance, "Truly I tell you, wherever the gospel is preached throughout the world, what she has done will also be told, in memory of her" (14:3–9). The section concludes with women buying spices so that they might go to anoint Jesus' body, but when they arrive at the tomb, they learn the good news that is to be preached throughout the world: "You are looking for Jesus the Nazarene, who was crucified. He has risen!" (16:6).

1.2.5.5 Bracketing or Intercalation

One piece of tradition is bracketed by two halves of another, creating an outside story and an inside story. Achtemeier states: "By bracketing one tradition within another, he tells us he thinks they share some point, clearer, usually, in one of them than the other."[268]

In 3:20–35, Jesus' family goes to seize Jesus because they think he was beside himself (3:20–21), which is interrupted by the story of the teachers of the law coming from Jerusalem and claiming that Jesus casts out demons by the power of Beelzebul (3:22–30). Then Jesus' mother and brothers arrive and call for Jesus (3:31–35).

In 5:21–43, Jesus heeds the entreaty of a synagogue ruler to come lay hands on his gravely ill daughter (5:21–24). This story is interrupted by a woman with a flow of blood who touches Jesus' garments and is made well (5:25–34). He then arrives at the home and raises the girl, who had died during the interval, back to life (5:35–43).

268. Paul J. Achtemeier "Mark as Interpreter of the Jesus Tradition," *Int* 32 (1978): 346. See also James R. Edwards, "Markan Sandwiches: The Significance of Interpolations in Markan Narratives," *NovT* 31 (1989): 193–216; Geert Van Oyen, "Intercalation and Irony in the Gospel of Mark," in *The Four Gospels 1992: Festschrift Frans Neirynck* (ed. Frans Van Segbroeck et al.; BETL 100; Leuven: Leuven University Press, 1992), 2:949–74; Tom Shepherd, *Markan Sandwich Stories: Narration, Definition, and Function* (Andrews University Doctoral Dissertation Series 18; Berrien Springs, MI; Andrews University Press, 1993); idem, "The Narrative Function of Markan Intercalation," *NTS* 41 (1995): 522–40.

In 6:7–32, Jesus sends out the disciples to preach repentance (6:7–13). Mark then narrates the beheading of John the Baptist (6:14–29). The apostles return from their mission and report on their success (6:30–32).

In 11:12–25, Jesus' protest in the temple, driving out those who were selling and buying in the temple, overturning the tables of the money changers and the seats of those selling doves, and stopping anyone from carrying vessels in the temple (11:15–19), is bracketed by the account of his cursing the barren fig tree (11:12–14, 20–25).

The chief priests' plot to put Jesus to death and Judas's perfidiously joining the intrigue (14:1–2, 10–11) wraps around the account of a woman who anoints Jesus' head with costly perfume (14:3–9).

Peter's denial of Jesus outside in the courtyard of the high priest (14:53–54, 66–72) brackets Jesus' grilling inside before the chief priests and the council (14:55–65)

The two halves of the story help to interpret each other, illumine the message, or have some rhetorical effect, such as heightening the dramatic tension, creating irony, or adding emphasis.

1.2.5.6 Threefold Repetition

Threefold repetition occurs throughout the gospel. Jesus predicts his destiny privately to the disciples (8:31; 9:30–31; 10:32b–34). Each time the disciples manifest their lack of understanding in some way (8:32–33; 9:32–34; 10:35–41). This misunderstanding gives Jesus an opening for making a statement about the requirements of discipleship (8:34–38; 9:35–37; 10:42–45). There are also three boat scenes (4:35–41; 6:45–52; 8:13–21). In his discourse on the Mount of Olives Jesus exhorts the disciples three times to keep awake and watch (13:33, 35, 37). In the Passion Narrative in Gethsemane, Jesus leaves his disciples three times to pray, and three times he returns and finds the disciples sleeping at the hour of crisis (14:37, 40, 41). Peter denies Jesus three times (14:66–72). Pilate asks Jesus three questions (15:9, 12, 14). There are three scenes in which Jesus is mocked: by some after his trial before the chief priests and the council (14:65), by the Roman soldiers after his interrogation by Pilate (15:16–20), and by three different groups during his crucifixion (15:29–32). The hours during his crucifixion are tolled three times (15:25, 33, 34). There are three lists of female witnesses of Jesus' crucifixion, burial, and resurrection (15:40–41, 47; 16:1). The repetitions serve to draw attention to things in the story, emphasize their importance, create expectations, encourage reflection of what has happened previously, and build associations.[269]

269. See Aune, *The Westminster Dictionary*, 399.

1.2.5.7 *Two-Step Progression*

Mark uses a two-step progression to get the hearer to notice something. The first step consists of a generality, while the second step, the repetition, gives more specific detail and usually contains a crucial element.[270] Examples occur in 1:28, "everywhere, throughout the whole countryside of Galilee"; 1:32, "when it was evening, when the sun set," which emphasizes that people brought their sick to Jesus as soon as the Sabbath was over; 1:45, "outside, in deserted places"; 6:53, "to the other side, to Gennesaret"; 7:26, "a Greek, a Syrophoenician"; and 14:3, "in Bethany, at the house of Simon the leper" (all pers. trans.).

1.2.5.8 *Delayed Use of Explanation Clauses*

Mark sometimes delays the clause that provides an explanation for something. Bird notes that it hardly explains the preceding sentence or sometimes obscures the meaning.[271] Thrall explains that writers who frequently use explanatory clauses "tend to set down the conclusion first and then to explain in a series of γάρ [explanatory] clauses the considerations which led up to it. In narrative they mention first the important or striking points in the story, and then fit in the explanatory details afterwards by using γάρ ['for'], whether or not these details should logically precede the main points."[272]

Evans cites examples that impact interpretation. In 1:34, Mark narrates that Jesus "drove out many demons, but he would not let the demons speak because they knew who he was." Evans notes that the sentence leaves the impression "that Jesus perhaps would have allowed the demons to speak had they not known him."[273] But it is an example of a misplaced explanatory clause. The demons think that knowing Jesus' identity will give them the upper hand in preventing him from exorcising them. Evans comments that Jesus "had no intention of wrangling with these spirits, so he did not permit them to speak."[274] His command for them to keep quiet has nothing to do with the so-called messianic secret. He is not trying to conceal his identity but to thwart any challenges from the demons (see also 5:7–8 [and sec. 5.2.3]).

Mark narrates in 3:20–21, "Then Jesus entered a house, and again a crowd gathered, so that he and his disciples were not even able to eat. When his family heard about this, they went to take charge of him, for they said, 'He is out of his mind.'" The delayed explanatory clause could lead the reader to conclude that Jesus' family sought to take charge of him because they heard that the large crowd prevented him from being able to eat. The real reason is given in the delayed explanation that they were saying he was out of his mind.

In 11:13, the delayed explanatory clause, "because it was not the season of figs," is

270. David Rhoads, "Jesus and the Syrophoenician Woman in Mark: A Narrative-Critical Study," *JAAR* 62 (1994): 352–53.

271. C. H. Bird, "Some γάρ Clauses in St. Mark's Gospel," *JTS* 4 (1953): 171–87.

272. Margaret E. Thrall, *Greek Particles in the New Testament: Linguistic and Exegetical Studies* (NTTS 3; Grand Rapids: Eerdmans, 1962), 47.

273. Evans, "How Mark Writes," 136.

274. Ibid., 137.

not intended to modify the phrase "he found nothing but leaves." Rather, it explains "Seeing in the distance a fig tree in leaf, he went to find out if it had any fruit . . . because it was not the season for figs." Evans comments, "Leafy trees in the spring may indicate the presence of edible buds. But when Jesus examined the tree, he found none, despite the encouraging signs of the early foliage."[275]

In 16:4, the women who went to the tomb "see that the stone is rolled back: for it was exceeding great" (ASV). Mark does not mean that the stone rolled away because it was so large. The delayed explanatory clause modifies the women's earlier question, "Who will roll the stone away from the entrance of the tomb? . . . which was very large." What are perceived to be Mark's stylistic flaws probably contributed to the gospel falling into neglect.

Evans concludes his analysis of how Mark writes with these words:

> The Marcan evangelist found ways to arrange and connect his materials that would develop and advance a compelling plot and at the same time would instruct his readers in important aspects of Christology, discipleship, and eschatology. For all the evangelist's shortcomings in matters of literary style and polish, it must be admitted that his literary achievement is nonetheless remarkable and should be viewed as successful. In that the Matthean and Lucan evangelists adopt approximately 95 percent of the Markan text between them, it seems that they would agree with this assessment.[276]

That Matthew and Luke did adopt most of Mark and in many cases improved on Mark's style meant that Mark was viewed as less effective by Christians in the second century and later. The result was that for centuries Mark was overlooked.

1.2.6 Reception of the Gospel of Mark

It is well known that Mark's gospel was dwarfed by the other three gospels and fell into disuse in the early church. This fact can be interpreted as pointing to the initial success of Mark's gospel in the earliest Christian circles, which inspired Matthew and Luke to compose their own gospels. Matthew incorporated almost the entire gospel into his own.[277] The result was that Mark was spoiled by its overwhelming success.

Schildgen titles her chapter on Mark's reception from AD 130–430 as "Present but Absent."[278] This neglect of Mark was due in part to its overlap with Matthew and Luke. It added nothing to their storylines and did not include an infancy and a resurrection narrative, any motivation for why Judas would want to betray Jesus, any explicit reconciliation between Peter and Jesus after Peter's threefold denial of him, any extensive teaching like that found in the Sermon on the Mount, nor any captivating parables like those found in Luke or the allegories found in Matthew.[279]

275. Ibid.

276. Ibid., 148.

277. J. Andrew Doole, *What Was Mark for Matthew?: An Examination of Matthew's Relationship and Attitude to his Primary Source* (WUNT 2/344; Tübingen: Mohr Siebeck, 2013).

278. Brenda Deen Schildgen, *Power and Prejudice: The Reception of the Gospel of Mark* (Detroit: Wayne State University Press, 1999), 35.

279. Ibid., 21.

Mark's gospel also did not seem to prove useful in the theological skirmishes with the Gnostics. Schildgen cites Irenaeus's concern that Mark was "less decisive on the divine nature of Jesus than the other Gospels."[280] It contributed to confusion over the relationship between Jesus and the Christ. Irenaeus (*Haer.* 3.11.7) asserts: "Those who separate Jesus from the Christ and wish this 'Christ' to remain 'impassable,' so that Jesus alone would have suffered, give their preference to the Gospel according to Mark; but if they read with the love of truth, they have the possibility to correct themselves." Mackay adds that the "early interests were not so much historical as doctrinal," and the other gospels proved to be more valuable for the various doctrinal battles.[281]

Believing that Matthew was the first gospel, Augustine (*Cons.* 1.2) described Mark as Peter's follower and abbreviator. Black states, "Early on, in both common worship and constructive theology, Mark's gospel became something of the stepchild among the canonical four. By focusing on Mark's diminished status among the Evangelists, Augustine thus may have indirectly rationalized and to that degree unintentionally ratified what had been, and would long continue to be, a practical reality."[282] Matthew had "pride of place as the first in the collection because of its supposed apostolic connection, its greater detail and completeness, and its references to specific ecclesiastical and sacramental practices that were central to the discussions of the age."[283] Augustine had little or no Greek to discern textual characteristics and little interest in doing so. He wanted to show the unanimity of the four Gospels to produce a universal Christian story as he and other church fathers wanted "to create a unified and uniform Church with as little variety in ecclesiastical belief and practice as possible."[284] Mark added little to Matthew—only around 40 of Mark's 675 verses are not found in Matthew—and its gaps in its version of the story and theological ambiguity made Augustine incapable of considering "that Mark's narrative style was a dimension of what constitutes the gospel's understanding of the events it retells."[285] Schildgen summarizes:

> For the Fathers, trained in the requirements of classical rhetoric, the gospel was anomalous. In contrast to Matthew, it lacks many of the desirable details for a harmonized and "complete" life of Jesus. It provides no clear material for any of the Fathers' doctrinal interests (for example, primacy of the authority of the disciples, legitimacy of the Church of Rome, the Trinity, the sacraments); to the contrary, it is close to silent on these issues. In terms of literary style, the gospel appears on the surface to be the least sophisticated. It is paratactic, has redundancies, pleonasms, and even grammatical flaws. Its narrative is disjunctive because its presentation of the story includes embedded narratives, juxtapositions, intercalations and parallelisms, and folktale simplicity (trebling, journey motif, and wonder-working hero). All of these complement the gospel's

280. Ibid., 52–53.
281. Mackay, *John's Relationship*, 46–47.
282. Black, *Images*, 131.
283. Schildgen, *Power and Prejudice*, 38.
284. Ibid., 49.
285. Ibid., 59.

> paradoxical content, which our own era, trained to be sophisticated readers of prose fiction in an intellectual culture thriving on suspicion, relativity, and ambiguous open-endedness, has found so interesting.[286]

Consequently, Oden and Hall note that "there are no complete commentaries of Mark that have survived the patristic period," and that the commentary wrongly attributed to Victor, presbyter of Antioch (ca. AD 500), is basically a catena of quotes from homilies on Matthew by Chrysostom, Origen, Cyril of Alexandria, Titus of Bostra, and Theodor of Heraclea.[287] One may surmise that Mark survived this indifference only because of its traditional connection to Peter.

In the modern period, the proposal that Mark was the first gospel brought it fresh attention as it was mined as the primary source for the historical Jesus. Holtzmann judged it to be crucial for providing the historical framework for the life of Jesus.[288] Mark's primary value was deemed to be its historical aspect, and most assumed that the gospel had no significant theological message of its own.[289] Black writes that in contrast to John and Paul, championed as the pivotal theologians in the NT, Mark "has been stereotyped as little more than an unsophisticated storyteller whose interests were more historical, or historicist, than theological."[290]

The work of Wrede on the messianic secret and the advent of redaction criticism radically changed the perspective on Mark. Mark is no longer recognized as a recorder who simply passes on the tradition but as a theologian who reinterprets and rearticulates it. Mark is no longer read as a simple, straightforward account of Jesus' life; instead it has become "widely regarded as one of the subtlest, most enigmatic of the Gospels."[291] There is an increasing fascination with its plethora of paradoxes.[292] Kelber runs through the main ones:

> Jesus announces the Kingdom but opts for the cross; he is King of the Jews but condemned by the Jewish establishment; he asks for followers but speaks in riddles; he is identified as Nazarene but rejected in Nazareth; he makes public pronouncements but also hides behind a screen of secrecy; he saves others but not himself; he promises return but has not returned; he performs miracles but suffers a non-miraculous death; he is a successful exorciser but dies overcome by demonic forces; he is appointed by God in power but dies abandoned by God in powerlessness; he dies but rises from death. His beginning is nebulous and his future status is indefinite, and at the moment of Messianic disclosure he still speaks enigmatically of himself in the third person (14:62; cf. 8:31; 9:31;

286. Ibid., 136.

287. Thomas C. Oden and Christopher A. Hall, eds., *Mark* (ACCS NT 2; Downers Grove, IL: InterVarsity Press, 1998), xxxi. Michael Cahill, ed. and trans., *The First Commentary on Mark: An Annotated Translation* (New York: Oxford University Press, 1998), 3–4, identifies the first commentary written on Mark as written in the sixth century and was possibly of Irish provenance.

288. Heinrich J. Holtzmann, *Die synoptischen Evangelien: Ihr Ursprung und geschichtlicher Charakter* (Leipzig: Engelmann, 1863).

289. Mackay, *John's Relationship*, 52.

290. Black, "Christ Crucified in Paul and in Mark: Reflections on an Intracanonical Conversation," 184.

291. Carl R. Holladay, *A Critical Introduction to the New Testament: Interpreting the Message and Meaning of Jesus Christ* (Nashville: Abingdon, 2005), 104.

292. Laura C. Sweat, *The Theological Role of Paradox in the Gospel of Mark* (LNTS 492; London: Bloomsbury T&T Clark, 2013), 13–27, establishes a definition of paradox in Mark.

10:33–34). If there is one single feature that characterizes the Mkan [*sic*] Jesus it is contradiction or paradox. It might therefore be argued that "Mk presents not two conflicting views of Jesus" but one complex "paradoxical view" (Dewey).[293]

Sweat explains why paradox is so important in Mark theologically:

> ... describing God's activity in paradoxes is due both to human finitude and to God's transcendence and mystery. Using paradoxical language mirrors how humans perceive God's mystery. In other words, paradoxes reveal something concrete about the nature and activity of God in ways that can be somewhat understood by human senses and reason. Concurrently, they preserve and prevent complete comprehension. In other words, paradoxical language highlights the mysterious character of God's action in the Gospel of Mark.[294]

Schildgen comments that "our own era finds Mark's gaps and silences precisely the source of its interest, as commentators seek to understand these absences literarily or intellectually."[295] The different evaluation of Mark in our era is strikingly expressed by Price, who says that the gospel of Mark "has proved the most enduringly powerful narrative in the history of the Western civilization, perhaps in the history of the world."[296] Cranfield states that Mark exercised "self-restraint and respect for his sources" and describes him as "an extremely honest and conscientious compiler" rather than "a creative literary artist."[297] In his supplementary notes, he clarifies that this evaluation is not intended to imply "that Mark was not a theologian." He asserts that he intended to suggest that Mark

> possessed, to an outstanding degree, that without which one cannot begin to be a true theologian, namely, a deep humility before God's self-revelation, and that he tried to state the facts of what he believed to be God's self-revelation as accurately as he could, refraining from all attempts at improving on them by artistry, precisely because he was a serious theologian—too good a theologian not to recognize the folly of trying to paint the lily or (to borrow an expression of B. L. Manning's) to varnish sunlight.[298]

In my view, Mark records the tradition he learned from Peter about what Jesus said and did and what others said and did in their response to him. Bruce asks, "What did the Roman Christians know of the origin of their faith? Were they able to answer current misrepresentations with a confident account of the real facts? Was it true their Founder had been executed by sentence of a Roman magistrate?"[299] Mark does not engage in apologetics for a non-Christian audience in providing

293. Werner H. Kelber, "Conclusion: From Passion Narrative to Gospel," in *The Passion in Mark: Studies on Mark 14–16* (ed. Werner H. Kelber; Philadelphia: Fortress, 1976), 179.

294. Sweat, *The Theological Role of Paradox*, 177.

295. Schildgen, *Power and Prejudice*, 21.

296. Reynolds Price, "Foreward" to *Mark as Story: An Introduction to the Narrative of a Gospel*, by David Rhoads and Donald Michie (Philadelphia: Fortress, 1982), xi.

297. C. E. B. Cranfield, *The Gospel According to St Mark* (3rd ed.; CGTC; Cambridge: Cambridge University Press, 1966), 16.

298. Ibid., 479.

299. Bruce, "The Date and Character of Mark," 78.

his written account. Tcherikover makes the case that marginalized groups would have had great difficulty attracting the attention of the larger culture and that the group's self-defense usually would not have resonated with the larger group since they "had differing value systems and authoritative literature."[300] Mark provides his fellow Christians with information that could dispel their misgivings and boost their faith during perilous times. He does so in a narrative that more importantly unfolds the divine identity of Jesus, the theological significance of his death and resurrection, and the mysterious presence and action of God's kingdom in the world. In addition, he presents what is required of those who submit to God's reign and become followers of Jesus, the Messiah, the Son of God.[301]

300. See Victor Tcherikover, "Jewish Apologetic Literature Reconsidered," *Eos* 48 (1956): 171–79, noted by Kelli S. O'Brien, "Innocence and Guilt: Apologetic, Martyr Stories, and Allusion in the Markan Trial Narratives," in *The Trial and Death of Jesus: Essays on the Passion Narrative in Mark* (ed. Geert van Oyen and Tom Shepherd; CBET 45; Leuven: Peeters, 2006), 210.

301. Perkins, "Mark as Narrative Christology," 75–78.

Chapter 2

A LITERARY AND THEOLOGICAL READING OF MARK'S GOSPEL

BIBLIOGRAPHY

Dewey, Joanna. "Mark as Interwoven Tapestry: Forecasts and Echoes for a Listening Audience." *CBQ* 53 (1991): 221–36. Eadem. "Mark as Aural Narrative: Structures as Clues to Understanding." *STRev* 36 (1992): 45–56. Eadem. "The Survival of Mark's Gospel: A Good Story?" *JBL* 123 (2004): 495–507. **Malbon, Elizabeth Struthers.** *In the Company of Jesus: Characters in Mark's Gospel*. Louisville: Westminster John Knox, 2000.

2.1 A GENERAL OUTLINE OF MARK

Dewey insists,

> Mark is telling a story for a listening audience, not presenting a logical argument. Arguments may be clouded by the lack of a clear linear outline, but stories gain depth and enrichment through repetition and recursion.[1]

Because of Mark's oral nature, many argue that the gospel does not lend itself to outlines.[2] Outlines are visual and are constructed for a reading audience, not a listening audience. Williams compares Mark's gospel to a path, a road "on which readers can travel, walking with Jesus and experiencing his life, death, and resurrection."[3] As an "episodic narrative,"[4] it winds its way this way and that. To change the metaphor, Mark is much like a kaleidoscope from which scholars discern various patterns.[5]

In my view, a threefold division of the gospel is most appealing. The problem is that this threefold division can be sliced in different ways. The option that I favor charts the gospel, after the incipit and introduction in 1:1–13, this way:

1:14–8:21 Jesus' Ministry in Galilee and Surrounding Areas
8:22–10:52 Jesus on the Way to Jerusalem

---

1. Joanna Dewey, "Mark as Interwoven Tapestry: Forecasts and Echoes for a Listening Audience," *CBQ* 53 (1991): 224.

2. Kee, *Community*, 64, contends, "It would appear that Mark no more lends itself to analysis by means of a detailed outline developed by simple addition of components than does a major contrapuntal work of music." The great motifs are repeated again and again (75).

3. Joel F. Williams, "Does Mark's Gospel Have an Outline?" *JETS* 49 (2006): 505.

4. Gundry, *Mark*, 1046.

5. Malbon, *Mark's Jesus*, 24–55, presents four different and expanded outlines and four schematic diagrams that are designed to show the narrative's "enacted Christology."

11:1 – 16:8 Jesus in Jerusalem: The Temple, the Cross, and the Resurrection

The first section (1:14 – 8:21) contains three subsections (1:14 – 3:6; 3:7 – 6:6a; 6:6b – 8:21). Each begins with a summary (1:14 – 15; 3:7 – 12; 6:6b), which is followed by the calling of the disciples or a commission that sends them out (1:16 – 20; 3:13 – 19; 6:7 – 13). Each ends with an account of opposition to or unbelief in Jesus (3:6; 6:1 – 6a; 8:14 – 21).

The second section (8:22 – 10:52) recounts Jesus' journey to Jerusalem as he teaches his disciples on the way about his upcoming death and resurrection and about the nature of discipleship. Teaching material dominates over narrative. Only four narratives, the healing of a blind man (8:22 – 26), the transfiguration (9:2 – 8), the healing of the demon-possessed boy (9:14 – 29), and the healing of blind Bartimaeus (10:46 – 52), appear. The teaching emphasizes that to follow Jesus on the way does not mean that one simply treks after him but that one takes up a cross and follows his way of life.

The third section (11:1 – 16:8) recounts Jesus' theatrical entry into the city, an audacious demonstration against the temple and a confrontation with the temple hierarchy, teaching in the temple and fending off malicious inquisitors, and private instructions about the temple's impending doom and its relation to the end. It reaches a denouement with an account of the plotting by his nemeses, his last meal with the disciples, his arrest, his interrogation by the religious and secular authorities, and his crucifixion. The report of his resurrection from death is the culmination of the narrative. All of these events occur within the time frame of one week.

The first section can be broken down further into three units. Marcus notes that after three transitional summaries of Jesus' activity (1:14 – 15; 3:7 – 12 and 6:6b), narratives of calling and commissioning disciples follow (1:16 – 3:6; 3:7 – 6:6a; 6:6b – 8:21), marking these off as three literary units: 1:14 – 3:6; 3:7 – 6:6a; 6:6b – 8:21.[6]

The second section (8:22 – 10:52) is noteworthy for narrating the healing of a blind man at Bethsaida at the beginning (8:22 – 26) and the healing of a blind man in Jericho at the end (10:46 – 52). Three times in this section (8:31 – 38, 9:30 – 37, 10:32 – 45), Jesus predicts to his disciples his impending death and his resurrection. Significantly, he tells them these things "plainly" (8:32), not in parables (4:33 – 34). Each time, the disciples demonstrate in some way that they are blind to all of this talk of suffering and death. Each time, Jesus responds by expounding on the nature of discipleship. He tries to get them to understand that the cross is necessary not only as a means of redemption but also as a way of life, which they are to share if they want to follow him as disciples. A particular fate awaits anyone who faithfully follows this suffering leader.

The placement of the healing of the blind men at the beginning and end of this section is intentional, not coincidental. They frame Jesus' announcement of his suffering, death, and resurrection and his instructions about the true nature of discipleship,

6. Marcus, *Mark 1 – 8*, 177.

which involves the willingness to suffer. These incidents have something to say about the blindness of the disciples who do not yet fully grasp who Jesus is or that it is necessary for him to suffer and die. The disciples are like blind men who will also be given sight.[7]

The third section begins with a triumphal procession into the city with Jesus' followers hailing his arrival. This section can be divided into two units. In the first unit (11:1–13:37), the promising pageantry of his entry is disturbed by his actions in the temple and their interpretation from Scripture that highlight the temple's dysfunction from God's point of view and foreshadow its ultimate demise. It concludes with Jesus' exit from the temple and his announcement of its total destruction in chapter 13. In the second unit (14:1–16:8), the priestly hierarchy plot Jesus' death and a woman anoints Jesus' head, which he interprets as anointing his body for burial beforehand. It concludes with the success of the chief priests' plot when Jesus dies on a cross and when the women followers of Jesus buy spices intending to anoint Jesus' corpse. Jesus, however, has been raised from the dead and has left Jerusalem to go before the disciples to Galilee, where they will regather.

2.2 The Incipit: "The Beginning of the Good News about Jesus Christ, the Son of God" (1:1)

The opening line functions as a title or incipit of the gospel (1:2–16:8).[8] The word "beginning" recalls the opening words of Genesis, and Mark writes about a new beginning in salvation history that God inaugurates. The story does not end with the suffering, death, and resurrection of Jesus, nor does it end with the fear of the women who flee the tomb. The gospel's curious conclusion does not narrate the women eventually sharing the news of the resurrection or any resurrection appearances of Jesus to the disciples, let alone the promised rendezvous with the disciples in Galilee.[9] It introduces another aspect of the good news: "The church exists because of what God has done in Christ, not because of any outstanding abilities in its first members."[10] The story of God's good news will not be stopped

7. Evans, "How Mark Writes," 144–47, argues for a bipartite structure that sandwiches 8:27–9:1:

A 1:1–8:26
    B 8:27–9:1
A' 9:2–16:8

The heavenly voice declaring Jesus to be "my Son" appears at the beginning of both halves (1:11; 9:7). He contends that the first half "dramatically illustrates Jesus' divine authority and power thus justifying the bold assertion in the incipit that Jesus is the Son of God" (p. 146). In the middle section, Peter only partially understands the works of power and concludes that Jesus is the Christ. Jesus corrects him by speaking of his suffering, death, and resurrection and thus redefines what the Messiah does. The second half narrates Jesus on the way to Jerusalem and his suffering, death, and resurrection. While this division is attractive, it separates the three passion and resurrection predictions from one another.

8. The absence of a verb makes it more likely that this opening line serves as a title rather than a verbless sentence (compare the beginnings of Prov 1:1; Cant 1:1; and Eccl 1:1 without predicates; and Rev 1:1).

9. Contrast Matt 28:1–10, 16–20; Luke 24:1–53; John 20:1–29; 21:1–25.

10. Leon Morris, "Disciples of Jesus," in *Jesus of Nazareth Lord and Christ: Essays on the Historical Jesus and New Testament Christology* (ed. Joel B. Green and Max Turner; Grand Rapids: Eerdmans, 1994), 124.

by human failures or satanic opposition. The open-ended narrative points to yet another beginning when the gospel is proclaimed throughout the world (13:10; 14:9; see Acts 28:31).

Three key terms in the title represent important themes in Mark: "the good news," "Christ," and the "Son of God." The "good news" ("gospel," 1:14, 15; 8:35; 10:29; 13:10; 14:9) is the story of Jesus' words, deeds, death, and resurrection through which God acts to save humankind. The narrative that follows is good news for all who have been waiting for the fulfillment of God's promises to bring redemption, and makes clear that this redemption comes through Jesus as God's anointed Messiah, who is also the Son of God.[11]

The title "Messiah" ("Christ") is used reservedly in Mark (1:1; 8:29; 9:41; 12:35; 13:21; 14:61; 15:32). The term could conjure up a constellation of different notions for Jews, and its meaning in Mark can only be understood after Jesus' death and resurrection. He is David's Lord and more than an earthly deliverer. He is the one who will not use his power to save himself and come down from the cross (15:32) and who will be seated at the right hand of the Mighty One ("Power") and will return on the clouds of heaven (14:62).

The references to Jesus as the "Son of God" also appear infrequently in the gospel, but they do appear at pivotal junctures: at the baptism (1:11), the transfiguration (9:7), and the crucifixion (15:39). Demons use this title to refer to Jesus (3:11; 5:7). The high priest asks Jesus if he is the "Messiah, the Son of the Blessed One" (14:61), and Jesus responds unambiguously, "I am" (14:62).

2.3 THE INTRODUCTION (1:2–13)

The introduction divides into three parts: (1) the citation of Scripture and the introduction of John the Baptist (1:2–8); (2) the baptism of Jesus (1:9–11); and (3) the testing of Jesus by Satan (1:12–13). Each incident takes place in the same vicinity, the wilderness and the river Jordan (1:4, 5, 9, 12, and 13), and each contains a reference to the Spirit (1:8, 10, 12). This introduction presents the reader with privileged information from a divine perspective that is unavailable to the characters in the story.

2.3.1 The Ministry of John the Baptist (1:2–8)

Mark begins his narrative with Scripture, and this passage is the only place in the gospel where the narrator tells the reader that Scripture is being fulfilled. The scriptural citation discloses that this account is about the continuation of God's salvific work in history. Mark ascribes this reference to Isaiah, because Isaian themes form an

11. This passage and the introduction (1:2–13) are discussed in greater depth below.

important backdrop for understanding this narrative.[12] The reference, however, is a mixture of texts from Exod 23:20; Isa 40:3; and Mal 3:1. Mark uses a familiar technique in postbiblical Judaism of blending texts that originally had nothing to do with each other. Together, they represent the Law and the greater and lesser prophets.[13]

Three individuals are mentioned in 1:2: the one who will send the messenger, the messenger who will prepare the way, and the one whose way is prepared ("your way"). The "I" who makes the announcement is God. "My messenger" is John the Baptist. The pronouns in the phrases "before *your* face" ("ahead of you," NIV), "*your* way," and "paths for *him*," which are to be made straight, refer to Jesus. The original prophecy in Mal 3:1 refers to God who suddenly comes to his temple. In Mark, it is applied to Jesus, reflecting the high Christology of this gospel. The "way" (or "road") is a key term in Mark that refers to the way on which Jesus will lead his followers (8:27; 9:33–34; 10:17, 32, 52).

Mark offers no background information about John the Baptist except to present him as an Elijah figure preparing for the imminent coming of God (Mal 4:5–6).[14] He is represented as the new Elijah, who preaches a "baptism of repentance for the forgiveness of sins."[15] Repentance, which entails changing one's heart and mind about what is ultimately important and changing one's life accordingly, is required of all Israel. John acknowledges that his water baptism is only preparatory; the Spirit baptism will be definitive. In his only speaking part in Mark, John proclaims that one who is more powerful than he is coming after him, who will baptize with the Spirit and who will execute God's will. Mark continually drives the focus to Jesus.

2.3.2 Jesus' Baptism (1:9–11)

Mark provides no information about Jesus' genealogy or birth (contrast Matt 1–2; Luke 1–2; 3:23–38; John 1:1–5) and only informs the audience that Jesus came from Nazareth in Galilee (1:9).[16] He also does not tell the audience why Jesus went to be baptized but only what occurs at his baptism. Jesus sees (1) the heavens "being torn open"; and (2) the Spirit "descending on him like a dove"; and (3) he hears a

12. Joel Marcus, *The Way of the Lord: Christological Exegesis of the Old Testament in the Gospel of Mark* (Louisville: Westminster John Knox, 1992), 20; Rikki E. Watts, *Isaiah's New Exodus and Mark* (WUNT 2/88; Tübingen: Mohr Siebeck, 1997). In Isa 40:9–10, the immediate context of Isa 40:3 that is cited in Mark 1:3, there is a reference to preaching the gospel and the Lord God coming with might. The tearing of heavens (1:10) is mentioned in Isa 64:1. The heavenly voice (1:11) echoes Isa 42:1. Living at peace with animals (1:13b) can be found in Isa 11:6–9 and 65:25. The forgiveness of sins is prominent throughout Isaiah. Isaiah is also cited as the explanation for the people's incomprehension of the kingdom of God appearing in Jesus' ministry (4:12, citing Isa 6:9–10) and provides the key details of the end time (13:24–26, citing Isa 13:10; 34:4).

13. J. Duncan M. Derrett, *The Making of Mark: The Scriptural Bases of the Earliest Gospel* (Shipston-on-Stour, UK: Drinkwater, 1985), 46–47.

14. Contrast Luke 1:5–25, 39–45, 57–80.

15. One need not interpret 1:4 to mean that baptism effects the forgiveness of sins. One can translate, "a baptism of repentance on the basis of the forgiveness of sins." The divine action of forgiveness of sins would precede any human action (see Isa 40:2; Jer 31:34; Mic 7:18). Swete, *Mark*, 4, comments that baptism is "the expression and pledge of repentance," which responds to this forgiveness. The baptism purified the faithful (Isa 4:4; Zech 13:1) and marked them out as members of the faithful Israel. It also prepared them to receive the Holy Spirit (Ezek 36:25–27; see also 1QS 4:20–21; 1:21–25).

16. An indirect reference to Jesus' background appears in the question raised by those in the synagogue at Nazareth, "Isn't this the carpenter? Isn't this Mary's son and the brother of James, Joseph, Judas and Simon? Aren't his sisters here with us?" (6:3).

voice from heaven announce, "You are my Son, whom I love; with you I am well pleased." With the tearing of the heavens, Isaiah's hope that God "would rend the heavens and come down" (Isa 64:1) is being fulfilled. The descent of the Spirit on Jesus confirms him as the Messiah (Isa 11:1–2) and as the one who will launch a new beginning and a new creation (Gen 1:2). With the announcement from the heavens, Jesus is identified as the Son of God.

2.3.3 Testing in the Wilderness (1:12–13)

The Spirit drives Jesus into the wilderness, a thematic focal place in Mark's gospel,[17] where he encounters Satan. Mark does not describe the testing that Jesus underwent for forty days or Jesus' besting of Satan in their confrontation, but when Jesus is served by angels, the implication is that Satan is beaten. Mark's emphasis is not on Jesus' testing but on the clarification of his identity. As Gundry construes it, "All that we have is a dignifying of Jesus, a series of acknowledgments—a backhanded acknowledgment by Satan, a pacifistic acknowledgment by the wild beasts, and a ministerial acknowledgment by the angels—in recognition of the status of Jesus as God's beloved Son."[18]

2.4. JESUS' MINISTRY IN GALILEE AND BEYOND (1:14–8:21)

The first large section (1:14–8:21) recounts Jesus' ministry to Israel in which he announces the coming of the kingdom of God, calls disciples, teaches with authority, exorcises demons, heals the sick, and preaches to throngs. He is shown to be all powerful, overcoming opposition from supernatural demons to tumultuous storms to earthly adversaries.

2.4.1 The Beginning of Jesus' Ministry as One with Authority (1:14–3:6)

2.4.1.1 Summary of Jesus' Preaching (1:14–15)

When the drama begins, John the Baptist has been removed from the stage. Despite the crowds swarming to receive his repentance baptism, John's popularity does not prevent him from being arrested. He has been "handed over" ("put in prison," NIV) and eventually will be executed. Mark gives no details about his imprisonment so that the term "handed over" stands out. The same verb is used to describe what will happen to Jesus (3:19; 9:31; 14:10, 11, 18, 21, 41, 42, 44; 15:1, 10, 15). John the Baptist is Jesus' forerunner in more ways than one. He paves the way in preaching repentance to Israel, in his conflict with the powerful, established order, and in

17. Marcus, *Way*, 22. See Ulrich W. Mauser, *Christ in the Wilderness: The Wilderness Theme in the Second Gospel and Its Basis in the Biblical Tradition* (SBT 39; Naperville, IL: Allenson, 1963), 51–52.

18. Gundry, *Mark*, 60.

his suffering and death. John's arrest is the first hint that the coming of God's kingdom will be resisted. Those who are faithfully obedient to God will suffer for their faithfulness.

The preposition "after" in the phrase "after John was put in prison" may be more than simply a chronological marker. It may have an eschatological connotation that hints at the end of an old era and the beginning of the new era.[19] John preached that something will happen: "After me comes the one more powerful than I" (1:7).

When Jesus returns to Galilee[20] and preaches good news, he proclaims that something has happened: "The time has come.... The kingdom of God has come near" (1:15).[21] John came "preaching a baptism of repentance for the forgiveness of sins" (1:4). Jesus comes "proclaiming the good news of God," and repentance is based on this prior act of God in sending Jesus to preach this good news. The narrative that follows reveals that he is not merely a herald who simply announces the coming of God's kingdom. His coming does not simply coincide with the nearness of the kingdom of God; rather, it brings it about. He is not told what he is to say as the prophets were, but he speaks on his own authority as the Son of God about what God is doing in the world.

The kingdom of God is a central theme in the gospel (4:11, 26, 30; 9:1, 47; 10:14–15, 23–25; 12:34; 14:25; 15:43).[22] The presence of the kingdom of God requires immediate repentance. According to Moore, "To the Jewish definition of repentance belong the reparation of injuries done to a fellow man in his person, property, or good name, the confession of sin, prayer for forgiveness, and the genuine resolve and endeavor not to fall into the sin again."[23] For Jesus, it means "to let [God's] reign form a sustaining and guiding pattern for their lives."[24] For Mark, believing the gospel means also believing in Jesus, since the good news of God is the good news about Jesus Christ (1:1).

2.4.1.2 Calling of the First Disciples (1:16–20)

Mark sets the pace and rhythm of his narrative with the key word "at once," "immediately," "without delay," or "straightway" (1:18, 20, 21, 23, 28, 29, 30, 42, 43).[25] Jesus immediately speaks and acts with God's authority by calling two sets of brothers, Peter and Andrew, and James and John, to leave their fishing occupations to come and follow him. Unlike the prophets, who called people to turn back to

19. Stein, *Mark*, 70. According to John 3:22–4:2, the ministries of John the Baptist and Jesus overlapped.

20. Galilee is the place from which Jesus hails and will be the place where he first proclaims the good news (1:14, 39). He calls his disciples there, and his followers come from there (15:41). His mighty works and authoritative teaching result in his reputation spreading throughout Galilee and beyond (1:28) so that he draws huge crowds (3:7–8). He promises to regather his scattered disciples in Galilee after his resurrection (14:28; 16:7).

21. James M. Robinson, *The Problem of History in Mark* (SBT 21; London: SCM, 1957), 72.

22. Its meaning in the gospel will be developed below.

23. George Foot Moore, *Judaism in the First Centuries of the Christian Era* (Cambridge, MA: Harvard University Press, 1927; repr., New York: Schocken, 1971), 1:117.

24. Hartman, *Mark*, 49.

25. Also 1:10, 12; 2:8, 12; 3:6; 4:5, 15, 16, 17, 29; 5:2, 29, 30, 42; 6:25, 27, 45, 50, 54; 7:25; 8:10; 9:15, 20, 24; 10:52; 11:2, 3; 14:43, 45, 72; 15:1, which is oftentimes translated "at once" and "without delay"; it does not consistently appear in the NIV translation.

God, Jesus calls them to "follow *me*" (cf. 1 Kgs 19:15–21).[26] Jesus does not wait for would-be followers to come to him to learn from him, as other teachers did; he takes the initiative in calling his own disciples (1:16–20; 2:14; 3:12–14, "those he wanted"). His claim on their lives is absolute, and they follow "immediately" (1:20; "without delay" NIV). Through the power of his call they are destined to "fish for people" (1:17). The metaphor was used in the OT for gathering people for judgment (Jer 16:14–16; Ezek 29:4; 47:10; Amos 4:2; Hab 1:14–17), but Jesus uses it in a positive sense. They will gather people for salvation.

2.4.1.3 Casting Out an Impure Spirit in the Synagogue and Teaching with Authority (1:21–28)

The good news that Jesus preaches is lethal news for the demons, who immediately recognize who he is. Mark distinguishes those who suffer from impure spirits from those who are sick (1:32, 34). The term "impure spirit" has a religious connotation indicating that what is impure or unclean has evaded God's control. The victim requires a greater power to expel what has him under its thrall, and the demons recognize that they have met their match in Jesus and usually howl their alarm (1:24; 5:7). They have caused their victim to suffer violently (5:5; 9:22) and produce some kind of damage, harm, or noise when driven out.

The impure spirit's panicked query, "What do you want with us?" (1:24; lit., "What [between] us and you"), appears in the OT in a context "of combat or judgment."[27] "The impure spirit" is singular, but the use of the plural "us" suggests that the spirit speaks on behalf of the entire realm of demonic powers. It makes a futile attempt to gain the upper hand and to ward off the impending exorcism by shouting out, "I know who you are—the Holy One of God!" (1:24).[28] Since Jesus is *the* Holy One of God, imbued with the Holy Spirit (1:10), it is understandable why these impure (the opposite of holy) spirits would be threatened.[29] Their cry of distress rams home that Satan's realm is under assault by a more powerful one (1:7). The impure spirit recognizes that Jesus possesses the power of God, and Jesus exercises that power by muzzling it. At his command, the spirit departs. This exorcism reveals that God's holiness is not repelled by impurity and tries to be shielded from it, but instead comes to expel it.

26. Boring, "Markan Christology," 465, comments: "The call of the disciples is what God does to make people prophets, not what rabbis do to make people disciples. The claim is absolute, asking what only God can ask, idolatrous if not ultimately God's claim (cf. 8.34; 10.17–22; 12.44; 14.3–9)."

27. William L. Lane, *Commentary on the Gospel of Mark* (NICNT; Grand Rapids: Eerdmans, 1974), 73. See Judg 11:12; 2 Sam 16:10; 19:22; 1 Kgs 17:18; 2 Kgs 3:13; 2 Chr 35:21. Similarly, in the L.A.E. 11:2, Eve says to the devil, "What have you to do with us? What have we done to you, that you should pursue us with deceit? Why does your malice fall on us?"

28. The unclean spirit assumes that knowledge is power and tries to fend off its impending defeat with the exorcist's technique of pronouncing the name of the opponent. In the ancient magical papyri, names were used as incantations because it was believed that pronouncing the name of the power or enemy gave one a tactical advantage in manipulating and defeating them.

29. The definite article is significant. Horace Jeffery Hodges and John C. Poirier, "Jesus as the Holy One of God: The Healing of the *Zavah* in Mark 5.24b–34," *JGRChJ* 8 (2011–12): 169–70, argue, "The article thus elevates Jesus above various holy men." They continue in n. 60, "The motif of the *fear* that Jesus inspires by virtue of his holy power also goes beyond the reactions inspired by the prophets, and this also distinguishes the Markan Jesus from these other charismatic leaders." The contrast is evident by a comparison with 1 Kgdms 17:18 (LXX), where the widow of Zarephath uses that same question, "What between me and you?" and addresses Elijah as "man of God," not "the Holy One of God."

The amazed reaction of the synagogue worshipers stresses the authority of Jesus' teaching: "What is this? A new teaching—and with authority! He even gives orders to impure spirits and they obey him" (1:27). Their declaration links his teaching to his mighty deeds. The result is that the *power* of his teaching is emphasized rather than its content. It echoes Elihu's pronouncement, "God is exalted in his power. Who is a teacher like him?" (Job 36:22). Mark in a subtle way presses home Jesus' divine authority, which explains the power of his teaching.[30] He is not dependent on some external authority but expounds the law by directly laying claim to the will of God.[31]

Hurtado highlights another theme that runs through the early sections of Mark: "The response of the people ... involves surprise and wonder but not faith. They notice the demonstration of authority but seem unable to identify its source and nature."[32] Only the impure spirits and the readers who know Mark's introduction understand why Jesus' teaching and deeds are so powerful. He is the Son of God, the mightier One filled with God's Spirit, who comes to destroy Satan's minions.

The NIV opts to translate the word normally rendered "scribes" as "teachers of the law." In this scene, they make their first appearance in the gospel as ones who teach but not with authority (1:22). They are authorities only in expanding and interpreting traditions derived from the law, and, as those competing for stature with the people, they will engage in a power game with Jesus and will try to stifle his soaring stock with them. They are mentioned alone elsewhere in the gospel in 2:6; 3:22; 9:11, 14; 12:28, 32, 35, 38; with the Pharisees in 2:16; 7:1, 5; with the chief priests in 10:33; 11:18; 14:1; 15:31; and with the chief priests and elders in 8:31; 11:27; 14:43, 53; 15:1. In 12:28, a teacher of the law responds favorably to Jesus in his sparring with the Sadducees over the resurrection.

The teachers of the law assume that Jesus is guilty of blasphemy for pronouncing the forgiveness of sins (2:6–7) and publicly accuse him of being in collusion with Beelzebul, the prince of demons, in casting out demons (3:22). With the Pharisees they are disturbed that he eats with sinners (2:16) and that his disciples eat with unwashed hands and ignore the traditions of the elders (7:1–2, 5). They collude with the chief priests in orchestrating his death (8:31; 10:33; 11:18; 14:1, 53; 15:1). With the chief priests they also question Jesus' authority to act as he did in the temple (11:27), join the mob who arrest him (14:43), and chime in during the mockery as he dies on the cross (15:31).

Their teaching that Elijah must come first (9:11) and that the Messiah is to be the son of David (12:35) is assumed to be correct. One teacher of the law appears in a positive light when he commends Jesus' defense of the resurrection and his interpretation of the greatest commandment. Jesus, with matchless authority, pronounces him, in turn, to be near the kingdom (12:28–34). Jesus then proceeds

30. Jesus has authority as a teacher (1:21–22) to offer forgiveness of sins (2:5–12), over the Sabbath (2:27–28), over impure spirits (3:22–27), over the mystery of the kingdom of God which he gives to others (4:10–11), over nature (4:35–41; 6:45–52), over the law (7:1–13, 14–23), and over the temple (11:12–33).

31. Rainer Riesner, *Jesus als Lehrer* (WUNT 2/7; 3rd ed.; Tübingen: Mohr Siebeck, 1988), 499.

32. Larry W. Hurtado, *Mark* (NIBC 2; Peabody, MA: Hendrickson, 1989), 27.

to castigate the teachers of the law as a class for walking around in flowing robes and hankering to be greeted with respect in the marketplaces, for seeking the chief seats in the synagogues and places of honor at banquets, and for devouring widows' houses while making a pretense of piety with their lengthy prayers (12:38–40). These charges reveal that their problem is more than not teaching with authority. They are condemned as well-to-do, who gain their wealth in rapacious ways. Their actions betray their evil character, which they try to mask with a show of piety.

2.4.1.4 Healing of Simon's Mother-in-Law and Many Others (1:29–34)

When Jesus leaves the synagogue and enters Simon and Andrew's home, he is told that Simon's mother-in-law is laid low by a fever. Jesus does not initiate healing; instead, he "heals as a response to the initiative of others."[33] Rather than being a symptom of a disease, fever was considered by many Jews to be an illness with theological significance.[34] Fevers could be regarded as a punishment sent by God for violating the covenant (Lev 26:14–17; Deut 28:20–22), and they were believed to be curable only by divine intervention (*b. Ned.* 41a). Jesus' ability to heal her fever showed that he was able to do that which only God could do.

The immediate and full recovery of Simon's mother-in-law with no aftereffects is confirmed when she takes over her duties as hostess and "waits on them" (1:31; lit., "she was serving them"). She serves Jesus as the angels served him in recognition of his authority (1:13). The summary of his healing many of the various diseases and driving out many demons when the whole town gathered at his door reveals that the exorcism in the synagogue and the healing of Simon's mother-in-law are not unique events. They reveal a pattern in which Jesus responds with divine power to those who need deliverance from demons and to those who need healing.[35]

2.4.1.5 Praying before Going Out to the Whole of Galilee (1:35–39)

Jesus prays three times in Mark: here at the beginning of his ministry, in the middle (6:46), and before the end (14:32–40)—always alone, at night, and at times of tension. While praying in the wilderness,[36] Jesus is pursued by Simon and his companions,[37] who are ignorant of his divine commission and his greater plans to "go somewhere else—to the nearby villages" to preach. They want him to return to Capernaum to bask contentedly in the glories of the previous day.

33. Tolbert, *Sowing the Gospel*, 135.

34. Julius Preuss, *Biblical and Talmudic Medicine* (trans. and ed. Fred Rosner; New York: Sanhedrin, 1978), 160–63. See John 4:52 and Acts 28:7–10 ("fever and dysentery") for other instances of fever as a disease in the New Testament.

35. Joel F. Williams, *Other Followers of Jesus: Minor Characters as Major Figures in Mark's Gospel* (JSNTSup 102; Sheffield: JSOT, 1994), 95.

36. NIV translation of "solitary place" is the same word for "wilderness" that appeared in 1:3–4, 12–13. "Wilderness" is an inappropriate term to describe any geographical area around Capernaum.

37. NIV translation of "look for him" (1:36) does not properly capture the meaning of the verb that is used. It is better translated in this context as "hunted down." In a good sense, they sought him zealously.

2.4.1.6 Healing of a Leper (1:40–45)

A man with leprosy begs Jesus, if he is willing, to cleanse him of his plague. Philo (*Posterity* 47) describes "leprosy" as "that changeful disease which assumes so many different forms." The translation "scale disease" rather than "leprosy" is more accurate.[38] It was considered by many Jews before and after Jesus' day to be a punishment for sin.[39] After the victim is pronounced cleansed of the malady, the law requires that he make a "sin offering" in the temple as an atonement (Lev 14:13, 19, 22, 31). Since the disease was deemed to be a major source of defilement, akin to that of a corpse, the victims were excluded from the community (Lev 13:45–46; Num 5:2–4).

It was widely assumed that God inflicted this punishment and that only God could heal the disease.[40] When the king of Aram sent a letter to the king of Israel soliciting that his commander-in-chief Naaman be cured of his leprosy, upon reading the request, the king of Israel "tore his robes and said, 'Am I God? Can I kill and bring back to life? Why does this fellow send someone to me to be cured of his leprosy? See how he is trying to pick a quarrel with me!'" (2 Kgs 5:7). The leper's petition assumes that Jesus has the power of God to cleanse him, and, like God, Jesus can do as he wills (Wis 12:18).

Jesus responds with compassion and affirms that he not only has this divine power, "I am willing" (1:41), but he also has the grace to touch and to heal the man. Immediately, the disease leaves him, but he cannot be reintegrated back into society and resume a normal life until a priest has examined him and pronounced him free of the disease, and the healed person has performed the prescribed purification rites in the temple. For this reason, Jesus orders this leper to tell no one, but to go show himself "to the priest and offer the sacrifices that Moses commanded for your cleansing, as a testimony to them" (1:44; see Lev 14:1–32). Josephus (*Ant.* 3.11.3 §264) comments that Moses banished lepers from the city and claims that they were no different from a dead person because they could not interact with others: "But if their supplication to God caused them to be released from the disease and they recovered a healthy skin they gave thanks to God through various sacrifices." Though Jesus orders the man to tell no one about this, the leper is the first of a number of persons who cannot keep quiet about what Jesus has done for him. The result is that Jesus' surge in popularity means that he "could no longer enter a town openly but stayed outside in lonely places. Yet the people still came to him from everywhere" (1:45).

38. Jacob Milgrom, *Leviticus 1–16* (AB; New York: Doubleday, 1991), 816–20.

39. See Lev 14:34 ("I put a leprous disease in a house," NRSV); Num 12:1–15; Deut 24:8–9; 28:27; 2 Kgs 5:20–27; 15:5; 2 Chr 26:20. In a fragment of the Dead Sea Scrolls, lepers are listed in a category of transgressors (CD 4Q270; see also the later traditions in *b. ʿArak.* 15b–16a and *Lev. Rab.* 17:3). The tattered clothing prescribed for the leper in Lev 13:45 was interpreted in *Targum Onkelos* as a sign of mourning, presumably for the leper's sin for which he was being punished.

40. The title of the tractate in the *Mishnah* covering leprosy signs, *Negaʿim*, means "plagues" or "smitings."

2.4.1.7 Controversies Settled by Jesus' Pronouncements (2:1–3:6)

Jesus is not only pitted against the kingdom of Satan and the mayhem it inflicts on human lives; he also is set in opposition to religious leaders and their traditions, which impair rather than improve human lives. Jesus has healed and delivered a variety of victims so far in the narrative and will continue to do so. Bolt's comment is apropos and helps put Jesus' healing activity in theological perspective. The assortment of disorders depicts

> a world in great need, a world under the shadow of death. They also show that the Jewish religion was completely unable to help them in their need. In fact, it probably even made their situation worse by excluding them as unclean and so making God seem even further away. By coming to Jesus, this group shows the reader that faith means turning to Jesus Christ in the midst of real physical needs in this world under the shadow of death, and being prepared to follow him into the kingdom.[41]

The failure of the religious system and its interpreters is illustrated in the controversy scenes that follow. Jesus flouts and thereby corrects the traditional expectations of proper behavior as defined by a particular group of religious watchdogs. He responds to challenges from opponents with pronouncements:

"Who can forgive sins but God alone?" (2:7)	"The Son of Man has authority on earth to forgive sins." (2:10)
"Why does he eat with tax collectors and sinners?" (2:16)	"I have not come to call the righteous, but sinners." (2:17b)
"How is it that John's disciples and the disciples of the Pharisees are fasting, but yours are not?" (2:18)	"How can the guests of the bridegroom fast while he is with them? They cannot, so long as they have him with them." (2:19)
"Why are they doing what is unlawful on the Sabbath?" (2:24)	"The Son of Man is Lord even of the Sabbath." (2:28)

In the last scene, Jesus is the one who raises the challenge with his own question, "Which is lawful on the Sabbath: to do good or to do evil, to save life or to kill?" (3:4). The healing of the man's withered hand (3:5) turns the question mark into an exclamation point. On the Sabbath, one *may* not only do good and save life; rather, one *must* do good and save life! Jesus assumes the authority to decide what is "lawful" to do on the Sabbath, which was instituted by God and observed by God at creation (Gen 2:2).

Throughout this unit Jesus also offers proverbial sayings as part of his defense:

41. Peter G. Bolt, *The Cross from a Distance: Atonement in Mark's Gospel* (NSBT 18; Downers Grove, IL: InterVarsity Press, 2004), 38.

"It is not the healthy who need a doctor, but the sick." (2:17a)
"No one sews a patch of unshrunk cloth on an old garment." (2:21)
"No one pours new wine into old wineskins." (2:22)
"The Sabbath was made for man, not man for the Sabbath." (2:27)

The controversies reveal two discordant approaches to religious practices. The one represented by the Pharisees and teachers of the law leads to unresolved guilt, exclusion, legalistic burdens, spiritual paralysis, and ultimately death. The treacherous plotting of the Pharisees and Herodians to eradicate Jesus (3:6) reveals that "the withered hand of the man is nothing compared to the withered souls of these religious examiners."[42] The other represented by Jesus leads to forgiveness, fellowship with God and others, joy, mercy, and life.

2.4.1.7.1 Healing of a Paralytic and the Son of Man's Authority to Forgive Sins (2:1 – 12)

Mark has stressed that Jesus' fame has spread throughout Galilee (1:28) and that he is unable to enter a town openly without attracting attention. Despite retreating to lonely places, people flock to him from everywhere (1:45). When Jesus returns to Capernaum and is speaking the word in a home, it is no surprise that the house is teeming with so many people who have gathered to hear him that access to him through the door is cut off.[43] The friends of a paralytic want to bring him to be healed by Jesus, as others in Capernaum had brought their sick to him (1:32). They have no recourse but to carry him up to the roof, determinedly dig through it, and lower him down dramatically to Jesus.[44]

When Jesus sees "their faith," rather than immediately healing the paralytic, he announces that his sins are forgiven (2:5). Their faith is evinced by their dogged determination to get to Jesus. Marshall comments,

> At no point does the sick man or his friends verbalise their desire for healing or their trust in Jesus. Yet Jesus "sees" in the trouble they take to reach him an internal posture of faith (v. 5a). This is evidently because the men were driven by the overriding goal of reaching Jesus, and had refused to be deflected from doing so, either by the human obstacles that blocked the door or by the physical barrier of the roof that separated him Jesus from them.[45]

Since moderns tend to dissociate sin from sickness, what Mark narrates may be

42. David E. Garland, *Mark* (NIVAC; Grand Rapids: Zondervan, 1996), 108.

43. Parallels exist between the healing of paralytic and the exorcism of an unclean spirit in the synagogue (1:21 – 28): (a) both occur in Capernaum (1:21; 2:1); (b) Jesus is interrupted while he is teaching (1:21; 2:2); (c) a group questions among themselves what Jesus says or does (1:27; 2:6 – 7); (d) a reference to the teachers of the law (1:21 – 22; 2:6); (e) the issue of Jesus' authority is raised (1:22, 27; 2:10); (f) the crowd responds with amazement (1:22, 27; 2:12).

44. This detail is realistic. The archaeology of Capernaum reveals that the homes did not have large windows, and the walls were made of rough basalt without mortar. Without true foundations, the buildings could support little more than a sloping, flat thatch roof (see Ps 129:6). The men could easily dig through the earthen roof without causing irreparable damage.

45. Christopher D. Marshall, *Faith as a Theme in Mark's Narrative* (SNTSMS 64; Cambridge: Cambridge University Press, 1989), 86.

disconcerting.[46] One commentator states that the men brought their friend to Jesus to be healed, not to have his sins forgiven.[47] In Jesus' world, however, many people assumed that a connection existed between sickness and sin (see John 5:14; 9:2).[48] Most assumed that reconciliation with God must occur before healing could come. Jesus' announcement that the paralytic's sins are forgiven without any evidence of his repentance or confession of his sins (2:4–5) is as abrupt as it is unexpected.

The teachers of the law could have said, "God does not forgive sins so easily! Where are the signs of his contrition and repentance?" Instead, their indignant question, "Who can forgive sins but God alone?" (2:7), assumes that Jesus has presumptuously forgiven the man's sins. Since sin is an offense against God, only God can forgive sins.[49] Davis comments, "In this text, Jesus seems to be giving himself such authority as to be setting himself on a par with God."[50] One can only draw two conclusions from this scene: the coming of God's kingdom brings the forgiveness of sins and healing (Isa 33:22, 24; see also Jer 31:3; and Mic 7:18–19) and Jesus has divine authority to forgive sins, or Jesus is guilty of blasphemy for usurping God's authority to forgive sins, which warrants death (Lev 24:15–16; see Mark 14:64).[51] The teachers of the law assume the worse: Jesus is guilty of blasphemy.

Knowing their thoughts, something that only God is able to do,[52] Jesus asks them whether it is easier to make a theological pronouncement that the man's sins are forgiven or to provide empirical proof that the man's sins have been forgiven by virtue of being able to get up and walk.[53] Jesus' question presumes that forgiveness of sin and healing are interconnected (2 Chr 7:14; Ps 103:3). By forgiving the sin, he removes the effects of the sin, the paralysis. Jesus then commands the paralytic to get up and walk to prove that the Son of Man has the authority to forgive sins on earth.[54] Bolt states, "The long-awaited forgiveness of sins promised by the prophets (e.g. Isa. 40:1–2; Jer. 31:31–34; Zech. 13:1), and anticipated by John's baptism, has now arrived. Jesus, the Son of Man, is authorized to bring forgiveness to the land."[55]

46. Jesus does not overcome through power of positive thinking "a misplaced and exaggerated sense of guilt" (see Hartman, *Mark*, 114) that caused some kind of psychosomatic paralysis.

47. Ernst Haenchen, *Der Weg Jesu* (Berlin: Töpelmann, 1966), 101.

48. See also Exod 15:26; Deut 7:15; 28:22–28; 32:39; Job 2:5–6; Pss 41:3–4; 103:3; 107:17; Isa 19:22, 38:16–17, 57:17–19; Acts 12:20–23; 1 Cor 11:30; Jas 5:16.

49. Daniel Johansson, "'Who Can Forgive Sins but God Alone?' Human and Angelic Agents, and Divine Forgiveness in Early Judaism," *JSNT* 33 (2011): 351–74, establishes that pardoning sin was a divine prerogative that only God exercises and shares with no other. See Exod 34:7; 2 Sam 12:13; Pss 32:1–5; 51:1–4; 103:2–3; 130:4; Isa 6:7; 43:25; 44:22; Dan 9:9; and Zech 3:4.

50. Steven T. Davis, "'Who Can Forgive Sins but God Alone?' Jesus, Forgiveness, and Divinity," in *The Multivalence of Biblical Texts and Theological Meanings* (ed. Christine Helmer; SBLSymS 37; Atlanta: Society of Biblical Literature, 2006), 123. The appalled reaction of the teachers of the law to Jesus' announcement makes it unlikely that Jesus only conveys that the man's sins have been forgiven *by* God, as Nineham, *St. Mark*, 93, would have it. Otfried Hofius, "Vergebungszuspruch und Vollmachtsfrage. Mk 2,1–12 und das Problem priesterlicher Absolution im antiken Judentum," in *Neutestamentliche Studien* (WUNT 132; Tübingen: Mohr Siebeck, 2000), 57–69, shows that the priest cannot on his own authority pronounce the forgiveness of sins. What Jesus does here is unparalleled.

51. Marshall, *Faith as a Theme*, 185. The question of blasphemy is unspoken now, but it will resurface in Jesus' interrogation before the high priest and will lead to his condemnation to death.

52. See 1 Sam 16:7; 1 Chr 28:9; Ps 139:1–2; Jer 17:9–10; Sir 42:18–20; Luke 16:15; Acts 1:24; 15:8; Rom 8:27; 1 Thess 2:4; Rev 2:23.

53. This response accords with the scriptural guideline for verifying a true prophet and pinpointing a false prophet, who presumes to utter in God's name what the Lord has not commanded him to speak (Deut 18:22).

54. Jesus first refers to himself as the Son of Man here, and the meaning of this term will be dealt with below.

55. Bolt, *The Cross*, 20.

The crowd's amazement when the man picks up his mat and strolls away leads them to glorify God, because they had never seen anything like this.

2.4.1.7.2 Calling a Tax Collector and Eating with Sinners (2:13–17)

Another dispute arises after Jesus calls Levi, a tax collector, who immediately abandons his toll office to follow him.[56] Levi then hosts him in his house with what can only be understood as a celebratory meal to which he has invited "many tax collectors and sinners" (2:15). Tax collectors were renowned for their dishonesty and extortion. They habitually collected more than they were due, did not always post up the regulations, and made false valuations and accusations (see Luke 3:12–13). The teachers of the law, who were Pharisees, observe this scene and believe that Jesus has ignored purity boundaries by breaking bread with sinners who were beyond the pale.

The name "Pharisee" basically means "separatist," and the Pharisees were known for trying to avoid associating with sinners and evildoers, as Ps 1:1 advises. The Pharisees figure significantly in the narrative as Jesus' opponents. They are mentioned along with John's disciples as being known for their fasting (2:18). They alone are concerned about Jesus' disciples' violations of the Sabbath (2:24), and they plot with the Herodians to kill Jesus (3:6). In 8:15, Jesus lumps them together with the Herodians in warning his disciples against their leaven. In 12:12–15, they and the Herodians are sent by the chief priests, teachers of the law, and elders to try to trap him into saying something that would incriminate him in some way, and they pose the set-up question about paying taxes to Caesar. They are mentioned with the Jews as concerned about the washing of hands (7:3). They test him about a sign from heaven (8:11). They also test him with the question about divorce (10:2).

In this incident, their penchant to separate themselves from known sinners surfaces. Those identified as sinners, according to the standards of the Pharisees, were those who lived contrary to their interpretations of the law; and godliness, as defined by the Pharisees (see Luke 18:11–12), was unachievable for most. An extreme expression of this sentiment is found in a rabbinic commentary on Exodus (*Mekilta Amalek* 3.55–57 to Exod 18:1): "Let not a man ever associate with a wicked person, not even for the purpose of bringing him near to the Torah." Another expression of this attitude is found in the *Mishnah*: "Keep thee far from an evil neighbor and consort not with the wicked and lose not belief in retribution" (*m. ʾAbot* 1:7). These monitors of virtue assume that "birds of a feather flock together" and are offended by Jesus' choice of associates. They are not simply aggrieved that his fraternizing with sinners gives the impression that he condones their sin. The fear was that their impurity and rebellion might contaminate the righteous observer

56. Levi is called in the same way as the four fishermen, but his name does not appear in the list of disciples in 3:16–19. One called "Matthew" is summoned from his toll booth according to Matt 9:9, and that name does appear in all four lists of the Twelve (Mark 3:18; Matt 10:2–4; Luke 6:13–16; Acts 1:13). It is possible that the same person went by two names, Levi and Matthew. If the Levi mentioned here in Mark is not to be identified as the Matthew who is one of the Twelve, it means that the call to follow Jesus is not limited to the Twelve. The statement in 2:15 explaining the presence of these other guests, "for there were many who followed him," reinforces this interpretation.

of the law, since godliness was considered to be "an abomination to a sinner" (Sir 1:25). It is telling that they think that Jesus should agree with them that sinners and tax collectors should be shunned.

Jesus responds with proverbial wisdom that it is those who are sick who need a physician. By eating with sinners, Jesus embodies God's love and mercy. As Dodd puts it:

> His championship of the disreputable is not to be interpreted as the kindly tolerance of a broadminded humanist. It expresses the sovereign mercy of God in calling whom He will into his Kingdom, as in the parable the king's messengers gather his guests from the highways and hedges [Matt 22:9; Luke 14:23].[57]

The power of God will take away their sins and their shame and heal their infirmities and sin-sickness.

2.4.1.7.3 Not Fasting While the Bridegroom Is Here (2:18–22)

Someone notices that Jesus' disciples did not fast, unlike the disciples of the Pharisees (see Luke 18:12) or those of John the Baptist. Fasting was associated with grieving over the death of a loved one (1 Sam 31:13; 2 Sam 1:12; 3:35; 12:21), grieving over sin (1 Sam 7:6; 2 Sam 12:16–23; 1 Kgs 21:25–27), and making a petition to God. Jesus does not speak disapprovingly of the practice but responds with a parable that makes clear that it is a time to celebrate, not to put on sackcloth and fast. In this first response, he implicitly identifies himself as a bridegroom, which the prophets use as an image for God.[58] He hints at his upcoming death by saying that the time for mourning lies in the future when the bridegroom is taken away. When that happens, the celebratory merriment of his ministry (see 13:9–10) will be turned into a time of fasting and a yearning for his return.[59]

Two comparisons from everyday life stress how the new (Jesus' teaching) is incompatible with the old (Pharisaic teaching). One does not repair an old garment with new, unshrunken cloth. The two pieces of cloth are fundamentally mismatched, and a worse rip will be made when the new patch pulls apart from the old cloth when it is washed. One also does not put new wine into old wineskins, because their stiff and weakened fibers are not strong enough to contain the new wine that continues to ferment. They will burst, and one will lose both the wineskin and the wine. The implication is that the "new" that Jesus introduces, with its emphasis on the inclusion of those who are labeled outcasts, is beyond the capability of the old forms of Judaism to contain. The old garment is in need of repair, but Jesus has not come to do repairs. What are needed are new wineskins for this new wine. Mali remarks, "This means Jesus' ministry can neither be confined within the limits of

57. C. H. Dodd, *History and the Gospel* (London: Nisbet, 1938), 124.

58. Isa 50:1; 54:5–8; 62:4–5; Jer 2:2, 32–33; 3:1, 14; 31:32; Ezek 16:8.

59. 1 Macc 9:37–42 records an actual event in which a wedding celebration turns into a massacre and mourning.

Pharisaic Judaism, nor does it fit into Pharisaic ideals."[60] The theological mismatch between the new and the old will ultimately lead to Jesus' violent death when he will be taken away (2:20).

2.4.1.7.4 Plucking Grain on the Sabbath: The Son of Man Is Lord of the Sabbath (2:23–27)

This unit concludes with two Sabbath controversies.[61] The Pharisees spy Jesus' disciples plucking heads of grain as they pass through grainfields on the Sabbath. The Pharisees considered their plucking the grain heads to be equivalent to harvesting, a violation of the Sabbath (*m. Šabb.* 7:2). They direct their concern to Jesus as the one responsible for his disciples' behavior.

Jesus gives three responses. First, he cites the precedent of David when he and his companions were on the fly trying to escape Saul's wrath. They were hungry, and David entered the house of the Lord and ate the sacred bread of the presence permitted only to the priests (1 Sam 21:1–6; cf. Lev 24:5–9). The Pharisees would hardly see any connection between Jesus and his disciples and David and his companions. Only those already committed to Jesus would assume that the comparison holds true. For Mark, Jesus is the son of David but is far greater than David (12:35–37), and he is on a far more urgent mission. Second, he makes a humanitarian appeal by noting that God created the Sabbath for the well-being of humans. The purpose was not to create Sabbath rules to weigh down humans. Third, the statement that the Son of Man is the Lord of the Sabbath is a christological trump card that settles the whole matter. Jesus determines God's intention for the Sabbath and how the rules are to be interpreted.

2.4.1.7.5 Healing on the Sabbath (3:1–6)

In the second Sabbath controversy, Jesus' opponents menacingly lie in wait in the synagogue to see if he will heal on the Sabbath. His power to heal is taken for granted, and they remain unimpressed. He had healed on the Sabbath before (1:21–28), but no one raised an objection then. Jesus seizes the initiative by taking a man with a withered hand and placing him in the center. He then reframes the issue by asking them if it is lawful to do good or to do evil on the Sabbath, to save life or to destroy it. Apparently, doing nothing is not an option. The question contains its own answer. To avoid doing good when good can be done is to do evil. Doing good, healing the afflicted, then, can and should be done on the Sabbath.

The opponents' silence stems from their hardness of heart, and it condemns them. Their evil intent emerges when these Pharisees immediately take counsel

60. Joseph F. Mali, *The Christian Gospel and Its Jewish Roots: A Redaction-Critical Study of Mark 2:21–22 in Context* (Studies in Biblical Literature 131; New York: Peter Lang, 2009), 101.

61. The Sabbath signified many things for Jews in Jesus' day. Observing the Sabbath was a way to honor the holiness of Yahweh (Exod 20:8–11; Deut 5:12–15); a sign of Israel's sanctification among all the nations and therefore a national identity marker and safeguard against absorption by pagan culture; and a joyful entry into sacred time, the time of the beginning before human work.

with the Herodians to plot Jesus' death on the very same Sabbath. The religious and political figures align, and the audience already acquainted with the story should recognize that any involvement with Herod's camp means danger. Herod is the one who arrested John the Baptist and will put him to death.

2.4.2 Jesus' Ministry around the Sea of Galilee and Rejection in Nazareth (3:7–6:6a)

2.4.2.1 Summary Statement of Jesus' Ministry (3:7–12)

Crowds come to Jesus from Galilee, Judea, Jerusalem, Idumea, across the Jordan, and Tyre and Sidon—a geographical area that matches that of the Israel of old (see Isa 43:5–6), because they have heard what Jesus was doing. Mark's summary repeats earlier themes. Jesus' popularity brings a crush of people, and it is so overwhelming that he needs to have a boat ready to escape. While the crowd falls on him to receive the benefits of his healing power, the demons fall before him and are muzzled by the power of his word. As in the first exorcism of an impure spirit (1:23–28), the impure spirits recognize that he is the Holy One of God.

2.4.2.2 Choosing Twelve Disciples to Be With Him (3:13–19)

Jesus whittles down the large crowd to a limited group of twelve, whom he calls to be with him. Henderson points out the parallel with God calling Moses from the mountain (Exod 19:3). When Jesus "calls" from the mountaintop, "he assumes a similar mantle of sovereign authority."[62] These elected disciples will become the "entrusted leaders among God's people," who will expand his ministry as he sends them out to preach and to have authority over impure spirits (3:13–19).

Mark logs their individual names, with Simon Peter heading the list and Judas named last. The nickname "Peter" is added to the name "Simon," by which he was first introduced in the story (1:16, 29–30), but Mark does not expand on its significance.[63] Nor does Mark explain why James and John are dubbed the "sons of thunder" (3:17). Judas is identified as the one who handed Jesus over, and this ominously points toward Jesus' passion, but Mark does not explain why Judas was chosen by Jesus nor will he explain in detail why Judas would be moved to such treachery. The emphasis falls on Jesus' sovereign choice and not on the qualities of the disciples chosen.

2.4.2.3 Attempts to Obstruct Jesus' Ministry by His Family and the Teachers of the Law (3:20–35)

This segment is the first example of the Markan technique of bracketing (intercalation or "sandwiching"), where the narration begins with one story but is interrupted

62. Suzanne Watts Henderson, *Christology and Discipleship in the Gospel of Mark* (SNTSMS 135; Cambridge: Cambridge University Press, 2006), 80.

63. Presumably, Mark assumes that the original audience would know and understand the significance of the sobriquet "rock."

by another before it is concluded. In 3:20–21, Jesus' family went out to seize him because they said he was "out of his mind." Their action breaks off with the description in 3:22–30 of teachers of the law who come down from Jerusalem, claiming that Jesus is possessed by Beelzebul and Jesus' rebuttal of the charge. In 3:31–35, the storyline returns to Jesus' mother and brothers who arrive and call for him, and Jesus reinterprets who his mother and brothers are according to spiritual criteria. The bracketing fills in time in the narrative for Jesus' mother and his brothers to arrive, but, more importantly, the technique allows the two separate stories to make a similar point. The point is that any attempt to hinder or to redirect Jesus' ministry and mission is a serious sin, whether it is instigated by Jesus' intimate family or by his bitter enemies. These two incidents, put side by side, present two profoundly different choices: blaspheming against the Holy Spirit or doing the will of God.

The teachers of the law who came down from Jerusalem seek to slander Jesus by spreading gossip: "He is possessed by Beelzebul! By the prince of demons he is driving out demons" (3:22). They do not deny his success in casting out demons but attribute it to a strange confederacy with Satan. Since this charge has not arisen from any particular incident, it seems that they are motivated by envy over Jesus' remarkable success and his sway over the crowds, which diminishes their standing with the crowd (see 1:22) and generates their malevolence toward him (see 15:10).

The origin of the term "Beelzebul" is vague, but Mark clearly understands him to be "the prince of demons" (3:22). The translation that he "is possessed by Beelzebul" is not precise. He is charged literally with "having Beelzebul" (3:22) and having an impure spirit (3:30), which could mean, "having such a spirit under his control (i.e. being a sorcerer or spirit-medium)."[64] This charge is a malicious claim that Jesus has diabolical power and works by a different spirit than the Holy Spirit.

Jesus no longer responds to opponents with direct statements (2:10, 27–28) but speaks to them in parables (3:23). He exposes how ludicrous this charge is. He does not profit from his work or use it to gain some advantage. The victims of the demons are never harmed by his exorcisms but are set free. If he were in collusion with Satan, who willingly gives up these demonic minions who are cast out, then Satan's "kingdom would be in a state of civil war and accordingly on the point of collapse."[65] Looked at from another perspective, Jesus' success suggests that the strong man's (Satan's) house has been raided, and he has been bound so that Jesus can plunder his possessions; that is, he set free those victims who have been demonized. The audience can now reflect back on his encounter with Satan in the wilderness as a battle in which Satan was defeated (1:13).

To identify the work of the Holy Spirit as the working of the power of evil with the malicious intent of destroying another's reputation to safeguard one's own sphere of influence is an unforgivable sin. These critics reveal themselves to be the ones in league with Satan, the great defamer.

---

64. Eric Eve, *The Jewish Context of Jesus' Miracles* (JSNTSup 231; London/New York: Sheffield Academic Press, 2002), 328.

65. Ibid., 330.

Jesus' family came to "seize" ("to take charge of," NIV in 3:21) him. The Greek verb that is used is the same verb used when the posse seizes Jesus at his arrest (14:44, 46). His family either has heard that the people were saying that he was "out of his mind" (3:21) or have drawn that conclusion themselves. But they are not able to get through because of the crowd that surrounds him, and someone informs Jesus that his mother and brothers are outside. He looks at the crowd around him and asks pointedly, "Who are my mother and my brothers?" He gives the answer to his own question: "Here are my mother and my brothers! Whoever does God's will is my brother and sister, and mother" (3:34–35). "Father" is not mentioned because only God can serve that role.

Jesus insists that one's commitment to God is to be even greater than one's commitment to family, the greatest human bond. Jesus' mother is left outside with her other sons, excluded from the circle of Jesus' intimates. Kee comments, "All genetic, familial, and sex distinctions are eradicated in this new concept of the true family."[66] Biological family relationships are not based on choice but on birth. Belonging to the family of God, however, is a matter of choice. One can choose to be obedient to God's will and thereby be joined to others in a family comprised of those who accept God's rule. In the family of God, obedience and membership are completely voluntary. Those who are deprived of traditional family relationships can therefore become members of a greater family (see 10:30).

2.4.2.4 Teaching by the Sea in Parables (4:1–34)

This lengthy discourse is bracketed by the phrase "many parables": "He taught them many things by parables" (4:2); "with many similar parables Jesus spoke the word to them" (4:33). Key terms appear throughout the discourse. "Sowing" appears in 4:3 [2x], 4, 14 [2x], 15, 16, 18, 20, 31, 32 and is defined as "sowing the word" in 4:14. "Word" appears in 4:14, 15, 16, 17, 18, 19, 20, 33 (see 2:2; 5:36). The noun "seed" appears in 4:26–27 and is referred to in 4:4, 5, 7, 8, 15, 16, 18, 20, 31 ("mustard seed"). "Soil" ("earth") appears in 4:1, 5 (2x), 8, 20, 26, 28, 31 (2x).

The verb "to hear" occurs fourteen times (4:3, 9 [2x], 12 [2x], 15, 16, 18, 20, 23 [2x], 24, 33). It brackets the parable of the Sower: "Listen!" (4:3); "Whoever has ears to hear, let them hear" (4:9). It appears twice in the quote from Isa 6:9, explaining why everything comes in parables (4:12). It is therefore the crucial word in the interpretation of the parable. Each type of soil hears the word but reacts differently (4:15, 16, 18, 20). The command to hear concludes the parable of the Lamp, "If anyone has ears to hear, let them hear" (4:23) and precedes the parable of the Measure: "Consider carefully what you hear" (4:24). The discourse concludes with the summary statement that Jesus "spoke the word" to them in many parables "as they were able to hear it" (4:33, ASV; "understand" NIV).

66. Kee, *Community*, 109.

2.4.2.4.1 Introduction (4:1 – 2)

Mark has mentioned that Jesus taught (1:21, 27; 2:13), but this chapter provides a lengthy report of his teaching. Jesus teaches the crowd "by parables" (4:2),[67] and the first parable is a parable about his teaching. In the opening scene, Jesus teaches the entire crowd (4:1 – 2), but in the closing scene a split has occurred among the hearers (4:33 – 34). He "spoke the word" to them in many parables "as they were able to hear it" (4:33, ASV), but he privately explained all things to his disciples when he was alone with them.[68] This discourse explains how and why that division occurred.

2.4.2.4.2 Parable of the Sower (4:3 – 9)

In the first parable, a sower successfully sows the seed. The success of the seed, however, depends on the nature of the soil. The parable emphasizes the disparity of the results in different soils. Seeds that fall on the pathway get no chance to take root before the birds snatch them. Seeds grow rapidly on rocky ground, but with little depth of soil they quickly wither in the heat. The seeds that sprout in ground infested by thorns cannot compete and eventually are choked out. The three different verbs describing the differing failures, "ate" (4:4), "withered" (4:6), and "choked" (4:7), are matched by three verbs describing the fruitfulness of the success of the seed in good soil, "came up, grew and produced a crop" (4:8). The differing yields, "some multiplying thirty, some sixty, some a hundred times" (lit., "one ... one ... one ...") refers to the different yields of different seeds (4:20).

The parable by itself has no meaning. A farmer goes out to sow and meets with failure and a good yield. It only has significance if one has a faith commitment in the teller of the parable. The two longer parables in Mark, this parable of the Sower and the allegory of the Wicked Tenants (12:1 – 12), are similar in that they both serve as summaries that help the listener to get his or her bearings on the significance of what has happened in the story and to prepare for what is to happen.[69] The parable of the Sower explains Jesus' lack of success in his mission but also gives the assurance of a successful harvest.

Sowing is a metaphor for God's work. God promises to sow Israel (Jer 31:27 – 28; Ezek 36:9; Hos 2:21 – 23; 2 Esd 8:6; 9:31; *2 Bar.* 70:2). To sow the seed of the word is God's work. God does this to begin the renewal of Israel. The reference to sowing represents a new beginning for Israel. This eschatological image appears in *1 En.* 62:8: the community of saints and elect will be sown, and all the elect will stand before him on that day.

67. Of "the many ... parables" (4:33), we get only five and only one interpretation. The term "parable" is related to the Hebrew *māšal* in the OT, which could be used for short popular sayings, ethical maxims, oracles, wisdom discourses, short utterances, scornful, satirical sayings, allegories, riddles, fables — sometimes obvious, sometimes obscure. See further Klyne R. Snodgrass, "Parable," in *DJG*, 591 – 601.

68. The explanations, which are given "when he was alone" (4:10), are bracketed by the parables, which are given in public (4:1 – 9, 21 – 32).

69. Mary Ann Tolbert, "How the Gospel of Mark Builds Character," *Int* 47 (1993): 350.

2.4.2.4.3 General Statement about Hearing and Seeing (4:10 – 12)

Parables do not always make something obscure clearer. They can befuddle. They require interpretation from Jesus (see 3:22 – 30; 6:51 – 52; 8:14 – 21). Jesus' serious followers will come to inquire of him what he means, and that is what Jesus' disciples do. They ask him about the parables (4:10). How one responds to Jesus' teaching determines whether one is an insider or an outsider, whether one will be fruit-bearing or unfruitful.[70]

Jesus' explanation conveys that the parables are like a two-edged sword that reveals the mystery of the kingdom to disciples who come to Jesus for understanding, but they deepen the blindness in others.[71] The disciples are given "the secret of the kingdom of God" (4:11). The "secret" or "mystery" refers to a heavenly truth concealed from human understanding but known by God.[72] Humans cannot grasp the mystery through their own intellectual capacity. God gives it only to those who are willing to open themselves up to the truth. Jesus' charge to hear only occurs in the public parables and not in the private explanations, because insiders have already heard and have responded by coming to Jesus to hear more.

The citation from Isaiah 6 recalls God calling of a faithful prophet to preach to faithless people. The prophet Ezekiel also had to endure a people who had eyes to see but did not see, and ears to hear but did not hear (Ezek 12:2 – 3). He laments that the people think that his preaching is unclear, only riddles and allegories (17:2; 20:49).

2.4.2.4.4 Explanation of the Parable of the Sower (4:13 – 20)

The interpretation of the parable stresses that all of the soils have heard the word (4:15, 16, 18, 20). The seed that lands on the path cannot get into the ground to grow, and the birds that devour them are likened to Satan. Satan, though bound, is still a danger to those who hear indifferently. The seed that lands in the rocky ground and springs up immediately is compared to those who initially receive the word joyfully, but only superficially. Their faith shrivels when tribulation and persecution arrive. The seed that falls among the weeds grows until it is finally suffocated by the choking thorns, which are identified as "the worries of this life, the deceitfulness of wealth and the desire for other things." As the seed landing in bad soil fails in three different ways, it succeeds in three different ways in good soil. The interpretation does not expand on the reasons for this varying success.

70. Bearing fruit is a rich image in Scripture; see Isa 27:6; Ezek 17:23; John 15:8, 16; Rom 7:4; Phil 1:11, 22; Col 1:6, 10; Titus 3:14; Heb 6:7; 12:11; 2 Pet 1:8.

71. Joel Marcus, "Mark 4:10 – 12 and Marcan Epistemology," *JBL* 103 (1984): 566.

72. Joel Marcus, *The Mystery of the Kingdom of God* (SBLDS 90; Atlanta: Scholars Press, 1986), 46. Behind this concept is the OT idea of God's secret (Job 15:8; Ps 25:14; Prov 3:32; Amos 3:7). Cranfield, *Mark*, 153, writes: "The idea that God's thoughts and ways are not men's, but that they are his secret, which is not obvious to human wisdom but which he may reveal to those whom he chooses, was familiar to everyone who listened attentively in the synagogue."

2.4.2.4.5 General Truths about Hearing and Seeing in Parables (4:21–25)

The complementary parables about the lamp and the measure supplement the explanation about parables in 4:10–12. They express in parabolic form what Jesus said plainly to the Twelve and to those around him when they asked him privately about the meaning of the parables. If things seem hidden, it is not because there is anything wrong with the lamp but because God intends it.[73] Faith is born in the tension between the revealing and the veiling of the truth. God's purpose is ultimately to make it manifest to all. The parable of the Measure conveys that those who fail to hear well will ultimately lose everything. Those who hear well will get richer through greater explanations of God's purposes and will have a superabundance of understanding.

2.4.2.4.6 Two Seed Parables (4:26–32)

The second pair of parables, the seed cast on the earth (4:26–29) and the mustard seed sown on the earth (4:30–32), are counterparts to the parable of the Sower who sows the seed (4:3–9). They complement each other in developing the theme of the hiddenness of the kingdom.[74] In deciding the meaning of the parables, one should allow their context in Mark to be a key factor.[75]

Both parables touch on the deceptive insignificance of the kingdom's presence before its final manifestation. The results of the growth of the seed in both parables have eschatological overtones: the sickle sent to gather the harvest (4:29; Joel 3:13) and the birds of heaven nesting in the greatest of all bushes (4:32).[76] Despite unpromising appearances, God's purposes will be fulfilled in God's timing and in ways that humans will not initially understand or appreciate.

2.4.2.4.7 Narrative Conclusion (4:33–34)

The narrative summary concludes the parable discourse as it began by stating that Jesus "spoke the word to them" (the disciples and the crowds) in many parables (4:2) but adds the phrase "as much as they could understand" (4:33). How is one to understand? Verse 34 explains that one can only understand if one comes to Jesus for the explanation. Otherwise, one will remain in the dark and be destined for eternal darkness.

73. Four purpose clauses (with *hina*) appear in 4:21–22, which are translated "is meant to."

74. When Jesus begins with the statement, "the kingdom of God is like," he assumes divine authority to explain what God's rule is. The kingdom of God is present with the coming of Jesus.

75. Claude N. Pavur, "The Grain is Ripe: Parabolic Meaning in Mark 4:26–29," *BTB* 17 (1987): 21, highlights the wide variety of titles given to the parable in 4:26–29, which reveal how open it is to diverse interpretations.

76. The nesting of the birds in the branches of the mustard bush is an eschatological image that symbolizes the incorporation of the Gentiles into the people of God in *Jos. Asen.* 15:6: "And no more will you be called Aseneth, but your name will be 'City of Refuge,' for in you many nations will take refuge and will lodge [same verb as in Mark 4:32, which means "nest"] under your wings, and many nations will find shelter through you." See also Ps 104:12, 16–17; Ezek 31:3, 6; Dan 4:9–12, 21–22.

2.4.2.5 Demonstrations of Power on Both Sides of the Sea of Galilee That Meet with Faith and Rejection (4:35–6:6a)

In this large unit (4:35–6:6a), Jesus continues to spend time by the Sea of Galilee and ventures across the lake. The incidents Mark records demonstrate that Jesus is sovereign over the potent forces of nature and of death. Despite the mighty works that Jesus performs, the conclusion for this unit (4:35–6:6a) is similar to the conclusion for the first unit (1:14–3:6). Just as he was rejected by the Pharisees and the Herodians (3:6), he is rejected in his hometown (6:1–6a).

Several themes emerge. Death looms large in the miracles. The disciples are in peril on the sea. A demoniac lives in tombs, the realm of death. A woman's constant hemorrhaging puts her life in danger of death, and the young daughter of a synagogue ruler passes away. The characters are motivated by desperation to seek out Jesus. In the case of the Gerasene demoniac, the demons control him and are desperate to ward off being driven out of the man, later pleading to be cast into pigs grazing on the hillside so that they might stay in the same region. As a result of the exorcism of these demons, the local townspeople are desperate to get Jesus to leave their district.

The characters also experience reverent awe when they witness the different miracles of Jesus. The disciples feared a great fear after Jesus stilled the storm (4:41). The townspeople became afraid when they saw the man who had been possessed by a legion of demons dressed and sitting in his right mind at Jesus' feet (5:15). The woman who was immediately healed from her flow of blood when she touched Jesus' garment fell down before Jesus in fear and trembling (5:33). There is also a contrast between a doubting anxiety and a confident faith (4:40; 5:36). Faith brings healing. The absence of faith leads to the rejection of Jesus.

2.4.2.5.1 Stilling the Storm (4:35–41)

The calming of the storm in the Sea of Galilee[77] is the first nature miracle in the gospel of Mark. The miracle is not against nature so much as it is against Satan, who would destroy Jesus' followers and their faith. In contrast to the disciples' abject fear in the face of a sudden squall that threatens to swamp their boat, Jesus sleeps, seemingly indifferent to their plight. His sleep is a sign of his trust in God (Job 11:18–19; Pss 3:5; 4:8; 121:3–4; Prov 3:23–26) and a mark of his divine sovereignty. The disciples' vexed plea, "Teacher, don't you care if we drown?" ("are destroyed," 4:38), uses the same verb as in 1:24 when the demons ask, "Have you come to destroy us?" The question reflects a nascent trust that Jesus somehow is able to save them in their hour of need.

Jesus does not pray to God for deliverance but rebukes the wind and waves himself, and they stop. The sea is calmed, but the disciples' terror does not abate.

77. The Sea of Galilee was known as the Sea of Tiberias (John 21:1, NRSV) and "the Lake of Gennesaret" (Luke 5:1; "Sea of Kinnereth," see NIV text notes in Num 34:11; Josh 12:3; 13:27). Going across to the other side of the lake is mentioned in Mark 4:35; 5:1, 21; 6:45; 8:13.

They recognize that they are in the presence of one who has divine control of the sea. He is able to transform a "furious [*megalē*] squall" (4:37) into a "complete [*megalē*] calm" (4:39) with just a word.[78]

The disciples pose the key christological question when they ask, "Who is this?" and declare, "Even the wind and the waves obey him!" (4:41). He is something more than a charismatic, miracle-working prophet. The answer to their question comes from Scripture, which reveals that Jesus has power to do what only the God who created the sea can do (see Gen 8:1; Job 26:12; Pss 65:7; 74:13–14; 89:9; 93:3–4; 104:5–9; 106:9; 107:23–32; 114:3; Isa 50:2; Nah 1:4; cf. Isa 43:1–10). When Jesus asks them, "Why are you so afraid? Do you still have no faith?" (4:40), it is a gentle rebuke. Faith refers to trust in the divine power that is evident in Jesus' person. This miracle provides a significant piece of the puzzle that will help the disciples recognize Jesus' full identity as the Son of God.

2.4.2.5.2 Exorcism of the Gerasene Demoniac (5:1–20)

Jesus crosses the lake to the opposite shore, which is opposite in many other ways. It is an idolatrous region teeming with demons. When Jesus disembarks, he is immediately assailed by a demoniac. In comparison to Matthew's and Luke's accounts (see Matt 8:28; Luke 8:26–27), Mark alone gives a vivid account of the man's condition and how he had been treated. He had been chained and beaten as if he were a wild animal, but people were unable to tame him. He broke the chains and now lived alone in tombs, the unclean place of the dead, mutilating himself and screaming into the night. In the NT, demonized individuals are victims of an evil power, and it requires a stronger divine power to liberate them from the demonic oppression. Jesus never rebukes those who are demonized, never tells them to repent, and never tells them that their sins are forgiven. They need deliverance.

Jesus has been successful in casting out individual demons with ease. Now, he confronts a huge force of demons in one screeching person. Three different characters encounter Jesus in this story: the impure spirits (5:9–13), the townspeople (5:17), and the demoniac (5:18–19). Each makes a request of him. Jesus grants the appeals of the impure spirits to enter into the pigs that are feeding on the hillside, but when they enter them, the pigs stampede into the lake and are destroyed. He also grants the request of the troubled townspeople who beg him to leave their region. The demonized man, who is now fully clothed and in his right mind and sitting at Jesus' feet, begs him to allow him to be with him, the role of a disciple (3:14). Jesus does not grant his request. Instead, he tells him, "Go home to your own people and tell them how much the Lord has done for you, and how he has had mercy on

78. Antiochus Epiphanes is accused of "superhuman arrogance" for assuming that he could command the waves of the sea, and had imagined that he could weigh the high mountains in a balance (2 Macc 9:8). It is labeled "superhuman arrogance" because it is presumed that only God could stir up the sea and calm it. Augustus claimed to make the sea peaceful by ridding it of pirates (*Res Gestae* 4.25), and Philo (*Embassy*, 145–46) reiterates that boast in lauding Augustus for bringing an end to grievous wars over sea and land and bringing peace: "This is the Caesar who calmed the torrential storms on every side, who healed the pestilences common to Greeks and barbarians.... This is he who cleared the sea of pirate ships and filled it with merchant vessels." This incident reveals how much greater power Jesus possesses than Caesar.

you" (5:19). Jesus not only restores the man to his right mind, he restores him to his family. Jesus will leave the region but he leaves a witness. The man responds with obedience and tells the good news to everyone in the Decapolis. Jesus' next venture into this area will meet with far greater success (7:31–37).

A christological subtlety emerges in 5:19–20. Jesus tells the man to "tell [your own people] how much the *Lord* has done for you, and how he has had mercy on you" (5:19), but instead the man announces "how much *Jesus* had done for him" (5:20). For Mark, Jesus is synonymous with the Lord (1:3; 12:36–37). This proclamation modifies the demons' recognition of Jesus as "the Son of the Most High God" (5:7) because it is made in faith.

2.4.2.5.3 Healing a Woman with a Hemorrhage and Raising Jairus's Daughter (5:21–43)

When Jesus returns from the other side of the lake, he is immediately met by a synagogue leader named Jairus, who prostrates himself before Jesus and pleads with him to come and lay hands on his dying daughter so that she might live. On the way to Jairus's home, he is touched by a woman plagued by vaginal bleeding. Mark's second use of the bracketing technique to narrate a story connects the miraculous healing of a woman with a flow of blood for twelve years to the raising to life of a twelve-year old girl. The woman who touches Jesus' garment for healing and the father of the young girl who pleads for his daughter both exhibit the one thing that will bring them deliverance: their faith in Jesus.

The woman, who surreptitiously touches Jesus as he passes by in the crowd, suffers from an irregular discharge that makes her impure (Lev 15:25–30). She is not to touch any holy thing or enter the sanctuary (Lev 12:4). She is therefore isolated and could not attend religious festivals (Num 5:1–4). Her furtive touch is mentioned four times (Mark 5:27, 28, 30, 31), and that touch causes the hemorrhaging immediately to stop. Jesus suddenly stops the procession to ask who touched him, because he knew that someone had accessed his power. What the woman hoped might be quick and impersonal so that she could slip back into the crowd is turned into something personal when Jesus calls her out, and she is forced to make a public acknowledgment of what happened. Like Jairus, she prostrates herself before him, but she trembles in fear in the presence of one with such power. Jesus then addresses her as "Daughter" and announces that her faith has healed her and then tells her to go in peace (5:34).

The law stipulates regarding one who has suffered a discharge:

> When she is cleansed from her discharge, she must count off seven days, and after that she will be ceremonially clean. On the eighth day she must take two doves or two young pigeons and bring them to the priest at the entrance to the tent of meeting. The priest is to sacrifice one for a sin offering and the other for a burnt offering. In this way he will make atonement for her before the LORD for the uncleanness of her discharge. (Lev 15:28–30)

Unlike the leper, whom Jesus sent to the priests because he could not return to society without a priestly bill of health (1:44), he does not order the woman to go through the required rites for her cleansing and atonement. Her faith has "healed" her (5:34), but the verb also can be translated "saved"—her faith has "saved" her. She need do nothing else and can go in peace.

In the meantime, the bad news comes that Jairus's daughter has died. When Jesus arrives and says that she is not dead but sleeping, he meets with cynical incredulity from the mourners who had already assembled. He takes only the parents and three disciples, Peter, James, and John, to the young girl and raises her up. He then orders the parents to give her food to strengthen her and to prove that she is not some vaporous ghost.

The two main characters in this story occupy opposite ends of the economic, social, and religious spectrum. Jairus is a male and distinguished as a leader of the synagogue. He is named. He has honor so that he can openly, if deferentially, approach Jesus with a direct request. As a man of some means, Jairus would have a large household. By contrast, the woman is female and nameless, and her ailment renders her ritually unclean. She is walking pollution as the life force drains from her. This care-worn woman has become impoverished from the fruitless attempts by physicians to heal her.[79] Her condition makes childbearing hopeless and marriage next to impossible. She has no honor and believes she must sneak up to Jesus from behind, thinking that she has to purloin healing because Jesus would never grant a direct request from the likes of her.

What these two persons share in common is that both have heard about Jesus and both are desperate. They have run out of options. Dovetailing together the stories of two such disparate individuals conveys that neither being male, ritually pure, religiously well-regarded, nor having means provides any advantage in approaching Jesus. Being female, impure, dishonored, and destitute does not present insurmountable barriers that prevent Jesus from helping.

The religious leaders seem to be Jesus' archenemies in Mark. Malbon comments that, in Mark's characterization of the Jewish leaders, whether one is "a foe of the Markan Jesus is a matter of how one chooses to relate to him, not a matter of one's social or religious status and role."[80] The only thing that avails is exhibiting one's faith in Jesus. Faith enables all, honored and dishonored, clean and unclean, male and female, to tap into the merciful power of Jesus that brings both healing and salvation. Despite their seemingly hopeless situations, both the woman and Jairus display complete trust in him to deliver them.

Another noteworthy feature of the two accounts is that both pertain to matters of uncleanness. The laws concerning impurity sought to prevent it from infringing on the realm of God's holiness, but Jesus' ministry shows that God's holiness is

79. A negative attitude toward physicians appears in 2 Chr 16:12; Tob 2:10; Sir 10:10; and *m. Qidd.* 4:14.

80. Elizabeth Struthers Malbon, *In the Company of Jesus: Characters in Mark's Gospel* (Louisville: Westminster John Knox, 2000), xiii.

unaffected by human impurity. Jesus does not need to purify himself from the pollution of a person with a flux or from contact with a dead body (*m. Ḥag.* 2:13). This incident shows that Jesus is incapable of being defiled and that he has the power to overcome and to reverse the defilement of ceremonial uncleanness (bleeding and death). Hodges and Poirier conclude that Mark

> presents Jesus as *the* holy one of God—a source of inexhaustible power—and yet approachable even by those in a state of impurity. This suggests that Mark intends to present God as judging according to his mercy rather than his justice (to use the rabbinic terminology). This fits with the interpretation of Mark's portrayal of Jesus' mission as being motivated primarily by the politics of compassion rather than that of purity. This also signifies an increased emphasis in Mark upon the very *personal* nature of the divine. Destruction no longer occurs automatically when the impure comes near or even into contact with the holy, despite the fact that the impure and the holy remain antithetical forces characterized by their dynamic opposition. From a history-of-religions perspective, this means that in Mark's portrayal of Jesus as the *approachable* holy one of God, a new relation between the holy and the profane is emerging.[81]

Those who carry impurity (a leper, the sinners, a woman with a flux, a young female who is dead) are not destroyed by contact with Jesus, the Holy One of God (1:24). Quite the opposite happens. They are purged of their impurity and healed or raised to life by contact with him. This reality directly bears on Jesus' teaching about impurity in 7:1–23 and his interactions with Gentiles that follow (7:24–8:10).

2.4.2.5.4 Rejection of Jesus at Nazareth (6:1–6a)

Jesus encounters a surprisingly negative response when he returns to his hometown, Nazareth, and teaches in the synagogue. His teaching prompts them to ask, "Where did this man get these things?... What's this wisdom that has been given him? What are these remarkable miracles he is performing?" (6:2). Their questions are the third in a series of questions raised by those who have been bewildered by his teaching and his deeds in a synagogue. First, a synagogue gathering asked, "What is this?" (1:27). Next, some teachers of the law asked themselves, "Why does this fellow talk like that?" (2:7; cf. "Who is this?" in 4:41). Now, the question centers on the source of his deeds and teaching, "Where did this man get [this]?" While demons cry out Jesus' identity, humans still question it.[82] Only the audience of the gospel, however, knows that Jesus is the Son of God (1:1, 11), imbued with the Holy Spirit (1:10).

Jesus' response to reservations of the people of his hometown about him marks the first time in the gospel that the term "prophet" is applied to him. He has come like a prophet and is rejected like one. This rejection is therefore ominous because

81. Hodges and Poirier, "Jesus as the Holy One of God," 182–84.

82. Jack Dean Kingsbury, *The Christology of Mark's Gospel* (Philadelphia: Fortress, 1983), 86–87.

of Israel's history in mistreating prophets (1 Kgs 19:10; 2 Chr 36:16; Jer 11:21; 12:6; Matt 5:12; 23:37). Hartman comments,

> If one takes seriously the fact that "were offended" is in the imperfect tense, the attitude of Jesus' fellow citizens does not appear as a snooty reaction at the synagogue meeting but instead becomes a wider background of Jesus' maxim in v. 4 and something that characterizes their relationships during his stay for some time in Nazareth.[83]

The observation that Jesus could do no mighty works there except "lay his hands on a few sick people and heal them" (6:5) implies that Jesus' healings are intended to lead persons to faith, and this transformation from obduracy to faith is often overlooked as a mighty work. Marshall comments that unbelief does not make the performance of a miracle "impossible." Jesus does perform miracles (6:2, 5), but they are "meaningless" without faith. He writes: "A miracle leads nowhere if the externally astonishing event is not received and experienced in faith as a sign of salvation."[84]

2.4.3 The Expansion of Jesus' Ministry beyond Galilee (6:6b–8:21)

2.4.3.1 The Mission of the Twelve and the Execution of John the Baptist (6:6b–30)

Jesus will not enter a synagogue again in the narrative but now moves to open places where crowds come to him from all over. This new larger unit begins with a summary and a topographical note in 6:6b–13 as did the previous units in 1:14–15 and 3:7–12.

The disciples' commissioning by Jesus (6:6b–13) and their reporting back to Jesus about their mission (6:30–32) wraps around the grisly account of Herod's beheading of John the Baptist (6:14–29) and is another example of Mark's use of bracketing. Jesus invests the disciples with his authority over unclean spirits (see 3:15) and sends them out two by two, which satisfies the requirement of two or three witnesses (Deut 17:6; 19:15; Num 35:30; 2 Cor 13:1; 1 Tim 5:19), to preach repentance. Jesus heals with his word and touch, but the disciples will only have the use of oil to anoint and heal others (6:13). He allows them to take some measure of protection by taking a staff and wearing sandals, but he forbids them from taking along bread, knapsack, money, or an extra garment (6:8–9).

These details say more about the character of the disciples' mission than its

83. Hartman, *Mark*, 209. Mark is not clear what caused the people to move from amazement (6:2) to offense (6:3). The statement that they know Jesus' mother, brothers, and sisters might suggest that their familiarity with Jesus or his undazzling family bred their contempt. Jesus' father is not mentioned, and identifying him as "Mary's son" suggests that she is now widowed. Jesus' brothers are mentioned in Acts 1:14 (along with his mother); 1 Cor 9:5; Gal 1:19; Jas 1:1; and Jude 1:1 as believers.

84. Marshall, *Faith as a Theme*, 194, citing Richard Glöckner, *Biblischer Glaube ohne Wunder?* (Sammlung Horizonte, NF 14; Einsiedeln: Johannes, 1979), 81.

logistics. The staff may have a symbolic connection to the staff of the twelve tribes (Num 17)—a symbol of a tribal leader's authority, a symbol of readiness to be on the move as during the Passover (Exod 12:11), and/or a symbol of God's intention to renew the covenant with Israel (Ezek 37:15–28; 20:37). Not taking provisions forces the disciples to be entirely dependent on God for their support. Shaking the dust from their feet and leaving when they get no response conveys the urgency of the need for the people to repent. It becomes a prophetic warning of the dangers of failing to act. There can be no wavering, no middle ground.

As Jesus' mission began after John's imprisonment (1:14), the disciples' mission begins after John's death. These two events may appear to be unrelated to each other, but Mark deliberately links them together. John's beheading casts the shadow of death over the disciples' mission. Jesus has been rejected in his hometown of Nazareth and John the Baptist has been executed, and it becomes clearer that the disciples will preach repentance in a hostile world that not only resists reforming their lives around God but also will deal out death to the preachers of repentance.

The lengthy account of how Herod beheaded John the Baptist begins when Herod hears news about Jesus' miraculous powers. Rumors were rife that he was John the Baptist raised from the dead. Others said he was Elijah, and still others one of the prophets. The question "Who is this?" was first raised in the narrative by Jesus' disciples (4:41), and this misinformed speculation that Jesus was John the Baptist or Elijah brings to the fore the Elijah motif. The account has intertextual connections with the story of Elijah and Jezebel. Jezebel incited her husband, King Ahab, to do what was evil and sought to destroy Elijah, their prophetic nemesis.[85] In both stories a prophet confronts the king and his wife about their sinful ways. John publicly reproached Herod for marrying Herodias, his niece and the wife of Philip, Herod's brother, which is mentioned twice for emphasis (6:17–18).[86] This public denunciation of the marriage is identified as the cause for his imprisonment. The marriage smacks of incest (Lev 18:16; 20:21), and the odor of scandal also wafts over the dancing of his stepdaughter that so captivates Herod during his birthday banquet.[87] King Herod offers her half of his kingdom, which as a Roman vassal king was not his to give, but it is a proverbial expression for generosity (Esth 5:3, 6; 7:2; 1 Kgs 13:8).[88]

Herodias schemes to use her daughter to silence once and for all an obnoxious

85. David M. Hoffeditz and Gary E. Yates, "Femme Fatale *Redux*: Intertextual Connection to the Elijah/Jezebel Narratives in Mark 6:14–29," *BBR* 15 (2005): 199–221.

86. Herodias was the daughter of Herod Aristobulus, who was one of the sons of Herod the Great with Mariamne, and therefore the half-brother of Herod Antipas. She is therefore the half-niece of Herod Antipas.

87. Birthdays were viewed as pagan celebrations (*m. 'Abod. Zar.* 1:3), and Herod's celebration is further sullied by the hints of debauchery.

88. Herod Antipas is identified as a "king" (6:14), which may reflect a less technical, popular usage, or it may be intentionally ironic. The emperor Augustus specifically refused to bestow that royal title on Herod when his father, Herod the Great, died, and his former kingdom was broken up and parceled out to the surviving sons (see Josephus, *J.W.* 2.2.3 §§20–22; 2.6.3 §§93–95; *Ant.* 17.18.1 §188; 17.9.4 §§224–271; and 17.11.4 §318). Some in the audience may know the story of how his wife Herodias encouraged him to petition the emperor Gaius (Caligula) to name him king after he had granted that title to his nephew, Herod Agrippa. The request ultimately backfired and led to his exile when his enemies denounced him for stockpiling weapons.

prophet. She outfoxes her husband, who feared John as a righteous and holy man and listened gladly to him (6:20), by inducing her daughter to demand that John's head be presented to her on a platter. Herod is trapped by his rash vow and has the prophet executed. The account of John's beheading, as the Elijah-like forerunner of the Messiah, foreshadows what will happen to Jesus. As John was "handed over" (1:14), so Jesus will be "handed over" (3:19; 9:31; 10:33). As John was executed by a political ruler who was hesitant to do so but caught in the web of the behind the scenes plotting of his wife (6:14–29), so Jesus will be sentenced to death by a reluctant Pilate at the instigation of hostile leaders who have plotted his death behind the scenes (14:1–2; 15:1–2, 6–15).[89]

The disciples' mission enfolds this gruesome tale when it concludes with their report to Jesus about what they had done and taught (6:30). The flashback of John's execution does more than provide an interlude for the disciples to complete their mission; it interprets the flanking halves.[90] The disciples, now identified as "apostles" (6:30), were able to do what Jesus commissioned them to do, casting out demons and healing the sick (6:13). They might be tempted to revel in their success. The story of John's murder, however, "dispels any glamorous notion concerning discipleship."[91] The authority over impure spirits (6:7) does not invest them with invulnerability. They, too, will be imperiled by the machinations of those who violently resist God's reign. They, too, will be handed over (13:9, 11–12). They, too, will have to stand before kings (13:9). The prevalence of murderous evil in the world means that disciples who proclaim the message are likely to suffer and die in carrying out their commission.

2.4.3.2 Retreat to a Deserted Place and the Feeding of the Five Thousand (6:31–44)

After the disciples' mission, Jesus seeks to take them to a deserted place across the lake so that they might escape the crowds and have some rest. His popularity is such that the crowds race ahead of them by land and reach the spot before they arrive. Jesus does not begrudge this relentless pursuit but instead has compassion on the crowds because "they were like sheep without a shepherd" (6:34). This observation decries the malfeasance of Israel's religious leadership (see Zech 11:5, 15–17). Jesus' first response to their need is to teach them.

After long hours of teaching, the disciples set up the circumstances of the miraculous feeding that follows by fretting about finding provisions for all the people. They urge Jesus to send them off to buy food for themselves because it is late, they are stuck in a remote place where food is hard to get, they only have a meager amount of food for themselves, and it would take "more than half a year's wages"

89. As Herodias seized an opportune time (6:21) to do away with John, so Judas will look for an opportune time (14:11) to hand Jesus over to the high priests.

90. Edwards, "Markan Sandwiches," 196; Francis J. Moloney, "Mark 6:6b–30: Mission, the Baptist, and Failure," *CBQ* 63 (2001): 647–63.

91. Hoffeditz and Yates, "Femme Fatale *Redux*," 221.

(two hundred denarii) to buy food for such a large number (6:37). Undaunted by the immensity of the task, Jesus orders the disciples to feed the hungry throng.

Jesus has them organize the shepherdless multitude into orderly rows, which suggests the grouping of an army and recalls Israel's encampment in the wilderness.[92] There are also echoes of Psalm 23 as Mark notes that he has them recline on a carpet of green (6:39; Ps 23:2a, "He makes me lie down in green pastures"). As their shepherd, Jesus finds good pasture for his flock beside "quiet waters" (Ps 23:2b), and he has restored their souls and guided them in right paths with his teaching (Mark 6:34; Ps 23:3). As the good shepherd, he also feeds them (Ps 23:5; Ezek 34:23). Five thousand people are filled from five loaves and two fish, and the disciples pick up twelve basketfuls of leftover pieces of bread and fish (Mark 6:42–44).

This feeding in the wilderness sounds several biblical themes. First, it recalls God's miraculous provision of food to the people of Israel in the wilderness. The disciples' astonished question when asked to feed the crowd parallels Moses' consternation when he is prevailed upon to feed the people in the wilderness: "Would they have enough if flocks and herds were slaughtered for them? Would they have enough if all the fish in the sea were caught for them?" (Num 11:22). The few small fish may recall the bitter grumbling of Israel in the wilderness, "We remember the fish we ate in Egypt at no cost" (Num 11:5). The collection of an abundance of leftovers reveals that Jesus provides bread that does not decay overnight. The miraculous feeding also harkens back to Elijah feeding the widow of Zarephath and her son (1 Kgs 17:8–16) and Elisha feeding the company of prophets (2 Kgs 4:42–44). The intertextual echoes show that Jesus is incomparably greater than Moses, Elijah, and Elisha. The feeding scene also foreshadows the eschatological banquet envisioned by Isaiah (Isa 25:6–8; 55:1–2). Moreover, Jesus will offer people far more than physical bread when at the Last Supper he compares his death to bread that is broken and given to others (14:22).

2.4.3.3 Jesus Walking on the Water and Healing the Sick in Gennesaret (6:45–56)

Jesus sends off his disciples in the boat to Bethsaida, dismisses the crowd, and ascends a mountain to pray. He sees the disciples struggling against the wind through the night and getting nowhere, and he comes to them in the early morning walking on the sea. Treading the waves is something that only God can do (Job 9:8; 38:16; Ps 77:19; Isa 43:16; 51:10; Hab 3:15; Sir 24:5–6). Jesus wants to pass by them, which, in the OT, is phraseology that is connected to an epiphany (Exod 33:19–34:16; 1 Kgs 19:11–12). The purpose of passing by is to allow them to witness his transcendent majesty as a divine being. In the past, God could not be fully seen, but now God can be fully seen in Jesus Christ. The disciples, however, are overcome by fear

92. Exod 18:21, 25 (officers over thousands, hundreds, fifties, and tens); 1QS 2:21–22; 1QSa 1:14–15; 1:27–2:1; 2:11–22; 1QM 4:1–5:16; CD 13:1.

and cry out, thinking that they are seeing a phantasm. Jesus greets them with the divine formula of self-revelation as God ("It is I" translates *egō eimi*, "I am") and gets in the boat with them (Isa 43:2).[93]

The disciples' hardened hearts, however, prevent them from understanding the miracle of the loaves or grasping the significance of this epiphany. Van Iersel comments, "One would expect greater signs to cause greater understanding, but this is definitely not so with Jesus' followers." In fact, the reverse seems to happen: "the greater the signs, the greater their misunderstanding."[94] Mark's utilization of OT background texts and images, however, leads the audience via an indirect allusive path into the awesome mystery about who Jesus is.

Jesus had sent the disciples to Bethsaida (6:45), but they land in Gennesaret, between Capernaum and Tiberias. Mark either assumes that the audience will infer that the contrary wind forced them off course or, without narrating it, that the disciples landed at Bethsaida but immediately left for Gennesaret. That region lent its name to the lake (see Luke 5:1, "the Lake of Gennesaret"). The summary in 6:54–56 reiterates previous themes. Mark has highlighted Jesus' extraordinary popularity so that he is immediately recognized wherever he goes (see 6:33). His presence prompts people to make urgent appeals for him to heal their sick, carrying them to him on mats (see 2:4), or to seek to touch his cloak for healing (see 5:28).

2.4.3.4 Controversy over the Tradition of the Elders and Declaration about Purity (7:1–23)

The Pharisees and some of the teachers of the law again come from Jerusalem (see 3:22) and surround Jesus. They do not come to be healed or to be taught as the crowds do. As guardians of their tradition, which they would impose on all Israel, they come to scrutinize him and his followers. A controversy is sparked when they spy Jesus' disciples eating with "hands that were defiled [*koinos*], that is, unwashed." What is "common" (*koinos*) is the opposite of "holy" and refers to something that is ceremonially impure (Acts 10:14). The issue revolves around purity, not hygiene, and Mark offers an explanation about Jewish ritual washings for a Gentile audience unfamiliar with these customs (7:3–4).

Jesus' response divides into three parts. First, he excoriates these opponents for their hypocrisy, which he ties to their using their traditions to nullify the word of God (7:6–13). Second, he announces to the crowd that defilement only comes from within and not from contact with anything external (7:14–15). Third, he explains to his disciples in private what truly defiles a person, and Mark's parenthetical aside says, in effect, "Jesus declared all foods clean" (7:19).[95]

---

93. See Gen 17:1; 26:24; 31:13; Exod 3:6, 14; 14:4, 18; Deut 32:39; Isa 41:2–14; 43:1–13; 46:4; 48:12; 51:9–16; 52:6; John 8:58; 18:5–8.

94. Bas van Iersel, *Reading Mark* (Collegeville, MN: Liturgical Press, 1988), 88–89.

95. This rendering of the verse is not literal. It reads in Greek, "cleansing all foods," and the phrase "Jesus declared" is not present.

The Pharisees' traditions of the elders had no explicit scriptural basis. The tradition developed to fill in the gaps and silences in the regulations found in Scripture. Furstenburg describes the rules related to ritual contamination as a "tricky issue": "Impurity can flow from one object to another, from food to body and then again to other food, and it can pass through many stages before dying out."[96] The tradition of the elders mapped out purity boundaries that enabled one to classify when impurity had died out and who is impure and susceptible to impurity and who is not.[97]

That the Pharisees' rules concerning the washing of hands had no basis in the law is even admitted in the Talmud (*b. Ber.* 52b).[98] Washing was the normal means of removing most impurities. The examples cited in the parenthetical explanation, the washing of hands, cups, pots, and bronze vessels (7:3–4), reveal a religious mind-set that is primarily concerned with external purity. It is unfair to dismiss these concerns as "sham religion devoid of inner conviction."[99] The creators of this tradition were driven by an inner conviction that uncleanness belongs to the realm of death and demons and a wish to maintain holiness and to purge impurities lest the people's impurity drive God's presence from their midst (Lev 18:24–30). Brown clarifies the operating principle: "Impurity is hateful to God, and the unclean are excluded from God's presence (Lev. 11:43–47). It was therefore necessary to separate from whatever defiled God's dwelling place (Lev. 15:31; Ezek 11:21–23)."[100]

The problem is that overly scrupulous attention to such things allows one to major in minors while ignoring the weightier matters of the law (Matt 23:23). Jesus therefore does not simply quibble with the Pharisees over minutiae, such as the washing of hands. He rejects their whole approach to God's law. This explains why the disciples ignore this tradition of the elders. It has no relevance for them or for Mark's audience.[101]

Jesus cites Isaiah as specifically prophesying against them with his words, "These people honor me with their lips, but their hearts are far from me. They worship me in vain; their teachings are merely human rules" (7:6–7; Isa 29:13). The statement in 7:13, "And you do many things like that," means that the Corban example in 7:11–12 represents a whole system in which their tradition ultimately cancels out the direct commands of God. It is not just one exceptional misuse of their tradition; it reflects a pattern of abuse.

Jesus affirms the continuing validity of the law, but it needs to be interpreted rightly. God commands children to honor their parents (Exod 20:12; Deut 5:16),

96. Yair Furstenberg, "Defilement Penetrating the Body: A New Understanding of Contamination in Mark 7.15," *NTS* 54 (2008): 188.

97. Jerome H. Neyrey, "The Idea of Purity in Mark's Gospel," *Semeia* 35 (1986): 100.

98. Another rabbinic tradition in the same tractate insisted that washing the hands was in fact commanded by God: "When he washes his hands, he should say, 'Blessed is He who has sanctified us with his commandments and commanded us concerning the washing of hands'" (*b. Ber.* 60b).

99. Van Iersel, *Reading Mark*, 104.

100. Colin Brown, "The Jesus of Mark's Gospel," in *Jesus Then and Now: Images of Jesus in History and Christology* (ed. Marvin Meyer and Charles Hughes; Harrisburg, PA: Trinity Press International, 2001), 26.

101. Rainer Kampling, "Das Gesetz im Markusevangelium," in *Der Evangelist als Theologe: Studien zum Markusevangelium* (ed. Thomas Söding; SBS 163; Stuttgart: Katholisches Bibelwerk, 1995), 128–29.

and, in Jewish tradition, that entailed giving them physical necessities. A rabbinic tradition has it:

> Our rabbis taught: What is "reverence" [for parents] and what is honor? Reverence [refers to one who] does not sit in his parent's place and does not stand in his [parent's] place, he does not contradict his [parent's] opinions, and does not judge [his parent's disputes]. "Honor" [refers to one who] feeds [his father or mother] and gives him (or her) drink; he clothes him (or her) and covers him (or her), and helps him (or her) to enter and exit. (*b. Qidd.* 31b)

The Scripture also commands that one honor one's vows (Deut 23:21–22). The Pharisees' tradition overrules God's command to honor one's parents by allowing the sanctity of a Corban vow, no matter how unworthy its intention to evade the responsibility of giving support to parents, to supersede the command to honor one's parents by giving them support. Honoring vows does not absolve one from honoring parents, or, for that matter, from any other moral obligation.

Jesus follows up this attack by explaining the nature of purity and impurity to his disciples, who ask him what it all means (7:17). He does more than challenge the validity of the traditions of the elders; he seems to challenge the very legitimacy of the food laws. Jesus insinuates that God does not really care about surface impurity. God cares only about internal impurity that cannot be washed away by external rituals. Jesus gets to the heart of the matter: Defilement "has to do with the heart not the hands, with evil thoughts that leak out from within a person, not food that ends up in the latrine."[102] Jesus goes on to give a sampling of evil actions that stem from evil thoughts: "sexual immorality, theft, murder, adultery, greed, malice, deceit, lewdness, envy, slander, arrogance and folly" (7:21–22). A little water poured over cupped hands (7:3) does not cleanse these impurities,[103] nor does it soften "stubborn hearts" (3:5).

2.4.3.5 Exorcism of a Syrophoenician Woman's Daughter (7:24–30)

Jesus retreats to the region of Tyre and wants to remain incognito. Mark does not explain why, but his reputation has preceded him (3:8), and once again it is impossible for him to stay hidden. A woman, who is identified as "a Greek, a Syrophoenician by race" (7:26, ASV), beseeches him to cast out a demon from her daughter. She is a Gentile pagan who hails from a city that Scripture rails against as a tormentor of Israel (Ps 83; Isa 23; Jer 25; Ezek 26–28; Joel 3; Amos 1:9–10; Zech 9:3–4).

Jesus initially refuses this request by asserting the priority of Israel in a parabolic saying: "First let the children eat all they want ... for it is not right to take the children's bread and toss it to the dogs" (7:27). This response is deliberately scandalous and highlights the desperate mother's reply.[104] The overt affront does not embitter

102. Garland, *Mark*, 276.

103. Ibid., 277.

104. Jesus' response has puzzled many; Pablo Alonso, *The Woman Who Changed Jesus*, 2–51, offers a history of interpretation from the patristic period to the second half of the twentieth century.

her. Instead, she concedes Israel's precedence over Gentiles. She is willing to accept the role of a dog if it means getting fed. She asks only for a crumb of Jesus' power, and it will not deprive the children of their bread. She discerns that "God's care does not stop with the boundaries, dividing Jew from Gentile, but extends to all who call on God."[105]

Jesus commends her reply, which has nothing to do with it being quick-witted. It refers to her willingness to humble herself, which is a key requirement for discipleship (9:35; 10:44). The disciples have trouble learning to receive the kingdom "like a little child" (10:15); this woman has no qualms about receiving the kingdom as a little dog. Without coming into direct contact with her daughter to exorcise the demon, Jesus announces that the demon has left her daughter. Trusting his word, the mother leaves him and finds her daughter lying in bed and the demon gone.

After the controversy with the Pharisees over clean and unclean in the previous episode and Jesus declaring all foods clean, this incident shows Jesus ultimately erasing another boundary, the division between Jew and Gentile. Rhoads maintains that it "challenges the audience not to set limits on the universality of the good news of the kingdom of God."[106]

2.4.3.6 Healing a Deaf Mute (7:31–37)

Returning from the district of Tyre by way of Sidon to the Sea of Galilee through the district of Decapolis is a circuitous route. Mark places Jesus in a culturally pagan territory, and a Gentile crowd brings to him a man who is deaf and can hardly talk, just as the Jewish crowds in Galilee have brought or will bring their sick to Jesus (1:32; 8:22; 9:20). This man must be brought to Jesus because he could not have heard about him, nor could he ask him for help. They beg him to place his hand on him (see 5:23; 6:5; 8:22, 25). The healing of this deaf man who cannot talk parallels the healing of the blind man in 8:22–26. In both instances others bring the men to Jesus, and they ask him to lay his hand on the men (7:32; 8:22). Jesus performs the miracles apart from the crowds and uses his spittle (7:33; 8:23). Both miracles occur in stages: first the ears, then the tongue in 7:33; first partial sight, then full vision in 8:23, 25. Jesus then commands them not to tell anyone (7:36) or not to enter the village (8:26).

Opening up a person's ears is crucial since Jesus places so much emphasis on hearing his words (4:3, 9, 12, 15, 18, 20, 23, 24, 33; 7:14; 8:18; 9:7). Once again, it becomes clear that Gentiles will be included in God's renewal of the world (see Isa 29:18; 35:5).

105. Mary Cotes, "Following Jesus with the Women in Mark," in *Mark's Gospel of Action* (ed. John Vincent; London: SPCK, 2006), 81.

106. Rhoads, "Jesus and the Syrophoenician Woman in Mark," 370.

2.4.3.7 Feeding of the Four Thousand (8:1–10)

The phrase "during those days" loosely connects the feeding miracle with the preceding events (7:24–37) and places the feeding of the four thousand in the same Gentile setting (7:31). Like the first miraculous feeding in 6:31–44, this one also occurs in a deserted place (6:35; 8:4). Again, Jesus has compassion on the crowds (6:34; 8:2). His concern that they have had nothing to eat for three days and have journeyed a long distance (8:2–3) provokes the disciples' consternation about how to feed such a large crowd in a remote area (6:37; 8:4). Jesus asks the disciples, "How many loaves do you have?" (6:38; 8:5). Jesus orders the crowd to sit, blesses what the disciples have, and has them distribute it to the crowd (6:41; 8:6). The crowd eats its fill, and the disciples collect an abundance of leftovers (6:42–43; 8:8). The number fed decreases from five thousand (6:44) to four thousand (8:9), the number of loaves and fishes increase from five loaves and two fishes (6:41) to seven loaves and a few small fish (8:5, 7), and the number of baskets of leftover fragments decreases from twelve (6:43) to seven (8:8). Nothing should be made of the different numbers. They simply mean that, once again, Jesus' miraculous power produces something great from something small.

2.4.3.8 The Pharisees' Demand for a Sign (8:11–13)

The Pharisees demand that Jesus give them a "sign from heaven" (Exod 4:8; Judg 6:17–23; 2 Kgs 19:29; 20:8). This request reveals that they do not see Jesus as the sign from God, do not recognize any of his mighty works as signs, and are looking for something else. It may be that they are still thinking that he works by the power of Beelzebul. Or, they may be looking for some definitive eschatological sign of deliverance from God as various false prophets promised.[107]

The sharp edge of Jesus' refusal to produce a sign is difficult to translate. The text reads literally, "If a sign shall be given to this generation." It is part of an oath formula that leaves unexpressed a curse, "May God strike me down" or "May I be accursed of God." This oath fragment does more than say that no sign will be given this generation. It conveys with some vehemence that Jesus would like to prevent it from happening at all costs. His question, "Why does this generation ask for a sign?" (8:12), links this generation to the wilderness generation, who constantly put God to the test and badgered Moses for signs that God was with them (Exod 17:7; Num 14:11; Deut 6:16; 29:2–6; Pss 78:11–32; 95:8–10). Jesus' deep sigh indicates that they are trying his patience,[108] just as the wilderness generation tried God's patience. His refusal to comply with their request is because they do not have "a mind that understands or eyes that see or ears that hear" (Deut 29:4; see Mark 4:10–12). The scene harkens back to God's bitter vow, "They shall never enter my rest" (Ps 95:11; Heb 3:11; 4:3, 5).

107. Jeffrey B. Gibson, "Jesus' Refusal to Produce a 'Sign' (Mk 8.11–13)," *JSNT* 38 (1990): 37–66.

108. Jeffrey B. Gibson, "Mark 8.12a: Why Does Jesus 'Sigh Deeply'?" *BT* 38 (1987): 122–25.

2.4.3.9 Warning about the Leaven of the Pharisees and Herod (8:14–21)

The disciples have also failed to discern the signs, and Mark records a third sea incident in which the disciples' failure to understand becomes painfully obvious. Jesus warns them against the "leaven," or the corruption and poison, of the Pharisees and that of Herod.[109] "Leaven" is something that can spoil and spread a dangerous contagion. Jesus does not specify what he means by their "leaven." Is it their hypocrisy (7:6), their judgmental spirit (2:16), their malicious plotting to put Jesus to death (3:6), their blasphemy against the Holy Spirit (3:28–29), their elevating their traditions over God's word (7:13), or their demand for a confirming sign (8:11)? In the context, it seems to be related to a hardened heart that fails to recognize Jesus' miracles for the signs that they are (8:17–18).

The warning is precipitated by the disciples having forgotten to bring loaves, except, Mark notes, they had one loaf with them in the boat (8:14). Without any clear antecedent in the Greek text, the next verse continues (lit.), "And he warned them" about the leaven of the Pharisees (8:15). The word "Jesus" does not appear in verse 15; it has been added by translations for sake of clarity. What Mark originally wrote would suggest that he understands the one loaf with them in the boat to be Jesus, an idea developed fully in John 6.

The disciples are obliviously engaged in a discussion about having no bread (8:16). They forgot what Jesus had done previously in feeding five thousand and four thousand. It is not that they need never worry about a shortage of bread as long as Jesus is with them. The problem is that they still do not grasp the divine identity of the one who is with them. His question, "Do you still not understand?" (8:21), holds out hope that things will get better. Eventually, they *will* understand. Unlike the Pharisees and Herod, their problem is not a refusal to see but an inability to see. The veil over their eyes will be lifted after Jesus' death and resurrection.

2.5 ON THE WAY TO JERUSALEM AND THE CROSS (8:22–10:52)

Mark slows down the pace of the narrative in this section.[110] The bulk of material contains Jesus' private instruction to the disciples (8:27–9:13; 9:28–29, 30–50; 10:23–45). Major themes are developed related to Jesus' suffering, his death and

109. The translation "yeast" can be misleading. In the Old Testament, leaven symbolizes corruption and the infectious power of evil. The ancient world used a dangerous type of leaven that was produced by keeping back a piece of the previous week's dough, storing it in suitable conditions, and adding juices to promote the process of fermentation. This homemade rising agent was fraught with health hazards, because it could easily become tainted and would then spread its poison when baked with the rest of the dough. It, in turn, would infect the next batch. Plutarch wrote that leaven "is itself also the product of corruption, and produces corruption in the dough with which it is mixed ... and altogether the process of leavening seems to be one of putrefaction; at any rate if it goes too far, it completely sours and spoils the dough" (*Quaest. rom.* 289F; see also Pliny, *Nat.* 18.26).

110. The word "immediately" has appeared thirty-one times in 1:1–8:21 but appears only four times in 8:22–10:52; three of the occurrences crop up in the healing of the boy with the demon (9:15, 20, 24).

resurrection, the requirements of discipleship, the relationship between power and weakness, and Jesus' identity as the Son of God.

In the previous section, intimations appear in 2:20 and 3:6 that Jesus will suffer an untimely end. Now, Jesus no longer speaks in parables (4:33) but plainly (8:32). Three times he divulges his destiny to his disciples and tells them that suffering and death await him and that he will be raised after three days (8:31; 9:30–31; 10:32–34).[111] In each instance, the disciples in some way demonstrate their incomprehension, and Jesus takes the opportunity to instruct them about what discipleship entails (8:34–38; 9:35–37; 10:42–45). In the previous section, Jesus and his disciples were often in a boat or in a house. Now, they follow Jesus along the way (8:27; 9:33–34; 10:32, 52), which is revealed in 10:32 to be the way leading to Jerusalem. In other words, they learn about discipleship on the way with Jesus. Best sums up the gist of this section: "The main purpose of his teaching is to bring his followers to an understanding of his own Cross, not only as redemptive, but also as a way of life for themselves; they must take up their crosses as he did and serve as he served."[112]

Near the beginning of this section, Peter proclaims Jesus as the Messiah (8:29). At the end, blind Bartimaeus hails him as "son of David" (10:47). Both are right, but not completely. Accounts of Jesus restoring sight to two blind men in 8:22–26 and 10:46–52 serve as bookends that frame this section. Their healings represent Jesus' attempts to open the eyes of his disciples. The question "Who is Jesus?" is now connected to another question, "What has God sent him to do?" The disciples need to see that this Messiah must suffer and die and be vindicated in his resurrection.

2.5.1 Healing of a Blind Man in Bethsaida (8:22–26)

The incident of blind man's healing is not placed by chance between two examples of the disciples' blindness in 8:14–21 and 8:31–33. The Markan context, which portrays Jesus' struggle to get his disciples to see anything, gives this unusual two-stage healing added significance. After Jesus spat on the man's eyes and put his hands on him, he asked if he saw anything (8:23). Three verbs describe the man's progressive restoration of sight. He opened his eyes, but he only saw a blurred impression of people looking like trees walking around (8:24). A second touch results in his sight being restored and seeing everything clearly (8:25). This physical healing of blindness serves as a paradigm for the spiritual healing of the disciples' sight, which also comes gradually and with difficulty.

111. Matt 16:21; 17:23; 20:19 and Luke 9:22 and 18:33 have "on the third day." Hans F. Bayer, *Jesus' Predictions of Vindication and Resurrection* (WUNT 2/20; Tübingen: Mohr Siebeck, 1986), 206, makes the case that the Greek word translated "after" (*meta*) can mean "on" when it is used in reference to something that "comes to a conclusion without mentioning further activities."

112. Ernest Best, *The Temptation and the Passion: The Markan Soteriology* (2nd ed.; SNTSMS 2; Cambridge: Cambridge University Press, 1990), 190.

2.5.2 Peter's Declaration that Jesus is the Messiah and Jesus' First Passion and Resurrection Prediction (8:27–9:1)

Jesus teaches his disciples by asking them probing questions. He asks, "Who do people say I am?" and then asks them directly, "Who do you say I am?" The disciples' inability to recognize who Jesus is seems to come to an end in a blinding flash when Peter answers, "You are the Messiah." Jesus surprisingly rebukes him to tell no one. The secret is not that Jesus is the Christ but what he is destined to do as Messiah—or, rather, what will be done to him. The Son of Man must suffer, be rejected, be killed, and after three days be risen again (8:31).[113] The verb "must" expresses God purpose. This passage marks a shift between the first half of the gospel, where Jesus' power is so prominent, and the second half, where his weakness becomes predominant.

Peter wants to get out in front of Jesus to lead the way for him by rejecting this destiny. Jesus brings him back in line and addresses the requirements for following him to everyone, not just to select disciples. To be his disciple they need to say "no" to self, take up their cross, and follow him in his way of life (8:34). He then offers a rationale why one would want to accept these demands and the way of suffering. Trying to save one's life will lead only to ruin (8:36). The unspoken premise is that giving one's life to Jesus will result in life from God when this earthly life ends. A solemn warning follows. Failure to be loyal to Jesus will result in eschatological shame at the end of time (8:38). One's loyalty to Jesus determines one's participation in eschatological salvation. The warning is followed by a promise in 9:1. Some will see the kingdom of God come with power, which refers to Jesus' death and resurrection.

2.5.3 The Transfiguration of Jesus (9:2–8)

A transition occurs in 9:2. It takes place six days later in a different locale, a high mountain, with a different audience, the three disciples, Peter, James, and John. In Mark's gospel, the greater the revelation, the smaller the number of people who serve as witnesses (see 5:37; 16:1–8). The high mountain is the traditional place for special revelation in Scripture, and the three disciples see Jesus being transfigured. The passive voice, "he was transfigured" (9:2), implies that God is the agent. The transfiguration conveys that Jesus is far more than a Spirit-filled prophet (8:28) and far more than an earthly messianic liberator (8:29). Moses and Elijah appear as "heavenly figures, inhabitants of the heavenly dwelling-places." They are "the two best-known figures of this type."[114] The disciples get a glimpse of Jesus' true identity as a heavenly figure from a celestial perspective.

The transfiguration is tied chronologically to Jesus' announcement of his passion and resurrection ("after six days"). It reveals that Jesus' announcement of his suffering and death indeed corresponds to the divine will. His humiliating suffering and death are not incompatible with his divine glory. The parallels between the

113. "After three days" is a standard phrase for the time when God intervenes (see Gen 22:4; 42:17; Exod 15:22; 2 Kgs 20:5; Hos 6:2; Jonah 1:17–2:1).

114. Armand Puig i Tàrrech, "The Glory on the Mountain: The Episode of the Transfiguration of Jesus," *NTS* 58 (2012): 164.

transfiguration and the crucifixion connect his glory and his inglorious death. In the transfiguration, Jesus is exalted, surrounded by saints and clothed with radiance. In the crucifixion, he is humiliated, ringed by sinners and "wrapped in a garment of darkness."[115] In both scenes he is identified as the Son of God. It means that to see Jesus in all his glory one must see how it merges with his suffering and powerlessness.

The auditory element supplements the vision. The voice from heaven affirms Jesus' identity as the Son of God, and the command to listen to him means that God is now speaking directly through him.

2.5.4. Announcement that Elijah Has Already Come and Was Mistreated (9:9–13)

Jesus commands his three disciples to keep mum about what they have seen and heard until the Son of Man has risen from the dead (9:9). He is not referring to a general resurrection but to his own resurrection "after three days" (8:31). The disciples are confused by this reference (9:10). It is not that they do not understand or believe in the resurrection; it has not sunk in that Jesus will die.

The disciples ask about the coming of Elijah. Does he not come first? Jesus announces that Elijah has come, but his return does not mean the advent of blissful days. Elijah has gone before the Messiah in the way of suffering and death. The audience knows that Elijah in the person of John the Baptist has come and has been executed (6:14–29). The same fate awaits Jesus.

2.5.5 Exorcism of a Boy with an Impure Spirit (9:14–29)

This fourth and last of Jesus' exorcisms consists of four scenes. Jesus descends the mountain to land in the midst of a hubbub with his disciples squabbling with the teachers of the law. The disciples had failed to cast out the demon from a young lad whose father brought him to Jesus. Jesus laments over a faithless generation and tells him to bring the boy to him (9:14–19). In the second scene, Jesus meets the father, and the man begs him to have compassion and help "if you can do anything." Jesus takes umbrage at the expression of doubt in his power as illustrated in the phrase "if you can." The father confesses his uncertain faith and begs him to help his unbelief. This exorcism focuses on the struggle for faith, not a struggle with a demon (contrast 5:1–13). In the third scene, Jesus drives out the spirit that has tormented the boy, but when it departs, it strikes him down as if he were dead. Jesus raises him and restores him to his father (9:25–27). In the last scene, the disciples ask Jesus why they were unable to exorcise the demon. Jesus implicitly connects their failure to the failure to pray (9:28–29).

The disciples have been engaging in arguing with their nemeses rather than praying. Jesus does not pray himself before performing the exorcism. He has in mind an enduring activity, not a one-time invocation of God's power. Prayer is total

115. Davies and Allison, *Saint Matthew*, 2:706.

openness to God's action in and through us. Prayer would stop them from looking to themselves and asking, "Why couldn't *we* drive it out?" Prayer "hands over the battle with this evil to God alone."[116]

2.5.6 Jesus' Second Prediction of His Passion and Resurrection and Teaching on Discipleship (9:30–50)

2.5.6.1 Jesus' Second Prediction of His Passion and Resurrection (9:30–32)

Jesus' second announcement of his coming suffering and resurrection flies right by the disciples. As before, they do not understand its significance but now are afraid to ask. Perhaps they remember how Jesus had rebuked Peter as Satan earlier when he challenged him after the first prediction of his passion and resurrection (8:33). Jesus adds a new detail to his previous announcement of his suffering (8:31): "The Son of Man is going to be delivered into the hands of men" (9:31).[117]

The disciples apparently pay no attention to this ominous intimation of looming treachery, because they are caught having shamelessly bickered with one another when they were on the way about which of them was the greatest. Their self-absorption and self-importance does not bode well for how they will fare in the difficult days that lie ahead. The question at that time will be, which of them will be guilty of the *greatest* breakdown during the period of crisis?

2.5.6.2 True Greatness (9:33–37)

Jesus uses the disciples' competition among themselves as an opening to teach them about true greatness. Earlier, he presented them with the paradox that "whoever wants to save their life will lose it, but whoever loses their life for me and for the gospel will save it" (8:35). He now presents them with a second paradox: "Anyone who wants to be first must be the very last, and the servant of all" (9:35). He takes a child in his arms to serve as an example. The point of comparison is the insignificance of the child on the honor scale. Children in Jesus' culture had no power, no status, and few rights. Their vulnerability made them utterly dependent on others for survival. The saying about welcoming a little child means that those who want to be great should shower attention on those who are regarded as powerless and insignificant.

2.5.6.3 The Unfamiliar Exorcist (9:38–41)

John tells Jesus that they stopped someone casting out demons in his name because "he was not following us" (9:38, NRSV). Mark has no interest in the details about the strange exorcist, who is simply identified as "someone [a certain one]," but focuses on Jesus' correction of the disciples' attitude. Their desire to be the kingpins would have them disqualify someone who does not follow them. The irony is that they had

116. Hartman, *Mark*, 385.

117. The verb "delivered" has a double meaning. God ultimately is behind Jesus' deliverance unto death because it fulfills God's plan. But the verb is also used for Jesus' betrayal (3:19; 10:33; 14:10–11, 18, 21, 41, 42, 44).

only recently failed in an exorcism themselves (9:14–29), yet they are quick to hinder someone who is successful but who does not belong to their group. Jesus rejects their exclusivism that leads to unnecessary conflict and impedes the battle against the real enemy, Satan.[118] He encourages a spirit of generosity, which has practical benefits. Others cannot use his name to do mighty works and speak ill of him later.

Jesus later will warn them that they will be persecuted and hated by all (13:13). "Whoever is not against us is for us" has in view a future situation when they will be facing bitter opposition and will need all the allies they can get. Their circumstances will be so critical that those who give them something as basic as a cup of water because they belong to Christ will receive a reward (9:41).

2.5.6.4 Warnings against Causing Others to Stumble (9:42–48)

Jesus uses stark hyperbole to warn the disciples against causing a little one who believes in him to falter and to fall away from their faith. The little ones are assumed to have fragile faith and are to be looked after with special care (see 1 Cor 8:1–13). Those who cause them to stumble would be better off drowning at the bottom of the sea with a millstone hung around their necks than facing God's judgment for this sin. The disciples imagine themselves to be great ones, but to be great they must serve those who are imagined to be little.

The severity and finality of God's judgment is highlighted in the next series of warnings, in which Jesus refers to "hell, where the fire never goes out" (9:43) and "where 'the worms that eat them do not die, and the fire is not quenched'" (9:48). The warnings are connected to sins caused by one's hand, eye, or foot. To "cut off" is not to be taken literally but means that one should cut off everything in one's life that leads one to sin.[119]

2.5.6.5 Three Sayings Related to Salt (9:49–50)

Three sayings using salt as a figure conclude this segment of Jesus' teaching. The first, "Everyone will be salted with fire," appears only in Mark. It may be a reference to the suffering of the end time: "But who can endure the day of his coming? Who can stand when he appears? For he will be like a refiner's fire or a launderer's soap" (Mal 3:2; see *Sib. Or.* 2:252–255). A textual variant presents an early interpretation of this saying: "Season all your grain offerings with salt" (Lev 2:13).[120] It is possible that since salt is used for purification (2 Kgs 2:21–22; Ezek 16:4; 43:24), the copyist concluded that Christians would be purified by the fire of persecution "in the

118. Harry Fleddermann, "The Discipleship Discourse (Mark 9:33–50)," *CBQ* 43 (1981): 66.

119. The "eye" is the cause of covetousness, stinginess, jealousy, and lust; and *b. Nid.* 13b speaks of adultery with the hand (masturbation) and with the foot (a euphemism for the *membrum virile*). See M. H. Pope, "Bible, Euphemism and Dysphemism," *ABD*, 1:721, on the use of the euphemism "feet" to refer to genitalia (Exod 4:25; Ruth 3:7; 2 Sam 11:8; Isa 6:2).

120. D it[b, c, d, ff2, i]. Bruce M. Metzger, *A Textual Commentary on the Greek New Testament* (Rev. ed.; New York: United Bible Societies, 1994), 87, suggests that an early copyist found Lev 2:13 as a clue to the statement's meaning and wrote it in the margin. Later copyists either substituted the gloss for the words of the text or added it to the text.

way that salt purified a sacrifice."[121] The implication is that Jesus' disciples will be purified through the fiery trials they will endure (1 Pet 1:6–7; 4:12–19).

The second salt saying, "Salt is good, but if it loses its saltiness, how can you make it salty again?" (9:50a), assumes that one recognizes salt by its distinctive tang. If salt fails to salt food, it is not worth its salt.[122] The same principle applies to disciples. If they fail to exhibit the distinguishing traits that Jesus requires of disciples, they are worthless to him.

The third saying, "Have salt among yourselves, and be at peace with each other" (9:50b), is in synonymous parallelism. To have salt among yourselves can mean to have meals together (see Acts 1:4, where the Greek verb *synalizō* can mean "to eat salt with"). The disciples are not only to live in harmony with others (9:38–41), but it is important for them to live in peace with one another and not to engage in self-centered, political gamesmanship to boost their status over others (9:34).[123]

2.5.7 Jesus' Teaching about Divorce (10:1–12)

Jesus has laid out stringent requirements for discipleship, and his teaching on divorce dramatizes further the radical claims that God's reign makes on individuals. It is set up by the Pharisees asking him whether it is lawful for a man to divorce his wife. Mark adds that they were testing him, which implies that their question is intended to trap him in some way. Jesus is now in "the region of Judea and across the Jordan" (10:1), where John the Baptist had preached and baptized (1:4–5). John's public denunciation of Herod Antipas's divorce and remarriage to Herodias, his brother's wife, led to his arrest and violent death (6:17–29). The Pharisees have been identified as allies with the Herodians (3:6; 12:13), and their question may have been intended to ensnare Jesus with the same issue.

Most Jews believed that a man had an inalienable right to divorce a wife. The later debates centered on the proper grounds for divorce, not whether it was lawful. Malachi's lone protest against divorce in the OT, "I hate divorce, says the LORD, the God of Israel" (Mal 2:16, NRSV), is turned on its head by the Aramaic translation in *Targum Jonathan*: "If you hate her, divorce her."

Jesus responds to their question with a question, "What did Moses command you?" Jesus makes it personal with the "you." They respond that "Moses permitted a man to write a certificate of divorce and send her away" (10:3–4).[124] The regulations in Deut 24:1–4 do not delineate possible justifications for seeking a divorce but simply place restrictions on the husband if he should put away his wife. If the wife finds no favor in her husband's eyes because she is guilty of some indecency, or if he simply dislikes her, he is to give her a bill of divorce and may never remarry her after she becomes the wife of another man.

Jesus declares, "It was because your hearts were hard that Moses wrote you this

121. Hooker, *Mark*, 233.

122. According to Pliny, *Nat.*, 31.44.95, salt could spoil, which means that it was not pure NaCl but contaminated.

123. Fleddermann, "The Discipleship Discourse," 73.

124. The Mishnaic tractate *Giṭṭin* focuses on the legalities surrounding the preparing and delivering of a writ of divorce.

law" (10:5). He wanted to prevent greater evil from occurring. If the Mosaic legislation on divorce is only a concession to human hardness of heart, a condition that leads to willful defiance of God, then it cannot reflect the will of God. Divorce cannot be God's will for marriage. Jesus says that God's intention for marriage is to be found in the creation account in Gen 1–2, which is also a "Book of Moses" (Mark 12:26). Jesus' opponents have misunderstood the Scripture and, consequently, God's will for marriage. In marriage, male and female become one flesh, joined together by God, and no one is to undo that union (10:8–9).

Jesus reveals the mind of God on this issue and implies that one can no longer deal with God based on what Moses may have "permitted." God's will invades all areas of life, including what is culturally accepted and legally allowed. Jesus declares privately to the disciples that divorce and remarriage is akin to adultery and therefore is forbidden (10:10–12).

2.5.8 Blessing the Children (10:13–16)

The concern for children follows immediately after Jesus' statements about divorce. Parents were bringing their children to Jesus for him to lay hands on them, but the disciples sullenly rebuke them and try to block their access to Jesus. Their bullying provokes Jesus, who angrily tells them that "the kingdom of God belongs to such as these" (10:14). Children are regarded as insignificant and easily pushed aside, but the disciples need to learn not only to welcome little ones (9:37), but also to take on the attitude of littleness if they are to enter the kingdom of God (10:15).

2.5.9 Inviting a Rich Man to Sell All and to Follow (10:17–31)

A man runs up to Jesus, kneels before him, addresses him as "good teacher," and wants to learn from him what he must do to inherit eternal life. Jesus deflects the honorific title "good" by declaring that God alone is good.[125] Jesus directs him to the Ten Commandments and cites in random order the commands that pertain to how humans are to relate to others: murder, adultery, stealing, bearing false witness, defrauding, and honoring your father and mother. "Do not defraud" instead of "You shall not covet" (Exod 20:17; Deut 5:21) may be tied to the man's wealth, since many believed that riches were attained by defrauding others of their fair share, and the rich were often guilty of defrauding the poor (Sir 4:1; Jas 5:4).[126] This seemingly commonplace answer prompts the man to respond with great self-assurance that he has kept all these since he was a boy (10:20). If he expects Jesus to commend him, "Well done, thou good and faithful servant," and to confirm that he is a shoe-in for eternal life, he is in for a major disappointment.

Observing the commandments should do it, according to Deut 30:15–16. But

125. Incigneri, *Gospel*, 169–70, notes that Nero enjoyed the title "the Good God."

126. George W. E. Nickelsburg, "Riches, the Rich, and God's Judgment in *1 Enoch* 92–105 and the Gospel According to Luke," *NTS* 25 (1979): 327.

Jesus looks on this man with love (10:21), and this love "tries to bring sinners to a consciousness of their real condition in the sight of God."[127] He tells this man that he lacks one thing. He does not identify specifically what the one thing is but gives him four directives: Go, liquidate your assets, give to the poor, and follow me. Two implications can be inferred from these directives. First, the best thing to do with money is to invest it in heavenly treasure by divesting oneself of it to aid the poor.[128] Second, receiving eternal life depends entirely on one's response to Jesus and one's care for others, not on one's obedience to some external code of conduct.

Mark initially does not introduce the man as a rich man, but he explains that he balks at Jesus' demand and turns away "because he had great wealth" (10:22). He was concerned about securing his future destiny, but he also wanted to hold on to his present possessions and status to secure his present life on earth. Jesus insists that any human attachments that stand in the way of one's decision to commit to Jesus must be cast aside. One gains life by losing it, not by clutching to it. Hartman comments, "It is a particularly common human attitude to see one's identity as substantiated by what one possesses. So Jesus' demand here can be said to imply that this man should deny himself."[129] Jesus has warned about "the deceitfulness of wealth and the desires for other things" that can choke the word (4:19). He calls this man to free himself from the clutches of self-concern and worries about his wealth and status in order to enter God's reign as a little child.

When the man leaves, Jesus declares that those who are rich will find coming under God's reign more difficult than a camel trying to squeeze through the eye of a needle. The opening of a needle is the smallest passage imaginable, and the camel was the largest animal in Palestine.[130] The disciples react to this bombshell with shock and consternation. If those who seem to have everything going for them find salvation unattainable, "Who then can be saved?" (10:26). If it depends on humans, on what humans can do, the answer is that it is impossible, but all things are possible with God (10:27). The man asked, "What must I do?" (10:17), and asserted, "All these I have kept" (10:20), but that is not enough. One cannot do anything "to inherit." One either is an heir as a member of the family or is not. Salvation comes as a gift from God to those who belong to Christ's family.

Peter reminds Jesus that he and the disciples have done as Jesus asked: "We have left everything to follow you" (10:28). Jesus' response shifts from Peter's "we" to apply it to any who have "left home or brothers or sisters or mother or father or children or fields for me and the gospel" (10:29). This answer includes the audience of Mark's gospel. Jesus assures all that those who have had to cut family ties and earthly attachments for the sake of the gospel will receive "a hundred times as much

127. I. Howard Marshall, *A Concise New Testament Theology* (Downers Grove, IL: InterVarsity Press, 2008), 31.

128. References to God's storehouse are found in Deut 28:12; 32:34–35; Tob 4:7–11; 12:9; Sir 3:3–4; 2 Esd 7:77; and 1 Tim 6:17 is an apt commentary on this passage: "Command those who are rich in this present world not to be arrogant nor to put their hope in wealth, which is so uncertain, but to put their hope in God, who richly provides us with everything for our enjoyment."

129. Hartman, *Mark*, 434.

130. This statement does not mean that the destitute have an easier time of it. It can be hard for them to give up possessions as well.

in this present age: homes, brothers, sisters, mothers, children and fields" (10:30). As part of the Christian community, they become members of a new family. "Father" is missing from this list because there is only one Father, the Father of their Lord Jesus Christ. As adopted children and co-heirs with Christ, they will inherit eternal life in the world to come (Rom 8:14–17). But in this life, these rewards will come "with persecutions" (see Rom 8:18–39).

2.5.10 Jesus' Third Prediction of His Death and Resurrection (10:32–45)

Mark now identifies the "way" that Jesus and the disciples were journeying as the way going up to Jerusalem. Jesus leads the way to his passion as he will later lead the way to Galilee after his resurrection (14:28; 16:7, where the verb "to lead the way" appears again). Mark notes that the disciples following him are afraid, but he does not spell out what they fear or whether their fear is reverential awe. Jesus does not allay their fear but predicts for the third time his impending death and subsequent resurrection. The details now become specific. He will be handed over (betrayed) to the chief priests and teachers of the law. They will condemn him to death and hand him over to the Gentiles, who will mock him, spit on him, flog him, and kill him. Jesus will suffer utter degradation, but when humans have done their worst, he will be handed over to God, who will resurrect him.

What is even more shocking than this announcement is the response of James and John, who immediately beseech him with a selfish request. They want the privilege of being seated on his right and his left in his glory. It is likely that their petition assumes that Jesus will have a royal enthronement and will sit between two persons who hold a lofty rank. Josephus (*Ant.* 6.11.9 §235) describes Jonathan, King Saul's son, taking the seat to the right of the king and Abner, the commander of the army, taking the one on the left. James and John seem to envision an earthly reign and privileged positions that will allow them to bask in earthly glory. They have not understood a word of Jesus' three predictions that he will suffer and be resurrected. Neither have the other ten disciples, who respond to the quest of the sons of Zebedee with indignation. They are not upset over the brothers' callous insensitivity to Jesus' announcement of his shameful treatment and approaching death. Their anger is an expression of envy. There are only two seats at Jesus' right and left, and they will be left out.[131] They covet the seats of honor for themselves, but James and John have jumped the queue.

Jesus does not reproach them but responds by saying, "You don't know what you are asking" (10:38). He is not in charge of the seating arrangements in the kingdom. The audience may realize that when Jesus comes into his glory, the two on his right and his left are robbers who are being crucified. Jesus asks James and John if they think

131. Anselm C. Hagedorn and Jerome H. Neyrey, "'It Was Out of Envy That They Handed Jesus Over' (Mark 15.10): The Anatomy of Envy and the Gospel of Mark," *JSNT* 69 (1998): 49.

they can drink the cup he will drink and be baptized with the baptism with which he will be baptized. The cup is a metaphor for suffering (Isa 51:17, 22), and baptism is a metaphor for being plunged into calamity (see Ps 42:7; 69:1). The path to glory goes through the valley of death and requires taking up a cross, drinking to the dregs a cup of suffering, and undergoing a deluge of sorrow.[132] James and John naïvely answer that they are able to do so without fully recognizing that the thrones they imagine will be crosses and that to share in Jesus' glory, they will have to share in his suffering.

These disciples' confusion opens the door for Jesus to expound a third time on the prerequisites of discipleship. The cross is central to discipleship, and he reiterates that to be great one must take the role of a servant, and to be first one must be a slave of all. This imagery would have been far more graphic and arresting in the first century. Dio Chrysostom (*1 Serv. lib.* 14.16) defines a slave as one whose owner is free to whip, bind, and kill and to do whatever else might come to his mind.[133]

Jesus has told his disciples that he must die, but he has not told them yet why he must die. The soteriological interpretation of his death appears here, at the conclusion of his warnings to his disciples about his impending death and resurrection and its implications for discipleship, and prior to his entry into Jerusalem. Jesus will expound on it further at the climax of the Last Supper (14:24). Here he states that he gives his life as "a ransom for many" (10:45). In extrabiblical sources, the word "ransom" is frequently used to refer to the amount paid to set free someone in captivity or to redeem a pledge.

In Exod 30:12, the "ransom" is related to the annual half-shekel dues, which in the time of Jesus went to support the daily temple sacrifices for the people's sins. In Tosefta *Šeqalim* 1:6, the half-shekel offering is tied directly to the sin atonement between Israel and God. The concept of ransom is therefore connected to ideas of cost, substitution, and atonement. One can infer from the narrative that follows that his death serves as an expiatory offering for others. Isaiah was important to Mark for interpreting Jesus' ministry, and Isaiah speaks of making the life of the Suffering Servant "a guilt offering" that brings forgiveness for the many (Isa 53:10). I consider Isaiah 53 to be in the foreground of Jesus' interpretation of his death, but Mark does not feel any need to make Jesus' words coincide exactly with the LXX.

2.5.11 Healing of Blind Bartimaeus in Jericho (10:46–52)

The healing of two blind men bracket this section (8:22–26; 10:46–52). Blind Bartimaeus begs along the side of the road in Jericho, and when he is told that Jesus of Nazareth is passing by in a large crowd, he somehow recognizes him as the son of David, the only time this title appears in Mark, and cries out for mercy. In this episode the title "son of David" is shorn of its nationalistic and militaristic associations (see *Pss. Sol.* 17:21–25) as Jesus exercises his royal authority through giving sight to the blind.

132. Paul understands baptism theologically to be being "buried with him through baptism into death" (Rom 6:4).

133. Cited by Hartman, *Mark*, 441.

The rich man asked Jesus how he could ensure that he would receive eternal life for himself. James and John asked for positions of power. Bartimaeus only asks for mercy and to see again. Jesus answers Bartimaeus's insistent cries for help with an urgent call of his own that is repeated three times: Jesus tells the crowd to "call him"; "they called to the blind man," 'Cheer up! On your feet! He's calling you.'" The blind man sitting along "the way" (10:46; "roadside," NIV) is transformed into one who sees and follows Jesus on "the way" (10:52; "roadside," NIV). The calling and decision of Bartimaeus to leave behind his cloak (10:50), probably his sole worldly possession, to follow Jesus reveals that discipleship is open to all who identify with Jesus in faith and is not just confined to Jesus' specific call to follow.[134]

2.6 Jesus in Jerusalem: The Temple, the Cross, and the Resurrection (11:1–16:8)

Jesus no longer avoids the crowds or maintains secrecy but openly teaches in the temple after entering Jerusalem. His presence invites confrontations with his opponents, who are threatened by his popularity and secretly wish to do away with him. Jesus then moves to the Mount of Olives, where he predicts the destruction of the temple and then gives his disciples instructions on what to do during the time leading up to its destruction and how it relates to the timing of the end. The next scenes shift to the upper room, where Jesus has his last meal with his disciples, explains the meaning of his death, and warns of the disciples' failures. Then he moves to Gethsemane, where he is betrayed and arrested, then to the high priest's palace, where he is interrogated and pronounced worthy of death, then to Pilate's praetorium, where he is condemned to death, and then to Golgotha, where he dies. The last scene is at the tomb, where faithful women followers discover that it is empty and learn that he has been raised and gone before his disciples to Galilee.

2.6.1 Jesus in the Temple (11:1–12:44)

Day one of this last week begins with a crowd cheering his dramatic arrival on a coronation animal and hailing the coming kingdom of David (11:1–10). The scene ends when Jesus enters the temple and surveys it (11:11).

The second day is marked by Jesus' prophetic action of entering the temple and driving out those who were selling and buying, overturning the tables of the moneychangers and the seats of those who sold doves, and not allowing anyone to carry a vessel through the temple. This event is sandwiched by his cursing of a fig tree (11:12–25).

On his third visit to the temple, he faces challenges from various opponents. The high priests ask by what authority he does such things, and Jesus only responds to them with questions and a parable (11:27–12:27). The Pharisees and Herodians collaborate in an attempt to catch him with a question about whether it is right

134. Marshall, *Faith as a Theme*, 124–25.

to pay taxes to Caesar (12:13–17). The Sadducees then pose a gag question about the resurrection (12:18–27). When Jesus answers them well, a teacher of the law questions him about what is the greatest commandment (12:28–34). Jesus then goes on the offensive by asking a riddle about how the Messiah can be David's son (12:35–37). He suggests that the Messiah is greater than David, and that the Messiah's kingdom will be greater than David's kingdom. He then condemns the teachers of the law for their knavery and abuse of widows, which is masked by a cloak of piety (12:38–40). The temple scenes conclude with Jesus observing a widow who contributes all that she had to the temple coffers (12:41–44).

2.6.1.1 Jesus' Entry into Jerusalem (11:1–11)

Jesus' choice to enter Jerusalem riding on a colt rather than walking becomes an enacted symbol that daringly broadcasts his claim to be the king of Israel. The word translated "colt" refers to a horse when it "stands alone without indication that it is a foal," and "it can refer to any age from the time of being a foal to a grown working animal."[135] Matthew specifically identifies it as a donkey (Matt 21:2, 5, 7), which is understood as a royal animal in Zech 9:9. Jesus orders his disciples to impress the animal as a king would, having them declare to the owner who might object to their taking it, "The Lord needs it" (11:3). The reference to "need" recalls David's justification for eating the consecrated bread "when he had need" (2:25, ASV).

That the animal had never been ridden fits a royal motif. According to *m. Sanh.* 2:5, no one else may ride a king's horse, and it also makes it suitable for a sacred purpose (see Num 19:2; Deut 21:3; 1 Sam 6:7). The colt is bound and must be untied (11:2, 4), and an audience versed in Scripture would recognize allusions to Gen 49:10–11, a passage that was interpreted as a messianic prophecy. The disciples saddle the animal with their own garments, and people pave the way by spreading their cloaks on the road, while others spread branches (11:8). Spreading cloaks recalls the time when Jehu was anointed king. Every man took his garment and put it under him on the steps and proclaimed, "Jehu is king" (2 Kgs 9:12–13).

The spreading of branches recalls the triumphant entry of the Jews into Jerusalem after Simon Maccabaeus defeated the enemy and brought peace to the land. They entered "with praise and palm branches, and with harps and cymbals and stringed instruments, and with hymns and songs, because a great enemy had been crushed and removed from Israel" (1 Macc 13:51). Jesus enters Jerusalem as Israel's king, and an audience conversant with Scripture would have recognized the echo from Zech 9:9.

The messianic theme is noised abroad by those who went ahead and those who followed shouting, "Hosanna! Blessed is he who comes in the name of the Lord! Blessed is the coming kingdom of our father David! Hosanna in the highest heaven!" (11:9–10). The excitement surrounding Jesus' arrival ends with a seeming anticlimax, when he enters the temple only to look around and leave. The hour was "already late." But this detail sets the stage for what will happen the next day when

135. BDAG, 900.

Jesus' actions and words pronounce God's judgment on the temple. Malachi 3:1, which is cited in the gospel's introduction (Mark 1:2), provides the backdrop for understanding this aspect of the entry to Jerusalem. There God states, "'I will send my messenger, who will prepare the way before me. Then suddenly the Lord you are seeking will come to his temple; the messenger of the covenant, whom you desire, will come,' says the LORD Almighty." The passage continues, however, "But who can endure the day of his coming? Who can stand when he appears?" (Mal 3:2). Jesus inspects the temple as Lord, and the next day's events reveal that he finds it wanting. The reference to it being "already late" (Mark 11:11) may be taken as more than a reference to the lateness of the hour but also as a fateful nod to God's timetable for the temple. It is already too late.

2.6.1.2 Jesus' Prophetic Action in the Temple and the Cursing of the Fig Tree (11:12–25)

Mark brackets the temple incident with an account of Jesus' cursing the fig tree. Jesus' last miracle in Mark is bewildering because it brings death, not life. The fig tree has leaves and seems to promise a breakfast of figs, but it has none. Jesus curses it even though it was not the season for figs. Those familiar with Scripture know that trees are frequently used as symbols and are portrayed as sensitive to their moral surroundings (Jer 8:13; Isa 28:3–4; Hos 9:10, 16; Mic 7:1; Joel 1:7, 12). Fruitfulness was a symbol of Israel's covenant relation to God; lack of fruitfulness was a symbol of Israel's unfaithfulness in that relationship (Jer 8:13; Hos 9:10, 16, Mic 7:1). The term for "season" is the same word that is used in Jesus' opening proclamation, "The time has come" (1:15), for the tenants' failure to produce the fruit of the vineyard "at harvest time" (12:2), and in Jesus' last instruction on the Mount of Olives, "Be on guard! Be alert! You do not know when that time will come" (13:33). The barren fig tree represents the temple that is unprepared for the coming of its Lord. Jesus pronounces a withering curse on it: "May no one ever eat fruit from you again" (11:14).

Jesus' interpretation of driving out those buying and selling in the temple, overturning the moneychangers' tables and the benches of those selling doves, and not allowing anyone to carry a vessel through the temple (11:15–16), suggests that he does not intend to reform the temple.[136] His actions would have only a temporary result as the buyers and sellers would soon return, the moneychangers and dove sellers would soon pick up their tables and benches, and the temple traffic would soon return to normal. Jesus engages in a prophetic action to communicate God's rejection of the temple.[137] The passage cited from Isa 56:7, "My house will be called a house of prayer for all nations," means that God did not plan for the temple to become a national shrine only for Israel.

The reference to the "den of robbers" from Jer 7:11 has nothing to do with

136. "Vessel" is used in the LXX for the sacred temple vessels for the consecrated bread, lamp oil, and incense censers (see Isa 52:11, "the vessels of the LORD," NRSV).

137. Examples of prophetic representative actions are recorded in 1 Kgs 22:11; Isa 20:1–6; Jer 13:1–16; 19:1–15; 28:10–11; Ezek 4:1–3; Acts 21:11.

dishonest trade in the temple. Instead, it recalls a context where the prophet denounces the false security that deceptive shibboleths and the sacrificial cult have bred. The abuses that tarnished the temple cult in Jeremiah's day prompted God's threat, "Therefore, what I did to Shiloh I will now do to the house that bears my Name, the temple you trust in, the place I gave to you and your ancestors" (Jer 7:14). Jesus will tell his disciples that the temple will be destroyed (Mark 13:1–2), and his threats against the temple emerge as a charge at his trial (14:58) and as a taunt at the cross (15:29). "The cleansing of the temple," therefore, is not an apt title for this incident, particularly when it is interpreted by the cursing of the fig tree that surrounds it.[138]

On the next day, the disciples saw the fig tree withered to its roots, and Peter remembered Jesus' words. Withered to the roots, there is no hope for this fig tree's renewal. The blighted tree is a symbol of God's judgment (Isa 28:3–4; Jer 8:13; Hos 9:16; Mic 7:1; Joel 1:7, 12; Hab 3:17–18), and it portends the temple's utter desolation. But those who have faith in God (Mark 11:22), which also entails having faith in Jesus, will not be without a place of prayer or a means of atonement. Jesus assures his disciples, "And when you stand praying, if you hold anything against anyone, forgive them, so that your Father in heaven may forgive you your sins" (11:25). The temple will no longer be the focal point of God's presence among the people.

2.6.1.3 A Challenge to Jesus' Authority (11:27–33)

The chief priests and the teachers of the law, the ones whom Jesus prophesied would reject him (8:31) and condemn him to death (10:33), fully understand the implications of his actions and words and begin looking "for a way to kill him" (11:18). They oppose him because he threatens their position of religious and political power, and they are interested in preserving their role as the ones who dispense God's forgiveness.

They, along with the elders, ask Jesus to tell them the source of his authority to do and say what he did in the temple. Jesus seizes control of the situation by asking them about John's baptism: "Was it from heaven, or of human origin?" (11:30). John's ministry was linked to Jesus' ministry from the beginning of the gospel (1:14; 6:14–29; 9:11–13). These leaders did not approve of John the Baptist either but are afraid to admit that his authority was from heaven, because Jesus will condemn them for not believing him, and they are afraid to disparage his authority as merely human, because the people revered him. Jesus gets them to admit that they cannot tell the difference between what is from God and what is from men.

138. Jesus is not trying to clear away space for Gentiles to pray in the outer court. The outer court was not viewed positively as the place where Gentiles could worship. It was the place beyond which Gentiles could not go. The balustrade surrounding the sanctuary warned any Gentile from entering upon the threat of death (see Acts 21:27–30).

2.6.1.4 The Allegory of the Wicked Tenants of the Vineyard (12:1–12)

Despite the chapter division, the allegory of the wicked tenants continues Jesus' response to the leaders' challenge of his authority (11:27–33). A man plants a vineyard, puts a fence around it, digs a pit for the winepress, and builds a watchtower—a clear allusion to Isaiah 5:1–7, which declares that "the vineyard of the Lord Almighty is the nation of Israel" (Isa 5:7a; see Ps 80:8).[139] The Isaiah passage goes on to lament the bad fruit the vineyard produces and threatens its destruction.

The vineyard owner leases the vineyard to tenants and goes to another country.[140] When the season came for the tenants to pay him his share of the harvest, he sends servants to collect. The tenants drove off some and killed others, an allusion to Israel's mistreatment of God's prophets (2 Chr 24:18–19; 36:15–16; Neh 9:26).[141] The climactic moments in the parable are marked by direct discourse. The incensed landlord has one person left to send, his beloved son, and says, "They will respect my son" (12:6). The tenants, who are wise in their own eyes and shrewd in their own sight (Isa 5:21), say, "This is the heir. Come, let's kill him, and the inheritance will be ours" (12:7).[142] Recognizing who the son is only intensifies the gravity of the crime.

Jesus concludes the parable with a question, "What then will the owner of the vineyard do?" and then provides the answer, "He will come and kill those tenants and give the vineyard to others" (12:9). This answer emphasizes how self-defeating it was to attempt to outmaneuver the owner of the vineyard. The parable should remind the audience of what Jesus said in 9:37, "Whoever welcomes me does not welcome me but the one who sent me." The allegory conveys that the tenants have not won the day when they kill the son. They still have to deal with the owner, God.

Jesus ends this indirect indictment of the high priests and teachers of the law by capping off the parable with a citation from Ps 118:22–23: "The stone the builders rejected has become the cornerstone" (12:10).[143] Moyise comments, "Read without

139. Since the fence, winepress, and tower have no significance in the later development of the parable, these details were only included to link it to the context in Isaiah. See Wim J. C. Weren, "The Use of Isaiah 5,1–7 in the Parable of the Tenants (Mark 12,1–12; Matthew 21,33–46)," *Bib* 79 (1998): 1–26. In *t. Me'il.* 1:16 and *t. Sukkah* 3:15, the tower is taken as a figure for the temple and the winepress for the altar.

140. Craig A. Evans, "Jesus' Parable of the Tenant Farmers in Light of Lease Agreements in Antiquity," *JSP* 14 (1996): 65–83, notes that the tenants need not be regarded as impoverished peasants. His analysis of agricultural lease agreements in the Zenon Papyri and related documents indicates that they could be commercial farmers of means and standing in society. Martin Goodman, *The Ruling Class of Judaea: The Origins of the Jewish Revolt against Rome A.D. 66–70* (Cambridge: Cambridge University Press, 1987), 55–75, notes that the ruling priests in Jerusalem were the major landlords in Israel and would have naturally sympathized with the plight of a landowner dealing with deadbeat tenants. Jesus' parable cleverly turns the tables on his priestly inquisitors by putting them in the role of mutinous and murderous tenants.

141. The prophets are frequently identified as God's servants (1 Kgs 18:36; 19:10; 2 Chr 24:19–24; 36:15; Neh 9:26; Jer 2:30; 7:25–26; 26:20–23; Amos 3:7).

142. These are the same words used by Joseph's brothers who want to kill him (Gen 37:20a, LXX). When the tenants kill the beloved son, they throw his corpse out without burying it. To be refused an honorable burial underscores the humiliating treatment of the son (see Deut 28:26; Jer 7:33; 8:1; 22:19; Ezek 6:5; 29:5; 39:17).

143. Hartman, *Mark*, 480, notes that while some Christians identified the house built on this cornerstone as the church (1 Cor 3:9–16; 2 Cor 6:16; Eph 2:20–22; 1 Pet 2:4–10; Heb 3:6), he thinks that it might be "too far-reaching" to make this identification. If one believes that Mark was influenced by Pauline and Petrine traditions, however, these passages would suggest that Mark would have made this connection as well.

the closing quotation, the parable is a terrible tragedy."[144] This passage illuminates the meaning of Jesus' death from Scripture and sees it as the fulfillment of God's purposes. The psalm explains that the one who is "rejected" (the same verb used in Jesus' first prediction in 8:31) and murdered will be vindicated. Mark's audience can only understand Jesus to be the stone that the psalmist talked about.

This allegory reflects Jesus' consciousness of his sonship in relation to the Lord of the vineyard and his full awareness of his impending death at the hands of the authorities. The final quotation, "The Lord has done this, and it is marvelous in our eyes" (12:11), also gives God's endorsement to Jesus' condemnation of the temple and its hierarchy.

The leaders regard neither the ministry of John the Baptist nor that of Jesus as the Lord's doing and certainly do not regard it as marvelous (12:11). They know that Jesus "had spoken the parable against them" (12:12) and are all the more determined to do away with him, but they are temporarily deterred by their fear of the crowd. In Mark, the temple leaders are the ones who reject Jesus and have him killed, not the people of Israel. This allegory is not about God's rejection of Israel, but about God's rejection of these leaders.

2.6.1.5 Jesus' Authoritative Teaching in the Temple (12:13–37)

Mark presents a triad of Jesus' teachings in response to questions posed by insincere and sincere questioners. Jesus is identified as "teacher" in each encounter (12:14, 19, 32). The answers reveal his divine authority to interpret the law and to do more than simply resolve sticky dilemmas. They reveal something about the nature of God and what God demands.

2.6.1.5.1 The Pharisees and Herodians' Question about Paying Taxes to Caesar (12:13–17)

The chief priests continue their intrigue by sending some Pharisees and Herodians as their brokers to try to trap Jesus in his words. They hypocritically lavish praise on Jesus as "a man of integrity. You aren't swayed by others, because you pay no attention to who they are; but you teach the way of God in accordance with the truth" (12:14). The translation obscures christological implications. Donahue comments, "Three of these attributes are rather surprising when applied to a human being, that Jesus is true used as an unmodified attribute (*alēthēs ei*), that he has care for no one and is not a respecter of persons. The latter expression is applied in biblical writings normally to God."[145]

Jesus, like God, knows their inner thoughts (12:15; see 2:8, 8:16–17; cf. 11:31) and knows that they are putting him to the test (see 8:11) with their question about whether paying taxes to Caesar compromises one's fidelity to the God of Israel.

144. Steve Moyise, "Is Mark's Opening Quotation the Key to His Use of Scripture?" *IBS* 20 (1998): 148. The crowd chanted from Ps 118:25 when they cheered Jesus' entrance into the city (Mark 11:9–10).

145. John R. Donahue, "A Neglected Factor in the Theology of Mark," *JBL* 101 (1982): 572. See Lev 19:15; Acts 10:34; Rom 2:11; Eph 6:9; Col 3:25; Jas 2:9.

The question was politically and religiously loaded.[146] When Herod Archelaus was deposed in AD 6 at the insistence of the Jews, Judea became an imperial province, which meant that the people had to pay a poll tax that went to Rome. Josephus reports that it sparked a revolt led by Judas the Galilean, who upbraided the people as "cowards for consenting to pay tribute to the Romans and tolerating mortal masters, after having God for their lord" (*J.W.* 2.8.1 §118). The leaders hope that they might catch Jesus making a rash, treasonous statement that they can use against him with the Roman governor.

Mark is not concerned simply to show how Jesus evades their trap and solves this dilemma with a clever riposte. The central issue is what Jesus teaches about God. Before answering, Jesus asks them for a denarius and asks them to identify whose image it bears. Coins functioned as propaganda placards for the Roman Empire. He asked them whose image is on the coin, and they answer, "Caesar's." Assuming that they show him a Tiberian denarius, the obverse side bore the image of the emperor with the superscription: "TI[berius] CAESAR DIVI AVG[usti] F[ilius] AVGVST[us]." It proclaims Emperor Tiberius to be a divine or semidivine being as the son of the divine Augustus.[147] Jesus now answers their question: "Give back to Caesar what is Caesar's and to God what is God's" (12:17). Caesar's coins belong to him. Since they possess Caesar's money and do business with it, they should pay Caesar's taxes. One owes to God much more—what bears God's image and name. Since Jews believe that humans are created in the image of God (Gen 1:26–27; Isa 44:5; Ezek 18:4) and bear his name as children of God, they owe their whole selves to God.[148] Caesar's claim on people pales next to God's absolute claim on people. Jesus will teach that humans owe God love from all their heart, soul, mind, and strength (Mark 12:30, 33), and the widow who gave all she had to live on (12:44) becomes an example of that.

Jesus does not intend to imply that there are two separate and equal realms. God's rule "embraces all reality."[149] God is Caesar's Lord. Governments are not given a blank check to go their own way. Those that flout God's law in the end will be destroyed.

The reaction of amazement to Jesus' teaching (12:17) should hardly be surprising to the audience. Others have reacted this way to his teaching before (1:22; 6:2; 10:24, 26, 32; 11:18), and it is the same as the reaction to his miracles (1:27; 2:12; 4:41; 5:15, 20, 33, 42; 6:51; 7:37; see also 9:6; 16:5). Like Pilate's amazement at Jesus' silence (15:5), however, it is not an amazement that will cause them to bow to Jesus' divine authority.

146. Luke 20:20 makes explicit the intention of the trap: "They hoped to catch Jesus in something he said, so that they might hand him over to the power and authority of the governor."

147. The reverse side had a female figure facing right, seated on a throne, with a crown and holding a scepter in the right hand and a palm or olive branch in the left. The superscription reads: "P[ontifex] M[aximus], high priest." The woman possibly represents a priestess or Livia, the wife of Augustus, and the coin promotes the *Pax Romana* that places all peoples in subjection.

148. Tertullian (*Idol.* 15; *Marc.* 4.38.3) interpreted this passage to mean: "Render unto Caesar, the image of Caesar, which is on the money, and unto God, the image of God, which is in man; so that thou givest unto Caesar money, unto God thine own self." See Charles Homer Giblin, "'The Things of God' in the Question Concerning Tribute to Caesar [Lk. 20:25; Mk 12:17; Mt 22:21]," *CBQ* 33 (1971): 522–23.

149. Donahue, "A Neglected Factor in the Theology of Mark," 573.

2.6.1.5.2 The Sadducees' Question about the Resurrection (12:18–27)

The Sadducees appear for the first time in the gospel, and Mark introduces them as those who do not believe in the resurrection.[150] Jesus has predicted his resurrection three times (8:31; 9:31; 10:34). If there is no resurrection, then Jesus will not be vindicated by God.

They present Jesus with a conundrum based on the law of levirate marriage.[151] A woman married to seven brothers in succession bore no children: "At the resurrection whose wife will she be, since the seven were married to her?" (12:23). Jesus' response fits a chiastic pattern:

A You are deceived.
  B You do not know the Scriptures.
    C You do not know the power of God.
    C′ [The power of God] raises the dead and they become like angels.
  B′ [The Scripture is cited] in the bush passage, the God of Abraham, Isaac and Jacob.
A′ You are much deceived.

He dismisses the Sadducees' crassly materialistic picture of the resurrection life. The resurrected life is not comparable to life on earth, but Jesus does not go into details. He only says that those who are resurrected will be like the angels in heaven and neither marry nor be given in marriage. He then corrects their biblical ignorance by reminding them of the "bush passage" that identifies God as the God of Abraham, Isaac, and Jacob (Exod 3:6).[152] The living God would hardly identify himself as the God of corpses. Death annuls the covenant of marriage (Rom 7:2–3), but Jesus' answer assumes that death does not annul the covenant of election that God made with Abraham, Isaac, and Jacob. Finally, Jesus upbraids the Sadducees for failing to take into account God's power (or God's love, see 1 Cor 6:14) to give life again to those who die. God is able to conquer death.

2.6.1.5.3 A Scribe's Question about the Greatest Commandment (12:28–34)

A teacher of the law admires Jesus' rejoinder of the Sadducees and asks him, without any hint of hostility, what the greatest commandment is. He implicitly grants Jesus' authority to interpret the law. Jesus gives a conventional reply from the daily confession of Israel from Deut 6:4–5 (see Deut 11:13): "Hear, O Israel: The Lord our God, the Lord is one. Love the Lord your God with all your heart and with all your soul

150. Josephus (*Ant.* 18.1.4 §16) describes the Sadducees as believing that the soul perishes with the body. According to Acts 23:8, they also did not believe in angels.

151. Levirate marriage was prescribed when a man died with no heirs. One of his surviving brothers was to take the widow in marriage to provide the deceased with an heir (Deut 25:5–10; see Gen 38:6–26; Ruth 3–4). One attained a measure of immortality through the procreation of descendants to continue one's name. But the law was primarily motivated by the desire to keep the brother's inheritance in the family—"his widow must not marry outside the family" (Deut 25:5).

152. Prior to chapter and verse divisions, one cited Scripture by describing a distinguishing word or phrase in a passage. For example, in Rom 11:2 Paul uses the phrase "in Elijah" ("about Elijah," NIV) to refer to the passage about Elijah in 1 Kgs 19.

and with all your mind and with all your strength" (Mark 12:29–30). One cannot love God in isolation from our other relationships in life, and Jesus couples the command to love God with the command to love one's neighbor as oneself (Lev 19:18; see also Rom 13:10; 15:1–2; Gal 5:14; Jas 2:8).[153] Tacitus claimed that Christians were persecuted because of "their hatred of the human race" (*Ann.* 15.44), but Jesus' emphasis on loving the neighbor would discredit that vilification of his followers.

The teacher of the law commends Jesus' answer, reiterates it, and unexpectedly adds that obeying these commandments is "more important than all burnt offerings and sacrifices" (12:33). This supplement to Jesus' answer echoes 1 Sam 15:22 and Hos 6:6 and essentially diminishes the temple's religious significance. His answer occurs in the context of Jesus' prophetic condemnation of the temple when he overturned the tables (Mark 11:15–17) and provides a scribal endorsement of Jesus' position.

Jesus boldly states that the teacher of the law is not far from the kingdom. This statement takes the audience back to the beginning and Jesus' opening proclamation, "The kingdom of God has come near. Repent and believe the good news!" (1:15). To enter the kingdom the teacher must do more than simply approve of Jesus' teaching. He must accept the lordship of the Messiah, that Jesus is the Messiah that David spoke about, and that he should now follow him.[154] Simply approving, admiring, and even venerating the teaching of Jesus does not make one a follower. One must submit entirely to his authority and follow him on the way, which requires doing the will of God (3:35), denying oneself and taking up a cross (8:34), abandoning riches and helping the poor (10:21), becoming a servant to all (10:43–44), and enduring suffering for the sake of the gospel and being hated by all (13:9, 13). Mark does not record the man's response to Jesus' affirmation, but it effectively silences him and everyone else who questioned Jesus in the temple.

2.6.1.6 Jesus' Question about How the Messiah is David's Son and David's Lord (12:35–37)

The title "son of David" does not play a prominent role in Mark, but it was assumed by many that the Messiah was to be the son of David. This point is emphasized in Jesus' question, "Why do the teachers of the law say that the Messiah is the son of David?" (12:35). The real question is, What does this title mean when it is applied to Jesus? Bartimaeus called out to Jesus as the son of David when he was passing through Jericho (10:47, 48), and Jesus did not attempt to silence him as the crowd did. The crowd of followers also hailed "the coming kingdom of our father David" when Jesus entered into the city (11:10).

Jesus answers his first question about why the teachers of the law say that the Messiah is the son of David with a question about the meaning of Ps 110:1: "The Lord said to my Lord: 'Sit at my right hand until I put your enemies under your

153. John insists that those who do not show love to others can hardly claim to love God (1 John 3:14–18; 4:8, 10–12, 20–22).

154. George Keerankeri, *The Love Commandment in Mark: An Exegetico-Theological Study of Mk 12,28–34* (AnBib 150; Rome: Pontifical Biblical Institute, 2003), 173–79.

feet' " (Mark 12:36).[155] How can David call him Lord if he is his son? Jesus leaves the answer to this conundrum in the air, and the audience has to fill in the blanks. The kingdom that he brings is greater than that of "our father David"; it is the kingdom of the Father. Jesus does not wield military might as David did, but he is greater than the great king of Israel.

2.6.1.7 The Denunciation of the Teachers of the Law (12:38–40)

Surprisingly, after commending a particular teacher of the law (12:34), Jesus then proceeds to denounce them as a class. He reviles them for their religious preening, their parading about in flowing robes, their courting human adulation and seats of honor, and their praying long prayers. Their religious pomp and ceremony are exposed as sham piety by their failure to love their neighbor. They close their eyes to the needs of the poor, and, worse, they greedily appropriate the property of powerless widows. In the OT, widows symbolize the vulnerable, who are to be helped and defended, and those who abuse them will be severely judged by God (Isa 10:1–4).

2.6.1.8 The Commendation of the Widow Who Gave Her Whole Livelihood as an Offering (12:41–44)

The counterfeit virtue of the teachers of the law is contrasted with the genuine piety of an impoverished widow. Jesus observes the wealthy placing large sums into the temple's offering boxes and a widow contributing two small copper coins worth a few cents.[156] He notes that she gave out of her poverty, "all she had to live on" (12:44), which was not much. The only wealth she possessed was her openness to God, whom she manifestly loves with all her heart, soul, mind, and strength. She offers no sacrifices or burnt offerings because she could not afford any.

One might deplore the waste that one who was so impoverished would give so sacrificially to a religious institution run by those who oppressed the poor and a religious institution that Jesus implies will soon be destroyed and replaced.[157] Her devotional giving, however, parallels that of another unnamed woman who will extravagantly pour out precious nard to anoint Jesus head (14:3–9).[158] Malbon comments:

> Both the women give money, although the amounts differ greatly: two lepta (about a penny) and more than three hundred denarii (about a year's wages for a laborer). But money is only their literal gift. Their symbolic gift is, for the anointing woman, acknowledgment of Jesus' approaching death—that is, the gift of his life, and, for the poor widow, the gift of her whole life as exemplary of Jesus. The two healed blind men are suppliants/exemplars. The Bethsaida man

155. This passage is alluded to in Acts 2:34–35; Rom 8:34; 1 Cor 15:25; Col 3:1; Heb 1:13; 8:1.

156. The two *lepta* (Greek) are said to be worth a *quadrans*, the smallest Roman coin.

157. Addison G. Wright, "The Widow's Mites: Praise or Lament?—A Matter of Context," *CBQ* 44 (1982): 256–65.

158. See Elizabeth Struthers Malbon, "The Poor Widow in Mark and Her Poor Rich Readers," *CBQ* 53 (1991): 589–604.

and Bartimaeus request literal sight and seem to receive metaphorical insight. The two giving women are simply exemplars, asking for nothing. The poor widow and the anointing woman give literally their money, and metaphorically the one gives her acceptance of Jesus' gift of his life, while the other gives her own life.[159]

2.6.2 Teaching on the Mount of Olives about the Temple's Looming Destruction and the Timing of the End (13:1–37)

This second lengthy discourse in the gospel creates a pause in the action. The theme of the first discourse in chapter 4 is "hearing"; in this discourse the theme is "watching." As Jesus sat in a boat on the sea in 4:1 to teach about the sowing of the seed, he sits on the Mount of Olives opposite the temple to teach about the final harvest that will come. After the introduction where Jesus predicts the destruction of the temple (13:1–4), the discourse divides into three units. A double warning to watch out for false prophets and messiahs brackets the first unit (13:5–23). Jesus specifies three temporal signposts of things that will happen leading up to this catastrophe: "when you hear of wars and rumors of wars" (13:7); "whenever you are arrested and brought to trial" (13:11); and "when you see 'the abomination that causes desolation'" (13:14). The command not to be alarmed accompanies the first two warnings (13:7, 11). The third warning, however, signals that it is time to flee Judea for the mountains (13:14). These signs, however, are not harbingers of the end.

The second unit deals with the coming of the Son of Man and the end of the age (13:24–27). It happens with no warning, and the celestial collapse both announces and accompanies the event.[160] It will culminate in the gathering of the elect "from the ends of the earth to the ends of the heavens" (13:27).

The third unit concludes the discourse with two parables and a chain of warnings to watch (13:28–37). The parable of the Budding Fig Tree applies to the prophecy of the temple's downfall (13:5–23) and helps answer the question, "When will these things happen?" (13:4). Jesus asserts that "all these things" will happen before this generation passes away (13:30).

The phrase "but about that day or hour" in 13:32 marks a shift in the subject to the coming of the Son of Man. Jesus now speaks about something that can occur at any time during any generation. Its timing is unknown to *all* except the Father, and there will be no forewarning. The parable of the man who leaves home and puts his servants in charge and commands the doorkeeper to be on the watch is intended to convey that disciples are to be at their posts and constantly alert. A string of commands to "be on guard" and to "keep watch" surrounds the parable to reinforce the point.

159. Malbon, "'Reflected Christology,'" 140.
160. Edward Adams, *The Stars Will Fall from Heaven: Cosmic Catastrophe in the New Testament and its World* (LNTS 347; London/New York: T&T Clark, 2007), 159.

2.6.2.1 *Departure to the Mount of Olives and Prediction of Temple's Destruction (13:1–4)*

This discourse results from the disciples gawking over the temple's "massive stones" and "magnificent buildings" as they depart. Jesus responds by prophesying, "Not one stone here will be left on another; every one will be thrown down" (13:1–2). What was implicit in Jesus' prophetic actions in the temple now becomes explicit. This prophecy prompts the first four disciples Jesus called, Peter, Andrew, James, and John (1:16–20), to ask in private, "Tell us, when will these things happen? And what will be the sign that they are all about to be fulfilled?" (13:4).[161] The first question asks about the timetable for the temple's ruin. The second question asks about the sign that will warn about the eschatological finale.

2.6.2.2 *Warnings Connected to the Temple's Destruction (13:5–23)*

The unit forms a chiasm:

A Deceivers (13:5–6, "Watch!")
  B International Wars (13:7–8, "When you hear.")
    C Persecution of Christians (13:9–13, "Watch!")
  B′ War in Judea (13:14–20, "When you see.")
A′ Deceivers (13:21–23, "Watch!")

The central theme is that the disciples should not be deceived and led astray by the false prophets and pseudo-messiahs who will arise, nor should they be staggered by the frightening events that will occur throughout the world. Jesus speaks of things that the disciples and their contemporaries will "see," "hear," or "endure" during their lifetimes, and the warnings consistently use the second person plural. The upheaval throughout the world will feed apocalyptic furor, but the disciples must remain level-headed and not be perplexed by the persecution they will endure in carrying out their mission to preach the gospel to all nations (13:10).

When they see the desolating sacrilege, however, any who are in Jerusalem and the vicinity should take immediate action and flee to the mountains (13:14). This reference to the abomination that causes desolation links the reference in Dan 12:11 to the blasphemous object, possibly a pagan altar that Antiochus Epiphanes set up in the temple (see also 1 Macc 1:54, 59). The phrase "standing where it does not belong" suggests some personal presence or idolatrous statue, but there is no agreement as to what it might have been. Whatever it was, the original hearers would have recognized it and also would have recognized its dangerous implications that would lead to the desolation of the temple and the Holy City.

Wright interprets this warning to be the answer to the disciples' first question:

161. The disciples have consistently inquired of Jesus when they have witnessed something or he has said something provocative (4:10; 7:17; 9:28; 10:10).

"When will these things happen?" (13:4). The answer is that "when you see the desecrating abomination standing in the sanctuary this is the signal that the temple and the city's destruction are close at hand."[162] Jesus warns the disciples not to be crushed in the military onslaught that will accompany the temple's dying days.

The distress associated with the temple's destruction will be unequaled and almost unbearable. But the Lord will cut short the days for the sake of the elect (13:19–20). These are only preliminary signs and should not be interpreted as meaning that the end of the world is just around the corner. It is only the end of the world of the temple.

2.6.2.3 The Coming of the Son of Man (13:24–27)

The second unit deals with the coming of the Son of Man (see 8:38), which Marshall defines as "the coming of the exalted Jesus from heaven to earth" that is coupled with the final judgment of God and the end of human history.[163] Jesus does not give any specific information about how long it will take before the Son of Man comes "following that distress" (13:24). The end of the temple will happen before the end, but it does not mean the end is nigh. The second person plural is absent in these verses, which suggests that the disciples may not "be around to see these things happen."[164]

The coming of the Son of Man will not be preceded by any premonitory signs to help one prepare. When it happens, it will be unmistakable, with a cosmological upheaval accompanying the Son of Man's return in power and glory (13:24–26). Then, he will send angels to gather the elect (13:27). His coming means salvation for the elect—those who have faithfully responded to the gospel and who remain faithful to the end. Jesus does not give any details about what will happen next.

2.6.2.4 Final Warnings to Watch (13:28–37)

The third unit concludes with the parables of the budding fig tree (13:28–29) and the doorkeepers (13:33–37). These parables surround Jesus' declaration that no one, not even the Son, knows the hour (13:30–32). The parable of the Fig Tree refers to the events leading to the abomination of desolation, and we can know something—"when you see these things happening, you know that it is near, right at the door" (13:29). "These things" (13:29) refer to the war in Judea and the destruction of the temple. This parable sums up the warnings in 13:5–23. The second parable about the doorkeeper applies to the coming of the Son of Man. It emphasizes that no one knows when he will return (13:35). Jesus offers no deadline. It may come during the lifetime of the disciples, or it may happen in a far-distant future. Consequently, the discourse that began as a private explanation for four disciples ends addressed to all

162. N. T. Wright, *Mark for Everyone* (London: SPCK, 2001), 182. On the meaning of the phrase "let the reader understand," see §13.3.5.2.4.1.

163. I. Howard Marshall, "The Parousia in the New Testament—and Today," in *Worship, Theology and Ministry in the Early Church: Essays in Honor of Ralph P. Martin* (ed. Michael J. Wilkins and Terence Paige; JSNTSup 87; Sheffield: JSOT, 1992), 194.

164. Adams, *The Stars*, 146.

(13:37). It is impossible to compute how much time remains before the end comes, so the only alternative is always to be ready.

2.7 The Way to the Cross (14:1–15:47)

2.7.1 The Plot to Kill Jesus and the Anointing (for Burial) by an Anonymous Woman (14:1–11)

A woman's act of supreme devotion to Jesus is sandwiched between the murderous conspiracy of the high priests and teachers of the law on how to seize Jesus and kill him and Judas's voluntary offer to betray Jesus to them. Each scene—the plotting, the anointing, the betrayal contract—foreshadows Jesus' death.

2.7.1.1 The Plot to Kill Jesus (14:1–2)

The temple hierarchy had decided that Jesus must be seized and killed after his audacious prophetic action in the temple (11:18) and is all the more determined to eradicate him after the leaders recognized that the allegory of the wicked tenants of the vineyard was aimed at them (12:12). They have been thwarted from carrying out their wishes because of Jesus' popularity with the crowd and their fear that such action would stir up a hornet's nest of unrest. They still fear that seizing Jesus will cause a riot among the people (see Acts 17:5) who have flocked to Jerusalem for the Passover festival.

The word "festival" may refer to the festival crowd (see John 7:11) or the time of Passover. The leaders may fear seizing Jesus when he is surrounded by the crowd since their Roman overlords expected them to keep the peace and to prevent any uproar.[165] Arresting Jesus in the dead of night in the more secluded Gethsemane allowed them to avoid any public commotion. If it means "during the festival," then they do not want to kill Jesus at this season. Judas's offer to betray Jesus would have prompted them to change their minds. The events reveal that they are not ultimately in charge of what happens despite their evil scheming. Jesus will be executed during the Feast, and his death will transform the meaning of the Passover festival for Christians. They will not remember it simply as the time when God struck down the firstborn in the land of Egypt and liberated Israel from bondage. Instead, they will associate it with the death of God's beloved Son, who was struck down to ransom many (Mark 10:45; 1 Cor 5:7) and to inaugurate a new covenant.

2.7.1.2 The Anointing of Jesus (for Burial) by an Anonymous Woman (14:3–9)

Jesus is dining in the home of Simon the leper in Bethany when an unidentified woman brings an alabaster jar of costly nard, breaks it open, and pours the ointment

165. Pesch, *Markusevangelium*, 2:321.

on his head.[166] Mark does not explain her intention, but one can infer that her action is evidence of an ardent devotion to Jesus that will hold back none of her possessions in service to him. Mark emphasizes the high value of the perfume by noting in detail that it was contained in "an alabaster jar," that it was "pure nard" (14:3), and that it was worth "more than a year's wages" (14:5). The gathering, also unnamed, regards it as a profligate waste, and they harshly censure her and imagine that it could have been better used had it been sold and the proceeds given to the poor.[167] One can always imagine that one will do something noble for others, but the woman takes concrete action with what she has for Jesus.

Jesus interprets her gesture as anointing his body beforehand for burial and reveals that he has accepted his death. The disciples of John the Baptist claimed his body after his execution and buried it (6:29), but Jesus' disciples are nowhere to be seen when he dies, according to Mark. Jesus is hastily buried by a stranger in a borrowed tomb, and no mention is made of the anointing of the corpse. The women who observe the burial return to anoint the body after the Sabbath was over, but they discover that Jesus has been raised and is not there. Jesus' foreknowledge again is highlighted, and this announcement, which strongly hints at his impending death, provokes no outburst of protest. His prophecy that her devotion will be remembered wherever the gospel is preached throughout the world also strongly hints of the triumph of the resurrection. Only Mark's audience, after Jesus' death and resurrection, can fathom the implications of this statement.

Jesus' citation from Deut 15:11, "The poor you will always have with you" (14:7), does not justify callous neglect of the poor because nothing can be done to eliminate the problem of poverty. Jesus reproaches those who decried the waste of precious perfume, and the context of Deut 15:11 expands that reproach. God declares in Deut 15:4–5, "there need be no poor people among you, for in the land the Lord your God is giving you to possess as your inheritance, he will richly bless you, if only you fully obey the Lord your God and are careful to follow all these commands I am giving you today." That the poor are with you always is an incriminating reality that will not be improved by using the proceeds from this jar of perfume. Those who respond to Jesus wholeheartedly, however, as this woman does, love God and their neighbor wholeheartedly. Their care for the poor will not be a one-time charitable gift but a regular undertaking that will also address the structures of injustice that foster and perpetuate poverty.

2.7.1.3 Judas Iscariot Joins the Plot (14:10–11)

After the anointing, Mark narrates Judas's duplicity as he offers to betray Jesus to the chief priests. What did Judas betray? Judas does not appear in Jesus' interrogation

166. As "the leper," this Simon is distinguished from Simon Peter (1:16), Simon the Zealot (3:18), Simon the brother of Jesus (6:3), and Simon of Cyrene (15:21). It is possible that his name is preserved because he is the source of this tradition.

167. Petronius, *Satyricon*, 78:3, describes the fabulously rich freedman, Trimalchio, anointing his guests from a small flask of nard, and he portrays it as excessive extravagance.

as a witness for the prosecution. In light of the high priests' desire to avoid a protest among the people (14:2), their joy over Judas's offer to hand him over is probably connected to their expectation that as an insider he could help them be successful in their goal, and they pay him off. Mark makes no mention of Judas's soliciting payment from them or of the amount they shell out. Compared to the value of the perfume that the woman has poured out on Jesus' head, the sum paid out to hand him over is hardly worth mentioning. She has done a "beautiful thing" (14:6); he will do an abominable thing. That Judas "watched for an opportunity to hand him over" (14:11) makes it likely that what he betrays is the time and location where they can arrest Jesus without creating the riot the leaders fear.

2.7.2 The Last Supper (14:12–25)

Mark's account of the Last Supper divides into three scenes: the preparations for the supper (14:12–16), Jesus' words at the meal predicting his betrayal by one of the Twelve (14:17–21), and his interpretation of the meaning of his death from the bread and the cup of wine (14:22–25). In each scene Jesus demonstrates his foreknowledge of what will happen. He foreknows that they will find a man carrying a jar of water who will lead them to the place where they can prepare for the meal, that Judas will be the one to betray him, and that he is going to die. His foreknowledge underscores that what happens is not some tragic miscarriage of justice. His death is the fulfillment of God's predetermined plan in Scripture (14:21), and the disciples have been forewarned.

2.7.2.1 Preparation for the Supper (14:12–16)

The disciples ask Jesus where they should go to prepare to celebrate the Passover.[168] Jesus' instructions on how to find a room are similar to those he gave for them to find the animal that he would use to enter the city (11:1–6) and emphasize his authority. They will secure a room simply by identifying Jesus as "the Teacher" (14:14). They will find a man carrying a water jar, which would have been an unusual spectacle since women normally fetched water, and they are to follow him to the place. Mark's narrative stresses that it is Jesus' Passover. The disciples ask where they are to go to "make preparations *for you* to eat the Passover" (14:12). His answer is that when they follow the man with the water jar and meet the owner of the house where he enters, they are to ask, "Where is *my* guest room where *I* may eat the Passover with my disciples?" (14:14).

168. According to Exod 12:3–4, 7 the Passover meal was considered a family sacrifice to be eaten at home, while Deut 16:2 states that the Passover was sacrificed and eaten "at the place the LORD will choose as a dwelling for his Name," that is, at the temple, as Josiah did (2 Chr 35:1–19). *Jubilees*, clearly early, devotes a long passage (*Jub.* 49:16–21) to stress that this sacrifice must be eaten within the precincts of the sanctuary. According to rabbinic sources, the sacrifice offered in the temple could be eaten throughout Jerusalem (*m. Pesaḥ.* 5:10; cf. *m. Zebaḥ.* 5:8).

2.7.2.2 The Prediction That One of the Twelve Would Betray Jesus (14:17–21)

The Twelve eat and drink at this last meal in a doom-laden atmosphere of sorrow and worry, when Jesus announces during the meal that one of them will betray him. Mark draws attention to the dreadfulness of this act by narrating that Jesus identifies the betrayer as "one who is eating with me" (14:18), "one of the Twelve" (14:20a), and "one who dips bread into the bowl with me" (14:20b). To betray the one who has given you his bread was a horrendous act (see Ps 41:9; John 13:18). The central question preoccupying their minds is not the fatal consequence of this betrayal of Jesus but whether they might be the turncoat. Each asks him the self-centered question, "Surely you don't mean me?" (14:19), a translation that accurately conveys the Greek grammar, which expects the answer "No, it is not you."

Jesus gives no answer except to reiterate that it is one who dips with him in the common bowl. He then declares that what happens to him follows the plan laid out in Scriptures, but the Scriptures do not dictate that he must be betrayed by one of his intimates. He therefore pronounces a woe, perhaps a last warning to the betrayer, that "it would be better for him if he had not been born" (14:21) than to follow through on his plan.

2.7.2.3 The Interpretation of Bread and Cup as Pointing to Jesus' Death (14:22–25)

Jesus takes two basic elements of their meal together, the bread and the wine, and gives them a dramatic application that illustrates the meaning of his imminent death. When Jesus says of the bread, "This is my body" (14:22), and of the cup, "This is my blood of the covenant, which is poured out for many" (14:24), he is saying that his death is a new sacrifice offered to God. Senior comments, "Jesus' redemptive death effects the new and definitive covenant renewal awaited by Israel" that is expressed in Jer 31:31–34.[169]

The phrase "the blood of the covenant" derives from Exod 24:8, when Moses took the blood of sacrificed young bulls, dashed it on the people, and said, "This is the blood of the covenant that the LORD has made with you in accordance with all these words." As the blood of sacrificial animals is "poured out," so is Jesus' blood. It is implied that no more sacrificial victims will need to be killed after his death. Only his death, represented by the bread broken and shared and the wine poured out and shared, is efficacious for the forgiveness of sins (see Zech 9:11).

169. Donald Senior, *The Passion of Jesus in the Gospel of Mark* (Wilmington, DE: Michael Glazier, 1984), 61.

2.7.3 On the Mount of Olives (14:26–52)

2.7.3.1 The Prediction That All the Disciples Will Fall Away and of Peter's Threefold Denial (14:26–31)

After singing a hymn,[170] Jesus and the disciples make their way to the Mount of Olives. Along the way, Jesus again demonstrates his foreknowledge of what will soon happen. He announces that the disciples will all fall away and supports this prophecy with a citation from Zech 13:7 that the shepherd will be struck and all the sheep will be scattered.[171] The verb "to fall away" first appeared in the parable of the Soils in 4:17, referring to the seed growing in rocky soil that has no depth. The plant that grows up with no root lasts only a short time, withered by the heat of the sun. When it is applied to persons it means, "When trouble or persecution comes because of the word, they quickly fall away." The explicit citation from Scripture implies what will happen is attributable to God's initiative and therefore is under God's sovereign control. This fact is emphasized by the slight alteration from a command, "Strike the shepherd" in Zechariah's text, to a declaration, "I will strike the shepherd." Jesus will be the one to regather his scattered sheep and predicts his resurrection for the fifth time (8:31; 9:9; 9:31; 10:34) with his promise, "after I have risen, I will go ahead of you into Galilee" (14:28).[172]

The disciples respond to this dire prediction with arrogance combined with ignorance. Peter does not shrink from contradicting Jesus' citation from Scripture that they will all fail. He insists that he will prove himself more trustworthy than the rest. Only then does Jesus give a precise prediction: "Truly I tell you ... today—yes, tonight—before the rooster crows twice you yourself will disown me three times" (14:30). Unbowed, Peter insists, "Even if I have to die with you, I will never disown you" (14:31).[173] The disciples all follow suit in swearing their loyalty to Jesus even if it leads to death. Moments before, each was not sure whether he would be the one to betray him and needed reassurance from Jesus. It is an example of their presumptuous conceit that they now think that they can swear faithfulness to death. This attitude dramatically contrasts with that of Jesus on the Mount of Olives as he prostrates himself in prayer to his Father.

2.7.3.2 Jesus' Anguished Prayer in Gethsemane and the Disciples' Quiet Repose (14:32–42)

Jesus could have saved himself by going into hiding. Instead, he goes to Gethsemane and waits for his enemies to come to arrest him by wrestling in prayer. Mark's

170. Raymond E. Brown, *The Death of the Messiah: From Gethsemane to the Grave: A Commentary on the Passion Narratives in the Four Gospels* (ABRL; New York: Doubleday, 1994), 1:122–23, contends that singing a hymn conveys the "prayerful context as the meal closed." The first readers were likely to connect it to hymns they were familiar with singing in their worship.

171. This quotation caps a number of allusions to Zech 9–14 in the context: "my blood of the covenant" (14:24/Zech 9:11); "that day," "the kingdom of God" (14:25/Zech 14:4, 9); "the Mount of Olives" (14:26/Zech 14:4); "strike the shepherd" (14:27/Zech 13:7); resurrection and restoration of the sheep (14:28/Zech 13:8–9).

172. Brown, *Death*, 1:130, avers that this promise implies that Jesus will resume his shepherding role, leading them and calling them together.

173. In Pauline literature, "dying with" Christ refers to participation in his saving death (Rom 6:8; Col 2:20; 2 Tim 2:11), which is necessary for salvation.

Gethsemane scene is the darkest of the four gospels. He describes Jesus going through psychological horror as he faces the prospect of unimaginable physical and mental suffering. He is "deeply distressed and troubled" (14:33) and cites Scripture to verbalize his distress, "My soul is overwhelmed with sorrow to the point of death" (14:34/Pss 42:6, 11; 43:5). He falls to the earth in prayer. Sommer comments that Mark regards the suffering Jesus underwent to be as important as his remarkable miracles of raising the dead and his glorious transfiguration.[174]

Schweizer notes that Jesus does not undergo his suffering stoically but biblically with loud lament.[175] Jesus' prayer expresses an intimacy with God that allows him to speak his mind honestly.[176] Ahearne-Kroll observes, "Obedience to God's will gives way to a desire to understand God's will and even challenge it."[177] The only answer that Jesus gets is what he voices in his own prayer, "Yet not what I will, but what you will" (14:36). What is important is doing the will of God (3:35). The silence that follows reveals what he already knew. He knows that he is the one God sent to plunder Satan's kingdom (3:23–24) and to free people from his evil power. It is God's will for him to die "to redeem humanity and all of creation from these forces of evil."[178] The cross is the only option. Donahue comments, "Jesus is not simply a model to be followed on the way of suffering, but a model of one who in the midst of suffering can address God as *abba*, and who can see in suffering the will of God, even with the awareness that this will could be otherwise (14:34–36)."[179]

Mark reports the content of Jesus' prayer only once but reports the sharp commands Jesus gives when he finds his disciples asleep the three times he returns to them. The first time he asks, "Simon ... are you asleep? Couldn't you keep watch for one hour?"[180] and commands, "Watch and pray so that you will not fall into temptation" (14:37–38). The second time they are still sleeping. Mark does not record what Jesus says but only notes, "They did not know what to say to him" (14:40). The third time, when the betrayer approaches, he rouses them from sleep with a sharp command, "Rise! Let us go!" (14:42). These are the last words he speaks directly to them in Mark, and the command echoes his first words to them, "Come follow me!" (1:17). This time they do not come after him but scatter in different directions. While Jesus modeled faithful "watching," his disciples failed miserably to watch and pray. Their sleep during Jesus' struggle in prayer reveals that "the disciples, like others, require redemption and liberation."[181] The "flesh" of all humanity is weak and is the bridgehead "through which Satan moves to distract people from God's plan; it

174. Urs Sommer, *Die Passionsgeschichte des Markusevangeliums: Überlegungen zur Bedeutung der Geschichte für den Glauben* (WUNT 2/58; Tübingen: Mohr Siebeck, 1993), 105.

175. Eduard Schweizer, *The Good News according to Mark* (trans. Donald H. Madvig; Richmond, VA: John Knox, 1970), 311.

176. Addressing God with the familiar *Abba* that a child might use expresses this trusting, intimate relationship and his confidence in his Father's loving care.

177. Stephen P. Ahearne-Kroll, *The Psalms of Lament in Mark's Passion: Jesus' Davidic Suffering* (SNTSMS 142; Cambridge: Cambridge University Press, 2007), 187.

178. Collins, *Beginning*, 72.

179. Donahue, "A Neglected Factor in the Theology of Mark," 587.

180. Simon is not his apostolic name (3:16). He is identified as Peter everywhere in Mark except in 1:16, 29, 30, 36, before his nickname is mentioned in 3:16.

181. Donald H. Juel, *Mark* (ACNT; Minneapolis: Augsburg, 1990), 197.

represents the vulnerability of the human being."[182] They need to be baptized with the Holy Spirit (1:8) to be able to fend off Satan's onslaughts.

2.7.3.3 The Betrayal and Arrest of Jesus and the Flight of the Disciples (14:43–52)

Judas leads a crowd brandishing swords and clubs to Jesus and identifies him with a traitorous kiss, and they seize him. Someone, identified only as one "standing near," draws his sword and cuts off the ear of the servant of the high priest. Jesus says nothing to the sword-buckling disciple but chides the arresting party instead for coming after him as if he were someone leading an armed rebellion. Jesus' response makes clear before his trial that Jesus is no seditious firebrand, and his statement that Scripture is being fulfilled reminds the audience once again that the Son of Man is handed over in accordance with God's will.

The scene closes with the disciples shamelessly deserting Jesus and fleeing for their lives. When one is almost seized, he leaves his garment behind and speeds away naked. The mad dash to escape reveals that it is now every man for himself and lays bare how flimsy their pledges of never-ending loyalty were.

2.7.4 Jesus' Hearing before the Sanhedrin and Peter's Denial (14:53–72)

Mark's trial scene pins the primary responsibility and initiative for Jesus' death on the high priest and his Sanhedrin. Mark has told us that the high priests, teachers of the law, and elders have been "looking" for how they might "kill him" (11:18), how they might "arrest him" (12:12), and how they might "arrest Jesus" and "kill him" (14:1). Jesus may have been crucified as if he were guilty of sedition, but the trial scenes make it clear that he was not.

The four scenes that follow, Jesus' interrogation by the high priest and the council (14:53–72), his hearing before Pilate (15:1–22), his crucifixion (15:23–33), and his death and burial (15:34–47), reveal some structural parallels.[183]

1. The Hearing before Sanhedrin (14:53–72)
   a. 14:53–64 Jesus is led to the high priest for the hearing
   b. 14:65 Some mock Jesus as a prophet
   c. 14:66–72a Peter denies Jesus three times
   d. 14:72b Exit
2. The Hearing before Pilate (15:1–22)
   a. 15:1–15 Jesus is led to Pilate for trial
   b. 15:16–20 The soldiers mock Jesus as the King of the Jews
   c. 15:21 Simon of Cyrene carries Jesus' cross
   d. 15:22 Exit

182. Brown, *Death*, 1:199.

183. Olivette Genest, *Le Christ de la Passion—perspective structurale: analyse de Marc 14,53–15,47, des parallèles bibliques et extra bibliques* (Recherches 21; Montréal: Bellarmin, 1978), 116.

3. The Crucifixion (15:23–33)
    a. 15:23–27 Jesus is crucified between two robbers
    b. 15:29–32a Priests and passersby mock Jesus as Savior, Messiah, and king of Israel
    c. 15:32b The ones crucified with him revile him
    d. 15:33 Darkness covers the whole land
4. The Death and Burial (15:34–47)
    a. 15:34–38 Jesus dies
    b. 15:39 The centurion confesses Jesus to be the Son of God
    c. 15:40–41 The women followers of Jesus watch from afar
    d. 15:42–47 Joseph of Arimathea buries Jesus in a tomb

In the first component, the focus falls on what happens to Jesus. The second component highlights christological titles: prophet, King of the Jews, Savior, Messiah, king of Israel, and the Son of God. The third component reveals the stance toward or response of others to Jesus: denying knowing him, carrying his cross, reviling him, and watching from afar. The conclusion of each scene is marked by a transition that leads to the next scene.

2.7.4.1 Peter Follows from a Distance to the High Priest's Courtyard (14:53–54)

Jesus is led to the high priest, and Peter follows from a safe distance and enters the high priest's courtyard. By introducing the two settings, Mark intends to show that Peter's denial of Jesus takes place at the same time that Jesus makes his bold acknowledgment before the high priest and the council. While Jesus is under fire inside, Peter warms himself by the fire outside in the courtyard.

2.7.4.2 Jesus Affirms his Identity before the Sanhedrin (14:55–65)

Jesus is taken before a hastily gathered council of the high priest. They have sought witnesses to provide testimony that will enable them to condemn him to death, but even those suborned to commit perjury cannot get their stories straight. They claim to have heard him say, "I will destroy this temple made with human hands and in three days will build another, not made with hands" (14:58). Jesus never said that in Mark's gospel, but Mark may not want to discredit entirely this statement. In 11:17, Jesus alluded to Jer 7:11, which appears in a context that threatens the destruction of the temple. He also told the allegory in the hearing of the chief priests, teachers of the law, and the elders about the wicked tenants who will be destroyed and the vineyard given to others with the conclusion from the citation of Ps 118:22–23, "The stone the builders rejected has become the cornerstone" (12:10). Privately, to his disciples, he expressly prophesied that the temple will be destroyed in 13:1–2.[184]

184. Donald H. Juel, *Messiah and Temple: The Trial of Jesus in the Gospel of Mark* (SBLDS 31; Missoula, MT: Scholars Press, 1977), 138.

The temple leaders misconstrue what they heard Jesus say about its destruction. They probably think in terms of some kind of sorcery, which makes their accusation false. Mark assumes that his audience will recognize the truth, that the Romans will be the ones who will destroy the temple, and that God will be the one who will raise up another temple not made with hands.

Jesus remains silent before his false accusers (see Isa 53:7; Pss 38:12–15; 39:9). The Jewish leaders are stalled in their plan to condemn Jesus to death until the high priest intervenes and confronts Jesus directly in frustration: "Are you the Messiah, the Son of the Blessed One?" (14:61). Jesus makes his bold confession, saying "I am" and prophesying that they will see him "sitting at the right hand of the Mighty One and coming on the clouds of heaven" (14:62). Jesus incriminates himself and provides all the testimony they need to confirm their bias that he is guilty of blasphemy. He claims to be divine and implies that he not only has permanent access to the Most Holy Place but also that a second throne will be placed beside God's throne for him. Shepherd comments on the irony: "But in bringing him to death, removing his power, they actually bring him to power at God's right hand."[185] What they considered to be blasphemy is the truth; ironically they are the ones who have the greatest guilt.

Further irony arises. After the decision to take deadly action against Jesus, certain ones spit on him as a sign of repudiation (Num 12:14; Deut 25:9), slap him around, cover his face, and goad him to prophesy. They are not asking him simply to guess who struck him (see Matt 26:68 and Luke 22:64). Some assumed that the Messiah would have prophetic gifts (Isa 11:2–4), and Mark uses this taunt to remind his audience that Jesus has prophesied about what would happen to him, and all his prophecies are coming true.

Jesus told his disciples, "The Son of Man will be delivered over to the chief priests and the teachers of the law. They will condemn him to death and will hand him over to the Gentiles, who will mock him and spit on him, flog him and kill him" (10:33–34). He prophesied that the disciples would be scattered when the shepherd was struck (14:27), and this prophecy was unhappily fulfilled when the disciples fled at his arrest (14:50–52). He also prophesied that Peter would deny him three times this very night. The KJV translation effectively captures: "Before the cock crow twice, thou shalt deny me thrice" (14:30), and that prophecy is being fulfilled as these who are mocking Jesus speak. The audience also knows that he prophesied that the temple would be destroyed (13:2), and it soon will be (or was). He prophesied that after he is raised, he will go before the disciples to Galilee (14:28), and that too is fulfilled (16:7). What is yet to be fulfilled is this prophecy, "And you will see the Son of Man sitting at the right hand of the Mighty One and coming on the clouds of heaven" (14:62), but Jesus' prophecies have been fulfilled to the letter and his followers trust that this momentous prophecy also will be fulfilled.

185. Tom Shepherd, "The Irony of Power in the Trial of Jesus and the Denial by Peter—Mark 14:53–72," in *The Trial and Death of Jesus: Essays on the Passion Narrative in Mark* (ed. Geert van Oyen and Tom Shepherd; CBET 45; Leuven: Peeters, 2006), 241.

The irony of this taunt, then, presses the audience to affirm that Jesus is the true prophet whose "words will never pass away" (13:31).

2.7.4.3 Peter Denies Jesus Three Times in the Courtyard (14:66–72)

Peter pledged to Jesus that he would not "fall away," that he was ready to die with him, and that he would never disown him (14:29, 31). When he faces the weakest of pressure from a persistent servant girl who recognizes him as having been "with that Nazarene, Jesus," he shows himself to be cowardly and weak. He claims not to understand what she is talking about, denies being "one of them," and then invokes a curse and denies knowing Jesus. Trying to save his own life, he denies Jesus rather than himself (8:34–35). When the rooster crows a second time, he awakens to what he has done and remembers Jesus' prophecy. He bursts into tears. Mark does not narrate what he did next and leaves it to the audience's imagination.

2.7.5 Jesus' Hearing before Pilate and the Mockery by the Soldiers (15:1–39)

Pilate's investigation is marked by indecision. If Jesus claims to be king, he is guilty of a crime against the sovereign power of Rome. Mark has emphasized Jesus' greater authority throughout the gospel. The emphasis is on Jesus' innocence, but Jesus refuses to do anything that might help rescue him from this position and accepts his divine destiny, knowing that it leads to a glorious end.

2.7.5.1 Pilate's Failed Interrogation of Jesus (15:1–5)

The high priest and the leadership handed over Jesus to Pilate "very early in the morning." The reader can only infer from Pilate's first question to Jesus, "Are you the king of the Jews?" that the leaders had substituted the religious charge of blasphemy, which was their concern, with a political charge that would grab the Roman governor's attention. The term "king" appears six times (15:2, 9, 12, 18, 26, 32). The Romans, according to Tacitus (*Hist.* 5.9), considered any king not appointed by them to be a threat. By sending Jesus to Pilate "bound" (15:1) and presumably with an armed guard, the Jewish leaders give the impression that they regard him to be a dangerous agitator.

Jesus' enigmatic answer to Pilate's question, "You have said so," has a defiant edge to it. This phrase can have a variety of meanings, depending on the inflection, but it seems to mean here, "Whatever you say." Jesus refuses to defend himself, and his silence in response to the charges brought against him by the chief priests evokes Pilate's amazement. Pilate may recognize that it is ludicrous to think that Jesus is a threat to Roman hegemony, and he wants to release him, but he cannot let go someone who refuses to deny serious charges.

2.7.5.2 Pilate's Failed Attempts to Release Jesus (15:6–15)

Mark introduces the next scene by explaining that at the festival time one prisoner, whom the crowd requested, would be given amnesty. The governor mostly could do whatever he liked, and releasing a prisoner once a year could serve to appease a restless people. Pilate's ploy to release Jesus by asking the crowd if they wanted him to release "the king of the Jews" (15:9) backfires. Stirred up by the high priests, this crowd (probably made up of their supporters) cries out instead for the release of a certain Barabbas, whom Mark identifies as having connections to insurrectionists that had committed murder during an uprising. Mark does not describe the nature of the uprising, but Josephus cites many disturbances leading up to the Jewish revolt against Rome in an increasing spiral of violence. When Pilate asks what to do "with the one you call the king of the Jews," he is caught off guard even more. They cry out for him to be crucified.

Two points deserve notice as they touch upon Mark's theology. First, Mark narrates that Pilate knew that "it was out of self-interest that the chief priests had handed Jesus over to him" (15:10). The word translated "self-interest" is more accurately translated as "envy." Jesus' reputation has spread far and wide (1:28; 3:7–8; 6:14), and it would not escape the Jewish leaders that when he taught in the temple "the large crowd" that gathered around him "listened to him with delight" (12:37). In their extensive treatment of envy in the ancient world and in Mark, Hagedorn and Neyrey argue that the honor that Jesus has garnered prompted the leaders' envy, which inevitably "ushers in conflict and hostility."[186] Their envy ironically concedes Jesus' superiority. One does not envy someone who is pitiful.

Second, Pilate underscores Jesus' innocence when he asks the crowd, "Why? What crime has he committed?" (15:14). This question goes unanswered, and the roar of the crowd increases in volume as they cry out for Jesus to be crucified. Pilate concedes his authority to a boisterous crowd and orders that an innocent man to be put to death.[187] Jesus is not guilty of anything and is substituted for a brigand who is guilty of sedition and murder. The crowd not only chooses Barabbas over Jesus, they choose crucifixion for Jesus. Bird comments, "The tragedy is that what the Jewish leaders and the crowd want to do with *their* Messiah is hang him on a *Roman* cross."[188] As a result, Barabbas will go free, and Jesus will take his place on a cross that was intended for him.[189]

---

186. Hagedorn and Neyrey, "'It Was Out of Envy,'" 16.

187. He could have declared Jesus insane, scourged him, and then let him go as the governor Albinus did in the case of Jesus, son of Ananias, who was brought to him by Jewish leaders for speaking stridently against the temple (Josephus, *J.W.* 6.5.3 §§300–309).

188. Michael F. Bird, *Jesus Is the Christ:The Messianic Testimony of the Gospels* (Downers Grove, IL: Intervarsity Press, 2012), 40.

189. Schweizer, *Mark*, 338, states, "Without any dogmatic statement, the idea of vicarious suffering is suggested by placing side by side Barabbas who was set free and Jesus who was handed over to be crucified." Edwards, *Mark*, 461, comments, "It is not difficult to see in this exchange a reflection of the substitutionary understanding of atonement."

2.7.5.3 The Soldiers' Mockery of Jesus as the King of the Jews (15:16–20)

Pilate has Jesus flogged and then hands him over to the soldiers who will crucify him. The whole cohort of soldiers gather around him in the courtyard of Pilate's praetorium to make sport of the seemingly ridiculous charge that Jesus is the king of the Jews.[190] They robe him in purple, plait a crown of thorns, jokingly salute him as if he were Caesar, "Hail, king of the Jews," and kneel before him in false homage, perhaps pretending to sue for justice or to consult him on state affairs. The soldiers mix mockery with physical abuse by striking him on the head with a staff (or reed) and spitting on him, a detail that evokes Isaiah 50:6: "I offered my back to those who beat me, my cheeks to those who pulled out my beard; I did not hide my face from mocking and spitting."

2.7.6 The Crucifixion (15:21–32)

Mark is restrained in describing the horrors of the crucifixion.[191] The details are related sparingly so that the focus falls on the theological significance of Jesus' death. Simon carries Jesus' cross. Jesus rejects the offer of myrrhed wine. Soldiers cast lots to see who will get to take his clothes that have been stripped from him, leaving him with only a loincloth. The hours are chimed as they pass by to signify the progression of events and "the purposefulness of divine providence in bringing about Jesus' death."[192] He is crucified between two bandits.[193] He is executed as the king of the Jews. The various taunts recall the charges at the trial and unintentionally proclaim the truth about Jesus.

2.7.6.1 The Conscription of a Passerby to Carry the Cross (15:21–22)

Normally, the condemned man carried the crossbeam (*patibulum*) to the site of his crucifixion, where it was fastened to a vertical beam already firmly embedded into the ground. Simon, coming from the country into the city, is conscripted to carry this cross as the weakened Jesus is led outside the city to the place of execution.[194] Coming from the country makes it clear that he has not participated in any of the events surrounding Jesus' condemnation.[195] He is further identified as being from

190. Thomas E. Schmidt, "Mark 15.16–32: The Crucifixion Narrative and the Roman Triumphal Procession," *NTS* 41 (1995): 1–18 (pp. 6–7), suggests that the reference to the Praetorium may be intended to make the audience think of the imperial guard in Rome. He interprets this gathering of troops as intending to evoke images of a Roman procession. A Roman audience particularly would be able to perceive the allusions.

191. Contrast the gruesome details of the scourging of the elderly Eleazar on the orders of Antiochus in 4 Macc 6:3–11.

192. Joel Marcus, *Mark 8–16* (AYB; New Haven/London: Yale University Press, 2009), 1043.

193. The "bandits" are not likely to be petty thieves, who would not normally be crucified, but insurrectionists. Martin Hengel, *The Zealots: Investigations into the Jewish Freedom Movement in the Period from Herod I until 70 A.D.* (trans. David Smith; Edinburgh: T&T Clark, 1989), 382, n. 9, notes that Josephus uses the term with one exception to refer to insurgents who led the revolt against Rome, which justifies the NIV translation "rebels." The rebels often lived off the land.

194. Brown, *Death*, 2:914–15.

195. Andreas Bedenbender, "Der Epilog des Markusevangeliums–Revisited," *Texte & Kontexte* 81/82 (1999): 40.

Cyrene in North Africa and as the father of Rufus and Alexander.[196] He may be perceived as a model for disciples who must take up their cross and follow Jesus (8:34), even though Simon has not chosen to do so but was commandeered. Gill comments: "One of the profound paradoxes of Christianity is to be found in the fact that the one who was not able to carry his own cross (15:21) is the one who enables us to carry ours."[197]

The execution takes place on Golgotha, which Mark interprets for his audience as "the place of the skull." Mark does not interpret why it was named that, but it reinforces that it was a place of death. We can only assume that it refers to a prominent place outside the wall of the city where Jesus would hang on a cross, exposed for all to see (see Heb 13:12–13).

2.7.6.2 The Offer of Wine Mixed with Myrrh (15:23)

The reasons for offering Jesus wine mingled with myrrh is much debated.[198] The emphasis falls, however, on Jesus' refusal to drink. He made a vow of abstinence at the Last Supper that he will not drink from the fruit of the vine until he drinks it new in the kingdom of God (14:25). The wine may have had a certain narcotic property that might dull the pain, but Jesus chooses to scorn the pain and drink instead the cup of suffering that God has given to him (10:38; 14:36).

2.7.6.3 Jesus' Crucifixion at the Third Hour between Two Bandits and the Division of His Garments (15:24–27)

Mark tolls the hours during the crucifixion. It is the third hour (9:00 a.m.) when they crucify him. Darkness covers the land at the sixth hour, high noon, and Jesus cries out in a loud voice at the ninth hour, the Jewish hour of prayer (15:34–35). He laconically reports that Jesus is crucified with two others, one on his left and one on his right. This detail evokes the request of James and John to sit at Jesus' right and his left in his glory (10:37). These circumstances are hardly what they had in mind. The inscription on the placard placed on the cross announces to all Jesus' crime: he is "the King of the Jews" (15:2, 9, 12, 18). Was Pilate lampooning the Jewish leaders as well as Jesus with what he thought to be a sarcastic taunt? If so, it says more than he realizes.

Mark reports the division of his garments among the soldiers as they cast lots "to see what each would get" (15:24). It was customary for the executioners to split the minor personal belongings of the person being executed (Justinian, *Digest* 48.20.6). Mark mentions this detail because the division of garments also appears in Ps 22:18. The connection guides the audience to recognize that Jesus' humiliation

---

196. I concur with Bauckham's, *Eyewitnesses*, 52, suggestion that Simon is mentioned because he is the eyewitness behind this tradition. His sons are mentioned because it was "known in the early Christian movement not from his own firsthand account but through his sons."

197. Athol Gill, *Life on the Road: The Gospel Basis for a Messianic Lifestyle* (Scottdale, PA: Herald, 1992), 63.

198. See Collins, *Mark*, 740–44.

is fully consonant with God's will. As Jesus said, "The Son of Man will go just as it is written about him" (14:21a). The textual variant in 15:28 reveals that some early copyist saw this detail as fulfilling Isa 53:12. Gnilka points out that the verb translated "to see what each would get" is the same verb that is used in 15:21 to describe Simon taking the cross. The contrast is striking. Simon takes up the cross; the soldiers take what they can get.[199] Jesus, now stripped of his clothes, suffers utter public degradation, which starkly contrasts with the transfiguration when "his clothes became dazzling white" (9:3). But both paradoxically represent moments of glory from Mark's theological perspective.

2.7.6.4 The Mockery of Jesus by the Passersby, the High Priests, and Those Crucified with Him (15:29–32)

Jesus has become a laughingstock as the passersby, the high priests, and bandits crucified with him mock him. Their mockery, however, recalls the Scripture: "All who see me mock me; they hurl insults, shaking their heads" (Ps 22:7; see 109:25). The scoffing recalls the charges introduced during his interrogation before the high priest and his council. The passersby raise the charge that he supposedly said that he would destroy the temple and build it in three days (14:58; 15:29). They goad him to come down from the cross and save himself (15:30). The mockery reinforces a truth beyond their range of vision that only Mark's audience recognizes. Jesus' death does in effect destroy the temple made with hands and becomes the foundation for a new one not made with hands.

The chief priests and the teachers of the law join in the mockery next. They sneer that he saved others, but nailed to a cross he cannot save himself. The reference to saving others recalls the verb used when Jesus healed many during his ministry (3:4; 5:23, 28, 34; 6:56; and 10:52). He taught that whoever wants to save his own life will ultimately lose it (8:35). Their taunt ironically expresses the truth. Were he to save himself now and miraculously come down from the cross, he would not be able to save others. Marshall comments, "They thus evaluate divine power purely in human, self-serving terms, according to their own standards of practice."[200] They can only see things from the human point of view and not from God's perspective (8:35), and therefore they would see and believe nothing were he to come down from the cross. Things get worse when the bandits crucified with him even join in the mockery, but it makes clear that Jesus was not allied with insurgents.

2.7.7 Jesus' Death on the Cross (15:33–39)

2.7.7.1 Jesus' Cry to "My God" and His Death (15:33–37)

Darkness shrouds the whole land for the next three hours from the sixth to the ninth hour (noon until 3:00 p.m.). The darkness can signify many things: mourning

199. Joachim Gnilka, *Das Evangelium nach Markus* (EKKNT; Zurich: Benziger/Neukirchener Verlag, 1978–1979), 2:317.

200. Marshall, *Faith as a Theme*, 206.

(Jer 4:27–28); the death of great men;[201] God's judgment (Exod 10:21–23; Isa 13:9–13; Jer 13:16; Joel 2:10; 3:14–15; Amos 5:18, 20; 8:9–10); the great day of the Lord (13:24); and a new beginning (Gen 1:2; Job 38:17; Ps 74:12–20). It does not indicate God's absence.

At the ninth hour, Mark records Jesus' cry in Aramaic, "*Eloi, Eloi, lema sabachthani*?" and translates it, "My God, my God, why have you forsaken me?" (15:34). The cry echoes the opening lines of Psalm 22. There are other parallels to the psalm in the crucifixion account, and Winn insists that this cry underscores those connections:

> Through the parallels with the psalm, Mark not only focuses on Jesus' death but also points forward to Jesus' imminent resurrection and exaltation. Therefore, Jesus' words spoken on the cross are not merely indicators of Jesus' total rejection and isolation, but rather they help the reader to understand Jesus' death in terms of Ps 22 ... they also remind the alert reader that this suffering is only temporary and that power and glory are imminent.[202]

Juel objects to the view that this lament expresses confidence in God, since other texts "would have been far more suitable for such purposes." Notably, Luke has Jesus cite Psalm 31:5 as his last words: "Father, into your hands I commit my spirit" (Luke 23:46).[203] That a positive reading of the psalm expresses "almost the opposite meaning of what Jesus is portrayed as saying!" as Brown notes,[204] would explain why it would not have been included in Luke. The psalm expresses a bitter lament and the feeling of total desolation "in which Jesus felt the horror of sin so deeply that for a time the closeness of His communion with the Father was obscured," as Taylor phrases it.[205] In my view, Jesus turns to a Scripture passage that describes his frightful circumstances and his intense feeling of abandonment, but also his faith in "my God." Jesus always addresses God as Father in Mark with this one exception, which suggests that Mark presents him as quoting the psalm. Ahearne-Kroll notes that the psalm seeks

> to elicit the saving response of God by (1) appealing to God's past relationship with Israel and with the psalmist, (2) vividly depicting the psalmist's sufferings, and (3) vowing praise that will bring untold glory to God. With this in mind, Mark 15:34 takes on a significance that does not fall into the either/or categories of despair or hope that have given rise to the polarization of scholarship on this verse.[206]

201. Virgil, *Georgics* 1.463–68, writes: "the Sun will give you signs. Who dare say the Sun is false? Nay, he oft warns us that dark uprisings threaten, that treachery and hidden wars are upswelling. Nay, he had pity for Rome when, after Caesar sank from sight, he veiled his shining face in dusky gloom, and a godless age feared everlasting night."

202. Adam Winn, *The Purpose of Mark's Gospel: An Early Christian Response to Roman Imperial Propaganda* (WUNT 2/245; Tübingen: Mohr Siebeck, 2008), 135.

203. Donald H. Juel, *Messianic Exegesis: Christological Interpretation of the Old Testament in Early Christianity* (Philadelphia: Fortress, 1988), 114.

204. Brown, *Death*, 2:1049–51.

205. Taylor, *Mark*, 594. Francis J. Moloney, *The Gospel of Mark: A Commentary* (Peabody, MA: Hendrickson, 2002), 326, comments that the cry should not be softened but interpreted as a straightforward expression of abandonment so as "to capture fully the Markan presentation of the crucified Christ."

206. Ahearne-Kroll, *Psalms of Lament*, 209.

The psalm is an expression of protesting faith, not despair. The first line captures the mood of the entire psalm that expresses "outrage, anger, accusation, questioning, and pain at the thought that God has abandoned him in his time of greatest need."[207] It is a cry to get God to do something that will deliver him from suffering.[208] God answers the prayer immediately to end the suffering, though the release comes through death. Jesus dies immediately, a surprisingly quick death.[209] And God will raise him from death and exalt him to the right hand of power. A Gentile confesses him to be the Son of God, and the good news will be proclaimed throughout the world.

The confusion of some who think that Jesus is calling Elijah makes a theological point for Mark. One dashes off to get some wine vinegar, puts it on a sponge, and lifts it up on a staff to offer it to him, but another stops him with a cynical taunt to wait and see if Elijah will indeed come to save him (15:36).[210] They represent the befuddled hearing and contemptuous attitude of the hostile world. Wanting to "see" if Elijah comes to take Jesus "down" parallels the speech of the chief priests and scribes who want Jesus to "come down" so that they might "see."[211] Jesus has said, however, that Elijah has already come, "and they have done to him everything they wished" (9:13). He had come in the person of John the Baptist, who was beheaded by Herod (6:14–29). Elijah will not come to rescue him, and Jesus dies with "a loud cry," breathing out his life (15:37).

2.7.7.2 The Splitting of the Temple Veil (15:38)

Mark adds another detail with theological implications. At Jesus' death, the temple veil splits from top to bottom (15:38). It is a divine sign, but what it signifies is open to many interpretations and is dealt with below. One thing is sure, the veil can no longer function to separate the Most Holy Place from the less holy and the profane. Its tearing makes it "vulnerable to the invasion of the profane."[212]

2.7.7.3 The Confession of the Centurion (15:39)

Seeing how he died, the centurion who oversaw the crucifixion makes the extraordinary confession, "Surely this man was the Son of God!" (15:39). For the first time in the gospel, a human being voices what God had announced at the beginning of the gospel, "You are my Son" (1:11).[213] The centurion's statement, like the father's

207. Ibid.

208. Ibid., 210.

209. When Joseph of Arimathea went to Pilate to request to bury the body, Pilate was surprised to hear that he was already dead and checked with the centurion to make sure that it was true (15:44).

210. In 1QH^a 8:9–11, vinegary wine is connected to deceivers who persecute the righteous of the Qumran community and give it for their thirst to mock them. Craig A. Evans, *Mark 8:27-16:20* (WBC 34b; Nashville: Thomas Nelson, 2001), 501, however, contends that the soldiers are offering their finest wine to "the king of the Jews."

211. Frank J. Matera, *The Kingship of Jesus: Composition and Theology in Mark 15* (SBLDS 66; Chico, CA: Scholars Press, 1982), 123.

212. Brown, "The Jesus of Mark's Gospel," 41.

213. See below on the interpretation of this statement. It is not a sarcastic snicker, as some have recently interpreted it, but a genuine affirmation of Jesus' true identity that comes at the climax of the gospel. The opening word, "truly" ("surely," NIV), confirms the centurion's sincerity. One would have expected an ironic taunt to have continued the mockery that Jesus was a king. If he were ridiculing Jesus' claims, he would have been more likely to say, "Ha! This one was the King of the Jews!" The appearance of the term "Son of God" is both a dramatic and unexpected shift and would not be spoken with disdain.

imperfect faith (9:24), needs bolstering and refinement. Christians would change the imperfect verb he "*was*" to he *is*. But his confession is tied to seeing how he died, and it underlines that the confession that Jesus is the Son of God cannot gloss over that he is the one who bore disgrace, was crucified, and died.

If one asks, "Why a centurion?" Davis provides a good answer:

> Mark wanted the truth about Jesus proclaimed at the moment of his death, but all the disciples had fled, the mocking scribes were obviously inappropriate for the task, and the women's ignorance had to be preserved for the sake of the tomb scene. Who else was left to witness and interpret the decisive saving event?[214]

That a Gentile makes this declaration, however, also is in line with the theme of universal acclamation from "all the families of the nations" in Ps 22:27.[215]

2.7.8 The Burial of Jesus (15:40–47)

The statement that it was already evening, the Day of Preparation, the day before Sabbath, provides part of the motivation behind the actions of Joseph of Arimathea to ask Pilate for Jesus' body (15:42–43). Corpses must not be allowed to hang beyond sundown so as not to defile the land (Deut 21:23).[216] The onset of the Sabbath, when work is prohibited, makes Joseph's request all the more urgent. Soon it will be too late to take down the body and carry it to the tomb, so this task had to be rushed.

Mark identifies Joseph as one who "was himself waiting for the kingdom of God" (15:43). He is not identified as a disciple, but Mark has applied the term "disciple" only to the Twelve and could not use it of Joseph of Arimathea.[217] He may be simply a pious man, like Simeon (Luke 2:25), who would be concerned about such things as unburied bodies and the defilement of the land (see Tob 1:16–20).[218] Mark's positive portrayal of Joseph's solicitude for Jesus and not the insurgents crucified with him suggests, however, some reverence for Jesus and that he may have considered him to have been unjustly executed.

Mark says that he went to Pilate "boldly" (15:43). Since Jesus was executed on the charge of claiming to be a king, even though it was trumped up, it would have been politically risky for anyone to make a request to bury him, lest they be suspected of being a sympathizer. Victims of crucifixion were given dishonorable burials if they were buried at all.[219] As a "prominent member of the Council" and

214. Philip G. Davis, "Mark's Christological Paradox," *JSNT* 35 (1989): 15.

215. Daniel Guichard, "La Reprise du Psaum 22 dans le récit de la mort de Jésus (Marc 15,21–41)," *FoiVie* 87 (1988): 64.

216. Philo paraphrases the text, "Let not the sun go down upon the crucified but let them be buried in the earth before sundown" (*Spec. Laws* 3.151–52).

217. Aloysius M. Ambrozic, *The Hidden Kingdom: A Redaction-Critical Study of the References to the Kingdom of God in Mark's Gospel* (CBQMS 2; Washington, DC: Catholic Biblical Association of America, 1972), 243, claims that he "had accepted Jesus' message of the kingdom."

218. When Stephen was stoned, pious men, *not* Christians, buried him and made great lamentation over him (Acts 8:2).

219. Horace quotes one saying to a slave, "You'll hang on the cross to feed crows" (*Epistles* 1.16.48), which reveals that victims could be left on their crosses for days after their death.

presumably a wealthy man, however, he is likely to be above suspicion.[220] Pilate consents after consulting with the centurion to make sure that Jesus is dead.[221] This detail emphasizes that Jesus was really dead. Joseph not only intervened with Pilate to bury Jesus, but he also bought a linen cloth to wrap his body for burial and placed him in a tomb carved from rock, rather than a shallow pit. These actions hint that Joseph is like the teacher of the law whom Jesus said was not far from the kingdom of God (12:34). What he may not (yet?) appreciate is that the kingdom of God he was waiting for already has come in Jesus and in his death.[222]

The women followers of Jesus rise to unexpected prominence at the end of the gospel as the Twelve have vanished. Three are named, Mary Magdalene, Mary the mother of James the younger and of Joseph, and Salome (15:40). They are identified as following Jesus from Galilee to Jerusalem and serving him, along with other women (15:41). It is most likely that these women are named because they are the source of the tradition. They stood far off and witnessed the crucifixion to the end, saw where Jesus was buried, and saw the stone rolled to shut the tomb's entrance. They apparently do not see if Jesus' body was anointed, which sets up their return to the tomb after the Sabbath to anoint him.

2.8 The Announcement of Jesus' Resurrection to the Women at the Tomb (16:1–8)

The Passion Narrative began with an anonymous woman lavishly anointing Jesus, which he interpreted as the preparation for his burial. The gospel ends with women seeking to anoint Jesus after his burial but finding the large stone rolled away from the entrance and Jesus gone. A young man dressed in a white robe sitting on the right side, an angelic figure, announces to them that they have the right tomb. They are looking for Jesus the Nazarene, who was crucified. "He has risen! He is not here" (16:6).

Van Iersel highlights the parallels between the introduction to the gospel and its ending.[223] In both scenes, messengers appear: John the Baptist and a young man. Their dress is described so as to identify their role. John the Baptist is dressed in clothing made of camel's hair, with a leather belt around his waist, clothing that is deliberately reminiscent of the prophet Elijah's (2 Kgs 1:8; see Zech 13:4). The young man is dressed in a radiant white robe, which is clothing that identifies him as a heavenly being (Dan 7:9; Acts 1:10; 10:30; Rev 4:4; 2 Macc 11:8–10; *1 En.* 62:15–16; 87:2; see also Rev 6:11; 7:9, 13). Both figures make announcements about Jesus that are not narrated by Mark: he will baptize with the Holy Spirit (1:8); he

220. See Raymond E. Brown, "The Burial of Jesus (Mark 15:42–47)," *CBQ* 50 (1988): 233–45, on the Roman practice regarding the burial of crucifixion victims. He contends that Jesus was given a dishonorable burial, but the positive aspects of Mark's account seriously weaken that conclusion.

221. The verb "he gave" can have a more formal meaning that means he confers a benefit on him by giving him the corpse (15:45).

222. Marcus, *Mark 8–16*, 1075.

223. Van Iersel, *Mark*, 21.

has been raised from the dead (16:6). In both scenes Jesus' movements are noted: he comes from Galilee (1:9), and he goes to Galilee (16:7).

Mark's account of the resurrection is terse. "He has risen" is expressed in one word in Greek, but it means that Jesus' predictions that he would be raised (8:31; 9:31; 10:34) have been fulfilled. Secrecy is over, and the command for the women to go tell the disciples the news and to tell them that he goes before them to Galilee is the first time that Jesus' followers are told to tell something about him. The news now can be spread abroad: Jesus, who was crucified, is raised.

Mark's gospel, however, ends suddenly with the strange statement that the women "said nothing to anyone, because they were afraid" (16:8). It seems to end with utter failure. The issues related to the ending will be dealt with in depth below. Suffice it to say that I take this ending to mean that the women said nothing to the general public but did relay the news to the disciples, who then regathered in Galilee, where they were first chosen.[224]

224. See Larry W. Hurtado, "The Women, the Tomb, and the Climax of Mark," in *A Wandering Galilean: Essays in Honour of Seán Freyne* (ed. Zuleika Rogers, Margaret Daly-Denton, and Anne Fitzpatrick McKinley; JSJSup 132; Leiden: Brill, 2009), 427–50.

Part 2

Major Themes in Mark's Theology

Chapter 3

THE INTRODUCTION TO THE GOSPEL AND TO JESUS AS THE MESSIAH AND SON OF GOD (MARK 1:1–13)

BIBLIOGRAPHY

Bacon, Benjamin Wisner. "The Prologue of Mark: A Study of Sources and Structure." *JBL* 26 (1907): 84–106. **Bauckham, Richard.** "Jesus and the Wild Animals (Mark 1:13): A Christological Image for an Ecological Age." Pp. 3–21 in *Jesus of Nazareth: Lord and Christ: Essays on the Historical Jesus and New Testament Christology*. Ed. Joel B. Green and Max Turner. Grand Rapids: Eerdmans/Carlisle: Paternoster, 1994. **Becker, Eve-Marie.** "Mk. 1:1 and the Debate on a 'Markan Prologue.'" *FN* 22 (2009): 91–106. **Best, Ernest.** *The Temptation and the Passion: The Markan Soteriology*. SNTSMS 2. 2nd ed. Cambridge: Cambridge University Press, 1990. **Boring, M. Eugene.** "Mark 1:1–15 and the Beginning of the Gospel." *Semeia* 52 (1990): 43–81. **Caneday, A. B.** "Mark's Provocative Use of Scripture in Narration: 'He Was with the Wild Animals and Angels Ministered to Him.'" *BBR* 9 (1999): 19–36. **Cranfield, C. E. B.** "Baptism of Our Lord—A Study of St. Mark 1.9–11." *SJT* 8 (1955): 53–63. **Dixon, Edward P.** "Descending Spirit and Descending Gods: A 'Greek' Interpretation of the Spirit's 'Descent as a Dove' in Mark 1:10." *JBL* 128 (2009): 759–80. **Earl, Donald.** "Prologue-Form in Ancient Historiography." Pp. 842–56 in *ANRW*, Vol. 1/2. Ed. H. Temporini; Berlin/New York: de Gruyter, 1972. **Edwards, James R.** "The Baptism of Jesus according to the Gospel of Mark." *JETS* 34 (1991): 43–57. **Evans, Craig A.** "Mark's Incipit and the Priene Calendar Inscription: From Jewish Gospel to Greco-Roman Gospel." *JGRChJ* 1 (2000): 67–81. **Feneberg, Wolfgang.** *Der Markusprolog: Studien zur Formbestimmung des Evangeliums*. Munich: Kösel, 1974. **France, R. T.** "The Beginning of Mark." *RTR* 49 (1990): 11–19. **Giblin, Charles Homer.** "The Beginning of the Ongoing Gospel (Mk 1,2–16,8)." Pp. 975–85 in *The Four Gospels 1992: Festschrift Frans Neirynck*. Vol. 2. BETL 100. Ed. Frans van Segbroeck et al. Leuven: Leuven University Press, 1992. **Gibson, Jeffrey B.** "Jesus' Wilderness Temptation according to Mark." *JSNT* 53 (1994): 3–34. **Guelich, Robert A.** "'The Beginning of the Gospel': Mark 1:1–15." *BR* 27 (1982): 5–15. **Guijarro, Santiago.** "Why Does the Gospel of Mark Begin as It Does?" *BTB* 33 (2003): 28–38. **Heil, John Paul.** "Jesus with the Wild Animals in Mark 1:13." *CBQ* 68

(2006): 63–78. **Hooker, Morna D.** "Beginnings and Endings." Pp. 184–202 in *The Written Gospel*. Ed. Markus Bockmuehl and Donald A. Hagner. Cambridge: Cambridge University Press, 2005. Eadem. "This Is the Good News: The Challenge of Mark's Beginning." Pp. 30–44 in *Preaching Mark's Unsettling Messiah*. Ed. David Fleer and Dave Bland. St. Louis: Chalice, 2006. **Keck, Leander E.** "The Introduction to Mark's Gospel." *NTS* 12 (1965–66): 352–70. **Klauck, Hans-Josef.** *Vorspiel im Himmel? Erzähltechnik und Theologie im Markusprolog*. BibS(N) 32. Neukirchen-Vluyn: Neukirchener Verlag, 1997. **Lambrecht, Jan.** "John the Baptist and Jesus in Mark 1.1–15: Markan Redaction of Q?" *NTS* 38 (1992): 357–84. **Marcus, Joel.** *The Way of the Lord: Christological Exegesis of the Old Testament in the Gospel of Mark*. Louisville: Westminster John Knox, 1992. **Marshall, I. Howard.** "Son of God or Servant of Yahweh?—A Reconsideration of Mark 1.11." *NTS* 15 (1968–69): 326–36. **Matera, Frank J.** "The Prologue as the Interpretative Key to Mark's Gospel." *JSNT* 34 (1988): 3–20. **Mauser, Ulrich.** *Christ in the Wilderness: The Wilderness Theme in the Second Gospel and Its Basis in the Biblical Tradition*. SBT 39. Naperville, IL: Allenson, 1963. **Peppard, Michael.** "The Eagle and the Dove: Roman Imperial Sonship and the Baptism of Jesus (Mark 1.9–11)." *NTS* 56 (2010): 431–51. **Pesch, Rudolf.** "Anfang des Evangeliums Jesu Christi: Eine Studie zum Prolog des Markusevangeliums (Mk 1,1–15)." Pp. 108–44 in *Die Zeit Jesu: Festschrift für Heinrich Schlier*. Ed. Günther Bornkamm and Karl Rahner. Freiburg/Basel: Herder, 1970. **Sankey, Paul J.** "Promise and Fulfilment: Reader-Response to Mark 1.1–15." *JSNT* 58 (1995): 3–18. **Seitz, Oscar Jacob Frank.** "Praeparatio Evangelica in the Markan Prologue." *JBL* 82 (1963): 201–6. **Shepherd, Tom.** "The Narrative Role of John and Jesus in Mark 1.1–15." Pp. 151–68 in *Biblical Interpretation in Early Christian Gospels*. Vol. 1, *The Gospel of Mark*. Ed. Thomas R. Hatina. LNTS 304. London/New York: T&T Clark, 2006. **Stegner, William R.** "The Baptism of Jesus and the Binding of Isaac: An Analysis of Mark 1:9–11." Pp. 331–47 in *The Answers Lie Below: Essays in Honor of Lawrence Edmund Toombs*. Ed. Henry O. Thompson. Lanham, MD: University Press of America, 1984. **Stock, Augustin.** "Hinge Transitions in Mark's Gospel." *BTB* 15 (1985): 27–31. **Ulansey, David.** "The Heavenly Veil Torn: Mark's Cosmic *Inclusio*." *JBL* 110 (1991): 123–25. **Van Henten, Jan Willem.** "The First Testing of Jesus: A Rereading of Mark 1.12–13." *NTS* 45 (1999): 349–66. **Voorhis, John Winfield.** "The Baptism of Jesus and His Sinlessness: An Outline Discussion." *EvQ* 7 (1935): 39–53. **Wasserman, Tommy.** "The 'Son of God' Was in the Beginning (Mark 1:1)." *JTS* 62 (2011): 20–50. **Watts, Rikki E.** *Isaiah's New Exodus in Mark*. WUNT 2/88. Tübingen: Mohr Siebeck, 1997.

3.1 The Title of Mark's Gospel (Mark 1:1)

Mark does not begin his narrative like a normal biography by introducing Jesus' home and family background, though he knows this information (3:31; 6:1–6), or by describing his appearance. He focuses instead on the facets that form the basis of the belief that Jesus is the Christ and the Son of God.[1] In this introduction, the audience alone receives vital, behind-the-scenes information that remains hidden in various degrees to all of the human characters when the rest of the drama begins. Lohmeyer writes that Mark's opening section (1:1–13) is like a prologue[2] that comes from heaven, but at the same time it is more than a prologue because it begins the eschatological event.[3] Klauck entitles his monograph on this curtain-raiser *Vorspiel im Himmel?* ("Prelude [or Overture] in Heaven") and concludes that the prologue presents the inbreaking of heaven into earthly reality and fleetingly unveils the mystery to the audience.[4] It expresses central aspects of Mark's theology in a nutshell and therefore deserves special attention.

How the opening line of the gospel relates to what follows is ambiguous, and there are at least ten options for explaining its relationship to what follows.[5] Three basic options have received the most attention among interpreters. It serves as (1) a heading for 1:2–8 or 1:2–13 (15); (2) a heading combined with the scriptural citation (1:2–3) introducing 1:4–8 or 1:4–13 (15); or (3) the title or incipit for the entire gospel.

3.1.1 A Heading for 1:2–8 or 1:2–13 (15)

The phrase could introduce the description of the role of John the Baptizer in 1:2–8.[6] Based on this reading, the gospel story begins with the fulfillment of Isaiah's promise of a coming herald preaching in the wilderness and John's call for a repentance baptism for the forgiveness of sins. This interpretation accords with the apostles' preaching in Acts that traces the beginning of the story to the baptism of John (Acts 1:21–22; 10:37; 13:24–25).

The phrase could also be the heading for 1:2–13 and include Jesus' baptism accompanied by the descent of God's Spirit, the announcement from heaven identifying Jesus as the beloved Son, and his testing in the wilderness. If verses 14–15 are to be included in the introduction, it would also introduce Jesus' preaching about the kingdom of God in Galilee.

1. Erich Klostermann, *Das Markus-Evangelium* (HNT; Tübingen: Mohr Siebeck, 1926), 1.

2. The term "prologue" to describe 1:1–13 was first used by Benjamin Wisner Bacon, "The Prologue of Mark: A Study of Sources and Structure," *JBL* 26 (1907): 84–106. This terminology has since become prevalent. Eve-Marie Becker, "Mk 1:1 and the Debate on a 'Markan Prologue,'" *FN* 22 (2009): 96–97, questions the historical accuracy of this term since, according to Aristotle (*Poetics* 12.1452b), it introduces a tragedy right before the *parodos* of the choir. A *prooemium* introduces a prose text. To use the term "prologue" basically redefines the ancient literary terminology. She believes that the terms "introduction" or *Vorgeschichte* (prehistory) are more apt.

3. Ernst Lohmeyer, *Das Evangelium des Markus* (KEK; 2nd ed.; Göttingen: Vandenhoeck & Ruprecht, 1963), 9. Rikki Watts, "The Psalms in Mark's Gospel," in *The Psalms in the New Testament* (ed. Steve Moyise and Maarten J. J. Menken; London/New York: T&T Clark, 2004), 27–28, infers that Mark's "opening mixed citation, the rent heavens, and descent of the Spirit already indicate his story's eschatological setting and the imminence of the Lord's saving intervention (cf. 1:15)."

4. Hans-Josef Klauck, *Vorspiel im Himmel? Erzähltechnik und Theologie im Markusprolog* (Biblisch-theologische Studien 32; Neukirchen-Vluyn: Neukirchener Verlag, 1997), 113.

5. Cranfield, *Mark*, 34–35.

6. So ibid.; Lane, *Mark*, 42; Hooker, *Mark*, 33; Klauck, *Vorspiel*, 27–30; France, *Mark*, 50–51.

3.1.2 A Heading Combined with the Scriptural Citation (1:2–3) Introducing 1:4–8 or 1:4–13 (15)

This initial phrase could be read as the beginning of a clause that ends with the scriptural citation in verses 2–3 and serves as a subtitle that introduces the following prefatory account in 1:4–13 or 1:4–15.[7] Verses 2–3 serve as "a scriptural comment on v. 1" rather than beginning a new section introducing John the Baptizer.[8] Guelich translates it: "The beginning of the gospel of Jesus Messiah, Son of God, as written by Isaiah the prophet."[9] Since the adverb "as" (*kathōs*) in v. 2 does not normally begin a new sentence and usually connects what comes before to what follows (see 4:33; 9:13; 11:6; 14:16, 21; 15:8; 16:7),[10] this interpretation relieves Mark of writing clumsy grammar that begins the narrative with an adverb.

Giblin disputes these first two interpretations by asking why a work would begin with a subtitle but not have any other subtitles in the rest of the gospel.[11] Since no other subtitle appears in the rest of the work to introduce a section of the narrative, this phrase would seem to have a more far-reaching function. Wikgren adds that it would be "a rather pretentious title for so short a section," and if "the good news of Jesus Christ" includes a subjective genitive idea, the good news preached by Jesus Christ, it would be "an inappropriate title for the section on John the Baptist."[12] The Scripture quotation provides the biblical background that discloses John's significance, which in turn leads into the introduction of Jesus, who is the central figure in the story. It has a "programmatic force" that encourages the reader to view everything that follows as the fulfilment of these promises.[13] It is more likely, then, that "the beginning of the good news" is meant to extend beyond vv. 2–13 (15).

3.1.3 The Title or Incipit for the Entire Gospel

Another option for interpreting this opening line, which I favor, reads it as the title, or incipit, of the whole gospel (1:2–16:8).[14] An incipit is a brief phrase that

7. Gerhard Arnold, "Mk 1:1 und Eröffnungswendungen in griechischen und lateinischen Schriften," *ZNW* 68 (1977): 123–27, argues that Mark follows the examples of Greco-Roman authors and refers to the beginning of his work so that 1:1 is not a title but linked to vv. 2–3. Klauck, *Vorspiel*, 22–23, identifies 1:1–3 as a superscript and motto and divides the rest of the prologue into two sections: the appearance of the Baptizer (1:4–8) and the appearance of Jesus (1:9–15).

8. Gundry, *Mark*, 30–33; France, *Mark*, 50. Watts, *New Exodus*, 56, claims that the "as written" is "epexegetical of v. 1: the 'gospel' of Jesus Christ is that gospel about which Isaiah wrote."

9. Robert A. Guelich, "'The Beginning of the Gospel': Mark 1:1–15," *BR* 27 (1982): 6, n. 26.

10. See also J. K. Elliott, "καθώς and ὥσπερ in the New Testament," *FN* 4 (1991): 55–58.

11. C. H. Giblin, "The Beginning of the Ongoing Gospel (Mk 1,2–16,8)," in *The Four Gospels 1992: Festschrift Frans Neirynck* (ed. Frans van Segbroeck et al.; BETL 100; Leuven: Leuven University Press, 1992), 2:984.

12. Allen Wikgren, "ΑΡΧΗ ΤΟΥ ΕΥΑΓΓΕΛΙΟΥ," *JBL* 61 (1942): 13, 15.

13. See Ambrozic, *The Hidden Kingdom*, 20.

14. So Klostermann, *Markus*, 4; Lohmeyer, *Markus*, 10; Taylor, *Mark*, 152; Leander E. Keck, "The Introduction to Mark's Gospel," *NTS* 12 (1965–66): 359–60; Pesch, *Markusevangelium*, 1:74–75; Detlev Dormeyer, "Die Kompositionsmetapher 'Evangelium Jesu Christi, des Sohnes Gottes' Mk 1.1: Ihre theologische und literarische Aufgabe in der Jesus-Biographie des Markus," *NTS* 33 (1987): 454–55; M. Eugene Boring, "Mark 1:1–15 and the Beginning of the Gospel," *Semeia* 52 (1990): 47–53; idem, *Mark*, 29–32; Marcus, *Mark 1–8*, 143, 145; Giblin, "The Beginning of the Ongoing Gospel," 2:984–85; John R. Donahue and Daniel J. Harrington, *The Gospel of Mark* (SP; Collegeville, MN: Liturgical, 2002), 59–60; Collins, *Mark*, 129–32; Craig A. Evans, "Mark's Incipit and the Priene Calendar Inscription: From Jewish Gospel to Greco-Roman Gospel," *JGRChJ* 1 (2000): 67–81; Malbon, *Mark's Jesus*, 59–61. See Edwards, *Mark*, 23. Arnold, "Mk 1,1," argues strongly against this possibility from comparisons with other

introduces a document (or selection of a document). It could be used as an ancient form of title and "introduce and define or describe the document as a whole."[15] Becker contends that the phrase is multivalent and can refer to the title of the book, the beginning of the book, and the beginning of the description of events.[16] It can introduce the beginning of the appearance of the good news while at the same time serve to describe the content of the entire narrative as the beginning of the good news. Marcus is of the same opinion that it "probably has a double reference, encompassing both the first thirteen or fifteen verses of the Gospel, its prologue ... and Mark's work as a whole." He cites Gen 1:1 (LXX) as "the prototype for such double referents." The first words of the book, "In the beginning," state the theme of the first chapter of Genesis as well as of the whole book, which is a book of beginnings.[17] Cook allows that even if John were the beginning of the gospel with his preaching and baptism, the rest of the text is the continuation of that beginning, and 1:1 applies to it also as "a descriptive title."[18]

For the following reasons, I regard the opening line's primary function as the title or incipit for the whole gospel and not limit it to a heading for the introductory section. First, it helps a reader identify quickly the subject and contents of the book. Earl observes that the physical nature of ancient book production "did not allow the reader easily to scan the body of the work to ascertain its subject. The first sentence and first paragraph performed much of the function of the title page and list of contents in a modern codex."[19]

In this vein Collins comments, "If the author intended the work to be read by a wider public, if it was to be produced in multiple copies for wider circulation, usually in the context of the book trade, the author would be quite likely to give the work a title right from the start."[20] She does not use this point to argue that 1:1 is a title, but if Mark intended his book to be read more widely than in his local community, as I propose, it makes it more likely that he would have used the

writers. Helmut Koester, "From the Kerygma-Gospel to Written Gospels," *NTS* 35 (1989): 370, boldly asserts, "There is no indication whatsoever by any of the authors of the New Testament Gospels that *euangelion* would be an appropriate title for the literature they produced." He thinks it is possible a copyist added the phrase "the beginning of the gospel of Jesus Christ" to indicate the point in his manuscript where a new writing began; so Walter Schmithals, *Das Evangelium Markus* (ÖTK; Gütersloh: Gütersloher Verlaghaus, 1979), 1:73–74; but, if not, it refers to the message introduced by John's preaching of repentance and Jesus' preaching of the kingdom.

15. Dennis E. Smith, "Narrative Beginnings in Ancient Literature and Theory," *Semeia* 52 (1990): 5; see Donahue and Harrington, *Mark*, 59.

16. Becker, *Das Markus-Evangelium*, 112.

17. Marcus, *Mark 1–8*, 145.

18. John G. Cook, *The Structure and Persuasive Power of Mark: A Linguistic Approach* (Semeia Studies; Atlanta: Scholars Press, 1995), 151–52. France, *Mark*, 50–51, accepts that the opening line can be the "heading for the whole book" though it is not a mere "title" for the book because of its connection to what follows in vv. 2–13. But he also maintains that its contents point "far beyond the first part of chapter 1" and that it "sets forth themes which the whole book will explore." Gnilka, *Markus*, 1:42–43, concludes that it is not the title of the book but the designation of its contents.

19. Donald Earl, "Prologue-Form in Ancient Historiography," in *ANRW* 1/2 (ed. H. Temporini; Berlin/New York: de Gruyter, 1972), 856. See Paul L. Danove, *The End of Mark's Story: A Methodological Study* (BIS 3; Leiden: Brill, 1993), 136, n. 9 and Raymond C. Barber, "Mark as Narrative: A Case for Chapter One" (GTU diss; Berkeley, CA: Graduate Theological Union, 1987), 228, who claim that no other gospel begins with a title and that regarding 1:1 as a title is "an anachronistic projection of a modern narrative device onto the text." Van Iersel, *Mark*, 89, n. 3, however, cites the titles that Josephus (*History of the Jewish War* and *About the Destruction*) and Philo (*On the Life of Moses* and *On the Decalogue*) give their books, so it is wrong to regard it as an anachronistic device.

20. Collins, *Mark*, 2.

opening line to indicate the subject of his work.[21] Later on, as other gospels were written, copied, distributed, and used in different communities, Mark's gospel would have needed another title to distinguish it from the others. "According to Mark" and the "Gospel according to Mark" would have been added to the volume to identify it.[22]

Second, this opening line stands out grammatically for several reasons. It lacks a verb, and it seems best to read it as something separate from what follows.[23] Why begin a work with a verbless sentence were it not an incipit? If the phrase is grammatically connected to what follows, one must supply a verb ("was") or go to v. 4 to find a predicate. The sound quality of v. 1 with six consecutive Greek words ending with the "*ou*" sound also sets this phrase off from what follows.[24] It also omits the definite article before the word "beginning," and headings tended to be anarthrous.[25] In addition to Gen 1:1, other OT precedents exist for works that describe their contents in the first line (Neh 1:1; Prov 1:1; Eccl 1:1; Song 1:1; Isa 1:1; Jer 1:1; see also Tob 1:1; *1 En.* 1:1–2; Rev 1:1–3; *Did.* 1:1).[26] Finally, Davies and Allison argue that Matt 1:1, "book of the history" (*biblos geneseōs*), is a general title for the entire gospel. They note as part of their argument that "it was a custom in the prophetic, didactic, and apocalyptic writings of Judaism to open with an independent titular sentence announcing the content of the work."[27]

Third, to read this opening line as an incipit that describes the contents of the narrative conforms to how another evangelist, who used Mark, understood the subject matter of the gospel narrative as a beginning. Luke writes in Acts 1:1–2 that in his former book he "wrote about all that Jesus began to do and to teach until the day he was taken up to heaven."[28]

Finally and most important, interpreting 1:1 as the title of the gospel or incipit makes sense of the narrative's inconclusive termination in 16:8. Giblin suggests that one can understand the beginning of this work from its ending, where Mark abruptly stops the story: the women flee from the tomb trembling in astonishment and say nothing to anyone.[29] The gospel is open-ended, and the reader knows that the narrative's end was not the end of the story. Something else happened or else no one would have heard this gospel.[30] It "requires subsequent recourse to oral tradition to understand the *whole*, ongoing gospel story."[31]

---

21. Loveday Alexander, *The Preface to Luke's Gospel* (SNTSMS 78; Cambridge: Cambridge University Press, 1993), 29, notes that the earliest Greek historians "use the opening words of the first sentence to indicate the subject of their work."

22. These secondary labels probably contributed to the word "gospel" being used as a term for the literary gospels. See *Did.* 11:5; *2 Clem.* 8:5; Justin Martyr, *1 Apol.* 66.3; Irenaeus, *Haer.* 4.20.6; Clement of Alexandria, *Strom.* 1.136.

23. Malbon, *Mark's Jesus*, 59.

24. Philip Ruge-Jones, "Omnipresent, not Omniscient: How Literary Interpretation Confuses the Storyteller's Narrating," in *Between Author and Audience in Mark: Narration, Characterization, Interpretation* (ed. Elizabeth Struthers Malbon; NTM 23; Sheffield: Sheffield Phoenix, 2009), 33, cited by Malbon, *Mark's Jesus*, 61.

25. James Hope Moulton, *A Grammar of New Testament Greek.* Vol. 1, *Prolegomena* (3rd ed.; Edinburgh: T&T Clark, 1908), 81–82.

26. "Beginning" is the first concept in Gen 1:1; Hos 1:2; John 1:1 (see also 1 John 1:1).

27. Davies and Allison, *Saint Matthew*, 1:151.

28. The statement in Heb 2:3 that salvation "was first announced by the Lord" and then "confirmed to us by those who heard him" would support the view that what Jesus did was a beginning that his disciples carried on.

29. See below on the interpretation of this silence.

30. Giblin, "The Beginning of the Ongoing Gospel," 975–85. See also van Iersel, *Reading Mark*, 31.

Marcus explains that "the movement from hiddenness to revelation that took place in the events of Jesus' life, death and resurrection ... was, Mark implies, the *beginning* of a manifestation that continues in Mark's own time, and will continue until the Parousia (1:1)."[32] Boring avers that Mark "as a whole narrates the beginning of a story that continues in the readers' own day and of which they are a part. The open 'ending' of the story at 16:8 suggests that the whole of Mark's story is only a beginning, that 'the *beginning* of the gospel story is over on Easter morning,' and that every reader is challenged to continue the story in his or her own time."[33]

The beginning of the gospel concludes on the morning of the resurrection, but the story will recommence when the disciples, baptized with the Holy Spirit (1:8), follow Jesus anew and continue his ministry. What began with Jesus' life and ministry, death, and resurrection now "makes discipleship and mission possible."[34] Van Iersel puts it this way: "When the readers see the title again at a second reading, they realize that it has more than one meaning."[35] This first page introduces the beginning of the story about Jesus, but, reading or hearing it again, they can recognize that the entire book is only the beginning of the proclamation about Jesus as the Messiah and Son of God that continues to their day.

3.1.4 The Theological Affirmations in the Title

3.1.4.1 The Beginning

The term "beginning" in Greek can refer to "the commencement of something" or the "foundation," "origin," "norm," "rule," or "governing principle."[36] Mark uses the word, however, in a chronological sense in 10:6; 13:8, 19 (see Luke 1:2; Phil 4:15; and *2 Clem.* 14:2), which suggests that this meaning best fits here. Hartman maintains that if 1:1 is the title, then "the contents of the Gospel are the beginning or the point of departure of the proclamation of Christ by the church, that is, of the church's gospel."[37] The use of the temporal "beginning" and the historical present throughout the gospel reveal that Mark is not a mythic work but a historical one.[38] The origins of the good news are traceable historically to the start of Jesus' ministry

31. Giblin, "The Beginning of the Ongoing Gospel," 985. N. Clayton Croy, "Where the Gospel Text Begins: A Non-Theological Interpretation of Mark 1:1," *NovT* 43 (2001): 119–27, argues that the gospel was a codex and its beginning and ending were damaged and lost and a copyist added v. 1 at a later time. See also his *The Mutilation of Mark's Gospel* (Nashville: Abingdon, 2003), 113–36. See also W. A. Craigie, "The Beginning of St. Mark's Gospel," *Expositor* 8th Series 24 (1922): 303–5; R. Way-Rider, "The Lost Beginning of St. Mark's Gospel," *SE VII* (Berlin: Akademie, 1982), 553–56; and J. K. Elliott, "Mark 1.1–3–A Later Addition to the Gospel?" *NTS* 46 (2000): 584–88, who considers 1:1–3 to be a later addition. Croy claims that the nine textual variants in the opening line and its syntactical and interpretive problems suggest that it was a second century-gloss. I would counter that if 1:1 were a later gloss to fix a mutilated beginning to the gospel, why would the glosser not have added details from the infancy narratives in Matthew and Luke to reconstruct an improved beginning as a later copyist did in adding 16:9–20 by gleaning various resurrection details from the other gospels to fix what was perceived to be a truncated ending.

32. Marcus, *Mystery*, 231.

33. Boring, *Mark*, 31.

34. Geddert, *Mark*, 31.

35. Van Iersel, *Mark*, 90.

36. See Wikgren, "ΑΡΧΗ ΤΟΥ ΕΥΑΓΓΕΛΙΟΥ," 15–20. Boring, "Mark 1:1–15," 53, argues for the meaning "norm" or "rule" and maintains that the narrative that follows is the "normative statement for preaching" the gospel about Jesus Christ.

37. Hartman, *Mark*, 2.

38. Becker, *Das Markus-Evangelium*, 115.

in Galilee (Mark 1:14–15; Luke 23:5; Acts 10:37–38), but also before that to the baptism of John the Baptizer, and long before that to the plan of God that Isaiah revealed in his prophecy.

3.1.4.2 Good News

Matthew identifies his work as a "book" (*biblos*, Matt 1:1); Luke identifies his work as a "narrative" (*diēgēsis*, Luke 1:1); and John identifies his work as a "testimony" (*martyria*, John 1:19). Only Mark uses the term "good news" (*euangelion*) to describe the contents of his book, which means that he does not regard the narrative that include Jesus' death to be a tragedy.[39] It is meant to be read as a joyous proclamation by or about Jesus Christ, the Son of God. The term "good news," however, could evoke differing connotations in the context of Mark's world.

3.1.4.2.1 Backgrounds for the Usage of the Term "Good News"

3.1.4.2.1.1 The Old Testament and Isaiah

In the LXX, the noun "good news" appears rarely and is used for the tidings from the battlefield and the messenger's reward, which can be death if the messenger relays bad news instead of good (2 Kgdms 4:10; see also 18:20, 22, 25, 27; 4 Kgdms 7:9). The verb form is also used for tidings, good and bad, from the battlefield (1 Kgdms 31:9; 2 Kgdms 1:20; 4:10; 18:19–20, 26, 31; 3 Kgdms 1:42; 1 Chr 10:9; Ps 67:12[11]) or for the tidings to a father of his child's birth (Jer 20:15). It is also used theologically for the good news of God's saving deliverance from evils and iniquities (Ps 39:10) and for the declarations that the Lord is king and brings salvation (Ps 95:2 [96:2]), is a stronghold who destroys the adversaries (Nah 2:1 [1:15]), and saves those whom he calls (Joel 3:5 [2:32]).

Isaiah's use of the verb form "to announce good news" (*euangelizomai*) is more relevant for Mark.[40] Isaiah uses it for announcing the good tidings ("Here is your God!" Isa 40:9; "Your God reigns!" 52:7), for announcing good news to the oppressed (61:1), and for announcing that the nations will proclaim the praise of the Lord (60:6). Watts contends that Mark's usage of the term "good news" derives primarily from the Isaianic announcement of comfort from the good news that God will come to assert his kingly rule and lead his people on a new exodus.[41]

---

39. The noun "good news" does not appear in John or Luke, though it does appear in Acts 15:7 and 20:24. It derives primarily from the Isaianic announcement. Luke uses the verb "to proclaim good news" ten times for the activity of preaching the good news. Matthew qualifies the noun as the "gospel/good news of the kingdom" (Matt 4:23; 9:35; 24:14) or "this gospel" (Matt 26:13). Since Mark uses the term "gospel" to describe his literary work, its meaning will become altered when others use it later to identify a narrative that deals with the life and teaching of Jesus, which the apostles transmitted in "their memoirs called gospels" (see Justin, *1 Apol.* 66.3; see also *Did.* 15:3–4; *2 Clem.* 8:5; Irenaeus, *Haer.* 1.7.4; 1.8.4). For Matthew and Luke, who do not use the term to describe their works, it did not yet designate a collection of traditions about Jesus' life and teaching.

40. It translates the Hebrew *bāśar* (see also Isa 41:27).

41. Watts, *New Exodus*, 119.

3.1.4.2.1.2 Paul

The term "good news" appears some sixty times in Paul's letters (forty-eight in the undisputed letters, nine of these in Romans). Paul never defines it and therefore must assume that his audience understands what he means by it. One can infer from his usage that it refers to "the plan of salvation conceived by God, promised by the prophets, and realised in the death and resurrection of Christ."[42] It also is tied to God's election and calling of those who accept this plan. The message did not come to the communities of Christians in just words but in power (1 Thess 1:5; 1 Cor 2:1–5), and not just in a series of propositions about Jesus as Lord but in a narrative about his ministry, death, and resurrection (1 Cor 11:23–26) that was a fulfillment of Scripture (1 Cor 15:1–8). Some argue that Paul's usage of the term derives from Christian Jews who extended Isaiah's usage of the term, employed for the message about God's salvation of his people, to its fulfillment in Jesus. The gospel about Jesus is the completion or resolution of the story of Israel with the fulfillment of God's promises.[43]

Paul reviews the trajectory of the gospel from Jesus' passion to the resurrection to the consummation of the age in 1 Cor 15:1–28.[44] It is the gospel tradition that Paul preached to the Corinthians, which they received, and which he received from the earliest apostolic tradition. It is not a collection of abstract doctrines about Jesus and salvation that he dreamed up but an account of the significant events in the life of Jesus that *fulfilled* the Scriptures; that is, they brought the story of Israel to completion and unleashed salvation (15:1–11). After making arguments that Christ was raised bodily (15:12–19), the apostle then draws out the repercussions of his resurrection (15:20–28). Believers will be resurrected in Christ. Every ruler, authority, and power, even death, will be destroyed. Then, all things will be subjected to the Son; the Son himself will also be subjected to the God who put all things in subjection under him; and the goal will be reached: God will be all in all (15:27–28).

Mark is not writing in a vacuum, and, in my view, Paul's usage of the term fundamentally informs Mark's usage. Mark applies the keyword "gospel" that was used in missionary preaching to his narrative of "the path of the earthly Jesus from his baptism by John through his ministry in Galilee up to his passion, his death on the cross and his resurrection in Jerusalem."[45] This application of the term gospel to the record of the significant events in the life of Jesus that fulfill Scriptures explains why Mark can identify his gospel as only a beginning. When he writes his gospel, Mark recognizes that many events that Jesus prophesied would happen are yet to come to pass.

42. James Everett Frame, *Epistles of Paul to the Thessalonians* (ICC; Edinburgh: T&T Clark, 1912), 80; see also Joseph A. Fitzmyer, "The Gospel in the Theology of Paul," *Int* 33 (1979): 343.

43. Darrell Bock, *Recovering the Real Lost Gospel* (Nashville: B&H, 2010), 7–21.

44. Scot McKnight, *The King Jesus Gospel: The Original Good News Revisited* (Grand Rapids: Zondervan, 2011), 45–62.

45. Karl Kertelge, "The Epiphany of Jesus in the Gospel (Mark)," in *The Interpretation of Mark* (ed. William R. Telford; 2nd ed.; Edinburgh: T&T Clark, 1995), 107.

3.1.4.2.1.3 Roman Imperial Propaganda

The meaning of the term "good news" in the Greco-Roman world must also be taken into account.[46] While it was also used for a reward given for the messenger of good news (Homer, *Od.* 14; 152, 166), Cranfield notes that most of the inhabitants of the Roman Empire would have associated the word that represented the announcements of such events as the birth of an heir to the emperor, his coming-of-age, and his accession to the throne, as glad tidings or gospels with the emperor-cult.[47] Koester claims that this usage during the time of Augustus was new and earned the term a "particular dignity" that would have influenced Christian missionaries who lived a few decades later.[48] Fears underscores the triumphal ring of the good tidings of imperial propaganda. It proclaimed the dawning of a new age of peace, concord, and abundance on earth, and the emperor as a divinely sent savior who brought these benefits to humankind with the advent of his reign.[49]

This usage is most clearly exhibited in a frequently cited calendrical inscription from Priene in southwestern Asia Minor dated to 9 BC, which decrees that the birthday of Emperor Augustus (September 23) would now mark the beginning of the year when persons assumed civil office. It is filled with exaggerated praise:

> it is a day which we may justly count as equivalent to the beginning of everything—if not in itself and in its own nature, at any rate in the benefits it brings—inasmuch as it has restored the shape of everything that was failing and turning into misfortune, and has given a new look to the Universe at a time when it would gladly have welcomed destruction if Caesar had not been born to be the common blessing of all men.

The decree resolves:

> Whereas the Providence (*pronoia*) which has ordered the whole of our life, showing concern and zeal, has ordained the most perfect consummation for human life by giving to it Augustus, by filling him with virtue for doing the work of a benefactor among men, and by sending in him, as it were, a saviour for us and those who come after us, to make war to cease, and to create order everywhere ... and whereas the birthday of the God [Augustus] was the beginning for the world of the glad tidings [in the Greek the 'Evangel'] that have come to men through him ... Paulus Fabius Maximus, the proconsul of the province ... has devised a way of honouring Augustus hitherto unknown to the Greeks,

46. Winn, *Purpose*, 99, claims that Mark's incipit proclaims the good news "by bringing together the language of both Deutero-Isaiah and the Roman imperial cult."

47. C. E. B. Cranfield, *A Critical and Exegetical Commentary on the Epistle to the Romans* (ICC; Edinburgh: T&T Clark, 1975), 1:55. Fronto (in Seneca, *Ep.* 4.12) claims that images of the emperor were found "anywhere and everywhere," so that "the emperor—especially Augustus" could be called "the only Empire-wide god in the Roman pantheon" (noted by Peppard, *The Son of God in the Roman World*, 91).

48. Helmut Koester, *Ancient Christian Gospels: Their History and Development* (Philadelphia: Trinity Press International, 1990), 4.

49. J. Rufus Fears, "Rome: The Ideology of Imperial Power," *Thought* 55 (1980): 103–4.

which is, that the reckoning of time for the course of human life should begin with *his* birth.[50]

What constitutes good news in this edict is the cessation of wars and the bringing of worldly benefits and social order. It reflects an ideology that worshiped political power as divine.[51]

Evans boldly asserts, "There can be little doubt that when the Markan evangelist began his Gospel with the words, 'The beginning of the good news of Jesus Christ, the Son of God' (Mark 1:1), he deliberately imitated the language used in reference to the Roman emperors."[52] If this assertion is correct, then Mark used the term "good news" for the title of his Christian message about Jesus as the Son of God to hurl defiance at Roman imperial claims about the good news associated with their emperors.[53] Bolt writes:

> Mark's Gospel proclaimed an alternative kingdom: the kingdom of God. It spoke of Jesus in terms associated with the Caesars, and, by so doing, proposed an alternative view of reality which offered an alternative set of hopes for the future. Mark's Gospel was subversive in that it undermined the claims of the *imperium* to be the source of life for the world and so joined forces with those critics who suggested that Rome had instead extended the shadow of death across many nations. It proposed that the true source of life for the world was found in the gospel of Jesus Christ, and that he brought life to those who found themselves living under death's shadow.[54]

In the Hellenistic tradition (and the LXX), the plural "gospels" (*euangelia*, "good news") was sometimes used,[55] but, like Paul, Mark employs exclusively the singular form of "gospel" (*euangelion*). Strecker suggests that the singular "gospel" deliberately "distinguishes the Christ-event as a unique eschatological fact from all *euangelia* [gospels] in the non-Christian world."[56] This distinction is generally lost in the English translation "good news" or "good tidings."

50. Cited by Ernest Barker, *From Alexander to Constantine: Passages and Documents Illustrating the History of the Social and Political Ideas 336 B.C.–A.D. 337* (Oxford: Clarendon, 1956), 211–12. The full Greek inscription is found in OGIS II, 458. Josephus (*J.W.* 4.10.6 §618) uses "good tidings" (in the plural) in connection with the news of the arrival of Vespasian, who was newly proclaimed as emperor, and the festivals and sacrifices offered on his behalf in "every city" (see also *J.W.* 4.11.5 §656). Its usage is related to the announcement of imminent deliverance with the emergence of a new emperor and celebratory sacrifices to the gods.

51. See the papyrus rejoicing in the tidings of the accession to the throne by G. Julius Verus Maximus Augustus in AD 238, cited by Deissmann, *Light from the Ancient East*, 367.

52. Craig A. Evans, "Jesus and the Dead Sea Scrolls from Qumran Cave 4," in *Eschatology, Messianism and the Dead Sea Scrolls* (ed. C. A. Evans and P. W. Flint; Grand Rapids: Eerdmans, 1997), 93.

53. Boring, *Mark*, 30. Evans, *Mark 8:27–16:20*, lxxxii–lxxxiii, lists various divine titles given to the emperors from Julius Caesar to Vespasian that are echoed in the NT ("son of god," "savior," "lord," "benefactor"). Evans, "Mark's Incipit and the Priene Calendar Inscription," 70, asserts that Mark makes the claim that only Jesus Messiah, not Julius Caesar or any of his descendants, can be rightly regarded as the Son of God. Watts, *New Exodus*, 119, argues for the Isaianic background of the word but admits that it may have "polemical edge" in terms of its "Hellenistic connotations."

54. Peter G. Bolt, *Jesus' Defeat of Death: Persuading Mark's Early Readers* (SNTSMS 125; Cambridge: Cambridge University Press, 2003), 42–43.

55. The only clear use of the plural is in 2 Sam 4:10; there is some debate regarding the use of *euangelia* in 2 Sam 18:20, 22, 25, 27; 2 Kgs 7:9.

56. Georg Strecker, "εὐαγγελίζω, *euangelizō*," *EDNT*, 2:71.

3.1.4.2.2 The Meaning of "Good News" for Mark

Mark applies the term "good news" to the Christian message about God's reign and salvation that is brought by Jesus (13:10; 14:9). It differs from other tidings of good news, first because it has its origins in God (1:14; Rom 1:1; 15:16; 2 Cor 11:7; 1 Thess 2:2, 8; 1 Pet 4:17), who is the beginning and end of all things and the true source of blessing for humankind. The term implies an announcement that is new and heretofore unknown, but the news that Mark relates does not come out of the blue. It arises out of God's blueprint for the salvation of humanity. The quotation from Isaiah that immediately follows 1:1 reveals that "what happened in Jesus followed the plan of salvation laid out by God in the prophecies of the Scriptures."[57] This narrative "is good news precisely because it is the fulfilment of scripture."[58] Caneday points out, however, that Mark suppresses explicit mention of the fulfillment of Scripture, but the "juxtaposition of scriptural allusions and citations with the actions and words of Jesus within his Gospel pericopes indicates that he is convinced that Jesus fulfills the full array of scriptures used in his narrative."[59]

Second, this good news is not the starry-eyed hype of a propaganda campaign trying to puff up a new leader. Christianity does not offer a series of gospels, as was the case with the good tidings of imperial propaganda that was broadcast with every succeeding emperor, but only *the one gospel* about *the one true Lord*.

Third, the good news is tied to Jesus' death. In 14:1 – 9, Jesus defends the action of the anonymous woman who poured the precious ointment of nard on his head by saying that she has anointed his body beforehand for its burial (14:8) and connects it to the good news: "wherever the gospel is preached throughout the world, what she has done will also be told, in memory of her" (14:9). The good news of the peace and the benefits that Jesus brings to the world derives from his sacrificial death on the cross as a ransom for many (10:45) and from his resurrection, not from terroristic military triumphs that crush everyone who gets in the way.

Fourth, Jesus' death is not the sum and substance of the gospel for Mark. It also includes the resurrection. What scholars often call "the passion predictions" in Mark neglects that in each one of them Jesus also foretells his resurrection (8:31; 9:31; 10:34; see also 9:9; 14:28). They are passion *and* resurrection predictions.

Fifth, the gospel also includes Jesus' exaltation to the right hand of the Father and his coming again on the clouds of heaven (14:62). Obviously, this chapter in the story cannot yet be narrated because it is yet to happen, but Jesus' vindication and return are integral to the whole story.

Sixth, the benefits of the gospel are extended without distinction to everyone who will believe and follow Jesus as Lord; they are not limited to just the privileged few who belong to a ruling circle. It includes Jew and Gentile, sinners and outcasts, the poor and seemingly inconsequential. This gospel is truly good news for the

57. Marcus, *Mark 1–8*, 147.

58. Morna D. Hooker, "Mark," in *It is Written—Scripture Citing Scripture: Essays in Honour of Barnabas Lindars, SSF* (ed. D. A. Carson and H. G. M. Williamson; Cambridge: Cambridge University Press, 1988), 220.

59. Caneday, "Mark's Provocative Use of Scripture," 23.

entire world, but humans must repent and believe it (1:15) to receive its benefits, and Jesus' followers must preach it throughout the world (13:10; 14:9).

3.1.4.3 The Good News of Jesus Christ

"The good news of Jesus Christ" may be an objective genitive, "the good news about Jesus Christ"; a subjective genitive, "the good news preached by Jesus Christ"; or a plenary genitive, which includes both subjective and objective ideas.[60] Marxsen chooses the last option: Jesus is both the proclaimer of the gospel and the proclaimed one.[61] What immediately follows 1:1, however, is the Isaian prophecy *about* the coming of the Lord (1:2–3) and the preaching of John the Baptizer *about* the coming of a stronger one (1:4–8). The baptism and testing scenes reveal Jesus' identity as God's beloved and faithful Son (1:9–13). The "good news of God" in 1:14 is clearly an objective genitive, the good news about God. Gundry notes that Jesus does not proclaim himself but "the nearness of God's rule."[62] He also points out that the objective genitive accords with the reality that by the time Mark wrote, Jesus Christ had long been the object of the apostolic preaching of good news.[63] The word "gospel" appears in 1:14, 15; 8:35; 10:29; 13:10; 14:9; aside from 1:14–15, it refers to the whole story about Jesus that not only is narrated in the text but also that is told in oral tradition that complements the text—the words, deeds, death, and resurrection of Jesus and what it all means as God's saving act. Mark's gospel is *about* Jesus; and Christology, the revelation of the person and deeds of Jesus, is one of the evangelist's fundamental aims as his introduction makes evident. Grindheim comments,

> When we read this usage of the term "gospel" against its Jewish background, we see that Mark has placed Jesus where Jewish eschatological expectations saw God himself. Whereas Isaiah's messenger merely proclaimed the good news of God (Isa. 40.9; 41.27; 52.7; 61.1), Mark sees Jesus as the content of the message. Jesus does not merely take the place of the messenger—he takes the place of God.[64]

It is misleading, however, to think that Jesus only proclaims the kingdom of God and does not *also* proclaim that God was bringing the resolution of Israel's story through him. He identifies himself as the center of God's plan. He understands that he has come with a special mission (1:38; 2:17) that gives him the authority to order persons to follow him (1:17, 20; 2:14). He has a cup to drink and a baptism with which to be baptized that has been given to him by God (10:38; 14:36). He is so bold as to say, "Whoever welcomes one of these little children in my name welcomes me, and whoever welcomes me does not welcome me but the one who sent

60. Daniel B. Wallace, *Greek Grammar beyond the Basics* (Grand Rapids: Zondervan, 1996), 119–20.

61. Marxsen, *Mark the Evangelist*, 148–50. This view is widely held. Henderson, *Christology*, 42, for example, states that the good news is "both personified and heralded by Jesus Christ."

62. Gundry, *Mark*, 32.

63. Gundry, ibid., 33, citing Josef Schmid, *The Gospel according to Mark* (trans. Kevin Condon; RNT; Staten Island, NY: Alba House, 1968), 17

64. Sigurd Grindheim, *Christology in the Synoptic Gospels: God or God's Servant?* (London/New York: T&T Clark, 2012), 36.

me" (9:37). He has a special identity and mission that he will clarify for his disciples (8:29). He has divine authority to take dramatic action in the temple (11:15–17, 27–33). He declares that his words will not pass away (13:31). He proclaims his death and interprets its meaning for his disciples (10:45; 14:6–9, 22–25), asserting that Scripture specifically applies to what will happen to him (14:21, 27). As the Son of Man, he has the authority to forgive sins (2:10), is Lord of the Sabbath (2:28), gives his life as a ransom for many (10:45), and will be seated at the right hand of the Power and will come with the clouds of heaven (14:62). In that regard, Marshall is correct that Jesus is both "the theme and author of good news."[65]

3.1.4.4 Jesus Christ

"Jesus" is the Greek form of "Joshua" and is one of the most common names in the first century (see Matt 27:16–17 [according to Θ]; Luke 3:29; Acts 7:45; 13:6; Col 4:11). Four of twelve first-century Jewish high priests had this name. Mark is interested in undergirding the historical truth that the risen Jesus, proclaimed and worshiped by the church, is firmly tied to the historical Jesus who came from Nazareth in Galilee (1:9). The OT gives witness to God's mighty acts in history, and the gospels affirm God's incarnation in a human life in the person of Jesus.[66]

Mark introduces Jesus as "Christ" ("Messiah," "Anointed One"). The answer to the question, "Anointed by whom?" quickly emerges in the narrative of Jesus' baptism (1:9–11). He is anointed by the Spirit sent by God.[67] What he is anointed to do will be revealed by the narrative.

The title "Christ" ("Messiah") appears twice on the lips of Jesus' enemies, which offers insight on how they understood the title. The high priest, Caiaphas, connects Christ to "the Son of the Blessed One" in his direct question to Jesus (14:61). The high priests and teachers of the law mock Jesus on the cross as "the Christ, the king of Israel" (15:32), which reveals their understanding of what the title "Christ" means. They assume that Jesus is a royal pretender, but their taunt unwittingly testifies to the truth that they cannot fathom. Jesus is the Christ, the king of Israel. His answer to the high priest indicates that Jesus sees himself as the Christ, the Son of the Blessed One (14:62). But the title can be misleading because of its associations with imperial power and establishing an earthly regime.[68] Jesus' warning in 13:21–22 that many false "christs" ("messiahs") will come and lead many astray indicates how problematic the title could be. Mark's narrative about "Jesus Christ the Son of God" defines what he thinks these titles mean when applied to Jesus.

65. I. Howard Marshall, "Jesus as Messiah in Mark and Matthew," in *The Messiah in the Old and New Testaments* (ed. Stanley E. Porter: Grand Rapids: Eerdmans, 2007), 118.

66. See William L. Lane, "From Historian to Theologian: Milestones in Markan Scholarship," *RevExp* 75 (1978): 613.

67. Brown, "The Jesus of Mark's Gospel," 31.

68. Herbert W. Bateman, IV, "Defining the Titles 'Christ' and 'Son of God' in Mark's Narrative Presentation of Jesus," *JETS* 50 (2007): 537–59, concludes that the use of the titles "Christ" and "Son of God" in Mark simply "speak of the divine authentication, commissioning, and empowerment of Jesus for ministry as 'the Christ' (1:1)" (p. 557). Looking only at the use of titles in Mark misses the most significant aspect of Mark's Christology, because they do not fully disclose his divinity.

The narrative provides the evidence for the correct evaluation of what it means for Jesus to be the Christ, the anointed Messiah/King. It will reveal, as Matera puts it: "Jesus is the expected Messiah in a most unexpected manner."[69] The messianic expectation found, for example, in the *Psalms of Solomon* 17:21–25, about the son of David who would "destroy the unrighteous rulers, to purge Jerusalem from gentiles who trample her to destruction; in wisdom and in righteousness to drive out the sinners from the inheritance; to smash the arrogance of sinners like a potter's jar," is the polar opposite of what the audience learns about Jesus as Christ and the son of David (12:35–37) in Mark. Those who share such militaristic ideas about the Messiah's role[70] will use the title "Christ" without the slightest conception of what it means for this Jesus of Nazareth to be the Christ (see 8:29; 12:35; 13:21; 14:61; 15:32). Since Jesus gathers no army, wins no military battles, ascends no earthly throne to rule a great empire, and dies ignominiously on a cross on the orders of a Roman ruler, all preconceptions of what this title means must be revised. Only *after* Jesus' death and resurrection can one begin to understand the momentous nature of the news that God has acted decisively in and through Jesus, who is the true Christ of God (see Luke 9:20; 23:35).

3.1.4.5 Son of God

3.1.4.5.1 A Textual Variant

The additional title "Son of God" is absent in a handful of manuscripts, most notably the original hand of Codex Sinaiticus (א*).[71] Head concedes that the numerical superiority, geographical diversity, and conjunction of Western and Alexandrian texts that have the longer reading provide a strong case for it.[72] Nevertheless, he favors the shorter reading because of "the total absence of Greek witnesses to the long reading until c. A.D. 400, in contrast to the wide spread of Greek witness to the short reading from the second century onwards."[73] It also seems more likely that a copyist would add the title "Son of God" rather than intentionally delete it. Head cites a number of NT variants where "Son of God" is reverentially added to the text.[74] It is also deemed improbable that the title would have been omitted

69. Matera, *Kingship*, 145.

70. See Jer 23:5–8; 30:9–10; 33:14–26; Ezek 34:20–31; 37:15–28; *Pss. Sol.* 17–18; *2 Bar.* 39:7; 70:9; *1 En.* 48:10; 52:4; and *Jub.* 31:18–20.

71. א* Θ 28^c 255 geo^1 arm^{9mss}. The phrase is included in $א^c$ B D L W 2427 and the majority of texts have the definite article *tou* before "God" (A K Δ Π f^1 f^{13} 33 565 700, Cyril). See C. H. Turner, "A Textual Commentary on Mark 1," *JTS* 28 (1927): 150; and Alexander Globe, "The Caesarean Omission of the Phrase 'Son of God' in Mark 1:1," *HTR* 75 (1982): 210–15, on how to assess the patristic evidence. They note that many contract the openings of the gospels rather than give exact citations of the texts. The "Son of God" without any definite article appears in Mark 15:39; Luke 1:35; and Rom 1:4. Globe ("The Caesarean Omission," 217) contends that this anarthrous use suggests Markan rather than scribal authorship, since a copyist adding the title for reverential reasons would have been likely to add the definite article.

72. Peter M. Head, "A Text-Critical Study of Mark 1.1: 'The Beginning of the Gospel of Jesus Christ,'" *NTS* 37 (1991): 623.

73. Ibid., 626. See also Jan Slomp, "Are the Words 'Son of God' in Mark 1.1 Original?" *BT* 28 (1977): 143–50; Pesch, *Markusevangelium*, 1:74, n.1; Bart D. Ehrman, "The Text of Mark in the Hands of the Orthodox," *LQ* 5 (1991): 143–56; Elliott, "Mark 1:1–3—A Later Addition to the Gospel?" 584–88; Heinrich Greeven and Eberhard Güting, eds., *Textkritik des Markusevangeliums* (Theologie, Forschung und Wissenschaft 11; Münster: LIT Verlag, 2005), 41–46; Marcus, *Mark 1–8*, 141; and Collins, *Mark*, 130, who regard "Son of God" as a secondary addition.

74. Head, "A Text-Critical Study of Mark 1.1," 627.

accidentally by a copyist when he first started to copy the text, presumably in an alert state.[75]

Arguments that the title was not original to Mark are not conclusive.[76] Codex Sinaiticus was corrected by the original corrector before it left the scriptorium, so the omission can be attributable to an accidental error by the copyist.[77] *Nomina Sacra*[78] were used by Christian copyists out of reverence; and the omission could have been caused by the copyist becoming confused by the string of genitive endings in 1:1, which looks like this in Greek without a break between words: ΑΡΧΗΤΟΥΕΥΑΓΓΕΛΙΟΥΙΥΧΥΥΥΘΥ.[79] Three other manuscripts besides Sinaiticus that omit ΥΥΘΥ ("Son of God") have been corrected (582, 820, 1555), and 28 omits ΧΥ ("Christ"). The copyist of Sinaiticus omits one in a string of genitives in other passages (Acts 28:31; Col 2:2; Heb 12:2; Rev 12:14; 15:7; 22:1), so an accidental omission is possible.[80] Since Mark is not the first book in the codex, the copyist may not have just started his copying with Mark 1 but continued on after copying sections of Matthew. The recurrence of the same letters may well have played tricks on the copyist's eyes causing him to omit these last letters.

If it were a deliberate omission, Gundry suggests as one explanation that the copyist may have thought it "otiose" or "linguistically ugly" to have the repetition of the *ou* sound.[81] Hartman offers that a copyist may have been influenced by Paul's use of the phrase "gospel of Christ" eight times without the phrase "the Son of God."[82] If a copyist added this title, however, why would he not have added the title also to Peter's confession in 8:29, "You are the Messiah" (see Matt 16:16)?[83]

I would argue for the originality of the reading "Son of God" on internal grounds. First, the title is taken up in the baptism scene with the announcement from heaven (1:11). Second, the centurion's confession in 15:39 is textually undisputed, and Donahue and Harrington note that it "favors its inclusion here since Mark is fond of both foreshadowings and overarching interconnections."[84] Third, it is customary to identify the subject of a work as the son of someone (see Tob 1:1; Bar 1:1; Matt 1:1).[85] Fourth, the elements of the title, "the good news," "Jesus the Messiah," and "Son of God," all appear in Paul's creedal introduction in Romans 1:2–4, which

75. Ibid., 629.

76. A majority of commentators accept the longer reading, see Globe, "The Caesarean Omission," 209–18; Taylor, *Mark*, 152; Cranfield, *Mark*, 38; Lane, *Mark*, 41, n. 7; Carl R. Kazmierski, *Jesus, the Son of God: A Study of the Markan Tradition and its Redaction by the Evangelist* (FB 33; Würzburg: Echter, 1979), 1–9; Guelich, *Mark 1–8:26*, 6; Witherington, *Mark*, 69, n. 8; Hartman, *Mark*, 3. See also the conclusions of Tommy Wasserman, "The 'Son of God' Was in the Beginning (Mark 1:1)," *JTS* 62 (2011): 20–50.

77. T. C. Skeat and H. J. M. Milne, *Scribes and Correctors of the Codex Sinaiticus* (London: British Museum, 1938), 40. Peter Malik, "The Earliest Corrections in Codex Sinaiticus: A Test Case From the Gospel of Mark," *BASP* 50 (2013): 214–19, suggests that Sinaiticus attests to both readings, because it was possible that the correction was made using another exemplar.

78. *Nomina Sacra* are abbreviations of divine names in Greek (predominantly the words for "God," "Lord," "Jesus," and "Christ") with lines drawn over the abbreviations.

79. Guelich, *Mark 1–8:26*, 6; Gundry, *Mark*, 33; France, *Mark*, 49; Dean P. Deppe, "Markan Christology and the Omission of υἱοῦ θεοῦ in Mark 1:1," *FN* 21 (2008): 60–64; and Wasserman, "The 'Son of God.'"

80. Kurt Aland and Barbara Aland, *The Text of the New Testament* (trans. Erroll F. Rhodes; 2nd ed.; Grand Rapids: Eerdmans, 1989), 107, cite various careless errors in Sinaiticus.

81. Gundry, *Mark*, 33.

82. Hartman, *Mark*, 3.

83. Jens Dechow, *Gottessohn und Herrschaft Gottes: Der Theozentrismus des Markusevangeliums* (WMANT 86; Neukirchen-Vluyn: Neukirchener Verlag, 2000), 25.

84. Donahue and Harrington, *Mark*, 60.

85. Davies and Allison, *Saint Matthew*, 1:152.

preceded Mark's gospel and would have been well known to the audience. Fifth, Gundry argues that identifying Jesus from the outset as Christ and Son of God "changes his coming crucifixion from the shameful death of a common criminal into the awe-inspiring death of a divine being who is God's appointed agent."[86]

Sixth, Guijarro contends that Mark omitted sketching Jesus' origin and education, a topic found at the beginning of other Hellenistic lives, "because the available data were not suited to reveal his ascribed honor."[87] The introduction reveals that "Jesus' honor derives, not from his human ancestry, but from his intimate relationship to God."[88] His true ancestry goes back to God. The importance of this point for Mark makes it likely that he would have included the title "Son of God" in his incipit.

Seventh, if Mark deliberately contrasted his portrait of Jesus with the Roman Emperor, who was hailed as the son of god (see, e.g., the Priene inscription cited above; Virgil, *Aen.* 6:791–93), it seems likely that in his incipit he would specifically identify Jesus as the true Son of God, who brings a different sort of good news, what is genuinely good news, to the world.

3.1.4.5.2 Jesus as "the Son of God" Set against the Roman Emperor as "a Son of God"

Barrett asserts, "Among the Romans the distinction between man and god was not a sharp one."He contends that this "blurring is usually associated with the phenomenon of emperor worship in the Imperial age," but "its origins go back to the republic."[89] Virgil refers to Augustus restoring the golden age: "This, this is he whom so often you hear promised to you, Augustus Caesar, son of a god, who shall again set up a golden age in Latium amid fields where Saturn once reigned, and shall spread his empire past Garamant and Indian, to a land that lies beyond the stars" (*Aen.* VI.791–95). When Virgil refers to Octavian as one of the "gods among us" (*Ecl.* 1.41), or Scribonius Largus refers to Claudius as "our god Caesar" (*Praef.* 60, 163), these expressions probably conveyed to Romans that in this extraordinary case, this human exceptionally had divine qualities normally associated with a god.

Barrett points out that this "fine line" was "easily crossed" in the eastern provinces: "Many of the eastern peoples, notably, but not exclusively, the Greeks, had long been accustomed to honouring their rulers with the tokens of divinity and to identifying them during their lifetimes quite explicitly as gods made manifest on earth. When Roman officials replaced these rulers, they in turn became the object of worship."[90] In Mark's era, the imperial cult pervaded every aspect of life. Through religious rituals, it vaunted the power structure that the Romans had imposed on the world.[91]

86. Gundry, *Mark*, 33.

87. Santiago Guijarro, "Why Does the Gospel of Mark Begin as It Does?" *BTB* 33 (2003): 36.

88. Ibid., 37.

89. Anthony A. Barrett, *Caligula: The Corruption of Power* (New Haven, CT/London: Yale University Press, 1989), 140. See also Adela Yarbro Collins, "Mark and His Readers: The Son of God among Greeks and Romans," *HTR* 93 (2000): 85–100; Peppard, *The Son of God in the Roman World.*

90. Barrett, *Caligula*, 140

91. Simon R. F. Price, *Rituals and Power: The Roman Imperial Cult in Asia Minor* (Cambridge: Cambridge University Press, 1984).

After Caesar had been recognized as a god, "his successor, while outwardly foreswearing any desire for divinity, could at least present himself in his public pronouncements, on his coins and on his inscriptions, as son of a god."[92] The Romans in the first century did not officially worship the seated emperor but only his *genius*, which was the daemon or god or spirituality that animated his rule. Philo's *On the Embassy to Gaius*, however, paints a picture of the emperor expecting divine honors during his lifetime and complaining that the Jews offered sacrifices on his behalf but not to him.

When Mark refers to Jesus as "Son of God" in the incipit, the audience most likely would realize that Jesus is being presented as a challenger to the Roman emperor. The narrative that follows will reveal that Jesus is the "Son of God" on a totally different level. The term "Christ" ("Messiah") designates a human who came from Nazareth and died on the cross, but it will be shown that Mark understands the title "Son of God" to be a metaphysical term that designates Jesus' preexistent deity. He has not become the Son of God posthumously, as was the case for the Roman emperors.[93] As the Son of God, he did not come *from* the world but came *into* the world.[94]

3.2 The Introduction (Mark 1:2–13)

LaVerdiere argues that the title and introduction must be read in light of the entire gospel and vice versa. He advises rereading the introduction, which he calls a prologue, after reading each section in the gospel and "asking how the prologue introduced each section." He compares the introduction to

> the overture of an opera, which gathers the major themes of the opera in an orchestral introduction. Those who are unfamiliar with the opera can enjoy the music. Many overtures are performed apart from their operatic context. But only those that are familiar with the opera can recognize how its basic themes have been gathered into a new musical synthesis.[95]

He concludes that Mark's introduction prepares the way of his gospel like John the Baptizer prepared the way of the Lord. Since visions from heaven do not occur frequently in Mark—the exception is the transfiguration—and since the Holy Spirit does not appear frequently either, from an omniscient perspective, Mark has packed vital christological information into these opening verses that helps the reader put what follows in perspective. Hooker comments, "It is as though Mark

92. Barrett, *Caligula*, 142.

93. The satire *Apocolyntesis (The Pumpkinification of [the Divine] Claudius)*, attributed to Seneca the Younger, turns the deification of the Emperor Claudius upon his death into a farce. The Emperor Vespasian's flippant mockery of the idea of apotheosis is displayed by his supposed death-bed declaration, "Oh! I think I'm becoming a god!" (Cassius Dio, *Rom. Hist.* 66.3).

94. Otfried Hofius, "Ist Jesus der Messias? Thesen," in *Neutestamentliche Studien* (WUNT 2/132; Tübingen: Mohr Siebeck, 2000), 122–23.

95. Eugene LaVerdiere, *The Beginning of the Gospel: Introducing the Gospel according to Mark* (Collegeville, MN: Liturgical, 1999), 1:21.

were allowing us to view the drama from a heavenly vantage-point (whence we see things as they really are) before he brings us down to earth, where we find characters in the story totally bewildered by what is going on."[96] Lightfoot declares, "We find placed in our hands at the outset the key which the evangelist wishes us to have, in order that we may understand the person and office of the central Figure of the book."[97] We also are let in on the key figure who is operating behind the scenes, God. In many ways, Mark's introduction is comparable to John 1:1–18. Hooker sketches out the similarities:

> Both evangelists tell us of the special relationship between Jesus and his Father, describing Jesus as the "beloved" or "only" Son, and both term him "Christ," i.e. "Messiah." Both refer to the work of John the Baptist as the witness to Jesus, and stress the latter's superiority. Both describe Jesus' confrontation with evil: in Mark this is termed "Satan," in John, "darkness." Both indicate the source of the power with which Jesus is to work: in Mark, this is expressed in terms of the Holy Spirit; in John, Jesus is said to be the Word made flesh.[98]

3.2.1 The Extent of the Introduction

The extent of the introduction is debated. Does it include the summary of Jesus' preaching when he returns to Galilee (1:14–15), or does it end with the conclusion of Jesus' testing by Satan (1:13)?

3.2.1.1 Arguments to Extend the Introduction to 1:14–15

Those who argue that the introduction extends to 1:15 do so primarily on literary grounds.[99] Keck contends that the word "good news" in 1:1 and 1:14 forms an *inclusio* that marks off the introduction as a unit.[100] If 1:1 functions as an incipit, however, it would not provide the first element of a frame for the first unit, as Keck contends. Nor should it be surprising, if 1:1 describes the content of the entire gospel, for the word "good news" to reappear at the beginning of Jesus' public ministry.[101] Gundry argues that "the differences between 'of Jesus Christ' and 'of God' and between the Christological content of John's preaching and the theocratic content of Jesus' preaching rule out an inclusion that would clamp together vv 1–15 into a single pericope."[102] It seems better to take 1:14–15 as a new heading

96. Hooker, *Mark*, 32.

97. R. H. Lightfoot, *The Gospel Message of St. Mark* (Oxford: Clarendon, 1950), 17.

98. Morna D. Hooker, "Beginnings and Endings," in *The Written Gospel* (ed. Markus Bockmuehl and Donald A. Hagner; Cambridge: Cambridge University Press, 2005), 190.

99. So Anderson, *Mark*, 63–64; Gerhard Dautzenberg, "Die Zeit des Evangeliums: Mk 1, 1–15 und die Konzeption des Markusevangeliums," *BZ* 21 (1977): 219–34; Gnilka, *Markus*, 1:39–40; Pesch, *Markusevangelium*, 1:71–73; Guelich, *Mark 1–8:26*, 4; Marcus, *Mark 1–8*, 137–76; Witherington, *Mark*, 68; P. J. Sankey, "Promise and Fulfilment: Reader-Response to Mark 1.1–15," *JSNT* 58 (1995): 3–18; Richard J. Dillon, "Mark 1:1–15: A 'New Evangelization'?" *CBQ* 76 (2014): 5–7. Augustine Stock, "Hinge Transitions in Mark's Gospel," *BTB* 15 (1985): 27–31, takes a mediating position and argues that 1:14–15 is an "inverted hinge" so that v. 14 looks forward to Jesus' ministry and v. 15 looks back to the fulfillment of the Scripture and John's prophecy. See also Watts, *New Exodus*, 93–95.

100. Keck, "The Introduction to Mark's Gospel," 359–60. See also Boring, "Mark 1:1–15," 60–61.

101. Frank J. Matera, "The Prologue as the Interpretative Key to Mark's Gospel," *JSNT* 34 (1988): 6.

102. Gundry, *Mark*, 32.

for a new section that repeats a key word from the heading of the gospel to describe the preaching of Jesus. The repetition of the word "good news" "serves as a literary device to encourage retrospection or flashback to v 1 after the parenthetical digression in vv 2–13."[103]

Klauck argues that the introduction extends to v. 15 from what he discerns to be parallel introductions of John and Jesus.[104]

John (1:2–8)	Jesus (1:9–15)
Identified by an off-stage transcendent voice (1:2–4)	Identified by an off-stage transcendent voice (1:10–11)
In the wilderness: baptizing (1:5–6)	In the wilderness: being tested (1:12–13)
Preaching: repentance in terms of promise (1:7–8)	Preaching: repentance in terms of fulfillment (1:14–15)

This imagined parallelism, however, falls through in the middle term.

John	Jesus
Immersing	Immersed
	Tested
Preaching	Preaching

John is not tested by the cosmic power of evil. The balanced outline of parallels also mistakenly places John on an equal footing with Jesus, which is not Mark's intention. The introduction is not an introduction to the ministry of John but an introduction of John as the fulfillment of divine prophecy who prepares the way for Jesus. He bears prophetic witness that after him comes the mightier one. A better schematic analysis of 1:2–8 and 1:9–11 highlights the end stress in each of these segments and reveals what is most important to Mark, namely, the christological announcements.[105] John the Baptizer announces, "After me comes the one more powerful than I" (1:7). God announces, "You are my Son" (1:11). The testing by Satan and the ministrations of the angels in 1:12–13 confirm that these announcements are true.

Boring contends, however, that the introduction cannot close leaving Jesus in the wilderness (1:13). The reader needs to know the outcome of the testing.[106] Keck argues similarly that Jesus' proclamation of good news in Galilee follows naturally as a fitting announcement of a battle victory over Satan in the wilderness. Jesus

103. Marshall, *Faith as a Theme*, 37.

104. Klauck, *Vorspiel*, 21–27. Guelich, *Mark 1–8:26*, 4, claims that a threefold division occurs in both sections:

1. An identifying word from God (1:2b–3, 11)
2. A reference to their person and work (1:4–6, 12–13)
3. A climax in the summary of their preaching (1:7–8, 14–15)

See also Christian Rose, *Theologie als Erzählung im Markusevangelium: Eine narratologisch-rezeptionsästhetische Untersuchung zu Mk 1,1–15* (WUNT 2/236; Tübingen: Mohr Siebeck, 2007), 64–65. J. Ramsay Michaels, *Servant and Son: Jesus in Parable and Gospel* (Atlanta: John Knox, 1981), 44, presents 1:1–15 as a chiasm.

105. Hartman, *Mark*, 13.

106. Boring, "Mark 1:1–15," 57–58.

appears in vv. 14–15 as "the victorious Son of God who returns from the testing-ground with the [good news]."[107] Klauck also claims that an appropriate closure to the introduction is to be expected and maintains that dividing 1:14–15 from the preceding verses makes the beginning of the narration unnecessarily abrupt rhetorically (citing Quintilian, *Inst.* 4.1.79).[108]

I question, however, whether Mark was governed by classical rhetoric. The end of the introduction matches the end of the gospel, which is also abrupt and does not offer a clinching conclusion to the narrative. There is only the promise of Jesus going to Galilee before his disciples, and the reader is not told the outcome. The story of how word gets out about Jesus' resurrection is left hanging. I therefore agree with Sankey that Mark invites the reader in these opening verses "to play a highly creative role in making determinate what is left unsaid."[109] Mark seems to be partial to ambiguity in his narrative. For example, while he does not explicitly narrate Jesus vanquishing Satan in the wilderness testing, it may be inferred from the title of the gospel and from what follows in the narrative when Jesus expels Satan's demons time and time again.

Van Iersel adds that 1:14–15 has "the same structural function" at the beginning of the gospel as 15:40–41 does at the end of the gospel. Both serve as hinges, and "each provides a concise summary of a major part of the book: 1.14–15 looks forward to Jesus' ministry in Galilee, while 15.40–41 looks back on everything that the book has told about Jesus before."[110]

3.2.1.2 Arguments to Limit the Introduction to 1:2–13

I argue on narrative grounds that the introduction ends in v. 13.[111] First, each of the three incidents in vv. 2–13 takes place in the same region, the wilderness and the Jordan River (1:3, 4, 5, 9, 12, 13). A shift in location occurs in 1:14–15 as Jesus begins his ministry in Galilee. The summary of Jesus' preaching serves as the introduction to a sequence of episodes there, beginning with the call of disciples by the Sea of Galilee (1:16–20). Mark introduces new sections of Jesus' ministry in Galilee with summary statements in 3:7 and 6:6b.

Second, a clear time marker, "after John was put in prison," separates 1:14–15 from what precedes.[112] In 1:5, 6, 7, 9, 10, 11, 12, and 13, the clauses are connected by "and" (*kai*), but that pattern is broken with "after" (*meta de*) in 1:14.[113]

107. Keck, "The Introduction to Mark's Gospel," 361–62.

108. Klauck, *Vorspiel*, 34–35.

109. Sankey, "Promise and Fulfilment," 5.

110. Van Iersel, *Mark*, 104.

111. So Lightfoot, *The Gospel Message*, 15–20; Cranfield, *Mark*, 33; Lane, *Mark*, 39–40; France, *Mark*, 54–60. Becker, "Mk 1:1 and the Debate on a 'Markan Prologue,'" 97–105, argues that no visible narratological, semantic, or syntactic shift justifies dividing 1:1–13/15 from the rest of the narrative. She instead limits the introduction to 1:1–3 and contends the narrative begins in 1:4. I argue that there is a significant narratological shift in 1:14.

112. Marshall, *Faith as a Theme*, 37.

113. Gundry, *Mark*, 62, comments that Mark normally makes connections with *kai* ("and") and seldom uses *de* ("and"), and that when he does "we can see an adversative meaning that sets off the following material more radically than usual." He notes that it marks a transition from synagogues in 1:39 to deserted places in 1:45; from Galilee to Tyre in 7:24; from Galilee to Jerusalem in 10:32; from the eschatological discourse to the Passion Narrative in 14:1; from the trial to the crucifixion in 15:16; and from the crucifixion to the burial in 15:40.

Third, Mark reintroduces the name of the chief character, Jesus, in v. 14. It is best to take 1:14–15 as a resumption of the reference to the good news in 1:1 as Jesus' ministry in Galilee begins. Jesus has been a passive recipient of the action to this point and now takes the initiative in returning to Galilee to proclaim the kingdom of God. It seems best to take these verses as a concise introduction to Jesus' public ministry when the time of expectation outlined in 1:2–13 shifts to a new era, the time of fulfillment with the beginning of the gospel of Jesus Christ.[114]

Fourth, each of the three units in the previous verses contains a reference to the Spirit (1:8, 10, 12), but no mention is made of the Spirit in vv. 14–15 (contrast Luke 4:14–15). The Spirit is not prominent in the rest of the gospel and is mentioned only in 3:29; 12:36; 13:11.

Fifth, each of the three scenes presents the reader with privileged information that is unavailable to the characters in the narrative world—a transcendent voice off-stage making announcements about John and Jesus, visions of the heavens ripping and the Spirit descending, and a bird's-eye view of Jesus being tested by Satan and angels ministering to him.[115] Verses 14–15 mark a shift in narrative perspective.[116] As Hooker vividly describes it:

> In v. 14 we come down to earth with a bump, and the characters in the story become the normal, everyday inhabitants of Galilee. It is as though in vv. 1–13, Mark has allowed us to see Jesus from God's angle, and now the curtain falls, and we are among men and women who stumble around, wondering what is happening.[117]

For example, the baffled crowds ask, "What is this?" (1:27). Awestruck disciples ask, "Who is this?" (4:41). Threatened Pharisees brashly assert that he is in league with the ruler of demons (3:22). Herod's best guess is that he is John the Baptizer come back to life to haunt him for his sins, while others conjecture that he must be a recycled prophet (6:14–16; 8:27–28). The high priest and his council consider him guilty of blasphemy for passing himself off as the Messiah, the Son of the Blessed One, and mock him as a deluded fraud (14:61–65). His executioners poke fun at him as a farcical king (15:16–20). Even when Peter thinks he has Jesus pegged as the Messiah, Jesus' sharp response reveals that he is still off base and needs further instruction about his identity and mission (8:29–38). If the audience did not have the leads from the introduction that identify who Jesus is, they would be as clueless as the characters in the story who hear the good news of God but veer toward false inferences. The audience knows the truth about Jesus from the outset, but not the whole truth. Matera comments, "As in all good narratives, the narrator does not reveal everything to the readers at the beginning."[118]

114. Marshall, *Faith as a Theme*, 37, n. 3, suggests "that 'Galilee' in 1:14 could represent his public ministry as a whole."

115. Boring, *Mark*, 33, must concede, "The reader, but not the participants in the body of the narrative, is party to these extraordinary scenes, events, and voices, and is prepared to understand the story in a way that they cannot—until after the cross and resurrection."

116. Matera, "Prologue," 6.

117. Morna Hooker, *The Message of Mark* (London: Epworth, 1983), 16.

118. Matera, "Prologue," 4.

Finally, Marcus, who argues that the introduction extends to 1:15, undermines his argument by examining how Mark composes the first half of the gospel. Mark deliberately places narratives of Jesus commissioning his disciples (1:16–20; 3:13–19; 6:7–13) at the beginning of three literary units (1:16–3:6; 3:7–6:6a; 6:6b–8:21). These commissioning narratives follow "a transitional summary of Jesus' activity" (1:14–15; 3:7–12; 6:6b).[119] This structural feature reveals vv. 14–15 to be a "transitional summary" that does not belong to the introduction (1:1–13), any more than the summaries in 3:7–12 and 6:6b belong to the previous literary units. It functions as a hinge that links the introduction in 1:2–13 to the narrative that follows.

3.2.2 The Prophecy from Scripture (Mark 1:2–3)

The introduction contains three prophecies. The first two, in vv. 2–3, are about John. They confirm that he is the one who prepares the way in the wilderness for the coming of the Lord. John's validation from Scripture prepares for the third and climactic prophecy, his prediction about the mightier one who comes after him (vv. 7–8).

If the introduction begins in v. 2, it means that the adverb "just as" (*kathōs*) must begin the next sentence, and the main verb ("appeared") is to be found in v. 4. This solecistic beginning is little different from the nonstandard grammar of the ending in 16:8, where the sentence concludes with "for" (*gar*). As noted above (§3.1.2), the adverb "as" does not normally introduce a new sentence but links what follows with what precedes (see 9:13; 14:21).[120] Exceptions to grammatical norms, however, always exist in languages, and the adverb is used to begin a sentence in Luke 17:26; John 3:14; and 1 Cor 2:9. The phrase "as it is written" is common in Paul, appearing fourteen times in Romans alone (Rom 1:17; 2:24; 3:4, 10; 4:17; 8:36; 9:13, 33; 10:15; 11:8, 26; 15:3, 9, 21; see also 1 Cor 1:31; 2:9; 2 Cor 8:15; 9:9). This citation is the only time that Mark has the narrator appeal explicitly to Scripture,[121] and I would argue that he places the phrase "as it is written in Isaiah" at the starting point of the introduction for emphasis. It means that Mark intends for the story of the gospel of Jesus Christ to be understood in light of the OT story.

The citation of Scripture links the gospel story to that of Israel's history and God's promises, which reaches a turning point with John's preaching of a repentance baptism. The quotation from Scripture reveals that the good news extends back into the long history of God's dealing with Israel. Watts argues "that the prologue is indeed replete with textual icons derived from Israel's ideologically shaped recounting of her history."[122]

119. Marcus, *Mark 1–8*, 177.

120. Arnold, "Mk 1,1," 123–24; Guelich, "'The Beginning of the Gospel,'" 6, 12; Marcus, *Way*, 17–18; Watts, *New Exodus*, 55–56; Klauck, *Vorspiel*, 27.

121. The other references to Scripture appear on the lips of characters in the story.

122. Watts, *New Exodus*, 120.

3.2.2.1 A Composite Text

Mark cites Isaiah as the source of the quotation in vv. 2–3, but it is a mixed text that fuses Exod 23:20; Mal 3:1; and Isa 40:3.[123] How these three texts came together is difficult to unpack.[124] In introducing John the Baptizer, Matthew only cites Isa 40:3 (Matt 3:3), and Luke only cites Isa 40:3–5 (Luke 3:4–6). In Matt 11:10 and Luke 7:27, "This is the one about whom it is written: 'I will send my messenger ahead of you, who will prepare your way before you,'" the composite texts of Exod 23:20 and Mal 3:1 are applied to John the Baptizer without citing Isa 40:3. Regardless of how these texts may have been joined,[125] the result in Mark's setting is that "the Isaiah ascription together with the Isaiah 40:3 text provides the framework into which the Exodus/Malachi conflation is inserted."[126]

[Isaiah]	As it is written in Isaiah the prophet,
[Exodus and Malachi]	"I will send my messenger ahead of you, who will prepare your way."
[Isaiah]	"A voice crying in the wilderness, 'Prepare the way for the Lord, make straight paths for him.'"

Why does Mark identify Isaiah as the source?[127] It is not because he intends to give credit to the source as modern writers do in footnotes. Isaiah is the only prophet named in the gospel, and the book is cited in Mark more often than all the other OT books put together.[128] Isaiah is also the prophet connected to the messianic time and the new exodus. Mark is "hinting more broadly that his whole story of 'the beginning of the gospel' is to be understood against the backdrop of Isaian themes."[129] Watts's explanation that Mark "may have intentionally sandwiched the Exodus/Malachi text between the Isaiah ascription and quotation to ensure that

123. Mark fuses texts in 1:11 (Isa 42:1/Ps 2:7); 11:1–11 (Zech 9:9/Ps 118:25–26); 11:17 (Isa 56:7/Jer 7:11); 13:24–25 (Isa 13:10/Isa 34:4/Joel 2:10/Ezek 32:7–8); and 14:62 (Dan 7:13/Ps 110:1).

124. Modern printing expedients that can put scriptural references in the margins or footnotes were unavailable to ancient writers. Instead, conflation of Old Testament texts was a familiar technique in postbiblical Judaism. It is characteristic of Qumran exegesis to juxtapose Scriptures that originally had nothing to do with each other. Exodus 23:20 and Mal 3:1 could have been connected using the principle of *gezerah shawah* (verbal analogy), an interpretive method in which two passages with similar vocabulary are joined together so that each text clarifies or augments the meaning of other (see *Exod. Rab.* 32.9; *Deut. Rab.* 11.9, where the texts are joined). This linking would have been done in a Semitic milieu since the verbal parallels are present in the Hebrew but not in the LXX. See Marcus, *Way*, 12–17.

125. I think it unlikely that Mark drew from a testimonium (like a responsive reading in a hymnal that combines various texts) that wrongly attributed the text to Isaiah. Contra Krister Stendahl, *The School of St. Matthew and Its Use of the Old Testament* (ASNU 20; Lund: Gleerup, 1968), 50–51; Schweizer, *Mark*, 29; Lane, *Mark*, 45–46. Guelich, "'The Beginning of the Gospel,'" 14, n. 24, observes, "we do not have any examples of composite quotations ascribed to a single person, such as Isaiah in Mark 1.2–3 (cf. Matt 27:9)."

126. Watts, *New Exodus*, 89.

127. Some early Bibles (A K P W [NA] f^{13} part of Syriac Old Latin and Coptic) omit the name "Isaiah" and identify the source as "the prophets."

128. See 1:2–3 (Isa 40:3); 4:12 (Isa 6:9–10); 7:6 (Isa 29:13); 9:48 (Isa 66:24); 11:17 (Isa 56:7); 12:1 (Isa 5:1–2); 12:32 (Isa 45:21); 13:24 (Isa 13:10); and 13:25 (Isa 34:4). Compare 1:2 (Exod 23:20; Mal 3:1); 11:17 (Jer 7:11); 13:26 and 14:62 (Dan 7:13); and 14:27 (Zech 13:7).

129. Marcus, *Way*, 20, citing Guelich, "'The Beginning of the Gospel,'" 8–10.

130. Watts, *New Exodus*, 57.

it was understood within an Isaianic framework" is compelling.[130] The quotation from Isa 40 derives from a context of comfort and good news as the end of Israel's exile in Babylon is in sight. God will return to deliver the people, and a messenger comes to announce the good news of Israel's redemption (Isa 40:9–11).[131]

By contrast, the context of the quotation from Malachi is one of threatened judgment (Mal 3:1–9). God will send a messenger to prepare his way, but God's coming will not inaugurate a time of blessing. Instead, God comes in judgment to refine the faithless and disobedient and to purge the priests who have been derelict in their duties. The prophet asks, "But who can endure the day of his coming, and who can stand when he appears?" (Mal 3:2). The structure of Mark's quotation sandwiches an ominous threat with promise and comfort. The context of Exod 23:20 is the middle term. It is set in an account of Israel's founding when the way of the Lord is being prepared. Israel must be ready and listen to the voice of the messenger who comes to them to guide them through the wilderness to the Promised Land (Exod 23:21–22). But the angel/messenger of Exod 23:20 also comes as God's covenant enforcer because of "Israel's faithless rebellion."[132]

Isaiah 40:3 refers to God's coming and the inauguration of the new exodus. The exodus of the past in which God delivered Israel is projected into the future when a more glorious deliverance will transpire. Watts uses the Isaian exodus theme as a template to interpret all of Mark. The schema involves three stages:

A Yahweh's deliverance of his exiled people from the power of the nations and their idols.
B The journey along the "Way" in which Yahweh leads his people from their captivity among the nations.
C The arrival in Jerusalem, the place of his presence, where Yahweh is enthroned in a gloriously restored Zion.[133]

This template may be a Procrustean bed that stretches the text too far to fit the thesis at points, but there is no question that Isaian themes are prominent throughout Mark.

3.2.2.2 God as the One Who Initiates the Action

By citing the Scripture texts at the beginning of the narrative, Mark reveals that this is no ordinary story designed simply to entertain or to enrich the reader. God is the one who initiates the action behind the scenes as the promise-filled preaching of Isaiah is now realized in the coming of Jesus.[134] The long story of God's saving acts is reaching its climax.

131. Thorsten Moritz, "Mark," in *The Theological Interpretation of the New Testament* (ed. Kevin J. Vanhoozer; Daniel J. Treier and N. T. Wright; Grand Rapids: Baker, 2008), 42–43.

132. Watts, *New Exodus*, 67.

133. Ibid., 135.

134. Derrett, *The Making of Mark*, 46–47, asserts that by quoting this mixed text Mark certifies that the Torah (Exodus), the greater prophets (Isaiah), and the lesser prophets (Malachi, the last of the prophets) confirm what he is about to tell.

3.2.2.3 Jesus as the Lord

Three characters appear in 1:2: the one who sends the messenger, the one who will cry out in the wilderness and construct the way, and the one whose way is prepared ("your way"). Mark's meaning is elusive. He does not make it explicit that the messenger in the cited Scripture is John the Baptizer. One can only infer from 1:3 and the narrative that follows that John is the voice preaching in the wilderness and the one who prepares the way through his repentance baptism. John mentions that someone mightier than he comes after him, but he never identifies who that one is. Mark provides clues for the attentive reader from his alterations of the quotations. He changes "*my* face" in Mal 3:1 (LXX), which refers to God, to "*your* face," which in Mark's context can only refer to Jesus.[135] The explicit "the paths of our God" in Isa 40:3 (LXX) has become "*his* paths" in Mark. The antecedent is "the Lord," and the ambiguity of who "the Lord" is has significant christological implications.

Broadhead argues that "Lord" refers "first and foremost" and only to God, and that Jesus will become Lord only at the Parousia.[136] Johansson successfully counters this view. Mark deliberately uses the title "Lord" ambiguously so that in the context it can refer to God *and* to Jesus.[137] Implicit in the application of the citation to Jesus is that he is the manifestation of God. Isaiah anticipated a majestic procession led by God himself. Mark sees that God has turned this task over to Jesus. Jesus' appearance reveals that John is not paving the way for the appearance of God but for Jesus. "Our God's way" becomes "Jesus' way"; these are not two separate paths.[138] Boring avers, "In Mark's own view, the figures of God and Jesus modulate into each other under the designation 'Lord.'"[139] Collins also concludes, "In the context of Mark as a whole, to prepare the way of Jesus as Lord is also to prepare a way for the Lord God."[140] God's plans for the salvation of Israel and the world are centered in Jesus of Nazareth: "God's advent in salvation and judgement has taken place in Jesus."[141]

Marcus highlights the christological paradox that the juxtaposition of "your way" (Jesus' way) and "the way of the Lord" recognizes "the separateness of the two figures with a recognition of their inseparability."[142] Jesus remains dependent on

135. Christopher D. Stanley, *Paul and the Language of Scripture: Citation Technique in the Pauline Epistles and Contemporary Language* (SNTSMS 74; Cambridge: Cambridge University Press, 1992), 338–50, shows how combining different texts into a single quotation was not uncommon in Paul's time and that would apply to Mark's time. Writers felt free to adapt quotations to fit the point they wanted to make in citing a passage. Since these changes were obvious, such practices can be assumed to have been accepted by the audience.

136. Edwin K. Broadhead, *Naming Jesus: Titular Christology in the Gospel of Mark* (JSNTSup 175; Sheffield: Sheffield Academic Press, 1999), 141–43. See also Taylor, *Mark*, 153–54, who says that "Lord" is possibly only used of Jesus in the vocative in 7:28 and 11:3 in the sense of "the Master."

137. Daniel Johansson, "*Kyrios* in the Gospel of Mark," *JSNT* 33 (2010): 101–24. This ambiguity is striking in 5:19–20. "The Lord" of v. 19 becomes "Jesus" in v. 20. See also 11:3, where the colt for the Lord is brought to Jesus (11:3–7). Kingsbury, *Christology*, 59, contends that "the four genitives of the pronoun 'you' and 'he' and of the noun 'Lord' refer exclusively to Jesus Messiah, the Son of God."

138. Johansson ("*Kyrios* in the Gospel of Mark," 104) best explains the change in pronouns in vv. 2–3 from the second person to the third person: "In 1.2, speaking directly to Jesus, God promises to send a messenger before him; in 1.3 the messenger himself speaks about Jesus in the third person—hence the change of pronouns. 'Your way' is also 'the way of the Lord.' The Isaiah passage clarifies who the second person of 1.2 is."

139. Boring, *Mark*, 154.

140. Collins, *Mark*, 137. See also Watts, *New Exodus*, 87.

141. Hooker, *Mark*, 36.

142. Marcus, *Way*, 39.

God in the narrative (5:19; 10:18, 40; 13:32; 14:36; 15:34). The distinction between Jesus and the Father remains. Jesus does not come triumphantly from heaven on chariots of fire but inconspicuously and enigmatically from Nazareth, and few, therefore, will recognize his appearance as the coming of God. They also will not recognize that "Jesus' apparent defeat" on the cross "is the occasion for God's victory (cf. 15:33–39)."[143]

3.2.2.4 The Meaning of the Way

The citation from Isa 40:3 (see also Isa 42:16; 43:19; 48:17; 49:11; 51:10) introduces the theme of "the way," which will become prominent in the gospel. Garrett asserts that to "follow straight paths" means to avoid idolatry and other wicked behaviors, but the "cry in the wilderness" is not a cry to *follow* straight paths. Rather, it is an exhortation to "make straight paths for him" (1:3). This exhortation means "to assist ones who strive to walk in 'the way of the Lord'—to ensure their unhindered travel."[144] John may prepare the way by leveling the playing field in demanding that one and all repent and be immersed, but this demand should be read in light of the entire narrative.

In Mark, disciples do not prepare the way for Jesus. More often than not, they get in the way (8:33). Instead, it is Jesus who leads them on the way, and the disciples must follow him on the way. In Isa 40:3–4, "everything in the nature of the desert which is troublesome for the journey of the redeemed will be transformed into a condition insuring an easy passage."[145] As Jesus leads the way and teaches about it (12:14), however, it seems to be anything but easy. It is the way to the cross and the way of the cross. Stumbling blocks abound, and Jesus himself will strew them along the way (see 7:24–30). Boring comments that to follow Jesus "is not a call to adopt his 'way of life' in the sense of adopting his ideals and principles, but to follow behind him in the path he himself walked."[146] The citation from Isaiah, then, "establishes the theme of salvation for God's people, and the progression of the story develops the nature of that salvation."[147]

3.2.2.5 Beginning in the Wilderness, Not in Jerusalem or the Temple

Mark's account of the beginning starts in the wilderness, on the fringe of civilized existence that is alien to human habitation, *not* in the holy temple in Jerusalem, as in Luke (Luke 1:8–23), nor in the heavenly council of God before creation, as in John

143. Ibid., 41.

144. Susan R. Garrett, *The Temptations of Jesus in Mark's Gospel* (Grand Rapids: Eerdmans, 1998), 53. Josephus (*J.W.* 3.6.2 §118) uses this image quite differently for the advancing Roman army under the general Vespasian, who would later become the emperor and Josephus's patron. Some of the soldiers were assigned "to make the road even and straight, and if it were anywhere rough and hard to be passed over, to plane it, and to cut down the woods that hindered their march, that the army might not be in distress, or tired with their march."

145. Mauser, *Wilderness*, 51.

146. Boring, *Mark*, 38.

147. Elizabeth E. Shively, *Apocalyptic Imagination in the Gospel of Mark: The Literary and Theological Role of Mark 3:22–30* (BZNW 189; Berlin/New York: de Gruyter, 2012), 262.

(John 1:1–5). The wilderness held deep symbolic significance for Jews from their long history with God. For example, it was the place of new beginnings and renewal (Exod 2:15; 1 Sam 23:14; 1 Kgs 19:3–4). It was the place to which God led the people and from which they crossed over Jordan and took the land promised them (Exod 13:18; 16:32). God seeks to appeal to the wayward people to return to the wilderness so that they might be renewed (Hos 2:14). It was also the place where heroes fled iniquitous authorities and their web of cunning to avoid sharing in their defilement (2 Macc 5:27). According to the *Martyrdom and Ascension of Isaiah* 2:7–11, the prophets Isaiah, Micah, Ananias, Joel, Habakkuk, and his son Josab abandoned the corruption of Judah for the mountainous wilderness where they clothed themselves in sackcloth, lamented bitterly over straying Israel, and ate wild herbs.

The wilderness was also regarded as "the staging ground for Yahweh's future victory over the power of evil."[148] The covenanters who settled in Qumran took Isa 40:3 as their foundational text and formed a community in the wilderness to segregate themselves from the rest of Israel. Their aim was to "open there His path" and to prepare for God's coming deliverance with the study of the law (see 1QS 8:12–16; 9:17–20). It is also the place where they believed that the holy war would be fought and won (1QM 1:2–3). Many thought that the Messiah would appear in the wilderness (Matt 24:26), and it was the haunt of messianic insurrectionists like the Egyptian false prophet (Acts 21:38). Others believed it was the place where a second exodus would occur that would surpass the first, because there would be no need for haste or fearful flight. The wilderness would be changed into a paradise (Isa 41:18–19; 44:3–4; 51:3). The wilderness with all its associations is therefore an apt setting for "the drama of God's eschatological salvation" to begin.[149] The wilderness reappears in Mark's narrative as a retreat for prayer (1:35), solitude (1:45), and rest (6:31–32), and as the place where a miraculous feeding occurs (6:34–44).

3.2.3 John the Baptist the Prophetic Forerunner (Mark 1:4–8)

Mark has no interest in John except as the forerunner of Jesus. He does not give us any information about John, who his parents were, the circumstances of his astonishing birth, or the contents of his ethical teaching (see Luke 1:5–25, 39–80; 3:7–18). All Mark is concerned about is John's preaching, which "serves only one purpose—to point forward to Jesus."[150] He appears in the introduction solely to flag "his successor as the Coming One."[151] He is a witness to Jesus. For this reason, "the narrative proper only begins with the account of the Lord's activity in verses 14 and 15, when He comes into Galilee with the announcement that the time is ripe, and God's promises are now in process of accomplishment."[152]

148. Marcus, *Way*, 22.
149. France, *Mark*, 58.
150. Hooker, *Mark*, 38.
151. Ibid., 34.
152. Lightfoot, *The Gospel Message of St. Mark*, 19.

3.2.3.1 John as Elijah Redivivus

Mark gives us two seemingly superfluous details about John's diet and clothing. A diet of locusts and wild honey, "the harsh staples of desert hospitality," reflects that he lived simply and took no provisions for his tour of preaching and baptizing, as Jesus will later command the disciples to do (6:8–10).[153] But this detail also confirms that John is in the wilderness.[154]

His clothing, however, is intended to conjure images of the prophet Elijah's dress (2 Kgs 1:8; see Zech 13:4). Mark does not notify the reader explicitly that John is Elijah as do Matthew (Matt 17:13) and Luke (Luke 1:17) but assumes the reader can infer it from the allusions to Scripture and from the narrative (9:11–13). John's prophetic garb intimates that John is Elijah *redivivus*, and this inference should prevent readers from confusing Jesus with Elijah, as some of the crowds do (8:28).[155]

According to 2 Kgs 2:11, Elijah did not die but ascended into heaven in a whirlwind, and this miraculous departure fostered anticipation of a no less miraculous return (see Sir 48:10; *L.A.B.* 48:1; *Sib. Or.* 2:187–89; *Apoc. El.* 5:32–33). Elijah's return was assumed to herald the appearance of God himself, not the Messiah.[156] Stein is correct that no evidence exists to confirm "that first-century Judaism believed that Elijah would serve as a precursor for the Messiah."[157] This idea first surfaces in the Gospels and appears in later Christian writers, for example, Justin Martyr (*Dial.* 8.4; 49.1). It is likely that the idea that John the Baptizer was the forerunner of the Messiah derives from Jesus, who identified John as Elijah who must come first (9:11–13). Mark modifies the assorted expectations about Elijah's future eschatological role in the light of his Christology (6:14–16; 8:27–30; 9:2–8; 9:11–13; 15:33–39). John the Baptizer is Elijah, and his only role is to serve as the Messiah's forerunner and herald. Grindheim asserts, "the reason that Elijah was seen as Jesus' forerunner was that he was the one who would prepare for the coming of God himself."[158] Mark understands Jesus to come in the place of God.

3.2.3.2 A Baptism of Repentance for the Forgiveness of Sins

The Jordan River evoked for Israel associations of hope, as it later did for the New World slaves who sang about "Marching down to Jordan," having "One more river to cross," and "Deep River, My home is over Jordan." It was a place to "look over" to see the longed-for redemption. Josephus records how several prophet figures led people into the wilderness to the Jordan during this era (*J.W.* 2.13.4–5 §§259–63;

153. LaVerdiere, *The Beginning*, 1:31–32.

154. James A. Kelhoffer, *The Diet of John the Baptist: "Locusts and Wild Honey" in Synoptic and Patristic Interpretation* (WUNT 2/176; Tübingen: Mohr Siebeck, 2005), 121–23, 132–33. John's withdrawal into the wilderness may be a protest against the corruption in Jerusalem. See Jerry Camery-Hoggatt, *Irony in Mark's Gospel: Text and Subtext* (SNTSMS 72; Cambridge: Cambridge University Press, 1992), 95.

155. Frank J. Matera, *New Testament Christology* (Louisville: Westminster John Knox, 1999), 8. The privileged information also prevents readers from confusing Jesus with John the Baptizer raised from the dead, as Herod does and some others do (6:14, 16; 8:28).

156. Markus Öhler, "The Expectation of Elijah and the Presence of the Kingdom of God," *JBL* 118 (1999): 461–76.

157. Stein, *Mark*, 48.

158. Grindheim, *Christology*, 38; see also Sigurd Grindheim, *God's Equal: What Can We Know about Jesus' Self-Understanding?* (LNTS 446; London/New York: T&T Clark, 2011), 53–58.

Ant. 20.5.1 §§97–98; 20.8.6 §§167–168). The difference between their agenda and John's is that, according to Josephus, the (false) prophets intended to show the people "unmistakable signs and wonders." According to the Gospels, John called them out there to lead them to repentance in preparation for God's arrival.

Edwards argues that John's calling the people to baptism is "a symbol of moral and spiritual regeneration."[159] It "recalls and revives" God's covenant with Israel at Sinai that summoned the entire people to be a "kingdom of priests and a holy nation" (Exod 19:6; see 1 Pet 2:9), which the Israelites acknowledged "by washing their clothes and purifying themselves before entering into the covenant at Sinai (Exod 19:10)."[160] Donahue and Harrington cite Ezek 36:25–26 as the biblical background where God declares that he will cleanse the people from their idolatry by sprinkling clean water on them and give them a new heart and a new spirit (see also Isa 44:3; Ezek 39:29; Joel 2:28).[161]

Mark does not spell out the relationship between baptism, repentance, and the forgiveness of sins. When did the forgiveness of sins occur? When one repented? When one came out to John in the wilderness? When one was immersed? At the end of the age? Marcus asserts that it is a hope that resides in "the eschatological future" because the baptism of the Spirit awaits the future coming of the stronger one.[162] Mark, however, does not delve into these questions, because he believed John's baptism was only preparatory and temporary. What awaits is a more intense renewal by the Holy Spirit that the Mightier One who comes after John will bring (see Acts 18:24–26, 19:1–7). Mark's narrative will clarify that Jesus has the authority to forgive sins on earth (2:5, 7, 9–10) and that "the true remission resulted from Jesus' death as a 'ransom for many' (10:45)."[163]

3.2.3.3. Confession of Sins

John was not a lone wolf howling in the wilderness. His plea to repent and to submit to his repentance baptism incited a train of pilgrims from all Jerusalem and the whole Judean countryside to flock to him. They came confessing their sins as part and parcel of being immersed by him. Confession of sins is presumed to be a necessary precondition to forgiveness of sins. Boring observes, "The fundamental human problem is here conceived to be not ignorance or inherent human imperfection, but sin, understood as corporate active rebellion against the creator."[164] Many do not know their condition, which is why God sends prophets to warn them.

159. Edwards, *Mark*, 29.

160. Ibid., 30.

161. Donahue and Harrington, *Mark*, 64.

162. Marcus, *Mark 1–8*, 156. The baptism of the Spirit is associated with the forgiveness of sins (Ezek 36:25–26; Zech 12:10–13:1; and 1QS 4:20–21).

163. Marcus, *Mark 1–8*, 156.

164. Boring, *Mark*, 41. Collins, *Mark*, 144–45, argues that the confession of sins "was communal and general and that it signified acceptance of John's prophetic mission and a plea for forgiveness and thus for being spared from or in the eschatological judgment and punishment of God."

3.2.3.4 The Mightier One

What John says last is the crucial element in this report of his preaching. One more powerful than he is coming who will baptize the people with the Holy Spirit, not just with water. John's ministry is simply preparatory. He is only a subordinate figure, unworthy to stoop down and untie the thongs of the sandals of this one who is more powerful than he is (1:7). After John has performed his prophetic role, he can pass off the scene. The good news is not about him, and Mark is not interested in simply passing on historical information about John's fate. Mark therefore delays the fuller account of his arrest and death until a point in the narrative where he can use it to good effect to serve another purpose (6:7–30).

The reference to "the Mightier One" (the literal translation of the word translated by the phrase "the one more powerful") has christological significance, since God is identified as "the Mighty One" in Gen 49:24; Ps 132:2; Isa 1:24; 49:26. God is also the One whose coming is marked by power and strength (Isa 40:10, 26, 29, 31; 45:24; 50:2; 52:1; 63:1, 15; see also Rev 18:8). Again, the title is deliberately ambiguous. "Mighty One" refers to God in Scripture, but in the context of Mark's narrative, it refers to Jesus who comes after John and displays divine power (see 1:27; 3:20–27).

3.2.3.5 The One Who Bestows the Holy Spirit

The promised baptism in the Holy Spirit (1:8) is fulfilled after Easter and is not plotted in Mark.[165] Paul assumes that it is the experience of every Christian (1 Cor 12:13). Since Mark does not describe it occurring in the lives of the disciples (cf. Acts 1:5; 11:16), it is another facet of the story that he assumes his audience would recognize as already having happened. This statement also has christological significance because in the OT God alone dispenses the Holy Spirit. In Mark's context, this role is transferred to Jesus.

3.2.4 The Clarification of Jesus' Divine Identity at His Baptism (Mark 1:9–11)

The phrase "it happened in those days" ("at that time," NIV) serves as a transition that introduces the appearance of Jesus on the scene. It is biblical language that may have eschatological reverberations (see Jer 3:16, 18; 31:29; 33:15–16; Joel 3:1; Zech 8:23; see also Mark 13:17, 19, 24; Rev 9:6),[166] but its usage in 8:1 suggests that it may only point to the past from the perspective of the narrator.[167] Jesus joins the throngs from Jerusalem and Judea, but he comes from Nazareth in Galilee.[168] Paradoxically, the one who is to bring a baptism in the Holy Spirit comes instead to receive John's baptism in water.[169]

165. Juel, *Mark*, 55.

166. Sankey, "Promise and Fulfilment," 11.

167. Gnilka, *Markus*, 1:51.

168. On the historicity of Jesus' baptism, see R. L. Webb, "Jesus' Baptism: Its Historicity and Implications," *BBR* 10 (2000): 261–309.

169. R. T. France, "The Beginning of Mark," *RTR* 49 (1990): 15.

The "Mightier One" comes incognito from the periphery of the Jewish landscape, Galilee, and is found first among sinners who have come to repent from their sins. Three signs occur at his baptism, however, that confirm his identity as the Son of God: the heavens rip apart, the Spirit descends into ("on," NIV) him, and a heavenly voice announces, "You are my Son, whom I love; with you I am well pleased."[170]

3.2.4.1 Reasons for Jesus to Submit to John's Baptism for the Forgiveness of Sins

As one who is confessed as knowing no sin (2 Cor 5:21; Heb 4:15), Jesus' submission to a repentance baptism for the forgiveness of sins may seem puzzling. Mark apparently is untroubled by any theological problem that this report might create and offers no explanations.[171] Since no protest comes from John (cf. Matt 3:14), one can infer from Mark's text that John did not single out Jesus from any of the others who came for baptism. Mark's narration of this event may be rooted in a theological purpose. His aim is to present the reader with infallible divine testimony rather than human testimony about Jesus' identity (cf. John 1:29, 32–34).

Two proposals cogently explain Jesus' decision to submit to John's water baptism. (1) Jesus did not come to purify himself of sin but to identify himself with sinful Israel. He accepted John's repentance baptism as God's means for restoring Israel.[172] In this light, Craddock explains, "baptism is not a private act for private spiritual gain, but an acceptance of membership in the historic family of God and a participation in the continuing narrative of God's unfolding purpose."[173] Israel would emerge from the waters of John's baptism prepared for God's coming. LaVerdiere takes this view a step further:

> Jesus did not have to be a sinner to accept John's baptism. All he needed was to be in personal solidarity with men and women who are sinners and in need of salvation. Jesus' baptism by John revealed Jesus' humanity and his solidarity with all human beings, and it demonstrated his willingness to bear the weight of our sins on his own sinless shoulders.[174]

At the beginning of the gospel, Jesus joins the ranks of sinners and takes his stand with them. At the end, isolated and alone, he will die for them, going through

170. Translating the phrase "the Son of Man whom I love" instead of "beloved Son" may cause the reader to miss the intertextual connections with Jacob as a beloved Son.

171. In Luke, Jesus' baptism is placed *after* the baptism of the multitude as something special, but the report of it is passed over in haste with a participial clause (3:21). John 1:19–34 describes parallel events but omits any reference to Jesus being baptized. In the *Gospel of the Nazarenes*, Jesus himself protests: "What sin have I committed that I should go to him to be baptized?" (Jerome, *Pelag.* 3.20).

172. Armand Puig i Tàrrech, *Jesus: An Uncommon Journey: Studies on the Historical Jesus* (WUNT 2/288; Tübingen: Mohr Siebeck, 2010), 154.

173. Fred B. Craddock, *The Gospels* (Nashville: Abingdon, 1981), 76.

174. LaVerdiere, *The Beginning*, 1:34. Ignatius (*Eph.* 18:2) goes even further by claiming that Jesus purified the water for future baptism. But John's baptism is not a model for Christian baptism (Acts 19:1–6).

a different baptism (10:38, 45). The three events at Jesus' baptism have their counterparts at Jesus' crucifixion, and they frame the gospel story. Marcus notes that when Jesus dies on the cross, he "breathes out his *spirit* [he expires], the curtain of the Temple is *ripped apart*, and the centurion acclaims Jesus as *the Son of God* (15:37–39)."[175]

(2) By submitting to John's baptism, he acknowledges that John is God's messenger and that his ministry is sanctioned by heaven (see 11:30). He sides with the one who provides a way for people in Israel to receive divine acceptance outside of the temple cult.

3.2.4.2 Three Signals of Jesus' Divine Identity

The elements of later trinitarian doctrine appear in the description of what happens when Jesus comes up from the water with the mention of God, the Holy Spirit, and the Son. But Mark is only interested in telling what occurred at Jesus' baptism to reveal his divine identity to the audience. Jesus alone witnesses the three signs. Jesus comes "up out of the water," [176] and "he," not John, sees "heaven being torn open."[177] The direct address, "You are my Son" (1:11) rather than "This is my Son" (9:7; Matt 3:17; 17:5), indicates that the voice from heaven was audible only to Jesus, not the onlookers. John is not portrayed as a witness to these events. In Mark's account of the baptism, there is no evidence that John is privy to what the audience learns from these heavenly manifestations. For Mark, humans cannot fully grasp Jesus' identity as the Son of God until after his death. Navone contends that the human reaction in Mark's narrative to the beloved Son moves from nonrecognition at his baptism to incipient recognition at the transfiguration (9:2–8) to full recognition at the crucifixion (15:39).[178]

3.2.4.2.1 The Ripping Apart of the Heavens

The ripping apart of the heavens signifies a breach in the fixed partition between heaven and earth that only occurs in exceptional, revelatory moments. The opening of the heavens occurs elsewhere in the context of visions (Ezek 1:1; *2 Bar.* 22:1; *T. Levi* 2:6; 5:1; 18:6–8; *T. Jud.* 24:1–3; John 1:51; Acts 7:56; 10:11; Rev 11:19; 19:11), but the verb that Mark uses is not "opened" but "ripped," "split," or "torn." The same verb is used to describe the splitting of the temple veil, from top to bottom, when Jesus dies (Mark 15:38). What is opened may be closed, but what is ripped cannot easily return to its former state. The ripping of the heavens is a violent metaphor that lends itself to various interpretations. Three options commend themselves and are not mutually exclusive.

(1) The ripping of the heavens may refer to the divine penetration of the human

175. Marcus, *Mark 1–8*, 164.

176. Klauck, *Vorspiel*, 91, suggests that perhaps Jesus' baptism may be a prelude to his sinking in the flood-tide of death and his coming out of the water to his resurrection.

177. One is not to interject John 1:32–33 into Mark's account.

178. John J. Navone, "Spiritual Pedagogy in the Gospel of Mark," *TBT* 39 (2001): 231–38.

realm. Welker describes Jesus' baptism as a revolutionary act of humility that broke down the division between heaven and earth and made possible a direct encounter with God.[179] As Hartman claims, "it is through Jesus that a new connection between heaven and earth, between God and humans, is established."[180] Juel qualifies this interpretation by saying, "More accurate than referring to our access to God would be to speak of God's access to us. God comes whether we choose or not. That presence may turn out to be genuinely dangerous. Only the story will tell." The verb "being torn open" is in the present tense, which "suggests something dramatic in the process of taking place."[181] Boring writes, "the time of waiting and longing is over, the ultimate act of God's revelation is already beginning."[182]

(2) The ripping of the heavens may point to the fulfillment of the last plea found in Isaiah that God would not delay but descend through rent heavens to bring redemption: "Oh, that you would rend the heavens and come down, that the mountains would tremble before you" (Isa 64:1 [LXX 63:19b]).[183] This last great lament in Isaiah triggers God's response, which concludes the book. Watts states: "For Mark, Jesus is Yahweh's answer to that cry: he has indeed come, 'in strength,' to announce and to effect Israel's long-awaited NE [new exodus]."[184]

(3) Like the quotation in 1:2–3 that joins Mal 3:1 and Isaiah 40, the ripping of the heavens may also convey a threat. God is no longer safely ensconced in heaven but is loose in the world, reviewing and judging it.

3.2.4.2.2 The Descent of the Holy Spirit

What Mark narrates in Jesus' baptism is the converse of what John announced. Jesus does not baptize with the Holy Spirit (1:8) but is himself baptized in the Holy Spirit (1:10). The outpouring of God's Spirit was a meaningful expectation in the OT (Isa 32:15; 44:3; Ezek 36:26–27; 39:29; Joel 2:28–32, which is cited in Acts 2:17–21 in Peter's Pentecost sermon).[185] It was to be a general outpouring of God's Spirit on the house of Israel, but what occurs here is an outpouring of the Spirit only on Jesus. It conforms to the expectations found in the prophecies of Isa 11:1–2; 42:1; 61:1, which in the NT are interpreted messianically. Collins notes that the Spirit of God coming on a human endows them with different capacities: supernatural strength (Judg 14:6, 19), ecstasy (Num 11:25; 1 Sam 10:6, 10), miraculous transport to another place (1 Kgs 18:12; 2 Kgs 2:16; Ezek 3:12, 14; 8:3; 11:1, 24; 43:5), leadership charisma (Judg 3:10; 1 Sam 16:13), prophetic power (Mic 3:8; Neh 9:30), and the qualities of the ideal king (Isa 11:1–9).[186] What is most important for Mark is that this event reveals to the reader that Jesus is empowered and directed by God's Spirit so that the Spirit's role need not be explicitly mentioned in the scenes that follow.

179. Michael Welker, "Revolutionäre Demut: Mit Jesu Taufe erfüllt sich Gottes Gerechtigkeit," *EvK* 30 (1997): 280–82.

180. Hartman, *Mark*, 32.

181. Donald H. Juel, *A Master of Surprise: Mark Interpreted* (Minneapolis: Fortress, 1994), 34.

182. Boring, *Mark*, 45.

183. See the arguments in Watts, *New Exodus*, 102–7.

184. Ibid., 107.

185. France, *Mark*, 55.

186. Collins, *Mark*, 148–49.

Mark uses an unusual preposition to describe the Holy Spirit descending *into* (*eis*) Jesus rather than *upon* (*epi*) him. It suggests that Jesus possesses the Holy Spirit or that the Holy Spirit possesses him.[187] Either way, Jesus is permanently endowed with the Spirit. The Spirit does not come and go (cf., e.g., 1 Sam 10:6, 10; 11:6). Since the Spirit abides with him, Jesus is not suddenly empowered when the Spirit comes upon him to accomplish his exorcisms and healings and to teach. He does not need to appeal to the Lord or to inquire of the Lord.[188]

The descent of the Spirit as a dove into Jesus is not adverbial, a dovelike descent, but adjectival, the descent of a dovelike Spirit.[189] John Chrysostom asked, "But why in the form of a dove?" and his answer was that the dove was "gentle" and "pure" (*Hom. Matt.* 12.3). But the dove is also characterized in Scripture as silly and without sense (Hos 7:11). Those who think that the simile's literary home is in the OT propose various connections.

It may allude to Noah's dove (Gen 8:8 – 12),[190] but how the audience would connect this passage to the baptism scene and draw meaning from it is unclear. Others propose from Hos 11:1 – 12 that the dove represents Israel.[191] The idea may be that Jesus would epitomize the ideal Israelite. Or, Jacobson notes the image of the dove in *L.A.B.* 21:6, and, assuming that doves are faithful to their mates, contends that the point is that "one day Israel will be like a dove in its devotion to God."[192] The problem with these views is that they apply the dove simile to something about Jesus or about Israel, but in the text it pertains to the Spirit.

More plausible is the connection with Genesis 1:2 and the image of the Spirit hovering over the face of the water at the beginning of creation.[193] Marcus expounds on the possible meaning:

> The heavens that have been shut up since the youth of humanity are reopened; the Spirit that hovered over the primeval waters once more descends to liberate the earth from the stranglehold of chaos; and a voice unheard for age upon age sounds forth, announcing a decision made long ago in the eternal counsel. The words of that decision lay mysteriously hidden and uncomprehended in the scriptures of Israel, but now, with their fulfilment in Jesus' baptism, they can be understood by Mark's readers, who are privileged to witness the epiphany of 1:9 – 11.[194]

Allison, citing 4Q521, interprets the hovering dove to betoken the new creation

187. Juel, *Mark*, 59.

188. Collins, *Mark*, 40.

189. Contra Leander E. Keck, "Spirit and Dove," *NTS* 17 (1970): 41 – 67. Pesch, *Markusevangelium*, 1:91, contends the particle "as" is a "specific apocalyptic particle of comparison" that explains how what is heavenly and unobservable becomes observable. The particle "as" uses an earthly comparison to approximate heavenly realities and frequently appears in Revelation.

190. Paul Garnet, "The Baptism of Jesus and the Son of Man Idea," *JSNT* 9 (1980): 49 – 65.

191. Alfred Edersheim, *Life and Times of Jesus the Messiah* (London: Longmans & Green, 1883), 1:287.

192. Howard Jacobson, *A Commentary on Pseudo-Philo's Liber Antiquitatum Biblicarum* (Leiden/Köln/New York: Brill, 1996), 2:685.

193. Taylor, *Mark*, 161; Cranfield, *Mark*, 54; C. K. Barrett, *Holy Spirit and the Gospel Tradition* (London: SPCK, 1966), 38 – 39; Keck, "Spirit and Dove," 63; Marcus, *Mark 1 – 8*, 159 – 60.

194. Marcus, *Way*, 75.

of the eschatological new age.[195] The parallel with Gen 1:2 breaks down, however, because at creation the Spirit hovers over the waters of the formless void, but at Jesus' baptism the Spirit descends on/into him.

Dixon finds the literary home of the image in Greek mythology. He claims that the simile is modeled on Homer's depiction of the "descents of gods from the heavenly realm to earth."[196] Collins cites his view approvingly: "In relation to the transfiguration in 9:2–8, members of the audience familiar with Greek mythology would understand v. 10 to mean that the earthly Jesus, from the time of his baptism, was a divine being walking the earth."[197] The problem with this view is that the birds associated with divine activity were normally birds of prey, such as eagles or falcons, not doves, so the simile of the Spirit descending as a dove on Jesus needs further fine-tuning.

Peppard, to my mind, offers the best solution. He argues that the dove should be "interpreted as an omen and counter-symbol to the Roman eagle, which was a public portent of divine favor, election, and ascension to imperial power."[198] This simile would have been easily understood by a Roman audience who would be familiar with bird omens, especially those involving eagles, which "indicated providential favor for the accession to power of the person on or near whom they alighted."[199] A casual reading of Tacitus's *Histories*, for example, reveals how significant omens were to the Romans, particularly as they related to the rise and fall of aspirants to the throne after the death of Nero.

According to 2 Esd 5:23–27, God chose the dove above all other birds, and it, along with other things, is used to express Israel's special election over all others. The dove descending on Jesus when connected to the announcement from heaven can signify that he is specially chosen to be God's unique instrument. But there is a marked contrast between the eagle in Roman lore and the dove. In recounting the advance of the Roman army under Vespasian to quash the Jewish revolt, Josephus describes the sacred ensigns that accompanied every Roman legion. They had an image of an eagle, which, he says, is "the king and the most warlike of all birds, which seems to them a sure sign of empire, and an omen that they shall conquer all against whom they march" (Josephus, *J.W.* 3.6.2 § 123). Peppard establishes that "the bellicose eagle was the primary symbol of Roman military might and concomitantly of Roman imperial ideology, while the dove was a contrasting symbol of fear or nonviolence."[200] The descent of the dove from the heavens ripped open conveys that Jesus receives absolute power from God, but he would exercise that power quite differently from the way the warlike, tyrannical Roman emperors did.[201] His power

195. Dale C. Allison Jr., "The Baptism of Jesus and a New Dead Sea Scroll," *BAR* 18 no. 2 (March-April 1992): 58–60.

196. Edward P. Dixon, "Descending Spirit and Descending Gods: A 'Greek' Interpretation of the Spirit's 'Descent as a Dove' in Mark 1:10," *JBL* 128 (2009): 759–80.

197. Collins, *Mark*, 149.

198. Michael Peppard, "The Eagle and the Dove: Roman Imperial Sonship and the Baptism of Jesus (Mark 1.9–11)," *NTS* 56 (2010): 433.

199. Ibid., 445.

200. Ibid., 447.

201. It also differs from Isaiah's picture of the heavens being torn and God coming down so that the nations might tremble and the mountains quake before God's presence (Isa 64:1–3).

would embody a spirit of forgiveness, gentleness, and amity (see 2 Esd 5:26; *L.A.B.* 39:5; *Let. Aris.* 144–48).[202] This understanding is conveyed in Peter's preaching in Acts 10:36–38:

> You know the message God sent to the people of Israel, announcing the good news of peace through Jesus Christ, who is Lord of all. You know what has happened throughout the province of Judea, beginning in Galilee after the baptism that John preached—how God anointed Jesus of Nazareth with the Holy Spirit and power, and how he went around doing good and healing all who were under the power of the devil, because God was with him.

3.2.4.2.3 The Voice from Heaven

The tearing of the heavens and the vision of the Spirit are accompanied by an auditory revelation (see Rev 21:1–4) as a voice from heaven declares, "You are my Son, whom I love; with you I am well pleased." Edwards comments, "Only here and in the transfiguration (excepting John 12:28) do we see direct divine discourse with Jesus in the Gospels, and in each instance God addresses Jesus as 'my Son.' "[203]

3.2.4.2.3.1 The Combination of Psalm 2 and Isaiah 42

This declaration again combines texts. It begins with a royal psalm from Ps 2:7, "I will tell of the decree of the LORD: He said to me, 'You are my son; today I have begotten you' " (NRSV), and concludes with a servant song from Isa 42:1, "Here is my servant, whom I uphold, my chosen, in whom my soul delights; I have put my spirit upon him; he will bring forth justice to the nations" (NRSV).[204] Psalm 2 is addressed to the king on the day of his enthronement. Since David (and Davidic kings) is installed as the "son of God," this title only has a functional sense. The divine voice that speaks again in Mark's transfiguration scene (9:7), however, makes it clear that the voice calling Jesus "my Son" does not mean that he was simply being installed into some office at his baptism.[205] The citation of this psalm elsewhere in the NT (Acts 13:33; Heb 1:5; 5:5; 7:28; 2 Pet 1:17) reveals that early on it was understood by Christians as having a christological magnitude far beyond some appointment to a position, such as royal Messiah. The adoptive phrase in Ps 2:7, "today I have begotten you" (NRSV), is absent, so Mark does not present the scene as a messianic installation.[206] If the idea of Jesus' messiahship is present in the account, it would "appear that Jesus is the Messiah because he is the Son of

202. Peppard, "The Eagle and the Dove," 448–51.

203. Edwards, *Mark*, 37.

204. Hartman, *Mark*, 8, argues that since Mark's wording differs so totally from the LXX of Isa 42:1 that readers in Greek would not make the connection that Jesus is the servant of the Lord mentioned in Isaiah 42. Collins, *Mark*, 150, counters, "These passages suggest that 'chosen' and 'beloved' are synonyms."

205. I. Howard Marshall, "Son of God or Servant of Yahweh?—A Reconsideration of Mark 1.11," *NTS* 15 (1968–69): 335, n. 7.

206. Dillon, "Mark 1:1–15," 9–10.

God rather than vice versa."[207] The declaration "you are" is not a commission but recognition of what he already is.

Stein also contends that "my Son" does not refer to a " 'functional' sonship": "He is not the Son of God because he does certain things; he does certain things because he is the Son of God. Who he *is* determines what he does, not vice versa."[208] Compared to the call stories in the OT when a voice from heaven speaks (Isa 6; Jer 1–2; Ezek 1–2), this voice from heaven does not tell Jesus what he is to say or do. Instead, it identifies who Jesus is in relation to God.[209] The phrase "I am well pleased" suggests that Jesus will be God's obedient servant (see 2 Sam 22:20; Ps 147:10–11; Isa 42:1). Jesus' consciousness of his unique Father-Son relationship with God determines his life, message, and obedience (see 14:36).

3.2.4.2.3.2 The Echo from Genesis 22

The word "beloved" (translated "whom I love") in the Greek "often translates the Hebrew *yāḥîd* 'only' (as in Gen 22:2, 12, 16), and points to the uniqueness of Jesus as Son of God."[210] This echo from Gen 22:2, 12, 16, where God tells Abraham to take his son, "your only son, whom you love—Isaac—and ... sacrifice him there as a burnt offering on a mountain I will show you," adds a new wrinkle. Further hearings of the gospel may lead the audience to catch the hint that being God's "beloved" is connected to Jesus' sacrificial death.[211]

3.2.4.2.3.3 Not Adoptionist Christology

Does this announcement reflect an adoptionist Christology that excludes any attribution of intrinsic divinity or preexistence? Wellhausen, for example, comments that Jesus "went into the water as a mere human being and came out as the Son of God."[212] Boring states categorically that Mark "has no doctrine of preexistence." He comes from Nazareth (see also 1:24; 10:47; 14:67; 16:6), not from heaven, and no miraculous birth is narrated.[213] But this view should be challenged.

Davis counters that first, "Mark specifically identifies John's baptism as the beginning of the gospel, not of Jesus; there is no denial of Jesus' personal preexistence, a

207. I. Howard Marshall, "The Divine Sonship of Jesus," in *Jesus the Saviour: Studies in New Testament Theology* (Downers Grove, IL: InterVarsity Press, 1990): 143. He also argues (pp. 138–39):

> What is of especial importance is that this use of the category of Sonship would be based upon Jesus' consciousness of a unique filial relationship to God rather than upon the conviction that as the Messiah he was the Son of God. The evidence strongly suggests that the fundamental point in Jesus' self-understanding was his filial relationship to God and that it was from this basic conviction that he undertook the tasks variously assigned to the Messiah, Son of Man and Servant of Yahweh, rather than that the basic datum was consciousness of being the Messiah. If this is so, the argument that "the Son" was not a current messianic title becomes irrelevant. In any case, the Synoptic Gospels indicate that Jesus used this title only in his private teaching to his disciples, so that the question whether the people at large would have understood him to be using a current messianic title is further shown to be an irrelevant one.

208. Stein, *Mark*, 58.

209. Van Iersel, *Mark*, 100.

210. Boring, *Mark*, 45. Also C. H. Turner, "ὁ υἱός μου ὁ ἀγαπητός," *JTS* 27 (1925–26): 123–24, suggests that it alludes to Gen 22:2, 12, 16, where Isaac is offered up as beloved son.

211. Kazmierski, *Jesus, the Son of God*, 67–68, 71.

212. Julius Wellhausen, *Das Evangelium Marci* (Berlin: G. Reimer, 1903), 7, cited and translated by Boring, *Mark*, 46, n. 17.

213. Boring, *Mark*, 44.

necessary corollary of divinity."[214] Second, the citation from Ps 2:7, as already noted, omits the adoptionistic element of the verse, "Today, I have begotten you" (NRSV). Third, Mark begins with a biblical citation to show that the events narrated "are part of God's longstanding plan (1:2–3)." God is pleased with Jesus not because of his exemplary life before his baptism, which merits the reward of adoption, but because of his preexistence.[215] Fourth, since "there was already a strong body of Christian tradition by the time he wrote,"[216] if Mark were making an adoptionistic christological point that goes against these earlier Christian traditions, he would have made it more aggressively.[217] If the declaration of the heavenly voice alludes to Gen 22:2, Isaac did not suddenly "become" Abraham's beloved son. He already was. In the same way, Jesus does not become God's beloved Son at his baptism. God announces what he already is, and it could not be otherwise since Mark presents the coming of Jesus as the coming of God in 1:2–3.[218]

Schenke adds a fifth argument that Mark presents Jesus as both divine and preexistent, in which Paul's christological schema in Phil 2:6–11 and Rom 1:3–4 is presupposed.[219] He maintains that Jesus, the hero of the history, has a prehistory ("Vorgeschichte") stretching back to eternity that is played out in heaven, as well as a posthistory ("Nachgeschichte") that reaches beyond his earthly life to the eschaton.[220] Jesus neither becomes the Son of God, nor is he endowed with divine gifts at his baptism. Instead, Mark reveals to the audience at the outset of the gospel who Jesus really is: the Son of God who comes from the heavenly sphere. This explains why supernatural beings immediately recognize his divinity (1:24; 3:11; 5:6–7). In the transfiguration scene, which occurs at the midpoint of the gospel, Jesus again is revealed to human disciples as he really is, if only momentarily.[221] A similar heavenly pronouncement appears in the scene, "This is my Son, whom I love" (9:7). The order of what happens—Jesus' transfiguration, and then the heavenly voice—reveals that he is shown to be "the divine Son quite apart from the word spoken to him."[222]

The divine Son of God is also Jesus of Nazareth. The demons recognize him as "Jesus of Nazareth," who is "the Holy One of God" and is someone who has come to destroy them (1:24). Bartimaeus hears that Jesus of Nazareth is passing by and cries out to him as the son of David who can have mercy on him and restore his sight (10:47). Jesus returns to his hometown but is summarily rejected (6:1–6). Peter is identified as the follower of the man from Nazareth (14:67). The angel reassures the women who have come to the tomb that Jesus of Nazareth, who was crucified, has been raised (16:7). Mark does not explain the inner workings of this mystery. Broadhead argues that the occurrence of this seemingly nondescript designation of

214. Davis, "Mark's Christological Paradox," 12–13.
215. Ibid.
216. Ibid., 17, n. 27.
217. Ibid., 13.
218. Grindheim, *Christology*, 64.
219. Ludger Schenke, "Gibt es im Markusevangelium eine Präexistenzchristologie?" *ZNW* 91 (2000): 45–71.
220. Ibid., 67–68.
221. Ludger Schenke, *Das Markusevangelium* (Urban-Taschenbücher; Stuttgart: Kohlhammer, 1988), 109–10.
222. Ned B. Stonehouse, *The Witness of Matthew and Mark to Jesus* (2nd ed.; Grand Rapids; Eerdmans, 1958), 19.

Jesus paints a finely etched Christology in Mark.[223] He is a miracle-worker who teaches with authority but whose destiny is to be rejected and to suffer. I would add that it reinforces the christological distinction that Jesus is fully human and fully divine. LaVerdiere sums up well the points that Mark intends to make in this account:

> In three short verses (1:9–11), Mark has introduced the major lines of his Christology. Baptized by John the Baptist, Jesus is human. Anointed by the Spirit, Jesus is divine. Jesus is both the Son of Man and the Son of God. In the royal line of David, Jesus is royal Messiah. But as the Son of God, Jesus far transcends David's line and will reign with God in the kingdom of God. Jesus is the Christ, the anointed embodiment of a new Israel. Like Isaac, Jesus is a beloved Son that would be handed over but saved on the third day. Jesus is also God's suffering Servant.[224]

3.2.5 The Testing of the Son of God (Mark 1:12–13)

The testing follows the baptism as its "organic sequel." The Spirit who descends at the baptism takes hold of Jesus and sends him out into the wilderness.[225] Many translations render it, "The Spirit drove [or forced] him out," but this verb need not have a violent connotation, because it can also mean "send out" (Matt 9:38/Luke 10:2; John 10:4). Since it is repeatedly used for the expulsion of demons in Mark (1:34, 39, 43; 3:15, 22, 23; 6:13; 7:26; 9:18, 28, 38), however, it may convey that Jesus does not go quietly to the wilderness to meditate (contrast Philo, *Alleg. Interp.* 2.85) but is thrust there by the Spirit. Mark does not identify what role the Spirit plays during this sojourn, but since the Spirit is connected to Jesus' exorcisms in 3:22–30, one can infer that the Spirit helped Jesus in resisting Satan.[226] Since Mark does not narrate a series of temptations, as do Matthew (Matt 4:1–11) and Luke (Luke 4:1–13), the upshot is that the testing in the wilderness serves primarily to clarify further Jesus' divine identity.

3.2.5.1 Tested by Satan for Forty Days

Mark reports that Jesus was in the wilderness for forty days and is tested by Satan. The description of what happens during this period is so sparse that it lends itself to multiple interpretations. The verb means "to put to the test," "to ascertain or to demonstrate trustworthiness."[227] It communicates that a person "was undergoing an experience in which his character or fidelity was being 'put to the proof.' "[228] In the context of being tested, the reference to forty days, a biblical round number

223. Edwin K. Broadhead, "Jesus the Nazarene: Narrative Strategy and Christological Imagery in the Gospel of Mark," *JSNT* 52 (1993): 3–18.

224. LaVerdiere, *The Beginning*, 1:35.

225. Jeffrey Gibson, "Jesus' Wilderness Temptation according to Mark," *JSNT* 53 (1994): 7–8.

226. Best, *Temptation*, 14–15.

227. Joachim Hans Korn, *PEIRASMOS: Die Versuchung des Gläubigen in der griechischen Bibel* (Stuttgart: Kohlhammer, 1937), 18–20, 24–48, 87–88; and Birger Gerhardsson, *The Testing of God's Son (Matt 4:1–11 & Par.)* (ConBNT; Lund: Gleerup, 1966), 25–35.

228. Gibson, "Jesus' Wilderness Temptation," 12.

during which time something significant happens,[229] may bring to mind Israel's forty-year wilderness wanderings under Moses when they were tested by God and failed miserably (Deut 8:2). Forty days is specifically equated with the forty years of wandering in Numbers 14:34 (see Ezek 4:6).

Satan has a variety of aliases, and this name represents the ruler of the evil powers (see 3:22–27). Satan's malevolent purposes are evident from the few references to him later in the gospel. Satan is behind demonic possession (3:23, 26), steals the word that is sown on the path (4:15), and, through Peter, would deter Jesus from heading for the cross (8:33). Mark does not identify the nature of the testing, but we may infer that Satan attempts to undermine Jesus' faithfulness to God and to usurp the role of the Holy Spirit to lead him down a different path. Jesus' testing by Satan reveals that there are unseen, hostile powers at work in the world, which are engaged in a cosmic struggle against God, and Mark "uniquely portrays Jesus as the one whom God has sent to engage in a conflict with Satan."[230]

Mark does not narrate how the testing turns out. Is Satan vanquished or not? The lack of a definitive conclusion leads some to argue that further conflicts will occur (something that is explicitly stated in Luke 4:13) as Satan brings all his forces to bear against Jesus. Robinson interprets the testing as the first round in a contest, and this "diabolic antagonism" culminates in his crucifixion and is "conclusively broken" in the resurrection.[231]

Since the narrative begins immediately after this face-off, with Jesus exultantly proclaiming the advent of God's reign (1:14–15), it is more reasonable to assume that Jesus overcomes Satan in this encounter. Later, Jesus is identified as the stronger one who plunders Satan's house and routs demonic forces (3:22–27). Best concludes that Jesus is successful in overpowering demons because "for Mark, Satan was thus defeated and rendered powerless at the very beginning of the ministry of Jesus." He regards the exorcisms as "mopping-up operations of isolated units of Satan's hosts and [they] are certain to be successful because the Captain of the hosts of evil is already bound and immobilised."[232]

The general thrust of the introduction is to give the readers clues about Jesus' divine identity. Gundry is correct in his conclusion that this testing scene is another that dignifies Jesus as the Son of God. He contends:

> His being tempted by none less than Satan, the archdemon, carries an acknowledgment of Jesus' stature as the very Son of God. The wildness of the

229. Forty also represents the number of the days of the flood (Gen 7:4, 12, 17); the time that the people were handed over to the Philistines for their disobedience (Judg 13:1); the amount of time before the judgment of Nineveh (Jonah 3:4); the time Ezekiel lay on his side to symbolize the judgment of Israel (Ezek 4:6); and the time Abraham fasted (*Apoc. Ab.* 12:1–2). It is also the amount of time Jesus spent with the disciples after the resurrection (Acts 1:3). It also matches the time Moses spent on the mountain when he received the stone tablets of the covenant from God (Exod 24:18; Deut 9:11), when he pleaded for God not to destroy the people for their disobedience (Deut 9:25; 10:10), and when he fasted for forty days and nights before receiving the ten commandments (Exod 34:28; Deut 9:9; see also Deut 9:18). Elijah fasted for forty days and forty nights on Horeb, the mount of God (1 Kgs 19:8).

230. Shively, *Apocalyptic Imagination*, 155. She argues that Mark is unique, because he places this conflict with Satan at the beginning of his gospel and the Beelzebul conflict in 3:22–30 as part of Jesus' first discourse.

231. Robinson, *Problem of History*, 53.

232. Best, *Temptation*, 15.

beasts with which Jesus is present without harmful consequences bears witness to his being God's Son, the stronger one of whom John the Baptizer spoke. That even the angels serve Jesus adds a final touch to Mark's portrayal of him as no less a personage than the Spirit-endued Son of God.[233]

3.2.5.2 With the Wild Animals

The word for "animals" is often applied to "wild" beasts, but it can refer to any living creature, excluding humans. This detail may simply be an incidental reference that signals that Jesus has left the inhabited world and withdrawn to the inhospitable and menacing wilderness.[234] Bauckham contends, however, that in "so concise an account, where otherwise every feature is charged with theological significance," this reading seems "doubtful."[235] Does this detail represent something more?

Wilderness animals can be dangerous (see Deut 8:15). Many therefore assume that the animals represent the dangers that lie in ambush in a feral wilderness and that they are aligned with Satan in opposition to Jesus (see Ps 22:11–21).[236] Incigneri connects the reference to the actual history of Mark's first audience and the brutal barbarism that Nero unleashed against them. According to Tacitus (*Ann.* 15.44), they "were covered with the hides of wild beasts and torn to pieces by dogs."[237] The *Epistle to Diognetus* 7:7 reminds the readers of this continuing terror: "Do you not see that they are thrown to wild beasts to make them deny the Lord, and how they are not vanquished?" Incigneri concludes, "To be 'with the beasts' meant only one thing to a person in Rome—to be executed horribly as a criminal before cheering crowds."[238] Mark, he argues, included this detail for his Roman audience "to evoke a strongly emotional response in his reader."[239] Unlike those Christians torn to shreds in the Roman amphitheater, Jesus is untouched by the animals.

But how would this detail encourage readers who face the prospect of being torn to shreds? The structure of the scene suggests that the animals are not aligned with Satan:[240]

and he was in the wilderness
    being tested by Satan

and he was with the wild animals
    and the angels were ministering to him. (pers. trans.)

---

233. Gundry, *Mark*, 59.

234. So Jan Willem van Henten, "The First Testing of Jesus: A Rereading of Mark 1.12–13," *NTS* 45 (1999): 350, 352–56, 362, 366.

235. Richard Bauckham, "Jesus and the Wild Animals (Mark 1:13): A Christological Image for an Ecological Age," in *Jesus of Nazareth: Lord and Christ: Essays on the Historical Jesus and New Testament Christology* (ed. Joel B. Green and Max Turner; Grand Rapids: Eerdmans/Carlisle: Paternoster, 1994), 5.

236. Mauser, *Wilderness*, 37, 100–101.

237. Incigneri, *Gospel*, 111.

238. Ibid., 112.

239. Ibid., 113.

240. The seeming parallel in *T. Naph.* 8:4, "If you achieve good, my children, men and angels will bless you, and God will be glorified through you among the Gentiles. The devil will flee from you; animals will be afraid of you, and the angels will stand by you," is only coincidental.

As Satan and the angels go together as supernatural beings, so the wilderness and the wild animals go together. The text says that Jesus was with the animals, not that Satan was with them.[241]

One expects to find wild animals in the wilderness, and some animals are a threat to humans, but most live in fear of humans and keep a safe distance unless humans invade and shrink their habitat. They usually attack only in defense when they are threatened. Nothing in the text suggests that the animals posed a threat, and Milton's interpretation of this scene as one of peaceful submission is memorable:

> Among wild beasts: they at his sight grew mild
> Nor sleeping him nor waking harm'd; his walk
> The fiery serpent fled and noxious worm,
> The lion and fierce tiger glar'd aloof.[242]

Bauckham argues that the phrase "to be with" can refer to proximity but frequently has a "strongly positive sense of close association in friendship or agreement or assistance" (citing 3:14; 5:18; 14:67; cf. 4:36).[243] If Mark intends to portray some hostile confrontation between Jesus and the animals, the phrase "with the animals" fails to communicate it, since it "could readily suggest peaceable and friendly association."[244]

Klauck interprets the scene as portraying "eschatological peace with animals as a reappearance of Paradise," and that "Jesus appears here as a new Adam, moving into Paradise."[245] The view that Jesus is presented as a second Adam is highly questionable,[246] and this episode does not imply the restoration of paradise. The world is still awry. Demons, for example, will enter pigs and destroy them (5:13). Caneday is more accurate in arguing that Jesus being with the animals foreshadows that the reign of God that comes with Jesus is intended to bring harmony in the created order.[247] This harmony is described in various prophecies that depict peace between the human world and domesticated and wild animals (Isa 11:6–9; 43:20; 65:25; Hos 2:18; *2 Bar.* 73:6). Bauckham points out in addition that Isa 11:6–9 appears in the "context of the account of the messianic king and his righteous rule (Isa 11:1–5)."[248] This detail in Mark's context can connote that Jesus is the Son of God, anointed with the Spirit, and the Messiah. "The peace with wild animals belongs to this Messiah's righteous reign."[249] This interpretation fits well with what

241. While animals can be used as metaphors for demons, see Werner Foerster, "θήριον," *TDNT,* 3:134, it does not mean that actual animals are demonic or allies of Satan. Bauckham, "Jesus and the Wild Animals," 6, cites Rev 5:5 where the lion is a symbol of the Messiah, but it does not follow that actual lions are allies of the Messiah.

242. John Milton, *Paradise Regained,* 1.310–13.

243. Bauckham, "Jesus and the Wild Animals," 5. Gibson, "Jesus' Wilderness Temptation," 30–31, claims that the animals are aligned with Satan, but he concedes that the phrase "to be with" in 3:14, 5:18; 14:67 implies "subordination of one to another" and argues that Jesus stood over them as master and Lord. See also Erich Fascher, "Jesus und die Tiere," *TLZ* 90 (1965): 561–70.

244. Bauckham, "Jesus and the Wild Animals," 5, n. 6.

245. Klauck, *Vorspiel,* 57–59.

246. Hans-Günter Leder, "Sündenfallerzählung und Versuchungsgeschichte: Zur Interpretation von Mc 1. 12f.," *ZNW* 64 (1963): 188–216, adequately refutes this interpretation. See also John Paul Heil, "Jesus with the Wild Animals in Mark 1:13," *CBQ* 68 (2006): 63–78; Van Henten, "The First Testing of Jesus."

247. Caneday, "Mark's Provocative Use of Scripture," 19–36.

248. Bauckham, "Jesus and the Wild Animals," 15.

249. Ibid., 19.

will happen in the rest of the gospel with the restoration of creation: illnesses will be healed; stormy seas will be calmed; death will be reversed; and multitudes will be fed abundantly in the wilderness.

3.2.5.3 Ministered to by the Angels

In the story of Daniel in the lions' den, God sent an angel to prevent the lions from devouring him, because he was "innocent in his sight" (Dan 6:22). In Jesus' case, the angels do not come to protect him from the dangers in the wilderness. Instead, they come "to minister to him" ("attend," or "serve") *after* he has already been confronted by Satan (cf. Bel 1:31–39). Jesus does not need angelic intervention to defend him against evil. He can defend himself. The appearance of the angels, then, serves a christological purpose. It establishes their subordination to him (see Heb 1:5–7, 14). In 8:38, they are identified as the angels of the Son of Man ("his holy angels");[250] and, at the end of the age, the Son of Man will send his angels to gather his elect (13:27).

250. This understanding reads the definite article in 8:38 and 13:27 with the nuance of a possessive.

Chapter 4

Christological Titles in Mark

Bibliography

Achtemeier, Paul J. "'He Taught Them Many Things': Reflections on Marcan Christology." *CBQ* 42 (1980): 465–81. **Ambrozic, Aloysius M.** "Jesus as the Ultimate Reality in St. Mark's Gospel." *Ultimate Reality and Meaning* 12 (1989): 169–76. **Bateman, Herbert W., IV.** "Defining the Titles 'Christ' and 'Son of God' in Mark's Narrative Presentation of Jesus." *JETS* 50 (2007): 537–59. **Begasse de Dhaem, Amaury.** "Sur les pas du fils de l'homme: la christologie selon saint Marc." *NRTh* 133 (2011): 5–27. **Bird, Michael F.** "'Jesus Is the Christ': Messianic Apologetics in the Gospel of Mark." *RTR* 64 (2005): 1–14. **Boring, M. Eugene.** "The Christology of Mark: Hermeneutical Issues for Systematic Theology." *Semeia* 30 (1984): 125–53. Idem. "Markan Christology: God-Language for Jesus?" *NTS* 45 (1999): 451–71. **Broadhead, Edwin Keith.** *Teaching with Authority: Miracles and Christology in the Gospel of Mark.* JSNTSup 74. Sheffield: JSOT, 1992. Idem. "Jesus the Nazarene: Narrative Strategy and Christological Imagery in the Gospel of Mark," *JSNT* 52 (1993): 3–18. Idem. *Naming Jesus: Titular Christology in the Gospel of Mark.* JSNTSup 175. Sheffield: Sheffield Academic. 1999. Idem. "Reconfiguring Jesus: The Son of Man in Markan Perspective." Pp. 18–30 in *Biblical Interpretation in Early Christian Gospels.* Vol. 1: *The Gospel of Mark.* London/New York: T&T Clark, 2006. **Brower, Kent E.** "'Who Then Is This?'—Christological Questions in Mark 4:35–5:43." *EvQ* 81 (2009): 291–305. **Brown, Colin.** "The Jesus of Mark's Gospel." Pp. 26–53 in *Jesus Then and Now: Images of Jesus in History and Christology.* Ed. Marvin Meyer and Charles Hughes. Harrisburg, PA: Trinity Press International, 2001. **Chapman, Dean W.** *The Orphan Gospel: Mark's Perspective on Jesus.* The Biblical Seminar 16. Sheffield: JSOT, 1993. **Chronis, Harry L.** "To Reveal and to Conceal : A Literary-Critical Perspective on 'the Son of Man' in Mark." *NTS* 51 (2005): 459–81. **Davis, Philip G.** "Mark's Christological Paradox." *JSNT* 35 (1989): 3–18. **Donahue, John R.** "A Neglected Factor in the Theology of Mark." *JBL* 101 (1982): 563–94. **Edwards, James R.** "The Authority of Jesus in the Gospel of Mark." *JETS* 37 (1994): 217–33. **Gathercole, Simon J.** "The Son of Man in Mark's Gospel." *ExpTim* 115 (2004): 366–72. Idem. *The Preexistent Son: Recovering the Christologies of Matthew, Mark, and Luke.* Grand Rapids: Eerdmans, 2006. **Grindheim, Sigurd.** *Christology in the Synoptic Gospels: God or God's Servant?* London/New York: T&T Clark, 2012. **Gurtner, Daniel M.** "The Rending of the

Veil and Markan Christology: 'Unveiling' the 'ΥΙΟΣ ΘΕΟΥ (Mark 15:38–39)." *BibInt* 15 (2007): 292–306. **Guttenberger, Gudrun.** *Die Gottesvorstellung im Markusevangelium*. BZNW 123. Berlin/New York: de Gruyter, 2004. **Hengel, Martin.** *The Son of God*. Trans. by John Bowden. Philadelphia, PA: Fortress, 1976. **Hurtado, Larry W.**, and **Paul L. Owen**, eds. *Who Is This Son of Man? The Latest Scholarship on a Puzzling Expression of the Historical Jesus*. LNTS 390. London/New York: T&T Clark, 2011. **Johansson, Daniel.** "*Kyrios* in the Gospel of Mark." *JSNT* 33 (2010): 101–24. **Johnson, David H.** "The Characterization of Jesus in Mark." *Didaskalia* 10 (1999): 79–92. **Juel, Donald H.** "The Origin of Mark's Christology." Pp. 449–60 in *The Messiah: Developments in Earliest Judaism and Christianity*. Ed. James H. Charlesworth. Minneapolis: Fortress, 1992. **Kazmierski, Carl R.** *Jesus, the Son of God: A Study of the Markan Tradition and its Redaction by the Evangelist*. FB 33. Würzburg: Echter, 1979. **Kee, Howard Clark.** "Christology in Mark's Gospel." Pp. 187–208 in *Judaisms and Their Messiahs at the Turn of the Christian Era*. Ed. Jacob Neusner, William Scott Green, and Ernest S. Frerichs. Cambridge: Cambridge University Press, 1987. **Kingsbury, Jack Dean.** *The Christology of Mark's Gospel*. Philadelphia: Fortress, 1983. **Kirchhevel, Gordon D.** "The 'Son of Man' Passages in Mark." *BBR* 9 (1999): 181–87. **Lambrecht, Jan.** "The Christology of Mark." *BTB* 3 (1973): 256–73. **Lee, Aquila H. I.** *From Messiah to Preexistent Son: Jesus' Self-Consciousness and Early Christian Exegesis of Messianic Psalms*. WUNT 2/192. Tübingen: Mohr Siebeck, 2005. **Marcus, Joel.** "Mark 14:61: Are You the Messiah-Son-of-God?" *NovT* 31 (1989): 125–41. Idem. "Identity and Ambiguity in Markan Christology." Pp. 133–47 in *Seeking the Identity of Jesus: A Pilgrimage*. Ed. Beverly Roberts Gaventa and Richard B. Hays. Grand Rapids: Eerdmans, 2008. **Marshall, I. Howard.** "Jesus as Messiah in Mark and Matthew." Pp. 117–43 in *The Messiah in the Old and New Testaments*. Ed. Stanley E. Porter. Grand Rapids: Eerdmans, 2007. **Martinez, Ernest R.** "Identity of Jesus in Mark." *Comm* 1 (1974): 323–42. **Matera, Frank J.** *New Testament Christology*. Louisville: Westminster John Knox, 1999. **Mkole, Jean Claude Loba.** "Mark 14:62: Substantial Compendium of New Testament Christology." *HvTSt* 56 (2000): 1119–45. **Schenke, Ludger.** "Gibt es im Markusevangelium eine Präexistenzchristologie?" *ZNW* 91 (2000): 45–71. **Tait, Michael.** *Jesus, The Divine Bridegroom in Mark 2:18–22: Mark's Christology Upgraded*. AnBib185. Rome: Gregorian & Biblical Press, 2010. **Williams, Catrin H.** *"I am He": The Interpretation of 'Anî Hû' in Jewish and Early Christian Literature*. WUNT 2/113. Tübingen: Mohr Siebeck, 2000.

4.1 JESUS AS THE SON OF GOD

Mark's introduction presents a high Christology with the testimony from Scripture and from heaven.[1] Boring asserts that Mark indeed

> is a theological document, and his theology is principally a christology. The equation 'the Christ is Jesus' is made in the first line of Mark, and the Jesus who appears in almost every paragraph of the Gospel is interpreted throughout as the one through whom God acts to bring his kingdom which is salvation. Jesus-as-the-act-of-God-for-our-salvation is the subject matter of the Gospel of Mark.[2]

Mark presents Jesus to the reader in multiple ways to show how he bridges the divide between heaven and earth. Mark's picture of who Jesus is is told in a story, and a systematic analysis of the titles used for Jesus in the gospel does not tell the whole story. The titles are not the key for unlocking Mark's Christology. The messianic titles and the concepts behind them were not fixed articles in the time of Jesus.[3] Nevertheless, the titles applied to Jesus in the story deserve scrutiny, recognizing that Jesus is the one who best interprets what they mean when applied to him.

The title "Son of God" provides the primary category for understanding Jesus' identity in Mark's gospel since this is how God identifies him in the narrative.[4] A voice from heaven twice salutes Jesus as the Son of God (1:11; 9:7), and one may assume that Mark regards God to be a reliable witness. When Jesus crosses the paths of impure spirits, who presumably possess supranormal comprehension, they immediately recognize him as the "Son of the Most High God" who has come to destroy them (3:11; 5:7). The truth of this defensive recognition of Jesus as the Son of God is borne out immediately when he drives them out of their victims. Jesus silences their disclosure of his identity, however, because it is primarily intended to ward off the impending exorcism by pronouncing his name,[5] and he wants to stifle any public sparring with demonic spirits (see 5:1 – 20). These demonic cries, however, provide the audience with further supernatural testimony that Jesus is the Son of God. To be sure, their testimony is quite different from God's, but it does confirm God's announcement at Jesus' baptism. Since the human characters in the narrative never react to these demonic shouts, they presumably do not hear or understand them.

1. Larry W. Hurtado has shown that a high Christology can find its roots in the late Second Temple period; see *One God, One Lord: Early Christian Devotion and Ancient Jewish Monotheism* (London: SCM, 1988; new ed.: Edinburgh: T&T Clark, 2003); *Lord Jesus Christ: Devotion to Jesus in Earliest Christianity* (Grand Rapids: Eerdmans, 2003); and *How on Earth Did Jesus Become a God? Historical Questions about Earliest Devotion to Jesus* (Grand Rapids: Eerdmans, 2005).

2. M. Eugene Boring, "The Christology of Mark: Hermeneutical Issues for Systematic Theology," *Semeia* 30 (1985): 127. Dechow, *Gottessohn und Herrschaft Gottes*, 42, claims that the primary purpose of Mark is to confront the reader with the eschatological message of Jesus, and that the transcendent identity of the messenger plays a subordinate role. While Jesus' eschatological message is indeed important, its importance is attributable to the fact that it is delivered by the Son of God, and revealing Jesus' transcendent identity is vital to Mark.

3. See Howard Clark Kee, "Christology in Mark's Gospel," in *Judaisms and Their Messiahs at the Turn of the Christian Era* (ed. Jacob Neusner, William Scott Green, and Ernest S. Frerichs; Cambridge: Cambridge University Press, 1987), 187 – 208.

4. Kingsbury, *Christology*, strongly makes this case.

5. See the discussion of the exorcisms below. Their testimony is unclean and demonic, but that is not the reason Jesus muzzles them; see §8.2.1.2.

One may sort the episodes where Jesus is identified as the Son of God into two columns labeled "sympathetic" and "hostile." The pronouncements from God are approving, and the exclamations from the impure spirits are futile attempts to shield themselves from being expelled. Two declarations from human characters in the narrative can also be placed in the two columns. The high priest belts out a hostile question at the trial, "Are you the Messiah, the Son of the Blessed One?" (14:61).[6] When the centurion sees the manner in which Jesus died, he declares sympathetically, "Surely this man was the Son of God" (15:39).[7] The high priest perceives Jesus to be a threat and is set on destroying him. This enmity toward Jesus places him in the column of those who are in league with Satan. The centurion's apparent endorsement of Jesus after witnessing his death aligns him with God's point of view.

	Sympathetic	**Hostile**
Baptism:	"You are my Son, whom I love" (1:11)	Evil spirits: "You are the Son of God" (3:11)
Transfiguration:	"This is my Son, whom I love" (9:7)	Impure spirit: "Son of the Most High God" (5:7)
Centurion at the crucifixion:	"Surely this man was the Son of God!" (15:39)	High priest at the trial: "Are you the Messiah, the Son of the Blessed One?" (14:61)

It should also be noted that the centurion's declaration and the opening title from the author bracket the two declarations that come from God:

"Son of God" (1:1)
"My Son" (1:11)
"My Son" (9:7)
"Son of God" (15:39)[8]

4.1.1 The Centurion's Confession (Mark 15:39)

God declares Jesus to be "my Son" at Jesus' baptism prior to Jesus' beginning his public ministry. God again declares Jesus to be "my Son" at the transfiguration, which appears at the beginning of Jesus' way to Jerusalem. Jesus had just disclosed to his disciples that he will suffer, die, and be raised from the dead (8:31). After the transfiguration, he embarks on the way to the cross. Since God's will for Jesus' earthly ministry culminates in the crucifixion (14:36), it marks a fitting moment for a human being to utter what can be characterized as "the climactic christological statement of the Gospel."[9] The centurion's declaration "this man was" may mean

6. "Blessed One" is a circumlocution for God: "Blessed be He" (see Luke 1:68; Rom 1:25; 9:5; 2 Cor 1:3; 11:31; Eph 1:3; 1 Pet 1:3; *1 En.* 77:2; *m. Ber.* 7:3). Darrell L. Bock, *Blasphemy and Exaltation in Judaism and the Final Examination of Jesus: A Philological-Historical Study of the Key Jewish Themes Impacting Mark 14:61–64* (WUNT 2/106; Tübingen: Mohr Siebeck, 1998), 209–20, demonstrates the authenticity of the saying and that Mark did not create it.

7. On the centurion's confession, see §4.1.1.

8. Rose, *Theologie*, 240.

9. Boring, *Mark*, 434. Sonya K. Stockklausner and C. Anthony Hale, "Mark 15:39 and 16:6–7; A Second Look," *McMaster Journal of Theology* 1 (1990): 34–44, argue that the climax occurs in 16:6–7.

that only now, *after* he has died, can one discern that Jesus was truly the Son of God who suffers vicariously for others. That one of the executioners discerns this truth is surprising and means that *anyone* can do so.

Others, however, challenge the claim that this statement by a centurion is a christological confession. It seems *too* surprising to some that a Roman soldier would proclaim the central Christian confession. He is an improbable spokesman. Johnson maintains, for example; "A Roman soldier's allegiance to the Emperor was expected to be absolute and it is unlikely that Mark's readers would find it believable that a professional soldier would risk his career in order to worship a crucified man, especially if by such a confession he might be risking his own death for treason."[10] Johnson claims that the audience, knowing the Romans' scorn for foreign gods and their utter disdain for those who were crucified, would have assumed that this utterance belongs with the other derisive taunts during the crucifixion.

The inscription taunts him (and the Jews) as "THE KING OF THE JEWS" (15:26). The passersby heckle him as the one who would destroy the temple and rebuild it in three days (15:29). The chief priests and teachers of the law mock him as a Savior who cannot save himself (15:31) and taunt him as "this Messiah, this king of Israel" to come down from the cross that they might believe (15:32). Other bystanders ridicule the expectation that he would be rescued by Elijah (15:35–36).[11] Blount claims that the soldier caps off the mockery when he dies with a guffaw: " 'Yeah, right, this guy was the Son of God.' " What Son of God would be allowed to suffer such a wretched, disgraceful death?[12]

This interpretation is mistaken for a number of reasons. First, the previous statements from hostile bystanders are clearly flagged as derision. The passersby "hurled insults" (15:29);[13] the chief priests and teachers of the law "mocked" (15:31); and those crucified with him "heaped insults on" him (15:32).[14] The centurion's declaration is not characterized as mockery that inadvertently and ironically speaks the truth.

10. Earl S. Johnson, "Is Mark 15,39 the Key to Mark's Christology," *JSNT* 31 (1987): 13.

11. Ibid., 16.

12. Brian K. Blount, "Is the Joke on Us? Mark's Irony, Mark's God, and Mark's Ending," in *The End of Mark and the Ends of God: Essays in Memory of Donald Harrisville Juel* (ed. Beverly Roberts Gaventa and Patrick D. Miller; Louisville: Westminster John Knox, 2005), 16. Juel, *A Master of Surprise*, 74, n.7, states that he has come to read it as a taunt comparable to the other taunts in 14:61; 15:2, 18, 32. See also Geert van Oyen, "Irony as Propaganda in Mark 15:39?" in *Persuasion and Dissuasion in Early Christianity, Ancient Judaism, and Hellenism* (ed. Pieter W. van der Horst et al.; Leuven: Peeters, 2003), 136; and Ahearne-Kroll, *Psalms of Lament*, 220–21.

13. The verb translated "hurled insults" is the same verb that appears in 2:7, "He's blaspheming!" and in 3:29, "whoever blasphemes against the Holy Spirit." Mark's audience may assume that it has the same nuance here. By taunting Jesus in this way, they, not he (14:62), are the ones truly guilty of blasphemy. See Joel F. Williams, "Foreshadowing, Echoes, and the Blasphemy at the Cross (Mark 15:29)," *JBL* 132 (2013): 913–33.

14. Tae Hun Kim, "The Anarthrous υἱὸς θεοῦ in Mark 15,39 and the Roman Imperial Cult," *Bib* 79 (1998): 221–41, claims that an audience familiar with the imperial cult would have been accustomed to the anarthrous confession and would have interpreted it to mean that the centurion recognized Jesus to be the true Son of God rather than the revered figure of the cult, the Emperor Augustus. See also Collins, *Mark*, 768. Why the centurion would make this comparison with the emperor after seeing Jesus' suffering death is unclear. Whitney T. Shiner, "The Ambiguous Pronouncement of the Centurion and the Shrouding of Meaning in Mark," *JSNT* 78 (2000): 4, believes, "The soldier mistakes Jesus as a divine or divinely inspired person on a Hellenistic model, but Mark crafts the scene so that the centurion's mistake, like the mocking of the passersby (Mk 15.29–32), reinforces his audience's understanding of Jesus while reflecting the church's experience of existing within an uncomprehending world." He considers "the ambiguity of the centurion's pronouncement" to be "part of a consistent use of irony and misunderstanding throughout the crucifixion scene" (p. 16).

Second, and most important, the centurion's statement is prefaced by the adverb "surely" ("truly," [*alēthōs*]); see Mark 14:70; also Matt 14:33). This adverb never prefaces a sarcastic remark in the NT. It means that the statement to follow is "*matter-of-fact*, almost as if to say that doubt is impermissible."[15] Mark is not interested in the centurion's personal beliefs—whether he fully comprehends what he says or not—but is only attentive to his declaration as a crowning christological affirmation. As Davis puts it, the issue "is not what Mark's readers thought of the centurion and the equality of his faith; it is what they were to think of Jesus."[16] The centurion's declaration reveals that even pagans accord Jesus respect and recognize that he is not a criminal but one who is linked with God.[17]

The centurion's announcement parallels Peter's confession that Jesus is the Messiah (8:29) in that Peter was correct in his declaration but needed to come to a fuller understanding of what it meant for Jesus to be the Messiah. That deeper appreciation will come only *after* Jesus has been crucified. The Messiah is one who will suffer and die and who has come to serve and to give his life as a ransom for many (10:45). The centurion's statement that Jesus "*was* the Son of God" is also correct, but the use of the past tense reveals that this confession needs to be modified. That correction will come only *after* Jesus has been raised from the dead. The centurion only has seen the way he died; he is yet to see that he will be raised by God. The two confessions, Peter's and the centurion's, echo the incipit, which identifies this work as the beginning of the good news of *Jesus the Messiah, the Son of God* (1:1).

Third, the crucifixion scene connects to the baptism scene in Mark. The verb "to split" occurs in only these two passages in Mark. At Jesus' baptism, the heavens *split* and the Spirit comes down as a dove (1:10). At his crucifixion, the temple veil *splits* from top to bottom (15:38). The use of this verb may mark out an *inclusio* with pronouncements proclaiming Jesus' identity as the Son of God at the beginning of Jesus' earthly ministry and at its end.[18]

There are three further links between the two passages. (1) Jesus identifies his death as a baptism that he must undergo (10:38–39).[19]

(2) The eighty-foot-high outer curtain of the temple portrayed the heavenly firmament (see Isa 40:22). Josephus, who served as a priest, describes the tabernacle for his Greco-Roman readers as divided into three equal parts. The court and the Holy Place are likened to the land and the sea, which are accessible to humanity; the

15. Hans Hübner, "ἀλήθεια," *EDNT*, 1:56. Peter's suspicious accusers use the adverb in 14:70, because they think that, as a Galilean, he "surely" is one of Jesus' followers.

16. Davis, "Mark's Christological Paradox," 15.

17. See Lorenzo Scornaienchi, "The Controversy Dialogues and the Polemic in Mark and Matthew," in *Mark and Matthew I: Comparative Readings: Understanding the Earliest Gospels in their First-Century Settings* (ed. Eve-Marie Becker and Anders Runesson; WUNT 2/271; Tübingen: Mohr Siebeck, 2011), 317.

18. David Ulansey, "The Heavenly Veil Torn: Mark's Cosmic *Inclusio*," *JBL* 110 (1991): 123–25.

19. Stephen Motyer, "The Rending of the Veil: A Markan Pentecost," *NTS* 33 (1987): 155–57, also cites the presence of the Elijah/Elisha symbolism in both passages (1:6; 15:35–36) and the Spirit's coming down with the cognate verb "breathe out" describing Jesus' death (15:37, 39) to suggest that this represented a "Markan Pentecost."

third area, the Most Holy Place, represents heaven, which is accessible to God alone (*Ant.* 3.6.4 §123; 3.7.7 §181). He describes the veil as eighty feet high, a "Babylonian tapestry, with embroidery of blue and fine linen, of scarlet also and purple, wrought with marvellous skill. Nor was this mixture of materials without its mystic meaning: it typified the universe." It was embroidered with "a panorama of the heavens, the signs of the Zodiac excepted" (*J.W.* 5.5.4 §§212–214).[20] From this description of the veil, those who knew the nature of the veil in the temple would consider its rending of the veil as akin to the rending of the heavens.

(3) Gurtner adds further evidence for this reading that the downward splitting of the veil is the symbolic equivalent of the opening of heaven at the baptism by approaching it from an apocalyptic perspective.[21] Hofius has shown from rabbinic texts that the veil was believed to conceal divine secret plans, and it is only breached when the rare few are allowed to overhear what is said behind the veil or are permitted to catch a glimpse of what goes on behind it. Its rending could also have revelatory consequences.[22] Just as the rending of the heavens allows the audience to hear from the other side of the tear God's proclamation that Jesus is "my Son, whom I love" (1:11), the rending of the temple veil, with its panorama of the heavenly firmament, allows the centurion to see Jesus' death from a supernatural perspective and to recognize that the crucified Jesus is "the Son of God."[23]

Boring, among many, claims that the tearing of the curtain signifies that God is not to be regarded as localized or confined "either in an earthly holy place or in the heavens."[24] The rending lets God out from a symbolic perspective. Perhaps it is better to interpret the tearing of the veil as letting out the secret about Jesus' identity as God's Son.[25] Matera asserts that the tearing of the temple veil grants the centurion "access to the divine glory and allows him to make the first public proclamation of the gospel, by a human being, that Jesus is the Son of God."[26] The centurion is not more perceptive or sympathetic than others at the cross so that he is able to see what others do not. Rather, something miraculous that is external to him has happened that enables him to see, and God reveals this insight into Jesus' identity.[27]

Some point out that the centurion's confession lacks the definite article in Greek and argue that his statement should be translated more ambivalently, "This man was

20. Garland, *Mark*, 595.

21. Daniel M. Gurtner, "The Rending of the Veil and Markan Christology: 'Unveiling' The 'ΥΙΟΣ ΘΕΟΥ (Mark 15:38–39)," *BibInt* 15 (2007): 304.

22. Otfried Hofius, *Der Vorhang vor dem Thron Gottes: Eine exegetisch-religionsgeschichtliche Untersuchung zu Hebräer 6,19f und 10,19f* (WUNT 14; Tübingen: Mohr Siebeck, 1972), 24–25, cited by Gurtner, "The Rending of the Veil," 301–2.

23. For other reasons, Howard M. Jackson, "The Death of Jesus in Mark and the Miracle from the Cross," *NTS* 27 (1987): 16–37, argues that the tearing of the veil prompted the centurion's affirmation.

24. Boring, *Mark*, 432.

25. Shiner, "The Ambiguous Pronouncement of the Centurion," 4, wrongly contends that revelation is "veiled and ambiguous" throughout Mark and that the secret of Jesus' identity remains secret to the very end.

26. Matera, *Kingship*, 139.

27. Brian K. Gamel, "The Centurion's Confession as Apocalyptic Unveiling: The Death of Jesus as a Markan Theology of Revelation" (Ph.D. diss., Baylor University, 2014).

a son of God." The absence of the definite article, however, does not make "Son" indefinite, just as it does not do so in the gospel's title in 1:1.[28] Hurtado positively appraises the work of Collins for helpfully providing "background on the usage of divine sonship language in Jewish tradition and pagan culture of the first century."[29] But he criticizes her for "curiously" not considering

> whether Mark presents readers with a basis for reinterpreting such language in the light of the story of Jesus he conveys. That is, the intended audience of Mark was likely Christians, whether from Jewish or Gentile backgrounds; so their understanding of such language would also likely have been shaped by their Christian associations and usage, and not merely by their respective pre-Christian cultural backgrounds.[30]

If that is the case, one would expect Mark's Christian audience to hear the centurion's utterance as resonating with their own Christian conviction: Surely, this man, who has just died on the cross, is *the* Son of God.

4.1.2 The Allegory of the Wicked Tenants (Mark 12:1 – 12)

Jesus' implicitly identifies himself as the Son of God in the parable of the Tenants addressed to "the chief priests, the teachers of the law and the elders" (11:27; 12:1). A vineyard owner sends a series of servants to collect his share of the fruits of the vineyard, but each is successively brutalized and some are murdered. As a last resort,[31] the owner decides to send his "son, whom he loved" (12:6).[32] The parable's purpose is to warn the Jewish leaders that their iniquitous dereliction of duty will bring God's judgment, but it also has christological ramifications.[33] It is not happenstance that the description "beloved" resonates with God's recognition of Jesus as "my Son, whom I love" at the baptism and transfiguration (1:11; 9:7).

---

28. Wallace, *Greek Grammar beyond the Basics*, 250, cites "Apollonius' Canon" that as a general rule in Greek, "*both* the head noun and the genitive noun either have the article or lack the article," and "it makes little semantic difference whether the construction is articular or anarthrous." E. C. Colwell, "A Definite Rule for the Use of the Article in the Greek New Testament," *JBL* 52 (1933): 12–21, argued that the noun-phrase in 15:39 lacks the article because a predicate nominative lacks the article, even if it is definite, in order to distinguish it from the subject of the clause. Maximilian Zerwick, *Biblical Greek* (trans. Joseph Smith; Rome: Pontifical Biblical Institute, 1963), §175, p. 56, found that, throughout the New Testament, the predicate use of the title "Son of God" virtually always conforms to Colwell's rule. See also Robert G. Bratcher, "A Note on *huios theou* (Mark xv. 39)," *ExpTim* 68 (1956–57): 27–28; Philip H. Bligh, "A Note on *Huios Theou* in Mark 15:39," *ExpTim* 80 (1968–69): 51–53; T. Francis Glasson, "Mark xv.39: The Son of God," *ExpTim* 80 (1968–69): 286; Harold A. Guy, "Son of God in Mk 15:39," *ExpTim* 81 (1969–70): 151; and Brown, *Death*, 2:1146–50. Philip B. Harner, "Qualitative Anarthrous Predicate Nouns: Mark 15:39 and John 1:1," *JBL* 92 (1973): 75–87, challenges Colwell's conclusions, so that arguments from grammar have now become unpersuasive. Earl S. Johnson Jr., "Mark 15,39 and the So-Called Confession of the Roman Centurion," *Bib* 81 (2000): 407–48, rejects the reading "Son of God" in 1:1 as original to Mark, but see the arguments for its authenticity above in §3.1.4.5.1.

29. See Collins, "Mark and His Readers," 85–100. See also Peppard, *The Son of God in the Roman World*.

30. Hurtado, *Lord Jesus Christ*, 288, n. 69.

31. The word translated "last of all" (*eschaton*) in 12:6 is used numerous times in the New Testament in connection with the last days.

32. Aquila H. I. Lee, *From Messiah to Preexistent Son* (WUNT 2/192; Tübingen: Mohr Siebeck, 2005), 164, makes the point that if the son were not a significant part of the parable, "Jesus might have skipped directly from the sending of the slaves to the coming of the owner because the tenants' ill-treatment of the slaves would well have justified the owner's coming."

33. Lee, ibid., 165, asserts that it is "highly likely that in telling this parable Jesus implicitly revealed his self-consciousness of divine sonship and of divine mission, although this was not his primary intention." Mark would have understood and regarded as valid the christological implications.

The response of the chief priests, the teachers of the law, and the elders to this parable—"they knew he had spoken the parable against them" (12:12)—reveals that they understood Jesus' story to be a transparent allegory. The vineyard represents Israel (Isa 5:1–7); the vineyard owner is God; the bloody-minded tenants are the Jewish leaders; and the servants sent out to collect the owner's portion of the produce are the prophets (Matt 23:37; Acts 7:52; 1 Thess 2:15).[34] Jesus has referred to God as "the one who sent me" (9:37). He also has announced that he will "be rejected by the elders, the chief priests and the teachers of the law" and will be killed (8:31; see 9:31) and that he "will be delivered over to the chief priests and the teachers of the law" (10:33). Jesus is therefore the beloved son whom they will put to death through their calculating intrigue.[35] The only explanation in the narrative for the high priest's supposition that Jesus passed himself off as "the Messiah, the Son of the Blessed One" (14:61) comes from putting two and two together from this parable. The chief priests, the teachers of the law, and the elders correctly understand its gist, but it does not dissuade them from plotting to do away with him. Just the opposite, it steels their resolve.

The parable surveys the history of God's dealing with Israel. "Last of all" underscores the finality of the landowner sending his son. He is "the decisive figure in the whole of God's history of salvation."[36] The son has authority over the vineyard by virtue of his relation to his father. He too is the owner of the vineyard, and he should be accorded respect. The parable tacitly makes bold claims about Jesus' identity and status, but it also anticipates Jesus' shameful death at the hands of the Jewish leaders. The scriptural quotation from Ps 118:22–23 forecasts his ultimate vindication by God. He will become the cornerstone of a new, living temple (1 Cor 3:10–17; 2 Cor 6:16; Eph 2:19–22; 1 Pet 2:4–8), or perhaps the elevated capstone.[37] The "owner of the vineyard" who comes to destroy the treacherous tenants represents "the Lord Jesus returning as Son of Man in the glory of his *Father* (8:38)."[38] This exalted connection is confirmed by Jesus' response to the high priest that they will "see the Son of Man sitting at the right hand of the Mighty One and coming on the clouds of heaven" (14:62).

34. Roger David Aus, *The Wicked Tenants and Gethsemane: Isaiah in the Wicked Tenants' Vineyard, and Moses and the High Priest in Gethsemane: Judaic Traditions in Mark 12:1–9 and 14:32–42* (University of South Florida International Studies in Formative Christianity and Judaism 4; Atlanta: Scholars Press, 1996), 37, notes that in the MT, the prophets are often referred to as God's servants: "my servants the prophets" (9x); "his servant the prophets" (6x); and "your servants the prophets" (2x).

35. See Klyne R. Snodgrass, *Stories with Intent: A Comprehensive Guide to the Parables of Jesus* (Grand Rapids: Eerdmans, 2008), 294. Kingsbury, *Christology*, 115–16. Meinrad Limbeck, *Markus-Evangelium* (SKKNT; Stuttgart: Katholisches Bibelwerk, 1984), 174, notes that this parable comes at the end of his public freedom of action when the outcome of his sending has become increasingly clear.

36. Kingsbury, *Christology*, 117.

37. David Stern, *Parables in Midrash: Narrative and Exegesis in Rabbinic Literature* (Cambridge, MA: Harvard University Press, 1991), 195, who claims it is "the capstone or keystone in an arch, which must be irregularly shaped in order to fit its strategic position at the apex of the arch." The builder's initially rejected it "because it seemed misshapen" but it "proved in the end to be the perfect shape for the capstone."

38. Boring, *Mark*, 331.

4.1.3 The Son's Not Knowing the Timing of the End (Mark 13:32)

The central theme of the eschatological discourse in chapter 13 is that "*the timing of the Son of Man's return is not knowable in advance of his arrival*."[39] No one can or should chart out a timeline of end-time events. To score this point, Jesus states, "But about that day or hour no one knows, not even the angels in heaven, nor the Son, but only the Father" (13:32). He identifies himself as the Son of the Father.[40] The argument only has force if it is assumed that the Son would have the same access as the angels to heavenly intelligence about the final days. If the Son with such divine ties does not know this detail, then who else on earth could possibly know it?

4.1.4 Jesus' Use of Abba

In his ordeal in Gethsemane, Jesus addresses God in prayer as "*Abba*, Father" (14:36), the only time the transliteration of this Aramaic word appears in the Gospels.[41] The prayer that follows reveals Jesus intensely imploring his Father to do what would seem from his earlier prophecies of his destiny to be absolutely unthinkable, to permit him to skip the cross and its suffering. Fitzmyer asserts, "There is no evidence in the literature of pre-Christian or first-century Palestinian Judaism that *ʾabbā* was used in any sense as a personal address for God by an individual."[42] It does imply a special relationship and expresses "the respectful intimacy of a son in a patriarchal family."[43] Addressing God with such unique familiarity expresses the heart of Jesus' relationship to God.[44] This mode of address must have impressed the disciples

39. Timothy J. Geddert, *Watchwords: Mark 13 in Markan Eschatology* (JSNTSup 26; Sheffield: JSOT, 1989), 223.

40. Raymond E. Brown, *An Introduction to New Testament Christology* (New York/Mahwah, NJ: Paulist, 1994), 89, observes, "It is curious that the very passage that speaks of Jesus absolutely as the Son (of God) is the most famous passage in the Gospels for indicating that Jesus' knowledge was limited!"

41. Mark records Aramaic expressions spoken by Jesus in 5:41; 7:34; and 15:34.

42. Joseph A. Fitzmyer, "*ʾAbba* and Jesus' Relation to God," in *À cause de l'èvangile: études sur les Synoptiques et les Actes: offertes au P. Jacques Dupont, O.S.B. à l'occasion de son soixante-dixième anniversaire* (ed. F. Refoule; LD 123; Paris: Cerf, 1985), 1:28. The appeal to God as "Father" appears in Greek in 3 Macc 5:7; 6:3–4; Wis 14:3; and Sir 23:1; and 4Q46 and 4Q372 contain prayers uttered in distress that address God as *ʾabî* ("my father").

43. France, *Mark*, 584.

44. Joachim Jeremias, *The Central Message of the New Testament* (New York: Scribner's, 1965), 9–30; and *The Prayers of* Jesus (SBT 6; Naperville, IL: Allenson, 1967), 11–65. James Barr, "*ʾAbbā* Isn't 'Daddy,'" *JTS* 39 (1988): 28–47, corrects Jeremias. Jesus did not use a childish term and address God as "Daddy," but evidence shows that children used an adult term. Jeremias himself offers a qualification in *New Testament Theology: The Proclamation of Jesus* (New York: Scribner's, 1971), 67–68. Jesus is not addressing God in "the language of a tiny child," and he cautions against ascribing to Jesus from this usage any idea of preexistence. Jesus' intimate mode of invoking God in prayer, using family language instead of the more formal "Lord," "God," or "Master," simply implies that Jesus "was conscious of being authorized to communicate God's revelation, because God had made himself known to him as Father (Matt. 11.27 par.)." Mary Rose d'Angelo, "*Abba* and 'Father': Imperial Theology and the Jesus Traditions," *JBL* 111 (1992): 611–30, challenges all of Jeremias's conclusions, but they have been substantially upheld with qualifications by Georg Schelbert, "Sprachgeschichtliches zu '*Abba*,'" in *Mélanges Dominique Barthélemy: études bibliques offertes à l'occasion de son 60e anniversaire* (ed. Pierre Casetti, Omar Keel, and Adrian Schenker; OBO 38; Göttingen: Vandenhoeck & Ruprecht, 1981), 395–447; Fitzmyer, "*Abba* and Jesus' Relation to God," 1:15–38; and Lee, *From Messiah to Preexistent Son*, 122–36. Joseph A. Grassi, "*Abba* Father (Mark 14:36): Another Approach," *JAAR* 50 (1982): 449–58, argues that Jesus cries to his Father as an obedient Son, as Isaac did to his father Abraham (Gen 22:7).

enough that it was passed on and preserved in the tradition of the Greek-speaking early church (see Rom 8:15; Gal 4:6).[45]

4.1.5 Jesus' Response to the High Priest (14:61–62)

Jesus' response to the high priest during his interrogation before the council is another christological high point in the gospel. The high priest and his council sought witnesses to provide testimony that Jesus was guilty of blasphemous threats against the temple and therefore guilty of blasphemy against God. Whether the witnesses were suborned or not to give false testimony, Mark comments that it was false and adds that there was a bumbling failure on their part to get their testimonies to match, thereby stalling the plans to condemn Jesus to death. The vexed high priest, using a circumlocution for "God," breaks in to demand, "Are you the Messiah, the Son of the Blessed One?" (14:61).[46] The two titles that appeared in the incipit in 1:1, "Messiah," and "the Son of God," reappear together for the first time in the narrative. Also, for the first time, Jesus responds by openly confessing his identity, "I am" (14:62). Jesus incriminates himself and provides all the testimony they need to confirm their bias that he has committed blasphemy. It guarantees that the high priest and the council will seek some way to induce the Roman governor to execute him as Jesus had prophesied (10:33).

This reply is decisive for laying bare Mark's understanding of Jesus' messianic claim and his relationship to God. The shorter reading "I am" is to be preferred over the longer reading, "You have said that I am."[47] It has better external attestation[48] and makes the best sense of the high priest's reaction, "Why do we need any more witnesses?" (14:63). "I am" is an affirmative reply and should not be construed

45. Marianne Meye Thompson, *The Promise of the Father: Jesus and God in the New Testament* (Louisville: Westminster John Knox, 2000), 65, contends that "the persistent use of 'our Father' and the absence of 'my Father' from the rest of the New Testament may suggest that both could be traced back to Jesus, with 'our Father' as a form of address commended to his followers, and 'my Father' limited to Jesus himself."

46. Jean Claude Loba Mkole, "Mark 14:62: Substantial Compendium of New Testament Christology," *HvTSt* 56 (2000): 1121, asserts that it is "likely that the question of his [Jesus'] identity may have been at the center of his interrogation."

47. Against Taylor, *Mark*, 568, who thinks it accords with Jesus' reserve about his messiahship in Mark. See also James D. G. Dunn, "'Are You The Messiah?': Is the Crux of Mark 14.61–62 Resolvable?" in *Christology, Controversy and Community: New Testament Essays in Honour of David R. Catchpole* (ed. David G. Horrell and Christopher M. Tuckett; NovTSup 99; Leiden/Boston/Köln: Brill, 2000), 11–12; and Marcus, *Mark 8–16*, 1005.

48. Renatus Kempthorne, "The Marcan Text of Jesus' Answer to the High Priest (Mark xiv 62)," *NovT* 19 (1977): 197–208, who argues convincingly for the shorter reading. The longer reading is found only in Θ, f^{13}, 472, 543, 565, 700, 1071, two versions, Geo and Arm, and in Origen. See also Leroy A. Huizenga, "The Confession of Jesus and the Curses of Peter: A Narrative-Christological Approach to the Text-Critical Problem of Mark 14:62," *NovT* 53 (2011): 244–66, who argues that Jesus' positive answer dramatically contrasts with Peter's denial in this intercalated passage (14:53–72). Since Jesus gives this evasive answer "You have said so" to Pilate in 15:2, Marcus, *Mark 8–16*, 1005, considers it to be one of numerous doublets in Mark. Pilate's question, "Are you the king of the Jews?" however, is entirely different from the high priest's question. On Pilate's lips, the query implies that Jesus is an agitator intent on fomenting rebellion to attain political power. That question only deserves an evasive answer. It spurs the governor to prod him to give some reply, "Aren't you going to answer?" (15:4). Marcus also asserts that the scribes who copied the Scripture are "known for altering passages in the direction of a higher or more explicit Christology" and would change it to a more direct answer (Marcus, *Mark 8–16*, 1006); see also Bart D. Ehrman, *The Orthodox Corruption of Scripture: The Effect of Early Christological Controversies on the Text of the New Testament* (Oxford: Oxford University Press, 1993), xi, who argues that "scribes occasionally altered the words of their sacred texts to make them more patently orthodox." Ehrman assumes that a reading that is least orthodox is most likely to be original. In this case, however, copyists were more likely to assimilate Mark to agree with the more influential gospels of Matthew and Luke (see Matt 26:64; Luke 22:70; see Gundry, *Mark*, 910).

as Jesus applying to himself the ineffable name for God (Deut 32:39; Isa 43:10; 46:4 [LXX]).[49] God's previous declarations in the narrative, "You are my Son the Beloved" (1:11) and "This is my Son the Beloved" (9:7) (lit. trans. for both) now become Jesus' own testimony. He publicly confirms before his enemies what God has declared in private (1:11; 9:7).

This confession occurs at the single most appropriate moment for the truth to come out because Jesus' identity as the Christ and the Son of God cannot be detached from his destiny as the one who will be crucified and raised from the dead. The suffering and degradation that he predicted he must undergo (8:31) have already begun.[50] Brown comments, "To be able to see him as the Messiah, the Son of God, in *these* circumstances is to understand the mystery."[51] The high priest's rejoinder that Jesus' confession is blasphemy makes it clear that his death is precipitated by his *christological* claims and not by any imagined politically subversive activity. From the high priest's perspective, Jesus violated the fundamental demarcation between the human and the divine by laying claim to a seat at the right hand of power and sharing in God's authority.[52] Kingsbury maintains that Mark "desires to show that Jesus is condemned to death by the Sanhedrin for being exactly who he is, namely, the royal Son of God whom God sent to die on the cross and be vindicated in his resurrection (12:6, 10–11; 15:39; 16:6)."[53]

Boiling with outrage, the high priest tears his garment upon hearing Jesus' admission. Such "blasphemy" is worthy of death, he thunders (14:63–64).[54] What makes this confession blasphemous is not, as some claim, that he openly admits that he is the Messiah. Supposedly, Jesus' admission infringed on God's sole prerogative to make known the Messiah and to enthrone him. But most scholars agree that such a claim, however pretentious it might seem, would not have been labeled blasphemy—outrageous, perhaps, but not blasphemy.[55]

---

49. Catrin H. Williams, *"I am He": The Interpretation of 'Anî Hû' in Jewish and Early Christian Literature* (WUNT 2/113; Tübingen: Mohr Siebeck, 2000), 246–51. The answer "I am" alone does not spark the charge of blasphemy, contra Ethelbert Stauffer, *Jesus and His Story* (trans. Richard and Clara Winston; New York: Knopf, 1960), 124–25, 174–95.

50. Brown, *Death*, 1:489.

51. Ibid.

52. Morna D. Hooker, *The Son of Man in Mark: A Study of the Background of the Term "Son of Man" and Its Use in St. Mark's Gospel* (Montreal: McGill University Press, 1967), 172–73.

53. Kingsbury, *Christology*, 120. Hans Lietzmann, "Der Prozess Jesu," *Sitzungsberichte der Preussischen Akademie der Wissenschaften* 14 (1931): 313–22; Paul Winter, *On the Trial of Jesus* (Studia Judaica; Forschungen zur Wissenschaft des Judentums 1; ed. and rev. by T. Alec Burkill and Geza Vermes; 2nd ed.; Berlin: de Gruyter, 1974); Haim H. Cohn, *The Trial and Death of Jesus* (New York: Harper, 1971); and Ellis Rivkin, *What Crucified Jesus? The Political Execution of a Charismatic* (Nashville: Abingdon, 1984) variously argue that the Sanhedrin trial in Mark is a pro-Roman, anti-Jewish Christian fiction told tendentiously to shift the blame for Jesus' death from the Romans to the Jews in order to make life more tolerable for Christians in the Roman world. I would argue instead that Mark's purpose in this scene is entirely christological. It is not to give assurance to Romans that Jesus was framed by perverse Jewish opponents envious of his popularity, that his death was all a travesty of justice, and that he is no enemy of the state.

54. Tearing one's garments is an appropriate response to hearing blasphemy, according to *m. Sanh.* 7:5, though in that context it specifically applies to hearing the Tetragrammaton spoken. Barnabas and Paul tore their clothes and protested when the Lystrans called Barnabas, "Zeus," and Paul, "Hermes," and wanted to offer sacrifices to them (Acts 14:12–15).

55. Lane, *Mark*, 538, thinks "Jesus' open avowal of his messiahship" falls into the category of blasphemy. Craig A. Evans, "In What Sense 'Blasphemy'? Jesus before Caiaphas in Mark 14:61–64," in *Jesus and His Contemporaries: Comparative Studies* (AGJU 25; Leiden/New York/Köln: Brill, 1995), 407, points out, however, that Josephus disparaged "the many would-be kings and deliverers of first-century Israel" as "imposters and opportunists" but never accused them of blasphemy. Joel Marcus, "Mark 14:61: Are You the Messiah-Son-of-God?" *NovT* 31 (1989): 128–29, cites two Tannaitic traditions about Simon Bar Kozeba (Bar Kochba) where he was acclaimed as the Messiah by R. Akiba, who is only rebuked

Gundry argues that Jesus uttered the Tetragrammaton in his reply, "You will see the Son of Man seated at the right hand of Yahweh," and that any public report of blasphemy required using a substitute for the Divine Name (*m. Sanh.* 7:1–6)—hence, Mark's use of the circumlocution "the right hand of the Mighty One" (lit., "Power").[56] While Jesus may have used the name Yahweh, it is unlikely that it provoked the charge of blasphemy.[57] The wide-ranging opinions of what constituted blasphemy included assuming divine prerogatives (2:7), making divine claims, or affronting the law, the temple, or God's people (see Acts 6:11, 13).[58] Jesus himself labels offenses against the Holy Spirit as blasphemy and applied it to the Jerusalem scribes' accusation that he has Beelzebul and cast out demons through the prince of demons (3:22, 28–29).

Marcus makes the case that the question "Are you the Messiah, the Son of the Blessed One?" is not in nonrestrictive apposition and should not be separated by the comma so that it implies that the two terms "Messiah" and "the Son of the Blessed One" are to be understood synonymously as in 15:32, "this Messiah, this king of Israel."[59] This punctuation assumes that the term "Messiah" supplies the primary identification and "the Son of the Blessed One" simply fills it out. He asks why it would be considered blasphemous if "the Son of the Blessed One" were simply ancillary to the Messiah.[60] He argues instead that "the Son of the Blessed One" is a restrictive appositive and "indicates *what sort* of messianic expectation is in view: *not* the Messiah-Son-of-David, nor the Messiah as the son of any other human being, but rather the Messiah-Son-of-*God*."[61] Luke 22:67–71 confirms this reading of the text since Luke treats "Messiah" and "Son of God" as two separate titles by breaking the question into two parts. The chief priests and teachers of the law ask, "If you are the Messiah, tell us" (Luke 22:67). When he responds that they will see the Son of Man seated at the right hand of God (Luke 22:69), they ask, "Are you then the Son of God?" (Luke 22:70a). His ambiguous answer "You say that I am" (Luke 22:70b) confirms their suspicions and clinches the case against him.

In my view, the serious indictment of blasphemy was further prompted by Jesus' merging of two OT passages, Ps 110:1 and Dan 7:13, to make a high christological claim that he will share God's throne and will come to judge the high priest and all the others gathered with him.[62] A comparison of the texts reveals the connections:

for being rash (*y. Taʿan.* 4:5), and where he identifies himself as the Messiah and is expected to give authenticating signs (*b. Sanh.* 93b). The unwarranted claims are regarded as foolish and an indication that he was a false prophet worthy of death, but not blasphemous.

56. Gundry, *Mark*, 915–18.

57. Evans, "In What Sense 'Blasphemy'?" 413.

58. See ibid., 407–34; Bock, *Blasphemy and Exaltation*; and Adela Yarbro Collins, "The Charge of Blasphemy in Mark 14:64," in *The Trial and Death of Jesus: Essays on the Passion Narrative in Mark* (ed. Geert van Oyen and Tom Shepherd; CBET 45; Leuven: Peeters, 2006), 160–65. Mark does not regard the high priest's accusation to be some phony, trumped-up charge, contra Anderson, *Mark*, 331.

59. Marcus, "Mark 14:61: Are You the Messiah-Son-of-God?" 125–41.

60. Ibid., 127.

61. Ibid., 130. For example, this designation would distinguish him from the Messiah [Son] of Aaron and the Messiah [Son] of Israel (1QS 9:11; 1QSa 2:11–22).

62. The following summarizes and adds to the conclusions in my commentary, Garland, *Mark*, 561–64. Albert Vanhoye, *Structure and Theology of the Accounts of the Passion in the Synoptic Gospels* (Collegeville, MN: Liturgical, 1967), 25–27, recognizes that the basis for the blasphemy charge stems from the response from Ps 110:1 and Dan 7:13. See also Martin Hengel, "'Sit at My Right Hand!': The Enthronement of Christ at the Right Hand of God and Psalm 110:1," in *Studies in Early Christology* (Edinburgh: T&T Clark, 1995), 119–226 (esp. 185–89); and Evans, "In What Sense 'Blasphemy'?" 413–23.

Psalm 110:1

The LORD says to my lord: "Sit at my right hand until I make your enemies a footstool for your feet."

Daniel 7:13–14 (LXX)

And behold *on the clouds of heaven he came* (in appearance like a *son of man* [human]), and he was present like an Ancient of Days. And those who were standing in wait were with him, and authority was given to him and all the nations of the earth from every race and all glory waited upon him, and his authority is an eternal authority which will not be taken [from him] and his dominion will not be destroyed. (author's trans.).

Mark 14:62

"And you will see the *Son of Man* sitting at the right hand of the Mighty One and *coming on the clouds of heaven*."

Psalm 110 refers to the king of Israel being invited to take his seat at the right hand of God. Sitting at the right hand signifies the transfer of temporal, not divine, authority and judgment to the earthly king. The king is established on Zion and occupies the throne of God's reign over Israel as God's representative on earth (1 Chr 28:5, 29:23; 2 Chr 9:8). Jesus appealed earlier to Ps 110:1 in questioning how the teachers of the law can say that the Messiah is David's son if David called him Lord (12:35–37). This provocative question reveals that for Mark, the passage has messianic implications. The question goes unanswered, but in asking it Jesus insinuates that the Christ is something more than simply the son of David, an earthly king, since David himself acknowledged his supremacy. It insinuates that Jesus is the son of someone greater.[63]

No OT passage explicitly conferred on the Messiah full equality with God on a heavenly plane. Jesus extends the image from Ps 110:1 with the line from Dan 7:13, the "son of man" "coming with the clouds of heaven." Allusions to Dan 7:13–14 appear three times in Mark, which suggest its importance for the Evangelist:

Daniel 7:13–14	**Mark 8:38–9:1**	**Mark 13:26**	**Mark 14:62**
angels (7:10)	with the holy angels		
with the clouds of heaven		in clouds	with clouds of heaven
came	when he comes	coming	coming

63. See David M. Hay, *Glory at the Right Hand: Psalm 110 in Early Christianity* (Nashville: Abingdon, 1973), 116. The confession that Paul cites in Rom 1:3–4 that Jesus "was born of the seed of David according to the flesh, who was declared *to be* the Son of God with power, according to the spirit of holiness, by the resurrection from the dead" (ASV) confirms that "son of David" cannot fully convey Jesus' unique identity.

Daniel 7:13–14	Mark 8:38–9:1	Mark 13:26	Mark 14:62
one like a son of man	the Son of Man	the Son of Man	the Son of Man
to him was given ... glory and a kingdom	in the glory of his Father	glory	
	come in power	with great power	at the right hand of Power

In Dan 7:14, one like a son of man comes to the Ancient of Days and receives divine power. The vision of Daniel 7 has unique features when compared with other theophanies (e.g., Ezek 1:26–28). First, it is not a glorious manifestation of God on earth but a scene that takes place in the clouds of heaven on the divine level. Second, two characters appear, not one: the Ancient of Days, God, who is enthroned, and a being "like a son of man" who advances to the Ancient of Days. Third, in other theophanies, the almighty God is approached with fear and trembling (see Exod 3:6; Isa 6:5), but the one "like a son of man" boldly approaches God and receives divine power.

The vision never specifically identifies who this one "like a son of man" is.[64] Is he a real person or an abstraction? The interpretation of the vision in Dan 7:16–28 has the people of the Most High receiving and possessing the kingdom forever and ever (7:18, 22, 27). Is the one like a son of man who receives "authority, glory and sovereign power" (7:14) the saints of the Most High or only a symbol of them? Is he a human being or some divine being? The passage contains only subtle royal messianic overtones if the one like a son of man represents an individual king who represents the people he rules.[65] No mention is made of his enthronement at the right hand of God, and dominion is given to him alone with no reference to any descendants.[66]

Lust contends that the LXX with its free translation of the Hebrew text "wishes to identify the son of man with the Ancient of Days. He is God. Therefore they present him as riding 'on the clouds,' the clouds being known as a vehicle of the gods."[67] In the LXX, the authority of the one like a son of man "becomes identical to the authority of God and his dominion identical to God's dominion."[68] Lust claims that the throne vision in Daniel 7 forms a counterpart to the stone vision in Daniel 2. He writes, "The stone demolishing the statue in ch. 2 corresponds to the heavenly figure

64. One "like a son of man" contrasts with the preceding string of beasts in Dan 7:2–12, and he is given the dominion that is taken away from the beasts.

65. G. K. Beale, *A New Testament Biblical Theology: The Unfolding of the Old Testament in the New* (Grand Rapids: Baker Academic, 2011), 395, cites Dan 7:17 where the four beasts are interpreted to be "kings," and in 7:23 the fourth beast is described as "a kingdom." He concludes, "this suggests that the Son of Man is both an individual and also a representative for a community."

66. Contrast *Pss. Sol.* 17:4, "Lord, you chose David to be king over Israel, and swore to him about his descendants, that his kingdom should not fail before you."

67. Johan Lust, "Daniel 7,13 and the Septuagint," *ETL* 54 (1978): 64. Beale, *A New Testament Biblical Theology*, 192, cites the Old Greek, a major version of the LXX, that translates it that the one like Son of Man came "*as* the Ancient of Days," not "*up to* the Ancient of Days."

68. Hengel, "'Sit at My Right Hand!'" 185. He notes that Daniel 7 and Ps 110:1 are connected in *1 En.* 51:3; 55:4; 61:8; 62:2.

in ch. 7, called 'Son of Man' or 'Ancient of Days.' They represent a heavenly ruler and a heavenly kingdom which will abolish and replace the human dominions."[69]

By linking these two different traditions, Jesus' answer creates an explosive stew as they interpret each other.[70] On the one hand, the one like a son of man is no longer some mysterious apparition but a real man, a descendant of David, in whom the messianic prophecies are realized. On the other hand, sitting at God's right hand is no longer simply a symbol of royal splendor as God's earthly representative. It denotes divine power exercised on the heavenly plane and equality with God. Jesus understands his sonship to be on a far more exalted level than the Davidic king obtains in Ps 2:7 and 2 Sam 7:14. His affirmation therefore far surpasses any current conception about the Messiah. He implies that he has divine authority and that one day his accusers will see him riding the clouds as God rides the clouds and coming to judge them.[71] At this moment, however, the high priest can only see a blasphemous combination of Scripture passages that Jesus applies to himself.

The high priest is shocked because Jesus' confession confirms his suspicions that Jesus is guilty of hubris against God. He does far more than claim to be the Messiah, the Son of the Blessed One; he claims to have divine status with a transcendent future role. The implication is that this high priest will be judged by the very one who stands before him, but on that day he "will be full of the radiance of glory, surrounded by the clouds."[72] Jesus' response to the high priest answers the riddle that he posed in 12:37 about the Messiah as the son of David that was left hanging. David calls him "Lord" because he is far more than simply the son of David.[73] In 12:35–37, Jesus did not repudiate the Messiah's Davidic connections but intimates that the Messiah is not an earthly, royal figure but a divine, transcendent figure. It is one thing for Jesus to affirm that he is the Messiah, the Son of the Blessed One, but it is another to say that they will see him being given a throne, sitting beside the majestic God, and coming on the divine transport of clouds to judge them.

In his answer, Jesus shifts from the present to the future, "you will see," to refer to his future vindication.[74] The contexts of the allusions to Scripture in the trial

69. Lust, "Daniel 7,13," 69.

70. Hengel, "Sit at My Right Hand!" 187, asserts that this mixture of the texts "is certainly not a construct of the author of the gospel—who is sometimes incorrectly portrayed as the first 'Christian novelist'—but contains an 'old form' of christology which connects the exaltation to the right hand of God and the parousia for the purpose of the last judgement."

71. Only God travels on the clouds; see Ps 104:3; Isa 19:1; Jer 4:13; see also 2 Sam 22:10–12; Job 22:14; Ps 97:2–5. Evans, "In What Sense 'Blasphemy'?" 419–20, explains the odd juxtaposition of being "seated" and also "coming." It refers to being seated on "God's chariot throne" (Dan 7:9, "As I looked, thrones were set in place, and the Ancient of Days took his seat. His clothing was as white as snow; the hair of his head was white like wool. His throne was flaming with fire, and its wheels were all ablaze"). The image would have been understood by a Greco-Roman audience. A coin minted in AD 55 depicts Claudius sitting at the right hand of Augustus atop a chariot drawn by four elephants (see Harold Mattingly, *Coins of the Roman Empire in the British Museum*. Volume 1. *Augustus to Vitellius* [London: Trustees of the British Museum, 1936], 1:201 [plate 38]). The difference is that Jesus sits next to God, not the Roman emperor.

72. Simon Gathercole, "The Son of Man in Mark's Gospel," *ExpTim* 115 (2004): 371.

73. Evald Lövestam, "Die Davidssohnsfrage," *SEÅ* 27 (1962): 72–82.

74. Eduard Schweizer, *Lordship and Discipleship* (trans. David E. Green; SBT 38; London: SCM, 1960), 36, comments: "If Jesus did foresee suffering and rejection for himself and his disciples, then, of course, he saw it not as a catastrophe but as a gateway to the glory of the coming Kingdom. If he did call himself the Son of Man and connected this title with his lowly state on earth as well as with the glory to come, then he must in fact have expected something like his exaltation to the presence of God."

narrative (Mark 14:55/Ps 37:32; Mark 14:61/Isa 36:21; and Mark 14:65/Isa 50:6) express a consistent theme that God will protect and vindicate God's righteous agent and judge the wicked.[75] Jesus is shown to be obedient to God, and Scripture testifies that God will vindicate those submissive to God's will. The allusion to Ps 37:32 in Mark 14:55 augments this notion, "The chief priests and the whole Sanhedrin were looking [seeking] for evidence against Jesus so that they could put him to death."[76] Psalm 37:32–34 reads:

> The wicked lie in wait for the righteous,
> intent on putting them to death [the Greek reads lit., "and seek to put him to death"];
> but the LORD will not leave them in the power of the wicked
> or let them be condemned when brought to trial.
> Hope in the LORD
> and keep his way.
> He will exalt you to inherit the land;
> when the wicked are destroyed, you will see it.

The righteous will be protected, and the wicked will be judged. Jesus' answer, however, goes much further than asserting his trust in God's future vindication. He indicates that he will be the agent of divine vengeance against those who resist God's will. The one now being judged by them will be given divine authority as the ultimate judge. The roles will be reversed, but, unlike their judgment of him, the judgment he will pronounce will be eternal.

The upshot is that Jesus' affirmation far surpasses any current conception about the Messiah. He is the Son of God on a level with God and with divine authority. In the eyes of the high priest, this claim by a living human being is evidence of blasphemous audacity on Jesus' part.[77] Collins asserts: "The narrative of the trial is ironic in the sense that what is blasphemy for the members of the council is true from the perspective of those who accept Jesus as the agent of God."[78] To repeat the observation of Shepherd cited earlier, it is ironic that Jesus' confession gives the high priest and the council the power to take deadly action against him, but by doing so and thinking they are eradicating his power, "they actually bring him to power at God's right hand."[79]

4.2 JESUS AS THE MESSIAH (CHRIST)

Jesus is identified as "Messiah" ("Christ") in the incipit (1:1). Since this title appears so prominently, we must assume that Mark regards it as a fundamental category

75. O'Brien, "Innocence and Guilt," 217–24.

76. O'Brien, ibid., 218–19, notes how Psalm 37 is applied to "the teacher of righteousness" and "the wicked priest" in 4Q171.

77. Compare Philo's reactions to Emperor Gaius's claims to be a god (*Embassy* 45 §§352–357, 367; 46 §368).

78. Collins, "The Charge of Blasphemy in Mark 14:64," 151.

79. Shepherd, "The Irony of Power in the Trial of Jesus," 241.

for understanding Jesus' identity. The narrative that follows, however, suggests that this title is problematic. Five of the other six times the term "Messiah" appears in Mark, it is on the lips of "those who do not understand what Jesus' mission is, or who are hostile toward it" (8:29; 12:35; 13:21; 14:61; 15:32).[80] The one exception is when Jesus promises, "Truly I tell you, anyone who gives you a cup of water in my name because you belong to the Messiah will certainly not lose their reward" (9:41). Jesus warns that his followers will face persecution after his death and resurrection (13:9–13), but the phrase "bearing the name of Christ" ("you belong to the Messiah," NIV) in 9:41 seems anachronistic in the narrative. It can only apply in the situation of the early church when many are antagonistic toward the Christian movement and just a cup of water from others seems heaven-sent.[81] The title "Messiah," then, is applied to him only by others. Jesus does not reject it but does not use it publicly to refer to himself.

The probable reason for this reticence is that no fixed idea existed about the Messiah or his identity or role. For example, Green notes that in early Jewish literature, the term "messiah" is used twice for the patriarchs; six times for the high priests, once for Cyrus, and twenty-nine times for the Israelite king (Saul, primarily David, and an unnamed Davidic monarch). In *1 En.* 37–90 (*Similitudes*), it is used to refer to a "transcendent, heavenly figure." In *2 Apocalypse Baruch*, it refers to a warrior figure.[82] He concludes, "In early Jewish literature, 'messiah' is all signifier with no signified; the term is notable primarily for its indeterminacy."[83] The differing assumptions that this term might have evoked made it inadequate to communicate Jesus' identity. Jesus highlights this problem with the warning that in the days of extreme distress that are coming, false messiahs (christs) and false prophets will appear and perform deceptive signs and miracles.[84] Some will say, "Look, here is the Messiah!" or "Look, there he is!" (13:21–22). Jesus warns that even the elect will be targets of their deception, and they are not to be hoodwinked by their claims.

From Mark's point of view, what it means for Jesus to be the Messiah could be understood only in retrospect after his death and resurrection. "Messiah" and the complementary titles "son of David" and "king of Israel" fail to do justice to his cosmic identity, which Mark wishes to convey. While Mark identifies Jesus as the Messiah in 1:1, he qualifies it with the title "Son of God." This pattern is found elsewhere in Mark. Jesus asks his disciples, "Who do people say that I am?" and they tell him the various conjectures: John the Baptist, Elijah, or one of the prophets

80. Kee, "Christology in Mark's Gospel," 200.

81. Codex Sinaiticus has "in my name because you are mine" in the original text that has been corrected. "You are Christ's" may have been a scribal gloss to clarify a strange phrase in Greek "in the name that."

82. William Scott Green, "Introduction: Messiah in Judaism: Rethinking the Question," in *Judaisms and Their Messiahs at the Turn of the Christian Era* (ed. Jacob Neusner, William Scott Green, and Ernest S. Frerichs; Cambridge: Cambridge University Press, 1987), 1–14.

83. Ibid., 4.

84. The Pharisees asked Jesus for a sign from heaven, to test him (8:11). That Mark identifies their intentions as testing him exposes their impure motives. They are not seeking the truth (Deut 13:1–4). They expect him to certify his mission with a cosmic miracle. Jesus will give no sign (8:12) and will not turn his ministry into a carnival side show. That is what false messiahs and false prophets do. People do not believe in Jesus because he performs signs. If people already believe, they will see the signs.

(8:27–28). When Jesus asks his disciples, "But what about you? Who do you say that I am?" Peter acknowledges him to be the Messiah (8:29). Jesus responds by strictly ordering them to tell no one. It is not that this opinion is wrong, for Mark identifies Jesus as the Messiah in 1:1. Jesus also accepts the title in his response to the high priest's question, "Are you the Messiah, the Son of the Blessed One?" to which he responds, "I am." The problem is that Peter does not fully fathom what it means for Jesus to be the Messiah.

Malbon argues that in the gospel Jesus "refracts—or bends—the 'christologies' of other characters and the narrator. The image comes from the way a prism refracts 'white' light and thus shows its spectral colors. When a thing is bent and looked at from another angle, something different appears."[85] In this episode, Jesus bends Peter's understanding of him as the Messiah with the assertion that the Son of Man must suffer, die, and rise from the grave (8:31). In taking Jesus aside and rebuking him (8:32), it is obvious that this news was both disconcerting and disturbing to Peter. This dark destiny apparently did not match his messianic expectations.

The transfiguration that follows six days later (9:2), a chronological detail that connects it to Peter's confession, amends his acknowledgment that Jesus is the Messiah. God reveals that he is "my Son, whom I love," to whom they must listen (9:7). The close connection between these two events means that Jesus' identity as the Messiah *must be* accompanied by accepting his destiny of suffering and death while also recognizing his exalted, divine status as God's Son. In 14:61, the high priest connects the two titles, though he uses a circumlocution for God: "Are you the Messiah, the Son of the Blessed One?" Jesus answers "Yes," but he refracts his answer through a scriptural lens that makes this claim even more shocking to the high priest (14:62).

4.3 Jesus as the Son of David

The widespread assumption in this era that the Messiah was to come from the Davidic line is taken for granted in the NT (Matt 1:1–25; Luke 3:31; John 7:42; Acts 2:30–31; 13:22–23; Rom 1:3–4; 2 Tim 2:8; Rev 3:7; 5:5; 22:16). The title "son of David," however, appears infrequently in Mark (10:47–48; 12:35). It may be that Mark does not emphasize Jesus' Davidic lineage because it was a politically charged issue for the Romans during and after the Jewish War against Rome. The Romans associated it with Jewish nationalistic zeal and the messianic pretenders who fomented the revolt. After they conquered Jerusalem, Eusebius notes that Emperor Vespasian ordered that all of David's descendants should be hunted down "so that, among the Jews, not one of the royal house should remain." This concern about Jewish royal lineage continued into the reigns of Domitian and Trajan (*Hist. eccl.* 3.12.19, 32).[86]

85. Elizabeth Struthers Malbon, "Narrative Christology and the Son of Man: What the Markan Jesus Says Instead," *BibInt* 11 (2003): 374.

86. Christopher Bryan, *A Preface to Mark: Notes on the Gospel in Its Literary and Cultural Settings* (New York/Oxford: Oxford University Press, 1993), 165. See also Marcus, "The Jewish War," 456–60.

Mark may have prudently dampened Jesus' Davidic pedigree because it was politically hazardous, but it is more likely that his reticence is attributable to his Christology. This title, like the title "Messiah" ("Christ"), required a critical reorientation of expectations about David's heir. It is not that it is wrong to identify Jesus as the son of David, but it must be refracted through the lens that he is far more as the Son of God. Ahearne-Kroll comments,

> Never is Jesus simply the Suffering Servant, or the Danielic Son of Man, or King David. Mark takes certain aspects of each of these figures (and others) and creatively juxtaposes them to characterize Jesus. The result is a Jesus who is familiar because he is reminiscent of these traditional figures but who, upon closer examination, is also very unfamiliar because of Mark's creative collocation of the qualities of these figures.[87]

4.3.1 Jesus as Greater than David

After Jesus had been teaching in the temple courts, he raised the question, "Why do the teachers of the law say that the Messiah is the son of David?" (12:35). The problem is not that Scripture contradicts itself. Jesus presents the case as a contradiction between Scripture and the opinion of the teachers of the law. It is analogous to his refutation of the Sadducees' misreading of Scripture regarding the resurrection (12:18–27).[88] He immediately excoriates the teachers of the law for putting on religious airs, pious posturing, and exploiting widows (12:38–40). This scribal expectation that the Messiah will belong to the line of David (12:35) is supported by OT texts (Isa 11:1–5; Jer 23:5–6; 33:15; Ezek 34:23–24; 37:24; Zech 3:8; 6:12) and early Jewish texts (*Pss. Sol.* 17; 4QFlor). Jesus' answer to his own question (12:36–37) seems to call into question this connection:

> "David himself, speaking by the Holy Spirit, declared: 'The Lord said to my Lord: "Sit at my right hand until I put your enemies under your feet."' David himself calls him 'Lord.' How then can he be his son?"[89]

Since David calls the Messiah "Lord" and since fathers do not address their sons as "Lord," he cannot be the Messiah's father. Calling him "the son of David," therefore, misrepresents his full identity.

Despite references to David's descendant as God's son in Ps 2:7 and 2 Sam 7:14, he was never understood in Judaism to be a divine figure.[90] The "son of David" was a human ruler.[91] Thus, Jesus is not the son of David that the teachers of the law and others expected.

---

87. Ahearne-Kroll, *Psalms of Lament*, 173.

88. Thomas Römer and Jan Rückl, "Jesus, Son of Joseph and Son of David, in the Gospels," in *The Torah in the New Testament: Papers Delivered at the Manchester-Lausanne Seminar of June 2008* (ed. Peter Oakes and Michael Tait; LNTS 401; London/New York: T&T Clark, 2009), 71.

89. 11Q5 (11QPs[a]) 27:11 asserts that David wrote psalms and "spoke through (the spirit of) prophecy which had been given to him from before the Most High."

90. Ahearne-Kroll, *Psalms of Lament*, 137, notes that David is pictured in ancient literature as "king," "shepherd," "poet," "musician," "warrior," "sage," "father of a dynasty," "founder of the Temple and its cult," "messiah," "persecuted and pursued," "pious one," "prophet," and "judge."

91. Christoph Burger, *Jesus als Davidssohn: Eine traditionsgeschichtliche Untersuchung* (FRLANT 98; Göttingen: Vandenhoeck & Ruprecht, 1970), 16–24.

Jesus hints that the Messiah son of David is a divine, transcendent figure in his second reference to Ps 110:1 in Mark 14:62. It appears in his climactic response to the high priest's indignant question, "Are you the Messiah, the Son of the Blessed One?" (14:61). Jesus' answer, "I am," is followed by an explosive combination of Ps 110:1 and Dan 7:13, "And you will see the Son of Man sitting at the right hand of the Mighty One and coming on the clouds of heaven" (14:62). The amalgamation of these two texts provides an answer to the enigma that Jesus posed in 12:36–37. Sitting at the right hand of God implies more than reigning as a king of Israel as God's representative on earth. When applied to Jesus, it means reigning *with* God on a heavenly/cosmic level.[92]

That Jesus understands himself to be like David but also greater than David appears early on in the narrative in the first Sabbath controversy (2:23–28). To justify his disciples breaking the Sabbath by picking heads of grain while walking through a grain field, Jesus appeals to the precedent of David (2:25–26). David along with his companions ate the consecrated bread given to him by the priest of the sanctuary of Nob (1 Sam 21:1–7). Jesus implies that he is connected in some way to David. The audience, however, must infer what that relationship is. It is assumed that David did not take the liberties with the law regarding consecrated things capriciously, but his actions were based on his interpretation of the law. David is regarded as both a lawgiver (1 Sam 30:21–25) and an interpreter of the law.[93] Jesus' argument runs as follows:

David was God's chosen (implied).
As God's chosen, he could suspend the strict regulations regarding the bread of the presence on the table standing before God in the tabernacle (Exod 25:23–30; Lev 24:5–9).
Jesus is God's chosen (which only the audience knows from the baptism scene, 1:9–11).
As God's Son, Jesus' authority far outstrips David's authority.
Jesus, the Son of Man, is Lord of even the most sacred of biblical institutions, the Sabbath.
As Lord, Jesus does more than just suspend scriptural regulations. He can interpret and make authoritative pronouncements about their divine intention (2:27–28; see also 7:1–23; 10:1–12).[94]

From the beginning of the narrative, then, Mark communicates that Jesus is like David but greater than David.

92. See the discussion in §4.1.5.

93. Damiá Mondada Roure, "La figure de David dans l'évangile de Marc: des traditions juives aux interprétations évangéliques," in *Figures de David à travers la Bible* (XVIIe congrès de l'Association Catholique Française pour l'étude de la Bible [Lille 1er-5 septembre 1997]; ed. Louis Desrousseaux and Jacques Vermeylen; LD 177; Paris: Cerf, 1999), 399–401.

94. Camille Focant, *The Gospel according to Mark: A Commentary* (trans. Leslie R. Keylock; Eugene, OR: Pickwick, 2012), 113, follows Roure, "La figure de David," and argues, "If David could interpret the law concerning the loaves of shewbread, how much more can the Son of Man interpret that of the Sabbath, since he is its 'Lord' (*kurios*)."

4.3.2 Jesus as an Unmilitary Son of David

Collins's analysis of the texts from various strands of Judaism in the first century pictured "the Davidic messiah as the warrior king who would destroy the enemies of Israel and institute the era of unending peace."[95] This militaristic image associated with the son of David is expressed clearly in the *Pss. Sol.* 17:21–25:

> See, Lord, and raise up for them their king, the son of David, to rule over your servant Israel in the time known to you, O God. Undergird him with the strength to destroy the unrighteous rulers, to purge Jerusalem from gentiles who trample her to destruction; in wisdom and in righteousness to drive out the sinners from the inheritance; to smash the arrogance of sinners like a potter's jar; To shatter all their substance with an iron rod; to destroy the unlawful nations with the word of his mouth; At his warning the nations will flee from his presence; and he will condemn sinners by the thoughts of their hearts.[96]

While Mark does link Jesus to royal images, he "undercuts the military associations of David."[97] Jesus exhibits no political or martial aspirations as the Messiah.

The complex mixture of Scripture in Mark's account of Jesus' baptism provides the first subtle evidence that Mark will downplay or neutralize the militaristic images associated with King David. When Jesus rises from the water, the voice from heaven announces, "You are my Son, whom I love; with you I am well pleased" (1:11). The first part of this announcement echoes Ps 2:7 and calls to mind David as God's anointed king on earth installed on Zion, God's holy mountain (Ps 2:6). It communicates that the Davidic king reigns over Israel with God's authority. But God also promises, "I will make the nations your inheritance, the ends of the earth your possession" (Ps 2:8), and the next line envisions the violent subjugation of these nations, "You will break them with a rod of iron; you will dash them to pieces like pottery" (Ps 2:9).

Ahearne-Kroll points out that the image of King David's unrestrained brute power is tempered by the evocation of the sacrifice of Isaac in Gen 22 and the servant song in Isa 42.[98] The use of the phrase "my beloved Son" ("my Son, whom I love," NIV) appears in Gen 22:2, 12, and 16 and suggests that the sacrifice of a beloved son should be read alongside the baptism.[99] The phrase "with you I am well pleased" echoes Isa 42:1 (more closely the Hebrew text than that of the LXX).[100] It presents the image of a nonviolent and tender servant: "A bruised reed he will not break, and a smoldering wick he will not snuff out. In faithfulness he will bring forth justice" (Isa 42:3). Ahearne-Kroll argues that this scriptural medley presents a "complex image of Jesus."[101] He is a royal Davidic Messiah, but he will reign as a servant who will be sacrificed.

95. John J. Collins, *The Scepter and the Star: Messianism in Light of the Dead Sea Scrolls* (2nd ed.; Grand Rapids: Eerdmans, 2010), 78.

96. R. B. Wright, "Psalms of Solomon," in *The Old Testament Pseudepigrapha* (ed. James H. Charlesworth; Garden City, NY: Doubleday, 1985), 2:667.

97. Ahearne-Kroll, *Psalms of Lament*, 57.

98. Stephen P. Ahearne-Kroll, "The Scripturally Complex Presentation of Jesus in the Gospel of Mark," in *Portraits of Jesus: Studies in Christology* (ed. Susan E. Myers; WUNT 2/321; Tübingen: Mohr Siebeck, 2012), 49–52.

99. See §4.2.3.2.

100. Watts, *New Exodus*, 114–16.

101. Ahearne-Kroll, "The Scripturally Complex Presentation of Jesus," 52.

Notably, when Jesus implicitly compares himself to David appropriating the bread of the presence from the priest of Nob to assert his authority as the Son of Man (2:23–27), he recounts a story from a time when David was a "fugitive in need," not a combatant with sword in hand.[102] Jesus never mentions any of David's military exploits.

The revision of any militaristic associations that might be evoked by the title "son of David" is also evident in Mark's account of Jesus' healing of blind Bartimaeus, his entry into Jerusalem, his crucifixion as the king of Israel, and the Davidic individual lament psalms that are part of the warp and woof of the Passion Narrative.

When Jesus is leaving Jericho on the last leg of his journey to Jerusalem, a blind beggar named Bartimaeus urgently cries out to him to have mercy on him. Twice, he yells, "Jesus, Son of David, have mercy on me" (10:47–48). He is portrayed as a reliable witness because he not only recognizes and has faith in Jesus' miraculous power, but he also is the only person whom Jesus heals who then immediately leaves everything to follow him (10:52).[103] This blind man has more spiritual sight than the crowd. They apparently only know him as "Jesus of Nazareth" (10:47). He recognizes him to be the "Son of David."

The healing associates the title "son of David" with therapeutic mercy rather than the ruthlessness required in warfare.[104] More significantly, the petition "Have mercy on me" is directed only to God in Scripture.[105] This datum hints again that even though Jesus is the son of David, he is greater than David, for it is David who utters this plea to God in the psalms.

The healing of Bartimaeus who cries out for mercy from the son of David prepares for Jesus' approach to Jerusalem, where he meets a joyous clamor from the crowds crying out: "Hosanna!" "Blessed is he who comes in the name of the Lord!" "Blessed is the coming kingdom of our father David!" "Hosanna in the highest heaven!" (11:9–10). Jesus has walked everywhere during his ministry except for the times he crossed the lake in a boat. He departs from this normal pattern by stage-managing a grand procession to the city by riding on an animal. At Bethphage and Bethany, near the Mount of Olives, he directs two unnamed disciples to enter the

102. Michael Tait, *Jesus, The Divine Bridegroom, in Mark 2:18–22: Mark's Christology Upgraded* (AnBib 185; Rome: Gregorian & Biblical Press, 2010), 110.

103. Boring, *Mark*, 256, 305, thinks that Mark is "suspicious of 'son of David' Christology" and dissociates Jesus from the Davidic hope. In this instance, Bartimaeus calls out to Jesus as the son of David while he is still blind and only follows him after his blindness is cured. This reading, in my opinion, overly parses the text. Jesus responds to Bartimaeus's cry and affirms his faith (10:52). He does not tell him to be quiet, as the crowd does, or try to correct any supposedly mistaken view of his identity. Juan Carlos Ossandón, "Bartimaeus' Faith: Plot and Point of View in Mark 10, 46–52," *Bib* 93 (2012): 377–402, makes the case that for Mark Bartimaeus is a model of faith who confesses Jesus as the son of David and follows him promptly on the way to the cross.

104. Stephen H. Smith, "The Function of the Son of David Tradition in Mark's Gospel," *NTS* 42 (1996): 527–28. According to 2 Sam 5:8, the "blind and lame" are David's "enemies," forbidden entry into the palace.

105. Grindheim, *Christology*, 74, 80, n. 51. It can be translated "be gracious to me," and the petition appears in Pss 6:2; 9:13; 25:16; 26:11; 27:7; 31:9; 41:4, 10; 51:1; 56:1; 57:1; 67:1; 86:3, 16; 119:29, 58, 132; 123:3; Isa 30:19; 33:2. In the Apocrypha, it appears in Jdth 6:19; Sir 36:1, 17; Bar 3:2; 3 Macc 6:12. The only exception where this petition is addressed to a human is in 2 Macc 7:27, when the mother of the seven brothers tortured by Antiochus to get them to renounce their faith urges her last surviving son in her native language to have pity on her and to accept death rather than to yield.

village and secure a colt for the last phase of his journey. He manifests his supernatural foreknowledge by predicting that they will find a colt tied up near the village entrance (11:1–2). If they are challenged for taking the colt, he instructs them to say, "The Lord needs it and will send it back here shortly" (11:3). Jesus impresses the animal as a king would. The statement that the Lord needs it is a royal requisition formula.[106] It matches the justification for David's eating the consecrated bread: "when he had need" (2:25, ASV). Jesus, however, does not exploit subjects as kings are inclined to do but promises to return the animal immediately.

The animal has never been ridden, which makes it suitable for a sacred purpose and worthy of a king.[107] The colt could have been the foal of a donkey, horse, or mule. Kings rode mules (2 Sam 18:9; 1 Kgs 1:33–48), but donkeys are associated with the Messiah (*Gen. Rab.* 98:9; *b. Sanh.* 98a, 99a; *Qoh. Rab.* 1:9).[108] The allusion to Zech 9:9, "Rejoice greatly, Daughter Zion! Shout, Daughter Jerusalem! See, your king comes to you, righteous and victorious, lowly and riding on a donkey, on a colt, the foal of a donkey," which Matt 21:4–5 and John 12:14–16 directly quote as a fulfillment of prophecy, suggests that the gospel writers understand it to have been a donkey, a royal animal. That Mark twice notes that the colt is bound and must be untied (11:2, 4) alludes to Gen 49:10–11, which was also interpreted messianically (see *b. Ber.* 56b–57a; *Gen. Rab.* 99:8). The interpretation of Gen 49:11 in *Targum Neofiti* is telling:

> How beautiful is King Messiah who is to arise from among those of the house of Judah. He girds his loins and goes forth to battle against those that hate him; and he kills kings with rulers and makes the mountains red from the blood of their slain and makes the valleys white from the fat of their warriors. His garments are rolled in blood; he is like a presser of grapes.[109]

Jesus is not that King Messiah. His visit to the temple and condemnation of it by his prophetic actions the next day reveal that he has come for a far different purpose than to destroy the Roman occupiers of the Holy City. He will be bloody; the blood, however, is not that of his enemies but his own blood, "which is poured out for many" (14:24).

Schweizer contends that Jesus modeled his entry into Jerusalem after Zech 9:9 to counter "the general expectation of a Davidic Messiah who would drive out the Romans by force."[110] His agenda is totally different. He will not put others to death but instead will die in their place.[111] He therefore comes as a humble king, not as a violent, warrior king. He is "David's spiritual as opposed to his political heir."[112]

106. Ethelbert Stauffer, "Messias oder Menschensohn?" *NovT* 1 (1956): 85.

107. According to *m. Sanh.* 2:5, no one else may ride a king's horse.

108. The combination of Zech 9:9 and Dan 7:13 in *b. Sanh.* 98a is noteworthy: "R. Alexandri said: R. Joshua opposed two verses: it is written, "And behold, one like the son of man came with the clouds of heaven," whilst [elsewhere] it is written, [behold, thy king cometh to thee...] lowly, and riding on an ass." If they are meritorious [he will come] "with the clouds of heaven"; if not, "lowly and riding upon an ass." Mark suggestively applies both passages to Jesus.

109. Martin McNamara, *The Aramaic Bible Volume 1A: Targum Neofiti 1: Genesis* (Collegeville, MN: Michael Glazier, 1992), 220.

110. Schweizer, *Mark*, 227.

111. Grindheim, *Christology*, 54.

112. Smith, "The Function of the Son of David Tradition in Mark's Gospel," 532.

He does come as a king, however. The disciples saddle the animal with their own garments, and the crowd strewing the way with their garments alludes to the account of Jehu's anointing as king. The people took their cloaks and spread them before him and shouted, "Jehu is king" (2 Kgs 9:12–13). The references to the "many" who spread their cloaks on the road and branches (or cut straw) from the fields (11:8) and to "those who went ahead and those who followed" crying out (11:9) are indefinite. There is no indication that these enthusiastic greeters are made up of the inhabitants of Jerusalem. The "they" in 11:6–7 refers to Jesus' followers. Mark notes that a "large crowd" followed him out of Jericho (10:46), which then added Bartimaeus (10:52), who had proclaimed him the son of David, and these are the most likely persons to fill the air with a chorus of Hosannas ("Save us!"), "Hosanna! Blessed is he who comes in the name of the Lord!" (11:9), and to cry, "Blessed is the coming kingdom of our father David! Hosanna in the highest heaven!" (11:10). This jubilant cry dots the "i's" and crosses the "t's" for any tone-deaf reader who does not already perceive that Jesus' entrance into Jerusalem is deliberately messianic. Ambrozic comments, "Jesus is the Son of God bringing the kingdom of God, not the son of David introducing the kingdom of David."[113]

From the perspective of Greco-Roman conventions, what is notable about Jesus' dramatic approach to the city is that its leaders do not come out to welcome him. Josephus describes Alexander's entrance into the city. His followers anticipated being able to plunder it as conquerors, but when Alexander was still far away, he "saw the multitude in white garments the priests at their head clothed in linen, and the high priest in a robe of hyacinth-blue and gold, wearing on his head the mitre with the golden place on it on which was inscribed the name of God." Instead of plundering the city, their approach caused Alexander to prostrate himself in reverence to the God whom the high priest served, to give his hand to the high priest and enter the city with "the Jews running beside him," and to offer sacrifices to God in the temple (*Ant.* 11.8.5 §§329–339).

Kinman's analysis of the account of Jesus' approach in Luke 19:28–44 applies also to Mark's account.[114] He highlights the normal features of the reception of a royal figure or dignitary.

1. Welcome was commonly bestowed on kings and other ruling figures.
2. The welcome was normally extended when the dignitary approached the city.
3. The religious and political elite and other welcomers would meet the dignitary and escort him back to the city.
4. The large body of citizens would mark the occasion by wearing ornamental clothing.

113. Ambrozic, *The Hidden Kingdom*, 43.

114. Brent Kinman, "Parousia, Jesus' 'A-Triumphal' Entry, and the Fate of Jerusalem (Luke 19:28–44)," *JBL* 118 (1999): 279–94.

5. The dignitary would be lauded by speeches presented to him on behalf of the city, expressing their privilege at receiving his visitation.[115]

Given these conventions, Kinman concludes:

> Jerusalem's hardened spiritual condition is epitomized by its failure to recognize its king. He [Jesus] is not met by city officials, nor fêted by the leading citizens, nor escorted back to the city ... and the nonappearance of the high priests, other officials, and the citizens of Jerusalem is an affront.... Although he is the king, he is not received as one by Jerusalem.[116]

Jesus also is not accompanied by the high priest as might be expected when he finally enters the city and goes into the temple (11:11). Instead, the official indifference to his arrival points to the fact that he will be rejected, and the leaders will arrest him and turn him over to be crucified.

4.3.3 Jesus as the Son of David Who Suffers and Dies

Jesus' enemies use the terms "Messiah" and "king of the Jews" synonymously in one of the taunts hurled at him as he hangs on the cross: "Let this Messiah, this king of Israel, come down now from the cross, that we may see and believe" (15:32). The high priest asks Jesus if he is the Messiah (14:61), and after deciding his guilt, the council hands him over to the Roman governor. They must have accused him of claiming to be "the king of the Jews," because it is Pilate's first question to Jesus: "Are you the king of the Jews?" (15:1–2).[117] Jesus forthrightly admits to being the Messiah in his answer to the high priest: "I am" (14:62). He responds to Pilate ambivalently, "You have said so" (15:2). It can mean that he denies it, "*You* say that, I do not," or that he reluctantly affirms it but it needs to be qualified, "Yes, but."[118] The latter is more likely from what follows. Jesus rejects the political connotations that Pilate instinctively would have associated with the term "king of the Jews."

After his interrogation by Pilate, the soldiers mock him as a bogus king. He fits no category of kingship familiar to them, and the charge that he is a king seems comically absurd. He has no army to challenge the military might of Rome, no subjects to lord over (10:42), and no power to save himself, let alone any power to save the woeful Jewish people who have handed him over as an impostor. Consequently, they make fun of him as a faux Caesar, clothing him in royal purple, plaiting a crown of thorns for his head, and paying him simulated homage (15:16–19). The charge "the king of the Jews" (15:26), which they inscribe on the cross, continues the rude jesting as he is executed for the crime of lese majesty. From Pilate's and the soldiers' perspective, Jesus strikes a ridiculous figure as a king. From the audience's perspective, it is ridiculous to think that Jesus was an insurrectionist like the

115. Ibid., 280–84.

116. Ibid., 293–94.

117. "King of the Jews" is the way non-Jews like Pilate (15:2, 9, 12) and the soldiers (15:18, 26) would have phrased things. Jews use the appellation "Messiah" and understand it to denote "the king of Israel" (15:32).

118. France, *Mark*, 628. Edwards, *Mark*, 459, interprets the reply as suggestive, "You would do well to consider the question!"

agitators crucified on either side of him. He has not come to rout his enemies but to give his life for them.

Ahearne-Kroll reads the voice of the suffering David in the four lament psalms evoked in Mark's Passion Narrative as foreground. These lament psalms are not the source for the creation of the narrative but form "an integral part of the multifaceted characterization of Jesus and Markan theological concerns."[119] His study of the psalms of individual lament echoed in Mark's account of Jesus' passion is subtitled "Jesus' Davidic Suffering." These psalms help in part to disclose what it means when Jesus says "The Son of Man will go just as it is written about him" (14:21).

Jesus' identification of his betrayer as the one "who is eating with me" (14:18) evokes Ps 41:9 (40:10, LXX). [120] His extreme distress in Gethsemane, "I am deeply grieved, even to death" (14:34, NRSV), evokes Pss 42:6, 11; 43:5 (41:7, 12, and 42:5, LXX). The offer of wine mixed with myrrh (15:23) evokes Ps 69:21 (68:22, LXX). The division of his clothes by his executioners (15:24) evokes Ps 22:18 (21:19, LXX). The passersby who wag their heads and mock Jesus to save himself (15:29–30) evokes Ps 22:7 (21:8, LXX). Jesus' cry of forsakenness before he dies (15:34) evokes Ps 22:1 (21:2, LXX). The second offer of sour wine when someone thinks that he is calling Elijah (15:35–36) again evokes Ps 69:21 (68:22, LXX). These details come from four lament psalms (Pss 22; 41; 42–43; 69) that "attempt to persuade God in various ways to act on behalf of the psalmist as he experiences suffering." They deal with God's silence during a time of severe affliction and the impression that God is absent.[121] The use of these lament psalms links Jesus to David as one who suffers, and they clarify that Jesus is to be understood as the suffering Davidic Messiah. He conquers evil on a heavenly and cosmic level through his suffering.[122]

4.4 JESUS AS THE SON OF MAN

The literature on the subject of the Son of Man is massive.[123] After an exhaustive analysis of the research, Burkett concludes that no consensus exists about the background of the phrase and acknowledges that some questions may never be fully resolved.[124] His assessment of the research leads him to the conclusion that the

119. Ahearne-Kroll, *Psalms of Lament*, 1.

120. Ahearne-Kroll (ibid.) refers throughout his analysis to and interprets the LXX, but since the different numbering of the psalms in the LXX is confusing to many readers, I cite the relevant passages as they appear in the versification of the NIV.

121. Ibid., 135.

122. Ibid., 167. From Ahearne-Kroll's analysis, he also concludes that the suffering King David is more appropriate than the Suffering Servant in Isaiah as a model for Jesus' suffering in Mark and that Mark does not present Jesus as a divine warrior king, contra Marcus, *Way*, 196–98; and Paul Brooks Duff, "The March of the Divine Warrior and the Advent of the Greco-Roman King: Mark's Account of Jesus' Entry into Jerusalem," *JBL* 111 (1992): 55–71.

123. See Larry W. Hurtado and Paul L. Owen, eds., *"Who is This Son of Man?" The Latest Scholarship on a Puzzling Expression of the Historical Jesus* (LNTS 390; London/New York: T&T Clark, 2011).

124. Delbert Burkett, *The Son of Man Debate: A History and Evaluation* (SNTSMS 107; Cambridge: Cambridge University Press, 1999), 124. See also Mogens Müller, *The Expression "Son of Man" and the Development of Christology: A History of Interpretation* (London: Equinox, 2008), 419, who represents the view that in everyday usage in Aramaic "son of man" was a "colourless circumlocution" for "I" that had no special meaning. See also Richard Bauckham, "The Son of Man: 'A Man in My Position' or 'Someone,'" *JSNT* 23 (1985): 23–33. Maurice Casey, *Aramaic Sources of Mark's Gospel* (SNTSMS 102; Cambridge: Cambridge University Press, 1998), 111–37; and *The Solution to the "Son of Man" Problem* (LNTS 343; London/New York: T&T Clark, 2007), argues that Jesus used the term originally

phrase is best understood as a reference to Jesus and not to some other messianic personage.[125] No evidence exists that there was a well-defined notion of the "Son of Man" as a messianic figure or that the phrase was used as a messianic title. This assessment is supported by Mark's narrative.[126] The phrase appears only on the lips of Jesus. Neither human characters nor the narrator calls Jesus "the Son of Man." When Jesus asks his disciples, "Who do men say that I am?" the phrase "the Son of Man" is not one of the conjectures (8:27–30). The high priests also do not charge Jesus with claiming to be "the Son of Man" at his trial.

While "Son of Man" was not an established title, the figure was known from Dan 7:13–14, which I believe provides the backdrop for Jesus' usage and Mark's understanding of the phrase. Clear verbal connections between Dan 7:13–14 and Jesus' sayings appear in the references to the Son of Man coming "in his Father's glory with the holy angels" (8:38), "coming in clouds with great power and glory" (13:26), and "coming on the clouds of heaven" (14:62). Daniel refers to "one like a son of man," while Jesus in Mark's text refers to "the Son of Man" with a definite article. Gathercole contends that the problem caused by this variance "disappears if one sees Mark identifying Jesus as *that* Son of Man, i.e., the one in Daniel 7."[127] I am of the opinion that Jesus used the term publicly in reference to himself because it was sufficiently vague that he could fill it with his own meaning. On the one hand, it was unlikely to be tainted by any preconceived notions that his audience might have entertained about who this figure might be or what he would do. On the other hand, its use in Dan 7:13–14 made it suitably mysterious.[128]

It is striking that Jesus' first usage of this phrase to refer to himself appears in 2:10 without any preparation for the reader. Mark has identified Jesus in the incipit as "the Messiah" and "the Son of God" (1:1), but Jesus identifies himself as "the Son of Man." How does this title relate to these other two titles? Chronis offers the suggestion that "the Son of Man" functions in the narrative logic of Mark's gospel to enable Jesus to remain incognito.[129] Jesus uses this phrase to talk about

---

to refer to human beings in general or to a group of human beings, and this meaning was lost in translation. He contends that only those sayings that can be translated back into Aramaic with this meaning are authentic. The titular meaning, he claims, is the creation of the early church. But Mark did not understand "the Son of Man" to be a colorless circumlocution. Jack Dean Kingsbury, "The Christology of Mark and the Son of Man," in *Unity and Diversity in the Gospels and Paul: Essays in Honor of Frank J. Matera* (ed. Christopher W. Skinner and Kelly R. Iverson; Atlanta: Society of Biblical Literature, 2012), 69, however, considers it to be "a solemn and forceful self-referential term that is used exclusively by Jesus to point to himself."

The sayings that are the easiest to construe as a circumlocution for "I" (Matt 8:20; 13:37; Luke 11:29–30; Matt 11:18–19/Luke 7:33–34; Matt 12:32/Luke 12:10) do not appear in Mark. See Delbert Burkett, "The Nontitular Son of Man: A History and Critique," *NTS* 40 (1994): 514–21.

125. Burkett, *Son of Man*, 121.

126. Collins, *The Scepter and the Star*, 197, notes that *1 En.* 46:1 initially introduces the figure "as one whose face had the appearance of a man." When Enoch asks the angelic guide who it is, the angel responds that "he is 'the son of man' who has righteousness." This introduction assumes that "Son of Man" is not a well-known title. It is used here as a way of referring back to the figure "while simultaneously recalling Daniel 7."

127. Gathercole, "The Son of Man in Mark's Gospel," 368.

128. The phrase "one like a son of man" notably appears in Dan 7, but the differences are significant. In Daniel, the son of man may be a representation of God's people (7:27). He also comes on the clouds of heaven to the heavenly throne of God but not to earth (7:13). Hartman, *Mark*, 117, argues that the image in Daniel influenced the usage of the term in *1 En.* 37–71 in which "son of man" is a symbol of "the people of the Holy Ones of the Most High." The imagery "was changed into an individual, with whom different features of eschatological expectations could be associated." The image of the son of man in Dan 7 also inspires the usage of the term in 2 Esd 13, but it too is modified to refer to a man.

129. Harry L. Chronis, "To Reveal and to Conceal: A Literary-Critical Perspective on 'the Son of Man' in Mark," *NTS* 51 (2005): 459–81.

himself as the Son of God "without at the same time violating his own injunction to secrecy."[130] He claims that the phrase hides Jesus' "divinity as 'the Son of God' under a convenient contradiction, his humanity."[131] He refers to himself in the third person to speak of the heavenly authority of his ministry, his destiny to suffer, die, and rise from the grave on the third day, and his coming as the glorious figure at the end of time.

Jesus never says, "I am the Son of Man," but it is implied in the sayings. In Mark, this term most adequately expresses what Jesus does as the Son of God. He has authority to forgive sins (2:10). He is Lord of the Sabbath (2:28). He comes not to be served but to give his life as a ransom for many (10:45). He will be betrayed (14:21, 41), suffer ignominy and death, and be raised on the third day (8:31, 38; 9:9, 12; 10:33). He will be seated at the right hand of power and return on the clouds and will gather his elect (13:26–27; 14:62).

4.4.1 The Authority of the Son of Man on Earth

Jesus' assertion of his "authority" as the Son of Man to forgive sins (2:10) harks back not only to the theme of the arresting authority of his teaching (1:22, 27) but also to the majestic authority of the one like a son of man who is given "authority" (Dan 7:13–14). The two controversy stories in 2:1–12 and 2:23–28 reveal that Jesus' authority is his by right, and it outstrips any authority that an ordinary human might possess.

4.4.1.1 The Authority to Forgive Sins (Mark 2:1–12)

Jesus' exercise of authority seems brazenly to encroach on divine prerogatives. When a paralytic is brought to him, he boldly announces that his sins are forgiven (2:1–12). The teachers of the law who witness this pronouncement blanch and then presumably turn red with indignation over this blasphemous usurping of God's authority. Reading their minds, Jesus responds to their outrage by asking them, "Which is easier: to say to this paralyzed man, 'Your sins are forgiven,' or to say, 'Get up, take your mat and walk'?" (2:9). He then orders the man to take up his mat and go home, and he does so to the amazement of everyone (2:11–12). This command is intended to prove that "the Son of Man has the authority on earth to forgive sins" (2:10). Forgiving the paralytic's sin and healing him are not "two distinct acts, but are different aspects of one thing—the total restoration of the paralysed man."[132] "Since it would be incredible that a man with blasphemy on his lips should be able to effect such a miracle," this cure proves both his extraordinary power to heal and his extraordinary authority to forgive.[133]

The scandalized question of the teachers of the law, "Who can forgive sins but God alone?" (2:7), scores the point. Jesus not only has divine power to read their minds and to heal a paralytic, but he has divine authority here and now to

130. Ibid., 465.
131. Ibid., 477.
132. Hooker, *The Son of Man in Mark*, 89.
133. Ibid., 88.

pronounce the forgiveness for sins that anyone might commit against God. What is more, those who are forgiven do not need to go through the prescribed channels of the temple sacrificial cult or to give prerequisite evidence of their repentance. They need only exhibit faith in him. The crucial element of "faith" ("when Jesus saw their faith," 2:5)[134] rules out the possibility that his pronouncement applies to human beings in general. The men's faith is directed toward Jesus,[135] and it is he and he alone who has this divine authority to forgive sins.

4.4.1.2 The Authority Over the Sabbath (Mark 2:23–28)

In a second incident related to Jesus' authority as the Son of Man, the Pharisees object when they see his disciples picking some heads of grain as they amble through a field on the Sabbath. The law permitted anyone (particularly the needy, Lev 19:9–10; 23:22; Ruth 2:15–16) to pluck ears in a neighbor's field of standing grain as long as one did not use a sickle (Deut 23:25). The Pharisees interpreted the disciples' action as "harvesting," which made it a specific violation of the Sabbath restrictions against work (*m. Šabb.* 7:2). The Sabbath is grounded in creation when God rested on the seventh day (Gen 2:2). The rules prohibiting any semblance of work on the Sabbath (Exod 20:8–11; Deut 5:12–15) had burgeoned over the years. The disciples' disregard for the Sabbath rules reflected negatively on their teacher.[136] Teachers were responsible for the actions of their pupils, so their question, "Look, why are they doing what is unlawful on the Sabbath?" (2:24), is really a challenge.[137] "Does your teaching encourage Sabbath violations?" Or, "how could you overlook such behavior?"

The first part of Jesus' response recalls the biblical precedent of David violating the law during his outlaw years when he was fleeing from King Saul. The famished David asked the priest at Nob for bread. The only bread that the priest possessed was the consecrated bread of the Presence that was to be eaten in a holy place only by the priests (Lev 24:5–9; see *Lev. Rab.* 32:3).[138] To coax the priest to give him the loaves, David prevaricated that he was on an urgent mission from the king.[139]

---

134. While it is the friends of the paralytic who bring him to Jesus and overcome the logjam created by the crowd by breaking through the roof, one may also assume that the paralytic would have encouraged his friends to take these actions because of his faith in Jesus' power to heal him.

135. With the definite article in Greek, Mark could only understand "the Son of Man" to refer to a particular individual not to humans in general. When the phrase has a generic sense that applies to all humans, the plural is employed, as in 3:28, "All their sins shall be forgiven unto the sons of men" (ASV).

136. The penalties for desecrating the Sabbath are serious: being cut off from the people and death (Exod 31:12–17; 35:2; Num 15:32–36).

137. Sven-Olaf Back, *Jesus of Nazareth and the Sabbath Commandment* (Åbo: Åbo Akademi University Press, 1995), 79, n. 10, cites examples showing it was a common idea in the ancient world.

138. Jesus' answer refers to Abiathar instead of Ahimelech, who, according to 1 Sam 21:1–6, was the priest involved in this incident. Abiathar was Ahimelech's son who barely escaped the massacre of the priests that was ordered by King Saul when he discovered what had happened (22:6–23). The error may be attributed to confusion between these two priests that also surfaces in 22:20; 30:7; 2 Sam 8:17; 1 Chr 18:16; 24:6. The text, however, does not say that David came to Abiathar but that this event happened when Abiathar was high priest. Abiathar is specifically identified as the high priest while Ahimelech was only a priest. The reference to Abiathar reflects the convention of eponymous dating (see Luke 3:2), and this interpretation is reflected in the rendering of the Greek phrase (*epi Abiathar*) as "in the days of Abiathar" (2:26).

139. In recounting this episode, Jesus omits this detail but adds that David's companions were with him, that they were hungry and in need, and that he entered the house of God and ate the consecrated bread permitted only for priests instead of merely asking for bread.

Since the Scripture does not condemn him for this action, it is assumed that it tacitly approves it.[140]

The second part of Jesus' response declares, "The Sabbath was made for man, not man for the Sabbath" (2:27). The pronouncement in 2:28, "So the Son of Man is Lord even of the Sabbath," may be part of Jesus' direct speech as the third stage of his response, or it may be the narrator's concluding observation. It is more likely that Mark intends for it to be taken as the third part of Jesus' response.

David's violation of taking and consuming consecrated bread hardly seems to be an apt parallel to Jesus' disciples' violation of the Sabbath by plucking grain and rubbing it to eat as they travel. Both may have been hungry, but Mark does *not* mention the disciples' hunger (contrast Matt 12:1). Mark therefore does not understand the point to be that humanitarian concerns can override Sabbath rules. Hooker recognizes that the real parallel is that "regulations which were made to safeguard something which is holy were set aside for David, who enjoyed a special position, and for 'those who were with him'; he and they were allowed to eat what was normally permitted only to the priests."[141]

Jesus' answer concedes that the disciples had violated the strict interpretation of the Sabbath rules, but he does not try to justify it by quibbling with the Pharisees over their interpretation of Sabbath regulations. Instead, when one takes the entire narrative of Mark into account, the argument moves from the lesser to the greater. David was God's chosen one. He suspended the rules of the law to do what he thought necessary in the situation. Jesus is God's chosen one, and he ignores the rules of the law to do what he thinks is necessary. I comment, "If the strict regulations regarding the bread of the Presence could be set aside for David, who was fleeing for his life, how much more can holy regulations be set aside for Jesus (and his companions), whom Mark presents as David's Lord (Mark 1:2–3; 12:35–37) and who is in a situation of far greater urgency in proclaiming the coming of the kingdom of God."[142] Jesus ties his authority as the Son of Man to David's authority, but the implication is that his authority as the Son of Man is far greater and more far reaching as "Lord even of the Sabbath." For Mark, this incident conveys that Jesus "has authority to interpret and proclaim the will of God in the last days."[143]

While the humanitarian purpose of the Sabbath is affirmed (2:27), that is not the essential point for Mark. Gundry correctly sees that "the emphasis builds up Jesus' authority as Lord of the Sabbath to pronounce on its humanitarian purpose."[144] The Son of Man is the one who determines the meaning and application of God's law. The dispute begins with the Pharisees speaking to him (2:24), but Jesus has the final word in all things. As far as Mark is concerned, this word from

140. The priest acquiesces to David's request with the sole stipulation that David and his men must not have had sexual relations with women (1 Sam 21:4–5). When Josephus retells this story, he does not mention David and his men eating the bread of the Presence, which reveals his priestly sensitivity to such a violation (*Ant.* 6.12.1 §243).

141. Hooker, *The Son of Man in Mark*, 98.

142. Garland, *Mark*, 106–107. See also Back, *Jesus of Nazareth*, 84.

143. Collins, *Mark*, 205.

144. Gundry, *Mark*, 142.

Jesus settles the issue. It should be noted, however, that Jesus ignores the Sabbath commandment in this case "*in order to feed the hungry*."[145] Jesus does not set aside a commandment in the law capriciously to satisfy a whim.

4.4.2 The Passion and Resurrection of the Son of Man

In the three specific predictions of his passion and resurrection to his disciples, Jesus uses the term "Son of Man" to refer to what he must undergo (8:31; 9:31; 10:33–34). He also uses it four other times in reference to his suffering, death, and arrest (9:12; 10:45; 14:21, 41), and one other time to refer to his resurrection (9:9). All of the sayings reveal Jesus' genuine humanity as the Son of Man who is not insulated from the burdens and travails of his fellow Jews. An intimate will betray him to the priestly ruling class. He will be treated with contempt, undergo great physical suffering, and die at the hands of Israel's Roman masters. Neville vividly describes Jesus' physical ordeal: "Within a short time-frame, his burden of suffering is increased further by interrogation, false accusations, verbal abuse, torture and public humiliation. From the perspective of narrative development, by the time of his execution Jesus' resources are spent; this may explain the atypical detail in Mark 15:21 that Simon of Cyrene was commandeered to carry Jesus' crossbeam."[146] Jesus endures this suffering because of his subordination and obedience to his Father.

The term "the Son of Man" is not being used as a modest circumlocution for "I" but as a title. Peter, James, and John have witnessed Jesus' transfiguration and see the innate glory that will become manifest to all when he comes in glory at the end of the age (9:1–8). Jesus orders them "not to tell anyone what they had seen until the Son of Man had risen from the dead" (9:9). Jesus could only be referring to himself as the Son of Man who will be raised. The disciples have experienced a revelation with the declaration of the voice from heaven that Jesus is the Son of God (9:7). After his death and resurrection, the secret can be revealed to all.

The mystified disciples raise a question about Elijah coming first to restore all things as the teachers of the law have speculated (9:11; see Mal 3:1; 4:5). Jesus corrects any expectation that Elijah is a figure who is still to come from heaven at some future time to restore all things. As the Messiah's forerunner, he is an "earthly figure who has already lived on this earth and suffered a violent death at the hands of its authorities."[147] In the same way, the Son of Man, namely Jesus, is an earthly figure who will suffer at the hands of the earthly authorities who reject his authority and revolt against God. Twice, Jesus says what will happen to him is written about the Son of Man (9:12; 14:21). His destiny has been spelled out in Scripture. The Son of Man is no ordinary figure whose death was a tragic miscarriage of justice. When he is arrested, he says "the hour has come" (14:41). This "hour" does not simply refer to

145. Back, *Jesus of Nazareth*, 85, 90.

146. David Neville, "God's Presence and Power: Christology, Eschatology and 'Theodicy' in Mark's Crucifixion Narrative," in *Theodicy and Eschatology* (ed. Bruce Barber and David Neville; Hindmarsh: Australian Theological Forum, 2005), 22.

147. Boring, *Mark*, 263. Marcus, *Mark 8–16*, 644–45, translates 9:12 as a question, "Is it really the case that Elijah, when he comes first, restores all things?" He reasons, had Elijah restored all things before the Messiah, why would there be any need for the Son of Man's suffering?

an interval of time. It refers to the inevitable "hour" that is connected to the Father's will and is filled with divine purpose (14:35), namely, that the Son of Man came to give his life a ransom for many (10:45).

Jesus tells the disciples that he will be raised on the third day (8:31; 9:31; 10:34), which Mark narrates as being literally fulfilled. In comparison with the lengthier description of his suffering in these predictions, the resurrection gets less attention. As a result, Jesus' statements are frequently labeled "passion predictions," which is misleading. It ignores something that is crucial to Mark. After Jesus' suffering and death, he will be vindicated by God through his resurrection.[148] Carey proposes that "the concept of the suffering and death of the Christ would have been more problematic to Mark's readers than his resurrection, and would have thus required more preparation, explanation, and justification in the narrative."[149] One can only infer that the audience would know that Jesus is not putting his hope in a general resurrection at the end of the age (see 2 Macc 7:9, 14, 23), but his own resurrection. Being raised from death "after three days" would have been considered exceptional.

One can also only infer that the audience understood that Jesus' resurrection had positive consequences touching all believers. He is the "firstfruits of those who have fallen asleep" (1 Cor 15:20; see Col 1:18; Rev 1:5), but Mark does not delve into the full implications of Jesus' resurrection for others except that it will result in a regathering of the scattered disciples (14:28; 16:7).

4.4.3 The Future Exaltation and Coming of the Son of Man

Jesus warns that those who are "ashamed of me and my words in this adulterous and sinful generation, the Son of Man will be ashamed of them when he comes in his Father's glory with the holy angels" (8:38). The logic of this saying makes it clear that Jesus identifies himself with this glorious Son of Man and is not referring to some other yet greater eschatological figure.[150] Being "ashamed" of Jesus in this world is the opposite of denying oneself, taking up a cross, and following him (8:34). It avoids any identification with this one who died a shameful death. It will result in the Son of Man being "ashamed" of those ashamed of him. In the context of coming "in his Father's glory with the holy angels," this shame implies rejection at the final judgment. The Son of Man comes as the final judge and one's future salvation depends on both allegiance and obedience to Jesus. The one who has the authority to forgive sins on earth (2:10) will also be the one who judges sinners.

In 13:26–27, Jesus refers to the Son of Man "coming in clouds with great power and glory" and sending out his angels to gather his elect "from the four winds, from the ends of the earth to the ends of the heavens" (13:27). The image of coming

148. Bayer, *Jesus' Predictions of Vindication and Resurrection*, seeks to correct the tendency of past studies of Mark to overemphasize the aspect of Jesus' suffering and death to the neglect of his prediction of vindication in the resurrection.

149. Holly J. Carey, *Jesus' Cry From The Cross: Towards a First-Century Understanding of the Intertextual Relationship between Psalm 22 and the Narrative of Mark's Gospel* (LNTS 398; London/New York: T&T Clark International, 2009), 47.

150. Schweizer, *Mark*, 168, points out that it would have been unlikely for Jesus to use an obscure title that "was familiar only to small separatist groups" to designate this other heavenly figure.

in clouds appears again in his climactic declaration before the high priest and his council, "You will see the Son of Man sitting at the right hand of the Mighty One and coming on the clouds of heaven" (14:62). God will vindicate him after his death through his resurrection and exaltation, and the tables will be turned. He will be their ultimate judge. This last mention of the Son of Man in Mark reveals that, for him, the Son of Man refers to Jesus as a glorious figure enrobed with divine power.

4.5 JESUS AS LORD

The title "Lord" appears sixteen times in Mark (1:3; 2:28; 5:19; 7:28; 11:3, 9; 12:9, 11, 29 [2x], 30, 36 [2x], 37; 13:20, 35). Johansson argues "that the evangelist used it to communicate important aspects of the identity of Jesus."[151] Broadhead had argued that Mark represents a primitive form of the early Christology that maintained a clear distinction between the identity of Yahweh as Lord in the OT as exclusively divine and Jesus as the future agent of salvation.[152] Johansson counters that the line between God and Jesus in Mark is not as clear-cut as Broadhead maintains. Mark uses the title "Lord" ambiguously in the gospel, and it seems that he does so deliberately. It is difficult to decide where it refers to God or Jesus or in what sense it is used.[153] He makes the case "that the ambiguous use of *kyrios* [Lord] is intentional and serves the purpose of *linking Jesus to the God of Israel*, so that they *both share the identity* as *kyrios* [Lord]."[154]

A good example of this deliberate ambiguity is in 1:3 and the quotation from Isaiah 40:3: "a voice of one calling in the wilderness, 'Prepare the way for the Lord, make straight paths for him,'" which is discussed above.[155] In Isaiah, the "Lord" refers to God, but in the context, Jesus is the one for whom the voice in the wilderness prepares the way (1:9). Johansson argues that it is mistaken to try to resolve the ambiguity. It should remain. "Lord" refers to God and Jesus.[156] This ambiguity here and elsewhere in Mark (particularly in 5:19; 11:3, 9; 12:36) presents in a narrative the early Christian confession that Jesus is Lord (Rom 10:9; 1 Cor 12:3; Phil 2:11).[157]

4.6 JESUS AS TEACHER

Jesus is identified as "teacher" in Mark more than any other title, and teaching describes his predominant activity. "Teacher" is also the most common way Jesus is addressed. It is not surprising that his disciples address him as "teacher" four times (4:38; 9:38; 10:35; 13:1) since the term "disciple" in Greek means that they are in a

151. Johansson, "*Kyrios* in the Gospel of Mark," 101.
152. Broadhead, *Naming Jesus*, 143–44.
153. Johansson, "*Kyrios* in the Gospel of Mark," 102.
154. Ibid., 102–3.
155. See §3.2.2.3.
156. Johansson, "*Kyrios* in the Gospel of Mark," 105.
157. Ibid., 121.

learning role. But he is also addressed as "teacher" by one posing a question about how to attain eternal life (10:17, 20); by a member of a crowd who wants him to drive out a demon from his son (9:17); by opponents trying to trap him with loaded questions (12:14, 19); and by a teacher of the law who commends his answer about what is the greatest commandment (12:32). People who came from the house of Jairus call him "the teacher" (5:35), and Jesus identifies himself as "the teacher" (14:14).[158]

The term "Rabbi," which is normally transliterated rather than translated, means "my master" and was a respectful greeting for teachers (see Matt 23:7). Jesus is addressed as "Rabbi" three times—twice by Peter (9:5; 11:21), once by Judas (14:45)—compared with twice in Matthew and no instances in Luke.[159] Bartimaeus addresses him as *Rabbouni* (10:51), a term that appears elsewhere only in John 20:16, where "teacher" is added as a translation.[160]

The prominence of the references to Jesus as teacher in Mark becomes most evident when they are compared with Matthew and Luke.[161] Jesus is identified as "teacher" twelve times in Mark, compared with twelve times in Matthew and thirteen times in Luke.[162] Since Mark is the shortest by far of the Synoptic Gospels, these figures reveal the greater emphasis on this title in Mark. Also, most of the uses of "to teach" and "teaching" in Mark are editorial, appearing in summaries of Jesus' ministry or in the "seams" that link or introduce episodes rather than from material received from tradition.[163] In 10:1, Mark adds that Jesus teaches the crowds that came to him "as was his custom." Even his mortal enemies acknowledge, though hypocritically, that he teaches "the way of God in accordance with the truth" (12:14). They cannot deny his reputation as a teacher. Jesus indicates that obedience to his teaching will be a criterion of salvation in the judgment. Anyone who is ashamed of his words will be judged (8:38). He also asserts that heaven and earth will pass away but his words will not (13:31).

Mark also presents teaching as Jesus' characteristic activity. The verb "to teach" is used to describe Jesus' activity sixteen times in Mark, compared with nine times

158. Jesus sends two disciples into the city to find a room to prepare for the Passover. They are to follow a man carrying a water jar and then inform the owner of the house that he enters, "The Teacher asks: 'Where is my guest room, where I may eat the Passover with my disciples?'" Since Jesus has been teaching in the temple to large crowds for days, it makes sense that he would be known as and identify himself as "the Teacher" instead of identifying himself as "the Lord" (11:1–3).

159. In Matthew, only Judas addresses him as "Rabbi." At the Last Supper, he asks, "Surely you don't mean me, Rabbi?" (Matt 26:25), when the other disciples have addressed him as "Lord" (Matt 26:22). He also addresses him as "Rabbi" when he greets and kisses him to identify him to the captors at Gethsemane (Matt 26:49). For Matthew, the title "Rabbi" is connected to Jesus' and the church's adversaries, the teachers of the law and the Pharisees (Matt 23:2–8). Luke avoids Hebraic terminology.

160. The reading "Rabbi" accepted by the NIV appears only in D (Bezae) and in some old Latin versions. Gundry, *Mark*, 602–3, notes that it is used in rabbinic literature to address God and in the targums rarely to address human beings, so it is an exalted greeting address. Three of the usages of "Rabbi" and "Rabbouni" follow a miraculous event: the transfiguration, the healing of Bartimaeus, and the withering of the fig tree.

161. Taylor, *Mark*, 118–19; R. T. France, "Mark and the Teaching of Jesus," in *Gospel Perspectives: Studies of History and Tradition in the Four Gospels* (ed. R. T. France and David Wenham; Sheffield: JSOT, 1980), 1:101–36; Steve Dwinnels, "The Function of ΔΙΔΑΣΚΩ and ΚΗΡΥΣΣΩ in the Gospel of Mark: A Rhetorical-Critical Study of a Markan Emphasis on Jesus' Eschatological Ministry" (Ph.D. diss., The Southern Baptist Theological Seminary, 2002).

162. Mark 4:38; 5:35; 9:17, 38; 10:17, 20, 35; 12:14, 19, 32; 13:1; and 14:14.

163. France, "Mark and the Teaching of Jesus," 103–4. Best, *Temptation*, 71–72, notes that Mark's hand is evident in the use of the terms "teaching" in 1:22, 27; 4:2; 11:18; 12:38, and "to teach" in 1:21, 22; 2:13; 4:1, 2; 6:6; 8:31; 9:31; 10:1; 11:17; 12:35.

in Matthew and fifteen times in Luke.[164] In addition, the phrase "to speak the word" with Jesus as the subject appears three times (2:2; 4:33; 8:32).

France demonstrates that the commonly stated assumption that Mark's gospel contains little of Jesus' teaching and that Mark is uninterested in it is erroneous. He calculates that 40 percent of the gospel contains sayings of Jesus and around 12 percent consists of narrative contexts that lead to important sayings where Jesus' pronouncement is the raison d'être for the narrative. Over half the gospel, then, is devoted to Jesus' teaching.[165] Beavis notes a pattern in which Mark alternates between narrative and teaching throughout the gospel.[166]

Narrative (1:1–3:35)
Teaching (4:1–34)
Narrative (4:35–6:56)
Teaching (7:1–23)
Narrative (7:24–9:29)
Teaching (9:30–10:45)
Narrative (10:46–12:44)
Teaching (13:1–37)
Narrative (14:1–16:8)

The first appearance of Jesus as teacher occurs in 1:21–28. Mark introduces the episode as Jesus entering the synagogue to teach (1:21) and reports the results: "The people were amazed at his teaching, because he taught them as one who had authority, not as the teachers of the law" (1:22). Mark does not narrate what he taught but describes an exorcism that produces similar amazement from the people. They exclaim, "What is this? A new teaching—and with authority! He even gives orders to impure spirits and they obey him" (1:27). This exclamation makes clear that Mark considers Jesus' word and deed to be closely tied together.[167] The deliberate linkage of the two creates "the total impression of an unheard-of *exousia* [authority]."[168]

After teaching all day (4:1–34), Jesus set sail with his disciples for the other side of the lake. A sudden squall that was about to engulf and sink their boat prompts the disciples to implore Jesus frantically to wake from sleep, "Teacher, don't you care if we drown?" (4:38). In the Synoptic parallels, he is addressed as "Lord" in Matt 8:25 and "Master" in Luke 8:24. This is the first time he is addressed as "teacher" in the gospel. His power to control a raging storm is connected to his role as teacher. For Mark, Jesus' authority as a teacher cannot be separated from his power to perform mighty acts.[169]

164. Mark 1:21, 22; 2:13; 4:1–2; 6:2, 6, 34; 7:7; 8:31; 9:31; 10:1; 11:17; 12:14, 35; 14:49. Only once is the verb applied to the disciples (6:30), and they are teaching what Jesus taught them. The verb "to preach" occurs three times and is restricted to the initial announcement of the good news of God in 1:14, 38–39. It is probably not to be distinguished from his teaching, but the verb is more commonly used in the gospel to describe what others do (1:4, 7, 45; 3:14; 5:20; 6:12; 7:36; 13:10; 14:9).

165. France, "Mark and the Teaching of Jesus," 112–13.

166. Mary Ann Beavis, *Mark's Audience: The Literary and Social Setting of Mark 4.11–12* (JSNTSup 33; Sheffield: Sheffield Academic, 1989), 127.

167. Karl Kertelge, *Die Wunder Jesu im Markusevangelium: Eine redaktionsgeschichtliche Untersuchung* (SANT 33; Munich: Kösel, 1970), 56.

168. France, "Mark and the Teaching of Jesus," 110.

169. Paul J. Achtemeier, "'He Taught Them Many Things': Reflections on Marcan Christology," *CBQ* 42 (1980): 480.

Chapter 5

Enacted Christology in Mark

Bibliography

Ahearne-Kroll, Stephen P. "The Scripturally Complex Presentation of Jesus in the Gospel of Mark." Pp. 45–67 in *Portraits of Jesus: Studies in Christology*. Ed. Susan E. Myers. WUNT 2/321. Tübingen: Mohr Siebeck, 2012. **Camery-Hoggatt, Jerry.** *Irony in Mark's Gospel: Text and Subtext*. SNTSMS 72. Cambridge: Cambridge University Press, 1992. **Davis, Steven T.** " 'Who Can Forgive Sins but God Alone?': Jesus, Forgiveness, and Divinity." Pp. 113–23 in the *Multivalence of Biblical Texts and Theological Meanings*. Ed. Christine Helmer and Charlene T. Higbe. SBLSymS 37. Atlanta: Society of Biblical Literature, 2006. **Malbon, Elizabeth Struthers.** "The Christology of Mark's Gospel: Narrative Christology and the Markan Jesus." Pp. 33–48 in *Who Do You Say I Am? Essays in Christology in Honor of Jack Dean Kingsbury on the Occasion of His 65th Birthday*. Ed. David R. Bauer and Mark Allan Powell. Louisville: Westminster John Knox, 1999. Eadem. " 'Reflected Christology': An Aspect of Narrative 'Christology' in the Gospel of Mark." *PRSt* 26 (1999): 127–45. Eadem. *Mark's Jesus: Characterization as Narrative Christology*. Waco, TX: Baylor University Press 2009. **Martinez, Ernest R.** "Identity of Jesus in Mark." *Comm* 1 (1974): 323–42. **Naluparayil, Jacob Chacko.** *The Identity of Jesus in Mark: An Essay on Narrative Christology*. Studium biblicum franciscanum analecta 49. Jerusalem: Franciscan Printing, 2000. **Osborne, Grant R.** "Structure and Christology in Mark 1:21–45." Pp. 146–63 in *Jesus of Nazareth: Lord and Christ: Essays on the Historical Jesus and New Testament Christology*. Ed. Joel B. Green and Max Turner. Grand Rapids: Eerdmans, 1994. **Perkins, Pheme.** "Mark as Narrative Christology." Pp. 67–80 in *Who Is This Christ? Gospel Christology and Contemporary Faith*. Ed. Reginald Fuller and Pheme Perkins; Philadelphia: Fortress, 1983. **Tannehill, Robert C.** "The Gospel of Mark as Narrative Christology." *Semeia* 16 (1979): 57–95. **Trakatellis, Demetrios.** *Authority and Passion: Christological Aspects of the Gospel according to Mark*. Trans. George K. Duvall and Harry Vulopas. Brookline, MA: Holy Cross Orthodox Press, 1987.

5.1 INTRODUCTION TO ENACTED CHRISTOLOGY

Mark develops his Christology through narrative. That is, the audience learns Jesus' identity and significance for their lives from the story.[1] Jesus does not run about the Galilean countryside announcing, "I am the Messiah," or "I am the Son of God," and he does not use these titles that are normally associated with him.[2] Jesus did not easily fit into ready-made categories of Jewish messianic expectation, and trying to make him fit is like sewing a patch of unshrunken cloth on an old garment or putting new wine in stiff, old wineskins.[3] Malbon recognizes that Mark's narrative creates an "enacted Christology" that has to do with Jesus' actions. It reveals more about him than what others might say about him, which she labels "projected Christology."[4] Collins asserts, "Jesus is portrayed as Son of God narratively, by recounting his mighty deeds, his authoritative teaching, his prophecy, and his death for the benefit of others."[5] In this chapter, I intend to show how Mark conveys that Jesus is uniquely the Son of God by recording him doing things that only God can do or has the right to do. I fully agree with Moffat's conclusion:

> The theology of Mark ... is not a description of how a genial humanitarian Jesus went about doing good, unconscious of any specific divine functions. Mark's gospel is the story of Jesus as a supernatural figure, compelling homage from the invisible world of demons, and exercising the powers of divine forgiveness and authority on earth as Son of God and the Son of Man. Mark, as Wellhausen observes, is not writing *de vita et moribus Jesu*. He essays indeed to make His personality vivid, but that personality has a divine vocation which supplies the controlling interest of the story: Jesus is the Christ, the Son of God. In this respect the Christology of Mark is not so distant from the essential features even of the Fourth gospel.[6]

1. Tannehill, "The Gospel of Mark as Narrative Christology," 57. Marshall, "Jesus as Messiah in Mark and Matthew," 117, affirms this assessment: "The Gospels contain christological statements, but the Christology is revealed to the readers by the medium of a developing story." France, *Mark*, 24–25, noting the work of Richard V. Peace, *Conversion in the New Testament* (Grand Rapids: Eerdmans, 1999), 116–22, comments, "Mark's christological focus is located in the narrative development rather than in isolated sayings, resulting in an incremental revelation of who Jesus is and what he has come to do." Schenke, "Präexistenzchristologie?" 47–48, contends that Christology is a presupposition rather than a theme in Mark and that it is the characters of the story who ask who Jesus is, not the reader who already knows. In *Das Markusevangelium*, 108, Schenke observes that the Christology of Mark is presented in and as a story, not in a systematic way, and it is imperative to take this into account when interpreting it.

2. Eduard Schweizer, *Jesus* (trans. David Green; London: SCM, 1971), 13–22. But Tolbert, *Sowing the Gospel*, 122–23, n. 59, contends that "the practice of looking at 'titles' has come under increasing attack as the difficulty of establishing with certainty a fixed tradition of usage and meaning behind any of the 'titles' has become increasingly clear. Whether they should be called 'titles' at all is highly debatable.... In order to discover the specific understanding of Jesus guiding each of the canonical Gospels, instead of studying 'titles,' a truly narrative Christology must be developed that attempts to perceive the distinctive function and depiction of the character Jesus within the dynamics of each story.... Thus, the Christology of Mark is not established by looking at 'titles' provided for Jesus; rather, the meaning of the 'titles' is defined by the narrative itself."

3. Kee, "Christology in Mark's Gospel," 205–6. In addition to categories of "messianic expectation," he adds that Jesus does not fit the categories of "Jewish piety," "covenantal definition," or "eschatological hopes" either.

4. Malbon, "'Reflected Christology,'" 136–37.

5. Collins, "Mark and His Readers," 100. Ole Davidsen, *The Narrative Jesus: A Semiotic Reading of Mark's Gospel* (Aarhus: Aarhus University Press, 1993), 333, asserts, "The entire narrative is a christological proclamation; all the information serves to define Jesus of Nazareth."

6. James Moffatt, *The Theology of the Gospels* (New York: Scribner's, 1913), 12.

The term "enacted Christology" refers to how Mark presents Jesus' identity to his audience through his words and actions.[7] The images and narratives from Scripture provide the palette for painting the portrait of Jesus. In some cases, however, the result creates hues that may be too subtle for modern readers to discern the full depth of this enacted Christology. Johnson states:

> In Mark, Scripture is used to characterise Jesus, but it is a secret, allusive use. This is not often emphasised in the secondary literature on the topic, nor is the Christology of the New Testament studied from an Old Testament perspective in modern literature. But this is precisely how Mark conceives and writes Christology. It is truly a Christology from within, that is, from within the context of the canon.[8]

Scripture provides the warp and woof of Mark's presentation of who Jesus is: "The pre-text for the intertextual connections in Mark is the Bible."[9] Brower avers: "Thus, Mark's theological account of Jesus can only be understood if Mark's intertextual relationship with Israel's scripture is taken seriously. While Mark has fewer citations than Matthew, allusions to the Hebrew Bible are deep and all pervasive in Mark, and at least as significant as the direct citations."[10]

5.2 Jesus' Power to Call as God Calls (Mark 1:16–20)

One of Jesus' first actions is to call disciples to "follow *me*" (1:16–20). The narration of Jesus' call of the first disciples seems to be defectively condensed. Mark does not tell us why Jesus singled out the brothers, Simon and Andrew, and James and John, the sons of Zebedee, when he called them to follow him, nor why they decided to abandon their nets or their father immediately and obey his command. The accounts of the calling of these first disciples in John and Luke make more sense to the modern reader because they provide a narrative that explains why they would follow Jesus.[11] In the Fourth Gospel, John the Baptist tips off two disciples that Jesus is "the Lamb of God," and they leave John to spend a day with Jesus and see where he abides (John 1:35–39). One of these men, Andrew, then informs his brother Simon that they have found the Messiah. When he meets Jesus, he renames him "Cephas" (Peter), and he follows (1:40–42).

Jesus then summons Philip to follow him, seemingly out of the blue, but since

7. Broadhead, "Jesus the Nazarene," 3, recognizes, "Narratives create their own world, set their own rules, define their own terms. Seen from a formalistic literary perspective, the primary value of a christological title would no longer emerge from its pre-history or from authorial intent, but from the contours of its specific literary environment."

8. David H. Johnson, "The Characterization of Jesus in Mark," *Did* 10 (1999): 91.

9. Ibid., 92. Many early Christians came from a background that devoutly studied the Scriptures (see 2 Tim 3:15).

10. Brower, "'Who Then Is This?'" 292. See the essays in Thomas R. Hatina, ed., *Biblical Interpretation in Early Christian Gospels*; Vol. 1: *The Gospel of Mark* (LNTS 304; London: T&T Clark, 2006).

11. Boring, *Mark*, 60, asserts, "There is no parallel to such an unmotivated call story in ancient literature."

he is from the same town (Bethsaida) as Andrew and Peter, one might infer that they had previously alerted him about Jesus (John 1:43–44). Philip then informs Nathanael that they have found the one whom Moses and the prophets wrote about, and Jesus is able to dispel Nathanael's skepticism through his prophetic clairvoyance and promise that he will see "greater things," " 'heaven open, and the angels of God ascending and descending on' the Son of Man" (1:45–51).

In Luke's account of the calling of Simon (Luke 5:1–11), Jesus comes upon him and his companions cleaning their nets after an unsuccessful night of fishing. He sends them out into the lake again, and they haul in an overwhelming quantity of fish. Only after this remarkable miracle does he issue the command to follow. Simon along with James and John, who are silent partners in the story, then leave everything to follow Jesus.

By contrast, nothing in Mark's narrative prepares the reader to expect these fishermen to drop their nets or to leave their father to follow Jesus as disciples. Mark does not even say that they heard his stirring proclamation about the kingdom of God (1:14–15) so that the reader might infer that they were keen to follow him. Mark's seemingly undeveloped account prompts many to want to import the details from Luke and John into the interpretation of Mark's narrative or to introduce some extraneous psychological motivation to explain the disciples' action.[12] To do so causes one to miss Mark's point.[13]

The call of Levi, son of Alphaeus, as he sits at his tax booth, is similarly compressed (2:14). Levi responds to Jesus' call as instantly as the fishermen did. His obedience marks an even more radical break since he forsakes his post. The fishermen could always go back to fishing (see John 21:3), not so a toll collector who deserts his station.

In Mark's account, the emphasis falls on Jesus' authoritative call and its immediate effects. The rabbis of Jesus' day never called people to *follow them*, only to learn Torah from them and to obey it.[14] What makes Mark's narrative so distinctive is that Jesus' peremptory call resembles God's calling of humans in Scripture—a command with a promise that is followed by obedience (see Gen 12:1–4). These first disciples have witnessed nothing of Jesus' powers and have no idea what his battle plans might be. They do not take a few days to mull over their decision or to

12. Modern readers may be tempted to supply some psychological basis for the disciples' rapid response. Speculation about their having made a decision to repent and dedicate their lives to God after hearing his preaching about the kingdom of God (1:14–15) are unwarranted in the text. Even if they heard John the Baptist declare that "one more powerful than I" was coming and that he would "baptize you with the Holy Spirit" (1:7–8), they would have no clue that John referred to Jesus, who remains unknown to the throngs. Nor does Mark hint that they were longing for the Messiah to come to liberate Israel from foreign oppression or that they were going through a mid-life crisis and had an itch for action that primed them to jump at the chance to follow a would-be deliverer (see 13:21–22).

13. Ernest Best, "The Miracles in Mark," in *Disciples and Discipleship: Studies in the Gospel According to Mark* (Edinburgh: T&T Clark, 1986), 181, notes that Mark includes the call stories among "the wonderful events or miracles in his Gospel," since they "took place without any psychological preparation and as a result only of Jesus' simple word to them [the disciples]." The absence of any hint of motivation for them to follow Jesus serves Mark's Christology rather than to "facilitate the hearer's identification with the disciples" and experience "the disciples' call as their own call," as Whitney Taylor Shiner, *Follow Me!: Disciples in Markan Rhetoric* (SBLDS 145; Atlanta: Scholars Press, 1995), 185, contends.

14. Martin Hengel, *The Charismatic Leader and His Followers* (trans. James Greig; Edinburgh: T&T Clark, 1981), 50–53.

consult with a panel of experts. They do what many a modern reader may regard as overly rash. They obey someone who happens to pass by and imperiously beckons them to follow him.[15]

What it means to follow Jesus is *not* in the forefront of Mark's mind at this point.[16] Mark's focus falls only on Jesus as the one who calls, not on the disciples who leave their nets. Readers have been informed in the introduction that Jesus is the Son of God empowered by the Holy Spirit. The only explanation that readers can give for the sudden obedience of these disciples is that Jesus' call possesses a divine power that compels them to obey. In Mark's narrative, that power alone, not human calculations or circumstances, impels them to follow him.

The one who passes by (1:16; 2:14) may recall Elijah who passes by Elisha before throwing his mantle over him to commission him as a prophet (1 Kgs 19:19). But Mark uses this same verb in an epiphany scene in 6:48–50, that recalls Exod 33:18–23, where God "passes by" Moses, and 1 Kgs 19:11, where God "passes by" Elijah. Marcus suggests "it is possible that Jesus is being portrayed not only as Elijah-like but also as godlike."[17] I would suggest that Mark presents Jesus as far more than Elijah. Elisha put Elijah off until he could bid goodbye to his parents (1 Kgs 19:20). These disciples follow Jesus immediately, and James and John do not say farewell to their father. The verb "call" appears in the LXX in Isa 41:9; 42:6; 43:1; 45:3; 48:12, 15; 51:2, for God calling Abraham and Israel.[18]

The verb "I will make you" (ASV) in 1:17 occurs throughout the OT on the lips of God as a promise that God will make Israel a great nation or cause them to increase in number (Gen 12:2; 17:6; 22:17; 26:24; 32:12; 46:3; 48:3–4; Exod 32:10; Lev 26:9; Num 14:12; Deut 9:14; Isa 60:15), that God will make a covenant with David (1 Chr 17:8), or that God will make Israel desolate for their disobedience (Jer 17:4; 22:6; 30:11; 34:17; Ezek 5:14; 26:14; 26:20; 35:9, 14; Obad 2; Mic 6:16). When Jesus says to the first disciples, "I will make you to become fishers of men" (ASV), he is speaking as God speaks. In Jer 16:16, whether the image of fishers is used for the regathering of Israel from exile (see John 11:52) or for judgment, God says: "'But now I will send for many fishermen,' declares the Lord, 'and they will catch them.'" In Mark's context, the fishers would have a positive function. Jesus' choice of the Twelve in 3:13–19 has symbolic significance that points to the restoration of the twelve tribes of Israel (see Num 1:1–19, 44). Like God, Jesus chooses whom he wills (3:13), and Lohmeyer characterizes his call as coming like "a sharp military command" that produces obedience: "He commands as God commands.... He makes of the fisherman something new, that which he wills."[19]

Psalm 33 exalts the powerful force of God's utterances, "For he spoke, and it

15. Andrew and Simon presumably leave everything to follow Jesus, but they are found in their home in 1:29.

16. Contra Stein, *Mark*, 80–81.

17. Marcus, *Mark 1–8*, 179.

18. Karl Ludwig Schmidt, "καλέω," *TDNT*, 3:490.

19. Lohmeyer, *Markus*, 32. Haenchen, *Der Weg Jesu*, 80, ascribes the response to "the miracle of [Jesus'] compelling word" ("dem Wunder des zwingenden Wortes"). Hooker, *Mark*, 59, comments that the scene "conveys vividly the authority and power which he exercises," and Gundry, *Mark*, 67, declares, "how great must be the power of Jesus to induce that kind of conduct."

came to be; he commanded, and it stood firm" (Ps 33:9). The psalm provides the framework for understanding why these disciples respond as they do. Jesus speaks, and, like God, his command creates results. Here Jesus speaks, "Come, follow me!" and it produces immediate submission. This pattern continues in the narrative. Jesus speaks, "Be quiet! Come out of him!" and impure spirits are dispatched (1:25–26). Jesus speaks, "Quiet! Be still!" and a fierce wind stops and the sea becomes "completely calm" (4:39). Jesus speaks, "*Talitha koum*! Little girl ... get up!" and a dead child is raised (5:41–42). Jesus speaks, "*Ephphatha*! Be opened!" and a deaf man's ears are opened (7:34–35). Jesus speaks, "May no one ever eat fruit from you again!" and a fig tree is withered to its roots (11:14, 20). Jesus utters a great cry on the cross, and the temple veil splits from top to bottom (15:38). The power of the one who calls as God calls is the only explanation why these disciples respond immediately as they do. Instead of asking, "Why do the disciples leave everything to follow him so abruptly?" one should ask, "Who is this who generates such immediate obedience?"

5.3 Jesus' Power over the Demonic World

Mark's first detailed description of Jesus' public ministry has him teaching and exorcising a demon in the Capernaum synagogue on a Sabbath (1:21–28). The exorcism begins a series of mighty works in Capernaum that further reveal his divine power as the Son of God. The confrontation with Satan that occurred in the wilderness continues as a pitched battle, or, perhaps, a "mopping up" action, against Satan's demonic legions.[20] For Mark, the demonic realm represents a real power that invades the human realm. It seeks to take human minds and lives captive and to destroy them. The human realm therefore needs a divine power to be liberated from this satanic captivity.[21]

Jesus handily wins each encounter because of his unique authority. Mark records four individual exorcisms (1:21–28; 5:1–20; 7:24–30; 9:14–29), mentions the casting out of demons in three summaries of Jesus' ministry (1:32–34, 39; see 3:22–30), and records Jesus empowering his disciples to cast out demons (3:15; 6:7; see 6:12–13) and sanctioning a nondisciple who successfully casts out demons in his name (9:38–40).

5.3.1 Jesus' Supreme Authority as the Holy One of God (Mark 1:21–28)

In this opening scene, Jesus teaches in the synagogue, and the assembly is astounded by his teaching because he taught as one who had authority and not as the teachers of the law (1:21–22). Mark does not recount the content of his teaching but describes instead his "overpowering word of exorcism."[22] After his teaching, a demon-possessed man suddenly materializes in the midst of the synagogue. His

20. Best, *Temptation*, 15

21. Shively, *Apocalyptic Imagination*, 260.

22. As Gundry, *Mark*, 73, aptly titles this incident.

condition is described strangely by Mark. Literally, it reads "a man *in* an impure spirit."[23] Marcus argues that the phrasing suggests that "the man's personality has been so usurped by the demon that the demon has, as it were, swallowed him up." He notes that this sudden appearance of the demon after Jesus' teaching fits a pattern: like a bird, Satan swoops down immediately when people hear the word to snatch the seeds (4:15).[24]

In Mark's narrative, only spiritual beings — demons and angels (1:13) — fathom the divine mystery of Jesus' identity. The impure spirits always know who Jesus is (1:34). They recognize that he is not some run-of-the-mill, charismatic exorcist, but one who comes imbued with the power of God to crush Satan's regime.[25] The impure spirit in this scene yells out, "What do you want with us, Jesus of Nazareth? Have you come to destroy us? I know who you are — the Holy One of God!" (1:24).[26] This cry recalls the introduction where Jesus is identified as coming from Nazareth of Galilee to be baptized by John and a voice from heaven recognizes him as "my Son, whom I love" (1:9 – 11).

The impure spirit's nervous wail introduces one purpose of Jesus' coming and what it means that the kingdom of God has come near (1:15). He has come to preach (1:38), presumably "the good news of God" (1:14), to call sinners (2:17), and to give his life as a ransom (10:45). He has also come to free people from demonic bondage. The impure spirit, who is introduced as one demon, uses the plural in recoiling against Jesus' presence, "What do you want with *us*? ... Have you come to destroy *us*?" The spirit speaks for the demonic world in voicing their dread in God's presence. The impure spirit's declarative question draws attention to the prophecy in Zech 13:2: "On that day, says the LORD of hosts, I will cut off the names of the idols from the land, so that they shall be remembered no more; and also I will remove from the land the prophets and the unclean spirit" (NRSV). It sets this exorcism in the context of the eschatological battle that God has promised to wage against impure spirits.[27]

23. Guelich, *Mark 1 – 8:26*, 56 claims that the phrase "unclean spirits" "represents a common Jewish designation for demons." The expression, however, only occurs once in the OT (Zech 13:2); see Steffen Jöris, "The Markan Use of 'Unclean Spirit': Another Messianic Strand," *ABR* 60 (2012): 49 – 66. Collins, *Mark*, 167 – 68, suggests that the term may derive from the story of the fallen angels in Gen 6:1 – 4 and *1 En.* 6:1 – 11, who defiled themselves with "the daughters of men" (*1 En.* 15:3 – 4; see *Jub.* 7:21). "Unclean spirit" is a religious term and a spiritual diagnosis referring to moral impurity. G. B. Caird, *New Testament Theology* (ed. L. D. Hurst; Oxford: Clarendon, 1994), 109, notes that what is unclean in the Old Testament has "evaded the control of the divine holiness." It is the polar opposite of what is holy. Otto Bauernfeind, *Die Wörte der Dämonen im Markusevangelium* (BWANT 3.9; Stuttgart: Kohlhammer, 1927), 63 – 64, argues that they represent disembodied beings, able to perform screams, which could be perceived by humans.

24. Marcus, *Mark 1 – 8*, 192.

25. France, *Mark*, 100 – 101, E. F. Kirschner, "The Place of the Exorcism Motif in Mark's Christology, with Special Attention to Mark 3:22 – 30" (Ph. D. diss., London Bible College, 1988), 29, who notes that few exorcism narratives exist in ancient literature and even fewer stories about particular exorcists exist. We should not assume that Jesus was simply one of many exorcists running around the countryside casting out demons. France comments that readers would not have expected exorcisms from "a special religious figure" and would have responded with the same amazement as the synagogue congregation in Capernaum and concluded that this was "a new teaching."

26. Since the demon says much the same thing in 5:7, "What do you want with me?" but identifies him as "Jesus, Son of the Most High God," Bernd Kollmann, "Jesu Schweigegebote an die Dämonen," *ZNW* 82 (1991): 273, contends that "the Holy One of God" correlates with "Son of the Most High God." In John 6:69, Simon Peter confesses, "We have come to believe and to know that you are the Holy One of God."

27. See Graham H. Twelftree, *Jesus the Exorcist: A Contribution to the Study of the Historical Jesus* (WUNT 2/54; Tübingen: Mohr Siebeck, 1993), 173, 224.

I argue that Mark intends to present Jesus as the Son of God who acts with divine power and not simply as the appointed Messiah who is endowed with the Holy Spirit.[28] Lohmeyer forcefully asserts: "The Son of God is not in the first place a human but a divine figure. Demons see and know more than humans, and they immediately recognize him. He is not only endowed with the power of God, but is himself of God's nature; not only are his word and work divine, but his essence also."[29]

This interpretation is supported by the cumulative evidence of several details in the account of this exorcism. First, Jesus does not resort to any special techniques or instruments to expel the demon, such as preparing peculiar recipes, uttering secret incantations and prayers, interrogating the demon to gather information about it, or making use of the demon's name or appealing to its thwarting angel.[30] His supreme authority alone drives out the demon. He need only speak the word, "Be quiet! Come out of him!" (1:25).[31] Mark describes this command as a "rebuke" (*epitimaō*; the translation "said sternly" is far too weak). Jesus will also "rebuke" the wind and sea "to be still" (4:39). It is more than a word of reprimand. The term "rebuke" (Heb. root *gʿr*) is used in the OT for God's subjugating word that wrests control from enemies and completely dominates them.[32] Kee concludes that in Mark it becomes "a technical term for the commanding word, uttered by God or by his spokesman, by which evil powers are brought into submission, and the way is thereby prepared for the establishment of God's righteous rule in the world."[33] Gnilka goes so far as to say, "Jesus steps into Yahweh's place."[34]

Muzzling the impure spirit in this instance has nothing to do with the so-called messianic secret and silencing a premature confession about Jesus. The synagogue gathering appears to pay no attention to its cry. Therefore, Jesus does not silence the demon to check the danger of the crowd's premature idolization of Jesus that is

28. Contra Collins, *Mark*, 174.

29. Lohmeyer, *Markus*, 4 (author trans.).

30. The *Testament of Solomon* places great emphasis on knowing the demon's name and the name of the thwarting angel to exorcise it. Josephus (*Ant.* 8.2.5. §45) represents the view that successful exorcisms are tied to secret lore, techniques, and spells. He lauds Solomon's prowess in demonic exorcism: "And God granted him knowledge of the art used against demons for the benefit and healing of men. He also composed incantations by which illnesses are relieved, and left behind forms of exorcisms with which those possessed by demons drive them out never to return." He then describes an exorcism done by one Eleazar before the Roman general, Vespasian.

> He put to the nose of the possessed man a ring which had under its seal one of the roots prescribed by Solomon, and then, as the man smelled it, drew out the demon through his nostrils, and, when the man at once fell down, adjured the demon never to come back into him, speaking Solomon's name and reciting the incantations which he had composed. Then, wishing to convince the bystanders and prove to them that he had this power, Eleazar placed a cup or foot-basin full of water a little way off and commanded the demon, as it went out of the man, to overturn it and make known to the spectators that he had left the man. (*Ant.* 8.2.5. §§47–48).

By burning the liver and the heart of a fish, Tobias frightened off the demon Asmodeus, who had previously killed seven successive bridegrooms of Sarah on their wedding nights (Tob 8:2–3). This secret recipe was given to him by the angel Raphael (Tob 6:1–8).

31. T. A. Burkill, *Mysterious Revelation: An Examination of the Philosophy of St. Mark's Gospel* (Ithaca, NY: Cornell University Press, 1963), 74, states, "Unlike the demon, Jesus does not make an elaborate declaration; his supernatural power is such that he needs no sacred name, no mysterious formula, and no expression of special gnosis."

32. See 2 Sam 22:16; Job 26:11; Pss 9:5; 68:30; 76:6; 80:16; 106:9; 119:21; Zech 3:2.

33. Howard Clark Kee, "The Terminology of Mark's Exorcism Stories," *NTS* 14 (1967–68): 235. See John J. Kilgallen, "The Messianic Secret and Mark's Purposes," *BTB* 7 (1977): 60; and the refinement of Kee's assertions in Gordon J. Hamilton, "A New Hebrew-Aramaic Incantation Text from Galilee: 'Rebuking the Sea,'" *JSS* 41 (1996): 215–49; and Marcus, *Mark 1–8*, 193–94.

34. Gnilka, *Markus*, 1:81 (author trans.). Boring, *Mark*, 65, n. 12, thinks this statement goes too far, but the cumulative weight of the evidence suggests that Jesus does indeed step into God's role as God's Son.

incited by a demonic witness.[35] They are not impressed by the demon's disclosure of Jesus' identity but by Jesus' authority to expel it. To be sure, Jesus does not welcome demonic testimony, but by shouting out his name the demon attempts to stave off the exorcism by using a holy appellation (see 5:7).[36] The slave-girl, who had a spirit of divination and followed Paul and his companions in Philippi, crying out, "These men are servants of the Most High God, who are telling you the way to be saved," is also silenced by an annoyed Paul, who orders the spirit to come out of her (Acts 16:16–18). Names frequently appear as incantations in the ancient magical papyri because it was believed that knowing the name of the demon or power gave one a tactical advantage in defeating them. One can infer that the reverse was believed to be true. Demons are not simply raising the alarm but trying to foil exorcisms by using Jesus' divine names.[37] Jesus exerts his mastery over the demon by summarily telling it to shut up.[38] Evasive ploys will not save it.[39] Gagging demons in the same way he silences the storm, "Quiet! Be still!" (4:39), shows that he has defeated this malevolent power.

Second, the word "authority" (*exousia*) frames this scene (1:22, 27). Edwards's analysis "reveals that in the LXX and intertestamental literature *exousia* is used predominantly of supernatural powers and authorities, especially of God and God's works, representatives and emissaries."[40] The word "normally was reserved for or derived from supernatural authority."[41] In Mark, the word appears ten times, seven with clear reference to Jesus (1:22, 27; 2:10; 11:28, 29, 33). Twice it is found with reference to the authority that Jesus bestows on the apostles (3:15; 6:7). It also occurs in the simile of the man who leaves and "puts his servants in charge" (lit., "having given authority over to"), which alludes to Jesus' departure and the authority given to his disciples over his house (13:34).

The synagogue congregation recognizes the difference between Jesus' authority and that of the scribes. Teachers of the law did not claim direct revelation from God. Instead, according to Jesus, they substitute human traditions for the commands of God (7:7–8). While they stand in the tradition of the fathers (7:8–13), "Jesus

35. In my opinion, Jesus does not permit the demons he drives out to speak (1:34) for the same reason. Satan intends to suppress the secret of the kingdom of God (4:15), not to broadcast it. "Because they knew who he was" does not mean that Jesus is concerned that they will let the cat out of the bag prematurely. He will not permit them to use his name in futile attempts to fend off being vanquished and expelled. A textual variant (א^{2}, B, C, *f*^{13}) has "because they knew that he was the Christ." The reading "because they knew who he was" best explains how the variant arose. It is likely that copyists adapted the text to Luke 4:41. Paul J. Achtemeier, "Mark, Gospel of," *ABD*, 4:553, contends that Jesus stifles the demon because it sees him only as the victorious Son of God and not as one who must yet undergo suffering and death. While it is true that the final victory over Satan will be achieved through the cross and resurrection, and Jesus' self-giving death on a cross reveals him to be the Son of God (15:39; see Guelich, *Mark 1–8:26*, 148–49), these particular issues are not in play in these exorcisms. Jesus' mastery of demons also reveals him to be the Son of God.

36. The use of the challenge, "What do you want with us?" (lit. trans., "What between us and you?" 1:24), to "actual or potential aggressors" in Judg 11:12 and 1 Kgs 17:18 "has the force of 'Go away and leave me alone'" (France, *Mark*, 103).

37. See Bauernfeind, *Die Wörte der Dämonen im Markusevangelium*, 3–12; and Collins, *Mark*, 169–70, 172. The objections of Pierre Guillemette, "Mc 1,24 est-il une formule de défense magique?" *ScEs* 30 (1978): 81–96, are not strong enough to overturn this conclusion.

38. Lohmeyer, *Markus*, 36.

39. Kollmann, "Jesu Schweigegebote," 267–73.

40. James R. Edwards, "The Authority of Jesus in the Gospel of Mark," *JETS* 37 (1994): 217–33 (219). See also the review of the use of the word in the LXX in Klaus Scholtissek, *Die Vollmacht Jesu: Traditions- und redaktionsgeschichtliche Analysen zu einem Leitmotiv markinischer Christologie* (NTAbh 25; Münster: Aschendorff, 1992), 54–55.

41. Edwards, "The Authority of Jesus," 220.

receives his authority directly from the Father (1:11). The teachers of the law derive their authority from Torah, but Jesus appeals to a superior authority resident in himself."[42] This scene unveils the truth: "In both his word and work Jesus is endowed with the sovereign authority of God."[43] This divine authority has created an entirely new situation. Jesus' teaching, unlike that of the scribes, has divine authority, that is, divine power, to overthrow Satan's tyranny and to set free the captives.

Third, the audience's amazed response sounds a biblical pattern in which the following three elements appear: God's mighty work, human astonishment in response, and a question or exclamation in direct speech voicing this astonishment (see Gen 42:28; 1 Kgs 9:8; 2 Chr 7:21; Isa 52:13–53:4; Ezek 26:16–17; Dan 3:24–25; Wis 5:2–10).[44] Ambrozic concludes that the response of amazement to Jesus' miracles is understandable: The miracles "are concrete manifestations of God's eschatological power bringing about His kingdom in and through Jesus."[45] Only one with the power of God is able to accomplish this miracle.

In 2 Macc 3:24, God is identified as "the Sovereign of spirits and of all authority," whose manifestation of power astounds those who witness it.[46] In addition to having authority as a teacher (Mark 1:21–22), Jesus has authority over the forgiveness of sins (2:5–12), over the Sabbath (2:27–28), over impure spirits (3:19–27), over the mystery of the kingdom of God (4:10–11), over nature (4:35–41; 6:45–52), over the law (7:1–13, 14–20), and over the temple (11:12–33; 12:1–12). Only the Son of God could have such authority. Kelber remarks that this question, "*What* is this?" rather than "*Who* is this?" sets "the christological verbalization" into "the context of an apocalyptic power struggle."[47] The kingdom of God is attacking the satanic kingdom. This scene is a "programmatic prelude" to Jesus' public demonstration of his power and serves as a typical example of his authority (which is cited explicitly in 2:10, 28; 11:27–33).[48]

What is also new in this confrontation between the holy and impure is that "the human carrier of the impurity does not die, but rather undergoes purification by the holy."[49] Jesus' holy power destroys only the demon, not the one possessed by the demon. Even when the impure spirit leaves with an ear-splitting screech, the man is left unharmed. The carrier of the impurity is purged of this evil force, and the evil is eradicated. The cry of alarm when suddenly confronted by Jesus' holy presence becomes a death wail.

---

42. Ibid., 221. See Israel Abrahams, *Studies in Pharisaism and the Gospels* (Cambridge: Cambridge University Press, 1917), 1:14.

43. Edwards, "The Authority of Jesus," 222. Aloysius M. Ambrozic, "New Teaching with Power (Mk 1:27)," in *Word and Spirit: Essays in Honor of David M. Stanley, S.J., on His 60th Birthday* (ed. Joseph Plevnik; Willowdale, ON: Regis College, 1975), 121, also argues that the phrase "not as the scribes" refers to "the fundamental character and source of his [Jesus'] teaching." It is divine.

44. Ambrozic, "New Teaching with Power (Mk 1:27)," 127–28; Marcus, *Mark 1–8*, 189.

45. Ambrozic, "New Teaching with Power (Mk 1:27)," 128.

46. In this case, it refers to the foiled attempt of Heliodorus to plunder the temple treasury when he was struck down by angelic beings.

47. Kelber, *Kingdom*, 16.

48. Scholtissek, *Die Vollmacht Jesu*, 137.

49. Hodges and Poirier, "Jesus as the Holy One of God," 176.

5.3.2 Jesus as the Stronger One Who Raids Satan's Stronghold (Mark 3:22–30)

In chapter 3, Jesus' reputation has grown so much that he now draws large crowds from Judea, Jerusalem, Idumea, beyond the Jordan, and the region around Tyre and Sidon (3:8). His popularity and apparent violations of religious conventions set off alarm bells among the ranks of the religious authorities in Jerusalem. He comes from outside the system, and his success can only create envy and antipathy from those inside it.[50] The unidentified brass hats in Jerusalem send agents to descend on him to undercut any impression that his ministry is divinely sanctioned. They use the modern equivalent of the political attack ad. They do not deny that Jesus casts out demons but maliciously attribute this feat to an alliance with Satan and not with God.

The teachers of the law may have concluded that one who flouts hallowed traditions (2:24), flirts with blasphemy (2:7), and does not kowtow to their authority could only be an undercover agent for Satan. Satan is assumed to be the director of the spiritual forces that seek to obstruct God's purposes, eradicate God's ways, and despoil all humanity. They besmirch his reputation by claiming that he "is possessed by Beelzebul" (3:22) and an impure spirit (3:30).[51] They do not charge him with being possessed but claim that he is a sorcerer using diabolical power.[52] They refuse to consider what the demons know, that he is the Son of God empowered by the Holy Spirit or to concede that his exorcisms signify the collapse of Satan's realm, not its expansion.

The charge that Jesus colludes with Beelzebul, one of many aliases for Satan, is ominous. Such complicity merits the death penalty (see Lev 20:27; Deut 18:20). According to later rabbinic tradition, Jesus was condemned to death for practicing sorcery and misleading the people (*b. Sanh.* 43a; 107b; *b. Soṭah* 47a; and *t. Šabb.* 11:15; see also Justin, *Dial.* 69.7).[53] These mudslingers have been maliciously libeling Jesus behind his back, and Jesus summons them to confront them directly (3:23). He parries their smear campaign with two parables. As Boring notes, "Each image conceives of the demonic realm as a unified entity that is more than the aggregate of individual demons."[54] The first highlights how ludicrous their accusation is. Demonic powers ravage human life and alienate victims from God and others. Jesus' exorcisms bring liberation. Would a malignant power collaborate with him to engage in widespread deeds of mercy and abet the decimation of its minions? Satan

50. Garland, *Mark*, 131.

51. In the parable of the children playing in the marketplace and its interpretation (Matt 11:16–19; Luke 7:31–35), Jesus insinuates that the Pharisees, identified as "this generation," accused John the Baptist of having a demon (Matt 11:18; Luke 7:33).

52. Eve, *Context*, 328. Hartmut Stegemann, *The Library of Qumran: On the Essenes, Qumran, John the Baptist, and Jesus* (Grand Rapids: Eerdmans/Leiden: Brill, 1998), 238, suggests that because Jesus cast out demons without using "discernible tools," neither invoking the names of God or of angels, nor uttering Davidic or Solomonic texts of conjuration or employing magical prayers, rites, bowls, or rings, he must be using Satan's power.

53. Jonathan Z. Smith, "Good News Is No News: Aretalogy and Gospel," in *Christianity, Judaism and Other Greco-Roman Cults: Studies for Morton Smith at Sixty* (ed. Jacob Neusner; SJLA 12; Leiden: Brill, 1975), 23, explains that "the one, universal characteristic of magic" in the Greco-Roman world was its illegality, which carried penalties of death or deportation.

54. Boring, *Mark*, 107.

would recognize that a divided house cannot stand and would not sanction an attack on his own ranks. Satan's household, therefore, is not collapsing in on itself but is experiencing an assault that is bringing it to its knees.

The second parable follows up on this conclusion. If Jesus is not in league with Beelzebul, then it must be that a stronger one has invaded his house, bound him,[55] and is pillaging his goods. The more literal translation of 3:27 in the ASV captures a multistage process: "But no one can enter into the house of the strong *man*, and spoil his goods, except he first bind the strong *man*; and then he will spoil his house." It involves entering the strong man's house and binding him in order to spoil (or plunder) his goods (lit., "vessels") and his house. This parable is an allegory. The "strong *man*" represents Satan. His "goods" represent the hapless victims whom Satan has taken captive. His "house" is his domain that he seeks to hold secure. The stronger one is Jesus, who has come from God into this world to put an end to Satan's reign of terror. The allegory recalls the prophecy of John the Baptist in the introduction: "After me comes the one more powerful than I" (1:7). Jesus is not only stronger than John the Baptist, he is stronger than Satan.

Mark did not narrate in full detail the outcome of Jesus' testing by Satan in the wilderness (1:12–13), but the audience can now surmise that Satan met with defeat since Jesus must have bound Satan to be able to plunder his goods, that is, to drive out the demons from individuals. The one who comes to proclaim the arrival of the kingdom of God (1:14–15) also comes to destroy the kingdom of Satan. Jesus does not bind individual demons here and there (see Tob 8:3); he tethers the ruler of demons.

More importantly, the allegory prompts one schooled in Scripture to remember the promise in Isa 49:24–26 that God himself is the Mighty One who will overcome:

> Can plunder be taken from warriors,
>   or captives rescued from the fierce?
> But this is what the LORD says:
> "Yes, captives will be taken from warriors,
>   and plunder retrieved from the fierce;
> I will contend with those who contend with you,
>   and your children I will save.
> I will make your oppressors eat their own flesh;
>   they will be drunk on their own blood, as with wine.
> Then all mankind will know
>   that I, the LORD, am your Savior,
>   your Redeemer, the Mighty One of Jacob."[56]

55. Ironically, Satan is understood to bind his human victims (Luke 13:16). The verb "to bind" recurs in 5:3, where Mark narrates that the townspeople were powerless to "bind" the Gerasene demoniac even with chains. Only divine figures can bind Satan (Rev 20:1–3; see *T. Levi* 18:12).

56. For Jesus, Satan and the unclean spirits are the supreme tormentors that hold the people in bondage, not Babylon.

The binding of Satan is not being carried out by an amazing exorcist but by the very Son of God.[57]

5.3.3 The Destruction of Legion (Mark 5:1–20)

Jesus does not limit his miracles to one side of the lake. He declares God's rule and sows God's grace far and wide. In crossing the lake to an area where swine are kept, Jesus embarks on a daring invasion to claim alien turf under enemy occupation and reveals that there is no place in the world that God's reign does not intend to exert itself.

When Jesus steps ashore, he immediately grapples with another person in the grip of demons.[58] His holy presence activates a defensive reaction from the unholy as the demons controlling the man rush to Jesus.[59] Mark alone gives us a vivid account of this man's condition and how he had been treated. He is "as storm-tossed by the demons as the disciples' boat had been" storm-tossed by the waves.[60] His unruly behavior panicked the community in which he lived. All attempts to bind him failed because he was strong enough to break their fetters (5:3). The man's supernatural strength is reiterated in 5:4; no one had the power to "subdue" him. He is therefore banished as an outcast from society and dwells in the unclean place of the dead,[61] where he lacerates his body with stones and screeches through the night.[62] Malignant spirits always deface humanity and destroy life. Under the dominion of the demons, this man has become a formidable force, but he is self-destructive as he bruises himself with stones. His howling night and day (5:5) reveals him to be a microcosm of the whole of creation inarticulately groaning for redemption (Rom 8:22). Only a power more potent than the community's whips and chains will deliver him from this deadly demonic power.[63]

Mark presents a suspenseful confrontation between Jesus and the impure spirits that rule this ravaged man. The encounter shifts from the singular (5:7, 9a, 10) to the plural (5:9b, 10, 12, 13), and the story suggests "that the evil spirits are using him as a mouthpiece and that he is a miniature Pandemonium, the abode of all demons."[64] The impure spirits again recognize Jesus' divine identity (1:24; 3:11) and quake in his presence (see Jas 2:19). Even though they know that their doom

57. Walter Grundmann, "ἰσχυρός," *TDNT*, 3:401, contends that Isa 53:12 is also part of the background of Jesus' parable: "Therefore I will give him a portion among the great, and he will divide the spoils with the strong, because he poured out his life unto death, and was numbered with the transgressors. For he bore the sin of many, and made intercession for the transgressors." It links Jesus' overthrow of Satan's dominion to his death.

58. Boring, *Mark*, 150, asserts, "The length and placement of the story indicate the central importance of God's triumph over the demonic world in the Christ-event for Mark's theology."

59. The human hosts of the demons are like puppets with the demons pulling the strings.

60. Paul S. Minear, *Saint Mark* (Layman's Bible Commentary; London: SCM, 1962), 73.

61. Tombs were frequently located in caves and were known as haunts for demons, and the mountains were considered to be places of danger.

62. He is clearly one who would have been regarded as a demented soul screaming in his tortured isolation. The imbecile is one who goes out alone at night, sleeps in burial places, rips his clothes, and loses what he is given (*t. Ter.* 1:3; *y. Ter.* 1:1, 40b; and *b. Ḥag.* 3b), but if these things are done in an insane manner, he is considered to be deranged.

63. The Greek word used at the end of 5:4 is *damazein*; it is used for taming a wild animal and may be better translated, "no one was able to *tame* him" (5:4). The demoniac is beaten and chained like a wild animal but to no avail.

64. Garland, *Mark*, 203.

is sealed, they do not surrender without a struggle. They try to evade complete annihilation using tactics from an exorcist's bag of tricks. The dialogue between Jesus and the nervous and nervy impure spirits fearful of being tormented makes for an entertaining theatric skirmish, but, more importantly, it makes Jesus' ultimate victory all the more momentous.[65] The statement, "For Jesus had said to him, 'Come out of this man, you impure spirit!'" (5:8) is delayed. It is not intended to suggest that Jesus had been ineffectively trying to exorcise the demon. The imperfect verb is often translated as a perfect tense, "had said" (NIV, NRSV), and this accurately conveys Mark's delayed use of an explanation clause (see §1.2.5.8).[66] The impure spirits know that they will be expelled from their beleaguered quarry, but they attempt to avert hellish perdition.

First, the demonized man prostrates himself before Jesus (5:6), which should be deemed as a counterfeit submission that seeks only to beguile Jesus to leave them alone. Second, the man in their clutches cries out with a loud voice, as did the demon in 1:24, "What do you want with us?" They vainly attempt to place Jesus under their control by pronouncing his name, "Jesus, Son of the Most High God." By pronouncing his name, they are huffing and puffing, "We've got your number!" Third, they invoke the name of God to compel the Son of God not to torment them (5:7).[67] They have tormented their poor victim past endurance but want to elude suffering themselves. The verb "to torment" (*basanizein*) appears in Rev 20:10 for the everlasting torment of the devil in the lake of fire and sulfur.[68] Since they recognize that Jesus is the "Son of the Most High God," they should know that appealing to God for protection is useless. Adjuring God "merely makes Jesus' ultimate power the more obvious."[69]

Jesus seems to stall these defensive maneuvers by asking for the demon's name. The impure spirits dodge the question, however, by giving a number instead of a name: "My name is Legion ... for we are many" (5:9), the number in a Roman division (consisting of 5,000 to 6,000 foot soldiers and 120 horsemen). This number reveals that the man is captive to demons who, with military precision, have banded together (5:15) and are large enough in number "to drive 2,000 swine crazy."[70] It explains the switch to third person plural verbs and the use of the plural "impure spirits" (5:12–13).

Jesus' parable in Matt 12:43–45 and Luke 11:24–26 about demons going out of a person and wandering around until they find a place to inhabit suggests that impure spirits abhor a vacuum. A human host is best; wanting that, a bunch of pigs

---

65. Gundry, *Mark*, 251.

66. Donahue and Harrington, *Mark*, 165, argue that the verse is better translated to "connote a sense of past action that looks to the future": "for he was about to say to the man: 'Come out of this man, you evil spirit!'" Demons respond first to Jesus' presence (1:24; 9:20), and then he casts them out. This reading misconstrues Mark's confusing style of delayed explanations clauses.

67. The verb "to adjure" (*horkizein*) is used by some wandering Judean exorcists in Acts 19:13: "Some Jews who went around driving out evil spirits tried to invoke the name of the Lord Jesus over those who were demon-possessed. They would say, 'In the name of the Jesus whom Paul preaches, I command [adjure] you to come out.'" Gundry, *Mark*, 250, claims that the use of this word suggests that the demons are trying "to exorcise Jesus out of exorcising it."

68. See the use of cognates of this verb for eternal divine judgment in Matt 18:34 and Luke 16:23, 28.

69. Guelich, *Mark 1–8:26*, 279.

70. Minear, *Mark*, 74.

will do. The impure spirits therefore make a last-ditch attempt to avoid their fate by requesting to be sent into a huge herd of pigs feeding on the hillside. Jesus seems all too gracious in granting the request, but it leads to the surprise ending. Demons wreak havoc in whatever they inhabit, and the very thing the impure spirits wanted to prevent occurs. They "fall victim to their own designs and tumble headlong into chaos"[71] when the pigs "stampede, lemminglike, down the bank and into the waters, where both they and the evil spirits are destroyed."[72] The destructive power of the sea that almost swamped the disciples' boat now swallows up the pigs.[73] Jesus, who has just demonstrated his dominion over the sea (4:39, 41; cf. Pss 65:7; 106:9; 107:23–32), did not need to know the names of the impure spirits to drive them out. From a Jewish perspective, the pigs' plunge into the sea is fully merited.[74] A human being is cleansed, and impure spirits and unclean animals both are wiped out.[75]

After the destruction of the impure spirits, the focus turns back to the man, who now is fully clothed and quietly seated, the position of a disciple (5:15; see Luke 10:39; Acts 22:3). Informed about what had happened, the panicked community shows up and begs Jesus to leave their region. Perhaps they judge his continued

71. Robert G. Hamerton-Kelly, *The Gospel and the Sacred: Poetics of Violence in Mark* (Minneapolis: Fortress, 1994), 93.

72. Garland, *Mark*, 204–205. Some commentators provide a rationalistic explanation for the stampede by claiming it was caused when the demoniac began to scream and run frantically among the pigs causing them to scatter. The demons never leave quietly (1:26) and bring about self-destruction to whatever they inhabit. Lane, *Mark*, 186, comments: "It is their purpose to destroy the creation of God, and halted in their destruction of a man, they fulfilled their purpose with the swine." Some commentators also argue that the demons destroyed the pigs in a vengeful bid to turn the town against Jesus. If that were the case, they were successful.

73. Some have tried to make the account into a revolutionary moral tale about the Romans. Winter, *On the Trial of Jesus*, 180–81, pointed out that the ensigns of the tenth Roman legion, *Legio Decima Fretensis*, which was active in the Jewish War and destroyed Jerusalem in AD 70, bore the image of a wild boar. He suggested that the story derived from some Roman legionnaires taking a swim in the lake and drowning. John Dominic Crossan, *Jesus: A Revolutionary Biography* (San Francisco: Harper, 1994), 89–91, broadens this theory by arguing that the story derives from the colonial oppression of the Romans, which was incarnated individually as demonic possession. Markus Lau, "Die Legio X Fretensis und der Besessene von Gerasa: Anmerkungen zur Zahlenangabe 'ungefähr Zweitausend' (Mk 5,13)," *Bib* 88 (2007): 351–364, is the latest to make this argument. He offers a historical connection to the figure 2,000, describing the size of the herd of pigs, which was less than the normal complement of 5,000 to 6,000 soldiers in a legion. According to Josephus (*J.W.* 2.18.9 §§499–506), at the beginning of the Jewish War, a temporary task force of 2,000 soldiers was taken from the legions to deal with the threat of the Jewish insurgents. The twelfth legion is highlighted, however, and Josephus does not specifically mention the tenth legion. Lau nevertheless concludes that Mark portrays Jesus as a powerful warlord and liberator.

While it may be true that many in Israel chafed under the Roman oppression and would have liked nothing better than to see Roman legions driven into the sea, it is unlikely that Mark intended his story to convey such a point. If the striking parallel to this account in *T. Sol.* 11:1–6 was influenced by Mark, then the encoded political message was completely missed. "Legion" colorfully refers to a multitude (*T. Sol.* 5:1–13; 13:1–7). If it is independent of the gospels, then it provides evidence for the concept of a legion of demons without any hint of reference to Rome.

For Mark, the evil that the people of God face is far more serious than the colonial Roman powers, and Jesus is far more than a political emancipator. The clash is between God and Satan, not simply God and Rome, and this battle has cosmic and soteriological consequences. If the imagery is meant to be reminiscent of anything, Carey, *Jesus' Cry*, 76, takes it as alluding to "the conflict between the army of Pharaoh and the Israelite camp. In the Markan story, it is the demons who, like Pharaoh, enslave the Gerasene and meet their ruin by rushing down the hill and drowning in the sea."

74. In *T. Sol.* 5:11, a demon about to be exorcised pleads: "Do not condemn me to water." A land demon consigned to the sea presumably would be destroyed.

75. The Jewish antipathy toward pigs went deeper than simply the biblical injunction against eating pork (Lev 11:7–8). Antiochus Epiphanes brutally tried to eradicate peculiar Jewish practices (1 Macc 1:41–49) in a campaign of Hellenization, and pious Jews were forced to eat swine's flesh in a symbolic denial of their religion. A poignant account in 1 Macc 6:18–7:42 describes the valor of those who endured extreme torture, yet refused to yield to this demand. Swine became equated with paganism and persecution. Franz Annen, *Heil für die Heiden: Zur Bedeutung und Geschichte der Tradition von besessenen Gerasener (Mk 5,1–20 parr)* (FTS 20; Frankfurt am Main: Joseph Knecht, 1976), 107, 164, 173, notes that swine were linked to idolatry. Jews hearing this account would have hailed the pigs' destruction as a symbol of God's victory over evil, tyrannical powers but also would interpret it as Jesus' liberating a non-Jewish person from the evils of pagan idolatry.

presence to be bad for the pig business. Or, more likely, they are frightened by his holy power as were the disciples when they witnessed Jesus' divine power over the sea (4:40–41). Like Peter who implores Jesus to depart from him after witnessing the miracle catch of fish and cries, "Go away from me, Lord; I am a sinful man!" (Luke 5:8), the townspeople are uncomfortable in the presence of the holy (see Isa 65:5).[76] They are more like the pagan Philistines, however, who tried to rid themselves of the calamitous presence of the ark of God that was humbling their god Dagon and causing them all manner of afflictions (1 Sam 5:1–12). The Gerasenes tried to banish the suprahuman power of the demon-possessed man, and now they try to banish "the suprahuman power of Jesus."[77]

Jesus yields to the citizens' request to leave them, but he will not leave them without a witness to his power. The man begs Jesus to be allowed to be with him (5:18), which is the role of the disciple (3:14), but Jesus refuses him. It is the only request that he does not grant in this story. Mark gives no explanation for this refusal, but one can infer that Jesus intends to restore the man's identity by sending him back to his family (see Ps 68:6). He then reverses his customary demand of silence by giving him a commission. Apparently, Jesus did not fear stoking his popularity in this area and charges this man to proclaim how he has been delivered by God's mercy. Mark reports that in his obedience to this command he creates a bigger splash than the demons did, when they went careening into the sea, as the word about Jesus expands throughout the Decapolis and generates amazement (5:19–20).

A christological nuance that is easily overlooked appears in 5:19–20 over the ambiguity of the title "Lord." Jesus tells the man, "Go home to your own people and tell them how much *the Lord* has done for you, and how he has had mercy on you" (5:19). The exorcism is evidence of the power and mercy of the Lord God. Jesus is the one who delivered him, however, and the man announces "how much *Jesus* had done for him" (5:20). This change reflects Mark's Christology: where Jesus acts, God acts.[78] For Mark, both God and Jesus are Lord (1:3; 2:28; 11:3; 12:36–37).

5.3.4 Casting out the Demon of the Daughter of a Desperate Mother (Mark 7:24–30)

The report of Jesus' encounter with another pagan, a woman identified as a Greek hailing from Syrophoenicia (7:26), focuses on their dialogue (7:26–28). She worshipfully begs him to cast out a demon from her daughter. He gruffly refuses: "First let the children eat all they want ... for it is not right to take the children's bread and toss it to the dogs" (7:27). She comprehends the meaning of the parable, transcends any initial impulse to be scandalized by this presumed insult, accepts

76. Walter Schmithals, *Wunder und Glaube: Eine Auslegung von Markus 4, 35–6, 6a* (BibS[N] 59; Neukirchen-Vluyn: Neukirchener Verlag, 1970), 33, attributes their fear to being in the presence of the divine majesty.

77. Collins, *Mark*, 273.

78. Marcus, *Way*, 40. Marcus, *Mark 1–8*, 354, qualifies this statement that Mark does not mean that Jesus is God (see 10:18; 12:35–37; 13:32), but asserts, "neither can the two be absolutely separated."

Jewish priority—the bread rightly belongs to the children of Israel—and willingly humbles herself by assuming the status of a dog to get just a crumb of Jesus' saving power that will rescue her child from death. Like God, Jesus "reverses a previous decision"[79] and grants her petition. Mark concludes the scene by reporting that she went home and found the child lying in bed and the demon had been cast out (7:30). Jesus does not see the child, does not come into the presence of the demon, but is able to cast it out from a distance. Bovon claims that "in antiquity, miraculous healings were thought to be possible only through direct contact (cf. Luke 5:17 and 6:19)."[80] God, however, is able to heal by his word (Ps 107:20), and Jesus has the same power as God. Space and time make no difference for his great power.

5.3.5 Casting out the Demon of the Son of a Desperate Father (Mark 9:14–29)

Jesus' last exorcism is recorded in 9:14–29, when he descends from the mount where he was transfigured and reenters the everyday world of human and demonic discord. He finds his disciples embroiled in a quarrel with teachers of the law after the disciples have apparently bungled an attempt to cast out a demon in a young boy whose father had brought him to Jesus. The episode comprises four scenes. The first scene (9:14–19) begins with crowds gathered around the helpless disciples engaged in a debate and climaxes in Jesus' lament over this faithless generation. The second scene (9:20–24) brings Jesus face-to-face with a desperate father and culminates in the man's moving confession of his uncertain faith. In the third scene (9:25–27), Jesus wields divine power to drive out the impure spirit that has tormented the boy and raises him up after the demon has struck him down as dead. The final scene (9:28–29) returns to the disciples' failure to accomplish the exorcism themselves and connects that failure to their deficient life of prayer.

Jesus had deputized his disciples to cast out demons (3:15; 6:7), and they had success (6:13), but this difficult case thwarts them. Mark describes the boy's horrific afflictions in graphic detail four times. He is mute and racked by seizures that dash him to the ground, cause him to foam at the mouth and grind his teeth, and make him as stiff as a board. Often the impure spirit throws him into a fire or into water to destroy him (9:18, 20, 22, 26). The boy's father laments to Jesus, "I asked your disciples to drive out the spirit, but they could not" (9:18). The teachers of the law clashing with the disciples are no less impotent when confronted by the evil spirits that ruin human life, but the disciples' failure brings them public shame.

Jesus does not engage in dialogue with the spirit that possesses the boy since it is identified as, literally, "a mute spirit" (*pneuma alalon*, 9:17), which makes the boy both deaf and speechless (9:25). Jesus' presence throws demons into fawning submission or into a fury (1:26; 5:6–10). Upon seeing Jesus approach, this voiceless

79. Boring, *Mark*, 214.

80. François Bovon, *Luke 1* (trans. Christine M. Thomas; Hermeneia; Minneapolis: Fortress, 2002), 262.

spirit does not shout out Jesus' identity but reacts physically to the certainty of being cast out by throwing the lad into frightening convulsions (see 1:26) so that he falls to the ground and foams at the mouth.

Jesus directs questions to the distraught father who reveals the longtime severity of the problem that promised no cure. Witnessing his son's renewed torment, his belief that Jesus could do any better than his disciples falters. He has not lost all hope, however, and woefully entreats him, "If you can do anything, take pity on us and help us" (9:22). He believes that Jesus would like to do something if he could, but he does not firmly believe that he can do anything in such a grim case. His doubtful hope is similar to the leper's petition: "If you are willing, you can make me clean" (1:40). The leper considered Jesus' willingness the obstacle to healing; the father considers Jesus' lack of power to be the obstacle to healing.

The father's misgivings expressed in the phrase "If you can" meet with a sharp comeback from Jesus (9:23). Jesus repeats the doubt expressed by the father to challenge it.[81] Marshall paraphrases as follows: "So far as your 'if you can' is concerned, I tell you that all things are possible to the one who believes."[82] Jesus' expression of frustration, "You unbelieving generation ... how long shall I stay with you? How long shall I put up with you?" (9:19), echoes God's frustration with the wilderness generation (Num 14:11; Deut 32:20) and fits the pattern where Mark likens Jesus to God.[83]

Whom does Jesus have in mind when he speaks of "one who believes" (9:23)? Does he refer to the miracle worker's faith or to the faith of the one who seeks miracles? The answer is both, but Lane's paraphrase places far too much emphasis on the necessity of the father's faith: "As regards your remark about my ability to help your son, I tell you everything depends upon your ability to believe, not on mine to act."[84] Unlike the disciples, Jesus possesses unlimited power as God's Son.[85] It is Jesus' potent faith and divine power, not the father's admittedly flimsy faith, that accomplishes the exorcism. Boring is one of the few commentators, however, who recognizes, "The point is christological, not a general statement about the power of faith." He goes on to note that, typical of Mark, this outlook is expressed "dialectically, parabolically, ambiguously." He states:

> God is not one power among others, but the one God (2:7; 10:18; 12:29, 32), the Creator (10:6; emphatically 13:19) for whom nothing is impossible (10:27; 14:36).... As truly divine, God's power is at his [Jesus'] disposal. But also, as *truly* human, he is the one who manifests that ultimate trust in God that corresponds to human beings as their true selves, but which they have perverted as belonging to "this *un*believing generation."[86]

81. The literal rendering of the Greek reads "the if you can," with the definite article functioning either as the equivalent of a quotation mark or exclamation point.

82. Marshall, *Faith as a Theme*, 116–17.

83. Marcus, *Mark 8–16*, 653; Evald Lövestam, *Jesus and "This Generation": A New Testament Study* (trans. Moira Linnarud; ConBNT 25; Stockholm: Almqvist & Wiksell, 1995), 55.

84. Lane, *Mark*, 333.

85. Marcus, *Mark 8–16*, 652–53, observes that some ancient pagans identified similar symptoms as epilepsy and called it "the sacred disease" because they believed only a God could heal it (citing Aretaeus of Cappadocia, *Chronic Diseases* 1.4).

86. Boring, *Mark*, 274.

Jesus therefore chides the father for putting limits on what he can do to help.

The scene shifts in 9:25–27 to the exorcism. Jesus commands the demon to leave the boy and never enter him again (see Matt 12:43–45; Luke 11:24–26).[87] Demons never leave quietly. The impure spirit now is able to cry out, but Jesus has handled that before (1:23–24; 3:11; 5:7–8). It defiantly flails his young victim about in one last gasp of malice, and the boy became as dead so that many thought he had died. Jesus seizes his hand, as he did Jairus's dead daughter (5:41; see 1:31), and raises him up. Bolt highlights the twofold reference to his corpse-like state, "The boy looked so much like a corpse that many said, 'He's dead' " (9:26), which is balanced by a twofold reference to " 'resurrection' language," "he raised him" (*ēgeiren*, NIV, "lifted him to his feet") and "he was raised" (*anestē*, NIV, "he stood up"). He argues that after the raising of Jairus's daughter the audience would have "appreciated this scene, not just as an exorcism, but as an exorcism which brings the dead to life; a corpse to resurrection."[88] With divine power, Jesus drives the impure spirit out and raises up the boy to new life.

5.3.6 Casting out Demons in Jesus' Name: The Strange Exorcist (Mark 9:38–41)

In Mark 9:38–41, John jauntily announces to Jesus that they saw someone casting out demons in his name and "told him to stop, because he was not one of us" (or, "was not following us," 9:38). Mark has no interest in the details about the strange exorcist, who he was or how he came to know about the efficacious power of Jesus' name in casting out demons. He is simply identified as "someone."[89] Jesus chides the disciples not to hinder this one, and his explanation for condoning the exorcist's success in Mark's account is practical, not theological. They cannot use his name to do mighty works and then speak ill of him later or defame him for working by Beelzebul, as the teachers of the law from Jerusalem had done (3:22). The enemy is Satan, not those who are not one of us.

The name of Jesus is powerful, and Acts records several instances where persons are healed (Acts 3:6; 4:30; see Jas 5:14) or demons driven out (Acts 16:18) using the name of Jesus Christ. Mark does not clarify if there is a qualitative difference between the healing performed by a disciple in the name of Jesus and one by a nondisciple in the name of Jesus. The sons of a Jewish high priest named Sceva, however, failed to exorcise evil spirits when they tried to use the name of the Lord (Acts 19:13–17). They failed because the demons recognized that they were frauds who had no connection with Jesus.[90] The point is that Jesus' name is likened unto the name of God in its powerful efficacy to subdue demonic powers. But the passages in Acts reveal that it cannot be used as a magical incantation.

87. France, *Mark*, 369, notes that the Greek may be interpreted to draw attention to Jesus issuing an order, "It is *I* who command it."

88. Bolt, *Jesus' Defeat of Death*, 227–28.

89. Fleddermann, "The Discipleship Discourse (Mark 9:33–50)," 66.

90. Ernst Haenchen, *The Acts of the Apostles: A Commentary* (trans. R. McL. Wilson; Philadelphia: Westminster, 1971), 564, comments, "Jesus' name works only if he is called upon by a Christian."

5.4 Jesus' Power over Sin and Illness

Demons were able to cause illnesses, but demon possession is not to be equated with the illnesses that Jesus heals in Mark.[91]

5.4.1 Healing Fever (Mark 1:29–31)

After exorcising the impure spirit in the synagogue in Capernaum, Mark records Jesus immediately leaving and entering the house of Simon and Andrew. There he is informed that Simon's mother-in-law is in bed with a fever. The first four disciples Jesus called, Simon, Andrew, James, and John, are identified as present. The miracle receives short shrift in most commentaries. In the context of modern medicine, fever often can be remedied by taking a couple of aspirin, and some may wonder why something so seemingly insignificant and minor would be featured as Jesus' first recorded healing in the gospel.

Fever was not regarded simply as a symptom of a disease in Jesus' day but was considered to be an illness in and of itself.[92] In Lev 26:16 and Deut 28:22, fever is a punishment sent by God to those who violate the covenant. "Fevers" head the list of divine chastisements made by Philo (*Rewards* 143), and Philo regards it and other diseases as the wages of impiety and disobedience. A tradition appears in the Babylonian Talmud (*b. Ned.* 41a) from Rabbi Alexandri who said in the name of Rabbi Hiyya bar Abba:

> Greater is the miracle wrought for the sick than for Hananiah, Mishael and Azariah. [For] that of Hananiah, Mishael and Azariah [concerned] a fire kindled by man, which all can extinguish; whilst that of a sick person is [in connection with] a heavenly fire, and who can extinguish that?

The implied answer is that only God can extinguish this fire. This background heightens the significance of Jesus' first miracle of healing that otherwise might be dismissed as inconsequential. Jesus responds to Peter's mother-in-law's fever by seizing her hand and raising (*ēgeiren*) her up. The fever left her,[93] and she rose to serve them. He is able directly to extinguish a heavenly fire—something that only God can do.

91. See Reinhard von Bendemann, "Christus der Arzt. Krankheitskonzepte in den Therapieerzählungen des Markusevangeliums (Teil II)," *BZ* 54 (2010): 173–78.

92. Preuss, *Biblical and Talmudic Medicine*, 160. See John 4:52 and Acts 28:7–10 (which lists the illness as "fever *and* dysentery") for other instances of fever in the New Testament. See Konrad Weiss, "πυρέσσω, πυρετός," *TDNT*, 6:957. Bolt, *Jesus' Defeat of Death*, 76–88, cites numerous Greco-Roman sources that show "fever" to have been feared as a well-known killer. The rabbis also regarded fever as both demonic (caused, e.g., by dancing in the moonlight, *b. Ned.* 41a, *b. Giṭ.* 70a) and as a divine punishment (*b. Ber.* 34b = *y. Ber.* 9d, 21).

93. Weiss, "πυρέσσω, πυρετός," *TDNT* 6:958–59, thinks the language implies that a demonic element has been exorcised.

5.4.2 Healing Leprosy (Mark 1:40–45)

The healing of a leper by Jesus further illuminates Jesus' power as the Son of God.[94] He can overpower impure spirits and cleanse unclean diseases. A leper boldly approaches Jesus and declares, "If you are willing, you can make me clean."[95] A leper, like a corpse, was considered to be a prime source of ritual impurity and consequently was isolated. The law in Num 5:2–4 prescribes that lepers be put outside the camp to avoid defiling it. Josephus (*Ant.* 3.11.3 §264) confirms the widespread view that the leper was like a dead person. The cure of a leper was therefore akin to raising the dead.[96]

The OT accounts regarding leprosy imply that God is the one who causes this disease and that God alone can heal it (Exod 4:6). King Uzziah disobeyed God's laws, and the Lord smote him so that he was a leper to the day of his death (2 Kgs 15:5; 2 Chr 26:16–21). The king of Aram sent a letter, along with a considerable financial tribute, to the king of Israel asking him to heal his commander of his army, Naaman. When the king of Israel read the letter, he tore his robes and responded: "'Am I God? Can I kill and bring back to life? Why does this fellow send someone to me to be cured of his leprosy?'" (2 Kgs 5:7). This response, possibly alluding to Deut 32:39, assumes that only God can cure leprosy. Elisha intervened, "Have the man come to me and he will know that there is a prophet in Israel" (2 Kgs 5:8), but Elisha could not heal him either. As God's prophet, he can only send him to wash seven times in the Jordan river (5:10–14), assuming that God would intercede to heal. When the cure takes place, Naaman confesses: "Now I know that there is no God in all the world except in Israel" (5:15). He affirms that no god can cure leprosy except the God of Israel.

94. What is translated as "leprosy" in the Bible (Hebrew, *ṣāraʿat*; Greek, *lepra*) is not to be equated with what is now identified with leprosy (or Hansen's disease, named after the nineteenth-century Norwegian who identified the microorganism that causes it). The same term is applied to something affecting clothes (Lev 13:47–48) and houses (Lev 14:34–53), and the earliest physical evidence of this disease in Palestine is from the common grave of a Judean desert monastery dated around AD 600. Biblical leprosy included a number of curable and sometimes quite harmless skin diseases such as dermatosis, psoriasis, burns, alopecia (baldness that was suspicious), impetigo, eczema, gangrenous infections, favus, and leucoderma or white leprosy. Milgrom, *Leviticus 1–16*, 816–20, translates the Hebrew as "scale disease." See Wilhelm Ebstein, *Die Medizin im Neuen Testament und im Talmud* (Munich: Fritsch, 1903; repr. 1965); J. V. Kinnier-Wilson, "Leprosy in Ancient Mesopotamia," *RA* 60 (1966): 47–58; Calvin Wells, "Pseudopathology," in *Diseases in Antiquity: A Survey of the Diseases, Injuries and Surgery of Early Populations* (ed. Don Brothwell and A. T. Sandison; Springfield, IL: Charles C. Thomas, 1967), 17; E. V. Hulse, "The Nature of Biblical 'Leprosy' and the Use of Alternative Medical Terms in Modern Translations of the Bible," *PEQ* 107 (1975): 87–105; Gordon J. Wenham, *The Book of Leviticus* (NICOT; Grand Rapids: Eerdmans, 1979), 195–97; Joseph M. Baumgarten, "The 4Q Zadokite Fragments on Skin Disease," *JJS* 41 (1990): 159, 162; and Kenneth V. Mull and Carolyn Sandquist Mull, "Biblical Leprosy: Is It Really?" *BRev* 8 (April, 1992): 32–39, 62.

95. The primary concern about leprosy was the fact that it conveyed uncleanness. The phrase, "He is unclean," is a constant refrain in any Jewish text dealing with leprosy. It is the "uncleanness" that is contagious, not the disease. The tractate on leprosy in the *Mishnah* (*Negaʿim*) asserts that the rules concerning leprosy signs apply only to Israelites: "All can contact uncleanness from leprosy-signs excepting gentiles and resident aliens" (*m. Neg.* 3:1). The healing of leprosy in the gospels is not referred to as a healing but as a cleansing (see Matt 8:3, 10:8, 11:5; Mark 1:42; Luke 4:27, 7:22, 17:17). The only time the verb "to be healed" (ἰαθῆναι) is used to refer to a leper is in regard to the Samaritan in Luke 17:15. The Samaritan is not "cleansed" because his purity in relation to the Jewish ceremonial law would not have been recognized.

Only when a person is declared unclean after being examined by a priest is that one considered unclean. Therefore, in the *Sipra* to Leviticus 14:36, it is not recommended that a person be examined for the presence of the disease before a festival or a marriage celebration, or he or she could be forced to miss out. A wife of a leper was allowed to share exile with her husband, and they could and did cohabit (Uzziah's son, Jotham, was said to be born while Uzziah was leprous, according to *b. Moʿed Qaṭ.* 7b, *b. Ker.* 8b). Ideally, lepers were also permitted to come to the house of study as long as they entered first and left last and were separated from the rest by a wall ten handbreadths in height and four cubits in width (*m. Neg.* 13:12; *t. Neg.* 7:11). These measures were not designed to prevent catching the disease but to prevent catching the impurity.

96. Bolt, *Jesus' Defeat of Death*, 93–102, provides evidence from Greco-Roman sources that leprosy was suggestive of death.

Since it was also assumed that God is just and does not inflict injury to someone capriciously, leprosy was viewed as divine retribution for some sin.[97] One of the offerings required of the leper when cured of the disease was a guilt offering because of the guilt incurred by the sin that brought on the disease (Lev 14:10–32). The tattered clothing prescribed for the leper in Lev 13:45 identified one as a leper, but it was interpreted in the *Targum Onkelos* as a sign of mourning, presumably for the leper's sin that incurred this punishment.

The point of this brief excursus on leprosy is that before, during, and after the time of Jesus, Jews believed it to be inflicted by God as a punishment for sin. It had no medical remedy; it could only be healed by God. Josephus says that recovery from the distemper (whitening) comes from prayer to God (*Ant.* 3.11.3 §264). Priests had no power to heal it, only the know-how to identify it. This perspective highlights the christological features of this passage. When the leper implores Jesus, "If you are willing, you can make me clean," he must assume that Jesus is no ordinary mortal. He is not asking for him to declare him clean. This declaration required the consecration of temple rituals officiated by a priest (Lev 14:1–32). The leper believes that Jesus has the power of God to heal his disease because, like God (Wis 12:18), he is able to do as he wills.[98]

Jesus responds by stretching out his hand, reminiscent of the way God commands Moses and Aaron to stretch out the hand (see Exod 4:4; 7:19; 9:22; 14:16, 21, 26), touching him, saying, "I am willing," and commanding, "Be clean!" (1:41). He does not pray to God for healing, as Moses did in interceding to God to heal Miriam's leprosy (Num 12:13), nor does he send him to the Jordan to immerse himself seven times as Elisha commanded Naaman (2 Kgs 5:10). Instead, Jesus directly effects the cleansing of the leper by his word and touch. This scene shows that Jesus has the power of God.

Since leprosy was understood as a punishment for sin, the man's sin that brought about his condition also must be assumed to be forgiven by virtue of the fact that healing has taken place. Jesus could have said, "Your sins are forgiven," as "Be clean."[99] The cleansing is dependent on forgiveness.[100]

97. The conclusion of the Naaman story has Elisha's servant Gehazi stricken with leprosy and all of his descendants for wresting reward money from Naaman after Elisha had rejected it (2 Kgs 5:20–27). The rabbinic consensus was that the chief sin of which the leper was guilty was slander, which, according to one, was in the top four serious sins along with idolatry, immodesty, and bloodshed (*b. Sanh.* 74a). R. Joḥanan in the name of Joseph b. Zimri said, "Anyone who bears evil tales will be visited by leprosy." This saying contains a play on words between *mezora*, leper, and *mozi-shem-ra*, a slanderer before (*b. 'Arak.* 15b). The perception that a spiritual sin, such as slander, causes the affliction of leprosy derives primarily from the incident reported in Num 12:1–16, when Miriam and Aaron murmured against Moses because he had married a Cushite. God defended Moses, with whom God spoke face to face; and God's anger was kindled against both Miriam and Aaron. The result was that Miriam became leprous. Aaron interpreted this to be a punishment from God; she was as one who is stillborn (12:11–12). Moses beseeched God to heal Miriam (12:13); and God relented but required her to be shut out of the camp for seven days (12:14–15).

98. Pesch, *Markusevangelium*, 1:143.

99. Lev 14:18–22 prescribes a sin offering to make atonement for the one cleansed.

100. Edwin K. Broadhead, "Christology as Polemic and Apologetic: The Priestly Portrait of Jesus in the Gospel of Mark," *JSNT* 47 (1992): 24, misunderstands when he uses this passage to argue that Mark presents Jesus in a priestly role. He cites *m. Neg.* 3:1, "'All are qualified to inspect leprosy-signs, but only a priest may pronounce them clean or unclean.'" Jesus' command, "Be clean," does not pronounce him clean; it *cures* him of the disease. By contrast, priests have no power to heal, and Lev 13–14 does not describe a healing ceremony. It is a ceremony that is required *after* one has been cured, and it is the prerequisite for readmission into society (see *m. Neg.* 14:1–3). Priests can only determine whether one is free of the disease to reenter the camp and give their seal of approval after the obligatory sacrifices have been carried out.

Though the man is cured of his disease, he cannot go merrily on his way. He remains "unclean" until he is inspected and pronounced "clean" by a priest. He cannot be reintegrated into society until his cure is certified by prescribed temple sacrifices. Therefore, Jesus sends the man to the priest to be inspected and to go through the elaborate sacrificial rituals specified in Lev 14:1–32. Jesus adds that this sending to the priest is to be "a testimony to them" (Mark 1:44). Because leprosy was understood as a smiting dealt by God and that God alone could forgive and cleanse, the "testimony" conveys that Jesus possesses divine power to cleanse a leper by his own touch and his own word. One might place on the lips of the priests who hear this testimony the stunned question of the teachers of the law in the next scene (2:7), "Who can forgive sins and heal leprosy but God alone?"

5.4.3 Healing Paralysis and Forgiving Sins (Mark 2:1–12)

This passage forms a bookend with the exorcism of the impure spirit in the synagogue (1:21–28). Both miracles occur in Capernaum (1:21; 2:1), and Jesus is interrupted while speaking to the crowd (1:21; 2:2). The teachers of the law are mentioned in both scenes (1:22; 2:6–7). The issue of Jesus' authority comes to the fore in both passages (1:22, 27; 2:10), and the crowd responds to the miracle with amazement. They declare the newness of his authoritative teaching: "He even gives orders to impure spirits and they obey him!" (1:27). In 2:12, the crowds' amazement leads them to exclaim, "We have never seen anything like this!" and to glorify God. This refrain underscores the importance of the miracles Mark records in these opening chapters.

The healing of the paralytic is vividly depicted. His friends carry him to Jesus and are temporarily stymied by the crowd surrounding Jesus. The home is so jampacked that they cannot get through. Undeterred, they climb up on the roof, dig through it, and lower the man on his mat into the midst of the gathering. Jesus recognizes that only a determined faith (2:5) would have driven them to go to so much trouble. What is often overlooked is that faith in Mark is always faith in Jesus (5:34; 10:52). In the OT, however, faith is normally faith in God.[101]

Jesus responds to their faith by announcing to the paralytic, "Your sins are forgiven" (2:5). Haenchen comments that the four men did not bring their friend to have his sins forgiven him but to be healed.[102] This observation reflects a modern view of the relationship between sin and healing. No one in the narrative, however, expresses a belief that Jesus' declaration is irrelevant. The friends, the paralytic, and

101. Tait, *Jesus*, 97.

102. Haenchen, *Der Weg Jesu*, 101. Edwards, *Mark*, 77, argues that the phrase "your sins" means that Jesus is speaking of the man's specific sins and reflects Jesus' knowledge of his particular sins, which explains why he "explicitly correlates sin and infirmity" only in this healing. I would argue that the correlation between healing and forgiveness of sins is assumed in all of the healings, but it appears explicitly only here because the presence of the teachers of the law provides the occasion for Jesus' pronouncement that the Son of Man has the authority to forgive sins on earth. The worldviews and cultural practices found in the variety of extant Jewish literature, from the Old Testament, to intertestamental literature, to Qumran, to Josephus, to Philo, to the *Mishnah*, *Tosefta*, the halakic and haggadic *Midrashim*, the Jerusalem Talmud and the Babylonian Talmud—in other words, the Jewish foreground of the text—are crucial for understanding Jesus. Mark is not interested in explaining why people get sick but to present Jesus as the Son of God who has conquered principalities and powers, things present and things to come, things above the earth and things beneath the earth, and even death. He died for sinners so that their sins might be forgiven and receive salvation from God.

the crowd are silent. It was widely assumed that sin caused physical affliction and that God's forgiveness was required for healing (2 Chr 7:14; Pss 6:2; 30:2; 41:3–4; 103:3; Isa 19:22; 33:24; 38:16–17; 57:18–19; Hos 14:4; Sir 28:2–3; John 9:2–3). Mark records only the silent misgivings of the teachers of the law, who are aghast at the presumed blasphemy: "Why does this fellow talk like that? He's blaspheming! Who can forgive sins but God alone?" (2:6–7). They do not question what forgiving this man's sin might have to do with healing him, only Jesus' authority to do so.

The structure of the passage places the emphasis on the controversy:[103]

A Introduction: An overwhelming crowd gathered to hear Jesus speak the word (2:1–2)
 B Spiritual healing of a paralytic (2:3–5)
  C Controversy: Who can forgive sins but God alone? (2:6–10a)
 B′ Physical healing of a paralytic (2:10b–12a)
A′ Conclusion: An overwhelmed crowd giving glory to God (2:12b)

As experts in the law, the scribes' observation is not an interpretation open to debate.[104] It underscores the christological point Mark is making: God alone forgives sins (Exod 34:6–7; Isa 43:25; 44:22).[105] How dare Jesus presume to act in God's stead?

Jesus utters no intercessory prayer to God for forgiveness and healing. He completely bypasses any priestly atonement ritual. He is not taking the role of a priest who could pronounce the forgiveness of sins on the basis of repentance, restitution, and sacrifice.[106] He is not speaking on behalf of God as if he had "God's power of attorney."[107] Jesus remits sins on his own authority as if he were God.[108] Stegemann declares, "according to the Old Testament, no human being can grant forgiveness of sins, neither a priest nor a prophet, neither the Messiah nor the most righteous or holiest of all the pious, but always only God."[109] Jesus assumes this to be the case in 11:25: "When you stand praying, if you hold anything against anyone, forgive them, so that your Father in heaven may forgive you your sins." From the scribes'

103. Marshall, *Faith as a Theme*, 83–84.

104. The phrasing in Greek translated literally, "except the one God," is reminiscent of the Shema (Deut 6:4).

105. See Exod 34:9; Num 14:20; 2 Sam 12:13; 1 Kgs 8:30; Pss 32:1–5; 51:1–4; 103:2–3; 130:4; Isa 6:7; 55:7; Dan 9:9; Mic 7:18; Zech 3:4.

106. Contra Broadhead, "Christology as Polemic and Apologetic," 27. Jesus' pronouncement of forgiveness differs significantly from what appears, e.g., in Lev 4:26, 31, 35; 5:10, 13, 16, 18; 6:7. These passages describe a temple sacrifice and assert "the priest will make atonement on your behalf for the sin" (singular) and you will be forgiven. The priest does not forgive sins. A communal declaration of the forgiveness of sins occurs on the Day of Atonement (Lev 16:32–34; see also Ps 85:1–3), but it only comes after the sacrifice has been offered.

107. Davis, "'Who Can Forgive Sins but God Alone?'" 120, calls this "a christological minimalist way" of reading the text: "Jesus had little special status other than that of a passer-on of assurance of good news from God." He notes that this reading is belied by "the violent reaction of the scribes" in 2:7.

108. If Jesus is simply announcing the forgiveness of the man's sins, Collins, *Mark*, 185, notes that "there is no precedent for a human being making a simple declaration that God is at this moment forgiving another human being's sin." Edwards, "The Authority of Jesus," 223, notes that Nathan's announcement to David in 2 Sam 12:13, "The Lord has taken away your sin," invokes the power of God. By contrast, "Jesus presents himself as one who confidently stands in the place of God."

109. Stegemann, *The Library of Qumran*, 219. James D. G. Dunn, *Jesus, Paul, and the Law: Studies in Mark and Galatians* (Louisville: Westminster John Knox, 1990), 27, recognizes the "christological force" of the statements in 2:7 and 10 and maintains, "Jesus is able and has authority to forgive sins, not merely to declare them forgiven." No priest has that authority.

jaundiced perspective, presuming to forgive sins was a blasphemous arrogation of God's authority on Jesus' part.[110]

Jesus knows in his spirit that the teachers of the law are questioning and condemning his actions in their hearts (2:8). He does not simply read their body language; he reads their hearts. God is the one who knows hearts,[111] and Jesus does as well (see 8:17; 12:15). He perceives the faith of the ones conveying their friend, the sins of the paralytic, and the thoughts of his opponents. He does not refute their assertion that he acts in God's stead but answers their indictment with a riddling question of his own, "Which is easier: to say to this paralyzed man, 'Your sins are forgiven,' or to say, 'Get up, take your mat and walk'?" (2:9). One can "say" either easily, but the question is whether what one says has any concrete effect or not. Jesus is willing to demonstrate empirically that his words are valid.[112] The wording assumes a connection between sin and sickness and forgiveness.[113] It is not a matter of one being easier than the other.[114] The man cannot be healed without forgiveness of sin, and his healing is a sign of the forgiveness of his sins (see John 5:14).[115]

Jesus commands the paralytic to get up and walk so they might know that the Son of Man has authority to forgive sins on earth (2:10–11). The phrase "that you may know" (2:10, NRSV) is "used by God when about to perform his mighty acts before the obdurate Pharaoh."[116] When the man gets up and walks, the confirmation of his forgiven sins amazes everyone and prompts them to say, "We have never seen anything like this!" (2:12). They also have never read or heard anything like this from Scripture where a human on his own authority pronounces the forgiveness of sins. Jesus is shown to incarnate the words of Exod 15:26, "I am the LORD, who heals you," and Ps 130:3–4, "If you, LORD, kept a record of sins, Lord, who could stand? But with you there is forgiveness." Bultmann is right in stating that Mark presents Jesus as "the very Son of God walking the earth."[117] He is wrong, however, in concluding that Mark has dressed Jesus in a mythological garb borrowed from Hellenistic tradition. The issues in this story are Jewish issues with Jewish assumptions, and the miracles must have been the core of the traditions about Jesus from their beginning.

110. Blasphemy merits death (Lev 24:16), and the charge reappears at Jesus' interrogation before the high priest and the Sanhedrin and clinches his condemnation to death (14:64), a death that is a ransom for many (10:45).

111. Gundry, *Mark*, 113, lists a number of passages of Scripture to illustrate God's knowledge of human hearts to show that for Mark, "among Jesus' other powers is the power of clairvoyance which characterizes God himself." See 1 Sam 16:7; 1 Kgs 8:39; 1 Chr 28:9; Pss 7:9; 139:1–2; Jer 11:20; 17:9–10; Sir 42:18–20; Luke 16:15; Acts 1:24; 15:8; Rom 8:27; 1 Thess 2:4; Rev 2:23.

112. See Deut 18:22: "If what a prophet proclaims in the name of the LORD does not take place or come true, that is a message the LORD has not spoken. That prophet has spoken presumptuously, so do not be alarmed."

113. Paralysis also could be viewed as the punishment for sin (see Alcimus in 1 Macc 9:55 and Ptolemy IV Philopator in 3 Macc 2:21–23).

114. It is also not a matter of simply overcoming "a misplaced and exaggerated sense of guilt" that caused some kind of psychosomatic paralysis; see Hartman, *Mark*, 114.

115. This assumption is expressed in 4Q242, where Nabonidus, king of Babylon, was afflicted for seven years with a malignant inflammation, and an exorcist forgave his sin. This idea is also reflected in rabbinic literature. Rabbi Alexandri said in the name of R. Hiyya b. Abba: "A sick man does not recover from his sickness until all his sins are forgiven him, as it is written, 'Who forgiveth all thine iniquities, who healeth all thy diseases'" (quoting Ps 103:3; *b. Ned.* 41a). In a passage that seeks to explain why the prayer for forgiveness precedes the prayer for healing in the *Amidah*, Ps 103:3–4 is cited to prove "that redemption and healing come after forgiveness" (*b. Meg.* 17b).

116. Tait, *Jesus*, 98. See Exod 8:22; 9:14, 29; 10:2; 11:7; see 31:13. Tait concludes that Jesus "is here being presented as one who shares the divine functions if not the divine being itself."

117. Bultmann, *History of the Synoptic Tradition*, 240–41.

In the OT "healing was expected to accompany forgiveness and restoration of God's people."[118] Isaiah promised: "For the LORD is our judge, the LORD is our lawgiver, the LORD is our king; it is he who will save us.... No one living in Zion will say, 'I am ill'; and the sins of those who dwell there will be forgiven" (Isa 33:22, 24; see also Jer 31:34; Mic 7:18). The coming of the kingdom of God that Jesus preaches (Mark 2:2; cf. 1:14–15) ushers in the forgiveness of sins that brings this promised healing of the ill. This incident reveals once again that Jesus as the Son of God acts and speaks like God in announcing the forgiveness of sins and effecting healing. I agree completely with Davis's conclusion, which indirectly supports how vital it is to recognize enacted Christology in the narrative:

> There is nothing in this text that expresses the language of later creedal orthodoxy. There is nothing here about persons or natures or essences or hypostatic unions. Not everything that Christians want to say about Jesus is implicit in this text. Still, it is clear that Mark 2:1–12 is and ought to be one of the texts Christians take into consideration in doing Christology. In this text, Jesus seems to be giving himself such authority as to be setting himself on a par with God. His willingness to offer forgiveness was surely one of the things about Jesus that made such an impression on early believers that they reached the conclusion that he was divine.[119]

5.4.4 Raising the Dead (Mark 5:21–43)

When Jesus returns from a jaunt to the other side of the lake, a ruler of the synagogue named Jairus immediately falls before Jesus' feet and entreats him to come to lay hands on his sick daughter that she might be saved and live (5:22–23). Jesus consents, but the emergency dash to the girl's bedside is interrupted by an anonymous woman who touches Jesus' garments as he passes by in hopes that it would restore her to health. She has suffered from uterine bleeding for twelve years and has become impoverished and made worse by the fruitless remedies of physicians. Her hemorrhage makes her ritually impure (see Lev 15:25–30, which refers to an abnormal discharge of blood other than the regular menstrual cycle).[120] The story of Jairus and his daughter wraps around the story of the healing of this woman. The focus is on the faith of these two persons desperately seeking healing, who come from opposite ends of the social, economic, and purity scales, and not on the christological implications of the healing, though the healings do have a christological subtext.

The woman has wasted her living on futile cures from physicians. The reference to physicians may simply underscore her desperation and add another facet to her plight: she is destitute.[121] But references to physicians elsewhere in Jewish literature

118. Roy E. Ciampa and Brian S. Rosner, *The First Letter to the Corinthians* (Pillar; Grand Rapids: Eerdmans, 2010), 580, citing Deut 32:39; 2 Chr 7:14; Job 5:18; Pss 41:4; 103:3; 107:20; 147:3; Isa 6:10; 19:22; 29:18; 30:26; 35:5–6; 42:4–6; 53:5; 57:18–19; 58:8; 61:1; Jer 30:17; 33:6; Ezek 47:12; Hos 6:1; 7:1; 14:4; Mal 4:2; *2 Bar.* 73:1–2; and *1 En.* 96:1, 3.

119. Davis, "'Who Can Forgive Sins but God Alone?'" 123.

120. The tractate in the Mishnah on the menstruant is entitled *Niddah*, which means "banished." See Hodges and Poirier, "Jesus as the Holy One of God," 152–64.

121. According to Sir 10:10, "a long illness baffles the physician."

highlight their powerlessness to heal in contrast to the Lord's power. Among the many foibles of King Asa listed in 2 Chr 16, the last, which seems anticlimactic, notes that when he was severely diseased in his feet he did not seek the Lord, but sought help only from physicians (16:12). Tobit went to physicians to be healed from a white film on his eyes caused by sparrow droppings, "but the more they treated me with ointments the more my vision was obscured by the white films, until I became completely blind" (Tob 2:10). He turns to the Lord and prays, and the angel Raphael is sent by God to heal him (Tob 3:17).

Drained of whatever assets she had by the physicians, this destitute and forlorn woman turns to Jesus for healing and touches his garment, which is mentioned four times in 5:27, 28, 30, 31. She is not the first or the only one to do so (see 3:10; 6:56). When she touches Jesus, her hemorrhage stops at once. Just as immediately, Jesus knew that power had gone forth from him, and he mystifies the disciples by asking who in the throng pushing around him had touched him. She has a flow of blood that drains life; he has a flow of positive power that restores life.[122] Her touch does not contaminate Jesus but instead cures the woman. The power that heals her "had gone out from him"; it does not come "through him" or from his garments.[123] The grammar implies, as Boring comments, that Jesus "himself is the source of the power, not merely its vehicle—he does not pray to someone else buts acts on his own. It is not the 'power of faith' but the divine 'power of Jesus' that heals."[124]

This does not mean that Jesus experiences a sudden "loss of power" but that the power went out from him. That power is assumed by Mark to be inexhaustible simply because it is the power of God.[125] Jesus has the power to raise Jairus's daughter from the dead immediately after this miracle and does not need to recharge. Recognizing what had happened, the woman's "trembling with fear" (5:33) is the standard response to an epiphany in Scripture.[126] Hodges and Poirier argue that the woman's terror stems from the realization that as someone impure she has touched a holy object, which can result in destruction (see 1 Sam 6:13–20; 2 Sam 6:1–7/1 Chr 13:1–10; Isa 6:1–7). Miller contends that since Jesus is anointed by the Holy Spirit (1:10) and is the Holy One of God (1:24), "the woman risks her life in approaching Jesus." Because she is impure, "she may be destroyed by coming into contact with the holy."[127] But instead of being destroyed, she is healed. When she publicly admits that she was the one who touched him, Jesus tells her, "Your faith has healed you. Go in peace and be freed from your suffering" (5:34). Hodges and Poirier claim that her healing "signifies a new relation between impure humanity and the holy.

122. See Candida R. Moss, "The Man with the Flow of Power: Porous Bodies in Mark 5:25–34," *JBL* 129 (2010): 515–19.

123. Hodges and Poirier, "Jesus as the Holy One of God," 184, observe, "The way in which Jesus' healing power flows into the woman—even without his initially knowing it!—is similar to how her ritual impurity was imagined to flow from her into whomever she touched." Jesus' healing power as the Holy One of God (1:24) prevails over impurity.

124. Boring, *Mark*, 160. This does not mean that faith is inconsequential. Jesus' power and faith in Jesus' power go together (6:1–6a). See below on "faith."

125. Hodges and Poirier, "Jesus as the Holy One of God," 177, n. 79.

126. Lohmeyer, *Markus*, 130; Marcus, *Mark 1–8*, 359–60 (citing Gen 15:12; 28:17; Judg 6:22–23; 4 Macc 4:10; Phil 2:12).

127. Susan Miller, *Women in Mark's Gospel* (JSNTSup 259; London/New York: T&T Clark, 2004), 53.

One can approach the holy in an impure condition if one has the necessary faith. The holy still destroys the impurity, but faith preserves the one bearing impurity from destruction."[128]

The dreaded news comes to the frantic father that his daughter has died while Jesus was sidetracked by his attention to this woman. The bearers of the bad news add, "Why bother the teacher anymore?" (5:35). Meier comments: "The subliminal message here is that Jesus is only a teacher, and death marks the limit of whatever power he may have."[129] Jesus overhears the conversation and encourages the father to have faith as they continue on to the home. When he arrives, he reproaches the gathered mourners making a tumult, "Why all this commotion and wailing? The child is not dead but asleep" (5:39). They know death when they see it and can only laugh at his naïveté.[130] He calls it "sleep," however, because he "wills in this particular case to make death as impermanent as sleep by raising the girl to life."[131] With only the parents, Peter, James, and John allowed to be present, Jesus grasps the girl's hand to raise her up, saying "*Talitha koum.*" By translating this bit of Aramaic, "Little girl, I say to you, get up!"[132] Mark clarifies that it is an ordinary phrase and not some magical incantation. His words had an immediate effect: she "stood up."[133]

One puzzles why Marcus uses the phrase "restored to the land of the living by Jesus' strong, Orpheus-like grasp" to describe what Jesus does.[134] Orpheus tried to rescue his wife Eurydice, from Hades, but she slipped from his grasp back into the netherworld when he looked back just before reaching the sunlit world. Scripture provides more apt metaphors. God is the one who has power over life and death (Deut 32:39) and who raises the dead.[135] God seizes the hand: "For I am the LORD your God who takes hold of your right hand and says to you, 'Do not fear; I will help you'" (Isa 41:13; see 42:6; Ps 73:23). Sirach extols the wondrous deeds of the prophet Elijah, "You raised a corpse from death and from Hades, by the word of the Most High" (Sir 48:5). Elijah implored God to restore life to the son of the widow from Zarephath, stretching himself upon the child three times (1 Kgs 17:17–24). Jesus raises a corpse without appealing to God by seizing her hand and speaking his own word, "Get up." Like God (Acts 26:8; Heb 11:19), Jesus is able to raise people even from the dead.

Jesus commands them to give her something to eat so that it will be clear that she is not an apparition, but the "strict orders not to let anyone know about this" (5:43) seems most odd. How will they keep this miracle quiet? It is possible that those outside will conclude that Jesus was right and that indeed she was only asleep. But

128. Hodges and Poirier, "Jesus as the Holy One of God,"181. Jesus sends the healed woman, identified as "daughter," on her way, just as he sent the healed paralytic, identified as "son" (2:5), on his way (2:11).

129. John P. Meier, *A Marginal Jew: Rethinking the Historical Jesus* (New York: Doubleday, 1994), 2:786.

130. In Mark's day, when Christians confessed that Jesus is not dead but risen, they may have met with the same derision (see Acts 17:32; 26:8).

131. Meier, *A Marginal Jew*, 2:844, n. 26.

132. The verb translated "get up" is also used in Mark to refer to the resurrection from the dead (6:14, 16; 12:26; 14:28; 16:6).

133. The verb translated "stood up" also means "to raise" and is used elsewhere in Mark to refer to Jesus' resurrection (8:31; 9:9, 31; 10:34; see also 9:10; 12:25).

134. Marcus, *Mark 1–8*, 372.

135. See Acts 3:15; 4:10; 5:30; 10:40; 13:30, 37; Rom 4:24; 8:11; 10:9; 1 Cor 6:14; 15:15–20; 2 Cor 1:9; 4:14; Gal 1:1; Eph 1:20; Col 2:12; 1 Thess 1:10; Heb 11:19; 1 Pet 1:21.

the silence is necessary, because the timing for belief in the miracle of resurrection must wait until Jesus is himself raised from the dead (9:9). Now, the parents and their daughter receive a temporary reprieve from death. Mark would recognize with Paul that Jesus' death and resurrection is the firstfruits of the resurrection (1 Cor 15:20) that opens the door for others to be raised in Christ eternally.

Boring comments on the relationship of the two stories, the healing of the woman with flow of blood and the raising of the young girl whom Jesus raises up from death. Both incidents have to do with the human "condition of mortality."[136] This reflection is obvious in the case of the young girl. Understanding the Jewish perspective on the woman's chronic loss of blood, however, sharpens this observation that her illness is linked to death. Milgrom explains that the biblical laws on bodily impurities focus on four phenomena: death, blood, semen, and scale disease. The "common denominator is death." He comments, "Vaginal blood and semen represent the forces of life; their loss – death"; and "the wasting of the body, the common characteristic of all biblically impure skin diseases, symbolizes the death process as much as the loss of blood and semen."[137] Given this biblical viewpoint, both stories show that Jesus has the power to reverse the tide of death.

5.4.5 The Healing of a Deaf and Mute Man (Mark 7:31 – 37)

The healing of the man who was deaf and could hardly talk is one of the rare incidents that is recorded only by Mark. It may be that the graphic details of Jesus putting his fingers in the deaf man's ears, spitting and touching his tongue, looking up to heaven, sighing deeply, and uttering healing words in Aramaic, "*Ephphatha!*" which Mark translates, "Be opened!" led Matthew and Luke to omit this account because of the resemblance to magical techniques. For Mark, it is another miracle that shows Jesus' divine power as the Son of God.

The miracle of healing a deaf and mute man harks back to God's declaration, "Who gave human beings their mouths? Who makes them deaf or mute? Who gives them sight or makes them blind? Is it not I, the Lord?" (Exod 4:11). God alone gives hearing, speech, and sight. In Isa 35:4 – 6, God promises to come, save the people, and remedy their physical and spiritual disabilities: "Then will the eyes of the blind be opened and the ears of the deaf unstopped. Then will the lame leap like a deer, and the mute tongue shout for joy."[138] Jesus is portrayed as doing what God will do in his eschatological coming.

The people respond to this miracle with overwhelming amazement (see Isa 29:14). They score the point in their jubilation: "He has done everything well. He even makes the deaf hear and the mute speak" (7:37). This cry echoes Gen 1:31: "God saw all that he had made, and it was very good." Jesus again is to be seen doing what God does.

136. Boring, *Mark*, 157.

137. Milgrom, *Leviticus 1 – 16*, 893.

138. The Greek word translated "could hardly talk" (*mogilalos*) in 7:32 is a rare word that appears only here in the New Testament and in the LXX of Isa 35:6, and clearly echoes that passage.

5.5 THE MIRACULOUS FEEDING OF THOUSANDS (MARK 6:30–44; 8:1–10)

After the disciples report on their successful mission trip (6:7–13, 30), Jesus seeks to retreat to a deserted place with them to get some rest (6:31–32). The crowd races around the lake and beats the boat to its destination, further proof of Jesus' immense, superstar popularity (6:33). Jesus responds to their relentless pursuit with compassion "because they were like sheep without a shepherd," and he teaches them (6:34).

The simile of the lost sheep is unexpected. It is mentioned and then dropped. But it recalls Ezek 34.[139] God directly intervenes because the shepherds of Israel have fed themselves rather than the sheep and left them to fend for themselves against ravenous wild animals. The result is that they were scattered across the landscape (Ezek 34:2–10). The Lord God responds,

> "I myself will search for my sheep and look after them ... I will tend them in a good pasture, and the mountain heights of Israel will be their grazing land. There they will lie down in good grazing land, and there they will feed in a rich pasture on the mountains of Israel. I myself will tend my sheep and have them lie down, declares the Sovereign LORD." (Ezek 34:11, 14–15)

God will feed his flock like a shepherd (Isa 40:11). It is not an insignificant detail that Jesus commands that the scattered sheep be ordered in companies and made to recline on the "green grass" (6:39), which recalls Ps 23:1–2, the Lord as shepherd "makes me lie down in green pastures."

This background sets the scene for the miraculous provision of food. They begin with hardly anything and end up with enough to satisfy five thousand and with an abundance left over. Many, influenced by John, see the miraculous feedings as foreshadowing the Lord's Supper. The mention of the meager quantity of fish—two in 6:38, and "a few small fish" in 8:7—that were multiplied as part of the meal that fed the large crowd, however, would seem to call into question that connection. The fish, mentioned four times in the account of first feeding (6:38, 41, 43) and once in the second feeding (8:7), do not factor in the Lord's Supper. Achtemeier argues that Mark added the fish "to *de-emphasize* the eucharistic reflections in the two feeding accounts."[140]

In my opinion, the mention of the fish in the feeding of a Jewish crowd is made prominent because it would elicit memories of the Israelites' grumbling in the wilderness. They moan, "If only we had meat to eat! We remember the fish we ate in Egypt at no cost" (Num 11:4b–5a), and now we only see this manna (11:6). Moses complained to God about all the complaining and asked, "Where can I get meat for all these people? They keep wailing to me, 'Give us meat to eat!'" (11:13). God

139. See also Num 27:17; 1 Kgs 22:17; 2 Chr 18:16; Zech 10:2.

140. Paul J. Achtemeier, "The Origin and Function of the Pre-Marcan Miracle Catenae," *JBL* 91 (1972): 220. Richard Hiers and Charles Kennedy, "The Bread and Fish Eucharist in the Gospels and Early Christianity," *PRSt* 3 (1976): 21–48, contend that the fish motif was subsequently muted in the various accounts because it became an "embarrassment" to those who did not understand how fish were connected to the Eucharist.

repeats their grievance: "If only we had meat to eat! We were better off in Egypt!" and then says that they will get meat to eat and that Moses should make preparations (11:18–20). Moses raises objections: "Here I am among six hundred thousand men on foot, and you say, 'I will give them meat to eat for a whole month!' Would they have enough if flocks and herds were slaughtered for them? Would they have enough if all the fish in the sea were caught for them?" (11:21–22). The Lord then provided as he promised (11:31–32). Like God, Jesus miraculously provides food for the people in the wilderness in the face of the worried concerns of his disciples so that everyone is satisfied.[141]

5.6 MIRACLES OF DIVINE EPIPHANY

The miracles of divine epiphany on the sea are performed only for the benefit of the disciples and not for the uncommitted crowd.[142] Meier uses the word "epiphany" as an "umbrella-term signifying a striking, extraordinary, and temporary appearance of a divine or heavenly figure in the earthly realm, often to a select individual or group of people for the purpose of communicating a message."[143] The message is that Jesus is the divine Son of God, who belongs to both the human and celestial realm.

5.6.1 Power Over a Storm (Mark 4:35–41)

Jesus has chosen disciples to follow him, and they obey his command to embark on a small flotilla of boats to sail across to the other side of the lake.[144] Mark writes that the disciples "took him along ... in the boat." The fishermen were the skilled seafarers, but "ironically, they are the ones terrified by the unexpected storm, while Jesus, the carpenter (6:3), sleeps serenely on a sandbag used for ballast (translated 'cushion') in the stern."[145] Jesus' peaceful repose even during a raging storm churning the sea that fills the boat with water may be a sign of his trust in God (Job 11:18–19; Pss 3:5; 4:8; 121:3–4; Prov 3:23–26) and contrasts with the terror of the disciples. Batto, however, argues that rest is a divine prerogative and that sleeping is a symbol of divine rule in ancient Near Eastern literature. Isaiah 51:9–10 provides an interesting backdrop to this story:

> Awake, awake, arm of the LORD,
> clothe yourself with strength!
> Awake, as in days gone by,
> as in generations of old.

141. Ernest R. Martinez, "Identity of Jesus in Mark," *Comm* 1 (1974): 331, notes that the Western mind asks, "What happened?" but the Eastern mind asks, "What does it mean?" The disciples knew what happened at the two miraculous feedings, but they did not know what they meant (6:52; 8:14–21).

142. See Ernest Best, *Following Jesus: Discipleship in the Gospel of Mark* (JSNTSup 4; Sheffield: JSOT, 1981), 231.

143. Meier, *A Marginal Jew*, 2:996, n. 118.

144. The "other boats with him" (4:36) do not factor in the story, and their mention, according to Collins, *Mark*, 258, "may be inspired" by Ps 107:23: "Some went out on the sea in ships." If correct, the psalm provides important context for this miracle.

145. Garland, *Mark*, 191.

Was it not you who cut Rahab to pieces,
who pierced that monster through?
Was it not you who dried up the sea,
the waters of the great deep,
who made a road in the depths of the sea
so that the redeemed might cross over?[146]

Jesus' sleep is not simply a sign of exhaustion or trust in God but can indicate his divine sovereignty.[147]

The disciples misinterpret Jesus' sleep as indifference to their plight. They awaken Jesus with a wail of supplication. It takes the form of a question that expects the answer "Yes" as it is phrased in Greek: "You do care that we are perishing, don't you?" (4:38).[148] The disciples do not ask Jesus to call on God to save them as the frightened captain implored Jonah in the storm: " 'How can you sleep? Get up and call on your god! Maybe he will take notice of us so that we will not perish' " (Jonah 1:6).[149] Their cry to Jesus echoes the psalmist's exultation of God's steadfast love and redemption: "They cried out to the LORD in their trouble," and "he stilled the storm to a whisper; the waves of the sea were hushed" (Ps 107:28–30; see also Pss 65:7; 89:9; 93:3–4). Awakened, Jesus rebukes the wind in the same way he rebukes demons to be silent (1:25; 3:12; 9:25). The memorable phrase from the KJV, "Peace, be still," hardly captures the fierce potency of Jesus' word that transforms a great storm (4:37) into a great calm (4:39).[150] Waves do not suddenly stop after a storm passes, and the immediate calm is miraculous.

The disciples are terrified by the raging storm but are no less terrified by the calm. They ask, "Who is this? Even the wind and the waves obey him!" (4:41). The question "What is this?" (1:27) now shifts to "Who is this?" The disciples have seen Jesus' powerful miracles before, but the calming of the sea "strikes them with terror," which suggests that "this particular deed has implications for Jesus' identity that go far beyond his being a miracle worker or a prophet."[151] Collins avers that "Jesus is portrayed not so much as a human being who has trust in God's power to save, but

146. See also Ps 44:23–24.

147. Bernard F. Batto, "The Sleeping God: An Ancient Near Eastern Motif of Divine Sovereignty," *Bib* 68 (1987): 153–77.

148. Garland, *Mark*, 91, notes, "There is bitter irony that these same disciples will go to sleep on him in his hour of terror in Gethsemane unmoved by his pleas for them to watch and pray with him (14:37, 40, 41)."

149. Some see a closer connection to the Jonah story because of what I would consider coincidental parallels that are naturally part of stories of storms at sea. Gundry, *Mark*, 245–46, argues that "Mark uses the OT rather by way of analogy" and points out significant differences between the accounts in Mark and Jonah. Jesus is not fleeing the presence of the Lord, and there is no hint that the Lord sends the storm as some warning (Jonah 1:3–4, 10). Jesus is asleep in the stern not in the hold (1:5). The disciples do not battle the storm as the sailors on Jonah's boat did or cast lots to see who was the cause of the calamity (1:5, 7). The calm comes after Jonah is thrown overboard, not when he speaks (1:15). Jesus does not pray to God but addresses the sea directly, and his word creates the great calm. The sailors become frightened because this prophet serves the God who made the sea and the dry land (1:9–10). The disciples' fear stems from Jesus' Godlike control of the sea.

150. James Kallas, *The Significance of the Synoptic Miracles* (London: SPCK, 1961), 78, notes that the miracle is not against nature so much as it is against Satan, who would destroy Jesus' followers and their faith. Jesus' dominion over the wind and the sea points to what it will be like when "the rule of Satan is no more." In John's vision of the new heaven and earth, the sea is no more (Rev 21:1; see 4:6; 15:2; 20:13). On the historicity of the miracles, see Craig S. Keener, *Miracles: The Credibility of the New Testament Accounts* (2 vols.; Grand Rapids: Baker, 2011).

151. Watts, *New Exodus*, 156, n. 98.

as a divine being."[152] The audience schooled in Scripture can supply the answer to their awestruck question. He is the Son of God, who has mastery over the sea, the place of chaos and evil, as God does. He has divine power to do what only the God who created the sea can do (see Gen 8:1; Job 26:12; 38:8–11; Pss 65:7; 74:13–14; 89:9; 93:3–4; 104:5–9; 106:9; 107:23–32; 114:3; Isa 50:2; Nah 1:4; *Pr. Man.* 1:3; *T. Adam* 3:1).[153] Lane comments: "The subduing of the sea and the wind was not merely a demonstration of power; it was an epiphany, through which Jesus was unveiled to his disciples as the Savior in the midst of intense peril."[154]

Comparing Isa 43:1–10 with this story illuminates Mark's high Christology. Jesus is doing in Mark's story what Isaiah proclaims that God promises to do.

Isaiah 43	**Mark**
v. 1: But now, this is what the LORD says—he who *created* you, Jacob, he who formed you, Israel: "*Do not fear,* for I have redeemed you; *I have summoned you by name*; you are mine."	Jesus has *created* the twelve (Mark 3:14) and summoned disciples by name (1:16, 20; 2:14; 3:16–19). He said to his disciples, "*Why are you so afraid*? Do you still have no faith?" (4:40)
v. 2: "*When you pass through the waters,* I will be with you; and when you pass through the rivers, they will not sweep over you. *When you walk through the fire,* you will not be burned; the flames shall not set you ablaze."	Jesus is with them when they pass through the waters (4:36) and saves them from peril at sea (4:39). The assurance that they will not be harmed by fire is echoed in 9:49, "*Everyone will be salted with fire.*"
v. 3: "For I am the LORD your God, the Holy One of Israel, your Savior; I give Egypt for your *ransom*, Cush and Seba in your stead. v. 4: Since you are precious and honored in my sight, and because I love you, I will give people in exchange for you and nations in exchange for your life."	Jesus announces to the disciples that he gives his life as a *ransom* for many (10:45).

152. Collins, *Mark*, 260. Donahue and Harrington, *Mark*, 161, recognize that the resonances with God's power in the Old Testament "give a strong christological thrust to the passage. Jesus possesses the same power over the forces of chaos that characterizes the Lord of hosts."

153. It is presumed that only God (and in the Greco-Roman world, the gods) could stir up the sea and calm it (see Plutarch, *Def. orac.* 426C). The persecutor of the Jews, Antiochus Epiphanes, was struck by God "with a pain in his bowels, for which there was no relief, and with sharp internal tortures" and later fell out of his chariot and injured every limb of his body (2 Macc 9:5, 7). The author of 2 Maccabees contemptuously comments: "Thus he who only a little while before had thought in his superhuman arrogance that he could command the waves of the sea, and had imagined that he could weigh the high mountains in a balance, was brought down to earth and carried in a litter, making the power of God manifest to all" (9:8). This conviction may explain the odd grammar of the Greek text in Mark 4:1 that is covered up by the translation, "he got into a boat and sat in it out on the lake." It literally reads that Jesus "entered into a boat, and sat in the sea" (ASV). Marcus, *Mark 1–8*, 291, and John Drury, *The Parables in the Gospels: History and Allegory* (New York: Crossroad, 1985), 49, suggest an echo of Ps 29:3, 10 with its celebration of the voice of the Lord over mighty waters, and the Lord sitting "enthroned over the flood," and "enthroned as King forever."

154. Lane, *Mark*, 178.

Isaiah 43	Mark
v. 5: "*Do not be afraid*, for I am with you; I will bring your children from the east and gather you from the west."	Jesus tells the synagogue ruler not to be afraid for his daughter (5:36); he rebukes the cowardice of the disciples and tells them not to be afraid (6:50).
v. 8: "Lead out those who have eyes but are blind, who have ears but are deaf."	See 4:12; 8:18; Jesus heals two blind men (8:22–26; 10:46–52) and heals a deaf man (7:31–37).
v. 10: "You are my witnesses," declares the LORD, "and my servant whom I have chosen, so that you may know and believe me and understand that *I am he*. Before me no god was formed nor will there be one after me."	When Jesus comes to the disciples walking on the waves, he announces, "*It is I*!" (6:49–50).

The conclusion in Isa 43:11–12 proclaims, "'I, even I, am the LORD, and apart from me there is no savior. I have revealed and saved and proclaimed—I, and not some foreign god among you. You are my witnesses,' declares the LORD, 'that I am God.'" Mark would have the audience draw the same conclusion about Jesus as the Son of God. Jesus is the one who delivers his people, and in his hands they are safe.

5.6.2 Walking on the Sea and Intending to Pass By (Mark 6:45–52)

After feeding the five thousand, Jesus immediately compels the disciples to get into the boat to set a course for Bethsaida (6:45). Mark does not explain why Jesus made the disciples weigh anchor and leave (contrast John 6:15) and simply reports Jesus bidding farewell to them, sending the crowd away, and ascending the mountain to pray alone (6:45–46; see 1:35). Later, Jesus sees the disciples battling both fatigue and the wind as they ply their oars but make little headway on the lake. One must assume that Jesus has supernatural powers to see them so far away in the darkness (6:48). He then comes to them supernaturally during the fourth watch of the night (3:00 a.m. to 6:00 a.m.) by walking on the sea. The wind poses no obstacle to Jesus as he strides across the sea.

Jesus' appearance is not a frivolous stunt but recalls God's mastery over the waters of chaos as Creator and Savior. Walking on the sea is something that ordinary mortals do not do.[155] According to Scripture, only God is able to tread the waves (Job 9:8; 38:16; Ps 77:19; Isa 43:16; Sir 24:5–6).[156] Since many may not be familiar with these passages, it justifies citing them:

155. See David E. Garland, *Reading Matthew* (Macon, GA: Smyth & Helwys, 2000), 157–60, for an interpretation of Peter's failed attempt to walk on water in Matt 14:22–33.

He alone stretches out the heavens and treads on the waves of the sea. (Job 9:8)
Have you journeyed to the springs of the sea or walked in the recesses of the deep? (Job 38:16)
Your path led through the sea, your way through the mighty waters, though your footprints were not seen. (Ps 77:19)
This is what the LORD says—he who made a way through the sea, a path through the mighty waters. (Isa 43:16)
Alone I compassed the vault of heaven and traversed the depths of the abyss. Over waves of the sea, over all the earth, and over every people and nation I have held sway. (Sir 24:5–6, NRSV)[157]

The image of God trampling the sea with horses in Hab 3:15 conveys God's power to control the turmoil of the seas to save his people Israel (see also Isa 51:10).

When Jesus comes walking on the water to the struggling disciples, however, Mark adds that he "wanted to pass by them" (6:48, the literal rendering of the Greek). This curious detail causes much perplexity.[158] It seems rather callous of Jesus to spook his disciples by approaching them on the waves and then wanting to pass by them and leave them floundering in his wake. This mystifying phrase has elicited several attempts to understand it.

It is nonsensical to think that Jesus playfully overtakes them with the intention of surprising them by greeting them on the other side of the lake.[159] Some therefore interpret the verb *thelein* ("to wish, will") as an auxiliary verb like *mellein* ("to be about to") and render the phrase "he was about to pass by them" (NIV). The evidence for this use of the verb, however, is too slim to make this translation likely. The verb *thelein* does not mean "to be about to" do something, but in this context means "to resolve to" do something.[160] The translation "to be about to" also does not answer the question why he was about to pass by them. Some surmise that it was only the mistaken impression of the disciples in the boat,[161] but the text does not say, "They thought he was going to pass by them." Others assume that he intended to pass their way and go beside them, but do not explain why he would do so.[162]

The translation, "he would have passed by them," represented by the ASV, implies that Jesus wanted to pass by but did not do so when he heard the disciples' terrified cries (6:49–50).[163] The problem with this view is that he saw them in distress before

---

156. Adela Yarbro Collins, "Rulers, Divine Men, and Walking on the Water (Mark 6:45–52)," in *Religious Propaganda and Missionary Competition in the New Testament World: Essays Honoring Dieter Georgi* (ed. Lukas Bormann, Kelly del Tredici, and Angela Standhartinger; NovTSup 74; Leiden: Brill, 1994), 207–27; eadem, *Mark*, 328–33, following Wendy Cotter, "The Markan Sea Miracles: Their History, Formation, and Function in the Literary Context of Greco-Roman Antiquity" (Ph.D. diss.; Toronto: University of St. Michael's College, 1991), who places greater emphasis on Greek and Roman traditions than on Scripture.

157. See *Odes Sol.* 39:9–10, which refers to the "footsteps of the "Lord Messiah" standing firm on the water.

158. The McDonald Idiomatic Translation omits the phrase entirely.

159. Wellhausen, *Marci*, 52.

160. Albert-Marie Denis, "Jesus' Walking on the Waters: A Contribution to the History of the Pericope in the Gospel Tradition," *LS* 1 (1967): 288.

161. Taylor, *Mark*, 329; Cranfield, *Mark*, 226–27; France, *Mark*, 271–72.

162. Hendrik van der Loos, *The Miracles of Jesus* (NovTSup 9; Leiden: Brill, 1965), 652–53.

he set out on the sea (6:48). Why would he have wanted to pass them by? A curious interpretation links his actions to the so-called messianic secret. He wanted to be seen walking on the sea but wished to remain unrecognized.[164] Jesus does not try to keep his identity and role secret from his disciples, however, and he has no desire to frighten the hapless disciples and then disappear into the mist. Nor does he want to test their faith on this occasion, as Schweizer contends.[165] What would the test comprise?

Another view takes its cue from Amos 7:1–8:3 and interprets the phrase metaphorically: Jesus wanted to help the disciples in their difficulty.[166] Coming to them in the fourth watch may be significant since God is said to deliver the people early in the morning when dawn is about to break (see Exod 14:24; Pss 46:5; 130:6; Isa 17:14). Blackburn writes: "Thus Jesus, like Yahweh in the O.T. (and the New), manifests his saving power *prōi* [early]."[167] This last view has the virtue of interpreting Jesus' action from Scripture, but the account is not a rescue miracle. The disciples are not in peril on the sea but are simply stalled in their progress as they fight the wind.

In my view, the web of OT allusions strongly suggests that this episode is intended as an epiphany.[168] The verb "to pass by" occurs in two key theophany passages in the OT, Exod 33:19–34:7 and 1 Kgs 19:11–12. In Exod 33, Moses asks God to show him his glory, and God responds by passing before him and proclaiming his identity:

> And the LORD said, "I will cause all my goodness to pass in front of you, and I will proclaim my name, the LORD, in your presence. I will have mercy on whom I will have mercy, and I will have compassion on whom I will have compassion. But," he said, "you cannot see my face, for no one may see me and live."
>
> Then the LORD said, "There is a place near me where you may stand on a rock. When my glory passes by, I will put you in a cleft in the rock and cover you with my hand until I have passed by. Then I will remove my hand and you will see my back; but my face must not be seen." (Exod 33:19–23)

163. See Juel, *Mark*, 99. Bryan, *A Preface to Mark*, 96, comments that Jesus intends to pass the disciples, which communicates that he is not at their disposal, but when they cry out, "he *is* at their disposal."

164. Thierry Snoy, "Marc 6,48: '... et il voulait les dépasser': proposition pour la solution d'une énigme," in *L'évangile selon Marc: tradition et rédaction* (ed. M. Sabbe; BETL 34; Louvain: Leuven University Press, 1974), 347–63.

165. Schweizer, *Mark*, 142; see also Swete, *Mark*, 138.

166. Harry Fleddermann, "'And He Wanted to Pass by Them' (Mark 6:48c)," *CBQ* 45 (1983): 389–95. He interprets the verb "to pass by" in Amos 7:8 and 8:2 to express God's intention to avert catastrophe and argues: "A free, but accurate, translation would be: 'And he wanted to save them'" (p. 392).

167. Barry Blackburn, *Theios Anēr and the Markan Miracle Traditions* (WUNT 2/40; Tübingen: Mohr Siebeck, 1991), 146.

168. Martin Dibelius, *From Tradition to Gospel* (trans. Bertram Lee Woolf; New York: Scribner's, 1935), 95, was the first to categorize it as an epiphany. See also Ernst Lohmeyer, "'Und Jesus ging vorüber': Eine exegetische Betrachtung," in *Urchristliche Mystik: Neutestamentliche Studien* (Darmstadt: Hermann Gentner, 1956), 57–79; John Paul Heil, *Jesus Walking on the Sea: Meaning and Gospel Functions of Matt 14:22–33, Mark 6:45–52 and John 6:15b–21* (AnBib 87; Rome: Biblical Institute Press, 1981), 72–73, 118; Denis, "Jesus' Walking on the Waters," 294; Pesch, *Markusevangelium*, 1:361–63; Gundry, *Mark*, 336; Guelich, *Mark 1–8:26*, 350–51; Bas M. F. van Iersel, "Καὶ ἤθελεν παρελθεῖν αὐτούς: Another Look at Mark 6,48d," in *The Four Gospels 1992: Festschrift Frans Neirynck* (ed. Frans Van Segbroeck et al.; BETL 100; Leuven: Leuven University Press, 1992), 2:1065–76; W. Richard Stegner, "Jesus' Walking on the Water: Mark 6.45–52," in *The Gospels and the Scriptures of Israel* (ed. Craig A. Evans and W. Richard Stegner; JSNTSup 104; Sheffield: Sheffield Academic Press, 1994), 212–34; and Marcus, *Mark 1–8*, 423, 426, 430–34.

> Then the LORD came down in the cloud and stood there with him and proclaimed his name, the LORD. And he passed in front of Moses, proclaiming, "The LORD, the LORD, the compassionate and gracious God, slow to anger, abounding in love and faithfulness, maintaining love to thousands, and forgiving wickedness, rebellion and sin." (Exod 34:5–7a)

In 1 Kgs 19:11–12, the Lord tells Elijah to stand on the mountain, "for the LORD is about to pass by." In the LXX, the verb "to pass by" is used to refer to an epiphany.[169] In Gen 32:31–33 (LXX), the face of God "passed by" Jacob when he was wrestling with the angel (see 2 Kgdms 23:3–4 [LXX]). Job 9:8, 11 (LXX) reads, "he walks upon the waves of the sea.... If he goes by me, I will not see him, and if he passes by me, I will not recognize him." This biblical background suggests that Mark portrays Jesus wanting to pass by his disciples to reveal his transcendent, divine majesty to them. The disciples, however, are not given an advanced warning as Moses and Elijah were and are completely caught off guard. Nevertheless, the disciples' reaction of terror is a typical effect of an epiphany.[170]

This interpretation is supported further by Jesus' words of reassurance. His confirmation, "I am" (*egō eimi*), often translated "it is I," could simply mean that it is really he walking on the water and not some phantom (see Luke 24:39).[171] The assurance "Take courage!... Don't be afraid" (6:50), however, is the language of a divine being in the Scripture (see Gen 15:1; Josh 8:1; Dan 10:12, 19; Luke 1:13, 30; 2:10; Acts 23:11). Jesus' use of "I am" evokes OT texts and probably has a more numinous meaning. Jesus greets them with the divine formula of self-revelation, as God would: "I am."[172]

Isaiah 43:1–16 also is significant as a backdrop for interpreting this passage. God declares to Israel:

> "Do not fear, for I have redeemed you; I have summoned you by name; you are mine. When you pass through the waters, I will be with you... For I am the LORD your God, the Holy One of Israel, your Savior." (Isa 43:1a–3a)

169. Heil, *Jesus Walking on the Sea*, 70, considers the verb to have become "a 'technical term' for the appearance of a divine being, in the sense of his drawing near and showing himself before human eyes."

170. Collins, *Mark*, 334.

171. Jason Robert Combs, "A Ghost on the Water? Understanding an Absurdity in Mark 6:49–50," *JBL* 127 (2008): 345–58, argues that it would have been considered absurd that a ghost could walk on water.

172. See Exod 3:14; Deut 32:39; Isa 41:4; 43:10–11, 25; 46:4; 48:12; 51:12; 52:6; John 8:58. See David Daube, "The 'I AM' of the Messianic Presence," in *The New Testament and Rabbinic Judaism* (London: Athlone, 1956), 325–29. Williams, *"I am He,"* 225, asserts that "regardless of the possibility that Mark interprets Jesus' pronouncement in the light of divine 'I' declarations in biblical traditions (Exod 14:4, 18; Isa 43:10, 13), the fact that the expression *egō eimi* enables Jesus to make himself known as the one who exercises God's power to walk on the sea does suggest that this is a statement of profound significance in the Markan account." Williams (p. 220) cites parallels with motifs in Exod 14–15 that suggest that Mark "has consciously incorporated certain terms and motifs from Exod. 14–15 into his presentation of the event." In both passages there is a "strong wind" (Exod 14:21/Mark 6:48). The timing is similar; it is in the early morning (Exod 14:24/Mark 6:48). The location is in the midst of the sea (Exod 14:29; 15:8, 19/Mark 6:47). Fear appears in both passages (Exod 14:10, 31/Mark 6:50). The imperative "take courage" (*tharseite*) is used in both passages (Exod 14:13 [LXX]/Mark 6:50). The motif of making known that "I am the LORD" occurs (Exod 14:4, 18). Williams concludes from these parallels, however, that Mark's passage has salvific rather than epiphanic significance: "Mark depicts Jesus as exhibiting the salvific power of God, a power already made manifest on the occasion of the dividing of the Reed Sea, when he walks on the water and rescues his disciples." She likens it to a new exodus (see Ps 77:20). Heil, *Jesus Walking on the Sea*, 80, also affirms that Jesus identifies himself "with the revelation of Yahweh's will to save, which is now taking place in his action of walking on the sea."

> "You are my witnesses," declares the LORD, "and my servant whom I have chosen, so that you may know and believe me and understand that I am he. Before me no god was formed, nor will there be one after me." (Isa 43:10–11)
>
> "I am the LORD, your Holy One, Israel's Creator, your King." This is what the LORD says—he who made a way through the sea, a path through the mighty waters. (Isa 43:15–16)

The disciples who have been called by Jesus pass through the waters, and Jesus is with them and is the one who need only say, "I am." "The Holy One of God" (1:24), the "Son of the Most High God" (5:7), really is in their midst. For now, however, the answer sails by the disciples.

Against this interpretation, France contends that "I am" is not a deliberate use of the divine name because "a declaration of divinity does not seem appropriate at this point in the narrative where the focus is on the initial failure to recognize Jesus and his consequent self-identification, for which *egō eimi* is normal colloquial Greek (cf. Mt. 26:22, 25; Jn. 4:26; 9:9; 18:5)."[173] Jesus' identity is gradually being revealed to the disciples as the narrative progresses, and I would counter that it is indeed an appropriate point for Jesus to attempt to disclose his divine identity to his disciples. In a previous sea journey, Jesus calmed a severe storm, and the terrified disciples ask, "Who is this? Even the wind and the waves obey him!" (4:41). On this sea journey, Jesus provides an answer to that question. The disciples' eyes and minds, however, are not up to comprehending something so stunning. They only see a ghost, which throws them into a panic.[174] As they are making little progress on the lake in struggling to reach their destination, they are also making little progress in understanding who Jesus is. Jesus' intention to pass by is therefore frustrated by their fear and dullness. Marcus agrees: "This most 'divine' moment" is thwarted by the disciples' terror and incomprehension. As a result, Jesus "is called back to earth by the necessity of ministering to them."[175]

Mark offers a surprising explanation for the disciples' terror and amazement: "For they had not understood about the loaves; their hearts were hardened" (6:52). What is it that they did not understand about the loaves when they fed five thousand from two fish and five loaves that makes them clueless about the significance of Jesus walking to them on the water? Topel offers, "As they had failed to see the divine power in the preceding multiplication of loaves (6:30–44), so they fail to see the theophany of Jesus and are afraid of a (nondivine) supernatural ghost."[176]

173. France, *Mark*, 273, n. 71.

174. Consequently, Kertelge, *Die Wunder Jesu*, 150, classifies it as a "misunderstood epiphany." See also Hermann Josef Riedl, "Der Seewandel Jesu Mk 6,45–52 parr. Eine Epiphanieerzählung und ihre textpragmatische Intention," *SNTSU* 30 (2005): 16.

175. Marcus, *Mark 1–8*, 432. He argues that the spiritual lesson for the Markan community is this: "Jesus' followers' fear may stand in the way of a full divine self-disclosure to them, but the good news is that Jesus will come to them even when they are afraid." Jesus continues to be concerned that the disciples know who he really is, and he asks Peter point blank, "Who do you say I am?" (8:29). Peter's answer remains defective, and Jesus continues to fine-tune the disciples' understanding of his identity and purpose in coming.

176. John Topel, "What Were the Women Afraid Of? (Mark 16:8)," *JTI* 6 (2012): 88. Lane, *Mark*, 237–38, comments that they failed "to grasp that this event pointed beyond itself to the secret of Jesus' person. Because they were not truly open to the action of God in Jesus they had missed the significance of the miracle of the loaves for them, and saw only 'a marvel.'"

The one who comes to them striding on the sea is not merely another Moses who fills bread baskets in the wilderness. The disciples' lack of understanding of this experience because of their hardened hearts (6:52) becomes an invitation for the audience to understand. The one who comes to the disciples walking on the water is the transcendent Lord who comes to save, and not simply to save people from misadventures at sea.

Jesus displays his divine power to the disciples further when he gets into the boat with them. The wind ceases without any command from Jesus (6:51). Donahue and Harrington comment that Jesus' "simple presence in the boat calms the waves, which suggests that the main Markan focus here is on the epiphany rather than on the wondrous action."[177] Getting in the boat with the disciples enables them to continue their journey, though they reach a different destination, Gennesaret (6:53), rather than Bethsaida (6:45).

5.6.3 The Transfiguration (Mark 9:2–13)

The transfiguration is obviously an epiphany scene and marks a major transition in the gospel as Jesus enters a new phase of his ministry. He will leave Galilee on a journey to Jerusalem that will end with him hanged on a cross. Morrison identifies it as the pivot on which the entire narrative turns: "Based on linguistic and thematic links in the narrative ... the twin pericopae of Peter's confession (8:27–9:1) and the Transfiguration (9:2–13) together function as the turning point of the Gospel and serve in a Janus-like manner enabling the reader to see the author's true intention: the identity of Jesus and the significance of that reality for his disciples."[178] Heavenly portents and a divine announcement of his identity took place at Jesus' baptism. A divine voice rang out from the split heavens, "You are my Son, whom I love; with you I am well pleased" (1:11), as the gospel opens. This next stage in Mark's story begins in similar fashion with a divine voice resounding from a cloud: "This is my Son, whom I love" (9:7).[179] In Mark's account, only Jesus witnessed the divine display at his baptism. Now, three disciples witness his transfiguration and hear the divine declaration.

These three disciples, Peter, James, and John, were the first called (1:16–20), and their names head the list of the Twelve (3:16–17). They also have witnessed Jesus heal the fever of Peter's mother-in-law (1:29–31) and raise Jairus's daughter back to life (5:37–43). Jesus will take these three with him when he breaks away from the other disciples to pray during the dark hours on Gethsemane (14:33). They will drowsily see his great distress and agitation as he faces the cross. On the Mount of Transfiguration, however, they behold his glory as he is altered to reveal "a purer, brighter essence."[180]

Mark notes that the transfiguration occurs "after six days" (9:2). Such

177. Donahue and Harrington, *Mark*, 214.

178. Gregg S. Morrison, "The Turning Point in the Gospel of Mark: A Study of Markan Christology" (Ph.D. diss.; Washington, DC: The Catholic University of America, 2008), i.

179. Boring, *Mark*, 46, notes that this second announcement rules out any idea of an adoptionist Christology. Jesus is not adopted twice.

180. Tolbert, *Sowing the Gospel*, 204.

chronological markers are rare in Mark.[181] Its intent here is to connect the transfiguration to the preceding scene (8:27–9:1).[182] Peter confessed Jesus to be the Christ, and Jesus announced that the Son of Man will undergo brutal suffering and death at the hands of the priestly hierarchy and be resurrected. Peter vigorously objects to this prediction, and Jesus rebukes him, teaches about discipleship and the need to deny oneself and take up a cross, and promises that some standing there will not taste death before they see the kingdom of God coming in power. It makes the best sense of the flow of the narrative to view this saying in 9:1 as being fulfilled, however momentarily, in the transfiguration when three of the disciples witness the full manifestation of the kingdom's mighty presence in Jesus.

Jesus accuses Peter of not thinking as God does but as humans do; and worse, he castigates him as if he were in league with Satan (8:33). Peter's thinking needs to be corrected on three points. First, Puig i Tárrech contends, "Peter and the other disciples have lapsed into a kind of insubordination about what Jesus says concerning his future, apparently using what seems to be a decisive argument: God could not wish for Jesus' death! Jesus is mistaken when he proclaims for himself a future of suffering and death! The problem concerns, then, the interpretation of the will of God."[183] God must reveal to Peter and to the other disciples that Jesus' approaching suffering and death accord with God's will.

Second, God must reveal to Peter and to the other disciples that Jesus' earthly degradation is not incompatible with his inherent divine glory.

Third, God must reveal to Peter and to the other disciples that Jesus is much more than simply the Christ. He is God's Son, who belongs to the celestial realm.

Jesus chooses to take the three disciples up a high mountain with the expectation that they will have an encounter with God: "He does not know how it will occur but he is fully confident that the ascent of the mountain will be associated with an action of the Father, to which only three disciples will be privy."[184] What happens

181. The only other similar time reference in Mark appears in 14:1. In plotting Jesus' death, the high priests note that the Passover would arrive "after two days," that is, on the third day. See Ernst L. Schnellbächer, "*KAI META HEMERAS HEX* (Markus 9:2)," *ZNW* 71 (1980): 252–57. This specific registering of the time frame tangentially may recall Moses' six-day wait for God's revelation on Mount Sinai (Exod 24:15–16), contra Marcus, *Way*, 82, citing Joachim Jeremias, "Μωϋσῆς," *TDNT*, 4:867–73, n. 228. The parallels with Moses' encounter with God on the mountain break down, however.

Jesus chooses to go up to the mountain; he is not summoned as Moses was (Exod 24:12). Moses does not ascend the mountain with just three persons, Aaron, Nadab, and Abihu, but also with the seventy elders of Israel and Joshua (Exod 24:1, 9, 13). The cloud entirely covered the mountain, and God called to Moses out of the cloud (Exod 24:15–16). In Mark's account, Jesus is in the cloud. When Moses descended from the mountain, his face shone from being in the presence of God (Exod 34:29–35). His altered appearance frightened the people, but it was only a reflected glory that he covered with a veil and that soon faded. Jesus is transfigured, which is entirely different. The biblical account is retold in *L.A.B.* 11:15–12:1 with the added detail that Moses descended from the mountain with a transfigured appearance (Exod 34:29–35). Again, this is not what happens to Jesus. Finally, van Iersel, *Reading Mark*, 294, notes that God "makes visible who Jesus is by giving him, for a moment, the appearance of a figure that belongs to heaven" rather than showing himself (Exod 24:10–11).

Edwards, *Mark*, 269, correctly asserts: "The transfiguration of Jesus is a singular event in ancient literature. It has no analogy in the Bible, or in the extrabiblical literature from the Apocrypha, Pseudepigrapha, rabbinic literature, Qumran, Nag Hammadi, or in Hellenistic literature as a whole." Adrian Wypadlo, *Die Verklärung Jesu nach dem Markusevangelium* (WUNT 308; Tübingen: Mohr Siebeck, 2013), 392–95, makes the same point but argues that Exodus 24 and 34 provide the only background that makes Jesus' transfiguration comprehensible.

182. Morrison, "The Turning Point in the Gospel of Mark," 113–225, lists extensive linguistic and thematic parallels connecting the two accounts.

183. Puig i Tárrech, "The Glory on the Mountain," 163.

184. Ibid.

is "*for their benefit.*"[185] The passive verb he "was transfigured" (*metemorphōthē*) is a divine passive (9:2). Metamorphosis was known in Greco-Roman literature (see Ovid's *Metamorpheses*), but what happens to Jesus is not equivalent.[186]

It is best to interpret this event from Paul's exalted prose about Christ in Phil 2:5–11. He states that Jesus was "in the form [*morphē*] of God" (NIV "being in very nature God"), and he emptied himself "taking the form [*morphē*] of a servant," "being made in human likeness" (Phil 2:6–7, pers. trans.). Donahue and Harrington state, "In the transformation/transfiguration event the inner circle among Jesus' disciples receives a glimpse of Jesus' divine *morphē*."[187] The detail that his clothes "became dazzling white, whiter than anyone in the world could bleach them" (9:3), refers to an unearthly whiteness that can only belong to a divine being (see Dan 7:9). The garb of a Galilean teacher/prophet is transformed before their eyes into the transcendent raiment of the Son of God. As the implied agent of the transfiguration, God reveals that "the preexistent, heavenly Son (seen in his radiant glory in the transfiguration) is the very person sent by the Father into the world to be crucified by humankind and to give his life as a ransom for many."[188] Jesus' transfiguration is a revelation of the divine bound up in the material world.

Heil interprets this event to mean that Jesus is "temporarily transformed by God into a heavenly being while still on earth" and that his transfiguration anticipates "his future and permanent attainment of glory in heaven as promised to the righteous after their death."[189] I would interpret it instead as signaling the mystery of Jesus' divinity that is veiled by the incarnation. For Mark, Jesus' transfiguration does not reveal some future reality but his "true identity."[190] Jesus' glory that is only "briefly visible" to the disciples is "intrinsic to himself."[191] For a brief moment, the disciples catch sight of Jesus' being splashed in divine glory that only will be evident to all at the Parousia of the Son of Man (8:38).[192] Burkill's evaluation of the transfiguration in Mark is correct:

> It provides a dramatic demonstration of the glorious nature which properly belongs to Jesus as the Messiah, the Son of God, and affixes the seal of divine confirmation to Peter's recognition of the messianic secret in 8:29 and to the Master's interpretation of the secret in 8:31. For a few fleeting moments the veil of the flesh is withdrawn and the three disciples are privileged to behold their Master as he really is and as he will be made manifest to the world when he comes in clouds with great power and glory.[193]

185. Tolbert, *Sowing the Gospel*, 205.

186. Luke chooses to avoid the Greek verb for metamorphosis entirely and simply says "the appearance of his face changed, and his clothes became as bright as a flash of lightning" (Luke 9:29) to avoid any misunderstanding that what happened to Jesus was anything similar to what Greco-Roman writers portrayed.

187. Donahue and Harrington, *Mark*, 269.

188. Simon J. Gathercole, *The Preexistent Son: Recovering the Christologies of Matthew, Mark, and Luke* (Grand Rapids: Eerdmans, 2006), 20.

189. John Paul Heil, *The Transfiguration of Jesus: Narrative Meaning and Function of Mark 9:2–8, Matt 17:1–8 and Luke 9:28–36* (AnBib 144; Rome: Pontifical Biblical Institute, 2000), 260.

190. Boring, "Markan Christology," 268.

191. France, *Mark*, 351.

192. Randall E. Otto, "The Fear Motivation in Peter's Offer to Build τρεῖς σκηνάς," *WTJ* 59 (1997): 105, concludes, "It is not a vision of *what is to be*, but a revelation of *what already is*, a revelation of the unchanging divine glory which has been concealed beneath the lowliness of a human body."

193. Burkill, *Mysterious Revelation*, 164.

But why do Elijah and Moses show up with Jesus at this moment? Both had witnessed theophanies on Mount Sinai = Horeb (Exod 33:19–34:6 and 1 Kgs 19:8–18). Both were faithful servants who suffered because of their obedience, were rejected by the people of God, and were vindicated by God. Elijah and Moses were both regarded as eschatological figures. Moses was Israel's first deliverer, and people expected a prophet like Moses (Deut 18:15) to appear in the last days. Elijah was supposed to appear at the dawning of the end time when God would redeem Israel (Mal 4:4–6; see the following discussion about Elijah in Mark 9:9–13).[194] Their presence with Jesus may point to Jewish hopes about Israel's final redemption and suggest that the time is at hand.

It is more likely, however, that they appear as celestial beings. Jewish tradition claimed that both did not die. Elijah was caught up to heaven in a fiery chariot (2 Kgs 2:11), and later Jewish interpreters combined Deut 34:6, "no one knows where his grave is," with Exod 34:28, "Moses was there with the LORD," to conclude that Moses did not experience death."[195] Puig i Tárrech asserts that if Jesus is to be compared to Moses, it is to "the glorious, heavenly Moses, who accompanies Jesus in his transfiguration."[196] The same is true of Elijah. Their presence and Jesus' clothes that are now "whiter than anyone in the world could bleach them" (9:3) indicate that Jesus "now belongs to the heavenly world."[197] Ahearne-Kroll concurs: "The image of the transfigured Jesus on the mountain standing with the heavenly Moses and Elijah produces a highly exalted picture of Jesus that shows that he belongs in their company."[198]

Elijah is mentioned first, but he is identified as being with Moses. Moses, then, is the more noteworthy figure of the two.[199] It is unlikely that Moses and Elijah represent the Law and the Prophets, as Tertullian (*Marc.* 4.22) assumed, because Elijah was not a writing prophet. The clue to the order may go back to 8:27–31. Elijah's presence proves false the idle speculation that Jesus might be Elijah returned to life (6:15; 8:28). Wypadlo points a chiastic arrangement of the names in 9:4–5:

Elijah
    Moses
        Jesus
        Jesus
    Moses
Elijah

194. In *Deut. Rab.* 3:17 (on 10:1), God tells Moses: "When I will send Elijah, the prophet, you are to come both of you together." It is asserted in 2 Esdras that seeing "those who were taken up, who from their birth have not tasted death" is a sign of the end of the age (2 Esd 6:25–26).

195. So Philo, *QG* 1.86; *Moses* 2.288; Josephus, *Ant.* 4.8.48 325–26.

196. Puig i Tárrech, "The Glory on the Mountain," 155.

197. Ibid., 164. The clothing of the Ancient of Days in Dan 7:9, for example, was "white as snow." See also the vision of "a man dressed in linen" in Dan 10:4–11:1. In Mark 16:5, the young man at the tomb is dressed in a white robe; in Matt 28:3, the angel's "appearance was like lightning, and his clothes were white as snow;" and in Luke 24:4, the angels appear in "clothes that gleamed like lightning" (see also John 20:12). At the ascension, "two men dressed in white" appear (Acts 1:10; see also Rev 4:4; 15:6; 19:14). The language of brightness is reminiscent of Paul's account of his divine encounter with Christ on the Damascus road (Acts 9:3; 22:6, 9, 11; 26:13).

198. Ahearne-Kroll, "The Scripturally Complex Presentation of Jesus," 53.

199. John Paul Heil, "A Note on 'Elijah with Moses' in Mark 9,4," *Bib* 80 (1999): 115.

Wypadlo suggests that the prominence of Elijah's name serves as an entry into the theme of suffering, which becomes clearer in 9:9–13.[200] Jesus says, "Elijah has come, and they have done to him everything they wished, just as it is written about him" (9:13). In Mark, John the Baptist is presented as Elijah *redivivus* and is Jesus' forerunner in death. The last mention of Elijah in the gospel is in the crucifixion scene when the onlookers mistakenly think that Jesus was calling for Elijah when he cried out with a loud voice (15:34–35). The Elijah associations in the gospel imply that suffering and death cast their shadows over the glory of the transfiguration. The one whose garments became white beyond the power of any human fuller to make white (9:3) will suffer utter degradation when his garments are taken from him by those who raffle them off at the foot of his cross.

The dumbfounded Peter reacts to this glorious scene, "Rabbi, it is good for us to be here. Let us put up three shelters—one for you, one for Moses and one for Elijah" (9:5). The narrator adds parenthetically that the disciples were terrified and Peter did not know what to say (9:6). His desire to build tents ("tabernacles") for each one is clearly ill-considered because he puts Jesus on a par with Elijah and Moses and fails to recognize his true rank. Since Mark gives no explanation why Peter would consider building tents to be a good idea or necessary, what he intends to accomplish in building these tents is baffling.[201] It has elicited many explanations. Some assume that he wanted to build earthly counterparts to their heavenly dwelling-places appropriate to their honor and eternal dwelling-places[202] and that Peter also intends to prolong the experience. Puig i Tàrrech states that they "wish the state of happiness they are experiencing due to the glorious vision to continue."[203] But the text says that Peter and his companions are overcome with fear (9:6), not joy. Why would Peter want to extend this experience?[204]

In Matthew, the disciples fall to the ground terrified when they hear the voice (Matt 17:6); and in Luke, they are filled with fear when they enter the cloud (Luke 9:34). In Mark's account, the three disciples experience fear when they see Jesus' altered appearance and hear him conversing with Elijah and Moses. Fear is a proper and natural response when one is exposed to God's majesty, power, and holiness, or to those revealed to have a special relationship with God.[205] Otto suggests that Peter's statement "It is good for us to be here" could be punctuated instead as a

200. Wypadlo, *Die Verklärung*, 167–68, 172–91, 412–40, 444.

201. Mark gives an explanation for the obscure Jewish custom of washing hands, for which there is no biblical precedent, in 7:3–4, and the absence of any explanation here suggests to me that a biblical allusion lies behind this intention to erect the tents. Mark expects the audience to detect that allusion and to make the connection.

202. I. Howard Marshall, *The Gospel of Luke: A Commentary on the Greek Text* (NIGTC; Grand Rapids: Eerdmans, 1978), 386; Gundry, *Mark*, 460; Markus Öhler, "Die Verklärung (Mk 9:1–8): Die Ankunft der Herrschaft Gottes auf der Erde," *NovT* 38 (1996): 208–9; and Puig i Tàrrech, "The Glory on the Mountain," 167. See references to heavenly dwellings in *1 En.* 39:4–8; 71:16; *2 En.* 61:2; *T. Ab.* 20:14; Luke 16:9; John 14:2.

203. Puig i Tàrrech, "The Glory on the Mountain," 167.

204. Others connect the proposal to the Feast of Tabernacles (Lev 23:33–43; Num 29:12–38; Neh 8:14–17) and assume that Peter wants to build canopies of branches to shelter the three. The problem with this view is that "shelters" is not a technical term, and Mark gives no indication that this event occurs around the Feast of Tabernacles. If that were the case, they would need to build six canopies for all of the participants, not just the venerated three. See also Standaert, *L'évangile selon Marc. Deuxième partie*, 660.

205. Günther Wanke, "φοβέω," *TDNT*, 9:201–2.

question of alarm, "Is it good for us to be here?"[206] Gazing on the unveiling of Jesus' majestic, heavenly glory without having been consecrated or ritually purified may stir the disciples' fear. It may be similar to the people's fearful reaction to Moses' shining face after he talked with God (Exod 34:30). Peter's offer to build the tents may have been prompted by a desire to provide protection from being slain by this unapproachable glory. They may feel endangered by their proximity to the holy as Isaiah did, " 'Woe to me!' I cried. 'I am ruined! For I am a man of unclean lips, and I live among a people of unclean lips, and my eyes have seen the King, the LORD Almighty' " (Isa 6:5).

The tabernacles would shield the divine glory and prevent the three disciples, who knew themselves to be sinners (see Luke 5:8), from being destroyed.[207] The unveiled glory was "graciously brief," and the cloud covers Jesus, Moses, and Elijah and cloaks "that overwhelming glory from the disciples, thus obviating Peter's terrified proposal to build τρεῖς σκηνάς [three tents] and protecting the disciples from death."[208] Since the voice comes from *out of* the cloud, the disciples stand outside it.[209] The protective cloud assuages the disciples' fear.

What lies behind Peter's offer to build three tents may be difficult to discern, but the meaning of the words spoken from the cloud is of far greater importance and is clear. The voice from the cloud represents a higher authority than either Elijah or Moses, who do not speak. God identifies Jesus as "my Son, whom I love," and commands the disciples to listen to him (see Deut 18:15).[210] Jesus spoke plainly of his suffering and death (8:31–32). Now, God speaks plainly of Jesus' identity so that it is no longer a secret known only by angels and malevolent demons.[211] Unlike the declaration in 1:11, which is addressed to Jesus in the second person, "You are," this declaration about Jesus is addressed to the disciples using the third person, "This is." It is followed by a second person imperative, "Listen to him!"

This account can be compared with the giving of the Ten Commandments on Mount Sinai. God begins with the formula of self-introduction, "I am the LORD your God," and then gives the Decalogue (Exod 20:1–17). In this instance, God introduces his Son and demands that they listen to him. This command implies that "his instruction is to be seen on a level with God's commandments. His words, like God's word, 'will not pass away' (Mark 13,31)."[212] The command to listen also

206. Otto, "The Fear Motivation in Peter's Offer," 107. Alan Hugh McNeile, *The Gospel according to St. Matthew* (London: Macmillan, 1938), 250, allows reading this as an "awe-struck question" as a possibility, following Emil Wendling, "Die Äusserung des Petrus in der Verklärungsgeschichte (Mk 9,5)," *Theologische Studien und Kritiken* 84 (1911): 115. James Hope Moulton and Wilbert Francis Howard, *A Grammar of New Testament Greek* (Edinburgh: T&T Clark, 1920), 2:48, advise that in interpreting texts where modern punctuation has been inserted by editors who determine the meaning for us, "we must always be careful to realise our freedom to take our own line on sufficient reason."

207. Otto, "The Fear Motivation in Peter's Offer," 106–7, 110–12.

208. Ibid., 112. The cloud is both a veil and vehicle of divine glory that signifies God's presence (Exod 13:21–22; 16:10; 19:9; 24:15–18; 33:9–11; 34:5; 40:34–38; 2 Sam 22:12).

209. Moses could not enter the tabernacle because it was covered by the cloud, and the glory of the Lord filled it (Exod 40:34–35).

210. Tolbert, *Sowing the Gospel*, 206, notes the irony that this scene places so much emphasis on the sights—Jesus robed in glistening white, Elijah and Moses appearing with him, the overshadowing cloud—yet the voice does not command them "to look upon him" but to "listen to him."

211. Schweizer, *Mark*, 183.

212. Hanna Stettler, "Sanctification in the Jesus Tradition," *Bib* 85 (2004): 165.

resonates with the fundamental confession of Israel that begins, "Hear, O Israel" (Deut 6:4). Jesus is the Son of God, and humans must listen to him alone.[213] Jesus, then, is far more than simply a successor to Moses and Elijah.

Jesus says nothing during this scene. The close connection to what precedes suggests that the disciples particularly are to listen to his prediction about his suffering and teaching on discipleship (8:31–9:1). Peter and the rest of the disciples do not yet recognize that Jesus precedes Elijah and Moses in honor and in rank. They need to bend their minds around what he teaches them about his suffering, death, and resurrection and what it means to follow him.

5.7 Other Instances Where Jesus Is Closely Linked to God

5.7.1 Jesus as the Bridegroom (Mark 2:18–22)

Mark records that some came and asked Jesus, "How is it that John's disciples and the disciples of the Pharisees are fasting, but yours are not?" (2:18). The question about fasting is not an issue in the early church that requires a ruling from Jesus. Mark therefore is not "concerned with fasting regulations but with the divine identity and functions of Jesus Christ."[214] Jesus' answer draws on nuptial imagery that describes the relationship between God and Israel: "As a young man marries a young woman, so will your Builder marry you; as a bridegroom rejoices over his bride, so will your God rejoice over you" (Isa 62:5). He identifies himself as the bridegroom in his counterquestion and answer, "How can the guests of the bridegroom fast while he is with them? They cannot, so long as they have him with them. But the time will come when the bridegroom will be taken from them, and on that day they will fast" (2:19–20). Jeremias points out that the Messiah is nowhere presented as a bridegroom in the OT.[215] Tait maintains that in Isaiah, "it is always Yahweh who is the Bridegroom and never any of the possible messianic figures in the text. The Servant neither marries nor is given in marriage!"[216]

5.7.2 Jesus as Lord of the Temple (Mark 11:11)

Jesus' grandly staged arrival into Jerusalem generates excitement from his followers shouting, "Hosanna!" "Blessed is he who comes in the name of the Lord!" (11:9). The procession ends with somewhat of an anticlimax when Jesus enters the city and the temple courts only to look around and leave for Bethany. The readers' expectations may have been raised that Jesus would do something more memorable to cap his grand entry. Mark notes that it "was already late" (lit., "that it was already the hour of evening"; 11:11). Did time run out on Jesus before he could do anything?

213. Davis, "Mark's Christological Paradox," 13. Since Moses and Elijah fade from view when the voice from the cloud commands obedience to the Son, one could interpret the scene to mean that Jesus completes their work and surpasses them. As Lane, *Mark*, 321, puts it, "His word and deed transcend all past revelation."

214. Tait, *Jesus*, 133.

215. Joachim Jeremias, "νύμφη, νυμφίος," *TDNT*, 4:1101.

216. Tait, *Jesus*, 165.

This bland conclusion to Jesus' dramatic entry into Jerusalem depicts more than meets the eye, and its true significance can only be filled in by the OT. The verb Mark uses that is translated "to look around" or "to take a good look" (*periblepesthai*) does not mean that he is goggling at the temple's grandeur. It is used in 3:5, 34; 5:32; and 10:23 in the context of critically scanning his audience. One may picture Jesus reproachfully taking stock of the temple's operations. Jesus identified himself as the Lord who requires a mount to enter the city (11:3), and the Lord now enters his temple as prophesied by Mal 3:1–2, a passage that Mark cites in the Gospel's introduction (1:2):

> "I will send my messenger, who will prepare the way before me. Then suddenly the Lord you are seeking will come to his temple; the messenger of the covenant, whom you desire, will come," says the LORD Almighty.
>
> But who can endure the day of his coming? Who can stand when he appears? For he will be like a refiner's fire or a launderer's soap."

Jesus enters the temple to inspect it as the Lord, and the next day's events reveal that he comes not to restore it but to pronounce judgment on it.

After his actions in the temple, driving out the sellers and buyers, overturning the moneychangers' tables and the seats of those who sold doves, preventing persons from carrying vessels through the temple, and interpreting those actions with ominous biblical passages from Isaiah and Jeremiah, the priestly hierarchy immediately respond to this threat by plotting his death (11:15–18). When they confront Jesus face to face, they ask, "By what authority are you doing these things?... And who gave you authority to do this?" (11:27–28). The assumption is that no one possesses authority on his own to carry out such an outrageous sign of judgment on God's temple.

Jesus audaciously presumes to have divine authority. He refuses to answer directly until they respond to his question about the baptism of John, "Was it from heaven, or of human origin?" (11:30). Edwards comments that Jesus' answer is not evasive "for it was at the baptism by John that the heavens were parted, the Spirit of power descended into Jesus (*eis auton*, 1:10), and the voice from heaven declared him God's Son. The baptism of Jesus, in other words, was the event that inaugurated his *exousia* [authority], his conscious oneness with the Father, and his sovereign freedom and empowerment for ministry."[217]

5.7.3 Jesus as the One Who Gathers the Elect at the End of the Age (Mark 13:26–27)

Jesus refers to the coming of the Son of Man "in clouds with great power and glory" and sending out the angels to gather the elect in 13:26–27. What is noteworthy is that in the OT, God is assumed to be the one who gathers the dispersed people

217. Edwards, "The Authority of Jesus," 226–27. See Corrado Marucci, "Die implizite Christologie in der sogenannten Vollmachtsfrage (Mk 11, 27–33): Referat im Seminar 'Das Markusevangelium' beim SNTS-Kongress in Trondheim, 20. 8. 1985," *ZKT* 108 (1986): 292–300.

from the four corners of the earth (Deut 30:4; Isa 11:11–12; 43:5–6; 66:18; Jer 23:3; 32:37; Ezek 34:12–13; 36:24). Instead, Jesus says that the Son of Man will assume this role and direct angels, who are identified as *his* angels, to gather *his* elect. Hartman notes, "It is in keeping with the fact that here the Son of Man appears in place of God that the celestial phenomena which accompany this appearance are associated in the OT with theophanies on the Day of Yahweh."[218] Jesus follows this depiction of the coming of the Son of Man with an extraordinary assertion, "Heaven and earth will pass away, but my words will never pass away" (13:31).

A similar statement in Matt 5:18, "For truly I tell you, until heaven and earth disappear, not the smallest letter, not the least stroke of a pen, will by any means disappear from the Law until everything is accomplished," means that the law will be sacrosanct *until* the consummation when heaven and earth pass away. Jesus says that his words will endure beyond the end of heaven and earth.[219] This exalted imagery places Jesus and his words on the same level as God and God's words. God's words are imperishable: "The grass withers and the flowers fall, but the word of our God endures forever" (Isa 40:8; see Ps 119:89). The language also resonates with Isa 51:6, "Lift up your eyes to the heavens, look at the earth beneath; the heavens will vanish like smoke, the earth will wear out like a garment and its inhabitants die like flies. But my salvation will last forever, my righteousness will never fail."

Martinez comments regarding Jesus' identity in Mark that the evangelist "does not simply identify Jesus with Yahweh.... He leaves us with a greater mystery than a simple identification." He continues:

> He distinguishes Jesus from the Father and the Holy Spirit at the baptismal scene and at the transfiguration. Jesus prays to God and addresses him as "Abba" (Dad) in the scene at Gethsemane. And when he is questioned by the High Priest Jesus says that he will sit at the right hand of the Power—he places himself on an equality with God but distinguishes himself from God. What Mark clearly does is leave us with the beginnings of the problem of the Trinity.[220]

Jesus' concession, "But about that day or hour no one knows, not even the angels in heaven, nor the Son, but only the Father" (13:32), confirms this conclusion. This statement again distinguishes Jesus from God, but it contains a remarkable implication. Notably, it employs an absolute use of "the Son," and it assumes that "the Son" is also a heavenly being like the "the angels" and would seemingly know such things.[221] One should not parse this text, as Arius did, to mean that since Jesus does not know *all* things, he cannot be God. The point of the statement in its context is not to establish what the Son does or does not know. Mark includes it to forestall any presumptuous arrogance on the part of those who would claim to

218. Lars Hartman, *Prophecy Interpreted: The Formation of Some Jewish Apocalyptic Texts and the Eschatological Discourse Mark 13 Par.* (ConBNT1; Lund: Gleerup, 1966), 157. See the discussion in §2.6.2.3 above.

219. C. E. B. Cranfield, "St. Mark 13," *SJT* 7 (1954): 292–93.

220. Martinez, "Identity of Jesus in Mark," 338.

221. Gathercole, *The Preexistent Son*, 50. The ascending order of "no one," "the angels in heaven," "the Son," and "the Father" puts Jesus next to the Father in the divine hierarchy.

know more than Jesus or the angels about God's timetable for the end. No human knows or ever will know beforehand when the time will come (13:33). Only the transcendent God can know something like this.

This discourse is intended to exhort disciples during trying times to keep their wits about them and not to get swept up in end-time fervor and be deceived by false prophets forecasting God's imminent intervention. No one can know the timing of the end because there will be no preliminary signs. The statement serves to defuse any sense that the end lies just around the corner.

5.8 Jesus as the Final Arbiter of the Intention of the Law

Jesus' teaching reveals that he has divine authority that far surpasses that of a prophet. He determines what is God's intention regarding the law. The question about what is "lawful" (*exestin*) emerges in disputes with the Pharisees (2:24, 26; 3:4; 10:2; 12:14; see also 6:18). Kampling recognizes that Mark is not interested in academic debates about the validity of the law, but instead in Jesus' interpretation of the law related to specific cases.[222] What is permitted on the Sabbath (2:23–3:6)? What kind of defilement matters to God (7:1–23)? Is divorce permitted (10:1–12)? What are one's responsibilities to the Roman government (12:13–17)?[223] These are issues that would have relevance for Mark's Christian audience, and Jesus is assumed to be the ultimate judge in these matters (see 9:7).

5.8.1 Jesus' Ruling about the Sabbath (Mark 2:23–3:6)

God commands that the Sabbath be kept holy, which requires that one refrain from work. Josephus (*Ag. Ap.* 2:27 §3) claims that the word "Sabbath" "in the Jews' language denotes cessation from all work." The problem was defining what precisely classified as work. The *Mishnah* contains two tractates that address complex Sabbath regulations. Tractate *Šabbat* deals mainly with prohibitions of work and classifies objects that may or may not be carried from one domain to another. Tractate *ʿErubin* deals with extending the Sabbath boundaries beyond the 2,000 cubit limit so that one would not violate the prohibition of traveling too far on the Sabbath. In *Mishnah Ḥagigah* 1:8, it is admitted: "The rules about the Sabbath, festal offerings and sacrilege are as mountains hanging by a hair, for Scripture is scanty and the rules many." Observance of the Sabbath became more important as Jews became increasingly enveloped by their pagans. Caird contends, "The sabbath was therefore the chief, almost the sole, safeguard against the lapse of Jews into the beliefs and practices of their pagan neighbours, and to take away this safeguard meant the end of Judaism. The Pharisees believed they were fighting for the very existence of Israel."[224]

222. Kampling, "Das Gesetz im Markusevangelium," 125. He writes that according to Mark, Christian practice can have no other point of reference than the word of Jesus (143).

223. See §2.6.1.5.1.

224. Caird, *New Testament Theology*, 386–87.

The controversy about Jesus' disciples plucking grain on the Sabbath is dealt with above.[225] Jesus does make the point that the Sabbath has a humanitarian purpose, "The Sabbath was made for man, not man for the Sabbath" (2:27). He is not a scofflaw but assesses how the law is to be applied according to God's intention in creation. God did not create the Sabbath as a command simply to be obeyed.[226]

In a second controversy, Jesus heals a man with a withered hand on the Sabbath (3:1–6). Before his detractors, the Pharisees, who would like to police his activity, can utter an objection, he challenges them: "Which is lawful on the Sabbath: to do good or to do evil, to save life or to kill?" (3:4). Jesus' question implies that the Sabbath does not prevent one from doing what is good and saving life. Back states, "Without invoking scriptural or traditional support, he simply declares that it is necessary to heal on the Sabbath, since not healing is doing evil and killing, but healing is doing good and saving a 'soul.'"[227] His opponents may chafe over his actions, but they remain silent when he makes this pronouncement. Again, as the Lord of the Sabbath, he is the one who decrees what is lawful and unlawful.

5.8.2 Jesus' Ruling on Purity (Mark 7:1–15)

The Pharisees and some of the teachers of the law who had come from Jerusalem noticed that some of Jesus' disciples were eating with defiled hands, that is, without washing them. Washing the hands was judged to be sufficient to cleanse one of ritual impurity and made one fit to eat. The requirement to wash hands ritually before eating had no biblical basis, though later rabbinic tradition insisted that it did. According to *b. Ber.* 60b, "When he washes his hands he should say, 'Blessed is He who has sanctified us with his commandments and commanded us concerning the washing of hands.'"

The only command to wash hands in Scripture, however, appears in Exod 30:19–21 (see 40:12), which required priests engaged in the tabernacle service to wash their hands. Priests were also required to regard as holy the portion of the sacrifices that they were allowed to eat. They and everyone in their household could share in this food only when they were ceremonially clean (Num 18:8–13). The purity laws that distinguished between clean and unclean were primarily designed to protect persons and holy objects from becoming defiled by what is impure. The Pharisaic tradition extended these laws to apply to everyone anywhere in the land, not just to priests serving in the temple, and to all food, not just holy offerings.

"The tradition of the elders" (7:5) refers to unscriptural law that institutionalized the Pharisees' interpretation of proper religious practices.[228] The basic motivation was not sinister. As Hengel and Deines maintain, "since the basic *obligation to be holy* applied to the *entire people*, the Pharisees wanted to deduce what was involved from scripture and tradition, and then live this out as an example for the rest."[229]

225. See §4.4.1.2.

226. Gudrun Guttenberger, *Die Gottesvorstellung im Markusevangelium* (BZNW 123; Berlin/New York: de Gruyter, 2004), 129.

227. Back, *Jesus of Nazareth*, 119.

228. The phrase "the traditions of the fathers" appears in Gal 1:14 and in Josephus, *Ant.* 13.10.6 §§297–298; 13.16.2 §§408–409.

229. Martin Hengel and Roland Deines, "E. P. Sanders' 'Common Judaism,' Jesus, and the Pharisees," *JTS* 46 (1995): 47.

The later rabbis argue that this deposit of traditions derived from the oral tradition passed on from Moses to Joshua to the elders to the Prophets to the men of the Great Synagogue (*m. ʾAbot* 1:1).[230] Jesus lays into the tradition of the elders with a quote from Isa 29:13 that, he asserts, applies specifically to these opponents.[231] They are "hypocrites," those who honor God only with their lips while turning away from God with their hearts. They teach their innovations as if they were commandments from God (7:6–7). He refers to it as "human traditions" and "your own traditions" (7:9, 13) that cancel, nullify, and make void the commandment and the word of God (7:8, 9, 13).

Jesus also contrasts what "Moses says" (7:10) with what "you say" (7:11). Among the "many things" he could decry (7:13), Jesus provides one egregious example in the misuse of the Corban vow, a dedicatory vow that promises to give property (or persons) to God, which makes it sacred until it is sold to another or redeemed.[232] In the illustration, a son cunningly uses this vow to evade the responsibility of supporting his parents. The vow could have been phrased, "Any property of mine from which you could benefit is dedicated to the temple." A violation of temple property incurred serious guilt.[233] The tradition that facilitates dodging one's obligation to provide for one's parents exalts honoring a vow to the temple over honoring one's father and mother as God commands (Exod 20:12; 21:17; Deut 5:16; Lev 20:9). This outrage is symptomatic of their misreading of the law. Their tradition not only smiles on a son's plan to manipulate the law to his own advantage, but it abets his honoring God only with his lips and not his heart. Their adherence to their man-made traditions consistently prevents them from discerning God's intention in the law. Jesus essentially declares that the oral traditions of the elders have no binding force on Christians.

5.8.3 Jesus' Ruling on Dietary Laws (Mark 7:17–23)

When Jesus calls the crowd to him after his denunciation of the Pharisees' tradition, he proceeds to go much further and undermines scripturally based dietary laws because they can obscure what truly matters to God, namely, a person's internal purity rather than external purity. Again, the basic contrast is between the external, worship with the lips, and the internal, worship with the heart, which Isaiah makes clear is most vital to God (7:6). Jesus solemnly declares, "Nothing outside a person can defile them by going into them. Rather, it is what comes out of a person that defiles them" (7:15). When the disciples ask him the meaning of what they perceive is only a riddle, Jesus reveals that he is not talking about ritual impurity but only about moral impurity. What defiles a person are those toxic sins that begin with evil thoughts and progress to wicked deeds: "sexual immorality, theft, murder, adultery,

230. On the oral tradition from the perspective of the latter rabbis, see *m. ʾAbot* 1:1–18; 2:1–8; *b. Ber.* 19a; *b. ʿErub.* 54b; *b. Giṭ.* 60b; and *b. Menaḥ.* 29b.

231. This citation marks the third time that Mark quotes from Isaiah (see 1:2–3; 4:12).

232. Collins, *Mark*, 352. The property could be redeemed by the person who made the vow by paying for it plus 20 percent.

233. The casuistry involved in this vow is quite complicated, and Collins, *Mark*, 351–53, provides a succinct summary.

greed, malice, deceit, lewdness, envy, slander, arrogance and folly" (7:21–22). The moral demand to avoid these sins is found in the law and the prophets. God cares about what enters and comes from a person's heart, not a person's stomach.[234]

Dietary laws do not affect this kind of moral defilement and consequently are neither here nor there. What persons say and do is more important than what persons eat and how they eat. Mark adds a comment explaining the significance of Jesus' argument: "In saying this, Jesus declared all foods clean" (7:19).[235] It is significant in the narrative context that this statement appears before Jesus enters into Gentile territory and feeds a Gentile multitude. It is also significant in the mission context of the evangelist and his audience that this declaration makes it possible for Christians and pagans to have social dealings.[236] What is most important for Mark's Christology, however, is that he presents Jesus as the one who truly knows and declares God's will in the law.[237] Kampling insists that the statement in 7:15 reveals that, for Mark, "There is no difference between the teaching of Jesus and the command of God."[238]

5.8.4 Jesus' Ruling on Divorce (Mark 10:1–12)

The Pharisees seek to test Jesus with a question about divorce, "Is it lawful for a man to divorce his wife?" (10:2). Jesus turns the tables on them. He asks them what Moses *commanded* (10:3), and they respond with their interpretation about what Moses *permitted*: "Moses permitted a man to write a certificate of divorce and send her away" (10:4). They assume that Moses sanctioned a man's inalienable right to divorce his wife in Deut 24:1–4, a perspective that is taken for granted in Sir 25:26, "If she does not go as you direct, separate her from yourself." The primary concern of their interpretation of Deut 24:1–4 is how to apply the prescribed procedures in writing out and delivering the certificate of divorce (Deut 24:1–4).[239]

Moses does not spell out the legal grounds for putting away a wife but only gives rules for when it occurs. If the husband finds no favor in her because of some indecency or he simply dislikes her, he writes a bill of divorce. This certificate protects the wife, should she remarry. The husband gives up all rights to her forever if she should become the wife of another man.

Moses gave rules to regulate divorce, but Jesus interprets God's will for marriage. Jesus declares this legislation to be only a stopgap measure because "*your* hearts were hard" (10:5).[240] Guttenberger observes that Moses appears here not as the mediator

234. Broadhead, "Christology as Polemic and Apologetic," 29, comments, "Ethics, not eating, becomes the standard for clean/unclean."

235. The KJV presents Jesus as continuing his argument. The food does not enter the heart but the belly "and goeth out into the draught, purging all meats" (7:19). See Garland, *Mark*, 275–76.

236. Guttenberger, *Die Gottesvorstellung*, 144.

237. Ibid., 147. One may infer that the conclusion derives from Jesus' understanding of God's creation. The refrain, "And God saw that it was good," recurs in the creation account in Genesis 1:4, 10, 12, 18, 21, 25, and 31. One can reasonably conclude that one who consumes food that comes from God's good creation is not inherently defiled.

238. Kampling, "Das Gesetz im Markusevangelium," i, 130.

239. Cranfield, *Mark*, 319, notes that the word translated "certificate of divorce" (*apostasion*) is a legal term in the papyri that contains "the idea of giving up one's right to something." The divorce certificate read: "Behold, thou art permitted to marry any man" (*m. Giṭ.* 9:3).

240. This pointed reference to "*your*" hardness of heart incriminates Jesus' questioners.

of God's will, but as the administrator of the miscarriage of God's will.[241] If the Mosaic legislation on divorce is rooted in human hardness of heart, that is, stubborn rebelliousness against God's will, it cannot reflect God's will. Moses' legislation regarding the certificate of divorce may be legally recognized, but it does not reflect God's purpose for marriage. This law is a concession to the fallen world of humanity. Jesus goes back to God's intention for marriage in creation when God created male and female (Gen 1:27; 2:24).[242]

Because Jesus' opponents have consistently misread Scripture, they consistently misconstrue God's will—in this case, God's will for marriage. In marriage, the two become one flesh (Gen 2:24), and humans are not to tear apart what God has joined together (Mark 10:6–9). Jesus' understanding of God's intention for marriage is expressed even more dramatically when his disciples ask him in private about divorce. He brands remarriage to anyone after a divorce as adultery. The incident presents Jesus as an authoritative teacher who surpasses even Moses as the interpreter of God's will. He is the final arbiter for discerning God's intention in Scripture and how it is to be applied in life.

5.8.5 Jesus' Ruling on the Greatest Commandment (Mark 12:28–34)

When a teacher of the law appreciates Jesus' response to the Sadducees about the resurrection, he inquires which command is first of all (12:28). Jesus gives the expected answer from his Jewish tradition, citing Deut 6:4–5: "Hear, O Israel: The Lord our God, the Lord is one. Love the Lord your God with all your heart and with all your soul and with all your mind and with all your strength" (12:29–30). He adds a second from Lev 19:18, "Love your neighbor as yourself" (12:31). What is required is total commitment to God and total compassion for other humans. The implication is that Jesus considers that the commands of the law are to be understood as expressions of the love for one's neighbor.[243]

The teacher of the law validates Jesus' answer and repeats it. Jesus does not savor the honor of being affirmed by an expert in the law but instead assumes incredible authority by informing him that he is not far from the kingdom of God (12:34). Mark's audience would assume that the teacher of the law cannot enter the kingdom of God simply by approving of Jesus' teaching. One must obey it and follow him.[244]

---

241. Guttenberger, *Die Gottesvorstellung*, 149.

242. Ibid.

243. Ibid., 158.

244. John P. Meier, *The Vision of Matthew* (New York: Paulist, 1978), 43, concludes regarding Jesus' status as a teacher: "Christ is a teacher in a unique way, for what he teaches depends on his own person for its truth, validity, and permanence. Teacher and teaching become inextricably bound together. You do not fully understand what the teaching is unless you understand who the teacher is. You cannot fully accept the teaching as true unless you accept the teacher as your Lord, as Son of God and Son of Man."

5.9 THE HUMANITY OF JESUS IN MARK

Martin writes that Mark paradoxically depicts "a human Jesus who at the same time as revealing his frailty in embarrassing realism also exercises supernatural powers and strides majestically through the Markan stories," and that this paradox apparently poses no problem for the evangelist.[245] The narrative reveals Mark's complex Christology. Jesus is fully divine and fully human.

Jesus gets so exhausted that he sleeps through a storm (4:38). He shows human tenderness and care toward children (10:14–16) and love for one who is about to turn his back on him (10:21). He gets fed up and complains out loud, "You unbelieving generation, how long shall I stay with you?" (9:19). He needs and enjoys human companionship and has a close circle of intimates, Peter, James, and John, within a close circle of followers.

When Martin refers to "his frailty in embarrassing realism," however, he has in mind Mark's description of Jesus' human emotions and limitations that Matthew and Luke leave out or gloss over. Mark describes Jesus' emotional reaction of anger. When a leper begged of him, "If you are willing, you can make me clean" (1:40), the NIV accepts the reading in a textual variant in 1:41 that Jesus "was indignant," instead of being "moved with pity" (NRSV) or having "compassion" on him (NASB).[246] The principle that the hardest reading that best explains the others is the original text drives this choice rather than accepting the majority reading.[247]

The reading that Jesus was angry may also be supported by his immediately sending the leper on his way with a strong warning (1:43).[248] The participle translated "with a strong warning" is rendered "rebuked harshly" in 14:5, when some persons snap at the woman who poured precious perfume on Jesus' head as a huge waste (14:4–5). This verb can suggest anger (Lam 2:6, LXX; Dan 11:30, LXX), or it can express being deeply moved (John 11:33, 38). According to a tradition in *Lev. Rab.* 16:3, one particular rabbi, "when he saw a leper, would throw stones at him and shout: 'Go to your place and do not defile other people,'" but it seems unlikely that Jesus, who reaches out to touch this man to cleanse him of his leprosy, harbors the same attitude toward lepers. It is best to accept the reading of the majority of early texts that Jesus shows compassion on the leper and is deeply moved.[249] Nevertheless, it is telling that no mention of Jesus' human emotions, neither his compassion nor his anger, appears in the parallels in Matt 8:3 and Luke 5:13.

Mark also boldly records Jesus getting angry with his opponents, the Pharisees, when they clash over what is permissible to do on the Sabbath. Jesus had entered a

---

245. Martin, *Mark*, 139.

246. The variant appears in a handful of manuscripts (D, a, ff^2, r^{1*}) that represent the Old Latin. Codex Bezae, which has both the Greek and the Latin, is the only Greek manuscript that has this reading, and it is notoriously eccentric. All other texts read that Jesus has compassion on the man.

247. Bart D. Ehrman, *Misquoting Jesus* (San Francisco: HarperSanFrancisco, 2005), 133–35.

248. The verb translated "sent away" is used elsewhere in Mark to mean "to cast out" in the case of demons (1:34, 39; 3:15, 22–23; 6:13; 7:26; 9:18, 28, 38); "to drive out" in the case of humans (1:12; 5:40; 11:15); to "pluck out" an eye (9:47); or to throw out a dead body (12:8).

249. Peter J. Williams, "An Examination of Ehrman's Case for ὀργισθείς in Mark 1:41," *NovT* 54 (2012): 1–12, has clinched the case for the reading "moved with compassion."

synagogue on the Sabbath, and these nemeses monitored him carefully to see if he would attempt to heal a man with a withered hand. Presumably, they would then publicly censure him for violating the Sabbath (3:1 – 2). Undeterred by their hostility, Jesus tells the man to step forward and asks whether it is lawful to do good or evil on the Sabbath, to save life or to kill (3:4). They do not answer, and Jesus responds to their intransigence with anger, deeply distressed at their hardness of heart (3:5). He heals the man, and the Pharisees immediately conspire with the Herodians on how to do away with Jesus (3:6). These emotions of anger and grief again are omitted in the parallel accounts in Matt 12:9 – 14 and Luke 6:6 – 11.

This account also reveals the ambiguity in Mark's presentation of Jesus' humanity because it also lays bare flashes of his divinity. Once again, Jesus reads the hearts of his opponents (3:5) in the same way that God knows hearts. Tait comments that Jesus' wrath is like "God's reaction to his people's shortcomings in the Old Testament [Gen 6:5 – 7]" and that " 'hardness of heart' is almost a scriptural cliché for the disposition of those who frustrate God's redemptive work."[250] Jesus commands the man to stretch out his hand, and Mark uses the passive voice to report that the man's hand "was completely restored" (3:5; see also 8:25).

The Pharisees provoke another emotional response from Jesus when they argue with him and demand that he provide a sign from heaven to validate his ministry (8:11). They want some definitive proof. Mark records him "sighing deeply" in his spirit (absent from the parallels in Matt 12:38 – 39; 16:1 – 4; Luke 11:29) before giving his response (8:12; see 7:34).

Jesus also expresses indignation at his own disciples when they are guilty of rebuking and shooing away parents who have brought their little children for him to touch as a means of conveying blessing (10:13 – 14). His aggravation again is passed over in the parallel accounts in Matt 19:13 – 15 and Luke 18:15 – 17.

Jesus' emotions are even more candidly portrayed when he is on the Mount of Olives before his arrest. Mark vividly describes his mental anguish as he prepares himself for the suffering to come, and "Christian piety, both ancient and modern, has tended to find these passages offensive and distasteful."[251] He describes Jesus as "deeply distressed and troubled" (14:33). The first word (*ekthambeisthai*) portrays Jesus as being in the grip of a shuddering horror in the face of the dreadful prospect before him. The word translated "troubled" (*adēmonein*) conveys his distress (see Phil 2:26). In 14:34, Jesus evokes lament psalms by describing his grief as a "sorrow to the point of death" (Pss 42:6, 11; 43:5; 116:3). This statement could mean that he is sad to death, referring to the extent of his sorrow. Or, he refers to a sorrow so deep that it could kill, or a sorrow so great that death would be preferable.

This grim picture of his mental state is similar to the despair of Moses (Num 11:14 – 15), Elijah (1 Kgs 19:4), and Jonah (Jonah 4:3, 9), who all say they would

250. Tait, *Jesus*, 116 – 17.

251. Francis Watson, "Ambiguity in the Marcan Narrative," *King's Theological Review* 10 (1987): 14.

rather die than continue to live. Matthew does not attenuate Jesus' distress on the Mount of Olives (Matt 26:37–38) but all reference to Jesus' grief has been omitted by Luke. Jesus' suffering is an embarrassment to a theology that believes that Jesus must have been free from any internal turmoil. It is also embarrassing to those who think that his anguish might hint of an eleventh hour failure of nerve. Jesus apparently takes to heart his warning to Peter when he exhorts him to watch and pray to keep from falling into temptation (14:38), as he engages in persistent and arduous prayer during this time (14:35–36, 39).

Mark also implies that Jesus cannot do things and does not know things that one might expect a divine figure could do or would know. Mark alone comments that when Jesus returned to his hometown of Nazareth and they took offense at him (6:3), he "could not do any miracles there, except lay his hands on a few sick people and heal them" (6:5) and that "he was amazed at their lack of faith" (6:6). Matthew's version avoids any hint that Jesus was unable to do a mighty work or that he was amazed by their lack of faith: "And he did not do many miracles there because of their lack of faith" (Matt 13:58). He "*could* not do" in Mark becomes "he *did* not do" in Matthew, and this refusal to do any miracles is attributed to their skepticism. If Mark portrays Jesus' power being limited by the people's lack of faith, it is not completely suppressed. He does heal a few people.

The sneering dismissal of Jesus when he returns to his hometown of Nazareth also underscores his humanity. He is identified as a "carpenter" (6:3), not as "the carpenter's son" (Matt 13:55; see also Luke 4:22; John 6:42). The word (*tektōn*) could refer to a craftsman who worked in wood, metal, or stone. As a carpenter, he would have crafted ploughs, yokes, pieces of furniture, beams, window lattices, doors, and bolts. Campbell, however, concludes from his careful analysis of the linguistic and literary analysis that Jesus was not merely a carpenter but a "builder" who primarily worked in stone.[252] Meier asserts: "The airy weakling often presented to us in pious paintings and Hollywood movies would hardly have survived the rigors of being Nazareth's *tektōn* from his youth to his early thirties."[253] The elite in the Greco-Roman world assumed that craftsmen were uneducated and uncouth. This text created a problem for later Christians. In the late second century, Celsus scoffed that a humble carpenter could hardly be the mighty Son of God and mockingly connected his work to his crucifixion. Origen, apparently embarrassed by this charge, countered that the gospels never describe Jesus as working with his hands (*Cels.* vi.36).

It is also unusual to identify someone as the son of his mother rather than of his father (6:3).[254] Some have suggested that by identifying Jesus as the son of Mary, they maligned him and perhaps alluded to suspicions about his legitimacy (see Judg

252. Ken M. Campbell, "What Was Jesus' Occupation?" *JETS* 48 (2005): 501–19.

253. John P. Meier, *A Marginal Jew: Rethinking the Historical Jesus* (New York: Doubleday, 1991), 1:281.

254. Some copyists apparently tried to assimilate the text to Matt 13:55 and read "son of the carpenter and of Mary." This reading also removes the problem of Jesus being a carpenter.

11:1–2).[255] Possibly, they refer to him as "Mary's son" to distinguish him from Joseph's children by a previous wife.[256] More likely, they refer to him in this way because his father was no longer alive, and they were expressing their familiarity with his mother who still resides there. They further assert their acquaintance with his background by naming his brothers and mentioning that he also has sisters who live there. It means, "We know you. We go way back."

Mark first introduced Jesus in the narrative as coming from Nazareth in Galilee in 1:9. His mother and his family have already tried and failed to corral him because they thought he was out of his mind (3:21). The details Mark includes in the incident when his hometown repudiates him provide a reminder that Jesus is not some mythic hero, like Superman, who drops down to earth in a spacecraft from an alien planet. He is fully human with a mother, brothers and sisters, and a human occupation. But he is also much more, a prophet, who, like the prophets who came before him, is repudiated by his own people. Marshall asserts, "Their unbelief lies not in a failure to perceive the quality of Jesus' words or the reality of his miracles; it lies rather in a refusal to admit the true *source* of this wisdom and power (v 2) and to accept the unique *identity* of the one who manifests them (v 3)."[257]

Mark does not seek to resolve this paradox that he presents Jesus in his narrative as the fully divine Son of God and also as the fully human son of Mary. He slights neither. He simply provides the historical details in a narrative that Paul asserts in prose, "But when the set time had fully come, God sent his Son, born of a woman, born under the law, to redeem those under the law, that we might receive adoption to sonship" (Gal 4:4–5). As one who is fully human, Jesus suffers severe trials and dies on a cross. His corpse is buried in a tomb until God raises him from the dead.

255. Ethelbert Stauffer, "Jeschu ben Mirjam: Kontroversgeschichtliche Anmerkungen zu Mk 6.3," in *Neotestamentica et Semitica: Studies in Honour of Matthew Black* (ed. E. Earle Ellis and Max Wilcox; Edinburgh: T&T Clark, 1969), 119–28; and Marcus, *Mark 1–8*, 375.

256. Richard Bauckham, "The Brothers and Sisters of Jesus: An Epiphanian Response to John P. Meier," *CBQ* 56 (1994): 698–700, argues that outside of Nazareth, where the family was unknown, Jesus would have been identified simply as the son of Joseph.

257. Marshall, *Faith as a Theme*, 192.

Chapter 6

The Presentation of God in the Gospel of Mark

Bibliography

Carey, Holly J. *Jesus' Cry from the Cross: Towards a First-Century Understanding of the Intertextual Relationship between Psalm 22 and the Narrative of Mark's Gospel.* LNTS 398. London/New York: T&T Clark, 2009. **Gese, Hartmut.** "Psalm 22 und das Neue Testament: Der älteste Bericht vom Tode Jesu und die Entstehung des Herrenmahles." Pp. 180–201 in *Vom Sinai zum Zion*. BEvT. Munich: Chr. Kaiser, 1974. **Guttenberger, Gudrun.** *Die Gottesvorstellung im Markusevangelium*. BZNW 123. Berlin/New York: de Gruyter, 2004. **Kingsbury, Jack Dean.** " 'God' within the Narrative World of Mark." Pp. 75–89 in *The Forgotten God: Perspectives in Biblical Theology: Essays in Honor of Paul J. Achtemeier on the Occasion of his Seventy-Fifth Birthday*. Ed. A. Andrew Das and Frank J. Matera. Louisville: Westminster John Knox, 2002. **Smith, C. Drew.** " 'This Is My Beloved Son; Listen to Him': Theology and Christology in the Gospel of Mark." *HBT* 24 (2002): 53–86. **Sweat, Laura C.** *The Theological Role of Paradox in the Gospel of Mark*. LNTS 492. London: Bloomsbury T&T Clark, 2013.

6.1 Introduction

Mark does not delve into the nature of God. With the exception of 11:25, where Jesus refers to God as "your Father in heaven," the gospel contains no special attributes or ascriptions for God.[1] Most of the references to God in Mark's gospel occur on the lips of Jesus, and one can only know God fully through Jesus. Mark assumes that the audience knows the God of Scripture. God now is more fully known from the narrative, which describes what God has done through his Son, Jesus.

6.2 God as the Director of History

In the introduction to the gospel, God appears behind the scenes as the one directing human history to an intended end and inaugurating something new for the

1. See Donahue, "A Neglected Factor in the Theology of Mark," 565–70, for the statistics and citations and a comparison with the gospels of Matthew and Luke and the letters of Paul.

salvation of humanity. God can draw nigh to enter into the arena of history and change it. The Scripture citation in 1:2–3 reveals that God once again invades history, as foreseen by Isaiah, by sending his messenger to prepare the way for the Lord. Feldmeier and Spieckermann note that while God is "the principal player in Mark," God is "a secret principal player":

> God steps forward as the direct agent at Jesus' baptism, introducing the first half of the gospel when the heavens rip open, the Spirit descends, and a heavenly voice announces, "You are my Son, whom I love; with you I am well pleased" (1:9–11), and at the transfiguration, introducing the second half of the gospel, when Jesus is transfigured, Moses and Elijah meet him, and a heavenly voice announces, "This is my Son, whom I love. Listen to him!" (9:3–7).[2]

God reappears at the end of the narrative but again working behind the scenes. When Jesus dies, the temple veil is ripped from top to bottom (15:38). When the women arrive at an empty tomb, an angel announces that Jesus has been raised (16:6). God is the obvious agent of these events.

History is assumed to be permeable by the divine. God is not an apathetic observer of human affairs but the director of human history leading it to a predetermined destiny. Different slices of the divine plan can be discerned as being worked out in different segments of history so that it may seem at times that the evil powers are prevailing. According to Mark, the coming of Jesus marks a new age in salvation history when God's power has broken into the history in a new way, though it remains hidden to the eyes of most. The Spirit-filled Jesus announces that the time has been fulfilled (1:15). The word translated "time" (*kairos*) refers to an epoch or era that is defined by God's dealing with the world. An age has reached its end in God's plans, and something new is being ushered in. It is an era of good news and celebration, but the bridegroom soon will be taken away and brutally executed. What follows will be a time of mourning (2:19–20) and times of violent persecution for his followers (13:5–23).

But Mark conveys that as the Lord of history, God can and will cut short the days "for the sake of the elect, whom he has chosen," lest they not survive the perils of the tribulation (13:20). God also is in control of the end of history. Only God knows that day or hour, "not even the angels in heaven, nor the Son" (13:32), but the Son of Man will return in glory to gather his elect (13:24–27).

Humans do not set the agenda for the fulfillment of God's promises in history. They can only be receptive or unreceptive and antagonistic, as the case may be. They can understand God's plan for history from the Scriptures. The Scriptures hold the key, but they can be easily misinterpreted and twisted so that even the experts in the law can misread what God is doing and intends to do. For example, Jesus castigates the Pharisees and teachers of the law as "hypocrites" who allow

2. Reinhard Feldmeier and Hermann Spieckermann. *God of the Living: A Biblical Theology* (trans. Mark E. Biddle; Waco, TX: Baylor University Press, 2011), 72.

their tradition to nullify God's word (7:6–13). The Sadducees do not "know the Scriptures or the power of God" (12:24) and misjudge God's nature and purpose to raise the dead. God's reign and purposes are a mystery to most, but it has been revealed to Jesus' disciples (4:11).

6.3 GOD AS KING

In the summary of Jesus' first preaching he declares, "The kingdom of God has come near. Repent and believe the good news!" (1:14–15). The kingdom of God basically refers to God's dynamic reign as king. God's intention as king is to save. He offers protection to his people, guidance for a way of life, and ultimate vindication. The seed parables reveal, however, that God's ruling presence in the world does not overwhelm it (4:1–20, 26–29, 30–32). After the splitting of the heavens and the descent of the Holy Spirit into Jesus, God, as it were, withdraws in hiddenness, and God's revelation is made in the lowliness of his Son as an obedient human being. The revelation is hidden to those who do not have eyes to see or ears to hear beneath the familiar surface of things. It does not come spectacularly, and, consequently, it will be discerned only by the few to whom it is given.

To be sure, Jesus' ministry manifests an eruption of power that is attributable only to his divine empowerment. But false messiahs and false prophets will appear and perform signs and miracles that can deceive even the elect (13:22). As king, God has sent Jesus, as is made clear in 9:37b: "whoever welcomes me does not welcome me but the one who sent me" (see also 12:6). The culmination of sending Jesus will be both the ignominious death of God's Son on a cross, where the blood of the covenant is poured out for many, and his resurrection to sit at God's right hand. The cross and resurrection serve as the hallmark of God's transcendent rule:

> The symbol of God's sovereignty is not a scepter or a mace that God uses to break the bones of his opponents, but the cross, on which the blood of the Son of God is shed. Victory is hidden in the cross. Power is to be found in powerlessness.[3]

Chronis comments:

> Ostensibly, for Mark, suffering love paradoxically defines divinity, and hence it is Jesus' sacrificial suffering and death that demonstrate his Godness. Consequently, Mark finds it appropriate that Jesus' transcendent power and being should be recognized precisely in the depths of his powerlessness and ceasing-to-be, and that it should be ultimately in death (and not in mighty words or deeds) that he reveals his identity as divine *huios theou* [Son of God].[4]

3. Garland, *Mark*, 62.
4. Harry L. Chronis, "The Torn Veil: Cultus and Christology in Mark 15:37–39," *JBL* 101 (1982): 106.

6.4 God as Father

Mark takes for granted that God is the creator of the world and the human family (13:19; 10:6), but as creator God wills to enter into close relationship with humanity. When God announces "You are my Son" (1:11), it asserts Jesus' filial relationship to God. Mark refers to the Son of Man coming in the glory of "his Father" in 8:38, and again this filial relationship is assumed when Jesus says that the Son does not know the day or hour of the end, but only the Father (13:32). The intimacy of this relationship is expressed in Jesus' prayer to his Father on the Mount of Olives for the cup to be removed, if it is possible (14:36).

Mark records Jesus addressing God as "*Abba*," the Aramaic word for "father." The term was used both by children for their father and by disciples for an esteemed teacher. While the term can express intimacy, it does not mean "Daddy." Mark translates it for Greek readers with the regular word for "father" and does not use a diminutive form. While addressing God as "*Abba*" in prayer exhibits an informal intimacy, it is clear that God as Father requires obedience: "Yet not what I will, but what you will" (14:36). In almost an aside, Mark's Jesus notes in 11:25 that this intimate relationship will apply to his followers by telling them that "your Father in heaven" will forgive your sins (11:25). Hartman comments that since Jesus is the Son of God, the readers "are invited to see themselves here as the brothers, etc., of Jesus, because their life—both the biological and the spiritual—originates with this father; that he is 'in heaven' implies that he is the deepest and the highest being within, beyond, and under everything."[5]

6.5 God as All Powerful

Mark assumes God's sovereign power over the universe, and God endows Jesus with the Holy Spirit that empowers him to do his ministry (1:10). This power is evident in Jesus' ability to bind Satan (3:23–27) and to drive out demons as the Holy One of God (1:21–26; 3:11; 5:1–20; 7:25–30; 9:14–27). Jesus' private explanation to the disciples explaining why they were unable to cast out the demon of a young lad that a father had brought to Jesus (9:28–29) attributes the power to do so solely to God. Jesus had commissioned the disciples to exorcise demons (6:7); others were able to cast demons in his name (9:38), but Jesus explains that the power is not something they possess. They are completely dependent on the power of God, and they can only tap into that power through a spiritual relationship to God grounded in prayer (9:29). Donahue states, "Though Jesus empowered the disciples to exorcise, he is not the distributor of this power, only contact with God in prayer evokes it."[6]

Since "all things are possible" for God (10:27; 14:36), all things can be done for those who believe in God (9:23; 11:23). But this truth does not mean that God is at the believer's beck and call. What is requested of God must be in accordance with

5. Hartman, *Mark*, 475.

6. Donahue, "A Neglected Factor in the Theology of Mark," 589.

his purposes. Miraculous signs from heaven will not be given willy-nilly to anyone who demands them (8:11–12). James and John will not get to sit at Jesus' right and left hand as they request (10:35–37). The cup will not be removed from Jesus since it is not God's will (14:36). It is fascinating to note that these references to God's omnipotence, "everything is possible for you," do not "occur in the context of Jesus' successes, where its appearance would be plausible, but on the way to the Passion." Jesus declares God to be all powerful in the context of evil's apparent triumph (14:36).[7]

6.6 GOD AS THE ONE WHO BREAKS DOWN BARRIERS

The good news of God that Jesus preaches (1:14) declares that God is acting in a new way. Mark primes his audience to expect a dramatic development by narrating the tearing of the veil of heaven and the descent of the Holy Spirit into Jesus (1:10). Rhoads comments on this event: "For Mark, God shifts from being a God who stays in place to a God who crosses boundaries."[8]

Mark does not say that the heavens opened, as the KJV renders it, but uses the verb "to split" or "to tear open," which implies that it was done by use of force. The "opening" of the heavens usually indicates that God is about to speak or to act and that one will get a fleeting glimpse of God's intentions, and then they will close up again.[9] What is "ripped open," however, cannot easily return to its former state. Juel interprets the image as suggesting "that the protecting barriers are gone and that God, unwilling to be confined to sacred spaces, is on the loose in our own realm."[10] The ripping of the heavens and the descent of the Holy Spirit convey that God is not closed off but close up and that other barriers will be ruptured as Jesus begins his ministry.

God's love for humans and concern for their salvation is manifest in Jesus' healing of the sick and the forgiveness of sins. Liberation from guilt opens up the way to life. Jesus' statement "I have ... come" implies that God has sent him to sinners to be their physician (2:17). Jesus' merciful reaching out to sinners, however, perplex and provoke those who tend to have a defensive religious posture and prefer that the walls they have erected between the righteous and the sinners remain in place. Their traditions have erected fences that, intentionally or not, keep God sealed off lest those who are impure defile God's holiness in some way.

If one were to ask, "How do I approach Almighty God?" the psalmist answers, "With clean hands and a pure heart" (Ps 24:3–4). According to Jesus, the Pharisees' oral tradition placed an overemphasis on ritually clean hands (7:1–23). The Pharisaic rules related to purity "created the illusion of an ordered cosmos, with

7. Feldmeier and Spieckermann, *God of the Living*, 190.

8. David M. Rhoads, "Mission in the Gospel of Mark," *CurTM* 22 (1995): 343.

9. See Ezek 1:1; John 1:51; Acts 7:56; Rev 4:1; 11:19; 19:11; *Jos. Asen.* 14:2; *2 Bar.* 22:1; *T. Levi* 2:6; 5:1; 18:6; *T. Jud.* 24:2.

10. Juel, *A Master of Surprise*, 34–35.

carefully erected boundaries that kept every person and thing in its proper place."[11] They classified persons, things, places, and times as pure or polluted, as fit or unfit, as susceptible to impurity or as a cause of impurity.[12] The classifications helped one guard against uncleanness, because it is assumed that uncleanness belongs to the realm of death and demons.[13] Contact with that realm fractures fellowship with God because it is assumed from Scripture that God has the same aversion to dirt, disease, and death as humans do. Lindars comments that transgressing the Pharisaic taboos related to purity regulations "not only constitutes a formal disqualification for worship, requiring the proper procedure to restore the situation, but also stains the inner conscience, creating a barrier in one's personal relationship with God."[14] The Pharisees' concern for holiness meant that sinners were to be kept at arm's length until religiously decontaminated by concrete repentance and the proper ceremonial rites.

From the Pharisees' perspective, Jesus was out of control because he disregarded these rules and crossed their carefully drawn boundaries. He touches a leper (1:40–41). He eats with sinners (2:15–17). He is touched by a woman with a flow of blood (5:25–34). He touches a dead girl (5:35–42). He allows his disciples to ignore eating with ritually washed hands (7:1–23). He converses with a woman who is a Gentile Syrophoenician (7:25–30). In all these instances, he is not made unclean but instead cleanses and restores to life. His deeds manifest that God does not recoil from pollution but "spreads holiness and wholeness."[15]

The Pharisees' attitude toward the people was defined by Ezek 44, which lays down rules about who may enter the sanctuary and priestly service. It consists of closed gates (Ezek 44:2) and signs saying no admission to foreigners (44:9). The emphasis is on distinguishing between clean and unclean (44:23). Jesus' attitude toward people reflects the attitude of God as portrayed in Ezek 34, which describes the shepherd who seeks out the weak, the sick, and the lost sheep and feeds them in good pasture (34:12, 16). Mark's account of Jesus' ministry communicates that God's holiness did not need safeguarding. Instead, its numinous transforming power was being let loose on the world. It carries over into Mark's view of mission without boundaries that will preach the gospel through the world.

6.7 God's Involvement in Jesus' Death and Resurrection

Jesus' statement that the Son of Man goes as it is written of him (14:21) reveals that God wills his death. Jesus' alludes to this fact in the allegory of the wicked tenants (12:1–11). After the tenants maliciously seized, beat, treated shamefully,

11. Garland, *Mark*, 279–80.
12. Neyrey, "The Idea of Purity," 92.
13. Milgrom, *Leviticus 1–16*, 1002.
14. Barnabas Lindars, "All Foods Clean: Thoughts on Jesus and the Law," in *Law and Religion* (ed. Barnabas Lindars; Cambridge: James Clarke, 1988), 65.
15. Rhoads, "Mission in Mark," 344.

and killed the servants whom the owner sent to them to collect some of the fruit of the vineyard he had planted, he decides to send his beloved son last of all, saying, "They will respect my son." They do not respect him, but kill the heir, expecting to take over the inheritance. Jesus applies the allegory to himself as "the stone the builders rejected" that will become the cornerstone (12:10). The marvelous thing that the Lord has done (12:11) applies to both his death and his vindication.

When Jesus is arrested, he announces that what is happening is because "the Scriptures must be fulfilled" (14:49). The sentence is unfinished. It reads literally "but in order that the Scriptures be fulfilled," but Jesus clearly understands that God assigned this destiny to him. This purpose is captured in the three passion predictions. The Son of Man "must" suffer many things and be killed (8:31). The "must" reflects a divine necessity rooted in God's plan. The Son of Man will be handed over into the hands of men (9:31), who are identified as "the chief priests and the teachers of the law" in 10:33, "sinners" in 14:41, and "Pilate" in 15:1. This "handing over," then, does not simply refer to Judas's betrayal of Jesus to the Jewish authorities. It is God's hand that is behind Jesus' fate, and the evil stratagems of humans ultimately play into God's hands. God is not involved in Jesus' destiny as a remote, impersonal, and impassive divinity. God has sent his Son, whom he loves (12:6; 1:11; 9:7), to die. God will therefore transform the cross into a striking victory.

At the Last Supper, Jesus unambiguously states that God is behind his upcoming death. Quoting Zech 13:7, he refers to God as striking the shepherd (14:27). This text is solemnly introduced with the words "for it is written," and the quote is altered from 13:7 in a way that communicates God's direct involvement in what happens to Jesus. In that verse, God commands the sword to "awake ... against my shepherd" and to "strike the shepherd." Jesus' citation emphasizes God's agency: "*I* will strike the shepherd." God is the initiator of what is to come.[16]

6.8 GOD'S SILENCE IN THE FACE OF JESUS' SUFFERING

While Mark only specifies Zech 13:7 as a passage from Scripture that is being fulfilled by Jesus' death, echoes from the psalms of the righteous sufferer form a prominent backdrop for the Passion Narrative. Various allusions surface in the narrative.[17]

Mark	Psalms
14:1 Plot to kill Jesus by cunning	10:7–9
14:18 Betrayal by the one eating with me	41:9
14:34 Sorrow to the point of death	6:3; 42:5–6, 11; 43:5

16. This alteration is consistent with the phrase in the same verse, "I will turn my hand against the little ones" (Zech 13:7b).

17. Marcus, *Mark 8–16*, 984.

14:41 Delivered into the hands of sinners	140:4, 8
14:55 Seeking to put him to death	37:32; 54:3
14:57 False witnesses rising up	27:12; 35:11
14:61; 15:4–5 Silence before accusers	38:13–15; 39:9
15:24 Division of his garments	22:18
15:27 Encompassed by evildoers	22:16
15:29 Mockery and the wagging of heads	22:7
15:30–31 The taunt to save yourself	22:8
15:32 Reviling	22:6
15:34 The cry of forsakenness	22:1 (11, 19, 21)
15:36 Vinegar as a drink	69:21
15:40 Those looking on from a distance	38:11

Two passages in Mark reveal something about God that may be troubling. On the Mount of Olives, Mark vividly describes Jesus' distress as he faces the hour of his suffering. His spirit is strung taut to the breaking point. He cries out for the cup to be removed from him and seemingly reluctantly surrenders to God's will when God is silent (14:34–36, 39). At the moment before his death on the cross, Jesus cries out reproachfully to God for forsaking him (15:34). What do these two instances say about God?

6.8.1 Removing the Cup (Mark 14:35–36)

Of the four gospel accounts of Jesus on the Mount of Olives before his arrest, Mark's scene is darkest. Mark describes Jesus as "deeply distressed and troubled" (14:33), and in direct speech Jesus says, "My soul is overwhelmed with sorrow to the point of death" (14:34), an echo from Pss 42:5–6, 11; 43:5. In recounting Jesus' prayer, Mark first uses indirect narrative to depict his request for the cup to be removed: "Going a little farther, he fell to the ground and prayed that if possible the hour might pass from him" (14:35). It is then followed by direct speech, "'*Abba*, Father,' he said, 'everything is possible for you. Take this cup from me. Yet not what I will, but what you will'" (14:36). The third request is described in indirect narrative, "Once more he went away and prayed the same thing" (14:39). The cup may represent either the awful consequences of God's wrathful judgment on sinful humanity (Pss 11:6; 16:5; 23:5; 75:8–9; 116:13; Isa 51:17–23; Jer 16:7; 25:15–18; 49:12; 51:7; Ezek 23:31–34; Lam 4:21; Hab 2:15–16; Zech 12:2; Rev 14:10; 16:19; 17:4; 18:3, 6),[18] or simply the suffering and cruel death Jesus must endure.

Mark portrays Jesus as being less than stoically composed in the face of his

18. Matthew Black, "The Cup Metaphor in Mark xiv. 36," *ExpTim* 59 (1947–48): 195.

suffering and death, and he expresses his desire to escape it. Watson points out that "Christian piety, both ancient and modern, has tended to find these passages offensive and distasteful."[19] Those who might find this passage theologically offensive fail to recognize that his prayer fits the long tradition of Jewish lament. Lamentation to God is not prayer that is impassive, "fully controlled, or strained with politeness. In a rush of emotion, complaint, and even recrimination, the believers pour out their hearts to God."[20] Jesus' lament is not an insubordinate request to evade God's will but a demonstration of his trust that God listens to prayer and grants requests that can be reconciled "with overall Providence."[21]

Kelber judiciously warns, "The exegesis of Jesus' state at Gethsemane is habitually attended with the danger of being seduced into a psychological reading of the mind of Jesus."[22] It is unproductive to speculate if Jesus suddenly had a change of heart or what might have caused it. Tolbert notes that monologues in ancient literature "are not basically psychological but rather rhetorical."[23] The monologues typically occur at crucial points when a character is on the verge of battle or some other risky venture: "Why does my own heart dispute with me thus?"[24] Tolbert, citing Scholes and Kellogg, observes that monologues appear in those critical moments when "a character seems to be giving way to the promptings of his *thymos* [heart or mind] but pulls himself together in the formulaic mind ... and proceeds to do the right thing."[25]

When Mark allows the reader to hear Jesus' prayer at a moment of great crisis as the hour has come upon him, it strikes a chord in the audience. The audience can identify with Jesus' pain, and he therefore becomes an example. But Jesus' pain is not simply because death is staring him in the face. Marcus argues that the language of "keep awake," "hour," "cup," "sleeping," and "has come near" in the immediate context has "an apocalyptic nuance elsewhere in Mark, the rest of the NT, and ancient Jewish literature." Jesus' anguish reflects "an ongoing battle for the salvation of the world."[26]

Jesus' prayer brings to light several important theological points. First, Rindge sees a connection between Jesus as God's beloved Son and Isaac as Abraham's beloved son. He suggests, "Jesus attempts, perhaps, to convince God to intervene as God did to save Isaac."[27] God's silence reveals that there will be no ram caught in a thicket to be offered as a substitute sacrifice for this beloved Son. Jesus must undergo this suffering and die as the ransom for many (10:45). The cross is God's decision for him. It comes to him as a cup that needs to be drunk to the dregs,

19. Watson, "Ambiguity in the Marcan Narrative," 14.

20. Senior, *Passion*, 76.

21. Brown, *Death*, 1:167.

22. Werner H. Kelber, "Mark 14,32–42: Gethsemane: Passion Christology and Discipleship Failure," *ZNW* 63 (1972): 177.

23. Tolbert, *Sowing the Gospel*, 215; following Robert Scholes and Robert Kellogg, *The Nature of Narrative* (London: Oxford University Press, 1966), 177–94.

24. See Homer, *Il.* 11.402 (Odysseus); 17.97 (Menelaus); 21.562 (Agenor); 22.122 (Hector).

25. Tolbert, *Sowing the Gospel*, 215, citing Scholes and Kellogg, *The Nature of Narrative*, 180.

26. Marcus, *Mark 8–16*, 984.

27. Matthew S. Rindge, "Reconfiguring the Akedah and Recasting God: Lament and Divine Abandonment in Mark," *JBL* 130 (2011): 769.

and it cannot be passed on to others. Jesus becomes a model of one who faithfully obeys no matter what and lives out his trust in God in the face of God's inscrutable demands. As king, God gives commands (3:35; 7:8), and they must be obeyed and his will must be done. Those who do the will of God will be accounted as Jesus' brother, sister, and mother (3:35). Those who do not submit themselves to God's rule will be judged.

Second, Jesus does not pray for strength to endure what lies before him but for God to remove the cup entirely. By showing God's beloved Son grappling with the suffering in store for him through intense prayer, Mark presents him as an example of prayer for disciples. One only discerns God's will through prayer, and one can only meet and prevail over whatever test that might come through deep and passionate prayer. This scene reveals that answers to prayer accord only with God's providence, not with one's personal wishes. All things are possible for God (9:23; 10:27), but it is not possible for God to grant Jesus' request to remove this cup.

Third, what is most striking about this scene is that Jesus' intense prayer meets with the dreadful silence of heaven. No reassuring voice from heaven proclaims, "You are my beloved Son." The heavens are not torn open and the Spirit does not visibly descend on him as it did at his baptism (1:10). No ministering angels come to serve him as they did after his forty-day sojourn in the wilderness (1:13). God does not always speak through words of comfort in response to prayer. God can also speak through excruciating silence. Jesus knows that God has already spoken about his destiny and learns from the silence that nothing has changed. Jesus must obey and trust God. The disciples' continuing sleep, a token of human faithlessness and sin, is a palpable answer to Jesus' prayer.[28] Human sin means the cup cannot pass from him.

6.8.2 Abandonment by God (Mark 15:34)

The only words that Mark records Jesus speaking from the cross is his cry at the ninth hour, " '*Eloi, Eloi, lama sabachthani?*' —which means, 'My God, my God, why have you forsaken me?' " (15:34). Mark's text has Jesus cite the first verse of Ps 22 in the Aramaic vernacular rather than in the Hebrew original.[29] It suggests that "Jesus is not just quoting the psalm but has deeply assimilated these words of the psalm, making them genuinely his own."[30] What this cry is meant to convey, however, is subject to different interpretations.

28. Reinhard Feldmeier, *Die Krisis des Gottessohnes: Die Gethsemaneerzählung als Schlüssel der Markuspassion* (WUNT 2/21; Tübingen: Mohr Siebeck, 1987), 247.

29. See Douglas J. Moo, *The Old Testament in the Gospel Passion Narratives* (Sheffield: Almond, 1983), 264–68. Casey, *Aramaic Sources*, 88, suggests that Jesus read the Scriptures in Hebrew but expounded them in Aramaic, and he is using the language in which he "*expounded* the Scriptures." This suggestion may be a clue for interpreting this cry. The quotation from the Scripture may need to be expounded in light of the whole psalm.

30. Richard Bauckham, "The Gospel of Mark: Origins and Eyewitness," 166.

6.8.2.1 An Expression of Desolation over God's Abandonment

Many take this lament quite naturally as Jesus' cry of despair in the darkness over his divine abandonment. If one introduces the idea of God's holy wrath and the nature of sin that cuts the sinner off from God (see Isa 59:2) and assumes that Jesus takes the place of sinners to face the judgment on sin that is deservedly theirs, then one can interpret this cry to mean that Jesus experiences God's desertion when he drinks this bitter cup of God's wrath on the cross. He is totally forsaken. He cries out in acute agony as he bears the utmost penalty of the world's sin and is abandoned by God to the terrible abyss. This interpretation accords with Paul's assertions in 2 Cor 5:21, "God made him who had no sin to be sin for us, so that in him we might become the righteousness of God," and Gal 3:13, "Christ redeemed us from the curse of the law by becoming a curse for us—for it is written, 'Cursed is everyone who is hanged on a tree'" (ESV). Calvin reasoned: "If Christ had died only a bodily death, it would have been ineffectual.... Unless his soul shared in the punishment, he would have been the Redeemer of bodies alone."[31] Cranfield avers, "The burden of the world's sin, his complete self-identification with sinners, involved not merely a felt, but a real, abandonment by his Father. It is in the cry of dereliction that the full horror of man's sin stands revealed."[32]

Interpreting the darkness that covered the whole earth (the NIV translation interprets it as limited to the "land") from the sixth hour until the ninth hour as signifying God's judgment may support this reading. Amos 8:9–10 provides a significant backdrop:

> "In that day," declares the Sovereign LORD,
> "I will make the sun go down at noon
> and darken the earth in broad daylight.
> I will turn your religious festivals into mourning
> and all your singing into weeping.
> I will make all of you wear sackcloth
> and shave your heads.
> I will make that time like mourning for an only son
> and the end of it like a bitter day."[33]

Schweitzer also argues that Jesus uttered a human cry of desolation in the face of defeat and estrangement, but he famously gives it a twist. He claims that Jesus expected the kingdom of God to come, and Jesus as the Son of Man "lays hold of the wheel of the world to set it moving on that last revolution which is to bring

31. John Calvin, *Institutes*, 2.16.10 and 12, cited by John R. W. Stott, *The Cross of Christ* (Downers Grove, IL: InterVarsity Press, 1986), 81.

32. Cranfield, *Mark*, 458. He goes on to argue that it is "theologically important to maintain the paradox that, while this God-forsakenness was utterly real, the unity of the Blessed Trinity was even then unbroken" (459). Hooker, *Mark*, 375, comments, "These words provide a profound theological comment on the oneness of Jesus with humanity, and on the meaning of his death, in which shares human despair to the full." See also Best, *Temptation*, lxiv–lxviii.

33. See also Exod 10:21, which threatens Egypt with a "darkness that can be felt"; Jer 15:9; Joel 2:2, 10, 31; 3:15; Zeph 1:15.

all ordinary history to a close. It refuses to turn, and He throws Himself upon it. Then it does turn; and crushes Him."[34] He contends that Jesus died on the cross "with a loud cry, despairing of bringing in the new heaven and the new earth."[35] In Schweitzer's view, the darkness that had beset the land has now penetrated Jesus' heart. Since Mark presents Jesus castigating his disciples for their lack of faith (4:40) and encouraging others to have faith in the midst of woe (9:23) and when faced with insurmountable odds (11:23–24), it is highly unlikely that Mark intends to portray Jesus' faith faltering at the end and dying in surprised dereliction.

Others, who reject Schweitzer's explanation, nonetheless contend that Jesus' physical agony and mental anguish obscured his sense of communion with the Father. He *felt* utterly abandoned by God, but he refuses to let go and cries out to "my God." Broadus writes: "If it be asked how he could feel himself to be forsaken, we must remember that a human soul as well as a human body was here suffering, a human soul thinking and feeling within human limitations (Mark 13:32), not psychologically unlike the action of other devout souls when in some great and overwhelming sorrow."[36] It only seemed to Jesus that God was absent, but in reality was God never more fully and forcefully present than when Jesus dies on the cross.

Shipp challenges this interpretation with the question:

> What does it mean to say "It may *feel* as if God is absent, but he really is present," to the one who experiences God's absence in pain, loss, death, or persecution? To the one who laments, such abstractions are meaningless. So we are left with the honest and righteous cry of the one who laments—"Why are you so far away"—regardless of whether the absence and silence of God are "real" or only perceived. The introduction brings us immediately to the problem of all faithful people who suffer: the problem of the absence and silence of God.[37]

6.8.2.2 A Lament that Trusts in God's Deliverance

Others challenge the interpretation that Jesus' cry is an expression of despair in recognition that God has indeed turned away from him during his torment on the cross. Taylor asserts, for example, that the view that Jesus was forsaken by God because he was a substitute for sinners is "inconsistent with the love of God and the oneness of purpose with the Father manifest in the atoning ministry of Jesus."[38] It is therefore difficult for some to accept that Jesus, who has been betrayed, deserted,

34. Albert Schweitzer, *The Quest of the Historical Jesus: A Critical Study of its Progress from Reimarus to Wrede* (trans. William Montgomery; New York: Macmillan, 1961), 370–71.

35. Ibid., 255.

36. John A. Broadus, *Commentary on the Gospel of Matthew* (Philadelphia: The American Baptist Publication Society, 1886), 574.

37. R. Mark Shipp, "Psalm 22: The Prayer of the Righteous Sufferer," *Christian Studies* 25 (2011–12): 52. Watson, "Ambiguity in the Marcan Narrative," 15, interprets the cry to mean, "God who was once gladly addressed as 'Abba' has incomprehensibly turned away and hidden his face. In a moment of both bewilderment and insight, the reality of God-forsakenness as a characteristic of the world is recognized. No resolution to the problem is offered: only the question, "Why...?", and the equally eloquent though wordless 'loud cry' with which Jesus dies." Watson considers "God-forsakenness" to be "an inescapable aspect of reality." "Here, the story of Jesus makes the same point as the older story of Job: the world does not point unambiguously to a rational and loving providential care, and we must honestly accept this fact."

38. Taylor, *Mark*, 594.

denounced, denied, denuded, and derided by humans, is now abandoned by God in his hour of suffering and need.

Donahue and Harrington assert, "That these words are intended as a cry of despair on Jesus' part makes no sense at all. Why would Mark write a 'gospel' ('good news') about a tragic figure whose life ends in total despair? Such a work might qualify as a tragedy or a pathetic biography, but hardly as a gospel."[39] They argue that a literary and theological reading of Mark "would rightly place more emphasis on Psalm 22 taken as a whole as the prayer of a suffering righteous person and an important element in Mark's Christology."[40] It is unlikely that Mark would intend for the last words that Jesus speaks in the gospel to be a cry of despair. That Jesus' last words mimic the psalmist's (22:1) suggests that he intentionally resorts to Scripture to put his torment into words.[41] Dalman pointed out that the psalm was not an expression of despair, and Jewish interpretation of it did not explain it as such. Instead, "it exhibited the state of mind of one who even in the travail of death was conscious that He belonged to God, and now reminded His Father that He could not well leave Him in the lurch."[42]

Mark underscores that what was happening to Jesus fulfilled Scripture (14:21, 27, 49), and the details in Ps 22 tally well with what happens in a crucifixion as a matter of course. It was customary for the executioners to share out the minor personal belongings of the victim being executed,[43] and Mark presents the division of his garments and casting lots for them (15:24/Ps 22:18/LXX 21:19). The mocking of someone being executed was also normal, and Mark presents the passersby mocking and wagging their heads in derision (15:29/Ps 22:7/LXX 21:8).[44] The taunt for Jesus to save himself parallels the mockery of the sufferer in the psalm to let the Lord save him (15:30/Ps 22:8/LXX 21:9). Jesus' cry from the opening verse of Ps 22 would have cued an audience to read that psalm to find things that corresponded to what was happening when Jesus was crucified and to interpret his death in light of the psalm.[45]

Marcus contends that Mark's narrative from 15:20b to 16:6 "follows the course of the psalm in many significant details."[46]

---

39. Donahue and Harrington, *Mark*, 450.

40. Ibid., 451.

41. That he does not address God as "Abba" as he does in 14:36 may be due to his sense of alienation from God, or, more likely, it is attributable to his quoting Scripture.

42. Gustaf Dalman, *Jesus—Jeshua: Studies in the Gospels* (trans. Paul P. Levertoff; New York: Ktav, 1971), 207.

43. A. N. Sherwin-White, *Roman Society and Roman Law in the New Testament* (Oxford: Clarendon, 1963), 46; Justinian, *Digest* 48.20.6.

44. The details of Psalm 22, however, were not used to construct the crucifixion account. The psalm also mentions "bulls" (Ps 22:12), "lions" (Ps 22:13, 21), "dogs" (Ps 22:16), and "the horns of the wild oxen" (Ps 22:21), but no allusion to them appears in the crucifixion account. A threatening "sword" appears in Ps 22:20, but swords only appear when Jesus is arrested (Mark 14:48). Mark's laconic description of the crucifixion does not mention that Jesus' hands and feet were pierced (Ps 22:16).

45. Matthew adds the taunt "He trusts in the LORD ... let the LORD rescue him. Let him deliver him, since he delights in him" (Ps 22:8; Matt 27:43), and John adds the piercing of Jesus' body (Ps 22:16; John 19:34).

46. Marcus, *Way*, 182. Carey, *Jesus' Cry*, 142–50, identifies what she calls "fainter allusions" to Ps 22 in the larger narrative and in the Passion Narrative.

Psalm 22	Mark
Suffering (22:1 – 21)	15:20b – 27
Worship by Gentiles (22:27)	15:39
The kingdom of God (22:28)	15:43
Resurrection (22:29)	16:6
Proclamation to God's people (22:30 – 31)	16:7

Robbins objects that the "context of mockery and death into which Markan discourse places Ps 22 reverses the sequence of scenes in the psalm and subverts the rhetoric of confidence expressed in it."[47] This reversal of sequence, however, is coincidental and not rhetorical. The stripping of the victim and the division of the garments, the mockery of passersby, and the death cry of the victim follow the natural order of what would transpire at a crucifixion.

I would argue that this cry reflects the historical Jesus' intimate familiarity with Scripture that led him to this particular lament, the classic expression of the righteous person's anguish and vexation with God when undergoing torment. At the ninth hour, the Jewish hour of prayer (Acts 3:1), Jesus shouts out the prayer of the righteous sufferer who trusts fully in God's protection. His prayer is addressed to "my God," not to some remote and aloof deity. If he believed that God had truly forsaken him, why would he cry out to an absent God? The cry from Scripture assumes that Jesus (and Mark) believed that God was indeed there to hear and was able to deliver him. Senior maintains: "These words are, in effect, the final version of the prayer in Gethsemane where, also in a 'lament,' Jesus affirmed his unbroken trust in his Father while feeling the full horror of approaching death (cf. 14:32 – 42)."[48]

For Mark, the cry conveys that Jesus realizes that he has accomplished his mission and now cries to God for help. What Shipp writes about lament applies to the scene in Mark:

> Lament is much more than just complaint. It is the invocation of God into lament with the sufferer and is therefore an act of trust. It is to give to God everything we are and have. It is to cry out to God, suspended by our fingernails over the abyss.[49]

Psalm 22 begins with an anguished wail of pain, but in 22:19 there is a marked shift from lamentation to a burst in confidence that God would deliver the sufferer.[50]

47. Vernon K. Robbins, "The Reversed Contextualization of Psalm 22 in the Markan Crucifixion: A Socio-Rhetorical Analysis," in *The Four Gospels 1992: Festschrift Frans Neirynck* (ed. Frans van Segbroeck et al.; BETL 100; Leuven: Leuven University Press, 1992), 2:1164.

48. Senior, *Passion*, 124.

49. R. Mark Shipp, "'Smash Them against the Rocks'? The Christian Appropriation of Difficult Psalms," *Christian Studies* 26 (2013 – 14): 67.

50. The biblical lament begins by invoking God's name in a cry of distress and a frank expression of grievance against God. The mourner outlines the distress, expresses perplexity at the apparent triumph of enemies, and urgently prays for relief. The lamentation normally concludes with an expression of trust and thanksgiving and confidence that God has heard.

This deliverance will result in praising, honoring, and revering God for not despising or disdaining "the suffering of the afflicted one" and not hiding his face from those who cry for help (22:22–26). It concludes on a note of triumph with the affirmation that "all the families of the nations will bow down before him," and "future generations will be told about the Lord. They will proclaim his righteousness, declaring to a people yet unborn: He has done it!" (Ps 22:27–31).

Does Mark intend for the audience to interpret this cry in light of the entire psalm? Some ask reasonably why Mark should have Jesus quote only the beginning of the psalm if he was also alluding to its triumphant ending.[51] They insist on what Carey classifies as an "atomistic" reading of the citation that excludes allowing the context of the psalm to interpret Jesus' cry. But Mark has Jesus cite a single phrase from Isa 56:7 and from Jer 7:11 in Mark 11:17 that requires that these citations be read in light of their contexts to understand fully what Jesus intends. If Mark is recording what historically happened, it would be impossible for a crucified victim struggling for every breath to utter the entire psalm, but those who insist on an atomistic reading would only be convinced that the cry should be read in light of its context if Jesus spoke further words that were pointers to the psalm's conclusion.

Speaking the first words of the psalm, however, could allude to the entire context. The first line of a psalm could function like a title or incipit that invokes the entire context.[52] Chapter and verse divisions did not exist, and specific passages elsewhere in Scripture were cited by the first verse or key phrases. An example of this practice appears in 12:26, where Jesus cites Exod 3:6 and identifies it as from "the Book of Moses, in the account of the burning bush" (lit., "in the book of Moses at the bush"). Jews in Jesus' day were immersed in the Scripture the way moderns are immersed in television and the movies and can pick up rarefied allusions to them, and they would know that Ps 22 begins with despair but ends on a triumphant note. The Psalms were a regular part of Christian worship (Col 3:16), and the audience would have knowledge of them and could recognize the allusions.[53] The way Mark alludes to Scripture throughout his gospel suggests that he expects his audience to have familiarity with the Scriptures and the ability to connect the dots. If not all could do so, there were readers or members of the audience who could interpret passages for the others.[54]

Mark underscores that Jesus identifies himself with the righteous sufferer who

51. Gundry, *Mark*, 966, contends "the cry of despair in Ps 22:2(1) would be a singularly inapt pointer to a confidence spelled out in a wholly different kind of material many verses later in the psalm." France, *Mark*, 652–53, argues that "to read into these few tortured words an exegesis of the whole psalm is to turn upside down the effect which Mark has created by this powerful and enigmatic cry of agony."

52. Carey, *Jesus' Cry*, 106–11. See William F. Albright, "A Catalogue of Early Hebrew Lyric Poems (Psalm LXVIII)," *HUCA* 23 (1950): 1–39. *Mishnah Tamid* 5:2 describes the priests at the daily whole offering reciting a benediction, the Ten Commandments, and then passages identified by the first word or first line, the Shema (Deut 6:4–9); the *"And it shall come to pass if ye shall hearken"*(Deut 11:13–21); and the *"And the Lord spake unto Moses"* (Num 15:37–41). In *m. Tamid* 7:4, the seven songs sung by the Levites are all identified by the first verse of each psalm. A similar practice occurs in referring to gospel passages by the first word in Latin, the *Magnificat, Benedictus, Nunc Dimittis*, or, in German, *der Vaterunser*.

53. Carey, *Jesus' Cry*, 142–43.

54. Carey, ibid., 24, argues that the special level of biblical competency for interpreting Mark's use of Ps 22 in Mark 15:34 "has only to be located in the implied *reader*, not in the average first-century Christian."

feels the pain of his testing and complains stridently to God. This stridency attests to an intimacy with God that can complain boldly, but it also attests to an ultimate trust in God to intervene and to deliver. If one understands this cry as a prayer, then God immediately answers it in Mark's narrative sequence. The darkness that lasted from the sixth to the ninth hour immediately lifts, and Jesus is released from his suffering by his death. Mark notes that when Joseph of Arimathea boldly requested permission from Pilate to bury Jesus' body, Pilate "was surprised to hear that he was already dead" and summoned the centurion to make certain that he was dead (15:43–44). This detail may reinforce the hope for the audience that God will shorten the days of tribulation for sake of the elect lest no one survive the travail (13:20). The events that follow—the splitting of the temple veil, the confession of the centurion that Jesus is the Son of God, and the resurrection—reveal in overwhelming fashion that God has not hidden his face from Jesus but has listened to his cry for help (Ps 22:24).

Carey makes the case for a contextual reading of the citation from Ps 22. She argues this reading does not negate the real suffering Jesus experienced and shows that in Mark suffering and vindication go together as they do in the psalm.[55] In each passion prediction, Jesus refers to his vindication in his resurrection after three days (8:31; 9:31; 10:33–34).[56] Human violence will be countered by God's miraculous deliverance. This is the message of the psalm.[57] Carey contends that without the full context of Ps 22 in view, Mark's readers would fail to recognize the intention of the narrative to hold the two, suffering and vindication, in tension.[58] Mark's narrative sets up the expectation that something would happen beyond Jesus' death. God will intervene.

This passage is another where Mark leaves his audience to ponder an enigma and confront the question: How is it that God wills this suffering, compels Jesus to drink the cup to the dregs, and then have him endure being forsaken? Mark does not resolve the question of "Why," which Jesus himself asks. We are left to contemplate the truth that Jesus was tempted in every way as we are and lamented in every way as we do. What this lament can convey to an audience that faces persecution is that Jesus "enters into the Pit, he suffers the same persecution from enemies, the same physical distress, the same apparent silence and absence of God, that afflicts the psalmist in Psalm 22."[59] His blunt complaint to God reveals that God can be "accused, questioned and blamed,"[60] but the sequence of events after this cry also reveals that, as the psalmist in Ps 22 also believes, God is faithful to rescue. The righteous sufferer will be vindicated. This attitude of faith forms a striking

55. Carey, *Jesus' Cry*, 4–5, 45–69.

56. Ibid., 29.

57. Watts, "The Psalms in Mark's Gospel," 44, writes, "It is hard to see how anyone familiar with the 'righteous sufferer' psalms and Psalm 22 in particular could fail to expect that Jesus, David's messianic lord, will know Yahweh's vindication. It is intriguing to note that after Mark 15:37 and in keeping with the conclusion of Psalm 22, a representative of the Gentiles confesses Jesus to be the son of God (15:39; Ps 22:28), life is regained (16:6; Ps 22:30c), and proclamation encouraged (cf. 16:7; Ps 22:31–32)."

58. Ibid., 5.

59. Shipp, "Psalm 22," 58.

60. Rindge, "Reconfiguring the Akedah and Recasting God," 773.

contrast to that of the dying Hercules in Seneca's *Hercules Oetaeus* 1148–1150. After completing the twelve tasks assigned to him, Seneca has Hercules angrily fulminate against Jove by announcing that his death will bring about the collapse of the universe that will shake Jove's sovereignty:

> Yea, father [*genitor*], thy whole realm of air will my death put to hazard. Then ere thou art utterly despoiled of heaven, bury me father, 'neath the whole ruined world. Shatter the skies which thou art doomed to lose.[61]

Jesus' cry reveals the faith of one whose death saves a ruined world and establishes God's reign on earth. Mark may have intended to encourage his first readers, who also were experiencing a sense of abandonment in the midst of persecution and would identify with this anguish. Tolbert comments:

> The content of Jesus' cry from the cross, his expression of abandonment by God, stands as an assurance to his followers that the worst desolation imaginable, cosmic isolation, can be endured faithfully. What is separation from family and betrayal or denial by friends in comparison to that timeless moment of nothingness when God's Son is deserted by God?[62]

6.9 THE MYSTERY OF THE INCARNATION

Mark emphasizes that God is one, and he is the only author in the NT to quote the entire Shema (Deut 6:4) directly. When a teacher of the law asks Jesus to name the greatest commandment, he responds, " 'Hear, O Israel: the Lord our God, the Lord is one. Love the Lord your God with all your heart and with all your soul and with all your mind and with all your strength' " (Mark 12:29–30). Most references to God occur on the lips of Jesus, but the teacher of the law both affirms and reiterates Jesus' judgment, "You are right in saying that God is one and there is no other but him" (12:32). This answer combines Deut 4:35 ("You were shown these things so that you might know that the LORD is God; besides him there is no other") and Isa 45:21b ("Was it not I, the LORD? And there is no God apart from me, a righteous God and a Savior; there is none but me").

The oneness of God is also affirmed earlier by Jesus' antagonists, if peevishly, after Jesus announces that a paralytic's sins have been forgiven. The teachers of the law ask contemptuously, "Who can forgive sins but God alone?" (2:7). Jesus affirms the oneness of God in response to a man who runs up to him, falls on his knees before him and asks, "Good teacher, what must I do to inherit eternal life?" Jesus brusquely replies, "Why do you call me good? No one is good—except God alone" (10:17–18). The literal rendering of his answer is "except the one God." Mark's gospel shows God's goodness in sending his Son

61. Cited by Bilezikian, *The Liberated Gospel*, 129.

62. Tolbert, *Sowing the Gospel*, 287.

to fulfill God's purpose to ransom the many through his death so that they might have eternal life and in vindicating and exalting him in the resurrection.

If, as I have argued, Mark contains a high Christology and presents Jesus as a divine figure who also was fully human, the gospel offers little to help unpack the mystery of the incarnation and how it is that God is one and that Jesus is "the Lord" of the OT come in the flesh. Mark simply takes it for granted, but his Christology reveals that Christians have begun to redefine what it means to be a monotheist.[63] This theology presents the believer with a great paradox, and Mark is filled with paradoxes. Sweat contends that paradox, with its ambiguity and contradictions, is "the only way to express a sovereign God in a fallible, temporal world." She continues:

> Understanding God is more than Mark's audience can manage, and indeed, more than its author can pen. So this story takes winding turns and creative routes, marked by street-signs of enigmas, secrecy, and mystery. Contradictory statements are simultaneously true. In this way, the audience may find, in the words of Niels Bohr, that the opposite of one profound truth is not falsehood: it is another profound truth.[64]

63. See Hurtado, *How on Earth Did Jesus Become A God?*; idem, *God in New Testament Theology* (Nashville: Abingdon, 2010); idem, "'Ancient Jewish Monotheism' in the Hellenistic and Roman Periods," *JAJ* 4 (2013): 379–400.

64. Sweat, *The Theological Role of Paradox*, 27.

Chapter 7

THE KINGDOM OF GOD IN MARK

BIBLIOGRAPHY

Ambrozic, Aloysius M. *The Hidden Kingdom: A Redaction-Critical Study of the References to the Kingdom of God in Mark's Gospel.* CBQMS 2. Washington, DC: Catholic Biblical Association of America, 1972. **Beasley-Murray, George R.** *Jesus and the Kingdom of God.* Grand Rapids: Eerdmans, 1986. **Betsworth, Sharon.** *The Reign of God Is Such as These: A Socio-Literary Analysis of Daughters in the Gospel of Mark.* LNTS 422. London/New York: T&T Clark, 2010. **Dahl, Nils Alstrup.** "The Parables of Growth." Pp. 141–66 in *Jesus in the Memory of the Early Church.* Minneapolis: Augsburg, 1976. **France, R. T.** *Divine Government: God's Kingship in the Gospel of Mark.* London: SPCK, 1990. **Hiers, Richard H.** *The Kingdom of God in the Synoptic Tradition.* Gainesville, FL: University of Florida Press, 1970. **Hooker, Morna D.** "Mark's Parables of the Kingdom: (Mark 4:1–34)." Pp. 79–101 in *The Challenge of Jesus' Parables.* Ed. Richard N. Longenecker. MacMaster New Testament Studies. Grand Rapids: Eerdmans, 2000. **Kelber, Werner H.** *The Kingdom in Mark: A New Place and a New Time.* Philadelphia: Fortress, 1974. **Ladd, George Eldon.** *The Presence of the Future: The Eschatology of Biblical Realism.* 2nd ed. Grand Rapids: Eerdmans, 1974. **Maloney, Elliot C.** *Jesus' Urgent Message for Today: The Kingdom of God in Mark's Gospel.* New York: Continuum, 2004. **Marcus, Joel.** *The Mystery of the Kingdom of God.* SBLDS 90. Atlanta: Scholars Press: 1986. Idem. "Entering into the Kingly Power of God." *JBL* 107 (1988): 663–75. **Matera, Frank J.** *The Kingship of Jesus: Composition and Theology in Mark 15.* SBLDS 66. Chico, CA: Scholars Press, 1982. **Palu, Ma'afu.** *Jesus and Time: An Interpretation of Mark 1.15.* LNTS 468. London/New York: T&T Clark, 2012. **Scholtissek, Klaus.** "Der Sohn Gottes für das Reich Gottes: Zur Verbindung von Christologie und Eschatologie bei Markus." Pp. 63–90 in *Der Evangelist als Theologe: Studien zum Markusevangelium.* Ed. Thomas Söding. SBS 163. Stuttgart: Katholisches Bibelwerk, 1995. **Tuckett, Christopher.** "Mark's Concerns in the Parables Chapter (Mark 4, 1–34)." *Bib* 69 (1988): 1–26.

7.1 A SUMMARY OF JESUS' PREACHING OF THE KINGDOM OF GOD (MARK 1:14–15)

Mark 1:1–13 establishes Jesus' unique authority as the Messiah and the Son of God, whose coming fulfills OT prophecy and who is infused with the Holy Spirit, able to vanquish Satan, and worthy to be served by angels. Then Mark, in contrast to Matthew and Luke, immediately gets to Jesus' public ministry. After John was handed over, Jesus returns to Galilee and proclaims the good news of God: "The time has come. The kingdom of God has come near. Repent and believe the good news!" (1:14–15).[1] In contrast to John's preaching that something was about to happen—one more powerful than he was coming (1:7–8)—Jesus proclaims that something has happened.[2]

These words are not addressed to a specific audience, and the present tense of the participle "saying" (*legōn*) suggests that this proclamation was not a one-time event but something that was ongoing.[3] It means that this "initial proclamation is universal, embracing all the figures who appear in the narrative."[4] The repetition of key words and concepts from this message allows it to resound in the narrative that follows without the narrator having to repeat the exact content of it every time Jesus speaks. The kingdom of God, therefore, was central to Jesus' preaching and teaching even though it may not surface explicitly in every instance of Jesus' preaching and teaching that Mark records. Defining precisely what the kingdom of God denotes, however, is challenging.

7.2 Defining the Kingdom of God

The phrase "the kingdom of God" itself can foster misleading assumptions for modern readers as it might have for an ancient audience. The word "kingdom" for most English speakers implies a place, something fixed and immobile, the territory where some king or queen rules. But it is not a place, a community, or a state of affairs. In Mark, the term primarily is used as a way of talking about God's activity. Kingdom is a metonymical designation of God's reigning presence in which God intervenes in history and human experience, wielding his sovereignty to accomplish his purposes. It has a dynamic sense in affirming that God rules and is acting in his capacity as king. It can also refer to the condition that God's intervention obtains for those who submit to his rule. Ladd defines the kingdom of God as

> the redemptive reign of God dynamically active to establish his rule among men, and that this Kingdom, which will appear as an apocalyptic act at the end of the age, has already come into human history in the person and mission of Jesus to overcome evil, to deliver men from its power, and to bring them into

1. Sean P. Kealy, "Reflections on the History of Mark's Gospel," *Proceedings, Eastern Great Lakes Biblical Society* 2 (1982): 61, comments, "Mark, with little or no preliminary, literally thrusts Jesus *in media res* into the heart of things as was the ancient recommendation for a good writer. Jesus is put into sudden and direct contact with our suffering world and surrounded with human distress, ignorance, blindness and controversy from morning until night, from beginning to the end of his ministry."

2. W. D. Davies, *Jewish and Pauline Studies* (Philadelphia: Fortress, 1984), 231, asserts, "By setting the call to repentance in the context of the givenness and immediacy of the kingdom, Jesus freed it from mere moralism and utterly radicalized it."

3. The NIV rendering "he said" instead of "saying" may be misleading, if it is interpreted to mean that Jesus "said" this only once.

4. Marshall, *Faith as a Theme*, 38.

> the blessings of God's reign. The Kingdom of God involves two great moments: fulfillment within history, and consummation at the end of history.[5]

Since Jesus envisions the kingdom of God enfolding more and more people, God's reign also creates a domain where all things are put right as God intended things to be. The kingdom of God is therefore multidimensional.

- It has a *temporal* dimension. "After" John is arrested, a chronological reference (1:14), Jesus announces the kingdom of God is at hand and tangibly evident in his ministry (1:15). Yet it will be consummated only in the future (14:25).
- It has a *spatial* dimension: One can enter it (9:47; 10:15, 23–25) and be near it (12:34). Because he talks about "entering the kingdom," Schweizer suggests that "the kingdom is more like an area or a sphere of authority into which one can enter, so 'realm' would be a better translation (Mark 9:47; 10:15, 23–25; Matt 5:20; 7:21; 18:3; 19:23)."[6]
- It has a *communal* dimension. One can belong to it and be a part of its family (3:31–35; 10:30).
- Most importantly, the kingdom of God has a *supernatural spiritual* dimension that makes the earthly categories that are normally associated with kingdoms inapplicable.

7.2.1 The Kingdom of God in the Old Testament and Intertestamental Literature

In the OT, God is king of his chosen people, king of the surrounding nations (whether they acknowledged it or not), and king of the created order. God does not reign as a tyrant but in order to save, and God's reign is expressed in images that emphasize God's saving activity. God is unlike all other gods, majestic in holiness and power, awesome in splendor, and wondrous in leading a redeemed people in steadfast love to his holy abode (Exod 15:6–7, 11–13). The psalmists and prophets proclaim that the Lord and no one else is king, and that the Lord reigns and draws near to save his people (Pss 96:4–6, 10; 97:1; 99:1; Isa 33:22; 44:6–8; and 52:7). "The Lord reigns for ever and ever" (see Exod 15:18; see 1 Chr 29:11; Pss 10:16; 29:10; 47:7–8; 93:1–5; 95:1–3; 145:10–13). Jesus, however, "rarely spoke of God as king, nor did he ever speak of the establishment of God's sovereignty over Israel or over the world."[7]

In intertestamental literature, the kingdom of God is associated with the son of David, the Lord Messiah, ruling over Israel, purging Jerusalem of tyrannous

5. George Eldon Ladd, *The Presence of the Future: The Eschatology of Biblical Realism* (2nd ed.; Grand Rapids: Eerdmans, 1974), 218. See further Bruce Chilton, ed., *The Kingdom of God in the Teaching of Jesus* (Philadelphia: Fortress, 1984); C. C. Caragounis, "Kingdom of God/Kingdom of Heaven," in *DJG*, 416–30. To capture this sense, the phrase is sometimes rendered "the reign of God" or "dominion of God."

6. Schweizer, *Mark*, 45–46.

7. Ibid., 45.

Gentiles, who will then serve under his yoke, driving out sinners and smashing their arrogance, destroying the unlawful nations with the word of his mouth, and gathering a holy people (*Pss. Sol.* 17:21–34). In *T. Moses* 10:1, Moses asserts that when God's kingdom appears "through his whole creation," "the devil will have an end. Yes, sorrow will be led away with him."

By contrast, Jesus does not realize the hopes of a political kingdom for which the writer of the *Psalms of Solomon* optimistically yearns. The kingdom of God transcends any nationalistic limits, and it does not come with war-fevered ferocity. It is not to be seen in the march of armies. Its operative principle has nothing to do with nepotism, military might, or political maneuvering (10:35–45). Nor does it bring an immediate end to Satan, as the *Testament of Moses* assumes would be the case. Satan continues to threaten, swiping the seed of the word when opportunity presents itself (4:15). Jesus' perspective on the kingdom does not match these expectations except that he shares the confidence that no threat will prevent God's coming triumph.

7.2.2 Jesus' Role in the Kingdom of God

Jesus did share the vision of the kingdom of God found in apocalyptic literature that God as king would decisively intervene in history to establish his rule over those who rejected it and who oppressed God's people. God would reign on earth as God reigns in heaven. The difference is that Jesus taught that God's reign was a *present* reality breaking into human history and lives and not something that will take place in some future time. It was already operative in his ministry, though its presence in his words, miracles, and particularly in his death and resurrection was mysterious and not readily evident to all. Nevertheless, Jesus' coming presses God's claim on humans and makes neutrality impossible. The world will be turned upside down.

7.2.2.1 The Time Is Being Fulfilled (Mark 1:15a)

Jesus is at the epicenter of the kingdom of God, and his presence creates a new situation in salvation history that requires the human response of repentance and belief. The announcement that "the time has come [is fulfilled] +" (1:15) asserts that Israel's long yearning for this moment has arrived. France comments, "The idea is not simply that an allotted time has elapsed (that would have been better expressed by *chronos*, as in Acts 7:23), but that the decisive moment (*kairos*) has now arrived."[8] In Mark 1:15, Jesus' announcement refers to "a time measured by God's design."[9] What God has decreed in the Scripture cited in 1:2–3 is now coming to pass.[10]

8. France, *Mark*, 91. Joel Marcus, "'The Time Has Been Fulfilled!' (Mark 1.15)," in *Apocalyptic and the New Testament: Essays in Honor of J. Louis Martyn* (ed. Joel Marcus and Marion L. Soards; JSNTSup 24; Sheffield: Sheffield Academic, 1989), 49–68, argues, however, for the meaning "span of time." He interprets it to mean "when the measure of time allotted to the old age is full, the new age will come" (53).

9. Moloney, *Mark*, 49. Anderson, *Mark*, 84, dubs it "time seen from the divine side" (see Dan 7:22; Ezek 7:12; 9:1 [LXX]; Gal 4:4; 1 Pet 1:11; Rev 1:3).

10. Mark's use of the word *kairos* suggests it is an "appointed time" filled with opportunity, like the reference to the "time" in 13:33 is a time filled with calamities.

The description of Joseph of Arimathea as one who was "waiting for the kingdom of God" (15:43) highlights this expectancy among pious Jews. Jesus declares that "some who are standing here will not taste death before they see that the kingdom of God has come with power" (9:1). Flusser writes that Jesus "was the only Jew of ancient times known to us who preached not only that people were on the threshold of the end of time, but that the new age of salvation had already begun."[11]

Since Mark notes that this time of fulfillment commences after John's activities have been completed, it may suggest a division of salvation history into periods.[12] This view is reinforced by Jesus' parable of the Wedding Guests (2:18–20). The time of asceticism, associated with John the Baptist in the wilderness, is contrasted with the time of celebration that comes with Jesus. The reference to the time when the bridegroom is taken away may imply a third period, but Mark does not emphasize such divisions of salvation history. The interpretation of the next phrase reveals that they may be misleading.

7.2.2.2 The Kingdom of God Has Come Near (Mark 1:15b)

A long dispute, which Beasley-Murray characterizes as resembling "a long drawn-out tennis match,"[13] centers on whether to translate the phrase that the kingdom of God "has come near" or that it "has already come."[14] The verb translated "has come near" by the NIV (*ēngiken*) is in the perfect tense. From what he labels "the paradigmatic shift in the study of Greek verbal aspect,"[15] Palu concludes that the use of the perfect tense in this context "implies events unfolding in the present time and not in the past."[16] What is taking place in time is governed by the principle of fulfillment as the kingdom of God "progressively" comes near.[17]

Mark uses this verb "has come near" elsewhere in the gospel with the clear connotation of motion that leads to spatial nearness, not temporal nearness. In 11:1, the verb describes Jesus' reaching the outskirts of Jerusalem. After his winding journey to Jerusalem, he has finally arrived at the staging ground in Bethphage and

11. David Flusser and R. Steven Notley, *Jesus* (Jerusalem: Magnes, 1997), 110.

12. So Gnilka, *Markus*, 1:65; Lane, *Mark*, 63.

13. George R. Beasley-Murray, *Jesus and the Kingdom of God* (Grand Rapids: Eerdmans, 1986), 73.

14. Both the verbs "fulfilled" and "has come near" are in the perfect tense. C. H. Dodd, *The Parables of the Kingdom* (rev. ed.; New York: Scribner's, 1961), 29–40, famously argues for a realized eschatology. Dodd identifies the kingdom of God with the person of Jesus. The kingdom is a matter of present experience, not something to come in the near future. This interpretation opened the way to viewing the kingdom of God as a timeless reality. "The absolute, the 'wholly other', has entered into time and space" (p. 82). Dodd's view has influenced the REB translation of 1:15, "The time has arrived; the kingdom of God is upon you," and the NEB rendering of 9:1, "There are some of those standing here who will not taste death before they have seen the kingdom of God already come in power."

15. Ma'afu Palu, *Jesus and Time: An Interpretation of Mark 1.15* (LNTS 468; London/New York: T&T Clark, 2012), 125–31, noting the work of Kenneth L. McKay, "On the Perfect and Other Aspects in New Testament Greek: An Aspectual Approach," *NovT* 23 (1981): 289–329; Stanley E. Porter, "In Defence of Verbal Aspect," in *Biblical Greek Language and Linguistics: Open Questions in Current Research* (ed. Stanley E. Porter and D. A. Carson; JSNTSup 80; Sheffield: Sheffield Academic, 1993), 26–45; Buist M. Fanning, *Verbal Aspect in the New Testament with Reference to Tense and Mood* (SBG 1; New York: Lang, 1989), 119–20; Trevor V. Evans, "Future Directions for Aspectual Studies in Ancient Greek," in *Biblical Greek Language and Lexicography: Essays in Honor of Frederick W. Danker* (ed. Bernard A. Taylor et al.; Grand Rapids: Eerdmans, 2004), 206; Constantine R. Campbell, *Basics of Verbal Aspect in Biblical Greek* (Grand Rapids: Zondervan, 2000).

16. Palu, *Jesus and Time*, 134. He understands that what is being fulfilled is "the restoration of Israel."

17. Ibid., 135.

Bethany near the Mount of Olives, where he will prepare for his entry into the city that immediately follows (11:2–11). In 14:42, the verb is used in the perfect tense, as in 1:15, to note that Jesus' betrayer has drawn near. It is followed by the immediate appearance of Judas "just as he [Jesus] was speaking" (14:43). This usage suggests that in 1:15 the verb means more than that the kingdom of God is imminent.[18] It is coming into view.

France notes that since John had the role of forerunner, "it would be odd if the one who succeeds him also turns out to be no more than a herald of something which lies still in the future."[19] His analysis is a helpful guide through the conundrum that the kingdom appears to have arrived but is also something yet to come (see 9:1). He asserts, "God's kingship is both eternal and eschatological, both fulfilled and awaited, both present and imminent."[20] He writes that for Mark to have Jesus "declare that God's kingship has come near is to say that God is now fulfilling his agelong purpose, rather than to point to a specific time or event which can be defined as either already present or still future, but not both."[21] Jesus' announcement "constitutes the threshold of the in-breaking kingdom. The sovereign action of God to transform the world has been initiated in his proclamation."[22] In this moment in history, the world's future is being molded forever. God is acting *now* in and through Jesus. This assessment would have been startling to the Jews of that time, since, according to Stegemann, they "generally held to the notion that all of God's active dealings, in heaven as on earth, were confined to the past and the future."[23]

Kümmel points out that if Jesus had "announced only God's future eschatological action," his preaching would have been no different from other Jewish expectations of salvation, which looked to the future in hope. Jesus did not announce a period of anticipation. The kingdom of God is "realizing itself already in his person, his actions, his message."[24] Ambrozic explains that in 1:15 the first clause, "the time has come," "enunciates clearly that the divinely decreed time of waiting has come to an end. The decisive manifestation of the saving God, promised in the prophecies quoted in vss. 2–3, must, therefore, be taking place." The second clause, which is parallel to the first, interprets it and "states the same truth": "the kingdom of God has come near." Ambrozic claims, "The only difference between the members: the

18. Werner Georg Kümmel, *Promise and Fulfilment: The Eschatological Message of Jesus* (trans. Dorothea M. Barton; 2nd ed.; SBT 23; London: SCM, 1961), 19–25; Ambrozic, *The Hidden Kingdom*, 21–23; France, *Mark*, 91. Similar wording appears in Ezek 7:4 (LXX; 7:7 in the MT): "The time [*kairos*] has come! The day is near [*ēngiken*]!"

19. France, *Mark*, 92; also, see his *Divine Government: God's Kingship in the Gospel of Mark* (London: SPCK, 1990), 8–25.

20. France, *Mark*, 93.

21. Ibid.

22. Marshall, *Faith as a Theme*, 35. Beasley-Murray, *The Kingdom of God*, 74, makes a similar statement and cites Jürgen Becker, *Das Heil Gottes: Heils- und Sündenbegriffe in den Qumrantexten und im Neuen Testament* (SUNT 3; Göttingen: Vandenhoeck & Ruprecht, 1964), 206: "God's sovereignty as the sovereignty which comes is now coming to pass."

23. Stegemann, *The Library of Qumran*, 233. He writes, "In the meantime, God does not directly intervene in world events, but governs them only indirectly, through angels, through the revelation of his will of old, and through his revelation of all future events in the books of Moses and the Prophets, which books are available on earth. God also rules, indirectly, through the establishment of systems of governance such as the successive foreign ruler over Israel as ongoing punishment meted out to the ever sinful people of God" (234).

24. Kümmel, *Promise and Fulfillment*, 153.

first looks backward, while the second looks to the present and future; the first announces the end of the old era, the second proclaims the beginning of the new."[25]

7.2.2.3 The Presence of the Kingdom of God Is Cloaked in Mystery

Jesus offers no proof that his announcement that the kingdom of God is at hand is true. Since it comes hard on the heels of the notice that John, God's messenger, has been handed over, it highlights the paradox associated with its appearance. John is imprisoned, yet Jesus, who also will be handed over, announces good news. Only God's revelation can unravel this enigma: How is suffering connected to the kingdom's manifestation? People will have to reevaluate their expectations of God's reign and how it reveals itself.

Most in Jesus' audience would have understood the arrival of the kingdom of God to mean that God visits the people to bring grace and judgment, to put things right in the world, to vanquish malevolent powers, to oust the tyrannical rulers of this world and their yoke of domination and to exalt Israel, to conquer sin and to eradicate sickness, and to vindicate the righteous. Jesus' exhortation for persons to believe in the good news gives the first hint that the kingdom's manifestation is "paradoxical."[26]

The kingdom "is not yet present in all its overwhelming glory."[27] Its observable signs are not evident to everyone, and its victory will be hidden in the cross. Those who cannot change their accustomed ways of thinking and accept this paradox will in the end disqualify themselves from the kingdom. This paradox leads to the theme of the kingdom's mystery and hiddenness. France clarifies that it is "not a mystery in the sense that it is incomprehensible, but it is a 'secret' in that not everyone yet knows it."[28]

7.3 THE ENIGMATIC PARABLES OF THE KINGDOM OF GOD (MARK 4:1–34)

The parable discourse in chapter 4 falls in the middle of the first act of the gospel's narrative as the eschatological discourse in chapter 13 falls in the middle of the third

25. Ambrozic, *The Hidden Kingdom*, 21–22. Palu, *Jesus and Time*, 136–42, offers a quite different explanation. He contends that the first phrase, which he translates, "the time is fulfilled," is primary, and the second phrase, "the kingdom of God has come near" is subordinated to the first. It does not present a second stage but clarifies that the fulfillment of the time is "an ongoing process." The time fulfillment, in his view, is tied to the restoration of Israel, and this restoration is manifested in the kingdom of God "progressing toward its full realization" (140). Since Mark notes that this time of fulfillment commences *after* John's activities have been completed, I am inclined to agree with Ambrozic's interpretation.

26. Ambrozic, *The Hidden Kingdom*, 45. The "in" (*en*) in the Greek is left untranslated in the NIV ("believe the good news," 1:15). It is the only example in the New Testament where the verb "to believe" is followed by the preposition "in" (*en*), but it does occur in the LXX. The preposition may connote believe "on the basis of the good news" (see John 16:30; Acts 24:16; 1 Cor 4:4, where the preposition has this connotation) and thus accords with Paul's usage where the gospel is the ground of faith, not its object. Thus, *en* more likely signifies the ground of faith. Marshall, *Faith as a Theme*, 44–49, recognizes that the command does not call for intellectual assent to what Jesus says about God's kingdom but enjoins faith that in his own person and activity the kingdom of God is actually being inaugurated.

27. Ambrozic, *The Hidden Kingdom*, 45.

28. France, *Divine Government*, 36–37.

act. France comments, "Each discourse provides an explanatory framework to help the reader gain a true perspective on the narrative which precedes and follows it."[29] Like speeches in OT narratives, it stops the action and "takes stock of the entire story so far and sets up what is to come."[30] This break in the action is filled with Jesus' teaching in parables that have to do with the varied reactions to his kingdom preaching and the assurance of its fulfillment despite its present hiddenness.

In English, the term "parable" may refer to a moral story, an allegory or an exemplum; however, in the LXX and in Jewish Hellenistic literature, the word translated "parable" covers a broad semantic range. In postbiblical Judaism, the word was used for "figurative forms of speech of every kind: parable, similitude, allegory, fable, proverb, apocalyptic revelation, riddle, symbol, pseudonym, fictitious person, example, theme, argument, apology, refutation, jest."[31] Boring comments that the parables are "not mere comparisons or analogies, supplementary illustrations of truth already known but in need of illustration. Parables bring the truth itself to expression, which cannot be expressed abstractly."[32] The mystery of the coming of the kingdom of God cannot be satisfactorily communicated except in parables that both reveal and conceal at the same time.

The language of parable, simile, and metaphor also is the best means to convey what is inherently paradoxical.[33] It also is the best means to open up new vistas that can subvert previous biases, assumptions, and predispositions, because it can draw from a "common stock" of "well-known narrative themes, characters, and actions" to sculpt a transformative view of reality. The kingdom of God is a present reality tied to Jesus' presence and activity and yet it is future. It is tangible and recognizable and yet it is hidden. It is glorious and yet it manifests itself in unpretentious lowliness.

The parable of the Sower and its interpretation (4:1–9, 13–20) explain the different responses evoked by Jesus' proclamation of the kingdom: skepticism, puzzlement, hostility, superficial enthusiasm, and deep-rooted fruitfulness among those who submit to the kingdom of God made manifest in Jesus. The motifs of successful harvests and the growth of seeds (4:8, 20, 26–29, 30–32) provide encouragement that the kingdom of God will inevitably triumph. Opposition will arise, but it will not prevail. There will be a harvest, which is the goal of sowing.[34] The farmer does not abandon the field and plant in another better one after encountering obstacles. God's kingdom will thrive despite resistance.

29. France, *Mark*, 182. He identifies it as "a discourse about God's kingdom, and it aims to explain the paradoxical fact that a proclamation of such ultimate importance can be ignored or even opposed by some who hear it. It reveals a fundamental clash between divine and human values, and the necessity of a more-than-human insight if the purpose of God is to be understood and welcomed."

30. Drury, *Parables*, 49. Marcus, *Mark 1–8*, 290, concurs that the collection of parables slows down the hectic pace, softens the building tension with opponents, and offers "a solemn commentary on what has happened so far and what is still to come."

31. Joachim Jeremias, *The Parables of Jesus* (trans. S. H. Hooke; rev. ed.; New York: Scribner's, 1963), 20.

32. Boring, *Mark*, 121.

33. Edwards, *Mark*, 46, asserts, "As a mystery (4:11) that cannot be deciphered and calculated, it is best spoken of in analogies or parables (4:26, 30)."

34. The expectation of fruitful agricultural years is a characteristic of the blessings of the coming age (Jer 31:12; Hos 2:21–22; Joel 2:22; Amos 9:13; Zech 8:12).

The parables also touch on the mysterious ways of the kingdom and its disarmingly small and inconspicuous appearance. They impart an assurance that what is now hidden will be disclosed in due course. The kingdom is present but concealed like a seed planted in the ground and ready to burst forth. It is yet to unfurl its eschatological glory.

While many find a concentric pattern to the structure of this discourse,[35] a linear progression is more likely.[36]

1–2 Setting
3–9 Seed Parable 1 (The Sower/Soils)
10–13 Parable Explanation 1
14–20 Explanation of the Seed Parable
21–25 Parable Explanation 2 (which takes the form of parables)
  21 Parable of the Light under a Bushel Basket
  22 Explanation ("for")
  23–24a Emphasis on Hearing
  24b Parable of the Measure
  25 Explanation ("for")
26–29 Seed Parable 2 (The Seed Growing to Harvest)[37]
30–32 Seed Parable 3 (The Mustard Seed)
33–34 Parable Explanation 3

7.3.1 The Themes of the Parable Discourse Related to the Kingdom of God

The parables in this discourse do not teach how humans should act but what the kingdom is like.[38] They make the point that "*Jesus' ministry has inaugurated a sequence of action leading to the fullness of God's kingdom just as surely as sowing sets in play a spontaneous process leading to harvest.*"[39]

7.3.1.1 Jesus as the Sower of the Kingdom (Mark 4:3–8)

The parable of the Sower reinforces the point that Jesus is at the center of the kingdom of God. I have argued that the parable

35. Among many, see Joanna Dewey, *Markan Public Debate: Literary Technique, Concentric Structure, and Theology in Mark 2:1–3:6* (SBLDS 48; Chico, CA: Scholars Press, 1980); Jan Lambrecht, *Once More Astonished: The Parables of* Jesus (New York: Crossroad, 1981), 86–87; van Iersel, *Mark*, 176–77; Beavis, *Mark's Audience*, 133–55; Greg Fay, "Introduction to Incomprehension: The Literary Structure of Mark 4:1–34," *CBQ* 51 (1989): 65–73; Donahue and Harrington, *Mark*, 143; Moloney, *Mark*, 85–86; Elian Cuvillier, *Le concept de ΠΑΡΑΒΟΛΗ dans le second évangile: son arrière-plan littéraire, sa signification dans la cadre de la rédaction marcienne, son utilisation dans la tradition de Jésus* (Paris: Gabalda, 1993), 117.

36. Slightly revised from Boring, *Mark*, 113.

37. The name given to a parable predisposes how it is interpreted. The diverse titles given to this parable (4:26–29) testifies to its ambiguity. Interpretations that focus on the seed result in these titles: "the growing seed," "the seed growing secretly," "the seed growing of itself," "the seed growing gradually," "the mystery of the seed." Those that focus on the soil have these titles: "the earth producing of itself," "the automatic action of the soil." Those that focus on the farmer have these titles: "the patient husbandmen," "the confident sower," "the carefree sower," "the unbelieving farmer." Those that focus on the harvest give the parable this title: "the grain is ripe."

38. Snodgrass, *Stories with Intent*, 186.

39. Ibid., 189.

> by itself has no meaning at all: A farmer goes out to sow and meets with failure and a good yield. So what? It could represent the effect that any teacher might have with an audience. But sowing in the Old Testament is a metaphor for God's work. God promises to sow Israel to begin her renewal (Jer. 31:27–28; Ezek. 36:9; Hos. 2:21–23; *4 Ezra* 8:6; 9:31).[40]

What makes this parable significant is Mark's faith commitment to the teller of the parable: "The astounding implication, which only a few will see, is that Jesus comes as the end time sower of God."[41] Jesus understands his mission as one who goes out to sow the word (1:38; 2:17). And he sows it generously and indiscriminately. The seed falls on hardened paths, stony soil, thorny soil, and good soil. How one responds to his teaching, the seed, decides whether one will enter or be excluded from the kingdom of God.

7.3.1.2 Jesus as the Mystery of the Kingdom

The "secret" (or "mystery") of the kingdom of God is not that it will arrive at any moment but that the bearer of the kingdom has come incognito. An account of the disciples' boat imperiled by a sudden tempest on the lake immediately follows the parable discourse. When Jesus restrains the storm and calms the sea, the shaken disciples ask, "Who is this? Even the wind and the waves obey him!" (4:41). Jesus' identity is a mystery. Cranfield explains,

> It is the secret that the kingdom of God has come in the person and words and works of Jesus. That is a secret because God has chosen to reveal himself indirectly and in a veiled way. The incarnate Word is not obvious. Only faith could recognize the Son of God in the lowly figure of Jesus of Nazareth. The secret of the kingdom of God is the secret of the person of Jesus.[42]

The problem is not that the kingdom of God is too complex to figure out. The kingdom of God has come with invisible power that must be revealed. No one would have guessed that the kingdom of God was at hand had Jesus not announced that it was. It is not something unmistakably evident. Later in the narrative, the mystery will also entail that the Son of God will be crucified and that he will be raised by God, that he will be exalted to God's right hand, and that he will come in glory in the judgment. Like the seed growing secretly, no one can see what is going on beneath ground or explain how it germinates and grows. The mystery therefore cannot be cracked by human intellect; it can only be revealed, and it is only revealed by Jesus to those who come to him for enlightenment.[43]

---

40. Garland, *Mark*, 156; see also *2 Bar.* 70:2; *1 En.* 62:8; Ign. *Eph.* 9:1.

41. Garland, *Mark*, 156.

42. Cranfield, *Mark*, 153.

43. France, *Mark*, 197, maintains that the message about the kingdom of God "is something so paradoxical, so totally opposed to natural human insight, that it takes nothing less than divine revelation to enable people to grasp it."

7.3.1.3 *Jesus as the Giver of the Mystery of the Kingdom (Mark 4:11)*

When Jesus was away from the crowd, the Twelve ask him about the parables (4:10). Jesus has only given one parable, the parable of the Sower, so the plural "parables" applies to all of his teaching that is parabolic. Marcus comments that Jesus' parables in Mark are not "a mode of speech distinguished by its power to convince," as they are in Aristotle (see *On Rhetoric* 2.1393b 3–7).[44] They require deciphering, and yet the key to decipher them is not something that humans can discover on their own. It has to be given to them. The entire ministry of Jesus could be cast as a kind of parable. Schweizer says that for Mark the parables are not simply "a didactic method"; they are "the form of God's revelation" in Mark.[45] They reveal the mystery and hide it at the same time.[46] This mysterious revelation has the effect of revealing the blindness of the world. This universal blindness, which leads to disobedience, "necessitates Jesus' course towards a representative expiatory death."[47]

Jesus gives his answer to the disciples' question, "Why parables?" in parables (4:10–13). His immediate response in 4:10–13 offers the first of three explanations that he gives in the discourse (see the outline). He cites Isaiah, but the response seems deliberately vague, elusive, and sparse in detail. He affirms, "The secret of the kingdom of God has been given to you," but for outsiders all things come in parables. Many, if not most, will miss it.

The citation of Isa 6:9–10 in Jesus' explanation for teaching in parables has long posed a quandary for interpreters. The NASV translation captures the harshness of the explanation: Everything is spoken to those outside in parables, "in order that while seeing, they may see and not perceive; and while hearing, they may hear and not understand lest they return and be forgiven" (4:12). It is difficult to conceive that Jesus would intentionally shroud his teaching in riddles to prevent people from understanding and repenting.

Several interpretations attempt to moderate the seeming callousness of this statement by amending the two conjunctives "in order that" (*hina*) and "lest" (*mēpote*). The NIV, for example, renders the Greek word *hina* to express the results, "so that," rather than the purpose, "in order that." Jesus speaks in parables to outsiders "so that, 'they may be ever seeing but never perceiving, and ever hearing but never understanding; otherwise they might turn and be forgiven!'" (4:12). This translation suggests that the parables have the effect of causing persons to go blind and deaf, but

44. Marcus, *Mark 1–8*, 291, citing Cuvillier, *Le concept de ΠΑΡΑΒΟΛΗ dans le second évangile*, 21–79. Hartman, *Mark*, 159, cites Quintilian, *Inst.* 8.373, "You must be careful, so that what you pick as a parable (*similitudo*) is not obscure or abstruse. What you use to shed light on something must be more obvious than what is to be explained."

45. Eduard Schweizer, "Mark's Contribution to the Quest of the Historical Jesus," *NTS* 10 (1964): 423.

46. Sweat, *The Theological Role of Paradox*, 28–62, takes this theme as the first great paradox in the gospel that she investigates and contends that it means that "God hides and reveals the kingdom, the divine presence, and the roles that Jesus, insiders, and outsiders play in this unfolding drama" (62).

47. Hengel, *Studies*, 35.

that is not their purpose.[48] Manson tries to circumvent the problem by interpreting the "in order that" (*hina*) as a mistranslation of the Aramaic relative particle *dĕ* meaning "who." Manson interprets it to mean that the "purpose of parables is not to harden the hearts of the hearers"; instead "it is the hardness of heart of the hearers that defeats the purpose of parables."[49] Jeremias interprets the "in order that" as shorthand for "in order that it be fulfilled." It refers to the purpose of God, not Jesus' purpose. He interprets "lest" (*mēpote*) as not a threat of final hardening but a promise of forgiveness.[50] Others catch a hint of sarcasm or irony in Jesus' response. The "lest" means "perish the thought that they would ever hear repent."[51]

France argues that even though the word *hina* lexically means "in order that" and refers to purpose, it is to be understood "within the context of Semitic thought which tends to suppress second causes, so that human decisions are attributed to the overriding providence of God."[52] God's word always meets with a divided response. The context of the parable of the Sower would reinforce this realism.[53] The sower's purpose is not to waste seed deliberately but to get a harvest. He sows liberally, but the harvest depends on the condition of the soil that receives the seed. Witherington also places Jesus' teaching in an apocalyptic context that is found, for example, in Dan 12:8–10, which maintains that none of the wicked will understand the mystery but only the wise will comprehend: "The purpose of such apocalyptic rhetoric was not simply to be mysterious or enigmatic but to communicate in a way that would elicit whether one was responding in faith or not."[54] Some either will remain indifferent to Jesus' teaching or become bitterly hostile. Others will come to Jesus for further clarification, which they will receive.[55]

Attempts to soften the harshness of the parable theory lose sight of how it functions in the entire narrative. Boring is correct: "The harsh Markan statement should stand; the initial impression is correct: in this text Jesus is portrayed as having taught in parables to keep people from understanding, and Mark found a saying of Jesus in his tradition, bolstered by a Targumic citation from Isaiah, that supported this

48. C. F. D. Moule, *An Idiom-Book of New Testament Greek* (2nd ed.; Cambridge: Cambridge University Press, 1968), 142–43, states "that the Semitic mind was notoriously unwilling to draw a sharp dividing-line between purpose and consequence." He argues that "the radical view" that interprets the phrase to mean "that parables are told *to prevent* any who are not predestined for salvation from hearing, too incongruous with any part of the N.T. period to be plausible." See also Lane, *Mark*, 156–59.

49. T. W. Manson, *The Teaching of Jesus: Studies in Form and Content* (2nd ed.; Cambridge: Cambridge University Press, 1935), 75–81 (79).

50. Jeremias, *Parables*, 17.

51. Bruce Hollenbach, "Lest They Should Turn and Be Forgiven: Irony," *BT* 34 (1983): 312–21, translated it "because the last thing they want is to turn and have their sins forgiven!" (320).

52. France, *Mark*, 199. He claims that it is intended as "a typological correspondence between two phases in the ongoing history of God's appeal to his people," in Isaiah's day and in Jesus' day. Josephus, *Ant.* 18.1.3 §13, encapsulates this paradox in his description of the Pharisees, who determine that all things are done by fate but also believe in free will. Humans can act viciously or virtuously. See also *m. 'Abot* 3:16: "All is foreseen, but freedom of choice is given." It is not a matter of predestination or free will; as Edwards, *Mark*, 134, recognizes, the two are held in juxtaposition. Drury, *Parables*, 41, comments that in Isa 6:9–10, "The peoples' unreceptivity is thus pre-empted by being presented as a thing foreseen, and even ordained, by God. So it was when God sent Moses to be his spokesman to Pharaoh, at the same time hardening Pharaoh's heart so that he paid no attention (Exodus 7–11 *passim*)."

53. Ezek 12:1–2 may reflect a similar situation. The Lord tells Ezekiel that he is "living among a rebellious people. They have eyes to see but do not see and ears to hear but do not hear, for they are a rebellious people."

54. Witherington, *Mark*, 167. God commands Ezekiel to speak to a hardhearted people who neither see nor hear (Ezek 12:1–2; see also Jer 5:21).

55. Compare the reaction to Jesus' discourse about the bread of life in John 6:59–71.

view."[56] It is not simply because people could not understand until after the cross and resurrection. The explanation in 4:22, "For whatever is hidden is meant to be disclosed, and whatever is concealed is meant to be brought out into the open," implies that the hiddenness serves the purpose of revelation. This implication may seem patently absurd. Marcus, however, insightfully explains how this paradox unfolds in Mark:

> God intends the outsiders to be blinded by Jesus' parables and his parabolic actions (4:11–12), so that they oppose him and eventually bring about his death; in his death, however, the new age of revelation will dawn. Thus the hiddenness of Jesus' identity (cf. the *hina* clause in 4:12) leads to his death, which in turn results in the open manifestation of his identity (cf. the *hina* clause in 4:22). The *hina* clauses in vv 21–22, like the one in 4:12, refer to *God's* intention, and all of these *hina* clauses intersect at the cross.[57]

In his commentary, Marcus adds:

> This rejection of the word leads inexorably to Jesus' death, a result that, from the divine perspective, is necessary (8:31; 9:31; 10:33–34); he is killed by those who cannot grasp his identity and who look and look but never see, hear and hear but never understand (see the echoes of 4:12 in the uses of the verbs "to see" and "to hear" in the trial and death scenes in 14:64; 15:32, 35, 36).... The obscurity of the word thus ultimately serves the purpose of its revelation by leading to Jesus' revelatory death; what was hidden was hidden only *in order that* it might come into the light.[58]

Evans concurs that the hardened heart of the outsiders is God's intention; yet, mysteriously, it does not lack "redeeming features." He reasons, "Without the hardened heart, Jesus would not have been rejected and put to death; and had he not been put to death, there could have been no resurrection and no Christian gospel."[59] Mark has a deterministic view of Jesus' rejection and death. The Isaian text reveals that the lack of receptivity to Jesus was inevitable and something that God had foreseen and even ordained (see John 12:37–41; Acts 28:25–28; Rom 9:18–19; 10:16–21; 11:7–10).[60] God's kingdom as manifest in Jesus was obscured deliberately to fuel the obduracy of those who were disinclined to repent and believe. Their murderous impenitence, however, ultimately served God's redemptive purpose.[61]

The classic example of this phenomenon in Mark is the parable of the Tenants and its scriptural elucidation directed at the high priests, teachers of the law, and elders (12:1–11). They understand the gist of the parable as a threat aimed at them

56. Boring, *Mark*, 127.

57. Marcus, *Mystery*, 147.

58. Marcus, *Mark 1–8*, 319.

59. See Craig A. Evans, *To See and Not Perceive: Isaiah 6.9–10 in Early Jewish and Christian Interpretation* (JSOTSup 64; Sheffield: JSOT, 1989), 102–3.

60. Wilfrid J. Harrington, *Mark, Realistic Theologian: The Jesus of Mark* (Dublin: Columba, 1996), 51–52.

61. A similar reverse logic appears in Paul's explanation of the mystery of Israel's hardening: "Israel has experienced a hardening in part until the full number of the Gentiles has come in" (Rom 11:25). And yet "all Israel will be saved" (11:26).

(12:12) and respond with bitter defiance rather than repentance. The parable only hardens their intransigence and opposition to God as these opponents become all the more determined to put Jesus to death. Their eyes see, but they are loathe to see the truth about Jesus and themselves. In the same way, the teachers of the law from Jerusalem may have understood the parable about the divided kingdom and the strong man in 3:23–27, but they do not repent. They may be silenced for the moment, but they will continue to deny Jesus' authority and malign his reputation.

7.3.1.3.1 The Insiders

The quotation from Isaiah and the interpretation of the parable of the Sower would suggest that "insiders" are insiders by virtue of God's sovereign grace and election.[62] The parable and its interpretation do not explain how to become good soil; good soil is simply assumed to be good soil. To argue that soil "is passive and cannot change,"[63] however, ignores that the analogy breaks down when it is applied to human beings. Humans are not dirt and can strive to understand, come to Jesus for clarification, and change. Otherwise, the commands to "listen" throughout the parable discourse would be hollow (4:3, 9, 23, 24; see also 7:14; 8:18; 9:7).

If Boucher is right that the parables "are the means both by which God judges the hearers, and by which the hearers bring judgment upon themselves,"[64] then the insiders are those who "listen" and "see." In the interpretation of the parable of the Sower, all "hear." The issue is how they hear (4:3, 9, 20, 23, 24, 33). Understanding comes from correct hearing (see Deut 6:4–5). Bad hearing leads to misunderstanding and failure (4:15, 16, 18; 6:2, 11, 20; 14:58, 64; 15:35). The division between outsiders and insiders, then, is based both on God's choice and the individual's choice, a paradox that Mark does not attempt to resolve. How this response transpires is as mysterious as the germination of a seed under the ground. We do not know how (4:27).

The sower sows, and it is part of the inherent power of the seed to germinate and grow into a plant, but the seed must fall on fertile soil to produce anything. The same potent seed can fail if it falls into useless ground. The explanation for the parables conveys, as Moule conjectures, that only those "who listened seriously and 'meant business' could get any further."[65] The parables sift out the nonchalant listener from the serious listener. For the irresponsible listeners, the parables fall on deaf ears. The serious ones who seek out Jesus for more instruction find that they have been given the mystery of the kingdom of God. This view, Moule offers, is suggested by the saying in 4:25: "Whoever has will be given more; whoever does not have, even what they have will be taken from them."[66]

The insiders in Mark are not restricted to "the Twelve" whom Jesus has just

62. Boring, *Mark*, 119.

63. Ibid., 132.

64. Madeleine I. Boucher, *The Mysterious Parable: A Literary Study* (CBQMS 6; Washington, DC: Catholic Biblical Association of America, 1977), 84.

65. Charles F. D. Moule, "On Defining the Messianic Secret in Mark," in *Jesus und Paulus: Festschrift für Werner Georg Kümmel zum 70. Geburtstag* (ed. E. Earle Ellis and Erich Grässer; Göttingen: Vandenhoeck & Ruprecht, 1975), 246.

66. Ibid.

selected (3:13–19). When Jesus enters into a house, a crowd gathered with him and the disciples (3:20). In 4:1, he teaches the large crowd "gathered around him" by the lake. This detail would refer the audience to the preceding scene where Jesus teaches those "around him" (3:32, 34), and he explains that those who do the will of God are "my brother and sister and mother" (3:35). "The Twelve and the others around him" also ask him about the parables (4:10). This detail suggests that insiders are those who have been stirred by Jesus' teaching and come to him for further elucidation to learn more.[67] What distinguishes the insider from the outsider is that the insider gathers around Jesus to inquire of him (4:10). Kermode's complaint that the outsider seems to be kept "outside, dismayed and frustrated" in a seemingly arbitrary manner is unjustified.[68] What makes the insiders different is that they do not walk away frustrated or dismayed but come to Jesus for further illumination. The outsiders hear only baffling parables and go their way.

Mark concludes the discourse by summarizing that Jesus "did not say anything to them without using a parable. But when he was alone with his own disciples, he explained everything" (4:34). This summary underscores "the notion that any true grasp of the nature of God's kingdom derives not from human speculation but from close affiliation with Jesus, from 'being with him' as followers and heirs to his mission."[69] Maloney claims, "The enigma about the Kingdom, its mystery, is that one must *become a member of it* to understand it and any parable about it."[70] Mark would view his audience as those who get insider knowledge and should have understanding (13:14). Those whom one might assume to be insiders, however, are not hermetically sealed off from the variety of satanic assaults. The narrative reveals that insiders can become outsiders. Insiders may have ears to hear and to understand, but they do not understand everything about the mystery of the kingdom of God (4:13; 7:14–21). They can only begin to fathom this mystery after Jesus' crucifixion and resurrection.

7.3.1.3.2 The Outsiders

Those who qualify as "the outsiders" obviously comprise Jesus' overt enemies in the narrative, like the Pharisees and Herodians who plot to kill Jesus (3:6), the teachers of the law from Jerusalem who slander him as a purveyor of black magic (3:22), the members of the temple hierarchy whose envious appraisal of Jesus as a threat lead them to engineer his demise (12:12), and those who gather at the cross to mock his suffering (15:29–32). Identifying specific persons as outsiders, however, is not constructive. The text leaves the issue vague with an indefinite pronoun: "*Whoever*

67. Marcus, *Mystery*, 101, adapts the insights of Eugene E. Lemcio, "External Evidence for the Structure and Function of Mark iv. 1–20, vii. 14–23 and viii. 14–21," *JTS* 29 (1978): 323–38, and argues that it reflects an Old Testament pattern (Ezek 17:1–24; Zech 4:2–14) in which the initial statement is ambiguous and not understood. The revealer then expresses surprise or rebukes the listener, which leads to a full explanation. The pattern in Mark is incomprehension and explanation, never explanation and then incomprehension.

68. Frank Kermode, *The Genesis of Secrecy* (Cambridge, MA: Harvard University Press, 1979), 27–29.

69. Henderson, *Christology*, 125.

70. Elliot C. Maloney, *Jesus' Urgent Message for Today: The Kingdom of God in Mark's Gospel* (New York: Continuum, 2004), 57.

has ears to hear, let them hear" (4:9). Insiders are those who hear and understand. Outsiders are those whose indifference and impenitence make the parables impenetrable. They do not understand anything Jesus says or does, and they exclude themselves from God's kingdom.

The focus in 4:14–20 falls on insiders, not outsiders, which suggests that Mark is more interested in illustrating for his audience how insiders can become outsiders rather than how outsiders fail to come inside. Lemcio comments: "The great irony in all this is that those who have been granted the ability to perceive the rule of God in the mystery and ambiguity of its historical manifestation and reception are in danger of finding themselves among its casualties."[71] If one of the Twelve, like Judas, who was specifically chosen by Jesus to be with him (3:13–19), can become an outsider, then anyone might do so. The division between insiders and outsiders is not an unbridgeable chasm. The boundaries are permeable, and the bridge across the divide can lead one in both directions.

Paul uses the term "outsiders" for nonbelievers (1 Cor 5:12–13; 1 Thess 4:12; Col 4:5; 1 Tim 3:7; see Rev 22:14–15), and they are not dismissed as irrevocably doomed. Mark would seem to have the same view. For example, Jesus' biological family who came "to take charge of him," thinking that he was "out of his mind" (3:21), are standing "outside" (3:31–32) when Jesus identifies those who are his "brother and sister and mother" as those who do the will of God (3:34–35). The kingdom of God creates a family that is not based on biological kinship that can whip up exclusiveness, selfishness, and rivalries.[72] This marginalization of Jesus' biological family is not permanent, however. The early church's development reveals that they became insiders. The Galatians know about James, the Lord's brother, reputed to be one of the pillar apostles (Gal 1:19; 2:9). The Corinthians know about "the Lord's brothers," who take their wives on missionary journeys (1 Cor 9:5). Luke knows that Jesus' mother and brothers devoted themselves to prayer with the disciples and others after the resurrection (Acts 1:14).

7.3.1.4 The Manifestation of the Kingdom of God is Deceptively Ordinary and Small

"The kingdom of God does not come with sirens blaring and bombs bursting in air, but quietly and inconspicuously."[73] The parables address the apparent insignificance of what is happening in Jesus' ministry from the perspective of the casual observer. As Ambrozic recognizes, "Jesus' activity was so unlike the expected kingdom, so unlike anything that might give the impression of being a preparation for the

71. Lemcio, "External Evidence for the Structure and Function of Mark iv. 1–20, vii. 14–23 and viii. 14–21," 333–34.

72. Louis Feldman, *Jew and Gentile in the Ancient World: Attitudes and Interactions from Alexander to Justinian* (Princeton: Princeton University Press, 1993), 196–99 observes that Christianity differs from Judaism "in its very essence." "Jews historically have defined themselves as a people, a nation, a family, whence we can understand the Talmudic formulation [*b. Qidd.* 68b] defining the born Jew as one who has a Jewish mother (a biological rather than a credal definition); religion is an accoutrement of the nation." Christianity, by contrast, was the "first religion devoid of nationalistic connection" and was attacked for it by ancient critics.

73. Garland, *Mark*, 54.

kingdom, that he had to emphasize the link between his coming and the arrival of the kingdom as well as the fact that the manner of this arrival is inscrutable and ineffable."[74] The parables caution against being disconcerted, discontented, or disbelieving by the seemingly modest impact of the kingdom's presence. It requires faith not to be put off by its humble appearance.[75] Perrin interprets seed parables to mean: "The small beginning contains within itself the promise of the particular glory of God's future, precisely because both the present and the future are God's."[76] But this beginning, shorn of glory, is necessary. Dahl is on the mark: "To urge that Jesus, if he was the Coming One, should engage in messianic activity would be as foolish as to press the husbandman to be active in order to make the grain grow or to urge him to reap it before the harvest time."[77]

Even after the glories of Jesus' resurrection, however, Mark's Christian community remains small and insignificant. The imagery of a mustard bush suppresses any tendency toward triumphalism. The parable highlights the contrast between "an insignificant beginning and an impressive final size."[78] But the image of the mustard that "becomes the largest of all garden plants, with such big branches that the birds can perch in its shade" (4:32), pales in comparison with the grandiose images associated with the noble cedar of Lebanon, which is portrayed in the OT as a glorious tree that is associated with earthly empires that have oppressed Israel and will be destroyed by God (2 Kgs 19:23; Pss 29:5; 37:35; Isa 2:13; 37:24; Jer 22:7, 23; Ezek 31:1–12; Amos 2:9; Zech 11:1–2). Ezekiel uses it in an allegory and proclaims:

> "This is what the Sovereign LORD says: I myself will take a shoot from the very top of a cedar and plant it; I will break off a tender sprig from its topmost shoots and plant it on a high and lofty mountain. On the mountain heights of Israel I will plant it; it will produce branches and bear fruit and become a splendid cedar. Birds of every kind will nest in it; they will find shelter in the shade of its branches. All the trees of the forest will know that I the LORD bring down the tall tree and make the low tree grow tall. I dry up the green tree and make the dry tree flourish.
>
> "I the LORD have spoken, and I will do it." (Ezek 17:22–24; see also Ps 104:16–17).

It may have been more heartening for Jesus to say that the kingdom of God of would grow like a cedar in Lebanon (Ps 92:12) instead of like a mustard bush, but

74. Ambrozic, *The Hidden Kingdom*, 119. Marcus, *Mark 1–8*, 323, comments, "For the dominion of God is like the word: paltry in appearance, but hiding a tremendous divine potency behind its apparent insignificance."

75. Ambrozic, *The Hidden Kingdom*, 165. Cédric Fischer, *Les disciples dans l'évangile de Marc: une grammaire théologique* (EBib 57; Paris: Gabalda, 2007), notes that the disproportionate contrast between the seed and the plant that grows from it points to the paradoxical aspect of the kingdom.

76. Norman Perrin, *Rediscovering the Teaching of Jesus* (New York: Harper & Row, 1967), 158.

77. Nils Alstrup Dahl, "The Parables of Growth," in *Jesus in the Memory of the Early Church* (Minneapolis: Augsburg, 1976), 157.

78. France, *Mark*, 216. So also Gundry, *Mark*, 233–34; Marcus, *Mark 1–8*, 324.

the kingdom of God manifests itself in improbable, disquieting ways that are easy for many to dismiss.

Pliny describes the mustard as "pungent ... fiery ... grows entirely wild, though it is improved by being transplanted: but on the other hand when it has once been sown it is scarcely possible to get the place free of it, as the seed when it falls germinates at once"[79] Beyond being a seasoning, he lists its benefits in helping to cure serious ailments, but its noxious characteristics should not be overlooked. Henderson comments, "Due to its rapid germination, the mustard bush threatens to encroach on existing vegetation and depicts God's kingdom as an annoying, ineradicable weed that can overtake other kingdoms sown on the earth."[80] Boring concludes that the mustard bush "is not a tree and not necessarily desirable."[81] Even though the point seems clear, the plant that is "the largest of all garden plants" (or "shrubs") comes from a seed that is proverbially small. Tiny seed, huge bush;[82] this image for the kingdom of God is jarring.[83]

While it may not be the case that Jesus is deliberately parodying the majestic cedar of Lebanon with the lowly mustard plant,[84] the simile does suggest that there is something disarming and disenchanting about the kingdom as represented in Jesus. Sabin comments:

> Surely nothing as awe-inspiring as a "noble cedar" or a tree whose top touches the vault of heaven would come from such common seed. And in fact, Mark does not use the word "tree" to describe its final growth, but rather λάχανα [*lachana*] which literally means "garden plants" or "vegetables." To the reader versed in all the great trees of Scripture, this surely comes as a jolt, even a joke. The birds of heaven are taking shelter here under a tree of about eight feet. The great tree of God's kingdom has gone domestic.[85]

Jesus' view of the kingdom shatters cherished hopes and delusions of grandeur that may have been in the minds of his contemporaries and those who have followed him down through the ages. For example, Peter's hope of swift triumph and world empire without the Son of Man enduring suffering and death (8:31–33), the disciples' hopes of achieving precedence and rank above others (9:33–35), and James's and John's hopes of sitting on thrones and basking in glory (10:35–45) will all be rudely dashed. The kingdom of God does not fulfill human dreams of earthly triumph.

79. Pliny, *Nat.* 19.170–71.

80. Henderson, *Christology*, 131.

81. Boring, *Mark*, 139–40.

82. Claus-Hunno Hunziger, "σίναπι," *TDNT*, 7:287–91; Pesch, *Markusevangelium*, 1:261–62; see Matt 17:20; *m. Nid.* 5:2; *m. Ṭehar.* 8:8; *m. Naz.* 1:5.

83. It is even more jarring when it is combined with the odd image of leaven in Matt 13:31–33 and Luke 13:18–21.

84. So Robert W. Funk, "The Looking-Glass Tree Is for the Birds, Ezekiel 17:22–24; Mark 4:30–32," *Int* 27 (1973): 3–9. See also Bernard Brandon Scott, *Hear Then the Parable: A Commentary on the Parables of Jesus* (Minneapolis: Fortress, 1989), 383–86, and John Dominic Crossan, *The Historical Jesus* (San Francisco: Harper, 1991), 277–79.

85. Marie Sabin, "Reading Mark 4 as Midrash," *JSNT* 45 (1992): 21. The mustard seed that grows into a plant "with such big branches that the birds can perch in its shade" (4:32) suggests that God's reign will encompass more and more people. Marcus, *Mark 1–8*, 324, states that the birds seeking shelter symbolize the nations (see *1 En.* 90:30; *Midr. Ps.* 104:10). As the disciples are successful in their commission as fishers of men and the gospel is proclaimed to all nations (13:10; 14:9), those from the nations will be included.

7.3.1.5 The Present Is a Time of Growth That Leads Inexorably to a Great Harvest

The seed parables affirm that God's kingdom has been sown (4:3–4, 14–20, 26, 31–32), that is, has arrived and is growing organically (4:8, 20, 27–28, 32). This affirmation would bolster the confidence of Jesus' followers. At the same time, however, the interim can be a time of disquiet because the growth of the seed into a bountiful harvest is not readily visible. Failures are often more obvious (4:4–7). Evil coexists with God's kingdom, which adds to the mystery. It produces a "harvest of death,"[86] and it often seems to be winning. The seed parables in the parable discourse express differently the same idea that is found in Paul's word to the wise, "So we fix our eyes not on what is seen, but on what is unseen, since what is seen is temporary, but what is unseen is eternal" (2 Cor 4:18).[87] The kingdom of God's inevitable victory can only be perceived by faith, which explains the repeated injunction to listen. Despite appearances and human ignorance about how the promised harvest happens, the kingdom has begun with Jesus and will result in an inevitable harvest.

H. H. Rowley's observation about the difference between the prophets and the apocalyptists is germane: "the prophets foretold the future that should arise *out of* the present, while the apocalyptists foretold the future that should *break into* the present."[88] Edwards notes that the Dead Sea Scrolls affirm that the kingdom ultimately depended on God, but they also give the strong impression that "its arrival was predicated on the prerequisites of human righteousness and obedience, which might be thought of as 'matching funds' to the bargain."[89] Jesus' preaching of the kingdom of God affirms that it has already come, and its coming had nothing to do with any preparatory human effort. Despite our eagerness to be useful in bringing about the kingdom of God, it is not established by human hands. Humans can only wait for it (15:43), receive it, and enter it (10:15). As a corollary, the kingdom of God also will not be built, completed, or controlled by humans, and its consummation will not be hastened by human religious devotion or activity.[90]

The brief parable in 4:26–29 affirms this truth, but its interpretation is challenging because it is difficult to pinpoint where exactly the stress falls. It mentions three mediators. (1) The farmer scatters seed on the ground (4:26), sleeps and rises night and day (4:27a) but does not know how the seed sprouts and grows (4:27c), and finally swings the sickle to the grain (4:29a) when the harvest has come. (2) The seed is scattered (4:26), sprouts and grows (4:27b)—stalk, head, full kernel in the head (4:28b)—and finally ripens for the harvest (4:29b). (3) The soil receives the seed (4:26) and produces the grain all by itself (4:28). The word translated "by itself" (*automatē*)

86. Marcus, *Mark 1–8*, 297.

87. Mark Seifrid, *The Second Letter to the Corinthians* (Pillar; Grand Rapids: Eerdmans, 2014), 219, comments, "The 'things seen' are those of the present, fallen world. The 'things unseen' are God's promises, which find their Yes in Jesus and the hope of the resurrection that is yet to come."

88. H. H. Rowley, *The Relevance of Apocalyptic* (2nd ed.; London: Lutterworth, 1944), 34.

89. Edwards, *Mark*, 46.

90. Schweizer, *Mark*, 102, notes that the parable does not mention "man's plowing, harrowing, or cultivating. Neither is there any reference to his struggle against drought and storm." These things are purposefully omitted to place greater emphasis on the seed growing miraculously and producing a harvest. The farmer has done his part and need not worry.

may mean "without visible cause" or "incomprehensibly" (4:28a) and refers to God's miraculous involvement.[91] The only other time this word occurs in the NT is in Acts 12:10, which refers to Peter being led out of prison and coming to an iron gate that opened "by itself." Iron gates do not open by themselves; it is a miracle that God effects. This marvel of the seed's growth implies God's miraculous working.

It is not simply the power of the seed to grow once it has been sown, however. The parable of the Sower makes it clear that the harvest requires a sower to sow the seed and the productive interaction with the soil to produce a harvest. All three elements — the sower, the seed, and the soil — combine to result in the harvest. Beasley-Murray asserts that what makes this parable distinctive from ideas in related apocalyptic literature is its assumption "that *a sowing has taken place with which the almighty working of God is conjoined and which must therefore inexorably issue in the final harvest of the judgment and kingdom of God.*"[92] Jesus affirms that what is happening now in the present in his ministry is inseparably fused with what God will accomplish in the future with the final harvest and judgment. The final line in the parable, "he puts the sickle to it, because the harvest has come" echoes Joel 3:13, which pictures the judgment. Ambrozic captures the point that Jesus is trying to make: "his coming and activity are intimately linked with the glorious manifestation of the kingdom in the future, that his ministry is the first step of its arrival."[93]

Paul uses the analogy of the seed that is sown and the plant that grows from it to argue for the bodily resurrection in 1 Cor 15:37 – 44: "As in nature the bare seed that is sown is not the plant that miraculously sprouts from the ground, so in the resurrection the earthly body that is sown is not the spiritual body that is miraculously raised."[94] The phrase, "God gives it a body as he has determined" (1 Cor 15:38), refers to the apparent laws established for plants in creation (Gen 1:11 – 12). Paul assumes that plants do not rise of their own volition or by chance but as God wills. Continuity exists between the bare seed and the plant, but the transition from the one to the other is accomplished by God's creative power. This analogy of the seed and the plant also applies to the presence of the kingdom of God in Jesus. It may be sown in dishonor and weakness in its present manifestation, but it will be raised in glory and power. Beasley-Murray states, "the sowing has been appointed by God, the harvest has been appointed by God, and the time between is subject to his will."[95] The future lies in the hands of God who will accomplish all things. The enduring link between the present and that future final salvation is Jesus.[96]

Older interpretations inferred from the seed parables that the kingdom of God

91. Rainer Stuhlmann, "Beobachtungen und Überlegungen zu Markus IV.26 – 29," *NTS* 19 (1973): 153 – 62. Paul asserts that God alone gives growth in 1 Cor 3:5 – 9. He planted; Apollos watered; but God, who is everything, gave the growth. The miracle of God's provision of a harvest is assumed in the wording of Luke 12:16, "The ground of a certain rich man yielded an abundant harvest."

92. Beasley-Murray, *The Kingdom of God*, 126.

93. Ambrozic, *The Hidden Kingdom*, 119.

94. Garland, *1 Corinthians*, 725.

95. Beasley-Murray, *The Kingdom of God*, 127.

96. Werner Georg Kümmel, "Noch einmal: Das Gleichnis von der selbstwachsenden Saat: Bemerkungen zur neuesten Diskussion um die Auslegung der Gleichnisse Jesu," in *Orientierung an Jesus: Zur Theologie der Synoptiker: Für Josef Schmid* (ed. Paul Hoffmann, Norbert Brox, and Wilhelm Pesch; Freiburg: Herder, 1973), 235.

would gradually evolve in human society.[97] In 1882, A. B. Bruce interpreted the parable as pointing to "progress according to natural law, and by stages which must be passed through in succession."[98] The horrors of World War One ravaged that conviction. Dahl wisely observes:

> We may say that the parables of growth teach that the kingdom has a "history," a period of its secret presence preceding its final revelation. But this does not mean that the kingdom is a spiritual or social entity, "growing" and developing. The kingdom is in itself always perfect; only the conditions of its presence change and are different in this world from what they shall be in the coming one.[99]

Comparing the kingdom of God with the sphere of the organic life of plants implies that God directs history in a series of events that leads to a divinely intended culmination, but the real emphasis in the seed parables is on the contrast between the sowing and the harvest, not on the process of growth.[100] The farmer does not know how the seed grows (4:27), but he does recognize when the crop is fully ripe and ready for the harvest (4:29).

7.3.1.6 Opposition Will Not Stymie the Kingdom

Jewish apocalyptic literature expected that the appearance of God's kingdom would bring immediate triumph to God's persecuted people against the formidable and potent kingdoms of this world. Manson stresses that Jesus taught that "victory would not come quickly or easily; but come it must."[101] In Mark, it is noteworthy that Jesus' preaching of the good news of the kingdom begins after John the Baptizer has been handed over. The NIV translation, "after John was put in prison" (Mark 1:14), may cause readers to miss the subtle connection between the fates of John and Jesus. The verb "deliver" is used as shorthand for Jesus' Passion. It appears three times in his passion predictions (9:31; 10:33): he "is going to be delivered/handed over." Judas is first identified in the narrative as the one who handed him over (3:19), and this handing over is narrated in 14:10–11, 41–42 (see also 14:18, 21). The chief priests hand over Jesus to Pilate (15:1, 10), and Pilate hands him over to be crucified (15:15). In Mark's view, the handing over of John foreshadows the handing over of Jesus. A second reading of the lengthy description of John's gruesome end at the hands of Herod Antipas (6:14–29)

> allows one to see that, unbeknownst to the earthly powers, who are blind to anything that is happening on the spiritual plane, John's arrest sets the stage for the proclamation of the gospel. Herod Antipas may have thought he was getting

97. See Snodgrass, *Stories with Intent*, 183.

98. A. B. Bruce, *The Parabolic Teaching of Christ* (London: Hodder & Stoughton, 1882), 120.

99. Dahl, "The Parables of Growth," 164.

100. Ibid., 154.

101. T. W. Manson, "Realized Eschatology and the Messianic Secret," in *Studies in the Gospels: Essays in Memory of R. H. Lightfoot* (ed. Dennis E. Nineham; Oxford: Oxford University Press, 1955), 217.

> his prophetic nemesis out of the way; but, in reality, it was all part of preparing the way for the coming of the kingdom of God.[102]

John "not only prepares, but goes the way of Jesus."[103]

The verb "to hand over" appears in the LXX of Isa 53:6, 12, and Paul's use of it in Rom 4:25, "He was delivered over to death for our sins," and in Gal 2:20, "The life I now live in the body, I live by faith in the Son of God, who loved me and gave himself for me," clarifies that Jesus is not the innocent victim of tragic circumstances. It implies that God's hand is behind all of these events. The kingdom of God therefore breaks out in a malevolent environment. Since trouble and persecutions lead some to fall away (4:17), this overt enmity is not what those who first received the word about the kingdom of God with joy expected.

The explanation for the parables in 4:10–12 explains why Jesus as the bearer of the kingdom does not meet with universal acclaim and, as noted above, indicates that hardhearted resistance is part of God's plan. Marcus explains that "the Semitic concept of 'mystery' includes the paradox that, in spite of God's sovereignty, some human beings continue to be under the dominion of sin and the devil."[104] The paradox becomes apparent in the narrative: "Redemption has come, but in the unbelief of the outsiders the shadow of the old age falls mysteriously on the dawning kingdom."[105] The parable of the Sower with its emphasis on the failures of the seed highlights that Satan wages war against God's kingdom. But this satanic opposition neither imperils nor "compromises the ultimate outcome of God's victory."[106] To the contrary, God is at work even in "the outbreak of opposition, and the violence of the opposition is actually a *sign* of his inbreaking."[107] Henderson concludes,

> though the gospel features an awkward tension between faithful and faithless following, Mark consistently affirms that, despite dogged opposition from within and without, God's eschatological triumph will bring life out of death. Indeed, only when the way of suffering is viewed as a constituent part of a more comprehensive whole can we read Mark's gospel not as tragedy but as victory, a victory that depends finally on God's radically transforming power.[108]

7.3.1.7 Hidden Revelation

The parable of the Lamp draws on an image from everyday life to impress on readers that the present hiddenness of the kingdom of God is not intended to be permanent. A lamp "comes" (literal translation) to be put on a lampstand, not to be hidden under a bushel basket or under a bed (4:21). The interpretation of the image asserts

102. Garland, *Mark*, 58.

103. Ambrozic, *The Hidden Kingdom*, 20.

104. Marcus, *Mystery*, 50. He cites (p. 50 n. 128) Karl Barth, *Church Dogmatics* (Edinburgh: T&T Clark, 1961), 4.3.1.188–91, who writes, "Contrary to every rule, intention, and hope ... the true and living and effective word of the kingdom does not accomplish in the world that which it should accomplish in accordance with its nature and the world situation created by its proclamation."

105. Marcus, *Mystery*, 56.

106. Henderson, *Christology*, 126.

107. Marcus, *Mystery*, 57.

108. Henderson, *Christology*, 23. This view resonates with Paul's description of success of the gospel in the face of deadly resistance (Phil 1:12–14). Instead of hindering the gospel, his imprisonment has "actually served to advance the gospel" (Phil 1:12).

that nothing is hidden except to be disclosed, and nothing is secret that will not eventually come to light (4:22).

Henderson comments: "the mystery of God's coming kingdom drives relentlessly toward disclosure."[109] She explains that from Jewish apocalyptic literature "mystery" typically refers to "the puzzlement" that God's assured reign is "not yet fully disclosed on earth." Paradoxically, God's dominion remains hidden while simultaneously pushing toward revelation (Dan 2:30). In Jewish apocalyptic, as the mystery becomes unveiled, it "gives way to apocalypse."[110] As a second explanation for the parables (see the outline above), the parable of the Lamp conveys that the parables are intended both to hide and to uncover the truth: "Concealment intends disclosure."[111] But what is concealed? Why is it hidden? And when is it revealed?

In the OT, the metaphor of the lamp is used in a variety of ways: as an illustration of God turning darkness into light (2 Sam 22:29), of the messianic figure promised to David and his descendants (2 Kgs 8:19; Ps 132:17), and of the word of God that lights the pathway (Ps 119:105). In Mark's context, it may be a reference to God's kingdom.[112] The lamp, however, is the subject of the verb "comes," which is not to be taken as passive, "is brought." The metaphor is to be understood in "personal, christological terms."[113] The "lamp" refers to Jesus who comes (1:38) as the manifestation of the kingdom of God. What is hidden is that Jesus is the Son of God who will be crucified in weakness and raised by God's power. God's plan, which is hidden in the Scriptures, calls for humiliation first, then vindication.

It is hardly surprising that the company of soldiers heaps scorn on Jesus as "the king of the Jews," draping a purple robe around him, placing a crown of thorns on his head, and offering him mock homage (15:17–19). A king who has no army, whose followers have deserted him, who, beaten and bloody, looks totally powerless is an easy target for jeers. These tormentors ironically testify to the truth: he is the king of the Jews and much more. Marcus writes: "So powerful is the kingdom that it reaches down even into the hate-filled minds and venomous lips of its foes, drawing unwitting testimony from those who look without seeing."[114] This king, who takes the role of a slave and obediently accepts his death, even death on a cross, as a ransom for many, will be exalted by God and given a name above every name and before whom every knee will bow and every tongue confess that he is Lord, to the glory of God the Father (Phil 2:9–11). How could this be anything but an impenetrable mystery to unbelievers?

The transition to the parable of the Measure stresses the need "to hear" and to "consider carefully what you hear" (4:23–24a). The parable of the Measure (4:24b) and its interpretation (4:25) indicate that hearing well will lead to insight that leads to greater insight. If one understands the mystery surrounding the kingdom of

109. Henderson, *Christology*, 115.

110. Ibid.

111. Edwards, *Mark*, 140.

112. Guelich, *Mark 1–8:26*, 231; Witherington, *Mark*, 169; Henderson, *Christology*, 127.

113. Boring, *Mark*, 135. He argues, "In its Markan framework, this saying no longer explains Christology, but must be explained from it."

114. Marcus, *Mystery*, 117.

God and its integral relationship to Jesus, one will be able to understand more. The spiritually rich will get spiritually richer, but the spiritually impoverished will only become more and more spiritually poverty-stricken.

Jesus asserts that the mystery is given to disciples (4:11) who listen and see. Cranfield observes that God decisively manifests the kingdom in Christ "but it was a 'veiled manifestation'; he revealed his kingdom, not in such a way as to make assent unavoidable, but in a way that still left room for men to make a personal decision."[115] For those who would become believers, this mystery is unveiled at the cross and resurrection; but for others, the truth remains cloaked in mystery. It will only become abundantly clear to all at the last judgment when Christ is fully manifest in his glory and power (13:26; 14:62).

7.4 Receiving and Entering the Kingdom

Mark's gospel contains references to receiving and entering the kingdom (9:47; 10:15, 23–24). France makes a distinction between "entering" as a reference to one's "eternal destiny" and "receiving" as a reference to "a person's attitude and response towards God's demands in this life." He writes, "To 'receive the kingdom of God' means to be God's willing subject, gladly embracing the radical values which Jesus has come to inculcate." Receiving the kingdom now in this way opens the door to " 'entry' hereafter."[116] What are the criteria for receiving and entering the kingdom?

7.4.1 Repentance and Faith

The kingdom of God confronts the world with demands. Jesus' announcement that the kingdom of God is at hand leads to the command to repent and to believe (1:15). John's baptism of repentance prepared for the coming of the one who was more powerful and who will baptize with the Holy Spirit. Jesus' call for repentance requires a response to the kingdom of God's presence. I write,

> No minister of an earthly sovereign would ever announce, "So and so has become king! If it pleases you, accept him as your king!" Such a blasé, noncommittal declaration certainly did not characterize the news of a Roman emperor's ascension to the throne. The very announcement that so and so is king contains an implicit demand for submission. Jesus' announcement that God is king contains the same absolute demand. The divine rule blazed abroad by Jesus, therefore, requires immediate human decision and commitment: repentance, submission to God's reign, and trust that the incredible is taking place.[117]

These are not separate acts, first repent and then believe. Both go together. A difference exists between rational belief and trusting faith. Marshall asserts,

115. Cranfield, *Mark*, 66–67.

116. France, *Mark*, 397. See Ambrozic, *The Hidden Kingdom*, 143–48. Schweizer, *Mark*, 45–46, notes that entering the kingdom is not like entering a place but is more like entering and submitting to "a sphere of authority."

117. Garland, *Mark*, 60.

> Rational belief is essentially involuntary; a person cannot arbitrarily choose to believe on the spot; it is something that happens to him or her in light of the evidence. Trust, however, is voluntary, an act of the will. Or, again, belief can exist without it immediately affecting one's conduct, whereas trust requires certain consequent actions in order to exist.[118]

Believing affects the core of one's being and results in a changed life. Repentance for Jesus requires not only turning from evil ways but drastically breaking from one's previous orientation to life, even if one might perceive it to be a godly, religious life. Repentance requires a change of one's way of thinking, one's outlook, one's value system and expectations, one's commitments, and one's behavior as one puts faith in God's sovereignty. The kingdom of God opens up a doorway to a new life, as the call of Simon, Andrew, James and John reveals (1:16–20). Their lives are turned in a new direction with new orders and priorities.

Jesus enunciates with hyperbole a different aspect of this radical change related to one's behavior in 9:47–48: "And if your eye causes you to stumble, pluck it out. It is better for you to enter the kingdom of God with one eye than to have two eyes and be thrown into hell, where 'the worms that eat them do not die, and the fire is not quenched.'" This statement reminds the audience of the consequences for the failure to repent. Jesus never addresses the subject of hell in a discourse but simply accepts that it is the place of post-mortem punishment. It means that Jesus' proclamation of good news also contains bad news. Humans will be held accountable for their moral and religious decisions.

7.4.2 Openness to Receiving Grace

When the disciples thoughtlessly tried to drive away the people who were bringing children to Jesus to be blessed by him (10:13), he became indignant and said, "The kingdom of God belongs to such as these" (10:14).[119] He solemnly announces, "Anyone who will not receive the kingdom of God like a little child will never enter it" (10:15).[120] The phrase "as a child" may be taken as a nominative and may mean "as a child receives."[121]

The children did not come on their own but are helpless and completely dependent on others. They are young enough for Jesus to take them in their arms to bless them. They have no stellar religious résumé. They have no preconceptions of what is possible or impossible (10:26). Analogously, one can only receive the kingdom with "the empty hand of a beggar."[122] This lowliness and humility are illustrated

118. Marshall, *Faith as a Theme*, 55; see the full discussion on pp. 51–56.

119. The incident lays bare the low status of children in Jesus' world. Collins, *Mark*, 472, cites rabbinic debates on whether children would be raised from the dead (*t. Sanh.* 13:1–2; *b. Sanh.*110b; *'Abot R. Nat.* 36; *y. Šeb.* 4.35c. 29).

120. One might also note that children do not yet contain a vault of human wisdom that predisposes their perceptions of what is possible and impossible for God. They are open to surprise.

121. Against Peter Spitaler, "Welcoming a Child as a Metaphor for Welcoming God's Kingdom: A Close Reading of Mark 10.13–16," *JSNT* 31 (2009): 439, who thinks that the simile means that one should "welcome the kingdom as one welcomes a child." Those who share Jesus' vision of God's kingdom will necessarily minister to the marginalized.

122. Schweizer, *Mark*, 207.

in the way the Syrophoenician woman pled with Jesus for help to save her little daughter. She humbled herself and accepted the role of a "dog," begging for just a crumb of Jesus' healing power.[123] The disciples' apparent unwillingness to take the role of a slave's lowly status (9:35–37) and their exclusionary hauteur (9:38–41) are examples of what debars one from receiving the kingdom as a child. Those who want to be first in status, first in glory, first in authority, and first in honor are the ones who will fail to receive the kingdom.[124]

7.4.3 Back to Basics: Obedience

Children are expected to be obedient as Jesus' prayer to "*Abba*" reveals (14:36; see also Eph 6:1; Col 3:20; 1 Pet 1:14). Receiving a divine gift "contains the idea of service and subjection to someone who is to be welcomed as being sent by God himself."[125]

This idea is conveyed in the last public mention of the kingdom of God in Jesus' teaching in Mark (12:28–34). A teacher of the law who is pleased by Jesus' rejoinder to the Sadducees about the resurrection asks him, "Which is the most important [commandment]?" Jesus responds by giving two: God is one, and we are required to love God with all our heart, soul, mind, and strength (Deut 6:4–5). This command has a corollary. We are also to love the neighbor as ourselves (Lev 19:18). The teacher of the law affirms Jesus' answer and repeats the commands but appends an additional commentary. Obedience to these commands transcends the burnt offerings and sacrifices in the temple (see Hos 6:6). Jesus affirms this answer as wise and announces, "You are not far from the kingdom of God." He is open to the demands God places on those who would enter the kingdom of God.

7.4.4 Failure and Success

The parable of the Sower highlights the fate of individual seeds in different portions of the field. It records three failures (4:4–7, 15–19) and three successes (4:8, 20). Greater detail is given to the failures, which occur at different phases of the growth process: when the seed is first scattered, after germinating and shooting up, after growing but being choked so that it produces no fruit. Success is tied to listening well, which allows the word of God to take deep root. In Paul's writings, Christians are to be "rooted and built up in" Christ (Col 2:7; Eph 3:17).

The word that falls on the hardened path is snatched away, eaten by birds, which is interpreted as the dirty work of Satan, before there is any chance of a positive response. Rootlessness, a well-known problem of the ungodly in wisdom literature (Sir 23:25; 40:15; Wis 4:3), is the second cause of failure. The word is accepted for a time but it withers under the scorching heat (see Jas 1:11), which is interpreted as a metaphor for the pressure from trouble or persecution. The third failure is attributed

123. Sharon Betsworth, *The Reign of God Is Such as These: A Socio-Literary Analysis of Daughters in the Gospel of Mark* (LNTS 422; London/New York: T&T Clark, 2010), 98, rightly contends that the healing stories in Mark provide illustrations of the kind of persons who are receptive to becoming members of the kingdom of God.

124. Tolbert, *Sowing the Gospel*, 224–27.

125. Ambrozic, *The Hidden Kingdom*, 157.

to the cares of the world, the deceit of wealth, and the craving for other things, which choke out the response to the word.

Jesus' bitter opponents, the Pharisees and the Jewish leaders, seem apt as representatives of the first category. Some argue that the disciples who desert Jesus and flee into the night when he is arrested (14:50–52) and Peter who denies Jesus three times under slight pressure in the high priest's courtyard (14:66–72) qualify as examples of the rocky soil. I would argue, however, that Mark understands Jesus' disciples to be far more deeply rooted. These failures are serious, but they are only temporary setbacks. King Herod (6:14–29, see 6:20) and the rich man who turns down Jesus' invitation to sell everything he has and give to the poor and follow him (10:17–25) provide classic examples of those debarred from the kingdom because of their attachment to their wealth.[126] They are enmeshed in earthly loyalties that they will not give up.

Resistance to the kingdom of God and the failure to produce fruit will result in ultimate punishment. The demons know that Jesus' appearance means their ruin (1:24). Those who blaspheme against the Holy Spirit by attributing Jesus' miracles to some conspiracy with Beelzebul are guilty of an eternal sin and will never be forgiven (3:29). The tenants who reject the messengers from God and with malice aforethought kill the beloved son will be destroyed (12:9).

All of these types of soil where the seed fails are forewarnings for Mark's audience. The seed has been sown, and, despite appearances, the hoped-for abundant harvest will come. The good soil in the narrative seems to be represented by the minor characters in the story who are in tenuous positions in society—"the disenfranchised, the weak, and the subordinate of society."[127]

7.5 The Revelation of the Kingdom of God

7.5.1 Seeing That the Kingdom of God Has Come with Power in the Present (Mark 9:1)

Jesus' declarations in 9:1, "Truly I tell you, some who are standing here will not taste death before they see that the kingdom of God has come with power," puzzles interpreters. What event corresponds to the kingdom of God coming in power (9:1)? Conclusions as to what Jesus refers vary widely.[128]

One option is that "the kingdom of God coming in power" refers to the end time since the previous verse mentions the Son of Man coming in the glory of his

126. The primary concern about the rich in the Old Testament (Jer 22:13–17; Amos 2:6–8) and intertestamental literature is that they place greater trust in their riches, with its illusory promise of security and well-being, rather than in God, and that they oppress the righteous, poor, and helpless (*1 En.* 96:4, 5, 8; 99:12–16; 103:15).

127. Betsworth, *The Reign of God*, 135.

128. See Martin Künzi, *Das Naherwartungslogion Markus 9, 1 par [und Parallelstellen]: Geschichte seiner Auslegung: Mit einem Nachwort zur Auslegungsgeschichte von Markus 13, 30 par.* (BGBE 21; Tübingen: Mohr Siebeck, 1977); Kent E. Brower, "Mark 9:1: Seeing the Kingdom in Power," *JSNT* 6 (1980): 17–41; John J. Kilgallen, "Mk 9, 1—The Conclusion of a Pericope," *Bib* 63 (1982): 81–83; Thomas R. Hatina, "Who Will See 'the Kingdom of God Coming with Power' in Mark 9,1—Protagonists or Antagonists?" *Bib* 86 (2005): 20–34.

Father with the holy angels (8:38; see 13:26–27).[129] If Jesus refers to the Parousia, however, he expresses a mistaken confidence that it would occur during the lifetime of the disciples. Mark may have shared this belief, and the statements in 13:26 about the people seeing the Son of Man "coming in clouds with great power and glory" and in 13:30 that "this generation will certainly not pass away until all these things have happened" might be evocative of 9:1. But these declarations are best taken as related to Jesus' prophecy about the temple's destruction.[130] Jesus declares, "But about that day or hour no one knows, not even the angels in heaven, nor the Son, but only the Father" (13:32). "That day" refers to a time distinct from "those days" (13:17, 19, 24) and distinguishes the events surrounding the temple's destruction from the Parousia. Jesus does not know when the latter will occur. Furthermore, the coming of the Son of Man (13:26; 14:62) in Mark is different from the coming of the kingdom of God.

Finally, Jesus assures his disciples that what the anonymous woman did when she anointed his head, which he interprets as preparation for his burial, will be told in memory of her wherever the gospel is preached throughout the world (14:8–9). This promise suggests that he envisions a protracted period of time that will not have run its course during the disciples' lifetime. It is unlikely, then, that Jesus suggests in 9:1 that the Parousia is imminent or that Mark thought it would happen before the ink was dry on his papyrus. Ambrozic believes that 9:1 was added "presumably to distinguish the future coming of the kingdom from its presence in the word and work of Jesus Christ, the Son of God."[131]

If Jesus is not referring to the Parousia in 9:1, what is it that he promises that some of his disciples will see in their lifetime? The phrase may refer to the transfiguration that Mark narrates in what immediately follows (9:2–8).[132] The statement in 9:1 serves as a bridge that concludes his prediction of his death and resurrection in 8:31–38 and prepares for his transfiguration in 9:2–8. The two passages are linked by an unusually specific time notice, "after six days" (9:2). The three whom Jesus selects to go with him up the mountain and who "see" Jesus' glistening appearance with Elijah and Moses in his heavenly glory may be the "some who are standing here" in 9:1. But why use such melodramatic language—some of you "will not taste death"—to describe something that will occur only a week later? Why not say "within a week"? Evans classifies it as "a touch of hyperbole," but it seems to be a rather heavy-handed touch.[133] The transfiguration makes more sense as pointing to the ultimate fulfillment of this promise rather than its actual fulfillment.

129. So Enrique Nardoni, "A Redactional Interpretation of Mark 9:1," *CBQ* 43 (1981): 373–74; Hooker, *Mark*, 212; Collins, *Mark*, 413; Marcus, *Mark 8–16*, 621–22, 630.

130. See §13.3.5.3.

131. Ambrozic, *The Hidden Kingdom*, 23.

132. Cranfield, *Mark*, 287–88; Lane, *Mark*, 313–14; Pesch, *Markusevangelium*, 2:67; Gundry, *Mark*, 469; David Wenham and A. D. A. Moses, "'There are Some Standing Here ...': Did They Become the 'Reputed Pillars' of the Jerusalem Church? Some Reflections on Mark 9:1, Galatians 2:9 and the Transfiguration," *NovT* 36 (1994): 146–63; Evans, *Mark 8:27–16:20*, 29; Stein, *Mark*, 411. Taylor, *Mark*, 385–86; Gnilka, *Markus*, 2:26; and France, *Mark*, 345, see the transfiguration as a partial fulfillment of the prediction. G. H. Boobyer, *St. Mark and the Transfiguration Story* (Edinburgh: T&T Clark, 1942), views the transfiguration as an anticipation of the Parousia. Second Peter 1:16–18 may support this interpretation.

133. Evans, *Mark 8:27–16:20*, 28.

Dodd argues that Jesus' prediction in 9:1 refers to the disciple's eventual awareness before his death that the kingdom of God has already come. He renders it: "There are some of those standing here who will not taste death until they have seen that the Kingdom of God has come with power."[134] It seems more likely, however, that the promise in 9:1 refers to some specific event that is narrated in the gospel.

I agree with Hogeterp that seeing the kingdom of God come with power is a "veiled reference to Jesus' resurrection."[135] The disciples will "see" the full truth only after Jesus' death. The structure of the narrative supports this conclusion. Again, Jesus' statement in 9:1 concludes the unit that began in 8:31 when he makes the first announcement of his approaching suffering, death, and resurrection. It promises that some will be able to see his powerless death transformed into glorious vindication and evidence of God's powerful reign in Jesus.[136] After three disciples witness his transfiguration, Jesus admonishes them as they descend the mountain not to tell anyone about it until after the resurrection of the Son of Man (9:9). This order points to the resurrection as the climactic event that sheds light on what happened to Jesus on the mountain.

The motif of seeing appears during Jesus' passion and in the announcement of his resurrection. Bystanders taunt him when he is dying on the cross to come down so that they might "see and believe" (15:32). They also hope to "see" Jesus rescued miraculously by Elijah (15:36). The centurion, however, "sees" how he dies but sees something more than the death of a crucified victim and proclaims him to be the Son of God (15:39). After his resurrection, the disciples are promised that they will "see" him when they go to Galilee (16:7). This seeing refers to something more than a temporary physical reunion in Galilee. They will also see what God's power has done. In 12:24–27, Jesus chides the Sadducees for denying the resurrection. They do not know the Scriptures or the power of God. Resurrection is integrally tied to a manifestation of God's power. God's kingdom power is evident in the ousting of the minions of the prince of demons in Jesus' exorcisms, but it is most gloriously manifest in conquering the power of death in the resurrection.

7.5.2 Seeing That the Kingdom of God Has Come with Power in the Future (Mark 14:25)

Jesus foreknows his own death and tells his disciples at the Last Supper that his blood will be poured out (14:24). The shepherd will be struck down (14:27). He has eaten

134. Dodd, *Parables*, 37–38.

135. Albert L. A. Hogeterp, *Expectations of the End: A Comparative Traditio-Historical Study of Eschatological, Apocalyptic and Messianic Ideas in the Dead Sea Scrolls and the New Testament* (STDJ 83; Leiden/Boston: Brill, 2009), 136–38. See also John J. Kilgallen, "Mark 9:1—The Conclusion of a Pericope," *Bib* 63 (1982): 81–83. If Jesus refers to the resurrection, it would explain why, when speaking to the disciples, he limits those who will see that the kingdom has come in power to "some who are standing here." Judas will not see it.

136. France, *Divine Government*, 66–76, argues that Jesus may not refer to a single event but a series of events, the transfiguration, death, resurrection, ascension, Pentecost, the destruction of the temple, and the development of the church. As one sees the seed develop into a stalk, head, and full kernel, some of Jesus' disciples will see the fulfilment of his prediction in stages. The kingdom's power will be undeniably visible.

(14:20, 22) and drunk wine, having given thanks for it (14:23), but he announces, "I will not drink again from the fruit of the vine until that day when I drink it new in the kingdom of God" (14:25), which is an implicit passion prediction.[137] Jesus' death will naturally mark the end of his earthly meals with his disciples, but it will not be the end of the story. The saying emphasizes the future fulfillment of the kingdom using the imagery of drinking wine and a banquet (see Isa 25:6–9; 55:1–2; Matt 8:11–12; Luke 13:28–29; 14:15; Rev 19:9; *1 En.* 62:13–16; *2 Bar.* 29:3–8; *m. 'Abot.* 3:20). The emphasis is not on his abstinence but on his assurance that God's purposes will be fully accomplished and he will be vindicated in glory.

Jesus does not clarify when this banquet will be. It is unlikely that it refers to the period between the resurrection and the ascension (Acts 10:41).[138] The phrase "in the kingdom" and the image of a banquet suggest an eschatological context. The word "until" stresses that there will be an interim period (see Mark 13:10) before he drinks it anew, and it is more likely that Paul captures its meaning in 1 Cor 11:26 with the declaration "until he comes."[139] Jesus looks beyond this world to another when he will drink again in future glory. The image recalls the feast of rich food for all peoples that Isaiah envisions when death will be swallowed up, the disgrace of his people will be removed, and those who trusted in the Lord will "rejoice and be glad in his salvation" (Isa 25:6–9).

Jesus' first words about the kingdom of God—"has come near" (1:15)—and his last words suggesting that the kingdom is not yet—"until that day" (14:25)—may seem confusing. But these last words tie the establishment of God's kingdom to Jesus' death and his "presence at the future manifestation of God's sovereign rule."[140] His death is not a shattering setback but sets off a chain reaction that will culminate in a victory celebration. The cup of death and lamentation mentioned in 14:24 will be replaced by the cup of triumph and rejoicing.

7.6 COSMIC OPPOSITION TO THE KINGDOM OF GOD

Satan's kingdom is coexistent with the kingdom of God, and these two kingdoms are engaged in a cosmic battle. Malbon argues, "The background conflict underlying Mark's gospel is that between the kingdom of God and the kingdom of Satan. The 'kingdom of God has come near' (1:15), and for Satan's kingdom the 'end has come' (3:26). Everything else that happens in Mark is to be understood against this transcendental background."[141] God's kingdom redeems; Satan's kingdom tyrannizes and destroys. Marcus asserts that Mark's eschatology assumes "the earth is

137. Ambrozic, *The Hidden Kingdom*, 195, citing other implicit predictions of Jesus' passion in 2:20; 9:12; 10:38; 14:3–8.

138. Contra Cranfield, *Mark*, 428.

139. The passage is noteworthy for not mentioning Jesus' Parousia or role at this meal.

140. Marinus de Jonge, "Mark 14:25 among Jesus' Words about the Kingdom of God," in *Sayings of Jesus: Canonical and Non-Canonical: Essays in Honour of Tjitze Baarda* (ed. William L. Peterson; Johan S. Vox; and Henk J. de Jonge; NovTSup 89; Leiden: Brill, 1997), 123.

141. Malbon, "'Reflected Christology,'" 130.

in subjection to cosmic forces of evil, which human beings are helpless to combat through their own efforts, and that the only hope for them is an eschatological act of God that will utterly transform the conditions of human existence and defeat the oppressive powers."[142]

The world still groans under satanic tyranny (Rom 8:22; Rev 6:10), and Mark testifies to this reality as Satan is still able to filch the seed of the word that is sown so that it cannot take root (4:15). As a result, individuals align with Satan and do not become a part of God's people. Satan is also behind Peter's attempt to talk Jesus out of the divine necessity of his suffering and death as the Messiah, which would stall the divine for the salvation of humans. Jesus consequently calls Peter "Satan" (8:33) because his human reasoning epitomizes Satan's norms. As Hedge's translation of Martin Luther's hymn "Ein Feste Burg ist unser Gott" reads:

> For still our ancient foe doth seek to work us woe;
> His craft and power are great, and, armed with cruel hate,
> On earth is not his equal.

The evil forces organized under the prince of the power of the air must be defeated before the kingdom of God can be fully established. Mark would assert that Jesus' coming into the world as a man from Nazareth means that a far stronger one than Satan has arrived. He is able to restrain Satan's power and thrash Satan's minions. Paradoxically, his death secures Satan's ultimate defeat. Golgotha is to Satan as Waterloo was to Napoleon.

Mark rather tersely describes Jesus' first encounter with Satan after the baptism: "He was in the wilderness forty days, being tempted by Satan. He was with the wild animals, and angels attended him" (1:13). Since Satan does not make a direct appearance in the narrative again, Mark enigmatically depicts this attempt to derail Jesus from the purpose for which he has been sent to be an utter failure. Jesus' argument in 3:27, "no one can enter a strong man's house without first tying him up," with its emphasis on "first" implies that he has already conquered Satan.[143] Jesus alone has the power of heaven at his side and drubs Satan in a single combat. Angels appear only to serve Jesus, not to join in the battle. Jesus' triumph in the wilderness explains why the impure spirits immediately recognize him as the victorious Son of God who has come to destroy them (1:24; 3:11; 5:7–8). The strife is not over, however. Satan does not simply retreat from this encounter to engage in rearguard resistance. The cross is still to follow, and many of Satan's captives still need to be released.

7.6.1 The Strong Man Assaulted and Bound (Mark 3:22–30)

The teachers of the law who come from Jerusalem try to blacken Jesus' reputation by attributing his success in casting out demons to an unholy alliance with Beelzebul,

142. Marcus, *Mark 1–8*, 72.

143. Klaus Scholtissek, "Der Sohn Gottes für das Reich Gottes: Zur Verbindung von Christologie und Eschatologie bei Markus," in *Der Evangelist als Theologe: Studien zum Markusevangelium* (ed. Thomas Söding; SBS 163; Stuttgart: Katholisches Bibelwerk, 1995), 75.

identified as the "prince [or ruler] of demons" (3:22). Jesus responds to this calumny with an argument that demonstrates how nonsensical their position is. Why would Satan drive out Satan? Is Satan a party to the self-destruction of his kingdom? Are Satan's pawns engaged in a civil war? If not, then the exorcisms are evidence that Satan's house is under direct assault from an outside, more powerful force. Jesus concludes his response with a pregnant allegory, "No one can enter a strong man's house without first tying him up. Then he can plunder the strong man's house" (3:27).

The allegory acknowledges Satan's power. He is a "strong man" (3:27). It also acknowledges that Satan's rule is still undivided and therefore still capable of doing harm. Satan still has a "house," representing Satan's organized hierarchy of evil, and it is filled with possessions, representing the possessed humans who have been made captive. Mark does not explain how Satan received this power. It is simply assumed that Satan's power over the world is real and not an imaginary illusion that so-called enlightened humans can safely discard. It is also assumed that the evil spirits or demons are Satan's willing soldiery. Mark also does not explain their origin or why they are permitted to ravage humans and animals (5:12–13).

The image of the strong man recalls John the Baptist's prophecy that one who was stronger than he would come (1:7). It turns out that the one who comes is also stronger than Satan. Jesus has raided Satan's kingdom, overrun it, and bound its lord so that he is unable to thwart the liberation of its prisoners. Watts argues that Mark presents Jesus as the divine warrior who is the agent of the new exodus (Exod 15:3; Isa 40:10–11; 42:13–15; 51:9; 52:10), delivering "the plundered, despoiled, and hidden away in the darkness of prisons" (see Isa 42:22–23; 49:9; 51:14; 52:2).[144] Yet the individual routing of demons does not cause the total destabilization or collapse of Satan's reign.[145] Satan is being restrained but can still inflict chaos until his final defeat at the end of the age.

The theme of defeating evil powers that can take various forms is a common theme in modern movies. The plot is often framed around an invasion of a different species from outer space. In this cinematic mythology, the world is saved through the heroic actions of a small cadre of intrepid humans who use their guile and military weapons to destroy the enemy by violent force. Mark's theology assumes that humans, even with their cleverness and their technology, are incapable of defeating evil powers on their own. In fact, they make matters worse with their violent schemes. Human impotence when confronting the cosmic forces of evil is also evident in the vain attempt of the jailors to shackle the Gerasene demoniac (5:3–4).

According to Mark, humans can only align with God, who alone will defeat evil. The victory will be won by the One who gives his life for others. Marcus points out that the verb "can" or "is able" in the phrase, "no one can enter a strong man's house without first tying him up" (3:27), along with the cognate adjective, "possible

144. Watts, *New Exodus*, 140–41. He contends that the imagery of the strong man "is associated in some contemporary Jewish traditions with God's eschatological deliverance of his people" (p. 147).

145. See Joel Marcus, "The Beelzebub Controversy and the Eschatologies of Jesus," in *Authenticating the Activities of Jesus* (ed. Bruce Chilton and Craig A. Evans; Leiden: Brill, 1999), 252.

(*dynatos*)," is used by Mark "to emphasize what God and/or Jesus alone can do (1:40; 2:7; 5:3; 8:4; 9:3, 22, 28; 10:26–27; 14:35–36) or what human beings can do only through the power of God (9:23, 29). The whole issue is summed up in the terse pronouncement in 10:26–27: salvation is impossible for human beings, but not with God."[146]

146. Marcus, *Mark 1–8*, 72.

Chapter 8

The Secrecy Motifs in Mark

Bibliography

Aune, David E. "The Problem of the Messianic Secret." *NovT* 11 (1969): 1–31. **Bedenbender, Andreas.** "Das 'Messiasgeheimnis' im Markusevangelium." *Texte und Kontexte* 27 (2004): 1–96. **Berger, Klaus.** "Die königlichen Messiastraditionen des Neuen Testaments." *NTS* 20 (1973): 1–44. **Burkill, T. A.** *Mysterious Revelation: An Examination of the Philosophy of St. Mark's Gospel.* Ithaca, NY: Cornell University Press, 1963. **Dunn, James D. G.** "The Messianic Secret in Mark." Pp. 116–31 in *The Messianic Secret.* Ed. Christopher Tuckett. Minneapolis: Fortress, 1983. **Ebeling, Hans Jürgen.** *Das Messiasgeheimnis und die Botschaft des Marcus-Evangelisten.* BZNW 19. Berlin: Töpelmann, 1939. **Fendler, Folkert.** *Studien zum Markusevangeliums: Zur Gattung, Chronologie, Messiasgeheimnistheorie und Überlieferung des zweiten Evangeliums.* GTA 49. Göttingen: Vandenhoeck & Ruprecht, 1991. **Focant, Camille.** "Un christologie de type 'mystique' (Marc 1.1–16.8)." *NTS* 55 (2009): 1–21. **Kelber, Werner, H.** "Narrative and Disclosure: Mechanisms of Concealing, Revealing and Reveiling." *Semeia* 43 (1988): 1–20. **Longenecker, Richard N.** "The Messianic Secret in the Light of Recent Discoveries." *EvQ* 41 (1969): 207–15. **Moule, C. F. D.** "On Defining the Messianic Secret in Mark." Pp. 239–52 in *Jesus und Paulus: Festschrift für Werner Georg Kümmel zum 70. Geburtstag.* Ed. E. Earle Ellis and Erich Grässer. Göttingen: Vandenhoeck & Ruprecht, 1975. **Räisänen, Heikki.** *The "Messianic Secret" in Mark's Gospel.* Trans. Christopher Tuckett. Edinburgh: T&T Clark, 1990. **Taylor, Vincent.** "Unsolved New Testament Problems: The Messianic Secret in Mark." *ExpTim* 59 (1948): 146–51. **Tillesse, G. Minette de.** *Le secret messianique dans l'évangile de Marc.* Paris: Cerf, 1968. **Tuckett, Christopher, ed.** *The Messianic Secret.* Philadelphia: Fortress, 1983. **Watson, David F.** *Honor among Christians: The Cultural Key to the Messianic Secret.* Minneapolis: Fortress, 2010. **Watson, Francis.** "The Social Function of Mark's Secrecy Theme." *JSNT* 24 (1985): 49–69.

8.1 The Wrede Detour

In 1901, William Wrede proposed in his book, *The Messianic Secret*, a theory that Bedenbender labels "a Copernican change in Markan research."[1] It has dominated

1. Andreas Bedenbender, "Das 'Messiasgeheimnis' im Markusevangelium," *Texte und Kontexte* 27 (2004): 16.

and vexed Markan scholarship for decades. Wrede contended that the first Christians believed that Jesus became the Messiah after his resurrection (see Acts 2:36; Rom 1:3–4; Phil 2:6–11).[2] Christians proclaimed Jesus to be the Messiah and believed that his earthly ministry must have had a messianic character, but there was little or no evidence for it in the received tradition. Wrede coined the term "the messianic secret" to argue that secrecy was read back into the story of Jesus to account for why he was not acknowledged as the Messiah during his ministry.[3] Jesus had shown himself to be the Messiah in a number of ways but had enjoined silence to keep it hidden. For Wrede, the unhistorical character of this apologetic device is most evident in the strict orders Jesus gives to Jairus and the others that they should keep secret the raising of his dead daughter back to life (5:43).[4] Since the mourners had already gathered in the house, such silence would have been impossible unless the parents were to keep their daughter permanently sequestered. Everyone would soon know what had transpired when, refreshed by food, the girl reenters village life. The command, he argues, must then be tied to Mark's theological purpose and is not historical.

Wrede maintains that the messianic secret motif is singularly Markan and emerges in various situations in the gospel.[5] (1) Jesus commands silence of demons who recognize his true identity (1:25, 34; 3:12), of those who benefit from his miraculous power (1:43–44; 5:43; 7:36; 8:26), and of the disciples who are on the verge of recognizing his true identity (8:30; 9:9). (2) Jesus attempts to keep his whereabouts secret (7:24; 9:30–31). (3) His teaching is incomprehensible to many, which is summed up in his explanation about parables in 4:10–12. He deliberately teaches in a cryptic way that veils his meaning so that outsiders will not perceive the secret of the kingdom. He only gives private explanations about what it means to his disciples.[6] (4) Despite giving the disciples this special instruction, they, too, fail to grasp his meaning.[7]

This secrecy motif explains why Jesus was not recognized as the Messiah during his earthly ministry. He kept it hush-hush by preventing anyone from divulging

2. Wrede, *The Messianic Secret*, 225–29.

3. Wrede (ibid., 145–46) believed that the secret messiahship theme originated in the early tradition but Mark amplified it and made it predominant in his gospel. Manson, "Realized Eschatology and the Messianic Secret," 220, acidly comments that, according to Wrede, Mark adopted "the hopeless contradiction that he [Mark] must record acts and words of Jesus that demand publicity and recognition of him as the Messiah within a framework that demands secrecy and non-recognition.... The evangelist cannot be given credit of having invented the lunatic structure by himself; and so we fall back on that ever-present help in critical difficulties, the anonymous group. They concocted the bulk of the farrago of nonsense, which Mark, with a few embellishments of his own, eventually put into writing."

4. Wrede, *The Messianic Secret*, 50–51, also cites the healing of the blind man (8:22–26) and asks, "How then is the sufferer to reach his house without going near the town and how is he to remain concealed from the people in his house?"

5. Matthew and Luke, who use Mark, do not contain the idea except when they take over traditions from Mark, and even then they omit the demands to secrecy that appear, for example, in 1:34; 3:11–12; 5:43; 7:36.

6. Wrede, *The Messianic Secret*, 62, following Adolf Jülicher's *Die Gleichnisreden Jesu*, assumes that Jesus used parables to elucidate his teaching without any allegorizing features. All of Jesus' parables are presumed to be self-explanatory, not cryptograms needing decoding, and were designed to enlighten the listeners, not to perplex them.

7. Public teaching (4:1–9)/private instruction (4:10–20); public teaching (4:21–34a)/private instruction (4:34b); public teaching (7:1–15)/private instruction (7:17–23); public teaching (10:1–9)/private instruction (10:10–12); public teaching (10:17–22)/private instruction (10:23–27); public teaching (12:27–40)/private instruction (13:1–37). The disciples' lack of understanding is emphasized in 6:52 and 8:17, 21 and imputed to their hardened hearts.

his messianic identity and by giving plain teaching only to insiders. Even then, the insiders remained in the dark. The command in 9:9, according to this theory, sums up the rationale behind all the other commands to silence: "As they were coming down the mountain, Jesus gave them orders not to tell anyone what they had seen until the Son of Man had risen from the dead." Jesus' identity will only be revealed after the resurrection.

A corollary to Wrede's theory is that Jesus did not present himself as the Messiah during his earthly ministry and was neither acclaimed nor recognized as such.[8] Wrede therefore judges the gospel to be an unreliable historical foundation on which to construct a life of Jesus. Not surprisingly, Wrede regards Peter's confession that Jesus is the Christ to be unhistorical. This corollary has captured much of the attention of scholars, and it is the easiest facet of his argument to refute. It fails to explain why Jesus would have been executed as a messianic pretender as "king of the Jews" (Matt 27:11, 29, 37; Mark 15:2, 9, 12, 18, 26; Luke 23:3, 37, 38; John 18:33, 39, 19:3, 12, 14, 21) were there not something messianic about Jesus' ministry.[9] The leaders know his claims and ask where he gets the authority to do what he does (11:28). His confession in 14:62 does not come as a surprise. The high priest asks him a leading question, expecting him to incriminate himself.

Most important is this theory's failure to explain why the disciples would want to transform their unmessianic master into the Messiah and heavenly Son of Man after the resurrection.[10] Albert Schweitzer asks:

> How can the appearances of the risen Jesus have suggested to the disciples the idea that Jesus, the crucified teacher, was the Messiah? Apart from any expectations, how can this conclusion have resulted for them from the mere "fact of the resurrection?" The fact of the appearance did not by any means imply it. In certain circles, indeed, according to Mark vi. 14–16, in the very highest quarters, the resurrection of the Baptist was believed in; but that did not make John the Baptist the Messiah. The inexplicable thing is that, according to Wrede, the disciples began at once to assert confidently and unanimously that He was the Messiah and would before long appear in glory.[11]

Juel contends, "The resurrection would have been understood as proof of his [Jesus'] messiahship only if a messianic claim were already an issue, only if messiahship were somehow at stake in his death."[12]

Finally, the secrecy motif is not a purely Markan fabrication because it is also found in John. For example, John, in comparison to Mark, *emphasizes* the glory of

8. Wrede, *The Messianic Secret*, 230.

9. Hengel, *Studies*, 44, boldly states that the tradition with which Mark worked "was still aware of Jesus' messianic claim, the reality of which should not be doubted, since otherwise, historically and in terms of their content, the whole of his activity up to his passion, which is without parallel in the history of ancient religion, not to mention the development of the earliest christology after Easter, would be incomprehensible."

10. Martin Hengel, "Jesus, the Messiah of Israel: The Debate about the 'Messianic Mission' of Jesus," in *Authenticating the Activities of Jesus* (ed. Bruce Chilton and Craig Evans; NTTS 28/2; Leiden/Boston: Brill, 1999), 327.

11. Schweitzer, *Quest*, 345.

12. Juel, *Messiah and Temple*, 25.

the unveiled Christ, but the secrecy theme emerges in Jerusalemites' demand, "How long will you keep us in suspense? If you are the Christ, tell us plainly" (John 10:24). This theme must have some root in the historical ministry of Jesus.

Weber notes that Wrede's messianic secret has been "variously accepted, rejected, supplemented, revised, extended, re-arranged, restricted."[13] Sanday was one of the first in English to reject Wrede's arguments and scornfully observed, "That any ancient should seek to cover the non-existence of certain presumed facts by asserting that they did exist, but that the persons affected were compelled to keep silence about them, is a hypothesis altogether too far-fetched to be credible."[14] Taylor offers, " 'The citadel has caved in; but the flag still flies.' "[15] After years of debate, most scholars do not believe that Wrede's hypothesis provides a sufficient description of or explanation for the secrecy or concealment motif that runs through Mark's narrative, but no consensus has arisen on how to interpret this theme. Luz declares, "The messianic secret is still a mystery."[16] In my view, Wrede's conclusions led Markan scholarship down a detour, which then became a well-paved highway by subsequent studies. What follows is an attempt to change course and to remedy the misrepresentation of Mark's theology.

8.2 THE SECRECY MOTIFS UNVEILED

8.2.1 The Inconsistency of the Pattern of Secrecy

A first step in trying to unravel the mystery of the secrecy motif is to recognize that the commands to silence in Mark's narrative do not produce a uniform response. No single overarching theory explains these disparate responses to the commands to silence in Mark's narrative. When Jesus silences the demons who shout out his identity, he is always obeyed (1:25, 34; 3:11–12). When Jesus commands the beneficiaries of his miracles not to tell anyone, he is usually disobeyed. This last response is also unpredictable and exhibits "a back-and-forth toggling between secrecy and disclosure to chosen persons."[17] For example, he tells the Gerasene demoniac to go home and tell his friends all that the Lord has done for him (5:19–20). He also does many miracles in public and makes no attempt to squelch the crowd from noising it abroad. Luz notes that in the healing summaries (1:32–34; 3:7–12; 6:54–56) the

13. Reinhard Weber, " 'Christologie' und 'Messiasgeheimnis': Ihr Zusammenhang und Stellenwert in den Darstellungsintentionen des Markus," *EvT* 43 (1983): 110. See the surveys of scholarship in James L. Blevins, *The Messianic Secret in Markan Research 1901–1976* (Washington, DC: University Press of America, 1981); Christopher Tuckett, "Introduction: The Problem of the Messianic Secret," in *The Messianic Secret* (ed. Christopher Tuckett; Philadelphia: Fortress, 1983), 1–28; Heikki Räisänen, *The 'Messianic Secret' in Mark's Gospel* (Studies of the New Testament and its World; Edinburgh: T&T Clark, 1990), 38–75; Maretha M. Jacobs, "Mark's Jesus through the Eyes of Twentieth Century New Testament Scholars," *Neot* 28 (1994): 53–85; Jacob Chacko Naluparayil, "Jesus of the Gospel of Mark: Present State of Research," *CurBS* 8 (2000): 191–226.

14. William Sanday, "The Injunctions of Silence in the Gospels," *JTS* 5 (1904): 324. France, *Mark*, 331, n. 43, is no less severe: "The longevity of Wrede's speculation, which has set (and perhaps skewed) the agenda for subsequent discussion, that the theme of secrecy is a Marcan apologetic invention, is one of the more remarkable phenomena of biblical scholarship." See also N. T. Wright, *Jesus and the Victory of God* (Minneapolis: Fortress, 1996), 529, n. 181.

15. Taylor, *Mark*, 123.

16. Ulrich Luz, "The Secrecy Motif and the Marcan Christology," in *The Messianic Secret* (ed. Christopher Tuckett; Philadelphia: Fortress: 1983), 75.

17. Ben Witherington III, *The Indelible Image* (Downers Grove, IL: InterVarsity Press, 2009), 1:611.

commands to silence have nothing to do with a messianic secret. What is to be kept secret is the miracle.[18] The commands to silence in the exorcisms of demons and in the healing miracles should not be lumped together. The commands to silence about his identity are obeyed; the commands to silence about something miraculous that he has done are not.[19] They should be interpreted under separate categories and should not be forced to fit into some imagined coherent theological straitjacket.[20]

Luz argues that the commands to demons and to the disciples fall into the category of an identity secret while the commands to those who are healed fall into the category of a miracle secret.[21] These classifications are too simplistic. The commands to demons differ from the commands to the disciples (8:29–30; 9:9), differ in their intent, and express dissimilar theological motifs. Silencing the demons, those who are healed, and the disciples should be dealt with separately to recognize how they convey distinct theological themes.

8.2.1.1 Silencing Demons

The clearest text that lends support to Wrede's theory is 3:11–12: "Whenever the impure spirits saw him, they fell down before him and cried out, 'You are the Son of God.' But he gave them strict orders not to tell others about him." This translation is misleading, and it is better to translate this last phrase literally: "he rebuked them not to make him known."[22] This passage and the other commands that muzzle the demons can be construed in a variety of ways. Not all of the interpretations are mutually exclusive.

First, with their supernatural knowledge the impure spirits perceive what the human characters in the narrative cannot. Mark appears to use their recognition of Jesus' divine identity as a literary device to reinforce for the audience that Jesus is the Son of God. The so-called secrecy motif, as Hooker recognizes,

> *functions in precisely the opposite way to what one expects*: it serves as a means of revelation to the hearers/readers of the gospel. When Jesus commands the impure spirits to be silent about his identity it is too late, since they have already spoken (1.24f.; 3.11f.). Yet no one in the story hears them, and the truth they utter remains hidden—as it must, to all whose eyes and ears have not been opened: their words are intelligible only to those who already believe that Jesus is what they declare him to be—the Son of God.[23]

18. Luz, "The Secrecy Motif," 80.

19. Grindheim, *Christology*, 73.

20. See William C. Robinson Jr., "The Quest for Wrede's Secret Messiah," in *The Messianic Secret* (ed. Christopher Tuckett; Philadelphia: Fortress, 1983), 97–115; Heikki Räisänen, "The 'Messianic Secret' in Mark's Gospel," in *The Messianic Secret* (ed. Christopher Tuckett; Philadelphia: Fortress, 1983), 132–40. Hengel, *Studies*, 45, points out that the tradition was disparate: "With so unique a figure as Jesus, who bursts all historical frameworks, there could be no 'one-dimensional tradition,' without tensions and apparent contradictions. His person and activity cannot be forced into the confines of ready-made christological theories."

21. Luz, "The Secrecy Motif," 86–88.

22. The word "others" is not in the text, and the same adjective ("known," *phaneron*) that is used here appears in 6:14, where King Herod hears of the miracles performed by Jesus' disciples, for his name had become "well known."

23. Hooker, *Mark*, 67.

Second, many assume that Jesus commands the impure spirits to be silent because identifying him as the Son of God before the cross and resurrection is premature.[24] Premature for whom? This declaration is not news to the audience, who knows the incipit and introduction (1:1–13). The declaration has already been made by God (1:11). The cat has already been let out of the bag when the demons shout out their recognition of Jesus in the synagogue (1:24), but it does not register with the worshipers. They must have heard the demon shriek to know that it had succumbed to Jesus' greater authority, but the content of what it yelled apparently made no impression on them. The emphasis is on the power behind this exorcism: "What is this? A new teaching—and with authority! He even gives orders to impure spirits and they obey him" (1:27).[25] The order for the impure spirit to be silent apparently has nothing to do with concealing the mystery of Jesus' identity.[26]

A third option understands that Jesus silences the demons to prevent creating speculation about his divine identity that would redirect attention from his preaching of repentance (1:15).[27] Jesus came to proclaim the message related to the kingdom of God and repentance (1:38), not to proclaim himself. Mark wants to emphasize the importance of Jesus' word and obedience to it.[28] This view founders on the same point noted above. No one takes up or wonders about the demons' acknowledgment of Jesus.

Fourth, others argue that the demons' confession is silenced because it springs from a dubious source.[29] Impure spirits belong to the forces of evil and are incapable of revealing the full truth even when they talk out of turn. Jesus does not want public testimony that is demonic. They can never align with Jesus; they are to be destroyed. The problem is that this testimony is not untimely for Mark's audience. Mark intends for them to know Jesus' divine origins from the beginning. That demons recognize Jesus' identity when they are hostile both to him and to God makes their declaration all the more compelling for the audience.

Fifth, Hooker claims that the secret is artificial as a technique to highlight for the audience the story's real significance and that it has no historical basis in Jesus' ministry.[30] I would contend that silencing the demons is part of the earliest tradition and that it is intrinsic to the exorcism.[31] Jesus does not silence the evil spirits because he fears that they will divulge to the public a secret known only to them and give the game away. They are irreconcilably opposed to Jesus and try to use their knowledge of his identity only for sinister purposes. The command to silence exerts his power over them.

24. Luz, "The Secrecy Motif," 82; Guelich, *Mark 1–8:26*, 148–49.

25. See §5.3.1.

26. Burkill, *Mysterious Revelation*, 74.

27. Kilgallen, "The Messianic Secret," 60–65.

28. Ibid., 65.

29. Schweizer, *Mark*, 56; Lane, *Mark*, 131; Witherington, *Mark*, 144.

30. Hooker, *Mark*, 68–69.

31. See Gerd Theissen, *The Miracle Stories of the Early Christian Tradition* (ed. John Riches; trans. Francis McDonagh; Philadelphia: Fortress, 1983), 140–52. He maintains, "The command to be silent is aimed at the apotropaeic power of miraculous knowledge, not against its manifestation" (144).

Those familiar with Jewish exorcism techniques represented, for example, in the *Testament of Solomon* appreciate that knowing the names of the demons and their thwarting angel are vital to mastering them. One may infer that the reverse is true. Knowing Jesus' true identity would seem to give the demons a tactical advantage over him.[32] The impure spirits howl out Jesus' sacred names as a preemptive defensive maneuver to control him and to fight off the exorcism.[33] The translation of Jesus' response, "be silent" (*phimōthēti*), is too subdued since the verb is also used for muzzling an animal (1 Tim 5:18; cf. Deut 25:4).[34] The rebuke that muzzles the demons is part and parcel of driving them out. Shutting them up shuts them down.[35] This fact explains why the audience is not told explicitly in 3:12 that Jesus drove out the demons. The audience can assume that he drove them out by virtue of his lordly command for them not to make him known.[36]

Dunn points out that the command to silence does not always appear in the exorcism stories (5:1–20; 7:24–30; 9:14–29), which would seem to undermine the argument that it is part of the exorcism.[37] I would counter, however, that the absence of the command in these reports is because the demons do not try to resist the exorcism by audaciously pronouncing Jesus' name as a magical counter-spell. When Jesus encounters the legion of demons bedeviling the Gerasene demoniac, they try to stave off the exorcism after Jesus was saying, "Come out of this man, you impure spirit!" (5:8). They adjure him, "What do you want with me, Jesus, Son of the Most High God? In God's name don't torture me!" (5:7). Jesus does not order them to be silent. It is not because there are no spectators to hear their shouts but for narratological reasons. The account contains a dramatic interchange between Jesus and the demons (5:9–13), and immediately silencing the demons would have ruined the story.

The demon cast out of the Syrophoenician woman's daughter is carried out from a distance, so the demon does not directly encounter Jesus and has no chance to try to put up a defense (7:24–30). The spirit that plagues the young boy by dashing him down to the ground and trying to destroy him by casting him into fire and into

32. Collins, *Mark*, 169, cites a magical papyrus where a magician expects to gain power over the moon because he knows its "good and great Majestic names" (*PGM* IV. 2251–53; 2289; 2343–45). Bolt, *Jesus' Defeat of Death*, 68, notes the long lists of names that appear in magical spells to gain control and to manipulate higher powers. It might be analogous to the English colloquial expression "I've got your number."

33. Cranfield, *Mark*, 77, asserts, "These 'confessions' (here and in iii. 11, v. 7) can hardly be explained as testimonies wrested from the demons against their will." Francis Watson, "The Social Function of Mark's Secrecy Theme," *JSNT* 24 (1985): 50, agrees: "In Mk 1.25, the command to silence is simply part of the means by which the exorcist defeats the evil spirit's use of 'the apotropaeic power of miraculous knowledge' ... and thus probably belongs to the pre-Markan tradition (cf. *siōpa*, *pephimōso* in 4.39, where nothing is said about keeping a secret)." But he claims that in 1:34 and 3:11 Mark redacted "this feature of the tradition" by turning it into "an injunction to secrecy about Jesus' messiahship." So also Gnilka, *Markus*, 1:135.

34. Bolt, *Jesus' Defeat of Death*, 65–66, refers to the use of the verb in the magical papyri to mean "to bring under control." According to James Hope Moulton and George Milligan, *The Vocabulary of the Greek Testament: Illustrated from the Papyri and Other Non-Literary Sources* (Grand Rapids: Eerdmans, 1976), 672, the verb and its cognate noun are "used in rude Egypto-Syrian Greek as equivalent to *katadein*, *katadesmos* in denoting the *binding* of a person by means of a spell, so as to make him powerless to harm."

35. The accounts in 1:34 and 3:10–12 simply reverse the order of 1:25 ("Be quiet ... come out of him"): "He also drove out many demons, but he would not let the demons speak because they knew who he was" (1:34). Mark does not state that Jesus ousts the demons in 3:11 but his rebuking them and silencing them in 3:12 necessarily implies their expulsion.

36. See Gnilka, *Markus*, 1:135.

37. James D. G. Dunn, "The Messianic Secret in Mark," in *The Messianic Secret* (ed. Christopher Tuckett; Minneapolis: Fortress, 1983), 116–31.

water immediately convulses the boy when Jesus appears (9:18, 20). It does not call out Jesus' name because it is a "deaf and mute spirit" (9:25). This demonic paroxysm, however, is a wordless but equally futile maneuver to prevail over Jesus. It cannot resist Jesus' power but exits violently with an inarticulate shriek and one last horrific convulsion that leaves the boy corpse-like (9:26). The impure spirit also parted from its victim in the Capernaum synagogue by shaking him violently and howling (1:26). Jesus is able to restore the boy back to life from this deadly body (9:26–27).

I would conclude that the demons' gasps of recognition are not truly confessions of Jesus' identity but desperate defensive measures that inevitably fail. Views one and four are closest to the mark. Mark has taken the historic tradition of Jesus' muzzling the demons to control and expel them and used it for his christological purposes. The supernatural impure spirits recognize Jesus' divine status and try to evade the exorcism, but Jesus is able to thwart them by his own greater power. The commands that gag them have nothing to do with a secrecy motif that keeps hidden Jesus' messianic, or in this case, divine identity. Instead, they reveal Jesus' divine power to crush "the strongest forms of demonic resistance by the utterance of the simplest commands."[38]

8.2.1.2 Silencing Those Who Are Healed

If Mark programmatically seeks to present Jesus quashing all hints of his identity, he critically fails in a number of episodes. Jesus has no qualms about doing miracles with enormous theological implications in public. He does not avoid the limelight when he pronounces the forgiveness of the paralytic's sins in the midst of a large crowd and says that the Son of Man has the authority to forgive sins (2:1–12). This announcement evokes outrage among the teachers of the law who question in their hearts: "Why does this fellow talk like that? He's blaspheming! Who can forgive sins but God alone?" (2:7).[39]

After Jesus exorcised the legion of demons from the Gerasene demoniac, the man, now in his right mind, pleads with Jesus that he might be with him (5:18). Jesus refuses his request and tells him, "Go home to your own people and tell them how much the Lord has done for you, and how he has had mercy on you" (5:19). The man proclaims throughout the Decapolis how much Jesus, not the Lord, had done for him, and everyone responded with amazement (5:20). Bolt interprets his actions "as an abundance of obedience: so overwhelmed was he by what had occurred that he was apparently convinced that Jesus could be equated with the Lord and he went even beyond the bounds of his mission."[40] The audience would not judge his actions negatively. Instead, they would be likely to recognize the miraculous transformation in one who "went from crying out in distress day and night, to preaching far and wide."[41]

38. Burkill, *Mysterious Revelation*, 76.

39. Luz, "The Secrecy Motif," 76, notes that the controversy with the teachers of the law requires "an element of publicity" and that disclosure further explains why the Pharisees conspired with the Herodians on how to destroy him (3:6).

40. Bolt, *Jesus' Defeat of Death*, 146.

41. Ibid., 147.

While Jesus forbade those who had witnessed the revival of Jairus's daughter to let anyone know about it (5:43), he is not reticent about making public the healing of the woman with the flow of blood (5:25–34), an incident that is sandwiched between the episode of raising of the young girl (5:22–24, 35–43). Jesus is aware that power had gone forth from him when the woman surreptitiously touched him and turns to the crowd to ask, "Who touched my clothes?" The woman is obliged to come forward and announce to one and all what had happened to her. Jesus pronounces that her faith, presumably her faith in Jesus' miraculous powers, made her well; and he tells her publicly to go in peace and be healed of her disease (5:30–34).[42]

When Jesus exits Jericho, Bartimaeus, a blind beggar sitting by the roadside, shouts, "Jesus, Son of David, have mercy on me!" Jesus does not try to silence him; instead, the crowd does. Jesus does not rebuke him for calling him "son of David" but heals him and proceeds on his fateful journey to Jerusalem with the man following in his train (10:46–52). Nor does he try to silence the crowd that greets him as he enters Jerusalem and links his arrival to "the coming kingdom of our father David" (11:10).

8.2.2 The Theological Significance of the Commands to Silence

The orders to keep the miracles quiet have nothing to do with Jesus' identity as the Messiah. The commands to silence go back to the historical Jesus, and Mark draws out several important theological motifs from them.[43]

8.2.2.1 Jesus' Miraculous Power Cannot Be Concealed

The command to secrecy reveals that despite Jesus' desire for his miracles to remain hush-hush, such divine healing power cannot be kept secret.[44] The command to silence after cleansing the leper would seem to be a prime example of this theme. Jesus tells him, "See that you don't tell this to anyone. But go, show yourself to the priest and offer the sacrifices that Moses commanded for your cleansing, as a testimony to them" (1:44). The leper disregards Jesus' orders to keep quiet and "proclaims" (*kēryssein*) many things and spreads "the word" (*ton logon*; 1:45). Bolt argues that "Jesus' 'command to silence' ought to be understood as an attempt to limit *when* he might tell others." He is to show himself first to the priest to get a clean bill of ritual purity health that readmits him into the community before he can give his testimony. Bolt argues that his "eager proclamation (v. 45) simply occurred *too early*."[45]

42. Jesus' strict orders not to let anyone know about raising Jairus's daughter (5:43) may be connected to the command to the disciples that places a time limitation on telling about the transfiguration until after the resurrection (9:9). Marcus, *Mark 1–8*, 373, contends that if raising the girl to life foreshadows Jesus' resurrection, it must "remain a secret until Jesus himself has arisen."

43. Hengel, *Studies*, 43, argues that the command to silence is not a theme imposed on the traditional material but goes back to the historical Jesus. Related to the demand that the disciples not tell anyone that Jesus is the Messiah (8:29–30), France, *Mark*, 331, notes that "a 'historicist' approach to the messianic secret has been widely undervalued in scholarly discussion."

44. Moule, "On Defining the Messianic Secret in Mark," 245, contends "it is not unreasonable to explain the secrecy motif in the healing stories in terms of privacy rather than of messianic or theological mystery."

45. Bolt, *Jesus' Defeat of Death*, 91–92.

Nothing in the text condemns the joyous reaction of the healed leper. In fact, it marks a progression in the reactions to Jesus' first miracles. The synagogue spectators reacted to the exorcism of a demon with amazement and identify it as "a new teaching—and with authority" (1:27). When Peter's mother-in-law was raised from her fever, she reacts by serving them (1:31). The leper reacts to his cleansing by spreading the news. However one interprets the leper's response, as the result of disobedience or the result of joy that cannot be contained, for Mark, Jesus' power and mighty deeds are too stupendous to be kept secret.

It makes no difference whether Jesus insists on secrecy or not; his deeds are extolled and his reputation magnified. Mark notes that Jesus' fame spread throughout the surrounding region of Galilee after the first exorcism (1:28). After healing Peter's mother-in-law, people brought to him all those who were sick or demon possessed so that the whole city was gathered around his door (1:32–33). After the leper noises abroad the news of his cleansing, Jesus is no longer able to enter a town openly, as people come from miles around seeking him out (1:45). When he returns to Capernaum, the crowd is so thick that they are practically hanging from the rafters of the house where he is speaking the word to them (2:2, 4). Jesus continues to be surrounded by a surge of people, as Mark notes that increasing numbers of supplicants come to him "from Judea, Jerusalem, Idumea, and the regions across the Jordan and around Tyre and Sidon" (3:7–8). The leper's disobedience may have forced Jesus to avoid the cities and to retreat to deserted places (1:45), but even there throngs continue to come from all over (6:32–33; 7:24).[46]

Jesus does not attempt to silence the crowd who flocks to him after they are healed of their various diseases (1:34; 3:10; 6:56), and his popularity swells exponentially. Jesus has to order the disciples to have a boat ready for him to escape being crushed by the crowd (3:7–9). He then teaches the large crowd that had gathered on the shore from the boat (4:1). When his family comes to seize him, they have to cool their heels outside the house where he is teaching, presumably because the packed crowd prevents them from entering (3:31–32). The crowd that accosts him is so relentless that he does not have leisure to eat (6:31). Even when he tries to retreat to a deserted place by crossing the sea, a crowd from all the towns hurtles around the shore to meet them (6:31–34). People recognize Jesus when he recrosses the sea and lands at Gennesaret, and wherever he went people brought their sick to him and begged to touch his cloak to be healed (6:54–56).

Jesus could not even escape notice when he hid himself in the region of Tyre (7:24–25). He fails to keep things low-key as the crowd gets wind of his works and proclaims his celebrity all the more, "He has done everything well" (7:36–37). A mass of people in the region of the Decapolis hangs on his every word for three days with next to nothing to eat (8:1–2). The crowd even swarms the disciples in his absence (9:14), and people bring their children to him for him to touch and

46. Williams, *Other Followers*, 135, notes that after the disobedience of the deaf man (7:36–37), the next scene also begins with a large hungry mob in the wilderness (8:1).

presumably to bless (10:13). On the fateful journey to Jerusalem, a large crowd follows him as he leaves Jericho (10:46), and many hailed his entrance into the Holy City (11:8–10). His teaching engrosses such a large crowd in the temple that the priestly hierarchy are determined to kill him, because the crowd seems to have been mesmerized by him (11:18). His enormous popularity, however, deters them from openly carrying out their plot to do away with him (12:12).

The handful of commands to secrecy after Jesus heals someone (1:43–44; 5:43; 7:36; 8:26) do nothing to suppress news of his power from mushrooming, to tamp down the excitement of the crowd that besieges him, or to impede their speculation about his identity (6:14–15; 8:28). Tolbert contends that "the author's intention in fashioning the secrecy passages is *not* to propose that Jesus remained unknown and did not attract crowds but rather to verify that Jesus did not seek renown for himself or glory, although the spread of his fame and the growth of multitudes around him was inescapable, given who he was and what he did. It was not his desire but his fate."[47] That the crowd mistakenly guesses that Jesus might be John the Baptist, Elijah, or one of the prophets, but not the Messiah (8:28), is not because Jesus shrouded his deeds in secrecy. These mistaken inferences are attributable to other reasons. People will fail to recognize the truth that Jesus is God's Son and the Messiah. But Isa 6:9–10, cited in 4:11–12, reveals that this was part of God's mysterious plan.

8.2.2.2 The Modesty of the Miracle-Worker

Tolbert's comment that Jesus "did not seek for himself renown or glory" leads to a second point. The commands to silence highlight Jesus' reserve in not calling attention to himself as a miracle worker.[48] Winn understands it to be a Markan modesty, not secrecy, motif. He argues that this portrayal fits a historical context in which the current Roman emperor Vespasian promoted the virtue of modesty. In presenting Jesus to his Roman readers as the true ruler of the world, Mark portrays Jesus manifesting the same imperial virtue.[49] He claims that the secrecy motif fits Roman imperial virtues and that Jesus "is portraying the modest behavior of an ideal Roman emperor."[50] This virtue is most clearly evident in Jesus' command to the man who has been delivered from his legion of demons, "Go home to your own people and tell them how much the Lord has done for you, and how he has had

47. Tolbert, *Sowing the Gospel*, 227–28,

48. Collins, "Mark and His Readers," 89, cites the philosopher and miracle worker Empedocles who lived in Sicily during the fifth century, and later in the Peloponnese. He played up his fame and once said:

> Friends, who live in the great city of the yellow Acragas, up on the heights of the citadel, caring for good deeds, I give you greetings. An immortal god, mortal no more, I go about honoured by all, as is fitting, crowned with ribbons and fresh garlands; and by all whom I come upon as I enter their prospering towns, by men and women I am revered. They follow me in their thousands, asking where lies the road to profit, some desiring prophecies, while others ask to hear the word of healing for every kind of illness, long transfixed by harsh pains.

Jesus' efforts to keep his identity secret contrast with Empedocles's self-promotion.

49. Winn, *Purpose*, 190–92.

50. Ibid., 191–92.

mercy on you" (5:19). The man, however, tells how much "Jesus" has done for him (5:20). Jesus' desire is to focus on God and not himself.

Watson approaches the issue from the ancient Mediterranean values of honor and shame.[51] He claims that Jesus deliberately resists receiving honor that he has merited through his acts of healing or exorcism (1:40–45; 5:21–24, 35–43; 7:31–37; 8:22–26) in an attempt to subvert the conventional expectations attached to it.[52] First-century readers would have regarded Jesus' commands to silence as a surprising resistance to honor. He has no interest in achieving wider public acclaim. Watson concludes, "Mark's Jesus is not keeping a secret regarding his messiahship, but demonstrating the standards for establishing honor within the new family of faith."[53] Mark develops this theme because he is intent on presenting a new context for receiving honor, namely, the surrogate family of those believers who obey the will of God (3:31–35), and new criteria by which honor is established, namely, taking up one's cross and following a crucified Savior (8:34). Mark's sole purpose in using the secrecy motif may not be to subvert the existing honor/shame value system and replace it with a different one determined by the cross, but this reading does fit a first-century cultural context that has much to commend it.

8.2.2.3 A Powerful Jewish Miracle-Worker Who Was Not an Agent Provocateur

Jesus warns that in a time of wars and rumors of wars wonder-working prophets and so-called Messiahs, claiming "I am he," will appear and will try to deceive even the elect (13:21–22). Jesus is not of their ilk. He did not do miracles to amaze people as false prophets would do or to rouse a rebellious rabble. He is not like Judas the Galilean, who rose up at the time of the census and enticed people to follow him, or Theudas, who appeared claiming to be somebody, and rallied a number of men around him playing a desperate game of sedition (Acts 5:36–37). Mark's narrative shows that Rome has no reason to fear him as the King of the Jews (15:2–5) who would foment an uprising of the people.

Hultin refashions this argument by pointing to possible political and social pressures behind Jesus' attempts to maintain secrecy about his miracles. He suggests that this motif was "meant to show that Jesus was concerned for how his activity might have endangered *others*."[54] He argues that Jews in the first-century Mediterranean world lived in precarious situations and argues with Slingerland that there was a pattern of "continuous imperial antipathy towards the foreign cult" of the Jews.[55] Jews

51. David F. Watson, *Honor among Christians: The Cultural Key to the Messianic Secret* (Minneapolis: Fortress, 2010). See a summary of his thesis in "The 'Messianic Secret': Demythologizing a Non-existent Markan Theme," *Journal of Theology* 110 (2006): 33–44.

52. For example, when Jesus heals the leper (1:40–45), the leper would be expected to repay his benefactor by singing his praise far and wide. Jesus' command for him to be silent topples that conventional expectation.

53. Watson, *Honor among Christians*, 44.

54. Jeremy F. Hultin, "Disobeying Jesus: A Puzzling Element in the Messianic Secret Motifs," in *Portraits of Jesus: Studies in Christology* (ed. Susan E. Myers; WUNT 2/321; Tübingen: Mohr Siebeck, 2012), 82.

55. Hultin, ibid., 83–92, citing H. Dixon Slingerland, *Claudian Policymaking and the Early Imperial Repression of Judaism at Rome* (SFSHJ 160; Atlanta: Scholars Press, 1997), 87.

were accused of being bent on causing agitation and fostering sedition throughout the world (see Acts 17:6–7) and therefore were regarded as a menace to society. He presents evidence "that the Romans saw a political threat to their order in miracles and in excessive charismatic popularity."[56]

Jews recognized that when the Romans felt threatened, they too were threatened (see John 11:47–51). Jesus' ministry attracted crowds and awakened hopes in them that the Romans and their Jewish proxies would have perceived as sinister. Hultin argues that Jesus sought to keep his miraculous deeds secret because he was aware of how dangerous it was to arouse the suspicions of the Romans and the Jewish aristocracy, who were charged with the task of keeping order. He wanted to keep at bay any threat of military intervention. He cites a quotation from Paula Fredriksen and adds the emphasis: "*The open dissemination of a Messianic message ... put the entire Jewish community at risk.*"[57] He concludes that if Jesus' supporters present him as trying to keep his miraculous deeds quiet, trying to avoid crowds, and trying to keep his messianic identity under cover, he "would appear less immediately responsible for his own fate and for the way he endangered other Jews."[58]

8.2.2.4 A Teacher on a Divine Mission

Mark offers a variety of explanations why Jesus wanted to avoid the crowd. Attending to their every need would interfere with his purpose in coming. When the disciples find Jesus after his wondrous miracles in Capernaum, they declare, "Everyone is looking for you!" (1:37). They want him to return to the village and build on his success. Jesus balks and declares his purpose is to proclaim the message in neighboring towns, "That is why I have come!" (1:38). In 6:31, Mark explains that Jesus wanted to get away to a deserted place in order to rest for a while because so many were coming and going they did not have a chance to eat.[59] Mark offers no reason why Jesus went off to the region of Tyre and did not want anyone to know he was there, but this detail reemphasizes that the word about Jesus had already spread to Tyre (3:8). "He could not keep his presence secret" (7:24).

In 9:30, Mark notes that Jesus passed through Galilee and did not want anyone to know it. Mark gives no reason why Jesus wanted to remain concealed, but many have inferred that Jesus may not have wanted to attract unnecessarily the premature attention of hostile authorities. More significantly, it is during this time that he teaches his disciples on the way privately and plainly about his impending death and resurrection and the nature of discipleship. It makes sense that he did not want to be distracted by the crowd, who would comprehend even less than his disciples did the necessity of his suffering and death. The secrecy theme noticeably fades after 9:13, and Jesus no longer bans his disciples from saying anything.

56. Hultin, "Disobeying Jesus," 92.

57. Ibid., 89, citing Paula Fredriksen, "Judaism, the Circumcision of Gentiles, and Apocalyptic Hope: Another Look at Galatians 1 and 2," *JTS* 42 (1991): 556.

58. Hultin, "Disobeying Jesus," 93.

59. John J. Pilch, "Secrecy in the Mediterranean World: An Anthropological Perspective," *BTB* 24 (1994): 155, offers a psychological reason for this retreat: "An existence that allows little or no privacy is very exhausting."

8.2.2.5 The Uselessness of Fostering a Faith Based on Miracles

While Mark's gospel heightens the emphasis on Jesus' miracles, it also reveals that God's power is not revealed solely through miracles. Divine power becomes manifest most clearly in the crucifixion, seemingly, the epitome of powerlessness, and in the resurrection, when God raises Jesus from the dead. Those who clamor only for miracles will see nothing as Jesus languishes on the cross (15:29–32). The significance of the miracles, therefore, can easily be misconstrued. They can evoke external awe but not transform inner existence. They can create astonishment, but they do not create belief in Jesus' messiahship unless one already has faith. Mark makes this spiritual reality clear when he states that in Jesus' hometown of Nazareth, "he could not do any miracles there, except lay his hands on a few sick people and heal them. He was amazed at their lack of faith" (6:5–6a).

Jesus does not trust faith that is based only on miraculous spectacles.[60] That kind of faith is built on only a half truth. It is likely to be repulsed by and to eschew the unpleasant fact that this powerful miracle worker will be crucified. It is therefore prone to avoid suffering and unable to persevere when it comes.

8.2.3 Silencing the Disciples

8.2.3.1 The Order to Tell No One that Jesus Is the Messiah

The disciples are in a privileged position because they receive private explanations of Jesus' teaching, and they participate in what Wrede labels, "the sublimest of revelations."[61] The disciples who ask, "Who is this? Even the wind and the waves obey him!" after the calming of the storm (4:41), appear to reach a major breakthrough when Peter, as the disciples' spokesman, confesses, "You are the Messiah" (8:29). Their eyes now seem to see; their ears now seem to hear; and they now seem to remember (8:18), and they put it all together to reach this verdict.[62] Surprisingly, this confession does not elicit joy from Jesus. Instead, he "warns" them to tell no one about him (8:30). The translation "warn" is rather colorless. It is the same verb (*epitimaō*) that Jesus uses to rebuke demons (1:25; 3:12; 9:25) and the raging wind (4:39).[63] This directive is the only one for which the tag "messianic secret" is apt, but why Jesus uses such strong language to silence the disciples at this point draws out multiple explanations.

(1) The command highlights the division between the disciples and the ill-informed crowd, to whom everything comes in riddles.[64] According to Hooker, "the

60. See John 4:48; 6:26; 12:37.

61. Wrede, *The Messianic Secret*, 115–16.

62. Wrede, ibid., 119, interprets this confession to mean only that the narrative is not telling us "so much about a moment in the life of the disciples as that it is telling us what Jesus is and yet cannot be in public."

63. The disciples "rebuke" the people who brought their little children to Jesus (10:13), and the crowd "rebukes" Bartimaeus to be quiet when he was crying out to Jesus (10:48).

64. The crowd gathers to hear Jesus teach (2:13; 4:1; 5:21; 7:14; 8:1; 10:1), and, at one point, Mark notes that they receive his teaching gladly (12:37). They follow him wherever he goes (5:27, 30–31; 9:15, 25; 10:46), and he has compassion on them, which results in his teaching them (6:34) and feeding them (8:2). It is notable that he instructs them along with the disciples on the requirements of discipleship (8:34). The picture one gets of the crowd in Mark is that they are generally sympathetic, even enthusiastic when it came to his miracles, but entirely undiscerning. Mark does not differentiate the crowd that he attracts in the temple from the crowd that comes to arrest Jesus armed with swords and clubs (14:43) and is stirred up by the priests to cry for Jesus to be crucified and for Barabbas to be released (15:8–15).

truth about his [Jesus'] identity can be grasped only by those who are his disciples."[65] The crowd may not be hostile to Jesus, but they are not distinguished by their discernment. Jesus' identity is to remain a secret to all those who are not committed to him.

(2) A historicist interpretation assumes that the term "Messiah" carried political freight. If the word got out that Jesus was the Messiah, it could ignite unwanted nationalistic expectations among the people. Taylor dubs it "a counsel of prudence" in a volatile atmosphere in which this claim might fan the flames of revolutionary hopes.[66] Berger disputes this common assumption, however, by showing that the title "Messiah" need not have involved a political and military meaning in the first century.[67]

(3) The command may simply mean that the time for public testimony has not yet arrived.[68] This interpretation finds confirmation in a second command for the three disciples to keep silence after they have witnessed the transfiguration. They are not to speak of it to anyone until after the resurrection (9:9). Watson argues that the secret creates a distinction "between two chronological epochs: the time of secrecy (Jesus' earthly ministry) and the time of revelation (Jesus' death and/or resurrection), at which his identity as Christ and Son of God is disclosed."[69] This chronological distinction makes sense when it is recognized that being "the Messiah" is not simply a title or a status that is conferred on Jesus but a task to be accomplished (see John 19:30). Jesus' reticence makes sense because he understood being the Messiah as a destiny that was to be fulfilled (9:12; 14:21, 27). It would have been ill-timed to proclaim that he was Messiah before that destiny had been realized.

(4) I would argue that although Peter's confession is technically correct, the full implications of what it means for Jesus to be the Messiah can only be understood in the context of Jesus' suffering, death, and resurrection.[70] The ensuing narrative reveals that Peter and the disciples are still in the dark. As Camery-Hoggatt puts it, "Peter's confession is accurate only in its vocabulary."[71] The disciples consistently misunderstand almost everything to this point, and one would not expect for the mist before their eyes suddenly to evaporate so that they now see with perfect vision. Jesus must continue to unveil the mystery of his identity to his disciples with private

65. Hooker, *Mark*, 203.

66. Taylor, *Mark*, 377.

67. Klaus Berger, "Die königlichen Messiastraditionen des Neuen Testaments," *NTS* 20 (1973): 1–44.

68. Juel, *Mark*, 120.

69. Watson, "The Social Function of Mark's Secrecy Theme," 55.

70. Jesus' response has nothing to do with Mark's attempt to amend a false Christology that understood Jesus as a divine man (*theios anēr*). This concept, now regarded as an artificial construct, arose in a Hellenistic setting and assumed that a heroic figure of the past could be regarded as a supernatural being endowed with divine wisdom and the divine power to perform miracles. The thesis of Weeden, *Mark: Traditions in Conflict*, is that Mark presents the disciples' false divine man Christology with Jesus' wondrous deeds of power in the first half of the gospel and then counters it in the second half by focusing on Jesus' death on the cross. See also Norman Perrin, "Towards an Interpretation of the Gospel of Mark," in *Christology and a Modern Pilgrimage: A Discussion with Norman Perrin* (ed. Hans Dieter Betz; rev. ed.; Missoula, MT: Scholars Press, 1974), 38. Otto Betz, "The Concept of the So-Called 'Divine Man' in Mark's Christology," in *Studies in New Testament and Early Christian Literature: Essays in Honor of Allen Wikgren* (ed. David E. Aune; Leiden: Brill, 1972), 229–40, has sufficiently discredited this view. His conclusions are confirmed by Carl R. Holladay, *Theios Anēr in Hellenistic-Judaism: A Critique of the Use of This Category in New Testament Christology* (SBLDS 40; Missoula, MT: Scholars Press, 1977); Jack Dean Kingsbury, "The 'Divine Man' as The Key to Mark's Christology—The End of an Era?" *Int* 35 (1981): 243–57; idem, *Christology*, 25–45. The assumption that Mark intends to combat some false christological view has done a disservice to understanding the gospel.

71. Camery-Hoggatt, *Irony in Mark's Gospel*, 157.

teaching before they can make it known to others. An essential element is missing: his divinely willed death on the cross. The question is not simply, "Who is the Messiah?" but "What is the Messiah?"[72] Jesus speaks "plainly" about his destiny, and this inconceivable, disconcerting, and disappointing fate of the Messiah is the real messianic secret, which is hard for his disciples, let alone others, to fathom.

The dialogue that follows reveals that "knowing *who Jesus is* does not guarantee knowing *what Jesus will do!*"[73] Taylor captures Mark's view: "Messiahship is a destiny; it is that which He does, that which the Father is pleased to accomplish in Him and which he fulfils in filial love.... The Messiah already, He would not be the Messiah until His destiny was fulfilled."[74] Hengel avers, "Only in suffering does the Marcan Jesus manifest his messianic status in the full sense. Messianic status and representative suffering belong indissolubly together."[75] If Peter refuses to accept Jesus' mission that will lead to his suffering and death, he does understand what it means for Jesus to be the Messiah.

After this confession, Jesus announces openly that the Son of Man must suffer many things and be rejected by the elders, the chief priests, and the teachers of the law, and that he must be killed and after three days rise again (8:31). Peter emphatically objects, rebuking Jesus in return (8:32). Jesus just as emphatically rebukes him because his vision of the Messiah's role stands in direct opposition to God's purpose (8:33).[76] Peter may recognize that Jesus is more than a recycled, wonder-working prophet, as rumored among the people (8:28), but he does not yet recognize that Jesus is more than a wonder-working Messiah sent to restore the Davidic kingdom to Israel (see 11:10; Acts 1:6). Disciples argue with one another on the way who was the greatest (9:34) and jockey for the privilege of being installed on Jesus' right and his left in glory (10:37). Peter's words may be correct, but Jesus must harshly correct him in 8:33. His thinking is not simply wrong-headed; it is worse. It is satanic thinking. It stems from an inherent human self-centeredness stoked by Satan that believes that our personal interests are identical with God's interests.

The audience knows that Jesus is the Messiah from the beginning of the gospel. For them, the mystery is not his identity but what he has come to do as the Messiah and how it affects God's relationship with the people of God.[77] The title of Messiah, as Peter presently understands it, is inadequate to express what it means for Jesus to be God's Messiah. For the disciples to circulate their personal opinions about Jesus at this point would only spread more error and confusion. The disciples' mind-set is fixed on human things and not on divine things (8:33), and Jesus sets out to transform their thinking.

72. Manson, "Realized Eschatology and the Messianic Secret," 221.

73. David L. Tiede, "Proclaiming the Hidden Kingdom: Preaching on the Gospel Lessons in Mark," *CurTM* 11.6 (1984): 327.

74. Taylor, *Mark*, 123.

75. Hengel, *Studies*, 42.

76. France, *Mark*, 25, contends, "In this the disciples represent not a particularly hostile or obtuse ideology, but the very natural human reaction to a divine plan which makes no human sense; their thoughts are, to use again the language of a saying which is crucial for understanding Mark's christological perspective, human rather than divine (8:33)."

77. Ernest Best, *Mark: The Gospel as Story: Studies of the New Testament and Its World* (Edinburgh: T&T Clark, 1983), 80, comments that by responding that the Son of Man must suffer many things (8:31), Jesus "turns a question of identity into an answer of activity."

The section that follows this confession (8:31 – 10:52) contains explicit teaching to the disciples and reveals that the disciples do not understand the necessity of the cross both for Jesus as the Messiah and for themselves as his followers. They are partially correct in their evaluation of Jesus and must now absorb that Jesus the Messiah must be a suffering Messiah. Mark explains exactly why Jesus passed through Galilee and did not want anyone to know it "*because*" he was teaching his disciples that the Son of Man is going to be delivered over to human hands. He will be killed, and "after three days he will rise" (9:30 – 31). The secrecy is not an apologetic device imposed on the material but goes back to the historical Jesus.

Mark spaces Jesus' passion and resurrection announcements strategically in the narrative (8:31; 9:30; 10:33 – 34) as he unfolds for his disciples the things of God regarding his role and destiny. This teaching requires the disciples to reexamine all of their presuppositions about the Messiah's role and destiny. Donahue and Harrington correctly identify Mark's purpose: "Mark sought to redefine the term 'Messiah' and other christological titles in the light of Jesus' death and resurrection, and so he puts off revealing Jesus' true identity until his death (see 15:39) and his resurrection (see 9:9)."[78] Jesus' identity as the Messiah can be understood only in terms of his death and resurrection, not simply his messianic power. It follows that a belief that God is acting through Jesus' suffering, death, and resurrection for human salvation can be understood only in retrospect. Marcus maintains, "until that time ... any revelation of it [Jesus' identity] must necessarily be veiled."[79] The commands to silence, then, alert the audience that what it means for Jesus to be the Messiah can only be conveyed after the predicted events unfold.

The command has nothing to do with an attempt to explain why Jesus was not recognized as the Messiah before the resurrection. Jesus partially unveils this secret in the temple to the chief priests, the teachers of the law, and the elders with the allegory of the wicked tenants (12:1 – 12), and he fully unveils when he makes his own bold confession before the high priest and the whole council that he is indeed the Messiah, the Son of the Blessed One (14:61 – 62).[80] With that confession, he signs his death warrant. Because he faithfully submits to the will of God (14:36), all of his prophecies about his suffering and death will come to pass. The command to silence in 8:30 serves to highlight that the disciples can only put things together and begin to understand the full implications of what it means for Jesus to be the Messiah after these events. As Watson insists: "Mark is not trying to *replace* a Christology of power with a Christology of suffering, as some have argued. His thought is genuinely dialectical: power and weakness must somehow be held together."[81]

78. Donahue and Harrington, *Mark*, 28. Eduard Schweizer, "Anmerkungen zur Theologie des Markus," in *Neotestamentica et Patristica. Eine Freundesgabe Herrn Professor Dr. Oscar Cullmann zu seinem 60. Geburtstag überreicht* (NovTSup 6; Leiden: Brill,1962), 45, argues that Mark's Jesus does not want to be known as simply an observable historical figure who may be evaluated by customary human norms that cloud his true identity as the crucified and risen Son of God, a fact that can only be recognized after the resurrection.

79. Marcus, *Mark 1 – 8*, 526.

80. The centurion essentially restates Jesus' confession at the cross when he sees how Jesus dies (15:39).

81. Watson, "Ambiguity in the Marcan Narrative," 12.

8.2.3.2 The Order to Tell No One about Jesus' Transfiguration Until after the Resurrection

After his transfiguration, Jesus orders Peter, James, and John, who witnessed it, to tell no one about what they had seen on the mountain "until the Son of Man had risen from the dead" (9:9). Hooker follows Wrede and thinks that this command is intended to resolve the question why ordinary persons were unaware of his heavenly glory during his lifetime and the disciples kept quiet about such an experience until after his resurrection.[82] I would argue instead that the transfiguration is so closely tied to Peter's confession that Jesus was the Messiah that Mark intends to show that both could only be appreciated after Jesus' death and resurrection. The suffering Messiah is the glorified Messiah.

Once again, the disciples are baffled by Jesus' words as they discuss among themselves what this "rising from the dead" meant (9:10). It is not that they have no concept of resurrection (see 5:35–43). They do not know what it means *for Jesus to be raised.*[83] The transfiguration is integrally connected to the previous episode in 8:27–9:1, and this statement connects back to Jesus' prediction that the Son of Man "must be killed and *after three days rise again*" (8:31). Their confusion has nothing to do with the possibility of a future general resurrection. The problem they have yet to untangle is the inevitability of Jesus' passion: "If the Son of Man is to be raised, he first must *die.*"[84]

After the second announcement of Jesus' passion and resurrection in 9:30–31, Mark comments that the disciples did not understand what he was talking about but were afraid to ask (9:32). Until they can accept the reality that the Son of Man must undergo suffering and death as part of God's plan, talk of Jesus' glory will only misrepresent his true glory. Like the command to keep mum that Jesus is the Messiah (8:30), this command not to tell anyone about what they experienced aims at deferring their proclamation until they can fully comprehend what it is that they are to proclaim. The time limitation reveals that only after Jesus' crucifixion and resurrection will they be able to grasp that Jesus as Messiah and the Son of God was destined by God to suffer and to be raised. This time limitation may also explain Jesus' bewildering orders that no one should know about his raising Jairus's daughter from the dead (5:43). Meier claims that this earlier command to silence "points forward to the death and resurrection of Jesus."[85]

8.3 CONCLUSION

In my view, Dahl helps put the issue of the secrecy motif in Mark in the right perspective:

82. Hooker, *Mark*, 219.
83. Manson, "Realized Eschatology and the Messianic Secret," 217; Lane, *Mark*, 323.
84. Edwards, *Mark*, 273.
85. Meier, *A Marginal Jew*, 2:779–80.

The concealing of Jesus' messiahship is not an apologetic theory intended to explain how Jesus was rejected. The case is just the reverse. In Mark, the historical fact that Jesus was spurned by the majority of Jews serves to illustrate the mysterious character of the revelation and salvation given in him. It has to do with "what no eye has seen, nor ear heard, nor the heart of man conceived, what God has prepared for those who love him."[86]

Since Jesus did not come "in his Father's glory with the holy angels" (8:38), the theme of hiddenness "is bound up with the innermost nature of the event that is described."[87] There is something inherently mysterious about Jesus, who he is and what he is doing, that is conveyed by the various questions of the disciples, the crowds, and the opponents throughout the narrative. Taylor writes:

> Mark has no theory of the Incarnation, but his assumption appears to be that Jesus is *Deus absconditus*, the Hidden God. This view is not docetism, since the humanity of Christ is conceived as real. It is rather the view that, behind a fully human life, Deity is concealed, but is visible for those who have eyes to see, in His personality, teaching, and deeds.[88]

Jesus' identity is not revealed by the titles that are given to him by others, whether they be demons or disciples, but by God, by what he does in healing, casting out demons and binding Satan, teaching with authority, and going to the cross to die as a ransom of many, and by how God vindicates him in raising him from the dead. The one who claimed no exalted name for himself was highly exalted and given "the name that is above every name" by God himself, not by humans (Phil 2:9–10).

There is another dimension to the messianic secret in Mark that few commentators take into account. Human blindness cannot see the truth even when it is staring them in the face. Wink writes:

> But there is a deeper truth to the messianic secret that Wrede and others did not see: It was not just a strategy to avoid arrest, or a literary technique to explain peoples' failure to acknowledge him. For the secret of Jesus' identity is the kind of secret that stays secret even when paraded openly before peoples' eyes. The crisis of Jesus' ministry is a crisis of epistemology: Why do people not recognize a revelation when it is stuck right under their noses? This secret is not a contrivance by a redactor to save the appearances. It is part and parcel of the human blindness that makes the coming of a revealer necessary in the first place. As Paul so eloquently put it, "The god of this world has blinded the minds of the unbelievers, to keep them from seeing the light of the gospel of the glory of Christ, who is the likeness of God" (2 Cor. 4:4).[89]

86. Nils Alstrup Dahl, "The Purpose of Mark's Gospel," in *The Messianic Secret* (ed. Christopher Tuckett; Philadelphia: Fortress, 1983), 30–31.

87. Hengel, *Studies*, 42.

88. Taylor, *Mark*, 121. Feldmeier and Spieckermann, *God of the Living*, 72, assert that the form of God's revelation "in the lowliness of this human being," Jesus, is part and parcel of God's hiddenness.

89. Walter Wink, "The Education of the Apostles: Mark's View of Human Transformation," *Religious Education* 83 (1988): 284.

It requires more than blatant announcements to make a breakthrough with this human blindness. Something more subtle, like telling parables, is required.

After Jesus told the parable of the Sower to the crowd, the Twelve and others who were around him asked him about the parables (4:10). As discussed above, Jesus' response that "the secret of the kingdom of God" has been given to them is as important as the statement that everything comes in parables to outsiders " 'so that, they may be ever seeing but never perceiving, and ever hearing but never understanding; otherwise they might turn and be forgiven!' " (4:11 – 12). According to Mark, Jesus did not say anything to the crowd without using a parable but explained everything to his own disciples when he was alone with them (4:33 – 34). The term "secret" or "mystery" (*mystērion*) is an apocalyptic concept that connotes "the disclosure by God of a truth hidden until a certain decisive point in the divine plan is reached (see Rom 11:25; 1 Cor 15:51; Col 1:26)."[90] Eyes that see and ears that hear (Mark 4:9, 23; 8:18) are conferred by God's grace and election alone. God reveals secrets and mysteries and will unlock the secret to all in due time: "For whatever is hidden is meant to be disclosed, and whatever is concealed is meant to be brought out into the open" (4:22). Mark's audience continues to live in a time of hiddenness when Jesus is still not acknowledged as the Messiah despite revelation. It remains a mystery (1 Cor 2:1 – 16), a scandal to Jews and foolishness to Gentiles (1 Cor 1:23).

Ebeling countered Wrede's conclusions by showing that when the disciples failed to understand, Jesus would always instruct them.[91] Jesus' teaching brings revelation. But Jesus cannot reveal the mystery of the kingdom of God carelessly to anyone, because to receive it and to become enlightened requires more than being a casual bystander who may pick up a random sampling of his teaching. Best comments, "if Mark sets out Jesus as one who reveals, it is not in the sense of one who admits the curious to see the mysteries of God, but of one who is only understood by his disciples as they enter on the hard path of discipleship."[92] The only ones who can understand the so-called "messianic secret" are those who faithfully follow Jesus as the Son of God who was crucified and raised.

90. Donahue and Harrington, *Mark*, 29. See also Garland, *First Corinthians*, 83 – 84, 95 – 96.

91. Hans Jürgen Ebeling, *Das Messiasgeheimnis und die Botschaft des Marcus-Evangelisten* (BZNW 19; Berlin: Töpelmann, 1939), 146 – 79.

92. Best, *Temptation*, 73.

Chapter 9

Mark's Theology of Discipleship

Bibliography

Barton, Stephen C. *Discipleship and Family Ties in Mark and Matthew*. SNTSMS 80. Cambridge: Cambridge University Press, 1994. **Bayer, Hans F.** *A Theology of Mark: The Dynamic between Christology and Authentic Discipleship*. Explorations in Biblical Theology. Phillipsburg, NJ: Presbyterian & Reformed, 2012. **Best, Ernest.** *Following Jesus: Discipleship in the Gospel according to Mark*. JSNTSup 4. Sheffield: JSOT, 1981. Idem. *Disciples and Discipleship: Studies in the Gospel of Mark*. Edinburgh: T&T Clark, 1986. **Black, C. Clifton.** *The Disciples according to Mark: Markan Redaction in Current Debate*. JSNTSup 27. Sheffield: JSOT, 1989. **Borrell, Agustí.** *The Good News of Peter's Denial: A Narrative and Rhetorical Reading of Mark 14:54.66–72*. Trans. Sean Conlon. International Studies in Formative Christianity and Judaism. Atlanta: Scholars Press, 1998. **Donahue, John R.** *The Theology and Setting of Discipleship in the Gospel of Mark*. Milwaukee: Marquette University Press, 1983. **Freyne, Seán.** *The Twelve: Disciples and Apostles: A Study in the Theology of the First Three Gospels*. London: Sheed and Ward, 1968. **Hawkin, David J.** "The Incomprehension of the Disciples in the Marcan Redaction." *JBL* 91 (1972): 491–500. **Henderson, Suzanne Watts.** *Christology and Discipleship in the Gospel of Mark*. SNTMS 135. Cambridge: Cambridge University Press, 2006. **Hurtado, Larry W.** "Following Jesus in the Gospel of Mark—and Beyond." Pp. 9–29 in *Patterns of Discipleship in the New Testament*. Ed. Richard N. Longenecker. Grand Rapids: Eerdmans, 1996. **Keerankeri, George.** *The Love Commandment in Mark: An Exegetico-Theological Study of Mk 12,28–34*. AnBib 150; Rome: Pontifical Biblical Institute, 2003. **Kertelge, Karl.** "Jüngerschaft und Nachfolge: Grundlegung von Kirche nach Markus." Pp. 151–65 in *Der Evangelist als Theologe: Studien zum Markusevangelium*. Ed. Thomas Söding. SBS 163. Stuttgart: Katholisches Bibelwerk, 1995. **Malbon, Elizabeth Struthers.** "Fallible Followers: Women and Men in the Gospel of Mark." *Semeia* 28 (1983): 29–48. Eadem. "Texts and Contexts: Interpreting the Disciples in Mark." *Semeia* 62 (1993): 81–102. **Marshall, Christopher D.** *Faith as a Theme in Mark's Narrative*. SNTSMS 64. Cambridge: Cambridge University Press, 1989. **Matera, Frank J.** "The Incomprehension of the Disciples and Peter's Confession (Mark 6,14–8,30)." *Bib* 70 (1989): 153–72. **Meye, Robert P.** *Jesus and the Twelve: Discipleship and Revelation in Mark's Gospel*. Grand Rapids: Eerdmans, 1968. **Mingo Kaminouchi, Alberto de.** *"But It Is Not So Among You": Echoes of Power in Mark 10.32–45*. JSNTSup 249. London: T&T Clark, 2003. **Moloney, Francis**

J. "The Vocation of the Disciples in the Gospel of Mark." *Salesianum* 43 (1981): 487–516. **Santos, Narry F.** *Slave of All: The Paradox of Authority and Servanthood in the Gospel of Mark*. JSNTSup 237. London/New York: Sheffield Academic, 2003. **Schweizer, Eduard.** "The Portrayal of the Life of Faith in the Gospel of Mark." *Int* 32 (1978): 387–99. **Shiner, Whitney Taylor.** *Follow Me!: Disciples in Markan Rhetoric*. SBLDS 145. Atlanta: Scholars Press, 1995. **Söding, Thomas.** "Leben nach dem Evangelium: Konturen markinischer Ethik." Pp. 167–94 in *Der Evangelist als Theologe: Studien zum Markusevangelium*. Ed. Thomas Söding. SBS 163. Stuttgart: Katholisches Bibelwerk, 1995. **Tannehill, Robert C.** "The Disciples in Mark: The Function of a Narrative Role." *JR* 57 (1977): 386–405. **Wiarda, Timothy.** *Peter in the Gospels: Pattern, Personality and Relationship*. WUNT 2/127. Tübingen: Mohr Siebeck, 2000. **Williams, Joel F.** *Other Followers of Jesus: Minor Characters as Major Figures in Mark's Gospel*. JSNTSup 102. Sheffield: JSOT, 1994.

9.1 Jesus' Call for Persons to Follow Him

The Greek word for disciple ("learner") occurs some forty times in Mark. It is always in the plural and usually with a possessive that distinguishes Jesus' disciples from others, the crowd, or the disciples of John the Baptist (2:18; 6:29) or the Pharisees (2:18). The gospel of Mark tells us not only who Jesus is and what God has done through him but also what it means to respond to the good news in becoming his disciple. Kelber states: "Kingdom theology and discipleship are closely interwoven."[1] Loving God with all of one's heart, understanding, and strength (12:33)—one's whole being—also demands obedience to Jesus with all of one's heart, understanding, and strength as his disciple.

Jesus' calling disciples to follow him in 1:16–20 occurs almost immediately after the gospel's introduction (1:1–13) and highlights the importance of discipleship for Mark.[2] This sudden calling of disciples while Jesus is passing by on the Sea of Galilee primarily has a christological purpose (see §5.2), but it also reveals that his disciples do not join themselves to him as pupils normally joined themselves to a teacher. Rabbis in this era never directed persons to become their disciples. Pupils were self-selecting and chose a rabbi they thought would best instruct them in the law.[3] Their goal was to acquire wisdom from study of the Torah, and one day they might even surpass their teacher in their mastery of the law.[4] The primary loyalty of the disciple was to the law, and he could join himself to another rabbi if he thought that he could learn more about the law from him. Hengel argues, therefore, that Jesus was not a rabbi and shows that there are no analogous stories of "calling" and "following after" in rabbinic literature.[5] Jesus does not call his disciples to study

1. Kelber, *Kingdom*, 11, n. 36.

2. Contrast Luke 5:1–11, where the calling of Peter, James, and John occurs after Jesus orchestrates a miraculous catch of fish.

3. See *m. ʾAbot* 1:6, which advises that one should "provide thyself with a teacher."

4. Hengel, *The Charismatic Leader*, 32.

the law with him but calls them to himself—to follow him! The primary loyalty of Jesus' disciples was to be to him, not to the law. Hengel asserts that Jesus' call and setting apart these first disciples are similar to "*the calls of the Old Testament prophets by God.*"[6]

Not only does Jesus choose his disciples, not vice versa, but his choice of followers seems to come out of the blue. The legend about how the famous Rabbi Hillel was accepted into the house of study is illustrative. He journeyed from Babylonia to study Torah and earned a starvation wage as a day-laborer. In the winter, he listened in to the rabbis teaching in the school at an attic window and almost froze to death in the snow. The rabbis, impressed by his fixity of purpose, took him in and praised him by saying that it was even worth desecrating the Sabbath for such a dedicated pupil (*b. Yoma* 35b).[7] No follower of Jesus in Mark shows this kind of keenness or initiative so that Jesus concludes that he is worthy to be taken on as a disciple. Jesus does not call individuals because they possess outstanding personal qualities or demonstrate extraordinary religious devotion or flair.[8] The calling is an act of grace that simultaneously imposes an enormous demand. He does not seek them out in some hallowed religious setting such as the synagogue or house of study but encounters them in the midst of their daily work.[9] The command to follow inescapably explodes their everyday world.

9.1.1 The Calling of Fishermen (Mark 1:16–20)

As Jesus passes by on the shoreline of the Sea of Galilee, he sees two fishermen, Simon and Andrew, who are in the midst of casting their nets, and calls them to follow him.[10] Mark notes that Jesus "saw" Simon and Andrew, James and John, and Levi, and Schweizer compares it to God "seeing" David (1 Sam 16:7) in order to call him.[11] The call comes as a command that demands an immediate response, not as invitation for them to mull over. The call also comes with the promise that Jesus will make them to become fishers of men (1:17). The disciples say nothing in response but immediately leave their nets to follow. Jesus next finds James and John, the sons of Zebedee, on their boat cleaning their nets and he calls them. They too leave their boat and their father with his hired hands and come after him.

The christological significance of the power of Jesus' call that creates immediate

5. Ibid., 42–57.

6. Ibid., 73.

7. Cited by Hengel in ibid., 31.

8. When John reports seeing a man successfully driving out demons in Jesus' name, Jesus does not seek to recruit this anonymous person as a disciple. He simply tells John, "Do not stop him" (9:38–39).

9. Schweizer, *Mark*, 48.

10. One should not presume that Peter and Andrew, in contrast to the Zebedee brothers, were too poor to own a boat (see Luke 5:1–11). Early church tradition suggests that this scene took place in the cove of Tabgha, west of Capernaum, where warm mineral springs flow into the lake attracting schools of fish. John J. Rousseau and Rami Arav, *Jesus and His World: An Archaeological and Cultural Dictionary* (Minneapolis: Fortress, 1995), 94, note that in the winter, a type of fish called musht "move closer to the shore in schools to seek warmer waters." These fishermen were probably taking advantage of this opportunity to catch fish from the shore. See also Mendel Nun, *The Sea of Galilee and Its Fishermen in the New Testament* (Kibbutz Ein Gev: Kinnereth Sailing Co., 1989); K. C. Hanson, "The Galilean Fishing Economy and the Jesus Tradition," *BTB* 27 (1997): 99–111.

11. Eduard Schweizer, "The Portrayal of the Life of Faith in Mark," *Int* 32 (1978): 390.

response is primary to Mark (see §5.2), but this first narrative in the gospel also reveals something about what discipleship involves.

9.1.1.1 Readiness to Leave and to Follow Jesus

The calling of these first disciples shows that one must not only repent and believe the gospel (1:15) but also be ready to leave and follow this particular proclaimer of the gospel. Since the disciples utter no words in this scene, discipleship is not based on some formal confession about Jesus but active obedience to him. It is not based on saying something but on doing something. Edwards asserts, "For Mark, the act of following Jesus entails a risk of faith, and faith must be an act before it is a content of belief. Only as Jesus is followed can he be known."[12] These first disciples obey Jesus' command and follow him, but they have no clue where following him will lead. It only becomes clear when Jesus begins teaching them about his destiny and the concomitant requirements of discipleship in 8:27 – 10:45.

9.1.1.2 Readiness to Engage in Missionary Activity for Jesus

Identifying Simon and Andrew as fishermen prepares for the promise to make them into fishers of men (1:16 – 17). The use of this metaphor in Jewish and Greek texts is wide-ranging.[13] The tenor of the image in the OT (Jer 16:16; Ezek 29:4 – 5; Amos 4:2; Hab 1:14 – 17), for example, is one of threat and judgment, which does not seem appropriate in this situation.[14] What the metaphor means for Mark is revealed by Jesus' activity of preaching and ministering to people indiscriminately. Mark's audience would most likely connect it to the missionary activity that is presupposed in Paul's discussion in 1 Corinthians 9: "I have made myself a slave to everyone, to win as many as possible" (1 Cor 9:19).

9.1.1.3 Readiness to Show Absolute Loyalty to Jesus

Jesus makes absolute demands on his disciples' loyalty and devotion. Identifying James and John as the sons of Zebedee and specifically noting that they leave their father in the boat with the hired hands (1:20) calls attention to the seemingly indispensable familial ties that one may have to break to follow Jesus. They break ties with their family to tie themselves to Jesus' destiny. That Jesus' family tried to round him up and bring him back under their control (3:21) shows that Jesus himself had cut ties with his family that would have constrained his ministry (3:31 – 34).

9.1.1.4 Readiness to Be Molded by Jesus

Jesus' promise in 1:17 to make them fishers of men suggests that becoming a disciple of Jesus is more a gift than an achievement.[15] Jesus is not only the initiator of discipleship but the one who will mold them to will and to act according to his

12. Edwards, *Mark*, 50.
13. See Wilhelm H. Wuellner, *The Meaning of "Fishers of Men"* (Philadelphia: Westminster, 1967), 64 – 133.
14. Shiner, *Follow Me!* 175.
15. Marshall, *Faith as a Theme*, 136.

purpose. Translating it literally "to become fishers of men" suggests that being a disciple of Jesus involves a process, and the narrative reveals that it is a slow one in which the disciples progress and regress in fits and starts. Söding observes that it is significant that before Jesus issues any ethical instructions, he proclaims the necessity of repentance, faith, and following after him (1:14–20). Söding claims that Mark wants to make it clear that ethical obedience grows only from one's close relationship to God and Christ and is grounded in the nearness of the kingdom of God. Doing right, which is the sign of the true Christian (as opposed to the hypocrite, 7:6–13; 12:38–40), is the fruit of repentance, faith, and following Jesus.[16] It is the proof that one is molded by Christ and governed by God's rule.

9.1.2 The Call of a Tax Collector (Mark 2:13–17)

The call of Levi, the tax collector, follows the same pattern as the call of the fishermen in 1:16–20. Jesus again comes to the sea, and passing by he spots Levi, the son of Alphaeus, in the middle of his workaday world sitting at his customs kiosk. Jesus also calls him to follow him, and, like the fishermen, he rises and wordlessly obeys.

Levi is not a tax baron like Zacchaeus (Luke 19:1–10) but a low-level official stationed at the intersection of trade routes in Capernaum.[17] He has the task of assessing and wresting tolls, tariffs, imposts, and customs from traveling merchants. Toll collectors were renowned for their dishonesty and extortion. They habitually collected more than they were due, did not always post up the regulations, and made false valuations and accusations (see Luke 3:12–13).[18] Levi does not seem to be a choice candidate for discipleship since most would have dismissed a tax collector as an example of someone who "craved money more than respectability or righteousness."[19] The account continues as the scene shifts to Jesus eating along with his disciples at Levi's house with a cluster of tax collectors and sinners (2:15–17). The teachers of the law and the Pharisees, who observe this assemblage, take exception to Jesus eating with tax collectors and sinners. Their objection triggers Jesus' pronouncement that he did not come to call the righteous but sinners (2:17). This declaration underscores that the call of Levi is an example of the inclusive call of sinners by Jesus.

9.1.2.1 Discipleship is Open to All

The call of Levi reveals that one's position or caste, even one's shady reputation, is

16. Thomas Söding, "Leben nach dem Evangelium: Konturen markinischer Ethik," in *Der Evangelist als Theologe: Studien zum Markusevangelium* (ed. Thomas Söding; SBS 163; Stuttgart: Katholisches Bibelwerk, 1995), 176–77.

17. Since Levi is stationed in Galilee, he is most likely in the employ of Herod Antipas, a client king of Rome.

18. See John R. Donahue, "Tax Collectors and Sinners: An Attempt at Identification," *CBQ* 33 (1971): 39–61. Toll collectors were also detested throughout the Greco-Roman world. Plutarch (*Curios.* 518E) wrote, "We are annoyed and displeased with customs-officials, not when they pick up those articles which we are importing openly, but when in the search for concealed goods they pry into baggage and merchandise which are another's property. And yet the law allows them to do this and they would lose by not doing so."

19. Minear, *Mark*, 60. One might assume that someone with the name Levi belonged to the tribe of Levi. In the *T. Levi* 13:1–2, Levi commands that his descendants learn to read and write so that they might read and understand the law. Levi the tax collector has chosen a different path to use his presumed literacy.

not a liability when it comes to receiving and responding to the call of Jesus. He does not first examine Levi's character, genealogy, expressed interest, or evidence of commitment, as others might. Shiner observes,

> Unlike the followers of philosophers and wisdom teachers, the disciples of Jesus are shown to have no apparent merit. While other teachers draw their students from an intellectual and moral elite, Jesus gathers an undistinguished group.... Yet the audience knows that this seemingly undistinguished group, because of its connection with Jesus, is the real elite, part of the elect of God whom the Son of Man will gather from the four winds when he returns from heaven (13.26–27). The disciples' real identity, like that of Mark's listeners, is hidden from ordinary perception.[20]

This interpretation is reinforced by the statement in 2:15, "for there were many who followed him." The call to follow Jesus will be extended to those who are stigmatized and assumed to be beyond the reach of religion's sanctification. They do not repent first and then receive the call. The call brings them to repentance when they respond. Instead of the Lord laughing *at* the wicked, "for he knows their day is coming" (Ps 37:13), the Lord laughs *with* the wicked who turn to him. The task of fishing for people is illustrated by the scene with Jesus eating with many other toll collectors and sinners. Had Levi invited them to come hear him as one who has already become a fisher of men?

9.1.2.2 Discipleship Requires a Radical Commitment

Levi responded to the force of Jesus' call as promptly as the fishermen did when he rose and followed him, but his obedience marks an even more radical break with his livelihood than that of the fishermen. They could always go back to fishing (see John 21:3). A toll collector who suddenly abandons his post would probably find it difficult if not impossible to return.

9.1.3 A Refusal to Follow: A Rich Man (Mark 10:17–31)

The story of a rich man who beseeches Jesus to give him the key that would unlock the secret for inheriting eternal life occurs in the section of the gospel, where the issues related to discipleship figure prominently (8:22–10:52). When Jesus is continuing on his way to Jerusalem, the man eagerly runs up, kneels before him, and asks, "Good teacher, what must I do to inherit eternal life?" (10:17). Jesus first deflects the honorific distinction of being "good" by asserting, "No one is good—except God alone" (10:18), perhaps better translated more literally "except the one God," which makes the echo of the Shema (Deut 6:4–5) more apparent. He distinguishes himself from the teachers of the law who love to be greeted in the marketplaces (12:38), but his objection to this salutation seems overly humble. As the ensuing dialogue reveals, however, this man understands "good" quite differently from the way Jesus

20. Shiner, *Follow Me!* 290.

does. His greeting "assumes that one can find goodness in human resources and accomplishments," and that "goodness" assures that one will inherit eternal life on the basis of one's own efforts.[21]

Jesus next reminds the man what he already knows. He reels off in random order the second table of the Ten Commandments, with an added commandment, "you shall not defraud" (10:19).[22] Most assumed that the rich became so only by defrauding others of their fair share.[23] This negative view of the rich may be behind the inclusion of this added commandment. The man avows that he has kept all of these commandments from his youth (10:20; cf. Paul's self-evaluation that he was faultless with respect to righteousness under the law, Phil 3:6). Jesus does not dispute his claim. Redolent with sanctity, this man seems to be a far more worthy candidate for discipleship than an odious tax collector like Levi. The narrator reports that Jesus looks at him and loves him. "One thing you lack," he said. "Go, sell everything you have and give to the poor, and you will have treasure in heaven. Then come, follow me" (10:21).

Jesus' love for the man is not to be likened to some feeling of affection. His divine love is expressed in discerning the man's deficiency, offering a remedy for it, and inviting him to follow him.[24] Hicks points out another feature of Jesus' call to discipleship: "The Markan Jesus does not seem inclined to call someone because they are obedient to the law; rather, he calls those who recognize their deficiencies (see 2:17; 8:35–38)."[25] Obedience to the law is pointless if it is not directed toward God and the kingdom of God.[26]

The surprising addition of "do not defraud" to the list of commandments may explain his "one" shortcoming. Hicks argues that a broader intertextual relationship exists between Mal 3 and Mark 10:17–22 and that Jesus alludes specifically to Mal 3:5, " 'So I will come to put you on trial. I will be quick to testify against sorcerers, adulterers and perjurers, against those who defraud laborers of their wages, who oppress the widows and the fatherless, and deprive the foreigners among you of justice, but do not fear me,' says the LORD Almighty."[27] We learn only at the end of the episode that the aspirant to eternal life had many possessions, when, in a state of shock, he despondently turns down Jesus' offer by departing, perhaps to seek out a second opinion (10:22).[28]

9.1.3.1 Eternal Life Is Tied to Following Jesus

Inheriting eternal life requires more than a professed obedience to the Ten Commandments. Eternal life is life under the eternal King[29] and therefore requires

21. Garland, *Mark*, 395.

22. The command not to defraud is absent from Exod 20:1–17; Deut 5:6–21; and the parallels in Matt 19:18–19 and Luke 18:20.

23. See Bruce J. Malina, *The New Testament World: Insights from Cultural Anthropology* (Atlanta: John Knox, 1981), 75–85; idem, "Wealth and Poverty in the New Testament," *Int* 41 (1987): 354–67; Nickelsburg, "Riches, the Rich and God's Judgment," 327.

24. Richard Hicks, "Markan Discipleship according to Malachi: The Significance of μὴ ἀποστερήσῃς in the Story of the Rich Man (Mark 10:17–22)," *JBL* 132 (2013): 194.

25. Ibid., 193.

26. Kampling, "Das Gesetz im Markusevangelium," 147.

27. Hicks, "Markan Discipleship according to Malachi," 179–99.

28. As a rich man, he probably has many fields, and he may exploit his laborers as James says the rich are wont to do (Jas 5:4).

29. Betsworth, *The Reign of God*, 101.

obedience to Jesus. Outside of the sphere of Christian discipleship, there is only death. Those who do not follow Jesus will miss out on real life in this age and eternal life in the age to come. Eternal life is tied solely to one's relationship to Jesus by following him.

In the discussion with the disciples that is precipitated by this exchange, Jesus declares how hard it is for the rich to enter the kingdom of God (10:23). The disciples are no less shocked than the man by Jesus' radical demand that he must sell all that he has and distribute it to the poor to receive treasure in heaven. Peter remonstrates, "We have left everything to follow you!" (10:28). Jesus responds, "No one who has left home or brothers or sisters or mother or father or children or fields for me and the gospel will fail to receive a hundred times as much in this present age: homes, brothers, sisters, mothers, children and fields—along with persecutions—and in the age to come eternal life" (10:29–30). The key is leaving things for his sake ("on account of") and for the sake of the gospel. Following Jesus will bring the reward of a greater community in this life and eternal life in the age to come.

9.1.3.2 Eternal Life Comes as a Divine Gift That Cannot Be Earned

Jesus' discussion with his disciples also reveals that salvation, which is tied to following Jesus, comes as a gift. The disciples fret that if Jesus' hyperbolic metaphor that it is easier for a camel to squeeze through the eye of a needle than for a rich man to enter the kingdom of God is true, "who then can be saved?" (10:23–26). The obvious answer is, "No one." It is utterly hopeless were it not for the power of God that saves those who seem to be beyond hope: "All things are possible with God" (10:27). This declaration offers insights on the ability of humans to be "good" disciples. Freyne comments, "The absolute and unconditional following of Jesus is impossible with men ... but with God all things are possible, and Peter and those who have followed with him can hope to receive their reward for answering the divine call (10:17–31)."[30] Obedience, like faith, is a gift of God, and one does not earn eternal life through an earthly life of good works.

9.1.3.3 Discipleship Is Costly and Comes with Persecutions

This incident, which records the only time in Mark that someone refuses Jesus' personal bidding to follow him, highlights the cost of following him: sell everything and give it to the poor; leave family; receive more in return but "with persecutions" (10:30). One must cut loose whatever it might be in this life that prevents one from giving oneself completely to God and from following Jesus. Usually, it is material possessions and the imagined material security they offer that prevent total commitment to Jesus. In this particular case, Boring notes that discipleship requires "placing one's

30. Seán Freyne, *The Twelve: Disciples and Apostles: A Study in the Theology of the First Three Gospels* (London: Sheed & Ward, 1968). 135. The hope is based on the faithfulness of God and not on their faithfulness to Jesus.

property at the disposal of others."[31] It would create a radical change in the man's status that he would naturally dread: "After divestment, the man can no longer fulfill the role of patron or benefactor, but joins the ranks of those dependent on others."[32] The particular example, however, extends to anything that might inhibit a would-be disciple and inheritor of eternal life from total commitment to following Jesus.

9.2 THE CREATION OF THE TWELVE (MARK 3:13–19)

In 3:13, the setting shifts from Capernaum and the seaside to a mountain which Jesus ascends and from where he summons "those he wanted." Here he appoints the Twelve. This event occurs so shortly after the Pharisees and Herodians plot how they might kill him (3:6) that being called to be with him places the Twelve in danger.

Jesus' ascent of a mountain is reminiscent of Moses climbing Mount Sinai with a company of priests and elders (Exod 24:1–4), but, unlike Moses, Jesus does not go in answer to God's summons. Instead, he is the one who beckons those whom he wanted, which may suggest God's sovereign calling of individuals in the OT (Exod 3:4–10; 1 Sam 3:4–11; Jer 1:5–10).[33] It also is reminiscent of God's choosing Israel (Deut 7:6–8; Isa 41:8–10; 45:4). Moloney notes that "Jesus wrests all initiative from them." Jesus is the subject of the active verbs: he went up the mountain, called those he desired, appointed the Twelve, commissioned them, and surnamed three of them. All that the disciples do is "come to him."[34] Since "came" translates a compound verb in Greek that means "to come away" and not simply "to come," Marcus suggests that the choice of this verb may serve as "a reminder that following Jesus means leaving other things behind (cf. 1:20)."[35]

Jesus "appointed" ("made" or "created") twelve (3:14). The verb "to make" occurs in 1:17 in the promise to "make" Peter and Andrew fishers of men. It also recalls biblical themes. The Lord "appointed" Moses and Aaron to lead Israel (1 Sam 12:6), and Moses "made" able men as heads over the people (Exod 18:25).[36] The initiative in creating and naming the Twelve ("those he wanted," 3:13) belongs to Jesus as it belongs to God in creating, naming, and choosing humans (Isa 43:1, the Lord "created" and "summoned you by name").[37] Those chosen are not voted on by other disciples. Jesus alone decides.

The creation of the Twelve sets up a distinction between those who indiscriminately follow him seeking healing or are caught up in the excitement of the moment

31. Boring, *Mark*, 295. Though most ignored it in practice, some in a Roman audience would have agreed, theoretically at least, that wealth was dangerous to one's spiritual health. Seneca, for example, wrote, "No one is worthy of God unless he despises wealth" (*Ep.* 14.18). He also concluded: "Our soul knows, I tell you, that wealth does not lie where it can be heaped together. It is the soul itself that we ought to fill, not our money chests. It is the soul that we may set above all other things, and put, God-like, in possession of the universe" (*Ep.* 92.32–33).

32. Boring, *Mark*, 295.

33. Stein, *Mark*, 168.

34. Moloney, *Mark*, 76.

35. Marcus, *Mark 1–8*, 266.

36. In both 1 Sam 12:6 and Exod 18:25, the same Greek verb ("made" or "created") appears in the LXX as appears in Mark 3:14.

37. See John 15:16; Isa 49:1; Jer 1:5; Amos 7:15; and Gal 1:15.

with his miracles and those who are to be close to him and to receive special instruction and revelation.[38] Most agree that the term "the Twelve" in Mark (3:14; 4:10; 6:7; 9:35; 10:32; 11:11; 14:10, 17, 20, 43) is interchangeable with the term "the disciples." This special group is highlighted in 1 Cor 15:5, where Paul passes on the tradition that after Jesus was raised "he appeared to Cephas, and then to the Twelve." After Judas betrayed him, they numbered only eleven, but the number twelve had become fixed as a symbolic number that goes back to Jesus.[39]

The choice of twelve has symbolic value recalling the twelve tribes of Israel.[40] After Mark has tallied the enormous response to Jesus by the multitude from Galilee, Judea, Jerusalem, Idumea, beyond the Jordan, and the region around Tyre and Sidon (3:7–8), it is likely that they represent the whole nation of Israel with Jesus at their head.[41] Hengel argues that the symbolism of twelve represents that Jesus "has come to call *all* Israel to repentance in the light of the nearness of God's rule, and to proclaim salvation to her."[42] Some point to the prevailing view in Jesus' era that only two and a half of the tribes of Israel (Judah, Benjamin, and one half of Levi) remained and the others were lost. The appointment of Twelve possibly anticipates the end-time restoration of Israel (see Isa 49:5–6; Ezek 47:13–14; Sir 36:10–13; 48:10; *Pss. Sol.* 17:26–32; *T. Jos.* 19: 1–7; *Sib. Or.* 2:170–76; Matt 19:28; Luke 22:29–30).[43] Lane states, "In proleptic fashion they represent the final form of the messianic community, the eschatological creation of God."[44] Stein contends, "Through the symbolism of choosing the Twelve, Jesus was proclaiming that he was bringing the long-awaited kingdom of God to Israel."[45] Mark does not develop the symbolism further. Instead, the Twelve in Mark represents the number of a fixed group of disciples whom Jesus gathered around him from the beginning of his ministry to the end.

9.2.1 The Names of the Twelve

The list of the twelve names provides few clues as to their previous status, background, or religious training. The first three are given descriptive nicknames. Simon (1:16) is dubbed Peter, "rock," in the list of names and identified by this name in the rest of the narrative (5:37; 8:29, 32, 33; 9:2, 5; 10:28; 11:21; 13:3; 14:29, 33, 37,

38. The text does not suggest that Jesus chose this group from a larger company of followers who become also-rans (like Joseph Barsabbas, when the lot to replace Judas fell to Matthias, Acts 1:20–26).

39. See E. P. Sanders, *Jesus and Judaism* (Philadelphia: Fortress, 1985), 106. The symbolic significance of the Twelve is underscored by Eph 2:20 and Rev 21:14.

40. See Gen 35:22–26; 49:1–28. In Num 1:1–19, 44, God commands Moses to take a man from each tribe to be "with you" (Num 1:4, ASV) as representatives of the "heads of the clans of Israel" (Num 1:16). The men were registered according to their clans (Num 1:18) to represent their "ancestral house" (Num 1:44, NRSV) in military service. According to the Community Rule from Qumran, there were to be twelve men and three priests in the community council. They were to be "perfect in everything that has been revealed about all the law to implement truth, justice, judgment, compassionate love and unassuming behavior of each person to his fellow to preserve faithfulness on the earth with firm purpose and repentant spirit in order to atone for sin, doing justice and undergoing trials in order to walk with everyone in the measure of truth and the regulation of time" (1QS 8:1–4).

41. Hooker, *Mark*, 111.

42. Hengel, *The Charismatic Leader*, 68.

43. The importance of the symbolic significance of twelve can be seen in the church's felt need to replace Judas (Acts 1:15–26). This symbolism vanishes in the *baraita* in the Babylonian Talmud (*b. Ber.* 43a) that states that Jesus (Yeshu) had five disciples (Mattai, Nakkai, Netzer, Buni, and Todah).

44. Lane, *Mark*, 133; see also Witherington, *Mark*, 151.

45. Stein, *Mark*, 169–70.

54, 66, 67, 70, 72; 16:7), except when Jesus chides him for sleeping and not keeping watch even for one hour on the Mount of Olives and he calls him Simon (14:37). Peter not only heads the list of the Twelve, but he is always mentioned first in the inner circle of three disciples before James and John (5:37; 9:2; 13:3; 14:33). He is the first disciple identified by name in the gospel (1:16, "Simon"), and Andrew is introduced as Simon's "brother," clearly suggesting his lesser status. Peter is also the last one named in the gospel (16:7).

Throughout the narrative, he acts as spokesman for the disciples. He makes the confession identifying Jesus as the Christ and then objects when Jesus says that the Son of Man must suffer and die (8:29–33). He is the only one to speak at the transfiguration besides the heavenly voice (9:5). He expresses his concern to Jesus that he and the other disciples have left everything to follow him (10:28). Jesus' answer implies that he was worried about what reward they might receive for their sacrifice. He is also the one who calls attention that the fig tree Jesus cursed had withered (11:21). He is also singled out as the first of the disciples at the Last Supper to vow that he will not fall away even if the others desert Jesus (14:29). Jesus singles him out on the Mount of Olives for sleeping and failing to watch even for one hour (14:37). The rest of the NT confirms Peter's eminence in both the Jewish Christian (Acts 2–12; 15:6–11) and Gentile Christian sectors of the early church. The Galatians and the Corinthians both know and esteem him.

James and John, formerly introduced as the sons of Zebedee, are named the "sons of thunder," "Boanerges" (3:17). Boanerges does not mean anything in Greek and is probably a rough transliteration of the Aramaic. Its origins are obscure. These nicknames are not derived from some distinctive character traits that Jesus detected in Peter, James, and John. Instead, they convey something about these disciples' future role.[46] They will have foundational significance as witnesses to the gospel. They along with Peter witness the healing of Peter's mother-in-law (1:29–31), the raising of Jairus's daughter (5:37), and the transfiguration (9:2). John is the one who informs Jesus that they saw someone casting out demons in his name and tried to stop him (9:38), and James and John also request that Jesus honor them by letting them sit on his right and his left in his glory (10:35–45). They also precipitate the apocalyptic discourse when they, along with Peter and Andrew, ask Jesus privately to tell them when his dire prediction of the temple's demise will come to pass. Jesus will also separate them along with Peter from the other disciples to watch and pray with Jesus on the Mount of Olives, and they groggily witness his distress and troubled spirit (14:33–34).

With the exception of Judas Iscariot, none of the rest of the disciples listed in this roll call of the Twelve plays any individual role in Mark's narrative. To distinguish the two Simons, one is identified as "the Cananaean" (NRSV). The

46. Marcus, *Mark 1–8*, 263. Some draw an analogy between Peter and Abraham, who is identified as "the rock" from which Israel is hewn (Isa 51:1–2). In the Dead Sea Scrolls, the Teacher of Righteousness is also regarded as the bastion of the community (1QH 7:7–9).

sobriquet transliterates an Aramaic word that means "zealot."[47] It could refer to his religious zeal.[48] Since the term is used here with a definite article, like "Matthew the tax collector" (Matt 10:3), without any further amplification such as "zealot for God," or "zealot for the law," it is likely that he belonged to a group that had the name "the Zealots" in Jesus' time.[49] It does not necessarily mean he belonged to a political movement of freedom fighters resolved to foment rebellion against Rome like the one Josephus describes as beginning in the war in AD 66–73, but it does suggest a rigorous nationalism.

"Iscariot" distinguishes Judas the disciple from Judas the brother of Jesus (6:3). What "Iscariot" means has been the subject of much speculation, and Mark does not pursue its significance.[50] It is most likely that it refers to "man of Kerioth." John refers to him as "Judas, the son of Simon Iscariot" (6:71; 13:2, 26), which suggests that this second name was passed on to the son and likely refers to the family's place of origin. It also suggests to Bauckham that the family left "Kerioth" and settled elsewhere. They could have moved to Galilee, which would mean that Judas was not the only disciple not from Galilee.[51] Mark accentuates the disgrace that one of the Twelve would wind up betraying his master. Judas is identified as "one of the Twelve" three times (14:10, 20, 43).

9.2.2 The Twelve Are to Be with Jesus

Jesus has many followers, but only the Twelve are given the unique privilege of being *with* Jesus.[52] This unique privilege is highlighted at the conclusion of the account of driving out the legion of demons from the man in the region of the Gerasenes (5:1–20). When the townspeople learn of the destruction of the pigs, they implore him to leave their territory (5:18). As Jesus complies with their request and prepares to depart for the other side of the lake, the man who had been possessed, now clothed and in his right mind, begs that he "might be with him" (lit. trans. of 5:18). Jesus denies this request and tells him to return to his family and proclaim what the Lord had done for him (5:19). "To be with Jesus," therefore, is reserved only for those chosen to be among the Twelve, and the man delivered from the legion of demons is not permitted to wrest the initiative of the call from Jesus.

This special intimacy brings with it a singular vantage point. The Twelve—and Peter in particular—will become the primary repository and guarantors of the memory of Jesus' ministry. They are his constant companions except when he sends

47. Luke avoids Aramaic terms and identifies him as "Simon the Zealot" (Acts 1:13) and "Simon who was called the Zealot" (Luke 6:15).

48. Paul describes himself as "extremely zealous for the traditions of my fathers" (Gal 1:14; Acts 22:3; see also 2 Macc 4:2).

49. Hengel, *The Zealots*, 70. Josephus describes Judaism for his Roman audience as divided into four philosophies. He cites the tradition from Hippolytus' *Philosophymena* that reports on the Essenes who refused to touch coins that had an image, refused to pass through a city gate where statues were placed, threatened with death an uncircumcised person who spoke about God and his laws, and then connects them to the name of Zealots and *Sicarii*.

50. See Brown, *Death*, 2:1410–16, on the various theories of the name's meaning.

51. Bauckham, *Eyewitnesses*, 106–107.

52. Having been with Jesus from the beginning is assumed to be an essential requirement for the one who would take Judas's place as a member of the Twelve in Acts. The disciples choose from "one of the men who have been with us the whole time the Lord Jesus was living among us" (Acts 1:21).

them out on a short mission (6:7–13, 30) and on the three occasions when he withdraws from them to pray (1:35; 6:46; 14:32, 35, 39).[53] Consequently, they share and observe closely his life and receive his instruction. They will see his nocturnal prayer in a deserted place (1:35), his eagerness to fulfill his divine commission (1:38), his method of dealing with conflict, his method of teaching through simple illustrations that are yet ambiguous and puzzling, his grief over hardheartedness, his care for the sick and demonized, his reliance on prayer, his humble submission to the will of God, and his cold evaluations of the earthly powers and fearless resistance to them. They will also witness all of his public miracles and are the only ones to experience two epiphanic miracles: Jesus' stilling of the storm (4:35–41) and his walking to them on the water (6:45–52). They become active participants in the two miracles of the feeding of five thousand (6:33–44) and the four thousand (8:1–10).

The Twelve repeatedly hear his teaching to the masses and share his daily life. At several points, they receive private instruction denied to outsiders (4:34; 6:31–32; 7:17–23; 9:2, 28; 13:3). Peter, James, and John, who comprise an inner circle of the Twelve, are also with Jesus at crucial points in the gospel: when he raises Jairus's daughter back to life (5:37–43), when he is transfigured on the mountain (9:2–13), and when he prays in Gethsemane (14:33–42). They also witness his healing Peter's mother-in-law of fever (1:29–31), and they come to him privately to ask what he meant when he said that the temple's great buildings will be totally destroyed and not a single stone will be left standing (13:2–3). The result of being with Jesus is that the Twelve learn about him and learn from him. They also ask him questions. Henderson classifies this as the "discipleship as inquiry." It is "divinely inspired pursuit of understanding" as being with him prompts them to they seek after God and God's ways.[54] With the special revelation that they are granted, they are accredited to pass on the authentic tradition about the gospel of Jesus Christ, Son of God (see Luke 1:2).

The appointment of the Twelve reveals that there is a sharp difference between being simply a hanger-on and truly being with him. To be with him means that "they must follow wherever he leads and share the toil of the ministry, the harassment of the crowds (3:20; 6:31–33), and the same bitter draught of suffering (10:39)."[55] Without any meaningful relationship with Jesus, their lives and mission in the future will be ineffectual. To be with Jesus ultimately has nothing to do with physical proximity. It means having a meaningful relationship with him that results in heeding his words and following his example.

53. C. H. Turner in J. K. Elliott, *The Language and Style of the Gospel of Mark: An Edition of C. H. Turner's "Notes on Marcan Usage" Together with Other Comparable Studies* (NovTSup 71; Leiden: Brill, 1993), 36–42, cites twenty-one instances in Mark where the plural verb is used to denote the coming and going of Jesus with the disciples or some other activity that is followed immediately by a singular verb with reference to Jesus alone (see, e.g., 1:21; 5:1–2, 38; 8:22; 9:30, 33; 10:32, 46; 11:1, 12, 15, 27; 14:18, 22, 26–27, 32). He notes that it would have saved space and been simpler to construct the sentence in the singular, and Matthew and Luke often do just that, as do later copyists. He asks if Mark is "repeating the story of one to whom the plural came natural as being himself an actor in the events he relates" and contends that it indeed derives from Peter. In telling the account, Peter used "we," and Mark, not being a participant in the events, changed it to the third person plural. Whether this conjecture is correct, this feature does convey that Jesus and his disciples are conjoined in their travels and activities.

54. Henderson, *Christology*, 110–12.

55. Garland, *Mark*, 129.

9.2.3 The Twelve Are to Be Sent Out

What it means to be fishers of men is clarified when Jesus sends the Twelve out on mission (6:7–13). The Twelve are not to be merely eavesdroppers and onlookers during Jesus' ministry but will themselves become agents of the kingdom of God. They will do what Jesus has done; they will go out, preach repentance, and have authority over demons. They are to join in the cosmic battle that God wages against Satan.

When Jesus commissions them to preach, they are to preach that people should repent (6:12). At this point in the narrative, they do not preach the gospel of the kingdom, as Jesus does (1:14–15), since they do not yet fully understand its meaning or the identity of Jesus. Since they preached "repentance," their preaching is comparable to that of John the Baptist. It is noteworthy that Jesus does not simply transfer to the Twelve a body of teaching and interpretation but his own authority over the demonic realm.[56]

The missionary success of the Twelve has "nothing to do with the skill, training or virtue of the disciple, a point the disciples themselves have forgotten in 6,30, but depends upon Jesus' appointing them to be closely associated with his person."[57] Jesus gave them authority to cast out demons, but they may have been "tempted to believe that the gift they had received from Jesus (Ch. 6:7) was in their control and could be exercised at their disposal."[58] Their failure to drive out the demon from the son of a desperate father (9:14–29) reveals that this authority was not under their control. It was Jesus' delegated authority that was only available to them through prayer.[59] In fact, the task of preaching and exorcising demons is not limited to the Twelve in Mark. Jesus tells the Gerasene demoniac, delivered from the scourge of a legion of demons, to go preach to his family in the Decapolis what the Lord has done for him (5:19–20; see 7:36). Others, who are identified only as certain ones who did not follow the disciples, are reported to be successful in casting out demons in Jesus' name (9:38–39).

9.2.4 Other Followers of Jesus

Meye strongly argues that Mark presents Jesus as having only twelve disciples from the beginning.[60] Henderson maintains, however, that Mark does not intend to emphasize a dichotomy between the Twelve and Jesus' followers but presents a "progressive continuity" between them.[61] Moloney agrees, "What is said of 'the Twelve' applies to all 'disciples,' including the Markan community and all subsequent readers/

56. Shiner, *Follow Me!* 188. Hengel, *The Charismatic Leader*, 53, maintains, "Jesus' aim was not to form tradition or to nurture exegetical or apocalyptic scholarship but to proclaim the nearness of God in word and deed, to call to repentance, and to proclaim the will of God understood radically in the light of the imminent rule of God, which indeed was already dawning in his activity; similarly, 'following after' him and 'discipleship' were orientated to this one great aim."

57. Francis J. Moloney, "The Vocation of the Disciples in the Gospel of Mark," *Salesianum* 43 (1981): 513.

58. Lane, *Mark*, 335.

59. Marshall, *Faith as a Theme*, 222–23.

60. Robert P. Meye, *Jesus and the Twelve: Discipleship and Revelation in Mark's Gospel* (Grand Rapids: Eerdmans, 1968), 97–191. See also Lane, *Mark*, 132.

61. Henderson, *Christology*, 86–87.

listeners."[62] I would concur with Meye that Mark does limit Jesus' "disciples" to the Twelve, but since discipleship necessitates a proper response to Jesus, Mark illustrates that response in the stories of other characters beside the disciples.[63] Malbon is correct, "what Mark has to say about discipleship is understood in reference not only to the disciples but also to other Markan characters who meet the demands of following Jesus."[64] This interconnection emerges at various points in the gospel.

When Jesus defines his family as those who do God's will (3:32–35), the audience is identified as "the crowd ... sitting around him" (3:32). In 4:10–11, "the Twelve and the others around him" ask him about the parables, and he affirms that the mystery of the kingdom of God has been given "to you." While Mark highlights the significant relationship of the Twelve with Jesus and their role as agents in preaching to others, these texts open the door to other followers of Jesus, and therefore Mark's readers, to serve in these roles as well.

This possibility is advanced by the case of Levi, the son of Alphaeus (2:13–14). He is called in the same way as the four fisherman (1:16–20), but his name is absent from the list of twelve disciples in 3:16–18. Is he excluded from the Twelve? Matthew's gospel gives the name of the one whom Jesus calls to follow him when he is sitting as his toll booth as "Matthew" (Matt 9:9). That name does appear in all four lists of the Twelve (Matt 10:2–4; Mark 3:18; Luke 6:13–16; Acts 1:13). Was this toll collector known by two names, Levi and Matthew, in the same way that Simon is known as Simon and Peter (Cephas)? If so, Mark uses one name and Matthew the other. The picture is complicated, however, by the inclusion of "James the son of Alphaeus" in all four listings of the disciples. His patronymic distinguishes him from James the son of Zebedee. Levi and James may have been brothers or, again, this may reflect the same person being referred to by two different names. Ancient scribes apparently sought to solve the problem by substituting the name of James for Levi in 2:14.[65]

If readers only have access to Mark's text, it is natural for them to conclude that even though Levi was called to follow Jesus just as dramatically as Peter, Andrew, James, and John were, he was not numbered among the Twelve. It allows the readers to infer that Jesus' call to follow him is not limited to the Twelve, and what he teaches them about discipleship is to be extended to all who would follow him in Mark's day.[66] This impression is confirmed by Jesus' announcement about the criteria for being his disciple in 8:34. It addresses *anyone* who wishes to come after him. The call to discipleship is not restricted only to the Twelve but is extended to anyone who wishes to align themselves with him through faith. What makes the Twelve unique is that they were with him throughout his earthly ministry. The role of being Jesus' disciple, however, is open to all who seek to follow Jesus.

62. Moloney, *Mark*, 78, n. 21. See Elizabeth Struthers Malbon, "Disciples/Crowds/Whoever: Markan Characters and Readers," *NovT* 28 (1986): 104–30.

63. This is the primary thesis of Williams, *Other Followers*, 15–17, 157.

64. Elizabeth Struthers Malbon, "Fallible Followers: Women and Men in the Gospel of Mark," *Semeia* 28 (1983): 30.

65. D, Θ, 565, f^{13} (except 346), Tatian.

66. This interpretation is reinforced by the statement in 2:15 that "many ... followed him."

The healing of Bartimaeus, a blind man reduced to begging for his living, borders on a call story (10:46–52) and provides another example of a follower of Jesus who is not one of the Twelve.[67] He sits by the roadside in Jericho hoping for alms from passersby, when he hears that Jesus is going by. He desperately cries out to him, "Jesus, Son of David, have mercy on me!" (10:47) and disregards the crowd's attempts to stifle him and shouts out all the more. Jesus heeds his cry, stops, and calls for him to come to him.[68] Jesus then asks him the same question he had earlier asked James and John (10:36), "What do you want me to do for you?" (10:51).

Williams identifies Bartimaeus as an exemplary character, and though he is not a disciple, he "possesses a number of traits that are normally associated with the disciples of Jesus."[69] Like the first disciples Jesus called, he is engaged in his everyday pursuit trying to earn a livelihood from alms when he encounters Jesus. He has insight into Jesus' messianic identity by calling him "son of David." He also addresses him reverently as his teacher, "Rabbouni," "my master" (elsewhere only in John 20:16). The detail that he throws aside his cloak when he jumps up to come to Jesus (10:50) is open to various interpretations. France contends that it "serves no purpose in the story except to make it more vivid."[70] Marcus maintains that it serves as a symbol of the later Christian baptismal rite.[71] If Bartimaeus serves as an exemplary follower, however, it is more likely that tossing aside his cloak is evocative of his readiness to abandon everything when Jesus calls.[72] Williams writes:

> In the broader narrative, those who have been called by Jesus leave something behind in order to follow him. Simon and Andrew abandon their nets to follow Jesus (1.18), while James and John leave their father in the boat with the hired servants (1.20). Levi walks away from his occupation to go with Jesus (2.14). Jesus commands the rich man to sell all of his possessions and give away what he has to the poor in order to follow (10.21). In view of the rich man's failure, Peter points out that the disciples have left everything in order to be with Jesus (10.28).[73]

In comparison to the many possessions that the rich man refused to give up to follow Jesus, Bartimaeus's cloak may seem insignificant, but, as a beggar, it is one of the few things that he possessed.[74] When Jesus heals him and he can see again, Jesus tells him, "Go, your faith has healed [or saved] you." Bartimaeus has the option to go on his way, but instead he does what disciples are required to do. He follows Jesus on the way (10:52).

67. Paul J. Achtemeier, "'And He Followed Him': Miracles and Discipleship in Mark 10:46–52," *Semeia* 11 (1978): 124–25; Michael G. Steinhauser, "The Form of the Bartimaeus Narrative (Mark 10:46–52)," *NTS* 32 (1986): 583–95. Since Bartimaeus is a suppliant, it is best to see it as functioning as both a miracle story and as a call story that shows one who has faith in Jesus and who follows him. To emphasize one over the other, as Williams, *Other Followers*, 169, notes, "would inevitably result in certain parts being ignored."

68. The verb "call" is repeated three times in 10:49: Jesus tells the crowd to "call him"; "they called" him, saying "Cheer up! On your feet! He's calling you." The verb (*phōneō*), however, is different from the one (*kaleō*) that Mark employs to describe Jesus calling the first the disciples.

69. Williams, *Other Followers*, 163.

70. France, *Mark*, 424.

71. Marcus, *Mark 8–16*, 760, 765.

72. Marshall, *Faith as a Theme*, 141.

73. Williams, *Other Followers*, 157.

74. According to Exod 22:26–27 and Deut 24:12–13, for the poor, the cloak could be taken in pledge but it must be returned by sunset since it was the only covering that a poor person has for his body.

9.3 The Disciples' Encouraging Performance in Mark's Narrative

Much has been made of Mark's portrayal of the disciples' many failures in his narrative. It is readily apparent that Jesus' disciples are not a perfect, sinless dream team. They are beset by the same sins that plague all humanity, and they range from presumptuous ambition, vain rivalry, lack of concern for others, to cowardice. They reach the nadir of their failures when individual disciples betray, desert, and deny Jesus. As Kingsbury describes it, "The disciples in Mark's gospel story are a pitiable lot. The trend with them is downhill, from ignorance to apostasy."[75]

Mark does not sugarcoat any of these failures but amplifies them more than any other gospel. Nevertheless, one may approach this downhill trend more optimistically. For example, when Jesus calls the first disciples, he promises, "I will make you to become fishers of men" (1:17, ASV). Edwards stresses the word "become" in the Greek text and observes, "The process of becoming disciples of Jesus is a slow and painful one for the Twelve; it is not easy to understand (8:14–21), to watch (14:37), to follow (14:50), to suffer persecution for the cause of Jesus (13:13)."[76] One does not become a mature disciple in year one, and Mark offers significant hints that despite being consistently obtuse prior to the resurrection, their future renewal and success as disciples are assured. It misrepresents Mark's intent to emphasize only the disciples' bumbling performance.

Positive signs point to the disciples' ultimate success. These first disciples who were called immediately respond to Jesus' summons by leaving their jobs and family to follow him. One can assume that this sacrificial zeal was true of all of the Twelve. When Peter wonders who could be saved if someone like the rich man who was obedient to the law from his youth might be excluded from the kingdom, he protests, "We have left everything to follow you!" (10:28). When Jesus set his destination toward Jerusalem, the disciples follow even though they may fear the worst (10:32–34). This devotion to Jesus, as frail as it proves to be before the resurrection, bodes well for their future obedience to Jesus after they absorb the good news of his resurrection and receive the baptism in the Holy Spirit promised in 1:8.

To be sure, the disciples have feet of clay. They will desert him when he is nabbed by his formidable adversaries from the temple (14:50–52), but this desertion has been divinely foreordained (14:27) and is overridden by Jesus' promise that they will be reunited in Galilee (14:28; 16:7). Mark offers further hints that after his death and resurrection they will prove to be faithful. Jesus assures James and John, "You will drink the cup I drink and be baptized with the baptism I am baptized with" (10:39). For this prophecy to transpire—and Jesus' prophecies in Mark are unfailing—they will have become faithful proclaimers of the gospel.

In the eschatological discourse that Jesus delivers only to the disciples, he forewarns

75. Jack Dean Kingsbury, "'God' within the Narrative World of Mark," in *The Forgotten God: Perspectives in Biblical Theology: Essays in Honor of Paul J. Achtemeier on the Occasion of his Seventy-Fifth Birthday* (ed. A. Andrew Das and Frank J. Matera; Louisville: Westminster John Knox, 2002), 86.

76. Edwards, *Mark*, 50.

them that they "will be handed over to the local councils and flogged in the synagogues" and *on account of* Jesus "will stand before governors and kings as witnesses to them" (13:9). This prophecy assumes that they will not wither under fire but will stand firm, even when betrayed by family and hated by all (13:12–13). Baptized with the Holy Spirit (1:8), they will be able to respond powerfully, "for it is not you speaking, but the Holy Spirit" (13:11). When Jesus says that "the gospel must first be preached to all nations" (13:10), he assumes that the disciples will be the first to carry out this preaching. Their preaching will meet with the same success that Jesus confidently guarantees will occur in the parables of the seeds (4:3–8, 26–29, 30–32). The preaching will be continued by those who will respond to their preaching.

Jesus also affirms that "the secret of the kingdom of God" has been given to them (4:11), and while they may be slow on the uptake when Jesus first utters his parables, the assumption is that eventually they will understand because they come to him for explanations. The upshot of these glimmers of hope about their future success is that they will prove not to be "ashamed" of Jesus and his words "in this adulterous and sinful generation." The Son of Man, then, will not be "ashamed" of them "when he comes in his Father's glory with the holy angels" (8:35–38). "His angels" will gather them as part of "his elect from the four winds, from the ends of the earth to the ends of the heavens" (13:27). Jesus' vow at the Last Supper that he will not drink again of the fruit of the vine until that day when he will drink it anew in the kingdom of God (14:25) anticipates that they ultimately will be celebrating with him.

9.4 The Disciples' Failing Performance in Mark's Narrative

Despite intimations of their ultimate success after the resurrection, the overall portrayal of the disciples' performance during Jesus' ministry seems unusually harsh to most readers.[77] Mark is faithful to the historical reality that the disciples were not

77. Some interpreters claim that Mark used the disciples as representatives of his own theological opponents who espouse a deviating divine man Christology. Mark discredited the view of the false teachers through the embarrassing failures of the disciples. The abrupt ending of Mark's gospel is assumed to seal the fate of the disobedient, faithless disciples. Since the women are silent, they would never tell the disciples and Peter to meet Jesus in Galilee. Since they do not go to Galilee, they are not restored. Weeden, *Mark: Traditions in Conflict*, 50–51, boldly claims: "Mark is assiduously involved in a vendetta against the disciples. He is intent on totally discrediting them. He paints them as obtuse, obdurate, recalcitrant men who at first are unperceptive of Jesus' messiahship, then oppose its style and character, and finally totally reject it. As the coup de grace, Mark closes his Gospel without rehabilitating the disciples."

See the earlier work of Johannes Schreiber, "Die Christologie des Markusevangeliums: Beobachtungen zur Theologie und Komposition des zweiten Evangeliums," *ZTK* 58 (1961): 154–83; Joseph B. Tyson, "The Blindness of the Disciples in Mark," *JBL* 80 (1961): 261–68. This view is also found in John Dominic Crossan, "Mark and the Relatives of Jesus," *NovT* 15 (1973): 109–10; idem, "Empty Tomb and Absent Lord (Mark 16:1–8)," in *The Passion in Mark: Studies on Mark 14–16* (ed. Werner H. Kelber; Philadelphia: Fortress, 1976), 149; Kelber, *Kingdom*, 144–47; idem, *Mark's Story of Jesus*, 83–87; and idem, "Apostolic Tradition and the Form of the Gospel," in *Discipleship in the New Testament* (ed. Fernando F. Segovia; Philadelphia: Fortress, 1985), 39–42.

This radical misreading of Mark's intent collapses for the following reasons. (1) It ignores Mark's assumptions that Jesus' predictions will come true to the letter. Since all of Jesus' predictions at the Last Supper and on the Mount of Olives come true, one would expect that his promise that he will go ahead of them to Galilee where the scattered sheep will be regathered will also be fulfilled (14:27–28), even if it is not narrated by Mark. (2) This theory assumes that Mark is trying to debunk a divine man Christology, but there is no historical evidence that it existed or that it would have created the problem that Mark needed to correct. (3) This view utilizes a mistaken model of mirror reading, as is done in Paul's letters to discover the position of Paul's opponents.

always steadfast and faithful. They failed. But the experiences of the twelve disciples typify the experiences of disciples in Mark's church, and describing that failure has theological and instructional purposes for Mark.[78]

According to *Barn.* 5:9, Jesus chose "apostles who were to preach his Gospel ... those who were iniquitous above all sin to show that 'he came not to call the righteous but sinners.'" Best explains, "If the power of Jesus is to be properly understood this can only be done in the light of the weakness of man; if Mark wishes to show Jesus' power he must show the weakness of his disciples."[79] The disciples are shown to be weakest in their understanding of Jesus during his ministry. Marcus mitigates this failure by explaining that for Mark "no human being can possess wholeness of sight until after Jesus has been crucified" is correct.[80] Moloney goes so far to assert that humans "can never understand the mystery of the Cross" unless "*given* the power to do so."[81] But the disciples' lack of perception "facilitates the presentation of Mark's Christology rather than scolding dull Christians of Mark's own community."[82] Hawkin argues that what the disciples fail to understand about the mystery of Christ "*specifies what the Church is to seek to understand.*"[83]

Mark does not present the disciples as models for the readers to imitate but as mirrors in which the audience can view their own foibles and failures as followers of Jesus. The disciples may appear to be dense and wrong-headed, but the audience "is never led to disengage his or her identification with them."[84] Mark does not intend for readers to be merely observers who look disdainfully at the disciples' ineptitude but to identify with them and recognize their own inadequacies as disciples and be moved to correct them. Best claims, "It is their weakness and failure to understand which gives Mark the opportunity of teaching what true discipleship is." He notes that this approach fits a pattern in literature of the ancient world, where "stories of philosophers depict them as teaching through the failure of their disciples to understand."[85] An episode of failure allows "the true ideal of discipleship to stand out more clearly by its non-attainment" and also "provides an opportunity for corrective teaching from Jesus and often for a demonstration of the power available to remedy the failing."[86] Tannehill is right that Mark's narrative methods bend the story into "a weapon for tearing apart and tearing open our comfortable assurance that we are adequate disciples."[87] In reality, all disciples, past, present, and future,

78. Hans-Josef Klauck, "Die erzählerische Rolle der Jünger im Markusevangelium: Eine narrative Analyse," *NovT* 24 (1982): 1–26.

79. Ernest Best, "The Role of the Disciples in Mark," *NTS* 23 (1976–77): 388.

80. Marcus, *Mystery*, 100.

81. Moloney, "The Vocation of the Disciples in the Gospel of Mark," 492.

82. Boring, *Mark*, 266, n. 46, contra Karl-Georg Reploh, *Markus, Lehrer der Gemeinde: Eine redaktionsgeschichtliche Studie zu den Jüngerperikopen des Markus–Evangeliums* (SBM 9; Stuttgart: Katholisches Bibelwerk, 1969), 81–86.

83. David J. Hawkin, "The Incomprehension of the Disciples in the Marcan Redaction," *JBL* 91 (1972): 500.

84. Alberto De Mingo Kaminouchi, *"But It Is Not So among You": Echoes of Power in Mark 10.32–45* (JSNTSup 249; London: T&T Clark, 2003), 34–35; John R. Donahue, *The Theology and Setting of Discipleship in the Gospel of Mark* (Milwaukee: Marquette University Press, 1983), 27.

85. Best, *Story*, 47.

86. Marshall, *Faith as a Theme*, 211.

87. Robert C. Tannehill, "Reading It Whole: The Function of Mark 8:34–35 in Mark's Story," *Quarterly Review* 2 (1982): 76.

are "fallible followers."[88] Mark knows that his audience also needs to be challenged, to be forgiven, and to be allowed new beginnings.

Iverson offers the intriguing hypothesis that Mark presents the disciples' shortcomings humorously as "a rhetorical and redemptive tool, intertwined with the theological underpinnings of the narrative and intended to evoke a dynamic audience response."[89] Their responses are often laughable, and this humor is best captured if the text is read aloud in a group, as it would have been originally shared. He makes his case from the incident about the loaves in 8:14–21 where the disciples are shown to be particularly thick-skulled. Iverson's conclusions are insightful:

> While the audience enjoys Mark's jocular probing of the disciples, the act of laughing guides audience perspective. Indeed, Mark has deliberately narrated the episode in order to bait the audience into temporarily dissociating from the disciples. The irresistibly silly depiction of the Twelve, debating what is readily discernible to the audience, forces the observer to stand apart from the Twelve. But at the very moment when the audience might be prone to exalt themselves over and against the disciples, Mark orchestrates a reversal that forces the audience to recognize their fidelity with the Twelve.[90]

This reversal comes in Jesus' direct rebuke of the disciples, which then becomes an indirect rebuke of the audience that needs to recognize that they too, even after the resurrection, have moments when they fail to see, fail to hear, fail to remember, and fail to understand. Their hardened hearts lead to their own absurd bungling of their duties as Jesus' followers. Humor helps the audience swallow this indirect censure more easily.

In the end, Mark's account of the disciples' manifold letdowns can serve as an encouragement to later disciples. If they fail to comprehend perfectly all of the mystery, so did these first disciples,[91] and Jesus did not discard them for a more insightful lot. Harrington concurs with this analysis in noting that the disciples "want to be loyal to Jesus, but not at the cost of giving up everything, least of all their lives. The fact remains that readers of the gospel are most likely to empathise with those same disciples. By doing so the readers come to discern their own inadequacies. They find comfort in the realisation that, although the disciples failed him, Jesus remained unflinchingly faithful to them."[92]

Peter is portrayed in Mark as the most prominent disciple and is dogged by failures that frequently take center stage. Timothy Wiarda's study of the characterization of Peter in all four Gospels adds another wrinkle to the interpretation of Peter's gaffes. He typically is driven by positive intentions and his loyalty to Jesus.[93]

88. Malbon, "Fallible Followers," 48.

89. Kelly R. Iverson, "Incongruity, Humor, and Mark: Performance and the Use of Laughter in the Second Gospel (Mark 8.14–21)," *NTS* 59 (2013): 19.

90. Ibid., 16–17.

91. James G. Williams, *Gospel against Parable: Mark's Language of Mystery* (Sheffield: Almond, 1985), 63.

92. Harrington, *Mark: Realistic Theologian*, 15.

93. Timothy Wiarda, *Peter in the Gospels: Pattern, Personality and Relationship* (WUNT 2/127; Tübingen: Mohr Siebeck, 2000).

For example, Jesus went out early in the morning to be alone in prayer, and Peter hunts him down to prevail on him to return to Capernaum because everyone was looking for Jesus (1:35–39). He wants Jesus to take advantage of his growing celebrity. This purpose demonstrates that he is "*enthusiastic about Jesus* and *insensitive to Jesus' priorities.*"[94] He is not alone in his enthusiasm and insensitivity, since he is also joined by "his companions."

I would add, however, they may seem indifferent to Jesus' priorities because they have yet to be apprised of what they are, namely, that he has come to preach the good news of God's kingdom throughout Galilee (1:38). Even so, this episode reveals a penchant on the part of Peter to want to direct Jesus' agenda, but what is often not noted is that Peter ultimately submits to Jesus' authority. When Jesus travels throughout Galilee, preaching in their synagogues (1:39), Peter (and the disciples who are called to be with him) accompany him on his mission.

The inclination to redirect Jesus to do what Peter thinks is in Jesus' own best interest emerges most notoriously in 8:31–33. When Jesus announces that the Son of Man must suffer many things, be rejected, and be killed, Peter rebukes him in trying, presumably, to get him to change his mind. He unwittingly becomes a satanic source of temptation by urging Jesus to consider his own welfare first (see Matt 4:10).[95] Only six days later after his rebuke of Jesus and Jesus' rebuke of him, Peter still enjoys a privileged position as one of three disciples Jesus brings with him up the mountain to witness his transfiguration (9:2). Peter again asserts himself inappropriately by proposing to build booths for Jesus, Moses, and Elijah. Once again, he is well intentioned but misguided, and he is silenced this time by God, who speaks from the cloud, identifies Jesus as his beloved Son, and orders all three disciples to listen to him.

Wiarda attributes the additional failures of Peter and the other disciples to a "*desire to be loyal to Jesus* and, to a lesser degree, a measure of *confidence in self* and *less than perfect confidence in Jesus' words.*"[96] Peter's pledge never to desert Jesus even though the others might (14:29) and to die with him if necessary (14:31) are attempts to affirm his loyalty to Jesus and perhaps to reinforce it with such a public vow. One can read some of the disciples' stumbles, particularly Peter's, more positively as primarily motivated by an impulsive devotion to Jesus. The problem is that enthusiastic zeal will go awry when understanding does not guide where it is aimed.

9.4.1 The Disciples' Incomprehension

The disciples consistently misunderstand Jesus' teaching despite the private tutorials and are mystified by his mighty works. As the story progresses, the disciples' dazed incomprehension (7:17–18; 8:14–21, 27–33; 9:9–13, 30–32; 10:23–31, 32–45; 11:20–25) and blindness (4:35–41; 6:45–52; 9:2–8; 14:17–25, 32–43) reveal that even they are at risk of moving from "insiders" to "outsiders." The life to which

94. Ibid., 72.
95. Ibid., 77.
96. Ibid., 80–81.

Jesus calls disciples to live requires a fundamental change of perspective, to think the things of God (8:33).

9.4.1.1 The Disciples' Failure to Understand the Parables

After Jesus spoke the parable of the Sower to the crowd and was alone with the Twelve, they asked him about the parables (4:3–10). Jesus expresses mild surprise at their incomprehension with a promise and a warning: "The secret of the kingdom of God has been given to you" (4:11). "Don't you understand this parable? How then will you understand any parable?" (4:13). Jesus draws a distinction between those who are outside and those who are inside. All things come in parables to those outside (4:11). If left to their devices, the Twelve would be as utterly clueless as the crowd, but Mark relates that Jesus explains everything to them privately (4:33–34). Even though the mystery has been given to them, the private instruction does not sink in, at least, not immediately.

The disciples' incomprehension suggests to some that they move from insiders to outsiders (4:11), but this reading is gratuitously negative. Freyne notes that the process of understanding "is a slow and painful one, but in the school of the divine teacher it is eventually destined to succeed."[97] The disciples may be no less in the dark than anyone else, but they do come to Jesus to ask for enlightenment. Marcus asserts, "part of faithful listening is asking questions appropriate to Jesus' teaching."[98] Jesus' teaching, like the seed growing secretly (4:26–29), will have its effect and will eventually produce a harvest of understanding.

9.4.1.2 The Disciples' Failure to Understand the Issues Related to Ritual Purity

In 7:1–23, the Pharisees and some of the teachers of the law from Jerusalem try to expose Jesus' incompetence as a teacher by pointing out how some of his disciples were eating without first ritually purifying their hands by washing them.[99] Eating with unclean hands has nothing to do with hygiene but ceremonial purity.[100] A quote in the Babylonian Talmud from one rabbi reveals how inflammatory this issue could be: "Whoever eats bread without previously washing the hands is as though he had intercourse with a harlot" (*b. Soṭah* 4b). It is likely that widespread disobedience to the rabbis' dictates concerning washing hands provoked such a harsh fulmination

97. Freyne, *The Twelve*, 131.

98. Marcus, *Mystery*, 91.

99. The Greek reads that they eat with "common" hands, that is, the opposite of "holy" or "devoted to God." The reference to "some" of the disciples may suggest that others did wash their hands before eating, and it may reflect a division in Mark's church (see Rom 14:1–23).

100. Mark includes a parenthetical discussion about Jewish ritual washings for readers who must be unfamiliar with these traditions. The reference to "all the Jews" hints at some sense of detachment and that much of Mark's audience may be Gentiles. The Levitical system treated uncleanness as something that could be transferred to persons, vessels, clothes, and even houses by touch, lying, sitting, or by an overhang. The impurity could be removed through ceremonial washings. The NIV leaves untranslated the phrase "with a fist." It probably refers to "a cupped hand" and may signify that they use a fistful of water. Later rabbinic traditions define the valid amount of water (*m. Yad.* 1:1–2, 2:3; *b. Ḥul.* 106ab) and the method of pouring (*m. Yad.* 2:1; *b. Šabb.* 62b) for the washing to be valid, see Garland, *Mark*, 272, n. 6.

against those who ignored their rulings. Jesus turns the tables on these would-be watchdogs by excoriating them as hypocrites who neutralize the word of God with their own legal traditions (7:6–13). He then makes a startling declaration to the crowd about the issue of clean and unclean: "Listen to me, everyone, and understand this. Nothing outside a person can defile them by going into them. Rather, it is what comes out of a person that defiles them" (7:14–15).

This statement seems unambiguous and clear-cut, but when the disciples are with him in private, they ask him about "this parable" (7:17). Since Jesus said that everything comes in parables to "outsiders," it may explain the note of exasperation in his reply: "Are you so dull? . . . Don't you see that nothing that enters a person from the outside can defile them?" (7:18). Jesus introduced his instruction with the exhortation, "Listen to me, everyone, and understand this" (7:14), and this appeal implies that what he says may be difficult to understand and requires careful consideration. If it is a "parable," as the disciples identify it, then it is something that requires additional explanation as did the parable of the Sower (4:13–20).

The slow-witted reactions of the disciples to Jesus' teaching reveal that they are not yet blessed with wisdom. Mark's purpose, however, is not to expose them as dunces. Aune points out, "In the ancient world, *misunderstanding* was understood as a characteristic human response to divine revelation. . . . In the Gospels, the ignorance and fear of those in contact with Jesus are literary devices emphasizing the revelatory character of his words and the supernatural power evident in his deeds."[101] Their incomprehension always allows Jesus to give further instruction that Mark aims at his own audience.

Their question prompts Jesus to give a lengthy exposition on the issue of clean and unclean, which is encapsulated in the conclusion that what comes out of a person defiles (7:20). This saying is amplified in 7:21–23, and the controversy shifts "from *how* to eat (washed vs. unwashed hands) to *authority* for making such decisions (word of God vs. tradition of the elders) to *what defiles* (what goes in vs. what comes out; the stomach vs. the heart; food vs. intentions and acts)."[102] The passage implies that those in Mark's community who might not accept this view align themselves with the hypocritical Pharisees, who twist the law for their own selfish purposes. They had better not ignore the evils that ooze out from the dark recesses of their souls because that is what ultimately defiles them and cuts them off from God. Jesus' disciples are to ally themselves with his interpretation of God's will in the Scriptures so that they honor God with their "hearts," not just their lips (7:6; Isa 29:13) or their ritual correctness.

---

101. David E. Aune, *The New Testament in Its Literary Environment* (LEC 8; Philadelphia: Westminster, 1987), 55–56.

102. Boring, *Mark*, 202.

9.4.1.3 The Disciples' Failure to Understand the Significance of Jesus' Mighty Works

9.4.1.3.1 Fear in a Storm (Mark 4:35–41)

After teaching the crowd in parables and evening had arrived, Jesus had ordered the disciples to cross over to the other side of the lake. They are caught in a furious squall, and the waves swamp the boat while Jesus snoozes in the boat's stern on a cushion. The disciples panic and reproachfully rouse Jesus, "Teacher, don't you care if we drown?" (4:38). Jesus rises to rebuke the wind and calm the sea. Then, he gently chides the disciples, "Why are you so afraid? Do you still have no faith?" (4:40). The disciples' faint-heartedness results from the failure to trust "the power of God unleashed in their midst."[103] The noun form of "afraid" or "cowardly" occurs in a list in Rev 21:8 that includes the "the unbelieving [those lacking faith], the vile, the murderers, the sexually immoral, those who practice magic arts, the idolaters and all liars" who are all destined for "the fiery lake of burning sulfur." This accusation of being cowardly is therefore ominous.

After witnessing Jesus calm the sea with just a word, the disciples are overcome by an even greater fear (4:41).[104] "Fear" in this context conveys a sense of awe. The disciples function as straight men in the narrative because their fear impels them to ask at this strategic moment in the narrative, "Who is this? Even the wind and the waves obey him!" (4:41). Their question serves to underscore Mark's Christology and is not intended to draw attention to their blinded theological vision.

9.4.1.3.2 Failure to Understand Jesus' Feeding of the Multitudes (Mark 6:52; 8:17–21)

The disciples' vision is blinkered, and this impairment emerges clearly when they fail to perceive the significance of Jesus feeding the multitudes. A large crowd races around the lake to meet Jesus and the disciples, when he attempted to withdraw to a solitary place for a brief respite. Jesus had compassion on the crowd and taught them until late in the day. The disciples fret that Jesus needs to disperse the crowd so that they can find something to eat. When Jesus instructs them to feed them instead, their misgivings serve to heighten the magnitude of the miracle. They stress that they are in a remote place (6:35), the same term translated "desert" or "wilderness" in 1:3, 4, 12, 13. They calculate the cost to feed such a number to be at least two hundred denarii, the equivalent of two hundred days' pay for a day laborer (Matt 20:2), which the NIV renders as "more than half a year's wages" (6:37).[105] Since Jesus ordered them to take no money with them on their recent mission tour (6:8),

103. Henderson, *Christology*, 4.

104. The Greek reads, they "feared a great fear."

105. Their outcry is a familiar one in Scripture. Moses objected when God told him to feed the people (600,000 soldiers) for a month: "Would they have enough if flocks and herds were slaughtered for them? Would they have enough if all the fish in the sea were caught for them?" (Num 11:22). When Elisha asks his servant to feed the company of prophets, he balked, "How can I set this before a hundred men?" (2 Kgs 4:43a).

they would still be penniless, and the potential outlay to feed this crowd was well beyond their means.

Jesus ignores their concerns and has them arrange the shepherdless throng into groups (6:39). They are divided into units of hundreds and fifties (6:40) that makes it easier to feed them in an orderly fashion.[106] Jesus then has the disciples feed the five thousand from five loaves and two fish, and they collect twelve baskets full of broken pieces left over.

Unlike the other miracles, Mark records no reaction to this miracle. The crowd is not astounded, and the disciples do not ask, "Who is this that can feed five thousand with next to nothing?" Instead, Jesus immediately commands the disciples to get back into the boat and to go ahead of him to Bethsaida. He then dismisses the crowd and departs up a mountainside to pray. As they try to cross the lake, the disciples fight the wind and make no progress. Jesus sees their struggle and comes to them walking on the water. His sudden appearance terrifies them, and they think that they are seeing a ghost. Jesus tries to calm their fears by announcing, "It is I," and he gets in the boat with them so that they continue their journey. The disciples do not calm down in his presence but remain stunned. Mark offers a surprising explanation for the disciples' terror and amazement: "for they had not understood about the loaves; their hearts were hardened" (6:52). The two incidents are somehow connected, but Mark does not explain what it is about the loaves that the disciples do not understand.

The disciples show no signs of having turned the corner in their understanding with the feeding of the four thousand in 8:1 – 10. Another large crowd has gathered around Jesus to hear his teaching. He has compassion on them because they have had nothing to eat for three days, and they would collapse on the way if he were to send them home hungry. They hesitate yet again at trying to feed this quantity of people, reminding Jesus that they were in an out-of-the-way location: "But where in this remote place can anyone get enough bread to feed them?" (8:4). By expressing the disciples' qualms once again, Mark underscores the magnitude of Jesus' miracle. Jesus ignores their hesitancy and commands the crowd to sit, takes seven loaves, gives thanks, breaks them, and gives them to the disciples to distribute among the people (8:6). A miracle once more happens. Seven loaves and a few fish fill and satisfy a crowd of four thousand (8:8 – 9), but in Mark's account this miracle again evokes no reaction.

The scene in 8:14 – 21 is introduced by the statement, "the disciples had forgotten to bring bread, except for one loaf they had with them in the boat" (8:14). Unconcerned, Jesus warns them about the leaven of the Pharisees and of Herod.[107] The point does not register with the disciples. In a previous scene, a Syrophoenician woman immediately caught Jesus' parabolic imagery about "the children's bread"

106. It possibly reflects the encampment of Israel (see Exod 18:21, 25; 1QS 2:21 – 22; 1QSa 1:14 – 15, 27 – 2:1; CD 13:1 – 2).

107. "Leaven" is a better translation than "yeast" because its over-fermentation can lead to corruption, and that corruption that can poison a whole batch of flour becomes a metaphor for the dangers of various kinds of evil influences (see 1 Cor 5:6 – 8; Gal 5:9).

and responded fittingly (7:24–30). The disciples, by contrast, farcically miss what Jesus is saying and take his metaphor quite literally. They quarrel among themselves that they have no bread at all! The narrator notes that they do have "one loaf" with them in the boat. Translating the text literally in English as "one loaf" or "one bread" opens the way to a subtle insight. Mark writes that the disciples forgot to bring "loaves" (plural) except that they had one loaf (singular) with them in the boat (8:14). Without any clear antecedent, 8:15 continues, "Be careful.... Watch out for the yeast of the Pharisees and that of Herod." The grammar suggests that Jesus is that one loaf with them in the boat.[108]

Focant argues that it parallels the statement in 9:8, they "saw no one with them anymore, except Jesus alone" (NASB 1995).[109] After this incident, the next and last time the word for "bread" (or "loaf") appears in Mark is at the Last Supper when Jesus takes bread, gives thanks, breaks it, and gives it to his disciples, saying, "Take it; this is my body" (14:22). Even if Mark does not intend to make this connection, the audience would know that the disciples do have Jesus with them, and he has demonstrated what he can do when there is a bread shortage. Matera asserts, "There is, of course, no rational explanation for their memory lapse, nor is there meant to be. It can only be attributed to their hardness of heart which paradoxically points to the unfathomable mystery."[110]

The disciples do not catch that Jesus is not giving consumer advice about what to avoid at the market in his warning about the leaven of the Pharisees and of Herod. He is not talking about leaven per se.[111] He therefore rebukes them for failing to see and understand because of their hardened hearts. He jogs their memories about the feeding of the five thousand and the four thousand, numbers that emphasize the remarkable scale of the miracles. They remember the details precisely. They picked up twelve baskets full of bread fragments on the first occasion (6:43) and seven basketfuls on the second (8:8). Jesus asks twice, "Do you not yet see or understand?" (8:17, NASB 1995); "Do you not yet understand?" (8:21, NASB 1995). They give no evidence that they do.

The disciples have witnessed in two incidents that a great mass of people "ate and were satisfied" (6:42; 8:8) with a huge amount left over. They should have some inkling that something divinely earth-shaking and memorable had taken place and that it indicated something about Jesus' divine power. They perceived nothing because their hearts were hardened. Identifying their condition as attributable to a case of hardened hearts may seem ominous because Mark also attributes this condition to Jesus' bitter enemies (3:5; see Rom 11:25; Eph 4:18). It does not mean,

108. See Quentin Quesnell, *The Mind of Mark: Interpretation and Method through the Exegesis of Mark 6:52* (AnBib 38; Rome: Pontifical Biblical Institute, 1969), 242; Pesch, *Markusevangelium*, 1:414; Garland, *Mark*, 310; Boring, *Mark*, 226. The idea is more overtly expressed in John 6:25–58 where Jesus says, "I am the bread of life." Paul uses the phrase "one loaf" in 1 Cor 10:17 to refer to the Lord's Supper and connects it to the church's unity. Mark, it seems, is more interested in reinforcing the miraculous power of Jesus than in foreshadowing the Lord's Supper in this incident.

109. Focant, *Mark*, 321.

110. Matera, "The Incomprehension of the Disciples," 161.

111. Ironic misunderstanding like this is used to great effect in the gospel of John where Jesus makes a statement; the listeners, whoever they might be, misconstrue it by taking him literally; and Jesus then gives an extended restatement or reflection on his original statement.

however, that the disciples are splintering off into the enemies' camp. In contrast to Jesus' opponents, the disciples are not hostile to him. Their minds may be foggy, but they are not closed. They may be temporarily blind to what Jesus' mighty works convey about his identity, but Matera correctly recognizes that it does not reflect some moral failure on their part. He contends, "Hardness of heart paradoxically points to God's revelation which cannot be grasped apart from divine assistance."[112] Their failure to grasp the significance of the feeding miracles underscores "the mystery of Jesus' person" that requires divine revelation before anyone can understand it.[113] Only in retrospect, after Jesus' death and resurrection, will they be able to piece together what these events meant.

What does "the yeast" of the Pharisees and of Herod represent? (1) Is it a hostile attitude toward Jesus that eventually infects Judas?[114] (2) Does it refer to their desire to kill Jesus (3:6; 12:13)? (3) Is it related, as Trocmé suggests, to showing only superficial interest in the affairs of the kingdom of God like Herod, who "incarnates, it would seem, the sterile curiosity of the immoral man, who refuses personally to repent despite his liking for the man sent from God"?[115] The disciples can nail down the exact number of the baskets of leftovers from the miracles, but remain clueless and seemingly incurious about what it all might mean. (4) Does "the yeast [leaven]" refer to the Pharisees' quest for signs in the immediate context (8:11–12)? (5) Does it refer to being unable to discern the meaning of the signs they do witness (6:14)? This last suggestion is the most likely interpretation in the context. It is the inability to recognize that the miracles point to God bringing in the new age through the power manifested in Jesus.[116] If the disciples remain heedless to the import of these signs, they will be in grave spiritual danger.

As he is wont to do throughout Mark, Jesus leaves the disciples hanging. Wink asks, "Why doesn't Mark just come out and tell us what he means? Why, for that matter, doesn't Jesus simply explain to the disciples what it is that they don't understand? What can be more frustrating than being made to understand that you don't even understand what it is that you don't understand?"[117] The answer is that Mark is concerned about what happens to the audience in experiencing the disciples' befuddlement. The disciples suffer from an epistemological failure that makes them unable "to think the thoughts of God."[118] Mark's audience must avoid the same failing.

112. Matera, "The Incomprehension of the Disciples," 158. He cites the conclusion of Brevard S. Childs, *The Book of Exodus: A Critical Theological Commentary* (OTL; Philadelphia: Westminster, 1974), 174, about Pharaoh's hardening: "Hardening was the vocabulary used by the biblical writers to describe the resistance which prevented the signs from achieving their assigned task."

113. Matera, "The Incomprehension of the Disciples," 159.

114. Jeffrey B. Gibson, "The Rebuke of The Disciples in Mark 8:14–21," *JSNT* 27 (1986): 35, claims, "According to Mark, Jesus' rebuke arises because the disciples have shown themselves to be opposed to the extension of Israel's inheritance of salvation to those not of Israel." The problem with this view is that it is hard to connect it to the Pharisees and Herod in the context of Mark.

115. Etienne Trocmé, *The Formation of the Gospel according to Mark* (trans. Pamela Gaughan; Philadelphia: Westminster, 1975), 93.

116. It is because of this failure that Jesus' enemies plot his downfall.

117. Wink, "The Education of the Apostles," 282. Wink thinks that Jesus' explanation would have been fruitless. It is difficult to convince those who think they see that they are blind. They would simply try to force any explanation into the procrustean bed of their old presuppositions.

118. Shiner, *Follow Me!* 232.

Mark contains subtle allusions to Scripture throughout the gospel. Jesus' seemingly exasperated question to the disciples, "Do you have eyes but fail to see, and ears but fail to hear?" (8:18) echoes Isa 6:9–10 (see also Ps 115:5–6; Jer 5:21; and Ezek 12:2). It also echoes Deut 29:2–4:

> Moses summoned all the Israelites and said to them: Your eyes have seen all that the LORD did in Egypt to Pharaoh, to all his officials and to all his land. With your own eyes you saw those great trials, those signs and great wonders. But to this day the LORD has not given you a mind that understands or eyes that see or ears that hear.

Jesus' question in 8:18, "And don't you remember?" (8:18),[119] echoes Deut 32:7, "Remember the days of old, consider the generations long past. Ask your father and he will tell you; your elders, and they will explain to you."[120] "Remembering" is a leitmotif that runs through Deuteronomy, and the implication of this echo is that the Lord will give the disciples eyes to see and ears to hear, and they will indeed remember and put two and two together. They do not *yet* understand (8:17, translated "still" by the NIV), but they will. Hartman asserts that this transformation "might also be prefigured in the next passage, which deals with a person who does not see—like the disciples in a spiritual sense, but who gradually regains his sight."[121]

But Mark requires the audience to figure out for themselves the meaning of these events.[122] The numbers "twelve" and "seven" for the leftovers of fragments from the two feedings may be the key to the puzzle. Of the many suggestions,[123] the proposal that these numbers point to eschatological completion seems best. Marcus concludes, "What the Pharisees and Herod do not realize, then, and what the disciples are in danger of forgetting, is that in Jesus God is bringing the new age into being."[124] Wessel and Strauss note that this episode where the disciples demonstrate their lack of comprehension sets the stage for the interaction between Jesus and the disciples in what follows.[125] He will try to drum into their heads that as the Messiah he must suffer and the corollary that those who follow him faithfully will also be called upon to suffer.

It is important to note that Mark never presents Jesus giving up on the disciples as hopeless. They are not, as Kelber contends, "about to forfeit their privileged position as insiders."[126] Jesus poses their hardness of heart and lack of understanding as a question, not as a settled fact (8:17). Mark has structured the narrative so that

119. The word "remember" occurs only here in Mark.

120. Noted by Ched Myers, *Binding the Strong Man: A Political Reading of Mark's Story of Jesus* (Maryknoll, NY: Orbis, 1988), 225; followed by Marcus, *Mark 1–8*, 513.

121. Hartman, *Mark*, 320.

122. See L. William Countryman, "How Many Baskets Full?: Mark 8:14–21 and the Value of Miracles in Mark," *CBQ* 47 (1985): 643–55. His conclusion, however, is flawed that the reduction in the numbers signifies a reduction in the significance of Jesus' miracles as signs and the inadequate basis of faith.

123. See Beavis, *Mark's Audience*, 111–13.

124. Marcus, *Mark 1–8*, 514. Collins, *Mark*, 388, objects, "There are insufficient indications in the text of Mark to associate the seven baskets with eschatological fulfilment." What she ignores is that the numbers are associated with the miraculous feedings that do point to eschatological fulfilment.

125. Walter W. Wessel, and Mark L. Strauss, "Mark" in *The Expositor's Bible Commentary* (ed. Tremper Longman III and David E. Garland; rev. ed.; Grand Rapids: Zondervan, 2010), 9:818.

126. Kelber, *Mark's Story of Jesus*, 41.

Jesus declares that his disciples are deaf and blind *between* the stories of the healing of a deaf mute (7:31–37) and a blind man from Bethsaida (8:22–26). The healings also occur at the end of cycles following the two miraculous feedings. Richardson charts the narrative development:[127]

Feeding of the 5,000 (6:31–44)	Feeding of 4,000 (8:1–9)
Crossing the sea and landing on the west shore (6:45–56)	Crossing the sea and landing on the west shore (8:10)
Controversy with the Pharisees about what defiles (7:1–23)	Controversy with the Pharisees about signs (8:11–13)
A reference to bread: Taking the children's bread and giving it to dogs (7:24–30)	A reference to bread: Warning about the leaven of the Pharisees and of Herod, and the disciples' concern that they have no bread (8:14–21)
Healing of a deaf mute (7:31–37)	Healing of the blind mute (8:22–26)

The implication is that the disciples eventually will be healed, not from some physical deafness and blindness, but from their spiritual deafness and blindness.

9.4.1.4 The Disciples' Failure to Understand the Necessity of Prayer

After a hugely successful day in Capernaum of healing and driving out demons, Jesus retreats early in the morning to a lonely place to pray (1:35–38). The Greek verb that describes the search for him by Simon and his companions is stronger than the NIV translation (they "went to look for him," 1:36). It means they "pursued" or "hunted him down." When they find him and disrupt his moments of private prayer, they excitedly announce that everyone in Capernaum is seeking after him. They hound him to return to Capernaum where he has the potential to build a vast following after so many triumphs.

The account reveals that the concerns of his followers and those of Jesus are diametrically opposed. The disciples have decided that this great miracle worker is missing a golden opportunity to build up his following. They want to extend the previous day's triumphs that will add to Jesus' fame. By contrast, Jesus seeks God's will in prayer. The result is that he will not be deflected from the purpose. He is prepared to head elsewhere to proclaim the gospel that in the end will result in his rejection and suffering.

When Jesus and the inner circle of disciples, Peter, James, and John, descend from the Mount of Transfiguration, they find the other disciples caught up in a commotion with the teachers of the law. A father had brought his son to Jesus to drive out a demon. From the boy's childhood the impure spirit had "often thrown him into fire or water to kill him" (9:22). Jesus had given them authority over the

127. Alan Richardson, *The Miracle-Stories of the Gospels* (London: SCM, 1959), 81–99.

impure spirits (6:7) but now their stab at exorcising the demon in Jesus' absences fails. Their failure apparently provokes a spat with the teachers of the law.

Jesus exhibits his frustration with everyone in a lamentation: "You unbelieving generation ... how long shall I stay with you?" (9:19). He then engages in a dialogue with the father before successfully casting out the demon. Afterward, when the disciples come to him privately, they ask why they were unable to drive out the impure spirit. Jesus responds, "This kind can come out only by prayer" (9:28–29).[128] Since Jesus did not offer up a prayer before exorcising the impure spirit, he does not have in mind some formulaic incantation to be used in exorcisms that becomes part of some secret lore. Though Mark provides only brief glimpses of Jesus engaged in prayer in his ministry (1:35; 6:46; 14:32–39), the reference to prayer must refer to the persistent spiritual discipline of prayer, not to a spur-of-the-moment, emergency prayer. Jesus' explanation for the disciples' failure to drive out the impure spirit therefore contains an implicit indictment that the disciples had not been praying.

Jesus presents a positive example that reveals that a life governed by faith and prayer can vanquish demonic threats. The disciples present a negative example of what happens to those who neglect prayer.[129] Marshall points out that the disciples' question reveals that they are guilty of an "anxious self-concern" and a "misplaced self-confidence." He comments:

> Presumably they had come to regard their power to heal and exorcise as their own autonomous possession rather than being a commission from Jesus to realise his delegated authority afresh each time through dependent prayer. Mark is suggesting then that self-confident optimism may "feel" like faith, but it is in fact unbelief, because it disregards the prerequisite of human powerlessness and prayerful dependence on God.[130]

The disciples do not possess any inherent power. The power belongs entirely to God. It "must be received anew each time from him through a life of prayer."[131] Prayer is necessary because it "hands over the battle with this evil to God alone."[132] Otherwise, they are predictably impotent in the face of malevolent powers.

Mark starkly records Jesus' grappling through intensive prayer to come to terms

128. A textual variant that adds "fasting" to the requirement of prayer has weak manuscript support and was probably added because fasting was an interest of the early church (Acts 13:2; 14:23). "Fasting" is added to "prayer" in some texts of Acts 10:30 and 1 Cor 7:5. There is also no mention of Jesus' fasting in Mark, even during his forty-day sojourn in the wilderness (1:12–13; cf. Matt 4:2; Luke 4:2). When some people asked him why his disciples did not fast like the disciples of John the Baptist and the Pharisees, Jesus insists with a parable that they should not be expected to fast while "the bridegroom" is with them, that is, during his ministry (2:18–20).

129. James and John ironically report to Jesus that they obstructed the successful exorcisms of an outsider who cast out demons in his name. They offer as their reason: "because he was not one of us" (lit., "because he was not following us," 9:38). Larry W. Hurtado, "Following Jesus in the Gospel of Mark—and Beyond," in *Patterns of Discipleship in the New Testament* (ed. Richard N. Longenecker; Grand Rapids: Eerdmans, 1996), 13–14, considers this account to be an example of how persons "might show their interest in Jesus without first being formally counted among his disciples," and that readers "should not close the circle of fellowship too tightly, but should be open to a variety of ways by which people might begin to register their devotion to Jesus." Discipleship, however, requires more than a positive attitude toward Jesus, and trying to exploit the power of his name without commitment to him can have disastrous results (Acts 19:11–16).

130. Marshall, *Faith as a Theme*, 223.

131. Garland, *Mark*, 359.

132. Hartman, *Mark*, 385.

with God's will on the Mount of Olives (14:32–42). His struggle contrasts sharply with the unwary torpor of Peter, James, and John, whom he has taken to be with him as he prays (14:33). He commands them to "keep watch." After acknowledging, "My soul is overwhelmed with sorrow to the point of death," he goes a little further away and falls on the ground to pray that "the hour might pass from him" if it is possible (14:34–35). Jesus interrupts his prayer to return three times to find the disciples not watching but napping (14:37, 40, 41). On his first return, he speaks a word of reproach and warning: "Simon, are you asleep? Couldn't you keep watch for one hour? Watch and pray so that you will not fall into temptation. The spirit is willing, but the flesh is weak" (14:37–38).

The second time Mark does not record what Jesus says to them, only that they were sleeping "because their eyes were heavy" and "they did not know what to say to him" (14:40). "Not knowing what to say" is how Mark has described Peter's reaction to the transfiguration in 9:6 and reflects a complete lack of understanding about Jesus. They were dumb in the face of his glory, and now they are numb in the face of his anguish.[133] They neither heed his words nor follow his example.

When Jesus returns a third time, he says, "Are you still sleeping and resting? Enough! The hour has come. Look, the Son of Man is delivered into the hands of sinners" (14:41). The summary of Jesus' prayer is recorded only once (14:36). In 14:39, Mark simply reports that he prayed "the same thing," and in 14:41, he simply returns a third time. The account's center of gravity therefore shifts from Jesus wrestling in prayer to face the hour that is coming to the failure of the three disciples to watch and pray.

The disciples fail because of the weakness of the flesh, and the narrator says because their eyes were heavy. Heavy eyes are a sign of the flesh's frailty (cf. Jacob's eyes that are heavy with age, Gen 48:10). To be sure, their slumber is caused by physical exhaustion, but on a spiritual level they have had a bad case of heavy eyes all along (see 8:18). The weakness of the flesh is a persistent human condition that can only be overcome through prayer. They do not watch or pray because they are oblivious that a time of trial is about to overtake them. They will be completely unprepared for it as Peter's threefold failure to watch and pray with Jesus on the Mount of Olives will result in his threefold denial of Jesus.

9.4.1.5 The Disciples' Failure to Understand Jesus' Passion and Resurrection Predictions

Peter's confession that Jesus is the Christ (8:29) marks a turning point in the gospel because from now on Jesus speaks openly about the divine necessity of his death and resurrection. The disciples' benightedness becomes ever more apparent when he teaches them about his upcoming suffering, death, and resurrection. Jesus predicts his passion and resurrection in a threefold pattern in 8:31–38; 9:30–37; and 10:32–45. Significantly, Mark states that when Jesus announces his passion he tells

133. Garland, *Mark*, 542.

them "*plainly*" (8:32), not in parables (4:33). Despite this plain speech, each time Jesus speaks about his death and resurrection, the disciples manifest in some way that it does not register with them.[134] Their uncomprehending response then gives Jesus an opportunity to expound on the requirements of true discipleship.

All of these encounters occur while they were "on the way" (8:27; 9:33–34; 10:17, 32, where it is finally clarified that they are on the way to Jerusalem). Jesus therefore teaches about discipleship on the way to the cross. The point is clear to the audience, if not yet to the disciples in the narrative, that if they are to enter into his kingdom, they have to share his suffering. The cross is not only necessary for Jesus as the Messiah who gives his life as a ransom for the many, but the way of the cross is necessary for Jesus' disciples as a way of life.

9.4.1.5.1 The First Announcement of Jesus' Passion and Resurrection (Mark 8:31–38)

The first announcement occurs in the area of Caesarea Philippi after Jesus asks his disciples, "Who do people say that I am?" The disciples report the latest chatter: "John the Baptist," "Elijah," or "one of the prophets" (8:27–28). When Jesus probes them directly, "Who do you say I am?" Peter takes center stage and declares, "You are the Messiah" (8:29). Jesus then "warned them not to tell anyone about him" (8:30).

The language here is surprisingly strong. The verb translated "warned" is the same Greek verb used when Jesus rebukes the demons to come out from their victims (1:25; 9:25) and to remain silent about his identity (3:12), and when Jesus commands the wind to be still (4:39). The verb is also used for the disciples "rebuking" the people for bringing their little children to Jesus to lay hands on them (10:13) and for the crowd "rebuking" Bartimaeus for crying out loudly to Jesus as the son of David to have mercy on him (10:48). Mark does not explain why Jesus would censure Peter so vehemently and then forbid all of the disciples to broadcast the news that he is the Messiah. Was this confession only a fleeting moment of apprehension on Peter's part, or was his understanding of what it means for Jesus to be the Messiah only partially correct? The audience can infer from what follows that Peter's understanding of what it meant for Jesus to be the Christ was indeed flawed and needed refinement.[135]

After admonishing the disciples to keep mum about his identity, he teaches them that it is necessary[136] for the Son of Man to "suffer many things and be rejected by the elders, the chief priests and the teachers of the law, and that he must be killed and after three days rise again" (8:31). Peter responds by taking Jesus aside and "rebuking" him (8:32, the same verb used in 8:30). Mark does not narrate why

134. Shiner, *Follow Me!* 292, contends that the disciples' incomprehension also represents "the inability of the world to penetrate the mask of the mundane to comprehend the reality of Jesus."

135. Schweizer, "The Portrayal of the Life of Faith in Mark," 389, says it is not a confession but "a misunderstanding."

136. W. J. Bennett, Jr., "The Son of Man Must ...," *NovT* 17 (1975): 128, argues that the verb translated "it is necessary" (*dei*) is an indirect way of saying "God has willed it" as part of the eschatological plan of salvation. Bayer, *Jesus' Predictions of Vindication and Resurrection*, 204, maintains that the divine necessity of suffering leads to the divine necessity of vindication.

Peter so emphatically objects to Jesus' prediction. One could hardly expect him to jump for joy at this news, but he brazenly rebukes Jesus for making this prediction. It may be that Mark knows that the message of the cross is regarded as foolishness to the Greeks and a scandal to the Jews (1 Cor 1:18, 23), and he need not explain why Peter would challenge it as God's will for the Messiah. The promise of the Son of Man's resurrection apparently is ignored by Peter (see 9:10).

Shiner observes that Peter's rebuke assumes "Jesus has a choice in the matter." He is correct, Jesus does have a choice. "His reply is not, 'I have no choice,' but that Peter is thinking incorrectly in wanting him to choose against suffering." Jesus rebukes Peter even more sternly by calling him Satan and telling him to get behind him (8:33). "The vehemence of Jesus' reaction indicates the vehemence of his choice."[137] Peter looks at things from a purely human perspective and cannot yet understand Jesus' role as the Messiah. He associates the Messiah, as nearly all did, with success and triumphalism. It tallies with all that he has experienced in following Jesus so far. Jesus has demonstrated astounding miraculous power and, despite some opposition, has met with one sensational success after another. Peter quite naturally has come to expect more of the same or even greater miraculous feats. If one imagines the Messiah to be a liberator, a defeated Messiah is no Messiah. Because of his fond hopes that preclude the paradox of a beaten Messiah, Peter presses Jesus to choose a different way. Because of his extreme loyalty to Jesus, he also would do all in his power to prevent him from suffering.

The transfiguration scene that follows in 9:2–8 implies that Peter accepts Jesus' censure and again attempts to follow his lead. Puig i Tárrech comments, "after an episode of disobedience, where Peter and the other disciples have come out openly against Jesus' words concerning his passion and death, it is likely that the two episodes should be viewed in combination."[138] The fundamental question for Peter, speaking for the disciples, is, "Can this really be God's will?" The answer from the transfiguration is yes. The disciples must reposition themselves *behind* Jesus and must also shift their position on their perception of God's will. The divine command to listen to Jesus (9:7) means to "accept his announcement of suffering and death."[139]

In 8:34, Jesus begins to instruct the disciples and the crowd what is expected of those who follow him. They must forsake themselves, take up their crosses, and lose their lives for the sake of the gospel and Jesus. Losing one's life means giving up the human desire for security as the controlling motivation in one's life.[140] Hooker notes, "In Mark's context, the sayings point to the fact that the crucial divide is not between those who acknowledge Jesus as the Messiah and those who do not, but between those disciples who are prepared to follow him on the way of suffering and those who are not."[141]

137. Shiner, *Follow Me!* 271.
138. Puig i Tárrech, "The Glory on the Mountain," 170.
139. Ibid., 152.
140. Tannehill, "Reading It Whole," 68.
141. Hooker, *Mark*, 208.

9.4.1.5.2 The Second Announcement of Jesus' Passion and Resurrection (Mark 9:30–37)

Jesus teaches the disciples about his passion and resurrection a second time: "The Son of Man is going to be delivered into the hands of men.[142] They will kill him, and after three days he will rise" (9:31). The word "delivered into" has multiple applications in the narrative. Judas delivers ("hands over," "betrays") Jesus into the hands of the high priests (14:10–11, 18, 21, 41–42, and 44). The high priest's council will deliver Jesus into the hands of Pilate, and they will force his hand so that the governor will decide to execute him (10:33; 15:1, 10). Pilate will deliver Jesus into the hands of the soldiers who will crucify him (15:15). Noting that he is to be "handed over" to the hands of men, however, pins the responsibility for Jesus' death on humanity, not just the individual participants in the deed. Killing is what humanity usually does. In 14:41, they are identified as "sinners": "Look, the Son of Man is delivered into the hands of sinners." All humanity falls into this category.

Marcus notes from the usage of the verb to hand over in the LXX, "it is therefore better to fall into the hands of God than into those of humans (see 2 Sam 24:14/1 Chr 21:13; Sir 2:18), since God is merciful, whereas human beings customarily are not."[143] But there is another hand behind all this handing over. It is the hand of God, whose purposes are being fulfilled unbeknownst to any of the actors in the drama.

The good news is that "after three days" he will be raised. This positive note that appears in all three of the passion predictions is likely to sail right by the disciples since the narrator has already noted that Peter, James, and John questioned "what 'rising from the dead' meant" when Jesus ordered them not to report what they had seen in his transfiguration "until the Son of Man had risen from the dead" (9:9–10). Resurrection presumes death, and the message that the Son of Man will be put to death has yet to sink in.

The narrator specifically comments that the disciples do not understand what Jesus is talking about, but they keep quiet (9:32). They neither protest nor dare inquire what he meant. Best interprets their silence to mean, "they understand enough to be afraid to ask to understand more."[144] Perhaps, they are in a state of denial and vainly hope that ignoring what Jesus has said will make it go away. When they reach Capernaum, the serious extent of their misunderstanding is brought into an embarrassing light. Jesus asks them what they were discussing on the way. They remain silent, but the narrator reveals what presumably Jesus already knew. They had been quarrelling about which of them was the greatest (9:33–34). Their dispute borders on tragi-comedy after Jesus' prophecy and makes it painfully apparent that they do not comprehend, or refuse to comprehend, the implications of Jesus'

142. Hans F. Bayer, *A Theology of Mark: The Dynamic between Christology and Authentic Discipleship* (Explorations in Biblical Theology; Phillipsburg, NJ: Presbyterian & Reformed, 2012), 101, notes the striking paronomasia when the Greek phrase "the Son of Man into the hands of men" is translated back into Aramaic, *bar ʾanaš bene ʾanašîm*.

143. Marcus, *Mark 8–16,* 667.

144. Best, *Following Jesus,* 73.

prediction. This juvenile squabble about where they rank in the pecking order also reveals their desire to set up a hegemonic power structure.[145] This misunderstanding presents Jesus with a second opportunity to discuss true greatness as it relates to discipleship.

In his instructions about discipleship after his first passion and resurrection prediction, Jesus presented them with the paradox that those who want to save their life will lose it, and those who lose their life for his sake, and for the sake of the gospel, will save it (8:35). After this second prediction, he presents another paradox: the one who wants to be first must be the last, and the servant of all (9:35). What it means to be a servant will be defined further in 10:45. Jesus emphasizes that they have the choice between grasping for power to dominate others and surrendering dominance over others to serve them. The first option will lead to their ultimate humiliation. The second option, humbling themselves for the sake of others, will lead to their ultimate exaltation (Matt 23:12; Luke 14:11; 18:14; Phil 2:8–9).

Jesus then takes in his arms a little child to teach them another lesson: "Whoever welcomes one of these little children in my name welcomes me; and whoever welcomes me does not welcome me but the one who sent me" (9:37). It is perhaps ironic that he uses a child since their quarrel was so childish. The word translated "child" can also be used for an infant (see Matt 2:8, 9, 11, 13, 20, 21; Luke 1:59, 66, 76, 80; 2:17, 27, 40). Children were not romanticized in the ancient world. A child was dependent and vulnerable. In the Greco-Roman world, unwanted infants were frequently exposed. Children had no power, no status, and few rights. Therefore, they represent those who are lowly, who do not count (see Matt 14:21). It is striking, then, that Jesus chooses a little child as an example of someone who represents him: those who welcome the child for his sake welcome him. The disciples show themselves once again to be dunderheads when they later rebuke and attempt to turn away the parents who were bringing their children to Jesus so that he could lay hands on them (10:13–16). Jesus' teaching always fails to impress itself on the disciples initially, which reinforces the impression that they are disciples in embryo.

9.4.1.5.3 The Third Announcement of Jesus' Passion and Resurrection (Mark 10:32–45)

Jesus predicts his impending death and his subsequent resurrection a third time (10:32–34). It occurs when Jesus walks ahead of his entourage on the way.[146] For the first time, Jesus identifies their destination as Jerusalem. Mark notes "the disciples were astonished," and "those who followed were afraid" (10:32). Focant proposes that the narrator underlines that fear occupies all who follow Jesus "to emphasize

145. According to the Community Rule from the Dead Sea Scrolls (1QS 5:23–24), the community was organized around the rankings of the members: "And they shall be recorded in order, one before the other, according to one's insight and one's deeds, in such a way that each one obeys another, the junior the senior. And their spirit and their deeds must be tested, year after year, in order to upgrade each one to the extent of his insight and the perfection of his path, or to demote him according to his failings."

146. As he "goes before" (*proagōn*) them to Jerusalem to the cross (10:32), he will "go before" them after the resurrection to Galilee (14:28; 16:7).

the dramatic scope of the third and last announcement of the passion."[147] The NIV translation correctly interprets the first pronoun as a reference to the disciples, "the disciples were astonished." "Those who followed," however, suggests a second group in Jesus' retinue, perhaps the women "who had come up with him to Jerusalem" (15:41), and they "were afraid."

This rendering pictures the disciples following in an astonished stupor and others with a sense of awe or dread. The only explanation from the text for these reactions is that they are heading *to Jerusalem*. It may have dawned on them that Jesus is heading into the lions' den of the powers that threaten to undo him. De Mingo Kaminouchi notes, "People used to be amazed by the wondrous deeds and powerful words of Jesus. Now they are astonished by a man who goes to face torture and death. His followers are scared."[148] Perhaps, but some of the disciples are still in a fog and have visions of a glorious outcome when Jesus reigns on his throne.

Jesus calls aside the Twelve to give the longest and the most specific prediction of his death and resurrection. It is the only one that begins with the solemn introduction "behold" (omitted in the NIV). They were called to be with him, and they are to be with him in this crucial time of suffering and death when he will be handed over (or betrayed) to the chief priests and teachers of the law who will condemn him to death and then hand him over to the Gentiles. These will mock him, spit on him, flog him, and kill him. Again, he promises that he will be raised from the dead after three days (10:33–34).

The third time is not a charm for the disciples to understand the implications of Jesus' prediction. James and John immediately sidle up to him to request audaciously that Jesus do whatever they ask (10:35).[149] Others have made or will make bold requests of Jesus — the leper to be cleansed, the Syrophoenician woman for her daughter to be healed, Bartimaeus to see. Jesus refuses to sign a blank check for the disciples without knowing specifically what they want and asks, "What do you want me to do for you?" (10:36). It is the same question he will ask Bartimaeus (10:51). His answer is a far nobler one, "I want to see" (10:51). James and John are still too blind to see that they too need to see. Their answer reveals that they salivate over the possibility of landing the prime positions in Jesus' glorious kingdom.

The text does not provide adequate clues about the role they might have in mind. It is a generic request. If they envision the Son of Man as a glorious figure, as pictured in Daniel,[150] they have not absorbed anything that Jesus said about the

147. Focant, *Mark*, 422. The audacious request of James and John to sit on Jesus' left and right when he comes into his glory (10:35–37) does not suggest that they are gripped with foreboding over the destination.

148. De Mingo Kaminouchi, *"But It Is Not So Among You,"* 64.

149. They are identified as "the sons of Zebedee," which may mean that Mark simply preserves what is in the tradition, so Best, "Mark's Preservation of the Tradition," 33. Mark has mentioned their patronym only at the time of their call (1:20) and at their appointment to the Twelve (3:17). It may be added here to remind the audience of their social status as part of a family that had hired hands working for them. They were privileged in the social power structure and might expect special favor, so ibid., 93–94; see Gnilka, *Markus*, 1:74.

150. I argue below (§12.2.1.1) that the Danielic vision in Dan 7 of thrones, the exaltation of the Son of Man, the nations submissively serving him, and a court sitting in judgment have ignited the disciples' imaginations, and they want to share in this future glory as major figures themselves.

Son of Man being rejected, suffering many things, and dying a humiliating death (8:31; 9:12, 31; 10:33–34). Visions of sugar plums still dance in their heads. They ask to bask in the same resplendence that Jesus will receive as a glorious figure (8:38; 13:26).[151] They do not yet recognize that Jesus' death on the cross will cause many to be ashamed of him and his words and to want to dissociate themselves from any connection to him (8:38). De Mingo Kaminouchi argues that the "lack of specification serves to highlight the pure thirst for power" that drives their request.[152]

The other disciples respond to their request with anger (10:41). They do not fume because James and John were so callous to make such a request when Jesus just spoke of his coming suffering and death. They are irate because these brothers might become the frontrunners for the power slots. All of the disciples reflect the same lust for power. They are "still clinging to the same values of the world in terms of power-seeking and self-assertion."[153] None of the disciples has yet learned the previous lesson, "Anyone who wants to be first must be the very last, and the servant of all" (9:35). They want to rank in the upper echelons so as to dominate others, not to serve them.

Jesus does not chastise James and John but simply states that they do not know what they are asking. He then asks them an enigmatic question in return: "Can you drink the cup I drink or be baptized with the baptism I am baptized with?" Without skipping a beat, the two disciples assure him, "We can" (10:38–39). They are as confident in their own abilities as the rich man was about his obedience to God's commandments (10:20) and as Peter and the other disciples will be about their gritty determination never to deny Jesus (14:31). But when Jesus talks about drinking his cup, he is not thinking about them becoming his wine-tasters (Xenophon, *Cyropaidia* 1.3.9–10). Nor is the cup the cup of victory (Pss 23:5; 116:13), though the disciples might hope that it were so. They will not be drinking from a silver chalice.

Their glib answer presents the opportunity for Jesus to drive home the point once again that discipleship requires radical commitment and ultimate sacrifice. Crossbearing is to be an integral part of discipleship, and disciples must follow Jesus on an arduous path. The cup is one of wrath (Ps 75:8; Isa 51:17–23; Jer 25:15–18; 49:12; 51:7; Ezek 23:31–34; Lam 4:21; Hab 2:16; Zech 12:2; Rev 14:10; 16:19; 18:6)[154] that contains a drink that causes one to stagger and fall. In the *Mart. Isa.* 5:13, the cup is used as an expression for the martyrdom a prophet has to endure

151. In Matthew, "glory" ("splendor," NIV) is associated with earthly kingdoms. Satan shows Jesus the kingdoms of the world basked "in their glory" (Matt 4:8), and Solomon also has glory (6:29). Jesus promises "at the renewal of all things, when the Son of Man sits on his glorious throne," that the disciples "who have followed me will also sit on twelve thrones, judging the twelve tribes of Israel" (19:28). The disciples in Mark, however, have in mind the eschatological glory pictured in Dan 7.

It is unlikely, having witnessed Jesus' glorious transfiguration when he was flanked by Moses and Elijah (9:2–8), that James and John want to replace these two figures, contra Josef Ernst, *Das Evangelium nach Markus* (RNT; Regensburg: Friedrich Pustet, 1981), 307. Nor is it likely that they think of places of honor at the messianic banquet, contra Joachim Jeremias, *The Eucharistic Words of Jesus* (trans. Norman Perrin; London: SCM, 1973), 205. It is even more unlikely that they expect a "messianic coup" when Jesus arrives in Jerusalem and want positions of power in the new government, as Myers, *Binding*, 278, imagines.

152. De Mingo Kaminouchi, *"But It Is Not So Among You,"* 102.

153. Dorothy A. Lee-Pollard, "Powerlessness as Power: A Key Emphasis in the Gospel of Mark," *SJT* 40 (1987): 180.

154. See also 1QpHab 11:14–15; 4 QpNah 4:6; *Pss. Sol.* 8:14; *2 Bar.* 13:8.

(see also *Mart. Pol.* 14:2), and that idea fits well the context in Mark. It can only be the cup of suffering and death that Jesus drinks in giving his life as a ransom for many. In 14:24, it represents the awful consequences of divine judgment on sinful humanity.[155] The baptism image reinforces the notion of suffering. The word "baptize" in the context means to "drown." The LXX of Isa 21:4 has the prophet lamenting that "the lawlessness baptizes me"; in other words, it "drowns" me. Jesus will be submerged in suffering.

Jesus bluntly refuses to promise James and John the preferential seating they want in glory. They do not know what they are asking, and the seating arrangements are out of his hands. He cannot promise for them to sit at his right or left: "These places belong to those for whom they have been prepared" (10:40). In the context of Mark, this statement contains some irony. The only other time that the words "left" and "right" appear in the gospel is when Mark notes that the bandits were crucified with Jesus, "one on his right and one on his left" (15:27). The Zebedee brothers, obviously, do not request to be crucified on either side of Jesus. Whether on Golgotha or in glory, the use of the passive voice attests that God ultimately controls everything, including seating assignments.

Jesus only guarantees that they drink the same cup that he drinks and will be baptized with the same baptism (10:39).[156] What may seem to be a dire threat actually expresses a glorious promise in the context of the rest of the NT. Paul assures the Romans that as God's children "we are ... heirs of God and co-heirs with Christ," but then adds the caveat, "if indeed we share in his sufferings in order that we may also share in his glory" (Rom 8:16–17; see 1 Pet 4:13). Those who share Christ's sufferings are guaranteed to participate in his glory. If God's Son must learn obedience through suffering (Heb 5:8), so must the disciples. While the disciples may envision glorious and heroic sacrifices that will be richly rewarded with positions of power, Mark is not primarily interested in portraying them unsympathetically. The implication from this promise is that James and John will snap out of their lust for power and will become faithful and that faithfulness will lead unavoidably to their suffering.

The disciples' continued misunderstanding gives Jesus another opening for instructions about discipleship, and, for the first time, he briefly explains the purpose and the significance of his death—why he must die (10:42–45). The lust for rank and privilege is characteristic of pagan potentates and their courtiers. They covet seats of power so that they can lord it over others. Among disciples, the standard instead is to be serving others. Whoever wants to be first is to be slave of all. Greatness comes through giving one's life for others. One cannot understand Jesus apart from the cross, where Jesus takes the form of a slave, obedient to death (Phil 2:7–8), and one cannot understand discipleship to Jesus apart from the willingness to follow him on a way that leads to the cross.

155. Cranfield, *Mark*, 338, comments, "whereas he was thinking of a shameful death under the curse of the Law and in abandonment by God (cf. xv. 34), they were thinking of heroic and glorious sufferings in the cause of the messianic kingdom, something which could be faced in the mood of the martyrs of Maccabean days."

156. The glorious vision of Dan 7 includes the dire prophecy of the rising of the four beasts who will inflict severe suffering on the holy ones of the Most High (Dan 7:15–25).

9.4.1.5.4 Repercussions for the Failure to Understand Who Jesus Is and the Necessity of His Suffering and Death

The disciples' misconceptions and misguided responses reveal that failing to understand or rejecting Jesus' fate will lead to miserable failure as a disciple.

9.4.1.5.4.1 Betrayal by One of the Twelve (Mark 14:10–11, 17–21, 43–46)

When Jesus arrives in Jerusalem, the high priests and the teachers of the law begin plotting how to capture him surreptitiously and to do away with him without stirring up a tumult during the Passover festival (14:1–2). Judas Iscariot, one of the Twelve, has been identified as a betrayer from the beginning (3:19), but even so, he unexpectedly and inexplicably approaches these leaders with the offer to hand Jesus over to them. For whatever reason, Judas has lost faith in Jesus. He does not believe that he is the bringer of the new age and conspires with the powers of the old age to hatch a plot to ensnare him. The priests rejoice at this unanticipated solution to their problem of how to get rid of Jesus and promise Judas money in return. He then seeks an opportune time and place to betray Jesus (14:10–11). Ironically, the account begins by noting that Judas "went away" (see John 6:66). As one of the Twelve, he was chosen "to be with [Jesus]" (3:14) but Judas "willfully separated himself from the source of all that he could be and all that he could do by handing Jesus over."[157]

At the Last Supper, the drama of betrayal intensifies when Mark records Jesus solemnly announcing at the beginning of the meal that one of the disciples eating with him would betray him (14:18). Jesus knows exactly what is to happen. All but one of the disciples are in the dark, and they ask him, one by one, "Surely you don't mean me?" (14:19). This translation captures the force of the Greek that expects the answer "No, I do not mean you." As one of these disciples, Judas asks Jesus the same question, assuming that he can bluff his way through the meal. Jesus reassures none of them and only adds that the betrayer is "one of the Twelve, one who dips bread into the bowl with me" (14:20).[158]

Mark does not sweep under the rug this embarrassing treachery by a trusted disciple but instead underscores that the betrayer is the one "eating with me" (14:18), "one of the Twelve" (14:20a), "one who dips bread into the bowl with me" (14:20b). Such perfidy provokes a bitter denunciation from Jesus: "But woe to that man who betrays the Son of Man! It would be better for him if he had not been born" (14:21). Since the woe is generic, it can apply to any follower who would betray him and not simply to Judas (cf. Matt 18:7).

Luke explains the betrayal by attributing it to Satan: "Satan entered Judas" (Luke 22:3). Matthew ascribes the betrayal to greed as Judas solicits money from the

157. Moloney, "The Vocation of the Disciples in the Gospel of Mark," 514.

158. The image suggests that they are eating from a common bowl.

high priests, "What are you willing to give me if I deliver him over to you?" (Matt 26:15). In John's gospel, Judas is identified as one who embezzled from the common purse (John 12:6), so avarice could be construed as an implicit motive behind the betrayal, but the narrator explicitly states, "the devil had already prompted Judas, son of Simon Iscariot, to betray Jesus" (John 13:2), and "Satan entered into him" after he took bread from Jesus' hand (13:27). Dissatisfied with these explanations, interpreters over the years have tried to provide more clear-cut motives for Judas's treachery, but they are all based on flimsy historical guesswork. Mark deliberately gives no motive whatsoever for the betrayal. The effect is that in his narrative Judas commits a horrific act that cannot be rationalized. It leads the audience to conclude, if one of the Twelve could betray the Lord for no obvious reason, then any follower of Jesus could potentially do the same thing for the multitude of reasons that might arise or because of the multitude of character flaws that Satan could exploit.[159]

Judas somehow slips away after the meal and has given the armed band that comes to arrest Jesus a signal as he leads them to Gethsemane on the Mount of Olives: "The one I kiss is the man; arrest him and lead him away under guard" (14:44). The word translated "under guard" means "securely." He wants them to make sure that the squad brandishing swords and wielding clubs would place Jesus under tight restraint. Did Judas so misunderstand Jesus that he worries that he would try to fight to the finish or try to escape? When he arrives, Judas addresses Jesus with the honorific title "Rabbi" and kisses him so that he betrays no sign that the bond between him and Jesus has been broken. He hands him over to a certain death with a warm gesture of love or the customary greeting of respect.[160] He then disappears completely from the narrative, but not from the memory of the church.

9.4.1.5.4.2 The Disciples' Bravado on the Way to the Mount of Olives (Mark 14:26–31)

After the supper and when they had reached the Mount of Olives, Jesus forewarns the disciples of their imminent failure by announcing that they will all "fall away" ("become deserters," NRSV; "be scandalized," 14:27). The meaning of the verb is spelled out in the interpretation of the parable of the Sower and the seed sown on rocky ground: "When they hear the word, they immediately receive it with joy. But they have no root, and endure only for a while; then, when trouble or persecution arises on account of the word, immediately they fall away" (4:16–17, NRSV). Jesus' citation from Scripture, "For it is written: 'I will strike the shepherd, and the sheep will be scattered'" (14:27; Zech 13:7), serves both to confirm what Jesus has predicted and to convey that the disciples' breaking down and then, temporarily,

159. Augustine Stock, *Call to Discipleship* (Wilmington, DE: Michael Glazier, 1984), 195.

160. One kissed the hand out of deference or the cheek if one considered oneself to be an equal (see Luke 7:45, "You did not give me a kiss"). The word Mark uses for "kiss" could picture affection (see Luke 15:20; Acts 20:37). A biblical precedent for a kiss veiling malevolent intentions appears in Joab's slaying of Amasa (2 Sam 20:9–10). Mark's readers would be familiar with the church practice of greeting one another with a holy kiss (Rom 16:16; 1 Cor 16:20; 2 Cor 13:12; 1 Thess 5:26; 1 Pet 5:14), which would have made this gesture seem all the more unspeakable.

breaking up are all in accordance with God's will.[161] He follows this prophecy with a promise that after he is raised up he will go before them to Galilee.[162]

The disciples, led by Peter, respond with a protest of undying loyalty (14:29–31). This is not the first time that Peter has disputed a divine plan. He challenged Jesus' announcement that the Son of Man *must* (implying a divine necessity) suffer (8:31–33). Now, however, he does not flinch at the shepherd being struck, but he does take exception to the assertion that he will be one of those who will falter and be scattered.[163] He ignores the implied promise of restoration and contests Jesus' prophecy in a competitive spirit: "Even if all fall away, I will not" (14:29). Peter suffers from the same overweening self-confidence as James and John, who are convinced that they could drink the same cup as Jesus and be baptized with the same baptism. This spirit of rivalry exposes the growing fissure in the disciples' ranks.

The other disciples follow Peter's lead and join in protesting that they will never be false to Jesus. Tolbert perceptively observes, however, "If they are not sure whether or not they will betray him, how can they possibly swear faithfulness to death?"[164] Such swaggering arrogance combined with ignorance about the enormity of the test that awaits them portends their collapse. Jesus called his followers to put to death their selfish ambition, which includes their cocksure vanity about their own strength of purpose.

Jesus responds with a prophecy that Peter will deny him three times before the cock crows twice (14:30), which may simply mean "before the next dawn."[165] Jesus utters a woe to condemn bitterly Judas's cold-blooded decision to betray him but passes over Peter's forthcoming denials without censure. It is attributed to human frailty (14:38), not malice aforethought.[166] Peter's denials of Jesus begin with his denial that Jesus could possibly be right. He brashly responds that if it is necessary, he will die with Jesus and never deny him (14:31). To his credit, he has grown in his understanding that as a disciple he has to be ready to lose his life (8:35). Peter's protest of loyalty, then, ironically, reveals how far he is from Jesus' spirit.[167] It also ironically highlights a core commitment of the Christian faith: the necessity of dying with Christ to be raised with him (see Rom 6:8, Col 2:20; 2 Tim 2:11). What is necessary, however, is not dying as a martyr on the battlefield but dying to self (Gal 2:19–20).

161. Agustí Borrell, *The Good News of Peter's Denial: A Narrative and Rhetorical Reading of Mark 14:54.66–72* (trans. Sean Conlon; International Studies in Formative Christianity and Judaism; Atlanta: Scholars Press, 1998), 20–21.

162. This promise along with 16:7, "There you will see him," is not a prophecy of the Parousia, as Lohmeyer, *Galiläa und Jerusalem*, 11–13, argued (see Collins, *Mark*, 658–67). Instead, it is a reference to a resurrection appearance and the regathering of the disciples after their dismal performance during Jesus' passion.

163. Brown, *Death*, 1:134.

164. Tolbert, *Sowing the Gospel*, 212.

165. Charles Masson, "Le reniement de Pierre: quelques aspects de la formation d'une tradition," *RHPR* 37 (1957): 24–35; David Brady, "The Alarm to Peter in Mark's Gospel," *JSNT* 4 (1979): 42–57; Brown, *Death*, 1:137, make the case that Jesus refers to a literal cock crow and not trumpeting of the end of one of the four night-watches.

166. Borrell, *Peter's Denial*, 161.

167. Ibid., 163.

9.4.1.5.4.3 The Disciples' Craven Abandonment of Jesus on the Mount of Olives (Mark 14:43–52)

The arrest scene on the Mount of Olives begins with the action of Judas in greeting and kissing Jesus (14:43–45). This signal prompts the arresting mob to spring into action and to lay hands on him, inciting a melee in which the high priest's servant's ear is cut off (14:46–47). Mark identifies the culprit only as "one of those standing near," *not* as Peter or one of the disciples. Jesus then calmly responds by condemning the violence of the armed band, and their swords and clubs are mentioned a second time as if they were coming to arrest some rebel bandit who was armed and dangerous. He announces that they could have seized him any day in the temple, but the Scriptures are being fulfilled (14:48–49). The scene closes with the scattering of the disciples as Jesus had predicted (14:50–52). They had forsaken family, livelihoods, and everything to follow Jesus (1:18, 20; 10:28–30). Now, they forsake him to escape and in effect temporarily disavow their discipleship. With the exception of Peter, who makes one last ignominious appearance, the disciples fade from the narrative.

Mark alone describes the specific escape of a young man who was following Jesus wearing a linen cloth. He wriggles free from the grasp of the arresting party and sprints away into the darkness stripped bare (14:51–52).[168] Cranfield asks, "Why should Mark insert such a trivial detail in so solemn a narrative?"[169] This incident fascinates many, but what is it intended to convey? It has stimulated many "imaginative flights of fancy" both novelistic and symbolic.[170] Vearncombe's study of the nature of the garment should help to rein in some of the wildest speculations. The *sindōn* was a more expensive rectangle of cloth that was draped around the body as an outer garment.[171] Such sleeveless rectangles of cloth without buttons, pins, or belts were embarrassingly prone to slip off when running,[172] and papyrological

168. Joan E. Taylor's argument in "The Garden of Gethsemane: Not the Place of Jesus' Arrest," *BAR* 21 (1995): 26–35, 62, that "Gethsemane," which means "oil press," refers to a spacious cave (about 55 feet long and 29½ feet wide) within a cultivated enclosure on the Mount of Olives where olives were pressed for oil. The press would have been in operation in fall and winter after the olive harvest, but it would have been idle and used only for storage in the spring. It would provide a "warm, dry, and roomy" shelter on a night when others were kindling fires for warmth (14:54). Jesus would have left the cave with the three disciples to go further away to pray by himself. If they were sheltered in a cave, it would also explain why the young man who fled was attired only in a linen garment. He presumably slept on his cloak. Were he out in the open and exposed to the frigid air, such a choice would have been unlikely.

169. Cranfield, *Mark*, 438.

170. Brown, *Death*, 1:299. See the critique of various proposals in Gundry, *Mark*, 603–23; Howard M. Jackson, "Why the Youth Shed His Cloak and Fled Naked: The Meaning and Purpose of Mark 14:51–52," *JBL* 116 (1997): 273–77. Mark is not putting his signature on the canvas, so to speak, by inserting his own personal involvement in this event. This view must ignore Papias's comments about Mark that "neither did he hear the Lord, nor did he follow him" (Eusebius, *Hist. eccl.* 3.39.15). The desperate flight is also not an allusion to Amos 2:16, which envisions people fleeing on the day of the Lord: "'Even the bravest warriors will flee naked on that day,' declares the LORD." Mark does not present this time as the day of the Lord. The interpretation that focuses on the linen garment (*sindōn*) as somehow prefiguring the linen cloth in which Jesus' body will be wrapped (15:46) and connects this "young man" with the "young man" at the tomb announcing the resurrection (16:5) is far-fetched. The young man who escapes the clutches of his would-be captors does not symbolize Jesus' escape from death through the resurrection. Nor is Mark reflecting the later baptismal practice of taking off one's garment before baptism and putting on a white one afterwards. The young man sheds his garment when he is abandoning Jesus, not confessing him, and he does not die with Jesus.

171. Erin Vearncombe, "Cloaks, Conflict, and Mark 14:51–52," *CBQ* 75 (2013): 683–703.

172. Jackson, "Why the Youth Shed His Cloak," 280.

evidence reveals that "the loss of a cloak in a situation of conflict was a fairly common experience."[173] This incident is not something fantastical but a realistic detail. Mark cites it, however, only because of its emblematic significance of the disciples' failure.

The immediate context should govern the interpretation. On the way to the Mount of Olives, Jesus cites Zechariah and tells his disciples that they will all become deserters: "You will all fall away, for it is written: 'I will strike the shepherd, and the sheep will be scattered' " (14:27). All the disciples vehemently protest that they will not desert him (14:31). When Jesus is about to be seized by the arresting party, he says, "The Scriptures must be fulfilled" (14:49). They are being fulfilled in multiple ways, one of which occurs in the next verse when all of the disciples forsake him and make a mad dash to safety as he had foretold (14:50). The disciples do not make good on their boasts to drink Jesus' cup (10:38–39) or to die with him (14:31), and their inglorious exit exposes their empty pledges. The young man's panicked getaway reflects the disciples' mind-set: "Every man for himself" and "Save yourself if you can."[174]

In contrast to Bartimaeus, who casts aside his cloak to follow Jesus (10:50–52), and those who spread their cloaks on the road before Jesus as he rode into Jerusalem (11:8), this young man *abandons* his cloak to flee naked from Jesus.[175] Vearncombe asserts, "Nakedness was associated in the ancient Mediterranean with poverty, death, defeat, and pollution."[176] Moloney's argument that followers who separate themselves from Jesus are left "naked in their nothingness" would seem to capture the theological gist for Mark.[177] He continues that the young man "would rather lose his clothes than lose his life."[178] Kuruvilla concludes that the naked runaway represents "every Disciple, shamefully feeble and fallible."[179]

9.4.1.5.4.4 Peter's Threefold Denial of Jesus (Mark 14:54, 66–72)

Peter alone follows after Jesus when he is arrested but only at a safe distance. He somehow gains entry to the high priest's courtyard, where he sits with the enemy, warming himself by the fire (14:54).[180] The light of the fire gives him away, and one of the serving girls fingers him as one who was "with that Nazarene, Jesus" (14:66–67). Jesus chose the Twelve particularly to be "with him" (3:14), but Peter

173. Vearncombe, "Cloaks, Conflict, and Mark 14:51–52," 696. She notes that it was more expensive than the coarser *himation*, that it was normal to wear next to the skin, and that translations should not add the phrase "nothing but," which does not occur in the Greek, before "linen garment" as if it were something unusual (690–91).

174. Schweizer, *Mark*, 319; Harry Fleddermann, "The Flight of a Naked Young Man (Mark 14:51–52)," *CBQ* 41 (1979): 412–18; Jackson, "Why the Youth Shed His Cloak," 278–86.

175. Jackson, "Why the Youth Shed His Cloak," 287–89. Vearncombe, "Cloaks, Conflict, and Mark 14:51–52," 702, notes that nakedness can simply refer to "an incomplete state of dress," which is no less embarrassing. In Rev 3:18, "nakedness" is considered to be "shameful."

176. Vearncombe, "Cloaks, Conflict, and Mark 14:51–52," 693.

177. Moloney, "The Vocation of the Disciples in the Gospel of Mark," 500.

178. Dean B. Deppe, "Charting the Future or a Perspective on the Present? The Paraenetic Purpose of Mark 13," *CTJ* 41 (2006): 96.

179. Abraham Kuruvilla, "The Naked Runaway and the Enrobed Reporter of Mark 14 and 16: What Is the Author Doing with What He is Saying?" *JETS* 54 (2011): 545.

180. That Mark notes that Peter is "below" in the courtyard implies that Jesus is being interrogated upstairs in the priest's home.

tries to evade the accusation by denying it and feigning an inability to understand what she was saying. Peter simply "denied it" (14:68, aorist tense).

Peter then attempts to slither away unobtrusively to the vestibule that leads into the courtyard. A complicated textual problem surfaces in 14:68. The statement "and a rooster crowed" after this first denial is absent from some significant manuscripts, and some contend that it was interpolated at a later date, perhaps to emphasize the literal fulfillment of Jesus' prophecy in 14:30 that Peter would disown him three times "before the rooster crows twice." It is possible, however, that since Matt 26:74 and Luke 22:60 only mention one cock crow, the copyists, with their penchant for harmonizing, would have expunged it from Mark. The reading that the rooster crowed "a second time" in 14:72, however, points to the rooster crowing a first time.[181] If the rooster crowing after the first denial is the original reading, which seems likely, Peter is unmindful of this early warning.

When the serving girl spots Peter in this new location, she announces to the bystanders that he is "one of them," which he again denies (14:69–70a), this time using the imperfect tense. Having caught the attention of others, they now recognize that he is a Galilean, presumably from his accent, and concur that surely he must be one of them. Peter denies the accusation this time by invoking a curse and swearing an oath that he does not know "this man you are talking about" (14:70b–71).

The transitive verb "to invoke a curse" has no direct object in the Greek text. It could be that he calls down curses on himself, as the NIV translates it. He denies Jesus under oath and curses himself if he is lying. It is also possible that he pronounces a curse on Jesus (see the use of a related noun in 1 Cor 12:3).[182] What makes this possibility plausible is the report that the younger Pliny, a special commissioner to Pontus-Bithynia (ca. AD 110), sent to the Emperor Trajan. He relates that when he interrogates those suspected of being Christians, he asks them three times, "Are you a Christian?" with threats of punishment. The accused proves his or her innocence by cursing Jesus, something, Pliny insists, "those who are really Christians cannot be made to do" (*Epistles* 10.96.3, 5).

In the mid-second-century *Mart. Pol.* 9:3, the proconsul tells the bishop Polycarp, "Swear and I will release you." He replies, "Eighty-six years I have served him, and he had done me no wrong. How can I blaspheme my King who has saved me?" According to Justin Martyr (*1 Apol.* 31.6), the Jewish rebel leader Bar Kochba (AD 132–135) gave Christians the choice between death and cursing Christ. In *Herm. Sim.* 8.6.4, the author refers to Christian defectors who "blaspheme the Lord." It is possible that Mark's community may have experienced the same kind of threats in their persecution in the first century, and Mark notes the similarities

181. France, *Mark*, 618, notes that the variants in 14:72 show evidence of attempts of harmonization.

182. Helmut Merkel, "Peter's Curse," in *The Trial of Jesus: Cambridge Studies in Honour of C. F. D. Moule* (ed. Ernst Bammel; SBT 2/13; Naperville, IL: Allenson, 1970), 66–71; G. W. H. Lampe, "St. Peter's Denial and the Treatment of the *Lapsi*," in *The Heritage of the Early Church: Essays in Honor of Georges Vasilievich Florovsky* (ed. David Neiman and Margaret Schatkin; OrChrAn 195; Rome: Pontifical Oriental Institute, 1973), 113–33. This is the only time the verb is used in Scripture without an object or reflexive pronoun (see Acts 23:12, 14, 21), and it is likely that Jesus' name was suppressed out of piety.

in Peter's experience. The difference is that Peter is not under arrest or threatened with his life. That Peter cannot bring himself to utter Jesus' name, "I don't know this man you're talking about," makes it less likely that he cursed "Jesus" by name. He may have cursed "this man," whoever he is.

Peter's threefold denial of knowing Jesus is cut short by the crowing of the rooster a second time, just as Jesus had predicted. It jars his memory of what Jesus had told him. Remembering is key to understanding (see 8:18; 11:21), and it is the beginning of Peter's implied repentance. Bockmuehl, writing on the prominence of the rooster in early Christian iconography, notes, "Greco-Roman antiquity saw the rooster as symbolizing the arrival of light, of victory, and occasionally of immortality. For Christians, on the other hand, that same motif proved highly conducive to a link with the resurrection of Christ.... The cock's crow projects into the dark night of Maundy Thursday the bright daylight of Easter Sunday."[183]

In the narrative, however, the cockcrow awakens Peter to his shame, and he flees into the darkness. The violence of his sorrow is emphasized by the verb translated "broke down" (14:72). The meaning of the verb here, however, is difficult to decipher.[184] It literally means "to throw over" or "to cast upon." The context records Peter's physical movement further away from where Jesus is being interrogated by the high priest and company as he slinks from the inner courtyard to the entryway. Rendering the verb he "dashed outside" or "threw himself out" seems to fit this situation. He takes wing from the probing bystanders and their unspoken threats (see Matt 26:75; Luke 22:62). Away from their accusatory gaze, he could weep freely over his shameful cowardice and not give himself away.

The verb, however, can also be used to mean "to give one's attention to" or "to think on," and if that is the meaning here, Peter remembers Jesus' words and fastens his attention on them.[185] He had boasted of his fortitude (14:27–31), but when confronted with the slightest pressure, he caves in by denying any connection to Jesus. Auerbach eloquently describes his collapse: "Because his faith was deep, but not deep enough, the worst happened to him that can happen to one whom faith had inspired but a short time before: he trembles for his miserable life."[186] He now realizes just how weak the flesh is (14:38). In the narrative, "Peter has reached rock-bottom."[187] He flees the scene of Jesus' trial grieving but much sobered. Mark ignores telling the reader how Peter made good his escape because the story is not about Peter.

Peter's denial of knowing Jesus is reprehensible, but his ultimate restoration reveals that such disloyalty, even if it is tinged with blasphemy, is not irredeemable. The prophetic promise that Jesus will go before them to Galilee after he has

183. Bockmuehl, *Simon Peter*, 160.

184. Brown, *Death*, 1:609–10, lists nine options for translating it: (1) having broken down; (2) being thrown to the ground; (3) having rushed outside; (4) having begun to cry; (5) having thought of Jesus' prediction; (6) having cast his eyes on Jesus; (7) having answered; (8) having thrown a piece of clothing on him, or covering his head; (9) or having struck his chest.

185. Borrell, *Peter's Denial*, 110–11.

186. Erich Auerbach, *Mimesis: The Representation of Reality in Western Literature* (trans. Willard R. Trask; Princeton: Princeton University Press, 1953), 42.

187. Borrell, *Peter's Denial*, 114.

risen from the dead implies that the disciples' failures and their dispersal are only temporary (14:27–28). Tannehill concludes, "So the Gospel holds open the possibility that those who deserted Jesus will again become his followers, reinstating the relationship established by Jesus' call."[188] This promise is reinforced when the young man at the tomb specifies that the women are to "go, tell his disciples and Peter, 'He is going ahead of you into Galilee. There you will see him, just as he told you'" (16:7). This word is not simply an invitation to go to Galilee but an infallible prophecy that they *will* go.[189] This note, unique to Mark, reveals that Jesus' resurrection dramatically changes things. The failures of the past are canceled, and "a new and hopeful era" has dawned.[190] Those who were scattered will be regathered.

Lane comments, "The focus upon human inadequacy, lack of understanding and weakness throws into bold relief the action of God and its meaning."[191] The lesson for the disciples and for the audience is that they cannot rely on their own strength, resolve, or tenacity (see 2 Cor 12:9).

9.5 The Women Followers' Performance in Mark's Narrative

When Peter declared that Jesus was the Christ (8:29), Jesus admonished his disciples, "If anyone is ashamed of me and my words in this adulterous and sinful generation, the Son of Man will be ashamed of them when he comes in his Father's glory with the holy angels" (8:38). He also insisted that whoever wants to be his disciple must deny themselves (8:34). Peter denied Jesus instead of denying himself. The result of this final failure by a disciple is that, in Mark, Jesus goes to the cross surrounded by strangers. A passerby carries his cross (15:21), and one of the executioners will utter the confession that he is the Son of God (15:39). The disciples of John the Baptist claimed his body from Herod and laid it in a tomb (6:29), but Jesus will be buried by a member of the council that condemned him to death (15:43). The sad litany of the disciples' failures during Jesus' passion is counterbalanced by the loyalty of the female followers of Jesus who followed him to Jerusalem and stuck it out to the bitter end. Malbon points out, however, "Woman characters of Mark are 'good' or 'positive' because they are followers or exemplify followership—not because they are women."[192]

188. Robert C. Tannehill, "The Disciples in Mark: The Function of a Narrative Role," *JR* 57 (1977): 404.

189. Joel Marcus, "Identity and Ambiguity in Markan Christology," in *Seeking the Identity of Jesus: A Pilgrimage* (ed. Beverly Roberts Gaventa and Richard B. Hays; Grand Rapids: Eerdmans, 2008), 135, recognizes that all of "the negative features of the Markan disciples" must "be balanced with the recognition that their destiny as 'fishers of people' rests not on their worthiness but upon Jesus' call (1:16–20), that in spite of everything they remain Jesus' chosen companions up until the end of the story, and that even their abandonment of Jesus there cannot annul his promise that after his resurrection they will be reunited with him in Galilee (14:27–28; 16:7)."

190. David Catchpole, "The Fearful Silence of the Women at the Tomb: A Study in Markan Theology," *JTSA* 18 (1977): 4.

191. Lane, *Mark*, 592.

192. Malbon, *Company*, 66. Women can be no less villainous or antipathetic to Jesus than men. Herodias and her daughter instigate the beheading of John the Baptist (6:14–29), and a servant girl blows the whistle on Peter's presence in the high priest's courtyard (14:66–70).

9.5.1 The Women's Service

Females make surprising cameo appearances in the narrative, where they often seem to be superior to the Twelve in their service. When Simon's mother-in-law is cured of her fever, she begins to serve them (1:29–31). The audience would likely associate service with that of the angels who "served" Jesus when he was in the wilderness (1:13). Service is the fundamental characteristic of greatness (10:43). Jesus is the model of service as the one who "did not come to be served, but to serve, and to give his life as a ransom for many" (10:45). Though the disciples are to be known for service, the Twelve are never the subject of the verb in Mark. It is the women who followed Jesus from Galilee to the cross who are identified as serving him (15:40–41). Women will come to the tomb to offer him what they think will be their last service by anointing his dead body with spices (16:1).

9.5.2 The Women's Faith and Humility

A woman with an incurable uterine hemorrhage exhibits extraordinary faith in Jesus. She puts her faith in action by covertly touching Jesus' garment in the full expectation that she will be healed from her plague (5:25–34). A Syrophoenician Greek woman falls at Jesus' feet and shamelessly begs him to heal her demonized daughter. She then exhibits extraordinary humility in readily accepting the status of a dog to receive just a little crumb of his healing power (7:24–30). Both of these women are driven by absolute desperation that pushes them to persist in overcoming obstacles. Both would be classified as proscribed persons from the perspective of rigorous Jewish legalism.[193] Jesus extends grace and healing to both women because of their faith and humility. By contrast, the disciples are reproached by Jesus for their lack of faith (4:40) and never exhibit humility.

9.5.3 The Women's Devotion

The woman who anointed Jesus in the house of Simon the leper meets only with derision from the disciples (14:3–9). She broke an alabaster jar containing nard and poured the precious ointment on Jesus' head. The onlookers peg its value at three hundred denarii, which is more than enough to provide a meal for over five thousand people (6:37) and almost a year's wages for a day laborer (Matt 20:4, 10), and they complain bitterly about the waste of something so costly. "They rebuked her harshly" (14:5), because they fail to grasp the significance of her extravagant

193. The tractate on the menstruant in the *Mishnah* is entitled *Niddah*, which means "banished," because the impurity was transmissible to others. Josephus (*J.W.* 5.5.6 §227; *Ant.* 3.11.1 §261; *Ag. Ap.* 2.8 §103) reports that women in their menstrual period were banned from entering the temple. This woman's perpetual bleeding was abnormal and cut her off from normal social intercourse. She had suffered twelve years and had become destitute in her vain search for a cure from physicians. Mark describes the woman from Tyre as a Greek and a Syrophoenician (7:26). Rhoads, "Jesus and the Syrophoenician Woman in Mark," 352–53, describes this repetition as a two-step progression in which the first step expresses a generality, while the second step, the repetition, gives more specific detail and usually contains a crucial element. It conveys that she is a Gentile pagan who hails from a city that the Old Testament deems to be a wealthy and godless oppressor of Israel (see Isa 23; Jer 47:4; Ezek 26–28; Joel 3:4; Amos 1:9; Zech 9:2). Observant Jews in the first century (John 18:28; Acts 10:28) shared without question the prejudice that Gentiles defile by touch like a person with a flux.

gesture of devotion. Like the widow who gave her last penny to the temple coffers (12:41–44), this woman freely gives, out of her devotion to Jesus, all that is in her power to give. Malbon comments,

> Both the women give money, although the amounts differ greatly: two lepta (about a penny) and more than three hundred denarii (about a year's wages for a laborer). But money is only their literal gift. Their symbolic gift is, for the anointing woman, acknowledgment of Jesus' approaching death—that is, the gift of his life, and, for the poor widow, the gift of her whole life as exemplary of Jesus.[194]

Jesus intercedes on her behalf by saying that she has "wrought a good work on me" (KJV)[195] and interprets her action as anointing him for burial in advance of his impending death (14:6–8). Mark contains no mention of Jesus' body being anointed for burial after his death in the rush to take him down from the cross before the onset of the Sabbath. This anointing before his death would have to suffice. Her lavish devotion stands out because it is followed by the story of a false disciple, Judas, who sells out his master to those scheming to put him to death (14:1–2, 10–11). Jesus says that she will be remembered always for her act of love wherever the gospel is preached throughout the world (14:9). Judas, who ironically was one of the Twelve chosen by Jesus to be sent out to preach, will be remembered always for his act of treachery.

9.5.4 Service, Faith, and Devotion at the Cross and at the Tomb

The women seem to have taken over the role of the Twelve at the cross and the tomb. They also followed Jesus from Galilee to Jerusalem and were in the practice of ministering to him (15:40–41). They also followed him to the cross and watched from afar (15:40). Mark identifies them as Mary Magdalene, Mary the mother of James the younger and of Joseph, and Salome. Mark identifies Mary Magdalene and Mary the mother of Joseph as observing where Jesus was buried in a rush to get the task done before the commencement of the Sabbath (15:47). Mark identifies Mary Magdalene, Mary the mother of James, and Salome again as those who buy spices and come to the tomb seeking to carry out one last service to Jesus by anointing his body (16:1). The women are named three times!

Hurtado draws attention to the normal practice in the Roman era of not naming women in the public sphere out of a sense of respect for them, not because of some imagined misogyny. He reminds us that it is unprecedented to give prominence to women as observers at the cross and the burial, and as the ones who discover the

194. Malbon, "'Reflected Christology,'" 140.

195. David Daube, *The New Testament and Rabbinic Judaism* (New York: Arno, 1973; orig. 1956), 315, suggests that the phrase "good work" has a technical sense that connects to a rabbinic catalogue of good works: almsgiving, putting up strangers, visiting the sick, and burying the dead.

great stone rolled away and see the place where he had been laid in the tomb.[196] They are the first to hear of Jesus' resurrection from the young man (an angel) who explains why the tomb is empty. When they overcome their awed bewilderment over this stupefying miracle, they are the first to proclaim the message of the resurrection to the disciples (16:5, 8), although not in the plotted narrative of Mark.[197]

9.6 Hope for the Followers of Jesus

The disciples' failures were a historical reality that could not be whitewashed, and Mark had no intention of doing so. Their liability to error serves a theological purpose in Mark's narrative. Their fallibility not only reveals that one does not become a mature disciple in one year; it also reveals that even those closest to Jesus and chosen by him were part of universal human disobedience necessitating the cross and Jesus' representative expiatory death.[198] Mark expresses this truth through narrative; Paul, through prose: "For all have sinned and fall short of the glory of God, and all are justified freely by his grace through the redemption that came by Christ Jesus. God presented Christ as a sacrifice of atonement, through the shedding of his blood—to be received by faith" (Rom 3:23–25a).

The disciples' failures also show that no one can be a faithful disciple by dint of his or her own strength. What is impossible for humans, however, is possible for God (10:26–27). They are saved by God's grace, and Mark provides hopeful signs of the disciples' restoration. Jesus' teaching on his own suffering, death, and resurrection and on the requirements of discipleship in 8:27–10:45, which reveals the disciples' spiritual sightlessness, is set off by the technique of *inclusio*.[199] Jesus gives sight to a blind man in Bethsaida (8:22–26) and to a blind man, Bartimaeus, in Jericho (10:46–52). He therefore opens eyes of blind men at the beginning and at the end of this section, and he attempts to open the spiritual eyes of the disciples throughout this section.[200] Mark intends to record "real events" that are "not mere literary playthings,"[201] but Mark has arranged the presentation of his material to achieve his theological purposes.

One of the striking features of the healing of the blind man in Bethsaida, which has no parallel in Matthew or Luke, is that it occurs in two stages. After Jesus spits on the man's eyes and put his hands on him, he asked if he sees anything. The man responds that he sees people but they look like trees walking around. Jesus again puts his hands on the man's eyes, "Then his eyes were opened, his sight was restored,

196. Hurtado, "The Women, the Tomb, and the Climax of Mark," 430.

197. See §14.3.2.2.

198. Hengel, *Studies*, 35

199. Achtemeier, "'And He Followed Him,'" 115.

200. Walter Wink, "The Education of the Apostles," 278, contends, Mark "does not believe the disciples are basically in good shape, needing just a strong dose of Jesus' teaching to get them ready for their tasks. On the contrary, Mark, apparently on the authority of Jesus himself, regards the disciples as blind men who are incapable of understanding either who Jesus is or what he is about. No amount of learning can correct this. They are blind, and they must be healed. Faith for Mark is not then the opposite of doubt. It is blindness healed. It is having one's sight restored."

201. Bockmuehl, *Simon Peter*, 136.

and he saw everything clearly" (8:23–25). The partial vision of the man can parallel the blurred vision of the disciples who do not yet see clearly who Jesus is, even when they identify him as the Messiah, because they want to force their view of his identity into old pigeonholes and do not yet see that he must die. The second touch that will open the disciples' eyes to see things clearly is not narrated in Mark. It will begin when they go back to Galilee and experience the presence of the risen Christ (14:28; 16:7). This healing expresses hope that just as the blind man recovered his sight, the disciples will have their spiritual blindness removed.[202] Gaining full insight into Jesus' identity and role demands a second touch, so to speak.[203]

The incident of restoring the sight of Bartimaeus resembles a call narrative, which seems to come late in the narrative.[204] He has spiritual insight in identifying Jesus as the son of David when he cries for mercy. After his healing, Jesus announces that his faith has healed him, and he follows after Jesus on the way. Geddert comments that his healing "does not symbolize what *has happened* to the disciples on this journey. It symbolizes rather what *is possible* for disciples, what must yet happen."[205] The disciples cannot understand Jesus and the way of the cross prior to the resurrection.[206] Therefore, one can only expect them to fail until Christ's death and resurrection of Christ, which unleashes a new power in their lives. Only then could they see clearly to begin to piece together what everything meant. Brown offers,

> Mark is offering a pedagogy of hope based on the initial failure of the most famous followers of Jesus and a second chance for them. He may well have in mind readers who also failed initially or became discouraged by the thought of the cross. He is issuing parenetic warnings against the danger of being scandalized or falling away from faith and against overconfidence.[207]

The portrayal of the men and women in the gospel who are all fallible communicates "clearly and powerfully to the reader the twofold message: anyone can be a follower, no one finds it easy."[208]

202. Taylor, *Mark*, 370; Earl S. Johnson, "Mark VIII. 22–26: The Blind Man from Bethsaida," *NTS* 25 (1979): 383.

203. Marshall, *Faith as a Theme*, 140.

204. Achtemeier, "'And He Followed Him,'" 132; Steinhauser, "The Form of the Bartimaeus Narrative," 583–95; Maarten J. J. Menken, "The Call of Blind Bartimaeus (Mark 10:46–52)," *HvTSt* 61 (2005): 273–90.

205. Geddert, *Mark*, 418.

206. Cilliers Breytenbach, *Nachfolge und Zukunftserwartung nach Markus: Eine methodenkritische Studie* (ATANT 71; Zürich: Theologischer Verlag, 1984), 335–38.

207. Brown, *Death*, 1:141.

208. Malbon, *Company*, 67.

Chapter 10

The Requirements, Costs, and Rewards of Discipleship

Bibliography

Barton, Stephen C. *Discipleship and Family Ties in Mark and Matthew.* SNTSMS 80. Cambridge: Cambridge University Press, 1994. **Bayer, Hans F.** *A Theology of Mark: The Dynamic between Christology and Authentic Discipleship.* Explorations in Biblical Theology. Phillipsburg, NJ: Presbyterian & Reformed, 2012. **Best, Ernest.** "Discipleship in Mark 8.22–10.52." *SJT* 23 (1970) 323–37. Idem. *Following Jesus: Discipleship in the Gospel of Mark.* JSNTSup 4. Sheffield: JSOT, 1981. Idem. *Disciples and Discipleship: Studies in the Gospel of Mark.* Edinburgh: T&T Clark, 1986. **Black, C. Clifton.** *The Disciples according to Mark: Markan Redaction in Current Debate.* JSNTSup 27. Sheffield: JSOT, 1989. **Borrell, Agustí.** *The Good News of Peter's Denial: A Narrative and Rhetorical Reading of Mark 14:54.66–72.* Trans. Sean Conlon. International Studies in Formative Christianity and Judaism. Atlanta: Scholars Press, 1998. **Breytenbach, Cilliers.** *Nachfolge und Zukunftserwartung nach Markus: Eine methodenkritische Studie.* ATANT 71. Zürich: Theologischer Verlag, 1984. **Donahue, John R.** *The Theology and Setting of Discipleship in the Gospel of Mark.* Milwaukee: Marquette University Press, 1983. **Fleddermann, Harry.** "A Warning about the Scribes (Mark 12:37b–40)." *CBQ* 44 (1982): 52–67. **Freyne, Seán.** *The Twelve: Disciples and Apostles: A Study in the Theology of the First Three Gospels.* London: Sheed and Ward, 1968. **Hawkin, David J.** "The Incomprehension of the Disciples in the Marcan Redaction." *JBL* 91 (1972): 491–500. **Hays, Richard B.** *The Moral Vision of the New Testament.* San Francisco: Harper Collins, 1996. **Henderson, Suzanne Watts.** *Christology and Discipleship in the Gospel of Mark.* SNTMS 135. Cambridge: Cambridge University Press, 2006. **Hurtado, Larry W.** "Following Jesus in the Gospel of Mark—and Beyond." Pp. 9–29 in *Patterns of Discipleship in the New Testament.* Ed. Richard N. Longenecker. Grand Rapids: Eerdmans, 1996. **Keerankeri, George.** *The Love Commandment in Mark: An Exegetico-Theological Study of Mark 12,28–34.* AnBib 150. Rome: Pontifical Biblical Institute, 2003. **Kertelge, Karl.** "Jüngerschaft und Nachfolge: Grundlegung von Kirche nach Markus." Pp. 151–65 in *Der Evangelist als Theologe: Studien zum Markusevangelium.* Ed. Thomas Söding. SBS 163. Stuttgart: Katholisches Bibelwerk, 1995. **Lee-Pollard, Dorothy A.** "Powerlessness as Power: A Key Emphasis in Mark." *SJT* 40 (1987): 173–88. **Malbon, Elizabeth Struthers.**

"Fallible Followers: Women and Men in the Gospel of Mark." *Semeia* 28 (1983): 29–48. Idem. "Texts and Contexts: Interpreting the Disciples in Mark." *Semeia* 62 (1993): 81–102. **Marshall, Christopher D.** *Faith as a Theme in Mark's Narrative.* SNTSMS 64. Cambridge: Cambridge University Press, 1989. **Matera, Frank J.** *What Are They Saying about Mark?* New York/Mahwah, NJ: Paulist, 1987. Idem. "The Incomprehension of the Disciples and Peter's Confession (Mark 6,14–8,30)." *Bib* 70 (1989): 153–72. **Menken, Maarten J. J.** "The Call of Blind Bartimaeus (Mark 10:46–52)." *HvTSt* 61 (2005): 273–90. **Meye, Robert P.** *Jesus and the Twelve: Discipleship and Revelation in Mark's Gospel.* Grand Rapids: Eerdmans, 1968. **Miller, Susan.** *Women in Mark's Gospel.* JSNTSup259. London/New York: T&T Clark, 2004. **Mingo Kaminouchi, Alberto de.** *"But It Is Not So Among You": Echoes of Power in Mark 10.32–45.* JSNTSup 249. London: T&T Clark, 2003. **Moloney, Francis J.** "The Vocation of the Disciples in the Gospel of Mark." *Salesianum* 43 (1981): 487–516. **Perrin, Norman.** *Rediscovering the Teaching of Jesus.* New York: Harper & Row, 1967. **Santos, Narry F.** *Slave of All: The Paradox of Authority and Servanthood in the Gospel of Mark.* JSNTSup 237. London/New York: Sheffield Academic, 2003. **Schweizer, Eduard.** "The Portrayal of the Life of Faith in the Gospel of Mark." *Int* 32 (1978): 387–99. **Shiner, Whitney Taylor.** *Follow Me! Disciples in Markan Rhetoric.* SBLDS 145. Atlanta: Scholars Press, 1995. **Söding, Thomas.** "Leben nach dem Evangelium: Konturen markinischer Ethik." Pp. 167–95 in *Der Evangelist als Theologe: Studien zum Markusevangelium.* Ed. Thomas Söding. SBS 163. Stuttgart: Katholisches Bibelwerk, 1995. **Tannehill, Robert C.** "The Disciples in Mark: The Function of a Narrative Role." *JR* 57 (1977): 386–405. **Tolbert, Mary Ann.** *Sowing the Gospel: Mark's World in Literary-Historical Perspective.* Minneapolis: Fortress, 1989. **Wiarda, Timothy.** *Peter in the Gospels: Pattern, Personality and Relationship.* WUNT 2/127. Tübingen: Mohr Siebeck, 2000. **Williams, Joel F.** *Other Followers of Jesus: Minor Characters as Major Figures in Mark's Gospel.* JSNTSup 102. Sheffield: JSOT, 1994.

10.1 UNCONDITIONAL OBEDIENCE TO JESUS

Mark's portrayal of discipleship is told in a narrative, and converting narrative into an outline of requirements of discipleship cannot help but distort the picture in some measure. Nevertheless, it is useful to organize elements of what Mark's Jesus requires of his disciples into a more systematic listing. Throughout the narrative there are intimations that others, both men and women, become followers of Jesus and that there will come a time when "the distinction between the Twelve and other disciples will no longer be apparent."[1] What is required of the disciples in the narrative will be required of all those in his audience who seek to follow Jesus.

The first call to discipleship recorded in the gospel comes as a seemingly

1. Miller, *Women in Mark's Gospel*, 48.

unreasonable and scandalous claim on the lives of the brothers, Simon and Andrew, and James and John (1:16–20). Their immediate response to Jesus' call to follow him reveals that disciples are expected to accept unconditionally Jesus' demand for absolute obedience. The narrative that follows conveys that discipleship is not part-time volunteer work on one's own terms or at one's convenience. To follow Jesus means far more than trailing after him as he stuns the crowds with miracle after miracle; it means "imitating the pattern of his life."[2] He alone embodies the true model of what discipleship entails, and following him means following his example and obeying all his commands, especially his command to deny oneself and accept the shame of the cross (8:34).

10.2 Leaving Everything Behind

Those who are called must be ready to leave the old sources of their identity and security behind to follow him. Jesus does not call persons to become mendicants. Henderson cites the comments of Tertullian, "None of those whom the Lord chose said to him, 'I have no means to live'" (*Idol.* 12).[3] Jesus does call persons to be detached from anything they rely on for their earthly security that prevents them from depending entirely on God.

In the narrative, Simon and Andrew turn from their nets (1:18); James and John turn from their father and their boat (1:20). Levi abandons his post as a tax collector (2:14). The rich man who seeks the key to eternal life is told that he must give up his wealth for the service of the poor, and then, and only then, can he follow Jesus (10:21–22). This demand creates a shockwave among the disciples, and Peter speaks for all of them in announcing, "We have left everything to follow you!" (10:28). Jesus' response reveals that such sacrifices will receive a reward but not because he regards their sacrifice as a work of supererogation. Schweizer perceptively observes that "giving up of one's possessions is not a prerequisite for discipleship. It is the consequence of discipleship."[4]

Discipleship entails unreserved allegiance that holds nothing back. That is why Jesus does not offer a less rigorous category of auxiliary discipleship that promises the reward of eternal life while allowing one to continue the pursuit of money and success. Moloney notes that the first disciples abandon what marked them as a success in the eyes of their contemporary peer group: "tools of the trade (nets and boats), servants: the sign of their success, in having other men 'under their control.'"[5] Marshall remarks, "they dispossess themselves of all that gives them control or power over their own lives and over the lives of others."[6] What formerly

2. Donahue, *The Theology and Setting of Discipleship*, 15, citing the Venerable Bede.

3. Henderson, *Christology*, 63.

4. Schweizer, *Mark*, 212.

5. Moloney, "The Vocation of the Disciples in the Gospel of Mark," 502.

6. Marshall, *Faith as a Theme*, 138.

had supreme value suddenly fades next to the supreme worth of following the one who proclaims the kingdom of God.[7]

The account of the healing of blind Bartimaeus reveals that leaving everything to follow Jesus is expected of all, the poor as well as the rich. When Bartimaeus has his sight restored by Jesus, he promptly tosses aside his cloak, probably his most valuable and certainly his most essential possession, to follow him (10:50). As a blind beggar, he is unquestionably poor, and he may have laid out his cloak in front of him to collect the alms that passersby might toss to him. If he uses the cloak to receive alms, leaving it behind signifies both the abandonment of his occupation, which the first disciples did, and the abandonment of his possessions, wretched and meager as they might be.[8]

To follow Jesus requires forsaking any attachment to and reliance on possessions because they pose an obstacle to entering the kingdom of God. The interpretation of the parable of the Sower identifies the thorns that choked the plants as "the deceitfulness of wealth and the desires for other things" (4:7, 19). Jesus' diagnosis was that the rich man, who came to him seeking the key to inheriting eternal life, lacked one thing and invited him to sell everything he had and give it to the poor (10:21). When he balks at this demand, Jesus comments that it is easier for a camel to go through the eye of a needle than for a rich man to enter the kingdom of God (10:24–25).

It is important to note that Jesus does not try to make the rich man feel guilty for his wealth. Instead, he tries to make him feel responsibility to the poor. The man's question to Jesus is totally self-centered, "What must *I* do to inherit eternal life?" (10:17). Jesus' command to "sell everything you have and give to the poor" (10:21) is not simply concerned about the redistribution of goods. It requires him to turn the focus of his life outward to others.

There are three assumptions behind this command. First, humans are interdependent. Those with power and wealth cannot receive eternal life from God if they regard others as belonging to the expendable class whose sole purpose in life is to serve the needs of the powerful. Second, Jesus assumes that everyone could have the necessities of life if others did not hoard their wealth or exploit others. Third, material wealth is something that should be fluid. The interconnectivity of life in God's kingdom means that should the man who has given away his wealth to help the poor ever be in need himself, there would be those who would help him. The saying that God helps those who help themselves is not true, particularly if they help themselves to too much. God helps those who help others.

The rich man's quest is prompted by his fear of death. He wants assurance that he will be safe in the life to come. Bolt writes:

7. Compare Phil 3:4–11 for a similar evaluation of the comparative value of "know[ing] Christ—yes, to know the power of his resurrection and participation in his sufferings, becoming like him in his death," versus the gain one might achieve that is prized by the world's standards.

8. Menken, "The Call of Blind Bartimaeus," 277–78.

> The fear of death is the most basic of all fears. It introduces a profound anxiety into human existence. This existential anxiety provokes us to undertake a quest for security. Lucretius [*de rerum natura*] echoes what we find in the Scriptures, that human beings seek after greatness, status, importance, possessions, friendship, pleasure—all in the vain attempt to bring some security to an existence that is constantly undermined by the grave.[9]

Security cannot be found in the shaky structures of this world that breed false aspirations and a false religion that imagines that God blesses selfish materialism and avarice. These things must be left behind. Obedience to God's will requires breaking with the mores and standards that the world judges to be the marks of success or failure. One cannot balance accommodation to the world's values with devoted service to God.

Mark's gospel provides numerous examples of those who will not enter into the kingdom of God because of their greed. If the Gerasenes drive Jesus away from their region because they imagine that he will cause the revenues from the pig business to plunge, then they reveal themselves to be more concerned about profits than the deliverance of demonized people (5:11–17). Greedy sons, abetted by the casuistry of the teachers of the law and Pharisees, maneuver around the law to avoid helping their parents financially while pretending to be devout (7:10–13). Greedy teachers of the law "devour widows' houses" while making a show of piety with long prayers (12:40).[10]

Mark also offers positive examples of persons (women) who give sacrificially. Jesus contrasts these teachers of the law and the well-heeled contributors to the temple with a poor widow (12:41–44). The wealthier donors tossed in large sums into the temple treasury, probably one of thirteen shofar-chests (shaped like a trumpet bell) that stood around the Court of the Women in the sanctuary. Presumably, they gave what they could spare and did so ostentatiously, as their larger gifts made a loud clang. The widow is described as a "poor widow," and she put in two trifling coins. Jesus praises her gift because the rich stayed rich after donating their money. The widow gave "all she had to live on." The rich gave a proportion out of their wealth; she gave out of her destitution, holding nothing back. She foreshadows the woman who held nothing back and extravagantly anoints Jesus' head with expensive perfume made of pure nard that was calculated to be worth over three hundred denarii, approximately a year's wages (14:3–9). Those who leave everything behind or give up everything represent what it means to love God with all one's strength (12:30).

9. Bolt, *The Cross*, 41–42.

10. Widows epitomize the helpless in the Old Testament, and abusing them is harshly condemned (Exod 22:21–23; Deut 10:17–18; 24:17; Isa 1:17, 23; 10:1–4; Ezek 22:7).

10.3 POTENTIALLY SEVERING FAMILY TIES

For James and John to leave their father so abruptly to follow Jesus not only marked a profound change in their lives, but the rupture would have transgressed accepted cultural values that cherished belonging to a family and clan and the identity that it brings.[11] One's family of birth was primarily devoted to preserving its genealogical line, its wealth, and its honor (see Sir 26:19–21). Jesus insists that the call of God surpasses the call of family, and that discipleship in the kingdom of God outweighs any familial obligations that would obstruct obedience to that calling. Jesus' own family is displeased with what he is doing, thinking him mad (3:21, 31–35), and Mark will report that his hometown synagogue in Nazareth will be both unresponsive to his teaching and dismissive of him (6:1–6). After the apathetic response in Nazareth, Jesus states a prophet is without honor in his own country, among his relatives, or in his own house (6:4).

When Jesus' mother and brothers come to seize him forcibly, he does not welcome them warmly.[12] They are left to cool their heels outside the crowded house. They literally have become "outsiders" who oppose the will of God by wanting to constrain his ministry. Jesus dissociates himself from them in announcing to the gathering, "Here are my mother and my brothers! Whoever does God's will is my brother and sister and mother" (3:34–35). While becoming Jesus' disciple may cause the fabric of the family to rip, this pronouncement reveals that Jesus does not call people to be completely bereft of family. Disciples become a part of a greater family of faith whose first allegiance is to do the will of God.[13] He declares that those who may have left "home or brothers or sisters or mother or father or children or fields for me and the gospel" will receive "a hundred times as much" (homes, brothers, sisters, mothers, children and fields) in this present age (10:28–30). Father is not mentioned because God remains the one Father (see 8:38; 11:25; 13:32; 14:36; cf. Matt 23:9) and cannot be supplanted. "Biological family relationships are not based on choice, but becoming a member of the family of God is. The only membership requirement in this new messianic family is obeying God, whose commands are defined by what Jesus taught and did."[14]

11. See Exod 20:12; Deut 5:16; Prov 23:22–25; Tob 5:1; Sir 3:1–16, where it is declared in the last verse, "Whoever forsakes a father is like a blasphemer, and whoever angers a mother is cursed by the Lord."

12. Lane, *Mark*, 139, thinks Jesus' family is concerned for his welfare since he has not eaten (3:20). The verb translated "to take charge" elsewhere in Mark means "to seize" (6:17; 12:12; 14:1, 44, 46, 49, 51), and would suggest that they want to bring a complete halt to his ministry, not to bring him some chicken soup. Jesus has feasted with Levi (2:15), so his ministry does not force him to fast, but there are times when the press of the crowd prevents him from eating (6:31). Myers, *Binding*, 167–68, suggests that they are worried that Jesus might be in danger. The Pharisees and Herodians indeed have plotted together on how to destroy him (3:6), but how could his family know what was planned in secret?

The intercalation of this incident with the teachers of the law who come from Jerusalem to malign his reputation (3:22–30) connects the two groups converging on Jesus and suggests that Jesus' family's arrival should be perceived as negative in intent. Jesus' family, for whatever reason, thinks he is out of his mind (3:21), and the teachers of the law claim he has an evil spirit (3:30). Both his family and the teachers of the law want to put him out of commission, but he will not be turned away from his commission from God, and he stymies both of their missions.

13. Stephen C. Barton, *Discipleship and Family Ties in Mark and Matthew* (SNTSMS 80; Cambridge: Cambridge University Press, 1994), 85.

14. Garland, *Mark*, 140–41.

Situations therefore might arise when disciples are faced with the choice between allegiance to family and allegiance to God. Fidelity to God must always take primacy. This requirement does not mean that Jesus intends to destroy the biological family. He sends the healed Gerasene demoniac, who had been living alone in the tombs, back to his family (5:18–19). He does not mention leaving spouses for him and the sake of the gospel (10:29). He condemns divorce for any reason as a violation of God's intention for marriage (10:2–12). He also condemns those who might try to sidestep their financial responsibilities to their parents by using the legal casuistry of Corban that declared what they could use to help them as forbidden because it was devoted to God (7:6–13). The command to honor father and mother remains valid, but because greater loyalty is to be given to God as Father and to his Son rather than to an earthly father, estrangement in families may arise. Some disciples tragically will be betrayed and handed over to death by their most intimate family members (13:12). The language echoes Mic 7:6, "For a son dishonors his father, a daughter rises up against her mother, a daughter-in-law against her mother-in-law—a man's enemies are the members of his own household."

10.4 FOLLOWING ON THE WAY WITH JESUS

The command to "follow me" (1:17, 20; 2:14; 8:34; 10:21) implies that Jesus is on the move, and Mark shows him as an itinerant who wandered from place to place. Jesus was known even by his opponents as someone who taught "the way of God" (12:14). He did not set up headquarters in a fixed school building where disciples could come and study with him. They had to learn the way of God while on the way with him. The original disciples had to follow him on the way (8:27; 9:33, 34; 10:17, 32). Discipleship to Jesus is not a sedentary, scholastic enterprise. Best writes,

> The call is not one to accept a certain system of teaching, live by it, continue faithfully to interpret it and pass it on, which was in essence the call of a rabbi to his disciples; nor is it a call to accept a philosophical position which will express itself in a certain type of behaviour, as in Stoicism; nor is it the call to devote life to the alleviation of suffering for others; nor is it the call to pass through certain rites as in the Mysteries so as to become an initiate of the God, his companion—the carrying of the cross is no rite! It is a call to fall in behind Jesus and go with him.[15]

Discipleship, then, is not an idle academic exercise, and learning the way of God does not come from walking around in one's own thoughts. It requires imitating what they see in the model of Jesus' life so that disciples might continue his practices, exercise his authority, and share his destiny.

15. Ernest Best, "Discipleship in Mark 8.22–10.52," *SJT* 23 (1970): 329.

10.5 Denying Oneself/Taking Up a Cross/ Losing One's Life

The sequence of Peter's confession that Jesus is the Christ followed by Jesus' rebuke and demand that all those who want to be his disciple must deny themselves and take up a cross and follow him in 8:27–9:1 reveals that discipleship involves more than miming doctrinally correct confessions. Lambrecht writes that Jesus' "true nature cannot be learned from notions or titles, but it is existentially experienced in the following of Jesus, more concretely, in the carrying of the cross and in self-denial."[16] Discipleship manifests itself in a life that is to be lived, not in words that are merely spoken.

10.5.1 Denying Oneself

On the way to Jerusalem and the cross, Jesus reveals that to be his disciple, followers must deny themselves and take up a cross and be willing to lose their lives for his sake and for the sake of the gospel (8:34–35). Schweizer clarifies for a modern audience what "denying oneself" means. It is "not the same as repressing everything which would make us happy, and taking up one's cross is not the same as bearing patiently all kinds of aches and problems."[17] It is not denying something to oneself but denying the self.[18] Self-denial is not to become an end in itself. The goal is to serve God obediently, which requires surrendering the direction of one's life to God. "Those who deny themselves have learned to say, 'Not my will but thine be done.' "[19] It keeps in check the human proclivity to put self at the center of the universe, which expresses itself in self-absorption, self-admiration, self-pity, self-indulgence, self-reliance, self-seeking, self-assertion, and selfishness.

Jesus uses forceful hyperbole to describe the spiritual self-discipline expected of disciples. If the hand, foot, or eye causes one to sin, it is better to cut it off or pluck it out and be maimed than to go to hell where the fire never goes out (9:43–48).[20] These images are associated with sexual sins, but Marcus is correct that they should not be limited to them: "the *hand* is the instrument for the commission of sin, the *foot* is the means of transport to the place of its commission, and the *eye* is the means by which the temptation to commit it enters in."[21] The eye is the cause of covetousness, stinginess, and jealousy.[22] The point is that God's reign "lays claim to the whole of existence,"[23] and disciples cannot be apathetic about the sin in their lives and assume that it would not jeopardize their salvation.

16. Jan Lambrecht, "The Christology of Mark," *BTB* 3 (1973): 273.

17. Schweizer, "The Portrayal of the Life of Faith in Mark," 392.

18. Hans Bayer, *Theology*, 102, points out that self-chastisement and self-abasement can be driven by egocentrism.

19. Garland, *Mark*, 327.

20. Mark uses the word *gehenna* (trans. "hell"), which is the Greek rendering of the Aramaic term that means the "valley of Hinnom." It refers to the valley south of Jerusalem that was used in ancient times as a crematorium where children were sacrificed to the gods of Canaan (2 Kgs 16:3; 21:6; 23:10; Jer 7:31; 32:35). It later became a refuse dump where fires were kept continually burning. The name became associated with the place of never-ending, fiery punishment. According to *b. 'Erub.* 19a, Gehenna has seven names: "Netherworld" (*Sheol*; Jonah 2:2 [2:3]); "Destruction" (Ps 88:11 12.); "Pit" (of destruction; Ps 16:10); "Tumultuous Pit" (Ps 16:10); "Miry Clay" (Ps 40:2–3.); "Shadow of Death" (Ps 18:9–10.); and "Underworld." According to *1 En.* 26:2, "this accursed valley is for those who are accursed forever."

21. Marcus, *Mark 8–16*, 697.

22. Garland, *Mark*, 369 n. 4.

23. Marshall, *Faith as a Theme*, 137.

10.5.2 Taking up a Cross

Jesus also demands that every disciple must take up a cross and follow him (8:34).[24] This would have been startling and grisly imagery in the first century when the cross had not been bestowed with a halo as "the old rugged cross" or its horror minimized by becoming an item of jewelry.[25] Green contends that the Romans chose crucifixion as their preferred method of executing brigands and agitators because "executed publicly, situated at a major crossroads or on a well-trafficked artery, devoid of clothing, left to be eaten by birds and beasts, victims of crucifixion were subject to optimal, unmitigated, vicious ridicule."[26] Plutarch uses the image negatively: "Every evildoer carries his own cross" (*Sera* 554a). Seneca (*Ep.* 101.14) writes to Lucilius:

> Can anyone be found who would prefer wasting away in pain, dying limb by limb, or letting out his life drop by drop, rather than expiring once for all? Can any man be found willing to be fastened to the accursed tree, long sickly, already deformed, swelling with ugly tumours on chest and shoulders, and draw the breath of life amid long-drawn-out agony? I think he would have many excuses for dying even before mounting the cross!

Cook notes that "Go to the cross" was a bitter taunt that was equivalent to "go to hell."[27]

Bearing one's cross requires a sustained relationship with Jesus.[28] It entails accepting humiliation, dishonor, public indignities, and dehumanizing suffering.[29] Mark, however, does not perceive carrying a cross to be simply a way of death but a way of life for the Christian who is committed to the kingdom of God and the way of Jesus (see Rom 6:6; Gal 2:20). As Manson writes, disciples "must steel themselves along with their master to endure hardships and privations, hatred and contempt, wounds and death, in the cause."[30]

10.5.3 Losing One's Life

Why would one voluntarily follow Jesus with the prospect of dying such a degrading death? The reasons are given in 8:34–38. Trying to save one's life in this life and gain "the height of human ambition and achievement"[31] has the paradoxical effect

24. Mark's audience would have interpreted this demand in light of Jesus' crucifixion (see 1 Cor 1:17–18; Gal 6:14; Phil 2:8; Col 1:20; 2:14; Heb 12:2; 1 Pet 2:24).

25. Evans, *Mark 8:27–16:20*, 25, notes, "In rabbinic parlance, a disciple is urged to take up the yoke of the Torah or the yoke of the commandments (e.g., *m. 'Abot* 3:5; *m. Ber.* 2:2), never to take up the cross." David W. Chapman, *Ancient Jewish and Christian Perceptions of Crucifixion* (WUNT 2/244; Tübingen: Mohr Siebeck, 2008), 217–19, notes that in ancient Judaism the shame and horror of crucifixion were associated with punishment for brigandage, magic, or blasphemy, but it was also associated with the death of the innocent martyr.

26. Joel B. Green, "Crucifixion," in *The Cambridge Companion to Jesus* (ed. Markus Bockmuehl; Cambridge: Cambridge University Press, 2001), 91.

27. Cook, *Roman Attitudes*, 71.

28. Taylor, *Mark*, 381.

29. Normally, the condemned person carried the cross bar (*patibulum*) to the sight of crucifixion (see Plautus, *Carbonaria frag.* 2; Plutarch, *Sera* 9.554). Cicero (*Rab. Post.* 5.16) mentions an executioner's hook used to drag the condemned to the place of execution.

30. Manson, "Realized Eschatology and the Messianic Secret," 217.

31. France, *Mark*, 341.

of causing one to lose one's very soul. Losing one's life for Christ and the gospel paradoxically results in experiencing what true life means and saving one's soul eternally. Nothing in this mortal life can ransom the soul (Ps 49:7–9). Disciples must be mindful of the coming judgment with the coming of the Son of Man. Those who are ashamed of Christ and disown him in this world will be shamed and disowned before the heavenly court in the age to come. One has two options: to choose to risk death in this life at the hands of the henchmen of earthly kingdoms who would coerce one to deny one's faith in Christ, which brings eternal life in the age to come in God's kingdom, or to choose to cave-in to the earthly kingdoms in this life, which will result in eternal death.[32]

These stark directives bring to light that following Jesus is unlikely to lead down a path to success as the world defines it. It is more apt to lead instead to persecution and possible execution. Persecution, from Mark's perspective, is normative for Christians. To proclaim in Mark's Roman world a gospel that acclaims another king and an alternative kingdom "would inevitably lead to conflict with imperial power."[33] But Christian disciples can expect hostility whenever and wherever they bear witness in a world that is in rebellion against God. They can never cozy up to a world that is hostile to God.

Jesus tells Peter that those who leave everything to follow him will "receive a hundred times as much in this present age: homes, brothers, sisters, mothers, children and fields—along with persecutions—and in the age to come, eternal life" (10:30). In a list of blessings, "persecutions" seems out of place. It probably reflects Mark's context. Mark's original audience did not live in a paradise filled with bliss and joy. Since persecutions are mentioned with blessings, including "eternal life," Mark communicates that they are not an anomaly. Their ultimate gain comes with present pain. Suffering and hope in God paradoxically belong together (see Rom 5:3–5). In 9:49, Jesus warns enigmatically, "Everyone will be salted with fire," which is probably an allusion to persecution (see 1 Pet 1:6–7; 4:12–13, referring to a fiery ordeal; Rev 3:18).[34] Again, the point is made that the persecution should not be misinterpreted as some unfortunate irregularity but rather as par for the course. Since discipleship is forged in the furnace of confrontation with evil powers, it cannot help but be costly. France comments, "Their dedication to the service of their suffering Messiah is like that of a burnt offering, total and irrevocable."[35]

The account of Herod beheading John the Baptist (6:14–29) provides the first inkling in the narrative that discipleship may result in literally losing one's life.

32. Tia Park-Kim, in a private correspondence, suggests that Mark's narrative exhibits another reason why one would want to risk one's life to follow Jesus: because one has been a recipient of God's mercy through Jesus' healing power. The Gerasene demoniac wants to follow Jesus because of the mercy that he has been shown in being freed from the legion of demons (5:18–20). Bartimaeus begs Jesus for mercy and receives his sight, and he also wants to follow Jesus (10:46–52).

33. Bolt, *Jesus' Defeat of Death*, 50.

34. An early interpretation of this saying appears in a textual variant that connects it to Lev 2:13: "Season all your grain offerings with salt. Do not leave the salt of the covenant of your God out of your grain offerings; add salt to all your offerings." Since fire (Num 31:23; Mal 3:2; Matt 3:11; Luke 3:16) and salt (Ezek 16:4; 43:24) had a purifying power, it may be that this textual gloss associated fire with persecution that would purify the Christian community.

35. France, *Mark*, 383–84.

This account is mortised between the instructions Jesus gives to the Twelve before sending them out to preach repentance, to drive out demons, and to heal the sick on 6:6b–13 and the apostles' report about "all they had done and taught" when they returned in 6:30. The interlude with the sordid tale of Herod's birthday party excess that turns into the bloody butchery of John does more than fill a time gap between the commissioning of the disciples and their return.[36] On the one hand, John's fate foreshadows Jesus' fate.[37] On the other hand, as a Markan intercalation, it is a precursor of the danger that Jesus' disciples will face when they go on mission. As Tolbert comments, the beheading of John the Baptist, God's messenger, emphasizes "the lethal omnipresence of evil." She goes on to assert, "Tribulation and persecution in such a world as this are as inevitable as the rising of the sun (cf. 4:6)."[38] The gospel, Jesus declares, must be preached to all nations (13:10), but "when they become good news for others it will be bad news for them!"[39]

The account of Herod's ruthless violence, therefore, casts the shadow of death over the disciples' mission even though they meet with astounding success. In fact, it is the reports of the sensational success of Jesus' and the disciples' ministries that brings them to Herod's attention (6:12–16). This intercalation presages the suffering that unavoidably comes to God's messengers who are sent out to preach repentance to a hostile, sin-sick world. They can expect to be handed over to the local councils, to be flogged in the synagogues, and to stand before governors and kings (13:9). They can also expect to be betrayed by intimates (13:12). This ominous future explains why the primary teaching on discipleship in Mark occurs in the narrative section where Jesus announces three times his death and resurrection. Best explains that Mark arranges his narrative in this way because "the nature of discipleship becomes apparent only in the light of the cross, and not in light of Jesus' mighty acts."[40]

10.6 FAITH AND TRUST IN JESUS

The summary of Jesus' first preaching involves the double command to repent and to believe the good news (1:15). The divine initiative with the coming of the kingdom of God is to be met with the positive human response of repentance and faith. As the narrative develops, it becomes clear that the faith required is faith in Jesus. Marshall comments, "In Mark's story, the attachment of disciple to master is ... more than commitment to his teaching, and more even than fierce loyalty to his person (cf. 6:29); the bond is one of religious faith."[41] This bond of faith involves

36. So Taylor, *Mark*, 307; Cranfield, *Mark*, 206; Hooker, *Mark*, 158. What happens to John who goes out to preach (1:4) foreshadows what is going to happen to Jesus who goes out to preach (1:14). As John was "arrested" and "bound" (6:17), so Jesus will be "seized" (14:44, 46, 49) and "bound" (15:1).

37. Christian Wolff, "Zur Bedeutung Johannes des Täufers im Markusevangelium," *TLZ* 102 (1977): 857–65.

38. Tolbert, *Sowing the Gospel*, 198.

39. Blount, "Is the Joke on Us?" 27.

40. Best, *Following Jesus*, 13–14.

41. Marshall, *Faith as a Theme*, 139.

believing in Jesus as God's Son and Messiah, accepting the scandal of his destiny in the cross, and faithfully following him should it lead to persecution and death.

The disciples in Mark are not good models of this faith. Jesus chides them early on for their panic and paucity of faith when they are caught in a sea squall when he was asleep in the stern: "Why are you so afraid? Do you still have no faith?" (4:40). When Jesus calms the storm, the disciples ask, "Who is this? Even the wind and the waves obey him!" (4:41). Recognizing who Jesus is is connected to having faith, which is faith in him and his divine power and authority. The minor characters who appear in the healing miracles are the ones who display an intuitive awareness that God's power is working in and through him, and they exercise absolute trust in him by seeking healing from him.

Unlike John's gospel, people do not come to faith *after* Jesus performs a miracle. In Mark's accounts of healing, faith in Jesus *precedes* the miracle. Determined faith is a characteristic of those who seek some kind of healing from him, and it propels them to overcome whatever obstacles might prevent access to him (2:1 – 12; 5:21 – 43; 7:24 – 30; 10:46 – 52). With astounding persistence, the friends of a paralytic maneuver around a large crowd surrounding Jesus and break through the physical barrier of a roof to lower him in front of Jesus so that he can be healed. When Jesus saw their faith, he forgave the sins of the paralytic, and he was restored to health (2:1 – 12). The woman with an incurable flow of blood bridges the gulf of ritual taboos and dares to touch Jesus' garment for healing, and Jesus announces that her faith has saved her (5:25 – 34).[42]

Jairus beseeches Jesus to heal his gravely ill daughter and receives the bad news that his daughter has died as he and Jesus are on the way to his home. Despite this tragic news, Jesus urges him not to fear but only to believe (5:36). This exhortation reveals that faith is the opposite of fear (see 4:40). Jairus manages to muster enough faith that Jesus is right — his daughter is not dead but only sleeps — to proceed, and Jesus raises her back to life (5:22 – 23, 35 – 43). The Syrophoenician mother will not take "no" for an answer when she requests Jesus to cast out a demon from her daughter. Because of her humble faith, Jesus relents and the daughter is set free from the demon (7:24 – 30). The blind beggar Bartimaeus ignores the crowd's attempt to stifle his cries when he calls out to Jesus, as he is passing by, to have mercy on him. Jesus announces that his faith has made him well, when he says that he wants to see again (10:46 – 52).

In various ways, the faith these persons had that Jesus could and would deliver them from their various maladies required an unwavering doggedness. This persistent faith is vital because Jesus says that only those who persevere to the end will be saved (13:13). These persons were also desperate. Marshall concludes, "For in Mark, faith is the power of those without power, and it is experienced as power only in relation to human powerlessness."[43]

42. Perrin, *Rediscovering the Teaching of Jesus*, 132 – 36, notes that the element of faith as expressed, for example, in this declaration, "Your faith has saved you," is completely absent in parallel miracle stories in Hellenistic literature and in the rabbinic traditions.

43. Marshall, *Faith as a Theme*, 175.

This truth becomes clear in the account of the fragile faith of a father whose son is being tormented by a demon (9:14–29). The father had brought his son to Jesus to expel a demon that regularly cast him into the fire and into the water in an attempt to destroy him. In Jesus' absence, the disciples had botched an attempt to drive out the demon, and the father's faith that Jesus could do any better falters. Nevertheless, he begs Jesus to have pity on them and, if he is able, to help them. Jesus bristles at this expression of doubt, "Everything is possible for one who believes" (9:23). Jesus possesses divine power to do miracles because of his potent faith and reproaches the father for putting limits on that power with his faint-hearted entreaty "if you can do anything" (9:22). The father, however, must also have complete faith in Jesus. The father's reply, "I do believe; help me overcome my unbelief!" (9:24), reveals that faith comes as a gift from God. Success does not depend on the amount of faith that one can generate within oneself but depends on recognizing one's own inadequacy and that one requires divine help. Best writes: "The strength of God can only be seen when it can enter into and work out through human weakness. The grace of God only appears when men and women fail."[44]

Disciples must not only have faith in Jesus to perform mighty acts, but they too have been given authority over demons if they engage in prayer (9:28–29). If they have faith in God, they will be able to drive mountains into the sea: "Truly I tell you, if anyone says to this mountain, 'Go, throw yourself into the sea,' and does not doubt in their heart but believes that what they say will happen, it will be done for them. Therefore I tell you, whatever you ask for in prayer, believe that you have received it, and it will be yours" (11:22–24). Faith opens the way for the believer to receive divine power and to use it.[45]

The assurance that it will happen, however, comes only on the condition that it is God's will, and that will is revealed through prayer. Jesus is not talking about hopeful optimism that something will be done, nor is he encouraging disciples to expect God to do whatever they wish. Marshall states, "The certainty of faith ... presupposes revelatory insight into the divine intention, though this must be actualized by the believer's volitional commitment to refuse doubt and seek undivided faith (cf. 5:36; 9:22–24)."[46] He adds, "Just as the command of faith moves mountains, so the prayer of faith receives answers."[47]

10.7 LIVING IN COMMUNITY

Matera comments, "Disciples do not live as isolated individuals but as member of the new community which Jesus has established, the Church."[48] Mark writes for a

44. Best, *Story*, 47.

45. Marshall, *Faith as a Theme*, 166.

46. Ibid., 168.

47. Ibid., 170. Marshall (171) cites Johannes Schreiber, *Theologie des Vertrauens: Eine redaktionsgeschichtliche Untersuchung des Markusevangeliums* (Hamburg: Furche-Verlag, 1967), 241: "Prayer is therefore for Mark the final and ultimate expression of faith because as dialogue with God it implies an unconditional commitment to the divine will."

48. Matera, *What Are They Saying about Mark?* 54.

community of faith and presents different images of it as a "house" (7:17; 9:28, 33; 10:10), a "boat" (4:35–41; 6:45–52; 8:14–21), a flock (14:27), and a "temple ... not made with hands" (14:58; cf. 15:29). He also offers instruction on how disciples are to live in this new community of faith gathered around Jesus.

10.7.1 Humble Service

Jesus' interchanges with the disciples who vie for top seeding in their imagined hierarchy (9:30–35), with Peter who wonders what they will receive for having left everything to follow him (10:28), and with James and John who try to wheedle him to grant them the seats of honor when he comes into his glory (10:32–45) reveal that discipleship cannot be motivated by "what one hopes to get out of it either in this life or in the life to come." It "entails suffering and service."[49] This message carries over into how those who become leaders in the community of faith are to wield their power. They are not to duplicate the way the potentates of this world use their power. Hays observes, "Those who exercise power to dominate others, to kill and oppress, are shown not only as villains but also, surprisingly, as pawns of forces beyond their control."[50] Jesus gives a blistering critique of the way the world's "recognized rulers lord it over their subjects, and their great men make them feel the weight of authority" (10:42, NEB).[51] The rulers of this world exert power to serve their own interests. Carter notes, "In the imperial system the exercise of power benefits a few at the oppressive expense of most."[52] But this perspective also is found in the fond hopes of Jewish apocalyptic writings. Watson asserts:

> Apocalyptic expresses the desire of the lowly and oppressed for the power and glory which are at present denied them. Because it is impossible for this dream to be fulfilled within the existing world-order, a miraculous transformation is hoped for in which the great and the powerful will be humbled and the lowly exalted. Since the disciples have now recognized Jesus as the Christ, the bringer of the new age, they expect him to accomplish this miraculous transformation for their benefit.[53]

By contrast, the life and death of Jesus reveal a different way: "God's power is the power to *renounce* power."[54] This use of power comes off as powerlessness, and no more so than when Jesus hangs on a cross, but it demonstrates the power of God and the wisdom of God that are stronger than human strength (1 Cor 1:24–25). It

49. Wessel and Strauss, "Mark," 9:869.

50. Richard B. Hays, *The Moral Vision of the New Testament* (San Francisco: Harper Collins, 1996), 90.

51. Some interpreters detect a subtle irony in the use of the verb translated as "regarded" or "recognize." It can also be translated as "seem." The power belongs to God, and their sovereignty is nothing compared to God's, so Cranfield, *Mark*, 340; Anderson, *Mark*, 256; Gnilka, *Markus*, 2:103; De Mingo Kaminouchi, *"But It Is Not So Among You,"* 119–23. Lane, *Mark*, 382, claims that they give the "illusion of ruling" particularly on their coins. The mention of the "great ones" recalls the great ones, translated "high officials," invited to Herod's ghoulish birthday party (6:21).

52. Warren Carter, "Toward an Imperial-Critical Reading of Matthew's Gospel," *SBLSP* 37 (1998): 322.

53. Watson, "Ambiguity in the Marcan Narrative," 14. For an example, see Rev 2:26–27: "To the one who is victorious and does my will to the end, I will give authority over the nations—that one 'will rule them with an iron scepter and will dash them to pieces like pottery'—just as I have received authority from my Father."

54. Dorothy A. Lee-Pollard, "Powerlessness as Power," 173–74.

disarms the powers and authorities, makes a public spectacle of them, and triumphs over them through the cross (Col 2:15).

This divine paradigm for the use of power in the community produces this rule: "Whoever wants to become great among you must become your servant, and whoever wants to be first must be slave of all" (10:43–44). It explains why those in authority should serve those who are insignificant (9:37; 10:14–15). But this principle rubs against the grain of conventional wisdom and seems self-contradictory. The word translated "slave" (also rendered "servant") would have been a jarring metaphor for Mark's audience. De Mingo Kaminouchi notes, "The impact of the metaphor for most modern readers who have no direct experience of treatment of slaves cannot be the same as for ancient readers for whom slavery was an everyday reality."[55] To become "last, and the servant of all" (9:35) means that those who want to be great must willingly accept the lowest ranking on the social scale.[56] It is not surprising that this teaching meets with incomprehension and resistance, but Santos notes that the goal of this striking teaching is to lead the disciples "to re-evaluate their value system in a thought-provoking and decisive way."[57] It sabotages the idea that power comes from status.

Disciples are to follow the example of their Lord Jesus, who "did not come to be served, but to serve, and to give his life as a ransom for many" (10:45). The teachers of the law epitomize the opposite of Jesus' example (12:38–40).[58] They are on a ceaseless quest for honor and prestige and parade about in long robes to flaunt their status. They install themselves in the places of honor by snatching "the most important seats in the synagogues and the places of honor at banquets" (12:39). As Bird reminds us, "Honour was a limited commodity in ancient societies and it was attained through the social competition of challenge and response."[59] Jesus' disciples are not to be conformed to the relentless drive to attain honor for oneself and one's own that permeates their culture. They are to become unpretentious servants who attend to the needs of others because they are driven, instead, by the love of God, the commitment to Jesus and his teaching, and the love of neighbor. Fuller sums up well Jesus' teaching on servant leadership:

> Servanthood is not the negation of authority; servanthood is authority of a unique kind, an authority which is not inherent in the person of the office-bearer, but an authority which depends on being nothing oneself, in being powerless in order that the power of God may be manifested in human weakness.[60]

55. De Mingo Kaminouchi, *"But It Is Not So Among You,"* 134.

56. Paul uses this image to define his own role as an apostle in Rom 1:1; 1 Cor 9:19; Gal 1:10; Phil 1:1. The role of servant is reinforced in Mark by the parable of the household waiting for the master who has gone on a journey to return (13:34–36).

57. Santos, *Slave of All*, 16.

58. Harry Fleddermann, "A Warning about the Scribes (Mark 12:37b–40)," *CBQ* 44 (1982): 52–67.

59. Bird, *Jesus Is the Christ*, 43. What Jesus teaches in this passage is not totally foreign to the Greco-Roman culture. Bird cites the teaching of Plato, "that 'the man who has not been a servant (ὁ μὴ δουλεύσας) will never become a praiseworthy master (δεσπότης), and that the right way to gain honour is by serving (δουλεύω) honourably rather than ruling honourably'" (*Laws* 6.672e).

60. Reginald H. Fuller, "The Son of Man Came to Serve, Not to Be Served," in *Ministering in a Servant Church* (ed. Francis A. Eigo; Philadelphia: Villanova University Press, 1978), 57–58; cited by Santos, *Slave of All*, 183–84.

De Mingo Kaminouchi points out, "Jesus' commandment of service is not a gentle call to benevolence and kindness toward fellow human beings but a call to constitute a subversive community that proves possible ways of exercising authority other than dominion by the strongest."[61] James and John mention Jesus' "glory" (10:37), but his "glory" differs from the glory that the powerful of this world relish and from which they receive benefits. His glory will come from his service, and his service is to give his life as a ransom for many (10:45). If Jesus is the model for leading in the community of faith, it requires of those who would be great the willingness to make the extreme sacrifice for others.[62]

10.7.2 Forgiveness and Love for Neighbor

The disposition to put oneself last and to become servant of all is "an expression of the gospel's fundamental attitude" of loving the neighbor.[63] Mark does not place as much emphasis on the disciples' need to be merciful and forgiving as Matthew does (Matt 5:7; 6:12, 14, 15; 9:13; 12:7; 18:21, 33, 35; 23:23), but it does not make it less important for Mark as a crucial characteristic of the disciple. The community of faith is to be a house of prayer, and Jesus declares, "And when you stand praying, if you hold anything against anyone, forgive them, so that your Father in heaven may forgive you your sins" (Mark 11:25).

10.7.3 Not Causing Others to Stumble and to Lose Their Faith

Jesus roundly condemns anyone who causes "one of these little ones — those who believe in me — to stumble." He insists, "It would be better for them if a large millstone were hung around their neck and they were thrown into the sea" (9:42). The little ones are those members of the community who lack influence, authority, and any apparent importance. The sin is causing them to abandon their faith in Jesus altogether. Jesus does not specify how someone might cause these little ones to stumble. It can take many forms, but in the modern age, clergy sexual abuse has emerged as one of the most egregious examples of how those in authority not only destroy their victims' personal lives but also destroy their faith and that of a community of believers.

10.8 WATCHFULNESS AND PRAYER

The command to "watch" emerges as the key theme in the Olivet Discourse in chapter 13. A double warning to "watch out" (13:5) and to "be on your guard" (13:23) brackets the first unit (13:5–23). The danger is being deceived and led astray by false prophets and so-called messiahs. Disciples must beware of those who will

61. De Mingo Kaminouchi, *"But It Is Not So Among You,"* 155.

62. The word "ransom" was used frequently in the context of the price of redemption for a slave, and some early Christians applied this saying literally by taking another's place in enslavement to set them free, according to *1 Clem.* 55:2, "We know of many among ourselves who have given themselves to bondage that they might ransom others."

63. Keerankeri, *Love Commandment*, 145.

feed false hopes with lies (see Jer 14:14–16; 23:21–25; 29:8–9). Watching therefore requires spiritual discernment.[64]

The third unit concludes with the parables of the budding fig tree (13:28–29) and the watchful and indifferent doorkeepers (13:33–37). These parables warn *everyone* (13:37) and build on the premise that no one knows the day or hour of the Son of Man's coming, "not even the angels in heaven, nor the Son, but only the Father" (13:32). In case that piece of intelligence did not sink in, it is repeated: "Be on guard! Be alert! You do not know when that time will come" (13:33). "Watching" cannot apply to pinpointing the arrival of the end times. It must apply to an internal spiritual focus of readiness, alertness, and standing guard.

The command to watch reappears when Jesus returns to the Mount of Olives (14:34, 37, 38).[65] The disciples fail to watch, however, and sleep while Jesus prays.[66] Jesus returns three times and reproaches them for sleeping, and his reproach should remind the reader of his closing warning from his recent discourse on the Mount of Olives: "Therefore keep watch because you do not know when the owner of the house will come back—whether in the evening, or at midnight, or when the rooster crows, or at dawn. If he comes suddenly, do not let him find you sleeping" (13:33–37).[67] This contrast between sleeping and watching illuminates what watching must entail. To sleep is to stop praying because one is oblivious that at any moment one can be thrown into the midst of trial. To sleep means inevitable failure when adversity strikes because one is unsuspecting and unready. To watch is to pray as fervently as Jesus did in this episode. To watch is to be ever mindful that a willing spirit can always be sabotaged by the flesh's weakness. Prayer opens one up to a divine power that enables one to face any assault with confidence that whatever is God's will, the result will bring deliverance, either in this life or in the next (Phil 1:19–20). It yields trust in God to overcome fear and anguish in the face of looming suffering and death.

64. Geddert, *Watchwords*, 60, 146.

65. Gundry, *Mark*, 854; and Evans, *Mark 8:27–16:20*, 410, contend that Jesus wants them to stand watch as sentries to give him advanced warning of the approach of the arresting party. But why would Jesus need advanced warning? Jesus specifically says that they are to watch and pray so that they "will not fall into temptation" (14:38). This command refers to a different kind of watching than standing guard as sentries.

66. "Sleep" becomes a term for spiritual lassitude (Rom 13:11; 1 Thess 5:7).

67. Ronald J. Kernaghan, *Mark* (IVPNTC; Downers Grove, IL: InterVarsity Press, 2007), 297, notes that the references to "evening, midnight, cockcrow and dawn in that parable correspond to the major events of this night." Because they fail to watch and pray throughout this passion week, Garland, *Mark*, 543, comments "in the *evening*, when the Lord comes with his disciples for what will be his Last Supper, one of the Twelve at his table chooses to play into the hands of his enemies and betray him. At *midnight*, all the disciples flee into the darkness—one stark naked and each deserting his Lord to the enemy. At *cockcrow*, Peter disowns his Lord three times with curses. In the *morning*, Jesus is left alone—abandoned by all, condemned to death, and delivered into the hands of the Gentiles just as he prophesied."

Chapter 11

MISSION IN MARK

BIBLIOGRAPHY

Alonso, Pablo. *The Woman Who Changed Jesus: Crossing Boundaries in Mk 7,24–30.* BTS 11. Leuven: Peeters, 2011. **Annen, Franz.** *Heil für die Heiden: Zur Bedeutung und Geschichte der Tradition vom besessenen Gerasener (Mk 5,1–20 parr).* FTS 20. Frankfurt am Main: Joseph Knecht, 1976. **Dschulnigg, Peter.** "Grenzüberschreitungen im Markusevangelium: Auf dem Weg zu einer neuen Identität." *MTZ* 51 (2001): 113–20. **Harris, Geoffrey.** "Mark and Mission." Pp. 129–42 in *Mark: Gospel of Action: Personal and Community Responses.* Ed. John Vincent. London: SPCK, 2006. **Kato, Zenji.** *Die Völkermission im Markusevangelium: Eine redaktionsgeschichtliche Untersuchung.* Europäische Hochschulschriften: Theologie 23/252. Bern/Frankfurt am Main/New York: Lang, 1986. **Köstenberger, Andreas J., and Peter T. O'Brien.** *Salvation to the Ends of the Earth: A Biblical Theology of Mission.* NSBT 11. Downers Grove, IL: InterVarsity Press, 2001. **Rhoads, David M.** "Mission in the Gospel of Mark." *CurTM* 22 (1995): 340–55. **Senior, Donald P., and Carroll Stuhlmueller.** *The Biblical Foundations for Mission.* Maryknoll, NY: Orbis, 1983. **Wefald, Eric K.** "The Separate Gentile Mission in Mark: A Narrative Explanation of Markan Geography, The Two Feeding Accounts and Exorcisms." *JSNT* 60 (1995): 3–26.

11.1 THE DISCIPLES' MISSION

According to 1:16–20, Jesus immediately calls Peter, Andrew, James, and John away from their everyday vocations as fishermen to make them "fishers of men" (ASV). This call presumes that their primary task will be to engage in mission. Later, Jesus calls others who will make up the Twelve; they are commissioned to be with him, and he will send them out to preach (3:13–19). Their close association with Jesus will allow them to observe his deeds of power and receive his teaching, which will qualify them to carry on his mission.

Mark portrays Jesus on mission, and after performing remarkable miracles in Capernaum Jesus plainly tells Peter and his companions: "Let us go somewhere else—to the nearby villages—so I can preach there also. That is why I have come" (1:38). As the narrative progresses, the disciples increasingly are plugged into his mission as active participants rather than simply as observers.[1] After the disciples

1. Andreas J. Köstenberger and Peter T. O'Brien, *Salvation to the Ends of the Earth: A Biblical Theology of Mission* (NSBT 11; Downers Grove, IL: InterVarsity Press, 2001), 75.

had witnessed the stunning display of Jesus' power and listened to his private and public teaching, Jesus sends them out on a brief mission tour (6:6b–13, 30–31). One can extrapolate principles regarding Mark's view of mission from Jesus' commission to his disciples.

11.1.1 Mission as an Extension of Christ's Work

Jesus will not do everything by himself. He calls the Twelve to preach (3:14), and he sends them out to preach the same message he preached, namely, that all should repent (1:15; 6:12).[2] He bestows his divine authority on them to cast out demons (3:14) and to heal the sick (6:13) so that their preaching is also accompanied by deeds of power. When they return from their mission and report to Jesus all that they have done and taught, Mark underscores that he believes that Jesus intended for the disciples to extend his work by identifying them as "apostles," ones sent forth with orders (6:30).

The parable of the householder who goes away on a journey and leaves his servants in charge with their assigned tasks (13:33–37) confirms that Mark understood that disciples are to carry on Christ's mission during his physical absence. The parable has transparent allegorical features. The one who leaves on a journey, gives assignments to his servants, and may return at any moment represents Christ, who was resurrected (16:1–8), who ascended to the right hand of God (14:62), and who will return to gather his elect (13:26–27). Boring suggests that the "house" represents the house churches of Mark's community, and the "servants" represent the apostles and Christian ministers (10:43–44; Acts 4:29; Rom 1:1; Titus 1:1; Rev 10:7; 11:18) "who have received Christ's authority to represent him in Christian mission (cf. 3:15; 6:7)." He also notes that the Greek word *ergon* ("work," trans. "assigned task" in 13:34) is used to refer to the work of Christian mission.[3] He concludes: "It is a picture of the absent Lord of the church who has assigned it a missionary task involving the whole world."[4] One of the many ways for the servants to keep watch (13:35–37) for the return of their Lord is to keep on with their mission responsibilities.

11.1.2 Mission as Liberation

Jesus sends his disciples out with "authority over impure spirits" (6:7). Mark summarizes their success twice, more fully in 6:12–13: "They went out and preached that people should repent. They drove out many demons and anointed many sick people with oil and healed them" (6:12–13), and more briefly in 6:30, when they returned from their mission: "The apostles gathered around Jesus and reported to him all they had done and taught." It is important to recognize that their mission

2. Sending the disciples out in pairs provides them with mutual support, and the double witness validates the truthfulness of their message, which has life and death consequences (Num 35:30; Deut 17:6; 19:15).

3. See Acts 13:2; 14:26; 15:38; 1 Cor 16:10; Phil 1:22; 2 Tim 4:5.

4. Boring, *Mark*, 377.

involved more than simply preaching for people to repent of their ways. As Jesus cast off the demonic shackles that oppressed people, so did his disciples through his power. This detail discloses that mission is to encompass liberating people from the crippling forces that hinder life.[5] In the process, they manifest the power of God working in the lives of people.

11.1.3 Dependence on God for Provision

Jesus' instructions to the disciples to take nothing for the journey except a staff and sandals (6:8–9) recall the instructions given to the Israelites on the eve of their liberation from Egypt: "This is how you are to eat it: with your cloak tucked into your belt, your sandals on your feet and your staff in your hand. Eat it in haste; it is the LORD's Passover" (Exod 12:11). The command to take no bread, no bag, no money in your belts, and no extra tunic, however, is curious.[6] It means more than that Jesus expects them to travel light and to be ready to take off at a moment's notice. It requires them also to be completely dependent on God, who will engender hospitality in those to whom they preach.

To receive hospitality, the disciples will have to be about their task of proclaiming the message and healing and staying on the move.[7] They will have to depend entirely on the provision of God. They are not to try to be self-sufficient. The disciples cannot rely on themselves but only on the One who has given them the commission, who gives them the necessary sufficiency to discharge it, and who opens the hearts of others to receive them and hear their message.

11.1.4 Dedication to the Task

The disciples' mission requires utter devotion to the task rather than devotion to their own creature comforts. The instruction in 6:10, "Whenever you enter a house, stay there until you leave that town," implies that they are to accept whatever accommodations are first offered and not to move on if better lodgings are offered. Their mission is not a vacation excursion but a matter of life and death for others. They not only need to win their attention but also their confidence. No one will take seriously messengers who claim to bring an urgent message when it becomes evident that their first concern is to secure their own ease.

Since Jesus instructs the disciples to leave any place that refuses to listen to them and to shake the dust from their feet (6:11; see Acts 13:51), he does not expect that the disciples will always be successful, and they are not to fear rejection and failure. They are *not* sent out to change the world, because it is not in their power to do so. Their task is simply to go and preach, to sow the seed; God brings the harvest. The dramatic gesture of shaking the dust from their feet does not mean that they

5. Geoffrey Harris, "Mark and Mission," in *Mark: Gospel of Action: Personal and Community Responses* (ed. John Vincent; London: SPCK, 2006), 133.

6. Hans Dieter Betz, "Jesus and the Cynics: Survey and Analysis of a Hypothesis," *JR* 74 (1994): 453–75, rejects the argument that Jesus followed the model of wandering Cynic philosophers in the ancient world.

7. Rhoads, "Mission in Mark," 349.

consign those who might initially snub the rule of God to eternal condemnation.[8] But it does convey how serious it is for them to do so, and their unbelief will be used as incriminating testimony in the day of judgment if they do not repent and believe.

For disciples to shake the dust from their feet requires them to be free from any worldly entanglements. The more they become entrenched in the power structures of society and are at home with its values and pleasures, the harder it will be for them to dissociate themselves from a community, to warn of God's judgment, and to abandon the area when it is unresponsive. They will need to be prepared to leave "home or brothers or sisters or mother or father or children or fields" (10:29) and communities.

11.2 The Mission to the Gentiles

Unlike Matt 28:16–20 and Luke 24:44–49, Mark does not include a direct commissioning of the disciples to world mission. Kilpatrick contends that Mark had no interest in a universal mission: "There is no preaching the Gospel to Gentiles in this world and there is no interest in their fate in the world to come." He claims that Mark only recognizes that the gospel is to be preached outside of Palestine and that both Jews and Gentiles will need to read the signs of the times, "but that is as far as Mark goes."[9] According to Kilpatrick, this conservatism is all the more "striking" if the gospel were produced at Rome. He surmises that the entry of Gentiles into the church and the controversies it provoked "had not materially affected the Gospel tradition by the time Mark was written."[10]

I would evaluate the evidence differently. If Mark were written in Rome, and if both Peter and Paul had a significant influence on the author Mark, as I argue in the introduction, it is more than "striking" that Mark would not have been influenced by the Gentile mission that had already taken place for years; it is dumbfounding. In my view, Mark takes for granted that the Gentile mission is a fait accompli as the fulfillment of God's will and drops hints throughout his narrative that prepares for it. Senior and Stuhlmueller contend that all the gospels "are mission documents for the church itself, meant to justify, renew, and motivate the church's claim on the heritage of Jesus' own boundary-breaking ministry."[11] Mark presents Jesus' ministry as largely limited to Israel, but this is attributable to his "respect for the historical constraints of Jesus' mission and the limited degree to which Jesus himself elaborated on the implications of his own mission for the further development of his messianic community."[12] Nevertheless, his narrative not only foreshadows this mission, but it also lays the theological foundation for the inclusion of Gentiles in the community of disciples.

---

8. The Gerasenes spurned Jesus and asked him to leave their territory (5:14–17), but he sent the recovered demoniac to witness throughout the Decapolis what the Lord had done for him. The people responded with amazement (5:19–20).

9. G. D. Kilpatrick, "The Gentile Mission in Mark and Mark 13:9–11," in *Studies in the Gospels: Essays in Memory of R. H. Lightfoot* (ed. Dennis E. Nineham; Oxford: Blackwell, 1955), 157.

10. Ibid., 158.

11. Donald P. Senior and Carroll Stuhlmueller, *The Biblical Foundations for Mission* (Maryknoll, NY: Orbis, 1983), 211.

12. Köstenberger and O'Brien, *Salvation to the Ends of the Earth*, 85–86.

11.2.1 Foreshadowing the Mission to the Gentiles

When Jesus replaces blood ties with spiritual categories to determine who comprises his family, he opens the door for Gentiles who do the will of God to be included as his "brother and sister and mother" (3:31–35). The narratives of the exorcisms of the Gerasene demoniac (5:1–20) and the daughter of the Syrophoenician woman (7:24–30), the healing in the area of the Decapolis of the deaf man who could hardly talk (7:31–37), and the feeding of the four thousand in the same general area (8:1–10) all foreshadow that the gospel will include Gentiles. In addition, Jesus says that before the end, "the gospel must first be preached to all nations" (13:10). He also declares that the woman who anointed him beforehand was preparing for his burial and that it would be told in memory of her "wherever the gospel is preached throughout the world" (14:9). The implication is clear. He expects the gospel to be preached throughout the world to all people.

In his brief citation of Isa 56:7 in Mark 11:17, Jesus implies that God's ultimate purpose for the temple was for it to be "called a house of prayer for all nations." Herod's temple has failed to meet that purpose and will be destroyed and replaced by a temple not made with hands, where anyone anywhere who has faith and prays with a forgiving heart will have their sins forgiven by the Father, who resides in heaven (11:25).

11.2.1.1 The Gerasene Demoniac (Mark 5:1–20)

When Jesus crosses to the other side of the lake, he finds the region brimming with demons, swine, and pagan practices. After driving out a legion of demons from the Gerasene demoniac, the man, now fully clothed and in his right mind, begs Jesus to allow him to join him and the disciples as they prepare to leave the territory of Gerasa and return to the other side of the lake (5:18). Jesus refuses this request and instead sends him to his own people to tell them "how much the Lord has done for you, and how he has had mercy on you" (5:19). The result is that he is the first to spread the good news in Gentile territory. He heralds what *Jesus* had done for him throughout the Decapolis, and the people responded with amazement (5:20).[13]

Isaiah 65:1–5b provides a backdrop for understanding the missional thrust of this story.[14] God says to Isaiah:

> "I revealed myself to those who did not ask for me;
> I was found by those who did not seek me.
> To a nation that did not call on my name,
> I said, 'Here am I, here am I.'
> All day long I have held out my hands
> to an obstinate people,

13. The Decapolis refers to the distinctively Hellenistic region mostly east of the Jordan and the Sea of Galilee that included the cities of Gadara, Scythopolis, Pella, Gerasa, Hippos, Philadelphia, and Damascus.

14. Annen, *Heil für die Heiden*, 182–84.

who walk in ways not good,
  pursuing their own imaginations—
a people who continually provoke me
  to my very face,
offering sacrifices in gardens
  and burning incense on altars of brick;
who sit among the graves
  and spend their nights keeping secret vigil;
who eat the flesh of pigs,
  and whose pots hold broth of impure meat;
who say, 'Keep away; don't come near me,
  for I am too sacred for you!' "

The parallels with Mark's account include the mention of demons (5:2; Isa 65:3, LXX),[15] dwelling in tombs (5:3, 5; Isa 65:4a), the warning to keep away (5:7; Isa 65:5a), and the reference to the swine (5:11; Isa 65:4b). They do not seek the Lord (Isa 65:1), but Jesus' appearance there anticipates the mercy and grace God will extend to Gentiles. I conclude from this incident:

> The demoniac's incoherent cries are directed into the air to no god in particular. Not surprisingly, they receive no answer. He is not seeking God or even seeking healing. Caught in the web of demonic powers, he even resists healing when it comes. The region where he resides also resists it. Yet we see the power of God's mercy and love that captures and transforms those who do not even know that it exists and may initially resist it when it invades their lives.[16]

Though Jesus accedes to the townspeople's request to leave the region, he does not leave them without a witness. This incident reveals the power of the gospel to overcome initial hostility, and this man's preaching throughout the Decapolis prepares for a more positive response when Jesus returns (7:31).

11.2.1.2 The Woman Who Was a Greek, a Syrophoenician by Birth (Mark 7:24–30)

Jesus travels to the vicinity of Tyre (7:24), and Mark does not explain why he would do so. What Jesus does in this Gentile territory and in the next incidents in 7:31–37 and 8:1–10 in the region of the Decapolis provides the underpinnings for Mark's church to engage in mission, minister to human suffering, and feed the hungry in a cultural and religious milieu that may be foreign to them. Mark states that Jesus wanted to remain concealed in Tyre, but, earlier, people had streamed to him from this area when he began his ministry (3:8), and word of his presence there soon leaks out. He is approached by a woman who is identified as a Greek, which identifies

15. The LXX version of Isa 65:3 has them "sacrificing on bricks to demons."

16. Garland, *Mark*, 208.

her culturally and religiously, and as a Syrophoenician by birth, which identifies her geographically, but also may hint of her socioeconomic status.[17] This two-step description of her background serves to underscore that she is a Gentile (see Rom 1:16; 3:9; 10:12; 1 Cor 1:22–24; 10:32; Gal 3:28), not a Jew. She hails from a city that is reviled in Scripture as the wealthy, godless oppressor of Israel (see Isa 23; Jer 47:4; Ezek 26–28; Joel 3:4; Amos 1:9; Zech 9:2). Josephus states that "among the Phoenicians the Tyrians are notoriously our bitterest enemies" (*Ag. Ap.* 1§70). It is remarkable that even pagans from the detested city of Tyre seek out this Jewish miracle worker.

The woman falls at Jesus' feet (see 5:22, 33) and pleads with him to drive out a demon from her daughter, but he dismisses her appeal out of hand with a sharp insult: "First let the children eat all they want ... for it is not right to take the children's bread and toss it to the dogs" (7:27).[18] She can expect nothing from him. This gruff response diverts the attention of most modern readers who try to explain how Jesus could be so callous and offensive by comparing a suffering child to a dog. Does it also mean that he will not give what is holy to dogs (Matt 7:6)? What makes this response so troubling is that this woman is not some venomous Pharisee trying to trap him but a forlorn mother desperately pleading for her demonized daughter.

The multiple explanations that try to excuse Jesus' biting retort miss the point.[19] The key to this account is the word "first," which Marcus contends "is always used in Mark for events on the eschatological time line" (see 3:27; 4:28; 9:11–12; 13:10).[20] Its use here implies that Gentiles have some ray of hope, but for the time being this Gentile woman must wait patiently for her turn. Jesus asserts the priority of Israel in a parable, which Paul affirms in prose, "first to the Jew, then to the Gentile" (Rom 1:16; 2:9–10; see Acts 13:46).

The woman has no time to wait, however. She understands the parable (4:33; cf.

17. The women of Berea who believed are identified as "Greek" in Acts 17:12, the only other place in the New Testament where this particular Greek term occurs. Theissen, *The Gospels in Context*, 71–72, infers that she was relatively affluent from the reference to the "bed" in her home (7:30) instead of a straw pallet (2:4, 9, 11–12; 6:55) and the description of her as a "Greek," which connotes that she belonged to the privileged upper class (citing the analysis of the use of the term in Hermann Bengtson, "Syrien in der hellenistischen Zeit," in *Der Hellenismus und der Aufstieg Roms: Die Mittelmeerwelt im Altertum II: Bd. II* (ed. Pierre Grimal; Frankfurt: Fischer Taschenbuch Verlag, 1965), 252.

18. The verb translated "eat all they want" describes the results of the feeding of five thousand (6:42, "were satisfied") and of the four thousand (8:8). The term "dog" is not endearing (1 Sam 17:43; 24:14; 2 Sam 3:8; 9:8; 16:9; 2 Kgs 8:13; Isa 56:10–11; Matt 7:6; Phil 3:2; 2 Pet 2:22; Rev 22:15), and its diminutive form in the Greek text does not relieve the force of the insult. Because dogs did not discriminate in eating what would be regarded as filth and what is forbidden to Jews (Exod 22:31; 1 Kgs 14:11; 16:4; 21:24; 22:38; 2 Kgs 9:10, 36; Prov 26:11, cited in 2 Pet 2:22; Jer 15:3), it was natural for Jews to use "dog" as a slur for Gentiles. Such hostility is expressed in *b. Ḥag.* 13a: "As the sacred food was intended for men, but not for the dogs, the Torah was intended to be given to the Chosen People, but not to the Gentiles."

19. Frank G. Downing, "The Woman from Syrophoenicia and her Doggedness: Mark 7.24–31 (Matthew 15.21–28)," in *Making Sense in (and of) the First Christian Century* (ed. Frank G. Downing; JSNTS 197; Sheffield: Sheffield Academic, 2000), 109, comments,

> Most commentators are embarrassed by Jesus' response. Much of the discussion of other issues often seems at least in part aimed to reduce this harshness. Perhaps the harshness stems from the early church, from controversies then. Perhaps it is in thick quotation marks: "You know what they say." Perhaps Jesus is testing the woman's faith and/or demanding humility. Perhaps he is really just working things out in his own mind. Perhaps with his "Let the children be fed first" and perhaps, too, with his "puppies," "housedogs," he is already softening the harshness of what is to follow and providing a clue for the woman to pick up. There is no widespread agreement.

20. Marcus, *Mark 1–8*, 463.

4:13): the "children" represent Israel, the "bread" represents his saving work, and the "dogs" represent Gentiles. Her response reveals that she is not offended and accepts Jesus' premise that the children are to be fed first before "the dogs" get anything.[21] With a quick wit, however, she expands on the metaphors in the parable: "Lord, even the dogs under the table eat the children's crumbs" (7:28). She is the only person to address Jesus as "Lord" in Mark, and it means more than "Sir" (NRSV) in this context. She also accepts Jewish priority—the bread rightly belongs to the children, Israel. She does not accept being disqualified as a beneficiary of his saving power, as if it were reserved for Israel alone.[22] She does not ask for bread to be taken from the children and "tossed" her way but is willing to humble herself and accept the role of a devoted dog waiting under the table for just a crumb to drop, a tiny scrap of his saving power to drive the demon from her child.[23] This adaptation of Jesus' original image insinuates that she does not have to wait until all of the children have been satisfied before she can receive anything from him. Children (Israel) and dogs (Gentiles) can be fed simultaneously.[24] Jesus relents at this word, and she returns home to find her daughter delivered from the demon (7:30).

Many have speculated that this incident reflects Jesus' own struggle with the scope of his mission, which he believed was limited to Israel. The Gentiles would be brought into the fold only when God's purposes with Israel were consummated (see Isa 19:19–25; 66:19–20; Mic 4:1–2; Zech 8:20–22). Taylor, for example, imagines that there is "a tension in the mind of Jesus concerning the scope of His ministry, and ... in a sense He is speaking to Himself as well as to the woman. Her reply shows that she is quick to perceive this."[25] Her answer, it is claimed, opens his eyes to a wider extension of his mission to include Gentiles. Such speculation takes us far afield. Mark has no interest in portraying the inner workings of Jesus' mind or his personal struggle over the inclusion of Gentiles. This incident serves to explain why Jesus limits his earthly ministry primarily to Israel and introduces the order of salvation history: "first to the Jew, then to the Gentile." It also illustrates how Gentiles will *also* be recipients of God's grace and power. It requires them to accept the primacy of the Jews (see Rom 9:4–5; 11:17–21) and the recognition that "salvation is from the Jews" (John 4:22).

Surprisingly, Jesus says nothing about the woman's faith (contrast 2:5; 5:34; 10:52). Rhoads writes, "In Mark, faith is embodied in action," and he assumes that the woman put her faith in action by coming to Jesus and trusting that her "request will be granted."[26] But putting her faith in action does *not* suffice to get Jesus to

21. Zenji Kato, *Die Völkermission im Markusevangelium: Eine redaktionsgeschichtliche Untersuchung* (Europäische Hochschulschriften: Theologie 23/252; Bern/Frankfurt am Main/New York: Lang, 1986), 290.

22. Reinhard Feldmeier, "Die Syrophönizierin (Mk 7, 24–30): Jesus 'verlorenes' Streitgespräch?" in *Die Heiden: Juden, Christen und das Problem des Fremden* (ed. Reinhard Feldmeier and Ulrich Heckel; WUNT 1/70; Tübingen: Mohr Siebeck, 1994), 223.

23. Her abject humility in accepting this role is made clearer by comparing it to Judg 1:7, which records the boast of King Adoni-Bezek describing the mortification of his enemies: "Seventy kings with their thumbs and big toes cut off have picked up scraps under my table."

24. Jean-Noël Aletti, "Analyse narrative de Mc 7,24–30: difficultés et propositions," *Bib* 93 (2012): 370.

25. Taylor, *Mark*, 350; see also Cranfield, *Mark*, 247.

26. Rhoads, "Jesus and the Syrophoenician Woman in Mark," 359–60.

respond to her. Instead, it is her "reply" (*logos*), not her faith, that is stressed that gets a response.[27] Alonso believes that what is meant by "her reply" is "her argument in favour of the little dogs, her wit, her intelligence, and her resilient and dogged attitude."[28] I would place the emphasis only on "her argument in favour of the little dogs." This reply, however sharp-witted it might be, expresses astonishing self-effacement as she is willing to wait under the table for any crumb that might fall her way. It is not her ready wit with a quick retort that causes Jesus to relent but her humility. Her attitude is captured in a slight change of the wording of a well-known hymn, "Amazing grace ... that saved a dog like me." Neither Jew nor Greek is saved by their cleverness or their doggedness.

More important for Mark's theology of mission, the narrative context reveals that an abundance of "broken pieces of bread" were left over *after* Jesus had fed the children of Israel and they were all "satisfied" (6:42–43). This encounter with a Syrophoenician woman from Tyre prepares for the feeding of Gentiles in 8:1–10, which also results in a great quantity of leftovers. This incident from the ministry of Jesus validates the church's mission to the Gentiles and makes clear that accepting Gentiles does not deprive Israel from any blessing. Alonso concludes that one of the story's points is to function as a "mirror" for the audience that has relevance for today. It is a transformative encounter in which boundaries related to "gender, ethnicity, social class, culture, and religion" are crossed.[29] Jews were first at the table, but Gentiles are to be welcomed at the table as well. The reason is because God is good (10:18), and because love for God requires love for neighbor (12:28–34).

Feldmeier understands Jesus to have been "defeated" in the exchange.[30] I would argue that Jesus is deliberately scandalous—throwing stumbling blocks in people's way—as a mode of instruction. It is designed to confront and to move a person to the truth. He publicly affronts the Pharisees by calling them hypocrites to their face and scoffing at their beloved tradition (7:6–9), and he insults this Gentile woman by comparing her and her sick daughter to dogs. Most do not mind Jesus insulting Pharisees, but they do mind what seems to be a chauvinistic, if not racist, treatment of a desperate mother.

Regarding Jesus' confrontational manner that causes offense, McCracken writes, "The offense has a way of bringing the individual to a moment of crisis, revealing the heart's desire."[31] In response to the scandal, the person will stumble and reject Jesus or be led to change their view of Jesus, themselves, and the world. In the Pharisees'

27. Alonso, *The Woman Who Changed Jesus*, 213–16. Matthew 15:28 emphasizes her "great faith": "Woman, you have great faith! Your request is granted." Mark wants to emphasize her reply to make a different point.

28. Ibid., 215–16. This position is held by many others.

29. Ibid., 169, 343. It would have been rare for a woman to enter into the male domain of a private house. She also is a Greek, not a Jew, and probably a pagan, who comes from an affluent territory that imported Galilean agricultural products, which meant that the poor of the Jewish population of Galilee often had to go without.

30. Feldmeier, "Die Syrophönizierin," 226. So also Myers, *Binding*, 204, who thinks, "Jesus allows himself to be 'shamed' (becoming 'least') in order to include this pagan woman in the new community of the kingdom." He continues the sentence with how it applies to the Jewish mission to Gentiles, "so too Judaism will have to suffer the indignity of redefining its group boundaries (collective honor) in order to realize that Gentiles are now welcomed as equals."

31. See David McCracken, *The Scandal of the Gospels: Jesus, Story, and Offense* (New York: Oxford University Press, 1994), 33.

case, it hardened them and led them away from God. In the woman's case, it led her to the truth. Two basic human instincts collide: the gut reaction to recoil at the offense and to want to strike back and the gut reaction to do anything to help one's child. Pride stiffens the knees so that they will not bow down and muzzles the voice so that it will not call out for help. This woman swallows her pride and accepts Jesus' premise that the children are to be allowed to be fed first ("First let the children eat all they want," 7:27) before the dogs get anything. The word "first," however, gives her a ray of hope. She is not asking to be first. She can get a tiny scrap of mercy from the overflow (whether it falls from the table [see Luke 16:21] or is tossed), without depriving the children.

11.2.1.3 The Deaf Man Who Could Hardly Talk (Mark 7:31–37)

Mark records Jesus taking a curious detour that lands him back in the area of the Decapolis.[32] The mention of Tyre, Sidon, and the Decapolis emphasizes that Jesus passes through Gentile territory.[33] Just as Jewish crowds in Galilee brought their sick to Jesus (1:32–33; 8:22; 9:20), so a Gentile crowd brings a deaf and speechless man to him and begs Jesus to place his hand on the man to heal him (see 5:23; 6:5; 8:22, 25). The man's malady made it impossible for him to have heard about Jesus or to ask him for healing had he learned about him.[34] Others must intervene on his behalf.

This miracle is reminiscent of God's declaration, "Who gave human beings their mouths? Who makes them deaf or mute? Who gives them sight or makes them blind? Is it not I, the LORD?" (Exod 4:11). It also recalls God's promise to remedy the physical and spiritual disabilities of the people, including opening the ears of the deaf so that the mute tongue will shout for joy (Isa 35:5–6a). This miracle is a harbinger of God's promise to restore creation, but the surprise is that this restoration occurs in Gentile territory. The implication is that Gentiles will also have their ears unstopped to be able to hear the gospel and will have their tongues unloosed to be able to respond appropriately with adulation.

This indeed is what happens in this miracle. Jesus' command not to tell anyone is disobeyed, and they keep talking about the miracle with the result that Gentiles declare, "He has done everything well.... He even makes the deaf hear and the mute speak" (7:36–37). Hartman interprets their assessment of Jesus, which echoes Gen 1:25, 31, to mean "that Gentiles indirectly confess that God, the creator, is active in Jesus' work."[35] Gentiles are unexpectedly responsive to him, and this response

32. The location in the Decapolis has been challenged by Dietrich-Alex Koch, "Inhaltliche Gliederung und geographischer Aufriss im Markusevangelium," *NTS* 29 (1983): 145–66; and Collins, *Mark*, 369. France, *Mark*, 302, n. 50, responds that since Mark uses such a specific term as Decapolis immediately after a reference to Tyre in 7:24, it suggests that he intends to convey that this miracle also occurred in a Gentile context. Edwards, *Mark*, 223–24, explains the "horseshoe shaped itinerary" of 120 miles by citing the precedents for circuitous journeys in 2 Kgs 2:1–6 and 2:23–25. He suggests that it also may have been driven by Jesus' need to evade Herod Antipas as well as a desire to include the non-Jewish world in his ministry.

33. Dean W. Chapman, *The Orphan Gospel: Mark's Perspective on Jesus* (The Biblical Seminar 16; Sheffield: JSOT, 1993), 171–73, observes that since Mark lived in a "pre-map culture," he may be intending to locate Jesus "culturally, rather than coordinately." He is in the midst of a foreign ethos culturally.

34. Unlike Zechariah (Luke 1:63), he most probably could not read or write to communicate with others.

35. Hartman, *Mark*, 298.

portends that, as Isa 66:18–19 prophesies, "they will proclaim [God's] glory among the nations."

11.2.1.4 The Feeding of the Four Thousand (Mark 8:1–10)

The feeding of the four thousand is introduced by the phrase "during those days" and implies that Jesus has stayed on the eastern side of the lake in Gentile territory. This story parallels the feeding of the five thousand (6:31–44) with the same situation of a large crowd gathered around Jesus in a remote place (6:35; 8:4), his compassion on them (6:34; 8:2), the disciples' concern about feeding them because of their meager supply of provisions (6:35, 37; 8:4), and the crowd eating the multiplied loaves and fishes and being fully satisfied (6:42; 8:8). The differences in the two stories provide an accumulation of clues that the hungry crowd in the second feeding is made up of Gentiles.

(1) In the first feeding miracle, Jesus has compassion on the crowd because they are like sheep without a shepherd (6:34), which is a scriptural metaphor applied to Israel (Num 27:17; 1 Kgs 22:17; Ezek 34:5, 23). Having them sit on "the green" (Mark 6:39; "green grass," NIV) alludes to Ps 23:2a, "He makes me lie down in green pastures." The miracle presents Jesus as the good shepherd. This imagery is absent in the second feeding.

(2) Marshaling the crowd to sit in "groups of hundreds and fifties" in the first feeding (6:40) recalls the assembling of Israel company by company in the wilderness (Exod 18:21, 25). No mention is made of how the crowd is arranged in the second feeding.[36]

(3) In the second feeding, Jesus has compassion on the crowd because they had been with him for three days and have had nothing to eat. The crowd also is described as having "come from afar" (8:3, ASV). This phrase is used to refer to the non-Israelite nations in Scripture,[37] and the NIV translation ("have come a long distance") obscures this possible symbolic significance.[38]

(4) The different statistics of the two miracles stand out, and some see symbolic significance in them, especially since Mark draws particular attention to them in 8:19–20. On the one hand, it is possible that the five loaves that fed the Jewish crowd has a Jewish association and could evoke the five books of Moses or the five books of the Psalms. The collection of twelve baskets of leftover bread suggests the twelve apostles (3:13–19), who represent the tribes of Israel (Num 1:4–16). The seven loaves that fed the four thousand, on the other hand, might relate to the division

36. Eric K. Wefald, "The Separate Gentile Mission in Mark: A Narrative Explanation of Markan Geography, The Two Feeding Accounts and Exorcisms," *JSNT* 60 (1995): 3–26. In the first feeding, when Jesus tells the disciples to give the crowd something to eat, they ask if he expects them to go out and buy two hundred denarii worth of bread (6:37). They are willing to buy food for the Jewish crowd, but they make no such offer in the second feeding. He attributes this to their resistance to the Gentile mission. Most interpreters, however, assume that the disciples are incredulous and less than enthusiastic when Jesus asks them to feed both crowds.

37. Deut 28:49; 29:22; Josh 9:6, 9; 1 Kgs 8:41; 2 Chr 6:32; Isa 39:3; 60:4; Ezek 23:40; Joel 3:8; Acts 2:39; 22:21; Eph 2:13, 17.

38. The fear that they might faint "on the way" (8:3) may be a cryptic allusion to Gentile Christians who were followers of "the Way" (Acts 9:2; 19:9, 23; 22:4; 24:14, 22).

of the Gentile nations into seventy (Gen 10:1–32; *1 En.* 89:59; 90:22–25),[39] or it might reflect the seven deacons chosen to minister to the Hellenists in Acts 6:1–6. These numbers may simply be round numbers that have no deeper meaning except to convey the remarkable scale and superabundance of Jesus' miracle, but it is more likely that they reflect eschatological completion.

(5) The Greek word used for the baskets (*kophinos*, 6:43; 8:19) that are used to collect the leftovers in the first feeding was so unique that a person could be identified as Jewish just by carrying one (Juvenal, *Sat.* 3.14; 6.542).[40] The word used for the baskets in the second feeding (8:8, 20, *spyris*), by contrast, was used throughout the Mediterranean world for a large basket or hamper (see Acts 9:25).

This miraculous feeding of four thousand follows Jesus' brusque response to the Gentile Syrophoenician woman, "First let the children eat all they want" (7:27). In the feeding of the five thousand, the children of Israel *had* been fed first and were satisfied. The feeding of the four thousand anticipates the Gentile mission when they too will be fed. They will not have to scrounge for crumbs that might fall from the table, but they will receive food in abundance and also will be satisfied.[41] Mark's account of the feeding of the four thousand changes the question that is to be asked when it comes to the Gentiles. The disciples do not ask, "How can we eat with these people?" Instead, they ask, "Where in this remote place can anyone get enough bread to feed them?" (8:4). The answer to this question is from the power and beneficence of Jesus, the Son of God, and the narrative reveals that this power and beneficence ignores any artificial, ethnic boundaries.

11.2.1.5 Redefining What Causes True Defilement and Opening the Door to Fellowship with Gentiles (Mark 7:1–23)

Jesus' dispute with the Pharisees in 7:1–13 and the expansion of his teaching to his disciples in private in 7:17–23 prepares the way for his contact with Gentiles that Mark narrates in 7:24–8:10. The Pharisees publicly accuse Jesus' disciples of eating with hands that are defiled ("common," the opposite of "holy, devoted to God"). Mark explains for his audience unfamiliar with Jewish customs that "defiled hands" refers to "unwashed" hands (7:2), and he inserts a parenthetic explanation about Jewish ritual washings (7:3–4). The implication from a tradition recorded in *Mishnah Soṭah* 9:15 is that inattention to cultic cleanness has serious spiritual consequences:[42]

39. Pesch, *Markusevangelium*, 1:404.

40. Josephus (*J.W.* 3.5.5 §95) uses the same word, however, to describe the equipment issued to Roman infantry.

41. Boring, *Mark*, 219, concludes: "Both the macrostructure and Mark's general interest predispose the reader to think of one feeding as representing God's provision for Jews, the biblical and traditional people of God, and the other feeding as the extension of God's miraculous blessing to Gentiles, that is, a 'feeding' of a group that is primarily Gentile but includes Jews, representing the integrated inclusive Christian community of Mark's own time."

42. Noted by Bruce Chilton, Darrell Bock, Daniel M. Gurtner, Jacob Neusner, Lawrence H. Schiffman, and Daniel Oden, eds., *A Comparative Handbook to the Gospel of Mark: Comparisons with Pseudepigrapha, the Qumran Scrolls, and Rabbinic Literature* (Leiden/Boston: Brill, 2010), 240–42.

> R. Phinheas b. Jair says: Heedfulness leads to cleanliness, and cleanliness leads to purity, and purity leads to abstinence,[43] and abstinence to holiness. And holiness leads to humility and humility leads to the shunning of sin, and the shunning of sin leads to saintliness, and saintliness leads to [the gift] of the Holy Spirit, and the Holy Spirit leads to the resurrection of the dead.

Jesus' response to the Pharisees' criticism of his disciples is to vilify these opponents as "hypocrites" who are far from God (7:6), who worship God in vain (7:7a), who teach human traditions as if they were commands of God (7:7b) while ignoring God's commandments (7:8), and who evade God's commandments with hair-splitting, logic-chopping cunning (7:9–13).

The *Book of Jubilees* 22:16–19 reflects the scornful eye by which many Jews viewed Gentiles and cautions that all relationships with them should be avoided:

> And you also, my son, Jacob, remember my words, and keep the commandments of Abraham, your father. Separate yourself from the gentiles, and do not eat with them, and do not perform deeds like theirs. And do not become associates of theirs. Because their deeds are defiled, and all of their ways are contaminated, and despicable, and abominable. They slaughter their sacrifices to the dead, and to the demons they bow down. And they eat in tombs. And all their deeds are worthless and vain. And they have no heart to perceive, and they have no eyes to see what their deeds are, and where they wander astray, saying to the tree "you are my god," and to a stone "you are my lord, and you are my savior"; and they have no heart. But (as for) you, my son, Jacob, may God Most High help you, and the God of heaven bless you. And may he turn you from their defilement, and from all their errors.[44]

Table fellowship with the Gentiles remained a sore spot for many Jewish Christians as the emerging church engaged in their mission throughout the world (see Gal 2:11–14). Mark's narrative subtly presents Jesus' teaching and actions as the authoritative guide for resolving the issue and tearing down the walls that separated Jews and Gentiles. Jesus not only rejects the Pharisees' tradition of the elders regarding the washing of hands that has no explicit biblical basis (7:1–13),[45] but he also revokes dietary laws that do have an explicit biblical basis. The point is made twice, in public before the crowds and his Pharisaic nemeses, "Nothing outside a person can defile them by going into them. Rather, it is what comes out of a person that defiles them" (7:15), and in his private expansion of his teaching with the disciples (7:18b–23):

43. Herbert Danby, *The Mishnah* (Oxford University Press, 1933), 306, n. 14, notes that the Hebrew "*perishuth*," that is translated here as "abstinence," means "separatism."

44. O. S. Wintermute, trans., *The Old Testament Pseudepigrapha* (ed. James H. Charlesworth; Garden City, NY: Doubleday, 1985), 2:98.

45. The rabbinic tradition in *b. Ber.* 52b admits that the requirement to wash hands for ritual purification before eating ordinary food does not derive from the Torah, but the statement in *b. Ber.* 60b, "When he washes his hands he should say, 'Blessed is He who has sanctified us with his commandments and commanded us concerning the washing of hands,'" reveals that the rabbis would have insisted that their regulations did have divine authority behind them.

> "Don't you see that nothing that enters a person from the outside can defile them? For it doesn't go into their heart but into their stomach, and then out of the body." (In saying this, Jesus declared all foods clean.)
>
> He went on: "What comes out of a person is what defiles them. For it is from within, out of a person's heart, that evil thoughts come—sexual immorality, theft, murder, adultery, greed, malice, deceit, lewdness, envy, slander, arrogance and folly. All these evils come from inside and defile a person."

Food enters and leaves the digestive tract without touching the heart of a person. If nothing persons ingest makes them ritually impure, and if what defiles them is only what comes from their heart, and if Mark's parenthetical addition means that Jesus declares all foods clean (7:19), all of the food laws that were used to separate Israel from the Gentiles are now null and void.[46]

One might presume that Mark understands these laws to have been overridden by the greater commission for the disciples to bring the gospel of Jesus Christ to the world after his death and resurrection. This declaration that all foods are clean correlates with the later account of Peter's vision in Acts 10. The message that came to him regarding clean and unclean food is repeated three times, "Do not call anything impure that God has made clean" (Act 10:15–16). How this message about food is to be applied is clarified by the immediate appearance of the men from Cornelius, which leads to Peter's subsequent preaching to his household.

In Acts, the issue is highlighted by Peter when he first greets the gathering in the house of Cornelius the centurion in Caesarea: "You are well aware that it is against our law for a Jew to associate with or visit a Gentile" (Acts 10:28). The members of the circumcision party in Jerusalem lay emphasis on it when they call Peter to account for his actions: "You went into the house of uncircumcised men and ate with them" (11:2–3). Peter summarizes his vision in Joppa and his experience in Caesarea (11:4–17), which silences (temporarily, see Acts 15) the critics and inspires the gathering to praise God and declare, "So then, even to Gentiles God has granted repentance that leads to life" (11:18). Jesus' declaration about food also accords with Paul's lengthy argument regarding food in his letter to the Romans and his statements, "I am convinced, being fully persuaded in the Lord Jesus, that nothing is unclean in itself" (Rom 14:14a), and "All food is clean" (14:20).

Mark arranges his narrative so that Jesus' response to the Pharisees concerning the defilement that really matters to God applies to the Gentile mission. The audience can infer from the narrative and from Jesus' teaching that Christians need not separate themselves from Gentiles, fearing defilement from them, and that the Mosaic dietary laws need not be made compulsory for Gentile converts. Immediately after this unit, Jesus ministers to a Gentile Syrophoenician woman in the regions of Tyre (7:24–30), passes through the Gentile regions of the Decapolis

46. If Jesus declared all foods clean, then the food laws outlined in Lev 11:1–47; 19:26; Deut 12:21–25; 14:1–21, for example, would no longer be in force for Christians, and that would open the doors for Jews to have fellowship with Gentiles.

(7:31), and miraculously feeds a crowd of four thousand "during those days," which suggests that the crowd that was fed (8:1–10) was composed of Gentiles.

11.2.1.6 Incidental Statements Implying a Global Mission That Includes Gentiles

11.2.1.6.1 My House Will Be Called a House of Prayer for All Nations (Mark 11:17)

Jesus interprets his prophetic protest in the temple by citing God's intention, "My house will be called a house of prayer for all nations" (11:17; see Isa 56:7). Herod's temple has become a cave of refuge for brigands and does not fill this role. The context of this quote from Isaiah is important. It speaks of the foreigner joined to the Lord (Isa 56:3, 6), and God promises to gather not only the outcasts of Israel "but will gather still others" (Isa 56:8).[47] Since God's purposes will be fulfilled, Jesus' protest anticipates that the Gentile nations will be incorporated into Israel, and they will worship the one true God together in a restored temple that is an edifice, but not one made with hands.

11.2.1.6.2 The Gospel Must Be Preached to All Nations (Mark 13:10)

The various English translations of 13:9–10 make it seem obvious that the gospel is to be preached to all nations: "You must be on your guard. You will be handed over to the local councils and flogged in the synagogues. On account of me you will stand before governors and kings as witnesses to them. And the gospel must first be preached to all nations." Kilpatrick, however, musters grammatical arguments that challenge both the translation of the phrase "to all the nations" and the punctuation of verse 10. He argues that it should be translated, "And the gospel first must be preached *among* all nations."[48] He also contends that the phrase should be taken with the preceding sentence rather than the succeeding one and translated, "On account of me you will stand before governors and kings as witnesses to them and among all nations."[49]

Kilpatrick seriously misreads the text. The statement is best translated, "It is necessary first for the gospel to be preached," and it is included to explain parenthetically that the events mentioned in 13:6–9 do not herald the end (13:7). God provides time for worldwide mission before the end comes, and this implies that God intends for the world to have the opportunity to hear the gospel before the end.[50] As part of Jesus' warning that disciples are not to be misled by false messiahs

47. Köstenberger and O'Brien, *Salvation to the Ends of the Earth*, 82, contend that this allusion "breathes the spirit of Isa 40–66" and assumes that the Gentiles will respond.

48. Kilpatrick, "The Gentile Mission in Mark," 146–49.

49. Ibid., 149, following F. Crawford Burkitt, "Note on the Text and Interpretation of Mk. XIII 10," in *Christian Beginnings* (London: University of London Press, 1924), 145–55.

50. The interim is the period of God's "kindness, forbearance and patience" that is intended to lead people to repentance (Rom 2:4). Karl Kertelge, "Jüngerschaft und Nachfolge: Grundlegung von Kirche nach Markus," in *Der Evangelist als Theologe: Studien zum Markusevangelium* (ed. Thomas Söding; SBS 163; Stuttgart: Katholisches Bibelwerk, 1995), 161, comments that in its context, the declaration in 13:10 makes preaching the gospel to be "an eschatological 'necessity.'"

or cowered by political upheaval, natural disasters, threats to sacred institutions like the temple, or persecution, the statement in 13:10 implies that disciples should not allow anything to divert them from their mission to the nations. Adams points out, "Here, Mark's Jesus makes clear that the unknown timing of 'that day' must not be an excuse for inertia."[51] Standing before governors and kings because of their faith (13:9) gives them unique access to leaders and an extraordinary opportunity to give their testimony (see Acts 4:1–21; 5:17–42; 25:13–26:32; Phil 1:12–13).

11.2.1.6.3 Wherever the Gospel Is Preached throughout the World (Mark 14:9)

An anonymous woman shows her love and devotion to Jesus in anointing his head with precious ointment. Onlookers rebuke her for wasting something that could have been sold and the proceeds used to feed the poor (14:3–5). Jesus rebukes them for censuring her and explains, "She has done a beautiful thing to me" by anointing "my body beforehand to prepare for my burial" (14:6, 8). He then prophesies that this act of sacrificial love will not be forgotten: "Truly I tell you, wherever the gospel is preached throughout the world, what she has done will also be told, in memory of her" (14:9).

This prophecy assumes two ideas. First, the significance of her deed can only be recognized in retrospect, after his death and burial. Second, it affirms that the gospel will be preached to all the nations (14:9). This gospel is not a tragedy but the good news of Jesus' death and resurrection, and it will not be confined to a small corner of the world. Jesus' followers will proclaim it among the Gentiles throughout the world.

Jesus' prophecy is buttressed by another assurance that the returning Son of Man will "send his angels and gather his elect from the four winds, from the ends of the earth to the ends of the heavens" (13:27). Believers will be gathered wherever they are, and one can infer that this prophecy in 13:27 must imply that the gospel will have been preached throughout the world, and that persons throughout the world, including Gentiles, have responded to it.

11.2.1.7 The Confession by a Roman Centurion That Jesus Is the Son of God (Mark 15:39)

A Roman centurion, who witnesses how Jesus died on the cross, declares, "Surely this man was the Son of God!" (15:39). What is significant for Mark's view of mission is that this confession is made by the Gentile commander of the execution squad and not by a Jew.[52] His confession stands in stark contrast to the mockery of the Jewish scoffers who taunt Jesus to perform a miraculous feat by coming down from the cross (15:29–32) or jeer about a miraculous rescue by Elijah to save him (15:35–36). Jesus' ignominious death confirmed for the bystanders that his

51. Adams, *The Stars*, 166.

52. Kato, *Die Völkermission*, 80, 193.

claims were false (see Wis 2:17–20). This pagan outsider saw his powerless death and drew a different conclusion. "Seeing" is a metaphor for faith in Mark, and the centurion's faith was not produced by some display of power but by a revelation from God. Betz and Riesner contend that this confession conveys through narrative an extraordinary theological truth:

> The vicarious expiating death of the Christ and Son of God had an effect which extended beyond the boundaries of Israel, precisely because he revealed eschatologically the love of God for both just and unjust. The forgiveness of sins and the righteousness which stands before God are now no longer earned by fulfilling the law but through faith alone.[53]

Jesus' death will result in bringing others, Jews and Gentiles, to faith and confession. This confession conveys that his death is indeed "a death on behalf of the many (10:45; 14:24)."[54]

53. Otto Betz and Rainer Riesner, *Jesus, Qumran and the Vatican: Clarifications* (New York: Crossroad, 1994), 134.

54. Senior and Stuhlmueller, *Mission*, 225.

Chapter 12

Mark's Theology of Atonement and Salvation

Bibliography

Ådna, Jostein. "Jesus' Symbolic Act in the Temple (Mark 11:15–17): The Replacement of the Sacrificial Cult by His Atoning Death." Pp. 461–75 in *Gemeinde ohne Tempel*. Ed. Beate Ego, Armin Lange, and Peter Pilhofer. WUNT 2/118. Tübingen: Mohr Siebeck, 1999. Idem. *Jesu Stellung zum Tempel: Die Tempelaktion und das Tempelwort als Ausdruck seiner messianischen Sendung.* WUNT 2/119. Tübingen: Mohr Siebeck, 2000. **Ahearne-Kroll, Stephen P.** *The Psalms of Lament in Mark's Passion: Jesus' Davidic Suffering.* SNTSMS 142. Cambridge: Cambridge University Press, 2007. **Backhaus, Knut.** "'Lösepreis für viele' (Mark 10,45): Zur Heilsbedeutung des Todes Jesu bei Markus." Pp. 91–118 in *Der Evangelist als Theologe: Studien zum Markusevangelium*. Ed. Thomas Söding. SBS 163. Stuttgart: Katholisches Bibelwerk, 1995. **Bennett, Wilbert J., Jr.** "The Son of Man Must...." *NovT* 17 (1975): 113–29. **Best, Ernest.** *The Temptation and the Passion: The Markan Soteriology.* 2nd ed. SNTSMS 2. Cambridge: Cambridge University Press, 1990. **Bolt, Peter G.** *Jesus' Defeat of Death: Persuading Mark's Early Readers.* SNTSMS 125. Cambridge: Cambridge University Press, 2003. Idem. *The Cross from a Distance: Atonement in Mark's Gospel.* NSBT 18. Downers Grove, IL: InterVarsity Press, 2004. **Brown, Raymond E.** *The Death of the Messiah: From Gethsemane to the Grave: A Commentary on the Passion Narratives in the Four Gospels.* 2 vols. ABRL. New York: Doubleday, 1994. **Donahue, John R.** *Are You the Christ? The Trial Narrative in the Gospel of Mark.* SBLDS 10. Missoula, MT: Society of Biblical Literature, 1973. **Edwards, J. Christopher.** *The Ransom Logion in Mark and Matthew: Its Reception and Its Significance for the Study of the Gospels.* WUNT 2/327. Tübingen: Mohr Siebeck, 2012. **Gamel, Brian K.** "Salvation in a Sentence: Mark 15:39 as Markan Soteriology." *JTI* 6 (2012): 65–77. **Gray, Timothy C.** *The Temple in the Gospel of Mark: A Study in its Narrative Role.* WUNT 2/242. Tübingen: Mohr Siebeck, 2008. **Gurtner, Daniel M.** "The Rending of the Veil and Markan Christology: 'Unveiling' the 'ΥΙΟΣ ΘΕΟΥ (Mark 15:38–39)." *BibInt* 15 (2007): 292–306. **Hengel, Martin.** *The Atonement: The Origins of the Doctrine in the New Testament.* Trans. John Bowden. Philadelphia: Fortress, 1981. **Huys, Marc.** "Turning the Tables: Jesus' Temple Cleansing and the Story of Lycaon." *ETL* 86 (2010): 137–61. **Juel, Donald H.** *Messiah and Temple: The Trial of Jesus in the*

Gospel of Mark. SBLDS 31. Missoula, MT: Scholars Press, 1977. **Kingsbury, Jack Dean.** "The Significance of the Cross within Mark's Story." Pp. 95–105 in *Gospel Interpretation: Narrative-Critical and Social-Scientific Approaches*. Ed. Jack Dean Kingsbury. Harrisburg, PA: Trinity Press International, 1997. **Kirk, J. R. Daniel.** "Time for Figs, Temple Destruction, and Houses of Prayer in Mark 11:12–25." *CBQ* 74 (2012): 509–27. **Neusner, Jacob.** "Money-Changers in the Temple: The Mishnah's Explanation." *NTS* 35 (1989): 287–90. **O'Brien, Kelli S.** *The Use of Scripture in the Markan Passion Narrative*. LNTS 384. London/New York: T&T Clark, 2010. **Oyen, Geert van, and Tom Shepherd**, eds. *The Trial and Death of Jesus: Essays on the Passion Narrative in Mark*. CBET 45. Leuven: Peeters, 2006. **Riesner, Rainer.** "Back to the Historical Jesus through Paul and His School (The Ransom Logion—Mark 10.45; Matthew 20.28)." *JSHJ* 1 (2003): 171–99. **Senior, Donald.** *The Passion of Jesus in the Gospel of Mark*. Wilmington, DE: Michael Glazier, 1984. **Stuhlmacher, Peter.** "Vicariously Giving His Life for Many, Mark 10:45 (Matt. 20:28)." Pp. 16–29 in *Reconciliation, Law, and Righteousness: Essays in Biblical Theology*. Trans. Everett R. Kalin. Philadelphia: Fortress, 1986. **Telford, William R.** *The Barren Temple and the Withered Fig Tree: A Redaction-Critical Analysis of the Cursing of the Fig-Tree Pericope in Mark's Gospel and Its Relation to the Cleansing of the Temple Tradition*. JSNTSup 1. Sheffield: JSOT, 1980. **Watts, Rikki.** "The Psalms in Mark's Gospel." Pp. 25–45 in *The Psalms in the New Testament*. Ed. Steve Moyise and Maarten J. J. Menken. London/New York: T&T Clark, 2004.

12.1 THE DIVINE MUST

In Jesus' first prediction of his passion and resurrection, he states the Son of Man *must* suffer many things, be rejected by the elders, the chief priests, and the teachers of the law (scribes), and be killed (8:31). Jesus' death is not a tragic accident, a miscalculation, or an unhappy twist of fate. The use of "must" means that his death conforms to the divine will and plan.[1] Mark calls into question the religious categories of the age by narrating how God's salvation comes to the world through the crucifixion and resurrection of Jesus. Smith asserts, "The three Passion predictions (8:31; 9:31; 10:33–34), even though they are heavy with the foreboding of death, contain a theology of providence. These sayings declare that it is not merely sinful men who lead Jesus to the cross but the Father who is working out His predetermined plan."[2]

This point is repeated when Jesus descends with his three disciples from the Mount of Transfiguration. He responds to the disciples' question asking why the teachers of the law say that Elijah must come first with another question: "To be sure, Elijah does come first, and restores all things. Why then is it written that the Son of Man must suffer much and be rejected?" (9:11–12). The implication is that

1. Bennett, "The Son of Man Must . . . ," 113–29.

2. Robert H. Smith, "Darkness at Noon: Mark's Passion Narrative," *CTM* 44 (1973): 332.

what happened to Elijah, who has come in the person of John the Baptist, and what will happen to the Son of Man fulfill what is written about them in Scriptures.

This point emerges again at the Last Supper with the grim announcement that one of those eating with him would betray him. Jesus declares, "The Son of Man will go just as it is written about him. But woe to that man who betrays the Son of Man! It would be better for him if he had not been born" (14:21). This statement again assumes that God's plan for the Son of Man is revealed in the Scriptures, but Jesus does not identify which Scriptures. No single verse emerges that reveals that it is necessary, let alone why it is necessary, for the Messiah to suffer and die. While it is much debated, it seems to me that the Suffering Servant Songs in Isaiah, particularly Isa 53, provide the primary background for understanding this divine purpose. Bolt comments, "Once Jesus took on the role of the servant, suffering was inevitable, and the passion predictions now make that explicit."[3]

Mark's narrative accords with Paul's view in "the centrality that they both assign to the cross of Jesus as the definitive saving event performed by the God of Israel."[4] The divine imperative behind Jesus' death tempers the disgrace of his crucifixion. Since Jesus' death fulfills Scripture, it reveals that God's intention for that death is to provide salvation for the world. The crucifixion not only clarifies his identity as the Messiah who must die as a king,[5] but it also achieves an atoning sacrifice for people fettered by the chains of their sin and guilt.

12.2 The Soteriological Significance of Jesus' Death

Though Jesus frequently alludes to his looming death in the narrative, he remarks on its soteriological significance only twice in Mark. The two occasions take place at climactic points in the narrative. In the first, Jesus announces that the Son of Man came not to be served but to serve, and to give his life as a ransom for many (10:45). This declaration serves as the conclusion of the section that begins in 8:27 and contains Jesus' instruction to his disciples about his impending death and resurrection and its implications for discipleship.[6] The second declaration occurs at the climax of the Last Supper in 14:24, when Jesus interprets the meaning of the cup that he distributes to the disciples: "This is my blood of the covenant, which is poured out for many."

12.2.1 To Give His Life as a Ransom for Many (Mark 10:45)

Jesus has stated that he must die in 8:31 and 9:31, but he does not explain why he must die. The third and final announcement of his passion and resurrection in

3. Bolt, *The Cross*, 50.

4. Bird, "Mark: Interpreter of Peter and Disciple of Paul," 39. Jack Dean Kingsbury, "The Significance of the Cross within Mark's Story," in *Gospel Interpretation: Narrative-Critical and Social-Scientific Approaches* (ed. Jack Dean Kingsbury; Harrisburg, PA: Trinity Press International, 1997), 95, dubs Mark "the Gospel of the cross."

5. Donald H. Juel, "The Origin of Mark's Christology," in *The Messiah: Developments in Earliest Judaism and Christianity: The First Princeton Symposium on Judaism and Christian Origins* (ed. James H. Charlesworth; Minneapolis: Fortress, 1992), 458.

6. Norman Perrin, "The Son of Man in the Synoptic Tradition," *BR* 13 (1968): 24, affirms that "its position as the climax of the section 8:27–10:52 alone guarantees its immense importance for the Marcan theology."

10:33–34 provides the fullest statement of his suffering and death, and the conclusion of the unit in 10:45 provides an explanation: "For even the Son of Man did not come to be served, but to serve, and to give his life as a ransom for many."[7] Evans comments that in contrast to the great men who lord it over others and turn them into slaves (10:42), "Jesus is willing to give his life in exchange for their freedom from bondage."[8] The image of ransoming those in bondage gives an entirely different picture of how the strong man (Satan) will lose his possessions (3:27). There is no violent assault on hell to lead a great escape. The violence will be done to Jesus, who gives his life as payment to set the prisoners free.

12.2.1.1 The Old Testament Background of the Saying

Mark rarely cites the OT texts verbatim though he is heavily influenced by Isaiah in composing his gospel. Though Isa 53:10–12 is not quoted verbatim, the verbal echoes from Isa 53 in the LXX make it evident to many that it provides the backdrop for the idea of Jesus' vicarious death for the sins of the many. Both texts also refer to the "many" (five times in 52:13–53:12) who will benefit from the death. The one who came to serve and not to be served resonates with the righteous one "who serves many" (53:11, LXX). The benefit for "many" is repeated twice: the righteous servant will "serve *many*" ("justify many," 53:11, MT) and "bore the sin of many" (53:12), as the Son of Man gives his life as a ransom for *many*. The idea of the Son of Man giving his life (soul) in Mark's text also appears in 53:12, though it is expressed differently: "His soul was delivered to death" (LXX); or "he poured out his soul to death" (MT). Making the suffering servant an offering for sin in 53:10 is akin to the idea of giving his life as a "ransom" in Mark.

Although the noun "ransom" does not appear in Isa 53, the Greek verb form of the word, usually translated "to redeem," does surface frequently (35:9; 41:14; 43:1, 14; 44:22–24; 51:11; 52:3; 62:12; 63:9), and the noun appears in 45:13. The connection to Isa 53 should be clear when one recognizes, as France asserts, "the whole thrust of Is. 53 is to present the servant as one who suffers and dies for the redemption of his people, whose life is offered as a substitute for their guilt."[9] The question posed by Watts, "where else if not here in the OT can we find any concept of a 'serving' figure who, in an eschatological context, gives his life for 'the many'?" points persuasively to Isa 53. There is no other passage.[10]

Daniel 7:13–14 is also an important text in Mark (see 8:38–9:1; 13:26; 14:62), and Beale makes the case that most commentators have failed to notice sufficiently

7. See Max Wilcox, "On the Ransom-Saying in Mark 10:45c, Matt 20:28c," in *Geschichte—Tradition—Reflexion: Festschrift für Martin Hengel zum 70. Geburtstag. Bd. 3: Frühes Christentum* (ed. Hubert Cancik, Hermann Lichtenberger, and Peter Schäfer; Tübingen: Mohr Siebeck, 1996), 173–86; Rainer Riesner, "Back to the Historical Jesus through Paul and His School (The Ransom Logion—Mark 10.45; Matthew 20.28)," *JSHJ* 1 (2003): 171–99, for strong arguments that the saying originates with Jesus.

8. Evans, *Mark 8:27–16:20*, 122.

9. France, *Mark*, 420.

10. Rikki E. Watts, "Jesus' Death, Isaiah 53, and Mark 10:45: A Crux Revisited," in *Jesus and the Suffering Servant* (ed. William H. Bellinger Jr. and William R. Farmer; Harrisburg. PA: Trinity Press International, 1998), 143. The image of the cup that Jesus must drink recalls the bitter cup of the Lord's wrath that has caused Israel to stagger (Isa 51:17, 22). What follows in Isaiah suggests that the servant of the Lord will exhaust the bitter cup of God's wrath on behalf of Israel. Bolt, *The Cross*, 67, maintains that with the ransom saying, Jesus alludes that "as the servant of the Lord, he will drink the cup of God's wrath."

the Danielic complexion of Mark 10:45. The question about the ranking of persons when Jesus comes into the glory of his eschatological kingdom (10:37, 40) prompts him to teach that status in the kingdom of God will be completely opposite from the way rankings manifest themselves in earthly kingdoms (10:42–44). Jesus illustrates the ironic path to eminence in God's kingdom by saying the Son of Man has come to serve (10:45). Beale sees the connection between Mark 10:45 and Dan 7:13–14 in the reference to the Son of Man's "coming" and to all the nations "serving" him.[11] In my opinion, the ransom saying in 10:45 weaves Isaian themes with Dan 7:13–14 in much the same way Mark knits together biblical passages in 1:2–3 to interpret one another. The passage from Daniel is interpreted in light of the Suffering Servant of Isaiah 53 so that the Danielic Son of Man prophecy is being fulfilled in "a hitherto unexpected manner."[12] The Suffering Servant of Isa 53 redefines "the mission and destiny of the 'son of man' of Dan 7."[13]

The request of James and John that prompted Jesus' response also presumes the Danielic vision of the kingdom in which the Son of Man is exalted and "the sovereignty, power and greatness of all the kingdoms under heaven will be handed over to the holy people of the Most High. His kingdom will be an everlasting kingdom, and all rulers will worship and obey him" (Dan 7:27). The image of "thrones" set in place (7:9) and a court sitting in judgment (7:10, 26) may have stirred the Zebedee brothers' imaginations and their ambition to become imperial acolytes. The merging of the image of the Suffering Servant, who, in Isa 53, is executed, with the image of the Son of Man in Dan 7, which does not include this idea of suffering and death, turns this expectation upside down. It refashions the Son of Man's glory in the Danielic imagery from eschatological triumph with all the nations serving him to the imagery of a suffering servant whose glory will radiate from the cross on which he serves others by giving his life as a vicarious ransom for them.[14]

12.2.1.2 The Meaning of "Ransom"

The word "ransom" (*lytron*) only occurs here and in the parallel in Matt 20:28 in the NT. Deissmann argues that the popular usage of the word would have made the listeners of all classes connect it to the purchase money for manumitting slaves (see also Lev 25:47–55).[15] Ransom language is used frequently for God's redeeming Israel from their slavery in Egypt.[16] It was also used in reference to freeing prisoners of war and debtors.[17] Inscriptional evidence also exists that indicates the term was

11. Beale, *A New Testament Biblical Theology*, 196.

12. Ibid., 195.

13. Evans, *Mark 8:27–16:20*, 123.

14. De Mingo Kaminouchi, *"But It Is Not So Among You,"* 146.

15. Deissmann, *Light from the Ancient East*, 331–32. See J. Albert Harrill, *The Manumission of Slaves in Early Christianity* (HUT 32; Tübingen: Mohr Siebeck, 1995), 30–31. Marcus, *Mark 8–16*, 749, also cites Harrell and *1 Clem.* 55:2, "We know of many among ourselves who have given themselves to bondage that they might ransom others," to show that it can also be used to mean to take the place of another in enslavement.

16. See, e.g.,, Exod 6:6–8; Deut 7:8; 9:26; 13:5; 15:15; 24:18; 2 Sam 7:23; 1 Chr 17:21; Neh 1:10; Pss 74:2; 77:15; 78:42–55; 106:10; Isa 51:10–11; Mic 6:4.

17. Wilcox, "On the Ransom-Saying," 178, concludes that "the most promising choice of meaning is that of a payment for release of prisoners or hostages."

used in Hellenistic cults as an offering made to the gods to expiate some offense.[18] Kertelge defines it as "the 'price of release' for the liberation of a prisoner or debtor, in which the extent of the price of redemption and the manner of its payment follows certain conventions, but is commonly determined by the 'right of the sovereign.'"[19] This metaphor fits Jesus' rhetorical question, "What can anyone give in exchange for their soul?" (8:37). The implied answer is that humans are too insolvent to be able to offer anything to redeem their souls (see Ps 49:7–8).

Jesus' question explains why a ransom is required. He has already expressed his solidarity with sinners who need a physician (2:14–17), and now he identifies them as the many who need to be redeemed. His death pays the price to liberate spiritually bankrupt humans. Unlike Isa 53, the ransom saying in Mark 10:45 emphasizes the initiative of Jesus. He is not a scapegoat but actively gives his life in redeeming others.[20] This theological perspective resonates throughout the NT.[21]

Jesus does not specify to whom the ransom is paid. It is clearly not paid to Satan, since Satan is plundered, not paid off (3:27), and Satan tries in vain to forestall Jesus' death (8:33). Jesus also does not specify from what the many are ransomed. It could be from death, from sin, from the divine penalty of disobedience to God, from enslavement to satanic hostile powers, or from all of the above.

12.2.1.3 The Meaning of "For Many"

The Greek preposition in the phrase "to give his life a ransom *for* many" is predominantly translated as "for" (*anti*), meaning "in behalf of," but it can also mean "instead of" or "as an exchange."[22] If it is the latter, it means that Jesus takes the place of the many as a substitutionary offering for them.[23] He becomes their

18. G. H. R. Horsley, *New Documents Illustrating Early Christianity* (Sydney: Ancient History Documentary Centre, Macquarie University, 1982), 2:90; 3:72–75. See also Adela Yarbro Collins, "The Signification of Mark 10:45 among Gentile Christians," *HTR* 90 (1997): 371–82, who cites epigraphical evidence that the term could refer to an offering that releases a person from the consequences of a vow or a sin.

19. Karl Kertelge, "λύτρον, ου, τό," *EDNT*, 2:365.

20. Edwards, *Mark*, 328. In Judaism, a martyr's death could make atonement (see 2 Macc 7:37–38; 4 Macc 6:27–29; 17:21–22), but Mark views Jesus' death as far more than simply a martyrdom.

21. J. Christopher Edwards, *The Ransom Logion in Mark and Matthew: Its Reception and Its Significance for the Study of the Gospels* (WUNT 2/327; Tübingen: Mohr Siebeck, 2012), 30–53, provides a study of the reception of this saying in the NT. The following passages reflect on the theology of this saying: Luke 24:21; John 10:11, 15, 17–18; 15:13; Rom 3:24–25; 5:8; 1 Cor 1:30; 6:20; 7:23; Gal 1:4, 2:20; 3:13; 4:5; Eph 1:7; 5:2, 25; Col 1:14; 1 Tim 2:5–6; Titus 2:14; Heb 9:5, 12, 14–15; 1 Pet 1:18; 2:22–24; 1 John 2:2; 3:16; Rev 1:5–6.

22. It has this meaning in Matt 2:22; 5:38; Luke 11:11; Rom 12:17; 1 Thess 5:15; Heb 12:16; 1 Pet 3:9.

23. Hubert Frankemölle, "ἀντί," *EDNT*, 1:109, makes the point that "context determines the semantic structure of the prep., which contrasts the persons. In this way the death of Jesus is interpreted as a vicarious sacrifice of life, as a substitutionary offering for the life of the many which has been forfeited through their own guilt." A. T. Robertson, *A Grammar of the Greek New Testament in the Light of Historical Research* (Nashville: Broadman, 1934), 573, argues that the preposition means "in the place of" or "instead," which supports "the substitutionary conception of Christ's death." See also Nigel Turner, *Grammatical Insights into the New Testament* (Edinburgh: T&T Clark, 1965), 173; Rupert E. Davies, "Christ in Our Place—The Contribution of the Prepositions," *TynBul* 21 (1970): 76; Murray J. Harris, *Prepositions and Theology in the Greek New Testament* (Grand Rapids: Zondervan, 2012), 52–54. Wallace, *Greek Grammar beyond the Basics*, 365–68, cites the work of Bruce K. Waltke, "The Theological Significations of Ἀντί and Ὑπέρ in the New Testament" (Th.D. dissertation; Dallas Theological Seminary, 1958), 1:127–28, and concludes that it means that Jesus "not only is the price paid for the redemption of the many, stressing the redemptive work on the cross, but also He did this by '... nothing less than to step into their places...,' enduring the divine wrath to make propitiation. The meaning *in exchange for* points to the results of His vicarious suffering; and the meaning *in the place of* points to the method in which this redemptive work is accomplished. The blending of two concepts into the one preposition is not unusual."

substitute by doing for them what they cannot do for themselves. The word "many" may refer to a restricted, privileged group—many, but not all,[24] or it may have an inclusive sense referring to "all," the many who cannot be counted. Paul's discussion of the repercussions of Adam's trespass and Christ's obedience in Rom 5:12–19 uses "many" and "all" interchangeably. In the same way, "the many" in Mark 10:45 likely represents the sum total of humanity.[25] The saying is interpreted in 1 Tim 2:6, "who gave himself as a ransom for all people," to mean that Jesus died for all without limitation (see 2 Cor 5:14–15, 19). The "many" refers to the lawless and ungodly and from a NT perspective includes all humanity.

Jeremias points out that this universal offer of atonement was unheard of in the rabbinic tradition.[26] While all humanity potentially could profit from Christ's sacrificial death, the reality is that the ransom only avails for those who believe in Jesus and accept his demands to deny themselves and to take up a cross and follow him (8:34–38). While "salvation has been prepared potentially for the *many* or for all ... it is realized only through acceptance of the offer."[27]

12.2.2 This Is My Blood of the Covenant, Which Is Poured Out for Many (Mark 14:24)

The Last Supper was remembered by the disciples and the tradition was passed on (1 Cor 11:23–26), "not simply because it was the last meal of Jesus with the Twelve, but because he did and said something memorable."[28] Jeremias notes that the meaning of the Last Supper does not center on the founding of a new rite but on the fact that Jesus "linked an announcement and interpretation of his coming suffering with the familiar rite of grace before and after the meal."[29] Mark offers only a terse summary of it.

Since one normally broke bread to distribute and eat it, breaking the bread does not necessarily signify what will be done to Jesus' body. But the imagery of blood being poured out (often translated "shed") points to a violent death (see Matt 23:35; Luke 11:50; Acts 22:20; Rom 3:15 [Isa 59:7]; Rev 16:6). In my opinion, this image echoes Isa 53:12, "Therefore I will give him a portion among the great, and he will divide the spoils with the strong, because he poured out his life unto death, and was numbered with the transgressors. For he bore the sin of many, and made intercession for the transgressors."[30]

Jesus does not attach an explicit soteriological interpretation to the bread. After blessing it, he simply gives it to the disciples and says, "Take it; this is my body" (Mark 14:22). This symbolic action is left vague, though 1 Cor 11:24 makes clear

24. "The many" is used in the Dead Sea Scrolls (1QS 6:1, 7–25; CD 13:7; 14:7) to refer to the community.

25. Joachim Jeremias, "πολλοί," *TDNT*, 6:536–45.

26. Jeremias, *Eucharistic Words*, 230–31.

27. G. Nebe, "πολύς, πολλή, πολύ," *EDNT*, 3:133.

28. Hooker, *Mark*, 338.

29. Joachim Jeremias, *New Testament Theology: The Proclamation of Jesus* (trans. John Bowden; New York: Scribner's, 1971), 290.

30. Ibid., 226–31; R. T. France, *Jesus and the Old Testament: His Application of Old Testament Passages to Himself and His Mission* (Downers Grove, IL: InterVarsity Press, 1971), 120–23; Pesch, *Markusevangelium*, 2:358–59. Jeremias, *New Testament Theology*, 291, claims, "without Isa. 53 the eucharistic words remain incomprehensible."

that it is "for you" ("in behalf of you"). The interpretation attached to the cup, however, helps explain what it means. After taking the cup, offering thanks, and giving it to his disciples for them all to drink from it, Jesus announces, "This is my blood of the covenant, which is poured out for many" (14:24). The Jewish aversion to blood is notorious, and one can only imagine the shocked horror of these Jewish disciples when Jesus announces, "This is my blood," *after* they drank the cup. The consumption of blood is forbidden to all persons, not simply those under Jewish law (Gen 9:4; see Acts 15:20, 29), because it represents "the life," and because it had been ordained by God as a means of atonement. The blood of the sacrificial animals was poured out by the priests on the altar as a sin offering to atone for the sins of the people (Exod 24:6; 29:12; Lev 4:17, 18, 25, 30, 34; 9:9; Deut 12:27). Any animals killed for human consumption, therefore, must be drained of all blood before being eaten.[31] Therefore, to drink blood was not only to break a universal commandment but to desecrate something that was holy (Lev 17:10–11).[32] This jolting announcement dramatizes Jesus' interpretation of what the cup of wine represents as a symbolic renewal of the covenant.[33] But it does so with a dramatic twist that connects his death to the expiation of sins with the phrase "for many" (see 10:45).

Mark does not identify Jesus' blood poured out for many as representing a "new" covenant (see Luke 22:20) as prophesied in Jer 31:31–34:

> "The days are coming," declares the Lord,
> "when I will make a new covenant
> with the people of Israel
> and with the people of Judah.
> It will not be like the covenant
> I made with their ancestors
> when I took them by the hand
> to lead them out of Egypt,
> because they broke my covenant,
> though I was a husband to them,"
> declares the Lord.
> "This is the covenant I will make with the people of Israel
> after that time," declares the Lord.
> "I will put my law in their minds
> and write it on their hearts.
> I will be their God,
> and they will be my people.

31. Hooker, *Mark*, 342.

32. W. D. Davies, *Paul and Rabbinic Judaism: Some Rabbinic Elements in Pauline Theology* (rev. ed.; New York: Harper & Row, 1967), 244–50, discusses this issue and how Paul refines his formulation of the tradition to refer to "the new covenant in my blood."

33. Elisabeth Rexeis, "Die symbolische Verletzung des jüdischen Bluttabus in Mk 14,23f. par Mt 26,27f.: Das Becherwort in Einsetzungsbericht aus historisch-kritischer Sicht," *SNTSU* 38 (2013): 73–96, shows how this saying is a scandalous breach of the Jewish taboo against blood and argues for its authenticity as a dramatic gesture on Jesus' part that intensifies his word about the renewal of the covenant.

No longer will they teach their neighbor,
    or say to one another, 'Know the LORD,'
because they will all know me,
    from the least of them to the greatest,"
                                        declares the LORD.
"For I will forgive their wickedness
    and will remember their sins no more."

It is more likely that the imagery is intended to assert a connection to the expiatory sacrifices under the old dispensation.[34]

When God delivered Israel from captivity in Egypt, the first covenant was sealed by the blood of a sacrificial animal (Exod 24:3–8). Jesus' sacrifice seals a covenant, but it brings about something that is completely new. It establishes a covenant that brings redemption for the many that now makes all other sacrifices unnecessary. Hebrews argues that the blood of sacrificial victims had always been insufficient and temporary by virtue of the fact that they had to be continually repeated (Heb 10:1–22). The forgiveness of sins is now accomplished through the sacrifice of Jesus' life, which is symbolized in the bread broken and shared and the wine poured out and shared. His sacrifice is for all and once for all. Ironically, it is at Golgotha, the place of the skull, not at the temple, that the ultimate sacrifice for the forgiveness of sins occurs. Jesus' statement at the Last Supper about his death means that it "*is the vicarious death of the suffering servant, which atones for the sins of the 'many,' the peoples of the world, which ushers in the beginning of the final salvation and which effects the new covenant with God*."[35]

"The many" again does not imply a "limited, select group.... It links Jesus' death to the idea of vicarious sacrifice for the lawless, sinners, and transgressors."[36] Jesus' vow that he "will not drink again from the fruit of the vine until that day when I drink it new in the kingdom of God" (14:25) basically asserts that this cup of death will lead to the cup of eschatological glory when all things will be fulfilled.

Mark identifies the meal as a Passover meal (14:1, 12, 14, 16), but the primary elements associated with Passover meal—the unleavened bread,[37] the bitter herbs, and the lamb—go unmentioned in the description of the meal. Leon-Dufour contends that this silence is attributable to the Christian belief that the Passover of Israel was fulfilled in Jesus (1 Cor 5:7).[38] They would never need a ritual lamb again. Consequently, the meal's Passover associations are downplayed, and the Passover simply serves as a chronological marker for Jesus' execution.

34. I. J. du Plessis, "The Saving Significance of Jesus and His Death on the Cross in Luke's Gospel—Focussing on Luke 22:19b–20," *Neot* 28 (1994): 534.

35. Jeremias, *Eucharistic Words*, 231.

36. Edwards, *Mark*, 427. See above on 10:45.

37. The Greek word for unleavened bread (*azyma*) is not used; instead, the regular word for bread (*artos*) is used.

38. Xavier Léon-Dufour, *Sharing the Eucharistic Bread* (trans. Matthew J. O'Connell; Mahwah, NJ: Paulist, 1987), 193.

Contrasts and Parallels between the Passover and the Lord's Supper	
Passover	**The Lord's Supper**
In the old dispensation of the law	In the new dispensation of the kingdom
The great festival meal celebrating the birth of God's people	The new celebratory meal of the birth of God's people
Commemorates the liberation of the people of Israel from enslavement in Egypt	Commemorates the liberation of believers from every nation from their enslavement to sin
Participants associated themselves with redemption and a covenant with God	Participants associated themselves with redemption and a covenant with God
Participants look back to the exodus and forward to God's salvation	Participants look back to the cross and resurrection and forward to the consummation of the kingdom of God

12.3 JESUS' DEATH REPLACES THE ATONING SACRIFICES IN THE TEMPLE

Jesus' redemptive death has implications for the status of the temple. Its system of sacrifices for the sins of the people will become obsolete. Because the temple's leadership also failed to make it become a "house of prayer" for all the nations as God intended, it will be destroyed. Jesus' sacrificial death provides atonement for all, and he becomes the meeting place between God and all human beings.

12.3.1 The Cursing of the Fig Tree (Mark 11:12–14, 20–25)

Jesus' grand entry into Jerusalem riding on a coronation animal (11:1–10) marks the end of the time when he sought to avoid the crowd because he was teaching his disciples about his impending death (9:30–31). It also marks the beginning of his open confrontation with opponents in the temple that will result in his death. Jesus' impressive debut in Jerusalem, where he is joyously greeted by a lustily cheering throng shouting "Hosanna" and chanting one of the Hallel (thanksgiving) psalms (Ps 118:25–26) about the coming of David's kingdom, ends anticlimactically. He enters the temple, looks around, and leaves (11:11). Mark reports that it was late, but one might expect something a bit more dramatic to happen.

However, "this colorless ending to Jesus' dramatic entry into Jerusalem depicts more than meets the eye. It sets the stage for what will happen on the next day, and its true significance can only be filled in by the Old Testament." Jesus does not visit Herod's grandiose temple as if he were "a tourist dazzled by its glittering gold, glistening white marble, and gigantic stones."[39] Mark's use of the verb "to look around" does not refer to goggling at the sights but to scrutinizing something

39. Garland, *Mark*, 428.

critically (see 3:5, 34; 5:32; 10:23). Jesus' visit to the temple is not driven by any pious devotion, since Mark does not report that he offered prayers or sacrifice. The vital clue that explains this visit emerges in 11:3, where Jesus identifies himself as "the Lord" who requires a mount (11:3). "The Lord," who also comes in the name of the Lord (11:9), enters the temple at the end of the grand procession. This stop-off is meant to recall Malachi's prophecy in 3:1–2, which is partially quoted in Mark's introduction (1:2):

> "I will send my messenger, who will prepare the way before me. Then suddenly the Lord you are seeking will come to his temple; the messenger of the covenant, whom you desire, will come," says the LORD Almighty.
>
> "But who can endure the day of his coming? Who can stand when he appears? For he will be like a refiner's fire or a launderer's soap."

Jesus enters the temple to inspect it as the Lord.[40] When Mark identifies it as "late," he may be ironically communicating that it is "late" in more ways than one. The next day's events reveal that Jesus is neither awed nor pleased by what he sees, and it is too late for this temple and its cult.

The next day is given over to Jesus' theatrical action in the temple (11:15–19). It is nestled between the cursing of a fig tree and the discovery that it has been withered to the roots (11:12–14, 20–25). To summarize, the next morning when Jesus leaves Bethany where he was staying, he is hungry and spots a fig tree in leaf in the distance. When he finds that it has no fruit but only leaves, he pronounces a curse on it (11:14a). The curse contains a double negative. A literal translation reads, "May no one eat fruit from you no longer forever," which highlights the severity of this condemnation. Mark reports that the disciples heard what he said (11:14b).

After the incident in the temple, Jesus and the disciples return to Jerusalem the next morning the same way and see that the fig tree Jesus cursed has withered from the roots. Peter's stunned remark to Jesus, "Rabbi, look! The fig tree you cursed has withered!" underscores the effectiveness of Jesus' curse (11:20–21). Jesus then responds by teaching the disciples about the effectiveness of faith and prayer (11:22–25).

This story, which seems so out of character for Jesus, is made all the more puzzling by the statement, "Because it was not the season for figs." Many bewildered readers ask, Why does Jesus vent such anger on an inanimate object that fails to produce fruit out of season? Why does one intent on restoring life throughout his ministry suddenly wreak his malice on a tree? Klausner called it "a gross injustice on a tree which was guilty of no wrong and had but performed its natural function."[41] Manson finds the story to be "not in keeping with what we otherwise know of the character of Jesus" and comments: "It is a tale of miraculous power wasted in the service of ill-temper (for the supernatural energy employed to blast the unfortunate

40. The allegory of the Wicked Tenants offers another picture of this visit to Jerusalem and the temple. The vineyard owner sends his beloved son to collect the overdue rent (12:1–2).

41. Joseph Klausner, *Jesus of Nazareth* (London: George Allen & Unwin, 1925), 269.

tree might have been more usefully expended in forcing a crop of figs out of season); and as it stands is simply incredible."[42]

Giesen asks several other questions: Why was Jesus and no one else hungry after enjoying hospitality in Bethany (11:12)? Why did Jesus curse a tree for not producing figs when it was not the season for figs (11:13–14)? Why does Mark record that the disciples "heard" the curse (11:14)? Why did the tree wither from the roots (11:20) when Jesus only said, "May no one ever eat fruit from you again"?[43] Giesen concludes that the answers to these questions indicate that Jesus' actions were intended to have symbolic implications.[44] The cursing of the fig tree is an enacted parable.[45]

12.3.1.1 The Bracketing of the Cursing of the Fig Tree around the Temple Incident

From a Greco-Roman perspective, Jesus' action in the Jerusalem temple would seem to be a gross sacrilege of a sacred temple. Mark offers no rationale to explain why Jesus did this, except to surround it by the even more mystifying fig tree incident. Understanding it is essential for interpreting the temple event rightly.[46] The account of Jesus' encounter with the fig tree incident is quite different from the parable of the fig tree in Luke 13:6–9, in which the gardener implores his master to give an unfruitful tree one more chance—perhaps it will bear next year if I give it a load of manure. The fig tree that Jesus curses for bearing no fruit gets no reprieve, and no attempt is made to make it more productive. What is most ominous is that this destructive miracle is the last one that Jesus performs in the gospel. The fig tree account interprets what Jesus does in the temple. He is not trying to purify the temple of its abuses, but in a calculated prophetic gesture he is pronouncing God's judgment on it (see Matt 23:38).[47] When he exits the temple for the last time a couple of days later, he will prophesy its total destruction (13:1–2).

42. T. W. Manson, "The Cleansing of the Temple," *BJRL* 33 (1951): 279.

43. Gerhard Münderlein, "Die Verfluchung des Feigenbaumes (Mk. xi. 12–14)," *NTS* 10 (1963–64): 103–4, notes that Jesus condemned it to eternal fruitlessness, which is why it is shriveled to its roots. In other words, it is utterly destroyed.

44. Heinz Giesen, "Der verdorrte Feigenbaum—Eine symbolische Aussage? Zu Mk 11, 12–14.20f," *BZ* 20 (1976): 95–111. He interprets the episode as an eschatological sign of the inbreaking of God's kingdom that brings God's judgment.

45. Cranfield, *Mark*, 356, notes that the earliest commentary on Mark by Victor of Antioch in the fifth century recognized it as an enacted parable symbolizing the destruction of Jerusalem. See also Craig L. Blomberg, "The Miracles as Parables," in *Gospel Perspectives*, Vol. 6: *The Miracles of Jesus* (ed. David Wenham and Craig L. Blomberg; Sheffield: JSOT, 1986), 332–33.

46. See William R. Telford, *The Barren Temple and the Withered Fig Tree: A Redaction-Critical Analysis of the Cursing of the Fig-Tree Pericope in Mark's Gospel and Its Relation to the Cleansing of the Temple Tradition* (JSNTSup 1; Sheffield: JSOT, 1980); Robert H. Stein, "The Cleansing of the Temple in Mark (11:15–19): Reformation or Judgment?" in *Gospels and Tradition: Studies on Redaction Criticism of the Synoptic Gospels* (Grand Rapids: Baker, 1991), 121–33; Marcus, *Mark 8–16*, 788–90; Timothy C. Gray, *The Temple in the Gospel of Mark: A Study in Its Narrative Role* (WUNT 2/242; Tübingen: Mohr Siebeck, 2008), 39. Collins, *Mark*, 524–25, demurs and draws attention to studies that suggest intercalation to be a function of the essentially oral nature of reading in the ancient world. She concludes from these studies that such literary techniques are the author's way of aiding the listener and that "critics should then be cautious about exaggerating the degree to which the intercalated stories are intended to interpret one another." She goes on to suggest that, however illuminating such connections might be to the modern reader, they are not likely to reflect the author's intention. See also Gundry, *Mark*, 671–82. J. R. Daniel Kirk, "Time for Figs, Temple Destruction, and Houses of Prayer in Mark 11:12–25," *CBQ* 74 (2012): 511–12, carefully refutes these objections. He concludes, "Like sentences in a common paragraph, the two stories should be understood and interpreted together."

47. See the examples of prophetic actions in 1 Kgs 22:11; Isa 20:1–6; Jer 13:1–16; 19:1–15; 28:10–11; Ezek 4:1–3; Acts 21:11.

12.3.1.2 The Image of the Fig Tree

The barren fig tree is a metaphor for Israel when it has turned away from God (Isa 28:4; Jer 8:13; Hos 9:10, 15–17; Mic 7:1).[48] While Mark's readers may not have been familiar with the extrabiblical practices of the Pharisees (7:3–4), the frequent allusions to OT imagery and passages in the gospel suggest that they were familiar with the OT and would have been able to make the connections.[49] The fruitless fig tree is a transparent metaphor for Jerusalem, which is inexorably linked with the temple, and it is the temple with its corruption and imminent obsolescence after Jesus' death that is the object of his wrath, not the nation.[50] Like the fig tree, the bustling temple is all leaves that seem to attest to its productiveness, but it is deceptive advertising because it has no fruit.[51]

12.3.1.3 Jesus' Hunger

Jesus' hunger (11:12) allows him to make a prophetic point that symbolically depicts the judgment of the temple. On a second reading, he alone of the group is hungry, and it need not be restricted to physical hunger (see John 6:35). The hunger could be understood metaphorically and apply to his hunger for righteousness (Mic 7:1), faith, or justice.[52] In Mark, fruitfulness is a metaphor for a believing response to Jesus' message (4:1–20; see 12:1–12).

12.3.1.4 Not the Season for Figs

The statement that "he found nothing but leaves, because it was not the season for figs" (11:13) gives the impression that Jesus' angry lashing out at a seemingly innocent fig tree was extreme, to say the least. The word translated "season" (*kairos*), however, is the term Mark has used for eschatologically qualified time (1:14–15; 10:30; 13:33).[53] The use of this word suggests that Mark is not interested in commenting about botanical seasons but something else related to God's timing.

The vision in Ezek 47:12 reports that trees grow on both sides of the river, and "their leaves will not wither, nor will their fruit fail. Every month they will bear fruit, because the water from the sanctuary flows to them. Their fruit will serve for food and their leaves for healing." The implication is that trees near the temple in the messianic age should be especially fruitful, and bearing fruit should not be seasonal but continual.[54] Its fruitlessness contrasts with the abundant fruitfulness of the seeds planted in good ground in Jesus' parable (4:8, 20). Focant comments,

48. Telford, *The Barren Temple*, 129–63.

49. Rikki E. Watts, "The Lord's House and David's Lord: The Psalms and Mark's Perspective on Jesus and the Temple," *BibInt* 15 (2007): 312. Luke assumes that his Gentile audience would understand the imagery connected to the parable of the fig tree (Luke 13:6–9).

50. Telford, *The Barren Temple*, 141, notes that horticulture imagery is also connected to the proper operation of the temple and the cult.

51. Pliny, *Nat.* 16.49, claims that the fig tree is unique in producing fruit before leaves.

52. Giesen, "Der verdorrte Feigenbaum," 103–4.

53. In the allegory of the Wicked Tenants, at "the proper time" (*kairos*, NAB), the owner of the vineyard sent messengers to collect the fruit (12:2).

54. Incigneri, *Gospel*, 142–43.

"It is a disaster for the fig tree-temple not to bear fruit at the moment in which Jesus proclaims the coming of the reign of God."[55] It is not only that the fig tree-temple falsely represents its fruitfulness while having no fruit, the coming of Jesus as the Son of God, who will give his life as a ransom, displaces the temple in God's plan for the salvation of humanity. The statement that it was not the season for figs when it is applied to the temple entails that its usefulness in God's salvation history has passed. That reality explains why the tree, representing the temple, is cursed never to produce fruit again.

Bracketing the cursing of the fig tree around Jesus' action in the temple signifies that the religious center of Israel is similarly judged to be fruitless and ultimately will be destroyed.[56] The prophets used the image of the withered fig tree as a symbol of judgment and punishment. In Jeremiah, God laments, "When I would gather them, declares the Lord, there are no grapes on the vine, nor figs on the fig tree; even the leaves are withered, and what I gave them has passed away from them" (Jer 8:13, ESV; see also Isa 34:4; Jer 29:17; Hos 2:12; Joel 1:7). Cursing the fig tree "enacts parabolically for the benefit of the disciples the terminal condition of the Jerusalem cultus."[57]

12.3.1.5 The Fig Tree Withered to Its Roots

In 8:18, Jesus rebuked the disciples for having eyes but failing to see, ears but failing to hear, and not remembering and therefore not understanding the miracles of the loaves. For the first time in the gospel, the disciples hear (11:14), see (11:20), and remember (11:21), which is required for discerning the narrative symbolism of the events. Jesus personifies the righteous wrath of God against the temple that refuses to reform its ways and condones and participates in the oppression of the alien, the fatherless, and the widow; sheds innocent blood; steals; murders; commits adultery; and lies under oath (Jer 7:5–6, 9): "Therefore this is what the Sovereign Lord says: My anger and my wrath will be poured out on this place—on man and beast, on the trees of the field and on the crops of your land—and it will burn and not be quenched" (Jer 7:20). Incigneri points out, "In Ezekiel's terms, the Temple is not life-giving and, in a dramatic allusion to the 'death' of the Temple, while Jesus stands in the Court of the Gentiles pronouncing judgement, the fig tree outside Jerusalem is dying."[58]

12.3.2 Jesus' Actions in the Temple (Mark 11:15–18)

Mark reports that when Jesus entered the temple on this second day, he drove out those who were buying and selling there, overturned the tables of the moneychangers

55. Focant, *Mark*, 455.

56. There will be no thirty, sixty, or even a hundredfold return on the seed here (4:8–9) or even a harvest (4:29). The temple's sterility is obviously attributable to its leaders, whose spiritual malfeasance will result in bringing about its physical destruction.

57. Marshall, *Faith as a Theme*, 161.

58. Incigneri, *Gospel*, 143. William R. Telford, "More Fruit from the Withered Tree: Temple and Fig-Tree in Mark from a Graeco-Roman Perspective," in *Templum Amicitiae: Essays on the Second Temple Presented to Ernst Bammel* (ed. William Horbury; JSNTSup 48; Sheffield: JSOT, 1991), 264–304, notes that the imagery of fig trees was also associated with Rome, and a withered fig tree was an ominous portent.

and the benches of those selling doves, prevented anyone from carrying vessels through the temple, and announced that what God intended to be a house of prayer for all nations had been made into a den of robbers (11:15–18). Wedderburn asserts, "Scholarly opinion is more deeply divided over the interpretation of this action than is the case with most other questions presented by the New Testament texts."[59]

The phrase "den of robbers" leads many to assume that Jesus protests against the exploitation of worshipers through inflated prices for sacrificial animals and bloated fees for changing money into ritually acceptable coinage, not Roman or Greek currency. Others assume that Jesus is dismayed to discover business being conducted in the temple precincts, which hindered the worship of Gentiles by turning the outer court into a noisy open market. Still others argue that Jesus attempts to resanctify the Holy Mount by stopping what he perceived to be unholy activity within it to prevent any "further profanation."[60] All of these assumptions are mistaken. This action was a prophetic performance designed to signal God's coming judgment on the temple. Mark takes it also to mean that the temple is no longer a place where one can receive atonement through ritual sacrifices but atonement now comes through faith in the atoning power of Jesus' death as a ransom for many (10:45).

12.3.2.1 Jesus Was Not Rectifying Economic Injustice

The assumption that Jesus is only concerned that the temple hierarchy was guilty of profiteering from their monopoly over sacrificial commodities is wrong for a number of reasons. First, Jesus called it a "den of robbers," but robbers do not do their robbing in their "den." After committing their crimes, they retreat to their "den" as a place of safety. To be sure, Josephus censures the high priest Ananias (AD 47 to ca. 55) as the "great procurer of money" (*Ant.* 20.9.2 §§205–207; see *Ant.* 20.8.1. §181),[61] and Jesus may have objected to "the way the financial side of the sacrificial system was run."[62] Turning over tables and momentarily interrupting business, however, does little to rectify the situation in the long run. The moneychangers will set up their tables again, pick up their coins, and soon be back in business.

Kirk recognizes that the "den of robbers" citation from Jer 7:11 actually "points away from the notion of corrupt business practices in the temple. The sermon in Jeremiah 7 rebukes the people of Israel for oppressing the orphan and the widow, shedding innocent blood, and idolatry—and warns such people against treating the temple as a good-luck charm that will preserve them against their enemies (vv. 1–15)." They treat the temple as a "place of safety to which they can flee after committing various forms of injustice in other spheres."[63]

Second, Mark describes the crowd's response to Jesus' action as being "amazed at his teaching" (11:18). Jesus has not yet taught in the temple, so "his teaching"

59. Alexander J. M. Wedderburn, "Jesus' Action in the Temple: A Key or a Puzzle?" *ZNW* 97 (2006): 5.

60. Ahearne-Kroll, *Psalms of Lament*, 154.

61. This wealth was probably acquired from being a landowner who rented to tenants.

62. Richard Bauckham, "Jesus' Demonstration in the Temple," in *Law and Religion: Essays on the Place of the Law in Israel and Early Christianity* (ed. Barnabas Lindars; Cambridge: James Clarke, 1988), 78.

63. Kirk, "Time for Figs," 519.

can only refer to his interpretation of his actions from the Scripture (11:17). The verb "amaze" appears elsewhere in Mark to describe people who are stupefied by what Jesus says or does (1:22; 6:2; 7:37; 10:26). If it were obvious to the crowd in the temple that his action was a protest against fleecing the worshipers, one would expect them to applaud rather than to be bewildered.

Finally, since Jesus throws out both the sellers *and* the buyers, he is not trying to bring about an economic reform on behalf of the buyers. Jesus is not concerned that the sellers are taking advantage of the buyers; his action is a judgment on the entire enterprise.

12.3.2.2 Jesus Was Not Creating an Area for Gentiles to Pray

The assumption that Jesus was concerned that this commercial activity was hindering the Gentiles from praying in the outer court[64] is wrong for several reasons. First, Mark does not mention where this act occurred, and it is unlikely that the activity of changing money and offering sacrificial doves for sale was spread out all over the outer court of the temple. The larger animals were kept in the markets in the north end leading out from the "Sheep Gate" (John 5:2). The small temple market for cultic provisions was probably located inside the Royal Portico (Stoa) along the south wall of the plaza.[65]

Second, if the commercial activity did perchance spill over into the outer court, it was not viewed positively as the area where Gentiles could worship and pray.[66] It was not called "the court of the Gentiles" in the time of Jesus. That is a modern designation.[67] This area of Herod's expansion of the temple setting was regarded simply as the place beyond which Gentiles could not go. They could never enter the sanctuary to worship, and a balustrade surrounding it warned that Gentiles who breached it would face the penalty of death (see Acts 21:27–30).[68] The recent analysis of the inscription by Lllewelyn and van Beek deserves quoting:

---

64. So Lightfoot, *The Gospel Message*, 60–65; Gundry, *Mark*, 674, 676.

65. Jostein Ådna, "The Attitude of Jesus to the Temple: A Critical Examination of How Jesus' Relationship to the Temple is Evaluated within Israeli Scholarship, with Particular Regard to the Jerusalem School," *Mishkan* 17–18 (1992–93): 68; and Benjamin Mazar, "The Royal *Stoa* in the Southern Part of the Temple Mount," in *Recent Archaeology in the Land of Israel* (ed. Hershel Shanks; trans. Aryeh Finkelstein; Washington, DC: Biblical Archaeology Society, 1984), 141–47. Josephus describes the Royal Stoa in *Ant.* 15.11.5 §§411–416.

66. It should be remembered that this court was the result of Herod's expansion of the temple's setting. The size of the sanctuary was dictated by Moses and was rather modest and could not be expanded. Herod, the great builder, undertook an ambitious project to enhance its significance by increasing the size of its setting. He did this by building a spacious plaza with retaining walls. Schweizer, *Mark*, 233, rightly compares this area of the temple platform with "the square before a church visited by pilgrims."

67. Lloyd Gaston, *No Stone on Another: Studies in the Significance of the Fall of Jerusalem in the Synoptic Gospels* (NovTSup 23; Leiden: Brill, 1970), 87, n. 2, notes that it is occasionally mentioned that Gentiles may enter the outer court but only in a negative sense.

68. Two tablets with the Greek inscriptions have been found. The text of the complete one is cited in Emil Schürer, *The History of the Jewish People in the Age of Jesus Christ* (ed. and trans. Geza Vermes, Fergus Millar, and Matthew Black; Edinburgh: T&T Clark, 1979), 2:222, n. 85; 285, n. 57. It reads: "No foreigner is to enter within the forecourt and the balustrade around the sanctuary. Whoever is caught will have himself to blame for his subsequent death." See also Elias J. Bickerman, "The Warning Inscriptions of Herod's Temple," *JQR* 37 (1946–47): 387–405. Cecil Roth, "The Cleansing of the Temple and Zechariah xiv 21," *NovT* 4 (1960): 174–81, cites Zech 14:21 as the justification for the exclusion of Gentiles from the inner courts. Josephus, *J.W.* 6.2.4 §§124–126, records the irate Roman general Titus commenting on the leniency of the Romans for allowing the Jews to put up the parapet around their sanctuary that shut out foreigners and to put up inscriptions threatening those who went beyond it with death, while committing atrocities within those walls during the revolt against Rome.

> The outer court was greatly expanded by the construction of a massive pediment and its external limits defined by the colonnades (eastern and western sides) and a stoa (southern side); in typical Herodian fashion, contemporary Roman architectural practice, as evidenced in many of the *agorae* and *fora* of the Mediterranean world, was followed. And the outer court was to continue the function as an *agora*, i.e. a place of trade, to conduct business and to have agreements drawn up, etc. However, it is in the *stoa basileia* at the southern end of the pavement that Herod gave full expression to his regal status before a temple from which he, unlike his Hasmonean predecessors, was excluded. Also it is likely that Herod intended to hear legal cases here. In other words, the splendour of the temple and its inner courts was matched by the king's own innovative constructions in the outer court, and it was through these that most people gained access to the temple. The new structure thus advertised both the temple and Herod's rule, and by juxtaposing in such splendour the divine and the secular it highlighted the need to differentiate the two. The erection of the balustrade with its warning inscriptions was necessitated by such changes.[69]

The barricade drew the boundary between the sacred and the profane, the sanctuary and the outer court, which was not perceived to be a place of prayer for Gentiles. It is hard to imagine that Jesus was simply interested in clearing a quiet place for Gentiles to pray while the partition that barred them from the sanctuary remained. It is also hard to imagine that Mark thought that what God intended to be "a house of prayer for all nations" would be segregated and shut out everyone but properly purified Jews from the sacred place of God's presence.

12.3.2.3 Jesus Was Not Resanctifying the Temple

The assumption that Jesus attempts to resanctify the temple and to halt its further profanation is wrong for the following reasons. First, what Jesus does is markedly different from the purification of the temple carried out by Josiah (2 Kings 23) and Judas Maccabeus (1 Macc 4:36–59; see also 13:51; 2 Macc 10:7). Hooker points out that "as an act of reforming zeal," what Jesus does "would have to be judged a failure: the money changers no doubt soon recovered their coins, and the place was restored to order."[70] It is far more likely that Jesus seeks to make a point through dramatic prophetic action "rather than to have a concrete result."[71] Wedderburn claims that since Jesus did not cleanse all evil from the cult and did not really expect the priestly hierarchy to repent and mend their ways, his actions were symbolic. Like so many prophetic acts before when prophets threatened God's judgment was nigh, it "would go unheeded and would therefore be followed by the disaster that the prophet foresaw." Wedderburn asserts that "Jesus' action would be better described as warning of the need for cleansing *and* threatening destruction if that were not done."[72]

69. Stephen R. Llewelyn and Dionysia van Beek, "Reading the Temple Warning as a Greek Visitor," *JSJ* 42 (2011): 8–9.

70. Hooker, *Mark*, 264–65.

71. Sanders, *Jesus and Judaism*, 70.

72. Wedderburn, "Jesus' Action in the Temple," 14.

Betz makes an excellent historical case for why Jesus might have opposed the temple by reminding us that it was Herod's temple, in that he was its architect and builder of the large, splendid stones and buildings (13:1). He argues that Herod sought to legitimize his rule over Israel by following the model of his friend, the emperor Augustus, by building magnificent monuments to project his power.[73] Betz maintains that Herod's goal was to change Judaism into a Hellenistic Jewish ruler cult, and the primary means of accomplishing this was in the reconstruction and enlargement of the temple in Jerusalem. As a result, the temple cult became "politicized and commercialized," but it also brought "prosperity, political security, and international fame" to Jerusalem.[74] He contends that Jesus reacted against this transformation of temple worship.

Mark's standpoint in history, in my opinion, would have resulted in a quite different perspective of Jesus' actions, and I think that Mark also accurately reflects the theological implications that Jesus sought to convey by his prophetic protest. If Mark believes, as he certainly does, that Jesus had the authority on earth to forgive sins and to bypass the temple cult completely (2:10) and that his death was a ransom for many that established a covenant, then it is unlikely that he also believes that if the temple hierarchy had only repented and reformed aspects of the cult, all would have been well. From Mark's perspective, it was too late for reform. Gray concludes that Mark believes "that Jesus could not possibly have tried to cleanse the temple, because there was simply no time to do so — the eschatological harvest time had come — and there was no time to wait for another season."[75] A new era in salvation history was about to dawn within days.

Second, this view fails to recognize that this supposedly "unholy" activity in need of reform was central to the administration of the sacrificial cult. The people saw the temple's primary purpose to be the offering of sacrifices to God (see Josephus, *Ant.* 15.6.8 §248). Sanders maintains: "Those who write about Jesus' desire to return the temple to its 'original,' 'true' purpose, the 'pure' worship of God, seem to forget that the principal function of any temple is to serve as a place of sacrifice, and that sacrifices *require* the supply of suitable animals."[76] They also require a convenient means for pilgrims to purchase sacrificial offerings and for them to change money into the acceptable coinage to pay their half-shekel dues that kept the daily sacrifice for the forgiveness of sins of the people. Even if these activities somehow were considered by Jesus to profane the temple complex, why would he attempt to reform or purify something that he predicts, only days later, will soon be destroyed (13:2)?

Third, this view ignores how the cursing of the fig tree that surrounds this incident impinges on how Mark expects Jesus' actions in the temple to be interpreted.

73. Hans Dieter Betz, "Jesus and the Purity of the Temple (Mark 11:15–18): A Comparative Religion Approach," *JBL* 116 (1997): 462–67.

74. Ibid., 465.

75. Gray, *The Temple*, 43.

76. Sanders, *Jesus and Judaism*, 63. See also his *Judaism: Practice and Belief 63 BCE–66 CE* (Philadelphia: Trinity Press International, 1992), 47–76, and *Jewish Law from Jesus to the Mishnah* (Philadelphia: Trinity Press International, 1990), 49–51.

As the fig tree is not cleansed but cursed, so the temple is not cleansed but, in effect, cursed by a prophetic gesture that betokens God's wrathful displeasure.

Fourth, Jesus' actions, which portend the demise of the temple, and the hostile reaction of the temple hierarchy in seeking a way to arrest him (12:12) have parallels with Josephus's description of what happened to Jesus son of Ananias prior to the rebellion against Rome (Josephus, *J.W.* 6.5.3 §§300–309). Both Jesus and Jesus son of Ananias "entered the precincts of the Temple at the time of a religious festival ... spoke of the doom of Jerusalem, and both apparently alluded to Jeremiah."[77] When the latter persistently cried out woes against the city and the temple in public, "a voice from the east, a voice from the west, a voice from the four winds, a voice against Jerusalem and the sanctuary, a voice against the bridegroom and the bride, a voice against all the people," Josephus reports that "the leading citizens" arrested him and brought him to the Roman governor. The governor interrogated him, but, perplexed by his silence, judged him to be insane and set him free after having him brutally scourged. This harsh punishment did not stop Jesus son of Ananias from continuing to utter woes against the city, and he was eventually killed. The parallel adds weight to the interpretation that Jesus was announcing the temple's doom and not calling for its resanctification as part of a prophetic renewal mission.

12.3.2.4 Jesus Was Portending a New Means of Atonement

The temple's destruction in AD 70 created an acute crisis for Jews. Not only did they ask despairingly, "How could this happen to God's house?" but another more pressing and depressing question arose: "How could the sins of Israel be atoned?" This exact question was raised by Rabbi Joshua, when, in the company of Rabbi Johanan ben Zakkai, he laments over the ruins of the temple as they departed from Jerusalem, "Woe unto us! ... that this, the place where the iniquities of Israel were atoned for, is laid waste!" Rabbi Johanan responds by citing Hos 6:6: "My son, be not grieved, we have another atonement, as effective as this. And what is it? It is acts of loving-kindness, as it is said, 'For I desire mercy and not sacrifice' " (*'Abot R. Nat.* 4).

Years earlier, Mark offers a similar yet different answer. The cursing of the fig tree and Jesus' actions in the temple present a narrative theology that both negatively assesses the temple sacrificial cult and hints that the community of believers gathered around Christ will have another atonement apart from the sacrificial cult. Jesus will tell his disciples, "And when you stand praying, if you hold anything against anyone, forgive them, so that your Father in heaven may forgive you your sins" (11:25). The reader would know that this forgiveness is made possible through Christ's sacrifice of his life as a ransom for many (10:45).

77. Craig A. Evans, "Jesus and the 'Cave of Robbers': Towards a Jewish Context for the Temple Action," in *Jesus and His Contemporaries: Comparative Studies* (Leiden/New York/Köln: Brill, 1995), 345–65.

12.3.2.4.1 Overturning the Tables of the Money Changers

The tables to change money were set up to receive the annual half-shekel tax (also known as the temple tax) that was levied on all males from age twenty (Exod 30:11–16; Neh 10:32–34; Matt 17:24–27; *m. Šeqal.* 1:3; *t. Šeqal.* 1:6). Women, slaves, Samaritans, and Gentiles were excluded from this duty. The annual tax was due by the beginning of Nisan. Announcements went out on the first of Adar, and the money was collected on the fifteenth (*m. Šeqal.* 1:1). The half-shekel, translated *didrachmon* (double drachma) in Exod 30:13 (LXX) and Neh 10:32–33 (LXX), no longer existed. It was equal to four Athenian drachmae (Josephus, *Ant.* 3.8.2 §§194–196), and a Tyrian silver shekel was substituted for it (*b. Bek.* 50b; *b. B. Qam.* 36b).[78] Tables were set up to change money into ritually acceptable coinage on the 15th of Adar in the provinces and on the 25th in the temple (*m. Šeqal.* 1:3). These shekel dues funded the *Tamid*, the daily sacrifice of lambs in the morning and evening (Exod 29:38–46), for the atonement of the sins of the people (*t. Šeqal.* 1:6). Philo calls this temple tax, which gave every Jewish adult male some share in the daily sacrifices for the forgiveness of sins, "ransom money" (*Spec. Laws* 1.77; *Heir* 186; see also *b. B. Bat.* 9b).[79]

Neusner contends that when Jesus overturned the tables of the moneychangers, it

> will have provoked astonishment, since it will have called into question the very simple fact that the daily whole offering effected atonement and brought about expiation for sin, and God had so instructed Moses in the Torah. Accordingly, only someone who rejected the Torah's explicit teaching concerning the daily whole offering could have overturned the tables—or ... someone who had in mind setting up a different table, and for a different purpose: for the action carries the entire message, both negative and positive.... Indeed, their presence made possible the cultic participation of every Israelite, and it was not only not a blemish on the cult but part of its perfection.[80]

This action has nothing to do with Jesus' ire over dishonest profiteering. Overturning the tables of the moneychangers is an attack on the means of funding the daily sacrifices for the atonement of the sins of the people. Huys shows that a Hellenistic audience would have understood that toppling the tables symbolized divine wrath over perverted practices in a cult with the implication that it would be

78. Peter Richardson, "Why Turn the Tables? Jesus' Protest in the Temple Precincts," *SBLSP 31* (1992): 507–23; Jerome Murphy-O'Connor, "Jesus and the Money Changers (Mark 11:15–17; John 2:13–17)," *RB* 107 (2000): 46–48, contend that Jesus protested against this coinage because it had images of the god Melkart and of an eagle and the inscription "Tyre the Holy and Inviolable," but Richardson (p. 518) concedes that there is "no explicit evidence ... that suggests Tyrian shekels were found to be repugnant" at that time even though he and Murphy-O'Connor think they should have offended pious Jews.

79. Jostein Ådna, "Jesus' Symbolic Act in the Temple (Mark 11:15–17): The Replacement of the Sacrificial Cult by His Atoning Death," in *Gemeinde ohne Tempel* (ed. Beate Ego, Armin Lange, and Peter Pilhofer; WUNT 2/118; Tübingen: Mohr Siebeck, 1999), 468–69.

80. Jacob Neusner, "Money-Changers in the Temple: The Mishnah's Explanation," *NTS* 35 (1989): 289; see also his "The Absoluteness of Christianity and the Uniqueness of Judaism: Why Salvation Is Not of the Jews," *Int* 43 (1989): 25. Marc Huys, "Turning the Tables: Jesus' Temple Cleansing and the Story of Lycaon," *ETL* 86 (2010): 154–55, agrees that "the table of the Eucharist" replaces the sacrificial cult.

replaced by a totally new moral and religious order.[81] Focant comments: "To turn over the tables amounts ... to contesting that the daily sacrifice had as an effect to expiate sins and that it was necessary to continue to pay for it."[82]

12.3.2.4.2 Overturning the Benches of Those Selling Doves

Since doves were the sacrificial offering for atonement of the poor who could not afford a lamb (Lev 5:7; 12:6–8 [after childbirth]; 14:22, 30; see Luke 2:24), overturning the benches of those selling doves may have been directed against the temple cult's impact on the subjugation of the poor. Myers asserts that this sacrifice "represented the concrete mechanisms of oppression within a political economy that doubly exploited the poor and unclean. Not only were they considered second-class citizens, but the cult obligated them to make reparation, through sacrifices, for their inferior status—from which the marketers profited."[83]

Doves, however, were not simply the sacrifice of the poor. They were also the prescribed sacrifice for a male's sexual discharge (Lev 15:13–14), for a female's flow of blood outside the time of her menstruation (Lev 15:29), for a leper who has been cleansed (Lev 14:22), and for the one who has taken a Nazirite vow and has come near a corpse (Num 6:10). Ådna points out, "The dove vendors provided Temple visitors with the kind of victims most in demand for individual burnt offerings and sin offerings."[84]

In my view, Jesus is not simply concerned about an economic injustice but takes action against a theology represented by the doves sold for sacrifices. This theological code "said that you are poor, suffering, and oppressed because you have sinned against God. To be forgiven you must offer sacrifice, which ultimately lined the pockets of those primarily responsible for the oppression of the poor."[85] Jesus would become a ransom for the many that brings forgiveness that is absolutely free.

12.3.2.4.3 Not Allowing Anyone to Carry Vessels through the Temple Courts

Jesus would not allow anyone to carry vessels through the temple (11:16). The NIV translates the Greek word "vessels" as "merchandise"; other translations, as "goods"; and still others, more generically as "anything." The assumption in these translations is that haulers were using the temple as a shortcut (see *m. Ber.* 9:5).[86] The word translated "merchandise" in the NIV is normally translated "vessel" in the NT and is used in the LXX for the various kinds of vessels or objects used in the cultic sacrifice.[87]

The translation "vessel" best fits the context of the passage. The previous verse

81. Huys, "Turning the Tables," 145–52.
82. Focant, *Mark*, 460.
83. Myers, *Binding*, 301.
84. Ådna, "Jesus' Symbolic Act in the Temple," 469.
85. Garland, *Mark*, 447.
86. Josephus, *Ag. Ap.* 2.8 §106, says it is not lawful to carry any vessel into "the holy house," but he refers to the inner sanctuary not the outer courts.
87. See also the references to "sacred vessels" used in the temple service by Josephus, *J.W.* 1.1.4 §39; *Ant.* 18.4.1 §85.

(11:15) describes Jesus disrupting things that were necessary for the normal operation of the temple cult, and it is likely that this theme is continued in 11:16. Jesus stops the transport of vessels within the temple related to the operation of the cult, such as vessels carrying sacrificial offerings or money that was to be deposited in the treasury.[88] A Gentile audience would be familiar with how pagan temples operated in their world and probably would assume that Mark refers to sacred vessels used in the cult rather than to delivery persons using the temple grounds as a shortcut through which to carry their goods.[89]

Ådna contends, I think rightly, that the vessels contained the money that had been changed and offering ingredients and were being transported from the Royal Stoa to the inner precincts. Jesus is symbolically interfering "with the most central function of the Temple, namely, the atoning cult."[90] By stopping the flow of traffic in cultic items in this part of the temple, Jesus brings sacrifices "to a virtual standstill."[91] But it is only a temporary stoppage. What is important is what these shock tactics are meant to convey.

12.3.2.4.4 Jesus' Interpretation of His Actions from Scripture, Isaiah 56:7 and Jeremiah 7:11

Jesus' quotation from Isa 56:7, "for my house will be called a house of prayer for all nations," in 11:17 has him assuming the first person address of the Lord![92] It is *his* house that is intended to be a place for all nations to pray. Isaiah 56:1–8 contains God's promise of blessing for all who for various reasons are shut out: the foreigner who has joined himself to the people (56:3), the eunuch (56:4, who was not allowed to enter the temple according to the regulations of Deut 23:1), and the outcasts of Israel (56:8).[93] Jesus expects Isa 56 to be fulfilled now, not in some distant future, and his ministry has manifested his compassion for the ritually impure, the physically maimed, and Gentiles. Jesus expects that God's temple would embody this inclusive love, but it does not. Purity restrictions keep multitudes at bay, and none of these persons listed in Isa 56 could enter the sanctuary.[94] Jesus has no interest in a segregated, separate, and unequal temple that claims to be a beacon that would draw the nations to God. In comparison with the parallels in Matt 21:13 and Luke 19:46 that quote Isa 56:7, only Mark includes the additional words "for all nations"

88. Jostein Ådna, *Jesu Stellung zum Tempel: Die Tempelaktion und das Tempelwort als Ausdruck seiner messianischen Sendung* (WUNT 2/119; Tübingen: Mohr Siebeck, 2000), 262–64; John Paul Heil, "The Narrative Strategy and Pragmatics of the Temple Theme in Mark," *CBQ* 59 (1997): 78, n. 5. Pesch, *Markusevangelium*, 2:198; Gnilka, *Markus*, 2:129.

89. Ådna, *Jesu Stellung zum Tempel*, 257–60, shows that it made no sense to use the outer court as a shortcut to get from one side of town to the other.

90. Ådna, "Jesus' Symbolic Act in the Temple," 469.

91. Gray, *The Temple*, 30.

92. Ibid., 32. The allegory of the Vineyard and the Wicked Tenants identifies the beloved son as the heir of the vineyard (12:6–7).

93. The blind and lame were barred access to the sanctuary of God's presence (see Lev 21:18–20; 2 Sam 5:8 [LXX]; 11QTemple 45:13; *m. Ḥag.* 1:1).

94. See Josephus, *Ant.* 15.11.4 §417. According to 4QMMT B 39–42, access would be allowed only to Israelites who were ritually pure and physically whole; and 4QFlor 3–4 insists that neither "the [ungodly nor defiled], the Ammonite, Moabite [Deut 23:3], half-breed [or bastard, Deut 23:2], alien, or sojourner will ever enter the house because my holy ones are there." Jesus has a quite different vision.

(11:17). The walls in this temple that had become a fiercely nationalistic symbol separating Israel from the hordes would have to crumble before it could ever become what God intended, a house of prayer for all nations (see Eph 2:11–22).[95]

Watts claims that "it would make little sense to speak of the Temple becoming a place of prayer (Isa 56:7) if it is already under sentence."[96] The phrase "my house will be called," however, does not require that it be fulfilled for this temple. It has failed to attain the purpose and will be judged for it. Nor is Jesus striving to make Isaiah's prophecy come to pass by his actions in the temple. This is Herod's temple, and it is doomed and will not be restored. Kirk concludes that the quotation from Isaiah means that Jesus is "declaring in the strongest terms that the current temple does not, and will not, attain to it," that is, Isaiah's vision of the eschatological role of the temple. He continues, "A day of judgment is coming that will entail the temple's destruction; something else will fulfill the role of 'house of prayer for all the Gentiles.' What that 'something else' is, however, the readers do not yet know."[97] The fulfillment of this prophecy will take place in a quite different way than expected.

It is significant that the temple is identified as a "house of prayer," not a place of sacrifice. Gray explains that the quotation is silent about this vital facet of the temple's functioning because "the only acceptable sacrifice and atonement in Mark's story is Jesus."[98] The downgrading of the temple's sacrificial cult is reinforced when a teacher of the law asks Jesus about the greatest commandment (12:28–31). He affirms Jesus' answer and then repeats it with an interpretive comment at the end: "To love him with all your heart, with all your understanding and with all your strength, and to love your neighbor as yourself is more important than all burnt offerings and sacrifices" (12:32–33). The scribe's supplement to Jesus' answer implies that obedience to the love commands *surpasses* sacrifices as the true worship to be offered to God. If one believes that Jesus' death is the definitive atoning sacrifice, then it is a small step to recognize that obedience to the love commands *supplants* sacrifices as the true worship to be offered to God.

Since this word is spoken within the temple precincts by a Jewish legal expert and just before Jesus' prophecy of the temple's destruction in 13:2, it adds weight to the developing theme in Mark that the temple cult is disposable. From this quotation in Isaiah, one can infer that if the temple is to become a house of prayer, not a place of atonement, then it is replaceable if it is true that anyone standing anywhere and praying to their Father in heaven (not in the temple) with a forgiving heart can receive forgiveness (11:25). The place of prayer will become the Christian

95. This nationalism is reflected in 1 Macc 7:37, where the priests in a time of dire crisis wept before the altar and said, "You chose this house to be called by your name, and to be for your people a house of prayer and supplication." The phrase "your people" assumes that the temple and the efficacy of prayer there was to be limited to Israel. In the *Pss. Sol.* 17:21–22, God is implored to raise up the king, the son of David, to come purge Jerusalem of Gentiles, who then may no longer sojourn with the people of God.

96. Watts, *New Exodus*, 326.

97. Kirk, "Time for Figs," 517.

98. Gray, *The Temple*, 32.

community gathered together in houses (3:20; see Acts 1:12–14; Rom 16:5; 1 Cor 16:19; Col 4:15) and doing God's will (3:35).

The quotation from Jer 7:11 comes from a passage that roundly condemns the abuses that blighted the temple cult and ensured its destruction if they were not remedied. By citing this passage, Jesus implies that the temple hierarchy in his day is guilty of the same sins that beset the people in the days of Jeremiah. Like the sliver of text quoted from Isa 56, the "den of robbers" citation from Jeremiah needs to be read in its entire context (Jer 7:1–15) to understand the point:

> This is the word that came to Jeremiah from the Lord: "Stand at the gate of the Lord's house and there proclaim this message:
>
> "'Hear the word of the Lord, all you people of Judah who come through these gates to worship the Lord. This is what the Lord Almighty, the God of Israel, says: Reform your ways and your actions, and I will let you live in this place. Do not trust in deceptive words and say, "This is the temple of the Lord, the temple of the Lord, the temple of the Lord!" If you really change your ways and your actions and deal with each other justly, if you do not oppress the foreigner, the fatherless or the widow and do not shed innocent blood in this place, and if you do not follow other gods to your own harm, then I will let you live in this place, in the land I gave your ancestors for ever and ever. But look, you are trusting in deceptive words that are worthless.
>
> "Will you steal and murder, commit adultery and perjury, burn incense to Baal and follow other gods you have not known, and then come and stand before me in this house, which bears my Name, and say, "We are safe"—safe to do all these detestable things? Has this house, which bears my Name, become a den of robbers to you? But I have been watching! declares the Lord.
>
> "'Go now to the place in Shiloh where I first made a dwelling for my Name, and see what I did to it because of the wickedness of my people Israel. While you were doing all these things, declares the Lord, I spoke to you again and again, but you did not listen; I called you, but you did not answer. Therefore, what I did to Shiloh[99] I will now do to the house that bears my Name, the temple you trust in, the place I gave to you and your ancestors. I will thrust you from my presence, just as I did all your fellow Israelites, the people of Ephraim.'"

The reference to the "den of robbers" has nothing to do with the trade in the temple but denounces the false security fostered by the sacrificial cult. It deludes worshipers into thinking that they are forgiven for their evil deeds and can continue to commit wickedness with impunity. The "robbers" are not swindlers but

99. See Ps 78:59–64. V. P. Hamilton, "שִׁילֹה," *Theological Wordbook of the Old Testament* (ed. R. Laird Harris, Gleason L. Archer Jr., and Bruce K. Waltke; Chicago: Moody, 1999), 919, suggests that Shiloh is chosen as an example because it had a temple to God where the ark of the covenant was kept, and the people "had attempted to exploit their relationship to God (via the ark and temple respectively) to achieve security in a time of political distress. Religion had become magic."

bandits.[100] By labeling the temple a robbers' lair, Jesus condemns them for turning God's sanctuary into a sanctuary for bandits who presume that they are safe and secure from all alarms within its confines. Jesus' prophetic action, accompanied by his teaching from the Scripture, attacks the efficacy of the temple cult for those who sin with a high hand. If, for example, they lie, steal, commit acts of violence, commit adultery (see 7:21–23), and rob widows' houses (12:40), they should not fool themselves into thinking that perfunctory temple sacrifices will exonerate them and bring forgiveness.

The phrase "I have been watching" in Jer 7:11 matches the description of Jesus' visit to the temple on the previous day when he "looked around at everything" (11:11). It confirms that Jesus' visit in reality was a divine inspection. Jesus shares God's perspective and pronounces God's judgment. In my view, Kirk rings the changes in concluding, "If Isa 56:7 tells us that the temple is falling short of Isaiah's depiction of the blessed precinct of the last days, Jer 7:11 tells us that it is like the cursed temple of old, awaiting divine destruction by the hands of Israel's enemies. Jerusalem is on the verge not of exaltation but of another coming judgment."[101] Jesus is not insisting that they call a halt to commerce in the temple complex but warning everyone that the temple and its sacrifices will not protect them from God's judgment.

When Jeremiah uttered his condemnation of the temple cult, it was met with outrage. The priests, the prophets, and all the people seized him and said, "You must die!" for prophesying against the house of the Lord. The priests and prophets turned him over to the officials and demanded that he should be sentenced to death (Jer 26:8–11). Jesus will get the same treatment as the chief priests and the teachers of the law immediately begin looking for a way to kill him (Mark 11:18). They were temporarily deterred from carrying out their evil purpose because of Jesus' popularity with the crowd, but only temporarily.

12.3.3 The Continuation of the Cursing of the Fig Tree Account (Mark 11:22–25)

"The barren fig tree represents the barrenness of temple Judaism that is unprepared to accept Jesus' messianic reign."[102] Fruitlessness now when the Messiah comes means fruitlessness forever.[103] When Peter remarks about the fig tree withered to its roots, Jesus' response in 11:22–25 seems to go off on a tangent:

100. Jeffrey B. Gibson, "The Function of the Charge of Blasphemy in Mark 14:64," in *The Trial and Death of Jesus: Essays on the Passion Narrative in Mark* (ed. Geert van Oyen and Thom Shepherd; Leuven: Peeters, 2006), 176–77, states that the temple had become the focal point of "religious exclusivism and revolutionary zeal." It was perceived as a "divine guarantee of security against Israel's enemies when Israel was beset by them and of God's ultimate subjugation of the nations to Israel." The temple literally became a refuge for bandits during the war with Rome when the Zealots retreated to it. According to Josephus, they committed all manner of vile acts: "For this reason, I think, even God Himself, hating their impiety, turned away from our city, and no longer judging the temple to be a clean house for Him, brought the Romans upon us and a cleansing fire on the city" (*Ant.* 20.8.5 §166). If the audience was aware of this, the reference to the "den of robbers" would have a double meaning.

101. Kirk, "Time for Figs," 519.

102. Garland, *Mark*, 440.

103. Tolbert, *Sowing the Gospel*, 193.

> "Have faith in God," Jesus answered. "Truly I tell you, if anyone says to this mountain, 'Go, throw yourself into the sea,' and does not doubt in their heart but believes that what they say will happen, it will be done for them. Therefore I tell you, whatever you ask for in prayer, believe that you have received it, and it will be yours. And when you stand praying, if you hold anything against anyone, forgive them, so that your Father in heaven may forgive you your sins."

These sayings are integrally related to the context. If it is the case, as Marshall argues, that Jesus' actions in the temple were "not merely a cleansing preparatory to its restoration, as anticipated in OT-Jewish tradition, but a definitive disqualification of its legitimacy,"[104] what does Mark understand to be its replacement?

Jesus' interpretation of the cursing of the fig tree begins with "Have faith in God" (11:22). The two verbs in the example of the mountain translated, "Go, throw yourself into the sea," are in the passive voice and may be more accurately translated, "Be lifted up and be thrown into the sea." Since God is the one who, according to Job, "moves mountains without their knowing it and overturns them in his anger. He shakes the earth from its place and makes its pillars tremble" (Job 9:5–6), I would interpret them as divine passives. Gundry comments: "Because of the command to have faith in God, the passive voice in 'be lifted up and be thrown into the sea' means, 'May God lift you up and throw you into the sea.'" He asserts that the destructiveness of this saying "makes the speaking to the mountain a curse, as much a curse as Jesus' speaking to the fig tree that no one should ever again eat fruit from it."[105]

The implication is that to bring a new order characterized by grace and forgiveness (11:25), God will overcome immense obstacles. Marshall comments, "The massive, institutionalized power of the existing religious establishment must give way to the kingdom community whose power lies solely in faith-borne prayer."[106] The disciples must have faith that this world-shattering turn of events reflects God's will and that they will "fill the role of the house of prayer and put their trust in prayer and forgiveness, and not in the sacrificial system of the temple, to obtain the divine pardon of their faults."[107]

If the saying about "this mountain" is generalized into a statement like "faith is able to move mountains" (see 1 Cor 13:2), it does not seem apropos to the context.[108] Jesus does not speak of "mountains," however, but specifies "this mountain." The demonstrative pronoun is "truly demonstrative" and not superfluous.[109] As it is a particular fig tree that withered, so this saying refers to a particular mountain.[110] In the context, it would most likely refer to the Temple Mount, Mount Zion, which would loom large before those walking from Bethany

104. Marshall, *Faith as a Theme*, 161.
105. Gundry, *Mark*, 653.
106. Marshall, *Faith as a Theme*, 176.
107. Focant, *Mark*, 457–58.
108. So Evans, *Mark 8:27–16:20*, 186.
109. Kirk, "Time for Figs," 523.
110. Gray, *The Temple*, 49.

to Jerusalem.[111] Josephus states that the temple "appeared to strangers, when they were at a distance, like a mountain covered with snow for, as to those parts of it that were not gilt, they were exceedingly white" (*J.W.* 5.5.6 §5). This saying, then, implies that the Temple Mount will not be exalted among the mountains as the highest (Isa 2:2; Mic 4:1) but will be cast down into the bottommost depths of the sea, where the demon-infested pigs drowned (5:13) and where those who cause little ones to stumble will be thrown (9:42).[112]

Kirk concludes, "The saying about the mountain being cast into the sea is not merely an appended statement on the efficacy of faithful prayer. It is tied to the particular actions that Jesus has performed, his own authority to speak a word of judgment against the house of God, and likely the authority that his own followers have to continue Jesus' prophetic ministry."[113] Ciampa's and Rosner's comment on 1 Cor 13:2 is pertinent: "The moving (or razing) of mountains is an eschatological motif associated with God's judgment and/or the removal of obstacles to the restoration of his presence to his people (Isa. 40:4; 41:15; 42:15; 49:11; 54:10; Luke 3:5; Rev. 6:14; 8:8; 16:20)."[114] The temple is not part of God's present or future salvific plans. As a consequence, Jesus and his followers will wage a " 'war of faith' " against "the 'mountain of unbelief' " represented by the temple system.[115]

The temple was not only the place where atoning sacrifices took place, it was also regarded as the place where prayer was particularly effective.[116] In 3 Macc 2:10, the high priest Simon declares to God: "And because you love the house of Israel, you promised that if we should have reverses and tribulation should overtake us, you would listen to our petition when we come to this place and pray." A late rabbinic commentary on Ps 91:7 reads: "When a man prays in Jerusalem, it is as though he prays before the throne of glory, for the gate of heaven is in Jerusalem, and a door is always open for the hearing of prayer, as it is said, 'This is the gate of heaven' [Gen 28:17]" (*Midr. Ps.* 91:7). Other rabbis said: "From the day on which the Temple was destroyed, the gates of prayer have closed, as it says, 'Yea, when I cry for help, He shutteth out my prayer' [Lam 3:8].... Since the day that the Temple was destroyed, a wall of iron divides between Israel and their Father in Heaven" (*b. Ber.* 32b). Jesus assures his disciples that the effectiveness of prayer has nothing to with the temple.[117] They can rest assured that their prayers will be effective whenever and wherever they pray with a forgiving heart.

The concluding explanation is explosive: "And when you stand praying, if you

111. Telford, *The Barren Temple*, 49–59; 119; Hooker, *Mark*, 270; Wright, *Jesus and the Victory of God*, 334–35; Evans, *Mark 8:27–16:20*, 188–89; Gray, *The Temple*, 50–53. The "holy mountain" is mentioned in the opening part of Isa 56:7; see also Ps 78:54; Isa 2:2–3; 10:32; 25:6–7, 10; 27:13; Zech 4:7; *b. Pesaḥ.* 87b; *b. Giṭ.* 56b. Kirk, "Time for Figs," 523, argues that even if this saying were "originally a generic, proverbial image of an impossible feat, the literary context established by Mark, within which the saying ties the cursed fig tree together with the judged temple, sustains Telford's argument."

112. Marshall, *Faith as a Theme*, 168–69.

113. Kirk, "Time for Figs," 523.

114. Ciampa and Rosner, *The First Letter to the Corinthians*, 577.

115. Marshall, *Faith as a Theme*, 169.

116. See 1 Sam 1:1–28; 1 Kgs 8:27–30, 31–51, where prayer is offered in or toward the temple; see also 2 Kgs 19:14–33; Jonah 2:7; Jdt 4:9–15.

117. Marshall, *Faith as a Theme*, 162–63; see also Stephen Hre Kio, "A Prayer Framework in Mark 11," *BT* 37 (1986): 323–28.

hold anything against anyone, forgive them, so that your Father in heaven may forgive you your sins" (11:25). It completely circumvents the temple cult. One can "appeal directly to the heavenly Father for mercy" and be forgiven.[118] The temple has been passed over as the place where atonement for sins and God's forgiveness transpires. These come from faith in God and forgiveness of others, which is within reach of anyone anywhere.[119] Focant's judgment is on target: "For the divine pardon of their [the disciples'] faults, they are invited to place their trust no longer in the expiatory rituals of the temple, but instead in a prayer that integrates their own forgiveness toward those who have offended them."[120] Guttenberger affirms that God wants all humans to worship him through prayer and faith and not through the temple cult or ritualistic patterns.[121]

It is noteworthy that this is the only passage in Mark where God is identified as the "Father in heaven." It is a reminder that God's true dwelling place is in heaven, and it is there where prayers are heard and forgiveness is granted, not from an earthly temple made with hands.[122]

12.3.4 The Challenge to Jesus' Authority to Take These Actions in the Temple (Mark 11:27–33)

Jesus returned to the temple the next day, and the troika of the chief priests, the teachers of the law, and the elders challenge him: "By what authority are you doing these things? . . . And who gave you authority to do this?" (11:27–28). Jesus' response seems evasive. Before he would answer, he asks them to tell him whether they believed John's baptism had its authority from heaven or from men (11:30). The question is not immaterial. John preached a baptism of repentance for the forgiveness of sins that completely bypassed the temple cult. If John's ministry was from heaven, then the temple has become passé.[123] Their answer, "We don't know" (11:33), reveals that they cannot tell the difference between what is from God and what is from men (or, for that matter, from Satan; see 3:22).

12.3.5 The Accusations That Jesus Threatened to Destroy the Temple (Mark 14:57–59; 15:29–30)

At his interrogation before the high priest and his council, charges were brought against Jesus that accused him of saying he would destroy this temple made with hands and build another not made with hands in three days (14:58). Only Mark describes the temple as "made with human hands" and the new temple as "not made with hands" (cf. Matt 26:61). The term "made with hands" is associated with idolatry in the OT (Lev 26:1; Ps 115:4; Isa 46:6; Acts 7:41; 17:23–24), and it subtly links the current temple to idolatry. Mark characterizes this testimony as "false" (14:56–57) and highlights that they could not get their stories straight (14:59). It

118. Marcus, *Mark 8–16*, 789.
119. Heil, "The Narrative Strategy," 80.
120. Focant, *Mark*, 458.
121. Guttenberger, *Die Gottesvorstellung*, 162.
122. Heil, "The Narrative Strategy," 80, n. 10.
123. Limbeck, *Markus-Evangelium*, 170.

is false because Jesus did not say or intimate that *he* would destroy the temple. It will be destroyed by the Romans, and it will be the result of God's judgment. He also never claimed that *he* would build another earthly sanctuary like the temple. In Mark's view, the temple was destroyed when Jesus died, making its atonement sacrifices superfluous. The temple God would rebuild without hands would not be a physical edifice (see Acts 7:48; 17:24).

The charge resurfaces in the taunts at the cross (15:29–30). The passersby assume that anyone who could destroy a temple and rebuild another one in three days would be able to come down from a cross. They testify to a truth beyond their range of vision. By staying on the cross, Jesus' death becomes a ransom for many that makes the temple made with hands obsolete. He saves others by *not* saving himself (15:30, 31). His death abolishes the need for any more temple sacrifices. His resurrection means that God will build a new temple from a community of believers with no walls and with no ties to any one geographical location.

12.3.6 The Tearing of the Temple Veil (Mark 15:38)

Mark is unrelenting in presenting Jesus' execution in the starkest of detail and highlighting "the brutal reality of Jesus' humiliation." His purpose is for the reader "to see that precisely in this brutal humiliation of Jesus the redeeming purpose of God comes to expression."[124] Two dramatic events occur at the moment of Jesus' death that are theologically earth-shattering. When Jesus dies with a loud shout, the narrator's camera suddenly shifts from the cross on Golgotha to zoom in on the sanctuary of the temple, where the curtain is ripped from top to bottom (15:38).[125] The narrator then quickly pans back to the crucifixion scene to record the exclamation of the centurion who heard Jesus' last cry and saw how he died: "Surely this man was the Son of God!" (15:39).[126] This abrupt transition from the crucifixion scene to the inner sanctuary of the temple conveys that Jesus' death has something to do with the tearing of the temple veil. Mark does not relate this detail to point out that the temple property and grounds committee had a serious problem but to convey a theological point. That point, however, is not immediately evident.

12.3.6.1 Which Veil of the Sanctuary Is Torn?

Interpreters debate over which curtain in the temple was rent.[127] The outer curtain that separated the sanctuary from the forecourt (Exod 26:36–37; 38:18; Num 3:26) is the only one that could have been seen from outside the sanctuary, but no one at the crucifixion site, which was blanketed in darkness from the sixth hour to the ninth (15:33), would have been able to see the temple let alone the curtain. The

124. Hurtado, *Mark*, 265.

125. Mark uses the word for the "sanctuary" (*naos*).

126. In Matt 27:51–54, after the centurion and those with him saw the events following Jesus' death, "the earthquake and all that had happened," they acclaimed Jesus as the Son of God. In Mark, the centurion only sees how Jesus died and nothing else.

127. See Harry E. Faber van der Meulen, "One or Two Veils in Front of the Holy of Holies," *ThEv* 18 (1985): 22–27; Daniel M. Gurtner, "The Veil of the Temple in History and Legend," *JETS* 49 (2006): 97–114.

sanctuary faced to the east, and Golgotha was outside the city to the west, which also would have made it impossible to see this curtain.[128] Priests could have reported this event at a later time, but Mark does not record anyone seeing it happen or responding to its tearing. It is not portrayed as a public event. The argument that Mark must have in mind the outer curtain because it was the only one visible to spectators is therefore irrelevant. As in the introduction when Jesus is baptized (1:9–11), the readers are given a privileged vantage point to see what God is doing when Jesus dies.

The inner veil that separated the Most Holy Place (or Holy of Holies) from the Holy Place had the greatest religious consequence.[129] Since the high priest could go past this veil only once a year on the Day of Atonement to offer sacrifice for the sins of the people (Exod 26:31–35; 27:16, 21; 30:6; 40:3, 21; Lev 4:17; 16:1–34; 21:23; 24:3; Josephus, *Ant.* 8.3.3 §§71–72), its splitting would have summoned the greatest theological significance for Mark.[130] The outer curtain, by contrast, had no critical religious connection.[131]

12.3.6.2 The Parallels with Mark 1:9–11

The tearing of the temple veil from top to bottom parallels the tearing of the heavens in Mark's introduction (1:9–11). First, both passages evoke the figure of Elijah. Mark introduces John the Baptist as an Elijah figure to whom Jesus comes to be baptized. Jesus now undergoes a different baptism (10:38) as he perishes on the cross. Just before his death, at the ninth hour (3:00 p.m.), he cries out in a loud voice, "'*Eloi, Eloi, lema sabachthani?*' (which means, 'My God, my God, why have you forsaken me?')" (15:34).[132] Bystanders mishear him and mistakenly think that he is calling for Elijah to rescue him (15:35–36). Some anticipate that Elijah may come at the last minute, but Jesus declared that Elijah had already come, and they had done to him whatever they pleased (9:11–13). There will be no last-second rescue.

Second, in both incidents, a rending of a holy place where God is presumed to dwell occurs.[133] The verb translated "torn" (*schizein*) occurs only in these two passages in Mark. When Jesus rose from the waters at his baptism, he saw the heavens, which are like a curtain according to Isa 40:22, rent asunder, and the Spirit descending upon him like a dove (1:10). The rending of the curtain of the temple is comparable. Josephus describes the tabernacle for his Greco-Roman readers as divided into three equal parts. The court and the Holy Place are compared to the land and the sea, which is accessible to humanity. The third area, the Most Holy

128. Collins, *Mark*, 760.

129. Hebrews 9:3 identifies it as the second curtain: "Behind the second curtain was a room called the Most Holy Place [or Holy of Holies]." According to *m. Yoma* 5:1, two curtains with a cubit space between them separated the Most Holy Place from the Holy Place.

130. Marcus, *Mark 8–16*, 1057, notes that both pagan and Jewish readers would have been familiar with this kind of curtain since deities in Hellenistic temples were "often curtained off from view."

131. Carl Schneider, "καταπέτασμα," *TDNT*, 3:629.

132. The moment of Jesus' death occurs at the ninth hour (3:00 p.m.), which is the same time as the afternoon Tamid sacrifice, the daily whole offering for the forgiveness of sins of the people.

133. Matt 3:16 and Luke 3:21 have variations of the verb "open." Motyer, "The Rending of the Veil," 155–57, and David Ulansey, "The Heavenly Veil Torn," 123–25, argue that this similarity in vocabulary links the two passages.

Place [Holy of Holies], represents heaven, which is accessible to God alone (*Ant.* 3.6.4 §§122–123; 3.7.7 §181).[134]

Third, the temple curtain is rent downward "from top to bottom" like the descent of the Spirit coming down from heaven (1:10). The verbs are both in the passive voice, which suggests they are divine passives that point to God as the agent of the actions.[135]

Fourth, in both the baptism and crucifixion scenes, there is a revelatory declaration. At the baptism, a voice from heaven announces, "You are my Son, whom I love; with you I am well pleased" (1:11). At the crucifixion, the centurion, "who stood there in front of Jesus, saw how he died," announces, "'Surely this man was the Son of God!'" (15:39). Gurtner observes, "as the rending of the heavens led to God's proclamation of Jesus as his 'beloved son' (1:11), so the rending of the veil led to the proclamation by the centurion of Jesus as the 'son of God' (15:39)."[136] It does not mean that the centurion saw the rending of the veil and that event triggered his confession. It means that the rending of the veil has mysteriously made it possible for a Gentile centurion to be able to recognize and to confess that Jesus is the Son of God.

The connection between the baptism and the crucifixion scenes, in my view, implies that the tearing of the temple veil should not be viewed primarily as a negative sign, a portent of the temple's destruction.[137] When the heavens are rent asunder, it is not a sign that they are going to be destroyed. Instead, their rending leads to a revelatory announcement. The torn veil is also intended to be revelatory. The God who hides himself (Isa 45:15) now stands revealed in the Son of God who gives his life on a cross. One would least expect death on a cross to be a means of revelation, but Matera affirms that in the crucifixion, "God has revealed his hidden glory to all."[138] That God's glory is revealed in his crucified Son is not obvious, and it will be a "stumbling block to Jews and foolishness to Gentiles" (1 Cor 1:23).

134. In his *Jewish Wars*, Josephus describes the outer veil in the Herodian temple as over eighty feet high, a "Babylonian tapestry with embroidery of blue and fine linen, of scarlet also and purple, wrought with marvelous skill. Nor was the mixture of materials without its mystic meaning: it typified the universe." He also says that it was embroidered with "the whole panorama of the heavens" excluding the signs of the Zodiac (*J.W.* 5.5.4 §§212–214). Ulansey, "The Heavenly Veil Torn," 123–25, believes that Mark must refer to this outer veil to create an inclusio with the rending of the heavens. Since Josephus must describe the veil to his Greco-Roman audience, it is unlikely that they would have made this connection without further explanation. Brown, *Death*, 2:1113, argues that it is unlikely that the audience would have understood "details of cosmic symbolism that are not contained in the biblical descriptions of the Temple." See his discussion of the veils in the temple of Jesus' time (1109–13). Because of the audience's own experience of temples, however, they would not have needed an explanation to understand that a curtain in a temple would shield something holy.

135. The views of Jackson, "The Death of Jesus in Mark," 16–37; Gundry, *Mark*, 947–50, 970; Thomas E. Schmidt, "Cry of Dereliction or Cry of Judgment? Mark 15:34 in Context," *BBR* 4 (1994): 151–52; and Evans, *Mark 8:27–16:20*, 509, that Jesus "breathing out" at his death somehow released a powerful wind that tore the temple curtain have not persuaded many.

136. Gurtner, "The Rending of the Veil," 293.

137. A rabbinic tradition in *b. Yoma* 39b records various portents of the temple's destruction—the lot not coming up in the right hand; the crimson colored strap not becoming white; the westernmost light not shining, and the doors of the temple opening by themselves until Rabbi Johanan b. Zakkai rebuked them. In addition to the doors of the eastern gate of the temple opening of their own accord, Josephus (*J.W.* 6.5.3 §§290–296) adds other portents, such as a heifer being led to sacrifice and giving birth to a lamb. These portents hardly compare to the religious significance of the veil before the Holy of Holies being ripped from top to bottom, and it cannot simply be reduced to an omen of the temple's destruction.

138. Matera, *Kingship*, 139.

Because this revelation is so astonishing, Mark records the tearing of the curtain of the temple as a confirmation of the divine significance of Jesus' death.[139]

12.3.6.3 The Tearing of the Temple Veil and Atonement

Mark presents visual theology: "the torn curtain unveils something of the mystery of the dying Christ."[140] The numerous and wide ranging proposals that attempt to explain the meaning of the splitting of the temple curtain reveal that its meaning is elusive, or that Mark may have intended for its meaning to be multivalent.[141] I would agree with Marcus that the "veil that previously hid the glory of God has been ripped in two, and that glory now begins to flood the universe."[142]

I would add that the curtain of the temple that shielded the Most Holy Place is also integrally connected to atonement, and an audience familiar with Scripture could make that connection. Hebrews describes the high priest entering the inner room only once a year, "and never without blood, which he offered for himself and for the sins the people had committed in ignorance" (Heb 9:7). Gurtner endorses I. Howard Marshall's suggestion that the tearing of the veil "opens the way for Jesus to ascend to God and offer his sacrifice there."[143] Because of the deep religious meaning of the temple veil with its association with the sacrifice on the Day of Atonement, this proposal makes sense. Hebrews 9:24–28 (see also Heb 6:19; 10:20) captures in elegant prose the theological truth that Mark seeks to convey through narrative:

> For Christ did not enter a sanctuary made with human hands that was only a copy of the true one; he entered heaven itself, now to appear for us in God's presence. Nor did he enter heaven to offer himself again and again, the way the high priest enters the Most Holy Place every year with blood that is not his own. Otherwise Christ would have had to suffer many times since the creation of the world. But he has appeared once for all at the culmination of the ages to do away with sin by the sacrifice of himself. Just as people are destined to die once, and after that to face judgment, so Christ was sacrificed once to take away the sins of many; and he will appear a second time, not to bear sin, but to bring salvation to those who are waiting for him.[144]

The regulations governing the arrangement of the tabernacle are a permanent symbol of its inadequacy. They draw attention to the things that obstruct any approach to God and thereby serve to reinforce the alienation between God and

---

139. Chronis, "The Torn Veil," 114, boldly asserts, "Certainly the significance of the fact that the torn veil reveals God's 'face' in the face of one *enthroned* not on the ark or the cherubim, but *on the cross,* would not be lost on cultically sensitive and discerning readers!" The problem is that modern readers are anything but cultically sensitive.

140. Gérard Rossé, *The Cry of Jesus on the Cross: A Biblical and Theological Study* (trans. Stephen Wentworth Arndt; Mahwah, NJ: Paulist, 1987), 20.

141. Geddert, *Watchwords,* 141–43, lists thirty-five interpretations, though some overlap.

142. Marcus, "Mark 4:10–12 and Marcan Epistemology," 571, n. 46.

143. Gurtner, "The Veil of the Temple in History and Legend," 113.

144. France, *Mark,* 656–57, asserts that "we cannot assume that Mark would have shared the theological symbolism of Hebrews." But we also cannot assume automatically that the two have nothing in common as if both were writing in a theological vacuum. Juel, *Mark,* 225, agrees that the reflection on Jesus' death in Heb 10:19–20 "fits well with Mark's narrative, which plays regularly on the theme of old and new: 'new skins for new wine' (Mark 2:22)."

humanity. The Scripture is clear; anyone who approaches the sanctuary and is not authorized to do so will die (Num 1:51, 3:10, 38; 17:13; 18:7). The curtain that separates the Most Holy Place from the rest of the sanctuary is even more forbidding. It broadcasts "No entry" (Heb 9:8) and ropes God off even from the priests. The veil is often described as a protective shield for the Most Holy Place (Exod 30:6; 35:12; 40:3, 21). It protects that place from being profaned, but it also protects individuals from being destroyed by God's overpowering glory. The tearing of the temple veil suggests that all barriers shielding God from the people are removed through Christ's death.[145] There is nothing to fear from the unveiling of God's presence. Even Gentiles, like the centurion, have access to God through Jesus. When Jesus dies on the cross, access to God is opened up for all. His death creates a new house of prayer, a temple not made with hands that will be without barriers or limitations

The daily sacrifices, morning and evening, ad infinitum (Heb 7:27), serve as a perpetual reminder that they are all in vain. Atonement is never attained. Guilt is never ultimately removed; otherwise, the sacrifices would have stopped (10:2–3). Sin remains like a weed that keeps getting its leaves cut while its roots only go deeper and sprout again and again. Mark's enigmatic portrayal of the devastation of the temple veil in connection to Jesus' death reveals that all of the provisional sacrifices in the temple are superseded by Christ's definitive sacrifice. His death not only establishes a covenant (Mark 14:24), but it secures eternal redemption (Heb 9:12) for both Jews and Gentiles who confess and believe in him.

If Jesus' death is an atoning sacrifice for many and his death is once for all, the temple sacrificial cult is now unnecessary. Cranfield asserts, "The sacrifices would no longer have any *raison d'être* when once the Sacrifice to which they pointed had been offered."[146] The Herodian temple is destined to be destroyed by the Romans. What happens to it, however, is irrelevant to Mark. As only a shadow of reality, it can have no influence on what is eternal. The problem is that it casts a large shadow, and its power and ostensible holiness may deceive followers. There will be a hesitancy to recognize that what seems to be so inviolable is only ephemeral, and some may be afraid to turn away from its sacrifices with their mystery and pageantry to a desolate cross. After the temple is destroyed, however, it will become clearer that a fruitless temple with its wicked leaders will be left desolate. It has no function in God's salvific plan.

The result is that nothing need separate humans from God. They are not kept at a distance, shut out, or curtained off. There is no such thing as wrong places to meet God. God cannot be identified with any place. God is in the midst of our common life.

---

145. From Josephus's description (*Ant.* 3.7.7 §181), the veil that screened the Most Holy Place would also have been regarded as the boundary between earth and heaven. Margaret Barker, "Beyond the Veil of the Temple: The High Priestly Origins of the Apocalypses," *SJT* 51 (1998): 1–21, cites a wide variety of texts supporting this view. She also contends that this idea was not new: "Texts such as Psalm 11 *The LORD is in his holy temple, the LORD's throne is in heaven*, suggest that the holy of holies was thought to be heaven at a much earlier period," and the LXX of Isaiah 6, which differs from the Hebrew, implies that the *hekhal* was the earth. The Glory of the LORD filled the house in v.1, and the seraphim sang that the Glory filled the earth, v.3 (pp. 1–2).

146. C. E. B. Cranfield, "St. Mark 13," *SJT* 6 (1953): 191.

12.3.6.4 The Allegory of the Wicked Tenants of the Vineyard and Atonement

The narrative of Jesus' death makes it clearer how Jesus' citation of Ps 118:22 at the conclusion of the allegory of the Wicked Tenants—"the stone the builders rejected has become the cornerstone"—has been fulfilled (12:10–11).[147] The echo from Isa 5:1–2 at the beginning of the parable forms the biblical backdrop for understanding it: "A man planted a vineyard. He put a wall around it, dug a pit for the winepress and built a watchtower" (Mark 12:1). The Isaiah passage was interpreted in contemporary Jewish exegesis as a reference to Jerusalem, its temple, and its cult, with the tower representing the sanctuary and the winepress, the altar where the sacrifice for the atonement for sins occurs (see 4Q 500 1; *Tg. Ps.–J.* Isa. 5:2; *t. Sukkah* 3:15; *1 En.* 89:50).[148]

In the parable, the servants sent to collect the fruit of the vineyard are either shamefully beaten and sent away empty handed or killed. Finally, the owner sends his beloved son. He is killed by the murderous tenants who believe that by doing so they will take ownership of the vineyard. An odd feature of Mark's version of the parable is that the tenants "took him and killed him, and threw him out of the vineyard" (12:8). In the parallels in Matt 21:39 and Luke 20:15, they first threw him out of the vineyard and then killed him, a more correct order historically, since Golgotha was outside the city wall. Brooke offers this intriguing suggestion to explain this difference: "Since the winepress is linked with the altar in some Jewish traditions, the fact that Mark has the son killed before he is cast out of the vineyard might enhance the cultic aspect of the son's death."[149]

Jesus continues the citation of Ps 118:22 with verse 23, "The Lord has done this, and it is marvelous in our eyes" (Mark 12:11). This rejection and murder do not seem to be "marvelous" but tragic. Only in retrospect after the resurrection can one begin to fathom the marvelous thing God has done. Only in retrospect can one also recognize that the structure built on this cornerstone is not a physical structure but the church; indeed this is how it is interpreted in the NT (Acts 4:10–12; 1 Cor 3:9–16; 2 Cor 6:16; Eph 2:20–22; 1 Pet 2:4–10; Heb 3:6).[150]

12.4 RECONCILIATION BETWEEN GOD AND HUMANITY AT THE CROSS

Gamel correctly recognizes that Mark is not a document full of "theological propositions to be sorted and categorized but rather a narrative whose aim is to proclaim 'The beginning of the good news about Jesus the Messiah, the Son of God'" (1:1). A narrative operates most effectively when it 'shows,' not when it 'tells.'"[151] Gamel

147. The same verb "rejected" appears in Jesus' first passion prediction (8:31).

148. George J. Brooke, "4Q500 1 and the Use of Scripture in the Parable of the Vineyard," *Dead Sea Discoveries* 2 (1995): 284.

149. Ibid., 289–90.

150. Hartman, *Mark*, 480.

151. Brian K. Gamel, "Salvation in a Sentence: Mark 15:39 as Markan Soteriology," *JTI* 6 (2012): 67.

elucidates how Mark shows that Jesus' death brings about reconciliation between humans and God (see Rom 5:10–11) through the centurion's confession, "Surely this man was the Son of God!"[152] The alienation and conflict between God and humans are evident in Mark. The "commands of God" are supplanted by "human traditions" (7:8–9). Jesus, in contrast to the teachers of the law, is a model of one who is not swayed by men but teaches the way of God (12:14). Peter tries to impede Jesus' fulfilling his mission from God because he has his mind set on "human concerns," not "the concerns of God" (8:33). By divorcing and justifying it through legal casuistry, humans separate what God has joined together (10:9). What is impossible for humans is possible only for God (10:27).[153]

It seems utterly impossible that a centurion, who embodies Roman oppression and who supervises the crucifixion, the quintessence of Roman brutality, would confess that Jesus is "the Son of God" after witnessing his death. It is almost as astonishing as the reality that this crucified victim *is* the Son of God. An enormous gap has been bridged, and the centurion *sees* things from God's point of view and believes. Since his confession conforms to the declarations by God that Jesus is the beloved Son (1:11; 9:7), Gamel argues that the cross "becomes the new meeting place of God and humanity, replacing the temple as the locus of divine-human encounter."[154] God and humanity are reconciled in the cross. He concludes from this narrative:

> The cross is salvific for Mark, then, as the place where the antagonism between God and humanity is overcome. The blood of the covenant poured out for many that Jesus anticipated during his last supper (14:24) has now ratified the binding relationship between God and humanity. No longer are they alienated and oppositional, for they have come together, aligned at last in the same direction.[155]

Humans, who are plagued by sin, cold-hearted legalism, hardened hearts, hypocritical religiosity, structural evil, demonic evil, the cares for this world, and a bundle of fears, now find the remedy through Christ alone. Jesus' mortal enemies taunted him on the cross, " 'He saved others,' they said, 'but he can't save himself!' " (15:31). That is because his death on the cross is his last and final saving deed.[156]

---

152. Ibid., 65–77. On the positive assessment of the centurion's confession, see §4.1.1.

153. Gamel, "Salvation in a Sentence," 73–74.

154. Ibid., 74.

155. Ibid., 75. A similar conclusion is stated by Reinhard Feldmeier, "Der Gekreuzigte im 'Gnadenstuhl': Exegetische Überlegungen zu Mk 15,37–39 und deren Bedeutung für die Vorstellung der göttlichen Gegenwart und Herrschaft," in *Le Trône de Dieu* (ed. Marc Philonenko; WUNT 69; Tübingen: Mohr Siebeck, 1993), 229.

156. Knut Backhaus, " 'Lösepreis für viele' (Mark 10,45): Zur Heilsbedeutung des Todes Jesu bei Markus," in *Der Evangelist als Theologe: Studien zum Markusevangelium* (ed. Thomas Söding; SBS 163; Stuttgart: Katholisches Bibelwerk, 1995), 117.

Chapter 13

MARK'S ESCHATOLOGY

BIBLIOGRAPHY

Adams, Edward. "The Coming of The Son of Man in Mark's Gospel." *TynBul* 56.2 (2005): 39–61. Idem. *The Stars Will Fall from Heaven: Cosmic Catastrophe in the New Testament and its World.* LNTS 347; London/New York: T&T Clark, 2007. **Balabanski, Vicky.** *Eschatology in the Making: Mark, Matthew and The Didache.* SNTSMS 97. Cambridge: Cambridge University Press, 1997. **Beasley-Murray, George R.** *Jesus and the Last Days: The Interpretation of the Olivet Discourse.* Peabody, MA: Hendrickson, 1993. **Brandenburger, Egon.** *Markus 13 und die Apokalyptik.* FRLANT 134. Göttingen: Vandenhoeck & Ruprecht, 1984. **Collins, Adela Yarbro.** "The Eschatological Discourse of Mark 13." Pp. 1125–40 in *The Four Gospels 1992: Festschrift Frans Neirynck.* Vol. 2. BETL 100. Ed. Frans van Segbroeck et al. Leuven: Leuven University Press, 1992. **Cranfield, C. E. B.** "St. Mark 13." *SJT* 6 (1953): 189–96; 287–303; 7 (1954): 284–303. **Deppe, Dean B.** "Charting the Future or a Perspective on the Present? The Paraenetic Purpose of Mark 13." *CTJ* 41 (2006): 89–101. **Dyer, Keith D.** *The Prophecy on the Mount: Mark 13 and the Gathering of the New Community.* International Theological Studies 2. Bern: Lang, 1998. **Geddert, Timothy J.** *Watchwords: Mark 13 in Markan Eschatology.* JSNTSup 26. Sheffield: JSOT, 1989. **Hartman, Lars.** *Prophecy Interpreted: The Formation of Some Jewish Apocalyptic Texts and the Eschatological Discourse Mark 13 Par.* ConBNT 1. Lund: Gleerup, 1966. **Lambrecht, Jan.** *Die Redaktion der Markus-Apokalypse: Literarische Analyse und Strukturuntersuchung.* AnBib 28. Rome: Pontifical Bible Institute, 1967. **Marcus, Joel.** " 'The Time Has Been Fulfilled! Mark 1:15." Pp. 49–68 in *Apocalyptic and the New Testament: Essays in Honor of J. Louis Martyn.* JSNTSup 24. Ed. Joel Marcus and Marion L. Soards. Sheffield: Sheffield Academic Press, 1989. **Pesch, Rudolf.** *Naherwartungen: Tradition und Redaktion in Mk 13.* KBANT 8. Düsseldorf, Patmos, 1968. **Shively, Elizabeth E.** *Apocalyptic Imagination in the Gospel of Mark: The Literary and Theological Role of Mark 3:22–30.* BZNW 189; Berlin/New York: de Gruyter, 2012. **Stein, Robert H.** *Jesus, the Temple and the Coming of the Son of Man: A Commentary on Mark 13.* Downers Grove, IL: InterVarsity Press, 2014. **Wenham, David.** " 'This Generation Will Not Pass ...' A Study of Jesus' Future Expectation in Mark 13." Pp. 127–50 in *Christ the Lord: Studies in Christology Presented to Donald Guthrie.* Ed. Harold H. Rowden. Downers Grove, IL: InterVarsity Press, 1982.

13.1 The Time Has Come

Jesus' preaching in Mark begins on an eschatological note: "The time has come. The kingdom of God has come near. Repent and believe the good news!" (1:15). Hays notes that Jesus' proclamation that the time has been fulfilled affirms that "all of human history hinges on this moment." It means, he continues, that "everything is happening fast, and there is a tremendous sense of urgency about action in the present."[1] Mark expresses this urgency with the word "immediately" that appears eleven times in chapter 1 out of the forty times it is used in the gospel. Many ascribe this use of "immediately" to a Markan stylistic idiosyncrasy that is intended to add vividness and drama to the action, but Hays rightly interprets it as reflecting Mark's eschatological perspective. He observes,

> This is not just a clumsy device to link separate pericopes; rather, it describes the breathless pace with which God's apocalyptic campaign is unfolding. The effect is like watching a multimedia presentation in which slides flash across the screen so rapidly that there is no time to absorb the details; we perceive the forward thrust of events and find ourselves caught up in them. Mark's Jesus has no time for leisurely discourses about the lilies of the field. This Gospel plunges us into the midst of a cosmic conflict careening forward; if we want to follow the story, we need to pick up the pace.[2]

The question then arises: What has reached its completion? It could refer to the reign of Satan.[3] Satan's time is up. This view might be confirmed by the response of the demons who cower when they encounter Jesus and declare him to be the "Son of God" (3:11). When Jesus is accused by the teachers of the law of being allied with Satan, he responds with a parabolic saying that a stronger one has come to bind up a strong man to plunder his house (3:22–30). The game is not over, but the outcome is not in doubt. All rebellion against God will be defeated.[4]

While the coming of the kingdom of God certainly entails the defeat of Satan, the citation of the prophecy from Isaiah in Mark 1:3 makes it more likely that Mark has in mind the fulfillment of the prophecy referring to God's saving action. Isaiah 49:8–13 captures the essence of what 1:15 declares is happening and what the narrative that follows reveals is happening:

> This is what the LORD says:
>
> "In the time of my favor I will answer you,
>   and in the day of salvation I will help you;
> I will keep you and will make you
>   to be a covenant for the people,
> to restore the land
>   and to reassign its desolate inheritances,

1. Hays, *Moral Vision*, 89. The perfect tense of the verb translated "has been fulfilled" reinforces that this is the decisive time.
2. Ibid.
3. So Joel Marcus, "'The Time Has Been Fulfilled!'" 49–68.
4. Hooker, *Mark*, 55.

> to say to the captives, 'Come out,'
> and to those in darkness, 'Be free!'
> They will feed beside the roads
> and find pasture on every barren hill.
> They will neither hunger nor thirst,
> nor will the desert heat or the sun beat down on them.
> He who has compassion on them will guide them
> and lead them beside springs of water.
> I will turn all my mountains into roads,
> and my highways will be raised up.
> See, they will come from afar—
> some from the north, some from the west,
> some from the region of Aswan."
> Shout for joy, you heavens;
> rejoice, you earth;
> burst into song, you mountains!
> For the LORD comforts his people
> and will have compassion on his afflicted ones.

Jesus' declaration in Mark 1:15 proclaims that the time of fulfillment is here and God's kingdom is present within history. It can be experienced in this world in Jesus' words and deeds. Osborne states, "Mark's eschatology is 'inaugurated' rather than final—i.e., it recognizes the 'beginning' of the 'end' and the fact that the believer lives in a state of tension between the two."[5] The coming of God's kingdom does not lead to a cataclysmic world-ending irruption. It manifests itself in individual acts of healing and exorcism. The mythic battle between God and Satan takes place in the battle for human souls. They either submit to God or continue to rebel, abandon all to follow Jesus or abandon him, worship him or betray him.

13.2 THE TIME WILL COME

Some people asked Jesus why the disciples of John the Baptist and the Pharisees fast while his disciples did not (2:18). His answer, using the image of the bridegroom, enigmatically affirms that his presence is cause for his followers to celebrate rather than to fast, but a time will come when he will be taken away, and that will occasion their fasting (2:19–20):

> "How can the guests of the bridegroom fast while he is with them? They cannot, so long as they have him with them. But the time will come when the bridegroom will be taken from them, and on that day they will fast."

5. Grant R. Osborne, "Mark, Theology of," *Evangelical Dictionary of Theology* (ed. Walter A. Elwell; 2nd ed.; Grand Rapids: Baker, 2001), 738.

Normally, the guests leave, not the bridegroom. Mark's audience can only understand the bridegroom being taken away as an allusion to Jesus' passion and death. This perception is confirmed by the scheming of the Pharisees and Herodians on how best to do away with him (3:6). This allegorical parable serves as a forewarning that after Jesus' death a time of mourning will descend on his disciples. The discourse in chapter 13 will reveal that their mourning will not be attributable simply to the loss of a loved one but because they will face bitter tribulation in the interim before the End.

The good news of Jesus' resurrection does not mean that all will be set right with the world and that his disciples will live happily ever after. Warnings throughout the gospel make it clear that they face a dark destiny when they proclaim the gospel to a hostile world. After the resurrection, this greatest of miracles, there will come a time of wars (13:7), persecution (13:9), betrayal and hate (13:12–13), tribulation (13:19), and deception (13:21–22). If disciples faithfully proclaim the good news, they will be hated by all (13:13). The mistreatment of Jesus suggests that his disciples will fare no better. As Chronis eloquently puts it:

> Jesus is spurned by his own family (6:1–6). He is scorned (2:24; 3:22), plotted against (3:6; 11:18; 12:12; 14:1–2, 10–11), and falsely convicted (14:53–65) by his religious elders. He is betrayed by one of his close friends (14:10–11, 43–45) and abandoned by the rest of them (14:50, 66–72). He is condemned by his own compatriots (15:13–15). He is unjustly sentenced to die (15:15), brutalized (15:16–20), and crucified (15:24) by the civil authorities. He is disparaged by persons unknown as he agonizes on the cross (15:29–32). He is cursed by his companions in death (15:32). Then, in his last dying moments, he is ostensibly forsaken even by his God (15:34).[6]

The way of Christian discipleship is not a triumphant procession with victory after victory but a way barbed by enmity and pocked by personal failures.

At the Last Supper, Jesus solemnly pronounces, "Truly I tell you, I will not drink again from the fruit of the vine until that day when I drink it new in the kingdom of God" (14:25). This statement promises that after his humiliating death there will be vindication, and Jesus implies that the disciples will also partake of this victory celebration. Jesus does not tell them when this will happen, only that it will happen sometime in the future. The danger is that when disciples find themselves caught in perilous circumstances, they may be duped by false prophets offering false hopes by telling people what they want to hear. Deliverance is at hand.

Jesus' discourse in Mark 13 lays out warnings so that disciples will not be deceived during this often terrifying interim. The time will come when the Son of Man will return "in his Father's glory with the holy angels." For those who are "ashamed" of him and his words in "this adulterous and sinful generation," it will bring judgment (8:38). There are only two options: loyalty to Jesus or disavowal of him. There is no middle ground. For those who have been faithful and endure to the

6. Chronis, "The Torn Veil," 99–100.

end, it means salvation. The Son of Man will "send his angels and gather his elect from the four winds, from the ends of the earth to the ends of the heavens" (13:27). In the meantime, however, the disciples will face hard times and can only patiently watch and wait until God's purposes for the world are fulfilled.[7]

13.3 Mark's Eschatological Discourse: Discipleship during Tough Times (Mark 13)

Mark's first discourse in 4:1 – 34 stops the action and provides a commentary on what has happened in 1:14 – 3:35 and what will happen in 4:35 – 8:31. This second discourse in 13:3 – 37 stops the action and provides a commentary on what has happened in 11:1 – 12:44 and prepares for what will happen in 14:1 – 16:8.[8]

13.3.1 The Further Clarification of the Events Recorded in Mark 11:1 – 12:44

This discourse in chapter 13 occurs after Jesus' prophetic entrance into Jerusalem to the acclamation of the crowd who hail him in terms of the expectations associated with a traditional Davidic Messiah (11:1 – 11) and after Jesus has intimated that he is more than the son of David but David's Lord (12:35 – 37). It also occurs after Mark has bracketed Jesus' cursing of the fig tree around Jesus' prophetic actions in the temple (11:12 – 25) that challenges the validity of a temple that has become a den of robbers and not a place of prayer for all the nations. Those actions portend that the temple will be destroyed. The tree appeared to have fruit but was barren and cursed, and it withered to its roots. With its breathtaking stones and buildings, the temple appears on the surface to be fruitful as a glorious tribute to the God of Israel, but it has become a petrified fossil useless to God.

This discourse also occurs after Jesus' parabolic challenge of the legitimacy of the priestly hierarchy (the chief priests, teachers of the law, and elders) in the allegory of the Wicked Tenants (12:1 – 12). The tenants refuse to yield the fruit of the vineyard to the owner, abuse those sent to collect the fruit, and finally murder the son of the Lord of the vineyard. The parable ends with the cautionary warning that the tenants will be destroyed and the vineyard given to others (12:9). Jesus' interactions with various hostile opponents in the temple that follow make clear that piety surrounding this temple is all show and no substance. Like the teachers of the law who parade about in long robes, secure the best seats in the synagogues and places of honor at banquets, prey upon poor widows, and pray long prayers for show, the temple and those linked to its spiritual root "will be punished most severely" (12:38 – 40).

7. Shively, *Apocalyptic Imagination*, 189, writes, "Mark presents the coming of the Son of Man as the eschatological judgment that includes the rejection of those who deny Jesus and the salvation of those who follow him. Jesus' followers must endure until he comes as the Son of Man in judgment, continuing to be faithful witnesses while imitating his suffering."

8. In the first discourse, the emphasis is on "hearing" (4:3, 9, 15 – 16, 18, 20, 23 – 24, 33); in this second discourse, the emphasis is on "watching" and "seeing" (13:2, 5, 9, 23, 33, 34 – 37).

The introduction to the discourse in 13:1–2 records Jesus departing from the temple. Combined with his ominous threats, his departure signals that the temple's "fate is sealed."[9] Its license as a house of prayer and the focal point of the identity of the people of God has expired. Jesus' prophecy that follows in 13:5–23 reveals that its desecration and demise is sure,[10] but it marks only the end of its world, not the End of the world.

13.3.2 The Prelude to the Events Recorded in Mark 14:1–16:8

This discourse also paves the way for Jesus' betrayal, arrest, trial, scourging, humiliating death, and ultimate vindication by God in the resurrection. The list of parallels between Mark 13 and Mark 14–15 highlights the connections.

Mark 13	Mark 14–15
The prediction of the temple's destruction (13:2)	The charge that Jesus threatened to destroy the temple (14:58) and the taunts of passersby, "So! You who are going to destroy the temple and build it in three days" (15:29)
The command for the disciples to watch (13:5, 9, 23, 33, 35, 37)	The command for the disciples to watch (14:34, 37–38)
The prediction that the disciples will be delivered up to religious councils and synagogues and political authorities, governors and kings (13:9)	Jesus is delivered up to a religious council and to the Roman governor (14:53–65; 15:1–15)
The prediction that the disciples will be betrayed by family members (13:12)	Jesus is betrayed by one of the Twelve (14:10, 11, 18, 21, 41–45)
Mention of the hour (13:23, 33)	Jesus states the hour has come (14:41)
The prediction that "in those days, following that distress, the sun will be darkened" (13:24)	Darkness came over the whole land from noon until three in the afternoon during Jesus' crucifixion (15:33)
The prediction that the Son of Man will come in clouds with great power and glory (13:26)	Jesus predicts before the council that they will see the Son of Man seated at the right hand of the Power, and coming with the clouds of heaven (14:62)
Warning to watch lest the master returns during the various watches of the night and find the servants sleeping (13:35–36)	The various watches of the night when the disciples fail: evening at the Last Supper (14:17); midnight when Jesus returns to find the disciples sleeping (14:37, 40); cockcrow at Peter's denial (14:72); early morning when Jesus is abandoned by all and condemned (15:1)

9. Vicky Balabanski, *Eschatology in the Making: Mark, Matthew and The Didache* (SNTSMS 97; Cambridge: Cambridge University Press, 1997), 58.

10. Mark 13:14 does not explicitly refer to the temple's destruction but its desecration, but the command to flee makes clear that this desecration is preliminary to its destruction. The disciples are to get out while they still can.

The darkening of the sun mentioned in 13:24 as a sign of the Parousia puts the darkness at noon over the whole land during Jesus' crucifixion (15:33) in cosmic perspective. Ultimately, the gloom of Jesus' death when the sun is darkened will be transformed when the Son of Man returns in glory and power, and creation, the sun, the moon, and the stars respond with trembling (13:24–26). The parallels between 13:33–37 and 14:32–42 suggest to Geddert that the discourse reflects "an eschatology *highly infused with Mark's passion theology* which must be correlated with the Gethsemane pericope, not an eschatology on the lookout for signs and apocalyptic phenomena."[11]

13.3.3 The Rhetorical Function of the Discourse

The study of Mark 13 has produced what Dyer calls "the labyrinth of scholarly interpretations."[12] Early on, research focused on the sources behind this discourse. Colani first designated it as a "little apocalypse." He contended that it was based on a Jewish or Christian Jewish apocalyptic flyleaf that was slightly Christianized and inserted into the narrative.[13] This conclusion was driven by the conviction that Jesus himself did not engage in such eschatological speculation, and, had he done so, he would not have been so mistaken to assert that "this generation will certainly not pass away until all these things have happened" (13:30). The errors in the predictions were attributable to the author of this flyleaf, who pieced together various traditions.

The search for an apocalyptic source for the discourse continues to exert its influence.[14] Beasley-Murray has successfully challenged these arguments by showing that Mark 13 is the evangelist's redactional compilation that utilizes independent sayings of Jesus.[15] "It is decidedly not an apocalypse," though it does exhibit an apocalyptic perspective.[16] It does not contain elements that normally belong to that genre: "It contains no tour of heaven or hell guided by an angel, no bizarre imagery,

11. Geddert, *Watchwords*, 106. Focant, *Mark*, 521, contends that Mark 13, inserted between Jesus' passion in Mark 11–12 and 14–16, represents the "passion of the community."

12. Keith D. Dyer, *The Prophecy on the Mount: Mark 13 and the Gathering of the New Community* (International Theological Studies 2; Bern: Lang, 1998), 24. See also Kenneth Grayston, "The Study of Mark XIII," *BJRL* 56 (1973–74): 371–87; Ferdinand Hahn, "Die Rede von der Parusie des Menschensohnes Markus 13," in *Jesus und der Menschensohn* (ed. Rudolph Pesch and Rudolf Schnackenburg; Freiburg: Herder, 1975), 240–66; David Wenham, *The Rediscovery of Jesus' Eschatological Discourse* (Gospel Perspectives 4; Sheffield: JSOT, 1984); George R. Beasley-Murray, *Jesus and the Last Days: The Interpretation of the Olivet Discourse* (Peabody, MA: Hendrickson, 1993).

13. Timothée Colani, *Jésus-Christ et les croyances messianiques de son temps* (2nd ed.; Strasbourg: Treuttel et Wurtz, 1864); Heinrich Wilhelm Weiffenbach, *Der Wiederkunftsgedanke Jesu nach den Synoptikern* (Leipzig: Breitkopf and Härtel, 1873), 69–171. The Christian additions are identified as 13:5–6, 9–11, 13a, and 23.

14. See, e.g., Egon Brandenburger, *Markus 13 und die Apokalyptik* (FRLANT 134; Göttingen: Vandenhoeck & Ruprecht, 1984), 41–42.

15. Beasley-Murray, *Jesus and the Last Days*, 1–376. Nevertheless, Hooker, *Mark*, 298, states, "The existence of the 'Little Apocalypse' cannot be either proved or disproved, but this is not of great importance, since the hypothesis in fact helps us little in understanding Mark 13 as it now is."

16. Shively, *Apocalyptic Imagination*, 218. Some argue that it functions as a "farewell discourse," in which a leader or patriarch of a family is nearing death and gives ethical exhortation and reveals heavenly secrets; see Balabanski, *Eschatology*, 70–71; Dyer, *Prophecy*, 233–66. See Gen 49:1–33; Deut 31:1–33:29; Josh 23:1–24:30; 1 Sam 12:1–25; 1 Kgs 2:1–9; 1 Chr 28:1–29:5; Tob 14:3–11; 1 Macc 2:49–70; *1 En.* 91–105; *Jub.* 23:9–32; and *T. 12Patr.* Evans, *Mark 8:27–16:20*, 289–90, counters that the problem with this view is that the discourse does not "review and comment on the past" as farewell discourses normally do, nor is it "cast in a much more formal setting" in which the dying patriarch or monarch summons his sons to address them. Jesus also makes no explicit mention of his death. See also Adams, *The Stars*, 135.

no division of history into different epochs to show the outworking of God's plan, no reference to a last great battle or war, no last-ditch demonic assault, a complete refusal to identify the time of the end, and no description of what happens after the Parousia."[17] It does employ, however, a cluster of apocalyptic motifs[18] and expects a cataclysmic coming of the Son of Man culminating in the salvation of the elect.[19]

Mark uses this apocalyptic language to exhort his audience.[20] Hurtado states that this discourse "quite transparently addresses the continuing concerns of disciples beyond the more immediate situation of Jesus and the Twelve."[21] Reading between the lines, then, suggests that Mark's first audience is "experiencing rejection, suffering, and death for the sake of the gospel," and Shively suggests that "some may be tempted to abandon the faith for an easier way" rather than to wait for God to break into history to deliver them. She argues, "The main rhetorical function of Mark's apocalyptic discourse is to persuade readers that it is precisely out of such rejection, suffering and death that God manifests redemptive power."[22] It does not disclose esoteric secrets related to the timing of the End because it is not intended to provide data to fill out a doomsday calendar. Instead, it is designed to encourage faithful endurance during the interim, before the Parousia, when the world is filled with strife and danger for Christian disciples.

Jesus issues eighteen imperatives in the discourse (13:5, 7, 9, 11 [2x], 14, 15 [2x], 16, 18, 21, 23, 28, 29, 33 [2x], 35, and 37). The essential directives are "understand," "watch out," "do not fear," and "escape." Bolt recognizes what is most vital in the series of instructions: "Rather than looking out for signs, rather than worrying about world events, the disciples should be looking out for *themselves* (v. 9)."[23] Only doing that will prevent them from falling sway to frothing messianism, wilting under persecution and falling away, or falling asleep and being unready when the Son of Man returns.

Jesus announces the future but offers no clues about precisely when things will end. Some events that will happen are predictable,[24] so disciples should not be panicked by wars and natural disasters, fooled by false prophets or messianic pretenders, or dispirited by persecution. The End, however, will come in God's timing when many may be lulled to sleep.

---

17. Garland, *Mark*, 504.

18. Many images and phrases are found in Daniel: the question about when all these things would be accomplished (Dan 12:6–7); the reference to threats of wars (Dan 9:26; 11:13, 40–42); the abomination that desolates (Dan 9:27; 12:11); the Son of Man coming in the clouds and given dominion and glory and kingship (Dan 7:13–14). Hartman, *Prophecy Interpreted*, 167, contends that what underlies the discourse is "an exposition or meditation based on texts in Daniel about the last things, especially 7,8–27; 8,9–26; 9,24–27; 11,21–12,13; and to some extent 2,31–35."

19. Shively, *Apocalyptic Imagination*, 186–88.

20. Focant, *Mark*, 521, contends that "parenesis would be the first aim of the evangelist, and it would be colored with apocalyptic teachings."

21. Hurtado, "Following Jesus in the Gospel of Mark," 15.

22. Shively, *Apocalyptic Imagination*, 257.

23. Peter G. Bolt, "Mark 13: An Apocalyptic Precursor to the Passion Narrative," *RTR* 54 (1995): 28. The literal translation of the phrase in 13:9 is "look to yourselves."

24. For example, C. E. B. Cranfield, "St. Mark 13," *SJT* 6 (1953): 192, writes that "there is no reason to doubt that Jesus had a sufficient measure of political insight to see that, if His fellow countrymen continued in their present mood, they would sooner or later bring down the wrath of the Romans upon their heads and that to a war between Rome and the Jews there could only be one outcome."

13.3.4 Theological Presuppositions of Mark's Eschatological Discourse

13.3.4.1 The Pattern of Suffering and Vindication

The discourse of Mark 13 corrects any false expectations that after the resurrection the disciples will be ever-victorious in their endeavors.[25] As John the Baptist was handed over and killed, and as Jesus was handed over and killed, so many disciples will be handed over and killed (13:9–11). The disciples must take up the cross, which ultimately leads to their vindication.[26]

It is noteworthy that the discourse is depicted as addressed to the three disciples who most openly resisted the way of the cross (13:3): Peter in 8:32b, and James and John in 10:35–37. Shively rightly asserts, "The aim of the Olivet discourse is to persuade followers to believe that suffering is God's will for the righteous, and to act self-sacrificially for Jesus' sake and the gospel's."[27] It instructs the audience that the persecutions they suffer must be suffered. The tribulation is part of God's plan leading to the end of history. Disciples must bear witness amidst intimidating enemies, and only those who endure to the end will be saved (13:13). Balabanski notes that the discourse contains "a glimpse of vindication, but it is the darkness of the tunnel rather than the light at the end of the tunnel which receives most attention."[28]

13.3.4.2 God's Sovereign Control

Mark assumes that history moves inexorably toward its predetermined goal (see Dan 8:26; 12:4, 9). The new age comes only by the direct intervention of God. Human actions might determine a person's own particular fate, but they do not affect the final fate of the world. That is entirely in God's hands. Translated literally, the phrase "from the beginning of creation, which God created" (13:19), was jettisoned by later scribes copying Mark because of its seeming redundancy and is avoided by most modern translations ("from the beginning, when God created the world," NIV). Marcus points out, however, that its repetitiveness "is purposeful: it emphasizes that despite the sufferings of the present time, God is not impotent and will soon reassert his control over the world he created."[29] God is in heaven, and, while all is not right with the world, it soon will be. God has already determined the destiny of the world and assures the ultimate deliverance of Jesus' faithful followers.

Disciples should not be alarmed when they hear about "wars and rumors of wars" (13:7) because "such things must happen."[30] The mayhem caused by war, therefore, is not out of the sovereign control of God. The phrase translated "nation will rise against nation, and kingdom against kingdom" (13:8) uses the passive voice, "Nation *will be*

25. Kelber, "Apostolic Tradition and the Form of the Gospel," 35.
26. Deppe, "Charting the Future," 93.
27. Shively, *Apocalyptic Imagination*, 219.
28. Balabanski, *Eschatology*, 61.
29. Marcus, *Mark 8–16*, 893. He continues by citing Michael E. Stone's, *Fourth Ezra* (Hermeneia; Minneapolis: Fortress, 1990), 290, translation of 2 Esd 9:2, "Then you will know that it is the very time when the Most High is about to visit *the world which he has made*" (emphasis added).
30. That they will "hear" about them suggests that they will not have experienced directly these conflicts.

raised against nation." Marcus interprets it as a divine passive meaning that *God* will raise up nation against nation (see Isa 19:2).[31] God also lengthens the days so that the mission might have the greatest results; God shortens the days to save the elect (13:20). God alone knows the day and the hour of the End (13:32). And God will also bring all things to an end at the consummation of the age. Evil will not have the last word. Therefore, they are not to be horrified or disheartened by what God has ordained.

13.3.4.3 The Hope of the Parousia and the Suddenness of the End

When one lives in the midst of a firestorm of persecution, one cannot always perceive how God's purposes are being accomplished in the world. Christians can endure the suffering facing them as they carry out their mission of taking the gospel to all people because of the hope of the return of the Son of Man in glory, who will gather the elect. They must not allow themselves to be deceived by false prophets, within or without the church, offering only counterfeit hopes centered on accomplishing the longings of humans rather than God's cosmic purposes. The End will come suddenly and without warning. Therefore, disciples must remain vigilant and not chart a timetable of the End but concentrate on their task in the world.

13.3.5 The Interpretation of Mark 13

Mark 13 is often understood as referring to two separate events: (1) the destruction of Jerusalem and the temple; and (2) the return of the Son of Man and the gathering of the elect at the end of history. Which verses are to be applied to which is much disputed, and some read this discourse as referring only to the destruction of the temple, and some read it as referring only to the Parousia and the end of history. My outline of the discourse interprets it as referring to the impending destruction of the temple (13:5–23) and the coming of the Son of Man in glory and the gathering of the elect at the End (13:24–27). It interprets the two parabolic conclusions, the lesson of the fig tree (13:28–32) as related to the destruction of the temple, and the unknown day and hour of the householder's return (13:33–37) as related to the separate event of the return of the Son of Man. This outline is offered in full awareness that widespread disagreement about this discourse will continue to exist.[32]

1. Introduction: Prediction of the temple's destruction and double questions (13:1–4)
   - 1.1 The disciples' observation of the temple's grandeur (13:1)
   - 1.2 Jesus' prediction of the destruction of the temple (13:2)
   - 1.3 The disciples' double question (13:3–4)
     - 1.3.1 When will this be?
     - 1.3.2 What will be the sign that all these things are about to be accomplished?

31. Marcus, *Mark 8–16*, 876–77.

32. Stein, *Jesus, the Temple and the Coming of the Son of Man*, 46–48, presents six different outlines proposed by various scholars.

2. Jesus' answer to the question about the destruction of the temple (13:5–23)
   2.1 Beware (*blepete*) of false messiahs (13:5–6)
   2.2 Hearing of wars and disasters, which do not portend the imminence of the end but only the beginning of the birth pains (13:7–8)
   2.3 Beware (*blepete*) not to fall away during the time of persecution (13:9–13)
   2.4 Seeing the desolating sacrilege, which brings tribulations and does portend the end of the temple (13:14–20)
   2.5 Beware (*blepete*) of false messiahs (13:21–23)
3. Jesus' answer to the question about when all these things are about to be accomplished (13:24–27)
   3.1 The unmistakable convulsion of the heavens accompanying the coming of the Son of Man in glory (13:24–26)
   3.2 The gathering of the elect (13:27)
4. Conclusion: Answers to the double questions (13:28–37)
   4.1 Parable of the Fig Tree related to the destruction of the temple (13:28–31)
   4.2 The unknown day or hour and the parable of the Watchman related to the coming of the Son of Man (13:32–37)

13.3.5.1 Introduction to the Discourse (Mark 13:1–4)

The awestruck reaction of anonymous disciples to the great stones of the temple prompts Jesus' prophecy that this magnificent edifice is destined to lie in ruins.[33] The disciples, as usual, have not grasped the significance of Jesus' action in the temple or the allegory of the Wicked Tenants, which concludes with the assurance that the Lord of the vineyard "will come and kill those tenants and give the vineyard to others" (12:9). This threat is divinely affirmed by the citation of Ps 118:22–23, "The stone the builders rejected has become the cornerstone; the Lord has done this, and it is marvelous in our eyes" (Mark 12:10–11).[34]

As in previous incidents when the disciples were slow on the uptake (8:16, 32b; 9:32; 10:35–37), this new example of their lack of discernment provides Jesus with the opportunity to spell things out more fully. What was implicit in Jesus' actions and words in the temple now becomes explicit when he unequivocally prophesies

33. Josephus, *J.W.* 5.5.6 §§222–224, rapturously describes the temple's grandeur:

> Now the outward face of the temple in its front wanted nothing that was likely to surprise either men's minds or their eyes: for it was covered all over with plates of gold of great weight, and, at the first rising of the sun, reflected back a very fiery splendor, and made those who forced themselves to look upon it to turn their eyes away, just as they would have done at the sun's own rays. But this Temple appeared to strangers, when they were at a distance, like a mountain covered with snow; for, as to those parts of it that were not gilt, they were exceedingly white.... Of its stones, some of them were forty-five cubits in length, five in height and six in breadth.

34. Michael Cahill, "Not a Cornerstone! Translating Ps 118,22 in the Jewish and Christian Scriptures," *RB* 106 (1999): 345–57, argues that the stone does not refer to a "cornerstone" but a capstone that is placed high in a prominent place at the completion stage of the building and offers the translation, "The stone rejected by the builders now crowns the castle."

its utter destruction.[35] Jesus reverses the prophet Haggai's rallying cry, "one stone was laid on another," which sought to kindle renewed commitment to the temple rebuilding project (Hag 2:15–19), and predicts, "Not one stone here will be left on another; every one will be thrown down" (Mark 13:2). Such a catastrophe would have been unthinkable to most, since the temple was regarded as the sacred dwelling place of God on earth. The ongoing construction of the temple complex made it not only breathtakingly grand but seemingly impregnable. Jesus warns the disciples not to be taken in by appearances.[36]

When Jesus leaves the temple, he crosses over to the Mount of Olives, where he sits down (13:3; see 4:1). The echo from Ezek 11:23, "The glory of the LORD went up from within the city and stopped above the mountain east of it," and its context of judgment on the people in Jerusalem "whose hearts are devoted to their vile images and detestable idols" (11:21), imply that Mark understands Jesus to be sitting in judgment of the temple and not simply shifting his teaching venue.[37] The temple's destruction is not the tragic result of foolish miscalculations of rebels thinking they could successfully revolt against Rome. Mark understands its impending destruction as attributable to God's judgment on the leaders' sinful rebellion in obstinately refusing to listen to God's prophets and rejecting and killing God's beloved Son (12:1–9). Stein adds, "There is also a sense in which Mark understands this prediction of Jesus not merely as declarative in nature but causative as well. Jesus not only predicts the destruction of Jerusalem and the temple, he brings it about!"[38]

Peter, James, John, and Andrew, the first disciples Jesus called, ask him privately to fill in the details attending this prophecy: "When will these things happen? And what will be the sign that they [these things] are all about to be fulfilled?" (13:4).[39] The phrase, "when these things are all about to be accomplished" (13:4, ASV), suggests that they have the End in mind. The question echoes Dan 12:6–7, when Daniel asks about how long until the end of these wonders he has been shown. The angel responds, "It will be for a time, times and half a time. When the power of the holy people has been finally broken, all these things will be completed." The same verb "completed" (*syntelein*), variously translated "fulfilled," "accomplished," and "come to an end," is used.

The disciples' second question assumes that the destruction of the temple would be tied to a series of events leading up to the end of all things. If Matthew is utilizing Mark as his source at this point, he certainly interprets their question in this way. The disciples ask, " 'Tell us when will this happen, and what will be the sign of your

35. The destruction of the temple is tied together with the destruction of Jerusalem in Old Testament prophecies (Jer 7:14; 26:6, 9, 16–19; Lam 2:7–9; Dan 9:26; Mic 3:12; and Tob 14:4).

36. The imposing architecture of the temple is like the fig tree in leaf that *appeared* to have figs but had none and was cursed (11:12–14, 20–21), and its ceremonial religiosity is like the teachers of the law who parade about and *appear* to be pious with their long prayers but who will receive the greater condemnation because it is all a façade that hides their greedy exploitation of widows (12:40).

37. Ezek 11:14–20 also contains God's promise to gather and renew the people scattered among the nations.

38. Stein, *Jesus, the Temple and the Coming of the Son of Man*, 65.

39. Seeking a sign is something Jesus' opponents do to put him to the test (8:11–12).

coming and of the end of the age?'" (Matt 24:3).[40] Jesus' response, in my opinion, drives a wedge between the two events. The temple's demise does not mean that the End is near, and the discourse will reveal that no sign will forewarn anyone of its approach.

13.3.5.2 The Beginning of the Birth Pains (Mark 13:5–23)

The disciples have asked their questions (13:4), and Jesus responds at the end of this unit, "I have told you all things beforehand" (13:23, ASV). But Jesus does not let the disciples in on the timing of the End. He only gives them warnings about the dangers that will take place in the near future related to the destruction of the temple. The key imperative in this section is "see" (*blepete*) in 13:5, 9, which is variously translated "be on your guard," "watch out," "take heed," "take care," and "beware," so that the disciples will not be taken in by frauds. In 13:9, the verb is best translated "take heed to yourselves" (RSV). The imperatives that follow the four temporal clauses in this section reveal that the primary concern is not to give the disciples information that will help them map out future eschatological events but to encourage them not to panic when the world seems to be falling apart or when they are being hounded by opponents. They are also warned not to become caught up in misguided messianic fervor that only leads down the road to ruin.

> When you hear of wars and rumors of wars, *do not be alarmed* (13:7).
> Whenever you are arrested and brought to trial, *do not worry beforehand* about what to say (13:11).
> When you see "the abomination that causes desolation" standing where it does not belong ... then let those who are in Judea *flee* to the mountains (13:14).
> At that time if anyone says to you, "Look, here is the Messiah!" or, "Look, there he is!" *do not believe it* (13:21).

These events must happen and should not divert disciples from their calling to preach the gospel.

13.3.5.2.1 Fraudulent Messiahs (Mark 13:5–6)

Jesus warns against being taken in by those who will come in his name saying, "It is I." Jesus used this phrase to identify himself to the terrified disciples when he approached them by walking on the sea (6:50). Does he refer to Christians who will come in Jesus' name and deceptively speak in his name? Boring argues that "I am" is part of a revelation formula used by charismatic Christian prophets who speak in the

40. Stein, *Jesus, the Temple, and the Coming of the Son of Man*, 75–76, shows that Luke, who also is believed to have used Mark as one of his sources, interprets "these things" as referring to the same event, the destruction of the temple: "As for what you see here, the time will come when not one stone will be left on another; every one of them will be thrown down." "Teacher," they asked, "when will these things happen? And what will be the sign that they are about to take place?" (Luke 21:6–7). He (pp. 78–79) cites other consecutive questions in Mark in which the second question is essentially a repetition of the first in 7:18; 9:19; and 14:37 and highlights the questions in 11:28 as parallels.

name of the risen Lord using the first person.[41] It is more likely, however, that false messianic figures promising divine deliverance are in mind.[42] "In my name" appears in 9:37, 38, 39, 41; 13:13 and refers to the authority of Jesus' messianic name. Those who claim "I am he" "usurp the name and lay claim for themselves divine authority that rightfully belongs only to Jesus."[43] These imposters make promises that God is an ally to their cause and will divinely intervene.[44]

13.3.5.2.2 Wars, Political Unrest, Earthquakes and Famines (Mark 13:7–8)

These dire predictions of unrest mesh with the Roman historian Tacitus's sober assessment of the upheaval in Rome during the period of the Jewish revolt (*Hist.* 1.2–3).[45]

Josephus (*J.W.* 1.1.2 §5) reports that the Jewish rebellion against Rome in AD 66 began in hopes that it would achieve success while the Romans were occupied with the Gauls and Celts and with the assistance of their fellow Jews beyond the Euphrates. Moreover, he says, "Nero's death ... brought universal confusion; many were induced by this opportunity to aspire to the sovereignty, and a change which might make their fortune was after the heart of the soldiery." It was a serious miscalculation. The rebels met with initial success that gave them false hope, but the formidable Roman army rallied and scorched its way through Galilee to besiege Jerusalem in AD 69 and ultimately sacked the city and burned the temple to the ground in AD 70. Josephus (*J.W.* 7.1.1 §§1–5) also says that after the Romans captured the city, "Caesar ordered that the whole city and the temple be razed to the ground, leaving only the loftiest of towers ... to indicate to posterity the nature of the city and the strong defences which had yet yielded to Roman prowess." The destruction was so total that Josephus said that future visitors would doubt that the place had ever been inhabited.

There were three earthquakes in Italy in AD 68[46] and an earthquake in Jerusalem in AD 67,[47] but wars and earthquakes were common images for coming doom (see Isa 13:13; Jer 49:21; 51:29; Joel 2:10; Amos 8:8). Famine inevitably results from the brutality of warfare (e.g., Isa 51:19; Jer 11:22; 14:12–18; 15:2; Rev 6:8). *Second*

41. See Boring, *Mark*, 362–63; and M. Eugene Boring, *The Continuing Voice of Jesus: Christian Prophecy and the Gospel Tradition* (Louisville: Westminster John Knox, 1991), 158–61.

42. Hengel, *The Zealots*, 229–45, 290–98, on Josephus's condemnation of the prophets who stirred up the people before the war against Rome and the messianic pretenders in the Jewish freedom movement, like Menahem and Simon bar Giora. For example, Josephus (*J.W.* 2.13.4 §§258–260) castigates a group whom he claims were worse than the violent revolutionaries during the war against Rome: "another group of scoundrels, in act less criminal but in intention more evil.... Cheats and deceivers, claiming inspiration, they schemed to bring about revolutionary changes by inducing the mob to act as if possessed and by leading them out into the wild country on the pretence that there God would give them signs of approaching freedom."

43. Garland, *Mark*, 492. It is ironic that Jesus announces, "I am [he]," in 14:62 (cf. 6:50), but his claim is dismissed.

44. See Rebecca Gray, *Prophetic Figures in Late Second Temple Jewish Palestine: The Evidence from Josephus* (Oxford: Oxford University Press, 1993), 112–44. From Josephus's accounts, some of their characteristics she lists are: (1) they were leaders of sizable popular movements; (2) they came from the ranks of the common people; (3) they presented themselves as prophets and were regarded so by their followers; (4) they promised imminent, miraculous divine intervention to bring deliverance from Roman rule.

45. See §1.2.2.2.1.1, above, for the full citation.

46. See the accounts in Suetonius, *Galba* 18.1; Pliny the Elder, *Nat.* 2.199; and Cassius Dio, *Rom. Hist.* 62.18.56.

47. Josephus, *J.W.* 4.4.5 §§286–287.

Baruch 70:8 captures all three images of war, an earthquake, and famine: "And it will happen that everyone who saves himself from the war will die in an earthquake, and he who saves himself from the earthquake will be burned by fire, and he who saves himself from the fire will perish by famine." The ravages of war overtake everyone unfortunate enough to be in its path. That the disciples will "hear" about these things may suggest some distance from the events.

13.3.5.2.3 The Persecution of Christians (Mark 13:9–13)

The disciples' allegiance to Christ will provoke opposition from Jews—being handed over to "local councils" (lit., "sanhedrins") and flogged in synagogues (see 2 Cor 11:24)—and from Gentiles—being brought before governors (see Acts 18:12–17; 24:10–27; 25:1–12) and kings (see 25:23–26:32). This persecution reveals that the disciples will be "conformed to the way of the cross that they are so consistently avoiding within the narrative."[48] They will be loathed by everyone (13:13). Tacitus's account of how Nero tried to pin the guilt for the devastating fire in Rome on the Christians describes them as "a class hated for their abominations ... by the populace" (*Ann.* 15.44.2, 4). The so-called abomination was their devotion to Jesus' name. The world's hatred will reach into the home (13:12) as family members will betray their closest kin.

According to 2 Esd 9:1–6, "earthquakes, tumult of peoples, intrigues of nations, wavering of leaders, confusion of princes" are signs of the end. Jesus contends, however, that such things are *not* true signs of the end but symptoms of a world still trampled by evil. Therefore they should not cause disciples to panic when they occur. His warning could not be clearer: "The end is still to come" (13:7); "these are the beginning of birth pains" (13:8).[49] Since the proclamation of the gospel to all nations *must* occur before the End, it implies that there will be time for this mission to be accomplished.[50] The emphasis on the gospel being preached reveals that this discourse is not driven by "despair over the evils of the world and a longing to escape them" but is a call to faithful discipleship in the midst of the evils of the world.[51]

13.3.5.2.4 The Abomination That Causes Desolation (Mark 13:14–20)

Since this discourse is not intended primarily to impart information but rather to exhort disciples, I would agree with Balabanski's proposal that 13:9–13 and 14–20 are not meant to be taken as "chronologically sequential, but as two distinct

48. Balabanski, *Eschatology*, 61.

49. The OT used the sharp pangs associated with childbirth as a metaphor for the pain of suffering that is inevitable (Isa 13:8; 26:17–18; 66:8; Jer 4:31; 6:24; 13:21; 22:23; Hos 13:13; Mic 4:9). It was not yet a technical term for the messianic woes, as can be seen from the variety of ways the imagery is used in the NT to refer to the pain from various troubles that give birth to something new and longed for (John 16:21–22; Rom 8:22; Gal 4:19; 1 Thess 5:3; Rev 12:2).

50. It is mistaken to interpret this statement to imply, as Tolbert, *Sowing the Gospel*, 265, does: "The sooner the gospel is preached to all nations, the sooner the kingdom will arrive and all suffering will cease," and preaching is "the one human act that can expedite the demise of this present evil, oppressive, and suffering-filled existence." The timing of the end depends entirely on God and not on any human activity. Humans can do nothing to hasten the end.

51. Dyer, *Prophecy*, 271.

glimpses of this period of persecution."[52] The disciples are warned to steer clear of hyper-messianism and volatile nationalism that inflame others, to stay calm, and not to worry about defending themselves but to allow the Holy Spirit to empower them to bear testimony to their faith. When they "see 'the abomination that causes desolation' standing where it does not belong" (13:14), they are *not* to take part in any resistance movement or to await God's intervention; rather, they must recognize it as the signal to flee to the hills. It is not the eschatological climax.

Jesus expresses pity for those trying to escape when they are pregnant or nursing children, which makes flight more difficult, and urges them to pray that it will not take place in the winter when the rains make the roads in Judea impassible. This command cannot refer to the end of the age when any attempt to run away will be fruitless. This segment has to do with the signs that portend the devastation that will consume Jerusalem and its temple. They point to the end of the temple's world, not the end of the world.[53]

The statement that "those will be days of distress unequaled from the beginning, when God created the world, until now" (13:19), strongly suggests that these warnings are applicable only to disciples in the first century. "Until now" is quite different from "until that day" (see Dan 12:1). Marcus believes that it exhibits a deliberate modification of Dan 12:1 and probably reflects Mark's situation: " 'that day' of eschatological tribulation, the like of which the world will never again see, has *now* become a terrifying reality."[54]

13.3.5.2.4.1 The Sign of the Desolating Sacrilege (Mark 13:14)[55]

The term "the abomination that causes desolation" derives from Dan 11:31: "His armed forces will rise up to desecrate the temple fortress and will abolish the daily sacrifice. Then they will set up the abomination that causes desolation" (see also Dan 8:13; 9:27; 12:11). Daniel does not specify what this abomination is and only affirms that this sacrilege will be accompanied by a time of severe tribulation for God's people, the occupation of the temple by foreign forces, the end of the regular temple sacrifices, the seduction of the people to false worship, and a king who exalts himself as greater than all the gods. What Antiochus Epiphanes did according to 1–2 Maccabees fits this description well. He erected a desolating sacrilege on the altar of burnt offering in the temple (1 Macc 1:54, 59, 6:7; see 2 Macc 6:3–6) and attempted to eradicate the Jewish religion (1 Macc 1:41–49). The use of this phrase in the Maccabean history suggests that it was evocative of horrors related to the temple that could be applied to a variety of situations.

The parenthetical instruction "let the reader understand" is mystifying. It is

52. Balabanski, *Eschatology*, 77.

53. Prophets had announced the temple's ruin before, and its destruction did not bring the end of the world (1 Kgs 9:7–8; Jer 7:14; 26:6, 9, 18; Mic 3:12).

54. Marcus, *Mark 1–8*, 29.

55. False messiahs and false prophets "perform signs and wonders" (13:22). Jesus does not. Focant, *Mark*, 522, states that the "Jesus of Mark teaches his disciples to live in incertitude as to times and seasons." But he does warn them that the desecrating abomination in the temple is a sign for them to break away or they will also perish in the devastation that will soon engulf Jerusalem. The desecration of the temple otherwise has no sign value.

unclear which reader is intended or what the reader is alerted to understand. Turner insists that it is an anachronism to think that Mark envisaged that his gospel would have been read in public worship and that the phrase means "my readers."[56] Since few individual Christians would have private copies of Mark to read, however, most interpreters understand "the reader" to be the lector who reads the gospel aloud to the church (1 Thess 5:27; Col 4:16; 1 Tim 4:13; Rev 1:3).[57] The Markan narrator interrupts what is presented as a private discourse to the four disciples (13:3) to address the audience of Mark's gospel (see also 13:37). Perkins argues against the view that "let the reader understand" is an editorial intrusion and maintains that it is intended to be taken as part of Jesus' discourse.[58] He contends that this third person singular imperative is comparable to the third person singular imperative, "Whoever has ears to hear, let them hear" (4:9, 23).

The verb "to read" occurs in three other Markan passages (2:25; 12:10, 26), where Jesus asks his opponents "Have you not read?" The question assumes that they have read the sacred Scriptures but have not understood or interpreted correctly what they have read.[59] Failure to "read" correctly is attributable to their obduracy. Perkins argues: "It is quite conceivable that in this context, as the author characterizes Jesus' prophesying about Israel's future and alluding to Jewish sacred texts in ways that would generate shock and dismay for any Jewish person, Jesus would think it necessary to warn them to understand these forecasted events as coherent with what they read in their sacred Scriptures."[60] The warning is to the person who reads the prophecy in Daniel, not the text of Mark, and to connect that prophecy to what they see happening. This instruction underlines the cryptic nature of the prophecy that requires interpretation.[61] It invites them to penetrate beneath the surface to discern "the significance of the prophecy"[62] in light of their experience.[63]

Mark assumes that his first audience would, upon reflection, understand the reference and would know that it has already happened or is about to happen. Current readers, however, are left in the dark. Several possibilities have been proposed. (1) In AD 40, the Emperor Gaius Caligula ordered that his statue be erected in the temple (see Josephus, *J.W.* 2.10.1 §§184–203; *Ant.* 18.8.2–9 §§256–309; Philo, *Embassy*; Tacitus, *Hist.* 5.9). The emperor had deified himself, but this particular mandate came in response to the Jews in Jamnia tearing down an imperial altar that had been recently erected.[64] A statue would ideally suit the image of "standing where it does not belong," but Mark has a masculine participle ("standing")

56. Elliott, *The Language and Style of the Gospel of Mark*, 32. Turner contends that Mark "reproduces ... the very phrase employed by Jesus, and adds to it parenthetically his own comment."

57. Beavis, *Mark's Audience*, 142–43, thinks that it signals the reader that the audience might need an explanation of the allusion's significance.

58. Larry Perkins, "'Let the Reader Understand': A Contextual Interpretation of Mark 13:14," *BBR* 16 (2006): 95–104.

59. Ibid., 99.

60. Ibid., 101.

61. Collins, *Mark*, 596.

62. Contra Marcus, *Mark 8–16*, 891.

63. Boring, *Mark*, 367. Given the similarity with Rev 13:18, "Let the person who has insight calculate the number of the beast, for it is the number of a man," it may conceal a reference to some figure in the Roman Empire.

64. See Theissen, *The Gospels in Context*, 125–65. He dates the apocalyptic leaflet, which he believes circulated in Jesus' name and was the source behind this discourse, to the year AD 40.

modifying the neuter noun ("the abomination"), and this disregard of grammar may suggest that the masculine participle is intended to make the abomination refer to a person rather than some idolatrous object.[65] Another problem with this option is that Caligula's order created only a temporary crisis because it was never carried out. Knowing that this directive would precipitate a violent uprising by the Jews, the legate of Syria, Petronius, stalled as long as he could. Caligula was assassinated in January of AD 41 before he could discipline his commander, and the calamity was averted.

(2) If "abomination of desolation" refers to something that occurred during the war with Rome, the heinous crimes of the rebels who occupied the temple precincts during the last years of the war are prime candidates (Josephus, *J.W.* 4.3.6–10 §§147–192; 4.5.4 §§334–344). Josephus (*J.W.* 4.6.3 §388) writes:

> For there was an ancient saying of inspired men that the city would be taken and the sanctuary burned to the ground by right of war, when it should be visited by sedition and native hands should be the first to defile God's sacred precincts. This saying the Zealots did not disbelieve; yet they lent themselves as instruments of its accomplishments.

The problem with this connection is that it would have been too late to flee the city. During the war, John of Gischala had shut the gates of Jerusalem, and Simon bar Giora, positioned outside the gates, murdered any fugitives seeking to flee John's reign of terror (Josephus, *J.W.* 4.9.10 §§564–565).

(3) "Abomination of desolation" could refer to something that occurred after the siege of Jerusalem and the temple's destruction. Josephus reports that the Roman soldiers set up their standards in the temple and sacrificed to them (*J.W.* 6.6.1 §316). Or, it may refer to the Roman general Titus, who entered the flaming temple to view the Most Holy Place (Josephus, *J.W.* 6.4.7 §§260–261). The problem with either of these possibilities is that, again, it would have been too late to flee the city.

(4) Snow argues that "abomination of desolation" does not have any historical referent. Instead, he contends that it evokes Jer 7, which was cited in Mark 11:17, and refers generally to the corruption of the elders, scribes, and chief priests that perverted the temple and brought about its judgment.[66] A similar tradition cited in 2 Thess 2:1–12, however, suggests that Mark would have understood it to refer to some historical occurrence (see 1 Macc 2:27–28).

65. Ernest Best, "The Gospel of Mark: Who Was the Reader?" *IBS* 11 (1989): 124–32, creatively suggests that the admonition instructs the lector reading in Greek not to correct the masculine participle with a neuter participle out of some mistaken grammatical sensitivity. What Mark has written, he deliberately wrote. He likens it to our modern *sic* that is placed after a word that seems odd or misspelled but is intentionally written: "But when you see that thing, the abomination of desolation, standing where he [*sic*] should not" (129). Collins, *Mark*, 597, counters, however, that this shift in gender would not have been read as a grammatical error, but it is a construction that is not infrequently used in Greek where the agreement of the words is with the sense, not the grammatical form (*constructio ad sensum*), and that Mark has used it in 9:20, 26.

66. Robert S. Snow, "Let the Reader Understand: Mark's Use of Jeremiah 7 in Mark 13:14," *BBR* 21 (2011): 467–77. Haenchen, *Der Weg Jesu*, 446–47, suggests that it refers to the imposition of emperor worship throughout the empire, but why would that require fleeing to the Judean hills?

13.3.5.2.4.2 *The Sign of the Desolating Sacrilege as Unrelated to the Imminence of the End*

The allusion remains inside information that can only refer to a first-century event when it made sense to flee Jerusalem and to pray that it not occur in winter. Modern readers can only guess what it might have been but can understand the point. It was not a sign of the End, since that event affects the entire world, not just Judea. The command to escape to the mountains (see Gen 19:17; 1 Macc 2:28) is irrelevant to those who do not live there. The mountains will provide no safe refuge in the face of God's wrath at the end of the ages (Hos 10:8; Rev 6:15–16). Who would be anxious to retrieve their garments or valuables at the end of the world? In the throes of that cataclysm, it also would make no difference whether one is pregnant or nursing or what the season and its weather conditions might be.

The sympathy for the plight of those trying to flee when travel is difficult or impossible only makes sense if they are trying to evade some looming savagery like that meted out by the advancing Roman army during the revolt.[67] During that war, many people fled *to* the temple fortress for refuge (cf. Jer 4:6).[68] Jesus counsels flight *away* from the temple (cf. Jer 6:1; Rev 18:4). The warning makes clear that Jerusalem and its temple will not be a stronghold of saving help, but God will allow it instead to become a death trap. The punishment that will come upon this generation in Jerusalem should not ensnare the disciples, and they are instructed to abandon all allegiance to the temple and to the city.[69] Geddert comments,

67. Josephus, *J.W.* 4.7.5 §§433–436, reports an incident when Gadarene refugees seeking shelter in Jericho could not cross the swollen Jordan and were slain by the Romans. Unlike the time of Joshua when the soles of the priests' feet touched the water and the river Jordan ceased flowing so that they could pass over on dry ground (Josh 3:13–17), the rivers will not part for them.

68. Josephus, *J.W.* 6.5.1 §§285–286, records that a large crowd met their deaths from giving heed to just such a charlatan:

> They owed their destruction to a false prophet, who had on that day proclaimed to the people in the city that God commanded them to go up to the temple court, to receive there the tokens of their deliverance. Numerous prophets, indeed, were at this period suborned by the tyrants to delude the people by bidding them to await help from God, in order that desertions might be checked and that those who were above fear and precaution might be encouraged by hope. In adversity man is quickly persuaded; but when the deceiver actually pictures release from prevailing horrors, the sufferer wholly abandons himself to expectation.

The Roman historian Cassius Dio (*Rom. Hist.* 66.6–2–3) expressed amazement over the Jewish resistance to the very end when obviously everything was lost:

> The Jews resisted [Titus] with more ardor than ever, as if it were a kind of windfall [an unexpected piece of luck] to fall fighting against a foe far outnumbering them, they were not overcome until a part of the Temple had caught fire. Then some impaled themselves voluntarily on the swords of the Romans, others slew each other, others did away with themselves or leaped into the flames. They all believed, especially the last, that it was not a disaster but victory, salvation, and happiness to perish together with the Temple.

69. Balabanski, *Eschatology*, 101–34, compellingly defends the historicity of the tradition that this oracle is connected to the Jewish Christians flight from Jerusalem to Pella sometime before the fall of Jerusalem. Eusebius, *Hist. eccl.* 3.5.3, writes,

> The whole body, however, of the church at Jerusalem, having been commanded by a divine revelation, given to men of approved piety there before the war, removed from the city, and dwelt at a certain town beyond the Jordan, called Pella. Here those that believed in Christ, having removed from Jerusalem, as if holy men had entirely abandoned the royal city itself, and the whole land of Judea; the divine justice, for their crimes against Christ and his apostles finally overtook them, totally destroying the whole generation of these evildoers form the earth.

See also Epiphanius, *Pan.* 29.7.7–8; 30.2.7; *On Measures and Weights* 15; Craig Koester, "The Origin and Significance of the Flight to Pella Tradition," *CBQ* 51 (1989): 90–106.

> The disciples are to flee, not because they fear what the enemy will do, but because God desires them to absent themselves when everything stands poised for the divine judgment to fall. When the judgment falls, all who will trust in themselves, their might, their leaders, their election or their temple will be judged along with the religious system they represent. All who take their stand with Jesus will leave the temple and the city to its fate.[70]

Whatever that abomination was, Mark intends for the audience to understand it as a fulfillment of Daniel's prophecy and another token of the beginning of the birth pains. The conflict will result in unprecedented suffering (13:19; see Exod 9:18; Joel 2:2; Dan 12:1).[71] This terrible affliction, however, is not outside the control of God, who can and will shorten the days (see 2 Sam 24:16; Isa 45:8). God does so for the sake of "the elect, whom he has chosen" (13:20; see Luke 18:7). The phrase "no one would be saved" (13:20) means that no one will be left alive (see 2 Esd 6:25; 7:27), not that they will not have salvation.[72]

13.3.5.2.5 The Relevance of the Warnings in Mark 13:5–23

What relevance did the evangelist think that this warning would have for his audience? I propose the following conclusions from this section.

(1) Marcus renders the conclusion in 13:23, "Look, I foretold all the things *that now have come upon you*."[73] If this is the correct rendering, it implies that the audience had witnessed the things that Jesus prophesied coming to pass. They therefore can place complete trust in all of Jesus' warnings and assurances.

(2) In the allegory of the Wicked Tenants, Jesus predicted that the owner of the vineyard would come and destroy the obdurate and vicious tenants (12:9), and the leaders of the temple "knew that he had spoken the parable against them" (12:12). Judgment follows because of their failure to receive the Son and their malicious complicity in having him killed. The warning also adds force to Jesus' threats that those who oppose him and his disciples will ultimately meet with God's vengeance, and that it is applicable to any opponent at any time and in any place.

(3) This unit begins and ends with warnings about deceivers and false prophets who will arise and exploit catastrophes for their own purposes (13:5–6, 21–22). Current readers must also be on their guard against their contemporary manifestations of those who speak what people want to hear. They are to watch themselves, not watch for signs of the End (cf. 1 Thess 5:1–11; 2 Thess 2:1–12).

(4) Current events should not be interpreted as signs of the End. Wars and persecution are "nothing other than the history of humanity being torn apart by hatred."[74] The slaughterhouse that wars produce has been repeated over and over

70. Geddert, *Watchwords*, 219.

71. Josephus provides gruesome accounts of famine and wholesale slaughter during the Roman siege of Jerusalem. In *J.W.* 6.3.5 §§214–219, he narrates a lurid tale of a prominent woman cannibalizing her son during the last stages of the siege of Jerusalem and describes it as "act unparalleled in the history whether of Greeks or barbarians and as horrible to relate as it is incredible to hear."

72. Hooker, *Mark*, 316.

73. Marcus, *Mark 8–16*, 903.

74. Focant, *Mark*, 537.

throughout history and will continue to do so until the End. What is important for Mark is that Christians are to be about their task of proclaiming the gospel regardless of world conditions and their circumstances.

(5) The command to take to the Judean hills when they see the abomination of desolation would seem to be limited only to a first-century situation. This command means that Herod's temple in Jerusalem no longer figured in God's plans, and God's people should move on and leave it behind. It requires clear-sighted courage to make painful breaks with cherished religious institutions that can also bring the heartbreaking termination of cherished relationships.

During the Jewish War, the flight of Christians away from Jerusalem branded them as unpatriotic, disloyal, and even treasonous.[75] Contemporary readers should learn from this historical disaster of the temple's destruction that they should not be blind to the corruption of their own sacred religious institutions and think that they are immune to God's wrath. Christians of any era can be deceived by appearances and fooled by the great stones of modern edifices that project the illusion of the invulnerability of a nation or of a hallowed organization or cause. They must not be deceived by appearances and also must be ready to read the signs and dissociate themselves from false ideologies even when they are attached to sacred institutions. Cranfield writes:

> If we imagine that every denominational tradition and every ecclesiastical vested interest and every bit of ecclesiastical pomp and circumstance are entitled to luxuriate behind the promise that "the gates of Hades shall not prevail against it," we are like those who fondly repeated "The temple of the LORD, the temple of the LORD, the temple of the LORD are these." In this connexion it is interesting that in Mark and Luke this passage is immediately preceded by the pericope of the widow's mites. In both passages Jesus calls in question the complacent assumptions of conventional piety.[76]

13.3.5.3 The Coming of the Son of Man and the Gathering of the Elect (Mark 13:24–27)

The use of the strong adversative "but" (*alla*) in 13:24 (see 14:27–28; 16:6–7) "denotes a break or shift in perspective from that which precedes it."[77] The parallels with 8:38 and 14:62 suggest that these verses switch from the destruction of the temple in the first century to the Parousia at the end of time. Adams effectively summarizes Mark's view of the End:

> The coming Son of Man is the exalted Jesus (14:62). He comes, at the close of history (13:24), from his heavenly seat of power (14:62), as the divine warrior (8:38), at the head of an angelic force (8:38; 13:27) to effect judgement (8:38;

75. Marvin R. Wilson, *Our Father Abraham: Jewish Roots of the Christian Faith* (Grand Rapids: Eerdmans, 1989), 76.

76. Cranfield, "St. Mark 13," *SJT* 6 (1953): 193.

77. Balabanski, *Eschatology*, 74–75.

> 14:62) and to rescue the elect (13:27). His coming is visible (13:26; 14:62) and its effects are global (13:27) and cosmic (13:24–25).[78]

Adams argues that this passage is a " 'Christologization' of the eschatological hope of the coming of God."[79] Bauckham writes that "much early Christian thinking about the Parousia did not derive from applying OT messianic texts to Jesus but from the direct use of OT texts about the coming of God."[80] Adams points out that it is God who "travels with clouds," whose "coming often issues in a revelation of his 'glory,' " who comes "with an angelic entourage," and who comes to gather a "dispersed people of Israel and Judah."[81]

13.3.5.3.1 The Response of Creation to the Coming of the Son of Man (Mark 13:24–26)

The disciples are not to pay attention to hearsay about hidden messiahs because when the Son of Man returns, it will be accompanied by celestial convulsions that will be visible to all. Creation reacts this way *because* the Son of Man appears, not as a sign that he is about to do so. These are effects that accompany the event. The description of the cosmic reactions echo passages from the OT:[82]

Mark 13:24 The sun will be darkened, and the moon will not give its light	Isa 13:10: The rising sun will be darkened and the moon will not give its light Joel 3:15: The sun and moon will be darkened, and the stars no longer shine
Mark 13:25a The stars will fall from the sky	Isa 34:4: All the stars will fall (LXX) Isa 13:10: The stars of heaven and their constellations will not show their light
Mark 13:25b And the heavenly bodies will be shaken	Joel 3:16: The LORD will roar from Zion and thunder from Jerusalem; the earth and the heavens will tremble

Beasley-Murray argues that the use of OT imagery "serves to underscore the nature of the parousia as a theophany."[83] He cites Judg 5:4–5 as representative of the fundamental pattern:

78. Edward Adams, "The Coming of the Son of Man in Mark's Gospel," *TynBul* 56 (2005): 60.

79. Adams, *The Stars*, 133. See Zech 14:5.

80. Richard J. Bauckham, *Jude, 2 Peter* (WBC 50; Waco, TX: Word; 1983), 97; cited by Adams, *The Stars*, 150.

81. Adams, *The Stars*, 151. On coming in clouds, see Exod 19:9; 34:5; Num 11:25; 12:5; 2 Sam 22:10–12; Pss 18:11–12; 97:2; 104:3; Isa 19:1; Jer 4:13; Nah 1:3; on coming with power and glory, see Pss 21:13; 46:1; 59:16; 66:3; Isa 59:19; 66:18; Hab 3:3; on coming with angels, see Deut 33:2; Ps 68:17; Zech 9:14–15; 14:5; on gathering the dispersed people of Israel, see Isa 11:11; 27:12–13; 43:6; 60:1–9.

82. Jozef Verheyden, "Describing the Parousia: The Cosmic Phenomena in Mk 13,24–25," in *The Scriptures in the Gospels* (ed. Christopher M. Tuckett; BETL 131; Leuven: Leuven University Press, 1997), 534–40, describes this "conflation" of related Old Testament texts as producing a quite different meaning from the original texts.

83. Beasley-Murray, *Jesus and the Last Days*, 424. He notes that "shaking" is "a standard term in OT descriptions of theophany (e.g., Judg. 5:5; Amos 9:5; Mic 1:4; Isa 64:11 [Theodotion]; Hab 3:6; Nah 1:5; Pss 18:7; 114:7; Job 9:6)."

When you, LORD, went out from Seir,
  when you marched from the land of Edom,
the earth shook, the heavens poured,
  the clouds poured down water.
The mountains quaked before the LORD, the One of Sinai,
  before the LORD, the God of Israel.[84]

These verses, he argues, do not describe the dissolution of the cosmos but picture it "in terror and confusion before the overwhelming might of the Lord of Hosts when he steps forth into the world to act in judgment and salvation. The language of cosmic convulsion is not to be taken literally but is intended purely to highlight the glory of that event."[85]

Adams argues, however, that these verses do describe the catastrophic end of the universe and compares them to Heb 12:25–29; 2 Pet 3:5–13; and Rev 6:12–17.[86] The reference to heaven and earth passing away in 13:31 suggests that Adams is correct. The universe is not everlasting. Though Mark's Jesus does not describe what happens next, Adams argues from Jewish eschatological thought that "the dissolution of creation is normally the prelude to its remaking, and we would expect this to be the case for the Synoptists, even if it is not explicitly indicated."[87]

The introduction, "but in those days, following that distress" (13:24), does not hint how long it will be after that tribulation before the Son of Man comes. Geddert contends that because Jesus neither affirms nor denies that there is a time gap between the desolation of the temple and the End in 13:24–27, he wants to prevent his followers from trying to nail down a specific chronology of end-time events.[88] Humans do not have control over the apocalyptic timetable, nor do they possess an early warning system to detect its coming. Unlike the rest of the discourse, this section lacks any imperatives because the End can come at any time, and when it does there is nothing that anyone can do.[89] These verses serve simply to depict the divine glory and cosmic convulsion that accompany the coming of the Son of Man.[90]

13.3.5.3.2 The Gathering of the Elect (Mark 13:27)

The description of the gathering of the elect focuses solely on the End as a day of redemption and ignores the judgment and punishment of the wicked. It is less likely that the elect refer to the faithful remnant of Israel[91] and more likely that it refers to the followers of Christ.[92] The elect are those who have faithfully responded to the gospel. Christians understood the idea of being gathered by the Lord to belong to the coming of the Lord (2 Thess 2:1–2).

84. Ibid., 307–8; see also Pss 18:3–19; 77:16–18; Amos 1:2; Mic 1:3–4; Nah 1:2–6; Hab 3:3–13; Sir 16:18–19.

85. Ibid., 425. Boring, *Mark*, 373, concurs that the imagery represents "the response of the creation to the advent of the Creator."

86. Adams, *The Stars*, 153–66, 253.

87. Ibid., 181.

88. Geddert, *Watchwords*, 234–35.

89. Boring, *Mark*, 373.

90. Beasley-Murray, *Jesus and the Last Days*, 309, 425.

91. Contra ibid., 420.

92. Adams, "The Coming of the Son of Man in Mark's Gospel," 58, notes that Deut 13:7; 30:4; and Zech 2:6 "refer to the gathering of Jewish exiles out of their far-flung places of captivity. But in Mark, 'the elect' extends beyond the elect of Israel."

13.3.5.4 Conclusion: The Lessons of the Fig Tree and of the Watchman (Mark 13:28–37)

The discourse concludes with two lessons to be gleaned from the everyday world of fig trees (13:28–29) and absentee masters (13:34–36). The parable of the Fig Tree (13:28) turns on the fact that, unlike most trees in Palestine, it loses its leaves in winter and comes into leaf in March and April, which makes it a harbinger of summer.[93] This illustration is followed by two pronouncements. In the first, Jesus declares that his prophecy would be fulfilled before this generation passes away (13:30). In the second, Jesus punctuates this assurance with a solemn declaration, "Heaven and earth will pass away, but my words will never pass away" (13:31).

In the parable of the Watchman, the master goes away and leaves his servants in charge of his house, each with an assigned task. The watchman is told to keep a sharp lookout because he does not know when "the owner of the house will come back" (13:34–35). It is followed by two warnings to "watch" because no one knows the day or hour or the appointed time (13:35–37).

If the two illustrations both refer to the coming of the Son of Man, they offer oddly contradictory perspectives. The lesson from the leafing out of the fig tree assumes that there will be an unmistakable sign indicating when "it is near, right at the door" (13:29). The lesson of the watchman assumes that the master does not announce when he will return and that he will arrive unexpectedly. The doorkeeper therefore must keep alert throughout the watches of the night when one is most prone to doze off.[94] In the first illustration, if it refers to the coming of the Son of Man, it is preceded by an unmistakable sign, "when you see these things" (13:29). In the second illustration, the coming of the Son of Man presents no advance warning. No one knows its timing (13:32), which consequently requires being ever vigilant lest he come suddenly and find you asleep (13:36).

It is unlikely that Mark intentionally holds these two perspectives in tension so that they interpret one another.[95] The best way to resolve this problem is to recognize that the two different illustrations provide answers to the two different questions broached at the beginning of the discourse. The parable of the Fig Tree is to be connected to the destruction of the temple and Jerusalem, "When will these things happen?" (13:4).[96] There are warning signs along the way, and Jesus confidently insists, "Truly I tell you, this generation will certainly not pass away until all these things have happened" (13:30). Throughout Mark "his generation"

93. Telford, *The Barren Temple*, 216–17, thinks the leafing fig tree is a counterpoint to the withered fig tree (11:21). Allan McNicol, "The Lesson of the Fig Tree in Mark 13:28–32: A Comparison between Two Exegetical Methodologies," *ResQ* 27 (1984): 200, writes: "Over and over again in the Old Testament, the conspicuous barrenness of the fig tree on the landscape became a metaphor for prophetic judgment against Israel (Hos. 2:12; Joel 1:7, 12; Hag. 2:19; Jer. 3:13); at other times the fresh foliage became a metaphor for the promise of the restored condition among the people of God at the day of Yahweh (Joel 2:22; Zech. 3:10)."

94. Troy W. Martin, "Watch during the Watches (Mark 13:35)," *JBL* 120 (2001): 685–701, argues that the names of the night watches, the "Evening," "Midnight," "Cockcrow," and "Morning" are not common designations of the night watches but "reflect Jewish practice in the environs of Jerusalem during the late Second Temple period" (701).

95. Contra C. E. B. Cranfield, "St. Mark 13," *SJT* 7 (1954): 299–300.

96. So also Stein, *Jesus, the Temple and the Coming of the Son of Man*, 151–59.

refers to Jesus' contemporaries (8:12, 38; 9:19), and it likely has that same meaning in this passage.

Attempts to avoid the problem that Jesus was mistaken in expecting the coming of the Son of Man and the End during this generation have prompted various suggestions that he refers to "the generation of believers who seek the Lord,"[97] the godless and wicked among humankind,[98] "the whole of humanity,"[99] the people of Israel,[100] or "the reader of Mark's gospel."[101] Those who accept that Jesus is referring to the End coming during "this generation" explain the miscalculation by appealing to prophetic foreshortening. Beasley-Murray, for example, contends:

> Intensity and certainty of prophetic convictions express themselves in terms of a *speedy* fulfilment.... The very intensity and sharpness of the vision of the end vouchsafed to Jesus added to the naturalness of his reckoning with nothing else in time but it alone, just as in clear atmosphere mountains appear far closer than they do on a dull day.[102]

It is most likely that the meaning of the term "this generation" remains consistent throughout Mark and refers to the generation of Jesus' day.[103] This does not mean that Jesus (or Mark) was mistaken. This discourse comments on *two* different events, the temple's desecration and destruction, and the coming of the Son of Man. Since no one, including the Son, knows when the latter will occur, it is unlikely that Jesus predicts that it must occur during the span of "this generation." If the parable of the Fig Tree refers to the destruction of the temple and Jerusalem, then the problem is solved. It did occur during "this generation," as Jesus foresaw, and it was preceded by discernible signs that could be seen and that set off alarm bells that signaled it was time to flee Jerusalem (13:14).

13.3.5.4.1 The Parable of the Fig Tree and Two Declarations about the Impending Destruction of the Temple and Jerusalem (Mark 13:28–31)

The budding fig tree would seem to be a meaningless sign for the advent of the Son of Man. Fig trees have been shedding their leaves and budding for thousands of years since this prediction. Beasley-Murray asserts that since 13:24–26 represent the "overwhelming and overpowering manifestation of the divine being who steps into creation to accomplish his purpose of judgment and salvation," the illustration

97. John Chrysostom, *Homilies in Matthaeum*, 58.701.

98. Walter Grundmann, *Das Evangelium nach Markus* (3rd ed.; THKNT; Berlin: Evangelische Verlagsanstalt, 1968), 270–71.

99. Evald Lövestam, "The ἡ γενεὰ αὕτη. Eschatology in Mk 13,30 parr.," in *L'Apocalypse johannique et l'apocalyptique dans le Nouveau Testament* (ed. Jan Lambrecht; BETL 53; Gembloux: Duculot, 1980), 403–13.

100. Franz Mussner, *Dieses Geschlecht wird nicht vergehen: Judentum und Kirche* (Freiburg/Basel/Vienna: Herder, 1991), 21–28.

101. Rudolf Pesch, *Naherwartungen: Tradition und Redaktion in Mk 13* (KBANT; Düsseldorf: Patmos, 1968), 185.

102. George R. Beasley-Murray, "The Eschatological Discourses of Jesus," *RevExp* 57 (1960): 160. See also idem, *Jesus and the Last Days*, 443–49; Lane, *Mark*, 480; Evans, *Mark 8:27–16:20*, 335.

103. Josephus uses the term "generation" similarly in lamenting the destruction of Jerusalem at the end of the war as "a city undeserving of these great misfortunes" except that "she produced a generation such as that which caused her overthrow" (*J.W.* 6.8.5 §408).

of the fig tree "cannot refer to the cosmic manifestation of vv. 24–25, but must refer to events that precede the advent of the Lord in his glory."[104] I would agree but argue instead that the events to which it refers are the desecration and destruction of the temple, and these events are not to be directly tied to the Lord's coming.

The Son of Man is more than right at the door; he has already come. The implied subject of the verb "is" in 13:29 could be "it," referring to an event, "it is near" (NIV), or "he," referring to a person, "he is near" (NRSV, NASB, ESV). If the predictions in 13:26 and 13:29 both refer to the coming of the Son of Man, the statement in 13:29 is quite pointless:

> "At that time people will see the Son of Man coming in clouds with great power and glory" (13:26).
>
> "Even so, when you see these things happening, you know that he [the Son of Man] is near, right at the door" (13:29).[105]

It is therefore best to translate 13:29 as not referring to the coming of the Son of Man but to an event, "it is near," namely, the destruction of Jerusalem and the temple.

The statement about this generation not passing away until all these things have happened (13:30) can only apply to the temple's desecration and destruction. If "all these things" refer to the series of catastrophes described in 13:5–23, then Jesus' prophecy was fulfilled. This generation did not pass away before the Romans laid waste to the temple and Jerusalem in AD 70. The next statement, "Heaven and earth will pass away, but my words will never pass away" (13:31), means far more than that Jesus' words will outlast creation. It implies that his words have destructive potency.[106] When these things have occurred, then "everything stands ready for God to bring his purposes to fulfilment."[107] The leafing out of the fig tree, however, gives no warning about when the End will occur.

13.3.5.4.2 The Parable of the Watchman and the Commands to Watch (Mark 13:32–37)

The phrase "but about that day or hour" in 13:32 marks a shift in the subject to the coming of the Son of Man.[108] Stein notes that "the expression 'that day' is a standard Old Testament expression for a theophanic event," so it most likely refers to the coming of the Son of Man in 13:24–27.[109] Jesus is no longer talking about something that will occur during this generation but something whose timing is unknown to *all* except the Father (13:32). There will be no preliminary sign to warn people before that hour strikes. That fact explains the battery of commands to "be

104. Beasley-Murray, *Jesus and the Last Days*, 309.

105. Adams, *The Stars*, 164–65; Stein, *Jesus, the Temple and the Coming of the Son of Man*, 154–55.

106. See Marcus, *Mark 8–16*, 918.

107. Geddert, *Watchwords*, 251.

108. The phrase "but about" (*peri de*) occurs throughout 1 Corinthians to mark a shift in topics being discussed (1 Cor 7:1, 25; 8:1; 12:1; 16:1, 12; see also 1 Thess 4:9; 5:1).

109. Stein, *Jesus, the Temple and the Coming of the Son of Man*, 164. See Isa 2:11–12, 20; 34:8; Jer 46:10; Ezek 13:5; Joel 3:18; Amos 5:18–20; 8:3, 9, 13; 9:11; Mic 4:6; 5:10; 7:12; Zeph 1:7–18; 3:16; Zech 9:16; 14:1–21.

on guard" (*blepete*, 13:33), to "be alert" (*agrypneite*, 13:33), and to "keep watch" (*grēgoreite*, 13:35, 37) that surround the parable of the Watchman. The doorkeeper in the parable is commanded to keep watch (13:34) because he will have no advance notice about the master's return. The same is true for those waiting for the coming of the Son of Man.

The upshot is that Jesus offers no clues about the timing of the End. It is certain to come, but its timing is unpredictable. It could be during any generation. Consequently, the discourse that began as private instruction to four disciples ends by addressing all with a command to watch (13:37). Disciples remain in the dark and must cope with it simply by constantly being on their guard.[110] Geddert sums up well what can be said about what we can know related to the End:

1. Jesus does not know when the End will come.
2. Mark does not know when the End will come.
3. The reader cannot know when the End will come.
4. No signs can help us predict when the End will come.
5. Coming catastrophes may or may not lead directly to the End; we don't know.
6. Discernment and faithfulness are *always* necessary precisely *because* we cannot know when the End will come.
7. Mark 13 teaches disciples what it means to be discerning, faithful disciples in various kinds of situations that will occur before the End, but Mark does not claim to know when the End will occur.[111]

The watchman illustration is intended to convey that disciples are to be at their posts doing their job and watching.[112] Geddert asserts, "If Mark is deliberately using the Passion narrative to help define what it means to watch (γρηγορέω) in the waiting period before the consummation, then 'watching' certainly has nothing to do with watching for portents. It has much more to do with faithful discipleship in a time of crisis."[113] The two stories of women who give extravagantly (12:41–44; 14:3–9) frame the discourse and also add another element of what "watching" entails, namely, the willingness to surrender all to God.[114]

110. Geddert, *Watchwords*, 283, n. 53. Cranfield, "St. Mark 13," *SJT* 7 (1954): 296, interprets 13:33 to mean "ignorance of the date of the End is not an excuse for being unprepared, but a reason (note the *gar* ["for"]!) for unceasing vigilance."

111. Geddert, *Mark*, 421.

112. Dyer, *Prophecy*, 271.

113. Geddert, *Watchwords*, 98.

114. Deppe, "Charting the Future," 98. He concludes, "The implications of this study suggest that preaching apocalyptic texts should climax in the ethical difference that this future teaching makes in the present lives of church members. Apparently there should be a lot fewer prophecy conferences and a lot more cross-bearing action on the part of the Christian community. Jesus, the gospel writers, and therefore the Christian community today should lay the primary stress upon discipleship activities such as the preaching of the gospel, our readiness to suffer, and the sacrificial lifestyle of the believer" (101).

13.4. THE HOLY SPIRIT AND THE INTERIM

In 1:7–8, John the Baptist predicts that the stronger one coming after him will baptize with the Holy Spirit. Mark does not develop what this Spirit baptism involves or when it will occur. One can infer that the Holy Spirit who descended into Jesus at his baptism (1:10) and drove him into the wilderness (1:12) was the source of his power in contending with Satan (1:13). One can also infer that the Spirit was the source of Jesus' power in driving out demons, because he condemns those who accuse him of casting out demons by Beelzebul, the ruler of the demons (3:22), for being guilty of blaspheming against the Holy Spirit, which he categorizes as an eternal sin (3:29).

Only in 13:11 does Mark give any hint of how the Holy Spirit works in the lives of believers who, presumably, will have received this Spirit baptism. The Holy Spirit will give disciples both the courage and the words to speak (see Exod 4:12; Jer 1:9) in times of persecution when they are standing in the dock before their accusers. Since the Holy Spirit inspired men like David with prophetic insight (12:36), one can infer that the Spirit continues to inspire persons with prophetic insight, but, again, Mark does not mention this facet of the Spirit's work. Jesus does not instruct disciples on how to evade or how to get out of trouble. He only gives instructions on how to learn from trouble and to bear witness through trouble. Jesus only promises "that they will receive divine help to preach, not divine deliverance, which comes only after death and after his final coming in glory."[115]

It is possible that Jesus' clarification of his exhortation to Peter on the Mount of Olives to "watch and pray so that you will not fall into temptation" (14:38) refers to the power of the Spirit: "the spirit is willing, but the flesh is weak." Most translations do not capitalize "spirit" and understand it to refer to Peter's spirit that controls his will and actions. Lane contends, however, that "the 'willing spirit' which stands in opposition to the weak flesh, is not a better part of man but God's Spirit who strives against human weakness."[116] This interpretation best explains why Jesus commands Peter to pray. Peter has no inner fortitude of spirit to call upon that will carry him through the testing that is to come. Through prayer, however, he opens himself up to the power of the Spirit, who alone can overcome the weakness of the flesh.

If this interpretation is correct, it is possible that Mark understands the Spirit's role in the same vein as Paul's command for the Galatians to "walk by the Spirit, and you will not gratify the desires of the flesh" (Gal 5:16). Paul explains this assertion in 5:17. It is because the Spirit and flesh are contrary to one another and pull in opposite directions. The Spirit, however, is far more powerful and is able to neutralize the flesh. One might then extrapolate from this possible connection that Mark may understand Jesus' saying to mean that the Spirit gives Christians the power to live the life of faith. Christians need more than willing spirits to overcome the power of the flesh; they need the divine power of the Holy Spirit.

115. Garland, *Mark*, 494.

116. Lane, *Mark*, 520. He cites Eduard Schweizer, "πνεῦμα," *TDNT*, 6:396–97, who contends, "the expression 'willing spirit' comes from the Heb. of Ps. 51:12, that it is identical there with God's Holy Spirit, and that it is here used in a prayer for endurance in temptation, it is plain that what is meant is the Spirit of God which is given to man and which strives against human weakness."

Chapter 14

The Ending of Mark's Gospel: A New Beginning

Bibliography

Aland, Kurt. "Bemerkungen zum Schluss des Markusevangeliums." Pp. 157–80 in *Neotestamentica et Semitica: Studies in Honour of Matthew Black*. Ed. E. Earle Ellis and Max Wilcox. Edinburgh: T&T Clark, 1969. Idem. "Der Schluss des Markusevangeliums." Pp. 435–70, 573–75 in *L'évangile selon Marc: tradition et rédaction*. Ed. M. Sabbe. 2nd ed. BETL 34; Leuven: Leuven University Press, 1988. **Black, David Alan, ed.** *Perspectives on the Ending of Mark: 4 Views*. Nashville: Broadman & Holman, 2008. **Boomershine, Thomas E., and Gilbert L. Bartholomew.** "The Narrative Technique of Mark 16:8." *JBL* 100 (1981): 213–23. **Hug, Joseph.** *La finale de l'évangile de Marc* (*Marc 16, 9–20*). EBib. Paris: Gabalda, 1978. **Hurtado, Larry W.** "The Women, the Tomb, and the Climax of Mark." Pp. 427–50 in *A Wandering Galilean: Essays in Honour of Seán Freyne*. Ed. Zuleika Rodgers, Margaret Daly-Denton, and Anne Fitzpatrick McKinley. (Supplements to the Journal for the Study of Judaism 132. Leiden: Brill, 2009. **Iverson, Kelly R.** "A Further Word on Final Γάρ (Mark 16:8)." *CBQ* 68 (2006): 79–94. **Juel, Donald Harrisville.** "A Disquieting Silence: The Matter of the Ending." Pp. 1–13 in *The Ending of Mark and the Ends of God: Essays in Memory of Donald Harrisville Juel*. Ed. Beverly Roberts Gaventa and Patrick D. Miller. Louisville: Westminster John Knox, 2005. **Kelhoffer, James A.** *Miracle and Mission: The Authentication of Missionaries and Their Message in the Longer Ending of Mark*. WUNT 2/112. Tübingen: Mohr Siebeck, 2000. **Lincoln, Andrew T.** "The Promise and the Failure: Mark 16:7,8." *JBL* 108 (1989): 283–300. **Magness, Jodi Lee.** *Sense and Absence: Structure and Suspension in the Ending of Mark's Gospel*. Semeia Studies. Atlanta: Scholars Press, 1986. **Meye, Robert P.** "Mark 16:8—The Ending of Mark's Gospel." *BR* 14 (1969): 33–43. **Stein, Robert H.** "The Ending of Mark." *BBR* 18 (2008): 79–98. **Thomas, John Christopher.** "A Reconsideration of the Ending of Mark." *JETS* 26 (1983): 407–19. **Topel, John.** "What Were the Women Afraid Of? (Mark 16:8)." *JTI* 6 (2012): 79–96. **Williams, Joel F.** "Literary Approaches to the End of Mark's Gospel." *JETS* 42 (1999): 21–35. **Williams, Travis B.** "Bringing Method to the Madness: Examining the Style of the Longer Ending of Mark." *BBR* 20 (2010): 397–417.

14.1 INTRODUCTION

The final chapter of Mark ends with Mary Magdalene, Mary the mother of James, and Salome rising early after the Sabbath was over, buying aromatic spices, and going to the tomb to anoint Jesus' body. They fret on the way about who might roll back the large stone that covered the tomb's opening, but when they arrive they find that it had already been rolled back. When they enter the tomb, they find a young man dressed in a white robe sitting on the right side, and they are amazed. The young man comforts them with news that Jesus of Nazareth, who was crucified, is risen and has gone ahead to Galilee. He then orders them to relay the news to the disciples and Peter and to tell them that they will see him in Galilee as Jesus had promised. The trembling and bewildered women flee from the tomb and tell no one, for they were afraid.

The witness of women was widely regarded as untrustworthy, but they are the only ones to see Jesus buried and the first to discover the empty tomb and to learn that Jesus was raised from the dead. Their prominence in the account of the resurrection is an argument for its historical accuracy. Women could not be witnesses in Jewish courts.[1] Josephus alleges that no evidence was to be accepted from women "because of the levity and temerity of their sex" (*Ant.* 4.8.15 §219). Origen says that Celsus scorned the Christian witness of the resurrection as coming from "a hysterical female" (*Cels.* 2.55). It is not surprising, then, that Luke's account of the male disciples' reaction to the women's report is dismissive: "But they did not believe the women, because their words seemed to them like nonsense" (Luke 24:11). It is highly unlikely that the women's role in the resurrection account was an invention. It is also theologically meaningful that women are the first recipients of the revelation that Jesus was raised from the dead and are commissioned to disclose that revelation to men.

For centuries, the Christians have read the continuation of the story in vv. 9–20 in their Bibles, and the canonical status of this passage has been assumed. But three other endings appear in the extant manuscripts of Mark's gospel. The advent of textual criticism has cast serious doubt on 16:9–20 as the original ending of Mark. The earliest and most reliable manuscripts end the gospel in 16:8 with the phrase "because they were afraid." Consequently, most modern-day translations end at v. 8, but they include vv. 9–20 in brackets or add special notes that remark on its spurious status as an authentic part of the gospel.[2] The other two readings are usually only included in the notes of study Bibles.

The textual evidence raises many questions. Did Mark intend to end his gospel at v. 8, or was the original ending damaged and lost, or was Mark somehow prevented from finishing his gospel? Did Mark write the longer ending in vv. 9–20, as a small minority still claim, and was it lost from early manuscripts, or did copyists deliberately excise it? Did someone else add the longer ending in the production

1. Martin Hengel, "Maria Magdalena und die Frauen als Zeugen," in *Abraham unser Vater: Juden und Christen im Gespräch über die Bibel: Festschrift für Otto Michel zum 60. Geburtstag* (ed. Otto Betz, Martin Hengel, and Peter Schmidt; AGSU 5; Leiden: Brill, 1963), 246.

2. By "authentic," I mean that it was written by Mark and reflects Mark's theology.

stage of the gospel, or did someone, unhappy with Mark's original ending, compose it many years later to provide a more satisfying finish that included Jesus' resurrection appearances to his disciples? Why did the other endings arise?

14.2 TEXTUAL EVIDENCE FOR FOUR ENDINGS TO MARK'S GOSPEL

14.2.1 The Ending at Mark 16:8

The gospel ends at 16:8 in the two oldest Greek manuscripts, deriving from the fourth century, Sinaiticus (א) and Vaticanus (B), and in 304, a manuscript deriving from the twelfth century. The reading is also found in various versions, the Sinaitic Syriac manuscript (Syr^{s}), a Coptic Sahidic manuscript (cop^{sa}), about one hundred Armenian manuscripts (arm^{mss}), and the two oldest Georgian manuscripts (geo^{1,a}).[3] Clement of Alexandria and Origen betray no knowledge of the longer ending. Eusebius in his explanations of gospel problems assumes that Mark ends at 16:8 and derides the behavior of the women at the tomb who did just the opposite of what the young man told them to do. He explains that these women belonged to a group that was different from the ones who are recorded as obedient in the accounts in Luke and John. They were "latecomers" who were

> not found worthy of seeing either the Saviour or the dazzlingly-bright angel, nor the two inside the tomb, nor the two men in Luke. It is merely some ordinary young man they saw, with a white robe on. The sight they see is one that corresponds to their own small-mindedness; yet even on seeing this person dressed in white for the festival, they were still amazed, as Mark attested of them, whereas at no point was there any mention of astonishment in the case of the earlier ones.[4]

Jerome, Ammonius, Victor of Antioch, and Euthymius also opt for it as the original reading.[5]

14.2.2 The Shorter Ending

A shorter ending adds to 16:8:

> Then they quickly reported all these instructions to those around Peter. After this, Jesus himself also sent out through them from east to west the sacred and imperishable proclamation of eternal salvation. Amen.

The Old Latin Bobiensis (it^{k}) is the lone manuscript to have only this shorter

3. See Kurt Aland, "Bemerkungen zum Schluss des Markusevangeliums," in *Neotestamentica et Semitica: Studies in Honour of Matthew Black* (ed. E. Earle Ellis and Max Wilcox; Edinburgh: T&T Clark, 1969), 157–80.

4. "Greek Fragments: To Marinus, Extracts from the Catena of Nicetas" in *Eusebius of Caesarea, Gospel Problems and Solutions: Quaestiones ad Stephanum et Marinum (CPG 3470)* (ed. Roger Pearse; trans. David J. D. Miller; Ipswich: Chieftain, 2010), 199.

5. William R. Schoedel, *The Apostolic Fathers.* Vol. 5. *Polycarp, Martyrdom of Polycarp, Fragments of Papias* (London: Thomas Nelson & Sons, 1967), 106, suggests that the muted critique of Mark's order by Papias "amounts to a complaint about its incompleteness."

ending. Some manuscripts have the shorter ending followed by the longer ending (L, Ψ, 099, 0112, 579).[6]

14.2.3 The Longer Ending, Mark 16:9–20, and an Addition

The longer ending (16:9–20) appears in the Textus Receptus ("received text"). It does not appear in any Greek manuscripts before the fifth century, but Irenaeus, who lived in the second century, knows it. The longer reading has various configurations. Most notably, Codex Washingtonianus (W) includes the following after 16:14, which, in effect, makes this a fourth extant ending to Mark:

> And they excused themselves, saying, "This age of lawlessness and unbelief is under Satan, who does not allow the truth and power of God to prevail over the unclean things of the spirits [or, does not allow what lies under the unclean spirits to understand the truth and power of God]. Therefore reveal your righteousness now"—thus they spoke to Christ. And Christ replied to them, "The term of years of Satan's power has been fulfilled, but other terrible things draw near. And for those who have sinned I was handed over to death, that they may return to the truth and sin no more, in order that they may inherit the spiritual and incorruptible glory of righteousness that is in heaven."

This reading was probably created to temper Jesus' harsh rebuke of the disciples in the previous verse: "Later Jesus appeared to the Eleven as they were eating; he rebuked them for their lack of faith and their stubborn refusal to believe those who had seen him after he had risen" (16:14). It would be an attempt to allay qualms that the disciples could not be trusted to "go into all the world and preach the gospel to all creation" (16:15) if they lacked faith and were stubborn. This addition, then, derives from a later scribe's attempt to absolve the disciples' guilt that is aired in 16:14.

14.2.4 The Evaluation of the External Textual Evidence

14.2.4.1 The Shorter Ending

The weak textual evidence for the shorter reading quickly excludes it as original. In addition, nine of the thirty-four words do not appear elsewhere in Mark, and the style noticeably differs from the rest of the gospel. Its existence gives evidence, however, that the gospel of Mark circulated at some point without the longer reading in vv. 9–20.

14.2.4.2 The Longer Reading: Mark 16:9–20 and the Application of the Principles of Textual Criticism

14.2.4.2.1 The Reading Found in the Oldest, More Reliable Manuscripts Is Preferred

The modern translations that continue to print the longer ending do not indicate

6. The reading is in the margin of the Harclean Syriac version, several Sahidic and Bohairic manuscripts, and some Ethiopic manuscripts.

that it first appears in manuscripts of the fifth century and much later and that these manuscripts are generally regarded as less reliable. Metzger points out that the early patristic evidence argues for the inauthenticity of 16:9–20: "Clement of Alexandria and Origen show no knowledge of the existence of these verses; furthermore Eusebius and Jerome attest that the passage was absent from almost all Greek copies of Mark known to them. The original form of the Eusebian sections (drawn up by Ammonius) makes no provision for numbering sections of the text after 16.8."[7] Also, some of the manuscripts include the longer reading with scribal glosses noting that older Greek copies lack it or with asterisks or obeli, the conventional signs used by copyists to indicate a spurious addition to a document.[8] An Armenian uncial version follows v. 8 with a blank space and vv. 9–20 is preceded by the line "from the priest Ariston." One wonders if this gloss identifies the author of this passage.[9]

Wallace refers to the evidence of the earliest manuscripts, the versions, and the early church fathers as "a threefold cord that is not easily broken."[10] I would add that the resurrection accounts of Matthew and Luke also provide evidence. They follow Mark closely in the Passion Narrative except where they add special material, which the two gospels do not share. They do not manifest any awareness of this longer ending, however, since they sharply diverge after Mark's account of the young man's (angel's) appearance to the women who came to the tomb. Matthew and Luke, then, may be considered the earliest evidence that the longer reading did not originally appear in Mark's gospel.

14.2.4.2.2 The Shortest Reading Is Usually Preferred

Since scribes were more likely to add than to delete, the shorter reading is typically preferred as original. The transcriptional probability is that the longer reading would have been added to the abrupt ending in Mark's original text.

14.2.4.2.3 The Reading That Does Not Betray the Tendency to Harmonize Texts Is Preferred

The reading that is less congruent with other texts in the NT is to be preferred over a reading that betrays evidence of harmonization. An analysis of the longer ending reveals that it contains a mélange of abstracts of fuller accounts found in the other gospels and Acts.[11]

---

7. Metzger, *Textual Commentary*, 123.

8. f^1, 22, 137, 138, 205, 1110, 1210, 1215, 1216, 1217, 1221, 1582.

9. See F. C. Conybeare, "Aristion, the Author of the Last Twelve Verses of Mark," *The Expositor*, Fourth Series 8 (1893): 241–54.

10. Daniel B. Wallace, "Mark 16:8 as the Conclusion to the Second Gospel," in *Perspectives on the Ending of Mark: 4 Views* (ed. David Alan Black; Nashville: Broadman & Holman, 2008), 15. See his analysis of the external textual evidence on pp. 14–29.

11. In his study of the reception history of the longer ending, James A. Kelhoffer, *Miracle and Mission: The Authentication of Missionaries and Their Message in the Longer Ending of Mark* (WUNT 2/112; Tübingen: Mohr Siebeck, 2000), 480, cites the critique of Celsus (AD 170) that Christians "go so far as to oppose themselves and *alter the original text of the Gospel* ... three or four or several times over, and they change its character to enable them to deny difficulties in the face of criticism" (Origen, *Cels.* 2.27).

Mark	Subject	Other gospels
16:9–11	The appearance to Mary Magdalene	John 20:11–18
16:12–13	The appearance to two disappointed disciples in the country	Luke 24:13–35
16:14	The appearance to the eleven	Matt 28:16–17; Luke 24:36–43; John 20:19–29; 1 Cor 15:5
16:15	The commissioning of the disciples	Matt 28:19; Acts 1:8
16:16	The declaration that belief and baptism lead to salvation; unbelief to condemnation	Acts 2:38; 16:31
16:17a	Casting out demons	Luke 10:17; Acts 5:16; 8:7; 16:18; 19:12
16:17b	Speaking in tongues	Acts 2:4–11; 10:46; 19:6
16:18a	Handling snakes	Luke 10:19; Acts 28:3–6
16:18b	Drinking deadly poison	(?)[12]
16:18c	Laying on hands to heal	Acts 3:1–10; 5:12–16; 9:12, 17–18; see also Jas 5:14–15
16:19a	The ascension of Jesus	Luke 24:50–53; Acts 1:9–11
16:19b	Sitting down at the right hand of God	Luke 22:69; Acts 2:33; 7:55; see also Rom 8:34; Col 3:1; Heb 10:12; 12:2; 1 Pet 3:22
16:20	Confirming the Lord's word by signs	Acts 14:3; see also Heb 2:3–4

Kelhoffer concludes from this list of parallels that 16:9–20 represents the author's "concentrated effort to reuse traditional materials in order to create the appearance of a passage that would be accepted as an authentic part of Mark."[13] He maintains that this deliberate imitation of the four Gospels earns the label "forgery" and that it is akin to the *Epistle to the Laodiceans*.[14] Forgers typically glean phrases and sayings from sources and place them in new contexts. Kelhoffer presumes that the author of the longer ending wrote before "the four-Gospel canon" had been fixed when Mark could be modified or expanded. He states: "Given that this individual wished

12. Drinking poison is the one sign that does not have NT antecedents (16:18b). Kelhoffer, *Miracle and Mission*, 417–72, shows that in the second century there was "a profound interest in the immunity of apostles and other holy people to the effects of harmful drugs and poison" (468). Notably, Eusebius speaks of wonderful events that Papias relates in his work, including the story of Justus, surnamed Barsabbas, who drank a deadly poison but, by the grace of the Lord, suffered no harm (*Hist. eccl.* 3.39.9). It is likely that this particular sign derives from interests that arose in the second century.

13. Kelhoffer, *Miracle and Mission*, 474

14. Ibid., 150–51. Joseph Hug, *La finale de l'évangile de Marc* (*Marc 16, 9–20*) (Ebib; Paris: Gabalda, 1978), argues that the passage was not a compilation of material from the other gospels but an independent tradition that was composed in the early second century. The striking list of parallels to the gospels in the passage, however, makes this theory unlikely. William R. Farmer, *The Last Twelve Verses of Mark* (SNTSMS 25; Cambridge: Cambridge University Press, 1974), attempts to prove the authenticity of these verses as part of his effort to defend Matthean priority. Among the many problems, including his conjectures about the activity of the early copyists in Alexandria and his use of the patristic evidence, the abrupt ending of Mark presents a significant stumbling block to his thesis. His work is biased by his prior commitment to his solution of the synoptic problem. David C. Parker, *The Living Text of the Gospels* (Cambridge: Cambridge University Press, 1997), 132, recognizes that those who believe that Mark used Matthew and Luke have difficulty in explaining why Mark would leave out the rich material in Matt 28 and Luke 24. J. N. Birdsall, "Review of William R. Farmer, *The Last Twelve Verses of Mark*," *JTS* 26 (1975): 151–60, offers a withering critique of Farmer's use of patristic evidence.

for newly-augmented copies of Mark to enjoy a lasting reception among future generations of Christians, he must have believed that he possessed the authority to interpret the NT Gospels in light of one another and, at least in the case of Mark 16:8, to modify an account that was perceived to be deficient (cf. Matt 28:8–10; Luke 24:9–11)."[15]

Since the longer ending agrees with what one finds in other canonical texts, it was not rejected as counterfeit. Sabin acidly comments, "It is not surprising that Tatian incorporated the longer ending into his harmonization of the Gospels, but it is somewhat perverse that the church that rejected the *Diatessaron* in the second century has nonetheless allowed this blurring of theological perspectives to continue for two thousand years."[16]

14.2.4.2.4 The Most Difficult Reading Is Preferred

The most difficult reading or the reading that best explains why the other variants would have appeared is usually to be preferred. One can understand why someone might want to add a more satisfying finish to a gospel that ends with the women seeming to fail to carry out their commission because "they were afraid"[17] and that has no account of Jesus' resurrection appearances to his disciples. No obvious reason surfaces to explain why a later copyist might have wanted deliberately to omit 16:9–20 had it been in the exemplar.

14.2.5 The Evaluation of the Internal Evidence

14.2.5.1 Vocabulary and Style

The longer reading contains a significant percentage of non-Markan vocabulary. So many words in the passage do not appear elsewhere in Mark that it is hard to imagine that this passage was written by the same author.[18] The style also is non-Markan.[19]

15. Kelhoffer, *Miracle and Mission*, 479–80.

16. Sabin, *Reopening*, 208.

17. Aída Besançon Spencer, "The Denial of the Good News and the Ending of Mark," *BBR* 17 (2007): 270, cites a note from the *Holy Bible, Pilgrim Edition* (New York: Oxford University Press, 1952), 1319, as an example of how the ending in 16:8 can be disturbing: "It hardly seems likely that the second Gospel would conclude with the words, 'for they were afraid.' The glorious Gospel of Christ does not leave His disciples in an attitude of fear."

18. Words that are unique to 16:9–20 when compared with the rest of Mark's Gospel include *pentheō* (v. 10); *theaomai* (vv. 11, 14); *apisteō* (vv. 11, 16); *heteros* (v. 12); *morphē* (v. 12); *hysteron* (v. 14); *hendeka* (v. 14), *parakoloutheō* (v. 17); *ophis* (v. 18), *thanasimos* (v. 18); *blaptō* (v. 18); *analambanō* (v. 19); *synergeō* (v. 20); *bebaioō* (v. 20); *epakoloutheō* (v. 20). Some unique phrases in 16:9–20 include *tois met' autou genomenois* (v. 10) as a description of the disciples, *meta tauta* (v. 12), and *kalōs hexousin* (v. 18). See James Keith Elliott, "The Text and Language of the Endings to Mark's Gospel," *TZ* 27 (1971): 255–62.

19. Joel F. Williams, "Literary Approaches to the End of Mark's Gospel," *JETS* 42/1 (1999): 23, n. 11, notes, "Mark always uses a compound form of *poreuomai* and not the simple verb. See the use of *eisporeuomai* in 1:21; 4:19; 5:40; 6:56; 7:15, 18, 19; 11:2; *ekporeuomai* in 1:5; 6:11; 7:15, 19, 20, 21, 23; 10:17, 46; 11:19; 13:1; *paraporeuomai* in 2:23; 9:30; 11:20; 15:29. In all these examples of compound forms of *poreuomai*, Mark never uses the aorist tense such as is found with the instances of *poreuomai* in 16:10, 15. *Ekeinos* functions as a pronoun in 16:10, 13, 20, whereas it is always used as an adjective elsewhere in Mark." Williams also cites "Other words in 16:9–20 that are used with a unique meaning or function when compared with the rest of Mark's Gospel include *phainō* (v. 9), *para* (v. 9), *phaneroō* (vv. 12, 14), *oneidizō* (v. 14), *ktisis* (v. 15), *sēmeion* (vv. 17, 20), *glōssa* (v. 17), *kan* (v. 18), *kyrios* (vv. 19, 20)" (p. 24). See also Travis B. Williams, "Bringing Method to the Madness: Examining the Style of the Longer Ending of Mark," *BBR* 20 (2010): 397–417. The evidence does not support the arguments of J. W. Burgon, *The Last Twelve Verses of the Gospel according to St. Mark: Vindicated against Recent Critical Objectors and Established* (London: John Murray, 1883), or of Maurice Robinson, "The Long Ending of Mark as Canonical Verity," in *Perspectives on the Ending of Mark: Four Views* (ed. David Alan Black; Nashville: Broadman & Holman, 2008), 40–79.

Anyone with intimate familiarity with the Greek of Mark quickly recognizes that the style of 16:9–20 marks a dramatic shift from the rest of the gospel.[20]

14.2.5.2 Literary Disruptions

The longer reading also introduces significant literary disruptions. (1) The subject of the action in 16:8 is the women who had come to the tomb, but in 16:9 the subject abruptly shifts to Jesus as the unexpressed subject of the main verb.

(2) Mary Magdalene is a primary character in the preceding scenes as one of the women who followed Jesus from Galilee (15:41), viewed his crucifixion from a distance (15:40), observed where he was buried (15:47), and came to the tomb to anoint him with the other women after the Sabbath (16:1). She is reintroduced in 16:9, however, with a descriptive phrase as the one "out of whom he had driven seven demons," as if the audience were meeting her for the first time. Why would Mark insert this detail at the fourth mention of Mary Magdalene? This background, by contrast, is revealed the first time she turns up in Luke's narrative (Luke 8:2). Also, why do the other women who were with Mary Magdalene at the tomb inexplicably disappear from the picture in 16:9–20? This gratuitous reintroduction of Mary Magdalene is a clue that someone has awkwardly added this next section by drawing on other traditions.

(3) It is odd to report in 16:9 that Jesus appeared first to Mary Magdalene when he rose "early" on the first day of the week. She came to the tomb with the other women to anoint the body "very early" (16:2). It is therefore confusing to determine when exactly this appearance occurred in Mark's timeline. Did she separate from the other women after visiting the tomb "very early"? It seems most likely that this tradition about Jesus' appearance to Mary Magdalene derives from John 20:1–18. If the statement in 16:8 means literally that the women told no one at all, then it is also odd that in the next episode Mary Magdalene does tell others (16:10).[21] Was she bolstered by renewed courage that overcame her fear, and if so, why is that not explained by the narrator? This detail, however, may be explained if telling no one means that the women told no one other than the disciples and if their fear is related to religious awe, not cowardice. Nevertheless, why is it only Mary Magdalene who reports the news to "those who had been with him" and the other women who were also commanded by the young man go unmentioned?

(4) The conclusion in 16:7 emphasizes telling "his disciples and Peter" about Jesus' resurrection and that he goes before them to Galilee where they will see him. Curiously, the narration in 16:9–20 mentions neither an appearance to the disciples in Galilee nor does it include any reference to Peter. Peter plays no role in the longer ending!

20. Robert H. Stein, "The Ending of Mark," *BBR* 18 (2008): 83, n. 19, makes a personal observation:

> Since my doctoral studies at Princeton Theological Seminary where I did my dissertation on Mark, I have had a continued love affair with this Gospel. I think that I can say with some measure of confidence that this is the book of the Bible of which I am least ignorant. I have become familiar with the style, vocabulary, and theological interests of the author of Mark 1:1–16:8, but I do not know the identity of the author of 16:9–20. He is a stranger to me.

21. In Matt 28:8, 10; Luke 24:9–11; John 20:1, 11–18, the women do tell others.

14.2.6 Conclusions about the Longer Ending

The longer ending most likely was composed in the second century to provide a more satisfactory ending to the text of Mark.[22] When the four Gospels were collected in the libraries of larger church communities in this era, Mark's abbreviated ending would have stood out more prominently. It probably would have generated the desire by someone, who knew the other gospels and Acts, to correct this perceived deficiency by composing the longer ending and producing a mosaic from other accounts. Ruling out 16:9–20 as the original ending of Mark, however, does not solve the problem of how this gospel ends.

14.2.7 The Problems with Ending the Gospel in Mark 16:8

The shorter ending also has notable difficulties that require explanation if it is to be accepted as Mark's intended conclusion to his gospel. First, it is disconcerting to have the gospel end with the women stupefied, reeling, frightened, and silent.[23] Instead of good news being proclaimed about the resurrection, it seems, we get no news. Many modern scholars are no less dissatisfied with this sketchy ending than the early scribes who tried their hands at counterfeiting a more detailed ending. For example, Stein asserts, "It is difficult to believe that Mark would have ended his Gospel of Jesus Christ, the Son of God, without an account of such an appearance." He continues: "There is no convincing reason why Mark would have wanted to end his Gospel at 16:8."[24]

Second, it is a grammatical oddity to end a sentence in Greek with "for" (the particle *gar*), not to mention ending an entire narrative with it. Something should normally follow after this clause.

Third, it is curious that Mark would emphasize in both 14:28 and 16:7 Jesus' prophecy that he would go before his disciples to Galilee after the resurrection but not narrate its fulfillment.

Fourth, Witherington argues that ancient biographies of other important public figures ended with their vindication beyond death.[25] He maintains, "They did not end like Mark" and infers that if Mark is a biography like these other biographies, then 16:8 could not be Mark's intended ending.[26]

14.2.8 Possible Explanations for the Seemingly Truncated Ending

14.2.8.1 A Mutilated Autograph?

Some argue that the gospel's ending was lost when it somehow became mutilated

22. Hengel, *Studies*, 168, n. 47, concludes that the addition of 16:9–20 "must be dated to the first decades of the second century." Kelhoffer, *Miracle and Mission*, 175, also fixes the time around AD 120–150.

23. Matthew 28:8 is more satisfying in narrating that the women left the tomb "afraid yet filled with joy, and ran to tell his disciples."

24. Stein, *Mark*, 735. He states in "The Ending of Mark," 90, "It is hard to imagine that a Gospel that begins with a bold, straightforward 'The beginning of the Gospel of Jesus Christ, the Son of God' (1:1) would end with a negative response of fear and fright by the women in 16:8."

25. Witherington, *Mark*, 42–45.

26. Witherington, *The Indelible Image*, 1:613.

in its early transmission. Croy tries to resuscitate this argument in a book length treatment.[27] He surmises that if the original copy of Mark had been a codex, both the ending and the beginning would have been mutilated. Since the beginning of the gospel is seemingly as glaringly abrupt as its ending, he suggests that both the beginning and the ending were lost. Witherington assumes, however, that the original copy of Mark was a scroll, and only a bit was included on this last page that vanished, something like what is found in Matt 28:9–10, 16–18.[28]

The mutilation theory is an improbable explanation for the abrupt ending. This hypothesis requires that the damage to Mark not only would have occurred shortly after its production but also that no one would have recopied it or could remember it well enough to restore it.[29] Textual damage normally results from long periods of use, and it is unlikely to have happened within a short time after Mark's composition. If it had suffered from such wear and tear, it was because it was valued and used, and if it was so highly prized, someone would have made an effort to restore its damaged last leaf. Also, other copies likely would have been made from the original over this period of time. Marcus concludes, "The mutilation thesis, then, combines two improbabilities—extremely rapid deterioration or dismemberment and mutilation precisely at the end of a pericope."[30]

14.2.8.2 An Unfinished Gospel?

Stein represents an alternative view that "Mark was never able to write his intended ending."[31] In supporting this assessment, Gundry claims that the last word in the Greek ("for," *gar*) is a particle that was meant to introduce another pericope.[32] Stein also contends that Jesus' promise to meet the disciples in Galilee after his resurrection (14:28; 16:7) would be the only unfulfilled prophecy of Jesus in the gospel, "other than the ones concerning the *Parousia*."[33] He thinks that Mark surely intended to record this reunion.

This argument fails to convince. First, other prophecies appear in Mark that the evangelist does not narrate but assumes will be fulfilled. For example, John the Baptist proclaims that a stronger one will come after him who will baptize with the Holy Spirit (1:8), but this prophecy is not narrated in Mark's story line. The audience, however, would have experienced this Spirit baptism (Acts 1:5; 2:38; 8:14–17; 11:15–17; 19:1–7; 1 Cor 12:13). The prediction that John and James will drink the same cup and be baptized with the same baptism as Jesus (10:39) also is not narrated, nor is the assurance that his anointing by the woman in the house of Simon the leper will be proclaimed wherever the gospel is preached (14:9). It does not present a problem for Mark not to recount the prophecy of Jesus' reunion with the disciples after his resurrection in the plotted narrative.

27. Croy, *The Mutilation of Mark's Gospel.*
28. Witherington, *Mark*, 48–49.
29. Marcus, *Mark 8–16*, 1091.
30. Ibid., 1092.
31. Stein, *Mark*, 737.
32. Gundry, *Mark*, 1011. We have seen, however, that Mark contains many instances of the delayed use of the explanatory clause with *gar*. See §1.2.5.8.
33. Stein, "The Ending of Mark," 97.

Thomas writes that in Mark, "whatever Jesus foretells comes to pass. On the basis of Jesus' past performances, the reader of Mark grows to expect fulfilment of 'prophecy.' Consequently, when the reader is faced with Mark 16:8 he naturally concludes that Jesus will indeed see his disciples in Galilee. Thus the gospel ends on a high note."[34] Mark has the young man repeat Jesus' prophetic assurance from 14:28 and then add the phrase "just as he told you" to reinforce that it came from Jesus.[35] Mark's audience consists of those who believe that Jesus' statement, "Heaven and earth will pass away, but my words will never pass away" (13:31), is true, and they would not only have believed that his prophecy would be fulfilled to the letter, they would have known from the proclamation of the gospel that it had been fulfilled.

Second, if Mark were like an unfinished symphony, it opens the door to all kinds of speculation as to why the evangelist did not bring his gospel to its planned conclusion. Did he become ill, get thrown into prison, or die? Such guesswork is pointless. The gospel somehow survived and was circulated, and one might wonder why no one from Mark's community took up the pen and added an epilogue during the first years of its circulation.[36] What happened after Jesus' resurrection was not a secret. Why did it take until the second century for someone to try his hand at finishing the gospel? Despite the existence of more influential gospels with their fully orbed endings, Mark survived as one of the four Gospels that were regarded as apostolic even with its supposedly disappointing ending. Only later did someone decide to emend it with a montage of details from the other gospel accounts of the resurrection. In the early years of Mark's circulation, however, no one saw any need to revise its ending, and one might assume they did not revise it because they recognized it to be the way Mark originally ended his gospel.

14.2.8.3 Literary Explanations for the Ending in Mark 16:8

Both the mutilation theory and the uncompleted gospel theory offer only historical guesswork as a solution to what is essentially a literary problem. If one can offer a literary solution that makes sufficient sense of the text as a meaningful closure to the gospel, then that answer should stand as a better alternative to historical conjecture. Burkill declares that the exegete's primary duty "is to elucidate the gospel as it stands, not as he thinks it ought to be."[37] Can 16:8 be read satisfactorily as Mark's intended ending?

14.2.8.3.1 Ending with the Particle *gar* ("for")

Iverson assesses the contention of many that because sentences ending with *gar* are less common in Greek narrative literature than, for example, in philosophical literature, that 16:8 could not be intended to be Mark's closing verse. He examines

34. John Christopher Thomas, "A Reconsideration of the Ending of Mark," *JETS* 26 (1983): 418.

35. Meye, "Mark 16:8," 42, comments, "*The evangelist is clearly concerned to stress that all that is happening is a fulfillment of Jesus' own word.*"

36. Compare the epilogue that was added to the Fourth Gospel (John 21).

37. Burkill, *Mysterious Revelation*, 5.

the use of a final *gar* ("for") in all extant ancient Greek literature and decides that the data is inconclusive. It can support the case for either a text that was intended to continue or for an intentionally abrupt ending.[38] Denyer makes a similar point after an analysis of the ending of Plato's *Protagoras*. Plato ends this work with "for," and Denyer maintains that because he chose to do so does not provide proof that Mark chose to do the same thing. He writes:

> It is, however, proof that there is no anachronism whatsoever in the hypothesis that Mark chose precisely such a means of leaving the reader in what is, after all, a proper frame of mind for someone who has just read a gospel: thinking that the story of the risen Christ cannot be over yet, and yearning to hear more. It was, no doubt, this yearning that generated the various conclusions that we find in manuscripts of the Gospel of Mark.[39]

One can conclude that it would not have been unheard of for Mark to end his gospel with "for."

14.2.8.3.2 The Genre of Biography

Witherington assumes that since ancient biographies of other important public figures ended with their vindication beyond death, Mark must have done so as well.[40] I would counter that the comparison is invalid because Mark's gospel is not like other ancient biographies of great men. It does not begin like a normal biography by introducing Jesus' home and family background, though he knows these things (3:31; 6:1–6), or by describing his appearance. Mark did not end like other ancient biographies because his gospel is not simply a biography of a great man.[41] Jesus is not merely another public figure, but the Son of God. The story cannot end with the account of his death and resurrection. It continues beyond the narrative because believers are to carry on his mission and to proclaim the good news until he returns.

14.2.8.3.3 The So-Called Obligation for an Author to Tie Up Loose Ends

It long has been argued that writers were expected to tie up loose ends. Knox, for example, argues that ancient stories required developed endings that left nothing to the imagination:

> To suppose that Mark originally intended to end his Gospel in this way implies both that he was totally indifferent to the canons of popular story-telling,

38. Kelly R. Iverson, "A Further Word on Final Γάρ (Mark 16:8)," *CBQ* 68 (2006): 79–94. Iverson caps his work by providing examples of the use of *gar* to end a sentence. See also Carl Hermann Kraeling, "A Philological Note on Mark 16:8," *JBL* 44 (1925): 357–58; R. R. Ottley, "ἐφοβοῦντο γάρ Mark xvi 8," *JTS* 27 (1926): 407–9; Morton Scott Enslin, "ἐφοβοῦντο γάρ, Mark 16:8," *JBL* 46 (1927): 62–64; Henry J. Cadbury, "Mark 16:8," *JBL* 46 (1927): 344–45; Lightfoot, *Locality and Doctrine*, 10–15; Frederick W. Danker, "Menander and the New Testament," *NTS* 10 (1964): 366; Pieter W. van der Horst, "Can a Book End with *GAR*? A Note on Mark XVI.8," *JTS* 23 (1972): 121–24; Steven L. Cox, *A History and Critique of Scholarship concerning the Markan Endings* (Lewiston, NY/Queenston, ON: Mellen, 1993), 223–27; Nicholas Denyer, "Mark 16:8 and Plato, *Protagoras* 328D," *TynBul* 57 (2006): 149–50.

39. Denyer, "Mark 16:8 and Plato," 150.

40. Witherington, *Mark*, 42–45.

41. See §1.2.4.2.

> and that by a pure accident he happened to hit on a conclusion which suits the technique of a highly sophisticated type of modern literature. The odds against such a coincidence (even if we could for a moment entertain the idea that Mark was indifferent to canons which he observes scrupulously elsewhere in his Gospel) seem to me to be so enormous as not to be worth considering. In any case the supposition credits him with a degree of originality which would invalidate the whole method of form-criticism.[42]

I would counter by citing Demetrius (*On Style* 222):

> Not everything should be given lengthy treatment with full details but some points should be left for our hearer to grasp and infer for himself. If he infers what you have omitted, he no longer just listens to you but acts as your witness, one too who is predisposed in your favour since he feels he has been intelligent and you are the person who has given him the opportunity to exercise his intelligence. In fact, to tell your hearer everything as if he were a fool is to reveal that you think him one.

Mark's ending in 16:8 forces the hearers to fill in the unnarrated events, and they are able to do so from the clues that Mark has offered in what precedes but also from knowing the tradition that they have heard preached. As one might infer from Paul's recitation of the creed in 1 Cor 15:3–5, the first audience of Mark were not virgin listeners. They knew the story. Blount uses the example of writing the tale of the sinking of the *Titanic* and to "end it at the moment the hull disappears beneath the icy waters of the North Atlantic as life boats drift solemnly at a distance." The "flesh-and-blood" reader knows what happens. A remnant will live to tell the tale of this disaster.[43] In the same way, Mark's audience knows what happens next in the story of Jesus, and in filling in the gaps they themselves become witnesses to the resurrection.

14.2.8.3.4 Unnarrated Endings in Mark

Boomershine and Bartholomew provide notable examples from the gospel that show that it is characteristic of Mark to leave his audience with "questions unanswered."[44] For example, Mark offers no narrative closure to the story of the temptation by Satan in the desert. Jesus is left in the wilderness being served by angels (1:12–13). The following scene, which begins a new section, shows him suddenly transported to Galilee where he begins to proclaim the good news of God (1:14–15). The audience can only infer that Jesus defeated Satan and will later have that inference confirmed by the series of exorcisms that suggest he is the stronger one who has plundered Satan's house (3:23–27). The audience therefore may be prepared subconsciously for the open-ended ending.

42. Wilfred L. Knox, "The Ending of St. Mark's Gospel," *HTR* 35 (1942): 22–23.

43. Blount, "Is the Joke on Us?" 29.

44. Thomas E. Boomershine and Gilbert L. Bartholomew, "The Narrative Technique of Mark 16:8," *JBL* 100 (1981): 213–23.

Once again, Jesus battles the forces of evil on the cross and has conquered death when he rose from the grave. An angel appears to report the news. The audience must again infer that Jesus did rendezvous with his disciples in Galilee, and once again the good news of victory will ring out, only this time it will be of an even greater and decisive victory.

14.2.8.3.5 Suspended Endings in Ancient Literature

Significant parallels to a suspended ending like Mark's exist in ancient literature. Hooker points out that, for various reasons, Homer's *The Illiad* and *The Odyssey* and Virgils's *Aeneid* leave their hearers "in suspense" at their end.[45] Magness provides evidence that it was normal literary practice in the ancient world to allude to well-known events that occurred after those being narrated in the text without actually narrating those events.[46]

14.2.8.3.6 Suspended Endings in Scripture

More significantly, the precedence of suspended endings is found in the OT. The ending in 2 Kgs 25:27–30 does not narrate Israel returning triumphantly from Babylon but only foreshadows it by citing King Jehoiachin's release from prison, taking a seat in the king's court, and being given an allowance that enables him to live well. The ending of Jonah 4:10–11 also leaves things hanging in the air. What will God do with "the great city of Nineveh, in which there are more than a hundred and twenty thousand people who cannot tell their right hand from their left—and also many animals"? Jonah does not narrate it.

In the NT, Luke's gospel ends with the disciples sent back to Jerusalem to tarry until they "have been clothed with power from on high" (24:49). Acts picks up the story with the ascension, but Peter, who has been a central figure in the beginning chapters, drops out of the narrative completely after Acts 15. The audience is given no clue what happens to him. Acts ends with Paul citing Isaiah that this salvation of God has been sent to the Gentiles and "proclaim[ing] the kingdom of God and teach[ing] about the Lord Jesus Christ—with all boldness and without hindrance!" (Acts 28:27–31). Luke does not narrate the results of Paul's appeal to Caesar. Instead, he concludes his work with the statement that Paul was preaching the kingdom of God and teaching about the Lord Jesus Christ with all boldness unhinderedly (the text in Greek ends with this adverb).

Luke concluded his gospel with a full account of Jesus' resurrection appearances and his ascension. Meye contends, "One could equally well find the narratives of Matthew and John unsatisfactory and abrupt in their conclusion, for they, unlike Luke, say not a word regarding Jesus' final separation from the disciples."[47] Luke also

45. Hooker, "Beginnings and Endings," 194.

46. Jodi Lee Magness, *Sense and Absence: Structure and Suspension in the Ending of Mark's Gospel* (Semeia Studies; Atlanta: Scholars Press, 1986), 30–31.

47. Meye, "Mark 16:8," 39.

continued the story with a history of what God continued to do in the lives of Jesus' followers for years after Jesus' resurrection. In the end, however, Luke faced the same question that confronted Mark. How does one end a story that does not end?

Jesus' parables in Luke frequently are left open-ended. They do not sort out what happens next in the story world of the parable, and Luke often does not record the response to the parable. For example, in the parable of the Samaritan (Luke 10:25–37), does the mugging victim that the Samaritan rescued recover from his wounds? Does he change his view toward Samaritans? How does the lawyer who posed the question that prompted the parable react? In the parable of the man who had two sons (Luke 15:11–32), what does the elder brother do? Does he respond to his father's entreaty to join the celebration over the recovery of his lost son, or does he boil with indignation after venting his spleen about the undeserved grace showered on his brother? How do the teachers of the law and Pharisees respond to the parables of the lost sheep, lost coin, and prodigal son (Luke 15)? How does Simon the Pharisee respond to the parable of the Two Debtors and Jesus' pronouncement that the sins of the woman who anointed his feet were forgiven (Luke 7:36–50)?

Like parables that do not recount what happens next, the question for Mark's account really is not what the women did or how long did they keep silent, but what will the auditors do upon hearing this story? Juel argues that the impact of reading an ending is more important than the ideas extracted from it: "An ending does things. It can achieve closure, pulling together loose threads from a story, or it can resist closure, refusing to answer burning questions posed in the course of the narrative."[48] Since most readers expect closure, Juel contends, "our need to overcome this experience of disappointment is the primary motor that drives interpretation."[49]

14.3 Mark 16:8 as the Intended Ending

14.3.1 The Young Man Dressed in a White Robe and Sitting on the Right Side (Mark 16:5)

14.3.1.1 A Follower of Jesus or an Idealized Disciple?

The figure in the tomb is identified as a "young man" (*neaniskos*), not as an angel. Wearing a white robe and sitting on the right does not suggest a heavenly origin to some interpreters. That Mark uses the term "angels" elsewhere in his gospel (1:13; 8:38; 12:25; 13:27, 32) but does not use it here has inclined some to identify this

48. Donald Harrisville Juel, "A Disquieting Silence: The Matter of the Ending," in *The Ending of Mark and the Ends of God: Essays in Memory of Donald Harrisville Juel* (ed. Beverly Roberts Gaventa and Patrick D. Miller; Louisville: Westminster John Knox, 2005), 4. Hooker, "Beginnings and Endings," 195, writes that the readers "are left pondering the moral of the story—can it really be true that God is concerned about the salvation of the Gentiles?" She contends, "It is precisely because the story told by the evangelists is only a part—though the crucial one—of a continuing narrative which began with the creation of the world and will end with its final restoration that the Gospels all end by pointing their hearers forward to what follows."

49. Juel, "A Disquieting Silence," 5. France, *Mark*, 671–73, strenuously objects to this kind of interpretation, ascribing it to postmodernism, and Stein, *Mark*, 735, dismisses it as the product of "twentieth-century existentialism." But if their view that the gospel was unfinished is true, it implies that we have been left with a regrettably curtailed gospel, in other words, a defective gospel of Mark.

figure as the same "young man" who was wearing nothing but a linen garment when Jesus was arrested on the Mount of Olives. When he was seized by Jesus' captors, he shed his linen garment and fled naked into the darkness (14:51–52).

Others suggest that the young man represents a "symbolic construction of the model disciple."[50] He embodies the baptized believer who has been "transformed through symbolic participation in, and identification with, the death and resurrection of Jesus."[51] This interpretation would replace any historic foundation for the resurrection account with symbolic fancy. Gourgues objects that the description of the young man's flight after the disciples' desertion (14:50) would hardly serve as a positive image for dying with Christ in baptism. Since Mark has no explicit reference to Christian baptism, this interpretation that the young man represents an initiate approaching baptism is implausible.[52] Fleddermann rightly interprets the flight of the young man to be "a symbol of those who oppose God's will in the passion."[53] The common vocabulary between 16:5 and 14:51–52 is merely coincidental, and Mark intends no literary/symbolic connection.[54]

If this young man were the same one who fled from Jesus and the arresting posse on the Mount of Olives, one would expect Mark to identify him as *the* young man (with a definite article) rather than as *a* young man (without an article).[55] If the young man were one of Jesus' followers, why would he not go tell the disciples himself instead of commanding the women to do so? Also, why would the women not have recognized him as one of his followers, and why would they be so alarmed by seeing him in the tomb? Why would he have come to the tomb in the first place, and why would he still be waiting around? Did he expect visitors? Since no male follower witnessed Jesus' burial, how does he know "where they laid him"? The answers to these questions lead to the conclusion that the young man is assumed by Mark to be a heavenly being, not an earthly disciple.

Moloney represents a more restrained interpretation of the verbal links to the incident of the young man who fled on the Mount of Olives. Jesus' dead body was wrapped in a "linen cloth" (15:46), the same word (*sindōn*) that is used to describe what the youth was wearing in 14:51–52. He suggests that this verbal link has symbolic meaning: "As God has transformed the death of Jesus by raising him from the dead, discipleship may be reestablished and nakedness covered."[56] He claims it is only "a hint that God's action can reverse failure."[57] It is far more likely, however, that Mark conveys this theological truth through the young man's restatement of

---

50. Robin Scroggs and Kent I. Groff, "Baptism in Mark: Dying and Rising with Christ," *JBL* 92 (1973): 531–48, identify the young man as the Christian initiate in baptism who has laid aside his garments and descended into the water naked and emerges clothed with a white garment. The young man who was stripped of everything is now restored, radiantly dressed and seated at the right hand, a fulfillment of Isa 40:30–31. "Jesus himself cannot appear, for he is already exalted to heaven and is already sitting at the right hand of God" (545). Focant, *Mark*, 657, also holds this position,

51. Steven R. Johnson, "The Identity and Significance of the *Neaniskos* in Mark," *Forum* 8 (1992): 129.

52. Michel Gourgues, "À propos du symbolisme christologique et baptismal de Marc 16.5," *NTS* 27 (1981): 675–76.

53. Fleddermann, "The Flight of a Naked Young Man," 417. See §9.4.1.5.4.3.

54. France, *Mark*, 679–80. See also Gourgues, "A propos," 672–78. Gnilka, *Markus*, 2:342, n. 20, dismisses this connection as "absurd."

55. Collins, *Mark*, 795.

56. Moloney, *Mark*, 345.

57. Ibid., 346.

Jesus' prophecy that he would meet the disciples in Galilee after his resurrection than through an overly subtle description of the messenger's attire.

14.3.1.2 A Heavenly Messenger

Christian art has tended to portray angels with large wings and haloes, and it may mislead modern readers about what angels should look like. That is not how angels are identified in Scripture.[58] Describing the occupant of the tomb as a "young man" does not mean that he is not a heavenly messenger, an angel. The angels who visited Abraham appeared like human beings (Gen 18:2, 16, 22; 19:1).[59] In 2 Macc 3:26, 33, angels are described as "two young men remarkably strong, gloriously beautiful, and splendidly dressed." In Tob 5:4–22, the angel Raphael appears as a man. In *L.A.B.* (*Pseudo-Philo*) 9:10, "a man in a linen garment" appears to Miriam in a dream, and he is a heavenly figure. Josephus describes the angel who appears to the wife of Manoah in Judg 13:13 as being in the likeness of a beautiful youth (*Ant.* 5.8.2 § 277). The *Shepherd of Hermas* (*Vis.* 3.1.6) describes six beings that he sees in a vision as "young men" who are later identified as angels (*Vis.* 3.4.1).[60] Matthew, who uses Mark, unambiguously understood this figure to be "an angel of the Lord [who] came down from heaven" (28:2–5).

The young man's greeting, "Don't be alarmed," is similar to the assurance, "Do not be afraid!" (Gen 15:1; Judg 6:23; Dan 10:12, 19; Luke 1:13, 30; 2:10). That is what heavenly beings say to frightened humans when they first reveal themselves. The "white robe" also is the customary attire of heavenly beings (Dan 7:9; Acts 1:10; 10:30; Rev 4:4; 2 Macc 11:8–10; *1 En.* 62:15–16; 87:2), and it matches the description of Jesus' garments in the transfiguration in Mark 9:3. In *L.A.B. (Pseudo-Philo)* 61:6, when Saul asked the witch of Endor about the appearance of Samuel, she responds that he is asking her about divine beings: "for behold his appearance is not the appearance of a man. For he is clothed in a white robe with a mantle placed over it, and two angels are leading him." Luke 24:4 also describes the clothing of the two men who appeared to the women who came to the tomb as "gleaming like lightning," which more clearly denotes the attire of heavenly beings. France observes, "for clothes to appear white in the darkness of the burial chamber they would need more than everyday whiteness."[61]

The young man in Mark also supernaturally knows why these women have come to the tomb: "You are looking for Jesus the Nazarene, who was crucified" (16:6).[62] More importantly, he discloses what only a divine being can know at this time: "He has risen!" (16:6). Humans had no part in nor did they witness the resurrection. This miracle, like the virginal conception, requires an interpreting angel to explain what has happened and what will happen next. Similarly, in Acts 1:9–11, two

58. Only the seraphim had wings, and they numbered six (Isa 6:2). The cherubim had animal and human features.

59. Tobias mistakes Raphael, the angel from God, as a human and addresses him as "young man" when he encounters him (Tob 5:4–22).

60. The apocryphal *Gospel of Peter* 9.36–37 describes the angels appearing in the resurrection scene as "men" and "young men."

61. France, *Mark*, 678.

62. Pesch, *Markusevangelium*, 2:532–33.

interpreting angels, identified as "two men dressed in white," explain the meaning of the ascension to the disciples and what will happen in the future.

The only time angels make an actual appearance in Mark's narrative is at the beginning when they came to minister to Jesus after his battle with Satan in the wilderness (1:13). One now appears at the end to announce the resurrection. In the beginning of the gospel, an earthly divine messenger clothed in rough camel's hair announces what God *is about to do*. John the Baptist says that one more powerful than he is coming who "will baptize you with the Holy Spirit" (1:2–8). At the conclusion of the gospel, a heavenly divine messenger clothed in a white robe reveals what God *has done*. In the beginning of the gospel, the way is to be prepared. At the end of the gospel, the way has been prepared.

14.3.1.3 The Function of the Heavenly Messenger

The heavenly messenger's greeting assures the women that they are at the right tomb: "See the place where they laid him" (16:6). They have not made a mistake.[63] He identifies the one they seek as Jesus the Nazarene (see 1:24; 10:47; 14:67), but he announces that his corpse is not there. The meaning of the empty tomb is not obvious and does not provide conclusive proof. Matthew reports that the Jewish leaders tried to explain it away with a rumor that the disciples came at night and stole the body (Matt 28:11–13). Only a divine messenger can explain why it is empty: Jesus the Nazarene, the very one who was crucified, has risen (16:6).[64] The one word announcement, "he has risen" (*ēgerthē*), is as terse as the two-word description of Jesus' execution: "they crucified him" (*staurousin auton*, 15:24).

By emphasizing that Jesus the Nazarene was crucified and is now risen, Mark underscores important theological points. God's power must be seen in *both* the crucifixion *and* the resurrection of Jesus. It also means that the historical Jesus who hailed from Nazareth is the same one as the Lord Jesus who was raised from the dead.[65]

The heavenly messenger finishes his revelatory task by giving the women the commission to tell the news to the disciples and Peter and to remind them of Jesus' promise (14:28), "He is going ahead of you into Galilee. There you will see him, just as he told you" (16:7). If disciples are to encounter the resurrected Lord, they are to follow him again in Galilee as he goes before them.[66]

14.3.2 The Women's Reaction to the Resurrection Message (Mark 16:8)

The final verse of the gospel describes the women's reaction to the news of Jesus' resurrection and the command to tell the disciples to go to Galilee to meet him: "Trembling and bewildered, the women went out and fled from the tomb. They

63. Incredibly, Kirsopp Lake, *The Historical Evidence for the Resurrection of Jesus Christ* (New York: Putnam, 1907), 252–53, contends that the women went to the wrong tomb and then misunderstood the directions of a bystander trying to help them.

64. Andreas Lindemann, "Die Osterbotschaft des Markus: Zur theologischen Interpretation von Mark 16:1–8," *NTS* 26 (1980): 305, notes that Mark argues that Jesus has been resurrected; therefore he is not here.

65. Stein, *Mark*, 731, n. 6.

66. Garland, *Mark*, 613.

said nothing to anyone, because they were afraid" (16:8). This ending provokes frustration, dismay, disappointment, surprise, and all kinds of questions in readers. What caused the women's fear and should it be regarded as a positive or negative emotion? Did they ever tell the disciples this news? If not, how did the word get out?

14.3.2.1 Fear in Mark and the Women's Numinous Awe

The verb "to fear" appears eleven other times in Mark, and it connotes different kinds of fear in differing contexts.[67] It is used to refer to reverential awe when the disciples are stunned after witnessing Jesus' divine mastery of the sea. With just a word he calms a storm that was about to sink their skiff and destroy them all (4:41). The woman who realizes her chronic flow of blood had been stanched after touching Jesus' garment is also overcome by fear and trembling when she fell at his feet (5:33). Her fear also is reverential awe over what has happened to her.

Reverential awe does not necessarily lead to reverence. After Jesus drove out a legion of demons from a man and they entered some pigs that triggered them to run, lemming-like, into the sea and drown, the townspeople from Gerasa came to investigate. They found the man, whom no one had been able to overpower even with chains, clothed and sitting calmly in his right mind alongside Jesus, and they were afraid (5:15). This divine power, however, makes them so uneasy that they beg Jesus to leave their region (5:17). Herod knew John the Baptist to be a righteous and holy man, and he was in fearful awe of him (6:20). But that fear did not prevent him from having him executed to honor an extravagant oath.

When the disciples saw Jesus walking to them on the sea, they thought they saw a phantasm and were terrified. Jesus gives them assurance that it is he and tells them not to fear (6:50). This fear is related to the dread over what a ghost might do to them in the middle of the sea in the middle of the night, but it is also an appropriate reaction to an epiphany. At the transfiguration, the disciples become "frightened" (the adjectival form, *ekphobos*) when they witness Jesus' transformation in the company of two heavenly figures, Elijah and Moses (9:6). Peter does "not know what to say" but blurts out something anyway. Again, their fear is a natural reaction to an epiphany. The point is made that they are not to speak themselves but to listen to Jesus (9:7).

The disciples are also afraid to ask Jesus what he meant when he uttered his second passion and resurrection prediction (9:32). This fear borders on wonder and amazement. The fear of those who followed Jesus as he makes his way to Jerusalem may be tinged by dread over what might happen when they arrive (10:32), but the audacious request of James and John to sit on Jesus' left and right when he comes into his glory suggests that these two disciples are not overcome with terrifying anxiety over what might transpire in Jerusalem (10:35–37). The fear expressed in 10:32, then, is like the majority of other instances of fear in Mark. It is not some

67. See the table of the vocabulary of fear in Mark in Edward L. Bode, *The First Easter Morning: The Gospel Accounts of the Women's Visit to the Tomb of Jesus* (AnBib 45; Rome: Pontifical Biblical Institute, 1970), 38.

ill-defined trepidation but an expression of wonderment that something divinely remarkable is about to happen.

Other uses of the word "fear" in Mark are related to fright over negative consequences. Jesus tells Jairus, for example, not to fear but only believe when word comes of his daughter's death. This fear is related to a father's natural pangs of distress over the death of his beloved child. The chief priests' hesitation to take overt action in putting Jesus to death is attributed to their fear of him (11:18). Their apprehension is not attributable to their reverential awe of a righteous and holy man (see 6:20) but reflects their nervousness about his influence over the Passover crowd that held him (and John the Baptist) in such high esteem (11:32; 12:12). Were they to take action against Jesus, they feared an angry and potentially violent backlash.

The description of the women's fear in 16:8 is linked to their response of "trembling" and "bewilderment" at the angel's announcement. The structure of the passage makes this clear in a more literal translation of 16:8:

> And going out they fled from the tomb
> for trembling and astonishment had come upon them;
> And they said nothing to anyone,
> for they were afraid.[68]

The related emotions of trembling, astonishment, and fear cause them to flee from the tomb and to say nothing to anyone.

Heavenly revelations frequently cause mental distress (Dan 7:15, 28; 8:27; 2 Esd 12:3).[69] Catchpole cites the combination of "fear and trembling" in Job 4:12–16 and Ps 2:11 and notes that they are not understood as negative emotions. They result from religious awe. In Paul's letters, "fear and trembling" are related to religious awe that leads to obedience (1 Cor 2:3; 2 Cor 7:15; Eph 6:5; Phil 2:12). This same understanding appears in the later rabbinic work *ʾAbot de Rabbi Nathan* 1:1 (16b). Catchpole states that fear and trembling "constitute the required response to divine manifestation and in particular to the word on which it is focussed. Obedience is an integral element of this awe."[70] Those familiar with this background might expect, then, that the women's fear and trembling at the word of a divine messenger would lead to their obedience.

The word translated "bewildered" (*ekstasis*, lit., "standing outside of one's self") appears in 5:42 to describe the reaction of those who witnessed Jesus raising Jairus's daughter from the dead, and there it is translated, "they were completely astonished." Topel notes that elsewhere in the NT, this noun "is always used in conjunction with a miraculous intervention or a theophany" (Luke 5:26; Acts 3:10; 10:10; 11:5; 22:17).[71] He contends that the women at the tomb are stupefied and overcome when they realized that they "have become participants in God's miraculous irruption into

68. Robert H. Smith, "New and Old in Mark 16:1–8," *CTM* 43 (1972): 525.

69. Noted by Pesch, *Markusevangelium*, 2:535.

70. Catchpole, "The Fearful Silence of the Women at the Tomb," 7–8.

71. Topel, "What Were the Women Afraid Of?" 90.

their history."[72] The fear that silences them is not apprehension over some imagined consequences from speaking the news of Jesus' resurrection. It is numinous awe in response to this dumbfounding miracle. The description of their fear combined with their "alarm," "trembling," and "bewilderment" all serve to accentuate the overpowering mystery of this news of the resurrection.[73]

Marcus fruitfully compares the ending of Mark to Gen 18:15. In this passage, three men (angels) pass by Abraham's tent by the oaks of Mamre, and he implores them to accept his offer of hospitality (18:1–9). One of the men promises that Abraham's wife Sarah will bear a son within a year (18:10). The aged Sarah, past menopause (18:11), was listening at the tent flap and indiscreetly laughs to herself in disbelief (18:12). When the Lord, through the angel, asks Abraham why Sarah laughed and expressed doubt (18:13), she denies that she had laughed. The narrator explains "for she was afraid" (18:15; the same Greek construction in the LXX as in Mark 16:8). Marcus connects this passage from Genesis to the ending of Mark since both passages report "a divine promise of life springing out of deadness, a promise that human incredulity, which is linked with fear, finds impossible to accept."[74] I would argue that Sarah's fear is not simply incredulity but also bewilderment, disorientation, and wonder at this news. Could it be so? If it is so, then it is true: nothing is "too hard for the LORD" (18:14). In my opinion, the women's trembling, astonishment, and fear when they receive the news of Jesus' resurrection from the heavenly messenger is similar. They are lost in wonder, not crippled by fright.

Paul makes an interesting connection between the birth of Abraham's son and the resurrection. The resurrection and the salvation that it brings are like God bringing forth a child from Sarah's barren and dead womb and from a man who "was as good as dead" (Rom 4:18–21). God raises Jesus from the realm of the dead (Rom 4:24). Against all reason and all hope, faith trusts in the promise of God and God's power to bring that promise to fulfillment. When it is accomplished, however, despite one's faith, it can leave one dazed and awestruck.

14.3.2.2 The Women's Limited Silence

This analysis of the women's fear influences how one interprets the statement that the women "said nothing to anyone, because they were afraid." Their fear is the normal response to divine revelation that cannot yet be fully understood.[75] As a consequence, I would argue that Mark understood the women's silence to be limited.[76] Hurtado interprets the phrase that they said nothing to anyone to mean that

72. Ibid.

73. It is completely unwarranted to argue that the disciples "never received the angel's message, thus never met the resurrected Lord, and, consequently never were commissioned," as Weeden, *Mark: Traditions in Conflict*, 50, does.

74. Marcus, *Mark 8–16*, 1082.

75. Pesch, *Markusevangelium*, 2:536. Horst Balz, "φοβέω . . . ," *TDNT*, 9:206, 208–12, discusses the theme of "epiphany fear" that results from "visionary revelations of God, His messengers, or other heavenly phenomena" in the Pseudepigrapha and in the NT. The women's fear can best be described as "epiphany fear."

76. I have changed my mind since writing my commentary on Mark. Many assumed that Jesus' death and resurrection is wreathed in human failure. At Gethsemane, the disciples "fled" in cowardice; at the tomb, the women "fled" in fear. In this reading of the text, it is not clear what the women were afraid of, and it is open to all manner of speculation.

they did not speak to the general public. It does not mean that they did not carry out the angel's command to tell the disciples the news.[77] For example, Jesus ordered the leper whom he cleansed not to tell anyone, but to go and show himself to the priests and offer the applicable sacrifices commanded by Moses as a testimony to them (1:44). Catchpole interprets this command as a "generalised instruction to keep silence." It "does not prevent disclosure to a specified individual. It simply relates to the broad mass of persons, the public at large."[78] The wording in the command to the leper parallels the wording in 16:8, and one may assume that the meaning is comparable.

> 1:44–45 "See that you don't tell this to anyone. But go, show yourself to the priest. . . ." Instead he went out and began to talk freely, spreading the news.
> 16:7–8 "But go, tell his disciples and Peter. . . ." They said nothing to anyone.

Unlike the leper who disobeyed and spread the news of his cleansing far and wide, the women did not broadcast the resurrection indiscriminately throughout Jerusalem, let alone go to the priests who orchestrated Jesus' death as a testimony to them. They delivered the message only to the disciples and to Peter as they were commanded.

This interpretation is supported by the grammar. Mark does not use "but" ("*but* they said nothing to anyone"),[79] which would express disobedience. Instead, he uses "and" ("*and* [*kai*] they said nothing to anyone"), which explains what they did not do.[80] This statement simply means that they did not shout the news from the rooftops but relayed it only to the persons the heavenly messenger specified.

Their silence makes theological sense. As Minear puts it incisively, "God does not disclose the Resurrection fact except to enlist people in a task."[81] The disciples are the ones Jesus enlisted in the task of proclaiming the news to the world at large. Focant classifies this explanation of the women's silence as "historico-psychological" and claims it is "unverifiable."[82] This reading, however, is indeed verified by the fuller accounts in Matthew and Luke that report that the women do inform the disciples about the resurrection and the empty tomb (Matt 28:8–11a; Luke 24:9–11; see John 20:18). They do not fail to carry out their commission; Mark simply does not, for whatever reason, narrate it.

Hurtado declares that Mark did not adopt a "sophisticated literary/rhetorical device intended to intrigue, disappoint, frustrate and 'trap' the intended Christian readers drawing them through a sophisticated process into some sort of existential completion of the story, thus compensating for the failures of the disciples in general

77. Hurtado, "The Women, the Tomb, and the Climax of Mark," 439.

78. Catchpole, "The Fearful Silence of the Women at the Tomb," 6.

79. The "but" (*alla*) occurs in 16:7 in the command "but go."

80. Hurtado, "The Women, the Tomb, and the Climax of Mark," 438–40.

81. Minear, *Mark*, 134. This insight is confirmed by Peter's sermon to the household of Cornelius: "We are witnesses of everything he did in the country of the Jews and in Jerusalem. They killed him by hanging him on a cross, but God raised him from the dead on the third day and caused him to be seen. He was not seen by all the people, but by witnesses whom God had already chosen—by us who ate and drank with him after he rose from the dead. He commanded us to preach to the people and to testify that he is the one whom God appointed as judge of the living and the dead" (Acts 10:39–42).

82. Focant, *Mark*, 664.

and the women of 16:1–8 in particular."[83] Instead, ancient practice supports the view that Mark adopted "the rather simpler technique of omitting further events/developments beyond those recounted, and *which the author expected readers to know and be fully able to supply*."[84] Mark's ending conforms to the tradition that Paul reminds the Corinthians that he passed on to them "as of first importance."[85]

1 Corinthians 15:3–6	Mark 16:6–7
Christ died for our sins (v. 3)	You are looking for Jesus the Nazarene, who was crucified (v. 6)
He was buried (v. 4)	See the place where they laid him (v. 6)
He was raised on the third day (v. 4)	He has risen! He is not here (v. 6)
He appeared to Cephas, and then to the Twelve (v. 5)	Tell his disciples and Peter, "He is going ahead of you into Galilee. There you will see him, just as he told you." (v. 7)

As the gospel begins with a prophecy that "he will baptize you with the Holy Spirit" (1:8), which from the audience's standpoint has been fulfilled, but its fulfillment is not narrated, so it ends with a prophecy, "He is going ahead of you into Galilee. There you will see him, just as he told you" (16:7). The audience knows that it has been fulfilled, but its fulfillment is not narrated by Mark. The assumption that the women did not obey the angel's command is therefore mistaken, and it has led to the many proposals that try to resolve the problem and explain Mark's intent.[86] I would agree with Lane's assessment that Mark chooses to end his gospel "by sounding the note by which he has characterized all aspects of Jesus' activity, his healings, miracles, teaching, the journey to Jerusalem. Astonishment and fear qualify the events of the life of Jesus." What happened in the resurrection "is an event beyond human comprehension and therefore awesome and frightening."[87]

83. Hurtado, "The Women, the Tomb, and the Climax of Mark," 437. Kermode, *The Genesis of Secrecy*, 68, a secular literary critic, opined that Mark's conclusion "is either intolerably clumsy; or it is incredibly subtle." Moloney, *Mark*, 350–51, among many modern interpreters, assumes the latter and claims, "Mark 16:1–8 is the masterstroke of a storyteller, who, up to this point, has relentlessly pursued the steady movement toward failure of all the male disciples." The evangelist subverted the tradition about the women reporting the Easter message to the disciples as found in Matthew, Luke, and John. By doing so, "he takes away all initiative from human beings and places it with God."

84. Hurtado, "The Women, the Tomb, and the Climax of Mark," 437–38. He cites the work of Magness, *Sense and Absence*, and continues that he knows of no other "ancient work with an 'open' ending intended to communicate the deep ambiguity that is attributed to the author of Mark 16:1–8 by some modern scholars" (438).

85. Garland, *Mark*, 622.

86. Stein, *Mark*, 86–88, cites an array of explanations for the abrupt ending. Alan H. Cadwallader, "The Hermeneutical Potential of the Multiple Endings of Mark's Gospel," *Colloquium* 43 (2011): 142, 145, 146, claims that "Mark's Gospel authorises hermeneutical tellings of later generational experiences of the resurrection of Jesus" and that the other endings "are all 'authentic' in that they testify to the efforts of various communities of faith to live in canonical connection with the Gospel of Mark." He maintains that "freezing of one particular ending as the only acceptable end to Mark's Gospel" would essentially "defeat Mark's purpose in his 'abrupt ending' and deny the validity of the variety of experiences of resurrection life throughout the church's history, a variety that is not yet exhausted." Does this interpretation not turn the ending into a Rorschach inkblot test, which supposedly tells more about the reader than what happened? Nothing could be further from Mark's intent.

87. Lane, *Mark*, 591–92.

14.3.3 Going to Galilee

The command for the disciples to go to Galilee where they will see Jesus is unique to Mark. It underscores that the disciples are not to look for him in an empty tomb, to linger there, or to erect a commemorative cenotaph. The grave is simply a transit point. If they do not follow him into Galilee, they will not see him. As Jesus went before the disciples when they journeyed to Jerusalem (10:32), so he goes before them into Galilee. The way of death in Jerusalem opens the way for the good news of the resurrection to be experienced in Galilee.

Five of the twelve references to "Galilee" in Mark occur in chapter 1 (1:9, 14, 16, 28, 39), so Galilee is "associated with the beginning of Jesus' ministry."[88] Galilee takes on a symbolic, more than literal or geographic, role. Symbolically, Galilee is the place where it all began — the proclamation of the kingdom of God, the routing of the demons, the healing of the sick, the pronouncement of the forgiveness of sins, and the eating with sinners. It is also the place where the disciples were first called and sent out by Jesus to preach and to cast out demons. When they return to Galilee, they will see him with new eyes. The audience cannot literally return to Galilee, but they can return to the beginning of the narrative that commences in Galilee (1:14–15). They, too, will see Jesus again with fresh eyes.

I have interpreted 1:1, "the beginning of the good news about Jesus the Messiah, the Son of God," as the incipit of the gospel, which I believe makes sense of the narrative's seemingly inconclusive termination in 16:8 (see §2.2). The gospel ends with news of Jesus' resurrection, but that news is only the beginning of the sequel that will be launched when the disciples return to Galilee and follow Jesus anew. For the audience, to turn back to the beginning in Galilee, however, is like reading a detective story a second time; "vital clues now reveal their significance."[89] The disciples and the audience now have the keys — Jesus' crucifixion and resurrection — that enable them to understand the mystery and to think the things of God rather than human things (8:33). The gospel becomes an endless loop. It must be reread and reheard with "20/20 hindsight."[90] The ultimate ending to this gospel transpires when the Son of Man comes "in clouds with great power and glory" and sends his angels to "gather his elect from the four winds, from the ends of the earth to the ends of the heavens" (13:26–27).

We can summarize what this command to go to Galilee means in Mark's context and ours. Best comments that it means:

> There is no resting place in the joy and triumph of the resurrection; we have always to return to the beginning in Galilee and advance forward again to the cross. It is a continual pilgrimage, and the Christ whom we follow is both the crucified and the risen Christ. In that way the story is rounded off and we realise its unity.[91]

88. Marcus, *Mark 1–8*, 171.
89. Hooker, *Mark*, 195.
90. Elizabeth Struthers Malbon, "Echoes and Foreshadowings in Mark 4–8: Reading and Rereading," *JBL* 112 (1993): 229.
91. Best, *Story*, 133.

The invitation is therefore to begin again where Jesus first called the disciples, taught them, and sent them out.[92] Geddert aptly uses the metaphors of a journey and a relay race, "*'Galilee' is the starting point for the discipleship road.* It is where a renewed journey to Jerusalem, carrying Christ's cross, has its beginning. It is the start of the disciples' lap around the track. The baton has now been passed on to them." Jesus is not simply "a step ahead" of his failing disciples but "a journey ahead." "Now that he has completed the journey, they will be enabled to make it themselves."[93] And Mark intends, in my view, for the baton to be passed on to each generation of believers and readers of his gospel.

92. Hooker, *The Message of Mark*, 120.

93. Geddert, *Watchwords*, 167.

Bibliography

Abrahams, Israel. *Studies in Pharisaism and the Gospels.* Cambridge: Cambridge University Press, 1917.

Achtemeier, Paul J. "The Origin and Function of the Pre-Marcan Miracle Catenae." *Journal of Biblical Literature* 91 (1972): 198–221.

———. " 'And He Followed Him': Miracles and Discipleship in Mark 10:46–52." *Semeia* 11 (1978): 115–45.

———. "Mark as Interpreter of the Jesus Tradition." *Interpretation* 32 (1978): 339–52.

———. " 'He Taught Them Many Things': Reflections on Marcan Christology." *Catholic Biblical Quarterly* 42 (1980): 465–81.

———. *Mark.* Proclamation Commentaries. 2nd ed. Philadelphia: Fortress, 1986.

———. "Mark, Gospel of." Pp. 541–57 in *The Anchor Bible Dictionary.* Vol. 4. Edited by David Noel Freedman. New York: Doubleday, 1992.

Adams, Edward. "The Coming of the Son of Man in Mark's Gospel." *Tyndale Bulletin* 56 (2005): 39–61.

———. *The Stars Will Fall From Heaven: Cosmic Catastrophe in the New Testament and its World.* Library of New Testament Studies 347. London/New York: T&T Clark, 2007.

Ådna, Jostein. "The Attitude of Jesus to the Temple: A Critical Examination of How Jesus' Relationship to the Temple is Evaluated within Israeli Scholarship, with Particular Regard to the Jerusalem School." *Mishkan* 17–18 (1992–93): 65–80.

———. "Jesus' Symbolic Act in the Temple (Mark 11:15–17): The Replacement of the Sacrificial Cult by His Atoning Death." Pp. 461–75 in *Gemeinde ohne Tempel.* Wissenschaftliche Untersuchungen zum Neuen Testament 2/118. Edited by Beate Ego, Armin Lange, and Peter Pilhofer. Tübingen: Mohr Siebeck, 1999.

———. *Jesu Stellung zum Tempel: Die Tempelaktion und das Tempelwort als Ausdruck seiner messianischen Sendung.* Wissenschaftliche Untersuchungen zum Neuen Testament 2/119. Tübingen: Mohr Siebeck, 2000.

Ahearne-Kroll, Stephen P. *The Psalms of Lament in Mark's Passion: Jesus' Davidic Suffering.* Society for New Testament Studies Monograph Series 142. Cambridge: Cambridge University Press, 2007.

———. "The Scripturally Complex Presentation of Jesus in the Gospel of Mark." Pp. 45–67 in *Portraits of Jesus: Studies in Christology.* Wissenschaftliche Untersuchungen zum Neuen Testament 2/321. Edited by Susan E. Myers. Tübingen: Mohr Siebeck, 2012.

Aland, Kurt. "Bemerkungen zum Schluss des Markusevangeliums." Pp. 157–80 in *Neotestamentica et Semitica: Studies in Honour of Matthew Black.* Edited by E. Earle Ellis and Max Wilcox. Edinburgh: T&T Clark, 1969.

———. "Der Schluss des Markusevangeliums." Pp. 435–70, 573–75 in *L'évangile selon Marc: tradition et rédaction.* 2nd ed. Bibliotheca ephemeridum theologicarum lovaniensium 34. Edited by M. Sabbe. Leuven: Leuven University Press, 1988.

Aland, Kurt, and Barbara Aland. *The Text of the New Testament.* 2nd ed. Translated by Erroll F. Rhodes. Grand Rapids: Eerdmans, 1989.

Albright, William F. "A Catalogue of Early Hebrew Lyric Poems (Psalm LXVIII)." *Hebrew Union College Annual* 23 (1950): 1–39.

Aletti, Jean-Noël. "Analyse narrative de Mc 7,24–30: difficultés et propositions." *Biblica* 93 (2012): 357–76.

Alexander, Loveday. *The Preface to Luke's Gospel.* Society for New Testament Studies Monograph Series 78. Cambridge: Cambridge University Press, 1993.

Allen, W. C. *The Gospel according to St. Mark.* Oxford Church Bible Commentary. New York: Macmillan, 1915.

Allison, Dale C., Jr. "The Baptism of Jesus and a New Dead Sea Scroll." *Biblical Archaeology Review* 18 no. 2 (March-April 1992): 58–60.

Alonso, Pablo. *The Woman Who Changed Jesus: Crossing Boundaries in Mk 7,24–30.* Biblical Tools and Studies 11. Leuven: Peeters, 2011.

Ambrozic, Aloysius M. *The Hidden Kingdom: A Redaction-Critical Study of the References to the Kingdom of God in Mark's Gospel.* Catholic Biblical Quarterly Monograph Series 2. Washington, DC: Catholic Biblical Association of America, 1972.

———. "New Teaching with Power (Mk 1:27)." Pp. 113–49 in *Word and Spirit: Essays in Honor of David M. Stanley, S.J. on His 60th Birthday.* Edited by Joseph Plevnik. Willowdale, ON: Regis College, 1975.

———. "Jesus as the Ultimate Reality in St. Mark's Gospel." *Ultimate Reality and Meaning* 12 (1989): 169–76.

Anderson, Hugh. *The Gospel of Mark.* New Century Bible. London: Oliphants, 1976.

Annen, Franz. *Heil für die Heiden: Zur Bedeutung und Geschichte der Tradition von besessenen Gerasener (Mk 5,1–20 parr).* Frankfurter Theologische Studien 20. Frankfurt am Main: Joseph Knecht, 1976.

Arnold, Gerhard. "Mk 1:1 und Eröffnungswendungen in griechischen und lateinischen Schriften." *Zeitschrift für die neutestamentliche Wissenschaft* 68 (1977): 123–27.

Auerbach, Erich. *Mimesis: The Representation of Reality in Western Literature.* Translated by Willard R. Trask. Princeton: Princeton University Press, 1953.

Aune, David E. "The Problem of the Messianic Secret." *Novum Testamentum* 11 (1969): 1–31.

———. *The New Testament in Its Literary Environment.* Library of Early Christianity 8. Philadelphia: Westminster, 1987.

———. *The Westminster Dictionary of the New Testament and Early Christian Literature.* Louisville: Westminster John Knox, 2003.

———. "Genre Theory and the Genre-Function of Mark and Matthew." Pp. 145–75 in *Mark and Matthew I: Comparative Readings: Understanding the Earliest Gospels in Their First-Century Settings.* Wissenschaftliche Untersuchungen zum Neuen Testament 2/271. Edited by Eve-Marie Becker and Anders Runesson. Tübingen: Mohr Siebeck, 2011.

Aus, Roger David. *The Wicked Tenants and Gethsemane: Isaiah in the Wicked Tenants' Vineyard, and Moses and the High Priest in Gethsemane: Judaic Traditions in Mark 12:1–9 and 14:32–42.* University of South Florida International Studies in Formative Christianity and Judaism 4. Atlanta: Scholars Press, 1996.

Avigad, Nahman. "A Depository of Inscribed Ossuaries in the Kidron Valley." *Israel Exploration Journal* 12 (1962): 1–12.

Back, Sven-Olaf. *Jesus of Nazareth and the Sabbath Commandment.* Åbo: Åbo Akademi University Press, 1995.

Backhaus, Knut. "'Lösepreis für viele' (Mark 10,45): Zur Heilsbedeutung des Todes Jesu bei Markus." Pp. 91–118 in *Der Evangelist als Theologe: Studien zum Markusevangelium.* Stuttgarter Bibelstudien 163. Edited by Thomas Söding. Stuttgart: Katholisches Bibelwerk, 1995.

Bacon, Benjamin W. "The Prologue of Mark: A Study of Sources and Structure." *Journal of Biblical Literature* 26 (1907): 84–106.

———. *Is Mark a Roman Gospel?* Harvard Theological Studies 7. Cambridge, MA: Harvard University Press, 1919.

Balabanski, Vicky. *Eschatology in the Making: Mark, Matthew and The Didache*. Society for New Testament Studies Monograph Series 97. Cambridge: Cambridge University Press, 1997.

Balz, Horst. "φοβέω." Pp. 205–19 in *Theological Dictionary of the New Testament*. Vol. 9. Edited by Gerhard Friedrich. Translated by Geoffrey W. Bromiley. Grand Rapids: Eerdmans, 1974.

Barber, Raymond C. "Mark as Narrative: A Case for Chapter One." GTU dissertation. Berkeley, CA: Graduate Theological Union, 1987.

Barker, Ernest. *From Alexander to Constantine: Passages and Documents Illustrating the History of the Social and Political Ideas 336 B.C.–A.D. 337*. Oxford: Clarendon, 1956.

Barker, Margaret. "Beyond the Veil of the Temple: The High Priestly Origins of the Apocalypses." *Scottish Journal of Theology* 51 (1998): 1–21.

Barr, James. "*'Abbā* Isn't 'Daddy.'" *Journal of Theological Studies* 39 (1988): 28–47.

Barrett, Anthony A. *Caligula: The Corruption of Power*. New Haven, CT/London: Yale University Press, 1989.

Barrett, Charles K. *Holy Spirit and the Gospel Tradition*. London: SPCK, 1966.

Barth, Karl. *Church Dogmatics*. Edinburgh: T&T Clark, 1961.

Bartlet, J. Vernon. *St Mark*. The Century Bible. Rev. ed. Edinburgh: T. C. & E. C. Jack, 1922.

———. "Papias's 'Exposition': Its Date and Contents." Pp. 15–44 in *Amicitiae Corolla: A Volume of Essays Presented to James Rendel Harris, D.Litt. on the Occasion of His Eightieth Birthday*. Edited by H. G. Wood. London: University of London Press, 1933.

Bartlet, Stephen C. *Discipleship and Family Ties in Mark and Matthew*. Society for New Testament Studies Monograph Series 80. Cambridge: Cambridge University Press, 2005.

Bateman, Herbert W. IV. "Defining the Titles 'Christ' and 'Son of God' in Mark's Narrative Presentation of Jesus." *Journal of the Evangelical Theological Society* 50 (2007): 537–59.

Batto, Bernard F. "The Sleeping God: An Ancient Near Eastern Motif of Divine Sovereignty." *Biblica* 68 (1987): 153–77.

Bauckham, Richard. *Jude, 2 Peter*. Word Biblical Commentary 50. Waco, TX: Word, 1983.

———. "The Son of Man: 'A Man in My Position' or 'Someone.'" *Journal for the Study of the New Testament* 23 (1985): 23–33.

———. "Jesus' Demonstration in the Temple." Pp. 72–89 in *Law and Religion: Essays on the Place of the Law in Israel and Early Christianity*. Edited by Barnabas Lindars. Cambridge: James Clarke, 1988.

———. "The Brothers and Sisters of Jesus: An Epiphanian Response to John P. Meier." *Catholic Biblical Quarterly* 56 (1994): 686–700.

———. "Jesus and the Wild Animals (Mark 1:13): A Christological Image for an Ecological Age." Pp. 3–21 in *Jesus of Nazareth: Lord and Christ: Essays on the Historical Jesus and New Testament Christology*. Edited by Joel B. Green and Max Turner. Grand Rapids/Carlisle/Paternoster: Eerdmans, 1994.

———. "For Whom Were Gospels Written?" Pp. 9–48 in *The Gospels for All Christians: Rethinking the Gospel Audiences*. Edited by Richard Bauckham. Grand Rapids: Eerdmans, 1998.

———. *Jesus and the Eyewitnesses.* Grand Rapids: Eerdmans, 2006.

———. "The Gospel of Mark: Origins and Eyewitness." Pp. 145–69 in *Earliest Christian History: History, Literature, and Theology: Essays from the Tyndale Fellowship in Honor of Martin Hengel.* Wissenschaftliche Untersuchungen zum Neuen Testament 2/320. Edited by Michael F. Bird and Jason Maston. Tübingen: Mohr Siebeck, 2012.

Bauer, Walter. *Orthodoxy and Heresy in Earliest Christianity.* Edited by Robert Kraft and Gerhard Krodel. Philadelphia: Fortress, 1971.

Bauernfeind, Otto. *Die Wörte der Dämonen im Markusevangelium.* Beiträge zur Wissenschaft vom Alten und Neuen Testament 3.9. Stuttgart: Kohlhammer, 1927.

Baumgarten, Joseph M. "The 4Q Zadokite Fragments on Skin Disease." *Journal of Jewish Studies* 41 (1990): 153–65.

Bayer, Hans F. *Jesus' Predictions of Vindication and Resurrection.* Wissenschaftliche Untersuchungen zum Neuen Testament 2/20. Tübingen: Mohr Siebeck, 1986.

———. *A Theology of Mark: The Dynamic between Christology and Authentic Discipleship.* Explorations in Biblical Theology. Phillipsburg, NJ: Presbyterian & Reformed, 2012.

Beale, G. K. *A New Testament Biblical Theology: The Unfolding of the Old Testament in the New.* Grand Rapids: Baker Academic, 2011.

Beasley-Murray, George R. "The Eschatological Discourses of Jesus." *Review & Expositor* 57 (1960): 153–66.

———. *Jesus and the Kingdom of God.* Grand Rapids: Eerdmans, 1986.

———. *Jesus and the Last Days: The Interpretation of the Olivet Discourse.* Peabody, MA: Hendrickson, 1993.

Beavis, Mary Ann. *Mark's Audience: The Literary and Social Setting of Mark 4.11–12.* Journal for the Study of the New Testament Supplement Series 33. Sheffield: Sheffield Academic Press, 1989.

———. *Mark.* Paideia Commentaries on the New Testament. Grand Rapids: Baker Academic, 2011.

Becker, Eve-Marie. *Das Markus-Evangelium im Rahmen antiker Historiographie.* Wissenschaftliche Untersuchungen zum Neuen Testament 2/194. Tübingen: Mohr Siebeck, 2006.

———. "The Gospel of Mark in the Context of Ancient Historiography." Pp. 124–34 in *The Function of Ancient Historiography in Biblical and Cognate Studies.* Edited by Patricia G. Kirkpatrick and Timothy D. Goltz. London/New York: T&T Clark, 2008.

———. "Mk. 1:1 and the Debate on a 'Markan Prologue.'" *Filologia Neotestamentaria* 22 (2009): 91–106.

Becker, Jürgen. *Das Heil Gottes: Heils- und Sündenbegriffe in den Qumrantexten und im Neuen Testament.* Studien zur Umwelt des Neuen Testaments 3. Göttingen: Vandenhoeck & Ruprecht, 1964.

Bedenbender, Andreas. "Der Epilog des Markusevangeliums-Revisited." *Texte & Kontexte* 81/82 (1999): 28–64.

———. "Das 'Messiasgeheimnis' im Markusevangelium." *Texte und Kontexte* 27 (2004): 1–96.

Begasse de Dhaem, Amaury. "Sur les pas du fils de l'homme: la christologie selon saint Marc." *La nouvelle revue théologique* 133 (2011): 5–27.

Bendemann, Reinhard von. "Christus der Arzt: Krankheitskonzepte in den Therapieerzählungen des Markusevangeliums (Teil II)." *Biblische Zeitschrift* 54 (2010): 162–78.

Bengtson, Hermann. "Syrien in der hellenistischen Zeit." *Der Hellenismus und der Aufstieg Roms: Die Mittelmeerwelt im Altertum II: Bd. II.* Edited by Pierre Grimal. Frankfurt: Fischer Taschenbuch Verlag, 1965.

Bennett, Wilbert J. Jr. " 'The Son of Man Must . . . .' " *Novum Testamentum* 17 (1975): 113–29.

Benoit, Pierre. *Jesus and the Gospel: Volume 1.* Translated by Benet Weatherhead. New York: Seabury, 1973.

Berger, Klaus. "Die königlichen Messiastraditionen des Neuen Testaments." *New Testament Studies* 20 (1973): 1–44.

Best, Ernest. "Discipleship in Mark 8.22–10.52." *Scottish Journal of Theology* 23 (1970): 323–37.

———. "The Role of the Disciples in Mark." *New Testament Studies* 23 (1976–77): 377–401.

———. *Following Jesus: Discipleship in the Gospel of Mark.* Journal for the Study of the New Testament Supplement Series 4. Sheffield: JSOT, 1981.

———. *Mark: The Gospel as Story: Studies of the New Testament and Its World.* Edinburgh: T&T Clark, 1983.

———. *Disciples and Discipleship: Studies in the Gospel according to Mark.* Edinburgh: T&T Clark, 1986.

———. "The Gospel of Mark: Who Was the Reader?" *Irish Biblical Studies* 11 (1989): 124–32.

———. *The Temptation and the Passion: The Markan Soteriology.* Society For New Testament Studies Monograph Series 2. 2nd ed. Cambridge: Cambridge University Press, 1990.

———. "Mark's Readers: A Profile." Pp. 839–58 in *The Four Gospels 1992: Festschrift Frans Neirynck.* Volume 2. Bibliotheca ephemeridum theologicarum lovaniensium 100. Edited by Frans van Segbroeck, Christopher M. Tuckett, Gilbert van Belle, and Joseph Verheyden. Leuven: Leuven University Press, 1992.

———. "Mark's Preservation of the Tradition." Pp. 153–68 in *The Interpretation of Mark.* 2nd ed. Edited by William R. Telford. Edinburgh: T&T Clark, 1995.

Betsworth, Sharon. *The Reign of God Is Such as These: A Socio-Literary Analysis of Daughters in the Gospel of Mark.* Library of New Testament Studies 422. London/New York: T&T Clark, 2010.

Betz, Hans Dieter. "Jesus and the Cynics: Survey and Analysis of a Hypothesis." *Journal of Religion* 74 (1994): 453–75.

———. "Jesus and the Purity of the Temple (Mark 11:15–18): A Comparative Religion Approach." *Journal of Biblical Literature* 116 (1997): 455–72.

Betz, Otto. "The Concept of the So-Called 'Divine Man' in Mark's Christology." Pp. 229–40 in *Studies in New Testament and Early Christian Literature: Essays in Honor of Allen Wikgren.* Edited by David E. Aune. Leiden: Brill, 1972.

Betz, Otto, and Rainer Riesner. *Jesus, Qumran and the Vatican: Clarifications.* New York: Crossroad, 1993.

Bickerman, Elias J. "The Warning Inscriptions of Herod's Temple." *Jewish Quarterly Review* 37 (1946–47): 387–405.

Bilezikian, Gilbert G. *The Liberated Gospel: A Comparison of the Gospel of Mark and Greek Tragedy.* Baker Biblical Monograph. Grand Rapids: Baker, 1977.

Bird, C. H. "Some γάρ Clauses in St. Mark's Gospel." *Journal of Theological Studies* 4 (1953): 171–87.

Bird, Michael F. "The Formation of the Gospels in the Setting of Early Christianity: The

Jesus Tradition as Corporate Memory." *Westminster Theological Journal* 67 (2005): 113–34.

———. "'Jesus Is the Christ': Messianic Apologetics in the Gospel of Mark." *Reformed Theological Review* 64 (2005): 1–14.

———. "The Markan Community, Myth or Maze? Bauckham's *The Gospel for All Christians* Revisited." *Journal of Theological Studies* 57 (2006): 474–86.

———. "Mark: Interpreter of Peter and Disciple of Paul." Pp. 30–61 in *Paul and the Gospels: Christologies, Conflicts, and Convergences.* Library of New Testament Studies 411. Edited by Michael F. Bird and Joel Willitts. London/New York: T&T Clark, 2011.

———. *Jesus Is the Christ: The Messianic Testimony of the Gospels.* Downers Grove, IL: Intervarsity Press, 2012.

Birdsall, N. "Review of *The Last Twelve Verses of Mark* by William R. Farmer." *Journal of Theological Studies* 26 (1975): 151–60.

Black, C. Clifton. "The Quest of Mark the Redactor: Why Has It Been Pursued, and What Has It Taught Us?" *Journal for the Study of the New Testament* 33 (1988): 19–39.

———. *The Disciples according to Mark: Markan Redaction in Current Debate.* Journal for the Study of the New Testament Supplement Series 27. Sheffield: JSOT, 1989.

———. "Was Mark a Roman Gospel?" *Expository Times* 105 (1993): 36–40.

———. *Mark: Images of an Apostolic Interpreter.* Columbia: University of South Carolina Press, 1994.

———. "Christ Crucified in Paul and in Mark: Reflections on an Intracanonical Conversation." Pp. 184–206 in *Theology and Ethics in Paul and His Interpreters: Essays in Honor of Victor Paul Furnish.* Edited by Eugene H. Lovering Jr. and Jerry L. Sumney. Nashville: Abingdon, 1996.

Black, David Allen, ed. *Perspectives on the Endings of Mark: 4 Views.* Nashville: Broadman & Holman, 2008.

Black, Matthew. "The Cup Metaphor in Mark xiv. 36." *Expository Times* 59 (1947–48): 195.

Blackburn, Barry. *Theios Anēr and the Markan Miracle Traditions.* Wissenschaftliche Untersuchungen zum Neuen Testament 2/40. Tübingen: Mohr Siebeck, 1991.

Blass, F. "On Mark xii.42 and xv.16." *Expository Times* 10 (1898): 185–87.

———. "On Mark xii.42." *Expository Times* 10 (1898): 286–87.

Blevins, James L. *The Messianic Secret in Markan Research 1901–1976.* Washington, DC: University Press of America, 1981.

Bligh, Philip H. "A Note on *Huios Theou* in Mark 15:39." *Expository Times* 80 (1968–69): 51–53.

Blomberg, Craig L. "The Miracles as Parables." Pp. 327–59 in *Gospel Perspectives.* Vol. 6: *The Miracles of Jesus.* Edited by David Wenham and Craig L. Blomberg. Sheffield: JSOT, 1986.

Blount, Brian K. "Is the Joke on Us? Mark's Irony, Mark's God, and Mark's Ending." Pp. 15–32 in *The End of Mark and the Ends of God: Essays in Memory of Donald Harrisville Juel.* Edited by Beverly Roberts Gaventa and Patrick D. Miller. Louisville: Westminster John Knox, 2005.

Bock, Darrell. *Blasphemy and Exaltation in Judaism and the Final Examination of Jesus: A Philological-Historical Study of the Key Jewish Themes Impacting Mark 14:61–64.* Wissenschaftliche Untersuchungen zum Neuen Testament 2/106. Tübingen: Mohr Siebeck, 1998.

———. *Recovering the Real Lost Gospel.* Nashville: Broadman & Holman, 2010.

Bockmuehl, Markus. *Simon Peter in Scripture and Memory*. Grand Rapids: Baker, 2012.

Bode, Edward L. *The First Easter Morning: The Gospel Accounts of the Women's Visit to the Tomb of Jesus*. Analecta biblica 45. Rome: Pontifical Biblical Institute, 1970.

Bolt, Peter G. "Mark 13: An Apocalyptic Precursor to the Passion Narrative." *Reformed Theological Review* 54 (1995): 10–32.

———. *Jesus' Defeat of Death: Persuading Mark's Early Readers*. Society for New Testament Studies Monograph Series 125. Cambridge: Cambridge University Press, 2003.

———. *The Cross from a Distance: Atonement in Mark's Gospel*. New Studies in Biblical Theology 18. Downers Grove, IL: InterVarsity Press, 2004.

Boobyer, G. H. *St. Mark and the Transfiguration Story*. Edinburgh: T&T Clark, 1942.

Boomershine, Thomas E., and Gilbert L. Bartholomew. "The Narrative Technique of Mark 16:8." *Journal of Biblical Literature* 100 (1981): 213–23.

Boring, M. Eugene. "The Christology of Mark: Hermeneutical Issues for Systematic Theology." *Semeia* 30 (1985): 125–53.

———. "Mark 1:1–15 and the Beginning of the Gospel." *Semeia* 52 (1990): 43–81.

———. *The Continuing Voice of Jesus: Christian Prophecy and the Gospel Tradition*. Louisville: Westminster John Knox, 1991.

———. "Markan Christology: God-Language for Jesus?" *New Testament Studies* 45 (1999): 451–71.

———. *Mark: A Commentary*. New Testament Library. Louisville: Westminster John Knox, 2006.

Borrell, Agustí. *The Good News of Peter's Denial: A Narrative and Rhetorical Reading of Mark 14:54.66–72*. International Studies in Formative Christianity and Judaism. Translated by Sean Conlon. Atlanta: Scholars Press, 1998.

Botha, Pieter J. J. "The Historical Setting of Mark's Gospel: Problems and Possibilities." *Journal for the Study of the New Testament* 51 (1993): 27–55.

Boucher, Madeleine I. *The Mysterious Parable: A Literary Study*. Catholic Biblical Quarterly Monograph Series 6. Washington, DC: Catholic Biblical Association of America, 1977.

Bouttier, Michel. "Commencement, force et fin de l'évangile." *Études théologiques et religieuses* 28 (1977): 465–93.

Bovon, François. *Luke 1*. Hermeneia. Translated by Christine M. Thomas. Minneapolis: Fortress, 2002.

Brady, David. "The Alarm to Peter in Mark's Gospel." *Journal for the Study of the New Testament* 4 (1979): 42–57.

Brandenburger, Egon. *Markus 13 und die Apokalyptik*. Forschungen zur Religion und Literatur des Alten und Neuen Testaments 134. Göttingen: Vandenhoeck & Ruprecht, 1984.

Brandon, S. G. F. "The Date of the Markan Gospel." *New Testament Studies* 7 (1960): 126–41.

Bratcher, Robert G. "A Note on *huios theou* (Mark xv. 39)." *Expository Times* 68 (1956–57): 27–28.

Breytenbach, Cilliers. *Nachfolge und Zukunftserwartung nach Markus: Eine methodenkritische Studie*. Abhandlungen zur Theologie des Alten und Neuen Testaments 71. Zürich: Theologischer Verlag, 1984.

———. "Current Research on the Gospel according to Mark: A Report on Monographs Published from 2000–2009." Pp. 13–32 in *Mark and Matthew I: Comparative Readings: Understanding the Earliest Gospels in Their First-Century Settings*. Wissenschaftliche

Untersuchungen zum Neuen Testament 2/271. Edited by Eve-Marie Becker and Anders Runesson. Tübingen: Mohr Siebeck, 2011.

Broadhead, Edwin K. "Christology as Polemic and Apologetic: The Priestly Portrait of Jesus in the Gospel of Mark." *Journal for the Study of the New Testament* 47 (1992): 21–34.

———. *Teaching with Authority: Miracles and Christology in the Gospel of Mark*. Journal for the Study of the New Testament Supplement Series 74. Sheffield: JSOT, 1992.

———. "Jesus the Nazarene: Narrative Strategy and Christological Imagery in the Gospel of Mark." *Journal for the Study of the New Testament* 52 (1993): 3–18.

———. *Prophet, Son, Messiah: Narrative Form and Function in Mark 14–16*. Journal for the Study for the New Testament Supplement Series 97. Sheffield: Sheffield Academic, 1994.

———. *Naming Jesus: Titular Christology in the Gospel of Mark*. Journal for the Study of the New Testament Supplement Series 175. Sheffield: Sheffield Academic, 1999.

———. "Reconfiguring Jesus: The Son of Man in Markan Perspective." Pp. 18–30 in *Biblical Interpretation in Early Christian Gospels*. Vol. 1: *The Gospel of Mark*. London/New York: T&T Clark, 2006.

Broadus, John A. *Commentary on the Gospel of Matthew*. Philadelphia: The American Baptist Publication Society, 1886.

Brooke, George J. "4Q500 1 and the Use of Scripture in the Parable of the Vineyard." *Dead Sea Discoveries* 2 (1995): 268–94.

Brower, Kent E. "Mark 9:1: Seeing the Kingdom in Power." *Journal for the Study of the New Testament* 6 (1980): 17–41.

———. " 'Who Then Is This?'—Christological Questions in Mark 4:35–5:43." *Evangelical Quarterly* 81 (2009): 291–305.

Brown, Colin. "The Jesus of Mark's Gospel." Pp. 26–53 in *Jesus Then and Now: Images of Jesus in History and Christology*. Edited by Marvin Meyer and Charles Hughes. Harrisburg, PA: Trinity Press International, 2001.

Brown, Raymond E. "The Burial of Jesus (Mark 15:42–47)." *Catholic Biblical Quarterly* 50 (1988): 233–45.

———. *The Death of the Messiah: From Gethsemane to the Grave: A Commentary on the Passion Narratives in the Four Gospels*. The Anchor Bible Reference Library. 2 vols. New York: Doubleday, 1994.

———. *An Introduction to New Testament Christology*. New York: Paulist, 1994.

———. *An Introduction to the New Testament*. New York: Doubleday, 1997.

Bruce, A. B. *The Parabolic Teaching of Christ*. London: Hodder & Stoughton, 1882.

Bruce, F. F. "The Date and Character of Mark." Pp. 69–89 in *Jesus and the Politics of His Day*. Edited by Ernst Bammel and C. F. D. Moule. Cambridge: Cambridge University Press, 1984.

Bryan, Christopher. *A Preface to Mark: Notes on the Gospel in its Literary and Cultural Settings*. New York/Oxford: Oxford University Press, 1993.

Buckwalter, H. Douglas. *The Character and Purpose of Luke's Christology*. Society for New Testament Studies Monograph Series 89. Cambridge: Cambridge University Press, 1996.

Bultmann, Rudolf. *Das Verhältnis der urchristlichen Christusbotschaft zum historischen Jesus*. Sitzungsberichte der heidelberger Akademie der Wissenschaften. Philosophisch-Historische Klasse 1960/3. Heidelberg: C. Winter, 1962.

———. *The History of the Synoptic Tradition*. Translated by John Marsh. New York: Harper & Row, 1963.

Burger, Christoph. *Jesus als Davidssohn: Eine traditionsgeschichtliche Untersuchung*. Forschungen zur Religion und Literatur des Alten und Neuen Testaments 98. Göttingen: Vandenhoeck & Ruprecht, 1970.

Burgon, J. W. *The Last Twelve Verses of the Gospel according to St. Mark: Vindicated against Recent Critical Objectors and Established*. London: John Murray, 1883.

Burke, Tony, ed. *Ancient Gospel or Modern Forgery? The Secret Gospel of Mark in Debate*. Eugene, OR: Cascade, 2013.

Burkett, Delbert R. "The Nontitular Son of Man: A History and Critique." *New Testament Studies* 40 (1994): 504–21.

———. *The Son of Man Debate: A History and Evaluation*. Society for New Testament Studies Monograph Series 107. Cambridge: Cambridge University Press, 1999.

———. *Rethinking the Gospel Sources: From Proto-Mark to Mark*. London/New York: T&T Clark, 2004.

Burkill, T. Alec. *Mysterious Revelation: An Examination of the Philosophy of St. Mark's Gospel*. Ithaca, NY: Cornell University Press, 1963.

Burkitt, F. Crawford. "Note on the Text and Interpretation of Mk. XIII 10." Pp. 145–47 in *Christian Beginnings*. London: University of London Press, 1924.

Burridge, Richard A. "The Gospels and Acts." Pages 507–33 in *Handbook of Classical Rhetoric in the Hellenistic Period, 330 B.C.–A.D. 400*. Edited by Stanley E. Porter. Leiden: Brill, 1997.

———. *What Are the Gospels? A Comparison with Graeco-Roman Biography*. 2nd ed. Grand Rapids: Eerdmans, 2004.

Byrskog, Samuel. *Story as History, History as Story*. Wissenschaftliche Untersuchungen zum Neuen Testament 123. Tübingen: Mohr Siebeck, 2000.

Cadbury, Henry J. "Mark 16:8." *Journal of Biblical Literature* 46 (1927): 344–45.

Cadwallader, Alan H. "The Hermeneutical Potential of the Multiple Endings of Mark's Gospel." *Colloquium* 43 (2011): 129–46.

Cahill, Michael, "Not a Cornerstone! Translating Ps 118,22 in the Jewish and Christian Scriptures." *Revue biblique* 106 (1999): 345–57.

Cahill, Michael, ed. and trans. *The First Commentary on Mark: An Annotated Translation*. New York: Oxford University Press, 1998.

Caird, George B. *New Testament Theology*. Edited by L. D. Hurst. Oxford: Clarendon, 1994.

Camery-Hoggatt, Jerry. *Irony in Mark's Gospel: Text and Subtext*. Society for New Testament Studies Monograph Series 72. Cambridge: Cambridge University Press, 1992.

Campbell, Constantine R. *Basics of Verbal Aspect in Biblical Greek*. Grand Rapids: Zondervan, 2000.

Campbell, Ken M. "What Was Jesus' Occupation?" *Journal of the Evangelical Theological Society* 48 (2005): 501–19.

Caneday, A. B. "Mark's Provocative Use of Scripture in Narration: 'He Was with the Wild Animals and Angels Ministered to Him.'" *Bulletin for Biblical Research* 9 (1999): 19–36.

Caragounis, C. C. "Kingdom of God/Kingdom of Heaven." Pp. 416–30 in *Dictionary of Jesus and the Gospels*. Edited by Joel B. Green, Scot McKnight, and I. Howard Marshall. Downers Grove, IL: InterVarsity Press, 1992.

Carey, Holly J. *Jesus' Cry from the Cross: Towards a First-Century Understanding of the Intertextual Relationship between Psalm 22 and the Narrative of Mark's Gospel*. Library of New Testament Studies 398. London/New York: T&T Clark, 2009.

Carlson, Stephen C. *The Gospel Hoax: Morton Smith's Invention of Secret Mark*. Waco, TX: Baylor University Press, 2005.

Carter, Warren. "Toward an Imperial-Critical Reading of Matthew's Gospel." *Society of Biblical Literature Seminar Papers* 37 (1998): 296–324.

Casey, Maurice. *Aramaic Sources of Mark's Gospel*. Society for New Testament Studies Monograph Series 102. Cambridge: Cambridge University Press, 1998.

———. *The Solution to the "Son of Man" Problem*. Library of New Testament Studies 343. London/New York: T&T Clark, 2007.

Catchpole, David. "The Fearful Silence of the Women at the Tomb: A Study in Markan Theology." *Journal of Theology for Southern Africa* 18 (1977): 3–10.

Chapman, David W. *Ancient Jewish and Christian Perceptions of Crucifixion*. Wissenschaftliche Untersuchungen zum Neuen Testament 2/244. Tübingen: Mohr Siebeck, 2008.

Chapman, Dean W. *The Orphan Gospel: Mark's Perspective on Jesus*. The Biblical Seminar 16. Sheffield: JSOT, 1993.

Chernow, Ron. *Alexander Hamilton*. New York: Penguin, 2004.

Childs, Brevard S. *The Book of Exodus: A Critical Theological Commentary*. The Old Testament Library. Philadelphia: Westminster, 1974.

Chilton, Bruce, ed. *The Kingdom of God in the Teaching of Jesus*. Philadelphia: Fortress, 1984.

Chilton, Bruce, et al., eds. *A Comparative Handbook to the Gospel of Mark: Comparisons with Pseudepigrapha, the Qumran Scrolls, and Rabbinic Literature*. Leiden: Brill, 2010.

Chronis, Harry L. "The Torn Veil: Cultus and Christology in Mark 15:37–39." *Journal of Biblical Literature* 101 (1982): 97–114.

———. "To Reveal and to Conceal: A Literary-Critical Perspective on 'the Son of Man' in Mark." *New Testament Studies* 51 (2005): 459–81.

Ciampa, Roy E., and Brian S. Rosner. *The First Letter to the Corinthians*. Pillar New Testament Commentary. Grand Rapids: Eerdmans, 2010.

Cohn, Haim H. *The Trial and Death of Jesus*. New York: Harper, 1971.

Colani, Timothée. *Jésus-Christ et les croyances messianiques de son temps*. 2nd ed. Strasbourg: Treuttel et Wurtz, 1864.

Collins, Adela Yarbro. *The Beginning of the Gospel: Probings of Mark in Context*. Minneapolis: Fortress, 1992.

———. "The Eschatological Discourse of Mark 13." Pp. 1125–40 in *The Four Gospels 1992: Festschrift Frans Neirynck*. Volume 2. Bibliotheca ephemeridum theologicarum lovaniensium 100. Ed. Frans van Segbroeck, Christopher M. Tuckett, Gilbert van Belle, and Joseph Verheyden. Leuven: Leuven University Press, 1992.

———. "Rulers, Divine Men, and Walking on the Water (Mark 6:45–52)." Pp. 207–27 in *Religious Propaganda and Missionary Competition in the New Testament World: Essays Honoring Dieter Georgi*. Novum Testamentum Supplements 74. Edited by Lukas Bormann, Kelly del Tredici, and Angela Standhartinger. Leiden: Brill, 1994.

———. "The Signification of Mark 10:45 among Gentile Christians." *Harvard Theological Review* 90 (1997): 371–82.

———. "Mark and His Readers: The Son of God among Greeks and Romans." *Harvard Theological Review* 93 (2000): 85–100.

———. "The Charge of Blasphemy in Mark 14:64." Pp. 149–70 in *The Trial and Death of Jesus: Essays on the Passion Narrative in Mark*. Contributions to Biblical Exegesis and Theology 45. Edited by Geert van Oyen and Tom Shepherd. Leuven: Peeters, 2006.

———. *Mark: A Commentary*. Hermeneia. Minneapolis: Fortress, 2007.

———. "Reflections on the Conference at the University of Aarhus, July 25–27, 2008." Pp. 411–14 in *Mark and Matthew I: Comparative Readings: Understanding the Earliest Gospels in Their First-Century Settings*. Wissenschaftliche Untersuchungen zum Neuen Testament 2/271. Edited by Eve-Marie Becker and Anders Runesson. Tübingen: Mohr Siebeck, 2011.

Collins, John J. *The Scepter and the Star: Messianism in Light of the Dead Sea Scrolls*. 2nd ed. Grand Rapids: Eerdmans, 2010.

Colwell, Ernest C. "A Definite Rule for the Use of the Article in the Greek New Testament." *Journal of Biblical Literature* 52 (1933): 12–21.

Combs, Jason Robert. "A Ghost on the Water? Understanding an Absurdity in Mark 6:49–50." *Journal of Biblical Literature* 127 (2008): 345–58.

Conybeare, F. C. "Aristion, the Author of the Last Twelve Verses of Mark." *The Expositor* Fourth Series 8 (1893): 241–54.

Conzelmann, Hans. *History of Primitive Christianity*. Translated by John E. Steely. Nashville: Abingdon, 1973.

Cook, John G. *The Structure and Persuasive Power of Mark: A Linguistic Approach*. Semeia Studies. Atlanta: Scholars Press, 1995.

———. *Roman Attitudes toward the Christians: From Claudius to Hadrian*. Wissenschaftliche Untersuchungen zum Neuen Testament 2/261. Tübingen: Mohr Siebeck, 2010.

Cotes, Mary. "Following Jesus with the Women in Mark." Pp. 79–97 in *Mark: Gospel of Action: Personal and Community Responses*. Edited by John Vincent. London: SPCK, 2006.

Cotter, Wendy. "The Markan Sea Miracles: Their History, Formation, and Function in the Literary Context of Greco-Roman Antiquity." PhD dissertation. Toronto: University of St. Michael's College, 1991.

Countryman, L. William "How Many Baskets Full?: Mark 8:14–21 and the Value of Miracles in Mark." *Catholic Biblical Quarterly* 47 (1985): 643–55.

Cox, Steven L. *A History and Critique of Scholarship concerning the Markan Endings*. Lewiston, NY/Queenston, ON: Mellen, 1993.

Craddock, Fred B. *The Gospels*. Nashville: Abingdon, 1981.

Craigie, W. A. "The Beginning of St. Mark's Gospel." *The Expositor* Eighth Series 24 (1922): 303–5.

Cranfield, C. E. B. "St. Mark 13." *Scottish Journal of Theology* 6 (1953): 189–96, 287–303.

———. "St. Mark 13." *Scottish Journal of Theology* 7 (1954): 284–303.

———. "The Baptism of Our Lord—A Study of St. Mark 1.9–11." *Scottish Journal of Theology* 8 (1955): 53–63.

———. *The Gospel according to St Mark*. Cambridge Greek Testament Commentary. Cambridge: Cambridge University Press, 1966.

———. *A Critical and Exegetical Commentary on the Epistle to the Romans*. International Critical Commentary. Edinburgh: T&T Clark, 1975.

Crossan, John Dominic. "Mark and the Relatives of Jesus." *Novum Testamentum* 15 (1973): 81–113.

———. "Empty Tomb and Absent Lord (Mark 16:1–8)." Pp. 135–52 in *The Passion in Mark: Studies on Mark 14–16*. Edited by Werner H. Kelber. Philadelphia: Fortress, 1976.

———. *The Historical Jesus*. San Francisco: Harper, 1991.

———. *Jesus: A Revolutionary Biography*. San Francisco: Harper, 1994.

Crossley, James G. *The Date of Mark's Gospel: Insight from the Law in Earliest Christianity*. Journal for the Study of the New Testament Supplement Series 266. London: T&T Clark, 2004.

Croy, N. Clayton. *The Mutilation of Mark's Gospel*. Nashville: Abingdon, 2003.

______. "Where the Gospel Text Begins: A Non-Theological Interpretation of Mark 1:1." *Novum Testamentum* 43 (2001): 105–27.

Cuvillier, Elian. *Le concept de ΠΑΡΑΒΟΛΗ dans le second évangile: son arrière-plan littéraire, sa signification dans la cadre de la rédaction marcienne, son utilisation dans la tradition de Jésus*. Paris: Gabalda, 1993.

D'Angelo, Mary Rose. "*Abba* and 'Father': Imperial Theology and the Jesus Traditions." *Journal of Biblical Literature* 111 (1992): 611–30.

Dahl, Nils Alstrup. "The Parables of Growth." Pp. 141–66 in *Jesus in the Memory of the Early Church*. Minneapolis: Augsburg, 1976.

———. "The Purpose of Mark's Gospel." Pp. 52–65 in *Jesus in the Memory of the Early Church*. Minneapolis: Augsburg, 1976.

———. "The Purpose of Mark's Gospel." Pp. 29–34 in *The Messianic Secret*. Edited by Christopher Tuckett. Philadelphia: Fortress, 1983.

Dalman, Gustaf. *Jesus—Jeshua: Studies in the Gospels*. Translated by Paul P. Levertoff. New York: Ktav, 1971.

Damm, Alex. *Ancient Rhetoric and the Synoptic Problem: Clarifying Markan Priority*. Bibliotheca ephemeridum theologicarum lovaniensium 252. Leuven: Peeters, 2013.

Danby, Herbert. *The Mishnah*. Oxford University Press, 1933.

Danker, Frederick W. "Menander and the New Testament." *New Testament Studies* 10 (1964): 365–68.

Danove, Paul L. *The End of Mark's Story: A Methodological Study*. Biblical Interpretation Series 3. Leiden: Brill, 1993.

———. *Linguistics and Exegesis in the Gospel of Mark: Applications of a Case Frame Analysis*. Journal for the Study of the New Testament Supplement Series 218: Sheffield: Sheffield Academic Press, 2001.

———. *The Rhetoric of the Characterization of God, Jesus, and Jesus' Disciples in the Gospel of Mark*. Journal for the Study of the New Testament Supplement Series 290. London: T&T Clark, 2005.

———. *Grammatical and Exegetical Study of New Testament Verbs of Transference: A Case Frame Guide to Interpretation and Translation*. Library of New Testament Studies 329. London: T&T Clark, 2009.

Daube, David. "The 'I AM' of the Messianic Presence." Pp. 325–29 in *The New Testament and Rabbinic Judaism*. London: Athlone, 1956.

———. *The New Testament and Rabbinic Judaism*. New York: Arno, 1973 [1956].

Dautzenberg, Gerhard. "Die Zeit des Evangeliums: Mk 1, 1–15 und die Konzeption des Markusevangeliums." *Biblische Zeitschrift* 21 (1977): 219–34.

Davidsen, Ole. *The Narrative Jesus: A Semiotic Reading of Mark's Gospel*. Aarhus: Aarhus University Press, 1993.

Davies, Meg. "Review of *What Are the Gospels?* by Richard A. Burridge." *New Blackfriars* 74 (1993): 109–10.

Davies, Rupert E. "Christ in Our Place—The Contribution of the Prepositions." *Tyndale Bulletin* 21 (1970): 71–91.

Davies, William D. *The Setting of the Sermon on the Mount*. Cambridge: Cambridge University Press, 1966.

———. *Paul and Rabbinic Judaism: Some Rabbinic Elements in Pauline Theology*. Rev. ed. New York: Harper & Row, 1967.

———. *Jewish and Pauline Studies*. Philadelphia: Fortress, 1984.

Davies, William D., and Dale Allison Jr. *The Gospel according to Saint Matthew*. Vol. 1. International Critical Commentary 26. Edinburgh: T&T Clark, 1988.

Davis, Philip G. "Mark's Christological Paradox." *Journal for the Study of the New Testament* 35 (1989): 3–18.

Davis, Steven T. "'Who Can Forgive Sins but God Alone?': Jesus, Forgiveness, and Divinity." Pp. 113–23 in *The Multivalence of Biblical Texts and Theological Meanings*. Society of Biblical Literature Symposium Series 37. Edited by Christine Helmer and Charlene T. Higbe. Atlanta: Society of Biblical Literature, 2006.

Dawsey, James M. *Peter's Last Sermon: Identity and Discipleship in the Gospel of Mark*. Macon, GA: Mercer University Press, 2010.

Dechow, Jens. *Gottessohn und Herrschaft Gottes: Der Thoezentrismus des Markusevangeliums*. Wissenschaftliche Monographien zum Alten und Neuen Testament 86. Neukirchen-Vluyn: Neukirchener Verlag, 2000.

Deissmann, Adolf. *Light from the Ancient East*. Translated by Lionel R. M. Strachan. Rev. ed. New York: Doran, 1927.

Denis, Albert-Marie. "Jesus' Walking on the Waters: A Contribution to the History of the Pericope in the Gospel Tradition." *Louvain Studies* 1 (1967): 284–97.

Denyer, Nicholas. "Mark 16:8 and Plato, *Protagoras* 328D." *Tyndale Bulletin* 57 (2006): 149–50.

Deppe, Dean P. "Charting the Future or a Perspective on the Present? The Paraenetic Purpose of Mark 13." *Calvin Theological Journal* 41 (2006): 89–101.

———. "Markan Christology and the Omission of υἱοῦ θεοῦ in Mark 1:1." *Filologia Neotestamentaria* 21 (2008): 45–64.

Derrett, J. Duncan M. *The Making of Mark: The Scriptural Bases of the Earliest Gospel*. Shipston-on-Stour: Drinkwater, 1985.

Dewey, Joanna. *Markan Public Debate: Literary Technique, Concentric Structure, and Theology in Mark 2:1–3:6*. Society of Biblical Literature Dissertation Series 48. Chico, CA: Scholars Press, 1980.

———. "Mark as Interwoven Tapestry: Forecasts and Echoes for a Listening Audience." *Catholic Biblical Quarterly* 53 (1991): 221–36.

———. "Mark as Aural Narrative: Structures as Clues to Understanding." *Sewanee Theological Review* 36 (1992): 45–56.

———. "The Survival of Mark's Gospel: A Good Story?" *Journal of Biblical Literature* 123 (2004): 495–507.

Dibelius, Martin. *From Tradition to Gospel*. Translated by Bertram Lee Woolf. New York: Scribner's, 1935.

Dillon, Richard J. "Mark 1:1–15: A 'New Evangelization'?" *Catholic Biblical Quarterly* 76 (2014): 1–18.

Dixon, Edward P. "Descending Spirit and Descending Gods: A 'Greek' Interpretation of the Spirit's 'Descent as a Dove' in Mark 1:10." *Journal of Biblical Literature* 128 (2009): 759–80.

Dodd, C. H. *History and the Gospel*. London: Nisbet, 1938.

———. *The Parables of the Kingdom*. Rev. ed. New York: Scribner's, 1961.

Donahue, John R. "Tax Collectors and Sinners: An Attempt at Identification." *Catholic Biblical Quarterly* 33 (1971): 39–61.

———. *Are You the Christ? The Trial Narrative in the Gospel of Mark*. Society of Biblical Literature Dissertation Series 10. Missoula, MT: Society of Biblical Literature, 1973.

———. "A Neglected Factor in the Theology of Mark." *Journal of Biblical Literature* 101 (1982): 563–94.

———. *The Theology and Setting of Discipleship in the Gospel of Mark*. Milwaukee: Marquette University Press, 1983.

———. "The Quest for the Community of Mark's Gospel." Pp. 817–38 in *The Four Gospels 1992: Festschrift Frans Neirynck*. Volume 2. Bibliotheca ephemeridum theologicarum lovaniensium 100. Edited by Frans van Segbroeck, Christopher M. Tuckett, Gilbert van Belle, and Joseph Verheyden. Leuven: Leuven University Press, 1992.

———. "Windows and Mirrors: The Setting of Mark's Gospel." *Catholic Biblical Quarterly* 57 (1995): 1–26.

Donahue, John R., and Daniel J. Harrington. *The Gospel of Mark*. Sacra pagina. Collegeville, MN: Liturgical Press, 2002.

Doole, J. Andrew. *What Was Mark for Matthew?: An Examination of Matthew's Relationship and Attitude to His Primary Source*. Wissenschaftliche Untersuchungen Zum Neuen Testament 2/344. Tübingen: Mohr Siebeck, 2013.

Dormeyer, Detlev. "Die Kompositionsmetapher 'Evangelium Jesu Christi, des Sohnes Gottes' Mk 1.1 Ihre theologische und literarische Aufgabe in der Jesus-Biographie des Markus." *New Testament Studies* 33 (1987): 452–68.

———. *Das Markus-Evangelium*. Darmstadt: Wissenschaftliche Buchgesellschaft, 2005.

Dormeyer, Detlev, and Hubert Frankemölle. "Evangelium als literarischer und als theologischer Begriff: Tendenzen und Aufgaben der Evangelienforschung im 20. Jahrhundert, mit einer Untersuchung des Markusevangeliums in seinem Verhältnis zur griechischen Biographie." Pp. 1541–1704 in *Aufstieg und Niedergang der Römischen Welt Vol. 1/2*. Edited by H. Temporini. Berlin/New York: de Gruyter, 1972.

Dowd, Sharon E. *Prayer, Power, and the Problem of Suffering: Mark 11:22–25 in the Context of Markan Theology*. Society of Biblical Literature Dissertation Series 105. Atlanta: Scholars, 1988.

Downing, F. Gerald. "Theophilus's First Reading of Luke-Acts." Pp. 91–109 in *Luke's Literary Achievement: Collected Essays*. Journal for the Study of the New Testament Supplement Series 116. Edited by Christopher M. Tuckett. Sheffield: Sheffield Academic Press, 1995.

———. "The Woman from Syrophoenicia and her Doggedness: Mark 7.24–31 (Matthew 15.21–28)." Pp. 102–21 in *Making Sense in (and of) the First Christian Century*. Journal for the Study of the New Testament Supplement Series 197. Edited by Frank G. Downing. Sheffield: Sheffield Academic Press, 2000.

Drury, John. *The Parables in the Gospels: History and Allegory*. New York: Crossroad, 1985.

Dschulnigg, Peter. *Sprache, Redaktion und Intention des Markus-Evangeliums: Eigentümlichkeiten der Sprache des Markus-Evangeliums und ihre Bedeutung für die Redaktionskritik*. Stuttgarter biblische Beitra¨ge 11. Stuttgart: Katholisches Bibelwerk, 1984.

———. "Grenzüberschreitungen im Markusevangelium: Auf dem Weg zu einer neuen Identität." *Münchener theologische Zeitschrift* 51 (2001): 113–20.

Duff, Paul Brooks. “The March of the Divine Warrior and the Advent of the Greco-Roman King: Mark’s Account of Jesus’ Entry into Jerusalem.” *Journal of Biblical Literature* 111 (1992): 55–71.

Dunn, James D. G. “The Messianic Secret in Mark.” Pp. 116–31 in *The Messianic Secret*. Edited by Christopher Tuckett. Minneapolis: Fortress, 1983.

———. *Jesus, Paul, and the Law: Studies in Mark and Galatians*. Louisville: Westminster John Knox, 1990.

———. *Colossians and Philemon*. The New International Greek Testament Commentary. Grand Rapids: Eerdmans, 1996.

———. “‘Are You The Messiah?’: Is the Crux of Mark 14.61–62 Resolvable?” Pp. 1–22 in *Christology, Controversy and Community: New Testament Essays in Honour of David R. Catchpole*. Novum Testamentum Supplements 99. Edited by David G. Horrell and Christopher M. Tuckett. Leiden/Boston/Köln: Brill, 2000.

Dwinnels, Steve. “The Function of [ΔΙΔΑΣΚΩ and ΚΗΡΥΣΣΩ] in the Gospel of Mark: A Rhetorical-Critical Study of a Markan Emphasis on Jesus’ Eschatological Ministry.” Ph.D. dissertation. Louisville: The Southern Baptist Theological Seminary, 2002.

Dwyer, Timothy. *The Motif of Wonder in the Gospel of Mark*. Journal for the Study of the New Testament Supplement Series 128. Sheffield: Sheffield Academic Press, 1996.

Dyer, Keith D. *The Prophecy on the Mount: Mark 13 and the Gathering of the New Community*. International Theological Studies 2. Bern: Lang, 1998.

Earl, Donald. “Prologue-form in Ancient Historiography.” Pp. 842–56 in *Aufstieg und Niedergang der Römischen Welt* 1/2. Edited by H. Temporini. Berlin/New York: Walter de Gruyter, 1972.

Ebeling, Hans Jürgen. *Das Messiasgeheimnis und die Botschaft des Marcus-Evangelisten*. Beihefte zur Zeitschrift für die neutestamentliche Wissenschaft 19. Berlin: Töpelmann, 1939.

Ebstein, Wilhelm. *Die Medizin im Neuen Testament und im Talmud*. Munich: Fritsch, 1903. Reprinted 1965.

Eck, Ernest van. *Galilee and Jerusalem in Mark’s Story of Jesus: A Narratological and Social-scientific Reading*. Hervormde Teologiese Studies Supplement Series 7. Pretoria: University of Pretoria, 1995.

Edersheim, Alfred. *Life and Times of Jesus the Messiah*. Vol. 1. London: Longmans & Green, 1883.

Edwards, J. Christopher. *The Ransom Logion in Mark and Matthew: Its Reception and Its Significance for the Study of the Gospels*. Wissenschaftliche Untersuchungen Zum Neuen Testament 2/327. Tübingen: Mohr Siebeck, 2012.

Edwards, James R. “Markan Sandwiches: The Significance of Interpolations in Markan Narratives.” *Novum Testamentum* 31 (1989): 193–216.

———. “The Baptism of Jesus according to the Gospel of Mark.” *Journal of the Evangelical Theological Society* 34 (1991): 43–57.

———. “The Authority of Jesus in the Gospel of Mark.” *Journal of the Evangelical Theological Society* 37 (1994): 217–233.

———. *The Gospel according to Mark*. Pillar New Testament Commentary. Grand Rapids: Eerdmans, 2002.

Ehrman, Bart D. “The Text of Mark in the Hands of the Orthodox.” *Lutheran Quarterly* 5 (1991): 143–56.

———. *The Orthodox Corruption of Scripture: The Effect of Early Christological Controversies on the Text of the New Testament*. Oxford: Oxford University Press, 1993.

———. *Misquoting Jesus.* San Francisco: HarperSanFrancisco, 2005.

Elliott, James K. "The Text and Language of the Endings to Mark's Gospel." *Theologische Zeitschrift* 27 (1971): 255–62.

———. "καθώς and ὥσπερ in the New Testament." *Filologia Neotestamentaria* 4 (1991): 55–58.

———. *The Language and Style of the Gospel of Mark: An Edition of C. H. Turner's "Notes on Marcan Usage" Together with Other Comparable Studies.* Novum Testamentum Supplements 71. Leiden: Brill, 1993.

———. "Mark 1.1–3–A Later Addition to the Gospel?" *New Testament Studies* 46 (2000): 584–88.

Ellis, E. Earle. "The Date and Purpose of Mark's Gospel." Pp. 810–15 in *The Four Gospels 1992: Festschrift Frans Neirynck.* Volume 2. Bibliotheca ephemeridum theologicarum lovaniensium 100. Edited by Frans van Segbroeck, Christopher M. Tuckett, Gilbert van Belle, and Joseph Verheyden. Leuven: Leuven University Press, 1992.

Enslin, Morton Scott. "ἐφοβοῦντο γάρ, Mark 16:8," *Journal of Biblical Literature* 46 (1927): 62–68.

Ernst, Josef. *Das Evangelium nach Markus.* Regensburger Neues Testament. Regensburg: Friedrich Pustet, 1981.

Esler, Philip F. "Community and Gospel in Early Christianity: A Response to Richard Bauckham's *Gospel for All Christians.*" *Scottish Journal of Theology* 51 (1998): 235–48.

———. *New Testament Theology: Communion and Community.* Minneapolis: Fortress, 2005.

Evans, Craig A. *To See and Not Perceive: Isaiah 6.9–10 in Early Jewish and Christian Interpretation.* Journal for the Study of the Old Testament: Supplement Series 64. Sheffield: JSOT, 1989.

———. "In What Sense 'Blasphemy'? Jesus before Caiaphas in Mark 14:61–64." Pp. 407–34 in *Jesus and His Contemporaries: Comparative Studies.* Arbeiten zur Geschichte des antiken Judentums und des Urchristentums 25. Leiden: Brill, 1995.

———. "Jesus and the 'Cave of Robbers': Towards a Jewish Context for the Temple Action." Pp. 345–65 in *Jesus and His Contemporaries: Comparative Studies.* Leiden/New York/Köln: Brill, 1995.

———. "Jesus and the Dead Sea Scrolls from Qumran Cave 4." Pp. 91–100 in *Eschatology, Messianism and the Dead Sea Scrolls.* Edited by C. A. Evans and P. W. Flint. Grand Rapids: Eerdmans, 1997.

———. "Jesus' Parable of the Tenant Farmers in Light of Lease Agreements in Antiquity." *Journal for the Study of the Pseudepigrapha* 14 (1996): 65–83.

———. "Mark's Incipit and the Priene Calendar Inscription: From Jewish Gospel to Greco-Roman Gospel." *Journal of Greco-Roman Christianity and Judaism* 1 (2000): 67–81.

———. *Mark 8:27–16:20.* Word Biblical Commentary 34b. Nashville: Nelson, 2001.

———. "How Mark Writes." Pp. 135–48 in *The Written Gospel.* Edited by Markus Bockmuehl and Donald A. Hagner. Cambridge: Cambridge University Press, 2005.

Evans, Trevor V. "Future Directions for Aspectual Studies in Ancient Greek." Pp. 199–206 in *Biblical Greek Language and Lexicography: Essays in Honor of Frederick W. Danker.* Edited by Bernard A. Taylor, John A. Lee, Peter R. Burton, and Richard E. Whitaker. Grand Rapids: Eerdmans, 2004.

Eve, Eric. *The Jewish Context of Jesus' Miracles.* Journal for the Study of the New Testament Supplement Series 231. London: Sheffield Academic, 2002.

Fanning, Buist M. *Verbal Aspect in the New Testament with Reference to Tense and Mood.* Studies in Biblical Greek 1. London/New York: Lang, 1989.

Farmer, William R. *The Last Twelve Verses of Mark.* Society for New Testament Studies Monograph Series 25. Cambridge: Cambridge University Press, 1974.

———. "Modern Developments of Griesbach's Hypothesis." *New Testament Studies* 23 (1977): 275–95.

Fascher, Erich. "Jesus und die Tiere." *Theologische Literaturzeitung* 90 (1965): 561–70.

Fay, Greg. "Introduction to Incomprehension: The Literary Structure of Mark 4:1–34." *Catholic Biblical Quarterly* 51 (1989): 65–81.

Fears, J. Rufus. "Rome: The Ideology of Imperial Power." *Thought* 55 (1980): 98–109.

Feldman, Louis. *Jew and Gentile in the Ancient World: Attitudes and Interactions from Alexander to Justinian.* Princeton: Princeton University Press, 1993.

Feldmeier, Reinhard. "The Portrayal of Peter in the Synoptic Gospels." Pp. 59–63 in *Studies in the Gospel of Mark.* Edited by Martin Hengel. London: SCM, 1985.

———. *Die Krisis des Gottessohnes: Die Gethesemaneerzählung als Schlüssel der Markuspassion.* Wissenschaftliche Untersuchungen zum Neuen Testament 2/21. Tübingen: Mohr Siebeck, 1987.

———. "Der Gekreuzigte im 'Gnadenstuhl.' Exegetische Überlegungen zu Mk 15,37–39 und deren Bedeutung für die Vorstellung der göttlichen Gegenwart und Herrschaft." Pp. 213–32 in *Le Trône de Dieu.* Wissenschaftliche Untersuchungen zum Neuen Testament 69. Edited by Marc Philonenko. Tübingen: Mohr Siebeck, 1993.

———. "Die Syrophönizierin (Mk 7, 24–30): Jesus 'verlorenes' Streitgespräch?" Pp. 211–27 in *Die Heiden: Juden, Christen und das Problem des Fremden.* Wissenschaftliche Untersuchungen zum Neuen Testament 1/70. Edited by Reinhard Feldmeier and Ulrich Heckel. Tübingen: Mohr Siebeck, 1994.

Feldmeier, Reinhard, and Hermann Spieckermann. *God of the Living: A Biblical Theology.* Translated by Mark E. Biddle. Waco, TX: Baylor University Press, 2011.

Fendler, Folkert. *Studien zum Markusevangeliums: Zur Gattung, Chronologie, Messiasgeheimnistheorie und Überlieferung des zweiten Evangeliums.* Göttinger theologischer Arbeiten 49. Göttingen: Vandenhoeck & Ruprecht, 1991.

Feneberg, Wolfgang. *Der Markusprolog: Studien zur Formbestimmung des Evangeliums.* Munich: Kösel, 1974.

Fernando, Ajith. *Acts.* NIV Application Commentary. Grand Rapids: Zondervan, 1998.

Fischer, Cédric. *Les disciples dans l'évangile de Marc: une grammaire théologique.* Études bibliques 57. Paris: Gabalda, 2007.

Fitzmyer, Joseph A. "The Gospel in the Theology of Paul." *Interpretation* 33 (1979): 339–50.

———. "*ʾAbba* and Jesus' Relation to God." Pp. 15–38 in *À cause de l'èvangile: études sur les Synoptiques et les Actes: offertes au P. Jacques Dupont, O.S.B. à l'occasion de son soixante-dixième anniversaire.* Vol. 1. Edited by F. Refoule. Lectio divina 123. Paris: Cerf, 1985.

Fleddermann, Harry. "The Flight of a Naked Young Man (Mark 14:51–52)." *Catholic Biblical Quarterly* 41 (1979): 412–18

———. "The Discipleship Discourse (Mark 9:33–50)." *Catholic Biblical Quarterly* 43 (1981): 57–75.

———. "A Warning about the Scribes (Mark 12:37b–40)." *Catholic Biblical Quarterly* 44 (1982): 52–67.

———. " 'And He Wanted to Pass by Them' (Mark 6:48c)." *Catholic Biblical Quarterly* 45 (1983): 389–95.

Flusser, David, and R. Steven Notley. *Jesus*. Jerusalem: Magnes, 1997.

Focant, Camille. "Un christologie de type 'mystique' (Marc 1.1–16.8)." *New Testament Studies* 55 (2009): 1–21.

———. *The Gospel according to Mark: A Commentary*. Translated by Leslie Robert Keylock. Eugene, OR: Pickwick, 2012.

Foerster, Werner. "θήριον." Pp. 133–35 in *Theological Dictionary of the New Testament*. Vol. 3. Edited by Gerhard Kittel. Translated by Geoffrey W. Bromiley. Grand Rapids: Eerdmans, 1966.

Foster, Paul, et al., eds. *New Studies in the Synoptic Problem: Oxford Conference, April 2008: Essays in Honour of Christopher M. Tuckett*. Bibliotheca ephemeridum theologicarum lovaniensium 239. Leuven: Peeters, 2011.

Fowler, Robert M. *Let the Reader Understand: Reader-Response Criticism and the Gospel of Mark*. Minneapolis: Fortress, 1991.

Frame, James Everett. *Epistles of Paul to the Thessalonians*. International Critical Commentary. Edinburgh: T&T Clark, 1912.

France, R. T. *Jesus and the Old Testament: His Application of Old Testament Passages to Himself and His Mission*. Downers Grove, IL: Intervarsity Press, 1971.

———. "Mark and the Teaching of Jesus." Pp. 101–36 in *Gospel Perspectives: Studies of History and Tradition in the Four Gospels*. Vol. 1. Edited by Richard T. France and David Wenham. Sheffield: JSOT, 1980.

———. "The Beginning of Mark." *Reformed Theological Review* 49 (1990): 11–19.

———. *Divine Government: God's Kingship in the Gospel of Mark*. London: SPCK, 1990.

———. *The Gospel of Mark*. The New International Greek Testament Commentary. Grand Rapids: Eerdmans, 2002.

Frankemölle, Hubert. "ἀντί." Pp. 108–9 in *Exegetical Dictionary of the New Testament*. Vol. 1. Edited by Horst Balz and Gerhard Schneider. Grand Rapids: Eerdmans, 1991.

Fredriksen, Paula. "Judaism, the Circumcision of Gentiles, and Apocalyptic Hope: Another Look at Galatians 1 and 2." *Journal of Theological Studies* 42 (1991): 532–64.

Freyne, Seán. *The Twelve: Disciples and Apostles: A Study in the Theology of the First Three Gospels*. London: Sheed & Ward, 1968.

Fuller, Reginald H. "The Son of Man Came to Serve, Not to Be Served." Pp. 45–72 in *Ministering in a Servant Church*. Edited by Francis A. Eigo. Philadelphia: Villanova University Press, 1978.

Funk, Robert W. "The Looking-Glass Tree Is for the Birds: Ezekiel 17:22–24; Mark 4:30–32." *Interpretation* 27 (1973): 3–9.

Furstenberg, Yair. "Defilement Penetrating the Body: A New Understanding of Contamination in Mark 7.15." *New Testament Studies* 54 (2008): 176–200.

Gamble, Harry Y. *The New Testament Canon: Its Making and Meaning*. Guides to Biblical Scholarship New Testament Series. Philadelphia: Fortress, 1985.

Gamel, Brian K. "Salvation in a Sentence: Mark 15:39 as Markan Soteriology." *Journal of Theological Interpretation* 6 (2012): 65–77.

———. "The Centurion's Confession as Apocalyptic Unveiling: The Death of Jesus as a Markan Theology of Revelation." PhD diss., Baylor University, 2014.

Garland, David E. *Mark*. NIV Application Commentary. Grand Rapids: Zondervan, 1996.

———. *Reading Matthew*. Macon, GA: Smyth & Helwys, 2000.

———. *First Corinthians*. Baker Exegetical Commentary on the New Testament. Grand Rapids: Baker, 2003.

———. *Luke*. Zondervan Exegetical Commentary on the New Testament. Grand Rapids: Zondervan, 2011.

Garnet, Paul. "The Baptism of Jesus and the Son of Man Idea." *Journal for the Study of the New Testament* 9 (1980): 49–65.

Garrett, Susan R. *The Temptations of Jesus in Mark's Gospel*. Grand Rapids: Eerdmans, 1998.

Gaston, Lloyd. *No Stone on Another: Studies in the Significance of the Fall of Jerusalem in the Synoptic Gospels*. Novum Testamentum Supplements 23. Leiden: Brill, 1970.

Gathercole, Simon J. "The Son of Man in Mark's Gospel." *Expository Times* 115 (2004): 366–72.

———. *The Preexistent Son: Recovering the Christologies of Matthew, Mark, and Luke*. Grand Rapids: Eerdmans, 2006.

Geddert, Timothy J. *Watchwords: Mark 13 in Markan Eschatology*. Journal for the Study of the New Testament Supplement Series 26. Sheffield: JSOT, 1989.

———. *Mark*. Believers Church Bible Commentary. Scottsdale, PA: Herald, 2001.

Genest, Olivette. *Le Christ de la passion—perspective structurale: analyse de Marc 14,53–15,47, des parallèles bibliques et extra bibliques*. Recherches 21. Montréal: Bellarmin, 1978.

Gerhardsson, Birger. *The Testing of God's Son (Matt 4:1–11 & Par.): An Analysis of an Early Christian Midrash*. Coniectanea biblica: New Testament Series 2. Lund: Gleerup, 1966.

Gese, Hartmut. "Psalm 22 und das Neue Testament: Der älteste Bericht vom Tode Jesu und die Entstehung des Herrenmahles." Pp. 180–201 in *Vom Sinai zum Zion*. Beiträge zur evangelischen Theologie. Munich: Chr. Kaiser, 1974.

Giblin, Charles H. " 'The Things of God' in the Question concerning Tribute to Caesar (Lk 20:25; Mk 12:17; Mt 22:21)." *Catholic Biblical Quarterly* 33 (1971): 510–27.

———. "The Beginning of the Ongoing Gospel Mk 1,2–16,8." Pp. 975–86 in *The Four Gospels 1992: Festschrift Frans Neirynck*. Volume 2. Bibliotheca ephemeridum theologicarum lovaniensium 100. Edited by Frans van Segbroeck, Christopher M. Tuckett, Gilbert van Belle, and Joseph Verheyden. Leuven: Leuven University Press, 1992.

Gibson, Jeffrey B. "The Rebuke of The Disciples in Mark 8:14–21." *Journal for the Study of the New Testament* 27 (1986): 31–47.

———. "Mark 8.12a: Why Does Jesus 'Sigh Deeply'?" *Bible Translator* 38 (1987): 122–25.

———. "Jesus' Refusal to Produce a 'Sign' (Mk 8.11–13)." *Journal for the Study of the New Testament* 38 (1990): 37–66.

———. "Jesus' Wilderness Temptation according to Mark." *Journal for the Study of the New Testament* 53 (1994): 3–34.

———. "The Function of the Charge of Blasphemy in Mark 14:64." Pp. 171–87 in *The Trial and Death of Jesus: Essays on the Passion Narrative in Mark*. Edited by Geert van Oyen and Thom Shepherd. Leuven: Peeters, 2006.

Giesen, Heinz. "Der verdorrte Feigenbaum—Eine symbolische Aussage? Zu Mk 11, 12–14.20f." *Biblische Zeitschrift* 20 (1976): 95–111.

Gill, Athol. *Life on the Road: The Gospel Basis for a Messianic Lifestyle*. Scottdale, PA: Herald, 1992.

Glasson, T. Francis. "Mark xv.39: The Son of God." *Expository Times* 80 (1968–69): 286.

Globe, Alexander. "The Caesarean Omission of the Phrase 'Son of God' in Mark 1:1." *Harvard Theological Review* 75 (1982): 209–18.

Glöckner, Richard. *Biblischer Glaube ohne Wunder?* Sammlung Horizonte, NF 14. Einsiedeln: Johannes, 1979.

Gnilka, Joachim. *Das Evangelium nach Markus*. 2 vols. Evangelisch-katholischer Kommentar zum Neuen Testament 2. Zurich: Benziger/Neukirchener, 1978–1979.

Goodacre, Mark S. "Fatigue in the Synoptics." *New Testament Studies* 44 (1998): 45–58.

———. *The Case against Q: Studies in Markan Priority and the Synoptic Problem*. Harrisburg, PA: Trinity Press International, 2002.

Goodman, Martin. *The Ruling Class of Judaea: The Origins of the Jewish Revolt against Rome A.D. 66–70*. Cambridge: Cambridge University Press, 1987.

Goulder, Michael D. "Did Peter Ever Go to Rome?" *Scottish Journal of Theology* 57 (2004): 377–96.

Gourgues, Michel. "À propos du symbolisme christologique et baptismal de Marc 16.5." *New Testament Studies* 27 (1981): 672–78.

Grant, F. C. "The Gospel according to St. Mark." Pp. 627–917 in *Interpreter's Bible*. Vol. 7. Edited by N. B. Harmon. Nashville: Abingdon, 1951.

Grassi, Joseph A. "*Abba* Father (Mark 14:36): Another Approach." *Journal of the American Academy of Religion* 50 (1982): 449–58.

Gray, Rebecca. *Prophetic Figures in Late Second Temple Jewish Palestine: The Evidence from Josephus*. Oxford: Oxford University Press, 1993.

Gray, Timothy C. *The Temple in the Gospel of Mark: A Study in Its Narrative Role*. Wissenschaftliche Untersuchungen zum Neuen Testament 2/242. Tübingen: Mohr Siebeck, 2008.

Grayston, Kenneth. "The Study of Mark XIII." *Bulletin of the John Rylands University Library of Manchester* 56 (1973–74): 371–87.

Green, Joel B. "Crucifixion." Pp. 87–101 in *The Cambridge Companion to Jesus*. Edited by Markus Bockmuehl. Cambridge: Cambridge University Press, 2001.

Green, William Scott. "Introduction: Messiah in Judaism: Rethinking the Question." Pp. 1–14 in *Judaisms and Their Messiahs at the Turn of the Christian Era*. Edited by Jacob Neusner, William Scott Green, and Ernest S. Frerichs. Cambridge: Cambridge University Press, 1987.

Greeven, Heinrich, and Eberhard Güting, eds. *Textkritik des Markusevangeliums*. Theologie, Forschung und Wissenschaft 11. Münster: LIT-Verlag, 2005.

Grindheim, Sigurd. *God's Equal: What Can We Know about Jesus' Self-Understanding?* Library of New Testament Studies 446. London/New York: T&T Clark, 2011.

———. *Christology in the Synoptic Gospels: God or God's Servant?* London/New York: T&T Clark, 2012.

Grundmann, Walter. "ἰσχυρός." Pp. 397–402 in *Theological Dictionary of the New Testament*. Vol. 3. Edited by Gerhard Kittel. Translated by Geoffrey W. Bromiley. Grand Rapids: Eerdmans, 1966.

———. *Das Evangelium nach Markus*. Theologischer Handkommentar zum Neuen Testament 2. 3rd ed. Berlin: Evangelische Verlagsanstalt, 1968.

Guelich, Robert A. "'The Beginning of the Gospel': Mark 1:1–15." *Biblical Research* 27 (1982): 5–15.

———. "The Gospel Genre." Pp. 183–219 in *Das Evangelium und die Evangelien 1982*. Wissenschaftliche Untersuchungen zum Neuen Testament 2/28. Edited by Peter Stuhlmacher. Tübingen: Mohr Siebeck, 1983.

———. *Mark 1–8:26*. Word Biblical Commentary 34a. Dallas: Word, 1989.

Guichard, Daniel. "La reprise du Psaum 22 dans le récit de la mort de Jésus (Marc 15,21–41)." *Foi et Vie* 87 (1988): 59–64.

Guijarro, Santiago. "Why Does the Gospel of Mark Begin as It Does?" *Biblical Theology Bulletin* 33 (2003): 28–38.

Guillemette, Pierre. "Mc 1,24 est-il une formule de défense magique?" *Science et Esprit* 30 (1978): 81–96.

Gundry, Robert. H. *Mark: A Commentary on His Apology for the Cross*. Grand Rapids: Eerdmans, 1993.

Gurtner, Daniel M. "The Veil of the Temple in History and Legend." *Journal of the Evangelical Theological Society* 49 (2006): 97–114.

———. "The Rending of the Veil and Markan Christology: 'Unveiling' The 'ΥΙΟΣ ΘΕΟΥ (Mark 15:38–39)." *Biblical Interpretation* 15 (2007): 292–306.

Guttenberger, Gudrun. *Die Gottesvorstellung im Markusevangelium*. Beiheft zur Zeitschrift für die neutestamentliche Wissenschaft 123. Berlin/New York: de Gruyter, 2004.

Gutwenger, Engelbert. "The Anti-Marcionite Prologues." *Theological Studies* 7 (1946): 393–409.

Guy, Harold A. "Son of God in Mk 15:39." *Expository Times* 81 (1969–70): 151.

Haenchen, Ernst. *Der Weg Jesu*. Berlin: Töpelmann, 1966.

———. *The Acts of the Apostles: A Commentary*. Translated by R. McL. Wilson. Philadelphia: Westminster, 1971.

Hagedorn, Anselm C., and Jerome H. Neyrey. "'It Was out of Envy That They Handed Jesus Over' (Mark 15.10): The Anatomy of Envy and the Gospel of Mark." *Journal for the Study of the New Testament* 69 (1998): 15–56.

Hahn, Ferdinand. "Die Rede von der Parusie des Menschensohnes Markus 13." Pp. 240–66 in *Jesus und der Menschensohn*. Edited by Rudolph Pesch and Rudolf Schnackenburg. Freiburg: Herder, 1975.

Hamerton-Kelly, Robert G. *The Gospel and the Sacred: Poetics of Violence in Mark*. Minneapolis: Fortress, 1994.

Hamilton, Gordon J. "A New Hebrew-Aramaic Incantation Text from Galilee: 'Rebuking the Sea.'" *Journal of Semitic Studies* 41 (1996): 215–49.

Hamilton, V. P. "שִׁילֹה." P. 919 in *Theological Wordbook of the Old Testament*. Edited by R. Laird Harris, Gleason L. Archer Jr., and Bruce K. Waltke. Chicago: Moody, 1999.

Hanson, K. C. "The Galilean Fishing Economy and the Jesus Tradition." *Biblical Theology Bulletin* 27 (1997): 99–111.

Harner, Philip B. "Qualitative Anarthrous Predicate Nouns: Mark 15:39 and John 1:1." *Journal of Biblical Literature* 92 (1973): 75–87.

Harrill, J. Albert. *The Manumission of Slaves in Early Christianity*. Hermeneutische Untersuchungen zur Theologie 32. Tübingen: Mohr Siebeck, 1995.

Harrington, Daniel J. *What Are They Saying about Mark?* New York/Mahwah, NJ: Paulist, 2004.

Harrington, Wilfrid J. *Mark: Realistic Theologian: The Jesus of Mark*. Dublin: Columba, 1996.

Harris, Geoffrey. "Mark and Mission." Pp. 129–42 in *Mark: Gospel of Action: Personal and Community Responses*. Edited by John Vincent. London: SPCK, 2006.

Harris, Murray J. *Prepositions and Theology in the Greek New Testament*. Grand Rapids: Zondervan, 2012.

Hartman, Lars. *Prophecy Interpreted: The Formation of Some Jewish Apocalyptic Texts and the Eschatological Discourse Mark 13 Par.* Coniectanea neotestamentica 1. Lund: Gleerup, 1966.

———. *Mark for the Nations: A Text- and Reader-Oriented Commentary.* Eugene, OR: Pickwick, 2010.

Hatina, Thomas R. *In Search of a Context: The Function of Scripture in Mark's Narrative.* Journal for the Study of the New Testament Supplement Series 232. Sheffield: Sheffield Academic, 2002.

———. "Who Will See 'the Kingdom of God Coming with Power' in Mark 9,1—Protagonists or Antagonists?" *Biblica* 86 (2005): 20–34.

Hatina, Thomas R., ed. *Biblical Interpretation in Early Christian Gospels.* Vol. 1: *The Gospel of Mark.* Library of New Testament Studies 304. London: T&T Clark, 2006.

Hawkin, David J. "The Incomprehension of the Disciples in the Marcan Redaction." *Journal of Biblical Literature* 91 (1972): 491–500.

Hay, David M. *Glory at the Right Hand: Psalm 110 in Early Christianity.* Society of Biblical Literature Monograph Series 18. Nashville: Abingdon: 1973.

Hay, Lewis S. "The Son-of-God Christology in Mark." *Journal of Bible and Religion* 32 (1964): 106–14.

Hays, Richard B. *The Moral Vision of the New Testament.* San Francisco: Harper Collins, 1996.

Head, Ivan. "Mark as a Roman Document from the Year 69: Testing Martin Hengel's Thesis." *Journal of Religious History* 28 (2004): 240–59.

Head, Peter M. "A Text-Critical Study of Mark 1.1: 'The Beginning of the Gospel of Jesus Christ.'" *New Testament Studies* 37 (1991): 621–29.

———. *Christology and the Synoptic Problem: An Argument for Markan Priority.* Society for New Testament Studies Monograph Series 94. Cambridge: Cambridge University Press, 1997.

Heil, John Paul. *Jesus Walking on the Sea: Meaning and Gospel Functions of Matt 14:22–33, Mark 6:45–52 and John 6:15b–21.* Analecta biblica 87. Rome: Biblical Institute Press, 1981.

———. *The Gospel of Mark as Model for Action: A Reader-Response Commentary.* Mahwah, NJ: Paulist, 1992.

———. "The Narrative Strategy and Pragmatics of the Temple Theme in Mark." *Catholic Biblical Quarterly* 59 (1997): 76–100.

———. "A Note on 'Elijah with Moses' in Mark 9,4." *Biblica* 80 (1999): 115.

———. *The Transfiguration of Jesus: Narrative Meaning and Function of Mark 9:2–8, Matt 17:1–8 and Luke 9:28–36.* Analecta biblica 144. Rome: Pontifical Biblical Institute, 2000.

———. "Jesus with the Wild Animals in Mark 1:13." *Catholic Biblical Quarterly* 68 (2006): 63–78.

Hemer, Colin J. *The Book of Acts in the Setting of Hellenistic History.* Edited by Conrad H. Gempf. Winona Lake, IN: Eisenbrauns, 1990.

Henderson, Suzanne Watts. *Christology and Discipleship in the Gospel of Mark.* Society for New Testament Studies Monograph Series 135. Cambridge: Cambridge University Press, 2006.

Hengel, Martin. "Maria Magdalena und die Frauen als Zeugen." Pp. 243–56 in *Abraham unser Vater: Juden und Christen im Gespräch über die Bibel: Festschrift für Otto Michel zum 60. Geburtstag.* Arbeiten zur Geschichte des Spätjudentums und Urchristentums 5. Edited by Otto Betz, Martin Hengel, and Peter Schmidt. Leiden: Brill, 1963.

———. *The Son of God.* Trans. by John Bowden. Philadelphia, PA: Fortress, 1976.

———. *Crucifixion in the Ancient World and the Folly of the Message of the Cross*. Philadelphia: Fortress, 1977.

———. *Acts and the History of Earliest Christianity*. Translated by John Bowden. Philadelphia: Fortress, 1980.

———. *The Atonement: The Origins of the Doctrine in the New Testament*. Translated by John Bowden. Philadelphia: Fortress, 1981.

———. *The Charismatic Leader and His Followers*. Translated by James Greig. Edinburgh: T&T Clark, 1981.

———. *Studies in the Gospel of Mark*. Translated by John Bowden. London: SCM, 1985.

———. *The Zealots: Investigations into the Jewish Freedom Movement in the Period from Herod I until 70 AD*. Translated by David Smith. Edinburgh: T&T Clark, 1989.

———. "Jesus, the Messiah of Israel." Pp. 1–72 in *Studies in Early Christology*. Edinburgh: T&T Clark, 1995.

———. " 'Sit at My Right Hand!': The Enthronement of Christ at the Right Hand of God and Psalm 110:1." Pp. 119–226 in *Studies in Early Christology*. Edinburgh: T&T Clark, 1995.

———. "Jesus, the Messiah of Israel: The Debate about the 'Messianic Mission' of Jesus." Pp. 323–49 in *Authenticating the Activities of Jesus*. New Testament Tools and Studies 28/2. Edited by Bruce Chilton and Craig Evans. Leiden/Boston: Brill, 1999.

———. *The Four Gospels and the One Gospel of Jesus Christ*. Translated by John Bowden. Harrisburg: Trinity Press International, 2000.

———. "Eye-Witness Memory and the Writing of the Gospels: Form-Criticism, Community Tradition and the Authority of the Authors." Pp. 70–96 in *The Written Gospel*. Edited by Markus Bockmuehl and Donald A. Hagner. Cambridge: Cambridge University Press, 2005.

———. *Saint Peter: The Underestimated Apostle*. Translated by Thomas H. Trapp. Grand Rapids: Eerdmans, 2010.

Hengel, Martin, and Roland Deines. "E. P. Sanders' 'Common Judaism,' Jesus, and the Pharisees." *Journal of Theological Studies* 46 (1995): 1–70.

Hicks, Richard. "Markan Discipleship according to Malachi: The Significance of μὴ ἀποστερήσῃς in the Story of the Rich Man (Mark 10:17–22)." *Journal of Biblical Literature* 132 (2013): 179–99.

Hiers, Richard H. *The Kingdom of God in the Synoptic Tradition*. Gainesville, FL: University of Florida Press, 1970.

Hiers, Richard, and Charles Kennedy. "The Bread and Fish Eucharist in the Gospels and Early Christianity." *Perspectives in Religious Studies* 3 (1976): 21–48.

Hill, Charles E. "Papias of Hierapolis." *Expository Times* 117 (2006): 309–15.

Hirsch, Eric D. *Validity in Interpretation*. New Haven, CT: Yale University Press, 1967.

Hodges, Horace Jeffery, and John C. Poirier, "Jesus as the Holy One of God: The Healing of the *Zavah* in Mark 5.24b–34." *Journal of Greco-Roman Christianity and Judaism* 8 (2011–12): 151–84.

Hoffeditz, David M., and Gary E. Yates, "Femme Fatale *Redux*: Intertextual Connection to the Elijah/Jezebel Narratives in Mark 6:14–29." *Bulletin for Biblical Research* 15 (2005): 199–221.

Hofius, Otfried. *Der Vorhang vor dem Thron Gottes: Eine exegetisch-religionsgeschichtliche Untersuchung zu Hebräer 6,19f und 10,19f.* Wissenschaftliche Untersuchungen zum Neuen Testament 14. Tübingen: Mohr Siebeck, 1972.

———. "Ist Jesus der Messias? Thesen." Pp. 108–36 in *Neutestamentliche Studien*. Wissenschaftliche Untersuchungen zum Neuen Testament 2/132. Tübingen: Mohr Siebeck, 2000.

———. "Vergebungszuspruch und Vollmachtsfrage: Mk 2,1–12 und das Problem priesterlicher Absolution im antiken Judentum." Pp. 57–69 in *Neutestamentliche Studien*. Wissenschaftliche Untersuchungen zum Neuen Testament 132. Tübingen: Mohr Siebeck, 2000.

Hogeterp, Albert L. A. *Expectations of the End: A Comparative Traditio-Historical Study of Eschatological, Apocalyptic and Messianic Ideas in the Dead Sea Scrolls and the New Testament*. Studies on the Texts of the Desert of Judah 83. Leiden/Boston: Brill, 2009.

Holladay, Carl R. *Theios Anēr in Hellenistic-Judaism: A Critique of the Use of This Category in New Testament Christology*. Society of Biblical Literature Dissertation Series 40. Missoula, MT: Scholars Press, 1977.

———. *A Critical Introduction to the New Testament: Interpreting the Message and Meaning of Jesus Christ*. Nashville: Abingdon, 2005.

Hollenbach, Bruce. "Lest They Should Turn and Be Forgiven: Irony." *Bible Translator* 34 (1983): 312–21.

Holmes, B. T. "Luke's Description of John Mark." *Journal of Biblical Literature* 54 (1935): 63–72.

Holtzmann, Heinrich J. *Die synoptischen Evangelien: Ihr Ursprung und geschichtlicher Charakter*. Leipzig: Engelmann, 1863.

Hooker, Morna D. *The Son of Man in Mark: A Study of the Background of the Term "Son of Man" and Its Use in St. Mark's Gospel*. Montreal: McGill University Press, 1967.

———. *The Message of Mark*. London: Epworth, 1983.

———. "Mark." Pp. 220–30 in *It is Written—Scripture Citing Scripture: Essays in Honour of Barnabas Lindars, SSF*. Edited by Don A. Carson and H. G. M. Williamson. Cambridge: Cambridge University Press, 1988.

———. *The Gospel according to Saint Mark*. Black's New Testament Commentary. Peabody, MA: Hendrickson, 1991.

———. "Mark's Parables of the Kingdom (Mark 4:1–34)." Pp. 79–101 in *The Challenge of Jesus' Parables*. McMaster New Testament Studies. Edited by Richard N. Longenecker. Grand Rapids: Eerdmans, 2000.

———. "Beginnings and Endings." Pp. 184–202 in *The Written Gospel*. Edited by Markus Bockmuehl and Donald A. Hagner. Cambridge: Cambridge University Press, 2005.

———. "This Is the Good News: The Challenge of Mark's Beginning." Pp. 30–44 in *Preaching Mark's Unsettling Messiah*. Edited by David Fleer and Dave Bland. St. Louis: Chalice, 2006.

Horsley, G. H. R. *New Documents Illustrating Early Christianity*. Sydney: Ancient History Documentary Centre, Macquarie University, 1982.

Horst, Pieter W. van der. "Can a Book End with *GAR*? A Note on Mark XVI.8." *Journal of Theological Studies* 23 (1972): 121–4.

———. *Ancient Jewish Epitaphs*. Contributions to Biblical Exegesis and Theology 2. Kampen: Kok Pharos, 1991.

Hübner, Hans. "ἀλήθεια." Pp. 57–60 in *Exegetical Dictionary of the New Testament*. Vol. 1. Edited by Horst Balz and Gerhard Schneider. Grand Rapids: Eerdmans, 1991.

Hug, Joseph. *La finale de l'évangile de Marc* (*Marc 16, 9–20*). Études bibliques. Paris: Gabalda, 1978.

Huizenga, Leroy A. "The Confession of Jesus and the Curses of Peter: A Narrative-Christological Approach to the Text-Critical Problem of Mark 14:62." *Novum Testamentum* 53 (2011): 244–66.

Hulse, E. V. "The Nature of Biblical 'Leprosy' and the Use of Alternative Medical Terms in Modern Translations of the Bible." *Palestine Exploration Quarterly* 107 (1975): 87–105.

Hultin, Jeremy F. "Disobeying Jesus: A Puzzling Element in the Messianic Secret Motifs." Pp. 69–97 in *Portraits of Jesus: Studies in Christology.* Wissenschaftliche Untersuchungen zum Neuen Testament 2/321. Edited by Susan E. Myers. Tübingen: Mohr Siebeck, 2012.

Humphrey, Hugh M. *From Q to 'Secret' Mark: A Composition History of the Earliest Narrative Theology.* London/New York: T&T Clark, 2006.

Hunziger, Claus-Hunno. "σίναπι." Pp. 287–91 in *Theological Dictionary of the New Testament.* Vol. 7. Edited by Gerhard Friedrich. Translated by Geoffrey W. Bromiley. Grand Rapids: Eerdmans, 1971.

Hurtado, Larry W. *One God, One Lord: Early Christian Devotion and Ancient Jewish Monotheism.* London: SCM, 1988. Revised edition. Edinburgh: T&T Clark, 2003.

———. *Mark.* New International Biblical Commentary 2. Peabody, MA: Hendrickson, 1989.

———. "Following Jesus in the Gospel of Mark—and Beyond." Pp. 9–29 in *Patterns of Discipleship in the New Testament.* Edited by Richard N. Longenecker. Grand Rapids: Eerdmans, 1996.

———. *Lord Jesus Christ: Devotion to Jesus in Earliest Christianity.* Grand Rapids: Eerdmans, 2003.

———. *How on Earth Did Jesus Become a God? Historical Questions About Earliest Devotion to Jesus.* Grand Rapids: Eerdmans, 2005.

———. "The Women, the Tomb, and the Climax of Mark." Pp. 427–50 in *A Wandering Galilean: Essays in Honour of Seán Freyne.* Supplements to the Journal for the Study of Judaism 132. Edited by Zuleika Rodgers, Margaret Daly-Denton, and Anne Fitzpatrick McKinley. Leiden: Brill, 2009.

———. *God in New Testament Theology.* Nashville: Abingdon, 2010.

———. " 'Ancient Jewish Monotheism' in the Hellenistic and Roman Periods." *Journal of Ancient Judaism* 4 (2013): 379–400.

Hurtado, Larry W., and Paul L. Owen, eds. *"Who Is This Son of Man?" The Latest Scholarship on a Puzzling Expression of the Historical Jesus.* Library of New Testament Studies 390. London/New York: T&T Clark, 2011.

Huys, Marc. "Turning the Tables: Jesus' Temple Cleansing and the Story of Lycaon." *Ephemerides theologicae lovanienses* 86 (2010): 137–61.

Iersel, Bas van. "The Gospel according to Mark—Written for a Persecuted Community?" *Nederlands theologisch tijdschrift* 34 (1980): 15–36.

———. *Reading Mark.* Collegeville, MN: Liturgical, 1988.

———. "Καὶ ἤθελεν παρελθεῖν αὐτούς: Another Look at Mark 6,48d." Pp. 1065–76 in *The Four Gospels 1992: Festschrift Frans Neirynck.* Volume 2. Bibliotheca ephemeridum theologicarum lovaniensium 100. Edited by Frans van Segbroeck, Christopher M. Tuckett, Gilbert van Belle, and Joseph Verheyden. Leuven: Leuven University Press, 1992.

———. *Mark: A Reader-Response Commentary.* Journal for the Study of the New Testament Supplement Series 164. Translated by W. H. Bisscheroux. Sheffield: Sheffield Academic, 1998.

Incigneri, Brian J. *The Gospel to the Romans: The Setting and Rhetoric of Mark's Gospel.* Biblical Interpretation Series 65. Leiden/Boston/Köln: Brill, 2003.

Iverson, Kelly R. "A Further Word on Final Γάρ (Mark 16:8)." *Catholic Biblical Quarterly* 68 (2006): 79–94.

———. "Incongruity, Humor, and Mark: Performance and the Use of Laughter in the Second Gospel (Mark 8.14–21)." *New Testament Studies* 59 (2013): 2–19.

Iwe, John Chijioke. *Jesus in the Synagogue of Capernaum: The Pericope and Its Programmatic Character for the Gospel of Mark: An Exegetico-Theological Study of Mk 1:21–28.* Tesi Gregoriana 57. Rome: Gregorian University Press, 1999.

Jackson, Howard M. "The Death of Jesus in Mark and the Miracle from the Cross." *New Testament Studies* 27 (1987): 16–37.

———. "Why the Youth Shed His Cloak and Fled Naked: The Meaning and Purpose of Mark 14:51–52." *Journal of Biblical Literature* 116 (1997): 273–89.

Jacobs, M. M. "Mark's Jesus through the Eyes of Twentieth Century New Testament Scholars." *Neotestamentica* 28 (1994): 53–85.

Jacobson, Howard. *A Commentary on Pseudo-Philo's Liber Antiquitatum Biblicarum.* Vol. 2. Leiden: Brill, 1996.

Jeffery, Peter. *The Secret Gospel of Mark Unveiled: Imagined Rituals of Sex, Death, and Madness in a Biblical Forgery.* New Haven, CT: Yale University Press, 2007.

Jenkins, Philip. *Hidden Gospels: How the Search for Jesus Lost Its Way.* Oxford: Oxford University Press, 2001.

Jeremias, Joachim. *The Parables of Jesus.* Rev. ed. Translated by S. H. Hooke. New York: Scribner's, 1963.

———. *The Central Message of the New Testament.* New York: Scribner's, 1965.

———. "Μωϋσῆς." Pp. 848–73 in *Theological Dictionary of the New Testament.* Vol. 4. Edited by Gerhard Kittel. Translated by Geoffrey W. Bromiley. Grand Rapids: Eerdmans, 1967.

———. "νύμφη, νυμφίος." Pp. 1099–1106 in *Theological Dictionary of the New Testament.* Vol. 4. Edited by Gerhard Kittel. Translated by Geoffrey W. Bromiley. Grand Rapids: Eerdmans, 1967.

———. *Prayers of Jesus.* Studies in Biblical Theology 2/6. Naperville, IL: Alec R. Allenson, 1967.

———. "πολλοί." Pp. 536–45 in *Theological Dictionary of the New Testament.* Vol. 6. Edited by Gerhard Friedrich. Translated by Geoffrey W. Bromiley. Grand Rapids: Eerdmans, 1968.

———. *New Testament Theology: The Proclamation of Jesus.* New York: Scribner's, 1971.

———. *The Eucharistic Words of Jesus.* Translated by Norman Perrin. London: SCM, 1978.

Jervell, Jacob. *Die Apostelgeschichte.* Kritisch-exegetischer Kommentar über das Neue Testament 3. Göttingen: Vandenhoeck & Ruprecht, 1998.

Johansson, Daniel. "*Kyrios* in the Gospel of Mark." *Journal for the Study of the New Testament* 33 (2010): 101–24.

———. " 'Who Can Forgive Sins but God Alone?' Human and Angelic Agents, and Divine Forgiveness in Early Judaism." *Journal for the Study of the New Testament* 33 (2011): 351–74.

Johnson, David H. "The Characterization of Jesus in Mark." *Didaskalia* 10 (1999): 79–92.

Johnson, Earl S., Jr. "Mark VIII. 22–26: The Blind Man from Bethsaida." *New Testament Studies* 25 (1979): 370–83.

———. "Is Mark 15,39 the Key to Mark's Christology." *Journal for the Study of the New Testament* 31 (1987): 3–22.

———. "Mark 15,39 and the So-Called Confession of the Roman Centurion." *Biblica* 81 (2000): 406–13.

Johnson, Steven R. "The Identity and Significance of the *Neaniskos* in Mark." *Forum* 8 (1992): 123–39.

Jonge, Marinus de. "Mark 14:25 among Jesus' Words about the Kingdom of God." Pp. 123–35 in *Sayings of Jesus: Canonical and Non-Canonical: Essays in Honour of Tjitze Baarda*. Novum Testamentum Supplements 89. Edited by William L. Peterson, Johan S. Vox, and Henk J. de Jonge. Leiden: Brill, 1997.

Jöris, Steffen. "The Markan Use of 'Unclean Spirit': Another Messianic Strand." *Australian Biblical Review* 60 (2012): 49–66.

Juel, Donald. *Messiah and Temple: The Trial of Jesus in the Gospel of Mark*. Society of Biblical Literature Dissertation Series 31. Missoula. MT: Scholars, 1977.

———. *Messianic Exegesis: Christological Interpretation of the Old Testament in Early Christianity*. Philadelphia: Fortress, 1988.

———. *Mark*. Augsburg Commentary on the New Testament. Minneapolis: Augsburg, 1990.

———. "The Origin of Mark's Christology." Pp. 449–60 in *The Messiah: Developments in Earliest Judaism and Christianity: The First Princeton Symposium on Judaism and Christian Origins*. Edited by James H. Charlesworth. Minneapolis: Fortress, 1992.

———. *A Master of Surprise: Mark Interpreted*. Minneapolis: Fortress, 1994.

———. "A Disquieting Silence: The Matter of the Ending." Pp. 1–13 in *The Ending of Mark and the Ends of God: Essays in Memory of Donald Harrisville Juel*. Edited by Beverly Roberts Gaventa and Patrick D. Miller. Louisville: Westminster John Knox, 2005.

Kähler, Martin. *The So-Called Historical Jesus and the Historic, Biblical Christ*. Translated by Carl E. Braaten. Philadelphia: Fortress, 1964.

Kallas, James. *The Significance of the Synoptic Miracles*. London: SPCK, 1961.

Kampling, Rainer. "Das Gesetz im Markusevangelium." Pp. 119–50 in *Der Evangelist als Theologe: Studien zum Markusevangelium*. Stuttgarter Bibelstudien 163. Edited by Thomas Söding. Stuttgart: Katholisches Bibelwerk, 1995.

Kato, Zenji. *Die Völkermission im Markusevangelium: Eine redaktionsgeschichtliche Untersuchung*. Europäische Hochschulschriften: Theologie 23/252. Bern/Frankfurt am Main: Lang, 1986.

Kazmierski, Carl R. *Jesus, the Son of God: A Study of the Markan Tradition and Its Redaction by the Evangelist*. Forschung zur Bibel 33. Würzburg: Echter Verlag, 1979.

Kealy, Sean P. "Reflections on the History of Mark's Gospel." *Proceedings, Eastern Great Lakes Biblical Society* 2 (1982): 46–62.

———. *A History of the Interpretation of the Gospel of Mark: Volume I: Through the Nineteenth Century*. Lewiston/Queenston/Lampeter: Mellen, 2008.

———. *A History of the Interpretation of the Gospel of Mark: Volume II: The Twentieth Century Book 1*. Lewiston/Queenston/Lampeter: Mellen, 2008.

———. *A History of the Interpretation of the Gospel of Mark: Volume II: The Twentieth Century Book 2*. Lewiston/Queenston/Lampeter: Mellen, 2008.

Keck, Leander E. "The Introduction to Mark's Gospel." *New Testament Studies* 12 (1965–66): 352–70.

———. "Spirit and Dove." *New Testament Studies* 17 (1970): 41–67.

Kee, Howard Clark. "The Terminology of Mark's Exorcism Stories." *New Testament Studies* 14 (1967–68): 232–46.

———. *Community of the New Age: Studies in Mark's Gospel*. Philadelphia: Westminster, 1977.

———. "Christology in Mark's Gospel." Pp. 187–208 in *Judaisms and Their Messiahs at the Turn of the Christian Era*. Edited by Jacob Neusner, William Scott Green, and Ernest S. Frerichs. Cambridge: Cambridge University Press, 1987.

Keener, Craig S. *Miracles: The Credibility of the New Testament Accounts*. 2 vols. Grand Rapids: Baker, 2011.

Keerankeri, George. *The Love Commandment in Mark: An Exegetico-Theological Study of Mark 12,28–34*. Analecta biblica 150. Rome: Pontifical Biblical Institute, 2003.

Kelber, Werner H. "Mark 14,32–42: Gethsemane: Passion Christology and Discipleship Failure." *Zeitschrift für die neutestamentliche Wissenschaft* 63 (1972): 166–87.

———. *The Kingdom in Mark: A New Place and a New Time*. Philadelphia: Fortress, 1974.

———. "Conclusion: From Passion Narrative to Gospel." Pp. 153–80 in *The Passion in Mark: Studies on Mark 14–16*. Edited by Werner H. Kelber. Philadelphia: Fortress, 1976.

———. *Mark's Story of Jesus*. Philadelphia: Fortress, 1979.

———. "Apostolic Tradition and the Form of the Gospel." Pp. 24–46 in *Discipleship in the New Testament*. Edited by Fernando F. Segovia. Philadelphia: Fortress, 1985.

———. "Narrative and Disclosure: Mechanisms of Concealing, Revealing and Reveiling." *Semeia* 43 (1988): 1–20.

———. *Conflict in Mark: Jesus, Authorities, Disciples*. Minneapolis: Fortress, 1989.

Kelhoffer, James A. *Miracle and Mission: The Authentication of Missionaries and Their Message in the Longer Ending of Mark*. Wissenschaftliche Untersuchungen zum Neuen Testament 2/112. Tübingen: Mohr Siebeck, 2000.

———. *The Diet of John the Baptist: "Locusts and Wild Honey" in Synoptic and Patristic Interpretation*. Wissenschaftliche Untersuchungen zum Neuen Testament 2/176. Tübingen: Mohr Siebeck, 2005.

Kempthorne, Renatus. "The Marcan Text of Jesus' Answer to the High Priest (Mark xiv 62)." *Novum Testamentum* 19 (1977): 197–208.

Kennedy, George. "Classical and Christian Source Criticism." Pp. 125–55 in *The Relationships among the Gospels: An Interdisciplinary Dialogue*. Edited by William O. Walker Jr. San Antonio: Trinity University Press, 1978.

Kennedy, George, ed. and trans. *Progymnasmata: Greek Textbooks of Prose Composition and Rhetoric*. Writings from the Greco-Roman World 10. Atlanta: Society of Biblical Literature, 2003.

Kermode, Frank. *The Genesis of Secrecy*. Cambridge, MA: Harvard University Press, 1979.

Kernaghan, Ronald J. *Mark*. InterVarsity Press New Testament Commentary. Downers Grove, IL: InterVarsity Press, 2007.

Kertelge, Karl. *Die Wunder Jesu im Markusevangelium: Eine redaktionsgeschichtliche Untersuchung*. Studien zum Alten und Neuen Testament 33. Münster: Kösel, 1970.

———. "λύτρον, ου, τό." Pp. 364–66 in *Exegetical Dictionary of the New Testament*. Vol. 2. Edited by Horst Balz and Gerhard Schneider. Grand Rapids: Eerdmans, 1991.

———. "The Epiphany of Jesus in the Gospel (Mark)." Pp. 105–23 in *The Interpretation of Mark*. Studies in New Testament Interpretation. 2nd ed. Edited by William R. Telford. Edinburgh: T&T Clark, 1995.

———. "Jüngerschaft und Nachfolge: Grundlegung von Kirche nach Markus." Pp. 151–65 in *Der Evangelist als Theologe: Studien zum Markusevangelium.* Stuttgarter Bibelstudien 163. Edited by Thomas Söding. Stuttgart: Katholisches Bibelwerk, 1995.

Kilgallen, John J. "The Messianic Secret and Mark's Purposes." *Biblical Theology Bulletin* 7 (1977): 60–65.

———. "Mark 9:1—The Conclusion of a Pericope." *Biblica* 63 (1982): 81–83.

Kilpatrick, G. D. "The Gentile Mission in Mark and Mark 13:9–11." Pp. 145–58 in *Studies in the Gospels: Essays in Memory of R. H. Lightfoot.* Edited by Dennis E. Nineham. Oxford: Blackwell, 1955.

———. "Galatians 1:18 ἹΣΤΟΡΗΣΑΙ ΚΗΦΑΝ." Pp. 144–49 in *New Testament Essays: Studies in Memory of T. W. Manson, 1893–1958.* Edited by A. J. B. Higgins. Manchester: Manchester University Press, 1959.

Kim, Tae Hun. "The Anarthrous υἱὸς θεοῦ Mark 15,39 and the Roman Imperial Cult." *Biblica* 79 (1998): 221–41.

Kingsbury, Jack Dean. *The Christology of Mark's Gospel.* Philadelphia: Fortress, 1983.

———. "The 'Divine Man' as The Key to Mark's Christology—The End of an Era?" *Interpretation* 35 (1981): 243–57.

———. "The Significance of the Cross within Mark's Story." Pp. 95–105 in *Gospel Interpretation: Narrative-Critical and Social-Scientific Approaches.* Edited by Jack Dean Kingsbury. Harrisburg, PA: Trinity Press International, 1997.

———. "'God' within the Narrative World of Mark." Pp. 75–89 in *The Forgotten God: Perspectives in Biblical Theology: Essays in Honor of Paul J. Achtemeier on the Occasion of his Seventy-Fifth Birthday.* Edited by A. Andrew Das and Frank J. Matera. Louisville: Westminster John Knox, 2002.

———. "The Christology of Mark and the Son of Man." Pp. 55–70 in *Unity and Diversity in the Gospels and Paul: Essays in Honor of Frank J. Matera.* Edited by Christopher W. Skinner and Kelly R. Iverson. Atlanta: Society of Biblical Literature, 2012.

Kinman, Brent. "Parousia, Jesus' 'A-Triumphal' Entry, and the Fate of Jerusalem (Luke 19:28–44)." *Journal of Biblical Literature* 118 (1999): 279–94.

Kinnier-Wilson, J. V. "Leprosy in Ancient Mesopotamia." *Revue d'assyriologie et d'archéologie orientale* 60 (1966): 47–58.

Kio, Stephen Hre. "A Prayer Framework in Mark 11." *Bible Translator* 37 (1986): 323–28.

Kirchhevel, Gordon D. "The 'Son of Man' Passages in Mark." *Bulletin for Biblical Research* 9 (1999): 181–87.

Kirk, J. R. Daniel. "Time for Figs, Temple Destruction, and Houses of Prayer in Mark 11:12–25." *Catholic Biblical Quarterly* 74 (2012): 509–27.

Kirschner, E. F. "The Place of the Exorcism Motif in Mark's Christology, with Special Attention to Mark 3:22–30." PhD dissertation. London: London Bible College, 1988.

Klauck, Hans-Josef. "Die erzählerische Rolle der Jünger im Markusevangelium: Eine narrative Analyse." *Novum Testamentum* 24 (1982): 1–26.

———. *Vorspiel im Himmel? Erzähltechnik und Theologie im Markusprolog.* Biblische-theologische Studien 32. Neukirchen-Vluyn: Neukirchener Verlag, 1997.

Klausner, Joseph. *Jesus of Nazareth.* London: George Allen & Unwin, 1925.

Kloppenborg, John S. "Evocatio Deorum and the Date of Mark." *Journal of Biblical Literature* 124 (2005): 419–50.

Klostermann, Erich. *Das Markus-Evangelium.* Handbuch zum Neuen Testament. Tübingen: Mohr Siebeck, 1926.

Knight, Jonathan. *Luke's Gospel*. New Testament Readings. London: Routledge, 1998.

Knox, Wilfred L. "The Ending of St. Mark's Gospel." *Harvard Theological Review* 35 (1942): 13–23.

Koch, Dietrich-Alex. *Die Bedeutung der Wundererzählungen für die Christologie des Markusevangeliums*. Beiheft zur Zeitschrift für die neutestamentliche Wissenschaft 42. Berlin: de Gruyter, 1975.

———. "Inhaltliche Gliederung und geographischer Aufriss im Markusevangelium." *New Testament Studies* 29 (1983): 145–66.

Koester, Craig. "The Origin and Significance of the Flight to Pella Tradition." *Catholic Biblical Quarterly* 51 (1989): 90–106.

Koester, Helmut. "From the Kerygma-Gospel to Written Gospels." *New Testament Studies* 35 (1989): 361–81.

———. *Ancient Christian Gospels: Their History and Development*. Philadelphia: Trinity Press International, 1990.

Kollmann, Bernd. "Jesu Schweigegebote an die Dämonen." *Zeitschrift für die Neutestamentliche Wissenschaft* 82 (1991): 267–73.

Korn, Joachim Hans. *PEIRASMOS: Die Versuchung des Gläubigen in der griechischen Bibel*. Beitra¨ge zur Wissenschaft vom Alten und Neuen Testament 72. Stuttgart: Kohlhammer, 1937.

Köstenberger, Andreas J., and Peter T. O'Brien. *Salvation to the Ends of the Earth: A Biblical Theology of Mission*. New Studies in Biblical Theology 11. Downers Grove, IL: InterVarsity Press, 2001.

Kraeling, Carl Hermann. "A Philological Note on Mark 16:8." *Journal of Biblical Literature* 44 (1925): 357–58.

Kümmel, Werner Georg. *Promise and Fulfilment: The Eschatological Message of Jesus*. Studies in Biblical Theology 23. 2nd ed. Translated by Dorothea M. Barton. London: SCM, 1961.

———. "Noch einmal: Das Gleichnis von der selbstwachsenden Saat: Bemerkungen zur neuesten Diskussion um die Auslegung der Gleichnisse Jesu." Pp. 143–56 in *Orientierung an Jesus: Zur Theologie der Synoptiker: Für Josef Schmid*. Edited by Paul Hoffmann, Norbert Brox, and Wilhelm Pesch. Freiburg: Herder, 1973.

Künzi, Martin. *Das Naherwartungslogion Markus 9, 1 par [und Parallelstellen]: Geschichte seiner Auslegung: Mit einem Nachwort zur Auslegungsgeschichte von Markus 13, 30 par*. Beiträge zur Geschichte der biblischen Exegese 21. Tübingen: Mohr Siebeck, 1977.

Kuruvilla, Abraham. "The Naked Runaway and the Enrobed Reporter of Mark 14 and 16: What Is the Author Doing with What He Is Saying?" *Journal of the Evangelical Theological Society* 54 (2011): 527–45.

Kuthirakkattel, Scaria, *The Beginning of Jesus' Ministry according to Mark's Gospel (1,14–3,6): A Redaction Critical Study*. Analecta biblica 123. Roma: Pontifical Biblical Institute, 1990.

Kyle, Donald G. *Spectacles of Death in Ancient Rome*. London: Routledge, 1998.

Ladd, George Eldon. *The Presence of the Future: The Eschatology of Biblical Realism*. 2nd ed. Grand Rapids: Eerdmans, 1974.

Lake, Kirsopp. *The Historical Evidence for the Resurrection of Jesus Christ*. New York: Putnam, 1907.

Lambrecht, Jan. *Die Redaktion der Markus-Apokalypse: Literarische Analyse und Strukturuntersuchung*. Analecta biblica 28. Rome: Pontifical Biblical Institute, 1967.

———. "The Christology of Mark." *Biblical Theology Bulletin* 3 (1973): 256–73.

———. *Once More Astonished: The Parables of* Jesus. New York: Crossroad, 1981.

———. "John the Baptist and Jesus in Mark 1.1–15: Markan Redaction of Q?" *New Testament Studies* 38 (1992): 357–84.

Lampe, G. W. H. "St. Peter's Denial and the Treatment of the *Lapsi*." Pp. 113–33 in *The Heritage of the Early Church: Essays in Honor of Georges Vasilievich Florovsky*. Orientalia christiana analecta 195. Edited by David Neiman and Margaret Schatkin. Rome: Pontifical Oriental Institute, 1973.

Lane, William L. *Commentary on the Gospel of Mark*. New International Commentary on the New Testament. Grand Rapids: Eerdmans, 1974.

———. "From Historian to Theologian: Milestones in Markan Scholarship." *Review and Expositor* 75 (1978): 601–17.

Lang, Friedrich Gustav. "'Über Sidon mitten ins Gebiet der Dekapolis': Geographie und Theologie in Markus 7,31." *Zeitschrift des Deutschen Palästina-Vereins* 94 (1978): 145–60.

Lau, Markus. "Die Legio X Fretensis und der Besessene von Gerasa: Anmerkungen zur Zahlenangabe 'ungefähr Zweitausend' (Mk 5,13)." *Biblica* 88 (2007): 351–64.

LaVerdiere, Eugene. *The Beginning of the Gospel: Introducing the Gospel according to Mark*. 2 vols. Collegeville, MN: Liturgical, 1999.

Leder, Hans-Günter. "Sündenfallerzählung und Versuchungsgeschichte: Zur Interpretation von Mc 1. 12f." *Zeitschrift für die neutestamentliche Wissenschaft* 64 (1963): 188–216.

Lee, Aquila H. I. *From Messiah to Preexistent Son: Jesus' Self-Consciousness and Early Christian Exegesis of Messianic Psalms*. Wissenschaftliche Untersuchungen zum Neuen Testament 2/192. Tübingen: Mohr Siebeck, 2005.

Lee-Pollard, Dorothy A. "Powerlessness as Power: A Key Emphasis in the Gospel of Mark." *Scottish Journal of Theology* 40 (1987): 173–88.

Lemcio, Eugene E. "External Evidence for the Structure and Function of Mark iv. 1–20, vii. 14–23 and viii. 14–21." *Journal of Theological Studies* 29 (1978): 323–38.

Léon-Dufour, Xavier. *Sharing the Eucharistic Bread*. Translated by Matthew J. O'Connell. Mahwah, NJ: Paulist, 1987.

Lietzmann, Hans. "Der Prozess Jesu." *Sitzungsberichte der Preussischen Akademie der Wissenschaften* 14 (1931): 313–22 .

Lightfoot, R. H. *Locality and Doctrine in the Gospels*. London: Hodder & Stoughton, 1938.

———. *The Gospel Message of St. Mark*. Oxford: Clarendon, 1950.

Limbeck, Meinrad. *Markus-evangelium*. Stuttgarter kleiner Kommentar, Neues Testament. Stuttgart: Verlag Katholisches Bibelwerk, 1984.

Lincoln, Andrew T. "The Promise and the Failure: Mark 16:7, 8." *Journal of Biblical Literature* 108 (1989): 283–300.

Lindars, Barnabas. "All Foods Clean: Thoughts on Jesus and the Law." Pp. 61–71 in *Law and Religion*. Edited by Barnabas Lindars. Cambridge: James Clarke, 1988.

Lindemann, Andreas. "Die Osterbotschaft des Markus: Zur theologischen Interpretation von Mark 16:1–8." *New Testament Studies* 26 (1980): 298–317.

Llewelyn, Stephen R., and Dionysia van Beek. "Reading the Temple Warning as a Greek Visitor." *Journal for the Study of Judaism* 42 (2011): 1–22.

Lohmeyer, Ernst. *Galiläa und Jerusalem*. Forschungen zur Religion und Literatur des Alten und Neuen Testaments 34. Göttingen: Vandenhoeck & Ruprecht, 1936.

———. "'Und Jesus ging vorüber': Eine exegetische Betrachtung." Pp. 57–79 in *Urchristliche Mystik: Neutestamentliche Studien*. Darmstadt: Gentner, 1956.

———. *Das Evangelium des Markus*. Kritisch-exegetischer Kommentar über das Neue Testament 2. 2nd ed. Göttingen: Vandenhoeck & Ruprecht, 1963.

Longenecker, Richard. "The Messianic Secret in the Light of Recent Discoveries." *Evangelical Quarterly* 41 (1969): 207–15.

———. "Acts." Pp. 663–1102 in *The Expositor's Bible Commentary*. Vol. 10. Rev. ed. Edited by Tremper Longman III and David E. Garland. Grand Rapids: Zondervan, 2007.

Loos, Hendrik van der. *The Miracles of Jesus*. Novum Testamentum Supplements 9. Leiden: Brill, 1965.

Lövestam, Evald. "Die Davidssohnsfrage." *Svensk Exegetisk Årsbok* 27 (1962): 72–82.

———. "The ἡ γενεὰ αὕτη. Eschatology in Mk 13,30 parr." Pp. 403–13 in *L'Apocalypse johannique et l'apocalyptique dans le Nouveau Testament*. Bibliotheca ephemeridum theologicarum lovaniensium 53. Edited by Jan Lambrecht. Gembloux: Duculot, 1980.

———. *Jesus and "This Generation": A New Testament Study*. Coniectanea biblica New Testament 25. Translated by Moira Linnarud. Stockholm: Almqvist & Wiksell, 1995.

Lust, Johan. "Daniel 7,13 and the Septuagint." *Ephemerides theologicae lovanienses* 54 (1978): 62–69.

Luz, Ulrich. "The Secrecy Motif and the Marcan Christology." Pp. 75–96 in *The Messianic Secret*. Edited by Christopher Tuckett. Philadelphia: Fortress, 1983.

———. "The Gospel of Matthew: A New Story of Jesus, or a Rewritten One?" Pp. 18–36 in *Studies in Matthew*. Translated by Rosemary Selle. Grand Rapids: Eerdmans, 2005.

Mack, Burton L. *Myth of Innocence: Mark and Christian Origins*. Philadelphia: Fortress, 1988.

Mackay, Ian D. *John's Relationship with Mark: An Analysis of John 6 in the Light of Mark 6–8*. Wissenschaftliche Untersuchungen zum Neuen Testament 2/182. Tübingen: Mohr Siebeck, 2004.

Magness, J. Lee. *Sense and Absence: Structure and Suspension in the Ending of Mark's Gospel*. Semeia Studies. Atlanta: Scholars Press, 1986.

Malbon, Elizabeth Struthers. "Fallible Followers: Women and Men in the Gospel of Mark." *Semeia* 28 (1983): 29–48.

———. "Disciples/Crowds/Whoever: Markan Characters and Readers." *Novum Testamentum* 28 (1986): 104–30.

———. *Narrative Space and Mythic Meaning in Mark*. San Francisco: Harper & Row, 1986.

———. "The Poor Widow in Mark and Her Poor Rich Readers." *Catholic Biblical Quarterly* 53 (1991): 589–604.

———. "Echoes and Foreshadowings in Mark 4–8: Reading and Rereading." *Journal of Biblical Literature* 112 (1993): 211–30.

———. "Texts and Contexts: Interpreting the Disciples in Mark." *Semeia* 62 (1993): 81–102.

———. "The Christology of Mark's Gospel: Narrative Christology and the Markan Jesus." Pp. 33–48 in *Who Do You Say I Am? Essays on Christology in Honor of Jack Dean Kingsbury on the Occasion of his 65th Birthday*. Edited by David R. Bauer and Mark Allan Powell. Louisville: Westminster John Knox, 1999.

———. "'Reflected Christology': An Aspect of Narrative 'Christology' in the Gospel of Mark." *Perspectives in Religious Studies* 26 (1999): 127–45.

———. *In the Company of Jesus: Characters in Mark's Gospel.* Louisville: Westminster John Knox, 2000.

———. "Narrative Christology and the Son of Man: What the Markan Jesus Says Instead." *Biblical Interpretation* 11 (2003): 373–85.

———. *Mark's Jesus: Characterization as Narrative Christology.* Waco, TX: Baylor University Press, 2009.

Mali, Joseph F. *The Christian Gospel and Its Jewish Roots: A Redaction-Critical Study of Mark 2:21–22 in Context.* Studies in Biblical Literature 131. New York: Peter Lang, 2009.

Malik, Peter. "The Earliest Corrections in Codex Sinaiticus: A Test Case from the Gospel of Mark." *Bulletin of the American Society of Papyrologists* 50 (2013): 207–54.

Malina, Bruce J. *The New Testament World: Insights from Cultural Anthropology.* Atlanta: John Knox, 1981.

———. "Wealth and Poverty in the New Testament." *Interpretation* 41 (1987): 354–67.

Maloney, Elliot C. "The Historical Present in the Gospel of Mark." Pp. 67–78 in *To Touch the Text: Biblical and Related Studies in Honor of Joseph A. Fitzmyer, S.J.* Edited by Maurya P. Horgan and Paul J. Kobelski. New York: Crossroad, 1989.

———. *Jesus' Urgent Message for Today: The Kingdom of God in Mark's Gospel.* New York: Continuum, 2004.

Mann, C. S. *Mark: A New Translation with Introduction and Commentary.* Anchor Bible 27. Garden City, NY: Doubleday, 1986.

Manson, T. W. *The Teaching of Jesus: Studies in Form and Content.* 2nd ed. Cambridge: Cambridge University Press, 1935.

———. "The Cleansing of the Temple." *Bulletin of the John Rylands University Library of Manchester* 33 (1951): 271–82.

———. "Realized Eschatology and the Messianic Secret." Pp. 209–22 in *Studies in the Gospels: Essays in Memory of R. H. Lightfoot.* Edited by Dennis E. Nineham. Oxford: Oxford University Press, 1955.

Marcus, Joel. "Mark 4:10–12 and Marcan Epistemology." *Journal of Biblical Literature* 103 (1984): 557–74.

———. *The Mystery of the Kingdom of God.* Society of Biblical Literature Dissertation Series 90. Atlanta: Scholars, 1986.

———. "Entering into the Kingly Power of God." *Journal of Biblical Literature* 107 (1988): 663–75.

———. "Mark 14:61: Are You the Messiah-Son-of-God?" *Novum Testamentum* 31 (1989): 125–41.

———. "'The Time Has Been Fulfilled!' (Mark 1:15)." Pp. 49–68 in *Apocalyptic and the New Testament: Essays in Honor of J. Louis Martyn.* Journal for the Study of the New Testament Supplement Series 24. Edited by Joel Marcus and Marion L. Soards. Sheffield: Sheffield Academic, 1989.

———. "The Jewish War and the *Sitz im Leben* of Mark." *Journal of Biblical Literature* 111 (1992): 441–62.

———. *The Way of the Lord: Christological Exegesis of the Old Testament in the Gospel of Mark.* Louisville: Westminster John Knox, 1992.

———. "The Beelzebub Controversy and the Eschatologies of Jesus." Pp. 247–77 in *Authenticating the Activities of Jesus.* Edited by Bruce Chilton and Craig A. Evans. Leiden: Brill, 1999.

———. *Mark 1–8.* Anchor Bible 27. New York: Doubleday, 2000.

———. "Identity and Ambiguity in Markan Christology." Pp. 133–47 in *Seeking the*

Identity of Jesus: A Pilgrimage. Edited by Beverly Roberts Gaventa and Richard B. Hays. Grand Rapids: Eerdmans, 2008.

———. *Mark 8–16*. Anchor Yale Bible 27A. New Haven, CT/London: Yale University Press, 2009.

Marshall, Christopher D. *Faith as a Theme in Mark's Narrative*. Society for New Testament Studies Monograph Series 64. Cambridge: Cambridge University Press, 1989.

Marshall, I. Howard. "Son of God or Servant of Yahweh?—A Reconsideration of Mark I. 11." *New Testament Studies* 15 (1968–69): 326–36.

———. *The Gospel of Luke: A Commentary on the Greek Text*. The New International Greek Testament Commentary. Grand Rapids: Eerdmans, 1978.

———. "The Divine Sonship of Jesus." Pp. 134–49 in *Jesus the Saviour: Studies in New Testament Theology*. Downers Grove, IL: InterVarsity Press, 1990.

———. "The Parousia in the New Testament—and Today." Pp. 194–211 in *Worship, Theology and Ministry in the Early Church: Essays in Honor of Ralph P. Martin*. Journal for the Study of the New Testament Supplement Series 87. Edited by Michael J. Wilkins and Terence Paige. Sheffield: JSOT, 1992.

———. "Jesus as Messiah in Mark and Matthew." Pp. 117–43 in *The Messiah in the Old and New Testaments*. Edited by Stanley E. Porter: Grand Rapids: Eerdmans, 2007.

———. *A Concise New Testament Theology*. Downers Grove, IL: InterVarsity Press, 2008.

Martin, Ralph P. *Mark: Evangelist and Theologian*. Grand Rapids: Zondervan, 1972.

———. *New Testament Foundations*. Vol. 1. Grand Rapids: Eerdmans, 1975.

Martin, Troy W. "Watch during the Watches (Mark 13:35)." *Journal of Biblical Literature* 120 (2001): 685–701.

Martinez, Ernest R. "Identity of Jesus in Mark." *Communio* 1 (1974): 323–42.

Marucci, Corrado. "Die implizite Christologie in der sogenannten Vollmachtsfrage (Mk 11, 27–33): Referat im Seminar 'Das Markusevangelium' beim SNTS-Kongress in Trondheim, 20. 8. 1985." *Zeitschrift für katholische Theologie* 108 (1986): 292–300.

Marxsen, Willi. *Introduction to the New Testament*. Translated by G. Buswell. Philadelphia: Fortress, 1968.

———. *Mark the Evangelist: Studies on the Redaction History of the Gospel*. Translated by James Boyce. Nashville: Abingdon, 1969.

Masson, Charles. "Le reniement de Pierre: quelques aspects de la formation d'une tradition." *Revue d'histoire et de philosophie religieuses* 37 (1957): 24–35.

Matera, Frank J. *The Kingship of Jesus: Composition and Theology in Mark 15*. Society of Biblical Literature Dissertation Series 66. Chico, CA: Scholars, 1982.

———. *What Are They Saying about Mark?* New York/Mahwah, NJ: Paulist, 1987.

———. "The Prologue as the Interpretative Key to Mark's Gospel." *Journal for the Study of the New Testament* 34 (1988): 3–20.

———. "The Incomprehension of the Disciples and Peter's Confession (Mark 6,14–8,30)." *Biblica* 70 (1989): 153–72.

———. *New Testament Christology*. Louisville: Westminster John Knox, 1999.

Mattingly, Harold. *Coins of the Roman Empire in the British Museum*. Volume 1. *Augustus to Vitellius*. London: Trustees of the British Museum, 1936.

Mauser, Ulrich W. *Christ in the Wilderness: The Wilderness Theme in the Second Gospel and Its Basis in the Biblical Tradition*. Studies in Biblical Theology 39. Naperville, IL: Alec R. Allenson, 1963.

Mazar, Benjamin. "The Royal *Stoa* in the Southern Part of the Temple Mount." Pp. 141–47 in *Recent Archaeology in the Land of Israel*. Edited by Hershel Shanks. Translated by Aryeh Finkelstein. Washington, DC: Biblical Archaeology Society, 1984.

McCracken, David. *The Scandal of the Gospels: Jesus, Story, and Offense*. New York: Oxford University Press, 1994.

McKay, Kenneth L. "On the Perfect and Other Aspects in New Testament Greek: An Aspectual Approach." *Novum Testamentum* 23 (1981): 289–329.

McKnight, Scot. *The King Jesus Gospel: The Original Good News Revisited*. Grand Rapids: Zondervan: 2011.

McNamara, Martin. *The Aramaic Bible Volume 1A: Targum Neofiti 1: Genesis*. Collegeville, MN: Michael Glazier, 1992.

McNeile, Alan Hugh. *The Gospel according to St. Matthew*. London: Macmillan, 1938.

McNicol, Allan. "The Lesson of the Fig Tree in Mark 13:28–32: A Comparison between Two Exegetical Methodologies." *Restoration Quarterly* 27 (1984): 193–207.

Meier, John P. *The Vision of Matthew*. New York: Paulist, 1978.

———. *A Marginal Jew: Rethinking the Historical Jesus*. Vol. 1. New York: Doubleday, 1991.

———. *A Marginal Jew: Rethinking the Historical Jesus*. Vol. 2. New York: Doubleday, 1994.

Menken, Maarten J. J. "The Call of Blind Bartimaeus (Mark 10:46–52)." *Hervormde teologiese studies* 61 (2005): 273–90.

Merkel, Helmut. "Peter's Curse." Pp. 66–71 in *The Trial of Jesus: Cambridge Studies in Honour of C. F. D. Moule*. Studies in Biblical Theology 2/13. Edited by Ernst Bammel. Naperville, IL: Alec R. Allenson, 1970.

Metzger, Bruce M. *A Textual Commentary on the Greek New Testament*. 4 Rev. ed. New York: United Bible Societies, 1994.

Meulen, Harry E. Faber van der. "One or Two Veils in Front of the Holy of Holies." *Theologica evangelica* 18 (1985): 22–27.

Meye, Robert P. *Jesus and the Twelve: Discipleship and Revelation in Mark's Gospel*. Grand Rapids: Eerdmans, 1968.

———. "Mark 16:8—The Ending of Mark's Gospel." *Biblical Research* 14 (1969): 33–43.

Michaels, J. Ramsay. *Servant and Son: Jesus in Parable and Gospel*. Atlanta: John Knox, 1981.

Milgrom, Jacob. *Leviticus 1–16*. Anchor Bible 3. New York: Doubleday, 1991.

Miller, Susan. *Women in Mark's Gospel*. Journal for the Study of the New Testament Supplement Series 259. London/New York: T&T Clark, 2004.

Minear, Paul S. *Saint Mark*. Layman's Bible Commentary. London: SCM, 1962.

Mingo Kaminouchi, Alberto de. *"But It Is Not So Among You": Echoes of Power in Mark 10.32–45*. Journal for the Study of the New Testament Supplement Series 249. London: T&T Clark, 2003.

Minor, Mitzi. *The Spirituality of Mark: Responding to God*. Louisville: Westminster John Knox Press, 1996.

Mitchell, Margaret M. "Patristic Counter-Evidence to the Claim That 'The Gospels Were Written for All Christians.'" *New Testament Studies* 51 (2005): 36–79.

Mitton, C. Leslie. *The Gospel according to St Mark*. London: Epworth, 1957.

Mkole, Jean Claude Loba. "Mark 14:62: Substantial Compendium of New Testament Christology." *Hervormde teologiese studies* 56 (2000): 1119–45.

Moeser, Marion C. *The Anecdote in Mark, the Classical World and the Rabbis*. Journal for the Study of the New Testament Supplement Series 227. Sheffield: Sheffield Academic Press, 2002.

Moessner, David P. "The Appeal and Power of Poetics (Luke 1:1–4)." Pp. 84–123 in *Jesus and the Heritage of Israel: Luke's Narrative Claim upon Israel's Legacy.* Edited by David P. Moessner. Harrisburg, PA: Trinity Press International, 1999.

Moffatt, James. *The Theology of the Gospels.* New York: Scribner's, 1913.

Moloney, Francis J. "The Vocation of the Disciples in the Gospel of Mark." *Salesianum* 43 (1981): 487–516.

———. "Mark 6:6b–30: Mission, the Baptist, and Failure." *Catholic Biblical Quarterly* 63 (2001): 647–63.

———. *The Gospel of Mark: A Commentary.* Peabody, MA: Hendrickson, 2002.

Moo, Douglas J. *The Old Testament in the Gospel Passion Narratives.* Sheffield: Almond, 1983.

Moore, George Foot. *Judaism in the First Centuries of the Christian Era.* Cambridge, MA: Harvard University Press, 1927. Reprinted New York: Schocken, 1971.

Morgenthaler, Robert. *Statistik des neutestamentlichen Wortschatzes.* Zürich: Gotthelf, 1958.

Moritz, Thorsten. "Mark." Pp. 39–49 in *The Theological Interpretation of the New Testament.* Edited by Kevin J. Vanhoozer, Daniel J. Treier and N. T. Wright. Grand Rapids: Baker, 2008.

Morris, Leon. "Disciples of Jesus." Pp. 112–27 in *Jesus of Nazareth Lord and Christ: Essays on the Historical Jesus and New Testament Christology.* Edited by Joel B. Green and Max Turner. Grand Rapids: Eerdmans, 1994.

Morrison, Gregg S. "The Turning Point in the Gospel of Mark: A Study of Markan Christology." PhD dissertation. Washington, DC: The Catholic University of America, 2008.

Moss, Candida R. "The Man with the Flow of Power: Porous Bodies in Mark 5:25–34." *Journal of Biblical Literature* 129 (2010): 507–19.

Motyer, Stephen. "The Rending of the Veil: A Markan Pentecost." *New Testament Studies* 33 (1987): 155–57.

Moule, C. F. D. *An Idiom-Book of New Testament Greek.* 2nd ed. Cambridge: Cambridge University Press, 1968.

———. "On Defining the Messianic Secret in Mark." Pp. 239–52 in *Jesus und Paulus: Festschrift für Werner Georg Kümmel zum 70. Geburtstag.* Edited by E. Earle Ellis and Erich Grässer. Göttingen: Vandenhoeck & Ruprecht, 1975.

Moulton, James Hope. *A Grammar of New Testament Greek.* Vol. 1: *Prolegomena.* 3rd ed. Edinburgh: T&T Clark, 1908.

Moulton, James Hope, and Wilbert Francis Howard. *A Grammar of New Testament Greek.* Vol. 2: *Accidence and Word-Formation.* Edinburgh: T&T Clark, 1920.

Moulton, James Hope, and George Milligan. *The Vocabulary of the Greek Testament: Illustrated from the Papyri and Other Non-Literary Sources.* Grand Rapids: Eerdmans, 1976 [1930].

Moyise, Steve. "Is Mark's Opening Quotation the Key to His Use of Scripture?" *Irish Biblical Studies* 20 (1998): 146–58.

Mull, Kenneth V., and Carolyn Sandquist Mull. "Biblical Leprosy: Is It Really?" *Bible Review* 8 (April, 1992): 32–39, 62.

Müller, Mogens. *The Expression "Son of Man" and the Development of Christology: A History of Interpretation.* London: Equinox, 2008.

Mullins, Terence Y. "Papias on Mark's Gospel." *Vigiliae Christianae* 14 (1960): 216–24.

Münderlein, Gerhard. "Die Verfluchung des Feigenbaumes (Mk. xi. 12–14)." *New Testament Studies* 10 (1963–64): 89–104.

Murphy-O'Connor, Jerome. "Jesus and the Money Changers (Mark 11:15–17; John 2:13–17)." *Revue biblique* 107 (2000): 42–55.

Mussner, Franz. *Dieses Geschlecht wird nicht vergehen: Judentum und Kirche*. Freiburg: Herder, 1991.

Myers, Ched. *Binding the Strong Man: A Political Reading of Mark's Story of Jesus*. Maryknoll, NY: Orbis, 1988.

Naluparayil, Jacob Chacko, *The Identity of Jesus in Mark: An Essay on Narrative Christology*. Studium biblicum franciscanum analecta 49. Jerusalem: Franciscan Printing, 2000.

———. "Jesus of the Gospel of Mark: Present State of Research." *Currents in Research: Biblical Studies* 8 (2000): 191–226.

Nardoni, Enrique. "A Redactional Interpretation of Mark 9:1." *Catholic Biblical Quarterly* 43 (1981): 365–84.

Navone, John J. "Spiritual Pedagogy in the Gospel of Mark." *The Bible Today* 39 (2001): 231–38.

Nebe, Gottfried. "πολύς, πολλή, πολύ." Pp. 131–33 in *Exegetical Dictionary of the New Testament*. Vol. 3. Edited by Horst Balz and Gerhard Schneider. Grand Rapids: Eerdmans, 1991.

Neusner, Jacob. "The Absoluteness of Christianity and the Uniqueness of Judaism: Why Salvation Is Not of the Jews." *Interpretation* 43 (1989): 18–31.

———. "Money-Changers in the Temple: The Mishnah's Explanation." *New Testament Studies* 35 (1989): 287–90.

Neville, David J. *Mark's Gospel: Prior or Posterior? A Reappraisal of the Phenomenon of Order*. Journal for the Study of the New Testament Supplement Series 222. London/New York: Sheffield Academic, 2002.

———. "God's Presence and Power: Christology, Eschatology and 'Theodicy' in Mark's Crucifixion Narrative." Pp. 19–41 in *Theodicy and Eschatology*. Edited by Bruce Barber and David Neville. Hindmarsh: Australian Theological Forum, 2005.

Neyrey, Jerome H. "The Idea of Purity in Mark's Gospel." *Semeia* 35 (1986): 91–128.

Nickelsburg, George W. E. "Riches, the Rich, and God's Judgment in *1 Enoch* 92–105 and the Gospel according to Luke." *New Testament Studies* 25 (1979): 324–44.

Niederwimmer, Kurt. "Johannes Markus und die Frage nach dem Verfasser des zweiten Evangeliums." *Zeitschrift für die neutestamentliche Wissenschaft* 58 (1967): 172–88.

Nineham, Dennis E. *St. Mark*. Westminster Pelican Commentaries. Philadelphia: Westminster, 1963.

North, J. L. "ΜΑΡΚΟΣ Ο ΚΟΛΟΒΑΔΑΚΤΥΛΟΣ: Hippolytus, *Elenchus* VII.30." *Journal of Theological Studies* 28 (1977): 498–507.

Nun, Mendel. *The Sea of Galilee and Its Fishermen in the New Testament*. Kibbutz Ein Gev: Kinnereth Sailing Co., 1989.

O'Brien, Kelli. "Innocence and Guilt: Apologetic, Martyr Stories, and Allusion in the Markan Trial Narratives." Pp. 205–28 in *The Trial and Death of Jesus: Essays on the Passion Narrative in Mark*. Contributions in Biblical Exegesis and Theology 45. Edited by Geert van Oyen and Tom Shepherd. Leuven: Peeters, 2006.

———. *The Use of Scripture in the Markan Passion Narrative*. Library of New Testament Studies 384. London: T&T Clark, 2010.

Oden, Thomas C., and Christopher A. Hall, eds. *Ancient Christian Commentary on Scripture. New Testament II. Mark.* Downers Grove, IL: InterVarsity Press, 1998.

Öhler, Markus. "Die Verklärung (Mk 9:1–8): Die Ankunft der Herrschaft Gottes auf der Erde." *Novum Testamentum* 38 (1996): 197–217.

———. "The Expectation of Elijah and the Presence of the Kingdom of God." *Journal of Biblical Literature* 118 (1999): 461–76.

Orchard, Bernard, and Thomas R. W. Longstaff, eds. *J. J. Griesbach: Synoptic and Text-Critical Studies 1776–1976.* Society for New Testament Studies Monograph Series 34. Cambridge: Cambridge University Press, 1978.

Osborne, Grant R. "Structure and Christology in Mark 1:21–45." Pp. 146–63 in *Jesus of Nazareth: Lord and Christ: Essays on the Historical Jesus and New Testament Christology.* Edited by Joel B. Green and Max Turner. Grand Rapids: Eerdmans, 1994.

———. "Mark, Theology of." Pp. 737–40 in *Evangelical Dictionary of Theology.* 2nd ed. Edited by Walter A. Elwell. Grand Rapids: Baker, 2001.

Ossandón, Juan Carlos. "Bartimaeus' Faith: Plot and Point of View in Mark 10, 46–52." *Biblica* 93 (2012): 377–402.

Ottley, R. R. "ἐφοβοῦντο γάρ Mark xvi 8." *Journal of Theological Studies* 27 (1926): 407–409.

Otto, Randall E. "The Fear Motivation in Peter's Offer to Build τρεῖς σκηνάς." *Westminster Theological Journal* 59 (1997): 101–12.

Oyen, Geert van. "Intercalation and Irony in the Gospel of Mark." Pp. 949–74 in *The Four Gospels 1992: Festschrift Frans Neirynck.* Volume 2. Bibliotheca ephemeridum theologicarum lovaniensium 100. Edited by Frans van Segbroeck, Christopher M. Tuckett, Gilbert van Belle, and Joseph Verheyden. Leuven: Leuven University Press, 1992.

———. "Irony as Propaganda in Mark 15:39?" Pp. 125–41 in *Persuasion and Dissuasion in Early Christianity, Ancient Judaism, and Hellenism.* Edited by Pieter W. van der Horst, Maarten J. J. Menken, Joop F. M. Smit, and Geert van Oyen. Leuven: Peeters, 2003.

———. "The Vulnerable Authority of the Author of the Gospel of Mark. Re-Reading the Paradoxes." *Biblica* 91 (2010): 161–86.

Oyen, Geert van, and Tom Shepherd, eds. *The Trial and Death of Jesus: Essays on the Passion Narrative in Mark.* Contributions in Biblical Exegesis and Theology 45. Leuven: Peeters, 2006.

Palu, Ma'afu. *Jesus and Time: An Interpretation of Mark 1.15.* Library of New Testament Studies 468. London: T&T Clark, 2012.

Parker, David C. *The Living Text of the Gospels.* Cambridge: Cambridge University Press, 1997.

Parker, Pierson. "Mark, Acts and Galilean Christianity." *New Testament Studies* 16 (1970): 295–304.

———. "The Posteriority of Mark." Pp. 67–142 in *New Synoptic Studies: The Cambridge Gospel Conference and Beyond.* Edited by William R. Farmer. Macon, GA: Mercer University Press, 1983.

Pavur, Claude Nicholas. "'As It Is Written': The Nature, Purpose, and Meaning of Mark's Gospel." M.S.T. thesis. Berkeley, CA: The Jesuit School of Theology, 1985. Revised 2011.

———. "The Grain Is Ripe: Parabolic Meaning in Mark 4:26–29." *Biblical Theology Bulletin* 17 (1987): 21–23.

Peabody, David B., Lamar Cope, and Allan J. McNicol. *One Gospel from Two: Mark's Use of Matthew and Luke.* Harrisburg: Trinity Press International, 2002.

Peace, Richard V. *Conversion in the New Testament.* Grand Rapids: Eerdmans, 1999.

Pearse, Roger, ed. "Greek Fragments: To Marinus, Extracts from the Catena of Nicetas." *Eusebius of Caesarea, Gospel Problems and Solutions: Quaestiones ad Stephanum et Marinum (CPG 3470).* Translated by David J. D. Miller. Ipswich: Chieftain, 2010.

Peppard, Michael. "The Eagle and the Dove: Roman Imperial Sonship and the Baptism of Jesus (Mark 1.9–11)." *New Testament Studies* 56 (2010): 431–51.

———. *The Son of God in the Roman World: Divine Sonship in Its Social and Political Context.* New York: Oxford University Press, 2011.

Perkins, Larry. "'Let the Reader Understand': A Contextual Interpretation of Mark 13:14." *Bulletin for Biblical Research* 16 (2006): 95–104.

Perkins, Pheme. "Mark as Narrative Christology." Pp. 67–80 in *Who Is This Christ? Gospel Christology and Contemporary Faith.* Edited by Reginald Fuller and Pheme Perkins. Philadelphia: Fortress, 1983.

Perrin, Norman. *Rediscovering the Teaching of Jesus.* New York: Harper & Row, 1967.

———. "The Son of Man in the Synoptic Tradition." *Biblical Research* 13 (1968): 3–25.

———. "Towards an Interpretation of the Gospel of Mark." Pp. 1–78 in *Christology and a Modern Pilgrimage: A Discussion with Norman Perrin.* Rev. ed. Edited by Hans Dieter Betz. Missoula, MT: Scholars Press, 1974.

Pesch, Rudolf. *Naherwartungen: Tradition und Redaktion in Mk 13.* Kommentare und Beiträge zum Alten und Neuen Testament. Düsseldorf: Patmos, 1968.

———. "Anfang des Evangeliums Jesu Christi: Eine Studie zum Prolog des Markusevangeliums (Mk 1,1–15)." Pp. 108–44 in *Die Zeit Jesu Festschrift für Heinrich Schlier.* Edited by Günther Bornkamm and Karl Rahner. Freiburg/Basel: Herder, 1970.

———. *Das Markusevangelium.* Herders theologischer Kommentar zum Neuen Testament. 2 vols. Freiburg/Basel: Herder, 1984.

Petersen, Silke. "Die Evangelienüberschriften und die Entstehung des neutestamentlichen Kanons." *Zeitschrift für die Neutestamentliche Wissenschaft* 97 (2006): 250–74.

Peterson, Dwight N. *The Origins of Mark: The Markan Community in Current Debate.* Biblical Interpretation Series 48. Leiden/Boston/Köln: Brill, 2000.

Pilch, John J. "Secrecy in the Mediterranean World: An Anthropological Perspective." *Biblical Theology Bulletin* 24 (1994): 151–57.

Plessis, I. J. du. "The Saving Significance of Jesus and His Death on the Cross in Luke's Gospel—Focussing on Luke 22:19b–20." *Neotestamentica* 28 (1994): 523–40.

Pope, M. H. "Bible, Euphemism and Dysphemism." Pp. 720–25 in *The Anchor Bible Dictionary.* Vol. 1. Edited by David Noel Freedman. New York: Doubleday, 1992.

Porter, Stanley E. "In Defence of Verbal Aspect." Pp. 26–45 in *Biblical Greek Language and Linguistics: Open Questions in Current Research.* Journal for the Study of the New Testament Supplement Series 80. Edited by Stanley E. Porter and D. A. Carson. Sheffield: Sheffield Academic, 1993.

Preuss, Julius. *Biblical and Talmudic Medicine.* Edited and translated by Fred Rosner. New York: Sanhedrin, 1978.

Price, Reynolds. "Foreword" in *Mark as Story: An Introduction to the Narrative of a Gospel* by David Rhoads and Donald Michie. Philadelphia: Fortress, 1982.

Price, Simon R. F. *Rituals and Power: The Roman Imperial Cult in Asia Minor.* Cambridge: Cambridge University Press, 1984.

Pryke, E. J. *Redactional Style in the Marcan Gospel: A Study of Syntax and Vocabulary as Guides to Redaction in Mark.* Society for New Testament Studies Monograph Series 33. Cambridge: Cambridge University Press, 1978.

Puig i Tàrrech, Armand. *Jesus: An Uncommon Journey: Studies on the Historical Jesus.* Wissenschaftliche Untersuchungen zum Neuen Testament 2/288. Tübingen: Mohr Siebeck, 2010.

———. "The Glory on the Mountain: The Episode of the Transfiguration of Jesus." *New Testament Studies* 58 (2012): 151–72.

Quesnell, Quentin. *The Mind of Mark: Interpretation and Method through the Exegesis of Mark 6:52.* Analecta biblica 38. Rome: Pontifical Biblical Institute, 1969.

Räisänen, Heikki. "The 'Messianic Secret' in Mark's Gospel." Pp. 132–40 in *The Messianic Secret.* Edited by Christopher Tuckett. Philadelphia: Fortress, 1983.

———. *The "Messianic Secret" in Mark's Gospel.* Studies of the New Testament and its World. Edinburgh: T&T Clark, 1990.

Ramsay, W. M. "On Mark xii.42." *Expository Times* 10 (1898–99): 232, 336.

Reiser, Marius. *Syntax und Stil des Markusevangeliums im Licht der hellenistischen Volksliteratur.* Wissenschaftliche Untersuchungen zum Neuen Testament 2/11. Tübingen: Mohr Siebeck, 1984.

Reploh, Karl-Georg. *Markus, Lehrer der Gemeinde: Eine redaktionsgeschichtliche Studie zu den Jüngerperikopen des Markus–Evangeliums.* Stuttgarter biblische Monographien 9. Stuttgart: Katholisches Bibelwerk, 1969.

Rexeis, Elisabeth. "Die symbolische Verletzung des jüdischen Bluttabus in Mk 14,23f. par Mt 26,27f.: Das Becherwort in Einsetzungsbericht aus historisch-kritischer Sicht." *Studien zum Neuen Testament und Seiner Umwelt* 38 (2013): 73–96.

Rhoads, David. "Jesus and the Syrophoenician Woman in Mark: A Narrative-Critical Study." *Journal of the American Academy of Religion* 62 (1994): 343–75.

———. "Mission in the Gospel of Mark." *Currents in Theology and Mission* 22 (1995): 340–55.

Rhoads, David, and Donald Michie. *Mark as Story: An Introduction to the Narrative of a Gospel.* Philadelphia: Fortress, 1982.

Richardson, Alan. *The Miracle-Stories of the Gospels.* London: SCM, 1959.

Richardson, Peter. "Why Turn the Tables? Jesus' Protest in the Temple Precincts." *Society of Biblical Literature Seminar Papers* 31. (1992): 507–23.

Riedl, Hermann Josef. "Der Seewandel Jesu Mk 6,45–52 parr.: Eine Epiphanieerzählung und ihre textpragmatische Intention." *Studien zum Neuen Testament und seiner Umwelt* 30 (2005): 5–18.

Riesner, Rainer. *Jesus als Lehrer.* Wissenschaftliche Untersuchungen zum Neuen Testament 2/7. 3rd ed. Tübingen: Mohr Siebeck, 1988.

———. "Back to the Historical Jesus through Paul and His School (The Ransom Logion—Mark 10.45; Matthew 20.28)." *Journal for the Study of the Historical Jesus* 1 (2003): 171–99.

———. "Martin Hengel's Quest for Jesus and the Synoptic Question." Pp. 171–90 in *Earliest Christian History: History, Literature, and Theology: Essays from the Tyndale Fellowship in Honor of Martin Hengel.* Edited by Michael F. Bird and Jason Maston. Wissenschaftliche Untersuchungen zum Neuen Testament 2/320. Tübingen: Mohr Siebeck, 2012.

Rindge, Matthew S. "Reconfiguring the Akedah and Recasting God: Lament and Divine Abandonment in Mark." *Journal of Biblical Literature* 130 (2011): 755–74.

Ritmeyer, Kathleen, and Leen Ritmyer. *Reconstructing Herod's Temple Mount in Jerusalem.* Washington, DC: Biblical Archaeology Society, 1990.

Rivkin, Ellis. *What Crucified Jesus? The Political Execution of a Charismatic.* Nashville: Abingdon, 1984.

Robbins, Vernon K. "The Reversed Contextualization of Psalm 22 in the Markan Crucifixion: A Socio-Rhetorical Analysis." Pp. 1161–83 in *The Four Gospels 1992: Festschrift Frans Neirynck.* Volume 2. Bibliotheca ephemeridum theologicarum lovaniensium 100. Edited by Frans van Segbroeck, Christopher M. Tuckett, Gilbert van Belle, and Joseph Verheyden. Leuven: Leuven University Press, 1992.

———. "The Claims of the Prologues and Greco-Roman Rhetoric: The Prefaces to Luke and Acts in Light of Greco-Roman Rhetorical Strategies." Pp. 63–83 in *Jesus and the Heritage of Israel: Luke's Narrative Claim upon Israel's Legacy.* Edited by David P. Moessner. Harrisburg, PA: Trinity Press International, 1999.

Robertson, A. T. *A Grammar of the Greek New Testament in the Light of Historical Research.* Nashville: Broadman, 1934.

Robinson, James M. *The Problem of History in Mark.* Studies in Biblical Theology 21. London: SCM, 1957.

Robinson, John A. T. *Redating the New Testament.* Philadelphia: Westminster, 1976.

Robinson, Maurice. "The Long Ending of Mark as Canonical Verity." Pp. 40–79 in *Perspectives on the Ending of Mark: Four Views.* Edited by David Alan Black. Nashville: Broadman & Holman, 2008.

Robinson, William C. Jr. "The Quest for Wrede's Secret Messiah." Pp. 97–115 in *The Messianic Secret.* Edited by Christopher Tuckett. Philadelphia: Fortress, 1983.

Römer, Thomas, and Jan Rückl. "Jesus, Son of Joseph and Son of David, in the Gospels." Pp. 65–81 in *The Torah in the New Testament: Papers Delivered at the Manchester-Lausanne Seminar of June 2008.* Library of New Testament Studies 401. Edited by Peter Oakes and Michael Tait. London/New York: T&T Clark, 2009.

Rose, Christian. *Theologie als Erzählung im Markusevangelium: Eine narratologisch-rezeptionsästhetische Untersuchung zu Mk 1,1–15.* Wissenschaftliche Untersuchungen zum Neuen Testament 2/236. Tübingen: Mohr Siebeck, 2007.

Roskam, Hendrika Nicoline, ed. *The Purpose of the Gospel of Mark in its Historical and Social Context.* Novum Testamentum Supplements 114. Leiden: Brill, 2004.

Rossé, Gérard. *The Cry of Jesus on the Cross: A Biblical and Theological Study.* Translated by Stephen Wentworth Arndt. Mahwah, NJ: Paulist, 1987.

Roth, Cecil. "The Cleansing of the Temple and Zechariah xiv 21." *Novum Testamentum* 4 (1960): 174–81.

Roure, Damiá Mondada. "La figure de David dans l'évangile de Marc: des traditions juives aux interprétations évangéliques." Pp. 397–412 in *Figures de David à travers la Bible.* XVIIe congrès de l'Association Catholique Française pour l'étude de la Bible (Lille 1er–5 septembre 1997). Lectio divina 177. Edited by Louis Desrousseaux and Jacques Vermeylen. Paris: Cerf, 1999.

Rousseau, John J., and Rami Arav. *Jesus and His World: An Archaeological and Cultural Dictionary.* Minneapolis: Fortress, 1995.

Rowley, H. H. *The Relevance of Apocalyptic.* 2nd ed. London: Lutterworth, 1944.

Ruge-Jones, Philip. "Omnipresent, not Omniscient: How Literary Interpretation Confuses the Storyteller's Narrating." Pp. 29–43 in *Between Author and Audience in Mark: Narration, Characterization, Interpretation*. New Testament Monographs 23. Edited by Elizabeth Struthers Malbon. Sheffield: Sheffield Phoenix, 2009.

Rüger, Hans-Peter. "Die lexikalischen Aramaismen im Markusevangelium." Pp. 73–84 in *Markus-Philologie: Historische, literargeschichtliche und stilistische Untersuchungen zum zweiten Evangelium*. Wissenschaftliche Untersuchungen zum Neuen Testament 33. Edited by Hubert Cancik. Tübingen: Mohr Siebeck, 1984.

Sabin, Marie Noonan. "Reading Mark 4 as Midrash." *Journal for the Study of the New Testament* 45 (1992): 3–26.

———. *Reopening the Word: Reading Mark as Theology in the Context of Early Judaism*. New York: Oxford University Press, 2002.

———. *Gospel according to Mark*. New Collegeville Bible Commentary. Collegeville, MN: Liturgical Press, 2005.

Sanday, William. "The Injunctions of Silence in the Gospels." *Journal of Theological Studies* 5 (1904): 321–9.

Sanders, E. P. *The Tendencies of the Synoptic Tradition*. Society for New Testament Studies Monograph Series 9. Cambridge: Cambridge University Press, 1969.

———. *Jesus and Judaism*. Philadelphia: Fortress, 1985.

———. *Jewish Law from Jesus to the Mishnah*. Philadelphia: Trinity Press International, 1990.

———. *Judaism. Practice and Belief 63 BCE–66 CE*. Philadelphia: Trinity Press International, 1992.

Sandmel, Samuel. "Prolegomena to a Commentary on Mark." Pp. 45–56 in *New Testament Issues*. Edited by Richard Batey. New York: Harper & Row, 1970.

Sankey, P. J. "Promise and Fulfilment: Reader-Response to Mark 1.1–15." *Journal for the Study of the New Testament* 58 (1995): 3–18.

Santos, Narry F. *Slave of All: The Paradox of Authority and Servanthood in the Gospel of Mark*. Journal for the Study of the New Testament Supplement Series 237. London/New York: Sheffield Academic, 2003.

Schelbert, Georg. "Sprachgeschichtliches zu *'Abba*.'" Pp. 395–447 in *Mélanges Dominique Barthélemy: études bibliques offertes à l' occasion de son 60e anniversaire*. Orbis biblicus et orientalis 38. Edited by Pierre Casetti, Omar Keel, and Adrian Schenker. Göttingen: Vandenhoeck & Ruprecht, 1981.

Schenke, Ludger. *Das Markusevangelium*. Urban-Taschenbücher. Stuttgart: Kohlhammer, 1988.

———. "Gibt es im Markusevangelium eine Präexistenzchristologie?" *Zeitschrift für die Neutestamentliche Wissenschaft* 91 (2000): 45–71.

Schildgen, Brenda Deen. *Power and Prejudice: The Reception of the Gospel of Mark*. Detroit: Wayne State University Press, 1999.

Schmid, Josef. *The Gospel according to Mark*. The Regensburg New Testament. Translated by Kevin Condon. Staten Island, NY: Alba House, 1968.

Schmidt, Karl Ludwig. "καλέω." Pp. 487–91 in *Theological Dictionary of the New Testament*. Vol. 3. Edited by Gerhard Kittel. Translated by Geoffrey W. Bromiley. Grand Rapids: Eerdmans, 1966.

Schmidt, Thomas E. "Cry of Dereliction or Cry of Judgment? Mark 15:34 in Context." *Bulletin for Biblical Research* 4 (1994): 145–53.

———. "Mark 15.16–32: The Crucifixion Narrative and the Roman Triumphal Procession." *New Testament Studies* 41 (1995): 1–18.

Schmithals, Walter. *Wunder und Glaube: Eine Auslegung von Markus 4, 35–6, 6a.* Biblische Studien 59. Neukirchen-Vluyn: Neukirchener Verlag, 1970.

———. *Das Evangelium Markus.* Ökumenischer Taschenbuch-Kommentar 2/2. Gütersloh: Gütersloher Verlaghaus, 1979.

Schneider, Carl. "καταπέτασμα." Pp. 628–30 in *Theological Dictionary of the New Testament.* Vol. 3. Edited by Gerhard Kittel. Translated by Geoffrey W. Bromiley. Grand Rapids: Eerdmans, 1966.

Schnellbächer, Ernst L. "*KAI META HEMERAS HEX* (Markus 9:2)." *Zeitschrift für die neutestamentliche Wissenschaft* 71 (1980): 252–57.

Schoedel, William R. *The Apostolic Fathers.* Vol. 5. *Polycarp, Martyrdom of Polycarp, Fragments of Papias.* London: Thomas Nelson & Sons, 1967.

———. "Papias." Pp. 235–70 in *Aufstieg und Niedergang der Römischen Welt* 2.27.1. Edited by Wolfgang Haase. Berlin: de Gruyter, 1992.

Scholes, Robert, and Robert Kellogg. *The Nature of Narrative.* London: Oxford University Press, 1966.

Scholtissek, Klaus. *Die Vollmacht Jesu: Traditions–und redaktionsgeschichtliche Analysen zu einem Leitmotiv markinischer Christologie.* Neutestamentliche Abhandlungen 25. Münster: Aschendorff, 1992.

———. "Der Sohn Gottes für das Reich Gottes: Zur Verbindung von Christologie und Eschatologie bei Markus." Pp. 63–90 in *Der Evangelist als Theologe: Studien zum Markusevangelium.* Stuttgarter Bibelstudien 163. Edited by Thomas Söding. Stuttgart: Katholisches Bibelwerk, 1995.

Schreiber, Johannes. "Die Christologie des Markusevangeliums: Beobachtungen zur Theologie und Komposition des zweiten Evangeliums." *Zeitschrift für Theologie und Kirche* 58 (1961): 154–83.

———. *Theologie des Vertrauens: Eine redaktionsgeschichtliche Untersuchung des Markusevangeliums.* Hamburg: Furche-Verlag, 1967.

Schürer, Emil. *The History of the Jewish People in the Age of Jesus Christ.* Edited and translated by Geza Vermes, Fergus Millar, and Matthew Black. Edinburgh: T&T Clark, 1979.

Schweitzer, Albert. *The Quest of the Historical Jesus: A Critical Study of Its Progress from Reimarus to Wrede.* Translated by William Montgomery. New York: Macmillan, 1961.

Schweizer, Eduard. *Lordship and Discipleship.* Studies in Biblical Theology 38. Translated by David E. Green. London: SCM, 1960.

———. "Anmerkungen zur Theologie des Markus." Pp. 35–46 in *Neotestamentica et Patristica: Eine Freundesgabe Herrn Professor Dr. Oscar Cullmann zu seinem 60. Geburtstag überreicht.* Novum Testamentum Supplements 6. Leiden: Brill, 1962.

———. "Mark's Contribution to the Quest of the Historical Jesus." *New Testament Studies* 10 (1964): 421–32.

———. "πνεῦμα." Pp. 389–455 in *Theological Dictionary of the New Testament.* Vol. 6. Edited by Gerhard Friedrich. Translated by Geoffrey W. Bromiley. Grand Rapids: Eerdmans, 1968.

———. *The Good News according to Mark.* Translated by Donald H. Madvig. Richmond, VA: John Knox, 1970.

———. *Jesus.* Translated by David Green. London: SCM, 1971.

———. "The Portrayal of the Life of Faith in the Gospel of Mark." *Interpretation* 32 (1978): 387–99.

Scornaienchi, Lorenzo. "The Controversy Dialogues and the Polemic in Mark and Matthew." Pp. 309–21 in *Mark and Matthew I: Comparative Readings: Understanding the Earliest Gospels in Their First-Century Settings.* Wissenschaftliche Untersuchungen zum Neuen Testament 2/271. Edited by Eve-Marie Becker and Anders Runesson. Tübingen: Mohr Siebeck, 2011.

Scott, Bernard Brandon. *Hear Then the Parable: A Commentary on the Parables of Jesus.* Minneapolis: Fortress, 1989.

Scroggs, Robin, and Kent I. Groff. "Baptism in Mark: Dying and Rising with Christ." *Journal of Biblical Literature* 92 (1973): 531–48.

Seifrid, Mark. *The Second Letter to the Corinthians.* Pillar New Testament Commentary. Grand Rapids: Eerdmans, 2014.

Seitz, Oscar Jacob Frank. "Praeparatio Evangelica in the Markan Prologue." *Journal of Biblical Literature* 82 (1963): 201–6.

Senior, Donald P. *The Passion of Jesus in the Gospel of Mark.* Passion Series 2. Wilmington, DE: Michael Glazier, 1984.

———. "'With Swords and Clubs . . .'—The Setting of Mark's Community and His Critique of Abusive Power." *Biblical Theology Bulletin* 17 (1987): 10–20.

———. "The Gospel of Mark in Context." *The Bible Today* 34 (1996): 215–21.

Senior, Donald P., and Carroll Stuhlmueller. *The Biblical Foundations for Mission.* Maryknoll, NY: Orbis, 1983.

Shepherd, Tom. *Markan Sandwich Stories: Narration, Definition, and Function.* Andrews University Doctoral Dissertation Series 18. Berrien Springs, MI: Andrews University Press, 1993.

———. "The Narrative Function of Markan Intercalation." *New Testament Studies* 41 (1995): 522–40.

———. "The Irony of Power in the Trial of Jesus and the Denial by Peter—Mark 14:53–72." Pp. 229–45 in *The Trial and Death of Jesus: Essays on the Passion Narrative in Mark.* Contributions to Biblical Exegesis and Theology 45. Edited by Geert van Oyen and Tom Shepherd. Leuven: Peeters, 2006.

———. "The Narrative Role of John and Jesus in Mark 1.1–15." Pp. 151–68 in *Biblical Interpretation in Early Christian Gospels.* Vol. 1: *The Gospel of Mark.* Library of New Testament Studies 304. Edited by Thomas R. Hatina. London/New York: T&T Clark, 2006.

Sherwin-White, A. N. *Roman Society and Roman Law in the New Testament.* Oxford: Clarendon, 1963.

Shiner, Whitney Taylor. *Follow Me!: Disciples in Markan Rhetoric.* Society of Biblical Literature Dissertation Series 145. Atlanta: Scholars Press, 1995.

———. "The Ambiguous Pronouncement of the Centurion and the Shrouding of Meaning in Mark." *Journal for the Study of the New Testament* 78 (2000): 3–22.

Shipp, R. Mark. "Psalm 22: The Prayer of the Righteous Sufferer." *Christian Studies* 25 (2011–12): 47–59.

———. "'Smash Them against the Rocks'? The Christian Appropriation of Difficult Psalms." *Christian Studies* 26 (2013–14): 65–74.

Shively, Elizabeth E. *Apocalyptic Imagination in the Gospel of Mark: The Literary and Theological Role of Mark 3:22–30.* Beihefte zur Zeitschrift für die neutestamentliche Wissenschaft 189. Berlin/New York: de Gruyter, 2012.

Sim, David C. "Matthew's Use of Mark: Did Matthew Intend to Supplement or to Replace His Primary Source?" *New Testament Studies* 57 (2011): 176–92.

Skeat, T. C., and H. J. M. Milne, *Scribes and Correctors of the Codex Sinaiticus*. London: British Museum, 1938.

Slingerland, H. Dixon. *Claudian Policymaking and the Early Imperial Repression of Judaism at Rome*. South Florida Studies in the History of Judaism 160. Atlanta: Scholars Press, 1997.

Slomp, Jan. "Are the Words 'Son of God' in Mark 1.1 Original?" *Bible Translator* 28 (1977): 143–50.

Smith, C. Drew. "'This is My Beloved Son; Listen to Him': Theology and Christology in the Gospel of Mark." *Horizons in Biblical Theology* 24 (2002): 53–86.

Smith, Dennis E. "Narrative Beginnings in Ancient Literature and Theory." *Semeia* 52 (1990): 1–9.

Smith, Jonathan Z. "Good News Is No News: Aretalogy and Gospel." Pp. 21–38 in *Christianity, Judaism and Other Greco-Roman Cults: Studies for Morton Smith at Sixty*. Studies in Judaism in Late Antiquity 12. Edited by Jacob Neusner. Leiden: Brill, 1975.

Smith, Morton. *Clement of Alexandria and a Secret Gospel of Mark*. Cambridge, MA: Harvard University Press, 1973.

———. *The Secret Gospel: The Discovery and Interpretation of the Secret Gospel according to Mark*. New York: Harper & Row, 1973.

Smith, Robert H. "New and Old in Mark 16:1–8." *Concordia Theological Monthly* 43 (1972): 518–27.

———. "Darkness at Noon: Mark's Passion Narrative." *Concordia Theological Monthly* 44 (1973): 325–38.

Smith, Stephen H. "The Function of the Son of David Tradition in Mark's Gospel." *New Testament Studies* 42 (1996): 523–39.

Snodgrass, Klyne R. "Parable." Pp. 591–601 in *Dictionary of Jesus and the Gospels*. Edited by Joel B. Green, Scot McKnight, and I. Howard Marshall. Downers Grove, IL: InterVarsity Press, 1992.

———. *Stories with Intent: A Comprehensive Guide to the Parables of Jesus*. Grand Rapids: Eerdmans/Leiden: Brill, 2008.

Snow, Robert S. "Let the Reader Understand: Mark's Use of Jeremiah 7 in Mark 13:14." *Bulletin for Biblical Research* 21 (2011): 467–77.

Snoy, Thierry. "Marc 6,48: ' ... et il voulait les dépasser': proposition pour la solution d'une énigme." Pp. 347–63 in *L'évangile selon Marc: tradition et rédaction*. Bibliotheca ephemeridum theologicarum lovaniensium 34. Edited by M. Sabbe. Louvain: Leuven University Press, 1974.

Söding, Thomas, ed. *Der Evangelist als Theologe: Studien zum Markusevangelium*. Stuttgarter Bibelstudien 163. Stuttgart: Katholisches Bibelwerk, 1995.

———. "Leben nach dem Evangelium: Konturen markinischer Ethik." Pp. 167–95 in *Der Evangelist als Theologe: Studien zum Markusevangelium*. Stuttgarter Bibelstudien 163. Edited by Thomas Söding. Stuttgart: Katholisches Bibelwerk, 1995.

Sommer, Urs. *Die Passionsgeschichte des Markusevangeliums: Überlegungen zur Bedeutung der Geschichte für den Glauben*. Wissenschaftliche Untersuchungen zum Neuen Testament 2/58. Tübingen: Mohr Siebeck, 1993.

Spencer, Aída Besançon. "The Denial of the Good News and the Ending of Mark." *Bulletin for Biblical Research* 17 (2007): 269–83.

Spitaler, Peter. "Welcoming a Child as a Metaphor for Welcoming God's Kingdom: A Close Reading of Mark 10.13–16." *Journal for the Study of the New Testament* 31 (2009): 423–46.

Standaert, Benoît. *L'Évangile selon Marc. Deuxième partie Marc 6,14 à 10,52*. Études bibliques. Pendé: Gabalda, 2010.

Stanley, Christopher D. *Paul and the Language of Scripture: Citation Technique in the Pauline Epistles and Contemporary Language*. Society for New Testament Studies Monograph Series 74. Cambridge: Cambridge University Press, 1992.

Stauffer, Ethelbert. "Messias oder Menschensohn?" *Novum Testamentum* 1 (1956): 81–102.

———. *Jesus and His Story*. Translated by Richard and Clara Winston. New York: Knopf, 1960.

———. "Jeschu ben Mirjam: Kontroversgeschichtliche Anmerkungen zu Mk 6.3." Pp. 119–28 in *Neotestamentica et Semitica: Studies in Honour of Matthew Black*. Edited by E. Earle Ellis and Max Wilcox. Edinburgh: T&T Clark, 1969.

Stegemann, Hartmut. *The Library of Qumran: On the Essenes, Qumran, John the Baptist, and Jesus*. Grand Rapids: Eerdmans, 1998.

Stegner, William R. "The Baptism of Jesus and the Binding of Isaac: An Analysis of Mark 1:9–11." Pp. 331–47 in *The Answers Lie Below: Essays in Honor of Lawrence Edmund Toombs*. Edited by Henry O. Thompson. Lanham, MD: University Press of America, 1984.

———. "Jesus' Walking on the Water: Mark 6.45–52." Pp. 212–34 in *The Gospels and the Scriptures of Israel*. Journal for the Study of the New Testament Supplement Series 104. Edited by Craig A. Evans and W. Richard Stegner. Sheffield: Sheffield Academic Press, 1994.

Stein, Robert H. "The Cleansing of the Temple in Mark (11:15–19): Reformation or Judgment?" Pp. 121–33 in *Gospels and Tradition: Studies on Redaction Criticism of the Synoptic Gospels*. Grand Rapids: Baker, 1991.

———. "Is Our Reading the Bible the Same as the Original Audience's Hearing It? A Case Study in the Gospel of Mark." *Journal of the Evangelical Theological Society* 46 (2003): 63–78.

———. "The Ending of Mark." *Bulletin for Biblical Research* 18 (2008): 79–98.

———. *Mark*. Baker Exegetical Commentary on the New Testament. Grand Rapids: Baker Academic, 2008.

———. *Jesus, the Temple and the Coming of the Son of Man: A Commentary on Mark 13*. Downers Grove, IL: InterVarsity Press, 2014.

Steinhauser, Michael G. "The Form of the Bartimaeus Narrative (Mark 10:46–52)." *New Testament Studies* 32 (1986): 583–95.

Stemberger, Günter. "Appendix IV: Galilee—Land of Salvation?" Pp. 409–39 in *The Gospel and the Land: Early Christianity and Jewish Territorial Doctrine*, by W. D. Davies. Berkeley: University of California Press, 1974.

Stendahl, Krister. *The School of St. Matthew and Its Use of the Old Testament*. Acta seminarii neotestamentici upsaliensis 20. Lund: Gleerup, 1968.

Stern, David. *Parables in Midrash: Narrative and Exegesis in Rabbinic Literature*. Cambridge, MA: Harvard University Press, 1991.

Stettler, Hanna. "Sanctification in the Jesus Tradition." *Biblica* 85 (2004): 153–78.

Stock, Augustine. *Call to Discipleship*. Wilmington, DE: Michael Glazier, 1984.

———. "Hinge Transitions in Mark's Gospel." *Biblical Theology Bulletin* 15 (1985): 27–31.

———. *The Method and Message of Mark*. Wilmington, DE: Michael Glazier, 1989.

Stockklausner, Sonya K., and C. Anthony Hale. "Mark 15:39 and 16:6–7: A Second Look." *McMaster Journal of Theology* 1 (1990): 34–44.

Stoldt, Hans-Herbert. *History and Criticism of the Markan Hypothesis*. Translated by Donald L. Niewyk. Macon, GA: Mercer University Press, 1980.

Stone, Michael E. *Fourth Ezra*. Hermeneia. Minneapolis: Fortress, 1990.

Stonehouse, Ned B. *The Witness of Matthew and Mark to Jesus*. 2nd ed. Grand Rapids: Eerdmans, 1958.

Stott, John R. W. *The Cross of Christ*. Downers Grove, IL: InterVarsity Press, 1986.

Strecker, Georg. "εὐαγγελίζω." Pp. 69–70 in *Exegetical Dictionary of the New Testament*. Vol. 2. Edited by Horst Balz and Gerhard Schneider. Grand Rapids: Eerdmans, 1991.

Stuhlmacher, Peter. "Vicariously Giving His Life for Many, Mark 10:45 (Matt. 20:28)." Pp. 16–29 in *Reconciliation, Law, and Righteousness: Essays in Biblical Theology*. Translated by Everett R. Kalin. Philadelphia: Fortress, 1986.

Stuhlmann, Rainer. "Beobachtungen und Überlegungen zu Markus IV.26–29." *New Testament Studies* 19 (1973): 153–62.

Styler, G. M. "Excursus IV: The Priority of Mark." Pp. 285–316 in *The Birth of the New Testament* by C. F. D. Moule. 3rd ed. San Francisco: Harper & Row, 1982.

Svartvik, Jesper. *Mark and Mission: Mk 7:1–23 in its Narrative and Historical Contexts*. Coniectanea biblica: New Testament Series 32. Stockholm: Almqvist-Wiksell, 2000.

Sweat, Laura C. *The Theological Role of Paradox in the Gospel of Mark*. Library of New Testament Studies 492. London: Bloomsbury T&T Clark, 2013.

Swete, Henry Barclay. *The Gospel according to Mark*. London: Macmillan, 1913.

Syreeni, Kari. *The Making of the Sermon on the Mount: A Procedural Analysis of Matthew's Redactional Activity: Part 1: Method and Compositional Analysis*. Annales academiae scientiarum fennicae dissertationes humanarum litterarum 44. Helsinki: Suomalainen Tiedeakatemia, 1987.

Tait, Michael. *Jesus, The Divine Bridegroom in Mark 2:18–22: Mark's Christology Upgraded*. Analecta biblica 185. Rome: Gregorian & Biblical Press, 2010.

Talbert, Charles H. *What Is a Gospel? The Genre of the Canonical Gospels*. Philadelphia: Fortress, 1977.

Tannehill, Robert C. "The Disciples in Mark: The Function of a Narrative Role." *Journal of Religion* 57 (1977): 386–405.

———. "The Gospel of Mark as Narrative Christology." *Semeia* 16 (1979): 57–95.

———. "Reading It Whole: The Function of Mark 8:34–35 in Mark's Story." *Quarterly Review* 2 (1982): 67–78.

Taylor, Joan E. "The Garden of Gethsemane: Not the Place of Jesus' Arrest." *Biblical Archaeology Review* 21 (1995): 26–35, 62.

Taylor, R. O. P. "The Ministry of Mark." *Expository Times* 54 (1942–43): 136–38.

Taylor, Vincent. "Unsolved New Testament Problems: The Messianic Secret in Mark." *Expository Times* 59 (1948): 146–51.

———. *The Gospel according to St Mark*. 2nd ed. London: Macmillan, 1966.

Tcherikover, Victor. "Jewish Apologetic Literature Reconsidered." *Eos* 48 (1956): 169–93.

Telford, William R. *The Barren Temple and the Withered Fig Tree: A Redaction-Critical Analysis of the Cursing of the Fig-Tree Pericope in Mark's Gospel and Its Relation to the Cleansing of the Temple Tradition*. Journal for the Study of the New Testament Supplement Series 1. Sheffield: JSOT, 1980.

———. "More Fruit from the Withered Tree: Temple and Fig-Tree in Mark from a Graeco-Roman Perspective." Pp. 264–304 in *Templum Amicitiae: Essays on the Second Temple Presented to Ernst Bammel*. Journal for the Study of the New Testament Supplement Series 48. Edited by William Horbury. Sheffield: JSOT, 1991.

———. *Writing on the Gospel of Mark.* Guides to Advanced Biblical Research 1. Dorset: Deo Publishing, 2009.

Telford, William R., ed. *The Interpretation of Mark.* 2nd ed. Edinburgh: T&T Clark, 1995.

Theissen, Gerd. *The Miracle Stories of the Early Christian Tradition.* Edited by John Riches. Translated by Francis McDonagh. Philadelphia: Fortress, 1983.

———. *The Gospels in Context: Social and Political History in the Synoptic Tradition.* Translated by Linda M. Maloney. Edinburgh: T&T Clark, 1992.

Thomas, John Christopher. "A Reconsideration of the Ending of Mark." *Journal of the Evangelical Theological Society* 26 (1983): 407–19.

Thompson, Marianne Meye. *The Promise of the Father: Jesus and God in the New Testament.* Louisville: Westminster John Knox, 2000.

Thrall, Margaret E. *Greek Particles in the New Testament: Linguistic and Exegetical Studies.* New Testament Tools and Studies 3. Grand Rapids: Eerdmans, 1962.

Tiede, David L. "Proclaiming the Hidden Kingdom: Preaching on the Gospel Lessons in Mark." *Currents in Theology and Mission* 11.6 (1984): 325–32.

Tillesse, G. Minette de. *Le secret messianique dans l'évangile de Marc.* Paris: Cerf, 1968.

Tolbert, Mary Ann. *Sowing the Gospel: Mark's World in Literary-Historical Perspective.* Minneapolis: Fortress, 1989.

———. "How the Gospel of Mark Builds Character." *Interpretation* 47 (1993): 347–57.

Topel, John. "What Were the Women Afraid Of? (Mark 16:8)." *Journal of Theological Interpretation* 6 (2012): 79–96.

Trainor, Michael. "The Women, the Empty Tomb, and *That* Final Verse." *The Bible Today* 34 (1996): 177–82.

Trakatellis, Demetrios. *Authority and Passion: Christological Aspects of the Gospel according to Mark.* Translated by George K. Duvall and Harry Vulopas. Brookline, MA: Holy Cross Orthodox Press, 1987.

Trocmé, Etienne. *The Formation of the Gospel according to Mark.* Translated by Pamela Gaughan. Philadelphia: Westminster, 1975.

Tuckett, Christopher. *The Revival of the Griesbach Hypothesis: Analysis and Appraisal.* Society for New Testament Studies Monograph Series 44. Cambridge: Cambridge University Press, 1983.

———. "Mark's Concerns in the Parables Chapter (Mark 4, 1–34)." *Biblica* 69 (1988): 1–26.

Tuckett, Christopher, ed. *The Messianic Secret.* Philadelphia: Fortress, 1983.

Turner, C. H. "ὁ υἱός μου ὁ ἀγαπητός." *Journal of Theological Studies* 27 (1925–26): 113–29.

———. "A Textual Commentary on Mark 1." *Journal of Theological Studies* 28 (1927): 145–58.

———. *The Language and Style of the Gospel of Mark: An Edition of C. H. Turner's "Notes on Marcan Usage" Together with Other Comparable Studies* by J. K. Elliott. Novum Testamentum Supplements 71. Leiden: Brill, 1993.

Turner, Nigel. *Grammatical Insights into the New Testament.* Edinburgh: T&T Clark, 1965.

———. *A Grammar of New Testament Greek. IV. Style.* Edinburgh: T&T Clark, 1976.

Twelftree, Graham H. *Jesus the Exorcist: A Contribution to the Study of the Historical Jesus.* WUNT 2/54. Tübingen: Mohr Siebeck, 1993.

Tyson, Joseph B. "The Blindness of the Disciples in Mark." *Journal of Biblical Literature* 80 (1961): 261–68.

Ulansey, David. "The Heavenly Veil Torn: Mark's Cosmic *Inclusio.*" *Journal of Biblical Literature* 110 (1991): 123–25.

Van Henten, Jan Willem. "The First Testing of Jesus: A Rereading of Mark 1.12–13." *New Testament Studies* 45 (1999): 349–66.

Vanhoye, Albert. *Structure and Theology of the Accounts of the Passion in the Synoptic Gospels.* Bible Today Supplementary Studies 1. Collegeville, MN: Liturgical, 1967.

Vearncombe, Erin. "Cloaks, Conflict, and Mark 14:51–52." *Catholic Biblical Quarterly* 75 (2013): 683–703.

Verheyden, Jozef. "Describing the Parousia: The Cosmic Phenomena in Mk 13,24–25." Pp. 525–50 in *The Scriptures in the Gospels.* Bibliotheca ephemeridum theologicarum lovaniensium 131. Edited by Christopher M. Tuckett. Leuven: Leuven University Press, 1997.

Via, Dan O. Jr. *The Ethics of Mark's Gospel—In the Middle of Time.* Philadelphia: Fortress, 1985.

Vines, Michael E. *The Problem of Markan Genre: The Gospel of Mark and the Jewish Novel.* Academia biblica 3. Atlanta: Society of Biblical Literature, 2002.

Voorhis, John Winfield. "The Baptism of Jesus and His Sinlessness: An Outline Discussion." *Evangelical Quarterly* 7 (1935): 39–53.

Votaw, Clyde Weber. "The Gospels and Contemporary Biographies." *American Journal of Theology* 19 (1915): 45–73, 217–49. Reprinted in *The Gospels and Contemporary Biographies in the Greco-Roman World.* Facet Books Biblical Series 27. Philadelphia: Fortress, 1970.

Waetjen, Herman C. *A Reordering of Power: A Sociopolitical Reading of Mark's Gospel.* Minneapolis: Fortress, 1989.

Wahlen, Clinton. *Jesus and the Impurity of Spirits in the Synoptic Gospels.* Wissenschaftliche Untersuchungen zum Neuen Testament 2/185. Tübingen: Mohr Siebeck, 2004.

Wallace, Daniel B. *Greek Grammar beyond the Basics.* Grand Rapids: Zondervan, 1996.

———. "Mark 16:8 as the Conclusion to the Second Gospel." Pp. 1–39 in *Perspectives on the Ending of Mark: 4 Views.* Edited by David Alan Black. Nashville: Broadman & Holman, 2008.

Waltke, Bruce K. "The Theological Significations of Ἀντί and Ὑπέρ in the New Testament." ThD dissertation. Dallas: Dallas Theological Seminary, 1958.

Wanke, Günther. "φοβέω." Pp. 197–205 in *Theological Dictionary of the New Testament.* Vol. 9. Edited by Gerhard Friedrich. Translated by Geoffrey W. Bromiley. Grand Rapids: Eerdmans, 1974.

Wasserman, Tommy. "The 'Son of God' Was In the Beginning (Mark 1:1)." *Journal of Theological Studies* 62 (2011): 20–50.

Watson, David F. "The 'Messianic Secret': Demythologizing a Non-Existent Markan Theme." *Journal of Theology* 110 (2006): 33–44.

———. "Beyond Suspicion: On the Authorship of the Mar Saba Letter and the Secret Gospel of Mark." *Journal of Theological Studies* 61 (2010): 128–70.

———. *Honor among Christians: The Cultural Key to the Messianic Secret.* Minneapolis: Fortress, 2010.

Watson, Francis. "The Social Function of Mark's Secrecy Theme." *Journal for the Study of the New Testament* 24 (1985): 49–69.

———. "Ambiguity in the Marcan Narrative." *King's Theological Review* 10 (1987): 11–16.

———. “Beyond Suspicion: On the Authorship of the Mar Saba Letter and the Secret Gospel of Mark.” *Journal of Theological Studies* 61 (2010): 128–70.

Watts, Rikki E. *Isaiah's New Exodus in Mark*. Wissenschaftliche Untersuchungen zum Neuen Testament 2/88. Tübingen: Mohr Siebeck, 1997.

———. “Jesus' Death, Isaiah 53, and Mark 10:45: A Crux Revisited.” Pp. 125–51 in *Jesus and the Suffering Servant*. Edited by William H. Bellinger Jr. and William R. Farmer. Harrisburg, PA: Trinity Press International, 1998.

———. “The Psalms in Mark's Gospel.” Pp. 25–45 in *The Psalms in the New Testament*. Edited by Steve Moyise and Maarten J. J. Menken. London/New York: T&T Clark International, 2004.

———. “The Lord's House and David's Lord: The Psalms and Mark's Perspective on Jesus and the Temple.” *Biblical Interpretation* 15 (2007): 307–22.

Way-Rider, R. “The Lost Beginning of St. Mark's Gospel.” *Studia evangelica VII* (1982): 553–56.

Webb, R. L. “Jesus' Baptism: Its Historicity and Implications.” *Bulletin for Biblical Research* 10 (2000): 261–309.

Weber, Reinhard. “‘Christologie’ und ‘Messiasgeheimnis’: Ihr Zusammenhang und Stellenwert in den Darstellungsintentionen des Markus.” *Evangelische Theologie* 43 (1983): 108–25.

Wedderburn, Alexander J. M. “Jesus' Action in the Temple: A Key or a Puzzle?” *Zeitschrift für die Neutestamentliche Wissenschaft* 97 (2006): 1–22.

Weeden, Theodore J. *Mark: Traditions in Conflict*. Philadelphia: Fortress, 1971.

Wefald, Eric K. “The Separate Gentile Mission in Mark: A Narrative Explanation of Markan Geography, The Two Feeding Accounts and Exorcisms.” *Journal for the Study of the New Testament* 60 (1995): 3–26.

Weiffenbach, Heinrich Wilhelm, *Der Wiederkunftsgedanke Jesu nach den Synoptikern*. Leipzig: Breitkopf and Härtel, 1873.

Weinacht, Harald. *Die Menschwerdung des Sohnes Gottes im Markusevangelium: Studien zur Christologie des Markusevangeliums*. Hermeneutische Untersuchungen zur Theologie 13. Tübingen: Mohr Siebeck, 1972.

Weiss, Konrad. “πυρέσσω, πυρετός.” Pp. 956–59 in *Theological Dictionary of the New Testament*. Vol. 6. Edited by Gerhard Friedrich. Translated by Geoffrey W. Bromiley. Grand Rapids: Eerdmans, 1968.

Welker, Michael. “Revolutionäre Demut: Mit Jesu Taufe erfüllt sich Gottes Gerechtigkeit.” *Evangelische Kommentare* 30 (1997): 280–82.

Wellhausen, Julius. *Das Evangelium Marci*. Berlin: G. Reimer, 1903.

Wells, Calvin. “Pseudopathology.” Pp. 5–19 in *Diseases in Antiquity: A Survey of the Diseases, Injuries and Surgery of Early Populations*. Edited by Don Brothwell and A. T. Sandison. Springfield, IL: Charles C. Thomas, 1967.

Wendling, Emil. “Die Äusserung des Petrus in der Verklärungsgeschichte (Mk 9,5).” *Theologische Studien und Kritiken* 84 (1911): 111–28.

Wenham, David. “‘This Generation Will Not Pass . . .’: A Study of Jesus' Future Expectation in Mark 13.” Pp. 127–50 in *Christ the Lord: Studies in Christology Presented to Donald Guthrie*. Edited by Harold H. Rowden. Downers Grove, IL: InterVarsity Press, 1982.

———. *The Rediscovery of Jesus' Eschatological Discourse*. Gospel Perspectives 4. Sheffield: JSOT, 1984.

Wenham, David, and A. D. A. Moses. "'There are Some Standing Here ...': Did They Become the 'Reputed Pillars' of the Jerusalem Church? Some Reflections on Mark 9:1, Galatians 2:9 and the Transfiguration." *Novum Testamentum* 36 (1994): 146–63.

Wenham, Gordon J. *The Book of Leviticus.* New International Commentary on the Old Testament. Grand Rapids: Eerdmans, 1979.

Weren, Wim J. C. "The Use of Isaiah 5,1–7 in the Parable of the Tenants (Mark 12,1–12; Matthew 21,33–46)." *Biblica* 79 (1998): 1–26.

Wessel, Walter W., and Mark L. Strauss. "Mark." Pp. 671–989 in *The Expositor's Bible Commentary.* Vol. 9. Rev. ed. Edited by Tremper Longman III and David E. Garland. Grand Rapids: Zondervan, 2010.

Wiarda, Timothy J. *Peter in the Gospels: Pattern, Personality and Relationship.* Wissenschaftliche Untersuchungen zum Neuen Testament 2/127. Tübingen: Mohr Siebeck, 2000.

Wikgren, Allen. "ΑΡΧΗ ΤΟΥ ΕΥΑΓΓΕΛΙΟΥ." *Journal of Biblical Literature* 61 (1942): 11–20.

Wilcox, Max. "On the Ransom-Saying in Mark 10:45c, Matt 20:28c." Pp. 173–86 in *Geschichte—Tradition—Reflexion: Festschrift für Martin Hengel zum 70. Geburtstag. Bd. 3: Frühes Christentum.* Edited by Hubert Cancik, Hermann Lichtenberger, and Peter Schäfer. Tübingen: Mohr Siebeck, 1996.

Williams, Catrin H. *"I am He": The Interpretation of 'Anî Hû' in Jewish and Early Christian Literature.* Wissenschaftliche Untersuchungen zum Neuen Testament 2/113. Tübingen: Mohr Siebeck, 2000.

Williams, James G. *Gospel against Parable: Mark's Language of Mystery.* Sheffield: Almond, 1985.

Williams, Joel F. *Other Followers of Jesus: Minor Characters as Major Figures in Mark's Gospel.* Journal for the Study of the New Testament Supplement Series 102. Sheffield: JSOT, 1994.

———. "Literary Approaches to the End of Mark's Gospel." *Journal of the Evangelical Theological Society* 42 (1999): 21–35.

———. "Is Mark's Gospel an Apology for the Cross?" *Bulletin for Biblical Research* 12 (2002): 97–122.

———. "Does Mark's Gospel Have an Outline?" *Journal of the Evangelical Theological Society* 49 (2006): 505–25.

———. "Foreshadowing, Echoes, and the Blasphemy at the Cross (Mark 15:29)." *Journal of Biblical Literature* 132 (2013): 913–33.

Williams, Peter J. "An Examination of Ehrman's Case for ὀργισθείς in Mark 1:41." *Novum Testamentum* 54 (2012): 1–12.

Williams, Travis B. "Bringing Method to the Madness: Examining the Style of the Longer Ending of Mark." *Bulletin for Biblical Research* 20 (2010): 397–417.

Wilson, Marvin R. *Our Father Abraham: Jewish Roots of the Christian Faith.* Grand Rapids: Eerdmans, 1989.

Wink, Walter. "The Education of the Apostles: Mark's View of Human Transformation." *Religious Education* 83 (1988): 277–90.

Winn, Adam. *The Purpose of Mark's Gospel: An Early Christian Response to Roman Imperial Propaganda*. Wissenschaftliche Untersuchungen zum Neuen Testament 2/245. Tübingen, Mohr Siebeck, 2008.

Winter, Paul. *On the Trial of Jesus*. Studia Judaica: Forschungen zur Wissenschaft des Judentums 1. Edited and revised by T. Alec Burkill and Geza Vermes. 2nd ed. Berlin: de Gruyter, 1974.

Wintermute, O. S. "Jubilees." Pp. 35-142 in *The Old Testament Pseudepigrapha*. Volume 2. Edited by James H. Charlesworth. Garden City, NY: Doubleday, 1985.

Witherington, Ben III. *The Gospel of Mark: A Socio-Rhetorical Commentary*. Grand Rapids: Eerdmans, 2001.

———. *The Indelible Image: The Theological and Ethical Thought World of the New Testament*. Vol. 1: *The Individual Witnesses*. Downers Grove, IL: InterVarsity Press, 2009.

Wolff, Christian. "Zur Bedeutung Johannes des Täufers im Markusevangelium." *Theologische Literaturzeitung* 102 (1977): 857–65.

Wrede, William. *The Messianic Secret*. Translated by J. C. G. Greig. London: James Clarke, 1971.

Wright, Addison G. "The Widow's Mites: Praise or Lament?—A Matter of Context." *Catholic Biblical Quarterly* 44 (1982): 256–65.

Wright, N. T. *Jesus and the Victory of God*. Minneapolis: Fortress, 1996.

———. *Mark for Everyone*. London: SPCK, 2001.

Wright, R. B. "Psalms of Solomon." Pp. 639–70 in *The Old Testament Pseudepigrapha*. Vol. 2. Edited by James H. Charlesworth. Garden City, NY: Doubleday, 1985.

Wuellner, Wilhelm H. *The Meaning of "Fishers of Men."* Philadelphia: Westminster, 1967.

Wypadlo, Adrian. *Die Verklärung Jesu nach dem Markusevangelium*. Wissenschaftliche Untersuchungen zum Neuen Testament 308. Tübingen: Mohr Siebeck, 2013.

Yarbrough, Robert W. "The Date of Papias: A Reassessment." *Journal of the Evangelical Theological Society* 26 (1983): 181–91.

Zerwick, Maximilian. *Biblical Greek*. Translated by Joseph Smith. Rome: Pontifical Biblical Institute, 1963.

Scripture Index

Joshua

Judges

Ruth

1 Samuel

2 Samuel

1 Kingdoms (LXX)

2 Kingdoms (LXX)

1 Kings

Proverbs

Ecclesiastes

Song of Songs

Isaiah

Mark

John

Acts

Romans

Index of Extrabiblical Literature

Subject Index

Author Index

BIBLICAL THEOLOGY OF THE NEW TESTAMENT

A Theology of Luke and Acts

God's Promised Program, Realized for All Nations

Darrell L. Bock; Andreas J. Köstenberger, General Editor

This groundbreaking work by Darrell Bock thoroughly explores the theology of Luke's gospel and the book of Acts. In his writing, Luke records the story of God working through Jesus to usher in a new era of promise and Spirit-enablement so that the people of God can be God's people even in the midst of a hostile world. It is a message the church still needs today. Bock both covers major Lukan themes and sets forth the distinctive contribution of Luke-Acts to the New Testament and the canon of Scripture, providing readers with an in-depth and holistic grasp of Lukan theology in the larger context of the Bible.

Available in stores and online!

BIBLICAL THEOLOGY OF THE NEW TESTAMENT

A Theology of John's Gospel and Letters

The Word, the Christ, the Son of God

Andreas J. Köstenberger; Andreas J. Köstenberger, General Editor

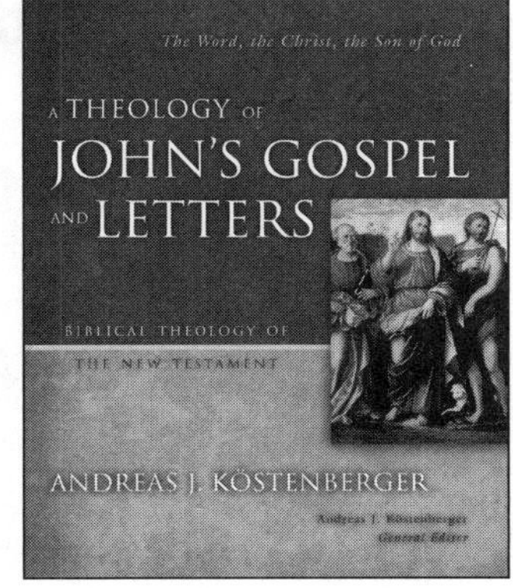

A Theology of John's Gospel and Letters introduces the first volume in the BTNT series. Building on many years of research and study in Johannine literature, Andreas Köstenberger not only furnishes an exhaustive theology of John's Gospel and letters, but also provides a detailed study of major themes and relates them to the Synoptic Gospels and other New Testament books. Readers will gain an in-depth and holistic grasp of Johannine theology in the larger context of the Bible.

Available in stores and online!

BIBLICAL THEOLOGY OF THE NEW TESTAMENT

A Theology of James, Peter, and Jude

Living in the Light of the Coming King

Peter H. Davids; Andreas J. Köstenberger, General Editor

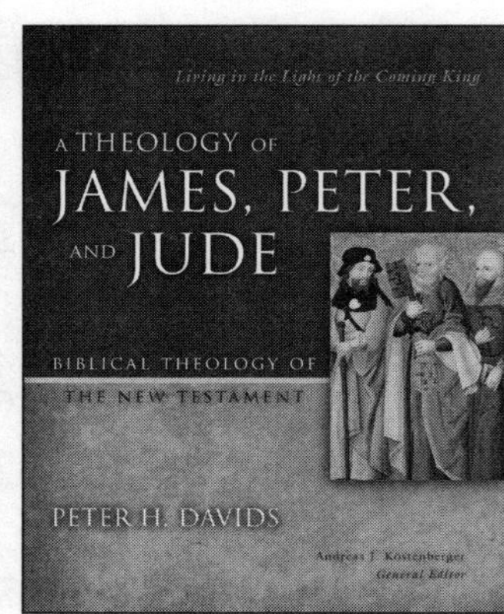

In this volume, Peter Davids offers a comprehensive study of the General or Catholic Epistles of James, 1-2 Peter, and Jude, which are often insufficiently covered in more general New Testament introductions, theologies, and surveys. Before discussing a theology of each of the four letters, Davids first deals with their common aspects—their shared background in the Greco-Roman world and a similar Christology, view of the source of sin, and eschatology—thus justifying their being treated together. In the chapters that follow, Davids embarks upon a theological reading of each letter informed by its social-rhetorical understanding—what they meant in the context of their original cultural settings—including: a survey of recent scholarship, a discussion of relevant introductory issues, a thematic commentary, a treatment of important theological themes, and a discussion of the place of the letter in the biblical canon and its contribution to New Testament theology.

Available in stores and online!